Brill's Encyclopedia of Global Pentecostalism

Brill's Encyclopedia of Global Pentecostalism

Executive Editor

Michael Wilkinson

Associate Editors

Connie Au
Jörg Haustein
Todd M. Johnson

BRILL

LEIDEN | BOSTON

Cover illustrations:
Culto in El Lugar de Su Presencia. Source: Wikimedia Commons, Photo: Cris12090823.

Members of the Pentecostal church praising the Lord. Chicago, Illinois. Library of Congress, Prints & Photographs Division, FSA/OWI Collection, LC-USF34- 038774-D. Photographer: Russell Lee.

Young pentecostals pray with hands up and speak in tongues at a meeting in Center of Faith Emanuel of Assemblies of God in Cancun (2012). Source: Wikimedia, Rayttc (CC BY-SA).

Service at Yoido Full Gospel Church Seoul (South Korea). Source: Center for the Study of Global Christianity.

Healing "laying on of hands" ceremony in the Pentecostal Church of God. Lejunior, Harlan County, Kentucky, 09/15/1946. Item from Record Group 245: Records of the Solid Fuels Administration for War, 1937–1948. Photographer: Russell Lee.

Water baptism of a pentecostal pastor (Assemblies of God). Cancún, Quintana Roo. Photographer: Wikimedia, Rayttc (CC BY-SA).

The Library of Congress Cataloging-in-Publication Data is available online at http://catalog.loc.gov
LC record available at http://lccn.loc.gov/

Library of Congress Cataloging-in-Publication Data

Names: Wilkinson, Michael, 1965- editor. | Ou, Keyin, editor. | Haustein,
    Jörg, 1975– editor. | Johnson, Todd M. (Todd Michael), 1958– editor.
Title: Brill's encyclopedia of global Pentecostalism / executive editor,
    Michael Wilkinson ; associated editors, Connie Au, Jörg Haustein, Todd M. Johnson.
Description: Leiden ; Boston : Brill, [2021] | Includes bibliographical
    references and index.
Identifiers: LCCN 2021000331 | ISBN 9789004297449 (hardback)
Subjects: LCSH: Pentecostalism—Encyclopedias.
Classification: LCC BR1644 .B75 2021 | DDC 270.8/203—dc23
LC record available at https://lccn.loc.gov/2021000331

Typeface for the Latin, Greek, and Cyrillic scripts: "Brill". See and download: brill.com/brill-typeface.

ISBN 978-90-04-29744-9 (hardback)

Copyright 2021 by Koninklijke Brill NV, The Netherlands.
Koninklijke Brill NV incorporates the imprints Brill, Brill Nijhoff, Brill Hotei, Brill Schoningh, Brill Fink, Brill mentis, Vandenhoeck & Ruprecht, Bohlau Verlag and V&R Unipress
All rights reserved. No part of this publication may be reproduced, translated, stored in a retrieval system, or transmitted in any form or by any means, electronic, mechanical, photocopying, recording or otherwise, without prior written permission from the publisher. Requests for re-use and/or translations must be addressed to Koninklijke Brill NV via brill.com or copyright.com.

This book is printed on acid-free paper and produced in a sustainable manner.

PRINTED BY DRUKKERIJ WILCO B.V. - AMERSFOORT, THE NETHERLANDS

Contents

Introduction   vii
Counting Pentecostals Worldwide   xiii
Pentecostals/Charismatics by Country, Region, Continent and Globe   xxxi
List of Authors   xlvi
Abraham, K.E. – Zschech, Darlene   1
Combined Bibliography   687
Index   756

Introduction

Pentecostal studies has developed and expanded worldwide with numerous conferences, publications, and papers presented on panels about Pentecostalism at major academic conferences like the American Academy of Religion. There are a number of scholarly societies that specifically focus on Pentecostalism like the Society for Pentecostal Studies, USA and the European Research Network on Global Pentecostalism (GloPent). There is a standard storyline that has developed and is crystalizing among scholars about the global Pentecostal movement. Typically, the storyline is that Pentecostalism began in the early twentieth century, expanded throughout the world rapidly, and is known for its incredible growth and success. There is some debate among scholars about the origins and whether or not it started in the United States at Topeka or Los Angeles. Some scholars argue that the origins are located in multiple sites found outside of, but inclusive of, the United States. The expansion and success of Pentecostalism is often described as phenomenal with figures and tables offering descriptions of that growth, especially in Africa, Asia, and Latin America. Missionaries, evangelists, apostles, prophets and a spirituality that revolves around experiences like healing, prophecy, speaking in tongues, and the miraculous are pointed to as the key factors for its success and growth. There is some debate about how Pentecostalism is defined. But overall, the general story is told with a certain amount of authority not only among scholars, but also by the general public, journalists, and popular websites. Pentecostalism, it is claimed, is expanding and growing and world Christianity is benefiting from its growth. This last point about the impact of Pentecostalism on world Christianity, however, needs some qualification.

There is a sort of triumphalism among some scholars and practitioners that Pentecostalism is growing and having a spectacular impact throughout the world with its evangelistic efforts, missionary activities, and social programs. Twenty-year growth numbers show the total number of Pentecostals/Charismatics increasing from about 454 million worldwide in 2000 to 694 million in 2019 (Zurlo, Johnson, and Crossing 2019). The numbers are often discussed by practitioners as signs of God's blessing or indicators for identifying the "winners" in a global religious market by some scholars. What is often missed is that while the number of Pentecostals is increasing, in some cases this is due to changes in definition and issues around what groups are to be included or excluded. Furthermore, while Pentecostals have increased their share of Christianity, the incredible growth worldwide has to be understood in the context of little to no growth for all sectors of Christianity combined (Zurlo, Johson, and Crossing 2019, 94–95). In 1900 there were 1.6 billion people worldwide growing to about 7.7 billion in 2019. The total number of Christians in the world in 1900 was 557 million increasing to 2.5 billion in 2019. Christianity, however, is just keeping up with the overall world population growth and Pentecostalism is not demonstrating enough religious innovation to make up for the declining rates more widely. In 1900 the total percentage of Christians in the world was about 34 percent. By 2000 it was 32 percent with no change in 2019. In other words, the 120 year trend for world Christianity is flat. Christianity is not growing or increasing its share of the global religious market and while Pentecostal churches have expanded, there is very little numerical impact on increasing world Christianity. While some types appear to be growing, Christianity is in fact not growing but only maintaining its share of the market.

These introductory observations raise two important issues that require some examination about Pentecostalism and world Christianity: what counts and who is counting?

What Counts? Defining Pentecostalism

Defining Pentecostalism is contested and scholars have spent considerable time debating this issue. The definition of Pentecostalism is partly related to debates among scholars about the definition of religion itself where a range of views about what it is or what it does or if it can even be studied empirically are especially important. Among Pentecostal scholars questions about definition are also related to debates among historians about origins. Standard textbooks on religion in America, for example, are increasingly taking the view that Pentecostalism began in America at the Azusa Street Revival and then quickly spread around the world (for example, Ahlstrom 2004; Bridges 2006; Williams 2008). Cecil M. Robeck, Jr (2006; 2013) offers one of the most appealing arguments for understanding the central role of Azusa and its leader, William Seymour, the African-American who was central to the revival from 1906–1909. Robeck's research on the American story is substantial and key for understanding that storyline. However, the assumption many scholars take from the American story about Azusa as the origin of Pentecostalism is contested, especially by post-colonial scholars and those who put forward a polycentric argument like Allan Anderson who argues for multiple sites of origin.

Anderson is a prominent scholar of Pentecostalism and his work has made an important contribution to the question about what counts and how Pentecostalism ought to be defined. In his book *An Introduction to Pentecostalism* (2004), Anderson offers a sustained critique of the central role of American Pentecostalism for launching the movement. Anderson argues that Pentecostalism is not an American invention and the historical evidence shows it is a far more global Christian event with revivals in places like India that were just as significant as Azusa for the emergence of the movement. Anderson focuses on the diversity of Pentecostalism culturally, theologically, and socially in an attempt to show that the movement has developed in unique ways outside of North America with little or no influence. Anderson does not deny that Azusa was an important event. He does, however, offer an interpretation that examines the polycentric origins of Pentecostalism opting for an explanation that counters the more American view of historical diffusion from a single place.

Anderson develops his argument further in his book *To the Ends of the Earth: Pentecostalism and the Transformation of World Christianity* (2013) where he expands on how world Christianity was transformed by Pentecostalism. Anderson argues that this transformation is not just about the growing numbers but highlights other key factors including the cultural and theological imperative to take the message to the whole world, the role of local missionaries, women, the cultural appeal of healing and deliverance, Pentecostalism's holistic approach, and its public role in politics. Anderson's work critiques the view of the emergence, growth, and development of Pentecostalism in North America that traditionally focuses on three movements or "waves" in the twentieth century. Much of the focus is upon American origins with little attention given outside of North America. The metaphor of "three waves" is employed by some scholars to discuss

Pentecostalism's historical development. The first wave emphasizes the role of Charles Parham's teaching on tongues as a sign or evidence of the baptism in the Holy Spirit and its primary teaching in Classical Pentecostal denominations like the Assemblies of God, USA and the Pentecostal Assemblies of Canada. The first wave explored this initial impulse of Spirit baptism that exploded during the Azusa Street Revival (1906–1909) in Los Angeles. The second wave referred to the role of renewal among the historical Protestant churches like the Methodists, Anglicans, Presbyterians, and Lutherans as well as the Roman Catholic Church beginning in the 1960s. The third wave referred to events beginning in the 1980s when renewal came to characterize a new movement among evangelical Protestants with the emergence of groups like the Association of Vineyard Churches and individuals like John Wimber and C. Peter Wagner. This three wave metaphor is criticized now for its American-centric focus neglecting the role of European revivals, as well as other important events that occurred in Africa, Asia, and Latin America that were indigenous and without influence by Americans. The inclusion of charismatic evangelicals by scholars has also increased the total number of Pentecostals worldwide since the 1980s demonstrating the role of redefinition and redistribution and its impact on the numbers more so than the actual evangelistic practices of Pentecostals. Furthermore, the many independent charismatic churches, non-denominational churches, and global movements networked through the leadership of Apostles has led to the critique of the classification system. The histories of Pentecostalism in China and many countries in Africa, for example, do not follow this pattern.

The globalization of Pentecostalism also raises questions about the definition of Pentecostalism (Wilkinson 2016). The challenge for scholars is to account for sameness and difference in defining a segment of Christianity that is worldwide and yet diverse theologically and culturally. Defining Pentecostalism is not simply about identifying key aspects or phenomenological characteristics. Definition is also highly polemical as "insiders" attempt to come to terms with so much variety raising questions about which groups are in or out. Debates about definition also reveal a number of issues about borders and boundaries, neo-colonial relations, economic liberalization, and concerns about the Americanization of the world. Globalization has the effect of relativizing Pentecostalism by bringing groups of people in close proximity in specific places but also in new spaces where they increasingly engage with one another through various exchanges, networks, organizations, and migration. These interactions raise questions about "who are the real Pentecostals" and what is an authentic expression of global Pentecostalism. There are certainly key cultural markers that identify Pentecostals from other types of Christians (Poewe 1994; Cox 1995). However, there are also unique histories and local practices that come to define Pentecostals from one region to another that reveal differences worldwide (Martin 2002; Beyer 2006). Growth is uneven throughout the world and there is a decline among charismatics in the Roman Catholic and the historical Protestant churches. Worldwide, Pentecostalism is fragmented and is now largely represented by a post-denominational form of Christianity that is located within many traditions or networked outside traditional Pentecostal denominations among major global megachurches. What Pentecostal studies needs are new methods for tracing a range of global flows of people, practices, liturgies, money, and power that does not neatly fit the three wave history.

Who is Counting? Pentecostals around the World

Defining Pentecostalism is not simply a matter of identification. It is largely related to the various ways different scholars across a range of disciplines from sociology to religious studies conceptualize religion generally and Pentecostalism particularly. It is also directly related to counting and the various problems with accounting for the numbers of Pentecostals worldwide. One of the challenges with conceptualizing and counting is that there are many different studies that use different measures from national censuses that ask a question about religious *identity* to self-reported denominational studies that focus on *attendance*, *adherents*, and *members* while other studies focus on the *practices* and *beliefs* of Pentecostals. Counting numbers of people who identify with a religion, attend religious services, or hold beliefs about a religion are all very different measures. Simply counting the number of Pentecostals worldwide is also problematic, even if the researcher was to focus simply on religious identification. The total number of Pentecostals worldwide does not address questions about beliefs or practices and assumes they are the same. Neither does it offer any explanation for understanding Pentecostals if we do not have other important data like gender, age, marital status, education, employment and a host of other variables to make important observations.

Furthermore, a numerical description of Pentecostals worldwide is not an explanation. For social scientists, statistics as a quantitative approach must also be theoretically driven and focus on offering an explanation about the relationship between variables. Even qualitative data that has a numerical or narrative form requires interpretation. Counting the total number of Pentecostals worldwide does not answer the questions about why they are growing or not growing, what they practice or believe, or for example, the age, gender, education, marital status or urban/rural context of Pentecostals. Every discipline from anthropology to history, religious studies and sociology has a range of theoretical options for observing and interpreting Pentecostalism including secularization theory, rational choice theory, cultural theories, intersectional theory, ethnography, diffusion theory, globalization theories, post-colonial theories, structural theories, feminist theories, and a wide range of other options, each with their own assumptions about how religion is defined and studied. What counts and who is counting complicates the scholarly understanding of global Pentecostalism over time and space, across disciplines, in congregational practices and daily life, with migration from one place to another, as well as ongoing research on a dynamic movement that is itself changing.

Brill's Encyclopedia of Global Pentecostalism and its editors recognize that Pentecostalism is a dynamic movement that has emerged, developed, and transformed over time and space, and impacted the character and culture of world Christianity. Pentecostal studies itself is also diverse and multi-disciplinary and in some cases interdisciplinary demonstrating just how quickly research has changed in the past twenty years. Explanations vary among the contributors and the encyclopedia includes a diverse representation of scholars, disciplines, and explanations for the various stories about Pentecostalism in our contemporary world. The contributors come from all over the world and the encyclopedia includes the most recent and current overview of the field of Pentecostal studies.

Reading the Encyclopedia

Brill's Encyclopedia of Global Pentecostalism is organized from A to Z and structured around four broad areas: regions and countries, themes and topics, biographies, and movements and organizations.

Regional and country entries account for local historical developments, national surveys, local studies, and numerical counts of Pentecostalism. The entries offer a range of interpretations rooted in different disciplines. Readers will find country specific reviews as well as regional coverage that includes some comments on those countries that do not have significant Pentecostal representatives or scholarly studies that still need to be completed. The overall coverage is excellent but also highlights where further studies need to be developed and far more complex analyses need to be offered.

The themes and topics include a wide range of entries that will be of interest for the study of Pentecostalism. Included under this broad area are the various disciplinary studies of Pentecostalism from anthropology to history, psychology, sociology and theology among others. Specialized topics like globalization, secularization, spirituality, experience, cosmology, gender, racism, and migration reflect the current literature on these issues.

The biographical entries focus especially on the worldwide individuals who made important contributions to Pentecostalism. The criteria for inclusion was based on two aspects including being born prior to the middle of the twentieth century and known for playing an important role in a region or country. The editors also focused on including those individuals outside of the traditional North American story with a large number of people from Africa, Asia, and Latin America in the encyclopedia. Biographies are representative of the diversity and range of Pentecostalism worldwide but is not exhaustive of all people who have shaped and influenced this type of Christianity.

Finally, the encyclopedia includes a large number of entries on Pentecostal movements and organizations that have influenced Pentecostalism regionally and worldwide. Movements are loosely organized events, activities, networks, and efforts among people for a specific goal. In this case, Pentecostal movements may revolve around renewal and revival, global social issues like the environment and ecological concerns, evangelism, worship and the practice of spiritual gifts, and public concerns that often intersect with local politics. Organizations more typically refer to Pentecostal denominations, congregations, universities and seminaries, media outlets and ministries, and scholarly societies that have specific purposes. Organizations are also key agents for shaping Pentecostal culture and distributing it worldwide while offering some sense of an identity.

The encyclopedia is aimed at summarizing the most important and current research in Pentecostal studies from around the world that attempts to accurately show the range and diversity of Pentecostalism but not necessarily the full story. Each entry includes recommended reading lists for the reader and we hope that users of the encyclopedia will build upon the works listed here. The encyclopedia will be of value for those just beginning their research as well as those scholars who are well into their careers in Pentecostal studies.

Bibliography

Ahlstrom, Sydney E. 2004. *A Religious History of the American People*. New Haven: Yale University Press.

Anderson, Allan. 2013. *To the Ends of the Earth: Pentecostalism and the Transformation of World Christianity*. New York: Oxford University Press.

Anderson, Allan. 2004. *An Introduction to Pentecostalism: Global Charismatic Christianity*. Cambridge: Cambridge University Press.

Beyer, Peter. 2006. *Religions in Global Society*. New York: Routledge.

Bridges, Lynn. 2006. *The American Religious Experience: A Concise History*. New York: Rowman and Littlefield.

Cox, Harvey. 1995. *Fire From Heaven: The Rise of Pentecostal Spirituality and the Reshaping of Religion in the Twenty-first Century*. Reading, MA: Addison-Wesley.

Martin, David. 2002. *Pentecostalism: The World Their Parish*. Oxford: Blackwell.

Poewe, Karla, ed. 1994. *Charismatic Christianity as a Global Culture*. Columbia, SC: University of South Carolina Press.

Robeck, Jr., Cecil M. 2013. "Launching a Global Movement: The Role of Azusa Street in Pentecostalism's Growth and Expansion." In *Spirit and Power: The Growth and Global Impact of Pentecostalism*, edited by Donald E. Miller, Kimon H. Sargeant, and Richard Flory, 42–64. New York: Oxford University Press.

Robeck, Jr., Cecil M. 2006. *The Azusa Street Mission & Revival: The Birth of the Global Pentecostal Movement*. Nashville, TN: Thomas Nelson.

Wilkinson, Michael. 2016. "Pentecostals and the World: Theoretical and Methodological Issues for Studying Global Pentecostalism." *Pneuma* 38 (4): 373–393.

Williams, Peter W. 2008. *America's Religions: From their Origins to the Twenty-First Century*. Urbana: University of Illinois Press.

Zurlo, Gina A., Todd M. Johnson, and Peter F. Crossing. 2019. "Christianity 2019: What's Missing? A Call for Further Research." *International Bulletin of Mission Research* 43 (1): 92–102.

Michael Wilkinson

Counting Pentecostals Worldwide

Over the past 120 years, the global Christian community has experienced a profound change in its cultural and linguistic composition. In 1900, over 80 percent of all Christians were European or North American. Today, that percentage has fallen to 33 percent (Johnson & Zurlo 2019b, 2). This demographic shift has formed the basis for most major analyses of world Christianity in the past 40 years. With the expansion of Christianity in the Global South there has been a proliferation of new denominations and networks, nowhere more apparent than in Africa (Barrett 1968). In 1900 there were approximately 5,000 denominations worldwide. This increased to 20,000 by 1970 and has now more than doubled to 45,000. The vast majority of these are Protestant and Independent (Barrett, et. al. 2001, 16–18). In this same period, a "renewal" movement has reached to virtually all traditions within Christianity. Alternately called the Pentecostal or Charismatic movement, it has grown from just over one million adherents in 1900 to over 640 million by 2020. This article outlines both the history and the research findings related to defining, categorizing, and counting Pentecostals. Subjects covered include early attempts to count Pentecostals, the development of taxonomies of Pentecostal denominations, the extent to which Pentecostalism has impacted mainline denominations, and statistical estimates of Pentecostals and Charismatics by type, by country, and by region. Demographics on national, regional, and global Pentecostalism provide an essential backdrop to almost every kind of quantitative or qualitative study done on other aspects of Pentecostalism. Virtually every article and book on Pentecostalism makes some allusion to demographics (Anderson, et. al. 2009). Composite figures reported in the tables below are calculated from individual denominational figures that are stored in the *World Christian Database* (Johnson & Zurlo 2019a).

Pentecostals and Charismatics considered together

The case for the Pentecostal and Charismatic Renewal as a single interconnected phenomenon can best be made by considering a 'family resemblance' among the various kinds of movements that claim to be either Pentecostal or Charismatic (Hollenweger 1972). The resemblance appears concerning the baptism of the Holy Spirit, the gifts of the Spirit, and the experiential nature of the Pentecostal tradition. Less clear, however, are the organic connections between various Pentecostal denominations and independent Charismatic networks. In addition, the modern movement appears to have no definitive, historical point of origin. From a demographic perspective, all forms of Pentecostalism and the Charismatic Movement are counted as part of the overall global Renewal phenomenon.

Early history of counting Pentecostals

In the mid-1960s, Anglican researcher David B. Barrett wrote an article on African Independent Churches for the *World Christian Handbook* (*WCH*), a publication that reported only on a portion of the Anglican and Protestant worlds (Grubb 1968). After contributing to the *WCH*, Barrett was determined to extend this kind of analysis to all Christian bodies and consequently produced the *World Christian Encyclopedia* (*WCE-1*, Barrett 1982) that documented, for 1980, the existence of over 20,000 Christian denominations worldwide. Barrett developed a seven-fold coded division among churches: Anglicans (A), Catholics (non-Roman) (C), Non-White indigenous (I), Marginal Christians (M), Protestants (P), Orthodox (O), and Roman Catholics (R). Each of these major traditions was subdivided into minor traditions (for example, Protestants as Lutherans (P-Lut), Baptists (P-Bap), Presbyterians (P-Ref), and so on) (Barrett 1982, 792–793, 820).

Pentecostals and Charismatics appeared in these listings in three ways. First, among Protestants were the classical Pentecostal denominations, such as the Assemblies of God or the Church of God (Cleveland, Tennessee) which could be coded with the single code "P-Pen." However, to illustrate the significant differences between them, sub-categories of Oneness (Pe1), Baptistic (Pe2), Holiness (Pe3), Perfectionist (Pe4), and Apostolic (PeA) were developed. Second, Pentecostals outside of the Western World who had split off from established Protestant denominations were labeled as Non-White indigenous (I-) with sub-category codes similar to those used for Protestant Pentecostals. Third, Barrett recognized the existence of Charismatic individuals within other traditions – designated "neo-Pentecostals" and evaluated by country as "pentecostals" (with a small "p"), illustrating renewal within an existing tradition (Barrett 1982, 820, 838).

It is important to note that the history of counting Pentecostals is directly related to that of counting Christians as a whole; that is, first, Christians are counted, and *then* certain Christians are identified as Pentecostals. This is the reason that virtually all estimates for the number of Pentecostals in the world are related to Barrett's initial detailed work. Barrett was, in fact, the only academic who produced estimates for global Pentecostalism based on individual denominational figures for every country in the world.

In 1988 David Barrett published a significant article in which he developed the Three Wave taxonomy (Barrett July 1988). This typology describes the twentieth-century "Pentecostal-Charismatic Renewal" as unfolding in three chronological waves. The First Wave included denominational "Classical" Pentecostals founded from 1900 on; the Second Wave, Charismatics in the mainline denominations in movements that started in and after 1960; and the Third Wave, independent Charismatic networks around the world, many emerging after 1980. The vast majority of independent Charismatics were placed in the First Wave (64 out of 75 million in 1970, 104 out of 169 million in 1980), as were all of the break-off groups from Protestant Pentecostalism. The Third Wave, at that time still in its infancy as a concept, was relatively small in size (see table 1 below).

In the second edition of the *World Christian Encyclopedia* (*WCE-2*), the Non-White indigenous category was changed to "Independents," and Catholics (non-Roman) were moved to "Independents," resulting in six major traditions instead of seven. In the assessment of the Pentecostal situation, independent schisms from classical Pentecostalism were moved to the Third Wave, which was now labeled as Independent Charismatic or Neocharismatic. This new taxonomy caused a major shift in the numerical sizes of the three waves; the First Wave, the largest category in the earlier surveys, was now much smaller (see table 1 below). Note that the three waves were collectively called "Renewalists."

Table 1. Estimates of Pentecostals and Charismatics by D. Barrett, 1970–2000

	WCE-1 1970	1988 survey 1970	WCE-2 1970	WCE-1 1980	1988 survey 1980
Pre-pentecostals	–	3,824,000	3,824,000	–	4,438,000
Pentecostals	36,794,000	64,335,000	15,382,330	51,167,000	104,546,000
Charismatics	1,588,000	3,789,000	3,349,400	11,004,000	45,545,000
Neocharismatics	–	50,000	53,490,560	–	4,000,000
Total Renewalists	38,382,000	71,998,000	76,046,290	62,171,000	158,529,000
Unaffiliated pentecostals	–	3,362,000	5,300,000	–	10,700,000
Total professing	–	75,360,000	81,346,290	100,000,000	169,229,000

	WCE-1 2000	1988 survey 2000	WCE-2 2000
Pre-pentecostals	–	7,300,000	7,300,000
Pentecostals	–	268,150,000	65,832,970
Charismatics	38,800,000	222,077,000	175,856,690
Neocharismatics	–	65,000,000	295,405,240
Total Renewalists	–	562,527,000	544,394,900
Unaffiliated pentecostals	–	56,800,000	78,327,510
Total professing	–	619,327,000	622,722,410

After the 1988 survey, Barrett published figures for Renewalists in many places. At the time he was finishing the *WCE-2*, he also updated the 1988 survey in the second edition of the *Dictionary of Pentecostal and Charismatic Movements* (Burgess & Van Der Maas 2002, 284–302). These continue to be the most widely-quoted figures of Renewalists (usually ranging from 500 to 600 million for 2000–10).

Critiques of taxonomy, methods, and results

Barrett's efforts to count Pentecostals have been critiqued in three ways: 1) general statements about inflated numbers or not trusting statistics, 2) the chronological inconsistencies of the three wave typology, and 3) which groups should be defined as Pentecostal or Charismatic.

The first critique – that his estimates were inflated or that statistics can't be trusted – was the most prevalent and the least helpful. These were almost always general statements that were not accompanied by any substantial evidence. Examples of unsubstantiated critiques include calling his estimates "wild guesses" (Anderson 2004, 1), "uncertain and contested" (Westerlund 2009, 20), "debatable", and "inaccurate and inflated" (Anderson 2013, 2). At the same time, leading scholars presented estimates with no documentation. For example, when David Martin (2002, 1) wrote that there were 250 million Pentecostals in the world he appeared to have no direct reference for the number, citing only "a conservative source".

Second, the three wave typology suffered from inconsistencies in its chronological sequence. For example, the third wave (independent Charismatics) predated the first two (Pentecostals, Charismatics) by 150 years. In addition, the three wave typology was used by some Pentecostals to promote the Renewal movement as God's initiative in the twentieth century. For these, and other, reasons "wave" terminology was abandoned for the current analysis.

From a demographic point of view, the third critique is the most important and helpful. Barrett's global figure is a composite of thousands of individual figures (denominations and networks) covering every country of the world. Because the global figure is a composite figure, the only way to 'critique' it is to dismantle the taxonomy by identifying which groups do not belong (or which groups have been left out). Despite all the critiques, such an analysis of the taxonomy has never been done. Anderson critiques the general number as too high ("considerably inflated by including such large movements as African and Chinese independent churches and Catholic Charismatics") and then goes on to rebuild a taxonomy of four types that appears to include all of Barrett's groups (Anderson 2010, Anderson 2013, 5).

Recent Efforts to Count Pentecostals

In 2006 the Pew Forum on Religion and Public Life published a report entitled "Spirit and Power: A 10-Country Survey of Pentecostals" reporting findings from 10 countries (Brazil, Chile, Guatemala, India (3 states only), Kenya, Nigeria, Philippines, South Africa, South Korea, and the United States). The report referred to Barrett's earlier work, even utilizing "Renewalists" for the overarching term. While the survey did not produce a new global total (citing instead Barrett's global figure), it performed the first extensive professional survey of Pentecostalism outside the Western World. The report revealed that Barrett's "inflated" figures were too low in some key countries. For example, the WCE (2001) reported that 47 percent of Brazilians identified with the Renewal while Pew's survey in 2006 said 49 percent. In Guatemala, WCE reported 22 percent and Pew 60 percent.

In 2010, in partnership with the Pew Forum on Religion and Public Life, the Center for the Study of Global Christianity (CSGC) embarked on a new assessment of Pentecostalism in every country of the world. While this project borrowed much from earlier attempts, a number of changes were made. First, the term "wave" was abandoned for the less prescriptive term "type." Thus, the three types are roughly approximate to the earlier "waves." Second, the methodology for calculating the number of Pentecostals was made more explicit. Third, the estimates were sourced for each denomination and for each percentage (as described below). The results of this survey were published in Pew's *Global Christianity* report (Pew 2011).

For this new project, the central research question remained, "How many Pentecostals are in each country of the world and how fast are they growing?" This question could not be answered by censuses or surveys because these are limited in scope (only half of the countries of the world ask a question on religion) and depth (most censuses and surveys do not ask about Pentecostals), or change over time (more than one date has not been surveyed) (Johnson & Grim 2013). Consequently, the only comprehensive method for counting Pentecostals builds on demographic data on Christian denominations. Every year Christian denominations collect and publish data on church membership in a variety of ways. The most extensive of these inquiries is that done by the Roman Catholic Church. All Roman Catholic bishops are required to answer 140 precise statistical questions concerning their work in the previous 12 months. The results are published in January each year as *Annuario Pontificio*, listing every diocese in the world. Many other denominations (such as Assemblies of God, Seventh-Day Adventists, and Presbyterians) also produce yearbooks of church membership. Some denominations publish their figures on their web sites. Other churches collect the data but then distribute the findings in limited form via printed documents.

Counting methodology based on denominational data

Starting in about 1960, David Barrett began to collect documents related to the demographics of Christian denominations. These documents accumulated and were archived, first in Kenya, and later in Richmond, Virginia. By the time the Center for the Study of Global Christianity was established at Gordon-Conwell Theological Seminary in 2003, the team had amassed over 8,000 books and one million documents including everything from unpublished manuscripts to articles from obscure journals in Africa, Asia, and Latin America. Since 2003, approximately 4,000 books and 200,000 additional documents have been added to the collection.

The major physical collection of documentation can be grouped under 13 headings. These are (1) around 10,000 statistical questionnaires returned by churches and national collaborators over the period 1960–2020; (2) field surveys and on-the-spot interviews in over 200 countries; (3) extensive correspondence with Pentecostal denominations and networks over the last 50 years; (4) unpublished documentation collected on the field, including reports, memoranda, facsimiles, photocopies, photographs, maps, etc.; (5) primary published documents of limited circulation; (6) 600 directories of denominations, Christian councils, confessions, and topics; (7) 4,500 printed contemporary descriptions of the churches, describing denominations, movements, countries, and confessions; (8) official reports of 500 government-organized national censuses of population; (9) unpublished reports and data concerning 50 government censuses of population by religion that were unprocessed or had remained incomplete, which the researchers then completed; (10) unpublished computer searches and surveys of 12,000 university doctoral dissertations or master's theses on Christianity and religion; (11) bibliographical listings from searches in a number of major libraries; (12) in-depth interviews with bishops, church leaders, theologians, and others, focusing specifically on the meaning, quantification, and interpretation of Pentecostalism; and (13) other documents including maps, charts, statistical tables, graphs, brochures, and so on. As this collection has grown, counting Pentecostals and Charismatics has become more firmly based on membership statistics of denominations in each country of the world, of which the CSGC has now identified approximately 45,000. Each of these denominations is now coded with one of four Christian traditions: Independents (I), Orthodox (O), Protestants (P), or Roman Catholics (R). These four are then broken down to a second level of approximately 70 minor Christian traditions. Some examples include Independent Baptists (I-Bap), Latter-day Saints (I-LdS), Russian Orthodox (O-Rus), Presbyterians (P-Ref), and Byzantine Catholics (R-Byz) (Barrett et. al. 2001, 16-18). This coding system provides the basis for analysis of subsets of Christianity, such as Pentecostals.

Three types of Pentecostals

For the purpose of understanding the diverse global phenomenon of Pentecostalism, it is still useful to divide the movement into three kinds or types. First are denominational Pentecostals, organized into denominations in the early part of the twentieth century. Second are Charismatics, individuals in the mainline denominations (primarily after the mid-twentieth century). Third are Independent Charismatics, those who broke free of denominational Pentecostalism or mainline denominations to form their own networks.

Pentecostals (Type 1)
Pentecostals are defined as Christians who are members of the explicitly Pentecostal denominations whose major characteristic is a new experience of the energizing ministry of the Holy Spirit that most other Christians have considered to be highly unusual. This is interpreted as a rediscovery of the spiritual gifts of New Testament times and their restoration to ordinary Christian life and ministry. Classical Pentecostalism usually is held to have begun in the United States in 1901 though most scholars have moved to a "multiple origins" theory of the birth of modern Pentecostalism, emphasizing early activity outside of the Western World (Anderson et al 2010, 22). For a brief period Pentecostalism expected to remain an interdenominational movement within the existing churches, but from 1909 onward its members increasingly were ejected from mainline bodies and so forced to begin new organized denominations (Synan 1972).

Pentecostal denominations hold the distinctive teachings that all Christians should seek a post-conversion religious experience called baptism in the Holy Spirit and that a Spirit-baptized believer may receive one or more of the supernatural gifts known in the Early Church: the ability to prophesy; to practice divine healing through prayer; to speak (glossolalia), interpret, or sing in tongues; to sing in the Spirit, dance in the Spirit, pray with upraised hands; to receive dreams, visions, words of wisdom, words of knowledge; to discern spirits; to perform miracles, power encounters, exorcisms (casting out demons), resuscitations, deliverances, or other signs and wonders.

From 1906 onward, the hallmark of explicitly Pentecostal denominations, by comparison with Holiness/Perfectionist denominations, has been the single addition of speaking with other tongues as the "initial evidence" of one's having received the baptism of the Holy Spirit, whether or not one subsequently experiences regularly the gift of tongues (Philips 2011). Most Pentecostal denominations teach that tongues-speaking is mandatory for all members, but in reality today not all members have practiced this gift, either initially or as an ongoing experience. Pentecostals are defined here as all associated with explicitly Pentecostal denominations that identify themselves in explicitly Pentecostal terms, or with other denominations that as a whole are phenomenologically Pentecostal in teaching and practice.

Among Protestants (coded as "P-") are Pentecostal denominations such as the Assemblies of God. Sub-categories of Oneness (Pe1), Baptistic (Pe2), Holiness (Pe3), Perfectionist (Pe4), and Apostolic (PeA) were retained from earlier research. Each minor tradition within Pentecostalism (currently limited to codes beginning with P-Pe) is considered to be 100 percent Pentecostal (all members of Pentecostal denominations are counted as Pentecostals).

Charismatics (Type 2)

Charismatics are defined as Christians affiliated to non-pentecostal denominations (Anglican, Protestant, Catholic, Orthodox) who receive the experiences above in what has been termed the Charismatic Movement. The Charismatic Movement's roots go back to early Pentecostalism, but its rapid expansion has been mainly since 1960 (later called the Charismatic renewal). Charismatics usually describe themselves as having been "renewed in the Spirit" and as experiencing the Spirit's supernatural and miraculous and energizing power. They remain within, and form organized renewal groups within, their older mainline non-pentecostal denominations (instead of leaving to join Pentecostal denominations). They demonstrate any or all of the *charismata pneumatika* (gifts of the Spirit) including signs and wonders (but with *glossolalia* regarded as optional). Concerning the key word, note that "In the technical Pauline sense charismata (AV, gifts) denote extraordinary powers, distinguishing certain Christians and enabling them to serve the church of Christ, the reception of which is due to the power of divine grace operating in their souls by the Holy Spirit" (Thayer 1977, 667).

Type 2 recognizes the existence of pentecostal individuals within the Anglican, Roman Catholic, Orthodox, and Protestant traditions. These are designated "Charismatic" and evaluated by country as Catholic Charismatics, Anglican Charismatics, and so on, designating renewal within an existing tradition. For example, the beginning of the Charismatic movement in Anglican churches is described by Episcopal priest Dennis Bennett in *Nine O'clock in the Morning* (1970). Traditions are assessed to determine what percentage of adherents identifies themselves as Charismatics, ranging from 0–100%. Self-identification percentages for Charismatics were calculated by contacting renewal agencies working within denominations.

Independent Charismatics (Type 3)

While the classification and chronology of the first two types is straightforward, there are thousands of churches and movements that 'resemble' the first two types but do not fit their definitions. These constitute a third type and often pre-date the first two types. For lack of a better term, these are called "Independent Charismatics." Part of the rationale for this term is the fact that they are largely found in the Independent category of Barrett's overall taxonomy of Christians. Thus, Type 3 includes Pentecostal or semi-pentecostal members of the 250-year-old Independent movement of Christians, primarily in the Global South, of churches begun without reference to Western Christianity. These indigenous movements, though not all explicitly Pentecostal, nevertheless have the main features of Pentecostalism (Hollenweger 1986). In addition, since the Azusa Street Revival, thousands of schismatic or other independent Charismatic churches have come out of Type 1 Pentecostals and Type 2 Charismatic movements. They consist of Christians who, unrelated to or no longer related to the Pentecostal or Charismatic denominations, have become filled with the Spirit, or empowered by the Spirit, and have experienced the Spirit's ministry (though usually without recognizing a baptism in the Spirit separate from conversion); who exercise gifts of the Spirit (with much less emphasis on tongues, as optional or even absent or unnecessary) and emphasize signs and wonders, supernatural miracles and power encounters; but also do not identify themselves as either Pentecostals (Type 1) or Charismatics (Type 2). In a number of countries they exhibit Pentecostal and Charismatic phenomena but combine this with rejection of Pentecostal terminology. These believers frequently are identified by their leadership as Independent, Postdenominationalist, Restorationist, Radical, Neo-Apostolic, or "Third Wave."

Thus, the third type is Independent Charismatics (also known in the literature as neo-charismatics or neopentecostals) who are not in Protestant Pentecostal denominations (Type 1) nor are they individual Charismatics in the traditional churches (Type 2). Type 3 is the most diverse of the three types and ranges from house churches in China to African Initiated Churches to white-led Charismatic networks in the Western world. It includes Pentecostals who had split off from established Protestant denominations (Type 1) and who were then labeled as Independent (I-), with sub-category codes similar to those used for Protestant Pentecostals (pen, pe1, pe2, and so on). Independent churches formed by Charismatic leaders (Type 2) who founded new congregations and networks are also included. Some Independent Charismatics speak in tongues, but healing and power evangelism are more prominent in this type than in the other two (Wimber 1986, 1987).

Three types together

One difficulty that has plagued all researchers and historians of Pentecostalism is what to call the overarching movement. Some have used "Pentecostalism" or "Global Pentecostalism," while others have used "Charismatic." Still others have used "Pentecostal and Charismatic." As noted earlier, Barrett originally used the lengthy phrase "the Pentecostal and Charismatic Renewal of the Holy Spirit," which he later shortened to "Renewal." He then coined the term "Renewalist" to refer to all three waves or types. In this study, we prefer the moniker "Pentecostal/Charismatics" to avoid using a neologism.

Pentecostal/Charismatics by tradition

Anglicans
In the early twentieth century there were numerous isolated "pentecostal" Anglican clergy and groups in several countries leading up to U.S. Episcopalian Agnes Sanford's healing ministry from 1953 (Sanford 1983), Dennis Bennett's well-documented experience of speaking in tongues in 1959 (Bennett 1970), and the Blessed Trinity Society (1961). Fountain Trust, founded by Church of England clergyman M. C. Harper in 1964 (Harper

1974), was present in 18 countries by 1978, expanding to 95 countries by 1987, with 850,000 active adherents in the UK served by Anglican Renewal Ministries (ARM); 520,000 (18 percent of all Episcopalians) in the USA served by Episcopal Renewal Ministries; and branches of ARM in other countries as well. More recently, however, the center of gravity of the Anglican Renewal movement has shifted to the Global South, especially to Africa. Much of this expansion is being tracked by a uniquely structured international Charismatic ministry body begun in 1979, SOMA (Sharing of Ministries Abroad), which now covers most Anglican Provinces worldwide.

Independents
Perhaps the most controversial of all questions related to counting Pentecostals is whether or not many of the indigenous and independent church movements around the world should be included. David Barrett, an expert on such movements, felt that they should and offered this rationale in 1988 (revised in 2001):

> indigenous denominations, which, though not all explicitly pentecostal, nevertheless have the main phenomenological hallmarks of pentecostalism (charismatic spirituality, oral liturgy, narrative witness/theology, dreams and visions, emphasis on filling with the Holy Spirit, healing by prayer, atmospheric communication [simultaneous audible prayer], emotive fellowship, et alia). Note that the term 'indigenous' as used here refers to the auto-origination of these movements, begun among Non-White races without Western or White missionary support (Barrett & Johnson 2001, 288).

Note that the Independent designation now includes large numbers of White-led movements such as the Vineyard churches. But the majority of the movements are found in Africa, Asia, and Latin America. It includes African Initiated Churches, Chinese house churches, Brazilian megachurches, and thousands of other groups. All Independent networks coded as 100 percent Charismatic exhibit these characteristics. In addition, networks that were not 100 percent Charismatic were interviewed to determine what percentage of their adherents self-identified as Charismatics.

Protestants
As mentioned earlier, denominational Pentecostalism is firmly rooted in the Protestant tradition, although virtually all Pentecostal denominations have spun off Independent groups of similar characteristics (for example, Independent Apostolic Pentecostals). In addition, all of the mainline (non-Pentecostal) Protestant groups (Presbyterians, Lutherans, Baptists, and Methodists) have experienced the Charismatic renewal, either in a positive fashion, with organized renewal agencies supporting growth, or in a negative fashion, with controversy, expulsions, and schisms. Some denominations have experienced both, either simultaneously or in chronological order. In the past, estimates for the size of the renewal in the mainline denominations have depended on informal surveys from the supporting agencies.

Roman Catholics

The best documented and organized of the various forms of the Charismatic movement can be found within the Roman Catholic Church. The origins of the movement trace back to both the United States and Colombia in 1967. Since 1978 there have been National Service Committees uniting Catholic Charismatics in over 120 countries. Streams of different emphasis in the USA and several other countries centered on (1) the Word of God Community (Ann Arbor, Michigan) with cohesive, authoritarian leadership, which originated as the International Catholic Charismatic Renewal Office (ICCRO) in Brussels, Belgium (and moved to the Vatican in 1987); and (2) People of Praise Community (South Bend, Indiana) and a wide international network of covenant communities, with a less-authoritarian structure and leadership style. Barrett and Johnson worked with ICCRO in 1997–8 to document the size of the Charismatic renewal among Roman Catholics. A second round of questionnaires was distributed, collected and analyzed in 2010–11 to chart changes over the past 10 years. Note, from table 2 below, that Catholic Charismatics make up about three-fourths of all Type 2 Charismatics in 2020.

Results of the methodology

After performing the research outlined above, results were compiled country by country for all denominations. The results are presented here in a series of tables with commentary. Table 2 is a summary of results in a global context from 1900 to projections for 2050 (Johnson & Grim 2013). The table reveals at least six interesting trends:

(1) Over the period 1900–2020, Pentecostal/Charismatics grew at four times the growth rate of both Christianity and the world's population. From 2020–50, it is expected to grow around twice as fast as world population.

(2) In 2020 Pentecostal/Charismatics make up over one quarter of all Christians. By 2050 this is expected to grow to 29.4 percent.

(3) Charismatics (Type 2) were the fastest growing of the types from 1900–2020, but Independent Charismatics (Type 3) are expected to grow faster than the other two types from 2020–50.

(4) In 2020 the largest of the three types are Charismatics (Type 2) at 268 million, but Independent Charismatics (Type 3) are not far behind at 252 million.

(5) Pentecostal/Charismatics are most numerous in Africa in 2020, with Latin America close behind.

(6) Pentecostal/Charismatics grew fastest in Oceania and Asia over the period 1900–2020, but Africa will likely be the fastest from 2020–50.

Table 2. Pentecostal/Charismatics in Global Context, 1900–2050

	1900	Rate % p.a. 1900–2020	2020	Rate % p.a. 2020–2050	2050
Global population	1,619,625,000	1.51	7,795,482,000	0.76	9,771,823,000
Global Christianity	558,346,000	1.52	2,518,834,000	1.03	3,421,107,000
Global Pentecostals/ Charismatics	981,400	5.97	644,260,000	1.58	1,031,500,000
as percentage of global Christianity	0.2	4.38	25.6	0.55	30.2
Pentecostals (Type 1)	20,000	7.99	123,687,000	1.68	203,681,000
Classical Pentecostals	20,000	7.93	118,865,000	1.57	189,907,000
Oneness Pentecostals	0	10.36	4,822,000	3.56	13,774,000
Charismatics (Type 2)	12,000	9.05	268,288,000	1.28	393,183,000
Catholic Charismatics	10,000	8.83	195,475,000	0.93	257,800,000
Protestant Charismatics	2,000	9.67	68,000,000	2.16	128,919,000
Orthodox Charismatics	0	9.67	4,813,000	0.99	6,464,000
Independent Charismatics (Type 3)	949,400	5.24	252,285,000	1.83	434,636,000
Apostolic	24,000	6.75	34,841,000	1.87	60,656,000
Charismatic (former Type 2)	12,000	7.69	39,729,000	2.65	86,991,000
Deliverance	0	7.37	330,000	1.46	510,000
Full Gospel	12,000	5.95	6,390,000	2.23	12,379,000
Hidden non-Christian believers in Christ	1,000	7.81	4,139,000	2.34	8,283,000
Media believers	0	8.76	1,273,000	2.11	2,384,000
Non-traditional, house, cell	4,000	7.76	26,980,000	0.52	31,500,000
Oneness	25,000	5.90	14,070,000	1.83	24,251,000
Pentecostal (former Type 1)	863,400	4.26	67,765,000	2.18	129,380,000
Word of Faith	0	8.67	1,328,000	1.64	2,164,000
Zion	8,000	6.22	8,230,000	1.01	11,123,000
Others in non-Charismatic networks	0	11.80	47,210,000	1.07	65,015,000

Table 2. Pentecostal/Charismatics in Global Context, 1900–2050 (*cont.*)

	1900	Rate % p.a. 1900–2020	2020	Rate % p.a. 2020–2050	2050
RENEWAL MEMBERS ON 6 CONTINENTS					
Africa	901,000	5.32	230,220,000	2.26	450,689,000
Asia	4,300	9.43	125,395,000	1.81	214,497,000
Europe	20,000	6.20	21,116,000	0.88	27,436,000
Latin America	10,000	8.78	195,222,000	0.74	243,225,000
Northern America	46,100	6.51	67,771,000	0.91	89,025,000
Oceania	0	9.69	4,536,000	1.27	6,627,000

Data source: Todd M. Johnson and Gina A. Zurlo, eds., *World Christian Database* (Leiden/Boston: Brill, accessed July 2019)

In 1900 the three largest Pentecostal/Charismatic populations were in South Africa, Nigeria, and the United States (see table 3 below). South Africa contained a much higher concentration of Pentecostal Christians than any other country (16.4 percent, see table 4 below) due to the growing presence of indigenous African movements with Pentecostal characteristics in the early twentieth century. In 2020, the countries with the most Pentecostal/Charismatics were Brazil, the United States, Nigeria and the Philippines. Wherever Christianity reached during the twentieth century, to a large extent Pentecostals and Charismatics did as well.

Table 3. Countries with the most Pentecostal/Charismatics, 1900 and 2020

Country	Pentecostal/Charismatics 1900	Country	Pentecostal/Charismatics 2020
South Africa	805,000	Brazil	108,000,000
Nigeria	96,000	United States	65,000,000
United States	46,100	Nigeria	60,000,000
Germany	20,000	Philippines	38,000,000
Trinidad & Tobago	10,000	China	37,000,000
China	2,000	Congo DR	28,000,000
India	1,800	South Africa	27,700,000
South Korea	500	India	21,000,000
		Mexico	17,450,000
		Kenya	17,300,000

Data source: Todd M. Johnson and Gina A. Zurlo, eds., *World Christian Database* (Leiden/Boston: Brill, accessed July 2019)

Table 4. Countries with the highest percentage of Pentecostal/Charismatics, 1900 and 2020

Country	Percent 1900	Country	Percent 2020
South Africa	16.4	Zimbabwe	52.3
Trinidad & Tobago	3.6	Brazil	50.5
Nigeria	0.6	Guatemala	50.1
United States	0.1	South Africa	47.2
Germany	0.0	Puerto Rico	45.2
South Korea	0.0	Eswatini	41.3
India	0.0	Vanuatu	37.4
China	0.0	Ghana	37.4
Russia	0.0	Chile	35.2
Japan	0.0	Philippines	34.6

(Limited to countries with over 100,000 Christians)
Data source: Todd M. Johnson and Gina A. Zurlo, eds., *World Christian Database* (Leiden/Boston: Brill, accessed July 2019)

Countries in which large populations held to animistic and spiritist traditions generally embraced Pentecostalism due to its emphasis on signs, wonders, and miracles – phenomena compatible with those in their former tribal religions. One example of this is sub-Saharan Africa, which moved largely from ethnoreligions to Christianity in the past century. Today, countries with the highest percentages of Pentecostal/Charismatics are found in the Global South, with a preponderance of countries in southern Africa and Latin America (table 4).

Pentecostal/Charismatics are currently growing the fastest where Christianity is relatively new, such as in Qatar and Bhutan (table 5). The fastest growth rates over the entire century (1900–2020) reveal those countries that now have some of the largest Pentecostal/Charismatic populations, such as Brazil, the Philippines, and DR Congo. Many regions saw up to 15–17 percent annual growth rates where both Christians and non-Christians embraced this form of Christianity. This huge influx of adherents comes from a variety of ethnicities and Christian backgrounds.

As outlined above, the demographics of Pentecostals and Charismatics are best understood by its constituent parts, namely, the three types: Pentecostals, Charismatics, and Independent Charismatics. Note that these tables show the results of adding up specific estimates related to Christian denominations that are categorized by each of the three types. Tables 6–8 show, for each of these types, the countries with the highest populations of Pentecostal/Charismatics, the highest percentages of Pentecostal/Charismatics in the over-all population, and the highest percentages of Pentecostal/Charismatics among all Christians. Thus one finds that while all Pentecostal/Charismatics are numerous in China, Brazil, and the United States (see table 3), Brazil has by far the most Pentecostals (table 6) and Charismatics (table 7), with the latter the largest bloc of Pentecostal/Charismatics in the country. In contrast, Independent Charismatics are most numerous in the United States and China (table 8).

Table 5. Countries with the fastest growth rates of Pentecostal/Charismatics, 1900–2020 and 2000–20

Country	1900–2020*	Country	2000–2020*
Brazil	17.27	Qatar	12.12
Philippines	15.80	Bhutan	9.74
Congo DR	15.35	Iran	9.50
Mexico	15.13	United Arab Emirates	7.40
Colombia	15.08	Cambodia	7.18
Kenya	14.71	Kuwait	6.92
Indonesia	14.40	Burkina Faso	6.56
Argentina	14.40	Algeria	6.45
Ghana	14.38	Saudi Arabia	5.96
Zimbabwe	14.33	Oman	5.74

* average annual growth rate, per cent per year, between dates specified. (Limited to countries with over 100,000 Christians)
Data source: Todd M. Johnson and Gina A. Zurlo, eds., *World Christian Database* (Leiden/Boston: Brill, accessed July 2019)

Pentecostals (Type 1)

Countries with the largest numbers of Pentecostals are Brazil, Nigeria, and the United States (table 6). Pentecostals in the Marshall Islands (population 53,300) constitute both the highest percentage of all Christians (70 percent) and of the population of the country (66 percent). Pentecostal denominations depend mainly on foreign missions and church planting as means of growth. Interestingly, Pentecostals make up a high percentage of all Christians in Cambodia, where Christianity as a whole has grown recently.

Table 6. Pentecostals (Type 1) in 2020

Highest population 2020		Highest percentage of country		Highest percentage of Christians	
Country	Adherents	Country	Percent of country	Country	Percent of Christians
Brazil	24,581,000	Marshall Islands	66.0	Marshall Islands	69.9
Nigeria	16,708,000	Vanuatu	28.8	Cambodia	42.1
United States	7,691,000	Dominica	24.9	Burkina Faso	31.2
Indonesia	5,425,000	American Samoa	22.4	Vanuatu	30.8
Ghana	5,078,000	Ghana	16.5	Mauritius	30.6
Kenya	4,717,000	Zimbabwe	15.4	Dominica	26.3
Angola	4,709,000	Papua New Guinea	15.2	South Korea	23.2
South Korea	4,006,000	Barbados	15.1	American Samoa	22.9
Congo DR	3,782,000	Angola	14.3	Ghana	22.7
South Africa	2,767,000	Nicaragua	13.8	Liberia	20.9

Data source: Todd M. Johnson and Gina A. Zurlo, eds., *World Christian Database* (Leiden/Boston: Brill, accessed July 2019)

Table 7. Charismatics (Type 2) in 2020

Highest population 2020		Highest percentage of country		Highest percentage of Christians	
Country	Adherents	Country	Percent of country	Country	Percent of Christians
Brazil	61,894,000	Guatemala	35.0	Mauritius	41.4
Philippines	26,732,000	Puerto Rico	31.7	Guatemala	36.0
United States	23,982,000	Brazil	28.9	Puerto Rico	33.2
Nigeria	16,573,000	Colombia	26.3	Brazil	31.9
Colombia	13,229,000	Philippines	24.4	Colombia	27.7
Mexico	11,852,000	Anguilla	17.6	Philippines	26.8
Ethiopia	10,815,000	Uganda	15.2	Qatar	24.6
China	7,491,000	Chile	14.8	Saudi Arabia	24.5
Uganda	7,166,000	Mauritius	13.4	United Arab Emirates	23.4
Kenya	6,668,000	Argentina	13.0	Kuwait	19.8

Data source: Todd M. Johnson and Gina A. Zurlo, eds., *World Christian Database* (Leiden/Boston: Brill, accessed July 2019)

Charismatics (Type 2)
Countries with the largest numbers of Charismatics include Brazil, the Philippines, and the United States (table 7). Guatemala is the country with the highest percentage of Charismatics in the total population, while Mauritius has the highest percentage in the Christian population. Charismatics typically grow by recruiting new members from within existing denominations. Roman Catholics in some countries have stagnant or declining numbers of Charismatics (United States), while others continue to grow rapidly (Brazil, Philippines).

Independent Charismatics (Type 3)
While found in many of the same countries as Pentecostals and Charismatics, Independent Charismatics are largest in the United States, China and Nigeria (table 8). Independent Charismatics experience growth by planting new churches and by schisms from traditional denominations. Of the three types, Independent Charismatics are most strongly concentrated in the Global South where new forms of Christianity have grown in the past 100 years.

Pentecostal, Charismatic, and Independent Charismatic churches continue to grow in Africa, Asia, and Latin America while slowing in Northern America and Europe. Exceptions to this trend can be found among Independents in the United States (still growing) and Charismatics in Europe (some growth among Roman Catholics). Another significant trend is the migration of Pentecostal/Charismatics from the Global South to the Global North. Thus, some of the largest congregations in Europe are African Independent charismatic in origin. In the USA, many recent Hispanic arrivals, both legal and illegal, are either Catholic Charismatics or Pentecostals (Pew Hispanic Center 2007, 27).

Table 8. Independent Charismatics (Type 3) in 2020

Highest population 2020		Highest percentage of country		Highest percentage of Christians	
Country	Adherents	Country	Percent of country	Country	Percent of Christians
United States	33,326,000	Eswatini	36.9	North Korea	90.0
China	29,450,000	South Africa	36.6	Nepal	62.8
Nigeria	26,719,000	Zimbabwe	34.7	Bhutan	50.6
Brazil	21,525,000	Botswana	30.5	Iran	48.0
South Africa	21,507,000	Congo DR	23.6	South Africa	44.6
Congo DR	21,138,000	Saint Vincent	20.8	Botswana	42.6
India	13,800,000	Chile	20.0	Zimbabwe	41.8
Philippines	9,665,000	Sao Tome & Principe	16.5	Eswatini	41.3
Zimbabwe	6,129,000	Ghana	13.8	Cambodia	32.2
Kenya	5,915,000	Nigeria	13.0	Algeria	28.5

Data source: Todd M. Johnson and Gina A. Zurlo, eds., *World Christian Database* (Leiden/Boston: Brill, accessed July 2019)

Conclusion

A demographic overview of Pentecostalism (all types) illustrates the complexities of both the spread of the movement across the countries of the world and the striking diversity of the churches themselves. While current ways of understanding Pentecostals, Charismatics, and Independent Charismatics reveal a global movement of immense proportions, perspectives on classification, counting, and assessment of the movement are likely to continue to evolve in the future. In the meantime, hundreds of millions of Christians across all traditions will continue to participate in the movement – bringing vitality in some denominations and schism in others. They will also promote social transformation in some communities and show little participation in others. What is certain is that, for the foreseeable future, Christianity as a whole will continue to experience the growth pains of this global phenomenon.

Bibliography

Anderson, Allan. 2013. *To the Ends of the Earth: Pentecostalism and the Transformation of World Christianity*. Oxford: Oxford University Press.

Anderson, Allan. 2004. *An Introduction to Pentecostalism: Global Charismatic Christianity*. Cambridge: Cambridge University Press.

Anderson, Allan, Michael Bergunder, André Droogers, and Cornelis Van Der Laan, eds. 2010. *Studying Global Pentecostalism: Theories and Methods*. Berkeley, CA: University of California Press.

Barrett, David B. 1988. "The 20th Century Pentecostal/Charismatic Renewal of the Holy Spirit, with its Goal of World Evangelization." *International Bulletin of Missionary Research* 12 (3): 119–29.

Barrett, David B. 1988. "Global Statistics." In *Dictionary of Pentecostal and Charismatic Movements*, edited by Stan Burgess and Gary McGee, 810-830. Grand Rapids, MI: Zondervan.

Barrett, David B. 1982. *World Christian Encyclopedia*. Nairobi: Oxford University Press.

Barrett, David B. 1970. "AD 2000: 350 million Christians in Africa." *International Review of Mission* LIX:233 (January): 39–54.

Barrett, David B. 1968. *Schism and Renewal in Africa: An Analysis of Six Thousand Contemporary Religious Movements*. Oxford: Oxford University Press.

Barrett, David B., and Todd M. Johnson, eds. 2001. *World Christian Trends*. Pasadena, CA: William Carey Library.

Barrett, David B., George Thomas Kurian, and Todd M. Johnson, eds. 2001. *World Christian Encyclopedia*, Second Edition. New York: Oxford University Press.

Bennett, Dennis. 1970. *Nine O'clock in the Morning*. Alachua, FL: Bridge-Logos.

Bülhmann, Walbert. 1976. *The Coming of the Third Church*. Maryknoll, NY: Orbis Books.

Burgess, Stanley, ed. 2002. *The New International Dictionary of Pentecostal and Charismatic Movements*. Grand Rapids, MI: Zondervan.

Grubb, Kenneth. 1968. *World Christian Handbook*. London: World Dominion Press.

Harper, Michael. 1980. *Charismatic Crisis: The Charismatic Renewal – Past, Present, and Future*. London: Hodder & Stoughton.

Harper, Michael. 1974. *As at the Beginning*. London: Hodder & Stoughton.

Hollenweger, Walter J. 1997. *Pentecostalism: Origins and Developments Worldwide*. Peabody, MA: Hendrickson.

Hollenweger, Walter J. 1986. "After Twenty Years' Research on Pentecostalism." *International Review of Mission* 75 (297): 3–12.

Hollenweger, Walter J. 1972. *The Pentecostals*. London: SCM Press.

International Catholic Charismatic Renewal Service. 2000. David B. Barrett, and Todd M. Johnson, eds., *"Then Peter Stood Up...": Collections of the Popes' addresses to the CCR from its origin to the year 2000*. Vatican: International Catholic Charismatic Renewal Service.

Johnson, Todd M. 2009. "The Global Demographics of the Pentecostal and Charismatic Renewal." *Social Science and Modern Society* 46 (6): 479–483.

Johnson, Todd M. 2014. "Counting Pentecostals Worldwide." *Pneuma* 36: 265–288.

Johnson, Todd M., and Brian J. Grim, eds. 2019. *World Religion Database*. Leiden: Brill.

Johnson, Todd M., and Brian J. Grim. 2013. *The World's Religions in Figures: An Introduction to International Religious Demography*. Oxford: Wiley-Blackwell.

Johnson, Todd M., and Kenneth R. Ross, eds. 2009. *Atlas of Global Christianity, 1910–2010*. Edinburgh: Edinburgh University Press.

Johnson, Todd M., and Gina A. Zurlo, eds. 2019a. *World Christian Database*. Leiden: Brill.

Johnson, Todd M. and Gina A. Zurlo. 2019b. *World Christian Encyclopedia*, Third Edition. Edinburgh: Edinburgh University Press.

Martin, David. 2002. *Pentecostalism: The World Their Parish*. Oxford: Blackwell.

Pew Forum on Religion and Public Life. 2011. *Global Christianity: A Report on the Size and Distribution of the World Christian Population*, www.pewforum.org.

Pew Forum on Religion and Public Life. 2006. "Spirit and Power: A 10-Country Survey of Pentecostals," www.pewforum.org.

Pew Hispanic Center. 2007. *Changing Faiths: Latinos and the Transformation of American Religion.* Washington, D.C.: Pew Research Center.

Phillips, Ron. 2011. *An Essential Guide to Speaking in Tongues.* Vol. 2, *Foundations of the Holy Spirit.* Lake Mary, FL: Charisma House.

Sanford, Agnes Mary White. 1983. *The Healing Light.* New York: Ballantine Books.

Synan, Vinson. 1972. *The Holiness-Pentecostal Movement in the United States.* Grand Rapids, MI: Eerdmans.

Thayer, Joseph Henry. 1977 [1886]. *Greek-English Lexicon of the New Testament.* Grand Rapids, MI: Zondervan.

Wagner, Peter C. 1988. *The Third Wave of the Holy Spirit: Encountering the Power of Signs and Wonders Today.* Ann Arbor, MI: Servant Publications.

Wagner, Peter C. 1987. *Signs and Wonders Today.* Portland, OR: Creation House.

Westerlund, David, ed. 2009. *Global Pentecostalism: Encounters with Other Religious Traditions.* London: I.B. Tauris.

Wimber, John, and Kevin Springer. 1987. *Power Healing.* San Francisco: Harper & Row.

Wimber, John, and Kevin Springer. 1986. *Power Evangelism.* San Francisco: Harper & Row.

Todd M. Johnson

Pentecostals/Charismatics by Country, Region, Continent and Globe

The following table contains data on Pentecostals/Charismatics in every country of the world. Each column includes an estimate for 1970 and 2020. Short explanations of each column are presented below.

Country/region
Short name of country (United Nations) and United Nations regions and continents
Year
1970 and 2020
Population
United Nations estimates for the country/region population
Christians
Christians of all traditions (Catholic, Orthodox, Protestant, Independent)
% Christians
Percentage of the country/region that are Christian
Pentecostals/Charismatics
Pentecostals/Charismatics of all types (1, 2, and 3)
% of Xns
Percentage of all Christians who are Pentecostal/Charismatic
Growth 1970–2020
Annual average growth rate of all Pentecostals/Charismatics from 1970 to 2020
Type 1: % of P/C
Percentage of all Pentecostals/Charismatics that are Type 1: Classical Pentecostals
Type 2: % of P/C
Percentage of all Pentecostals/Charismatics that are Type 2: Charismatics in non-Pentecostal traditions
Type 3: % of P/C
Percentage of all Pentecostals/Charismatics that are Type 3: Charismatics in Independent denominations and networks

Pentecostals/Charismatics by country, region, continent and globe

Country / Region	Year	Population	Christians	%	Pentecostals/ Charismatics	% of Xns	Growth 1970–2020	Type 1: % of Ren	Type 2: % of Ren	Type 3: % of Ren
Afghanistan	1970	11.126.000	5.000	0,0	30	0,6		0,0	0,0	100,0
	2020	38.055.000	7.500	0,0	3.000	39,8	9,65	14,7	14,1	71,2
Albania	1970	2.151.000	173.000	8,0	400	0,2		100,0	0,0	0,0
	2020	2.942.000	1.082.000	36,8	50.000	4,6	10,14	8,9	65,3	25,8
Algeria	1970	14.550.000	100.000	0,7	2.500	2,5		40,0	0,0	60,0
	2020	43.333.000	129.000	0,3	40.000	30,9	5,70	0,3	7,5	92,2
American Samoa	1970	27.300	27.000	99,0	1.600	5,9	5,53	94,0	0,0	6,0
	2020	55.800	54.400	97,5	23.500	43,2		53,1	24,8	22,0
Andorra	1970	24.300	24.100	99,1	0	0,0		0,0	0,0	0,0
	2020	77.200	69.500	90,0	800	1,2	9,16	0,0	86,9	13,1
Angola	1970	6.776.000	5.176.000	76,4	65.100	1,3		15,4	0,0	84,6
	2020	32.827.000	30.592.000	93,2	8.200.000	26,8	10,16	57,4	25,6	16,9
Anguilla	1970	6.400	6.200	96,1	0	0,0		0,0	0,0	0,0
	2020	15.300	13.600	88,9	2.800	20,6	11,93	0,0	95,9	4,1
Antigua & Barbuda	1970	67.100	65.700	97,9	830	1,3		97,0	0,0	3,0
	2020	105.000	98.000	93,2	16.800	17,2	6,21	51,1	37,8	11,1
Argentina	1970	23.973.000	22.937.000	95,7	366.000	1,6		26,8	0,1	73,1
	2020	45.510.000	40.431.000	88,8	9.300.000	23,0	6,68	17,4	63,4	19,2
Armenia	1970	2.525.000	865.000	34,3	2.100	0,2		0,0	0,0	100,0
	2020	2.939.000	2.774.000	94,4	120.000	4,3	8,43	25,9	46,1	28,0
Aruba	1970	59.100	57.200	96,9	160	0,3		93,4	6,2	0,4
	2020	106.000	102.000	95,6	8.000	7,9	8,13	14,0	67,6	18,4
Australia	1970	12.843.000	11.945.000	93,0	102.000	0,9		20,7	8,7	70,6
	2020	25.398.000	13.744.000	54,1	1.550.000	11,3	5,59	18,6	64,7	16,7
Austria	1970	7.516.000	7.268.000	96,7	13.600	0,2		14,7	0,0	85,3
	2020	8.782.000	6.278.000	71,5	270.000	4,3	6,16	8,1	84,4	7,5
Azerbaijan	1970	5.180.000	263.000	5,1	0	0,0		0,0	0,0	0,0
	2020	10.100.000	246.000	2,4	14.000	5,7	15,59	0,0	84,5	15,5
Bahamas	1970	169.000	164.000	97,1	11.500	7,0		78,1	6,9	14,9
	2020	407.000	378.000	93,0	52.000	13,7	3,06	38,5	35,7	25,7
Bahrain	1970	213.000	5.900	2,8	950	16,0		0,0	7,9	92,1
	2020	1.698.000	195.000	11,5	48.000	24,6	8,17	0,0	71,4	28,6
Bangladesh	1970	65.048.000	237.000	0,4	6.700	2,8		12,7	3,0	84,4
	2020	169.775.000	903.000	0,5	325.000	36,0	8,07	19,1	12,4	68,5
Barbados	1970	239.000	235.000	98,2	15.900	6,8		69,1	6,3	24,7
	2020	288.000	272.000	94,7	62.000	22,8	2,76	70,2	18,4	11,4
Belarus	1970	8.978.000	5.214.000	58,1	17.000	0,3		70,8	28,5	0,7
	2020	9.415.000	7.409.000	78,7	240.000	3,2	5,44	86,6	7,3	6,1
Belgium	1970	9.632.000	8.883.000	92,2	11.000	0,1		74,3	0,0	25,7
	2020	11.620.000	7.285.000	62,7	300.000	4,1	6,83	38,0	53,0	9,1

Pentecostals/Charismatics by country, region, continent and globe (*cont.*)

Country / Region	Year	Population	Christians	%	Pentecostals/ Charismatics	% of Xns	Growth 1970–2020	Type 1: % of Ren	Type 2: % of Ren	Type 3: % of Ren
Belize	1970	122.000	117.000	95,4	2.000	1,7		47,0	0,0	53,0
	2020	398.000	369.000	92,6	65.000	17,6	7,19	34,7	52,8	12,6
Benin	1970	2.912.000	515.000	17,7	42.900	8,3		30,3	0,0	69,7
	2020	12.123.000	5.631.000	46,5	2.250.000	40,0	8,24	29,0	11,2	59,8
Bermuda	1970	52.300	50.100	95,8	2.900	5,7		36,6	7,7	55,8
	2020	60.600	52.400	86,5	14.800	28,2	3,33	54,7	25,7	19,7
Bhutan	1970	298.000	950	0,3	380	40,0		0,0	0,0	100,0
	2020	835.000	19.500	2,3	11.300	57,9	7,02	4,4	8,2	87,4
Bolivia	1970	4.506.000	4.279.000	95,0	55.500	1,3		40,5	4,3	55,2
	2020	11.544.000	10.704.000	92,7	1.620.000	15,1	6,98	20,1	66,6	13,3
Bosnia-Herzegovina	1970	3.761.000	1.650.000	43,9	270	0,0		44,5	0,0	55,5
	2020	3.498.000	1.702.000	48,6	33.300	2,0	10,15	5,7	94,1	0,2
Botswana	1970	696.000	262.000	37,6	43.300	16,5		16,4	0,0	83,6
	2020	2.416.000	1.729.000	71,6	820.000	47,4	6,06	6,8	3,4	89,7
Brazil	1970	95.327.000	90.739.000	95,2	7.142.000	7,9		59,6	4,2	36,2
	2020	213.863.000	193.859.000	90,6	108.000.000	55,7	5,58	22,8	57,3	19,9
British Virgin Islands	1970	9.800	8.900	91,0	32	0,4		0,0	0,0	100,0
	2020	32.600	26.800	82,3	5.300	19,7	10,76	48,2	42,5	9,3
Brunei	1970	130.000	7.300	5,6	1.000	13,9		0,0	0,0	100,0
	2020	445.000	52.000	11,7	16.000	30,8	5,68	0,0	18,9	81,1
Bulgaria	1970	8.507.000	5.681.000	66,8	48.000	0,8		100,0	0,0	0,0
	2020	6.941.000	5.748.000	82,8	160.000	2,8	2,44	66,9	2,5	30,7
Burkina Faso	1970	5.625.000	523.000	9,3	89.500	17,1		92,3	0,4	7,3
	2020	20.903.000	4.965.000	23,8	2.048.000	41,2	6,46	75,7	19,5	4,7
Burundi	1970	3.456.000	2.577.000	74,6	98.000	3,8		99,4	0,1	0,5
	2020	11.939.000	11.220.000	94,0	2.000.000	17,8	6,22	52,8	31,5	15,7
Cabo Verde	1970	270.000	269.000	99,5	10	0,0		0,0	0,0	100,0
	2020	567.000	539.000	95,0	38.000	7,1	17,92	3,8	48,0	48,2
Cambodia	1970	6.995.000	33.300	0,5	2.000	6,0		0,0	0,0	100,0
	2020	16.716.000	471.000	2,8	365.000	77,5	10,96	54,3	4,2	41,6
Cameroon	1970	6.528.000	3.152.000	48,3	90.900	2,9		51,8	8,8	39,4
	2020	25.958.000	15.922.000	61,3	2.400.000	15,1	6,77	22,3	36,1	41,5
Canada	1970	21.453.000	20.264.000	94,5	709.000	3,5		37,8	27,8	34,4
	2020	37.603.000	23.519.000	62,5	2.750.000	11,7	2,75	16,0	71,8	12,2
Caribbean Netherlands	1970	10.400	10.000	96,6	22	0,2		45,5	54,5	0,0
	2020	26.200	23.900	91,3	1.600	6,7	8,95	51,9	34,6	13,6
Cayman Islands	1970	9.100	8.300	90,6	290	3,4		14,0	0,0	86,0
	2020	63.900	51.700	80,9	9.200	17,8	7,19	33,6	41,3	25,1

Pentecostals/Charismatics by country, region, continent and globe (*cont.*)

Country / Region	Year	Population	Christians	%	Pentecostals/ Charismatics	% of Xns	Growth 1970–2020	Type 1: % of Ren	Type 2: % of Ren	Type 3: % of Ren
Central African Republic	1970	1.829.000	1.162.000	63,6	99.900	8,6		50,0	0,0	50,0
	2020	4.921.000	3.691.000	75,0	930.000	25,2	4,56	14,0	32,5	53,5
Chad	1970	3.644.000	843.000	23,1	8.000	1,0		67,4	0,0	32,6
	2020	16.285.000	5.676.000	34,9	440.000	7,8	8,34	6,8	63,8	29,4
Channel Islands	1970	121.000	115.000	95,0	780	0,7		76,9	23,1	0,0
	2020	168.000	142.000	85,0	7.800	5,5	4,71	27,5	72,5	0,0
Chile	1970	9.564.000	8.861.000	92,7	1.495.000	16,9		2,3	5,3	92,4
	2020	18.473.000	16.203.000	87,7	6.500.000	40,1	2,98	1,2	42,1	56,8
China	1970	824.788.000	876.000	0,1	93.400	10,7		11,5	15,4	73,1
	2020	1.424.548.000	106.030.000	7,4	37.000.000	34,9	12,71	0,2	20,2	79,6
Colombia	1970	22.061.000	21.541.000	97,6	469.000	2,2		32,5	45,6	21,9
	2020	50.220.000	47.706.000	95,0	16.250.000	34,1	7,35	7,3	81,4	11,3
Comoros	1970	230.000	1.500	0,6	9	0,6		0,0	0,0	100,0
	2020	870.000	4.200	0,5	340	8,1	7,53	0,0	56,5	43,5
Congo	1970	1.365.000	1.253.000	91,8	86.000	6,9		16,3	0,0	83,7
	2020	5.687.000	5.109.000	89,8	1.050.000	20,6	5,13	5,6	42,1	52,3
Congo DR	1970	20.010.000	17.960.000	89,8	4.765.000	26,5		12,6	0,1	87,3
	2020	89.505.000	85.120.000	95,1	28.000.000	32,9	3,61	13,5	11,0	75,5
Cook Islands	1970	21.400	21.300	99,3	130	0,6		78,1	0,0	21,9
	2020	17.500	16.800	96,1	3.000	17,8	6,51	27,7	54,4	17,8
Costa Rica	1970	1.849.000	1.815.000	98,2	34.200	1,9		64,5	0,0	35,5
	2020	5.044.000	4.789.000	94,9	600.000	12,5	5,90	39,7	35,0	25,3
Côte d'Ivoire	1970	5.242.000	1.348.000	25,7	47.100	3,5		10,6	0,0	89,4
	2020	26.172.000	8.921.000	34,1	2.550.000	28,6	8,31	50,1	22,0	27,8
Croatia	1970	4.423.000	4.214.000	95,3	4.200	0,1		31,3	0,0	68,7
	2020	4.116.000	3.887.000	94,4	124.000	3,2	6,99	4,0	87,8	8,2
Cuba	1970	8.715.000	4.026.000	46,2	55.800	1,4		13,4	0,2	86,4
	2020	11.495.000	7.088.000	61,7	960.000	13,5	5,85	1,9	74,7	23,4
Curaçao	1970	144.000	139.000	96,9	180	0,1		100,0	0,0	0,0
	2020	163.000	152.000	93,1	7.200	4,7	7,66	38,1	57,5	4,4
Cyprus	1970	614.000	469.000	76,4	540	0,1		92,6	0,0	7,4
	2020	1.207.000	847.000	70,2	13.300	1,6	6,62	14,1	75,7	10,2
Czechia	1970	9.818.000	7.946.000	80,9	13.900	0,2		28,9	0,0	71,1
	2020	10.633.000	3.694.000	34,7	195.000	5,3	5,43	11,3	66,2	22,5
Denmark	1970	4.931.000	4.766.000	96,6	23.400	0,5		94,2	0,9	4,9
	2020	5.797.000	4.626.000	79,8	70.000	1,5	2,22	17,7	68,4	13,9
Djibouti	1970	160.000	12.000	7,5	0	0,0		0,0	0,0	0,0
	2020	1.000.000	10.800	1,1	500	4,6	8,14	0,0	47,8	52,2
Dominica	1970	71.100	70.000	98,4	330	0,5		90,9	0,0	9,1
	2020	75.100	70.900	94,4	21.000	29,6	8,66	88,9	8,3	2,8

Pentecostals/Charismatics by country, region, continent and globe (*cont.*)

Country / Region	Year	Population	Christians	%	Pentecostals/ Charismatics	% of Xns	Growth 1970–2020	Type 1: % of Ren	Type 2: % of Ren	Type 3: % of Ren
Dominican Republic	1970	4.503.000	4.381.000	97,3	64.400	1,5		57,6	0,3	42,1
	2020	11.108.000	10.506.000	94,6	1.500.000	14,3	6,50	21,0	68,9	10,2
Ecuador	1970	6.073.000	5.932.000	97,7	62.400	1,1		73,3	0,0	26,7
	2020	17.336.000	16.484.000	95,1	2.150.000	13,0	7,33	21,2	71,8	7,0
Egypt	1970	35.046.000	4.574.000	13,1	41.300	0,9		66,1	0,4	33,6
	2020	102.941.000	9.483.000	9,2	680.000	7,2	5,76	30,4	61,5	8,1
El Salvador	1970	3.669.000	3.642.000	99,3	149.000	4,1		76,3	0,7	23,0
	2020	6.479.000	6.243.000	96,4	1.700.000	27,2	4,99	40,8	15,2	44,0
Equatorial Guinea	1970	307.000	273.000	88,9	430	0,2		0,0	0,0	100,0
	2020	1.406.000	1.263.000	89,8	50.000	4,0	9,99	14,9	57,9	27,1
Eritrea	1970	1.812.000	857.000	47,3	700	0,1		0,0	0,0	100,0
	2020	5.432.000	2.552.000	47,0	130.000	5,1	11,01	0,0	92,6	7,4
Estonia	1970	1.360.000	614.000	45,1	2.100	0,3		82,1	1,0	16,9
	2020	1.301.000	474.000	36,5	26.000	5,5	5,19	40,2	43,8	16,0
Eswatini	1970	446.000	300.000	67,3	82.100	27,4		6,8	0,0	93,2
	2020	1.439.000	1.286.000	89,4	595.000	46,3	4,04	8,4	2,3	89,3
Ethiopia	1970	28.415.000	15.005.000	52,8	213.000	1,4		3,8	41,5	54,7
	2020	112.759.000	67.491.000	59,9	14.000.000	20,7	8,73	4,7	77,2	18,0
Faeroe Islands	1970	39.100	39.000	99,9	210	0,5		71,4	0,0	28,6
	2020	49.900	48.800	97,9	4.100	8,4	6,12	35,3	57,5	7,1
Falkland Islands	1970	2.000	1.900	93,0	0	0,0		0,0	0,0	0,0
	2020	2.900	2.300	80,0	300	12,8	7,04	0,0	100,0	0,0
Fiji	1970	521.000	263.000	50,5	20.800	7,9		96,0	0,3	3,7
	2020	925.000	598.000	64,6	200.000	33,5	4,63	38,1	23,1	38,8
Finland	1970	4.612.000	4.446.000	96,4	51.100	1,1		99,8	0,2	0,0
	2020	5.580.000	4.304.000	77,1	300.000	7,0	3,60	21,8	76,1	2,0
France	1970	50.844.000	42.644.000	83,9	149.000	0,3		42,6	0,1	57,4
	2020	65.721.000	41.497.000	63,1	1.000.000	2,4	3,89	12,5	54,0	33,5
French Guiana	1970	47.900	43.800	91,3	760	1,7		65,8	0,0	34,2
	2020	304.000	257.000	84,5	15.500	6,0	6,22	20,0	66,6	13,4
French Polynesia	1970	110.000	106.000	96,1	1.100	1,0		0,0	0,0	100,0
	2020	291.000	272.000	93,7	27.000	9,9	6,67	15,8	78,3	5,9
Gabon	1970	590.000	518.000	87,8	3.200	0,6		31,3	3,1	65,6
	2020	2.151.000	1.844.000	85,7	190.000	10,3	8,51	24,7	21,6	53,7
Gambia	1970	447.000	14.500	3,2	410	2,8		0,0	0,0	100,0
	2020	2.293.000	108.000	4,7	22.000	20,4	8,31	11,7	15,1	73,2
Georgia	1970	4.713.000	1.656.000	35,1	50	0,0		0,0	100,0	0,0
	2020	3.899.000	3.351.000	86,0	32.000	1,0	13,80	0,0	18,3	81,7
Germany	1970	78.573.000	70.516.000	89,7	811.000	1,1		13,1	1,3	85,6
	2020	82.540.000	54.411.000	65,9	1.250.000	2,3	0,87	18,2	43,7	38,1

Pentecostals/Charismatics by country, region, continent and globe (cont.)

Country / Region	Year	Population	Christians	%	Pentecostals/ Charismatics	% of Xns	Growth 1970–2020	Type 1: % of Ren	Type 2: % of Ren	Type 3: % of Ren
Ghana	1970	8.597.000	4.344.000	50,5	1.328.000	30,6		15,4	0,2	84,4
	2020	30.734.000	22.326.000	72,6	11.500.000	51,5	4,41	44,2	19,1	36,8
Gibraltar	1970	28.600	26.500	92,6	20	0,1		0,0	100,0	0,0
	2020	35.000	31.100	88,9	3.000	9,6	10,54	0,0	100,0	0,0
Greece	1970	8.660.000	8.510.000	98,3	10.700	0,1		29,1	41,3	29,6
	2020	11.103.000	9.872.000	88,9	132.000	1,3	5,16	2,0	78,1	20,0
Greenland	1970	46.100	45.300	98,3	500	1,1		100,0	0,0	0,0
	2020	56.800	54.300	95,7	6.200	11,4	5,16	36,1	56,1	7,8
Grenada	1970	94.400	93.500	99,0	1.900	2,1		56,7	5,7	37,6
	2020	109.000	105.000	96,3	18.000	17,1	4,56	42,5	32,6	24,9
Guadeloupe	1970	319.000	310.000	97,0	1.100	0,4		63,6	0,0	36,4
	2020	448.000	428.000	95,4	23.300	5,4	6,30	18,0	75,4	6,5
Guam	1970	83.900	80.700	96,2	2.700	3,4		51,4	36,7	11,9
	2020	169.000	158.000	93,6	12.000	7,6	3,01	25,2	52,0	22,8
Guatemala	1970	5.622.000	5.586.000	99,4	197.000	3,5		56,3	0,6	43,2
	2020	17.911.000	17.416.000	97,2	8.980.000	51,6	7,94	15,7	69,8	14,5
Guinea	1970	4.220.000	59.800	1,4	1.200	1,9		0,0	0,0	100,0
	2020	13.751.000	467.000	3,4	115.000	24,6	9,63	9,6	15,7	74,7
Guinea-Bissau	1970	712.000	66.800	9,4	0	0,0		0,0	0,0	0,0
	2020	2.001.000	257.000	12,8	65.000	25,3	19,20	1,9	17,0	81,2
Guyana	1970	705.000	387.000	54,9	24.900	6,4		31,4	4,0	64,6
	2020	791.000	430.000	54,4	180.000	41,9	4,04	45,4	14,1	40,5
Haiti	1970	4.709.000	4.551.000	96,6	184.000	4,1		66,6	0,3	33,1
	2020	11.371.000	10.697.000	94,1	2.000.000	18,7	4,88	27,8	47,2	24,9
Holy See	1970	640	640	100,0	0	0,0		0,0	0,0	0,0
	2020	800	800	100,0	80	10,0	4,25	0,0	100,0	0,0
Honduras	1970	2.717.000	2.664.000	98,1	30.500	1,1		71,1	0,7	28,3
	2020	9.719.000	9.305.000	95,7	1.700.000	18,3	8,37	43,1	40,8	16,1
Hong Kong	1970	3.873.000	623.000	16,1	82.300	13,2		27,3	40,5	32,2
	2020	7.548.000	1.146.000	15,2	320.000	27,9	2,75	11,3	60,1	28,6
Hungary	1970	10.366.000	8.813.000	85,0	25.400	0,3		36,2	0,8	63,0
	2020	9.621.000	8.397.000	87,3	350.000	4,2	5,39	1,1	67,8	31,1
Iceland	1970	204.000	200.000	98,0	3.300	1,7		59,9	4,6	35,5
	2020	343.000	316.000	92,2	20.000	6,3	3,64	12,1	68,9	18,9
India	1970	553.579.000	20.598.000	3,7	2.714.000	13,2		10,9	2,9	86,2
	2020	1.383.198.000	67.356.000	4,9	21.000.000	31,2	4,18	9,6	24,7	65,7
Indonesia	1970	114.835.000	11.233.000	9,8	2.179.000	19,4		26,7	0,0	73,3
	2020	272.223.000	33.192.000	12,2	11.000.000	33,1	3,29	49,3	11,7	39,0
Iran	1970	28.514.000	268.000	0,9	4.300	1,6		71,6	5,3	23,1
	2020	83.587.000	607.000	0,7	300.000	49,4	8,85	1,1	1,8	97,2

Pentecostals/Charismatics by country, region, continent and globe (*cont.*)

Country / Region	Year	Population	Christians	%	Pentecostals/ Charismatics	% of Xns	Growth 1970–2020	Type 1: % of Ren	Type 2: % of Ren	Type 3: % of Ren
Iraq	1970	9.918.000	401.000	4,0	340	0,1		0,0	50,9	49,1
	2020	41.503.000	175.000	0,4	40.000	22,9	10,03	0,0	8,9	91,1
Ireland	1970	2.950.000	2.934.000	99,4	450	0,0		66,7	6,7	26,7
	2020	4.888.000	4.433.000	90,7	410.000	9,2	14,60	3,2	91,3	5,5
Isle of Man	1970	55.400	51.600	93,1	400	0,8		25,0	50,0	25,0
	2020	85.900	71.000	82,7	6.000	8,4	5,57	3,8	90,8	5,4
Israel	1970	2.850.000	79.000	2,8	1.900	2,4		5,2	26,0	68,8
	2020	8.714.000	175.000	2,0	36.000	20,6	6,04	2,6	39,2	58,2
Italy	1970	53.579.000	47.360.000	88,4	354.000	0,7		89,3	0,4	10,3
	2020	59.132.000	44.865.000	75,9	1.220.000	2,7	2,51	16,6	46,9	36,5
Jamaica	1970	1.875.000	1.714.000	91,4	199.000	11,6		54,6	1,6	43,8
	2020	2.913.000	2.471.000	84,8	460.000	18,6	1,69	56,5	11,3	32,1
Japan	1970	104.926.000	3.100.000	3,0	349.000	11,3		7,4	1,1	91,5
	2020	126.496.000	2.665.000	2,1	430.000	16,1	0,42	15,3	30,0	54,7
Jordan	1970	1.719.000	83.400	4,9	2.000	2,3		35,8	0,0	64,2
	2020	10.209.000	129.000	1,3	11.000	8,5	3,52	16,4	49,5	34,2
Kazakhstan	1970	13.110.000	2.450.000	18,7	4.700	0,2		0,0	64,1	35,9
	2020	18.777.000	4.852.000	25,8	110.000	2,3	6,52	0,0	50,0	50,0
Kenya	1970	11.252.000	7.058.000	62,7	1.123.000	15,9		37,6	0,1	62,3
	2020	53.492.000	43.991.000	82,2	17.300.000	39,3	5,62	27,3	38,5	34,2
Kiribati	1970	51.200	50.000	97,7	540	1,1		92,6	7,4	0,0
	2020	122.000	119.000	96,9	10.000	8,4	6,01	28,1	68,9	3,0
Kosovo	1970	1.213.000	133.000	10,9	1.100	0,8		0,0	9,1	90,9
	2020	2.096.000	132.000	6,3	5.200	3,9	3,16	0,0	63,5	36,5
Kuwait	1970	747.000	38.600	5,2	1.300	3,3		0,0	19,0	81,0
	2020	4.303.000	513.000	11,9	105.000	20,5	9,22	0,0	96,7	3,3
Kyrgyzstan	1970	2.970.000	338.000	11,4	2.200	0,7		90,7	3,6	5,7
	2020	6.302.000	278.000	4,4	25.000	9,0	4,98	28,1	14,7	57,1
Laos	1970	2.688.000	62.400	2,3	40	0,1		0,0	25,0	75,0
	2020	7.165.000	199.000	2,8	18.000	9,1	13,00	15,3	84,4	0,3
Latvia	1970	2.378.000	918.000	38,6	10.000	1,1		60,0	30,0	10,0
	2020	1.893.000	1.552.000	82,0	102.000	6,6	4,75	4,3	92,1	3,6
Lebanon	1970	2.297.000	1.436.000	62,5	4.400	0,3		25,1	0,0	74,9
	2020	6.020.000	2.111.000	35,1	65.000	3,1	5,54	2,4	91,2	6,3
Lesotho	1970	1.033.000	842.000	81,5	50.000	5,9		17,0	5,0	78,0
	2020	2.322.000	2.161.000	93,0	375.000	17,4	4,11	5,6	37,4	57,0
Liberia	1970	1.417.000	392.000	27,7	91.500	23,3		32,8	0,4	66,8
	2020	5.104.000	2.169.000	42,5	820.000	37,8	4,48	55,2	6,3	38,5
Libya	1970	2.134.000	58.800	2,8	600	1,0		0,0	1,7	98,3
	2020	6.662.000	34.500	0,5	2.400	7,0	2,83	0,0	58,6	41,4

XXXVIII PENTECOSTALS/CHARISMATICS BY COUNTRY, REGION, CONTINENT AND GLOBE

Pentecostals/Charismatics by country, region, continent and globe (*cont.*)

Country / Region	Year	Population	Christians	%	Pentecostals/ Charismatics	% of Xns	Growth 1970– 2020	Type 1: % of Ren	Type 2: % of Ren	Type 3: % of Ren
Liechtenstein	1970	21.300	21.000	98,9	0	0,0		0,0	0,0	0,0
	2020	38.600	33.900	87,8	1.000	2,9	9,65	0,0	100,0	0,0
Lithuania	1970	3.137.000	2.212.000	70,5	4.600	0,2		21,7	34,8	43,5
	2020	2.852.000	2.547.000	89,3	49.000	1,9	4,85	10,5	56,2	33,3
Luxembourg	1970	340.000	324.000	95,3	540	0,2		0,0	17,9	82,1
	2020	604.000	463.000	76,7	23.200	5,0	7,83	5,5	85,6	8,8
Macao	1970	246.000	32.600	13,2	1.800	5,4		37,9	62,1	0,0
	2020	652.000	44.600	6,8	2.800	6,3	0,94	24,6	75,2	0,2
Madagascar	1970	6.576.000	3.326.000	50,6	46.700	1,4		1,3	0,0	98,7
	2020	27.691.000	16.205.000	58,5	1.750.000	10,8	7,52	13,4	51,1	35,5
Malawi	1970	4.604.000	2.664.000	57,9	88.200	3,3		23,3	0,1	76,7
	2020	20.284.000	16.406.000	80,9	3.300.000	20,1	7,51	33,0	29,6	37,4
Malaysia	1970	10.804.000	571.000	5,3	34.600	6,1		17,3	28,0	54,7
	2020	32.869.000	2.991.000	9,1	640.000	21,4	6,01	13,2	61,6	25,2
Maldives	1970	116.000	220	0,2	7	3,2		0,0	28,6	71,4
	2020	459.000	1.600	0,3	170	10,9	6,59	0,0	93,8	6,2
Mali	1970	5.949.000	85.200	1,4	120	0,1		0,0	0,0	100,0
	2020	20.284.000	467.000	2,3	50.000	10,7	12,82	10,0	49,8	40,2
Malta	1970	320.000	318.000	99,5	80	0,0		0,0	0,0	100,0
	2020	434.000	415.000	95,7	40.500	9,7	13,26	1,1	97,8	1,2
Marshall Islands	1970	20.400	19.200	94,1	4.000	20,8		100,0	0,0	0,0
	2020	53.300	50.300	94,4	37.500	74,6	4,58	93,7	5,5	0,8
Martinique	1970	325.000	320.000	98,4	250	0,1		0,0	0,0	100,0
	2020	385.000	370.000	95,9	20.000	5,4	9,20	22,8	35,9	41,3
Mauritania	1970	1.149.000	6.200	0,5	0	0,0		0,0	0,0	0,0
	2020	4.784.000	10.800	0,2	2.700	24,9	11,85	0,0	19,4	80,6
Mauritius	1970	826.000	296.000	35,9	1.300	0,4		63,7	31,9	4,4
	2020	1.274.000	411.000	32,3	300.000	73,0	11,58	42,0	56,7	1,3
Mayotte	1970	37.000	360	1,0	0	0,0		0,0	0,0	0,0
	2020	273.000	1.400	0,5	280	20,4	6,89	0,0	29,3	70,7
Mexico	1970	52.030.000	50.620.000	97,3	1.179.000	2,3		14,5	0,2	85,3
	2020	133.870.000	128.229.000	95,8	17.450.000	13,6	5,54	8,8	67,9	23,2
Micronesia	1970	61.400	57.600	93,8	260	0,5		100,0	0,0	0,0
	2020	108.000	102.000	94,5	10.800	10,6	7,71	23,0	68,3	8,7
Moldova	1970	3.595.000	1.665.000	46,3	6.600	0,4		90,9	6,1	3,0
	2020	4.018.000	3.915.000	97,5	60.000	1,5	4,51	26,4	59,2	14,3
Monaco	1970	23.500	23.100	98,2	0	0,0		0,0	0,0	0,0
	2020	39.300	33.400	85,0	1.100	3,3	9,86	0,0	100,0	0,0
Mongolia	1970	1.279.000	3.500	0,3	100	2,9		0,0	0,0	100,0
	2020	3.209.000	62.400	1,9	17.000	27,2	10,82	18,7	25,1	56,2

Pentecostals/Charismatics by country, region, continent and globe (*cont.*)

Country / Region	Year	Population	Christians	%	Pentecostals/ Charismatics	% of Xns	Growth 1970–2020	Type 1: % of Ren	Type 2: % of Ren	Type 3: % of Ren
Montenegro	1970	520.000	262.000	50,5	2.400	0,9		20,8	33,3	45,8
	2020	629.000	498.000	79,1	22.500	4,5	4,58	19,1	34,9	46,0
Montserrat	1970	11.600	11.300	97,6	1.300	11,0		100,0	0,0	0,0
	2020	5.200	4.700	89,5	1.400	28,8	0,15	48,1	23,2	28,7
Morocco	1970	16.000.000	109.000	0,7	380	0,3		13,2	0,0	86,8
	2020	37.071.000	31.500	0,1	4.500	14,3	5,07	2,9	25,2	71,9
Mozambique	1970	9.162.000	2.511.000	27,4	139.000	5,5		70,0	0,4	29,6
	2020	32.309.000	17.448.000	54,0	6.000.000	34,4	7,82	33,4	9,0	57,5
Myanmar	1970	26.381.000	1.350.000	5,1	86.900	6,4		69,1	0,0	30,9
	2020	54.808.000	4.362.000	8,0	1.160.000	26,6	5,32	37,4	22,9	39,7
Namibia	1970	780.000	709.000	90,9	34.600	4,9		10,4	0,6	89,0
	2020	2.697.000	2.462.000	91,3	365.000	14,8	4,83	13,0	50,6	36,4
Nauru	1970	6.500	5.300	82,3	0	0,0		0,0	0,0	0,0
	2020	11.200	8.300	74,2	1.600	19,5	10,71	15,5	44,7	39,8
Nepal	1970	11.998.000	7.400	0,1	3.500	47,0		2,9	1,2	96,0
	2020	30.260.000	1.285.000	4,2	900.000	70,0	11,76	6,9	3,4	89,7
Netherlands	1970	13.002.000	11.606.000	89,3	112.000	1,0		9,1	1,8	89,1
	2020	17.181.000	9.483.000	55,2	425.000	4,5	2,71	12,2	40,2	47,6
New Caledonia	1970	105.000	96.300	91,5	1.300	1,4		30,7	0,3	69,0
	2020	287.000	243.000	84,8	19.000	7,8	5,50	29,3	41,9	28,8
New Zealand	1970	2.818.000	2.688.000	95,4	28.200	1,0		46,9	32,3	20,9
	2020	4.834.000	2.619.000	54,2	420.000	16,0	5,55	21,0	61,5	17,5
Nicaragua	1970	2.398.000	2.383.000	99,4	42.200	1,8		69,6	8,0	22,3
	2020	6.417.000	6.082.000	94,8	1.400.000	23,0	7,25	63,2	22,7	14,1
Niger	1970	4.510.000	16.900	0,4	530	3,1		0,0	12,5	87,5
	2020	24.075.000	63.700	0,3	22.000	34,6	7,75	32,4	10,9	56,7
Nigeria	1970	55.981.000	21.318.000	38,1	3.365.000	15,8		17,1	13,7	69,2
	2020	206.153.000	95.358.000	46,3	60.000.000	62,9	5,93	27,8	27,6	44,5
Niue	1970	5.100	5.100	99,9	0	0,0		0,0	0,0	0,0
	2020	1.600	1.600	96,6	200	12,7	6,17	0,0	63,7	36,3
North Korea	1970	14.410.000	142.000	1,0	8.600	6,1		0,0	7,0	93,0
	2020	25.841.000	99.000	0,4	90.000	90,9	4,81	0,0	1,0	99,0
North Macedonia	1970	1.721.000	1.180.000	68,6	460	0,0		0,0	0,0	100,0
	2020	2.088.000	1.337.000	64,0	10.000	0,7	6,35	14,9	19,1	66,0
Northern Mariana Is	1970	13.100	12.900	98,0	0	0,0		0,0	0,0	0,0
	2020	55.300	43.100	77,9	8.000	18,6	14,30	23,4	30,5	46,1
Norway	1970	3.876.000	3.828.000	98,8	102.000	2,7		55,0	35,8	9,2
	2020	5.450.000	4.611.000	84,6	180.000	3,9	1,15	29,8	52,8	17,4
Oman	1970	724.000	2.700	0,4	150	5,5		0,0	40,0	60,0
	2020	5.150.000	185.000	3,6	36.000	19,4	11,58	0,0	44,2	55,8

Pentecostals/Charismatics by country, region, continent and globe (cont.)

Country / Region	Year	Population	Christians	%	Pentecostals/ Charismatics	% of Xns	Growth 1970–2020	Type 1: % of Ren	Type 2: % of Ren	Type 3: % of Ren
Pakistan	1970	58.091.000	1.156.000	2,0	148.000	12,8		13,0	1,3	85,7
	2020	208.362.000	4.052.000	1,9	900.000	22,2	3,67	35,6	31,9	32,4
Palau	1970	11.500	11.300	98,0	88	0,8		0,0	0,0	100,0
	2020	22.400	20.600	91,6	2.200	10,7	6,65	12,0	84,1	3,9
Palestine	1970	1.125.000	53.200	4,7	1.300	2,5		51,1	0,0	48,9
	2020	5.323.000	43.700	0,8	9.000	20,6	3,90	22,7	32,3	45,0
Panama	1970	1.519.000	1.447.000	95,2	39.500	2,7		78,9	0,9	20,2
	2020	4.289.000	3.866.000	90,1	580.000	15,0	5,52	33,9	53,4	12,7
Papua New Guinea	1970	2.528.000	2.390.000	94,6	109.000	4,6		91,9	1,5	6,6
	2020	8.756.000	8.338.000	95,2	1.950.000	23,4	5,94	68,2	18,8	13,0
Paraguay	1970	2.474.000	2.424.000	98,0	8.100	0,3		57,6	2,9	39,5
	2020	7.066.000	6.726.000	95,2	560.000	8,3	8,85	5,6	26,6	67,8
Peru	1970	13.341.000	13.079.000	98,0	147.000	1,1		74,3	0,7	25,1
	2020	33.312.000	32.131.000	96,5	4.300.000	13,4	6,99	12,6	68,8	18,6
Philippines	1970	35.805.000	33.607.000	93,9	1.182.000	3,5		16,1	1,7	82,2
	2020	109.703.000	99.577.000	90,8	38.000.000	38,2	7,19	4,2	70,3	25,4
Poland	1970	32.636.000	29.420.000	90,1	16.200	0,1		30,3	1,9	67,8
	2020	37.942.000	36.381.000	95,9	1.800.000	4,9	9,89	3,1	95,8	1,2
Portugal	1970	8.702.000	8.393.000	96,5	32.600	0,4		73,6	14,4	12,0
	2020	10.218.000	9.131.000	89,4	560.000	6,1	5,85	17,9	32,6	49,5
Puerto Rico	1970	2.710.000	2.667.000	98,4	177.000	6,7		49,1	15,4	35,6
	2020	3.651.000	3.488.000	95,5	1.650.000	47,3	4,56	13,5	70,1	16,4
Qatar	1970	110.000	3.900	3,6	270	7,0		0,0	24,9	75,1
	2020	2.792.000	367.000	13,1	98.500	26,9	12,50	0,0	91,6	8,4
Réunion	1970	462.000	446.000	96,6	800	0,2		100,0	0,0	0,0
	2020	897.000	777.000	86,7	44.000	5,7	8,34	5,3	87,1	7,6
Romania	1970	20.549.000	17.137.000	83,4	212.000	1,2		94,4	1,8	3,8
	2020	19.388.000	19.119.000	98,6	1.200.000	6,3	3,53	68,4	24,3	7,3
Russia	1970	130.123.000	49.731.000	38,2	1.269.000	2,6		5,1	13,3	81,5
	2020	143.787.000	117.848.000	82,0	3.400.000	2,9	1,99	23,5	38,7	37,8
Rwanda	1970	3.755.000	2.298.000	61,2	98.800	4,3		86,0	0,1	13,9
	2020	13.087.000	11.949.000	91,3	2.420.000	20,3	6,61	22,3	36,5	41,2
Saint Helena	1970	4.900	4.900	99,4	9	0,2		0,0	100,0	0,0
	2020	4.100	3.900	95,4	750	19,1	9,32	0,0	71,1	28,9
Saint Kitts & Nevis	1970	44.900	44.400	99,0	3.000	6,7		63,4	8,3	28,2
	2020	56.800	53.500	94,2	11.000	20,5	2,64	29,8	43,6	26,6
Saint Lucia	1970	104.000	102.000	98,4	940	0,9		26,6	5,3	68,1
	2020	181.000	173.000	95,6	15.000	8,7	5,70	54,5	36,9	8,5
Saint Pierre & Miquelon	1970	5.500	5.400	98,4	5	0,1		0,0	100,0	0,0
	2020	6.400	6.100	94,5	130	2,1	6,73	0,0	100,0	0,0

Pentecostals/Charismatics by country, region, continent and globe (*cont.*)

Country / Region	Year	Population	Christians	%	Pentecostals/ Charismatics	% of Xns	Growth 1970–2020	Type 1: % of Ren	Type 2: % of Ren	Type 3: % of Ren
Saint Vincent	1970	90.500	87.700	96,9	2.900	3,3		41,5	3,2	55,3
	2020	111.000	98.100	88,6	37.500	38,2	5,26	20,9	17,8	61,3
Samoa	1970	143.000	141.000	98,7	3.900	2,7		93,0	1,3	5,7
	2020	200.000	198.000	98,8	29.500	14,9	4,15	53,8	29,7	16,5
San Marino	1970	19.100	18.400	96,0	0	0,0		0,0	0,0	0,0
	2020	33.800	30.900	91,5	600	1,9	8,53	0,0	100,0	0,0
Sao Tome & Principe	1970	74.300	72.200	97,2	900	1,2		55,6	0,0	44,4
	2020	218.000	210.000	96,1	46.500	22,2	8,21	10,8	11,7	77,4
Saudi Arabia	1970	5.836.000	18.300	0,3	2.900	15,8		0,0	24,1	75,9
	2020	34.710.000	2.037.000	5,9	550.000	27,0	11,06	0,0	90,9	9,1
Senegal	1970	4.258.000	229.000	5,4	6.500	2,9		22,9	0,6	76,5
	2020	17.200.000	853.000	5,0	65.000	7,6	4,70	6,0	54,5	39,6
Serbia	1970	6.907.000	4.568.000	66,1	15.400	0,3		45,5	1,9	52,6
	2020	6.608.000	5.916.000	89,5	92.000	1,6	3,64	0,5	75,1	24,4
Seychelles	1970	52.400	51.500	98,3	10	0,0		0,0	100,0	0,0
	2020	96.100	90.900	94,6	5.200	5,7	13,32	21,5	74,3	4,2
Sierra Leone	1970	2.692.000	218.000	8,1	17.600	8,1		45,0	0,6	54,5
	2020	8.047.000	901.000	11,2	255.000	28,3	5,50	13,3	21,8	64,9
Singapore	1970	2.072.000	162.000	7,8	9.900	6,1		50,7	2,2	47,1
	2020	5.935.000	1.205.000	20,3	280.000	23,2	6,92	16,9	33,0	50,1
Sint Maarten	1970	6.900	6.700	97,8	4	0,1		0,0	100,0	0,0
	2020	41.400	36.700	88,8	3.100	8,4	14,23	52,7	32,3	15,0
Slovakia	1970	4.539.000	3.910.000	86,1	5.200	0,1		19,1	0,8	80,2
	2020	5.451.000	4.607.000	84,5	240.000	5,2	7,95	4,7	93,6	1,7
Slovenia	1970	1.670.000	1.549.000	92,8	1.100	0,1		4,8	28,6	66,7
	2020	2.082.000	1.713.000	82,3	47.000	2,7	7,90	1,8	82,2	16,0
Solomon Islands	1970	160.000	150.000	93,8	4.800	3,2		14,6	1,0	84,4
	2020	647.000	615.000	95,0	105.000	17,1	6,36	4,4	63,8	31,8
Somalia	1970	3.445.000	4.900	0,1	16	0,3		0,0	0,0	100,0
	2020	16.105.000	3.900	0,0	400	10,3	6,65	0,0	58,1	41,9
South Africa	1970	22.839.000	17.518.000	76,7	3.959.000	22,6		13,0	1,0	85,9
	2020	58.721.000	48.180.000	82,0	27.700.000	57,5	3,97	10,0	12,4	77,6
South Korea	1970	32.209.000	5.747.000	17,8	324.000	5,6		21,7	1,9	76,5
	2020	51.507.000	17.277.000	33,5	9.150.000	53,0	6,91	43,8	25,1	31,1
South Sudan	1970	3.648.000	721.000	19,8	2.200	0,3		0,0	7,4	92,6
	2020	13.610.000	8.405.000	61,8	950.000	11,3	12,94	14,2	67,1	18,6
Spain	1970	33.980.000	33.203.000	97,7	38.900	0,1		7,9	15,7	76,4
	2020	46.459.000	39.865.000	85,8	1.200.000	3,0	7,10	2,8	69,8	27,4

Pentecostals/Charismatics by country, region, continent and globe (cont.)

Country / Region	Year	Population	Christians	%	Pentecostals/ Charismatics	% of Xns	Growth 1970–2020	Type 1: % of Ren	Type 2: % of Ren	Type 3: % of Ren
Sri Lanka	1970	12.486.000	1.088.000	8,7	22.400	2,1		19,6	0,8	79,6
	2020	21.084.000	1.914.000	9,1	380.000	19,9	5,83	48,2	13,0	38,8
Sudan	1970	10.282.000	318.000	3,1	720	0,2		0,0	86,1	13,9
	2020	43.541.000	1.970.000	4,5	145.000	7,4	11,19	0,0	99,2	0,8
Suriname	1970	371.000	184.000	49,5	1.300	0,7		38,2	15,3	46,6
	2020	578.000	297.000	51,5	32.000	10,8	6,60	15,5	25,9	58,5
Sweden	1970	8.055.000	6.034.000	74,9	296.000	4,9		77,6	21,4	1,0
	2020	10.122.000	5.859.000	57,9	220.000	3,8	-0,59	38,3	54,3	7,4
Switzerland	1970	6.169.000	6.056.000	98,2	66.600	1,1		12,5	1,2	86,3
	2020	8.671.000	6.423.000	74,1	265.000	4,1	2,80	16,2	47,8	36,0
Syria	1970	6.351.000	667.000	10,5	480	0,1		0,0	79,0	21,0
	2020	18.924.000	677.000	3,6	20.000	3,0	7,76	0,0	91,9	8,1
Taiwan	1970	14.693.000	933.000	6,3	178.000	19,1		9,0	0,4	90,6
	2020	23.818.000	1.463.000	6,1	365.000	25,0	1,45	5,1	17,7	77,2
Tajikistan	1970	2.930.000	82.500	2,8	60	0,1		0,0	100,0	0,0
	2020	9.475.000	66.300	0,7	5.400	8,1	9,42	18,0	41,1	40,9
Tanzania	1970	13.606.000	5.008.000	36,8	326.000	6,5		38,5	0,2	61,3
	2020	62.775.000	35.520.000	56,6	6.400.000	18,0	6,14	38,5	43,0	18,5
Thailand	1970	36.885.000	240.000	0,6	55.000	22,9		13,6	1,3	85,1
	2020	69.411.000	906.000	1,3	145.000	16,0	1,96	29,4	40,7	29,9
Timor-Leste	1970	605.000	211.000	34,8	2.000	0,9		100,0	0,0	0,0
	2020	1.381.000	1.224.000	88,6	68.000	5,6	7,31	32,2	67,8	0,0
Togo	1970	2.116.000	584.000	27,6	37.000	6,3		13,5	0,0	86,5
	2020	8.384.000	4.030.000	48,1	980.000	24,3	6,77	49,9	32,4	17,7
Tokelau	1970	1.600	1.600	96,3	0	0,0		0,0	0,0	0,0
	2020	1.400	1.300	94,5	65	5,1	3,81	0,0	100,0	0,0
Tonga	1970	84.400	83.200	98,7	4.300	5,1		29,4	0,0	70,6
	2020	111.000	106.000	95,7	14.100	13,3	2,43	18,3	34,3	47,4
Trinidad & Tobago	1970	946.000	650.000	68,7	67.200	10,3		50,6	3,0	46,4
	2020	1.378.000	878.000	63,7	262.000	29,8	2,76	41,2	13,3	45,5
Tunisia	1970	5.060.000	27.300	0,5	560	2,1		17,7	1,8	80,5
	2020	11.903.000	23.100	0,2	2.400	10,4	2,94	1,0	31,3	67,7
Turkey	1970	34.876.000	290.000	0,8	2.100	0,7		0,0	94,3	5,7
	2020	83.836.000	171.000	0,2	8.500	5,0	2,82	0,0	66,8	33,2
Turkmenistan	1970	2.195.000	117.000	5,3	90	0,1		0,0	100,0	0,0
	2020	6.031.000	68.000	1,1	3.800	5,6	7,77	0,0	25,7	74,3
Turks & Caicos Is	1970	5.600	5.600	99,5	960	17,1		62,5	0,0	37,5
	2020	37.000	33.600	90,9	7.800	23,2	4,28	32,2	19,3	48,5

Pentecostals/Charismatics by country, region, continent and globe (cont.)

Country / Region	Year	Population	Christians	%	Pentecostals/ Charismatics	% of Xns	Growth 1970–2020	Type 1: % of Ren	Type 2: % of Ren	Type 3: % of Ren
Tuvalu	1970	7.300	7.200	98,6	7	0,1		0,0	100,0	0,0
	2020	11.500	10.900	94,8	1.900	17,4	11,74	7,7	73,2	19,1
Uganda	1970	9.446.000	6.429.000	68,1	293.000	4,6		26,9	0,1	73,0
	2020	47.188.000	40.040.000	84,9	10.000.000	25,0	7,31	18,9	71,7	9,5
Ukraine	1970	47.087.000	28.170.000	59,8	469.000	1,7		46,9	27,3	25,8
	2020	43.579.000	37.659.000	86,4	1.400.000	3,7	2,21	30,4	39,5	30,1
United Arab Emirates	1970	235.000	9.300	3,9	280	3,0		0,0	89,3	10,7
	2020	9.813.000	1.077.000	11,0	270.000	25,1	14,73	0,6	93,5	5,9
United Kingdom	1970	55.635.000	49.297.000	88,6	837.000	1,7		23,4	61,5	15,1
	2020	67.334.000	45.200.000	67,1	3.600.000	8,0	2,96	9,3	43,9	46,8
United States	1970	209.588.000	191.277.000	91,3	13.833.000	7,2		14,0	13,6	72,4
	2020	331.432.000	244.313.000	73,7	65.000.000	26,6	3,14	11,8	36,9	51,3
United States Virgin Is	1970	64.700	63.600	98,3	8.400	13,1		76,1	2,4	21,5
	2020	105.000	98.800	94,2	24.000	24,3	2,13	31,7	29,2	39,0
Uruguay	1970	2.810.000	1.904.000	67,8	42.500	2,2		43,0	0,5	56,4
	2020	3.494.000	2.174.000	62,2	360.000	16,6	4,36	13,9	67,6	18,5
Uzbekistan	1970	12.110.000	872.000	7,2	14.300	1,6		0,0	2,2	97,8
	2020	33.236.000	345.000	1,0	85.000	24,6	3,63	0,0	17,6	82,4
Vanuatu	1970	85.400	78.000	91,3	4.600	5,9		38,9	1,9	59,2
	2020	294.000	275.000	93,5	110.000	40,0	6,54	77,0	16,3	6,7
Venezuela	1970	11.588.000	11.184.000	96,5	245.000	2,2		19,3	43,6	37,1
	2020	33.172.000	30.542.000	92,1	6.300.000	20,6	6,71	22,6	63,8	13,6
Vietnam	1970	43.407.000	3.264.000	7,5	32.600	1,0		3,1	0,6	96,3
	2020	98.360.000	8.924.000	9,1	800.000	9,0	6,61	6,0	40,2	53,8
Wallis & Futuna Islands	1970	8.800	8.700	98,9	0	0,0		0,0	0,0	0,0
	2020	11.600	11.200	97,0	340	3,0	7,31	28,9	71,1	0,0
Western Sahara	1970	76.900	31.600	41,1	0	0,0		0,0	0,0	0,0
	2020	597.000	900	0,2	70	7,8	3,97	0,0	32,4	67,6
Yemen	1970	6.194.000	1.700	0,0	200	11,9		0,0	1,0	99,0
	2020	30.245.000	16.000	0,1	3.500	21,9	5,87	0,0	26,9	73,1
Zambia	1970	4.174.000	2.814.000	67,4	280.000	9,9		10,3	0,3	89,4
	2020	18.679.000	16.003.000	85,7	3.550.000	22,2	5,21	19,8	20,5	59,7
Zimbabwe	1970	5.176.000	2.688.000	51,9	599.000	22,3		14,6	0,2	85,3
	2020	17.680.000	14.653.000	82,9	9.250.000	63,1	5,63	29,4	4,4	66,3
Africa	1970	366.459.000	140.023.000	38,2	17.672.000	12,6		18,5	3,5	78,0
	2020	1.352.622.000	667.169.000	49,3	230.220.000	34,5	5,27	24,8	28,4	46,8
Eastern Africa	1970	110.292.000	54.770.000	49,7	3.310.000	6,0		31,8	2,8	65,3
	2020	457.440.000	303.183.000	66,3	77.401.000	25,5	6,51	23,7	43,2	33,1
Middle Africa	1970	41.122.000	30.409.000	73,9	5.120.000	16,8		14,2	0,3	85,5
	2020	178.959.000	149.426.000	83,5	41.307.000	27,6	4,26	22,5	17,3	60,2

Pentecostals/Charismatics by country, region, continent and globe (cont.)

Country / Region	Year	Population	Christians	%	Pentecostals/ Charismatics	% of Xns	Growth 1970–2020	Type 1: % of Ren	Type 2: % of Ren	Type 3: % of Ren
Northern Africa	1970	83.149.000	5.220.000	6,3	46.100	0,9		61,7	1,7	36,5
	2020	246.049.000	11.672.000	4,7	874.000	7,5	6,06	23,7	65,0	11,3
Southern Africa	1970	25.794.000	19.631.000	76,1	4.169.000	21,2		13,0	1,0	86,0
	2020	67.595.000	55.818.000	82,6	29.855.000	53,5	4,02	9,9	12,7	77,4
Western Africa	1970	106.102.000	29.994.000	28,3	5.027.000	16,8		18,4	9,3	72,3
	2020	402.579.000	147.070.000	36,5	80.783.000	54,9	5,71	32,5	25,4	42,1
Asia	1970	2.137.828.000	95.758.000	4,5	7.564.000	7,9		17,5	2,4	80,1
	2020	4.623.454.000	378.735.000	8,2	125.395.000	33,1	5,78	11,8	36,9	51,3
Central Asia	1970	33.315.000	3.859.000	11,6	21.300	0,6		9,4	16,6	74,0
	2020	73.821.000	5.609.000	7,6	229.000	4,1	4,86	3,5	33,6	63,0
Eastern Asia	1970	996.425.000	11.456.000	1,1	1.037.000	9,1		14,1	5,8	80,2
	2020	1.663.619.000	128.787.000	7,7	47.375.000	36,8	7,94	8,8	21,5	69,7
South Asia	1970	741.255.000	23.360.000	3,2	2.899.000	12,4		11,1	2,8	86,0
	2020	1.935.616.000	76.147.000	3,9	23.819.000	31,3	4,30	11,1	23,5	65,4
South-eastern Asia	1970	280.607.000	50.740.000	18,1	3.585.000	7,1		23,8	0,8	75,3
	2020	669.016.000	153.102.000	22,9	52.492.000	34,3	5,51	15,1	55,7	29,3
Western Asia	1970	86.226.000	6.343.000	7,4	21.200	0,3		14,5	21,2	64,3
	2020	281.382.000	15.090.000	5,4	1.480.000	9,8	8,86	2,8	80,3	17,0
Europe	1970	657.350.000	492.068.000	74,9	5.037.000	1,0		33,6	19,0	47,4
	2020	743.390.000	565.416.000	76,1	21.116.000	3,7	2,91	18,9	51,9	29,1
Eastern Europe	1970	276.197.000	157.688.000	57,1	2.082.000	1,3		27,4	14,8	57,9
	2020	290.776.000	244.778.000	84,2	9.045.000	3,7	2,98	27,3	50,1	22,6
Northern Europe	1970	87.354.000	75.455.000	86,4	1.332.000	1,8		42,6	46,6	10,8
	2020	105.863.000	74.184.000	70,1	4.995.000	6,7	2,68	11,8	52,2	36,1
Southern Europe	1970	127.677.000	111.584.000	87,4	461.000	0,4		77,1	3,9	19,0
	2020	151.553.000	120.547.000	79,5	3.541.000	2,9	4,16	10,1	57,4	32,5
Western Europe	1970	166.121.000	147.341.000	88,7	1.162.000	0,8		17,0	1,2	81,8
	2020	195.197.000	125.908.000	64,5	3.535.000	2,8	2,25	16,5	50,7	32,8
Latin America	1970	288.077.000	271.568.000	94,3	12.530.000	4,6		45,8	6,0	48,3
	2020	664.474.000	611.964.000	92,1	195.222.000	31,9	5,65	19,3	60,3	20,3
Caribbean	1970	25.310.000	19.798.000	78,2	798.000	4,0		54,1	4,5	41,4
	2020	44.679.000	37.719.000	84,4	7.179.000	19,0	4,49	22,7	56,5	20,8
Central America	1970	69.925.000	68.273.000	97,6	1.673.000	2,5		29,9	0,5	69,6
	2020	184.127.000	176.298.000	95,7	32.475.000	18,4	6,11	17,6	61,4	21,0
South America	1970	192.842.000	183.496.000	95,2	10.059.000	5,5		47,7	7,0	45,3
	2020	435.667.000	397.947.000	91,3	155.568.000	39,1	5,63	19,5	60,3	20,2
Northern America	1970	231.145.000	211.642.000	91,6	14.545.000	6,9		15,2	14,3	70,5
	2020	369.159.000	267.944.000	72,6	67.771.000	25,3	3,13	12,0	38,3	49,7
Oceania	1970	19.718.000	18.250.000	92,6	289.000	1,6		58,7	7,2	34,0
	2020	42.384.000	27.606.000	65,1	4.536.000	16,4	5,66	43,2	40,5	16,3

Pentecostals/Charismatics by country, region, continent and globe (*cont.*)

Country / Region	Year	Population	Christians	%	Pentecostals/ Charismatics	% of Xns	Growth 1970–2020	Type 1: % of Ren	Type 2: % of Ren	Type 3: % of Ren
Australia/ New Zealand	1970	15.661.000	14.633.000	93,4	130.000	0,9		26,4	13,8	59,8
	2020	30.233.000	16.363.000	54,1	1.970.000	12,0	5,58	19,1	64,0	16,9
Melanesia	1970	3.399.000	2.978.000	87,6	140.000	4,7		87,5	1,3	11,2
	2020	10.909.000	10.069.000	92,3	2.384.000	23,7	5,83	63,0	21,2	15,8
Micronesia	1970	248.000	237.000	95,6	7.600	3,2		80,9	13,7	5,4
	2020	541.000	501.000	92,5	82.100	16,4	4,87	55,8	33,6	10,6
Polynesia	1970	410.000	402.000	98,1	10.900	2,7		59,1	0,5	40,4
	2020	701.000	673.000	95,9	99.600	14,8	4,52	36,4	44,2	19,4
Global total	1970	3.700.578.000	1.229.309.000	33,2	57.637.000	4,7		25,0	8,0	67,0
	2020	7.795.482.000	2.518.834.000	32,3	644.260.000	25,6	4,95	19,2	41,6	39,2

Data source: Todd M. Johnson and Gina A. Zurlo, eds., World Christian Database (Leiden: Brill, accessed October, 2019)

List of Authors

Tom Aechtner (Science)
Obaji Agbiji (Ecology)
Rakel Alegre (Barratt, Thomas Ball)
Kimberly Ervin Alexander (Montgomery, Carrie Judd; Woodworth-Etter, Maria)
Dik Allan (Zhang, Rongliang)
Peter Althouse (Durham, William H.; Eschatology; Hawtin, George; Keswick Movement)
Reginald Alva (Cantalamessa, Raniero; Ranaghan, Kevin and Dorothy; Suenens, Leo Jozef; Velarde, Mariano)
Carmelo Alvarez (Venezuela)
Daniel Álvarez (Honduras)
Leonardo Marcondes Alves (Canadian Assemblies of God; Christian Assemblies in Argentina; Christian Congregation in Brazil; Francescon, Louis; International Fellowship of Christian Assemblies; Italian Transnational Pentecostal Movement; Petrelli, Giuseppe)
James N. Amanze (Botswana)
Linda M. Ambrose (Argue, Zelma; Garrigus, Alice Belle; Gender; McPherson, Aimee Semple)
Allan H. Anderson (Leatherman, Lucy; Missiology; Simpson, William Wallace; Sung, John (Song Shangjie))
Alexandre Antoine (France)
Kenneth J. Archer (Hermeneutics)
Torbjörn Aronson (Ekman, Ulf)
Amy Artman (Kuhlman, Kathryn)
J. Kwabena Asamoah-Gyadu (Africa; Ghana; Liberia)
William P. Atkinson (Copeland, Kenneth; European Pentecostal Theological Association)
Connie Au (Balcombe, Dennis; China; Harper, Michael and Jeanne; Hong Kong; Mok, Lai Chi; Morrison, J. Elmor; Pentecostal Mission, Hong Kong; Asia)
Daniela C. Augustine (Ethics)
Denise A. Austin (Greenwood, Charles L.; Mongolia; Brawner, Mina; Zschech, Darlene)
Diane J. Austin-Broos (Jamaica)
Esa Autero (Bolivia)
Bosco Bangura (Sierra Leone)
Lloyd Barba (Oneness Pentecostalism)
Stephen Barkley (Toronto Blessing (Catch the Fire))
Roscoe Barnes III (Bosworth, F.F.; Lindsay, Gordon)
Michael Bergunder (Definitions; History; India)
Jon Bialecki (Wagner, Charles Peter)
Candy Gunther Brown (Healing)
David Bundy (Dallière, Émile; Dallière, Louis; de Monléon, Albert; Evangelicalism)
Richard Burgess (Deeper Life Bible Church; Redeemed Christian Church of God; Winners Chapel)
Ewen Butler (Pentecostal Assemblies of Newfoundland and Labrador)
Mark J. Cartledge (Socialization)

Daniel Castelo (Mysticism)
Rafael Cazarin (Spain)
Paul Chang (Li, Changshou (Witness Lee); Nee, Watchman (Ni, Tuosheng); Yu, Cidu (Dora Yu))
Barry Chant (Cathcart, William; Harris, Leo Cecil)
Manase Kudzai Chiweshe (Zimbabwe)
Kyuhoon Cho (Pyongyang Revival; Yoido Full Gospel Church, Korea)
Terence Chong (Singapore)
Nikolaj Christensen (Bjørner, Sigurd and Anna Larssen; Denmark)
Brad Christerson (Networks)
Meehyun Chung (South Korea)
Corneliu Constantineanu (Bochian, Pavel; Bradin, Gheorghe; Codreanu, Teodor; Sandru, Trandafir)
Clayton Coombs (Planetshakers)
Travis Warren Cooper (Embodiment, Body)
Osvaldo Costantini (Eritrea)
Caleb Courtney (Johnston, Barbara; Lake, John G.; Price, Charles S.)
Benjamin Crace (Egypt; Jordan; Kuwait; Lebanon; Asia)
Jelle Creemers (Belgium)
David Daniels (Church of God in Christ; Mason, Charles Harrison; Racism)
Tommy Davidsson (Pethrus, Lewi)
Martin Dignard (Sanford, Agnes)
Dony K. Donev (Bulgaria; Ladd Bartleman, Anna; Nikolov, Nicholas; Voronaev, Ivan Efimovich; Zaplishny, Dionissy Michailovitch)
Lord Elorm Donkor (Anim, Peter; McKeown, James and Sophia; Onyinah, Opoku)
Tomas Sundnes Drønen (Cameroon; Conversion)
Dave Emmett (Burton, William Frederick)
Stian Sorlie Eriksen (Norway; Conversion)
Tibebe Eshete (Ethiopia)
Gastón Espinosa (López, Abundio and Rosa; Lugo, Juan León; Mexico; Olazábal, Francisco; Seymour, William)
Wilmer Estrada-Carrasquillo (Caribbean)
Steven Félix-Jäger (Aesthetics and Art)
Moritz Fischer (Bonnke, Reinhard; DR Congo; Osborn, T.L.)
Linda Flett (Bloomfield, Ray; Dallimore, A. H.)
Ambra Formenti (Portugal)
László Fosztó (Romania)
Simo Frestadius (Elim Pentecostal Church, UK)
Michael Frost (New Zealand)
Yvette D. Garcia (Aglow International)
Giuseppe Giordan (Italy)
Wanjiru Gitau (Kenya)
Henri Gooren (Paraguay)
Kellesi Gore (Page, Albert T. and Lou)

Junifrius Gultom (The Indonesian Pentecostal Fellowship of Churches (Persekutuan Gereja-gereja Pentakosta di Indonesia))
Tereza Halasová (Czech Republic; Slovakia)
Arto Hämäläinen (Sweden)
Jörg Haustein (Omahe, Chacha; Bonnke, Reinhard)
Tuija Hovi (Finland)
Keith Huey (Jesus People Movement)
James Huff (El Salvador)
Shin Fung Hung (Dzao, Timothy; Jing, Dianying; Wang, Zai (Leland Wang))
Stephen J. Hunt (Alpha; Holy Trinity Brompton; Politics)
Harold D. Hunter (King, Joseph H.; Taylor, George Floyd; Turner, William H.)
Mark Hutchinson (Adams, John Archibald Duncan; Australia; Davidson, Alexander Thomas; Houston, William Francis (Frank); Lancaster, Sarah Jane (née Murrell))
Monique Ingalls (Music)
Melissa Wei-Tsing Inouye (True Jesus Church)
Jerry M. Ireland (Glossolalia)
Daniel D. Isgrigg (Allen, A. A.; Luce, Alice Eveline)
Mark Jennings (Sexuality)
Todd M. Johnson (Counting Pentecostals Worldwide; Pentecostals/Charismatics by country, region, continent and globe)
Van Johnson (Spirituality)
Evangelos Karagiannis (Greece)
Veli-Matti Kärkkäinen (Ecclesiology)
William K. Kay (Europe; Gee, Donald; Higher Education; Jeffreys, George; Pentecostal European Fellowship; Pentecostal Missionary Union; Russia; United Kingdom; Welsh Revival; Wigglesworth, Smith)
Mimi Kelly (Ireland)
Johnny King (Haywood, G. T.; Philippines; Villanueva, Eddie)
Miranda Klaver (Netherlands)
Rony Chandra Kristanto (Indonesia; Purnomo, Petrus Agung; Sutanto, Adi)
James Kwateng-Yeboah (Migration)
Sang Yun Lee (Cho, Yonggi; Choi, Jashil; Lee, Yong Do; Ra, Woonmong)
Hui Li (Fangcheng Fellowship, China)
Scott Lim (Planetshakers)
Martin Lindhardt (Chile; Hoover, Willis Collins; Tanzania)
Peter Lineham (Oceania)
Yi Liu (Shouters, China; Weepers, China)
Hany Longwe (Zambia)
Andy Lord (House Church Movement, UK)
Wessly Lukose (Abrams, Minnie; Cook, Robert Felix; Mathews, Thomas; Mukti Revival; Ramabai, Pandita Saraswati)
Julie Ma (Prayer Mountain Movement, Korea)
Frank Macchia (Spiritual Gifts)
Giovanni Maltese (El Shaddai (Philippines); Jesus is Lord Church Worldwide, Philippines; Prosperity Gospel)

LIST OF AUTHORS

Bernice Martin (Secularization)
Paulo Ayres Mattos (Brazil; Macedo, Edir)
Michael McClymond (Apostles, Apostolic Ministry; Bethel Church; Hagin, Kenneth; International House of Prayer; Latter Rain; Neo-Pentecostalism; Revival; Roberts, Oral; Wimber, John)
Néstor Medina (Cuba; Guatemala)
John Gordon Melton (Assemblies of God, USA; Pentecostal Charismatic Churches of North America; United States of America)
Naar M'fundisi-Holloway (Cooper, Archibald; Hezmalhalch, Thomas; Le Roux, Pieter L.)
Martin W. Mittelstadt (Exegesis)
Steve Mochechane (Bhengu, Nicholas; Chikane, Frank; Letwaba, Elias)
S. David Moore (Shepherding Movement)
Eugene Mugisha (Rwanda)
Marius Nel (South Africa)
Peter D. Neumann (Experience; Pneumatology)
Eric Newberg (Palestine)
Abel Ngarsoulede (Chad)
Konstanze N'Guessan (Côte d'Ivoire)
Eloy H. Nolivos (Latin America)
Weanzana Wa Weanzana Nupanga (Central African Republic)
Caleb Nyanni (Otabil, Mensa)
Elijah Obinna (Nigeria)
Ryan Joseph O'Byrne (South Sudan)
Lois E. Olena (Society for Pentecostal Studies)
L. William Oliverio (Roman Catholic-Pentecostal Dialogue)
Kathleen Openshaw (Universal Church of the Kingdom of God)
Daniel Ortiz (Riubal, Julio Cesar)
Edward Pawlowski (Poland)
Jean Daniel Plüss (Hollenweger, Walter J.)
Devaka Premawardhana (Colonialism)
Katrien Pype (Media)
Sitna Quiroz-Uria (Benin)
Max Ruben Ramos (Cape Verde)
Ulrika Ramstrand (Sweden)
David Reed (Anglican Renewal Ministries; Berntsen, Bernt; Pentecostal Assemblies of the World; Wei, Paul (Wei, Enbo); Oneness Pentecostalism)
Tanya Riches (Hillsong)
Tony Richie (Inter-religious Relations)
Cecil M. Robeck (Azusa Street Revival; Ecumenism; Parham, Charles)
David G. Roebuck (Church of God, Cleveland)
David Rolles (Salt & Light)
Aaron Gabriel Ross (Hermeneutics)
Denise Ross (Myo Chit)
Joy Samuel (Abraham, K. E.; Dhinakaran, D. G. S.)
Norberto Saracco (Annacondia, Carlos; Argentina; Hicks, Tommy)

Paul Schmidgall (Germany)
Peter Schuurman (Megachurches)
Sally Jo Shelton (Branham, William Marrion)
Iâp Sian-chîn (Taiwan)
Florian Simatupang (Njotorahardjo, Niko)
Christopher A. Stephenson (Liturgy)
Lisa P. Stephenson (Farrow, Lucy)
Adam Stewart (Canada; Hebden, Ellen; McAlister, R. E.; Pentecostal Assemblies of Canada; Statistics)
Steven Studebaker (Soteriology)
Selena Su (Zhang, Rongliang)
Zexi (Jesse) Sun (Shandong Revival, China)
Geoffrey Sutton (Psychology)
Masakazu Suzuki (Coote, Leonard Wren; Juergensen, Carl Fredrick; Murai, Jun; Ryan, Martin Lawrence; Yumiyama, Kiyoma)
Donald S. Swenson (Charismatic Renewal in the Roman Catholic Church)
A.J. Swoboda (Ecology)
Karl Inge Tangen (Norway)
Fei Ya Tao (Jesus Family Church, China)
Allen Tennison (Buntain, D. Mark)
Joy Tong (Guneratnam, Prince)
John M. Usher (Polhill, Cecil)
Ilana Van Wyk (Anthropology)
Wolfgang Vondey (Baptism in the Holy Spirit; Full Gospel; Theology)
Rick Wadholm (Homiletics; Higher Education)
Timothy Wadkins (Mebius, Frederick E.)
Gavin Wakefield (Boddy, Alexander and Mary)
Brandon Walker (Miracles, Signs, Wonders)
Eunhee Zoe Wang (Ha, Young Jo; Kil, Seon Joo; Kim, Ik-du)
E. Janet Warren (Cosmology)
Cheong Weng Kit (Malaysia)
Michael Wilkinson (Introduction; Globalization; Sociology; Pentecostal World Fellowship; World Assemblies of God Fellowship)
Philip Wingeier-Rayo (Nicaragua)
Paulus Wong (Kong, Duen Yee (Mui Yee))
Daniel Woods (International Pentecostal Holiness Church)
Natalia Zawiejska (Angola)
Mary Zheng (House Churches, China)
Joshua Ziefle (Du Plessis, David)

Abraham, K.E.

K.E. Abraham was born to a Christian family on March 1, 1899 near Puthencavu, Chengannoor, Kerala. His parents were pious Christians and regularly participated in Christian activities. Thus, he grew up in a Christian atmosphere that shaped his calling of serving Jesus Christ. Hailing from a poor family, Abraham pursued his studies to earn his living as a school teacher. He did not continue his secular profession for long as he obeyed the calling of full-time ministry. Abraham was the disciple of a well-known Christian poet K.V. Simon of the Brethren Church in Kerala, South India. Simon was also the leader of a local Christian movement called Viyojitha Prasthanam.

During his early life, the family followed the Syrian Jacobite tradition. Although he became a school teacher at a young age, he dedicated his life to God's ministry. His personal experience with Jesus Christ took place during a gospel meeting conducted by Moothampackal Kochukunju Upadeshi of the Marthoma Church on December 1, 1912. Attendance at such gatherings indoctrinated him in the scriptural truths such as baptism in water and spirit baptism. He was baptized by water on February 27, 1916. Within a short period, he deliberately dissociated himself from the Jacobite church and joined the Brethren movement. He travelled as a young evangelist and preached the gospel in many gatherings. His own infilling of the Holy Spirit came on April 22, 1923, which compelled him to detach himself from the Brethren movement. He wrote that he travelled from his town to a remote place called Thiruvanathapuram to wait upon God to fill him with the Holy Spirit. He prayed with C. Manasseh and felt an electric shock passing through his body and a power filling him. He recorded in his autobiography that he was released to a spiritual realm beyond his control. Gradually he began to continually praise God in other unknown languages. According to Abraham, this experience is the baptism by the Holy Spirit, which dramatically changed Abraham's view of Pentecostal spirituality.

Abraham was associated with the Brethren Church as a gospel preacher in the early years of his ministry. After his baptism in the Holy Spirit, he led many people to faith in Jesus Christ and pioneered churches in Kerala. K.C. Oommen, P.T. Chacko, and K.C. Cherian are a few individuals who became leaders of the church later. He worked with Anderson Church of God that was led by Robert F. Cook, who was an American missionary. During the early years of ministry, Cook worked with the Assemblies of God under the leadership of Mary Chapman, but later started working with the Church of God in Cleveland, Tennessee. The disruptions in the relationship between Chapman and Abraham took place during Cook's absence. Cook supported Abraham's demand, that local congregations and leadership should be acknowledged and international mission agencies should not have power and property in India. Thereafter, Abraham and Cook worked together with the same vision in pioneering, developing, and strengthening churches. After the ministry flourished in the following years, including founding a Bible School in Mulakuzha, near Abraham's birthplace, Cook and Abraham were separated.

Malankara Full Gospel Church was a joint venture of Cook's and Abraham's ministry which was officially supported by Cook. This was during a fame of strong national spirit against the British colonial power in India, which led to the independence of the nation. The local leaders like Abraham were against the colonialism that tried to control local congregations.

Abraham was highly impressed by the way the Ceylon Pentecostal Mission functioned without any western support. He had already established relationship with Pastor Paul who founded the Ceylon Pentecostal Mission. Abraham and his coworkers were challenged by the faith life of Pastor Paul who lived like the first-century apostles. They concluded that the monthly support given by Cook would diminish their dependency on God, and they interpreted it as confidence in materialism. Consequently, the struggle between native leaders and western missionaries resulted in the emergence of new leadership by Abraham by 1930. Abraham was charismatic in nature and got the South Indian Church of God registered, which was later named as the Indian Pentecostal Church of God (IPC). This is the first indigenous Pentecostal organization in India. He served as the president for most times in the history of IPC. He penned several books, but *Mystery Babylon the Great Scarlet* is the classic. His contribution to plant and develop indigenous Pentecostal churches in India is unequalled. He was an enthusiastic and spiritual leader until his last breath. He died on December 9, 1974.

Bibliography

Amos, Ashish. 2011. *Pentecostal Churches in Kerala and Indigenous Leadership*. Delhi: ISPCK.
Anderson, Allan Heaton. 2014. *An Introduction to Pentecostalism: Global Charismatic Christianity*. Cambridge: Cambridge University Press.
Bergunder, Michael. 2008. *The South Indian Pentecostal Movement in the Twentieth Century*. Grand Rapids, MI: William B. Eerdmans.
Saju. 2011. *Kerala Pentecosthu Charithram* [The History of Kerala Pentecost in Malayalam]. Kochi: Sanctuary Media.

Joy Samuel

Abrams, Minnie

Minnie F. Abrams (1859–1912) was one of the most influential North American female missionaries to India, who became Pentecostal while there. She was born in Lawrenceville, Wisconsin, and grew up in Minnesota. Dreaming to become a teacher, she studied at the University of Minnesota. However, she was motivated by the life of Fidelia Fiske, a missionary educator, and dedicated her life for overseas missions. She then attended the Chicago Training School for City, Home and Foreign Missions.

In 1887 Abrams came to Bombay (now Mumbai), India as a missionary of Women's Foreign Missionary Society of the Methodist Episcopal Church. She began working as a religious instructor for Christian girls in a boarding school. She later learned the local language Marathi to directly engage with people. Although she intensely desired to engage in evangelism, she had to wait for ten years to receive the approval from her mission board to become a full-time evangelist.

During the summer of 1897 Abrams itinerated to villages beyond Bombay along with the local women. Urged by an inner voice to "go to Khedgaon," she visited Mukti Mission at Kedgaon, Pune, about 100 miles away from Bombay. Mukti was a home for young widows and famine victims, established by Ramabai, a Brahmin Hindu convert to Christianity. Abrams felt that the Lord wanted her to be a spiritual teacher to the young girls and the women

Minnie Abrams, 1859–1912 (right)

at the mission. As Ramabai felt it was an answer to their prayers, she welcomed Abrams. Abrams then left her service with the Methodist Mission to work at the nondenominational Mukti Mission.

Abrams was influenced by the Wesleyan-Holiness and Keswick Higher life teachings, and subsequently became interested in the Holy Spirit. She was encouraged by the reports of revivals in Australia (1903) and Wales (1904–05). Abrams went to Australia along with Manoramabai, the daughter of Ramabai, to investigate the revival. Realizing prayer as the chief cause of the revival, the Mukti community intensified their prayers for the outpouring of the Holy Spirit. Finally, the revival fire fell at Mukti in June 1905.

Desiring to spread the news of the Mukti Revival, Abrams gathered the young women to hold special meetings and conferences at various mission stations. Christian newspapers in India, including *The Bombay Guardian* and *The Christian Patriot* reported the activities of Abrams. She wrote the first edition of *Baptism of the Holy Ghost and Fire* in 1906. Her purpose was to motivate believers to seek the post-conversion experience of Spirit Baptism for sanctification, and the power to evangelize. In response to the teaching that the Spirit would teach the believers a clear language to preach (xenolalia), in the second edition of her book, Abrams made it clear that this was not the case in her understanding.

Abrams visited the United States in 1908 along with Manoramabai for promotional purposes. She preached at many Pentecostal centers, including Carrie Judd Montgomery's Home of Peace in Oakland, California, and the Upper Room Mission in Los Angeles. Believing that the evangelization of the world was not the role of men alone, she recruited six single women to accompany her for the task of evangelism among the unreached people of North India. They included Edith Baugh, Blanche Cunningham, Lillian Doll, Minnie Houck, "Miss Bristol," and "Miss Dempster." Ramabai called them the "Phillipus Class," as they were to be evangelists like the daughters of Philip (Acts 21:9). Two of them remained at Mukti, and others traveled to Uska Bazar, near the border of Nepal. Other American women including Bernice Lee and Jennie Kirkland who joined them later.

Abrams became a leading inspiration for the first Pentecostal revival in South America. In 1907 she sent a copy of her book *Baptism of the Holy Ghost and Fire* to Willis Collins Hoover and his wife, May Hoover, who were Methodist missionaries in Valparaiso, Chile. May was a classmate of Abrams at the Chicago Training School. The Hoovers' correspondence with her about the revivals created a desire to pray for a similar revival in Chile, and occurred in 1907.

Abrams believed that revival was not an end in itself, and the Great Commission would not be achieved without investing energy in evangelism. However, the intense opposition, the hot climate, and the lack of travel conveyance in North India made the work difficult. Abrams eventually became ill with fever, and so left to the United States, where later she died on December 2, 1912.

Abram's contribution to Pentecostalism is manifold. The *Baptism of the Holy Ghost and Fire* is one of the earliest books on Spirit Baptism. Her *Prayer Warfare* is considered the first Pentecostal discussion on intercessory prayer for world evangelization through signs and wonders. Abrams' cultural sensitivity enabled her to become an instrument of the revival as well as its promoter. Recognizing the need of women for the task of global evangelism, Abrams established Bezalel Evangelistic Mission, which was probably the first Pentecostal women's missionary society.

Bibliography

Abrams, Minnie F. 1908. "A Message from Mukti." *Confidence* (September 15).

Abrams, Minnie F. 1906. *The Baptism of the Holy Ghost and Fire*. Kedgaon, India: Mukti Mission Press.

Alexander, Estrelda. 2010. "Women as Leaders in Pentecostal/Charismatic Religions." In *Gender and Women's Leadership: A Reference Handbook*, edited by Karen O'Conner, 533–543. Thousand Oaks, CA: Sage Publications.

Dyer, Helen S. 1900. *Pandita Ramabai: The Story of Her Life*. New York: Fleming H Revell.

McGee, Gary B. 1999. "Baptism of the Holy Ghost and Fire: The Mission Legacy of Minnie F Abrams." *Missiology* 27 (4): 515–522.

Wessly Lukose

Adams, John Archibald Duncan

John Archibald Duncan Adams, 5 April 1844, Lessudden, Roxburgh, Scotland–8 Oct 1936, Dunedin, New Zealand. Second of 13 children born to Irish-born tailor, John James Adams (1818–1894), and his wife Elizabeth Ann nee Noble, John A.D. Adams emigrated from Scotland with his parents in 1848 to New Zealand as part of the first wave of settlers in the new Otago settlement. Farmers and labourers, in 1864 they sold their Taieri Beach farm and returned to Dunedin. Though Scots Baptists, many of the Adams children were christened at First Church (Presbyterian), Dunedin, and grew to become active in the temperance movement, particularly in the Sons and Daughters of Temperance, *The New Zealand Temperance Times*, the Good Templars (Dunedin) (where John was Grand Chief Templar in 1875), the Rechabites and local political "no licence" lobbying. His brother Alexander (1861–1937) was later national President of the Alliance for the Abolition of the Liquor Traffic, "enlivening" the "correspondence columns of the *Otago Daily Times* ... for years with his polemics." Numbers of his books were considered "temperance classics."

On 16 June 1870, John married Margaret Chalmers Dickie. A first child, Margaret Elizabeth, was born, but died young, and they later adopted a daughter, Archinia Stratford. In typical Scots fashion, John worked his way out of laboring pursuits through education and hard work. He entered the legal profession and gained admission to the bar in 1874, opening rooms with James Joyce. In 1883 John's brother Alexander, joined the firm, which also included A.C. Hanlan, "one of the most outstanding criminal advocates in New Zealand's history." (Knowles 2002). The firm still operates in Dunedin, under the name of Wilkinson Adams.

At some stage in the 1880s, John and Maggie moved from the Baptist Church to Methodist membership, possibly influenced by their temperance work. The influence of Wesley on Adams' thought would become apparent in his later teaching, particularly on "sinless perfectionism." Adams' attention was turned towards the issue of divine healing by the onset of a wasting palsy. "The doctors would give me no hope.... I should have died 39 years ago ... [but] I heard there was a man in Melbourne whom God was using in healing diseases." Before they could catch the boat to Melbourne, however, John Alexander Dowie arrived to campaign in their own town. [*Good News* 17.7, July 1926.] Dowie later claimed that his healing ministry "knocked all the Masonic devilry out of [Adams]". After prayer for healing, both he and his wife recovered (Chant, 1998: 170).

Dowie's visit to N.Z. in 1904 changed the direction of Adams' life. Dowie had stayed in their home while in Dunedin in 1888, and appears to have influenced him. The issue of divine healing eventually led to Adams's secession from the Methodist Church in 1900. Adams then opened his large home for prayer meetings, and he and others bought a block of land later that year for the building of the Roslyn City Road Mission. This early pentecostal assembly, which opened in 1903, modeled itself after the Plymouth Brethren, with the difference that there was "perfect liberty for the exercise of spiritual gifts." Adams insisted, however, on an open spirit. (*Good News* 19.3: 3–4)

Adams moved across Dowie-ite and missions circles, travelling to the USA on several occasions, including to Seattle, Vancouver, and possibly to Zion City. In a famous picture featuring early Pentecostal greats William Seymour, John G. Lake, F.F. Bosworth, and Tom Hezmalhalch, he can be seen standing among some of the most significant figures in early Pentecostalism. Adams was a clear and articulate writer and wrote numerous books, pamphlets, and articles dealing with evangelical and pentecostal theology ("The Voice of God Unheard and the Reason Why," "God's Ifs," "Optimists and Pessimists", etc). His book *The Church as revealed in Scripture* was published in the USA in 1904. Adams' legal training gave him a good ear for evidence, and an independent mind. He was also a prolific letter writer to the public newspapers, vigorously defending the pentecostal movement. Adams became an elder of the Pentecostal Church of New Zealand upon its formation after the campaigns of Smith Wigglesworth in 1922–23 and 1923–24. On moving to Melbourne after retirement, he spent three weeks in C.L. Greenwood's church without any invitation to speak. Turning, despite warnings about her unorthodoxy, to Sarah Jane Lancaster, he found a welcome into continued ministry. After his wife's death in 1926 in Dunedin, Adams remained active in the ministry of Good News Hall, elected in 1927 as the founding President of the Apostolic Faith Mission. He continued to travel, and though eventually re-settling in Dunedin, he acted as a father figure to fledgling congregations in both countries. In one visit to Perth in 1927, Edie Adams reported that folk were encouraged 'by [Adams'] deep and powerful Bible lessons', and healing ministry. In a visit to Florrie Mortomore's West End Mission in Brisbane in 1926, "more than one [reported] how his messages helped them" (*Good News*, 17. 11, November 1926: 11). Adams' ability to teach and expound doctrine in the new Pentecostal movement was an important part of the movement's ability to establish bases for unity.

Adams died at his home, 236 Highgate St, Maori Hill, Dunedin, on 8 October 1936, and was buried with his wife, Maggie, in the city's Southern Cemetery. He was survived by his adopted daughter, Archinia, who would marry Charles Hutton and live in Dunedin until her death in 1941.

Bibliography

Chant, B. 1998. "The Spirit of Pentecost." PhD diss., Macquarie University.

Cocker, J., and J. Malton Murray, eds. 1930. *Temperance and Prohibition in New Zealand*. London: Epworth Press.

Dowie, J. 1904. "Satan the Defiler." *Leaves of Healing* (14 May): 99.

Farrant, Edgar D. 1949. *The Taieri Plain: tales of the years that are gone*. Christchurch, N.Z.: Whitcombe & Tombs.

Greenaway, Richtard L.N. 2002. *Waimari Cemetery transcriptions*. library.christchurch.org.nz/Heritage/Cemeteries/Waimairi/WaimairiCemeteryWalk.pdf.

Hall, Geoffrey G. 2006. "Hanlon, Alfred Charles 1866–1944." *Dictionary of New Zealand Biography*. http://www.dnzb.govt.nz/.

Knowles, Brett. 2002. "Adams, J.A.D." In *New International Dictionary of Pentecostal and Charismatic Movements*, edited by S. Burgess and E. Van Der Maas. Grand Rapids: Zondervan.

Robeck, C.M. 2002. "Azusa Street Revival." In *New International Dictionary of Pentecostal and Charismatic Movements*, edited by S. Burgess and E. Van Der Maas. Grand Rapids: Zondervan.

Robeck, C.M. 2006. *Azusa Street Revival and Mission*. Nashville, TN: Nelson.

Worsfold, J.E. 1974. *A History of the Charismatic Movements in New Zealand*.

Mark Hutchinson

Aesthetics and Art

Pentecostals around the world have a paradoxical relationship with visual art. While Pentecostals and Charismatics are known for incorporating embodied expressions of the arts in liturgical worship services, they have historically veered away from a broader cultural engagement with visual art. As such, Pentecostals and Charismatics have developed a pragmatic approach to art that focuses on function rather than intrinsic qualities. Nevertheless, Pentecostals have made global contributions to the fields of visual art, especially how it pertains to its liturgical use.

The strong Protestant influence of Pentecostalism (Pietism, Holiness Movement, Keswick Movement) aided and abetted the general disdain that the Pentecostal and Charismatic movements have had towards visual art. In order to focus on Scripture, Protestants have historically adopted a simple aesthetic that spurned the ornate and grandiose visual style of Roman Catholicism. Pentecostals trace their roots theologically to the same Protestant traditions that distanced themselves from art. Pentecostalism, according to theologian Edmund Rybarczyk, has ignored art because of the corruption it might bring. Classical Pentecostalism has born a distrust of culture, and the ensuing incredulity towards the arts has come as an unfortunate consequence. This has caused many in and around the renewal movements to be out of touch with the surrounding culture's artistic expressions. Yet Rybarczyk believes that Pentecostals have some epistemic commitments to their worldview that lend themselves to artistic engagement, namely that Pentecostals are emotional and practice embodied pneumatocentric spirituality. Rybarczyk writes, "Pentecostals – because they are traditionally inspired by visceral, embodied, emotive, and intuitive characteristics of human nature – have a ready-made way of being for the presence of aesthetes and aesthetic flourish" (Rybarczyk 2012). Utilizing art in a context of worship, however, is a way that Pentecostals and Charismatics have effectively engaged the arts.

Pentecostalism and the renewal movements have approached visual art in the broader artworld in at least four distinct ways. First, an artist can view his or her Pentecostal/Charismatic upbringing as a formative source for art making. In other words, artists create from their own context and convictions, and if they are or have been devoted Pentecostals, then their art will implicitly represent their Pentecostal worldview. Artists like Nicholas Evans and Guy Kinnear fit in this category, as do de-converted artists, like Trenton Doyle Hancock, who still mine their contexts and upbringings for artistic inspiration.

Second, an artist can make explicit reference to his or her theological commitments, using art as a witnessing tool or vehicle for teaching. Untrained folk artists such as Sister Gertrude Morgan and William Thomas Thompson fit in this category. Their works read like polemical tracts, and they view their art as prophetic signals warning and informing the world of God's action on earth. Third, an artist can reconstruct biblical and traditional symbolism in abstracted or non-representational ways. Pentecostals tend to grasp onto particular biblical images, such as wind, fire, clouds, and the dove, that portray a Pentecostal's particular theological narrative. Kathy Self fits in this category as she paints abstract oil paintings mixed with wax, and often uses biblical images as a starting point.

Fourth and finally, an artist may not have come up in a Pentecostal tradition and still explores theologically rich biblical stories that are commonly associated with Pentecostalism. Tim Hawkinson's sculptural piece "Pentecost" is an example of this, where twelve figures surround a massive tree, and a motion detector senses movement, causing the figures to strike the tree creating a sound.

Paul Benney's piece, "Speaking in Tongues" is another example of a contemporary artist using a biblical image of glossolalia associated with Pentecostalism. "Speaking in Tongues" is a large 8'x12' oil painting which depicts twelve men posing with fire on their foreheads. Benney uses a theologically loaded biblical story that is commonly associated with renewal movements in order to express the issue of inclusion in a pluralistic world. Each of these examples represents ways in which Pentecostalism is engaged in the broader artworld through visual art.

Pentecostals commonly utilize various forms of music, dance, drama, and visual art in their worship services. Pentecostal churches often illustrate biblical scenes or symbols in order to emphasize their implicit theological commitments. For instance, one might find paintings of a dove, fire, or water adorning the church in order to represent the presence of the Holy Spirit in the people's midst. Furthermore, some churches have adopted the practice of so-called "spontaneous performance Jesus painting," which consists of impromptu visual art-making during a worship service (Félix-Jäger 2015). Here the visual artist typically stands at the side of the stage in the sanctuary and either illustrates sermon points, or paints intuited impressions inspired by musical worship. The artist follows the prompting of the Holy Spirit in hopes of adding a visual element to a holistic worship practice.

While Pentecostals and Charismatics have been slow in re-engaging visual art, important inroads have been paved. In an increasingly pluralistic world, the Pentecostal narrative is beginning to be heard with interest by the broader artworld. The Pentecostal's key to moving forward is to be fully aware and dialogical with the broader artworld in order to make relevant contributions therein.

Bibliography

Begbie, Jeremy. 2000. *Voicing Creations Praise: Towards a Theology of the Arts.* London: T&T Clark.

Félix-Jäger, Steven. 2015. *Pentecostal Aesthetics: Theological Reflections in a Pentecostal Philosophy of Art and Aesthetics.* Leiden: Brill.

Guthrie, Steven. 2011. *Creator Spirit: The Holy Spirit and the Art of Becoming Human.* Grand Rapids, MI: Baker Academic.

Harvey, John. 1997. "Image of God: Artistic Inspiration and Pentecostal Theology (A Case Study)." *Journal of Pentecostal Theology* 5 (10): 111–124.

Rybarczyk, Edmund. 2012. "Pentecostalism, Human Nature, and Aesthetics: Twenty-First Century Engagement." *Journal of Pentecostal Theology* 21 (2): 240–259.

Sherry, Patrick. 2002. *Spirit and Beauty: An Introduction to Theological Aesthetics*, Second Edition. London: SCM Press.

Wolterstorff, Nicholas. 1980. *Art in Action.* Grand Rapids: W.B. Eerdmans.

Steven Félix-Jäger

Africa

The rise, growth, and expansion of Pentecostalism is one of the key religious developments to occur within Christianity in post-missionary Africa. Pentecostal/charismatic Christianity is best defined through its core religious emphases of movements that in biblical fashion, aim to value, affirm and consciously covet and promote the experience of the Holy Spirit as normative to Christian spirituality. It is this experiential emphasis on encounters with the Holy Spirit that differentiates Pentecostal/charismatic movements from their historic mission counterparts. In the last three decades in particular, Pentecostal/charismatic movements have gained great public presence and recognition in Africa because they have the numbers. Besides, there has been some transitions from an initial emphasis on eschatological matters to more existential concerns that has seen Pentecostals now get directly involved in politics, education and other social developmental projects in Africa. Thus, in current African Pentecostalism, we encounter a movement that has transitioned from an "other-worldly" agenda to one that deals with "this-worldly" matters in ways that has established it as a critical religious force in African Christianity and society.

In Africa, the forms of pneumatic Christianity that we describe generally as "Pentecostal" started with the early twentieth century African independent/initiated/instituted churches (AICs). In South Africa, these would usually be called Zionist churches and in Nigeria, the Aladura, meaning people of prayer. In much of the rest of Africa they went by various indigenous names that simply translated as "churches of the Spirit." These were the first group of mass new religious movements in Africa whose main contribution to Christianity included the integration of charismatic renewal into spirituality and accounting for indigenous beliefs in supernatural evil. They responded to what was considered the "spiritual emptiness" of the mission churches, discounted the powers of local deities, and offered a new Christian spirituality with an interventionist theology that focused on ministering health and wholeness to adherents. The original AICs were inspired and constituted by converts of indigenous charismatic prophets such as William Wadé Harris and Garrick Sokari Braide of West Africa, Isaiah Shembe of South Africa, and Simon Kimbangu of Central Africa. In the first two decades of the twentieth century, these indigenous charismatic prophets converted masses to Christianity away from traditional religions and the testimonies of converts consisted of personal transformations, baptism in the Holy Spirit that manifested in speaking in tongues, healing, and receiving of prophetic dreams, visions and directions.

The development of the AICs was a sign for African theologians that the incalculable Holy Spirit had chosen to use the independent church movement for a spectacular advance of Christianity on the continent. The strength of the new movement lay in the fact that these indigenous Holy Spirit churches had proved to possess the raw materials out of which a dynamic church is made, and that is, spontaneity, total commitment, and the primitive responses that arise from the depths of life. Many AICs remained independent entities organized around the personal charisma of their founders and when these persons became incapacitated or passed on, many of the churches they started began to slip into oblivion. A number of AICs are still active, but except for South Africa, where Zionist churches are still strong as the Christianity of indigenous townships, they are no longer paradigmatic of African Christianity. Nevertheless, their religious and theological emphases of practical salvation, charismatic renewal, innovative gender ideology, and oral and interventionist theologies, have found new leases of life among contemporary Pentecostals on the continent. A few of the best-known Pentecostal churches in Africa originated from Europe and North America, but the AICs tilled the soils on which modern Pentecostalism thrives.

If we consider the AICs as belonging to their own class of Holy Spirit or charismatic movements, the rest which date from the 1920s to the present could be *typologized* as follows:

1. Classical Pentecostal denominations: This refers to the historically older and more doctrinally defined Pentecostal churches including the Assemblies of God, Elim Pentecostal Church, the Church of the Foursquare Gospel and various Apostolic faith churches that were established by foreign Pentecostal missions. Some like the Church of Pentecost and the Christ Apostolic Churches trace their origins to the work of missionaries but are considered historically indigenous as they severed ties with their Western sponsors quite early in their existence.

2. Neo-Pentecostals Movements: This refers to newer independent churches, para-church and trans-denominational movements that have been present across Africa mainly from the 1970s. There are three main neo-Pentecostal movements to be identified in Africa and these are:

a) Contemporary Pentecostal churches: these are urban-based charismatic churches of the prosperity and motivational preaching types. Although their spirituality has often been inspired by North American televangelists and charismatic figures, they are mainly indigenous movements started by a more educated and professional charismatic leadership. Their main features include media technology driven services, exuberant and expressive forms of worship, and their great attraction for Africa's upwardly mobile professionals disenchanted with the historic mission denominations of their parents and grandparents.

b) Trans-denominational charismatic fellowships: these include groups like the Full Gospel Businessmen's Fellowship International and Aglow International movements, para-church organizations that bring top professionals and businesspeople together for fellowship.

c) Renewal movements within historic mission denominations: these are groups that exist within non-Pentecostal churches and that aim to bring charismatic renewal into their denominations through intense and sustained prayer times, Bible study and the practice of spiritual gifts in their meetings.

At the present time therefore, the Christian religious atmosphere has been impacted greatly by the Pentecostals and their revivalist tendencies that are attributed to the presence and power of the Spirit, which tends to be present to various degrees even within non-Pentecostal churches. The trans-denominational fellowships have served as sources of charismatic renewal in the historic mission denominations leading to what may be described as the "pentecostalization" of Christianity in Africa. The changes brought to bear on African Christianity by the various forms of pneumatic Christianity on the continent since the early years of the twentieth century, have been seismic.

African classical Pentecostal churches share similar *theological emphases* as their

Western counterparts. Their basic theological teachings (Full Gospel) include Jesus as Savior; Jesus as baptizer with the Holy Spirit leading to speaking in tongues; Jesus as healer; and Jesus as the king who is coming again soon. The African religio-cultural context brings its own influence to bear on the expression of Pentecostalism and so healing, exorcism and prophetic ministries, which resonate strongly with African traditional worldviews are also important to classical Pentecostal churches on the continent. To that end, the various forms of Pentecostal/charismatic movements in Africa may represent fresh religious innovations, but at the same time, still share the orientation of their forebears – the AICs – in the amalgamation of the biblical and traditional worlds in the quest for and creation of contextually relevant forms of spiritual fulfilment and wholeness.

Pentecostal forms of worship have always proven very attractive for people on the margins of society and social anomie drives some in search of places to feel at home. In the 1970s, Africa experienced military interventions in its politics and the hardships brought upon the nations by collapsed economies due to military adventurism and corruption, were accompanied by the drought and hunger of those years that led many to read apocalyptic interpretations into the difficulties of the continent. The new Pentecostals stepped in with motivational messages of hope in times of despair. The sense of hope fostered by the Pentecostal emphasis on power, and the ability of God to prosper those who believe in him through empowering messages helped much in endearing the new preachers and their churches to Africans. There may well be other socioeconomic or even political factors that account for the growth of Pentecostalism in Africa. However, the religious factors accounting for their popularity far outweighs these other considerations. The new African Pentecostals moved charismatic experiences to new heights with contemporary gospel music and worship styles that looked very much like the Christian versions of secular entertainment that young people were abandoning through their born-again experiences.

The experience of the Holy Spirit is important for understanding Pentecostalism and also for explaining its growth in contexts like Africa where spirit-possession tends to be important for religious experience. In Pentecostalism, participants respond to a God who is active in their daily struggles beyond the cerebral confession of creeds and recitations of the Lord's Prayer and who can change destinies through open doors for riches, healing and general wellbeing. Testimonies of change and transformation involving high profile personalities delivered at trans-denominational charismatic meetings like those of the Full Gospel Businessmen's Fellowship International helped in no small way to move the membership of Pentecostal churches beyond those on the margins of society.

Furthermore, although the primary aim of African Pentecostals is to be biblical, the orientation towards the power of the Spirit, especially in the ministries of healing and deliverance take on added poignancy when understood within the context of the traditional spirit world in which religion is a survival strategy. At Pentecost, the Holy Spirit was "poured out" to reinvigorate the despondent disciples of Jesus by empowering them for witness (Acts 2), and if the words of Peter are anything to go by, then the promise of the Holy Spirit was for all generations including those "who are afar off" (Acts 2:38–39). Those who are afar off are the outsiders, those from Gentile territories who, as we know, came from "every nation under heaven" including Africa to benefit from the blessings of Pentecost.

The new sense of charismatic power available through an educated and gifted leadership, and the contemporary nature of the new Pentecostalism increased the drift of people from the historic mission churches into contemporary Pentecostal churches. When young Africans started migrating from historic mission denominations into new charismatic churches and fellowships from the early 1980s, they gave three mains reasons for their move:

a) That there was good teaching (rather than preaching) of Scripture as the authoritative Word of God. The new churches tended to apply Scripture in a way that spoke very forcefully to contemporary situations.
b) That the power of the Holy Spirit was affirmed in these churches. Young people for whom infant baptism and confirmation had lost their religious meaning yearned for something more experiential and many found it in the charismatic emphases on the power and experience of the Holy Spirit.
c) That worship was enjoyable and that you could feel it. People applauded the dynamic, exuberant, expressive and experiential nature of charismatic worship. Developments in worship in particular have been a critique of the liturgically ordered, staid and over-cerebral and ceremonial nature of worship in the historic mission churches.

The contemporary prosperity preaching Pentecostals with their mega size congregations and fashionable, trendy and media-savvy charismatic leaders, are now paradigmatic of what counts as Christianity in twenty-first century Africa. The leading names here would include Bishop David O. Oyedepo of the Living Faith Church Worldwide, also known as "Winners Chapel," Pastor Enoch A. Adeboye of the Redeemed Christian Church of God, both of Nigeria, and the Archbishop Nicholas Duncan-Williams of the Action Chapel International in Ghana. The references to Ghana and Nigeria must not be taken to mean these names and the movements they lead are known only nationally. The churches are very international with branches around the world making African Pentecostalism an important player in world Christianity.

The recurring emphases in the spirituality of Africa's contemporary Pentecostal churches are *success, prosperity, and internationalism* which are evident everywhere from the names of the churches to the physical symbols of wellbeing associated with the membership and leaders, but above all, also in their motivational messages of power for achieving breakthroughs in life. The contentious gospel of prosperity has very much been a part of African contemporary Pentecostal preaching with some of its leaders like Bishop Oyepedo following the lead of American counterparts in the purchase of personal jets. In spite of the criticisms against the prosperity gospel for its overly materialistic orientation that leaves the poor and marginalized stranded in faith, the preaching of a Christian message that directly addresses contemporary concerns of upward mobility has proven quite effective and popular. The contemporary Pentecostal preacher in Africa offers a gospel that speaks the language of social, political and economic opportunities; and the application of certain social and biblical principles for the realization of success in this life, and this is what has proven very attractive in an African context in which the political leadership is deemed to have failed the young people.

The emphasis on prosperity by contemporary Pentecostals means the preaching of heaven, hell, judgment and the Second Coming of Christ, associated with classical Pentecostal preaching is no longer emphasized. This is because of the motivational nature of contemporary Pentecostal theology and the existential nature of its salvation message. It does not make theological sense to encourage people in Wesleyan fashion to "gain all they can" in this world and then also preach in eschatological terms that Jesus could appear like a thief in the night. It is precisely because of its dominion theology and this-worldly emphasis, that eschatological issues remain marginalized in contemporary Pentecostal thought. Beyond prosperity and empowerment, however, this is a movement of discovery, recovery and restoration of pneumatic Christianity. For contemporary Pentecostals, as for their classical compatriots, the historical accounts of the activity of the Spirit in Acts of the Apostles, which are actually 'Acts of the Holy Spirit', provide a firm foundation for erecting a doctrine of the Spirit which has normative implications for the mission and religious experience of the contemporary church.

The reference to African Pentecostalism must now be understood to refer not simply to how indigenous Africans have embraced the Pentecostal faith, but also in how African charismatic leaders now lead some of the largest Pentecostal denominations in the West through *migration and expansion*. Ghana's Church of Pentecost which is a classical Pentecostal denomination and Nigeria's Redeemed Christian Church of God, which is a contemporary Pentecostal church both have branches in the northern hemisphere and across Africa too that are filled with migrants. They may be locally headquartered in Africa, but these are by no means African Pentecostal churches. They are international organizations that raise missionaries to serve in non-Western contexts in the same way that missionary agencies from the North evangelized Africa in the nineteenth century.

The single largest Pentecostal church in all of Western Europe is led by a Nigerian, the prosperity-preaching charismatic pastor, Matthew Ashimolowo of the Kingsway International Christian Center. There are many such African led mega-size Pentecostal/charismatic churches also in Eastern Europe which means, the proverbial shift in the presence of Christianity from its former heartlands in the northern to the southern continents including Africa, must be understood to include the impact of African Pentecostals in the modern West. African Pentecostalism is now a very transnational movement in which its charismatic leaders travel across continents to preach the gospel, hold mass evangelistic crusades and engage in healing and deliverance activities that only a generation ago was associated with names like Oral Roberts, T.L. Osborn and Morris Cerullo.

In conclusion, the heartlands of the Christian faith have shifted from its former centers of power in the north to new ones in the south including Africa. Pentecostalism with its younger and versatile progenies, the various neo-Pentecostal churches, and movements constitute an important indicator of this growth in Christianity. This is not a monolithic movement, but its religious core remains the experience of the Holy Spirit. In the experience and expression of the power of the Spirit, Pentecostalism has proven very adaptive and therefore in Africa, it has remained biblical while at the same time developing a spirituality that resonates very much with indigenous religio-cultural concerns, aspirations and experiences.

Bibliography

Anderson, Allan H. 2018. *Spirit-filled World: Religious Dis/Continuity in African Pentecostalism.* Cham, Switzerland: Palgrave Macmillan.

Asamoah-Gyadu, J. Kwabena. 2005. *African Charismatics: Current Developments Within Independent Indigenous Pentecostalism in Ghana.* Leiden: Brill.

Ludwig, Frieder, and J. Kwabena Asamoah-Gyadu. 2011. *African Christian Presence in the West: New Immigrant Congregations and Transnational Networks in North America and Europe.* Trenton, NJ: Africa World Press.

Gifford, Paul. 2004. *Ghana's New Christianity: Pentecostalism in a Globalizing African Economy.* Bloomington and Indianapolis: Indiana University Press.

Kalu, Ogbu. 2008. *African Pentecostalism: An Introduction.* Oxford: Oxford University Press.

Wariboko, Nimi. 2014. *Nigerian Pentecostalism.* Rochester, NY: University of Rochester Press.

J. Kwabena Asamoah-Gyadu

Aglow International

Aglow International is a women's parachurch organization in Pentecostal-Charismatic Christianity. The organization began in the context of the charismatic movement of the 1950s and 1960s by four wives of significant leaders of the Full Gospel Businessmen's Fellowship, an organization founded in 1953 to address the lack of male participation in religious revivals. Aglow began in 1967 under the name of the Full Gospel Women's Fellowship (FGWF). It holds international conferences, retreats, and has local groups in every state of the United States and almost 4,000 groups globally in nearly 170 nations.

The first FGWF meeting took place in 1967 in Seattle, Washington at a location that was intentionally accessible to women of various mainline Protestant denominations. Shortly thereafter, several meetings were organized throughout the Seattle area and then throughout the United States. In 1972, FGWF incorporated as Women's Aglow Fellowship International. By 1972, there were sixty groups in the United States, and by 1973–74 groups were formed in Canada, the Netherlands, and New Zealand. In 1974, Aglow held its first international conference in Seattle, and women attended from 25 states, Canada, Mexico, the Netherlands, and Nigeria. By 1979, Aglow had groups in all 50 states, and by 1987 there were groups in 75 nations. In 1980, Aglow held its first international conference outside of North America with over 700 women attending the conference in Jerusalem. In 1996 the organization's name changed to Aglow International.

With its roots in the Pentecostal-Charismatic tradition, Aglow members believe that the spiritual gifts listed in the New Testament are available to the modern believer, including miraculous healings and speaking in tongues. In November 1969 the FGWF released its first magazine under the name *Aglow*, taken from the Bible passage that says, "be aglow and burning with the Spirit" (Romans 12:11, Amplified version). The magazine was filled with women's testimonies recounting personal transformation in all aspects of life, spiritual, physical, and emotional.

Women's gatherings may include singing praise and worship songs, Bible study, and prayer. Prayers often focus on healing from physical and emotional ailments, including the healing of emotional wounds from past experiences of heartache and abuse. According to testimonies, healings often came after engaging demonic forces in a spiritual battle, for illness was viewed as part of the cosmic battle with Satan. Thus, all healing originates from God and is a form of spiritual victory. Meetings also took on a therapeutic tone, by facing issues such as abuse and addiction.

Aglow would generally be viewed as conservative in its beliefs, however, the organization has separated itself from conservative political groups, such as the Christian Coalition. Aglow's leaders believe their influence on society comes through prayer and evangelism.

Aglow was formed during the early days of the Women's Liberation Movement. Aglow authors often encouraged women to submit to their husbands, teaching that true freedom was to be found in submission. Housework was presented as sacred and an act of worship, a view that had the added benefit of boosting self-esteem. With the changing roles of women in society, the increase of women in the workplace, and higher divorce rates, the emphasis has shifted to mutual submission and the empowering of women through their participation in prayer and spiritual warfare.

Aglow's structure includes a group of advisors who, for the majority of the organization's existence, have all been men. The rationale for all male advisors comes from a view of Scripture that sees women needing a "covering" or male "headship."

Aglow's rationale for predominantly male advisors has transitioned to placing emphasis on the need for a balanced perspective that male advisors provide. Currently, there is one woman on the advisory board. Additionally, Aglow is not a ministry exclusively for women. Groups for men have been formed with the name Men of Issachar.

Along with prayer and evangelism, Aglow believes they have three God-given mandates: (1), gender reconciliation, (2), ministry to Muslims, and (3), support for Israel and Jews. Aglow also works against and advances awareness of human trafficking.

Although Aglow is generally considered to be comprised of middle-class white women, there is also a diverse group of women from various ethnic and racial backgrounds, along with efforts to increase diversity in the organization. Aglow has also worked toward racial reconciliation with Native American, African American, and Hispanic women speaking at Aglow meetings on their experiences of racism.

Aglow International, along with the Full Gospel Businessmen's Fellowship, have been credited with being influential on the rise of Pentecostal-Charismatic Christianity in Ghana, with Ghana having over 200 Aglow groups. Additionally, Aglow International has websites or Facebook pages for chapters in Malawi, Rwanda, South Africa, Japan, Korea, Canada, Curaçao, Dominican Republic, Jamaica, Belgium, Britain, Denmark, Finland, France, Germany, Iceland, Italy, Netherlands, Norway, Poland, Portugal, Russia, Spain, Sweden, Switzerland, Costa Rica, El Salvador, Guatemala, Honduras, Mexico, American Samoa, Australia, New Zealand, Argentina, Brazil, Chile, Paraguay, Uruguay, and Venezuela.

Bibliography

Asamoah-Gyadu, Kwabena. 1997. "'Missionaries Without Robes': Lay Charismatic Fellowships and the Evangelization of Ghana." *Pneuma* 19 (1): 167–188.

Griffith, R. Marie. 1999. "A Network of Praying Women: Women's Aglow Fellowship and Mainline American Protestantism." In *Pentecostal Currents in American Protestantism*, edited by Edith L. Blumhofer, Russell P. Spittler, and Grant A. Wacker, 131–151. Urbana: University of Illinois Press.

Griffith, R. Marie. 1997. *God's Daughters: Evangelical Women and the Power of Submission.* Berkely, CA: University of California Press.

Omenyo, Cephas. 1994. "The Charismatic Renewal Movement in Ghana." *Pneuma* 15 (2): 169–185.

Setta, Susan M. 1986. "Healing in Suburbia: The Women's Aglow Fellowship." *Journal of Religious Studies* 12 (2): 46–56.

Yvette D. Garcia

Allen, A.A.

Asa Alonzo Allen (1911–1970) was born in Sulphur Rock, Arkansas to impoverished parents who were subsistence farmers. After his father died from alcoholism during his teen years, Allen and his mother moved to Missouri. Allen was always hardworking, but because of his gregarious and entertaining personality, he developed the reputation for his excessive drinking and revelry. However, one day he wandered into a Methodist Church in Miller, Missouri, where he heard the gospel preached by evangelist Nina Depriest and came forward to receive Christ. From that point, Allen was radically changed and devoted himself to understanding the Bible. His hunger for truth led him to a small house meeting conducted by a Pentecostal who preached the baptism in the Spirit. Allen's Methodist pastor warned him to stay away from the "tongue talkers" because it was from the devil, but that only made him more interested in the Pentecostal experience and sought out meetings wherever he could. While attending a Tri-State Assemblies of God (AG) camp meeting in Miami, Oklahoma, Allen received the baptism in the Holy Spirit and spoke in tongues.

Shortly after, Allen was invited to come to Lamar, Colorado to work on a friend's farm. There he met his soon to be wife, Lexie Allen, who was one of the few Pentecostal women in the economically depressed farm community. Lexie felt called to ministry and even attended Central Bible Institute for one term in 1935 while they were courting. After they married in September 1936, they settled back in southern Missouri so that Allen could attend Bible school. But along the way, Allen instead began to launch revivals in churches and old school houses around southern Missouri, wherever he could gather a crowd. While pastoring in his first church in Towner, Colorado, he was ordained with the AG. Discouraged with the lack of miracles in his ministry, Allen became committed to fasting and prayer for God to reveal the secrets of miracle ministry. One such day, while praying, Allen received a revelation from God of eleven things that hindered him from seeing more miracles in his ministry. At the heart of this list was his commitment to healing the sick and seeing signs and wonders in his meetings. Allen began to hold small healing revivals while he pastored several different AG churches in Idaho and Colorado. As his success grew, Allen answered the call to pastor the AG church in Corpus Christi, Texas.

While pastoring in Corpus Christi, Allen attended the Oral Roberts healing crusade in his town and was convicted that he was not bringing healing to the church as he had been directed a decade before while in prayer. Allen immediately resigned the church and joined the growing number of healing evangelists who were conducting tent crusades. In July 1951, Allen held his first tent crusade in Yakima, Washington in a large tent which he purchased from William Branham. In 1953, Allen moved his growing ministry to Dallas, Texas and was closely associated with the Voice of Healing ministry begun by Gordon Lindsay. There he also launched his "Allen Revival Hour" radio broadcast and started his own publication, *Miracle Magazine*.

Allen was a captivating speaker and excelled in projecting an energetic stage presence. Through stories of his own humble beginnings, he was a master at connecting with common people and giving them faith to believe that miracles were possible. His message was clearly rooted in the Pentecostal full gospel. He denounced sin and preached the blood of Jesus. He was also very musical, playing guitar and enjoyed gospel music. He was one of the first healing evangelists who fully integrated his meetings during the era of segregation in America.

Allen had tremendous popularity, but he also became the subject of scandal. In 1955, Allen was arrested for drunk driving. Though he dismissed the incident as an unfounded attack by the enemy, others around him suspected that he had returned to drinking. This incident, coupled with concerns about some of his sensational claims and emphasis on prosperity, led to the AG withdrawing his credentials. In 1958, Allen was given a parcel of land in Arizona and moved his headquarters there and named it "Miracle Valley." As he became more isolated from other healing ministers, Miracle Valley was being transformed into a Christian community with a 4,000-seat church, a Bible training center, and residential homes.

During the mid to late 1960s, when most of the healing evangelists had folded their tents, Allen was still promoting the importance of tent revivalism. Allen focused on training young and talented ministers such as R.W. Shambach, Kent Rogers and Allen's eventual successor, Don Stewart to carry on this ministry. A few years before his death, Allen became more controversial as his life was seemingly spiraling out of control. Questions about his drinking resurfaced when he started to miss scheduled meetings and divorced his wife in 1967. Allen died in 1970, but his legacy as one of the most popular and gifted healing evangelists has remained.

Bibliography

Allen, Lexie E. 1954. *God's Man of Faith and Power: The Life Story of A.A. Allen*. Dallas: A.A. Allen.

Harrell, Jr., David Edwin. 1975. *All Things Are Possible: The Healing and Charismatic Revivals in Modern America*. Bloomington: Indiana University Press.

Sánchez Walsh, Arlene M. 2018. *Pentecostals in America*. New York: Columbia University Press.

Daniel D. Isgrigg

Alpha

The Alpha course has frequently been described as the most widely used Christian evangelising program of recent decades. This is not without good reason considering its application in thousands of churches worldwide. Alpha is noteworthy

because the course exemplifies state-of-the art church growth philosophies and the way that it engages with contemporary culture – not least of all the application of business techniques in spreading the gospel message. It is also striking because of the elements of Pentecostal/Charismatic theology and praxis that is central to the program.

Alpha has its origins in the Charismatic Anglican church, Holy Trinity Brompton, London (commonly referred to as HTB), one of the largest Anglican churches in the United Kingdom. HTB had long been a major advocate of the Charismatic renewal movement since the 1960s, growing to become a centre for revival in the capital. While, the course in its current form emerged in the late 1990s, Alpha had evolved over a number of years previously. The familiar program that came to be exported globally was the creative product of Nicky Gumbel who was to become the vicar of HTB. It was Gumbel who narrates Alpha's video presentations and who took the initiative to promote the course through nationwide large-scale poster and leaflet advertising.

The aim of Alpha is to reach unsaved and unchurched 'guests' in an increasingly secular environment where church attendance declines. This is perceived to be best achieved through exploring a number of questions believed to be of interest to those wishing to explore the Christian faith in a 'safe' environment. In this respect, Alpha generally amounts to weekly (lasting usually for 12 weeks) two-hour evening events. The precise content of Alpha is fairly standard; departure from the recommended structure is not encouraged by HTB. The usual site for the events is typically a local congregation. A communal meal is served, with the rationale of attempting to bring integration of 'guests' subscribing to the course and to be familiarised with the church environment. This is followed by a short worship period and prayers. A video on a weekly theme (15 in all) follows before discussion groups take place. Weekly topics included who was Jesus?, the significance of his death, the relevance of the Bible, the importance of prayer, and how to live the Christian life.

Many additional themes have a strong Pentecostal content such as the central importance of the Holy Spirit, 'spirit baptism' and spiritual 'gifts' (charismata), 'How can I be filled with the Holy Spirit', healing, and spiritual warfare. These themes inform the teaching of the weekend retreat that is generally planned some third of a way through the course in an aim to further bond the Alpha group. At some time during the weekend the Holy Spirit is evoked and in a way associated with the ministry of the California based Association of Vineyard churches and the teachings of its late leader John Wimber with which it had previous connections. Vineyard had become associated with the neo-Charismatic Third Wave movement with an emphasis on 'signs and wonders' such as miraculous healing that Wimber saw as a source of church growth.

The impact of Alpha has by no means be limited to the UK. By 1998, the year which marked the onset of the national campaign launch, Alpha was running in some 75 countries. By the year 2000 there was nearly 12,000 courses running internationally with over one million 'guests' passing through the program. In the USA alone, some 5,000 courses were organised during this time. The early 2000s probably marked the height of the popularity of Alpha with over 4 million people engaged. The course is also run in prisons and universities, suitably adapted, while a youth Alpha program is applied in many churches. Subsequently, many spin-off programs were designed such as the Alpha Marriage Course.

One strength of Alpha is that it attempts to be ecumenical and is adopted by different Christian denominations. The course in some respects has been successful where other evangelising programs have failed. Indicative of the success of Alpha is not just the number of courses run, the number of 'guests' who have passed through the program and the number of churches that have endorsed it, but the sale of books and other material supporting the course, many of which serve to aid in the spreading of Pentecostal/Charismatic beliefs and culture. It is, of course, impossible to conclude how many conversions have been achieved. Alpha has also drawn critics. Negative comments include the way that it endorses secular culture through its business techniques, its tendency to downplay sin and repentance, and not least of all the claim by more traditionally-minded Christians concerned with the spread of Pentecostal/charismatic theology and practice.

Bibliography

Brookes, A. ed. 2007. *The Alpha Phenomenon*. N.p.: Churches Together in Britain and Ireland.

Hocken, P.D. 2002. "Alpha Course." In *The New International Dictionary of Pentecostal and Charismatic Movements*, edited by Stanley M. Burgess. Grand Rapids, MI: Zondervan.

Hunt, S. 2005. "Alpha: The Theological Debate." *Pentecostudies*. asnws.scw.vu.nl/Pentecostudies.

Hunt, S. 2005. "The *Alpha* Programme: Charismatic Evangelism for the Contemporary Age." *Pneuma* 17 (1): 105–118.

Hunt, S. 2004. *The Alpha Enterprise: Evangelism in a Post-Christian Era*. Aldershot: Ashgate.

Stephen J. Hunt

Anglican Renewal Ministries

Anglican Renewal Ministries Canada is an independently incorporated, non-profit registered organization within the Anglican Church of Canada. Its primary purpose is to promote the movement of spiritual renewal within the Church, primarily the Anglican Church, but also other Christian traditions by invitation. It is rooted in the Charismatic Renewal of the last half of the twentieth century, beginning in the historic mainline Protestant and Catholic churches, and preceded by the earlier Pentecostal Movement. Its specific ministry reflects four distinctive charismatic priorities: discovering one's spiritual gifts, instruction on the gift of prophecy, ministry of healing, and the life of prayer and intimacy with God.

Pre-organizational history began with the influence of the Charismatic Renewal spreading from United States and England to Canada in the 1960s and 1970s. In 1973, a motion of support was passed at the 26th Session of General Synod of the Anglican Church of Canada in Regina, SK. It affirmed that Synod members recognized the need for spiritual renewal in the Church, and that they would commit the Church's resources to support the renewal, to further personal commitment to Jesus Christ, deepen relationships within the Fellowship, and sacrificially serve the wider community.

Growth and need for coordination by the leadership eventually required an organizational structure. This began in Western Canada where the Anglican renewal was initially stronger. Undoubtedly this was due in part to the West's proximity to St. Luke's Episcopal Church, Seattle, which was a major centre for renewal under the leadership of Dennis Bennett, a leading charismatic Episcopalian at the time.

The first organizational step occurred in 1978 under the leadership of Charles Alexander and John Vickers, two priests from Vancouver Island. At a meeting in Brooks, AB, they initiated Anglican Renewal West, with Alexander functioning as the first Chairperson. In 1980, the new organization hosted its first conference in Calgary. The international spread of the Renewal movement in Anglicanism was reflected in its choice of plenary speakers: Bill Burnett (South Africa), Michael Harper (UK), and Ted Nelson (US). Biennial conferences continued until 1985 when the national Anglican Renewal Ministries Canada was formed.

This entire process reflects Canada's distinctive demographics and the growing Anglican international network. Renewal in eastern Canada initially developed differently from the West, therefore requiring more time to build a national identity. In contrast to the United States, Canadian renewal parishes lacked the resources to release their leaders to travel in the interest of promoting spiritual renewal. Also, pressure was mounting from international leaders for increased cooperation and coordination within the Anglican Communion. This would minimally require a national body, a magazine, and a structure to communicate nationally and globally.

In 1983, 66 Canadian leaders attended a conference in Denton, TX, during which they were encouraged to form a national Canadian organization similar to Episcopal Renewal Ministries, formed in 1973. Very soon thereafter the Canadian leaders held their first national meeting in Ottawa, and the following year produced their first Newsletter. The formation of the Canadian organization in 1985 resulted in providing a national identity, a current mailing list, and a national office and secretary. Their first issue of a magazine, *Tongues of Fire*, appeared in 1986. In 1992, the name was officially changed to Anglicans for Renewal, Canada.

In 1994, Anglican Renewal Ministries widened its involvement in the Anglican Church of Canada by joining a coalition of theologically conservative leaders under the name, Anglican Essentials Canada. Tensions had been growing in the Church for some time over the issue of same-sex relations, especially proposals for offering blessings of unions and redefining the sacrament of marriage. To amplify their concerns, three conservative bodies entered into an alliance to provide a vehicle for influencing the future direction of the Church: Anglican Renewal Ministries, Barnabas Anglican Ministries, and The Prayer Book Society of Canada. What became known as Essentials '94 was a co-sponsored national gathering held in

Montreal in June, 1994, with 700 attendees. The leaders produced a manifesto called the Montreal Declaration of Anglican Essentials.

Strong support continued into 1997 when the leaders organized a national Essentials conference in Ottawa. Substantial papers were later published in an edited volume by George Egerton, *Anglican Essentials: Reclaiming Faith Within the Anglican Church of Canada*. The organization continued to build a national network with a part-time National Director and Secretary.

But weaknesses began to appear. In 1999 the Prayer Book Society left Essentials, and Barnabas Ministries eventually dwindled. Structurally, in 2004, Essentials Canada changed its Constitution from being an umbrella alliance to a separate legal entity. Given increased disillusionment with the direction in the Church on sexuality, many members were beginning to leave. So the Essentials Council divided into two separate groups: Essentials Federation for members who considered remaining, and Essentials Network for those who contemplated leaving. The consequence for Anglican Renewal Ministries is that, being the only partner remaining in the Federation, its role in Essentials Canada became diminished and distracting to its primary mission.

The current ministry of Anglican Renewal Ministries reflects the waning of the charismatic movement. It continues to be active in dioceses outside the major urban centres, such as Calgary, Central Newfoundland, Fredericton, Huron, Ottawa, Saskatoon, and Yukon. It functions with one national Board of twelve members, and four administrators. Its two publications appear quarterly, *Anglicans for Renewal Canada* and *Taste and See*.

Bibliography

Beatty, Don. "ARM – The Early Years." *Anglicans for Renewal Canada*. Issues: Oct 2002, Feb 2003, Sept 2003, Feb 2004, Aug 2004, May 2005.

Di Giacomo, Michael. 2009. "Pentecostal and Charismatic Christianity in Canada: Its Origins, Development, and Distinct Culture." In *Canadian Pentecostalism: Transition and Transformation*, edited by Michael Wilkinson, 15–38. Montreal and Kingston: McGill-Queen's University Press.

Hayes, Alan. 2004. *Anglicans in Canada: Controversies and Identity in Historical Perspective*. Urbana and Chicago: University of Illinois Press.

Kydd, Ronald A.N. 1996. "The Impact of the Charismatic Renewal on Classical Pentecostalism in Canada." *Pneuma* 18 (1): 55–67.

Reed, David A. 2009. "Denominational Charismatics – Where Have They All Gone? A Canadian Anglican Case Study." In *Canadian Pentecostalism: Transition and Transformation*, edited by Michael Wilkinson, 197–213. Montreal and Kingston: McGill-Queen's University Press.

David Reed

Angola

The appearance of Pentecostalism in Angola could be traced back to the 1930s; however, its early reception and later development faced many challenges. The current character and position of Pentecostalism in Angola is firmly embedded in the historical and political context, but it is also mediated by multiple geographical and theological connections.

The hegemony of the Roman Catholic Church, introduced in Angola's territory together with Portuguese political domination (1482), was an important factor determining the beginnings of the Pentecostal movement in Angola. Throughout the Portuguese colonial domination (until the mid-1970s), the relationship between the Pentecostals, among other Protestant denominations, and the political domain was ambiguous as they were frequently considered a threat to the country's political and religious order.

The 1930s to 1975 have to be considered for the role of missionaries in the formation of Pentecostalism, especially for the Assemblies of God and Church of God. However, in the late 1930s Swedish missionaries representing the Swedish Pentecostal movement also initiated evangelization in Cabinda province in northern Angola. Evangelical Pentecostal Church in Angola (EPCA) was the outcome of this missionary work. At the same time, the first Pentecostal missionaries appeared in the south. Edmond and Pearl Stark of the American Church of God (Cleveland, TN) started their mission in 1938 in Kwanza-Sul province (southern Angola), which was interrupted by the death of Edmond Stark (1939) and postponed due to the outbreak of World War II. A decade later Pearl Stark looked for missionary support among Portuguese Pentecostals. Joaquim Cartaxo Martins, a member of the Portuguese Assemblies of God, encouraged by Pearl's missionary call, disembarked in Benguela (southern Angola) in 1949. Together, they set up a missionary work named Missão Evangélica de Vista Alegre in Kwanza-Sul province, also known as the Pentecostal Mission. In 1952 the mission was granted permission for evangelization activities and teaching children. This date is now considered as the founding of the Assemblies of God in Angola. In 1953 Pearl Stark was granted a one-year leave and after returning back to Angola she continued establishing new congregations that were named the Evangelical Pentecostal Mission of Angola (EPMA, currently also a WCC member), after Angola's independence. In 1957 the Vista Alegre mission was closed because of political reasons. The followers spread throughout central Angola, creating congregations in Gabela and Porto Amboim amongst others. Some ended up in Luanda, where they started to evangelize in the African neighborhoods and set up small congregations, like Cazenga that were still supervised by Portuguese ministers. At the same time the Portuguese settlers and business owners staying in Luanda formed small congregations of a very mixed evangelical and Pentecostal background, with no institutional link to any foreign denomination. However, one of the congregations was legitimized by the Portuguese Assemblies of God in 1973, and renamed after 1975 the Assembly of God of Maculusso that gave rise to fourteen Assemblies of God congregations operating in Luanda and other provinces of Angola.

The post-independence period (the late 1970s and 1980s) changed the face of the Pentecostal movement. In the first phase, the communist political inclination of the dominating party (MPLA) was hostile to any religious organizations (especially in the 1975–79 period). However, for the established Pentecostal denominations such as the Assemblies of God this period was crucial for building up national and institutional structures. Their transnational links (with Brazil, the USA, and the Republic of South Africa) guaranteed the provision of basic resources, support of infrastructures and theological schooling. Ultimately, in 1987, religion was identified as a weighty social force by the Angolan government and the first twelve churches were officially recognized, among them a single Pentecostal denomination, the

Assemblies of God of Angola (EPMA in 1993, EPCA 1993).

The 1980s witnessed the diversification of the Pentecostal movement hitherto linked significantly to foreign missionaries. The missionary Pentecostal denominations gradually underwent an Africanization process. A significant wave of Pentecostal churches of Congolese origin (like Bom Deus Church) that appeared together with the return of *regressados*, the Angolan refugees fleeing the independence war in Congo, brought about multidimensional changes in the Angolan Pentecostal movement. Primarily different religiosity, theology and institutional models were introduced. Secondly, new models of Pentecostal churches appeared, combining Pentecostalism with African traditions, frequently inspired by prophetic or spiritual churches characteristic of the Congo region. Thirdly, new religious effervescence of the 1980s and 1990s resulted in the establishment of local, Angolan independent Pentecostal churches sometimes linked to foreign churches. At that time several churches with Pentecostal features were also founded in southern and central Angola, frequently linked to Zambia and South Africa.

With the introduction of the multiparty democracy (1992) and the renouncement of the socialist atheist ideology, the country faced a new wave of foreign Atlantic Pentecostal denominations of Neo-pentecostal/charismatic expression. The most prominent are the Brazilian Universal Church of the Kingdom of God in Angola since 1992, and Portuguese Maná Church (in Angola since 1989, which was banned due to political reasons in 2008 since then operating as Church of Josafat, and restored in Angola in 2018).

In recent years the pentecostalization of older evangelical denominations can be observed together with the development of a charismatic movement within the Catholic Church in Angola. Known currently as Movimento Apostólico do Renovamento Carismático, it started in the 1980s under Brazilian and Portuguese inspiration (father Ezio Tinazzo), but reached significant recognition only at the beginning of the twenty-first century after setting up a national charismatic centre, the Aldeia de Oração in Southern Angola in Lubango (2006). However, the initial development was linked to Luanda and Cabinda province.

Pentecostal denominations in contemporary Angola are subject to strict political control and are under pressure to abide by the local religious policy that is closely dependent on the political realm. According to the legal status and position in Angola's religious landscape, the Pentecostal churches, among other evangelical churches, are organized into two main groups: CICA (Council of Christian Churches of Angola) and CIRA (Council of Renewal Churches of Angola).

According to the 2014 country census, the Roman Catholic Church still represents the largest religious grouping in Angola (41 percent) over Protestant denominations (38 percent). It is difficult to estimate the number of adherents to Pentecostal, neo-Pentecostal and charismatic movements, since there does not exist any reliable data due to high rates of interdenominational mobility and a large number of factions within the Pentecostal and charismatic landscape.

Bibliography

Bahu, Helder Pedro Alicerces. 2017. "A Aldeia de oração do Lubango." In *Paisagens e Memórias Religiosas em Angola. Um Itinerário.* Vol. 1, *Currents of Faith, Places of*

History, edited by Ramon Sarró and Ruy Llera Blanes, 33–37.

Blanes, Ruy Llera. 2015. "Politics of Sovereignty: Evangelical and Pentecostal Christianity and Politics in Angola." In *The Anthropology of Global Pentecostalism and Evangelicalism*, edited by Simon Coleman and Rosalind I.J. Hackett, 197–213. New York: New York University Press.

Henderson, Lawrence W. 1990. *A igreja em Angola. Um rio com várias correntes*. Lisbon: Editorial Além Mar.

Viegas, Fátima. 1999. *Angola e as Religiões*. Luanda.

Wolff Swatowiski, Claudia. 2015. "Igreja Universal do Reino de Deus em Luanda." In *Ciências Sociais cruzadas entre o Brasil e Portugal: trajetos e investigações no ICS*, edited by Isabel Silva, Simone Frangella, Sofia Aboim, and Susana Viegas, 361–374. Lisbon: Imprensa de Ciências Sociais.

Zawiejska, Natalia, and Linda van de Kamp. 2018. "The Multi-Polarity of Angolan Pentecostalism: Connections and Belongings." *PentecoStudies* 17 (1): 12–36.

Natalia Zawiejska

Anim, Peter

Peter Newman Anim is known as the father of Classical Pentecostalism in Ghana. He was born to Simon Appiagyei and Hannah Lartebea on February 4, 1890 in Anum Bosso in the Volta region of Ghana. Anim attended the Boso Basel Mission School and the Anum Basel Mission School where he graduated in 1908. He worked briefly as a carpentry apprentice in his brother's workshop in Amanokrom in 1911. Then in the same year he became a weighing clerk at the Basel Mission's factory in Pakro, but only for one year due to serious illness. In 1914, he became a bricklayer. He married Dora Sakyibea in his hometown in 1916 and together they had four children. All of them suffered infant mortality in rapid succession. After four years of their marriage, Dora passed away and Peter married Esther Osimpo. She died in 1967.

Anim's early life was clearly characterized by many challenges: early mortality of his four children, widowhood, chronic stomach ulcers, and at some points, unemployment. Consequently, he was always exploring means to access a higher power that could liberate him. This spiritual hunger was evident in his interest in religious periodicals. Although he was a Presbyterian, he was noted for subscribing to international Christian periodicals that taught about other Christian traditions. In 1917, he read the *Sword of the Spirit*, a periodical that was edited by A. Clark, the founder of Faith Tabernacle Church of Philadelphia in the United States. Although the church was not Pentecostal, the magazine stressed the availability of divine healing through "prevailing prayers," which Anim believed he needed badly to fight his chronic illness.

In 1920, Anim converted and began to practice Faith Tabernacle's teachings, especially, divine healing. In 1921, he claimed he was miraculously healed from Guinea worm infection and chronic stomach ulcers (Larbi 2001). He then moved to Asamankese, which was larger than his hometown in the eastern region of Ghana, and organized prayer meetings that attracted many people. He was convinced of the authenticity of Clark's teachings, particularly, the teaching on divine healing, and named his congregation Faith Tabernacle Church in 1922. Although he never physically met Clark apart from correspondence, he received an ordination certificate from him in 1923, confirming the establishment of the Faith Tabernacle Church in Ghana. Anim was allowed to baptize converts and appoint workers in ministry (Larbi 2001). Many people were healed of all kinds of ailments in his prayer meetings and their testimonies spread across the eastern region of Ghana and neighbouring Togo.

Anim read about the baptism of the Holy Spirit evidenced by speaking in tongues from the periodical published by the Apostolic Faith, which was published by William Seymour's Azusa Street Revival in 1907. Anim adopted this teaching and ceased to be part of the Faith Tabernacle Church. He wrote a letter to the Apostolic Faith to state his desire to bring his congregation into affiliation with it in 1930. In 1932, Stephen Owiredu, a member of Anim's congregation in Brekumanso, received the baptism of the Holy Spirit and spoke in tongues while praying alone in the bush. When Anim heard the news, he and four of his members (two men and two women) in Asamankese went to verify the incident. Once they were confirmed, they held a prayer meeting in Owiredu's house. Owiredu's two sons and two women, Comfort Nyarkoah and Agnes Oparebea, also spoke in tongues (Larbi 2001). Anim's congregation began to practise glossolalia according to the teaching of Classical Pentecostalism derived from the Azusa Street Revival. Anim himself received Spirit baptism and spoke in tongues some years later.

After receiving the Pentecostal baptism, Anim sought a more direct relationship with an international Pentecostal body, the British Apostolic Church, which sent James McKeown to Ghana to work with his congregation. However, their teamwork only lasted for two years due to a disagreement over divine healing. Anim then separated from the Apostolic Church in 1939 and named his church Christ Apostolic Church. He ran it successfully, albeit with many further affiliations and secessions, until his death in February 1984. His church is a founding member of the [GPCC] Ghana Pentecostal and Charismatic Council (GPCC). It remains an important Pentecostal denomination which has spread to several countries, including Europe and North America.

Bibliography

Asamoah-Gyadu, Kwabena J. 2005. *African Charismatics: Current Developments within Independent Indigenous Pentecostalism in Ghana.* Leiden: Brill.

Larbi, Kingsley. 2001. *Pentecostals: The Eddies of Ghanaian Christianity.* Accra: Centre for Pentecostal and Charismatic Studies.

Leonard, Christine. 1989. *A Giant in Ghana: 3000 Churches in 50 years, the Story of James McKeown and the Church of Pentecost.* Chester: New Wine Press.

Lord Elorm Donkor

Annacondia, Carlos

Carlos Annacondia was born in Argentina on March 12, 1944. He was a successful businessman when he had his conversion experience on May 19, 1979. His parents of Catholic tradition had begun attending a small evangelical church of the Free Brethren in the suburbs of Buenos Aires. The pastor of this church, Jorge Gomelsky, came from an anti-Pentecostal tradition, but in those days, he had been impacted by the message of Puerto Rican evangelist Yiye Avila (Saracco 1989). In this condition he was willing to support an evangelistic campaign led by Panamanian evangelist and diplomat Manuel Ruiz. When Carlos Annacondia heard about the demonic liberations that were occurring in the campaign he decided to go and see what was happening motivated by curiosity after having read the book *The Exorcist*. Ten days after his conversion Annacondia received the baptism in the Holy Spirit and soon after that all the employees of his company were also converted. As they were not linked to any church, they decided to start one and invited Gomelsky as their pastor.

From his first days in the faith Annacondia shared the Gospel message. He did it with his friends, family, and clients. He also visited hospitals to pray for the sick (Saracco 1989). He decided to start a radio program as a means to make the gospel heard by as many people as possible. Unfortunately, his desire was met with the refusal of the radio stations, since during the military government they had Catholic priests as advisors. Because of this, the program was broadcast from Radio Real of the neighboring country of Uruguay. The name of the program was "Message of Salvation" which continued to be the name of Annacondia's ministry until today. His motto was: "Jesus loves you, saves you and heals you." It is interesting to note the order of the words, starting from God's love and ending with healing.

In addition to promoting the radio program Annacondia began to preach in the poor areas surrounding the city of Buenos Aires. His prayer was that God would give him the power of His Spirit so that the message would be accompanied by all kinds of signs and wonders. On April 12, 1982, three years after his conversion and while reading the Bible in Ezekiel 37, he lived an experience in which he considered that God spoke to him saying: "Everything you asked me, I give it to you. Start preaching." On April 30, 1982, a month after the start of the Falklands War, the first open-air campaign of Message of Salvation took place. From then on, the preaching places multiplied with attendance at the meetings in the tens of thousands. Thanks to a contact with Pastor Alti Viljanen, a missionary of the Finnish Pentecostal Mission in Uruguay, Annacondia preached for the first time in Finland and Russia.

One of the outstanding characteristics of Annacondia's ministry, beyond the healings, has been what are considered "demonic manifestations." These were revealed with people screaming, contorting their bodies and exhibiting unusual strength. This was not new to the Pentecostal churches that had these practices within their churches. What was new here was that these manifestations took place in public spaces, with thousands of people affected. Such was the magnitude of this phenomenon that it became necessary to have a special tent for deliverance during the event.

Concern for the unity of the church has been present since the beginning of Annacondia's ministry. So much so that in cities where the unity of the churches was not possible the campaign was not carried out. It is interesting to see that a movement with Pentecostal characteristics achieved the unity of most of the denominations in each city. This has been a legacy that has marked the Argentine church.

Carlos Annacondia's ministry triggered a new religious situation in Argentina. Its impact was greater than that caused by Tommy Hicks. From what Annacondia achieved, there has been a Pentecostalization of the religious experience, the practice of divine healing and prayers for deliverance and exorcisms have become widespread (Saracco 1989). Pastor Rogelio Nonini, a former president of the Christian and Missionary Alliance of Argentina has spoken of four benefits produced by the ministry of Annacondia: "1. People began to see God as a powerful and present reality; 2. The church felt challenged by the needs of the people; 3. There was a renewed desire to praise and bless God;

4. A more real and practical faith was awakened" (Nonini 1985).

Bibliography

Nonini, Rogelio. 1985. *Conclusiones sobre la campaña en San Justo*. Zona Oeste Jesús te ama, No1 (Mazo, 1985).

Saracco, Jose Norberto. 1989. "Argentine Pentecostalism: Its History and Theology." PhD diss., University of Birmingham, UK.

Wynarczyk, Hilario. 2014. *Tres evangelistas carismáticos. Omar Cabrera, Héctor Aníbal Giménez, Carlos Annacondia*. Buenos Aires: FIET/Prensa Ecuménica.

Norberto Saracco

Anthropology

At the inception of modern anthropology in the 1920s, anthropologists studied small, bounded communities on the margins of the world's political and economic centres. Since they treated local forms of religion as integral to the functioning of supposedly unchanging indigenous cultures, many early anthropologists either ignored missionaries, preachers and Christian conversion or described their corruptive influence. By the 1950s, anthropologists working in rapidly changing colonial contexts started describing how Christian conversion, especially in indigenous or independent Pentecostal churches, helped newly urbanised individuals to adapt to alienating urban environments. They were particularly interested in the symbolic, ritual and social continuities between these churches and the village or rural societies from which converts came.

This early work on Pentecostal Christianity, however, did not cohere into a thematic interest or subfield in anthropology until the 1990s. The resultant Anthropology of Christianity was heavily skewed towards the study of Pentecostalism, and especially its Pentecostal-Charismatic Church (PCC) expressions. On the one hand, this emphasis reflected global shifts in Christian adherence and growth, to PCCs and to the Global South. But on the other hand, it also reflected changes in anthropology itself. The discipline was no longer confined to studying small-scale communities and routinely studied social change at a global level. Due to a 'reflexive turn', anthropologists also realised that many of their analytical categories such as ideas of interiority and personhood, religion, ritual, sacrifice, symbol, belief, linear time, and the secular were shaped by the intellectual history of Christianity.

No longer a "repugnant cultural other" (Harding 1991) or anthropology's "repressed other" (Cannell 2006, 4), the study of Pentecostal Christianity in anthropology has clustered around the topics of conversion, Christian language use, materiality (Engelke 2007), gender, personhood, embodied ritual practice, popular media (Meyer 2009), globalization (Coleman & Hackett 2015), the nature of Christian social organisations (van Wyk 2014) and the intersections between economic and political practice (Corten & Marshall-Fratani 2001). In these fields, anthropological work is distinctive because of the discipline's emphasis on extended fieldwork and case-studies. Robbins (2004) also argued that anthropologists were uniquely interested in how Christians negotiated the relationship between their faith's transcendent ideals and their mundane daily lives.

In much of this work, anthropologists emphasised the radical social and cultural ruptures that accompanied Pentecostal conversion in the Global South (Robbins 2004). In Africa, scholars showed that

Pentecostalism fostered new kinds of individualism that allowed believers to extract themselves from socially and economically demanding extended kin relationships. In the Pacific and Latin America, anthropologists described shifts away from beliefs in community to individual salvation (Robbins 2004), radical changes in language ideologies (Keane 2007) and politics (Corten & Marshall-Fratani 2001) and emphasised the important role that Pentecostalism played in the formation of racial and gender identities (Burdick 1998). Culturally, anthropologists showed that Pentecostalism throughout the Global South often pitted itself against local traditions. This antagonism towards traditional beliefs and social ties found ritual expression in Pentecostal forms of spiritual warfare (Marshall 2009; van Wyk 2014), allowing Pentecostalism to both "localise" and, ironically, in many cases, to preserve indigenous spiritual ontologies. As such, local spirits were often translated into Christian "devils" (Meyer 1999) while believers continued to be centrally concerned with the material efficacy of their beliefs. These expectations impacted on the stability of otherwise close-knit religious communities as individual believers often shifted their religious loyalties between churches and religious leaders.

While the bulk of anthropological research on Pentecostalism focuses on its geographical centres of influence, namely on Africa, Latin America, Asia and the Pacific, a number of influential scholars have also looked at its expressions in Europe and the United States of America. Here, research is often divided between the work done on American or European-initiated churches and work on migrant churches. In the latter, scholars often describe churches as important nodes in transnational religious networks and as vital social institutions for migrants from the Global South who experience fundamental social and cultural dislocation (Butticci 2016). Research on American and European Pentecostal churches, on the other hand, often deal with the problem of belief in secularising contexts; how believers experience and understand conversion (Luhrmann 2012; Harding 2000), religious healing (Csordas 1994), miracles, the immanence of God (Bialecki 2017) and the technologies and promises of the prosperity gospel (Coleman 2000).

Closely tracking the initial growth and spread of Pentecostalism across the globe, recent anthropological work has also started to focus on the movement's "maturation" (Coleman & Hackett 2015, 16). In recent years, anthropologists started writing about the places and communities where Pentecostalism failed to take root (Premawardhana 2018), where it encountered stiff opposition from resurgent traditional religion and Islam, and where its believers accepted limits to the transcendent promises of its gospel (Haynes 2017) and its new sociality (van Wyk 2014).

Bibliography

Bialecki, Jon. 2017. *A Diagram for Fire Miracles and Variation in an American Charismatic Movement.* Berkeley, CA: University of California Press.

Burdick, John. 1998. *Blessed Anastacia: Women, Race, and Popular Christianity in Brazil.* New York: Roudedge.

Butticci, Annalisa. 2016. *African Pentecostals in Catholic Europe: The Politics of Presence in the Twenty-First Century.* Cambridge, MA: Harvard University Press.

Cannell, Fenella, ed. 2006. *The Anthropology of Christianity.* Durham, NC: Duke University Press.

Coleman, Simon, and Rosalind I.J. Hackett, eds. 2015. *The Anthropology of Global*

Pentecostalism and Evangelicalism. New York: New York University Press.

Coleman, Simon. 2000. *The Globalisation of Charismatic Christianity: Spreading the Gospel of Prosperity*. Cambridge: Cambridge University Press.

Corten, Andre, and Ruth Marshall-Fratani, eds. 2001. *Between Babel and Pentecost: Transnational Pentecostalism in Africa and Latin America*. Bloomington IN: Indiana University Press.

Csordas, Thomas. J. 1994. *The Sacred Self: A Cultural Phenomenology of Charismatic Healing*. Berkeley CA: University of California Press.

Engelke, Matthew. 2007. *A Problem of Presence: Beyond Scripture in an African Church*. Berkeley CA: University of California Press.

Harding, Susan F. 2000. *The Book of Jerry Falwell: Fundamentalist Language and Politics*. Princeton NJ: Princeton University Press.

Harding, Susan F. 1991. "Representing Fundamentalism: The Problem of the Repugnant Other. *Social Research* 58 (2): 373–393.

Haynes, Naomi. 2017. *Moving by the Spirit: Pentecostal Social Life on the Zambian Copperbelt*. Berkeley: University of California Press.

Keane, Webb. 2007. *Christian Moderns: Freedom and Fetish in the Mission Encounter*. Berkeley CA: University of California Press.

Luhrmann, Tanya M. 2012. *When God Talks Back: Understanding the American Evangelical Relationship with God*. New York: Alfred A. Knopf.

Marshall, Ruth. 2009. *Political Spiritualities: The Pentecostal Revolution in Nigeria*. Chicago IL: University of Chicago Press.

Meyer, Birgit, ed. 2009. *Aesthetic Formations: Media, Religion, and the Senses*. London: Palgrave Macmillan.

Meyer, Birgit. 1999. *Translating the Devil: Religion and Modernity among the Ewe in Ghana*. Edinburgh: Edinburgh University Press.

Premawardhana, Devaka. 2018. *Faith in Flux: Pentecostalism and Mobility in Rural Mozambique*. Philadelphia, PA: University of Pennsylvania Press.

Robbins, Joel. 2004. *Becoming Sinners: Christianity and Moral Torment in a Papua New Guinea Society*. Berkeley CA: University of California Press.

Van Wyk, Ilana. 2014. *The Universal Church of the Kingdom of God in South Africa: A Church of Strangers*. Cambridge: Cambridge University Press.

Ilana Van Wyk

Apostles, Apostolic Ministry

The so-called apostolic movement, apostolic-prophetic movement, or New Apostolic Reformation, has grown since the 1990s from small beginnings among pentecostal and charismatic Christians to become a significant factor in World Christianity. Demographers Todd Johnson and Gina Zurlo (2019, 934–5) estimated that some 44 million Christians belonged to "apostolic churches," defined as "pentecostal" communities stressing a "complex hierarchy of living apostles, prophets and other charismatic officials." Central to the apostolic movement is a revolution (Campos 2017) in understanding church leadership and structure, away from pastor-led congregations or denominations toward a different conceptuality. Adherents propose that the Christian church is "built upon the foundation of the apostles and prophets" (Eph. 2:20), and that apostles and prophets are not merely figures of the past but ought to be leading the present-day church. Some use the phrase "five-fold ministry" as essentially synonymous with "apostolic," since the biblical text that mentions five offices – apostles, prophets, evangelists, pastors, teachers

(Eph. 4:11) – places "apostles" first (cf. 1 Cor. 12:28). Because the "apostle" is "one who is sent forth" (Greek, *apostolos*), and who is thought prophetically to discern and follow God's will in a specific situation, proponents claim that apostolic leadership in the church injects elements of spiritual dynamism, missional orientation, and cultural adaptability that appear to be missing from traditional Catholic, Orthodox, and Protestant models of the church. In some contexts today, "apostolic" might be translated as "missional."

Proponents for modern-day apostles prior to the 1990s included: Edward Irving (1792–1834), whose followers formed the Catholic Apostolic Church; John Alexander Dowie (1847–1907), founder of the Christian Catholic Apostolic Church; D.P. (Daniel Powell) Williams, a leader of the Apostolic Church in Wales (est. 1916), Watchman Nee in China, leaders and authors of the Canadian Latter Rain Revival (1948–1950), and Derek Prince (1915–2003). Since the 1990s, advocates of contemporary apostleship included: Kenneth Hagin, C. Peter Wagner and Bill Hamon in the USA, David Cartledge in Australia, and Stefan Vatter in Germany. There are genealogical links between the apostolic teachings of Irving and of Dowie, the Canadian Latter Rain, and extending to Bill Hamon, who in turn influenced C. Peter Wagner. In apparent independence of developments elsewhere, Watchman Nee's "Little Flock" during the 1930s commissioned "apostles" (Chinese, *shi-tu*) as roving workers with a commission to establish new churches where none as yet existed (McNair Scott 2014).

Discussions of present-day apostles involve intricate debates over biblical exegesis and the assessment of traditional models of church governance (e.g. episcopacy, presbyterianism, congregationalism). Much of the controversy centers on questions of continuity and authority: Do apostles still exist in the church after the first century? And, if so, do they carry the sort of authority assigned to the original twelve? Roman Catholics – including Catholic Charismatics – understand Jesus' twelve apostles as having passed on their role and authority to bishops, who subsequently stand in an unbroken "apostolic succession" up to the present time. In Catholic theology there is thus no place for a "charismatic apostleship" whereby someone, who is not in the succession of bishops, might claim to be an apostle. Orthodox Christians and some Anglicans hold the same view. Protestant and Evangelical Christians typically deny an apostolic succession, yet they object to modern-day apostles for different reasons. They link apostleship to the foundational ministry – and authorship of the New Testament – accomplished in the first century and never to be repeated. They also stress the rarity of references to "apostle" after the first century or two. Protestants and Evangelicals are often troubled by an authoritarianism that they see as inherent in the notion of present-day apostles. If apostles existed today, would they not have unbounded authority? Some have proposed alternate terms that are less theologically charged (e.g., pioneer) as alternatives to apostle.

In response to these arguments, defenders of present-day apostleship argue that the New Testament does indeed apply the word apostle to numerous persons who were not among the original twelve chosen by Jesus (e.g., Paul, Barnabas, Epaphroditus, perhaps a woman named Junia in Rom. 16:7, etc.; cf. 2 Cor. 8:23). Furthermore, the Book of Revelation (Rev. 2:2) and the non-canonical Didache (ca. 90–120 CE) both suggest that itinerant preachers referred to as apostles were active in the early churches. Ancient

Christian sources also refer to some later figures as apostles (e.g., St. Patrick as the "apostle to Ireland"). Moreover, the Epistle to the Ephesians indicates that Christ established apostles subsequent to Jesus' ascension, and so these cannot be identified with Jesus' earlier choosing of the Twelve. Flowing from Jesus' ascension, the five-fold ministry promotes the upbuilding of the church and the training of each member to do his or her part (Eph. 4:7–16). This seems to be a ministry not limited to the first century but enduring to the present time. Jesus Christ is himself the "Apostle" (Heb. 3:1) who apportions from heaven the ministry gifts that are facets of his own continuing presence in his spiritual body. Some defenders of present-day apostleship, such as Kenneth Hagin, have distinguished foundational apostles from subsequent or functional apostles of the biblical era and of more recent times. This distinction allows for an intermediate position between those who categorically deny post-biblical apostles and those who affirm an essential identity between earlier and later apostles.

The global apostolic movement is manifold rather than unitary in character, and its literature is regionally and culturally contextualized. Against a backdrop of German church decline, Stefan Vatter calls his book on apostleship (2018) a "wake up call" for believers to discover a "church with a future". He stresses "apostolic teams" rather than individuals, and expatiates on the personal qualities needed in apostles (e.g., humility, faithfulness, perseverance, willingness to suffer, ability to effect signs and wonder s, etc.), as well as the traits found among false apostles (greed, pride, lust, hunger for power, desire to control). In Britain, Benjamin McNair Scott (2014) and William Kay (2007) regard apostolic ministry as a hopeful sign in a generally discouraging post-Christian environment.

They distinguish apostolic networks preoccupied with hierarchical authority and decision-making (R1) from those primarily concerned with evangelistic impact (R2). In Australia apostolic teachings affected the Assemblies of God as early as the 1970s – through Irvingite influences, Dowie's legacy, and the spread of the Canadian Latter Rain. David Cartledge (2000) attributed pentecostal growth in Australia since the 1980s to the apostolic movement, though he admits the existence of "pentecostal cessationists" who acknowledge many spiritual gifts but not that of contemporary apostleship. Perhaps because of Australians' unceremonious attitudes, those who affirm apostles today are still generally unwilling to apply this title to themselves or to other people.

Writing in Peru, Bernardo Campos (2017) depicts the ethos of Latin American apostolic ministry in terms of "prophetic worship", "royal ecclesiology", Old Testament models for the church, "high-level spiritual warfare", "victorious eschatology", and new patterns of church association ("chain-", "star-", and "mesh-networks"). Campos finds here an "ethic of impartation," "ethic of sending," and "ethic of earthly reign" that seeks to transmit spiritual fullness to believers and to send them out as agents of ecclesial and social change. Such a kingdom-based model of mission does not simply seek new church members but engages non-members alongside members in community transformation through varied activities.

In the USA, C. Peter Wagner (1930–2016) founded in 1999 what is known today as the International Council of Apostolic Leaders (ICAL), and formulated a charismatic dominion theology in which "workplace apostles" bring kingdom influence into the so-called "seven mountains" of culture (religion, family, education, government, media, arts, and business). Wagner stressed apostolic authority, commenting that: "In traditional Christianity, authority resided in groups such as church councils, sessions, congregations, and general assemblies. New Apostolic Christianity sees God entrusting the government of the church to individuals" (cited in McNair Scott 2014, 19). In response Douglas Geivett and Holly Pivec (2014) offered a stinging critique of Wagner's New Apostolic Reformation, which they saw as rife with prideful self-assertion and bad theology. Yet this critique focused almost exclusively on developments in the USA prior to Wagner's death in 2016, rather than on other global ministry networks self-designated as apostolic. Because of the differences among these, it may be best not to judge any such movement by its name alone but instead by a careful examination of its leaders, its teachings, and its effects (Mt. 7:16).

Bibliography

Campos, Bernardo. 2017. *¿Apóstoles Hoy? Historia y Teología del Movimiento Apostólico-Profetico*. Salem, Oregon: Publicaciones Kerigma.

Cartledge, David. 2000. *The Apostolic Revolution: The Restoration of Apostolic and Prophetic Ministry in the Assemblies of God in Australia*. Chester Hill, NSW, Australia: Paraclete.

Flegg, Columba Graham. 1992. *"Gathered Under Apostles": A Study of the Catholic Apostolic Church*. Oxford, UK: Clarendon Press.

Geivett, R. Douglas, and Holly Pivec. 2014. *God's Super-Apostles: Encountering the Worldwide Prophets and Apostles Movement*. Wooster, OH: Weaver Book Company.

Hamon, Bill. 1997. *Apostles, Prophets, and the Coming Moves of God*. Santa Rosa Beach, FL: Christian International.

Johnson, Todd M., and Gina A. Zurlo. 2019. *World Christian Encyclopedia*, Third edition. Edinburgh: Edinburgh University Press.

Kay, William K. 2007. *Apostolic Networks in Britain: New Ways of Being Church*. Milton Keynes: Paternoster.

McNair Scott, Benjamin G. 2014. *Apostles Today: Making Sense of Contemporary Charismatic Apostolates: A Historical and Theological Appraisal*. Eugene, OR: Pickwick Publications.

Vatter, Stefan. 2018. *Finden, Fördern, Freisetzen; Wirksam führen – die Wiederendeckung des apostolischen Dienstes*. 3. Auflage. Schwartzenfeld, Deutschland: Neufeld Verlag.

Walker, Andrew. 1998. *Restoring the Kingdom: The Radical Christianity of the House Church Movement*. Guildford, Surrey, UK: Eagle.

Michael McClymond

Argentina

The arrival of the first Pentecostal witness to Argentina occurred on 9 October 1909, when Louis Francescon, Giacomo Lombardi, and Lucía Menna arrived at the port of Buenos Aires from Chicago. Louis Francescon had founded the First Italian Presbyterian Church in Chicago. He had received the baptism in the Holy Spirit in the church of W.H. Durham and moved by a deep sense of mission to the Italian people went to Buenos Aires and contacted some families, but beyond some charismatic experiences, this first group was not significant. Five months later, on 8 March 1910, Francescon and Lombardi left for Brazil. On January 15 of that same year, Alice Wood had arrived in Buenos Aires. Wood had received training at the Christian and Missionary Alliance Institute in Nyack and had the strong spiritual influence of A.B. Simpson. Wood's importance lies in the fact that it was she who established the first Pentecostal church in Argentina and later trained the first Pentecostal pastors. In 1914, when the Assemblies of God were established, Wood requested membership from Argentina and her name is among the founders. Also, in 1910, Berger Jonson arrived from Norway. He carried out his ministry among the native peoples of the Argentine Northwest and he was so appreciated by them that at his death the natives requested that he be buried in their cemetery. In 1921, Charles Wortman, an obstetrician and the first missionary of the Pentecostal Assemblies of Canada, arrived. This denomination incorporated several independent missionaries who had left the mission field without institutional support and who were affected by the restrictions of the First World War. In 1947, the Assemblies of God, US plus the Pentecostal Assemblies of Canada and missionaries of the Pentecostal Holiness Church, established a legal organization under the name of Union of the Assemblies of God. Argentina is the only country where the Assemblies of God are called Union of the Assemblies of God. In addition to the American, Canadian and Norwegian currents there is a Swedish strand in the origin of Argentine Pentecostalism. The first Swedes arrived in 1920 sent by the Philadelphia Church in Stockholm, Sweden. Although their intention was to join the work of the Norwegian missionaries among the natives, they moved to Buenos Aires and in 1922 they opened the first Pentecostal church in the city and in 1926 they built the first temple. In the following decades, the rest of the Pentecostal denominations were established and indigenous churches were born. There have been three Pentecostal ministries that significantly affected society and the rest of the Evangelical churches. The first of these was the campaign of healing evangelist Tommy Hicks (1909–73). He arrived in Buenos Aires on 9 March 1954, when T.L. Osborn, the intended speaker, was unable to travel. His meetings extended uninterruptedly from April 14 to June 12. On the last night, there were 400,000 people in attendance for the mass evangelization event. The second of the ministries was that of Omar Cabrera. After being a pastor, he founded Visión de Futuro (Vision of the Future) in 1972 under the motto: "The greatest power in the world is the power of faith in God." His original intention was not to establish churches but to evangelize and integrate converts into existing congregations. However, his movement was so massive that there was no church capable of containing it and it ended up as another Pentecostal denomination. The third relevant ministry was that of Carlos Annacondia. He was a prominent metallurgist who was converted in 1979 and in 1981 founded Mensaje de Salvación (Message of Salvation). His ministry was characterized by an emphasis on the unity of the church, healings, and spiritual manifestations. During the first ten years of his ministry, the number of Evangelicals in Argentina went from 2 percent of the population to 6 percent.

In 1992, Argentina experienced another spiritual movement born within a Pentecostal church. It was called the "anointing" movement. In this case, the central figure was a pastor of the Assemblies of God, Claudio Freidzon. In the midst of a personal crisis, Freidzon began a spiritual quest and came into contact with the literature and ministry of Benny Hinn. Soon his ministry changed and different physical manifestations began to appear in participants, such as laughter. He had a special importance in the renovation of Baptist churches, he managed to gather crowds and his influence spread worldwide. Parallel to the Pentecostal movement there was another movement of spiritual characteristics known as the Charismatic Movement. On Monday, 20 March 1967, a small group of leaders hungry for a greater experience of God, met at the house of Alberto Darling, an executive of the Coca-Cola Export Corporation. Most of them, though not all, belonged to Free Brethren churches. From the beginning, they experienced a special joy, charismatic manifestations and a strong sense of spiritual renewal. Soon the movement grew and came to affect considerably not only the church in Argentina but throughout Latin America. Leaders such as Juan Carlos Ortiz, Jorge Himitian or Orville Swindoll have had a strong continental presence and influence. The main emphases of this movement have been the Lordship of Christ, the unity of the church, discipleship, the Gospel of the Kingdom and renewal in the liturgy.

In July 2003, Mateo Calissi, an Italian charismatic Catholic layman, visited Argentina. During his visit, he contacted some Argentine charismatic pastors. Out of this informal meeting came the idea of making a united convocation for a special day. This occurred on 1 July 2004, in the auditorium of the Catholic University. The following year the event was repeated and gave rise to CRECES (Renewed Fellowship of Evangelicals and Catholics in the Holy Spirit). CRECES convened a multitudinous gathering of Catholics and Evangelicals, which took place on 19 June 2006, at the Luna Park stadium. It had the decisive support of Cardinal Jorge Bergoglio, who years later was elected Pope Francis. He participated actively and at the end of the event, the pastors present on the platform prayed for him, laying their hands on him. A time of cooperation and unity began among Evangelicals, mostly charismatics, and Catholics. This marked the origin of a deep relationship between the pastors Jorge Himitian, Angel Negro, Omar Cabrera, Carlos Mraida, Norberto Saracco and the future Pope, a relationship that has continued during his pontificate.

Today, those who belong to some of the Pentecostal denominations, as well as those who consider themselves Pentecostals, not because of their belonging but because of their experience, constitute 13 percent of the population (5,460,000 people) of Argentina.

Bibliography

CONICET. 2019. Segunda encuesta nacional sobre creencias y actitudes religiosas en Argentina. Buenos Aires: CONICET.

Saracco, José Norberto. 2014. *Pentecostalismo argentino, origen, teología y misión (1909–1990)*. Buenos Aires: ASIT.

Swindoll, Orville. 2017. *Tiempos de restauración*. Buenos Aires: Logos.

Wagner, Peter, and Pablo Deiros, eds. 1998. *The Rising Revival: Firsthand Accounts of the Incredible Argentine Revival – and How it Can Spread Throughout the World*. Ventura, CA: Renew.

Norberto Saracco

Argue, Zelma

Zelma Argue (1900–1980) was a Canadian evangelist, musician, pastor and writer. The eldest daughter of Eva and A.H. Argue of Winnipeg, Manitoba, she was raised in a Pentecostal household after her father's baptism in the Holy Spirit in Chicago in 1907. The Argue family was well-known in North American Pentecostal circles, because of their travelling ministry and their

Zelma and A.H. Argue. Source: Pentecostal Assemblies of Canada Archives

leadership ties to William Durham, Aimee Semple McPherson, Maria Woodworth-Etter, and Charles S. Price, among others. As young adults, Zelma and her siblings (including Watson Argue and Beulah Argue Smith) regularly travelled with their father as musicians, teachers, and evangelists, becoming sought-after Pentecostal leaders in their own right.

Zelma Argue launched her ministry career as a travelling evangelist at the age of 20, working in partnership with her younger sister, Beulah. In step with Pentecostalism's focus on eschatology, when young women like the Argue sisters took to the platform at evangelistic meetings, they were seen to be fulfilling the prophecy declared by Joel and repeated in the book of Acts that, in the last days, both sons and daughters would prophesy (Holmes 2010). Indeed, when their family ministered together, A.H. Argue liked to point out that his daughters and his sons literally embodied that prophecy (Ambrose 2010).

As her young adult siblings married and established new ministry partnerships, Zelma continued to work and travel with her father throughout the 1930s on transcontinental campaigns that took them to San Diego during the winter of 1931, through southern Ontario in the spring of 1932, across Western Canada the following year, and into Kansas City, Missouri, and Ebenezer, New York, in the spring of 1934. Frequent reports of the Argues' campaigns and camp meetings filled the pages of Pentecostal periodicals and the frenetic pace at which the father-daughter team traveled was well documented. A report in February 1936 revealed that the Argues sometimes spent the winter in the American south. Florida offered a more comfortable winter climate than Winnipeg and allowed A.H. and Zelma to continue their travels for evangelistic work, but the fragile health of Zelma's mother, Eva, was another reason to escape the Canadian winter. In addition to Florida, the Argues sometimes held meetings in California where the family had maintained contacts from their days with Maria Woodworth-Etter and Aimee Semple McPherson, and where Zelma would eventually become a pastor.

Zelma Argue was a prolific contributor to several denominational magazines published in Canada and the United States between 1920 and 1969, with at least 235 articles appearing in *The Pentecostal Testimony* [Canadian], *The Latter Rain Evangel* and *The Pentecostal Evangel*. Indeed, American Pentecostal periodicals accounted for more than 70 percent of Argue's publications. She also published several books including *What Meaneth This?*, *Contending for the Faith*, *Garments of Strength*, *Strenuous Days*, *Prevailing Prayer*, and *The Beauty of the Cross*. Zelma's writing was described as being so popular among Canadian Pentecostals that at least one periodical launched subscription campaigns using her books as incentives. Indeed, the high number of Argue's publications made her one of the most prolific Pentecostal writers in North America, second only to the well-known C.M. Ward (Shearer 2002). Argue's writing established her as an authority figure in the Pentecostal movement, both because of her long-time service and her far-flung travels, and in spite of the fact that she was a woman. While it was common for women to write for religious periodicals, Argue's writing differs from the usual pattern, because she wrote for the general Pentecostal audience, not only for women or children as most female authors did (Ambrose 2009). As Zelma Argue's reputation grew because of her writing, travel, ministry experiences, and certainly because of her well-known extended family, she came to be regarded as one who had her finger on the very pulse of the developing North American Pentecostal movement.

Focused on her life as an evangelist, Zelma never married, but she did partner with another woman, Jeanette Jones, to pastor the Trinity Gospel Tabernacle in Los Angeles, California, beginning in 1948. After resigning from that church in 1957, Argue resumed her role as a travelling evangelist until she retired in 1964, supported by a pension from the American denomination, the Assemblies of God. Zelma Argue provides a fascinating case study in the gendered ministry of Pentecostalism because as a single woman she never did fill the role of "wife" to an evangelist or pastor, yet when she travelled with her father and brother, she acted almost as a "helpmeet" to them, while simultaneously establishing her individual ministry (Ambrose 2010). Well-known as an evangelist, a popular teacher, and a pastor, it was through her writings that Zelma Argue established her most enduring legacy among North American Pentecostals.

Bibliography

Ambrose, Linda M. 2009. "Establishing a Gendered Authority through Pentecostal Publications: The Writings of Zelma Argue, 1920–1969," in *Historical Papers: Journal of the Canadian Society of Church History*, 69–80.

Ambrose, Linda M. 2010. "Zelma and Beulah Argue: Sisters in the Canadian Pentecostal Movement." In *Winds from the North: Canadian Contributions to the Pentecostal Movement*, edited by Michael Wilkinson and Peter Althouse, 99–127. Leiden: Brill Academic Publishers.

Holmes, Pamela M.S. 2010. "Zelma Argue's Contribution to Early Pentecostalism." In *Winds from the North: Canadian Contributions to the Pentecostal Movement*, edited by Michael Wilkinson and Peter Althouse, 129–150. Leiden: Brill Academic Publishers.

Shearer, Sheryl. 2002. "Zelma Argue: Handmaiden of the Lord." *A/G Heritage* (Spring): 18–23.
Wilkinson, Michael, and Linda M. Ambrose. 2020. *After the Revival: Pentecostalism and the Making of a Canadian Church*. Montreal & Kingston: McGill-Queen's University Press.

Linda M. Ambrose

Asia

Pentecostalism has undergone vibrant growth in some areas of Asia at the end of the twentieth century, while in others it remains infertile. Both its growth and stagnancy deserve scholarly attention. This article will provide an overview of Pentecostalism in Asia from historical and sociological views in three sections. The first section includes East, Southeast, and South Asia, which share political, economic, and religious commonalities. The second section will focus on Central Asia and the third one on West Asia.

East Asia includes China, Hong Kong, Japan, Macao, Mongolia, North Korea, South Korea and Taiwan. Southeast Asia includes Brunei, Cambodia, Indonesia, Laos, Malaysia, Myanmar, Philippines, Singapore, Thailand, Timor-Leste, and Vietnam. South Asia includes Afghanistan, Bangladesh, Bhutan, India, Iran, Maldives, Nepal, Pakistan, and Sri Lanka.

Most countries in these three regions were colonies of Britain (Myanmar, Hong Kong, Malaysia, Singapore, Sri Lanka, India), the Netherlands (Indonesia), Japan (Taiwan and South Korea), France (Vietnam), or the United States (the Philippines). It was only Thailand that would be immune from colonialism. After WWII, colonial powers were gradually fading away, but self-governance did not necessarily render more freedom. In fact, there was worse oppression throughout the 1980s–1990s. For example, South Korea was under a dictator and military regime; Taiwan, the Nationalist government; Vietnam, the Communist government; and the Philippines, Ferdinand Marcos' rule. Besides political oppression, people of these authoritarian countries also suffered from corruption and a high crime rate due to media censorship which hindered close examination of the government and the privileged. In such unfavorable postcolonial circumstances, the vivid spiritual expression of Pentecostalism would sometimes bring hope to the oppressed. For example, the practice of divine healing echoed the Korean spiritual and physical suffering of han and realized the vision of the indigenous Minjung theology. In the Philippines, the Catholic Charismatic Renewal grew despite the oppressive regime of the 1970s.

Most of these countries became more democratic and respectful towards human rights and freedoms by the end of the twentieth century. However, in the twenty-first century, several authoritarian governments still exist, controlled either by the Communist party or fundamentalist Islamic power. In Communist countries, under the atheistic banner, all religions are oppressed bitterly. Although China and Vietnam (not North Korea) have been more tolerant towards religion since the 1980s, Pentecostalism, which emphasizes vibrant worship and vivid spiritual experiences promoting a sense of spontaneity and liberty, has been undergoing tighter surveillance and persecution. Evidence of Pentecostalism is mostly found in the underground house churches, although some official churches have been more open to it.

Some countries in this region have seen soaring economic growth since the 1970s. Capitalism has dominated their economies, and even some Communist countries like China and Vietnam opened their markets in the 1980s and joined the World Trade Organization. This economic motif directs the priority of life – focusing on quantity and money, especially because most of these countries were extremely poor. Pentecostalism first arrived in these regions as a new form of Christianity. It brought hope to the poor by opening schools, hospitals, and orphanages while also promoting divine healing and prophecy to concretely present the gospel. However, as the economic situation has improved, the prosperity gospel has begun to play a more significant role in the presentation of the gospel, together with the institutionalized practice of charisms, healing clinics, and prophet-training schools. The emphases on material wealth and institutionalized charisms fit the middle-class ethos of social prestige and professionalism. The use of high-tech visual and audio equipment and glamorous buildings become the visible symbols of divine blessing and rewards for the faithful's offerings. The competitiveness and high pressure in capitalist societies prompt people to seek inner healing more than the healing of their bodies and communities. The establishment of Pentecostal megachurches are mostly found in economically fast-growing countries like South Korea, Malaysia, Singapore, Taiwan, Hong Kong, and India. But there are exceptions: the Philippines and Indonesia whose economic progress has been slow. In the Philippines, huge Pentecostal and charismatic congregations not only exist in Protestant churches but also in the Roman Catholic Church.

Asia is the birthplace of four major religions that still dominate the region: Islam, Hinduism, Buddhism, and Christianity. As it took root in West Asia, Christianity spread across Central, South, and East Asia through missionaries for two millennia. Christianity, in general, has a long tradition of living with neighbors of other religions and facing pluralistic challenges. Some Pentecostals have managed to thrive and establish megachurches in some predominantly Islamic states like Malaysia and Indonesia, and in Hindu countries like India. But in countries where Buddhism has a strong foundation, like Thailand, Myanmar, and Sri Lanka, their growth seems to be moderate. But in both situations, due to Pentecostals' active evangelistic efforts, they are considered to be a threat to the state religion. Some governments adopt administrative and legal means to make new churches register. Some of the Pentecostal churches have been vandalized or burned by religious extremists.

In fundamentalist Islamic countries like Afghanistan, Pakistan, and Iran, Christianity can hardly exist. In Pakistan, although Christianity is tolerated, Christians can easily be accused of breaking blasphemy laws and be sentenced for life imprisonment or even execution. In such extreme circumstances, all Christians have to pay a high price to maintain their faith, including Pentecostals.

Pentecostalism has grown rapidly in some of the countries in these regions because Pentecostals acknowledge the operation of the spiritual world in the material world, which is coherent with the cosmology of other religions. Pentecostals, unlike other forms of Protestantism, do not deny that spiritual forces can manipulate human lives. Their faith and practices of physical and psychological deliverance have gained popularity in non-Christian countries. For example, in popular Hinduism, illnesses, infertility, family conflicts, unemployment, and other misfortunes are believed to be associated with evil spirits. While Hindu gurus or exorcists counter the evil spirits with their spiritual forces, Pentecostals deal with these problems with the power of the Holy Spirit.

Religion is often associated with national identity. In most of these countries, ethnic minorities and tribal multitudes face multifaceted deprivation of economic, political, and educational rights since they are not adherents of the state religions. Consequently, their social mobility is restricted across generations, like the Chinese in Malaysia and Indonesia, and the Chin in Myanmar. Pentecostalism's central message of hope, empowerment, and even prosperity, accompanied with tangible, physical manifestations, has attracted thousands of minorities. Intense experiences of spiritual empowerment strengthen them to face social injustice and inequality.

Central Asia includes Kazakhstan, Kyrgyzstan, Tajikistan, Turkmenistan, and Uzbekistan. It was under the Soviet control until 1989. These five states maintain a certain degree of restraint towards religion in order to develop patriotism and avoid religious extremism, especially because the region neighbors Afghanistan, the seedbed of twenty-first century Islamic extremism. All religious groups have to register and privately practice their faith. Islam is the major religion, co-existing with Buddhism (particularly Tibetan Buddhism), Christianity (particularly Russian Orthodoxy) and shamanism. Uzbekistan has the largest Muslim population of the five.

Christianity is in the minority in the region, but Kazakhstan and Kyrgyzstan are the exceptions. Besides Russian Orthodoxy, Catholic, Presbyterian, Baptist, Methodist, Mennonite, and Pentecostal churches can be found. Christians in these countries have reasonable relations with Muslims. Pentecostal churches are relatively new compared to other churches, and some of the Pentecostals are ethnically Koreans. Foursquare Missions International, a Pentecostal organization, has developed 27 communities in the country with Kazakhs as the local ministers. The Vineyard, a neo-Pentecostal denomination, has also been busy planting churches and training local pastors.

Pentecostals face persecution more frequently than other Protestant churches due to their zealous missionary approach. Some of the states like Tajikistan promulgates new laws to censor religious literature and restrict the venues of Christian meetings. Some states like Turkmenistan even view Pentecostals as sects and put them in the same category as Jehovah's Witness and Scientology.

West Asia is comprised of three main regions: the Levant, which includes the countries of Lebanon, Israel, Jordan, Palestine, Syria, and Cyprus; Eurasia, including Armenia, Turkey, Azerbaijan, and Georgia; and, finally, the Arabian Peninsula and the Arabian/Persian Gulf region with Kuwait, Oman, Qatar, Bahrain, Saudi Arabia, UAE, Yemen, and Iraq.

Most of the countries in West Asia have Islamic majorities. The exceptions to this are: Lebanon, Israel, Cyprus, Armenia, and Georgia. These countries have majority Christian and Jewish populations. The rest of the region is predominately Sunni Muslim with significant Shi'a populations scattered throughout with concentrations in Kuwait, Bahrain, Azerbaijan, Iraq, and Saudi Arabia.

Indigenous Apostolic Christianity remains somewhat intact in the region. Lebanon boasts significant Catholic Maronite and Melkite populations. Melkites can also be found in Syria, Iraq, Israel, Palestine, and Jordan. Cyprus, Georgia, and Armenia are mostly Orthodox, and the Assyrian Church of the East still survives in Syria and Iraq, though it has suffered much in recent years. Conclaves of Antiochian and Jacobite Orthodox are also present but in small numbers. The Egyptian Coptic Orthodox Church, too, has congregations throughout the region. These congregations, however, are typically associated with 20thcentury migration patterns rather than a local continuous presence. On the Arabian Peninsula, however, the ancient Church of the East did not survive past the 7th century. Nearly all current existing churches were begun by missionaries or migrants from other nations within the past hundred years.

In the early modern era, spurred by the Edinburgh Missionary Conference (1910) and a strong millenarianism promulgated at the Azusa Street Revival of 1906, evangelical and Pentecostal missionaries planted churches throughout the region. Some took root in Lebanon, Israel, Palestine, Syria, Cyprus, Kuwait and Jordan. Others did not last long against cultural and religious hegemonies. Only a few surviving congregations can claim continuity with these pre-WWI efforts.

WWI and WWII, together with the carving up of sections of the region between European powers, did a significant amount of damage to missionary activities and congregations. Subsequently, Armenia, Georgia, and Azerbaijan were effectively sealed behind the Iron Curtain. Petro-dollars and a puritanical form of Islam known as Wahhabism fuelled the rise of more stringently Islamic states thereby making missional activity prohibited and prosecutable. Through the second half of the twentieth century, many missionaries and fledging congregations emigrated to other countries to avoid violence and persecution.

As a region, West Asia's net Christian growth rate from 1970–2015 is –.55 percent, although this number is skewed due to the ongoing violence in Syria and Iraq, in particular. Nevertheless, in the postcolonial era, Pentecostal and evangelical churches are thriving in several of the countries in West Asia, following the general trend of the spread of global, pentecostalized Christianity. This is largely due to the influx of Christian migrant workers and greater connectivity through media between churches in the region and throughout the world. For example, many American and European congregations actively support Pentecostals financially. One success story is the Assemblies of God, which has been able to weather social and political change and maintain its denominational brand in most of West Asia either in missionary presence and congregations.

Anecdotally, the Pentecostal church is growing in the region through conversions. Actual numbers are difficult to assess given the dangerous climate many converts face from their families, friends, and governments. Conversion narratives often take the form of supernatural experiences. Many, if not most, conversions in the area occur after a significant dream or vision, through the undeniable answer to a prayer, or through healing. Pentecostal groups make much of these testimonies in their literature and media used to promote their missions in the West and elsewhere.

Bibliography

Anderson, Allan. 2007. *Spreading Fires: The Missionary Nature of Early Pentecostalism*. Maryknoll, NY: Orbis Books.

Anderson, Allan, and Edmond Tang, eds. 2011. *Asian and Pentecostal: The Charismatic Face of Christianity in Asia*. Oxford: Regnum.

Chong, Terence. 2018. *Pentecostal Megachurches in Southeast Asia: Negotiating Class, Consumption and the Nation.* Singapore: ISEAS Publishing.

Ross, Kenneth R., Mariz Tadros, and Todd M. Johnson, eds. 2018. *Christianity in North Africa-West Asia.* Edinburgh: Edinburgh University Press.

Connie Au
Benjamin Crace

Assemblies of God, USA

The American phase of the Pentecostal movement emerged within the Wesleyan Holiness movement, characterized by a belief in sanctification as a second critical event that followed justification in the believers' life. Holiness Pentecostals believed that the baptism of the Holy Spirit was a third critical event that followed sanctification. This understanding of the Christian pilgrimage was challenged by William H. Durham who in 1910 introduced the "Finished Work" perspective, reflecting his Calvinist theological background, and who suggested that the baptism of the Holy Spirit was immediately available to any Christian, without the necessity of a sanctifying event.

Over the next few years, the Finished Work perspective spread nationally and became a dominant view among Pentecostals, especially in Texas and the Midwest. Its supporters in the South Central states found a voice in the periodical, *Word and Witness*, based in Malvern, Arkansas, and its ministers were credentialed by a new loosely organized association, the Church of God in Christ (white). Seeing the need of greater organization, in 1913,*Word and Witness* editor Eudorus Bell joined with colleagues Howard Goss, Daniel C.O. Opperman, Archibald Collins, and Mack M. Pinson to issue a call to create a structure (short of a new denomination) that could deal with concerns such as doctrinal unity, ministerial education, and support for foreign missions.

The call resulted in a gathering at Hot Springs, Arkansas, in 1914 at which attendees approved the formation of the General Council of the Assemblies of God. Initially, headquarters were established in Findlay, Ohio, though within a few years the more permanent headquarters would be developed in Springfield, Missouri. As the organization evolved from a fellowship of ministers and began to welcome congregations into affiliation, they were allowed a degree of autonomy and maintained ownership of local church property, while placing control of ministerial education and ordination, the publishing of books and a periodical, and the coordination of overseas missions with the national organization. National leadership would be placed in the hands of a General Superintendent, and the national church was divided into a number of geographical districts, with additional districts serving a growing Spanish-speaking membership.

The Assemblies adopted the previously existing Gospel Publishing House as its own and the *Word and Witness* merged with a sister periodical, *The Christian Evangel* (1916) to create the still existing new periodical, the *Pentecostal Evangel.* The Assemblies moved to cooperate with several districts in setting up schools that could train leaders before designating Central Bible Institute as its primary institution of higher learning. As the Assemblies grew, it would develop more than a dozen colleges and universities across the United States along with a primary Assemblies of God Theological Seminary (opened in 1973).

The General Council appointed an initial missionary secretary, J.R. Flower, and backed the development of a systematic international mission with a coordinated sponsorship and support. Having inherited a host of missionary stations scattered around the globe, the Assemblies would, through the remainder of the century, turn its missionary effort into one of its most impressive accomplishments. By the 2010s, it reported more than 60 million adherents worldwide.

Initially the General Council refrained from adopting a statement of beliefs, but the task quickly assumed some importance with the emergence of the Oneness movement that replaced the traditional formula for baptism in the name of the Father, the Son and the Holy Spirit (derived from Matthew 28:19) with baptism in the name of Jesus only. The emerging Oneness movement, which found its support from among Finished Work Pentecostals, soon challenged the essential trinitarian view of God. In 1916 the Assemblies responded to the Oneness movement by passing a statement of beliefs that emphasized a traditional trinitarian Protestant Christian perspective. It affirmed belief in the Trinity, following which the Oneness believers in the Assemblies, feeling no longer welcome, withdrew, most ending up in the Pentecostal Assemblies of the World.

Having survived its first major theological challenge, the Assemblies would almost immediately encounter a second, when F.F. Bosworth, the pastor of the large congregation on Dallas, expressed his belief that speaking in tongues was not the singular evidence accompanying and verifying the baptism of the Holy Spirit. With the majority of Assemblies leaders unwilling to back away from their commitment to the necessity of tongues, Bosworth withdrew and moved on to a long career as a healing evangelist.

The decisions made through its first years of existence set the course of the Assemblies of God for a generation. It would not face further theological challenges until after World War II when several movements, each of which drew their early leadership from the ranks of the Assemblies' ministers, challenged the direction of the new generation of leadership. Beginning with the Latter Rain movement of the late 1940s and the Healing Revival of the 1950s, the Assemblies were repeatedly confronted with opposition to its move toward full denominational life. Dissenting voices complained of a loss of spiritual life while simultaneously offering innovative theological options. The Assemblies saw the need to respond to what it saw as extremes in behavior and beliefs.

Following the first popular movements of the post-war era, the Charismatic movement of the 1970s picked up the attack on the evidential nature of tongues while more recently the New Apostolic Reformation and the Prosperity Gospel/Word of Faith movements forced the Assemblies to defend its traditional theological commitments. These movements arose and were rejected even as the Assemblies found new life in cooperative endeavors with other Pentecostal denominations through the Pentecostal Fellowship of North America (PFNA) founded in 1948, and the larger world of Evangelicalism through the National Association of Evangelicals.

Through the last half of the twentieth century the Assemblies of God experienced a time of phenomenal growth both globally and across the United States. Even as mainline churches began a time of gradual decline, the Assemblies saw their fellowship surpass a million adherents, and reach two million (in the mid-1980s) and three million in 2010, with a continuing upward trajectory of numbers that as yet show no signs of slowing.

Even as the Assemblies grew, one problem in its life came into vivid focus, its acceptance into its fellowship of the segregated racial patterns that dominated American life. Steps to confront its failures in this regard became the subject of dialogue among members of the PFNA with several of the prominent African American Pentecostal denominations in the early 1990s. The immediate result of the discussions would be the disbanding of the all-white PFNA and its replacement in 1994 with the interracial Pentecostal Charismatic Churches of North America, which afforded an initial acknowledgement of the problem and has provided the Assemblies a long-term context for addressing this on-going problem.

Bibliography

Blumhofer, Edith L. 1993. *Restoring the Faith: The Assemblies of God, Pentecostalism, and American Culture*. Urbana and Chicago: University of Chicago Press.

Blumhofer, Edith L. 1989. *The Assemblies of God: A Chapter in the Story of American Pentecostalism*. Vols. 1–2. Springfield, MO: Gospel Publishing House.

Lewis, Paul W., ed. 2014. *All the Gospel to All the World: 100 Years of Assemblies of God Missiology*. Springfield, MO: Assemblies of God Theological Seminary.

McGee, Gary B. 2010. *Miracles, Missions, and American Pentecostalism*. Maryknoll, NY: Orbis Books.

Poloma, Margaret M. 1989. *The Assemblies of God at the Crossroads: Charisma and Institutional Dilemmas*. Knoxville, TN: The University of Tennessee Press.

Wacker, Grant. 2003. *Heaven Below: Early Pentecostals and American Culture*. Cambridge, MA: Harvard University Press.

John Gordon Melton

Australia

Australia is a highly plural, secularized federal Western democracy on the southern rim of the Asia-Pacific. It has a relatively small population (26 million) spread across a vast but largely uninhabitable landmass (and attendant islands). From 1788, British colonization over traditional Aboriginal land decisively shaped the first 160 years of religious culture, with 'the Big Four' traditions (Anglicanism, Catholicism, Methodism and Presbyterianism) dominating. Australia was thus an early recipient of the charismatic potentials within these traditions, broadly featuring primitivism and liturgical renewal, prophetic/millennialist, healing and sanctification/experiential movements. While census data would indicate c. 2 million PC members in the country, church attendance data suggests that there are over 400,000 Pentecostals in church on a weekly basis (Singleton 2017). If Catholic charismatics total one-third of Catholic church attenders, then non-pentecostal 'charismatics' in the country (including Anglicans and Uniting Church members) would total another 378,000. This suggests that there are probably not more than 1 million PC church members in Australia.

The first *organized* charismatic tradition in the country was the Catholic Apostolic Church, which sent one of its first 20 evangelists (Alfred Wilkinson) in 1853. After Edward Irving's son, Martin Howy, became Professor of Classics at the University of Melbourne, the CAC community in Carlton became the organizing point for CAC expansion around the region. Until at least the end of the nineteenth century, there is continuous evidence for charismatic ministries in these churches up to the rise of John Alexander Dowie's healing ministry (clearly influenced by CAC healing practices) and beyond. Other tongues movements broke out among holiness Methodists in rural Victoria, along with a number of internationally important healing ministries, particularly that of James Moore Hickson. Globalizing movements such as the liturgical revival in the Anglican Church, the Keswick Convention and faith missions movements, and transnational revivalism, spread these influences around the globe.

Classical Pentecostalism in Australia emerged largely from socially activist Methodist and Salvation Army people disappointed with liberalization and the declining experientialism. Important catalytic influences were the 1902 Torrey Alexander revival in Melbourne, connections to the Welsh Revival (1904), Alexander Boddy's *Confidence* magazine and reports of the South African work (often carried by former members such as the Braun/Brown family) of John G. Lake and other Zionists. Two active Methodists, Robert Horne (Southern Evangelical Mission) and Sarah Jane Lancaster (Good News Hall), established durable healing missions. Through magazines such as *Good News* and Thomas Ames' *Pentecostal Times*, and the work of women such as Florence Mortomore and Annie Dennis, similar missions sprang up in Sydney, Brisbane, and Perth. Around the same time, there is some evidence of Pentecostal-like phenomena among Indigenous peoples on the north coast of NSW and in Queensland. Much of this was prior to and uninfluenced by the Azusa Street Revival, which would have no real effect on Australia until the visit of Aimee Semple McPherson in 1922, and in reality until the Sunshine Revival under A.C. Valdez Sr and Kelso Glover from 1925. Indeed, prior to 1925, there is as much evidence for an Australian influence on American Pentecostalism as there was the reverse, and the majority international influence was (apart from Torrey, Chapman and Alexander) British.

Through the 1920s, local revivals such as Sunshine (1925) and Macknade (1924), and the visits of evangelists such as McPherson, Smith Wigglesworth (1921, and returns), J.M. Hickson, F.B. Van Eyk (from 1926) and later Stephen Jeffreys, Howard Carter, and Jean Darnell, the first Pentecostal denominations emerged as loose, underfunded networks – the Pentecostal Church of Australia (PCA), the Apostolic Faith Mission (AFM), the Assemblies of God in Queensland (AoGQ), The Elim Foursquare Churches (EF). These rationalized over time – the AFM splintered and eventually collapsed after the death of Lancaster, the PCA and the AoGQ combined in 1937 to form the Assemblies of God in Australia (AoGA), the EF collapsed after van Eyk's fall from grace and was largely absorbed into the AoGA and McPherson's International Church of the Foursquare Gospel. Struggles over orthodoxy were periodically an issue, and fuelled tensions between Good News Hall and the PCA, the PCA and Apostolic Church, and eventually led to divisions (over British Israelism) with a future founder of the Christian Revival Crusade movement, Leo Harris. The increasing influence of American models prior to and after World War II exacerbated such tensions, and while these movements grew slowly through until the late 1960s, they remained small and generally localized. Relatively, therefore, their success in missionary work among Indigenous communities was remarkable, with the emergence of both mission churches and Indigenous/Islander forms of Pentecostalism (among Bandjalung peoples in NSW, for example, and in the cane fields of northern Queensland) before similar trends in the mainline traditions. Papua New Guinea missions would absorb much of the attention of the AoGA, growing remarkably from the late 1950s onwards.

Through the 1950s, globalisation, the increase of non-British migration and a growing sense of separation from the State produced increasing mainstream interest in charismatic phenomena. The visits of Lester Sumrall, A.C. Valdez Jr., Oral Roberts, and others sparked a rediscovery of the healing resources in both Anglicanism and Catholicism. The Hickson tradition lived on in John Hope at Christchurch St Laurence in Sydney, and in the Order of Saint Luke/Camps Farthest Out influences returning from the USA. The Latter Rain and American Healing Revivals had a significant impact on both Australia and New Zealand, with the teaching of Ray Jackson and films by Oral Roberts and T.L. Evans provoking a range of Australian and New Zealand born leaders to revitalize the now ageing centres dominated by the founding generation. The return of the charismatic renewal through Alex Reichel to prayer meetings in Sydney (1969), and most importantly in Bardon, Queensland (around Vincent Hobbs and Brian Smith), sparked an upsurge of charismatic activity, both formal (through Alan Langstaff's Temple Trust) and formalizing (through intentional covenant communities, Life in the Spirit Seminars, etc). Not only would the Renewal spread throughout the mainstream (sparking backlash from reformed and more traditional gatekeepers), Smith, Langstaff and others would go on to have significant international careers.

By 1980, the Renewal was succumbing to mainstream reaction, and many of its members were either being drawn to (and some expelled to), the rising Pentecostal and charismatic churches. Though numbers of these (such as Paradise AoG, Garden City AoG, and Calvary Temple) grew markedly through the 1970s, some in the 1980s – such as Hills Christian Life Centre (later Hillsong Church), Christian City Church, Brookvale (later C3 Oxford Falls), Christian Outreach Centre, Mansfield, Riverview Church, and Crossway Baptist Church, Melbourne – broke the 2000 member level as megachurches. Though increasingly under pressure from an increasingly aggressive public culture, those churches with contingent networks (either suburban, linked to migration, or constructed through successful media and conference outreaches) continued to grow. Unlike "2000 plus" churches in the USA (of which there over 1600), most megachurches in Australia are Pentecostal/charismatic, and most of those are linked to the charismaticized 'new church' movement in the Assemblies of God in Australia (now the Australian Christian Churches). They are, as Singleton (2017) notes, uniquely successful in incorporating and engaging the large Majority World migration to Australia, producing widespread diversification in size and identity from the large Korean Full Gospel Church, Greenacre, to a myriad of small ethnically based churches (many with connections to international networks of their own).

By the early 1990s, these churches were proactively church planting, and beginning to spread to other parts of the world, producing compound growth and chain-multiplication. The three largest international networks – Hillsong, with around 150,000 members, C3 with over 500 churches in 64 countries, and the former Christian Outreach Centres (now INC) with over 300,000 in attendance around the world – are now a significant presence in Asia, the Pacific, North America and Europe. In some first world urban centres (such as London) these are among the largest Protestant churches in their settings. This international success has continued to build their Australian home churches, with their Colleges (such as Hillsong International Leadership College) attracting thousands of students. These churches have increasingly driven the cultural agendas of the loose-knit Pentecostal denominations in Australia, providing much of the training, strategy and innovation capital for what, by 2018, had become Australia's largest Protestant church movement.

Bibliography

Chant, Barry. 2011. *The spirit of Pentecost: the origins and development of the Pentecostal Movement in Australia, 1870–1939*. Lexington, KY: Emeth Press.

Elliott, Peter. 2018. "Four Decades of 'Discreet' Charismata: The Catholic Apostolic Church in Australia 1863–1900." *Journal of Religious History* 42 (1): 72–83.

Hutchinson, Mark. 2017. "Framing Australasia's Charismatic Past: Australian charismatic movements as a space of flows." *Pentecostal and Charismatic Christianities in Australia*, Conference Paper, University of Western Sydney, 11 August.

Ono, Akiko. 2012. "You gotta throw away culture once you become Christian: How 'culture' is Redefined among Aboriginal Pentecostal Christians in Rural New South Wales." *Oceania* 82 (1): 74–85.

Riches, Tanya. 2017. "(Re)imagining identity in the Spirit: Worship and Social Engagement in Urban Aboriginal-led Pentecostal Congregations." PhD thesis, Fuller Theological Seminary.

Singleton, Andrew. 2017. "Strong Church or Niche Market? The Demography of the Pentecostal Church in Australia." *Pentecostal and Charismatic Christianities in Australia*, Conference Paper, University of Western Sydney, 11 August.

Mark Hutchinson

Azusa Street Revival

The Apostolic Faith Mission, 312 Azusa Street in Los Angeles, California was the center of the Azusa Street Revival, which ran from April 1906 through 1909. It began in a cottage prayer meeting that quickly exploded into a global movement of churches highlighting the person and work of the Holy Spirit. Joseph Smale, formerly a Baptist pastor, had visited the Welsh Revival (1904–1905) and returned to Los Angeles, urging Christians to pray for revival. Christians in many churches joined him with great expectancy, as prayer meetings sprang up around the city. The African American preacher, William J. Seymour arrived in town just as these meetings were reaching their peak.

On April 9, 1906, a prayer meeting led by Seymour in the home of Richard and Ruth Asberry at 214 North Bonnie Brae Street sparked the revival that many believed was the answer to their prayers. Throughout the month of March Seymour had encouraged this largely African American prayer meeting to seek the Baptism in the Holy Spirit, which he told them, would be

Azusa leaders. Source: Oral Roberts University

evidenced by their ability to speak in other tongues as the Spirit gave them utterance (Acts 2:4). On the evening of April 9, first one and then another began to speak in tongues. With their ties to various congregations in Los Angeles, word of what was taking place at the Asberry home spread quickly.

That week, Seymour leased the former sanctuary of Stevens African Methodist Episcopal Church (now First AME Church) at 312 Azusa Street. The building was fire-damaged and in a sad state of repair. The people from Bonnie Brae began cleaning the building, spreading sawdust on the dirt floor, setting up chairs and benches in a circle. Seymour began services there on Easter Sunday, April 15. Three days later on April 18, the day of the San Francisco earthquake, the *Los Angeles Daily Times* announced its discovery of Seymour's congregation.

The Azusa Street Mission organized as a local congregation, soon purchased the building, incorporated with the State of California, elected a Board of Trustees, kept track of its membership, and advertised its annual business meetings in local newspapers. For the next three years, the Azusa Street revival, led by Seymour, would become a worldwide center of religious attention and the driving force behind the expansion of a movement that swept quickly through many parts of the world. Through the giving of its members and the philanthropy of Cecil Polhill, a wealthy English missionary, they paid off the building by February 1908.

Charles F. Parham, head of the Apostolic Faith Movement in Texas and Kansas, had taught Seymour about baptism in the Spirit. Both men had participated in the Holiness movement, where baptism in the Holy Spirit was a common topic. Leaders within Holiness circles debated the nature of this baptism. Many viewed it as synonymous with sanctification, a baptism of holiness or purity. Others argued that it was a baptism of power. Parham and Seymour agreed that baptism in the Spirit was a baptism of power bestowed on those living the sanctified life. Following their reading of Acts 2, Parham and then, Seymour asserted that the "Bible evidence" of a genuine baptism in the Spirit was the ability to speak in a language not learned in ordinary ways. For Parham, it was a foreign language given solely by the Holy Spirit, which enabled its recipients to engage in foreign missionary work. Seymour was committed to missionary work, but he was less convinced that the tongues that the Holy Spirit gave were for missionary use.

San Francisco's earthquake pushed Azusa Street off the pages of Los Angeles newspapers for several months, but in July 1906, they re-discovered Azusa Street. Most articles were critical of what they witnessed at the Mission. Titles such as "Women with Men Embrace," "Summer Solstice Sees Strenuous Sects Sashaying," and "Whites and Blacks Mix in Religious Frenzy" raised both the interest and the ire of the public. Yet, the Mission soon became a gathering place for many across the city and from around the world, who were interested in witnessing or experiencing this revival first hand. Many who came to the Mission received their baptism in the Holy Spirit. They returned to their homes or places of ministry intent upon bringing the revival to an ever-expanding group of churches and people. As a result, many new Pentecostal congregations were established, and newly "empowered" missionaries scattered across the globe.

There were no textbooks, courses, or seminars to explain what a Pentecostal congregation should do or how it should act, so Seymour encouraged discussion and dialogue. He also allowed some experimentation, such as "singing in tongues" and the practice of "writing in tongues." In the end, he approved of "singing in tongues" (1 Cor. 14:26), but he deemed "writing in tongues" not acceptable since Scripture did not mention it. He empowered those who came to the Mission encouraging full participation in its services regardless of age, gender, color, class, or previous condition of servitude, so long as they did so in a more or less orderly fashion. Their worship included old gospel songs, singing in tongues, extended times of testimony, and lengthy periods of prayer heard for blocks. Many took the opportunity to speak; others simply preached. People claimed to be converted, sanctified, baptized in the Spirit with the Bible evidence of speaking in tongues, and healed. The congregation flourished and for a time, the Mission served as many as 1500 people each Sunday, making it the largest African American led congregation in the city.

In September 1906, the Mission began to publish a paper called, *The Apostolic Faith*. It became an important means for expanding the revival, linking it with various outbreaks of the revival elsewhere, and raising funds for and connecting with missionaries. As the revival spread and new Pentecostal congregations appeared throughout the city, Seymour convened weekly meetings with their pastors, to strategize about the work and in some cases, to endorse pastors and missionaries.

The Mission took advantage of the streetcar system, sending street preachers and ordinary people to outlying areas, where they established yet more congregations. Others traversed the nation, traveling north to Portland and Seattle, east through Colorado Springs and Denver, Minneapolis, Chicago, Indianapolis, New York City, and Boston. By December 1906, the Mission had sent missionaries to Mexico, India, Sweden, Palestine, Liberia, and Angola. It had touched T.B. Barratt of Norway, who helped to spread the revival throughout Western Europe.

Seymour's first significant challenge came when Charles Parham visited Azusa Street in October 1906. Both Seymour and Parham had high expectations for Parham's visit. Yet, Parham's response to what he saw, created a crisis that led to a break between the two men – largely on what each viewed as culturally acceptable in these meetings. Parham condemned Seymour's work as fanatical "Negro spirituality" that white folk should not embrace, and criticized Seymour's staff, their methods, and his missionary appointments.

On May 13, 1908, William J. Seymour married Jennie Evans Moore. His trusted friend, Edward S. Lee performed the ceremony. The marriage sent ripples through the Mission, especially for two women, Florence Crawford and Clara Lum. Crawford had decided already to go into ministry on her own, and had just established her independent Apostolic Faith Mission, Portland, Oregon. Upset by Seymour's decision to marry Moore, Clara Lum, who had edited the Mission's newspaper since September 1906, left the Mission, taking with her a list of subscribers that crippled Seymour's ability to communicate with his worldwide following.

The third challenge came in 1911 in the person of William H. Durham, a feisty Chicago pastor and evangelist. Durham, a Baptist, had visited the Azusa Street Mission in February 1907, where he had received the baptism in the Spirit and spoken in tongues. He took that message back to his congregation in Chicago, where he made a significant impact. He led Italian, Iranian, and Swedish congregations into the Pentecostal Movement. Between 1907 and 1911, however, he rejected the Holiness version of sanctification as the second definite work of grace, and adopted a position he called the "Finished Work." In 1911, while Pastor Seymour was on an extended tour of other Pentecostal churches, Mrs. Seymour invited Durham to cover Seymour's absence. When Seymour returned and found him preaching what he believed to be heresy, he asked Durham to leave. Instead, Durham appealed to the people of Azusa Street to follow him. His action split the Mission, and many went with Durham to form a competing congregation.

By 1915, the revival had moved on, flaring up in many parts of the world. Seymour, having lost members to other congregations, and frustrated with race relations throughout the United States, published his *Doctrines and Discipline* in which he limited office holders to people of color, hoping that this action would be temporary, while admonishing Azusa's members to love all people. Seymour died in 1922, but the Mission continued until 1931 when it closed following the death of Mrs. Seymour.

Bibliography

Bartleman, Frank. *c.*1925. *How Pentecost Came to Los Angeles: As It Was in the Beginning.* Los Angeles, CA: F. Bartleman.

Borlase, Craig. 2006. *William Seymour: A Biography.* Lake Mary, FL: Creation House.

Corum, Fred T. 1981. *Like As of Fire: A Reprint of the Old Azusa Street Papers.* Wilmington, MA: Fred T. Corum.

Espinosa, Gastón. 2014. *William J. Seymour and the Origins of Global Pentecostalism: A Biography and Documentary History.* Durham, NC: Duke University Press.

Lawrence, B.F. 1916. *The Apostolic Faith Restored.* St. Louis, MO: Gospel Publishing House.

Martin, Larry. 1999. *The Life and Ministry of William J. Seymour and a History of the Azusa Street Revival.* Joplin, MO: Christian Life Books.

Robeck, Jr., Cecil M. 2006. *The Azusa Street Mission and Revival: The Birth of the Global Pentecostal Movement.* Nashville, TN: Thomas Nelson, Publishers.

Seymour, W.J. 1915. *The Doctrines and Discipline of the Azusa Street Apostolic Faith Mission of Los Angeles, California.* Los Angeles: no publisher.

Synan, Vinson, and Charles R. Fox, Jr. 2012. *William J. Seymour: Pioneer of the Azusa Street Revival.* Alachua, FL: Bridge-Logos.

Welch, Tim. 2013. *Joseph Smale: God's 'Moses' for Pentecostalism.* Milton Keynes, UK: Paternoster.

Cecil M. Robeck

Balcombe, Dennis

Dennis Balcombe (1945–) is an American Charismatic missionary to Hong Kong (HK) and China. He was born in El Centro, Southern California. According to his own account, the Methodist church which he was brought up in focused on the social gospel and politics. While thinking that it was the best and true church, his friend invited him to see miracles in the Assemblies of God. He was born again and felt called to China at sixteen years old. He was baptized by the Spirit and spoke in tongues at his Methodist grandparents' home, but they disapproved of his experience. He studied at Southern California Bible College (now Vanguard University) for one year. At the age of eighteen, he registered for the draft and three years later in 1966, he was sent to the Army. Whilst in the military camp in San Francisco, he joined Shiloh Church. After six months, he was posted to Vietnam for one year. His main duty was cooking, but he considered himself a soldier for Jesus. He evangelized fellow soldiers, the civilians, Vietnamese prostitutes and even prisoners-of-war. Although he had to carry a grenade and a pistol, he was allowed not to bring any ammunition. When he left Vietnam, he said he was the only one in his unit who was not wounded. After serving for another six months in the military base in California, he was sent by Shiloh Church as a missionary to HK in 1969.

In HK he founded the Revival Christian Church, whose primary goal is mission to China. He waited for the opportunity to enter China until April 1978 when the country reopened itself to foreigners. Balcombe's ministry to Chinese house churches was twofold. First, after seeing 40,000 Christians sharing one Bible in a house church in Guangxi Province, he decided to secretly bring Bibles into China. Second, he preached about Spirit baptism and evidential tongues, especially to house church leaders who had a strong evangelical background. Whenever Balcombe met with several hundred leaders, who represented hundreds of thousands of Christians, he spoke about Pentecostal messages for hours and prayed for their Spirit baptism. Some of them were laughing, crying, dancing, and speaking in tongues. These leaders became more courageous and miracles happened during their preaching. Balcombe reckons that thousands of Chinese are converted to Christianity because they are eye-witnesses or personally experienced miracles.

To serve the "illegal" house churches, Balcombe constantly put his life at risk. He started his ministry in Guangzhou in 1979. He was employed as an English teacher in 1985–1987 and used the Bible as a textbook. He baptized about 300 people. For this he was arrested but was soon released with a warning. A few years later, he was refused entry in Hangzhou airport and sent back to HK, but in twelve hours he returned back to China through another port. To enter villages, he sometimes pretended to be a dead corpse lying in a cart to be buried, or laid in a coffin for the local Christians to take him into villages. In 1994, when he visited Fangchen in Henan with six other foreigners for the Chinese New Year, the police raided the meeting place and detained all seven of them with some Chinese Christians for four days. They were accused of engaging in "illegal religious activities." Their arrest became international news and within a few days was reported by the Voice of America and other media. His arrest alarmed the US Congress and President Bill Clinton, who then sent the American ambassador to China to negotiate with the Chinese Ministry of Foreign Affairs.

Although Balcombe was finally released, the Chinese government annulled his visa for seven years from 1995. But this ban did not stop his influence on Chinese house churches. While Christians in the house churches could not speak for themselves to the outside world, Balcombe was invited to speak about their situation in many countries. His church in HK continued to send thousands of Bibles to Chinese Christians and organized mission trips to the mainland.

After the incident, Balcombe expanded his ministry in different directions. He began to serve Chinese migrants in Asia, North and South America, and Europe. In 1997 he founded the Revival Chinese Ministries International to serve house churches. Its branches in Australia and Germany work for the same goal. He also ministers to non-Han Chinese in China. As China became more tolerant of Christianity, he has been invited by pastors of the official Three-Self Patriotic Movement in China to teach about the Holy Spirit and revival.

Balcombe set out to be a missionary of an independent Charismatic church instead of working in a Pentecostal denomination. His military training and experiences during the Vietnam War prepared him to take any risk in his ministry for Chinese house churches. He brought his revival message to the house churches after they had undergone intense religious persecution from 1949 to 1978. He believes that persecution is the key to revival and evangelism in China, which remains true as persecution continues in the twenty-first century.

Bibliography

Balcombe, Dennis. 2014. *China's Opening Door: Incredible Stories of the Holy Spirit at Work in One of the Greatest Revivals in Christianity*. Lake Mary, FL: Charisma House.

Balcombe, Dennis. 2011. *One Journey, One Nation: Autobiography of Dennis Balcombe, Missionary to China*. Chambersburg: eGenCo. LLC.

Connie Au

Baptism in the Holy Spirit

Derived from biblical accounts surrounding the day of Pentecost, baptism in the Holy Spirit and its synonyms – Spirit baptism, baptism with (or in) the Holy Ghost, baptism with fire, baptism of love, the Pentecostal baptism and others – refers strictly speaking to the experience of the outpouring and reception of the Holy Spirit by the disciples of Jesus recorded in the New Testament. The original moment of this baptism, contained in the observation that the disciples "were all filled with the Holy Spirit" (Acts 2:4), is interpreted as the eschatological fulfillment of God's promise (v. 16–21; Joel 2:28), attributed to the resurrected and ascended Jesus (v. 33; Acts 11:16), and extended as a gift to all followers of Christ (v. 38; see Acts 10:44–46). Pentecostals interpret their own encounter with God as a continuation, repetition, or expansion of that original gift of the Spirit. Theological interpretations of Spirit baptism remain closely tied to the active language of "baptizing," "outpouring," and "filling" with the Spirit, the transitional language of the "coming" or "falling" of the Spirit, and the positional language of the Spirit's presence "in" and "on" the believer. The history and shape of the doctrine is dominated by debates about the place, purpose, and praxis of Spirit baptism in the Christian life.

The debate about the place of Spirit baptism emphasizes the process of the human awareness of God's saving grace along different moments of transformative experiences. Whereas some Christian traditions identify Spirit baptism with regeneration or sacramental initiation (Brand 2004), Pentecostals view the Christian life as several distinct crisis moments in which Spirit baptism is considered a second or third "blessing" subsequent to conversion. The interpretation of biblical events in light of their own experiences raises for most Pentecostals the question of a normative logical, or chronological, subsequence of Spirit baptism to conversion and regeneration (Fee 1985). Most Pentecostals highlight an initial experience of receiving the Holy Spirit for regeneration, an ongoing experience of being filled with the Spirit for sanctification, and a culminating experience of the baptism with the Holy Spirit for empowerment. The different experiences suggest a distinct manner of reception of the Spirit and a different soteriological purpose for Spirit baptism than for regeneration and sanctification (Petts 1998). Even when simultaneity of Spirit baptism and regeneration is granted, Pentecostals retain a logical distinction of progression in order to identify charismatic empowerment as a unique experiential dimension and continued spiritual progression of the Christian life.

The debate about the purpose of Spirit baptism emphasizes the fullness of human participation in the order of salvation. Traditionally seen as a baptism of holiness through sanctification given to those who already received a baptism of regeneration, the close association with Pentecost directed the doctrine primarily to the biblical rhetoric of power and charismatic endowment under which sanctification became assumed (Menzies 1994). The shift to the notion of charismatic endowment identifies the primary purpose of Spirit baptism with the reception of power for witness to the gospel (Acts 1:8). Although the doctrine remains identified at times exclusively in terms of prophetic and missiological implications and with little relation to the full experience and meaning of the Christian life (Perry 2017), conversion, sanctification, and charismatic empowerment can all function as metaphors for the purpose of Spirit baptism.

Classical Pentecostals, in particular, insist that Spirit baptism is manifested by speaking with other tongues as its initial (physical) evidence (Friesen 2013). Speaking with tongues highlights the observable and intensely personal nature of the experience: an audible call to holiness and proclamation of the gospel to the world, tongues speech confirms Spirit baptism as the source of the charismatic life and manifestation of the empowerment of the church in prophetic confrontation with the world (Friesen 2013, 154–93). While speaking with tongues has always functioned to justify the biblical precedence of Spirit baptism and the restoration of the apostolic life in the church, the emphasis on "initial" evidence points to a necessary openness to further charismatic manifestations. Reinterpretations of glossolalia as a sacramental sign (Macchia 1998) have provided theological grounds to view Spirit baptism less in evidential or causal categories than in existential and dialogical terms.

The debates on subsequence, empowerment, and initial evidence have marked the boundaries of doctrinal discussions on Spirit baptism for most of the history of Pentecostal theology. Isolated from a larger theological narrative and its spiritual realities, seeking an experience of the Spirit subsequent to conversion, manifesting charismatic empowerment, and speaking with tongues have become isolated, sometimes impoverished, ritual practices (Clifton 2007). Once the "crown jewel" (Macchia 2006, 20) of Pentecostal theological distinctives, this development threatens to stifle both the continuing experience and theological articulation of Spirit baptism as a central Pentecostal practice and doctrine, unless the theological discussion returns to the original practices and their reinterpretation and integration in the wider Christian spiritual tradition.

Bibliography

Brand, Chad, ed. *Perspectives on Spirit Baptism*. Nashville: B&H Publishing Group.

Clifton, Shane. 2007. "The Spirit and Doctrinal Development: A Functional Analysis of the Traditional Pentecostal Doctrine of the Baptism in the Holy Spirit." *Pneuma: The Journal of the Society for Pentecostal Studies* 29 (1): 5–23.

Fee, Gordon D. 1985. "Baptism in the Holy Spirit: The Issue of Separability and Subsequence." *Pneuma: The Journal of the Society for Pentecostal Studies* 7 (2): 87–99.

Friesen, Aaron T. 2013. *Norming the Abnormal: The Development and Function of the Doctrine of Initial Evidence in Classical Pentecostalism*. Eugene: Pickwick.

Macchia, Frank D. 2006. *Baptized in the Spirit: A Global Pentecostal Theology*. Grand Rapids: Zondervan.

Macchia, Frank D. 1998. "Groans too Deep for Words: Towards a Theology of Tongues as Initial Evidence." *Asian Journal of Pentecostal Studies* 1 (2): 149–73.

McGee, Gary B., ed. 1991. *Initial Evidence: Historical and Biblical Perspectives on the Pentecostal Doctrine of Spirit Baptism*. Peabody: Hendrickson.

Perry, David. 2017. *Spirit Baptism: The Pentecostal Experience in Theological Focus*. Leiden: Brill.

Petts, David. 1998. "The Baptism in the Holy Spirit: The Theological Distinctive." In *Pentecostal Perspectives*, edited by Keith Warrington, 98–119. Carlisle: Paternoster.

Wolfgang Vondey

Barratt, Thomas Ball

Thomas Ball Barratt (1862–1940) was a British-Norwegian pastor, evangelist, and writer who has become known as the "apostle of Pentecostalism to Europe," due to his important role in the revival's first years (Alegre 2019). Barratt was born in Albaston, in Cornwall, England, to devout Wesleyan Methodist parents. When he was five years old the family moved to Norway, as his father had accepted a position as the manager of a sulphur ore mine at Varaldsøy in Hardanger. From age eleven to sixteen he attended the Wesleyan College in Taunton, England, where he was strongly influenced by British Methodist Christianity. He excelled at music and drawing, and after finishing school he was able to study under pianist Edvard Grieg and painter Olaf Dahl in Norway. At seventeen years old Barratt started preaching in and around his local community in Western Norway, and he became an active participant in the temperance movement (Barratt 1927).

In 1882 Barratt passed his exam to become a local preacher in the Methodist Episcopal Church in Norway, and during the following twenty-four years he served as a minister in various positions. This included starting a Methodist mission at Voss (1886–1889), pastoring the Third Methodist Church in Christiania (1889–1892), serving as presiding Elder of Christiania district (1892–1898), and being the pastor of the First Methodist Church in Christiania (1898–1902) (Bundy

2009). During these years he was an active writer, preacher, lecturer, and temperance advocate, and among other things started a Methodist youth organization. In addition he served on the municipal board in Christiania as a candidate from the Temperance party. Barratt was one of the Methodist Episcopal Church's most dynamic, productive, and innovative leaders in Norway (Hassing 1980). Inspired by the Methodist Central Hall in London, Barratt started The City Mission (Bymissionen) in Christiania in 1902, in an attempt to reach marginalized groups and the working class population. In 1904 he started publishing the periodical, *Byposten*, in connection to this mission, and in this publication he demonstrated his strong interest in and desire for revival. In 1905 he went to the United States with the goal of raising funds for a building of the City Mission, which was to be called Haakonsborgen. This endeavor was not successful, and after a year with little results, he entered into a spiritual crisis (Bundy 2009).

While in New York during the fall of 1906, Barratt heard news of the Azusa Street Revival and read the first issues of *The Apostolic Faith*. After studying the Bible and corresponding with leaders at Azusa Street he became convinced of the Christian's need for Spirit Baptism with the sign of speaking in tongues and started seeking this. On November 15 he was baptized in the Spirit and reported having spoken and sung in eight different languages (Barratt 1927). On December 18, 1906, Barratt arrived home in Christiania, where a Pentecostal revival broke out under his leadership the following two weeks. The initially small revival received much press coverage from January 1907 and news of the revival soon spread internationally. It attracted visitors from England, Germany, Denmark, and Sweden. Some of the most notable visitors were Alexander A. Boddy, Jonathan Paul, and Lewi Pethrus (Bloch-Hoell 1956). During the first years of the revival Barratt was an important leader, preacher, apologist and theologian for the Pentecostal movement in several countries. He travelled extensively in Norway and abroad, and ministered in Sweden, Denmark, England, Switzerland, Germany, Palestine, and India. His influence also spread beyond this through his periodical, pamphlets and the book, *In the Days of the Latter Rain* (1909). His role as apologist and theologian was especially significant due to strong opposition against and ridicule of the revival, as well as internal problems such as excesses in physical manifestations and unfulfilled prophecies (Alegre 2019).

From 1910 Barratt focused increasingly on organizing and leading the Pentecostal movement in Norway. He had initially hoped that the Pentecostal revival would spread in all denominations, and did not wish to start a separate church or denomination. Therefore he also tried to avoid divisive issues such as baptism, but in 1913 he was convinced that infant baptism was unbiblical and both he and his wife, Laura, were baptized by Lewi Pethrus in Stockholm. In 1916 he founded a Pentecostal church in Christiania, which was later named as Filadelfia, and officially left the Methodist Church (Barratt 1927). During the 1920s and 1930s the Pentecostal movement in Norway grew steadily and became the largest free church in the country. (Bloch-Hoell 1956). During this period Barratt continued to publish books, pamphlets and articles on different theological topics, as well as a variety of songs, poems, and sermons. He was the most prominent and influential leader of Norwegian Pentecostalism from 1907 until he passed away in 1940 (Bloch-Hoell 1956).

Bibliography

Alegre, Rakel Ystebø. 2019. "The Pentecostal Apologetics of T.B. Barratt: Defending and Defining the Faith 1906–1909." PhD. diss, Regent University.

Barratt, Thomas Ball. 1927. *When the Fire Fell, and an Outline of My Life*. Oslo: Alfons Hansen & Sønner.

Bloch-Hoell, Nils. 1956. *Pinsebevegelsen: en undersøkelse av pinsebevegelsens tilblivelse, utvikling og særpreg med særlig henblikk på bevegelsens utforming i Norge*. Oslo: Universitetsforlaget.

Bundy, David. 2009. *Visions of Apostolic Mission: Scandinavian Pentecostal Mission to 1935*. Uppsala: Uppsala Universitet.

Hassing, Arne. 1980. *Religion and Power: The Case of Methodism in Norway*. Lake Junaluska, NC: General Commission on Archives and History, The United Methodist Church.

Rakel Alegre

Bartleman, Frank and Anna (Ladd)

Anna Ladd Bartleman was the wife of Azusa Street Revival historian Frank Bartleman. Born on November 7, 1876 in Tarnovo, Bulgaria she was one of the many orphans who lost their parents during the Russian-Turkish war and Bulgaria's liberation. Anna was adopted by a Methodist missionary couple, Rev. John Savillian Ladd (April 7, 1852–November 13, 1912) and Celia Rosette (Rosa) Doolittle (September 28, 1851–June, 29 1922). They were married on May 24, 1881 in Philippopolis (Plovdiv), Bulgaria and served as principals of the Literary Theological Institute in Svishtov. Anna was educated in a girls missionary school before the family returned to the US. In 1898, she became the matron of one of the eight homes for fallen and wayward girls in Pittsburgh, Pennsylvania.

Meanwhile, her future husband Frank Bartleman (b. December 14, 1871), had just returned from his second tour of the South to minister at the Hope Mission, part of which was the girls home where Anna worked. They were both assigned to a mission at McKees Rocks where following a "strong witness," Bartleman proposed to Anna and they were engaged. After a delay by Bartleman's complicated surgery, they were married on May 2, 1900 at the Methodist parsonage rented as their future home. With the help of his father-in-law, Bartleman secured a pastorate at a Methodist church in Corry, Pennsylvania. They were invited to return with the Ladds as missionaries to Bulgaria, but the arrival of their first child Celia Esther (b. April 30, 1901) changed their plans.

Their move westward started with a brief stay in Youngstown, Ohio and then working with Alma White and the Pillar of Fire Holiness Church in Denver. When they finally reached California, Frank was appointed director of the Peniel Mission. Their second daughter Ruth Margaret was born in Sacramento on August 11, 1903 while they lived in the rescue home. Anna often had to scrounge through garbage cans to feed her family before they finally left for Los Angeles on December 20, 1904.

By 1905, signs of revival were already evident in First Baptist and Lake Avenue Methodist Church in Pasadena. The Bartlemans attended meetings with Joseph Smale who had visited the Welsh Revival and corresponded with Evan Roberts. But only two months being in the new city, the Bartlemans were struck by the passing of their first-born daughter on January 7, 1905. His wife was unable to accompany Bartleman as he buried Esther among the graves of the foreign children at Evergreen Cemetery. There, Anna's spiritual strength ascended from sorrow as she worked at Bartleman's all-day meetings in Boyle Heights, Soto Street, Eagle Street and Oake's Lot (Pecan Playground) where most tent revivals were conducted and near the homes of many Slavic immigrants with whom Anna communicated freely. The Molokans and Pryguny among them spoke in tongues prior to arriving in the US and were baptised by the Spirit with other immigrants to Azusa.

The birth of the Bartleman's first son John on March 4, 1906 coincided with their first visit of the prayer meetings at Bonnie Brae. A month later, when Edward Lee spoke in tongues, Anna Ladd accompanied her husband as the meetings moved to Azusa Street. On August 12, 1906 the Bartlemans conducted meetings in a church at 8th and Maple Street. Anna would often wake up to pray for her husband's safety as services continued through the night.

Publishing revival chronicles and the *Apostolic Faith* newspaper, Frank Bartleman envisioned that Azusa Street Revival would be "a world-wide one without doubt." For two years beginning from March 1907, he travelled with his family to spread the Pentecostal message. Exhausted from laboring in 1909, they both became ill in Houston as did their son John while in Phoenix. The family had to return to Los Angeles and eight months later, their daughter Lois was born on October 14, 1909.

In March of the following year, Anna and the children stayed home at 163 South Gless Street (a mile from Azusa), while Bartleman undertook a worldwide journey. He returned home 11 months later, just a week before William Durham moved to Los Angeles in 1911. The Bartlemans relocated to Long Beach at 323 Short Street, but with W.H. Durham in Chicago and the Oneness debate following, they refused to join any of the newly established Pentecostal denominations. Instead, the whole family left for Europe on the Steam Ship Caronia on October 19, 1912 and ministered there for the next two years.

The Great War interrupted their plans to reach Anna's native Bulgaria with the Pentecostal message and forced them to leave for the US on the Steam Ship St. Paul on October 10, 1914. Anna was listed with the US citizens on the passengers list which stated "by virtue of husband's citizenship." After a brief stay in Philadelphia, they returned to Los Angeles for Bartleman's 43rd birthday on December 14, 1914. Their fourth child Francis Benjamin Bartleman was born there on December 9th in the following year. On his birth certificate addressed 323 E. Ave 60, both Frank and Anna were listed as missionaries.

In the next two decades Frank wrote his account of the Azusa Stree Revival, followed by books with his story, theology, and experience in missions. After his death on August 23, 1936, Anna and the children remained in Los Angeles at 434 Ebey Hv (sic). She passed away on August 14, 1953. Anna Ladd Bartleman's legacy remains not only as the first Bulgarian Pentecostal, but also as the first Bulgarian Spirit-filled minister and missionary.

Bibliography

Birth Certificate of Francis Benjamin Bartleman. December 9, 1915.
California Census, 1920, 1936, 1940. https://californiacensus.org/.
Frank Bartleman. 1925. *How Pentecost Came to Los Angeles As It Was in the Beginning.* Los Angeles: self published.
Annual Report of the American Bible Society, 1891ff.

James F. Clarke. 1885. *Missionary News from Bulgaria*, Issues 1–55. Harvard University.

Dony K. Donev

Belgium

Pentecostal/Charismatic Christianity in Belgium represents a small religious minority in a country that is historically Roman Catholic and today heavily secularized. Luther's protests in the early sixteenth century found fertile ground in the area today known as Belgium, as did the radical Anabaptist movement, but a repressive Spanish (and Catholic) regime soon extinguished virtually all Protestant presence. Only after the independence of the Kingdom of Belgium in 1830 did small revivals of Protestantism took place, in particular in the twentieth century through evangelical and Pentecostal missionaries coming from the Netherlands, the United Kingdom, Scandinavia, South Africa and North America. Pentecostalism came to Flanders first through Dutch pioneers Gerrit and Wilhelmina Polman, who held the first Pentecostal meetings in Antwerp in March 1911. A Pentecostal community was established there not long after World War I. The first Pentecostal churches were built in Hoboken and Damprémy in the early 1930s. At that time, the movement gained impetus in Francophone Belgium, kindled by the Elim Foursquare gospel message of British evangelist Douglas Scott. After Vatican II, the Catholic Charismatic Renewal took root in Belgium as well, key figures of which were Cardinal Leo Suenens (1996), King Baudoin (1993), and Queen Fabiola (2014). Since the 1990s, the growth of Pentecostal Christianity is particularly due to the establishment of migrant communities in the larger cities of Brussels, Antwerp, Ghent, and Liège, maintaining strong transnational relations with their countries of origin, such as Congo (DRC), Nigeria, and Brazil.

Pentecostal churches in Belgium self-identify as being part of the Protestant/evangelical minority. Belgium has no official census on religion, but different sociological surveys (SMRE) indicate that the Protestant/evangelical presence makes up less than 3 percent of the population. Arguably, the large majority of the Protestant presence in Belgium is characterized by a Pentecostal spirituality. In 2018, close to 400 Pentecostal congregations were members of the Administrative Council of the Protestant and Evangelical Religion (ACPER), the official organ representing these churches to the Belgian civil authorities. Pentecostal churches outside of the ACPER may well be close to 600, but calculations and estimations differ. Within the ACPER, Pentecostal churches cooperate closely with other (non-Pentecostal) evangelical free churches, just as they do in the Flemish Evangelical Alliance (member of the European Evangelical Alliance). It is estimated that about two-thirds of the Pentecostal churches have a non-European ethnic majority membership. Cooperation with and within this cultural diversity is limited. But the largest Pentecostal fellowships in Belgium, the Antioch Network (+100 churches) and the Vlaamse Verbond van Pinkstergemeenten (+80 churches) also count migrant churches among their members. Most Pentecostal churches have less than 100 members, but some migrant churches in larger cities count over 1000 visitors each Sunday, e.g., the (mostly Congolese) community of La Nouvelle Jérusalem (Church of God).

A complex and active network, Pentecostalism in Belgium is accounted for in a wide range of organisations, activities, and events, often bringing together individuals from a variety of churches for shared interests and goals. While recent initiatives are often the most energetic, we focus on a few established organisations and events, which have had considerable impact on the movement over time.

Since 1969, Flemish Pentecostal churches jointly organize annually a Meeting Day on November 11, a holiday in Belgium that celebrates the end of World War I. This yearly gathering attracts over 700 participants, which is slightly more than the annual meetings of Francophone Pentecostals on Pentecost Monday. The Catholic Charismatic movement in Belgium also holds annual joint celebrations, which demonstrate their remaining importance, although the movement has clearly aged.

The charismatic student association Pharos is active in the university town of Leuven and seeks cooperation with the evangelical student association Ichtus, member of IFES. Both aim to serve Christian students from a variety of backgrounds, including Pentecostals. In Francophone Belgium, the Assemblies of God affiliated Students for Christ bring together students in the larger university towns. The Pinkster Jongeren Vlaanderen (PJV), subsidized by the Flemish government, organizes over a dozen of camps every year, in addition to providing training and material for children and youth leaders in local Pentecostal congregations. Many Pentecostal churches, in particular the larger and international ones such as La Nouvelle Jérusalem and Igreja Videira, have their own educational programs equipping both adult and youth members for service in church. Academic Pentecostal theological education in English and French is offered at Continental Theological Seminary in Sint-Pieters-Leeuw (est. 1959 by the Assemblies of God).

Being a small religious minority, Pentecostalism is often looked at with suspicion in the Belgian media, which tend to label it suspiciously as a sect. Some churches and denominations also appeared on a highly publicized list of 189 potential sects in Belgium, the dubious work of a parliamentary commission in 1997. The growing Pentecostal membership of the ACPER (possible since 2003) helps to fight this label, as it implies official recognition by the Belgian state and compliance to an ethical code. Some Pentecostal churches – in particular the larger migrant communities – consciously seek to take up social responsibility and visiblility in the public sphere to counter negative perceptions. Pentecostalism is also present in about a dozen fully subsidized Protestant primary schools in Belgium.

Historical, theological, and empirical research on Pentecostalism takes place at the aforementioned Continental Theological Seminary and at the Evangelische Theologische Faculteit in Leuven. Archives of Pentecostal leaders and organizations are collected and archived by Evadoc, the Protestant Evangelical Archival and Documentation Center in Leuven. Research on Pentecostalism in Belgium is also sometimes conducted at faculties of social sciences, such as at the Université Catholique de Louvain, the Université Libre de Bruxelles, and the Université de Liège.

Bibliography

Bangura, Bosco. 2018. "Holding My Anchor in Turbulent Waters: God, Pentecostalism and the African Diaspora in Belgium." *Pneuma: The Journal of the Society for Pentecostal Studies* 40 (4): 498–516.

Brandt Bessire, Daniel. 1987. "Considérations historiques, théologiques et bibliographiques concernant directement ou indirectement le mouvement de Pentecôte Francophone Belge (1928–1982)." Master's thesis, Brussels: Faculté Universitaire de Theologie Protestante de Bruxelles.

Creemers, Jelle. 2017. "All Together in One Synod? The Genesis of the Federal Synod of Protestant and Evangelical Churches in Belgium (1985–1998)." *Trajecta. Religie, cultuur en samenleving in de Nederlanden* 26: 275–302.

Demaerel, Ignace. 1990. "Tachtig jaar pinksterbeweging in Vlaanderen (1909–1989): een historisch onderzoek met korte theologische en sociologische analyse." Master's thesis, Brussels: Universitaire Faculteit voor Protestantse Godgeleerdheid te Brussel.

Maskens, Maïte and Joël Noret. 2007. "La Nouvelle Jérusalem. Éléments d'histoire et de sociologie d'une Église pentecôtiste en Belgique." *Le Figueur* 1: 117–37.

Jelle Creemers

Benin

Located in West Africa, between Nigeria and Togo, lies the Republic of Benin and former French colony of Dahomey. In contrast to neighboring anglophone countries in West Africa, Pentecostals in Benin constitute a relative minority in relation to other religious affiliations. The relative effervescence of charismatic and Pentecostal churches in the late twentieth century can be seen as one chapter within the longer history of Christianity in this country. Yet, despite their relative low official numbers at a national level, the influence of Pentecostal churches in recent years cannot be underestimated.

People in Benin proudly claim an existing peaceful coexistence of diverse religious traditions. The National Constitution of 1990 guarantees freedom of religion. Geographically, the majority of Christians, particularly Pentecostals, are located in the south, around the major cities of Cotonou and Porto-Novo, whereas the majority of Muslims live in northern and south-eastern regions. According to the General Population and Housing Census 2016, there has been a shift in balance of representation from a former Catholic majority to a Muslim majority. In 2016, 27.7 percent of the population declared itself Muslim, compared to 24.4 percent in 2002. In contrast, the Catholic population decreased from 27.1 percent in 2002 to 25.5 percent in 2016. This is a remarkable trend considering the historical importance of Catholicism in the political history of Benin. Another feature of Benin's religious landscape is the widespread practice of vodun and other African rituals. Although, only 11.6 percent were registered as vodun practitioners, the majority of people observe rituals of African traditions alongside other religious affiliations. Other Christian denominations include 6.7 percent of the population that belong to the Celestial Church of Christ, 3.4 percent for Protestant Methodists, 9.5 percent belong to other Christian denominations; and 3.4 percent for other protestant churches. It is unclear which of these two latter categories include members of Pentecostal churches, which in this context, is broadly defined as evangelical.

Pentecostal churches in Benin hold a variety of theological positions and organizations. On the one hand, one can identify the so-called historical churches, such as the Assemblies of God church and Foursquare church, which place an emphasis on moral reform and biblical teachings. On the other, neo-Pentecostal churches, of more recent origin, have been influenced by the "Word of Faith Movement" or Prosperity Gospel. They often have a transnational character and their teachings proclaim that access to wealth and health are manifestations of divine blessings. The Pentecostal church with the largest membership at a national level is the Assemblies of God. However, the largest number of Pentecostal churches constitute those founded by independent pastors, with few members, that minimally represent a regional or national character. Nonetheless, all churches acknowledge the importance of the gifts of the Holy Spirit and conversion.

Pentecostal churches are part of a complex Christian landscape that has been shaped throughout Benin's history. Founded in 1872, the French colony of Dahomey was established after the defeat of the kingdom of Danxomé, which was famous for its armies of fearless amazons, its role in collaborating with European slave trade, and the power of its vodun religion. The first Christian contacts happened between the fifteenth and eighteenth centuries with Portuguese occupation in the coastal regions during the era of the trans-Atlantic slave trade. In the nineteenth century, with the formal establishment of the French, Catholic missions systematically expanded and founded educational establishments that formed an early colonial elite. By mid-twentieth century, African Independent Churches, such as the Celestial Church of Christ, were founded by African prophets in reaction to the rigidity of mission churches. These churches are often seen as preceding the expansion of African Pentecostal churches.

The introduction of the first Pentecostal missions, alongside other charismatic and Protestant churches, dates from the aftermath of the Second World War. Pentecostal missions of African origin arrived in Benin in the mid-1940s with churches such as the Apostolic Church from Nigeria, and the Ghanaian Church of Pentecost in the 1950s (de Surgy 2001). Missions of American origin, such as the Sudan Interior Mission (SIM) and the Assemblies of God, established themselves in the north of Benin in 1947 and 1946, respectively (de Surgy 2001; Claffey 2007). After the independence of Dahomey in 1960, churches such as Assemblies of God settled in Cotonou and started to evangelize the south (de Surgy 2001). However, Pentecostal expansion slowed down from 1972, when General Mathieu Kérékou orchestrated a *coup d'état* that led to the establishment of a Marxist-Leninist government. During the period between 1974–1980, Kérékou banned churches and religious groups that were considered enemies of the regime (de Surgy 2001). By the end of the 1980s, Benin faced a severe economic crisis, and with the signing of an IMF agreement in 1989, the Marxist-Leninist regime came to an end. Benin opened up to a liberal democratic transition after the National Conference (*Conférence Nationale des Forces Vives de la Nation*) held February 1990. Religious groups, in particular the Catholic Church, played a key role in summoning diverse interest groups to establish the terms of this transition. In December 1990, a new National Constitution was voted by public referendum. After winning the national elections of 1991, Nicéphore Soglo succeeded Mathew Kérékou, marking the end of a dictatorial regime. These changes enabled and legitimized the public presence of religious groups and actors. They also provided the conditions for the emergence of a vibrant plural religious landscape that flourished in reaction against the relative restriction of religion during Kérékou's regime.

One of the key features of the period between 1990–2016 was the strong presence and influence of Pentecostal discourses in mediating and legitimizing political changes and shaping the public sphere. In 1996, Kérékou was re-elected president after having experienced a Pentecostal conversion. During his electoral campaign, he presented himself as "Born Again" to distance himself from a sinful political past, characterized by corruption and the forces of evil (Mayrargue 2002; Stradsbjerg 2015). Kérékou's use of Pentecostal discourses presents a cultural continuity in the exercise of political power personalized by a single man, who infused with religious power, deploys them as a political strategy to accommodate to alternative centers of geo-political power, in this case, the United States (Strandsbjerg 2015). Its successor, Thomas Yayi Boni (2006–2016) followed a similar path. A former President of the West African Development Bank (BOAD), Yayi Boni was an active member of the Assemblies of God church. Although he did not explicitly exploit a Christian discourse during his campaign, during his presidency, he openly declared his Christian identity and several members of his cabinet and government offices were also members of the Assemblies of God.

During this period, neo-Pentecostal churches, mainly of anglophone African origin, flourished in urban areas, influencing so-called historical churches and fostering the creation of independent churches throughout the country. The influence of neo-Pentecostal discourse in the public sphere also contributed to shaping economic practices and the work of religious and non-religious organizations, creating what has been described as a profitable religious market (Amouzouvi 2005). In some cases, neo-Pentecostal discourse also contributed to legitimizing the fraudulent profit-making activities of organizations that operated under the lack of state regulation in the economy. The "ICC services affair" in 2010, one of the biggest scams in the history of the country, is an example of this (Quiroz 2016). This event and other incidents of corruption, during the government of Yayi Boni, seem to have contributed, in recent years, to a gradual delegitimization of Pentecostal churches in the public sphere.

Nonetheless, in the private domain, Pentecostal churches have played an important role in shaping new subjectivities, gender and family relations among their members (Quiroz 2013, 2016b). Reforming the African family has been the focus of missionary activity since the colonial period (Claffey 2007). Today, international organizations, in collaboration with the state, continue to focus on shaping modern forms of citizenship. It is also at the household level that economic and social changes have the widest impact. Pentecostal churches actively participate in shaping and mediating these changes, helping people to adapt to new challenges. As in many parts of Africa, Pentecostal preachers in Benin offer people deliverance from the spiritual "blood ties" that claim to hold people back. However, beyond fostering what has been interpreted as a form of "modern individualism", this ritual rupture, contributes to re-structuring patrilineal authority to reform and maintain the importance of consanguineal family and kinship relations, and to incorporate the authority of the church (Quiroz 2013).

Pentecostal Christianity in Benin needs to be understood in relation to the historical context that has shaped a plural religious landscape. Diverse religious traditions have created a space of mutual compromise and influence, but also of competition over membership and presence in the public sphere. The popularity of Pentecostalism during the past few decades can be considered as one episode in the longer history of religious revival movements in Benin. We should not underestimate, however, its impact. Pentecostal techniques of proselytization have often been adopted by contemporary movements of Islamic reform in the region. It is possible that Islam will continue to shape the public sphere in following decades.

Bibliography

Amouzouvi, Hippolyte D.A. 2005. *Le Marché de la Religion au Bénin*. Berlin: Verlag Dr. Koster.

Claffey, Patrick. 2007. *Christian Churches in Dahomey-Benin. A Study of their Socio-Political Role*. Leiden: Brill.

de Surgy, Albert. 2001. *Le Phénomène Pentecôtiste en Afrique Noire. Le Cas Béninois*. Paris: L'Harmattan.

Mayrargue, Cédric. 2005. "Dynamiques Transnationales et Mobilisations Pentecôtistes dans l'Espace Publique Béninois." In *Entreprises Religieuses Transnationales en Afrique de l'Ouest*, edited by Laurent Fouchard, André Mary and René Otayek, 243–265. Ibadan, Paris: IFRA, Karthala.

Mayrargue, Cédric. 2002. *Dynamiques Religieuses et Démocratisation au Bénin. Pentecôtisme et Formation d'un Espace Public*. Thèse de Doctorat en Science Politique, Bordeaux: CEAN, Université de Bordeaux.

Ogouby, Laurent O.A.G. 2011. *Le Développement du Protestantisme Évangélique et Pentecôtiste au Bénin de 1990 a nos Jours*. Thèse de doctorat en Sciences Religieuses. Paris: EPHE.

Quiroz, Sitna. 2016a. "Seeking God's Blessings: Pentecostal Religious Discourses, Pyramidal Schemes and Money Scams in the Southeast of Benin Republic." In *Neoliberalism and the Moral Economy of Fraud*, edited by David Whyte, and Jörg Wiegratz, 170–183. Abingdon, Oxon: Routledge.

Quiroz, Sitna. 2016b. "The Dilemmas of Monogamy: Pleasure, Discipline and the Pentecostal Moral Self in the Republic of Benin." *Religions* 7 (8): 102.

Quiroz, Sitna. 2013. *Relating as Children of God: Ruptures and Continuities in Kinship among Pentecostal Christians in the South-East of the Republic of Benin*. PhD thesis, Social Anthropology, The London School of Economics and Political Science.

Strandsbjerg, Camille. 2015. *Religions et Transformations Politiques au Bénin: Les Spectres du Pouvoir*. Paris: Karthala.

Sitna Quiroz-Uria

Berntsen, Bernt

Bernt Berntsen (1863–1933) was a Norwegian American and one of the earliest Pentecostal missionaries in China. He was the first missionary to introduce Oneness Pentecostalism to China, thereby becoming the critical link in the formation of the indigenous True Jesus Church.

Berntsen was born and reared in Larvik, Norway. Following his marriage to Magna Berg (1867–1935), together they migrated to the USA in 1893. Spiritually restless and searching for a deeper commitment in his faith, he volunteered as a missionary to China. In 1904 – the year he was granted US citizenship – Berntsen set sail with Magna and their two young sons. Their destination was the South Chihli Mission, a newly formed independent evangelical mission in Chihli (Hebei) Province, a rural region south of Beijing. The Mission's recruits and the churches that supported them were mostly Restorationist and Millenarian groups that were teaching the imminent return of Christ. This orientation was shaping Berntsen's predisposition toward what became known as the Latter Rain Revival.

A turning point soon came in Berntsen's ministry that would leave an indelible mark on his missionary legacy. He received a December 1906 issue of *The Apostolic Faith*, which was reporting on the controversial but captivating Azusa Street Revival occurring in Los Angeles. This new teaching and experience of "baptism in the Spirit" resonated so deeply with Berntsen that he began to explore it for himself. Undeterred by extensive negative reporting, he returned to the United States in 1907, eventually arriving at the Azusa Street Mission where on September 15 he received the baptism in the Spirit. Immediately upon returning to China, he resigned from the South Chihli Mission to open a new Pentecostal mission. This journey into Pentecostalism was to be Berntsen's first step in planting Pentecostal seed on China's soil.

In 1910 Berntsen made his second trip to the United States, this time to visit William Durham's North Avenue Mission in Chicago. There he heard and endorsed Durham's new "Finished Work of Calvary" teaching which was beginning to sweep through the Pentecostal movement, challenging the prevailing Wesleyan "Two Works" doctrine of sanctification. He began to build his network of supporters in Norway, Sweden, and Denmark, and consolidate his identity with the Finished Work fellowship, which in 1914 would become the Assemblies of God.

By 1912 Berntsen's ministry was expanding. He moved his center to Cheng Ting Fu, and his preaching points were flourishing throughout Chihli and Shandong Provinces. He was now ready to launch his own magazine in Mandarin, *Popular Gospel Truth* (*PGT*), with his Restorationist-millenarian vision emblazoned on the masthead: "Jesus will return soon." More important, *PGT* provided a platform for Berntsen to promote his developing ideas such as the Pentecostal Revival, baptism in the Spirit, eschatology, Oneness Pentecostalism, and his later Sabbatarian and foot-washing beliefs.

As Berntsen's ministry was thriving in China, an unanticipated crisis was developing within the Assemblies of God that would eventually deal a fatal blow to his mission. A new teaching that water baptism should be conducted in the name of Jesus Christ and that God is one without internal distinctions suddenly appeared. Later called Oneness Pentecostalism, the dispute raged for two years until in 1916 it ended in schism. Berntsen had become persuaded by the new teaching and affiliated with the first Oneness organization, the Pentecostal Assemblies of the World (PAW). His mission enjoyed support until the new fellowship itself split in 1924 over racial divisions. The white ministers eventually formed three organizations along regional lines, leaving the PAW predominantly black. The missionary support from the PAW was so diminished that Berntsen's mission dwindled into insignificance.

Remarkably, the same Oneness teaching that resulted in the demise of Berntsen's Chinese mission was also responsible for his name and legacy being indelibly etched in the doctrinal foundations of the True Jesus Church. Following a move to Beijing in 1916, he met a Chinese Christian businessman, Wei Enbo (1876–1919). Wei had experienced Pentecostal Spirit baptism just a year earlier and was becoming active in Berntsen's Apostolic Faith Church. As their friendship grew, Wei embraced Berntsen's Oneness teaching.

A crucial turning-point came in 1917 when Wei's friend, Zhang Zhongsan, also a member of the church, had apparently spoken against the missionaries. It was a signal that the tide was turning. Wei initiated his own baptism in a nearby river – his third which this time included the face-down ritual – thereby marking the break with western spiritual authority. With Zhang Lingsheng (1863–?), friend and church member, the three co-workers began what soon became the largest indigenous Christian body in China.

Bibliography

Huang, Ke-hsien. 2018. "Emergence and Development of Indigenous Christianity in China: A Class-Culture Approach." In *Transfiguration of Chinese Christianity: Localization and Globalization*, edited by Cheng-tian Kuo, Fu-chu Chou, and Sian-chin Iap, 153–193. Taipei: Chengchi University Press

Inouye, Melissa Wei-Tsing. 2018. *China and the True Jesus: Charisma and Organization in a Chinese Christian Church*. New York: Oxford University Press.

Melton, J. Gordon. 2017. "Pentecostalism Comes to China: Laying the Foundations for a Chinese Version of Christianity." In *Global Chinese Pentecostal and Charismatic Christianity*, edited by Fenggang Yang, Joy K.C. Tong, and Allan H. Anderson, 43–62. Leiden: Brill.

David Reed

Bethel Church

Bethel Church is a non-denominational charismatic megachurch based in Redding, California, USA, pastored by Bill Johnson, and as of 2019 attracting some nine thousand weekly attendees. On its website Bethel calls itself "a community of believers passionate about God's manifest presence," who "believe that God is good and our great privilege is to know and experience him," and who "exist to ignite individual hearts until Heaven meets Earth." The congregation exerts a global influence through its Bethel School for Supernatural Ministry (BSSM), which had more than 10,000 students from 1998 to 2019. The church and its school focus on Bible teaching, worship, music, healing, and international ministry. Bethel's worship gave birth to the Christian recording group, Jesus Culture. Bill Johnson is primarily known as a teacher and author, whose "revelational teaching" interprets scripture to bring out its deeper implications for living a "supernatural life" or "life of miracles," thus "making the supernatural natural" – to cite the language of Vineyard Church founder John Wimber.

Bethel Church was founded in 1952 and affiliated with the Assemblies of God (AG-USA) beginning in 1954. Bill Johnson's grandparents and parents served as leaders in the congregation before he did. The younger Johnson became pastor in 1996. In 2005, the membership of Bethel Church made a near-unanimous decision to withdraw from the AG-USA, to follow an independent path, and "to create a network that helps other networks thrive – to be one of many ongoing catalysts in this continuing revival."

Underlying the entire ministry of Bethel Church is a kingdom theology suggested by the petition of Matthew 6:10: "Your kingdom come, your will be done, on earth as it is in heaven." From this text follow an array of teachings and practices, and Bethel's mission is defined by God's kingdom-becoming-reality-on-earth (eschatology), as Johnson says: "When we pray for His kingdom to come, we are asking Him to superimpose the rules, order and benefits of His world over this one until this one looks like His. That's what happens when the sick are healing or the demonized are set free." There is "a conflict of kingdoms" and yet "His world always wins." Johnson deemphasizes "the gospel of salvation … focused on getting people saved and going to heaven" in favor of "the gospel of the Kingdom … focused on the transformation of lives, cities, and nations, bringing the reality of Heaven to earth."

Bethel's school – co-founded by Kris Vallotton – features a one-year curriculum, with an option for students to return for a second and third year. With its goal of training students for supernatural ministry, the program at BSSM is academically unconventional, and the school is unaccredited and offers no degrees but a certificate on completion. A Bethel-commissioned study by independent investigators – Eido Research – found that, after completing their studies, some 71 percent of BSSM graduates live in the USA and Canada, 18 percent in Europe, and 11 percent in the rest of the world. 97 percent of the graduates say that they are confident in their Christian faith, while some 10 percent disagree with BSSM core beliefs, and particularly the idea that God invariably answers prayers. 82 percent of graduates say that hear God's voice in some way each week.

Controversies involving Bethel Church have centered on miraculous claims. People associated with Bethel, including Bill Johnson, have made numerous statements about healings and other supernatural phenomena, including gold dust appearing in the auditorium, people brought back from the dead, and angels who purportedly spoke to individual visionaries. A multi-authored book with contributions from Bill Johnson and other Bethel Church staff – called *The Physics of Heaven* (2012) – suggests that God's presence in the universe is a kind of vibration to which believers must attune to receive God's blessings. Abigail Shuttleworth suggests that Bill Johnson's eschatology is "overrealized" in the sense that he interprets God's kingdom almost wholly as a present reality and not as a future hope. Another theological issue pertains to the role of human agency in advancing God's kingdom, and distinguishing the kingdom as a divine gift versus the kingdom as a human vocation.

Bibliography

Bethel Church. 2020. "You are Made for Revival." Accessed April 10, 2020. http://bssm.net/school/introduction/.

Eido Research. 2020. "The Story of Bethel School of Ministry Alumni." Accessed April 10, 2020. https://www.eidoresearch.com/report-bethel-school-of-supernatural-ministry-alumni/.

Franklin, Judy, and Ellyn Davis. 2012. *The Physics of Heaven: Exploring God's Mysteries of Sound, Light, Energy, Vibrations, and Quantum Physics*. Shippensburg, PA: Destiny Image Publishers.

Jesus Culture. 2020. "About Jesus Culture Music." Last accessed April 10, 2020. https://jesusculture.com/music/.

Johnson, Bill. 2018. "Bethel and the Assemblies of God." Accessed April 10, 2020. https://web.archive.org/web/20110701134709/http://www.ibethel.org/bethel-and-the-assemblies-of-god.

Johnson, Bill. 2003. *When Heaven Invades Earth*. Shippensburg, PA: Destiny Image.

Shuttleworth, Abigail D. 2015. "'On Earth as It is in Heaven': A Critical Discussion of the Theology of Bill Johnson." *Journal of the European Pentecostal Theological Association* 35 (2): 10–14.

Verbi, Samuel, and Ben Winkley. 2020. "The Story of BSSM [Bethel School of Supernatural Ministry] Alumni." Accessed April 10, 2020. https://www.eidoresearch.com/wp-content/uploads/2018/02/The-story-of-BSSM-alumni-Web-version.pdf.

Michael McClymond

Bhengu, Nicholas

Nicholas Bhekinkosi Hepworth Bhengu was born in 1909, in KwaZulu Natal, South Africa. He joined a conglomerate of missionary agencies, the Assemblies of God in South Africa (AGSA) in 1938 (Motshetshane 2016). He was converted in a tent meeting conducted by Full Gospel missionaries in 1929 in the Kimberley diamond mines of the Northern Cape. Earlier influences include political ideologies in the Industrial and Commercial Workers Union (ICU) in Natal led by AWG Champion (Hollenweger 1972). In the diamond mines he became a member of the Communist Party of South Africa (CPSA). Bhengu was only twenty years old when he started preaching.

Bhengu, while an enthusiastic evangelist, believed in the education and self-sufficiency of the African people (Balcomb 2005). Watt (2003) believes that he was the first architect of "Black Consciousness" in South Africa. His ministry was not limited to "saving the African soul," he empowered people to change their environment despite a political system that denied them a myriad of social and political rights.

These early ideological influences impacted his philosophy of ministry, overall, they guided his uneasy relationship with white colleagues in the AGSA, especially missionaries of the Assemblies of God USA (AGUSA). In 1955, in a meeting of the AGSA conglomerate in Witbank, South Africa, he imposed a moratorium on expatriate missionaries, especially missionaries of the AGUSA, forbidding them to work in African townships and villages. The contention revolved around funds, culture, and how the Americans seemed to exploit the situation of racial polarization to their advantage. He insisted that they should leave the ministry of African townships and villages to the indigenes because they understood their people better. He also wanted the funds raised in their name to be administered by African leaders with no strings attached. The American missionaries were not comfortable with this moratorium, especially because their unwritten mandate since the founding of the AGUSA in 1914 was to preach to the African "heathens."

Given the racial polarization of the time, the moratorium was more than a political strategy on his part, African townships were dangerous. In 1952, a female Catholic white medical missionary, Dr. Elsie Quinlan, was murdered and cannibalized for "strength" during a "Defiance Campaign" against apartheid in Duncan Village, East Cape. The doctor lived among the people, how much more American missionaries who lived in the white suburbs. Political radicals had repeatedly threatened to cook Bhengu in "boiling oil" if he continued to preach what was perceived then as a "white man's gospel". Thus, Bhengu vehemently insisted that white missionaries of the AGUSA should minister to other white people in the suburbs. He was not anti-missionary, in fact, appreciated the enormous educational contributions they had made in his life as a child at the Norwegian Lutheran missionary station of Entumeni (Lephoko 2010).

His moratorium on missionaries became a tense area of conflict between him and the AGUSA missionaries which led to a schism in 1964. When they could not adapt him to their demands or penetrate his work in the townships and villages, they tried to shut him down (Motshetshane 2016). They withdrew from the AGSA and immediately launch the International Assemblies of God (IAG). They were concerned with the loss of the economic benefits they accrued from their stay in South Africa; they were also not malleable to relocating to other parts of Africa when their principals suggested a relocation in the 1960s.

Bhengu was not the founder of the AGSA but was undeniably the embodiment of its vibrant African wing. It was his "Back-to-God" movement that saved the day in a fledgling AGSA in South Africa. He abhorred racial segregation; yet he found the principle conducive in moving his agenda forward (Hollenweger 1972). He believed that if black people were left to preach to their own, they would turn their incapacitating situation around to the point of not depending on white or expatriate missionary support.

He died in 1985, just four years short of his 80th birthday, and spanning more than five decades of ministry.

Bibliography

Hollenweger, Walter J. 1972. *The Pentecostals: The Charismatic Movement in the Churches*. Minneapolis: Augsburg Publishing House.

Lephoko, Daniel Simon Billy. 2010. *Nicholas Bhekinkosi Hepworth Bhengu's Lasting Legacy: A Study of the Life and Work of one of Africa's Greatest Pioneers*. Accessed July 15, 2019. https://repository.up.ac.za/handle/2263/27505.

Mager, Anne and Gary Minkley. 1990. "Reaping the Whirlwind: The Easter London Riots of 1952." Presented at History Workshop on February 6–10, 1990, available at the Wits Africana Library.

Watt, P., and W. Saayman. 2003. "South African Pentecostalism in Context: Symptoms of Crisis." *Missionalia* 31 (2): 318–333.

Steve Mochechane

Bjørner, Sigurd and Anna Larssen

The Bjørners were pioneers of the Pentecostal movement in Denmark and contributed to the spread of the Apostolic Church in Europe. Anna's fame as a former actress drew international attention to the early Pentecostal movement.

Anna Larssen Bjørner (1875–1955; née: Halberg) was born into a cosmopolitan family in Copenhagen with strong connections to the theatre. Anna made her theatrical debut at the age of seven and was soon recognized as a consummate talent. Her father died in 1888 and her mother subsequently sought comfort in the Christian faith, stimulated by the Lutheran pastor H.J. Mygind, who later became a Pentecostal missionary. From a young age, Anna moved in both Christian revivalist and radical modernist circles, but the influence from the latter was initially stronger. Anna married the author Otto Larssen in 1894. They had a son but were divorced in 1898.

At the height of her fame, she encountered the fledgling Pentecostal movement. Her latent faith was awakened and she experienced the baptism in the Spirit in

December 1908. She began to evangelize her fellow actors; the most significant fruit of this effort was Anna Lewini, who later became a Pentecostal missionary in Sri Lanka. Anna Larssen first spoke in tongues in the summer of 1909. During that time she decided to abandon her acting career. This decision led to consternation and threats of financial repercussions. She was persuaded to be admitted to a psychiatric clinic for observation, though she was eventually declared sane. The publicity garnered was harnessed by the Anglo-Norwegian preacher, T.B. Barratt, who held a tumultuous evangelistic campaign in Copenhagen later that year.

This series of events was publicized by Pentecostals across the world as one of the first great victories of the movement. Anna Larssen became a sought-after Christian speaker but only gradually found her voice as a preacher and singer. In 1912, two years after her former husband's death, she married a fellow evangelist, Sigurd Bjørner.

Sigurd Bjørner (1875–1953) was the son of a lecturer at the teacher training college in Ranum, and thus was born in the opposite end of Denmark from his future wife. He too lost his father when he was young, but his mother gave him a religious upbringing. His family was involved in the widespread Lutheran Evangelical movement known as the Indre Mission ("Home Mission"). After attending Bible school, Bjørner served in the army and rose to the rank of lieutenant, but then experienced a call to minister to the youth in Helsingør north of Copenhagen with the YMCA.

Bjørner formed a close and lasting friendship with his colleague, Carl Næser. They first heard news of the Pentecostal movement in 1910–1911, during which time Bjørner first met Anna Larssen. After their marriage, he was dismissed from his work as a YMCA secretary due to the interdenominational nature of the Pentecostal revival; the Danish YMCA was strictly Lutheran.

The Bjørners became itinerant evangelists across Scandinavia, but mainly in the area around Copenhagen and Helsingør where they held their meetings in a large tent. They remained members of the Lutheran state church until 1919, when the Swedish and Norwegian Pentecostals persuaded them to receive adult baptism. They then established their own Pentecostal congregation in Copenhagen, which quickly became the most influential in the country. They organized national conferences, edited a periodical, and strengthened contacts with Pentecostals abroad. Formally Sigurd was the congregation's pastor, with his wife's support, but in practice they worked as a partnership.

In 1923 the Bjørners encountered the Apostolic Church in Wales. Sigurd was appointed as apostle for Denmark, the denomination's first apostle outside the United Kingdom. The following year the Bjørners attempted to unify the scattered Danish Pentecostal churches under this banner, and over half of congregations joined. The Bjørners and their associates, including Næser, helped spread the denomination to other countries, including Italy and France. However, in 1936 they grew weary of being under foreign authority and left the Danish Apostolic Church to form their own independent congregation once again.

Even in later years, the Bjørners retained a more prominent public profile than any other Pentecostals in Denmark before or after them. They were evangelists rather than organizers at heart. Both remained open to new insights throughout their lives, to such an extent that some perceived them as overly fluctuating. They developed certain controversial eschatological views, but nonetheless also became more ecumenical in their outlook. Towards the end of their lives, they helped independent Pentecostals and the Apostolic Church in Denmark to begin to reconcile.

Bibliography

Bjørner, Anna Larssen. 1954. *Hørt, tænkt og talt*. Copenhagen: Facula.

Christensen, Nikolaj. 2017. "Flickering Flames: The Early Pentecostal Movement in Denmark, 1907–1924." PhD thesis, University of Birmingham, UK.

Jensen, Kristian. 1954. *Mindeskrift: Sigurd Bjørner*. Copenhagen: Vanløse Evangelieforsamlings Forlag.

Moberg, Jessica, and Jane Skjoldli, eds. 2018. *Charismatic Christianity in Finland, Norway, and Sweden: Case Studies in Historical and Contemporary Developments*. Cham, Switzerland: Palgrave Macmillan.

Worsfold, James E. 1991. *The Origins of the Apostolic Church in Great Britain: With a Breviate of Its Early Missionary Endeavours*. Wellington: Julian Literature Trust.

Nikolaj Christensen

Bloomfield, Ray

Ray Bloomfield (1924–) began his ministry alongside his father; a dedicated evangelist and preacher at the People's Worship in Freedom Mission in Auckland, New Zealand. After hearing news of a revival in the United States, his father wrote to discover the reason behind its success. In reply, he received a book by W.V. Grant on the nine spiritual gifts. Together father and son studied and implemented them one by one. Just as the church began to grow, Bloomfield suffered from a serious episode of osteomyelitis. Threatened with amputation, he and his wife, Anthea, prayed for healing. Bloomfield recovered fully and re-commenced preaching, but now with a fresh sense of compassion.

In 1957, Bloomfield established the Ellerslie-Tamaki Faith Mission (affiliated with the Assemblies of God) aiming to bring the Pentecostal message of deliverance to a needy area of Auckland city. Shortly after the work commenced, he was joined by Frank Houston, a former Salvation Army officer, who had recently been filled with the Spirit and healed (following two nervous breakdowns) at a Pentecostal meeting. Within six weeks, Bloomfield invited Houston to be his associate pastor; an offer only later ratified by the Assemblies of God executive council. Such spontaneity marked Bloomfield's ministry which was known to stop and shout gospel invitations at busy intersections or pause and help people so he could share Christ's love. Bloomfield's lively personality, remarkable faith, compassionate love for people, and simple but "gripping" sermons proved an attractive mix. Prayer lines lengthened as attendance at the meetings increased. Within six months one thousand decision cards had been signed, and on any one night, there were never less than thirty conversions for Christ. As the revival gathered momentum, chartered buses brought people from across the city and neighboring regions seeking salvation, healing, and deliverance.

The conversion of two Māori from Northland, New Zealand led to an opportunity to preach at Waiomio; an area locally known as "Drunkard's Valley". Following a formal welcome by Māori elders, Bloomfield preached salvation and healing. At the close of the meeting, eighty people received Christ. Within a short period, the move of God touched every home in the valley apart from the local Tohunga (literally, "priest" or "chosen expert"), who feared losing the powers entrusted to him by the gods. Bloomfield called on Houston for assistance, and the two travelled between Auckland and Waiomio preaching, following up converts and teaching.

Bloomfield and Houston faced significant opposition in the Auckland region, where they were accused of fanaticism and excesses. They also faced tension within the Ellerslie mission when some Māori pressed to establish independent meetings. In the midst of revival and challenge, Bloomfield received an invitation to conduct crusades in Canada for three months. Following his departure in 1958, Houston continued in his stead until relocating to Lower Hutt Assemblies of God in 1959. Although Bloomfield did not return to New Zealand, his ministry had a lasting impact on Houston. Houston became the General Superintendent of the Assemblies of God in New Zealand in December 1965, and significantly influenced the direction and expansion of the movement until his move to Sydney, Australia in 1977.

Bibliography

Clark, Ian. 2007. *Pentecost at the Ends of the Earth: The History of the Assemblies of God in New Zealand (1927–2003)*. Blenheim: Christian Road Ministries.

Houston, Hazel. 1989. *Being Frank*. London: Marshall Pickering.

Linda Flett

Bochian, Pavel

Pavel Bochian (1918–1996) was born on July 13 in Mocrea-Ineu, Arad district, and was baptized with water when he was 13 years old and baptized in the Spirit three years later. He married Ileana in 1942 and had three daughters and two sons. He became a pastor and later the leader of the Pentecostal denomination.

Like many Pentecostals believers and leaders in the early days of the church in Romania, Bochian suffered from the authorities. In 1938 he was imprisoned in Arad and Timișoara for preaching without having an "official" accreditation. In 1945, Bochian was ordained in pastoral ministry and in 1950 was elected as the president of the district of Arad (1951–1966). Bochian had been the national coordinator when he was elected the president of the Pentecostal denomination in 1962, a position which he held until 1990. He served as a pastor in several Pentecostal churches over the years: Mocrea (1945–1950); Gradiște, Arad (1950–1952); Bujac, Arad (1950–1962); Crângași, București (1962–1990); Emanuel, București (1990–1996). Internationally, Bochian served in the European Pentecostal Committee (1978–1990) and in the Consultative Committee of the Global Pentecostal Conference (1980–1990). Bochian taught courses at Seminarul Teologic Penticostal in Bucharest from its establishment in 1976 till 1990. He has written over 250 articles in the Romanian Pentecostal magazines and published four books.

Many people who knew him very well describe Bochian as a kind, soft, and joyful personality, with a great passion in everything he has done. Even though he was not too emotional, he was a loving, encouraging, and caring father and minister. He was a very good preacher and expositor of the Bible, with clear and profound teachings even though he was an autodidact. As the president of the denomination, Bochian helped organize communities attempting to unify different fractions of Pentecostal churches regarding four most common problems and controversies in particular: the official registration of believers in the church, the work of the Spirit, the structure and organization of the church, and foot washing. To accomplish these, Bochian travelled extensively throughout the country by train and walked for very long distances.

One very significant reality that needs to be highlighted is that Bochian has conducted most of his ministry and leadership of the Pentecostal denomination in Romania during one of the harshest communist regimes in Eastern Europe, so any assessment of his life and ministry must be placed in this context. There was, of course, enormous pressure from the state authorities on the leaders of all denominations to sign the "agreements of cooperation" and give reports on the activity of the churches. Like all churches during the communist era, the Pentecostal churches were also heavily controlled by the state through the Ministry of Denominations (Ministerul Cultelor) which was the only possible way for a recognized church to exist. Under the powerfully domineering communist regime that controlled all the officially recognized religious life in the country, Bochian and of all religious leaders endorsed and pleaded for an appropriate life within the system. This is excellently illustrated in Bochian's article, "The quality of citizen of the fatherland," published in the Pentecostal magazine.

As a leader of the denomination Bochian had to play a very agile role in reporting to the authorities and also contributed to the functioning, growing, and development of the Pentecostal church. With hindsight and a full understanding of the complexity of the situation, we can say that while he was a cooperant with the communist regime, he also succeeded in allowing and facilitating the development of the Pentecostal denomination through the difficult years of communism. A significant decision that Bochian took was to use and promote the intellectuals in the leadership of the Pentecostal churches, which was unlike his predecessor, Gheorghe Bradin, who did the opposite. Bochian mediated in Trandafir Sandru's case which enabled Sandru to be re-instated in pastoral ministry and in the leadership of the denomination. It is just an example of his contribution. Under his leadership, by 1989 there were some 800 authorized and 300 unauthorized Pentecostal churches in Romania, numbering a total of over 100,000 believers.

Bibliography

Andreescu, Valeriu. 2012. *Istoria Penticostalismului Românesc*, Two Vols. Oradea: Casa Cărții.

Bălăban, Ciprian. 2016. *Istoria Bisericii Penticostale din România (1922–1989): Institutie și Harisme*. Oradea: Scriptum.

Bochian, Pavel. 1997. *The Life of a Romanian Pastor*. București: Editura Privilegiu.

Bochian, Pavel. 1979. "Calitatea de cetățean al patriei." *Cuvântul Adevărului* 27 (2): 9–12.

Croitor, Vasilică. 2010. *Răscumpărarea Memoriei*. Medgidia: Succeed Publishing.

Corneliu Constantineanu

Boddy, Alexander and Mary

Alexander Alfred Boddy (1854–1930) and Mary Boddy (née Pollock) (1855–1928), a Church of England clergyman and his wife, played major roles in establishing the Pentecostal movement in the United Kingdom, its development in Western Europe, and encouraging it across the

Pentecostal leaders at the Sunderland Convention 1913: Standing: Cecil Polhill; George Jeffreys; Frank Bartleman; A.E. Saxby; Alexander Boddy. Sitting: Heinrich Vietheer; Eugen Edel; Jonathan Paul; Richard Geyer

English-speaking world. They also served for many years in a parish church amongst the industrial workers of one of the busiest shipbuilding ports in the world.

Both were raised in clergy families: Alexander was brought up in Red Banks, Cheetham, a poor district of Manchester, then rapidly expanding and industrialising. Mary was brought up in the countryside of North Yorkshire. Alexander initially trained as a solicitor but following a spiritual crisis and resolution at the Keswick Convention in 1876 he trained for ordination at the University of Durham. He was ordained deacon in 1880 and priest in 1881, and served a number of curacies in the Durham area. During this time he travelled in Europe, Russia and North Africa. A trip to one of the holy sites of Islam, Kairwan, resulted in a bestselling book and election as a Fellow of the Royal Geographical Society.

In 1884 he was sent to the industrial parish of All Saints', Monkwearmouth in Sunderland to restore a church that had been neglected by an alcoholic vicar. Through visiting, preaching and good organization the congregation grew rapidly and in 1886 he became the vicar. In the parish mission that year one of the assistants was Mary Pollock. She and Alexander married in 1891 and went on to have three children. They shared a commitment to the holiness teaching of the Keswick movement, worked out both in prayer and in practical support of the people in their parish. Mary's health was badly affected by the pollution in the area, though she was healed of asthma in 1899. After this she discovered a gift of divine healing through the laying on of hands.

Out of a desire for further spiritual renewal Alexander travelled to south Wales in 1904 to witness the Welsh Revival, with its emphases on prayer, singing, and confession of sin. This led to prayer meetings in the All Saints' vestry for a similar revival. Hearing news of the Pentecostal ministry of Thomas Ball Barratt in Christiana (now Oslo), Norway, Alexander attended these meetings in March 1907. He found them even more affecting than those of the Welsh Revival.

After repeated invitations Barratt visited Sunderland from 31 August 1907 for nearly two months. In public meetings Barratt spoke about and prayed for spiritual gifts. In the first two weeks seventeen people, including the Boddys' daughters, Mary and Jane, received the gift of speaking in tongues. Mary Boddy received this gift later, while Alexander was about the fiftieth person to do so in December 1907. This movement was highly controversial and attracted criticism from church circles, including the Pentecostal League, a prayer network with which Alexander had had strong links. It also received a skeptical response in national newspapers, a sign of the growing impact of the movement. The Boddys sought to counter this by emphasizing the importance of love, love for God and love for neighbor.

With a long experience of writing and denied access even to the Christian press, Boddy started his own magazine, *Confidence* (subtitled "A Pentecostal paper for Great Britain"). The paper contained a mix of news items, testimonies and theological reflection on Pentecostal themes. Mary was a regular contributor especially on healing and spiritual devotion. The 141 editions continuing until 1926 were widely distributed in the English speaking world and its news came from around the world. It remains a significant historical source in its own right.

The first edition of *Confidence* advertised a convention to be held at Whitsun 1908 at All Saints', Monkwearmouth. The programs for the Sunderland Conventions from 1908 to 1914 included Bible studies on speaking with tongues as "a sign of Pentecost", the second coming of Christ, and divine healing, as well as discussion about the leading of meetings where spiritual gifts might be exercised. As chairman Alexander had strict rules about behavior printed in the tickets and he firmly enforced them. Nonetheless the atmosphere was warm, building on personal relationships developed amongst like-minded leaders.

In January 1909 Alexander met Cecil Polhill, one of the original "Cambridge seven" who had gone out to China in the 1880s, to form the Pentecostal Missionary Union. This was probably the first Pentecostal missionary organization in the world, and modelled itself on Hudson Taylor's China Inland Mission. Polhill used his inherited wealth to underwrite the Pentecostal Missionary Union (PMU) and the magazine *Confidence*. In turn Alexander publicized PMU activities in *Confidence*. Further international perspective came from reports of the International Pentecostal Consultative Council (1912–1914), defending the new movement from attacks.

Up to the start of the First World War Alexander was the clear leader of the movement in the UK, being invited to speak in other Pentecostal centers and attracting Pentecostal leaders to Sunderland from the UK, Europe, the USA and India. All the key first generation leaders of the emerging Pentecostal denominations in the UK (Apostolic church, Elim, Assemblies of God) attended at least one convention. Smith Wigglesworth, an independent minister with a healing ministry, received the gift of tongues after prayer from Mary and he became a regular visitor, remaining friends with the Boddys throughout their lives.

Alexander visited Pentecostal conferences in Germany, the Netherlands, Canada and the USA helping to develop some common understanding of Pentecostal practice and theology. Alexander was committed to seeing this as a renewal movement within existing denominations but this had never been the view of everyone involved. Disagreements were seriously exacerbated over attitudes to the war: Alexander was a patriotic supporter and even travelled to battlefields, while most Pentecostal leaders were conscientious objectors, and some were imprisoned. The Boddys refused to leave the Church of England even as new denominations were formed and many relationships came to an end.

In 1923, partly as a result of Mary's poor health, Alexander became vicar of the rural parish of Pittington, near Durham. Mary died on April 25, 1928, Alexander on September 10, 1930 and they are buried together in the Pittington churchyard.

Bibliography

Cho, Kyu-Hyung. 2009. "The Move to Independence from Anglican Leadership: An Examination of the Relationship between Alexander Alfred Boddy and the Early Leaders of the British Pentecostal Denominations (1907–1930)." PhD thesis, University of Birmingham, UK.
Usher, John Martin. 2015. "For China and Tibet, and for World-wide Revival: Cecil Henry Polhill (1860–1938) and His Significance for Early Pentecostalism." PhD thesis., University of Birmingham, UK.
Wakefield, Gavin. 2007. *Alexander Boddy: Pentecostal Anglican Pioneer*. Milton Keynes: Authentic Media.

Gavin Wakefield

Bolivia

Pentecostalism arrived in Bolivia relatively late compared to neighboring Chile and Brazil. The first Pentecostal missionaries came from Sweden in 1920 (Johansson 1992, 74–75). The most important pioneer of the Swedish mission (*Misión Sueca Libre*) was Gustaf Flood (1895–1990) who settled in the town of Punata (near Cochabamba) in the early 1920s (1920 or 1921). He was soon accompanied by other Swedes and ministries sprung up in Santa Cruz and Villa Montes (Johansson 1992, 75–77). Swedish mission continued to pioneer Pentecostalism in Bolivia and Flood was instrumental in recruiting more missionaries through the 1950s (Johansson 1992, 77–79). Of the North American Pentecostal denominations, the International Church of the Foursquare Gospel was first to arrive (1929) pioneering work in Trinidad and the Amazon basin. The Assemblies of God established churches in Cochabamba, Oruro, and Santa Cruz starting in 1946. Evangelical Pentecostal Church of Chile (*Iglesia Evangélica Pentecostal de Chile*) sent pioneer missionaries to Cochabamba and Oruro by 1938 though it had less success in the beginning (Damen 2005, 341–344; Wightman 2008; Rivière 2007). Other Latin American Pentecostal missions followed suit soon after. According to Gustaf Flood's memoirs the early Pentecostal pioneers experienced many hardships including harsh climate, difficult travels, diseases, and even persecution (Johansson 1992, 76–78). Though initial years yielded only a few converts, the early 1960s began an era of growth that led to the nationalizing of classical Pentecostal denominations such as the Assemblies of God (Mercado 2002, 65–66). An important impetus for the growth was undoubtedly religious freedom that opened Bolivia for non-Catholic churches (Rivière 2007; Wightman 2008). In 1972 Bolivian evangelist Julio César Ruibal – the most important Pentecostal revivalist of Bolivia in the 1970s and 1980s – started healing campaigns in the major cities. In this endeavor he received help from dictator president Hugo Banzer Suàrez who gave him enormous logistical support for the healing campaigns, including the use of a large stadium in La Paz and air time on state TV. Similar favors were given to Argentine evangelist Luis Palau by Banzer's hand-picked successors in exchange for preaching submission to governing authorities (Stoll 1990, 121–122; Wightman 2008, 18; Villazón 2011, 23–24). Ruibal's healing campaigns are also considered to be the beginning of the neo-Pentecostal movement in Bolivia (Wightman 2008, 44; Villazón 2011, 23–24). Despite the successes of Ruibal's campaigns, neo-Pentecostalism did not gain significant momentum until the 1990s. *Ekklesía*, one of the most influential megachurches in Bolivia, had only 400–500 members in the early 1980s but reached 10,000 by 1995 in La Paz alone. An offshoot in Cochabamba boasted 1,600 members in early 2000 with plans to exceed 5,000 in the near future (Wightman 2008, 39). *Ekklesía* reaches major cities not only in Bolivia but also in Chile, Peru, Paraguay, Colombia, Central America, United States, Europe, and Asia. It also boasts TV and radio channels in eight major cities in Bolivia (Villazón 2011, 26) and according to Mandryk (2010, 154) it has 24,000 members and 48,000 affiliates in eight congregations. Another important megachurch in Bolivia is *Pare de Sufrir*, which is an offshoot of the Brazil-based Universal Church of the Kingdom of God (UCKG). The head quarter of Pare de Sufrir is located in Santa Cruz but has congregations in all the major cities in Bolivia (Villazón 2011, 28–29). The church is known for its aggressive form of prosperity theology.

From its inception Bolivian Pentecostals have found a way to connect with people's felt needs, especially the poor and the marginalized. More recently the urban middle classes have also flocked to Pentecostal churches. According to testimonies, Pentecostal faithful tell of being lifted out of poverty, (re)gaining a sense of dignity, and finding ways to cope with daily life. This is often coupled with a feeling of belonging to a group of believers who care and support one another (Rivière 2005, 343–347; 2007; Wightman 2008, 114–165; Chambe 2011, 45–84; Rosas 2011, 43–51).

One of the most important features of Bolivian Pentecostalism is "being saved" – or "having Jesus in heart" (Wightman 2008; Chambe 2011). The initial conversion experience is foundational for other Spirit-infused experiences, such as tongues speaking, healings, exorcisms, and other charismatic phenomena. Search for Spirit-experiences and supporting community also draw outsiders to Pentecostal churches in search of hope, healing, and prosperity. As such, an important aspect of Bolivian Pentecostalism is an infusion of hope and joy in the midst of everyday struggles (Wightman 2008; Chambe 2011). This is reinforced in celebratory services on Sundays and small group gatherings throughout the week. Though early Pentecostalism placed a heavy emphasis on Jesus' imminent second coming (Rivière 2007; Mansilla 2011, 9–11), the newer neo-Pentecostal congregations tend to focus on God's blessing and material prosperity in the here and now. The faithful are exhorted to give tithes (10 percent of income) as a demonstration of obedience and offerings (beyond 10 percent) to show love (Mansilla 2011, 14–18; Rosas 2011, 43–51). As one "sows seeds" (tithes and offerings), God grants well-being, blessing, and prosperity to the believer. Prosperity theology is perhaps the most distinctive feature of neo-Pentecostalism in Bolivia and elsewhere in Latin America. This is often connected to "victorious living" which promises health, wealth, and prosperity in every area of life – and sometimes includes a strong desire to conquer and take over societal institutions by faith (Mansilla 2011, 14–22). On the other hand, prosperity teaching has caused divisions among the classical Pentecostal denominations, such as the Assemblies of God. Many of the classical denominations and independent Pentecostal churches have tried to forge a middle path between an explicit prosperity theology and older more negative view of material well-being (Mansilla 2011, 7–11; Rosas 2011, 43–51). Closely related to material prosperity is faith healing. Though all Pentecostals believe in divine healing, the extent to which the faithful are entitled to it divides opinions. Chambe (2011) states that more traditional Pentecostals in Bolivia believe that sickness has many causes whereas neo-Pentecostals tend to view sickness and healing more closely related to spiritual cause and effect (Mansilla 2011, 7–22; Rosas 2011, 43–51). Autero's empirical research on the Bolivian Pentecostal use and interpretation of the Bible suggests that material prosperity and healing are part of larger theology of retribution. According to Pentecostals, God grants a believer well-being and blessing based on one's faith and actions (action-consequence theology). Though the equation at first appears simply causal, the data indicates that theology of retribution is more complicated than it first appears. For example, the church's distinct Pentecostal tradition and socio-economic status of its adherents play a significant role in how God's blessing is articulated (Autero 2016). Though theology of retribution is not unique to Bolivian Pentecostalism, it does resonate closely with the popular religious beliefs of the Bolivian low lands and the indigenous traditions of the Andean regions that emphasize reciprocity (Chambe 2011; 2006; Autero 2016; Esterman 2006). Another contested area for Bolivian Pentecostals is the relationship to ancestral beliefs, including Andean religious traditions and popular Catholicism. Some Pentecostals react vigorously against them while others retain practices that bear a resemblance to their old beliefs (Rivière 2007); however, often the existing similarities have more to do with form than the actual content (Autero 2016). Official Catholicism is often viewed with disdain as idolatrous and sometimes dismissed with harsh rhetoric. At the same time Catholic clergy and scholars tend to label Pentecostals as "charlatans", "sectarians", "fundamentalists", or "superstitious" (Mercado 2002, 61–80; Wightman 2008; Autero 2016). Another controversial topic is the extent to which Pentecostals in Bolivia contribute to social change. It is undoubtedly true that individuals, families, and even communities have been transformed by the help of Pentecostal faith (Rosas 2011, 43–51; Rivière 2007). Yet, it is less clear to what extent Bolivian Pentecostals contribute to broader social change. Wightman has argued that Pentecostals in Bolivia impact society as the faithful see themselves, individually and collectively, as change agents who "heal the land" (cf. 2 Chronicles 7:14). As such the goal of many Pentecostals is to infuse society with Christian values and practices. Yet, many of these values are often associated with political conservatism (PEW 2014). Many Pentecostal churches are also part of the National Association of Bolivian Evangelicals (*Asociación Nacional de Evangélicos de Bolivia* or *ANDEB*) that engages social and political issues such as abortion, women's rights, and religious liberty among others (Mercado 2002, 150–154). Recently ratified religious freedom in Bolivia is at least partly due to efforts of *ANDEB*. The current president of the association, Munir Chiquie, has deep roots in Pentecostal movement as a pastor and Bible college principal.

The number of Pentecostals in Bolivia is difficult to estimate. This largely depends on whether Catholic charismatics are included in the count. Also, many historic Protestant churches have been "pentecostalized"; that is, they exhibit Pentecostal worship patterns and spirituality. It is important keep in mind that many non-registered Pentecostal churches dot the landscape of Bolivia, both in the cities and the countryside (Rivière 2007). Some faithful do not even know what it means to be Pentecostal. They only know that their faith is directly from God and the Bible (Chambe 2011, 39–40). World Christian Encyclopedia (2001) indicates that Pentecostal/Charismatics form 14.3 percent of the population though does not take into a count Charismatic Catholics, despite its nomenclature (Barrett, Kurian, Johnson 2001, 120). According to PEW research (2014), 16 percent of Bolivians are Protestants and 49 percent of Protestants identify as Pentecostals. However, 30 percent of all Catholics are charismatics (77 percent of Bolivians are Catholic). Though Pentecostals are found in cities, villages, and rural areas, Charismatic Catholics hail mostly from urban middle and upper classes (Rivière 2007).

Bibliography

Autero, Esa J. 2016. *Reading the Bible Across Contexts: Luke's Gospel, Socio-Economic Marginality, and Latin American Biblical Hermeneutics*. Leiden: Brill Academic.

Barrett, David B., George T. Kurian, and Todd Johnson. 2001. *World Christian Encyclopedia. A Comparative Survey of Churches and Religions in the Modern World*. Second Edition. Oxford: Oxford University Press.

Chambe, Juan J. 2011. *Teologia pentecostal Popular. La fe en comunidades periurbanas y andinas*. Colección Teología y Filosofía Andinas, no. 6. La Paz, Bolivia: ISEAT.

Estermann, Josef. 2006. *Filosofía Andina: Un Visión para un Mundo Nuevo*. La Paz: ISEAT.

Johansson, Göran. 1992. *More Blessed to Give: A Pentecostal Mission to Bolivia in Anthropological Perspective*. Stockholm Studies in Social Anthropology 30. Stockholm: Gotab.

Klein, Herbert S. 2003. *A Concise History of Bolivia*. Cambridge: Cambridge University Press.

Mandryk, Jason. 2010. *Operation World*, Seventh edition. Colorado Springs, CO: Biblica Publishing.

Mansilla, Miguel, A. 2011. "El pentecostalismo clasico y el neopentecostalismo en America Latina." In *fe y pueblo. Nada es imposible para Dios. Una ventana a la fe neopentecostal*, no. 18, 6–22. La Paz, Bolivia: ISEAT.

Mercado, Moisés M. 2002. *Denominaciones cristianas no católicas en Bolivia: Una aproximación tipológica desde las divisiones del cristianismo del siglo XVI*. La Paz: Presencia.

Rivière, Gilles. 2007. "Bolivia: el pentecostalismo en la sociedad aimara del Altiplano". *Nuevo Mundo Mundos Nuevos*. Accessed May 8, 2019. https://journals.openedition.org/nuevomundo/6661.

Rivière, Gilles. 2005. "Cambios sociales y pentecostalismo en una comunidad aymara." In *De indio a hermano. Pentecostalismo indígena en américa latina*, edited by B. Jiménez, 329–354. Iquique, Chile: Ediciones Campus Universidad Arturo Prat.

Rosas, Yolanda. 2011. "Textos bíblicos en la celebración y teología neopentecostales." In *fe y pueblo. Nada es imposible para Dios. Una ventana a la fe neopentecostal*, no. 18, 43–51. La Paz, Bolivia: ISEAT.

Stoll, David. 1990. *Is Latin America Turning Protestant?: The Politics of Evangelical Growth*. Berkeley: University of California Press.

Villazon, Julio C. 2011. "El movimiento neopentecostal en Bolivia: Crisis economica, reorganizacion simbolica y conservadurismo social." In *fe y pueblo. Nada es imposible para Dios. Una ventana a la fe neopentecostal*, no. 18, 23–34. La Paz, Bolivia: ISEAT.

Wightman, Jill, M. 2008. *New Bolivians, New Bolivia: Pentecostal Conversion and Neoliberal Transformation in Contemporary Bolivia*. UMI Microfilm. Diss. University of Illinois at Urbana-Champaign. ProQuest.

N.a. *fe y pueblo. Nada es imposible para Dios. Una ventana a la fe neopentecostal*. 2011. No 18. La Paz, Bolivia: ISEAT.

Esa Autero

Bonnke, Reinhard

Reinhard Bonnke (1940–2019) was a German Pentecostal evangelist, best-known for his huge open-air meetings in Africa. Bonnke was born on April 19, 1940 in Königsberg (Kaliningrad), as the fifth child of a Pentecostal church organist and her husband, who was an army officer. His childhood was shaped by the Second World War, the family's dramatic escape from East Prussia, and four years in a Danish internment camp. Gradually, the family managed to rebuild their lives in Northern Germany, where Bonnke's father pastored a Pentecostal congregation mainly for refugees.

Reinhard Bonnke, 1940–2019. Source: Center for the Study of Global Christianity

Bonnke's autobiography depicts himself as a troubled and disobedient child, who was met with a rigid upbringing and outright dismissal from his parents and siblings. This was not resolved by his conversion, Spirit Baptism, or indeed his call to become a missionary in Africa, which he claimed to have received by the age of ten. Instead he narrates frequent struggles with feelings of inadequacy until well into becoming a successful minister, which he tended to turn into a message of empowerment about how God used a "zero" like him to great effect.

After an abortive attempt at a carpentry apprenticeship, he trained to become a retail merchant, before pursuing ministerial training at the Bible College of Wales. This was an unusual pathway to pursue for a German Pentecostal, not least because the school was steeped in the tradition of the Welsh Revival and did not allow Pentecostal practices. Initially, this held up his accreditation by the German Pentecostals, but here as in similar crossroads later on, Bonnke would overcome obstacles by insisting on his position and claiming that he was merely following God's guidance.

After marrying Anni Sülze in 1964, he pastored a small congregation of new converts in Flensburg and finally secured a placement with the Velberter Mission (VM) as missionary to South Africa, relocating there with his pregnant wife and first child in 1967. After serving a year as an apprentice with the Apostolic Faith Mission (AFM) in Ermelo, he was assigned his first placement in Lesotho. His travelling ministry with the existing Pentecostal churches there was not particularly successful, nor were his attempts at street evangelism. Bonnke now began to break the mould of a white missionary by inviting Africans into his house, preaching in urban night clubs, organizing a tract dissemination network by hiring Africans as bicycle couriers, training African preachers through correspondence courses, and teaming up with an African evangelist. Some success followed, but he also ran into difficulty with the VM for his expansion beyond his original brief. Once again, Bonnke stood his ground and resigned from the VM in 1974, while retaining a partnership with them as he built up his own evangelism ministry, called Christ for all Nations (CfaN).

Bonnke relocated to Whitfield in South Africa and now began to emulate the pattern of the "crusading" evangelist, which was already well-established at this time. This pattern had many advantages over the established missionary arrangement for Africans and evangelists alike. Firstly, by conducting short but major events centred on evangelism and healing, evangelists would make converts and direct them to the local churches while collecting visual material for their own fundraising operations. Secondly, their collaborations with local church leaders would enable them to build international networks, but claimed no oversight or guidance toward Africans apart from the organization of the "crusade." Finally, their events facilitated ecumenical cooperation without any structural commitments, as multiple churches would need to collaborate to host the evangelist, and Christians from all stripes would gather together during the event.

Bonnke soon acquired fame as a mass evangelist, at first buying ever larger tents to host the crowds (including one that could seat 34,000 people) and finally resorting to open fields with crowds in the 100,000s. From 1986 onward, Bonnke also ran the so-called annual "Fire Conferences," a multiplier event focused on ministering to African pastors and evangelists.

Arguably, Bonnke's success was driven by the miracles of healing attributed to him and showcased on his "crusade" stages as well as in CfaN campaign material – from regular displays of the blind seeing, the deaf hearing, and the crippled walking to claims of people being raised from the dead. Medical confirmation was not a regular part of his proclamation of miracles, and where it did happen, the evidence remained contested. Some campaigns came with tragic results. In Benin City 14 people were trampled to death when a mass panic erupted at an insufficient access road. When Bonnke secured a license to conduct an event in the predominantly Muslim city of Kano (Nigeria), resistance mounted and finally led to a riot after the CfaN team had arrived, leaving the city in flames and scores of people dead while Bonnke fled.

His political legacy was mixed. On the one hand, he visibly opposed and sought to mitigate the racism of apartheid, in the end moving his CfaN headquarters to Frankfurt in 1986 as part of the mounting pressure on the South African regime. On the other hand, he freely met with African autocrats and dictators such as Gnassingbé Eyadéma in Togo and Sani Abacha in Nigeria, perhaps motivated by a naïve pursuit of gospel opportunities, but certainly collecting political contacts he knew to leverage. In America he allied with the Pentecostal right, counting the conservative media mogul Pat Robertson among his strongest supporters as well as the controversial prosperity teachers [Copeland, G.] Kenneth and Gloria Copeland.

While Bonnke concentrated his work in Africa, he also held events in all other continents. His mass-mailing media campaign of a simple gospel tract (*From Minus to Plus*) in the UK, Germany, Hongkong, and Scandinavia was an ambitious undertaking, but with little tangible results. From around 2010 he began to hand over his CfaN empire to his successor, the American Daniel Kolenda. Bonnke died on December 7, 2019.

Bonnke's entire ministry was driven by a vision of mass conversions, culminating in ever larger counts of how many had prayed the "sinner's prayer" in his meetings. He saw these numbers as a fulfilment of his divine mission ("Africa shall be saved!") and called himself "God's combine harvester." This metaphor is revealing in its emphasis on effectiveness and industrial scale, and demarcates what Bonnke's critics see as flaws in his theology: a narrow understanding of salvation that neglects the wholeness of God's concern for the world and an obsession with the quantitative success of Christianity in Africa that neglects the ambivalent record of mission history and ignores the dialogical and complex character of the Christian witness.

Bibliography

Bonnke, Reinhard. 2009. *Living a Life of Fire: An Autobiography*. Orlando, FL: E-R Productions.

Bonnke, Reinhard. 1994. *Evangelism by Fire*. Eastbourne, UK: Kingsway.

Gifford, Paul. 1987. "'Africa Shall Be Saved': An Appraisal of Reinhard Bonnkes Pan-African Crusade." *Journal of Religion in Africa* 17 (1): 63–92.

Kürschner-Pelkmann, Frank. 2004. *Reinhard Bonnkes Theology: A Pentecostal Preacher and His Mission, a Critical Analysis*. Nairobi: All Africa Conference of Churches.

Steele, Ron. 1987. *Plundering Hell to Populate Heaven: The Reinhard Bonnke Story*. Melbourne, FL: DOVE Christian Books

Jörg Haustein
Moritz Fischer

Bosworth, F.F.

Fred Francis (F.F.) Bosworth (1877–1958) was a Pentecostal pioneer, musician, and famous healing evangelist whose ministry spanned several decades, beginning in the early years of the twentieth century. He played a prominent role in the Pentecostal movement in the United States. He also worked with the healing evangelists of the Voice of Healing during the post-World War II healing revival.

Bosworth was born on January 17, 1877, to Burton and Amelia Bosworth on a farm near Utica, NE. As a child, Bosworth discovered his talent for music, and he learned to sell. He was a teenager when he became a Christian. While still a youth, Bosworth contracted tuberculosis. Believing he would soon die, he travelled to Fitzgerald, GA to say farewell to his family. While there, he attended a service in a Methodist church that was held by an evangelist, Mattie Perry. She prayed for him and he was healed of his tuberculosis.

Bosworth was a founding minister and one of the first executive presbyters of the General Council of the Assemblies of God. In the 1920s and 1930s, he held citywide revival meetings that drew thousands of people in single services throughout the United States and Canada. It is believed that more than a million people came to Christ through his ministry. In addition to being a pioneer in radio broadcasting, he was the author of the widely-read book, *Christ the Healer* (1924). He was considered by some historians to be one of the most successful healing revivalists of his generation.

After learning about the healing ministry of John Alexander Dowie, Bosworth and his wife, Estella Hyde, moved north to live in Zion City, a town founded by Dowie as a Christian community. Dowie hired Bosworth to be his band director. In 1906, Pentecostal pioneer Charles Parham

Bosworth Evangelistic Campaign, Ottawa, 1924. Source: Pentecostal Assemblies of Canada Archives

visited Zion and shared the Pentecostal message. On October 18 of that year, Bosworth received the baptism of the Holy Spirit with the evidence of speaking in tongues. It was during that time that he received his call to preach. He and his family later moved to Dallas, TX, where they established a church that would become known as the First Assembly of God Church. Bosworth suffered hardships in Dallas. On one occasion a white mob held him at gun-point and brutally beat him because of his ministry at a black camp meeting.

In 1912, Maria Woodworth-Etter came to his church for a six-month revival meeting. During that time, Bosworth unleashed a flurry of press reports about conversions, miracles of healing and unusual events that occurred during her ministry. The news of the meetings attracted some of the biggest names in the Pentecostal movement. For several years, the meetings continued to grow. However, a conflict arose over the issue of speaking in tongues. While many in his assembly believed that speaking in tongues was the initial sign of Spirit baptism, Bosworth believed that it was only one of the signs of Spirit baptism. He also opposed the view that the tongues spoken in Acts were separate and distinct from the gift of tongues in First Corinthians. Because of his disagreement, Bosworth resigned from the Assemblies of God denomination and became an active minster in the Christian and Missionary Alliance. A few months following his resignation, Bosworth said farewell to his wife, Estella, who died of tuberculosis. Despite his grief, he continued to pray for the sick and preach divine healing. In 1920, he held successful healing campaigns in Lima, Ohio, and Pittsburg, Pa.

In the 1920s, Bosworth's ministry saw unprecedented growth. His biography, *Joybringer Bosworth*, appeared in 1921, and his book, *Christ the Healer*, in 1924. His 1924 campaign in Ottawa, Canada reportedly drew a massive crowd in which 12,000 sought salvation. This was also the decade in which he married Florence Naomi Valentine and launched his magazine,

Africa, Germany, and Japan, among other places. On January 23, 1958, he died of a heart attack in his home in Miami, FL. He was 81.

Bibliography

Barnes III, Roscoe. 2009. *F.F. Bosworth: The Man Behind 'Christ the Healer.'* Newcastle upon Tyne: Cambridge Scholars Publishing.

Bosworth, F.F. 2008. *Christ the Healer*. Grand Rapids, MI: Revell.

Harrell, David Edwin, Jr. 1979. *All Things Are Possible: The Healing and Charismatic Revivals in Modern America*. Bloomington: Indiana University Press.

King, Paul L. 2006. *Genuine Gold: The Cautiously Charismatic Story of the Early Christian and Missionary Alliance*. Tulsa, OK: Word & Spirit Press.

Perkins, Eunice M. 1921. *Joybringer Bosworth: His Life Story*. Detroit, MI: John J. Scruby.

Roscoe Barnes III

F.F. Bosworth, 1877–1958, taken from Eunice M. Perkins, *Fred Francis Bosworth (The Joybringer), Second Edition and Continued Story of Joybringer Bosworth, His Life Story* (First Edition, 1921; Second Edition, 1927).

Exploits of Faith. In the 1930s, Bosworth embraced the teachings of British Israelism and fell out of favor with his denomination. However, in the 1940s, he recanted his views and was welcomed back into fellowship.

Bosworth had all but retired when he learned of the healing ministry of William Branham, which was managed by Gordon Lindsay. After attending one of their meetings, Bosworth joined their staff. Despite being in his 70s, he taught and served as an advisor to Branham and other healing revivalists who were members of The Voice of Healing organization. Bosworth spent his final years of ministry as a missionary evangelist. He ministered in South

Botswana

Botswana is considered a Christian country though this assertion is not enshrined in the constitution which is secular. There is freedom of worship but religious societies are required to be registered by the Registrar of Societies in accordance with the Societies Act 1972. As a result, there are different types of Christianities in Botswana. One of these consists of Pentecostal-Charismatic Churches. These churches were introduced in the country as early as the 1930s but their impact began to be felt only from the beginning of the 1960s and 1970s. During this period missionaries from America and Europe planted Pentecostal churches in South Africa and eventually introduced them in

Botswana with the assistance of Botswana citizens working in South Africa as migrant labourers.

There are many Pentecostal-Charismatic Churches in Botswana today. They can be classified into two groups. The first group consists of traditional classical forms of Pentecostalism. The most well-known of these are the Assemblies of God Church, the Independent Assemblies of God, Apostolic Faith Mission of Africa in Botswana, Church of God in Christ, Pentecostal Holiness Church in Botswana, Holiness Union Church of Botswana, Full Gospel Church of God, Baptist Mission of Botswana, Africa Evangelical Church, Botswana Pentecostal Protestant Church, Church of God of Prophecy and the Church of the Nazarene Mission. Their emphasis is on conversion, baptism of the Holy Spirit and fire, and speaking in tongues.

From the early 1980s to the present Botswana has experienced a new wave of Pentecostal-Charismatic Churches with a different ethos. These include Winners Chapel International Church, Worldwide Family of God Churches, Forward in Faith International, Christ Citadel International Church, Prevailing Christian Ministries, End Time Ministries, Christ Embassy, Rhema Church, Bible Life Ministries, Living Waters, Zoe Ministries International, Good News Fellowship, Deeper Life, Temple of Love Ministries; Divine Healing Ministry to name a few. A number of these churches were introduced in Botswana by people from Ghana, Zimbabwe, Malawi, Nigeria and other parts of Africa. These churches are *sui generis* in that they are transnational, and are prominent in urban areas. They also emphasise conversion, spirit possession, speaking in tongues, faith healing, and the gospel of prosperity. There are claims that Pentecostal-Charismatic Churches are growing though there is very little research to support this assertion.

Modern Pentecostal-Charismatic churches are also known as "Fire Churches" and claim that they have a formula for success in material possessions and health generated by faith as expressed in the saying "what I confess, I possess." This claim attracts many people to the new churches looking for "miracle money" in order to be rich instantly. Believers are urged to pay "seed money" to the church in order to be rich. Poverty is considered as the work of the devil therefore sinful. Fire Churches claim they can heal all kinds of diseases including AIDS and cancer.

Pentecostal-Charismatic Churches contribute significantly to the overall development of the country through provision of scarce skills, employment creation and a good work ethic. They also promote stable family life, positive thinking and provide healing services. But they also face a great deal of criticism because their leadership is dominated by men and foreigners at the expense of women and citizens. Because of their emphasis on individual salvation, they are also accused of individualism which contrasts with the African philosophy of "personhood" as expressed in the saying "I am because you are."

Bibliography

Amanze, J.N., and T. Shanduka. 2015. "Glossolalia: Divine Speech or Man-made Language? A Psychological Analysis of the Gift of Speaking in Tongues in the Pentecostal Churches in Botswana." *Studia Historiae Ecclesiasticae* 41 (1): 3–19.

Tabalaka, A., and F. Nkomazana. 2009. "Aspects of Healing Practices and Methods among Pentecostals in Botswana – Part 1." *Boleswa Journal of Theology, Religion and Philosophy* 2 (3): 137–159.

Tabalaka, A., and F. Nkomazana. 2009. "Faith Healing and Reasoning: Aspects of Healing and Methods among Pentecostals in Botswana – Part 2." *Boleswa Journal of Theology, Religion and Philosophy* 2 (3): 160–169.

Togarasei, L. 2017. "The Place and Challenges of Modern Pentecostal Christianity in Botswana." *Botswana Notes and Records* 48: 225–235.

James N. Amanze

Bradin, Gheorghe

Gheorghe Bradin (1895–1962) was born to a rather modest family on February 3, 1895, in Ghioroc, the district of Lipova in Romania. Converted from an Orthodox family to the Baptist church where he met Persida, his future wife, he was baptized in water on May 10, 1914 at the age of 19. In 1915 Bradin was enrolled in the army and sent to the frontline in the Austro-Hungarian army, but was captured by the Russians and imprisoned in Russia until February 1918. On his return, he married Persida in 1918 and live in Păuliș where he eventually became the leader of a local Baptist church on January 1, 1922.

Just a few years after their marriage and serving in the church, Bradin's family went through a very difficult period of suffering and questioning, as their daughter died at only five weeks old and shortly after that, his wife was diagnosed with tuberculosis. Bradin came in contact with the Pentecostal teachings through reading a series of letters and booklets from the US, especially about healing and baptism in the Spirit. When his wife was miraculously healed from tuberculosis after his prayer in June 1922, they both embraced the Pentecostal faith. They opened the very first Pentecostal church in Romania in their home in Păuliș on September 10, 1922. This date remains in history the beginning of the Pentecostal churches in Romania. Even though historians have debated the exact circumstances and locations of the beginning and expansion of Pentecostalism in Romania, it is generally accepted that the Pentecostal movement established by Gheorghe and his wife Persida was the one that spread throughout the country.

Bradin and the first Pentecostal believers experienced baptism in the Spirit, speaking in tongues, and healings just as in the early church. This attracted many people and so the church grew rather quickly, but this also drew much opposition and harsh persecution. They could not hold their services during day time as there were informants everywhere, so they met in private homes after 9 pm and many times stayed till 5 am. Everything had to be done quietly and in great secret. They must fully cover their windows with pillows so that nothing could be seen or heard from the outside. Pentecostal churches met in secret for some 25 years. They were divided into three branches and the largest one was led by Bradin. Ironically, the communist Romanian government officially recognized the one and unified Pentecostal denomination under the leadership of Bradin for the first time in 1950. Prior to that, he sent a circular letter to all Pentecostal churches throughout the country, asking them to be loyal to the new communist regime based on Romans 13:1–2. Since the communists did not like speaking in tongues, Bradin removed its direct references from the denominational statutes and replaced them with biblical references. As one of his then young colleagues and co-workers, Trandafir Sandru, explained later, these actions of Bradin's played a key and strategic role in the official and legal recognition of the denomination by the communist state.

Many contemporary testimonies portray Bradin as a very rigid and legalistic person (he never wore a tie, for example) and he was rather against the intellectuals in the church. However, with his strong personality, great determination, and a keen instinctive intellectual capacity, Bradin was able to establish and lead the Romanian Pentecostal denomination through its early most difficult years during the communist era. When the church was heavily controlled by the state, he was rather cooperative with the regime. This explains some of Bradin's opinions and actions and even mistakes which facilitated the communist propaganda, promotion, and endorsement of some of the communist policies, such as collectivization. Considering all the challenges of leading a denomination under the communist regime, some history books credit Gheorghe Bradin regarding the establishment and development of the Pentecostal movement in Romania (1922–1937), the re-organization and the unification of the movement (1945–1950), and the leadership of Pentecostal denomination (1950–1962).

Bibliography

Andreescu, Valeriu. 2012. *Istoria Penticostalismului Românesc*, Two Vols. Oradea: Casa Cărții.

Bălăban, Ciprian. 2016. *Istoria Bisericii Penticostale din România (1922–1989): Institutie și Harisme*. Oradea: Scriptum.

Bradin, Gheorghe. 2010. "Autobiografie" (excerpt). *Cuvantul Adevarului*. 21 (1): 17–18.

Croitor, Vasilică. 2010. *Răscumpărarea Memoriei*. Medgidia: Succeed Publishing.

Sandru, Trandafir. 1997. *Trezirea Spirituală Penticostală din România*. București: Institutul Teologic Penticostal.

Corneliu Constantineanu

Branham, William Marrion

William Marrion Branham was born near Burkesville, Kentucky, on April 6, 1909. A lifelong mystic, he began having visions at age three. After his impoverished family moved to Indiana, Branham at the age of seven heard a voice from a treetop telling him not to smoke, drink, or defile his body as God had work for him in the future. Following an unhappy childhood and youth, Branham left Jeffersonville in his late teens to work on an Arizona ranch but eventually returned home to work for a local gas company where he suffered severe internal injuries from inhaling fumes. In a near-death experience, he heard a voice saying, "I called you and you would not go." Although not fully recovered, Branham began to seek God, eventually retreating to a secluded cabin where he saw a mystical light and a young man who identified himself as an angel of the Lord. Branham believed that this angel – which

William Marrion Branham, 1909–1965.
Source: Oral Roberts University

he also called a "pillar of fire" – accompanied him all his life, inspiring his visions.

Ordained by independent Baptists and healed through their prayers, Branham began a tent ministry. On June 11, 1933, during his first major revival, while he was baptizing converts in the Ohio River, the mysterious light appeared again, this time seen by a crowd that stood on the river bank. Soon afterward, he built Branham Tabernacle, which became his home church.

After marriage, Branham met some Oneness Pentecostals who impressed him with their spirituality and who, hearing him preach, asked him to hold revivals for them. However, succumbing to family pressure not to associate with "holy rollers," he canceled the meetings, a decision he later regretted. During the 1937 Ohio River flood, when both his wife and baby daughter died of spinal meningitis, Branham interpreted their deaths as divine punishment. Although heartbroken, Branham eventually re-married. During the Depression, he continued to preach but accepted no salary and instead worked as a game warden.

Branham's healing ministry was finally launched after an angelic encounter on May 7, 1946, in which he received a commission to take "a gift of healing to the people of the world." A few weeks after a minister's daughter was healed through his prayers, Branham held his first healing revival in St. Louis. From there he held healing meetings in Jonesboro, Arkansas, then in some small Oneness churches (Weaver 2000), then in Shreveport, Phoenix, and cities in California, and later in Canada. For the next decade, with the backing of, first, W.E. Kidson, then Jack Moore and Hal Lindsey, and later Ern Baxter and F.F. Bosworth, Branham's healing ministry surged. Using *The Voice of Healing* magazine, Lindsey promoted Branham's crusades in the USA and eventually in Finland and Norway, South Africa, Switzerland, and worldwide.

Several historians, including Walter Hollenweger, who interpreted for Branham in Zurich, observed his ministry and words of knowledge as he named the illnesses and discerned the unrepented sins of those to whom he ministered. Branham's success in the healing ministry was the catalyst for the postwar healing revival, inspiring several healing evangelists, including T.L. Osborn. His fellow ministers were impressed not only by the sensational miracles of his ministry – the restoration of sight and hearing, the healing of diseases, even cancer, and, on occasion, the raising of the dead – but also by his deep humility.

By the mid-1950s, Branham's ministry declined as more media-savvy ministers entered the healing arena. Added to financial shortfalls were tax evasion charges. Despite receiving only a minimal salary – due to a legal technicality – he was required to pay income tax on ministry donations. Not only did the volume of his mail shrink but the letters became critical of his teachings.

During his final decade, Branham's preaching became increasingly controversial. Whereas previously he emphasized evangelical unity, he began insisting on re-baptism in the name of Jesus only. Besides preaching a curious blend of Calvinism, anti-denominationalism, and dispensationalism, his rhetoric became offensive as he ranted against women preaching and wearing make-up and slacks. Most problematic was his teaching regarding the forerunner of the Second Coming, a composite figure drawn from the messenger of Malachi 4 and the angel of the Laodicean church age in Revelation 3. Once his followers became convinced that Branham was the end-time prophet, a personality cult developed that continued after his death.

In December 1965, as Branham was driving to Indiana from Arizona, a drunk driver crashed into his car. He died a few days later, on Christmas Eve. Some of those who believed Branham to be the end-time messenger expected him to rise from the dead before his burial, and even after his burial, some believed he would rise in time to usher in the Second Coming.

Although Kenneth Hagin (1983) stated that Branham erred in stepping out of his original calling of healing to teach prophecy – a task for which he had neither gifting nor training – his crucial role as initiator of the postwar healing revival is undeniable. As David E. Harrell comments, he was "preeminently the visionary of the healing revival" (Harrell 1975, 165).

Bibliography

Hagin, Kenneth. 1983. *Understanding the Anointing*. Tulsa, OK: K. Hagin Ministries.
Harrell, David E. 1975. *All Things Are Possible: The Healing & Charismatic Revivals in Modern America*. Bloomington, IN: Indiana University Press.
Liardon, Roberts. 2003. "William Branham: A Man of Notable Signs and Wonders." In *God's Generals: Why They Succeeded and Why Some Failed*. New Kensington, PA: Whitaker House.
Lindsay, Gordon. 1950. *William Branham: A Man Sent from God*. Jeffersonville, IN: W. Branham.
Weaver, C. Douglas. 2000. *The Healer-Prophet: William Marrion Branham: A Study of the Prophetic in American Pentecostalism*. Macon, GA: Mercer University Press.

Sally Jo Shelton

Brawner, Mina Ross

Mina Conrod Ross Brawner (1874–1960) was a medical doctor from the USA, who became one of the most influential female Pentecostal leaders in early twentieth-century Australia. Despite facing difficult personal challenges, she maintained an effective healing ministry, planted multiple churches, established a Bible training institute, and was a key spokesperson for the promotion of women in church leadership.

Mina was one of ten children born in the Sterling Valley (near Oswego), New York to poor Scottish migrants, Gerrard and Margaret (née Brebner) Ross. The family moved many times and eventually settled in Healdsburg, north of San Francisco. Her mother had been converted in a Charles Finney campaign in Scotland and became involved with the Seventh-day Adventists in the USA. While Mina's father struggled with alcoholism, her mother worked long hours as a nurse to put her children through school. Apart from one sibling who died in infancy, all of the nine surviving children completed college degrees, five of whom became medical doctors.

In 1896, Mina commenced at Adventist Healdsburg College and married Archelaus Stuttafor, an Adventist medical doctor. After an unsuccessful mission stint in Samoa, the couple moved to Australia as medical missionaries in 1900. However, in 1908 their daughter died, leading Mina to reject God. She left her husband and returned to the USA in 1911 and filed for divorce. She completed her studies at the Chicago Hospital Medical College in 1916 and purchased a property near Arvada, Wyoming. In 1922, Mina married a Baptist adherent, William E. Brawner, but a year later that marriage also ended and she moved to Reno, Nevada, then Carson City.

Through overwork and personal challenges, Mina's health broke down, manifested in serious heart problems. During this time, a friend gave her copies of the *Pentecostal Evangel*, as well as a tract by Aimee Semple McPherson, entitled "The Crucible of God." In 1924, Mina attended McPherson's Angelus Temple in Los Angeles and had such a significant baptism in the Holy Spirit and healing experience that she closed her medical practice and became a credentialed minister of the World's Faith Missionary Association (WFMA).

As a medical doctor, Mina did not deny the existence of sickness but held that God's supernatural power could heal physical infirmities. She led a number of tent meetings across the USA, including a 13-week evangelistic campaign with Carrie Judd Montgomery in Oakland. In 1926, Mina became the state evangelist for the Bible Standard Conference and was ultimately a long term member of the Open Bible Church network.

In 1927, Mina held a series of meetings in New Zealand, then travelled on to Australia. For the next five years, Mina worked on staff at Apostolic Faith Mission of Australasia which had been founded by Sarah Jane Lancaster. Besides preaching, she also published a controversial 14-part series on women in ministry in Lancaster's *Good News* magazine from January 1929 to March 1930. The collection was subsequently published as a book. Mina reasoned, "Charging God with the folly of anointing and equipping his handmaidens for service, and then disqualifying them because they are what he made them ... I must confess to ... impatience at such an archaic viewpoint."

Mina conducted campaigns across Queensland, New South Wales and Victoria. She claimed to have planted 14 churches during her 16 years in Australia. In 1932, she opened soup kitchens in Toowoomba and Brisbane, distributing around 800 meals a week for the unemployed during the Great Depression. Besides holding outreach and healing meetings, she also opened The Bible Standard Training School for Christian Workers for both residential and non-residential students, although it soon closed because of low enrolments.

Owing to the uncertainty of World War II, Mina returned to the USA in 1943. She settled on the family land in Healdsburg, California and her widowed twin sister Dr. Maggie Stewart came to live with her. Keen to continue her ministry, Mina embarked on a multi-city tour in 1944 with other Open Bible evangelists. During 1946–1947, she conducted a preaching tour of churches in Iowa, including Waterloo, Swea City and Mount Pleasant.

From her writings it appears that she became disillusioned with many Pentecostal churches that she felt had lost the initial fire of the Holy Spirit. In 1951, she resigned her membership of the Open Bible Standard churches, although she continued holding meetings with her WFMA credentials. Mina passed away sometime after July 1960.

Self-styled after the flamboyant McPherson, Mina Ross Brawner became renowned as a charismatic preacher, church planter, healing evangelist and educated spokesperson for gender equality in ministry. She revitalised the failing Apostolic Faith Mission after the death of Sarah Jane Lancaster, and founded a number of Bible Standard Churches across Australia. Her untiring commitment to ministry left a lasting legacy in Australia, New Zealand and the USA.

Bibliography

Brawner, Mina Ross. 1975. *Woman in the Word*. Dallas TX: Christ for the Nations.

Chant, Barry. 2011. *The Spirit of Pentecost: The Origins and Development of the Pentecostal Movement in Australia 1870–1939*. Lexington KY: Emeth Press.

Clifton, Shane. 2009. *Pentecostal Churches in Transition: Analysing the Developing Ecclesiology of the Assemblies of God in Australia*. Leiden: Brill.

Hutchinson, Mark P. "Mina Conrod Ross Brawner." *Australasian Dictionary of Pentecostal and Charismatic Movements*. Accessed February 26, 2019. https://sites.google.com/view/adpcm/a-d-top-page/brawner-mina-conrod-ross.

Hutchinson, Mark P. 2018. "Dissenting Preaching in the Twentieth-Century Anglophone World." In *The Oxford History of Protestant Dissenting Traditions Volume V: The Twentieth Century: Themes and Variations in a Global Context*, edited by Mark P. Hutchinson, 170–198. Oxford: Oxford University Press.

Denise A. Austin

Brazil

Since the early twentieth-century, Pentecostalism has had a growing presence in Brazil. The Brazilian religious landscape expresses an amazing and vital diversity. Such diversity is not a recent invention or even a re-invention of something forgotten in the past, but a continuous result of Brazilian cultural history that, through a process of the interpenetration and accommodation of various religious traditions, shaped the formation of the "Brazilian folk-religions" (Bastide 2007).

The Catholicism transplanted to Brazil by the Portuguese colonizers reflected the European "imaginary" of the medieval popular religion. It was a religion populated by good and evil spirits, saints, and demons, controlling everyday people's life. In the colonial context, such kind of religion was transfigured in and by the syncretistic encounter, first, with original native peoples of the land and, later, with African slaves (Rivera 2016). Pentecostalism has become a very important part of a such religious landscape.

Brought from Chicago a few years after the Azusa Street Revival, today's Brazilian Pentecostalism has become part of the religious life of more than 50 million Brazilians. As the three European immigrants that introduced Pentecostalism in Brazil belonged in their homeland to very poor and excluded sectors, as missionaries, they worked among poor sectors of the Brazilian society in the early twentieth century – Italian migrant workers in the factories and farms in the states of São Paulo and Paraná, and Northeast Brazil migrant rubber tappers in the Amazon forests. Since their very beginning, the two matrices of Brazilian Pentecostalism, the Christian Congregation and the Assemblies of God, came to be a religious-social phenomenon by, of, and among the poor – literally a Brazilian religion of the Brazilian migrant poor (Campos 2016).

Luigi Francescon, a former Presbyterian from Italy, and Gunnar Vingren and Daniel Berg, Baptists from Sweden, took Pentecostalism to Brazil, a few years after the beginnings of the Azusa Street Revival in Los Angeles. Francescon went to Presbyterians and Vingren and Berg to Southern Baptists and experienced rejection from those two evangelical churches. Soon, in Southern Brazil, Francescon formed his Christian Congregations, and, in the Northern Region, Vingren and Bergen established their Apostolic Missions that in a few years would be renamed as the

Assemblies of God. Both denominations, since their beginnings witnessed the plurality, diversity, and plasticity that in a near future would become a major characteristic of the Brazilian Pentecostalism (Campos 2016).

The movement did not expand in great numbers during the first half of the nineteenth century. However, after the Second World War, as a result of the rapid processes of industrialization and urbanization of the country, the two classical Pentecostal denominations experienced amazing numeric growth, especially in the peripheries of São Paulo, Rio de Janeiro, and other Brazilian large metropolitan regions (Campos 2016).

Besides the already two established denominations, in the 1950s new Pentecostal churches with a strong emphasis on divine healing were established throughout the country: The Foursquare Gospel Church and its offsprings – "Brazil for Christ" Evangelical Pentecostal Church, and "God is Love" Evangelical Pentecostal Church – firstly, were established in São Paulo, but soon spread to different regions (Miller, 2019).

At the same time, a process of pentecostalization of the mainline churches resulted in the formation of a different kind of Pentecostalism that affirmed the baptism of the Holy Spirit but preserved the order and the theology of the former denominations they split from. In a few years, Brazilian Pentecostalism would include "Spirit Renewed" Baptist, Methodist, Presbyterian, and Congregational Churches.

In the 1970s, having learned from the painful alienation process of the "Spirit Renewed" Churches, the mainline denominations tried to assimilate the influences of the North-American Charismatic Movement affirming in some ways the contemporaneity of the "so-called" spiritual gifts but, at the same time, relativizing the centrality of the Pentecostal teaching on the glossolalia. Today, those denominations, including the Roman Catholic Church, have large portions of their memberships professing Pentecostal experiences, but preserving the order, doctrine, and worship rituals of their own traditions.

In the late 1970s, Neo-pentecostalism, another sort of Brazilian Pentecostalism, begun to emerge in Rio de Janeiro. In fact, since then, Brazilian society has witnessed the extraordinary growth of this religious phenomena. The movement tries to present a religious response to human needs and desires imposed on most of the Brazilian population by the modern condition of Brazilian neoliberal capitalism (Campos, 2016).

Under such circumstances and the influence of the New Life Pentecostal Church (Rio de Janeiro upper-middle-class church, organized in the 1960's by Robert McAlister, a Canadian Pentecostal missionary), two of its former members, Romildo R. Soares and his brother-in-law Edir Macedo Bezerra, organized a new church that would become the matrix of the "so-called" Brazilian Neo-pentecostalism – the Igreja Universal do Reino de Deus [Universal Church of the Kingdom of God]. Edir Macedo, known now as Bishop Macedo, took over the control of UCKG, in a kind of a "coup-de-état" against Soares.

In the next two decades, Neo-pentecostalism spread all over the country with the establishment of many new denominations that propagate the famous "health and wealth" or prosperity gospel. Neo-pentecostal megachurches are impacting the Brazilian religious environment with their millions of members, enormous investments in mass-media communications, construction of megachurch buildings, mission work in many countries around the world, and strong participation in Brazilian political life (Machado Jr. 2018). Neo-pentecostalism challenges not only the secular predominance of Brazilian Catholicism and the presence of Afro-Brazilian religions, but also the major classical Pentecostal churches. On the other hand, Neo-pentecostal churches are playing a major social role in Brazilian society, providing the disadvantaged masses with religious responses, creating conditions for their survival in a violent and excluding socioeconomic context, and offering new spiritual and religious alternatives (Cunha 2018).

Bibliography

Campos, Leonildo Silveira. 2016. "Traditional Pentecostalism." In *Handbook of Contemporary Religions in Brazil*, edited by Bettina Schmidt and Steven Engler, 95–116. Leiden: Brill.

Cunha, Cristina Vidal. 2018. "Pentecostal Cultures in Urban Peripheries: A Socio-anthropological Analysis of Pentecostalism in Arts, Grammars, Crime, and Morality." *Vibrant: Virtual Brazilian Anthropology* 15 (1): e151401. Epub October 22.

Machado Jr., Celso. 2018. "Market as Religion: The Dynamics of Business Network of Megachurches." *Brazilian Business Review* 15 (3): 262–283.

Miller, Eric, and Ronald J. Morgan. 2019. *Brazilian Evangelicalism in the Twenty-First Century: An Inside and Outside Look*. Cham, Switzerland: Palgrave Macmillan.

Rivera, Paulo Barrera. 2016. "Pentecostalism in Brazil." In *Handbook of Contemporary Religions in Brazil*, edited by Bettina Schmidt and Steven Engler, 117–131. Leiden: Brill.

Roger Bastide. 2007. *The African Religions of Brazil: Toward a Sociology of the Interpenetration of Civilizations*. Baltimore: The John Hopkins University Press.

Paulo Ayres Mattos

Bulgaria

Pentecostalism was brought to Bulgaria by Russian immigrants to the United States, Ivan Voronaev and Dionessy Zaplishny, who undertook the difficult missionary journey to Eastern Europe with their families and coworkers on July 13, 1920. In just a short time after a center was established in the Congregational church in Bourgas on April 26, 1921, some 18 Pentecostal assemblies formed across the country. The movement grew rapidly even after Voronaev and his team left for Odessa on August 12, 1921. But a split over doctrine and practice within the newly established Pentecostal movement deepened when persecution forced the Zaplishnys to leave Bulgaria in May of 1924.

In September of 1926, the Assemblies of God, USA sent Bulgarian born Nikolas Nikolov to organize the churches in a Union of Evangelical Pentecostal Churches. Skeptical about the new organization, only four congregations (Bourgas, Rouse, Varna and Plovdiv) initially joined the Union during its first national assembly on March 28–31, 1928. The official government registration affirmed the previous division and by 1930 when the Zaplishnys returned to Bulgaria, many of the 58 Pentecostal congregations remained outside the Union. Meanwhile, several of the presbyters ordained by Zaplishny during his first visit (1920–1924), united many unregistered Pentecostals in the underground Church of God.

The Russian occupation of Bulgaria during World War II brought about a Communist regime, which heavily persecuted all evangelicals for the next 50 years. The 1948–49 trial of protestant pastors effectively beheaded the movement and the pulpits of the larger Pentecostal churches were filled with secret government agents acting as pastors. A similar trial in 1978–1979 ensured the elimination of a new generation of young and progressive evangelical vanguard and strengthened the government's grip on the church.

Half a century of continuous persecution had suppressed the Pentecostals to less than 5,000 nationwide until Easter of 1989, when Danish journalist Johny Noer prophesied the fall of Communism from the rooftop of the Pentecostal church in Varna. When the Berlin Wall fell seven months later, Bulgaria experienced one of the greatest revivals in Pentecostal history. Though the secular state still ostracized evangelicals as sectarian cults, the Bulgarian Pentecostal movement grew rapidly to over 150,000 strong. Several Pentecostal churches were started outside of Bulgaria too, following the ministry paradigm of the Bulgarian Church of God in Chicago established on July 16, 1995.

The Bulgarian Evangelical Alliance was restored in 1990 with Pentecostal denominations as the largest members. The early twentieth century *Pentecostal Evangel* was brought back to print and the *Morning Star* newspaper was renewed as published by the first American missionaries in 1865. The launching of Bulgarian Bible website Bibliata.com (1996) and Shalom TV (1997) set in course a Pentecostal presence in Bulgaria's media space. This helped the newly organized Bulgarian Christian Coalition gain 0.63 percent of the national vote in the 1997 parliamentarian elections. Consecutively, the Bulgarian Evangelical Theological Institute was granted government registration in 1999 with predominant Pentecostal participation, but never gained full accreditation and fractured after 2010. The Bulgarian Chaplaincy Coalition aimed to restore chaplaincy in the armed forces, but was suppressed by lack of legal precedent and government support (International Religious Freedom Report 2007, rel. Sept. 14, 2007 by U.S. Dept. of State).

In 2002, the new Acts of Confessions was voted by Bulgarian Parliament to replace the 1949 Communist Law of Religions and in just a few short years some one hundred evangelical denominations, predominantly Pentecostal/Charismatic in theology and liturgy, were registered. As a result of this, the Assemblies of God reported 50,000 members and many adherents, while the Church of God in Bulgaria reached 32,000 members nationwide and 28 local congregations in the capital Sofia alone.

After Bulgaria entered the European Union in 2007, the Pentecostal movement within the country began a steady decline in relation to large waves of immigration. The 2011 national census reported only 62,000 evangelical believers, but did not include over 70 new Pentecostal churches started in the United Kingdom, Germany, Spain, Cyprus, Canada, and the United States. Similar discrepancies were noted in large Roma communities with predominantly evangelical populations in cities across the country.

In 2019, new changes in the Legal Bill of Religions implemented restrictive measures toward religious minorities including evangelicals. Nevertheless, the influence of Pentecostal churches in Bulgaria continues to grow in numbers with some 1,000 congregations nationwide. In a setting of ever changing social realities and political unrest, the movement remains an important factor in maintaining an ethnic balance and equality. The largest Roma church in the Balkans is a Pentecostal congregation in the city of Samokov, home of American Missionary School during Bulgaria's National Revival of the nineteenth century. Pentecostal churches are an important factor in social involvement with migrant groups at the borders with Turkey and Greece. The Pentecostal movement of Bulgaria celebrated its centennial in 2020.

Bibliography

Bankov, Stefan. 2001. *Dossier: On Both Sides of the Iron Curtain*. Bourgas: self-published.
Diulgerov, D.V. 1932. "Pentecostals (Part 1)." In *Annual Publication of the Theological Faculty at Sofia University*. Vol. 9, *1931–1932*. Sofia: Gutenberg Press.
Dryanov, Yoncho. 1977. *History of the Evangelical Pentecostal Churches in Bulgaria (1920–1976)*. Unpublished manuscript, Varna.
Ignatov, Pavel. 2004. *The Bloodless Persecution of the Church*. Sofia: Lik.
Zarev, Ivan. 1993. *History of the Evangelical Pentecostal Churches in Bulgaria (1920–1989)*. Sofia: self-published.

Dony K. Donev

Buntain, D. Mark

Daniel Mark Buntain (1923–1989) served as a missionary in Calcutta, India where he, along with his wife Huldah Buntain, founded the Mission of Mercy. Together they planted a ministry that included a large congregation, a six-storey hospital, a feeding program providing daily meals for thousands, and dozens of schools for children and adults.

Buntain was born in Winnipeg, Canada, where his father, Daniel Newton Buntain, pastored a prominent Methodist congregation. His father opposed the early success of Pentecostalism in Canada until he attended a revival led by Charles S. Price. Daniel Buntain joined the Pentecostal Assemblies of Canada (PAOC) after he was asked to leave the Methodist Conference due to his support for Pentecostal doctrine. The church he founded became the largest in the PAOC. The family moved to Toronto when Daniel Buntain was elected as the general superintendent of PAOC. He served in that role from 1936 until 1944.

During his teenage years, Mark Buntain worked as an announcer on a radio station called CFCO (Coming From Chatham Ontario) in Ontario while preaching in churches around the area. He enlisted in the Royal Canadian Mounted Police after Canada instated the draft during World War II, though that enlistment was deferred when Buntain was assigned a pastorate in Watrous, Saskatchewan.

Buntain met Huldah Monroe after he accepted her father's invitation to preach at a revival meeting in Vancouver. Monroe was born in Tokyo where her parents, Alex and Gwendolyn Monroe, served as missionaries before returning to Canada. After marrying in 1944, Mark and Huldah Buntain joined the Assemblies of God in the United States and traveled the country as evangelists. The Buntains welcomed their only child, Bonnie, in 1953. That same year, they were invited to serve as missionaries in Calcutta, India.

The Buntains started holding tent meetings in 1954. They moved into a rented space above a popular nightclub by 1956 and named their new church the Calcutta Revival Center. Mark Buntain was able to purchase property on Royd Street from a Muslim family and dedicated the AG Church on Christmas Day, 1959. It was the first church building dedicated in Calcutta in over 100 years. Over the next 30 years they added language sections beginning with a Hindi section in 1965, a Teluga section in 1968, Bengali and Nepali in 1970, Tamil 1976, Oriya 1981, and Malayalam the year Mark Buntain died in 1989. In 1993, a larger building was dedicated as the Mark Buntain memorial Assembly of God Church.

Mark Buntain founded the Royd Street School in 1964 because many of the children attending the church were dismissed from their schools due to their association with the church. More schools soon followed including primary and middle schools offering an education in Hindi and Bengali both in Calcutta and in outlying villages. By 1982, they were operating 12 schools with over 2,000 students. Starting in 1979, they founded professional schools, including the school of nursing, West Bengal Bible College, the teacher's training college, and the Assembly of God Church Vocational School offering courses in tailoring, media design, catering, etc.

Perhaps the best-known aspect of Buntain's work is the emphasis on what the AG would later identify as "ministries of compassion." After the Bengali famine in 1964, the church started a feeding center for their students that gave a daily ration of milk, boneyed syrup, and paranthas. By 1987, more feeding centers were covering the daily needs of 15,000 people.

In 1970, Mark Buntain opened a two-bed outpatient clinic in the rear of the church building, manned by volunteer medical staff. The clinic grew to 16 beds in 1974, and within a year they began construction on a new six-story hospital and research center. In 1989, the Calcutta Mercy Hospital opened an Intensive Care Unit. Today, the 173-bed hospital serves around 100,000 patients a year, just under half free of charge.

Mark Buntain worked tirelessly to minister to the people of Calcutta. His boundless faith, energy, and generosity became a model for missionaries doing "compassion ministry" in the AG. His health suffered over the years but his passion for the city pushed him on.

Mark Buntain passed away in 1989 due to a cerebral brain hemorrhage. His death made headlines throughout India and 20,000 people came to pay respect at his funeral. Huldah Buntain was elected leader of the mission and became the first female living in India to be ordained.

In 2005, Calcutta Mercy Ministries was formed with an emphasis on feeding, educating, and medically assisting the poor. Today 35,000 students are educated in over 100 schools associated with Calcutta Mercy Missions. Dozens of Mercy Clinics can be found in rural villages surrounding Calcutta. Since the building of that first church on Royd Street, more than 900 associated churches have opened in 12 Indian states.

Bibliography

Anderson, Allan. 2007. *Spreading Fires: The Missionary Nature of Early Pentecostalism.* Maryknoll, NY: Orbis Books.

Breed, Sarah. 2014. "Mercy in Calcutta." *Charisma* (April): 20–25.

Donaldson, Hal, and Kenneth M. Dobson. 2012. *Huldah Buntain: Woman of Courage.* Calcutta, India: Devtech Publishers and Printers Pvt. Ltd.

Hembree, Ron. 1983. *The Mark Buntain Story.* Minneapolis, MN: Bethany House.

McGee, Gary B. 2010. *Miracles, Missions, and American Pentecostalism.* Maryknoll, NY: Orbis Books.

Allen Tennison

Burton, William Frederick

William Frederick Padwick Burton (1886–1971) was born in Liverpool in 1886. He was the son of a sea captain and grew up in a notable family in Surrey. He played football for the local Reigate team, trained as an engineer. He described himself as a teenager "getting into sin and sadness." He was converted after hearing R.A. Torrey's preaching in London in 1905.

Burton went to Preston to work as an engineer and was baptized in the Spirit in 1910. In 1911 he joined the Pentecostal Missionary Union (PMU) Bible school in Preston. He preached the gospel and prayed for the sick and saw some remarkable healings. He believed that God was calling him to be a missionary in Africa. Burton in a maverick way persistently provoked the PMU's leading figure, Alexander Boddy, over infant baptism. He was unsurprisingly rejected by the PMU in February 1914 and sailed to South Africa independently in June of the same year. As a gifted artist, he sold his artwork to pay for his ticket as no church supported him.

In South Africa he was impressed by an indigenous South African, Elias Letwaba. Burton described him baptizing converts in water with most of them "coming up out of the water speaking in tongues." He later wrote a biography on Letwaba in 1934 as one of the twenty-eight books that he authored.

In 1915 James Salter (from Preston and a former fellow PMU student of Burton's) travelled out to meet Burton in South Africa. The two had made a pact in the UK to work side by side in Africa. They set off together in June 1915 from South Africa to the Belgian Congo. They both went towards a plot of land just outside a town called Mwanza in the south-eastern Katanga province.

Burton and Salter initially struggled at learning the local language. Surrounded by what they described as "superstition" and "idolatry," they saw their circumstances as "trying in the extreme." Their efforts received a quantum leap forward in September 1916 due to thirty Congolese who had been taken into slavery from Congo to Angola years ago. These men and women had been converted in Angola in non-pentecostal settings. Having now been freed from slavery, they desired to return to Congo with the gospel. After a fifteen month journey on foot, they arrived unannounced in Mwanza while singing hymns as Burton and Salter were holding a service under some trees. The leader of these freed slaves was Shalumbo. Burton described them as "having a craving to preach."

In 1918, Shalumbo went to his home village of Kipushya (fifteen days on foot) and preached the gospel. Extraordinary healings followed. After Shalumbo returned, Burton travelled to Kipushya. This eventually led to a further missionary outpost being established there, which became a center for reaching out to the neighboring Kasai province. With their non-pentecostal background, the freed slaves were resistant to Burton's teaching on baptism in the Spirit for years. It was not until January 1920, a breakthrough for Burton and their baptism in the Spirit happened. Burton worked very closely with Shalumbo and other Congolese evangelists and pastors whom he trained. The Congolese established mission outposts and sometimes white missionaries followed. In 1922, Burton described two of the freed slaves, Kangoi and Ngoloma, as practically taking "the same place and responsibility with regard to the young native churches as the white missionaries." He continued by stating that if the white missionaries were to leave, "the native church would still have godly men to whom to look for help and direction." Burton wrote a biography on Shalumbo in 1929 before ever embarking on any history of the white missionary presence. He wrote that the missionary task at this time was to empower the Congolese pastors to govern the churches.

In 1929, Burton believed that his work was completed in this part of Congo and that he was ready to "move on" following his understanding of his own indigenous principles. However, a colonial Belgian government insisted on "white supervision" of Congolese churches. In 1933, he wrote that white missionaries were "a mere passing phase in the introduction of Christianity to a heathen people."

Describing the Congolese pastors to his own missionaries in 1959, he reckoned that they were "as good as we are and perhaps a lot better." By the time Burton left Congo in 1960, there were eighty missionaries serving in thirteen different missionary centers. Burton described the Congolese leaders in 1960 as "men to be wondered at." Independence came to Congo in 1960. Burton believed that the missionary society should close in 1964, but by this time he had less influence on it. He remained supportive of the missionary society, but was not effectively involved in any further decision making. He died in 1971 in South Africa.

Bibliography

Burton, W.F.P. 1933. *God Working with Them: Being Eighteen Years of Congo Evangelistic Mission History.* London: Victory Press.
Emmett, David. 2017. "W.F.P. Burton (1886–1971) and Congolese Agency: A Biographical Study of a Pentecostal Mission." PhD thesis., University of Birmingham, UK.
Garrard, David. 2015. "William F.P. Burton and the Birth of Congolese Pentecostalism." In *Pentecostalism in Africa: Presence and Impact of Pneumatic Christianity in Postcolonial Societies,* edited by Martin Lindhardt, 75–99. Leiden: Brill.
Garrard, David. 1983. "History of the Congo Evangelistic Mission/Communauté Pentecôtiste au Zaïre from 1915 to 1982." PhD diss., University of Aberdeen.

Dave Emmett

Cameroon

One of the most striking features of Christianity in Cameroon is the lack of African independent, or Aladura, churches throughout the country. There is a close connection between the development of independent and Pentecostal churches in other parts of sub-Saharan African, and the slow arrival of Pentecostalism to Cameroon is most probably linked to the absence of this vibrant type of African Christianity. Paul Gifford claims that this lack of Christian variation is a result of the state's preoccupation with security (1998, 292), a political tradition that is a legacy inherited from the laïcité policies introduced by the French colonial administration (1918–1960). The tight government control continued in new wrapping through both the Ahidjo (1960–1982) and the Biya (1982–) administrations, and has had the effect of creating a political culture of subordination also shared by the religious institutions. The religious leaders have been educated by an administrative system which to a large extent has been accepted and adopted by the religious communities, leaving little room for innovation in either religious or cultural terms. The africanization of Christianity has therefore developed at a much slower pace in Cameroon than in neighbouring countries, and the mainline churches have been granted privileged positions where they have to some extent joined forces with the government in order not to be challenged by competing churches (Akoko 2007; Gifford 1998). Even if the international community's pressure for democratization during the 1990s opened up for the establishing of new Pentecostal churches, it is estimated that less than 10 percent of the Pentecostal churches currently have government authorization.

The arrival and development of the Pentecostal churches in Cameroon followed the pattern of the mainline churches where the missionary influence was strong. The first church to be established was the Apostolic Church, of British origin, which was brought to Cameroon from Nigeria in the late 1940s, and gained a foothold and developed with the help of Swiss missionaries. For a long time the church was only present in the Anglophone part of the country, but after the Pentecostal boom following the 1990s, the church became a national church with congregations throughout the country. The largest Pentecostal church in Cameroon is the Full Gospel Mission, which was the result of a Pentecostal missionary initiative from Germany in the late 1950s. One of the missionaries originally sent to Nigeria, Werner Knorr, crossed the border to Cameroon and with help from his Nigerian assistants established the first Full Gospel Mission church at Mutengene in 1961. The church was legally recognised in 1969, and a Bible school was established in Bamenda in 1970. Later, English and American missionaries from the Assemblies of God worked with the German mission instead of creating a church of their own (Gifford 1998, 289–290; Akoko 2007, 68). The church was also the first Pentecostal church to gain a foothold in the Francophone part of Cameroon. Contrary to most Pentecostal churches, the Full Gospel Mission has been able to establish churches in big cities as well as villages, where the Catholic, and often one of the Protestant churches, have until recently been the only churches present. According to Robert Mbe Akoko, the Full Gospel Mission is also the first church to be exported from Cameroon to Nigeria, and congregations have also been established in Chad and the Central African Republic (Akoko 2007, 68). One of the first Pentecostal churches to be established without a foreign missionary initiative was Vraie Eglise de Dieu which was started by Nestor Toukea in 1959 (Gifford 1998, 290).

The Pentecostal churches mentioned thus far were traditional churches in the sense that they were a continuation of the holiness tradition they inherited from the European missionaries. Following the Pentecostal development from the 1990s, these theological ideas were to be seriously challenged. Akoko, in his doctoral thesis describing the changes within the Full Gospel Mission, the Catholic Church, and the Presbyterian Church in the Anglophone part of Cameroon, claims that two developments have significantly changed Cameroon Christianity during the last decades. The first is the move from ascetics to a gospel of prosperity; the second is what he calls a "pentecostalization" of the mainline churches. Akoko argues that the main reason behind these changes was the economic crises, which Cameroon experienced in the 1990s. Later research (Drønen 2013) has modified Akoko's claims, showing that the gospel of prosperity only to some extent has influenced Pentecostal churches in Cameroon, and that global influences, independent leadership and a redefinition of ethnic belonging and social organization are other important reasons behind the Pentecostal growth. The pentecostalization of mainline churches has continued with strength the last decade. As one example, Ludovic Lado's (2009) work on the Catholic Church gives interesting insight into how the healing movement of Meinard Hegba has influenced the Catholic community.

The Pentecostal boom in the 1990s was also related to the crusades held by famous prosperity preachers in the southern part of the country. The first major figure to visit Cameroon was Reinhardt Bonnke, who through his "Fire Conferences" and "Pastors Workshops" preached to both the masses and a selection of local pastors when he visited Kumba in 1989 and Bamenda in 1990. The Kumba crusade functioned as an appetizer for what was to come, and more than 65 churches and 250,000 people is said to have attended the five-day crusade in Bamenda. In the constant stream of preachers coming to Cameroon from Nigeria, two pastors in particular have made a lasting impact. The first is the late Benson Idahosa, who visited Cameroon several times until he passed away in 1999. Many Pentecostal leaders in Cameroon have been trained in the Idahosa Bible College and have been inspired by visits to the Church of God Mission International in Benin City. The other Nigerian worth mentioning here is Tunde Joda, the founder of Christ Chapel International Churches, which has several congregations in Cameroon. In addition to sharing the crusade-stage with preachers from all over the world, Joda's journal, Prosperity Now, did much to influence theological thinking in the Anglophone part of Cameroon. Recently, all the major Nigerian Pentecostal churches, Winners Chapel, Redeemed Christian Church of God, and Deeper Life Bible Church have a considerable network of congregations, both in the Anglophone and the francophone parts of Cameroon (Chewachong 2017).

An important person in the Cameroonian Pentecostal landscape is the unorthodox personality of Billy Lubansa. Originally from the Democratic Republic of Congo, Lubansa worked his way into the hierarchy of the Pan African Institute of Development (PAID), a job which gave him diplomatic status. He started his Flaming Fire of God Ministries in Zambia in 1986 before his professional office was moved to Cameroon, where he encountered what he later described as a dead Pentecostal movement. Due to the reluctant welcome in the country, Lubansa chose to work with the Apostolic Church and the Full Gospel Mission instead of establishing his own church, thereby changing Cameroon's Pentecostal churches from within. "Super Papa Billy" retired from his PAID position in 2003 and moved back to Zambia in order to take care of his church there, but he frequently returns to Cameroon to organise the fire conferences which regularly take place in Limbe.

The only Cameroonian to have reached the status of "stadium-pastor" is Zacharias Fomum, the former Presbyterian who after some time in the Full Gospel Mission created Communauté missionaire chrétienne internationale in Yaoundé. Fomum was a university professor and started the Christian Publishing House, which also has a branch in Nigeria. He has written numerous books, the most famous being *The Christian and the Money: Banking in Heaven Today* (1988).

From its origin as a theological revival in the Anglophone part of Cameroonian Christianity, Pentecostalism has gradually spread to other parts of the country. Recently several Pentecostal communities have been established through local initiatives also in the North, Iya Moussa being one central figure through the establishment of Eglise de la foi vivante in Ngaoundéré (Drønen 2013).

Bibliography

Akoko, Robert Mbe. 2007. "'Ask and You Shall be Given.' Pentecostalism and the Economic Crises in Cameroon." PhD thesis, Leiden, African Studies Centre.

Chewachong, Amos Bongadu. 2017. "Intra-African Pentecostalism and the Dynamics of Power: the Living Faith Church worldwide (Winners' Chapel) in Cameroon, 1996–2016." PhD thesis, University of Edinburgh.

Drønen, Tomas. 2013. *Pentecostalism, Globalisation, and Islam in Northern Cameroon. Megachurches in the Making?* Leiden: Brill.

Gifford, Paul. 1998. *African Christianity: Its Public Role*. London: Hurst & Company.

Lado, Ludovic. 2009. *Catholic Pentecostalism and the Paradoxes of Africanisation: Processes of Localisation in a Catholic Charismatic Movement in Cameroon*. Leiden: Brill.

Tomas Sundnes Drønen

Canada

Approximately 478,705 Canadians (about 1.5 percent of all Canadians) self-identify as Pentecostals. The majority of these individuals likely attend congregations affiliated with one of about a dozen explicitly Pentecostal denominations, the two largest being the Pentecostal Assemblies of Canada (established in 1919) and the Pentecostal Assemblies of Newfoundland and Labrador (established in 1925). The remainder attend other non-Pentecostal congregations or no congregations at all, but find meaning in self-identifying as

First Gospel Light Quatsino Village 1962
Source: Pentecostal Assemblies of Canada Archives

Pentecostal because the term represents either their beliefs in the operation of the gifts of the Holy Spirit or, for some, a sense of familial or religiocultural identity.

Most Pentecostals speak primarily English at home – 404,050 (84.4 percent) – while only a small minority speak mainly French – 22,950 (4.8 percent, compared with 20.7 percent of all Canadians) – indicating the lack of Pentecostal dissemination within Quebecois, Acadian, and other Canadian Francophone communities. The proportion of Canadians reporting immigrant statuses are slightly higher among Pentecostals at 24.7 percent than Canadians overall at 20.6 percent. The 118,120 Pentecostals reporting immigrant statuses originated from a wide variety of countries in the Americas (55,725), Africa (22,615), Asia (21,870), Europe (17,240), and elsewhere (665), with more than half originating from just eight countries – Jamaica (22,435), the Philippines (10,600), Nigeria (7,025), Trinidad and Tobago (5,025), the United Kingdom (4,555), the United States (4,505), Haiti (4,115), and Guyana (3,435). Approximately 153,970 Pentecostals (32.2 percent, compared with just 19.1 percent of all Canadians) reported visible minority statuses, 42,120 (8.8 percent, compared with 5.6 percent of all Canadians) reported

Spillenaar Wings of the Gospel – Northern Outreach. Source: Pentecostal Assemblies of Canada Archives

Aboriginal ancestry, and 36,360 (7.6 percent, compared with 4.3 percent of all Canadians) self-identified as Aboriginals. Significant visible minority Pentecostal congregations and networks exist – mostly in Canada's large urban centers – especially among the Black (97,005), Filipino (14,285), Latin American (13,650), South Asian (11,755), and Chinese (4,945) communities.

Canada's low population density (1.55 people per square mile in 1901), 8,891 kilometre border with the United States, and historically close cross-border ties to geographically corresponding American cities and regions make it difficult to identify a single point of Canadian Pentecostal origination. Scholars of Canadian Pentecostalism, however, generally agree that the earliest center of Canadian Pentecostalism was Toronto, Ontario, where British immigrants Ellen and James Hebden established the East End Mission in 1906 that experienced glossolalia without any apparent initial connection to the United States. The Hebdens – especially Ellen who primarily led the mission – played an important role in sending domestic evangelists and foreign missionaries to share their religious experiences, the most famous convert being the Canadian evangelist and founder of the International Church of the Foursquare Gospel, Aimee Semple McPherson. Another important early center of Canadian Pentecostalism was Winnipeg, Manitoba, where – after experiencing Spirit baptism at William Durham's North Avenue Mission in Chicago, Illinois – Andrew Harvey Argue established a Pentecostal mission in 1907. The Argue family's influence on Canadian Pentecostalism was, perhaps, more substantial than that of the Hebden's, but this was likely at least partially due to Ellen's experience of gender-based discrimination.

Despite their close cultural and geographical ties, Canadian Pentecostals historically exhibited some important differences from their American coreligionists. Early Canadian Pentecostals, for instance, were more greatly influenced by Great Britain and Anglicanism than were Pentecostals south of the border. This is evidenced by the impact that the British Keswick Movement had on the development of Canadian Pentecostal theology, the participation of Canadians in the Pentecostal Missionary Union established by British Anglican priest Alexander Boddy, and the enormously important role played by Canadian Anglican priest James Purdie as the principal of Canada's first Pentecostal Bible college and author of a Pentecostal catechism and statement of faith. Also, likely as a result of their proportionately smaller size of the overall national population compared with their American counterparts (1.5 percent compared with 5 percent in the United States), Canadian Pentecostals have, as a whole, been observed by scholars to be more irenic and ecumenical when compared with American Pentecostals. It was, for instance, Canadian Pentecostal Harry Faught who was the primary impetus behind the founding of the Evangelical Fellowship of Canada in 1964, and another Canadian Pentecostal Brian Stiller who, as Executive Director from 1983 until 1997, was responsible for transforming the association from what was essentially a ministerial that published a magazine and held occasional events into a national research and lobbying organization. Some scholars, however, have more recently noted that Canadian Pentecostalism is losing some of its denominational and national distinctiveness, possibly as a result of the increasing role played by transnational generically evangelical networks, which has served to homogenize Pentecostal identity, belief, and practice within and across Canada and the United States.

Canadians have made a number of important contributions to global Pentecostalism including Robert McAlister's – likely hagiographical, but still symbolically significant – role in the development of Oneness Pentecostalism in 1913, George Hawtin's, Percy Hunt's, and Herrick Holt's establishing of the Latter Rain Movement in 1948 that served as an important precursor to the Charismatic Movement, as well as the worldwide Charismatic revival known as the Toronto Blessing – again, likely hagiographically – said to have originated at the Toronto Airport Vineyard Church in 1994 led by John and Carol Arnott.

A survey of recent research reveals three pressing challenges facing contemporary Canadian Pentecostalism. These include the integration of a greater number of women within positions of congregational and denominational leadership, improving relationships with Indigenous Canadians who comprise one of Canadian Pentecostalism's fastest-growing demographics, and the restructuring of traditional denominational institutions in response to what appears to be their declining significance alongside competing transnational religious networks facilitated by expanding and deepening globalization.

Bibliography

Statistics Canada. 2011. *National Household Survey*. Statistics Canada Catalogue no. 99-010-X2011037. Ottawa: Statistics Canada.

Stewart, Adam. 2015. *The New Canadian Pentecostals*. Waterloo, ON: Wilfrid Laurier University Press.

Wilkinson, Michael, and Peter Althouse. eds. 2010. *Winds From the North: Canadian Contributions to the Pentecostal Movement*. Leiden: Brill.

Wilkinson, Michael, ed. 2009. *Canadian Pentecostalism: Transition and Transformation*. Montreal & Kingston: McGill-Queen's University Press.

Wilkinson, Michael. 2006. *The Spirit Said Go: Pentecostal Immigrants in Canada*. New York: Peter Lang.

Wilkinson, Michael, and Linda Ambrose. 2020. *After the Revival: Pentecostalism and the Making of a Canadian Church*. Montreal & Kingston: McGill-Queen's University Press.

Adam Stewart

Canadian Assemblies of God

Formerly the Italian Pentecostal Church of Canada, this Finished Work Pentecostal denomination began among Italian migrants in 1913. The CAG should not be confused with the other World Assemblies of God Fellowship (WAGF) affiliated groups in Canada: the Pentecostal Assemblies of Canada (PAOC) and the Pentecostal Assemblies of Newfoundland and Labrador (PANL).

The CAG traces its origins to a revival in a small independent Italian church in Hamilton, Ontario in 1913. This group, composed by families from the town of Racalmuto, Sicily, had left the Presbyterians one year before because the new pastor could not meet their spiritual needs. After initial contact with English-speaking Pentecostals, the Hamilton church entered into contact with the *Assemblea Cristiana* of Chicago, then the center for the Italian Pentecostalism. The Italian churches of the United States sent Agostino Lencioni and Massimiliano Tosetto to assist their Italian-Canadian brethren. Thus, it has established fellowship across the borders, based on their shared Italian migrant condition, Pentecostal experience, and many personal contacts, especially by itinerant speakers, joint missions, and family ties.

In the following years, believers from Hamilton went to Toronto and the revival spread quickly in the city's Little Italy. The building acquired for the first church also had apartments on the upper floors, where many converts lived. In 1921, one believer from Toronto, Eustachio D'Ercole, went to evangelize in Montreal. In the city, success among Italians repeated as in Toronto. In 1926, the Fabre Street Chiesa Cristiana Pentecostale received provincial recognition. Later, this church made amendments to provide a legal framework to cover other local Italian congregations so it effectively became the movement's headquarters.

The movement spread to other Italian communities in Canada with the early leadership of Ferdinando Zaffuto, Luigi Ippolito, Carlo Pavia, Felice Lisanti, Luca di Marco, Giuseppe DiStaulo, and Antonio DiBiase. In 1944, representatives from seven churches gathered at a convention in Toronto. This conference established permanent coordination for the churches, especially for a missionary program. Canadian authorities barred the initial attempt to incorporate as a district of the US-based Christian Church of North America. Thus, in 1959 the movement adopted a national-wide constitution as the Italian Pentecostal Church of Canada.

After World War II, Canada received another migrant wave from Italy, and the CAG worked among them. Different from their US counterpart, the Italian identity lasted longer and many second-generation ministers had cultural and linguistic skills to serve the Italian diaspora in northern Europe, USA, Australia, South America, and even in Italy. Bilingual periodicals and radio ministry have fostered a sense of fellowship as well as served for mission purposes. Onofrio Miccolis, a minister, launched a television and international humanitarian aid ministry. A Toronto based minister and entrepreneur, Elio Madonia, founded the Samaritan Foundation to alleviate poverty in the Dominican Republic, by helping build schools, churches, and clinics.

In 2005, the movement changed to its current name to reflect their multi-cultural outlook and the affiliation with the WAGF. Currently, nearly 40 congregations from Italian, French, and Anglo-Canadian, Haitian, Spanish, Portuguese, and other backgrounds, constitute it. Most churches are in Ontario and the metropolitan area of Montreal, with the headquarters in St-Leonard.

The CAG has an affiliation with the WAGF, the Pentecostal Fellowship of North America, and the Evangelical Fellowship of Canada. CAG has a close collaboration with the PAOC and other bodies with the same historical roots in the Italian Pentecostal movement, particularly with the International Fellowship of Christian Assemblies and the Assemblies of God in Italy.

Not all the Italian-Canadians are under the CAG umbrella. For reasons ranging from doctrinal controversies to personal preference to different institutional structures, individual members and congregations have followed other paths. The earlier disputes over the consumption of blood-made food and an anti-organization instance resulted in local churches splits. Despite the dismissal of most of those controversies over time, some congregations exist apart from the CAG. The Christian Congregation in Canada, organized in 1982, has about a dozen churches throughout the country, serving Canadians of Italian, Portuguese, and Brazilian background, maintaining many of the earlier times worship practices. Some churches became nondenominational, like the Oasis Community Church in Winnipeg and the River's Edge Community Church in Montreal, both with a remarkable membership size; or choose to affiliate with the PAOC, like the former Evangelical Pentecostal Church of Windsor, ON.

Theologically, the CAG is similar to other "Baptistic" Pentecostals in North America. The tensions of being multiple minorities (Protestant among Roman Catholics, migrants, Pentecostals among mainline Protestants, and speaking Italian beyond the English and the French language hegemony) and internal developments result in some ecclesiological nuances. Among these, there is a strong sense of valuing the local congregation and engagement to missionary activities. Another trait is cherishing religious literacy, with many ministers and lay members having published theological works by their expenses.

Bibliography

Cumbo, Enrico C. 2000. "Your Old Men Will Dream Dreams: The Italian Pentecostal Experience in Canada, 1912–1945." *Journal of American Ethnic History* 19: 35–81.

Di Giacomo, Michael. 2011. "Identity and Change: The Story of the Italian-Canadian Pentecostal Community." *Canadian Journal of Pentecostal-Charismatic Christianity* 2: 83–130.

Ippolito, Daniel. 2009. *Identity-Heritage-Destiny: A History of the Canadian Assemblies of God, Formerly the Italian Pentecostal Church of Canada*. Montreal: Canadian Assemblies of God.

Palma, Paul. 2019. *Italian American Pentecostalism and the Struggle for Religious Identity.* New York: Routledge.

Zucchi, Luigi. 1993. *The Italian Pentecostal Church of Canada: Origin and Brief History.* Montreal: Italian Pentecostal Church of Canada.

Leonardo Marcondes Alves

Cantalamessa, Raniero

Raniero Cantalamessa, O.F.M. Cap. was born in Colli del Tronto, in the province of Ascoli Piceno, Italy in 1934. In 1945, he made his first religious profession in the Order of Friars Minor Capuchin. He was then ordained as a Franciscan priest in 1958. He got the degree of Doctor in Divinity in 1962 from Fribourg University, Switzerland and in 1966, doctorate in Classical Literature from the Catholic University of Milan, Italy. Later from 1967, he taught History of Ancient Christianity at the Catholic University of Milan and served as the Director of the Department of Religious Sciences. In 1975, Pope Paul VI appointed him as a member of the International Theological Commission. He was a member of this Commission until 1980.

Cantalamessa encountered the Catholic Charismatic Renewal (CCR) in 1975. However, he had been very skeptical about its authenticity. In 1977, a woman from Milan offered one of his acquaintances, Professor Giovanni Saldarini, a plane ticket with all the expenses paid for him to attend an ecumenical Charismatic conference in Kansas City, Missouri. Professor Saldarini could not take this trip because of his mother's illness and so he offered his ticket to Cantalamessa. He readily accepted the offer, not because he was interested in the Charismatic conference, but because he wanted to learn English. However, in Kansas City, he was very impressed to see around 40,000 people belonging to different Christian denominations, praying together at the conference. As a scholar of Ancient Early Christianity, he could see a great similarity between the Charismatics and the early Christians. After the conference, he travelled from Kansas City to New Jersey and stayed in a retreat house, where he participated in Charismatic prayer meetings and realized that the Holy Spirit was truly working through the CCR. He asked the Charismatics gathered there to pray for his baptism of the Holy Spirit. After receiving it, he experienced a great joy in prayer and from reading the Bible, which was no longer an object to study but became the living Word of God. On his return to Italy, he began to participate in some Charismatic prayer meetings, which surprised the people who knew his animosity for the CCR.

Cantalamessa had a unique experience during his personal prayer. He felt Jesus was calling him to quit his academic profession and devote himself fully to preach the Word of God. Cantalamessa was perplexed with this experience and decided to talk to the Minister General of his Order, Pascal Rywalski. The Minister General asked him to wait for a year to discern the call. At the end of the year, both Cantalamessa and the Minister General were convinced that the calling was genuine. He therefore left the Catholic University of Milan in 1978.

In 1980, Pope John Paul II appointed Cantalamessa as the official preacher to the Papal Household. His task was to conduct meditations for the Pope, cardinals, prelates of the Curia and superior generals of religious orders every Friday during the liturgical seasons of Advent and Lent, usually at the Redemptoris Mater Chapel in Vatican. Pope John Paul II permitted some women to attend his sermons.

Cantalamessa continues to hold the office of preacher to the Papal Household until circumstances change, as there is no fixed term for this office. The Vatican allows him to freely choose the themes of meditations. Besides preaching to the Papal Household, Cantalamessa also preaches to bishops, clergy and the laity. He has preached in retreats and conferences in Italian, English, French, Spanish, and German in more than 70 countries. The core message is all about Jesus and the power of his Spirit working in the world.

Cantalamessa also has a great passion for Christian unity. He believes that his association with the CCR influences him to change his attitude towards other Christian denominations. He notes that it is not because of the theological arguments which causes him to long for spiritual unity, but because it is the gift of the Holy Spirit. Cantalamessa is convinced that no doctrinal differences between the Catholic Church and other Christian denominations can stop people from forming the bond of friendship. With the words of the great Indian poet, Rabindranath Tagore, Cantalamessa reflects upon his life as a reed flute, which the Lord Jesus carries through hills and dales to make people remember his words of the eternal life.

Bibliography

Cantalamessa, Raniero. 2018. *Jesus Christ: The Holy One of God*. Translated by Alan Neame. Eugene: Wipf & Stock.

Cantalamessa, Raniero and Aldo Maria Valli. 2015. *Serving the Word: My Life*. Translated by Marsha Daigle-Williamson. Cincinnati: Servant.

Cantalamessa, Raniero. 2012. *Sober Intoxication of the Spirit: Born Again of Water and the Spirit*. Part Two. Translated by Marsha Daigle-Williamson. Cincinnati: Servant.

Cantalamessa, Raniero. 2008. *Come, Creator Spirit: Meditations on the Veni Creator*. Translated by Dennis and Marlene Barrett. Collegeville: Liturgical Press.

Reginald Alva

Cape Verde

The relation between Cape Verde and Christianity goes back to the fifteenth-century and to the process of colonial occupation, settlement and spatial organization of the Islands. In other words, the establishment of Christianity in Cape Verde is inextricably connected into the historical period of Atlantic slavery and European colonialism. This period was marked by violence, compulsory conversions and resistance to racial hierarchy and repression of African religious practices. From this period onwards, Catholicism became the predominant religion in Cape Verde, benefiting from a range of institutional and material privileges granted by the colonial and postcolonial state (Ramos 2016). From the 1880s onwards, this archipelago had its first contact with the Protestantism. Firstly, with the presence of Anglicanism on São Vicente island, which was confined to the British community and ceased its mission in Cape Verde at the beginning of twentieth century. Secondly, with the coming of the Church of the Nazarene from the North America, in the 1900s, through the action of the missionary João José Dias, a Cape Verdean migrant in the USA, who paved what can be considered the first phase of Cape Verdean Protestantism (Monteiro 1997; Ramos 2015).

The first Pentecostal churches arrived in the beginning of 1990s. Since that period, many Pentecostal churches were established in the Islands, such as: Assemblies of God; God Is Love Pentecostal Church and the Universal Church of the Kingdom of God from Brazil (Laurent and Furtado 2008); Deeper Life Bible Church and Redeemed Christian Church of God from Nigeria; the Bom Deus Church from Angola; the Church of Pentecost from Ghana; Mana Church from Portugal; United Pentecostal Church of Cape Verde, initially United Pentecostal Church of Colombia, from Colombia; the USA Church Temple of Restoration; and many other churches and associations, including Chinese and Cuban evangelical groups. According to the last Census (2010), Catholic Church encompasses 77.4 percent of the population; 10.8 percent has no religion; 6.2 percent are Protestants (Evangelicals, Pentecostals and neo-Pentecostals); 1.9 percent belongs to Christian Rationalism; 1.9 percent is from other religions and 1.8 percent are Muslims. It is important to highlight that the 2010 Census does not include data on some Evangelical, Pentecostal and neo-Pentecostal churches. Despite the fact that Pentecostalism in Cape Verde is a "minority religion", the arrival of Pentecostal Churches, throughout the 1990s, changed the religious and Protestant landscape on the Cape Verde Islands. Those churches introduced many Christian practices of faith, some of them new, including "spiritual battle", "spiritual discernment", prophesies, prosperity, spiritual visions, speaking in tongues, authority and healin g, miracles, intercessory, and unceasing prayers – to name a few. These practices emerged not only among the Cape Verdean population, but also amongst classical and more established Protestant churches, where some members embraced the Pentecostal rituals and vocabularies. Pentecostal churches have gained some attention and visibility in public sphere. Some of them, in association with established Protestant churches, e.g. the Church of the Nazarene, have organized national campaigns, evangelical parade and gospel festivals, with music, dance choreography and preaching (Ramos 2018). The use of music and mass media has played an important role in disseminating the Pentecostal message, particularly to the Universal Church of the Kingdom of God from Brazil. This church uses the RecordTV Cabo Verde and the Crioula-FM, which belongs to the Brazilian media RecordTV, to diffuse narratives of miracles (emphasizing physical, financial and spiritual miracles).

Bibliography

Laurent, Pierre-Joseph, and Furtado, Cláudio. 2008. "Le pentecôtisme brésilien au Cap-Vert: L'Église Universelle du Royaume de Dieu." *Archives de sciences sociales des religions* 141: 113–131.

Monteiro, João Mateus. 1997. "The Church of the Nazarene in Cape Verde: a Religious Import in a Creole Society." PhD thesis, New Jersey, Drew University.

Ramos, Max Ruben 2018. "Cape Verde." In *Encyclopedia of Christianity in the Global South*, edited by Mark A. Lamport. Lanham: Rowman & Littlefield Publishers.

Ramos, Max Ruben. 2016. "Cape Verde." In *Anthology of African Christianity*, edited by Phiri, Isabel Apawo, and Werner, Dietrich. Oxford: Regnum Books.

Ramos, Max Ruben. 2015. "Missionários do Sul: evangelização, globalização e mobilidades dos pastores cabo-verdianos da Igreja do Nazareno." PhD thesis, Lisbon, Institute of Social Sciences, University of Lisbon.

Max Ruben Ramos

Caribbean

The Pentecostal landscape in the Caribbean is as complex and rich as the region itself. From afar, the Caribbean is a conglomeration of islands with tropical weather and beautiful beaches that expand throughout the Atlantic Ocean and the Caribbean Sea. However, as we move closer to this paradise-like region, we are quickly reminded of the undeniable influx of cultures, religions, and politics that are interconnected since the area became the first stop during the colonization era. A glance through the Caribbean literature affirms that the most pressing challenge within the region is the question of identity. For some, the people of the Caribbean suffer from questions about identity as if the influx of cultural and religious heritages represents a roadblock to their Caribbean identity. Others, rather than claiming such a negative view, understand that being a mulato, creole, jibaro or a garífuna represents a unique fluidity and richness in the region.

But the theme of identity is not the only complex topic. Beginning with the indigenous spirituality of the Arawak, Carib, and Taínos and moving through the experiential and integrative character of the African indigenous spirituality and the impact of the Western traditions such as Catholicism, Anglicanism, and Reformed, among others, the Caribbean region presents a multi-religious tapestry, which is central to its social imaginary. Moreover, these religious heritages may appear as mutually exclusive experiences but may overlap in some areas of the Caribbean. Therefore, the question of theological syncretism and cultural hybridization must always be present.

Another area of discussion is the political landscape of the region. For a region that seems minuscule, in contrast to other areas, the Caribbean presents a mosaic of political models such as independent and communist governments, sovereign republics, départments, associated territories, and colonial powers. What is interesting about this varied political landscape, is that each one is a product of a shared history that is shaped by the oppression of colonial powers.

Pentecostalism first arrived in the Caribbean in the early 1900s. To the surprise of many, what appeared as an insignificant movement, spread rapidly throughout the whole region and today claims close to five million adherents who come from different streams within the Pentecostal movement. The preference for the term arrival is intentional because the Caribbean is constructed by forms, values, and meanings brought by those who migrated willingly and forcefully to the region. Thus, whether Pentecostal, Charismatic, Neopentecostal, Indigenous Pentecostal or Independent, the movement arrived in two ways: (1) through Caribbean Pentecostals who returned to their homelands having experienced some Pentecostal manifestation abroad or (2) through the work of foreign missionaries who arrived in the region representing a North American Pentecostal form.

The first record of Pentecostalism arriving in the Caribbean among anglophone speakers is through a Bahamian couple who experienced the power of the Holy Spirit while visiting a revival campmeeting in Florida, USA. After such an experience, Rebecca and Edmond S. Barr felt some urgency to return to the Bahamas sometime in November of 1909, becoming among the first missionaries representing the movement. Several months later, the first Pentecostal foreign missionaries came to the same country. Ida and

R.M. Evans, who had invested financially in the Barr's trip to the Bahamas, now joined them in the Pentecostal work. During the same time that the Evans joined the Barrs (January 1910), on the island of Montserrat, there was some ministry work by Pentecostals, but it was not until 1912 when that work was fully recognized through the foreign missionary, Robert J. Jamieson.

The story of Pentecostalism in the Spanish-speaking region claims various starting points. On the one hand, contrary to the Anglophone region, the first Pentecostal-like experiences in the Spanish-speaking region occurred in Cuba by 1910 through the work of foreign missionary Sam C. Perry. Six years later, in 1916, the first recorded work of a local Pentecostal worker occurred in Puerto Rico. In 1916, Juan L. Lugo along with some Pentecostal companions, arrived at Puerto Rico after being evangelized in Hawaii by Azusa Street missionaries. On the other hand, Nélida Agosto Cintrón (1996) has challenged such history and offers a different reading by stating that there were signs of Pentecostal-like experiences within a Puerto Rican movement called Los Hermanos Cheos that might predate these accounts and the work of foreign missionaries.

The earliest arrival of Pentecostalism in the Francophone-speaking (Creole) Caribbean can be dated to 1929 in Haiti. According to the Church of God in Christ records, Haitian Paulcéus Léys, after receiving the gift of the Spirit, was sent to Haiti to begin the work for his denomination. Though there is little traceable history, it is believed that the arrival of Pentecostalism to this area was not through foreign missionary work. However, this is not to discredit the work of foreign missionaries. According to the Church of God of Prophecy, the first foreign missionary work in Haiti occurred in 1931. After their entrance, many other denominations came along.

The presence of Pentecostal adherents in the Dutch-speaking (Papiamentu) region of the Caribbean is slightly smaller when compared to its counterparts. One of the reasons may be due to its late arrival around the mid-twentieth century. In 1959, the Church of God of Prophecy recorded its first work, and in 1968 the Church of God began missionary work in Aruba. Though latecomers, it is estimated that over 10,000 people have identified with the different streams of Pentecostalism in this region.

To a certain extent, the Christian movements and denominations that were present in the region before the arrival of Pentecostals, entered with the assistance of their respective colonial powers. As a result, many of the social, political, and economic issues that affected the local population, were not challenged by these movements and denominations, but on the contrary, seeking the favor of the government, they attempted to maintain the status quo. However, in its early form, Pentecostalism's restorationist and resistive character arrived as an alternative Christian experience that recieved the attention of the local people. Pentecostalism was characterized as a movement that empowered, liberated, and adapted with some ease. These emphases served as a launchpad for the spread of Pentecostalism in a region where the majority of the people experienced oppression, abuse, exploitation, and the obligation of leaving behind their oral religious experiences, which were categorized as demon-possessed powers. This character and quality of Pentecostalism not only assisted them in taking root in the region, but moreover, it also helped the movement flourish and spread in a way that was unprecedented.

The arrival and spread of Pentecostalism in the Caribbean occurred in a time of political and economic shifts. During that time, the Caribbean economy depended on agricultural plantations like sugar, tobacco, and coffee. However, the region was also transitioning towards an industrial economy. Such a shift disrupted the traditional economy of the region creating a sense of hopelessness. It is within this context that Pentecostalism arrived with a message of hope and a vision for mañana (tomorrow). This message of hope, found good soil quickly, particularly among those for whom tomorrow was an unthinkable reality. Hence, many received the message of Pentecost as a gospel that liberated them from their present oppressive realities.

Furthermore, the impact of Caribbean Pentecostalism extended beyond its shores. Taking advantage of the colonial links with North America and Europe, many established churches in the region – foreign and indigenous – sent pastors from the Caribbean to support immigrant families and also to begin missionary work in so-called strange lands. For example, some of the largest Pentecostal churches in England came through migration and missionary efforts of English-speaking Caribbean churches. Additionally, many indigenous Spanish-speaking Pentecostal churches, like the Iglesia de Dios Pentecostal Movimiento Internacional (Pentecostal Church of God International Movement), became a missionary force in the USA and Latin America. As a result, that which was seen as a mission field became a mission force.

The present and the future of Caribbean Pentecostalism remains intrinsically connected to the region's colonial past. Though the first Caribbean country to celebrate its independence was Haiti in 1804, the region still manifests the cruel symptoms of colonialism. Hence, the challenge for Pentecostals is that of losing its prophetic voice against the forces of accommodation and institutionalization. The Caribbean is a culturally rich and complex region but it also suffers from insularity, that is, the lack of interest in other cultures and the preference of an ethnocentric experience. Such a myopic social imaginary has affected the development of healthy relationships among Pentecostals and with the wider Christian community.

Pentecostal theology also needs to reflect on the post-colonial experiences of Caribbean people and engage in post-colonial critical theory. One way this can be done is through the oral, experiential, and narrative characteristics of Pentecostalism that share something in common with Caribbean culture. Pentecostal theologians need to also engage the multicultural qualities of the Caribbean, diversity is not to be percieved as a problem but as an opportunity to engage its drich cultural history and practices. The reality is that Caribbean people and their identity is shaped by a multifaceted cultural tapestry. Furthermore, Caribbean Pentecostal theology needs to nurture voices that can construct theologies of exploration and emancipation. These theological approaches not only affirm the opportunity to critically engage a Caribbean reality in the light of Christian experience but also empowers the individual and their communities to express their understanding of God from a local perspective.

Some contexts will benefit greatly if their theological approaches intentionally engage the public sphere as a theological locus. The Caribbean context stands as a vivid example of such need. Since its arrival, Pentecostalism functioned as a quasi-public movement, yet, its institutionalization, upward movement, and close alliance with the state have silenced the prophetic voice of the Pentecostal church. Therefore, the future of Pentecostalism in the Caribbean stands in their ability to be a prophetic and public presence in its communities.

Bibliography

Agosto Cintrón, Nélida. 1996. *Religión y Cambio Social En Puerto Rico, 1898–1940*. Río Piedras, P.R: Ediciones Huracán: Ateneo Puertorriqueño.

Contreras-Flores, Jenniffer. 2015. "The Social Impact of the 1916 Pentecostal Revival in Puerto Rico." In *Pentecostals and Charismatics in Latin America and Latino Communities*, edited by Néstor Medina and Sammy Alfaro, 157–165. New York, NY: Palgrave Macmillan.

Estrada Adorno, Wilfredo. 2016. *El Fuego Está Encendido: Infancia Del Pentecostalismo Puertorriqueño Y Su Impacto En La Sociedad*. Cleveland, TN: CEL Publicaciones.

Estrada-Carrasquillo, Wilmer. 2018. "Entre El Templo Y La Ciudad: Constructing a Pentecostal Lived Ecclesiology." PhD diss., Asbury Theological Seminary.

González, Justo L., and Ondina E. González. 2007. *Christianity in Latin America: A History*. New York, NY: Cambridge University Press.

Luvis Núñez, Agustina. 2009. "Sewing a New Cloth: A Proposal for a Pentecostal Ecclesiology Fashioned as a Community Gifted by the Spirit with the Marks of the Church from a Latina Perspective." Dissertation, Lutheran School of Theology.

Marina, Peter. 2016. *Chasing Religion in the Caribbean*. New York, NY: Palgrave.

Wilmer Estrada-Carrasquillo

Cathcart, William

William Cathcart (1893–1988) was the founder of the Apostolic Church in Australia. He was tall and commanding in presence, quiet and serious in nature, and a competent teacher. Born of Scottish parents in Northern Ireland, he fought in France in World War One from which, being severely "shell-shocked" he was repatriated to a convalescent home where, while reading the New Testament, he believed God told him that he would be healed and preach in "the uttermost parts of the world." Not long after this, he attended an Apostolic congregation where he was cured of his condition. Twice he saw visions that indicated God was calling him to Australia.

The Apostolic Church drew its origins from the 1904–1905 Welsh Revival. It fully embraced the Pentecostal teaching on the baptism of the Holy Spirit and spiritual gifts. It was centralized and well organized. Its distinguishing feature was its focus on the ministry of apostles and prophets.

In 1929, the Apostolic Council decided to send Cathcart to Perth, Western Australia. The Great Depression was being felt across the land, and to survive, Cathcart and two others made their own mixture of tea and sold it door to door. They conducted street meetings and did what they could to help unemployed people. Cathcart taught "the Apostolic vision" and soon two small Pentecostal groups combined under his leadership, later to be joined by a third.

In 1932, Cathcart and his wife and son made the long 2,700 km journey east to the city of Adelaide, South Australia. Only eight people attended the first gathering but soon they were meeting in the Adelaide Town Hall for a six-week series and a new church was born. Not everyone was pleased; the two existing Pentecostal congregations lost people to the Apostolic venture. In 1932, the church purchased a building and named it Zion Temple.

In the meantime, the British Missionary Council appointed the amiable prophet Joshua McCabe of Edinburgh to Perth. Soon 200 people were attending regularly, and new assemblies were opened in the suburbs of Victoria Park, Claremont, and Fremantle.

Cathcart's teaching in Adelaide continued to attract people who were "materially poor but rich in spiritual goods." Local congregations were established in several suburbs. Bearing in mind a prophetic statement that Apostolic headquarters would be established in Melbourne, Victoria, Cathcart moved there. McCabe then transferred to Adelaide and AS Dickson, an apostle from England, took over the work in Perth.

Cathcart's strategy may have been partly shaped by his military experience: Advance; possess new ground; bring in reinforcements; secure the ground; make a further advance; and so on. To Apostolic believers, it was the outcome of a plan "prophetically revealed" to McCabe and Cathcart.

Cathcart arrived in Melbourne knowing only one person there. "I spent long hours in prayer," he claimed. But people began to gather – around 100 on weeknights and up to 300 on Sundays. On Easter Sunday 1933, the first communion service was conducted, with 160 in attendance.

Cathcart focused on the Apostolic approach to church government, explaining how they recognized the ministry of apostles and prophets. When the prophets began to call people to new spheres of ministry, and when apostles confirmed these actions, a deep impression was made, although there was strong criticism of this approach from some other Pentecostal groups.

Cathcart also taught on the second coming of Christ, using a huge chart nearly 12 metres (40 feet) long and 2.5 metres (eight feet) high, outlining in graphic form the destiny of humankind from creation to culmination.

In May 1933, Cathcart began overtly evangelistic campaigns with John Hewitt, a strongly-built Welshman, who had recently joined the movement. More than 1,000 people attended the first meeting, some 25 responded to an invitation to follow Christ and 100 or so sought physical healing. Within six weeks there were no empty seats. Dozens of handkerchiefs were prayed over and sent to the absent suffering. There were many testimonies of recovery, including that of Ensign Jenkins of the Salvation Army who walked almost instantaneously after 11 years with a walking stick, crutches, and ultimately a wheelchair.

Cathcart also visited New Zealand where "phenomenal success" was reported and where he was further assisted by John Hewitt and his brother Isaac. By the end of 1934, there were some 40 churches from every State of Australia and in New Zealand.

In 1935 Cathcart relocated to South Africa, returning to Australia in 1945, where Australians Leo Harris and Thomas Foster had launched the National Revival Crusade, with a strong focus on the fulfilment of biblical prophecies and British Israelism. After discussions with Foster in 1947, Cathcart, now 54 years of age, joined the new movement. In July 1948, they both preached to crowded meetings in Melbourne, Perth, Adelaide, and Sydney.

Soon the Cathcarts moved to New Zealand and then to the United States where they engaged in itinerant ministry before joining their son John in a pioneer church in Dallas. Cathcart died on November 13, 1988.

Bibliography

Chant, Barry. 1997. *Heart of Fire.* Unley Park, SA: Tabor.

Chant, Barry. 2011. *The Spirit of Pentecost: the Origins and Development of the Pentecostal Movement in Australia, 19870–1939.* Lexington, KY: Emeth Press.

Cooper, Dudley. 1995. *Flames of Revival.* Endeavour Hills, Vic: CRC.

Rowe, W.A.C., n.d. *One Lord, One Faith.* Bradford: Puritan Press.

Barry Chant

Central African Republic

A landlocked country located in the heart of Africa, Central African Republic (CAR) was a former French colony. With an estimated population of about 5 million, CAR is among the five poorest countries in the world according to the 2018 United Nations report on Human Development. In the absence of reliable data, the Christian population is estimated at 85 percent which is comprised of about 50 percent Protestant and 35 percent Roman Catholic.

Although Pentecostal missionaries from the Swiss Pentecostal Mission (SPM) and the Elim missions brought Pentecostalism around 1927, only in the last thirty years has there been an explosion of Pentecostal churches. These new churches are profoundly reshaping the face of the Protestant churches in CAR. The Union of Elim Evangelical Churches is the primary Pentecostal denomination from the mainline missionary work in CAR. Soon after the political independence in 1961, another Pentecostal church known as Churches of Evangelical Cooperation was founded from the work of The Open Door or Evangelical Cooperation in the World. Elim and Cooperation churches can be categorized among the moderate Pentecostal stream according to their practices. The Swedish Mission of Orebro established churches in the West of the country, The Baptist Churches in the West which became the Baptist Evangelical Churches. However in the 1970s, the Pentecostal presence became increasingly more visible due to the founding of the Apostolic Action which is linked to the work of The Church of the Candlestick (Eglise du Chandelier) in Grenoble, France. The Assembly of God, from Democratic Republic of Congo is the most recent Pentecostal church established in CAR.

The Apostolic Action which is now known as the Community of Apostolic Churches in Central African Republic emphasizes the predominant characteristic of the Pentecostal movement, the baptism of the Holy Spirit followed by and confirmed with speaking in tongues. Another main characteristic of the Apostolic Churches was their aggressive evangelism that led to the formation of many local Apostolic churches. As a result, no other denomination has experienced such growth in the last twenty years as the Apostolic Churches. The turn came at the end of the twentieth-century with the influence of Pentecostal preachers, who were for the most part, from Cameroon, Democratic Republic of Congo and Nigeria. The new Pentecostal preachers established independent churches such as Winners Chapel and Redeemed Christian Church of God from Nigeria. In practice, the emphasis is moving from the Baptism of Holy Spirit with speaking in tongues towards the "wealth and health" gospel also called the Prosperity Gospel. While previously speaking in tongues was considered the sign of God's blessing, now health, wealth, financial success, longevity, fertility and traveling abroad are perceived as God's approval in the life of the believer.

Prayer and fasting are the way to cast out the demons of poverty, unemployment, singleness, bareness, and sickness. The teaching on generational curses imported from the American Pentecostal churches has become another main characteristic of the Pentecostal churches. Witchcraft and deliverance are also among the prominent teachings. Wealth and health can be achieved by "sowing the seed." This idea is often embodied in the idea of giving to the church if one wants to reap bountiful harvest. Prophecy in the sense of prediction is increasing. Some Pentecostal preachers specialize in predicting the future such as employment, marriage, and healing. Biblical literalism and proof texts are often used to interpret the Bible.

The growth of the Pentecostal movement also gave birth to the Indigenous Pentecostal Churches. The advancement of the Pentecostal movement has undermined the mainline denominations by pulling away some of their members. There is now a kind of "pentecostalization" in the mainline denominations. Even some traditional Baptist churches have added a place for praise, dance and prayers for sick people for healing in their liturgy. Thus, the Pentecostal churches have brought a revival in the traditional churches that have been established for over century. Despite its fast growth, the Pentecostal movement remains mainly in urban settings and most the leaders have little or no formal theological training.

Bibliography

Anderson, Allan. 2004. *An Introduction to Pentecostalism: Global Charismatic Christianity*. Cambridge: Cambridge University Press.

Asamoah-Gbadu, J. Kwabena. 2006. *African Charismatics: Current Developments within Independent Indigenous Pentecostalism in Ghana*. Leiden: Brill.

Asamoah-Gbadu, J. Kwabena. 2013. *Contemporary Pentecostal Christianity: Interpretations from an African Context*. Eugene: Wipf and Stock.

Gifford, Paul. 2004. *Ghana's New Christianity: Pentecostalism in a Globalising African Economy*. London: Hurst.

Kalu, Ogbu U. 2008. *African Pentecostalism: An Introduction*. Oxford: Oxford University Press.

Weanzana Wa
Weanzana Nupanga

Chad

The history of Pentecostalism in Chad is as follows. Pentecostalism came to Chad through the missionary work of Albert Burkhardt who initally worked with a Baptist mission. He then joined l'Eglise de la Coopération Evangélique au Tchad (ECET) around 1965. Burkhardt was recommended by the "Mission porte ouverte de Châlons sur Saône." Burkhardt first settled in Sarh in southern Chad for his missionary work that developed over time. Churches in the Apostolic or Pentecostal tradition from other regions joined together to form what is called the "Alliance Evangélique des Eglises de Pentecôte du Tchad" (AEEPT) (Evangelical Alliance of Churches of Pentecost in Chad). AEEPT obtained authorization from the Ministry of the Interior to operate on 21 November 1991. There are now hundreds of local member churches of this Alliance, most of which are concentrated in the South.

The organization of the AEEPT is as follows: (1) the General Assembly of all the denominational members that is held periodically; (2) General Meetings with each denomination. The frequency and representation of meeting is determined by the Internal Rules of Procedure. The AEEPT executive committee is made up of members from each denomination. The Alliance coordinates the activities of its members and represents them before the State and other ecclesiastical and para-ecclesiastical organizations in the country. It operates according to a mandate with a fixed duration according to the Alliance and applied by the General Assembly.

It should be noted that the growth of Christianity in all its variations, both in Central Africa and in Chad, is largely due to the success of the Pentecostal churches. In Chad today it has 20 AEEPT member denominations and seven evangelical missions and ministries. The oldest are Eglise de Dieu au Tchad, Église Apostolique Tchadienne, Église de la Coopération Évangélique Tchadienne, Église Baptiste au Tchad, Église Messianique Évangélique au Tchad, Église de Christ Universel, Église Apostolique de Christ International, Église Maranatha, Église Biblique de la Vie Profonde, Église de la Famille Victorieuse, Heure de la Délivrance et Lumière du Monde, Action Évangélique pour le Réveil et Communauté de la Grâce de Dieu. These Pentecostal churches typically experience tensions that often lead to differences and the creation of new churches. All denominations have been able to draw upon a range of people with various traditional beliefs.

The number and diversity of AEEPT does not allow them to always formulate and agree upon a common vision. However, the mission is generally shared by all, which is to be a Christian witness through the proclamation of the Gospel. All members are characterized by a zeal for evangelism and a pragmatism in their work. The Pentecostal Churches in Chad share similar beliefs and practices with the member churches of the Entente des Eglises et Missions Evangéliques au Tchad (EEMET). However, some doctrinal points, notably the understanding of the Trinity and ecclesiology, constitute points of major differences preventing some collaboration.

The traditional religious background of Pentecostals is usually present in the everyday lives of its members, and is often in tension as an alternative and authoritative force with the Holy Spirit that affects their commitment to Christ. The role of the Holy Spirit is made less relevant to man. Pentecostalism in Chad and the role it plays in the life of the members of these churches is shaped by the following: the ecclesiastical traditions proposed by the missionaries, the influence of the tradition of the elders, openness to syncretism where space and time are rearranged according to local rituals, the phenomenon of "la multi-appartenance" (multi-belonging), and the influence of a diffuse form of communitarianism where the feeling of belonging takes precedence over Christian identity. To this list should be added the rejection of the dogmas and practices of other religions or families of churches, which often leads to conflict. Such an atmosphere does not allow for a broader collaboration among Protestants in the country.

The AEEPT has had discussions with "l'Entente des Eglises et Missions Evangéliques au Tchad" (EEMET) (Agreement of the Evangelical Churches and Missions in Chad), which is another Alliance of Evangelicals. It focuses on issues like food security, justice, social peace, and community health. Lately, there has been a sudden growth of Catholic and Protestant churches that are collaborating but the AEEPT has not joined them. An effort to approach the EEMET for cooperation has been initiated several times through a variety of Christian organizations and some individuals. But resistance is taken on the part of certain leaders of some denominational members of the EEMET where there has been a history of conflict that hampers any unity or cooperation between certain churches that are members of AEEPT. Chad is a secular and multi-faith state that at times raises some concern for the AEEPT. Maintaining a good relationship with the state authorities is important for social, cultural, political, and economic reasons. However, when the Christians in the country feel their integrety is threatened or compromised, the two Alliances, EEMET and AEEPT, often respond together by denouncing the state. This is done usually by the two groups in consulation that leads to a separate or joint statements that are communicated to the state authorities.

Bibliography

Denis, Philippe. 2015. "Bulletin d'Histoire du Christianisme en Afrique." *Revue d'Histoire Ecclésiastique* 110 (1/2): 288–301.

Ngarsouledé, Abel. 2016. *Enjeux sociologiques et théologiques de la sécularisation: Une étude de cas à N'Djaména en République du Tchad*. Langham Monographs.

Perrot, Etienne. 2008. "Les enjeux du Pentecôtisme africain." *Revue de Culture Contemporaine* 409 (7): 61–71.

Ribay, Jean-Marie, and Rebecca Redon. 2007. *'Toi, vas-y !': Albert Burkhardt, missionnaire, homme de Dieu*. Dijon: EMF.

Sébastien, Fath. 2002. "Réveil, and Petites-Églises." *Bulletin de la Société de l'Histoire du Protestantisme Français*, t. CILVIII (Oct.–Dec): 1101.

Abel Ngarsoulede

Charismatic Renewal in the Roman Catholic Church

The Catholic Charismatic Renewal (CCR) is an example of a mid-twentieth-century Christian movement of renewal. Christian renewal movements are generally popular expressions among participants who desire to see an increase in the spirituality of individuals and the church through activities like prayer, singing, the activation of spiritual gifts, and service to others (Swenson 2009a, 113–114). The CCR, in particular, was a renewal movement that was also characterized by its commitment to the Roman Catholic Church, its leadership, and its core beliefs. Much weight was given to the Vatican II Council (1962–1965) for the success of the movement. Peter Hocken, a scholar of the CCR, wrote, "Without the Second Vatican Council, it seems inconceivable that there could have been charismatic renewal in the Catholic Church" (2013, 16). Relying on the documents of Vatican II, leaders of the CCR made a case for legitimacy from the highest authority in the Roman Catholic Church, the bishops and the pope, who approved of the vitality and validity of the charismatic gifts. Studies by Swenson (1972), Anderson (2006) and Walsh (2006), support the view that the renewal was

Catholic Charismatics (Colombia). Source: Center for the Study of Global Christianity

related to the changes brought about through the Council.

The renewal commenced in 1967 in Pittsburgh at the College of the Holy Ghost (O'Connor 1971). Originally, a small group of college professors, a spouse, and a woman of the Presbyterian tradition came together for prayer. All witnessed a new Christian experience termed by the Pentecostals as the "Baptism of the Holy Spirit." A subsequent meeting included a person who visited a couple at the University of Notre Dame in South Bend, Indiana. This couple visited a local Assembly of God congregation where they also experienced the Baptism of the Holy Spirit. The movement gained momentum and within several years prayer groups emerged in Cleveland, Iowa, Portland, Boston, Orlando, Los Angeles, St. Louis and New York. The renewal movement went to the heart of Catholicism, the monastery and about twenty monasteries opened up to receive this new gift.

Anderson (2006) says that by 1976 the movement had approximately 300,000 adherents. It spread to France, Belgium, Italy, Spain, Portugal, Hungary, Czechoslovakia and Poland. It was notably strong in India (with perhaps five million) and the Philippines (about eleven million). By 2000 there were an estimated one hundred and twenty million Catholic Charismatics, some 11 percent of all Catholics worldwide. While the CCR appears to have come to an end in the United States and Canada, there are still Roman Catholics living in communities that continue to encourage and practice charismatic Christianity (Swenson 2009b, 2018).

Hocken (2013, 2016) expands our understanding of the CCR by situating it within dialogical encounters with Pentecostals, Protestant Charismatics, the new charismatic churches, and Messianic Jews. Participants in the early days of the renewal believed that they were experiencing the same grace that was exhibited in the prominence of spontaneous praise, a sensitivity to evil spirits, and the manifestation of the gifts as outlined in I Corinthians 12:8–10. All used a similar language of the experience, the Baptism of the Holy Spirit. Hocken acknowledged that the Baptism of the Spirit had been an identifying marker of the Pentecostal movement, the Protestant renewal, the Roman Catholic renewal, the New Charismatic Churches, and the Messianic Jewish movement.

The ecumenical relationship of the CCR to classical Pentecostalism, and particularly the Roman Catholic-Pentecostal dialogue, has been discussed at length (see Murphy 2018). What follows are some comments about the relationship of the CCR to the Messianic Jewish movement. According to Finto (2001), the Messianic Jewish movement in the United States had links with the CCR as early as 1967. A Jewish couple, Marty and Yohanna Chernoff, dedicated to retain their Jewish heritage as well as their belief in Yeshua, reached out to the Jewish youth who embraced Jesus as Messiah. They began to disciple them and to encourage them to combine their Jewish heritage along with their belief in Yeshua. In early 1970, Marty received a vision of the term Messianic Judaism and shortly after that started a Congregation called Beth Messiah in Cincinnati and later, in Philadelphia. By the end of 1999, there were 80 congregations in the United States and 81 in Israel. By the turn of the twenty-first century, there were 350 synagogues with about one million members. The relationship of the CCR to Messianic Judaism is one other area of research that requires more attention by scholars.

Bibliography

Anderson, A. 2006. "The Pentecostal and Charismatic movements." In *Christianity: World Christianities c.1914–c.2000*, edited by H. McCleod, 89–106. Cambridge: Cambridge University Press.

Finto, D. 2001. *Your People Will be My People*. Minneapolis: Chosen.

Hocken, Peter. 2016. *Azuza, Rome and Zion: Pentecostal Faith, Catholic Reform and Jewish Roots*. Eugene, OR: Pickwick Publications.

Hocken, Peter. 2013. *Pentecost and Parousia*. Eugene, OR: Wipf and Stock.

Murphy, Karen. *Pentecostals and Roman Catholics on Becoming a Christian: Spirit-Baptism, Faith, Conversion, Experience, and Discipleship in Ecumenical Perspective*. Leiden: Brill, 2018.

O'Connor, E. 1971. *The Pentecostal Movement in the Catholic Church*. Notre Dame: Ava Maria Press.

Rudolph, D. 2013. "Messianic Judaism in Antiquity and in the Modern Era." In *Introduction to Messianic Judaism*, edited by D. Rudolph and J. Willitts, 21–36. Grand Rapids, MI: Zondervan.

Swenson, Donald S. 2018. *Alleluia: An Ethnographic Study*. Lanham, MD: Lexington Books.

Swenson, Donald S. 2009a. *Society, Spirituality, and the Sacred. A Social Scientific Introduction*. Toronto: The University of Toronto Press.

Swenson, Donald S. 2009b. "The Canadian Catholic Charismatic Renewal." In *Canadian Pentecostalism*, edited by Michael Wilkinson, 214–232. Montreal & Kingston: McGill-Queen's University Press.

Swenson, Donald S. 1972. The Charismatic Movement within Denominational Christianity. Master's thesis: Calgary Alberta, The University of Calgary.

Walsh, M. 2006. "The Religious Ferment of the Sixties." In *Christianity: World Christianities c.1914–c.2000*, edited by H. McCleod, 304–322. Cambridge: Cambridge University Press.

Donald S. Swenson

Chikane, Frank

Frank Chikane (1951–) was raised in the Apostolic Faith Mission (AFM) and has served as a pastor and civil servant in South Africa. He is a member of the African National Congress. Chikane grew up in a racially polarized background both in church and country. He was later, as a pastor, victimized by the white leadership of the AFM and suspended from active participation in the church for his political activities against apartheid. He wrote of the difficulty of balancing the God he was confronted with in his own church and the God of biblical scripture. The tensions and contradictions were many and resonated with what was taking place across the socio-political landscape in South Africa. Opposing the system of apartheid involved many threats, including repeated incarceration, torture, poisoning, and the possibility of death, sometimes at the hands of fellow white Christians in the AFM.

In the 1970s he was part of the evolution of what was known as the Black Consciousness Movement along with Cyril Ramaphosa, Maurice Ngakane. All three were part of Pentecostal churches that did not encourage participation in the politics of the day. They could not support the sentiments propagated by their churches.

There was a difference between how black and white Pentecostals in the AFM practised their spirituality. He wrote: "Our spirituality was a holistic form of spirituality, with no differentiation between the spiritual and the social. Our services of worship, our spiritual activism, were launched within the very social dynamics of our society ... if a tragedy happens in a family. God must be involved negatively or positively. If someone is unemployed or dismissed from work, God must be involved. If an accident happens to a person, God must be involved. For the African, God cannot just be a spectator in the war that is raging between the evil spirits and the spirits of righteousness, between God and the devil" (Chikane 1988). He later became the General-Secretary of the Institute of Contextual Theology (ICT) in Braamfontein, Johannesburg. It was at the ICT where he and others like Fr. Albert Nolan of the Roman Catholic Church, facilitated discussions, and ultimately published *The Kairos Document* in 1986. Ironically, he later became the youngest general secretary of the South African Council of Churches (SACC) even though his church was not a member of the organization at the time.

The publication of *The Kairos Document* was the ultimate ecumenical expression in thought of Chikane and other theologians who were concerned about the situation of racism in South Africa. Their objectives were clear: "We as a group of theologians have been trying to understand the theological significance of this moment in our history. It is serious, very serious. For very many Christians in South Africa this is the KAIROS, the moment of grace and opportunity, the favourable time in which God issues a challenge to decisive action. It is a dangerous time because if this opportunity is missed, and allowed to pass by, the loss for the church, for the Gospel and for all of South Africa will be immeasurable" (The Kairos Document: A Theological Comment on the Political Crisis in South Africa 1988).

In 1994 he became part of Nelson Mandela's government and was vindicated in what many of the white AFM leaders had described as communist inspired theology. In 1996 the AFM repealed all racist policies and accepted black people into membership; before then they were described as a "mission field." He continues to participate in ecumenical structures around the world. He is a pastor in the AFM in Soweto and participates in the organization's international leadership structures.

Bibliography

Chikane, F. 2012. *Eight Days in September: The Removal of Thabo Mbeki.* Johannesburg: Picador
Chikane, F. 1988. *No Life of My Own.* Maryknoll, NY: Orbis Books.
Chikane, F. 1985. "Contextualisation and Indigenisation." Grahamstown: Unpublished.
Chikane, F. 1977. "Christianity and Black Consciousness." Unpublished.
Institute of Contextual Theology. 1988. *The Kairos Document: A Theological Comment on the Political Crisis in South Africa.* Grand Rapids, MI: Eerdmans.

Steve Mochechane

Chile

The case of Chile often occupies a prominent position in histories of Latin American and global Pentecostalism (Hollenweger 1997), in part because this was the first country in Latin America to witness the foundation of a Pentecostal church, but also, and mainly, because of the national roots of the Chilean Pentecostal movement. Whereas Pentecostalism was introduced to most other Latin American countries by foreign Pentecostal missionaries, the Methodist Pentecostal Church in Chile was founded in 1910 after a schism within the Methodist Episcopal Church and is known as the first autochthonous and financially and theologically independent Pentecostal denomination outside of Europe and North America (Lindhardt 2019).

The schism that eventually gave birth to the Methodist Pentecostal Church was preceded by a spiritual revival in the Methodist Episcopal Church in the city of Valparaíso and later the capital of Santiago. Inspired by readings of the Acts of the Apostles and under the guidance of the American Methodist pastor, Willis Collins Hoover, members of the congregation in Valparaíso started organizing daily prayer groups and all-night prayer meetings, during which they experienced manifestations described by Hoover as "laughing, weeping, shouting, singing, foreign tongues, visions and ecstasies" (Hoover 1977: 41; English translation taken from Lalive D'epinay 1969: 116). The Methodist authorities considered such phenomena to be anti-Methodist and saw the revival as a sectarian threat to the unity of the church. Eventually a division became inevitable and in April 1910 Hoover resigned and became the superintendent of the Methodist Pentecostal Church. He was followed by approximately 400 congregants from Valparaíso, and the new church further included two congregations from Santiago that had been separated from the Methodist Church in September 1909 because of their embracement of revivalism. Although the Pentecostal revival in Chile was remarkable for its absence of direct links to the Azusa Street Revival in Los Angeles in 1906 and the absence of foreign Pentecostal missionaries (Hoover had come to Chile as a Methodist, not a Pentecostal missionary and after resigning he lost all institutional and economic support from the Methodist Church) the events in Chile were not totally detached from revivals elsewhere in the world. There were strong revivalist tendencies within nineteenth-century American Methodism, which were to some extent imported to Chile, alongside a strong opposition to revivalism among many Methodist authorities (Lindhardt 2019). During a furlough in the United States in the 1890s Hoover visited a pre-Pentecostal church in Chicago which in his own words was "living in a constant state of revival," (Hoover 1977: 25) and in 1907 Hoover's wife received a pamphlet from a missionary friend in Mukti, India, describing a Christian revival. After reading this pamphlet Hoover started corresponding with Pentecostal leaders in different parts of the world.

The Methodist roots of Chilean Pentecostalism are not only manifest in the name of the first church, which despite numerous schisms, is still one of the largest Pentecostal denominations in the country. Many of Chile's autochthonous Pentecostal churches, most of which are offshoots or offshoots of offshoots of the Methodist Pentecostal Church still practice infant baptism and maintain aspects of a Methodist system of government and organization. A Methodist influence can also be identified in the way many Chilean Pentecostals from autochthonous churches understand glossolalia, namely as a spiritual gift which should be placed at the same level as other spiritual gifts but should not be seen as an indispensable sign of the baptism of the Holy Spirit.

After a couple of slow decades, Pentecostal growth took off in the 1930s with the total percentage of Chilean Protestants (most of who were Pentecostals) reaching 5.6 percent in 1960, compared to 1.5 percent in 1930. After a period of more modest growth in the 1960s, Pentecostalism again exploded during the Pinochet dictatorship (1973–1990) with the percentage of Protestants reaching 13.2 in 1990 (Gooren 2015, 209).

Most early converts belonged to the lower socioeconomic strata of society in both rural and urban areas, with many early urban Pentecostals being migrants from rural areas, struggling to get by in the informal economic sector or holding low-status jobs. Research has suggested that Pentecostalism appealed to lower class Chileans, who felt alienated from the Catholic Church, not only because they found new networks of mutual support in Pentecostal churches, but also because Pentecostal principles of lay responsibility and lay participation provided them with a sense of dignity and a social status that was at variance with their limited possibilities for upwards social mobility in the wider society (Willems 1967).

The 1930s and the decades that followed saw not only growth but also a beginning diversification of Pentecostalism. In 1934 a major schism occurred in the Methodist Pentecostal Church when Hoover and a large group of followers left and founded the Evangelical Pentecostal Church. Although these two churches have both experienced numerous subsequent schisms they remain the two largest denominations in the country. During the 1940s missionary Pentecostal churches such as the Assemblies of God and the Church of God, both of North American origin, were also founded in Chile.

For the better part of the twentieth century most Chilean Pentecostal churches maintained an insular stance towards the surrounding society, considering participation in political parties, labour unions and other secular organizations forbidden for the children of God. Theologically this stance has traditionally been framed in terms of strong dualism between the church or the children of God and the world. An attempt of Pentecostal leaders to move towards a more public, political, position in Chile occurred after the violent military coup in 1973 where the army, led by Pinochet, seized power. As the Catholic Church soon became a harsh critic of the military regime, an opening was provided for other churches, and in 1974 leaders of the Methodist Pentecostal Church invited Pinochet to the inauguration of the Cathedral, Jotabeche in Santiago. In July 1975 Council of Pastors was founded by leaders of the Methodist Pentecostal Church and other Evangelical denominations, and in September that same year, the first Evangelical *Te Deum* was held with the presence of Pinochet and other government officials. Up until then, the *Te Deum* had been a Catholic service in memory of Chilean independence. Newly installed governments were usually given an official welcome at the Catholic *Te Deum*, but the regime had received no such recognition. The Council of Pastors did not represent all Chilean Evangelicals. In 1982 the *Confraternidad Cristiana de Iglesias* (CCI) was founded by Evangelical churches that were critical of the regime including some smaller Pentecostal churches, The CCI made several public statements of critique against the regime and thus provided another public voice of Evangelicals-Pentecostals during the 1980s (Lindhardt 2012).

Relations between Pentecostalism and the world of politics continued to grow after the return to democracy in 1990 with politicians courting Pentecostals, especially during elections, and Pentecostal leaders putting pressure on political authorities in order to improve the legal status of churches. In 1999 a law of religious equality was finally passed, grating Evangelical churches the same status as the Catholic Church, and Chile's Evangelical population received further public recognition in 2008 when the government declared that the Friday closest to October 31 (the day of the Protestant Reformation) would be a public Evangelical holiday.

Pentecostalism has continued to grow after 1990, with the total percentage of Evangelicals reaching 15.1 in 2002. According to more recent estimates Evangelicals now make up about one fifth of the Chilean population, the majority of Evangelicals (an estimated 85–90 percent) being Pentecostals (Gooren 2015). Pentecostalism has also become increasingly diversified during the last three decades, in part due to schisms of autochthonous churches and the arrival of new foreign churches, for instance from Brazil, and in part because Pentecostals are adapting to popular culture, transformations in generational identities, a general boom in higher education and new class dynamics. The Chilean economy has improved since 1990, and although Pentecostals are still relatively poorer and less educated that the average Chilean, they too have been affected by overall economic growth and an increased access to higher education. Hence a growing number of Pentecostals, most of who are not ex-Catholics, but have been raised as Pentecostals, now study at tertiary educational institutions or hold degrees and have moved into the middle classes (Lindhardt 2016).

The gradual transformation of the social base of Pentecostalism has inspired revisions of the classical church/world dualism. This is particularly salient in some of Chile's newer neo-Pentecostal denominations (of both national and foreign origin) where the message of prosperity in the here and now is dominant. But other Pentecostal churches have also (gradually and to very different extents) reduced the theological emphasis on the need to be separated from the world. For instance, most Pentecostal churches have now abandoned or reduced previous restrictions on member's behaviour such as dress codes (for instance rules dictating that women should always wear skirts), prohibitions against wearing makeup, watching television, drinking an occasional glass of wine, going to the cinema, the beach. etc. Besides, whereas Hoover fiercely opposed the use of musical instruments in churches and saw them as something of a potential Trojan horse that would bring the contaminating influence of popular culture into congregations, many Pentecostal churches now have lively services with rock music (played on electric instruments) and power point shows in the background.

Furthermore, many Pentecostals are now being more open towards political participation than previous generations (Gooren 2016) although their actual political mobilization has been limited and mostly focused on securing Evangelical rights. But Pentecostals are increasingly participating in social and civic work without an explicit evangelistic agenda (Fediakova 2016) and both Pentecostal leaders and laypeople are increasingly raising their voices in public political debates, especially debates about a possible legalization of homosexual marriages, which they fiercely oppose. What their outspoken participation in such debates indicates is that while Pentecostals maintain elements of an oppositional identity and have highly critical opinions about the moral state of the Chilean society they live in, they also wish to become more involved as political citizens and exert a Christian influence in the society rather than separating themselves from it.

Bibliography

Fediakova, Evguenia. 2016. "To serve or to Save: The Social Commitment of Chilean Evangelicals (1990–2014)." In *New Ways of Being Pentecostal in Latin America*, edited by Martin Lindhardt, 151–164. Lanham: Lexington Books.

Gooren, Henri. 2016. "Pentecostal Conversion Careers, Generational Effects, and Political Involvement in Latin America." In *New Ways of Being Pentecostal in Latin America*, edited by Martin Lindhardt, 165–186. Lanham: Lexington Books.

Gooren, Henri. 2015. "The Growth and Development of Non-Catholic Churches in Chile." *Review of Relgious Research* 57 (2): 191–218.

Hollenweger, Walther. 1997. *Charismatisch-pfingstliches Christendum Herkunft, Situation ökumenische Chancen*. Göttingen: Vandenhoeck & Ruprecht.

Hoover, Willis Collins. 1977. *Historica del Avivamiento Pentecostal en Chile*. Santiago: Eben-Ezer.

Lalive d'epinay, Christian. 1969. *Haven of the Masses: A Study of the Pentecostal Movement in Chile*. London: Lutterworth.

Lindhardt, Martin. 2019. "Chilean Pentecostalism. Methodism Renewed." In *The Oxford History of Protestant Dissenting Traditions* vol. 4, edited by Jehu Hanciles. Oxford: Oxford University Press.

Lindhardt, Martin. 2016. "'We, the Youth, Need to be Effusive': Pentecostal Youth Culture in Contemporary Chile." In *New Ways of Being Pentecostal in Latin America*, edited by Martin Lindhardt, 135–150. Lanham: Lexington Books.

Lindhardt, Martin. 2012. *Power in Powerlessness: A Study of Pentecostal Life Worlds in Urban Chile*. Leiden: Brill.

Willems, Emilio. 1967. *Followers of the New Faith: Culture Change and the Rise of Protestantism in Brazil and Chile*. Nashville: Vanderbilt University Press.

Martin Lindhardt

China

Pentecostal missionaries from European and English-speaking Protestant countries were the earliest Pentecostal workers in China during the republican period (1910–1949). There were three types of missionaries in this period. First, some of them had been missionaries under different missionary societies like the Christian and Missionary Alliance (CMA) working in various parts of China but who adopted Pentecostal teachings and experiences through reading Pentecostal newspapers or participating in revival movements. Second, some felt the call to be missionaries in China after their revival experience in their home countries and set off to China without much preparation or knowledge of the culture. Third, some were sent by Pentecostal missions or churches, such as the Pentecostal Missionary Union from Britain and the Dutch Pentecostal Missionary Society stationed in Yunnan, the Finnish Free Foreign Mission in Manchuria, the Free Evangelical Assemblies of Norway in Shanxi and Hebei, the Pentecostal Holiness Church in Guangxi and Shanghai, the Pentecostal Assemblies of Canada in Guangdong, and the Pentecostal Assemblies of the World in Shanxi. (Tiedemann 2011) The General Council of the Assemblies of God (AG) was founded in 1914 and since then considerable independent American missionaries and those who had belonged to other mission societies affiliated with it. The AG became the largest Pentecostal missionary body in China and their missionaries worked in many parts of the country. In the first half of the twentieth century, all the streams of Classical Pentecostalism originating in the West were all planted in China: Trinitarian, Oneness, Holiness and Finished Work.

Pentecostalism swiftly spread through independent revivalists when the Chinese underwent a turbulent time of wars, banditry, and famine. During the Sino-Japanese War in 1937–1945, westerners were kept in concentration camps by the Japanese military then deported to the United States, Canada and other western countries through exchanging prisoners-of-war. The missionaries' churches were left to the Chinese to look after although some returned to China after the war. Moreover, most of the prominent Chinese revivalists were affiliated with Methodist, Baptist, Presbyterian, CMA and other Protestant churches. Their message of moral purification and millennialism gave hope to the masses to live through the sufferings. Their performances of miracles and eloquent sermons about hidden sins and eternal life convinced people of the living God. Watchman Nee was especially influenced by Plymouth Brethren's premillennial dispensationalism through Margaret Barber. Some of these revivalists travelled overseas to minister to the local Christians. For example, John Sung who founded the Bethel Band ministered in southeast Asia and Yu Cidao went to the Korean peninsula to conduct evangelistic meetings. Some of them founded their own churches like Nee's Little Flock and Timothy Dzao's Ling Liang Church, which still exist in Hong Kong, Taiwan, southeast Asia, and among the Chinese diaspora in North America.

Oneness Pentecostalism also took root through the effort of Chinese Pentecostals. Wei Enbo adopted the Oneness teaching from his Norwegian pastor Bernt Berntsen and developed his own True Jesus Church with other local Christians from non-Pentecostal denominations. Ever since it was founded in 1917 in Beijing, the church has been observing three sacraments: baptism in running water, foot-washing, and the Last Supper. Spirit baptism with evidential tongues is accompanied with water baptism. The main worship is conducted on Saturday morning. Currently, this Chinese-originated church has spread to Asia, North and South America, Europe, Australia, and Africa, reaching non-Chinese people.

Although the Boxer Rebellion broke out in Shandong in 1900 and brutally slaughtered thousands of missionaries, Chinese Christians and westerners in the country, this province also nourished some prominent Pentecostal churches. The Jesus Family was an indigenous Pentecostal community founded by Jing Dianying in Shandong in the 1920s. Lian Xi describes it as "an independent Christian mutual-aid community" featured by "a utopian pursuit of Christian communalism, one that found its triumph over poverty and wartime miseries in shared Pentecostal ecstasies." (Lian 2010) The Spiritual Gifts Society was founded in Shandong though was inactive during the 1940s. The famous Shandong Revival in the 1930s awoke the weary spiritual lives of missionaries and local Christians and produced uncountable anonymous Chinese evangelists to spread the gospel across the country and overseas. It also strengthened Chinese Christians to persevere through the Sino-Japanese War, civil wars between the Nationalists and Communists, and the Communist regime.

The Communists gained political power in 1949 and ended the period of religious freedom. The party has an innate "deep-seated fear of Western hostile forces [which] may attempt to use Christianity to incite domestic instability in China." (Koesel 2017) This fear drove the regime to expel all missionaries and many of them fled to Hong Kong, Taiwan and southeast Asia to continue their ministries. The regime also coerced Christians to follow the communist doctrines as a way to "love the country" through the Three-Self

Patriotic Movement. Revivalists like Nee and Jing, who refused to succumb to the power, were severely oppressed and died in prison. Political movements were launched one after the other, including the Anti-right movement and the Cultural Revolution, to eliminate any "anti-revolutionary" individuals, and Christians were always on their blacklists. The death of Mao Zedong in 1976 temporarily halted the unceasing massacres and the reformers within the party gained power.

Deng Xiaoping's strategy of "hiding power and biding time" guided the country to focus on internal economic development rather than provoking foreign powers. The country accordingly opened up its market for investments which paved the way for its entry into the World Trade Organization in 2001. Through engaging in global trade and becoming the "World's Factory," economic growth changed the landscape of Christianity in China. Urban educated Christians of both Three-self and house churches now engage in Christianity from an intellectual angle and are skeptical about ecstasy and the supernatural dimension. In rural areas, however, "the homegrown Christianity has been characterized by a potent mix of evangelistic fervor, biblical literalism, charismatic ecstasies, and a fiery eschatology" (Lian 2010). In coastal cities like Shanghai, Wenzhou, and Guangzhou, house churches grew rapidly in the 2000s under the leadership of "boss Christians", managers of factories and businesses (Cao 2010). Several networks of house churches spread across the country and some of them sent out missionaries to central Asia, Europe and the Middle East under the Back to Jerusalem Movement. Missionaries from Korea, Singapore, Hong Kong, and western countries entered the country through academic programmes, businesses, tourism, scientific and cultural exchanges, and conducted theological and worship training courses in urban, suburban, and rural areas. The enormous trading opportunities offered by China has attracted thousands of Africans to engage in formal and informal commercial activities. Most of the African migrants are Pentecostals mainly from Nigeria and Ghana. They form house churches and adopt their usual ecstatic worship style. Like the Chinese house churches, the African ones are also under surveillance and their leaders have to learn to skillfully communicate with the authorities for their safety and survival (Haugen 2013).

This thriving scenario of Christianity imbued the imagination of a China's Jerusalem but was soon dissolved under the leadership of Xi Jinping who is inclined to recover Mao's Communist doctrine. Thousands of crosses have been removed, and church buildings destroyed. Online communication between church members has been constantly spied on by security authorities. Missionaries were either expelled or their visa applications rejected. Authorities have tightly controlled the churches foreign connections and sponsorship. The setback to religious freedom proves that since the rule of law is not enacted in China, the destiny of both the Three-self and the houses churches still depends on the mercy of both the local authorities and the central government. This insecure situation has not changed since 1949.

Bibliography

Cao, Nanlai. 2010. *Constructing China's Jerusalem: Christians, Power, and Place in Contemporary Wenzhou*. Redwood City, CA: Stanford University Press.

Haugen, Heidi Østbø. 2013. "African Pentecostal Migrants in China: Marginalisation and the Alternative Geography of a Mission

Theology." *African Studies Review* 56 (1): 81–102.
Koesel, Karrie J. 2017. "China's Patriotic Pentecostals." In *Global Chinese Pentecostal and Charismatic Christianity*, edited by Fenggang Yang, Joy Tong, and Allan Anderson, 240–263. Leiden: Brill.
Lian, Xi. 2010. *Redeemed by Fire: The Rise of Popular Christianity in Modern China*. New Haven: Yale University.
Tiedemann, R.G. 2011. "The Origins and Organizational Developments of the Pentecostal Missionary Enterprise in China." *Asian Journal of Pentecostal Studies* 14 (1): 108–146.

Connie Au

Chit, Myo

Myo Chit was born to Baptist parents in Rangoon (now called Yangon) in Myanmar on October 23, 1930. His father was Burmese and a senior government official. His mother was German Burmese. His great grandfather was one of the initial converts of the well-known missionary, Adoniram Judson. Through the hardship of the Second World War, both of his parents had died by the time he was 13.

From 1948 to 1951, sent by the Burmese government, Chit studied aeronautical engineering in the UK. On his return to Rangoon, he married Daw Thein Swe on December 17, 1955, and they had four sons and one daughter. He attended a Plymouth Brethren church and his rekindled faith led him to become a lay-preacher. His passion for evangelism led him to start an interdenominational organization, "Gospel Youth," to evangelize young people.

Chit had a successful career. He was an air force instructor, a lecturer in a technical school, and translated technical documents from English into Burmese. He was a translator for the American Embassy's press department and wrote his own column in the technical section.

He opposed the loud and "crazy" Pentecostal meetings (Chit 1980, 18) in the ministry of the American Assemblies of God missionaries, Mabel Willets and Glenn Stafford. However, his conviction led him to question an elderly neighbor about the Holy Spirit. As they prayed together, he had an experience of Holy Spirit baptism and spoke in tongues for hours. Even though he initially stayed in the Brethren church, he faced opposition from the elders for his new enthusiasm. Subsequently, leaving the Brethren congregation coincided with an invitation from the American AG missionaries to help lead the Evangel Church.

Despite his hesitation, he became a full-time Pentecostal minister and joined the American AG missionary, Glenn Stafford, to minister in the Evangel Church in 1965. He took over as the pastor of Evangel and led the educational ministry when the American missionaries were expelled from Burma in 1966. After enduring initial financial struggles in the harsh political climate, church membership dwindled to only twelve, but subsequently grew successfully. The church experienced financial miracles and physical healings, which encouraged their faith and numbers to grow.

Chit experienced opposition to evangelism because Christianity was perceived as conflicting with Buddhist nationalism. However, starting in the 1970s, he took the opportunity to preach through the Far East Broadcasting Company's radio station, which broadcast via Manila. His preaching had the potential to reach a few million Burmese and those interested could follow up by applying for a Bible correspondence course.

Chit set up a short-term training programme as a "youth camp," known as "Evangel Bible Training School" on the site which was donated to him for the purpose of investing in youth development. This programme provided biblical trainings for new converts and young people, including practical evangelism, worship and fellowship (Chit 1981, 20). The graduates from this programme proceeded to evangelize and to plant AG churches in other areas of Myanmar (Chit 1981, 21). However, Chit perceived a need to provide a more substantial theological education for national AG ministers. On August 2, 1979, the short-term school was replaced by Evangel Bible College. It provided four-year programme and was organized in conjunction with the International Correspondence Institute (ICI, now Global University) and the American AG. Chit was the director and a professor of the College. Later on, Chit recommended short-term training and started a three to six-month Bible School of Evangelism in 1989, offering a combination of classroom and practical training for students throughout Myanmar.

He served as the general secretary of the AG Myanmar in 1968–1970 and 1972–1983, assistant general superintendent in 1984–1986 and was elected as the general superintendent of the AG Myanmar in 1990–2010.

He travelled to Chin State in the northern areas of Myanmar in the 1970s to preach in revival meetings, which led to many churches joining the AG. He promoted evangelism and church planting, thus spreading the Pentecostal message throughout Myanmar. In 1979, he preached in Sweden and America, and recounted the revival they had experienced in Myanmar. Meanwhile, Evangel Church continued to grow and planted daughter churches throughout Yangon and to send out ministers throughout Myanmar.

Bibliography

Chit, Myo. 1981. "The Youth Camp That Became a Bible School." *The Pentecostal Evangel* (29 November): 20–21.

Chit, Myo. 1980. "Even the Buddhist Monks Are Listening." *Pentecostal Evangel* (10 February): 18.

Khai, Chin Khua. 2003. *The Cross Among Pagodas: A History of the Assemblies of God in Myanmar*. Baguio: APTS.

Sann Oo, Saw Tint. 2014. "The History of the Assemblies of God Theological Education in Myanmar: Development of the Assemblies of God Bible School." *Asian Journal of Pentecostal Studies* 17 (2): 187–206.

Thureson, Birger. 2004. *The Fires of Burma: Biography of Rev. U Myo Chit*, translated by Jami Nordenstam. N.P.

Denise Ross

Cho, Yonggi

Yonggi Cho (1936–) was born in Ulju county in Gyeongnam province, South Korea. He was the second child and eldest son in his family among five brothers and four sisters in a typical Korean Buddhist family. During his childhood, he experienced huge adversities: the oppression of Japanese imperialism, the Second World War, and the Korean War. He could not have three meals a day because of extreme poverty and hardship of his family. When he was nine years old, he spent six months in bed due to lack of appetite and a high fever. In 1954, he realized that he had pulmonary tuberculosis and was told by a doctor that he could only live for less than three months. His physical condition became worse even though he prayed sincerely to the Buddha for healing. One day, he stopped praying to the Buddha and began to cry out to a heavenly god instead.

Dr. David Yonggi Cho. Source: Center for the Study of Global Christianity

At the time, he did not recognize that god as the Christian God, but as a supreme god in heaven based on his shamanic belief. He prayed that he would spend the rest of his life serving the supreme god if he was healed. He also prayed, "Jesus, you even healed lepers, can you heal my tuberculosis?" Then healing came upon him. Cho often said that this short prayer changed his life entirely. It is known as the first spiritual experience in his life.

In 1952, he entered a technical high school, hoping that he would support his large family after his graduation. As Cho developed friendships with the Assemblies of God (AG)'s missionaries, he changed his plan. He learned the Bible from two of the AG missionaries, Richard and Kenneth Tice. Cho became their interpreter when they preached to Korean congregations. Through studying the Bible with them, Cho came to understand more clearly about the AG beliefs and divine healing. After being trained by the missionaries for more than a year, he entered the Sunbogeum Theological Seminary in September 1956 and graduated in March 1958. He met Ja-Shil Choi at the Seminary, who later became his mother-in-law and a great partner as they developed the Yoido Full Gospel Church (YFGC).

In the winter of 1956, the first year of his seminary study, Cho became sick again with pneumonia. While he was in critical condition for several days, Choi, as an experienced nurse, took care of him. He recovered several days later. Since that moment, Cho and Choi became very close and started working together. Cho's personal experience of divine healing made him focus on healing ministry. In every service at the YFGC, Cho prays for the sick right after the sermon. He emphasizes on divine healing more than speaking in tongues in his ministry. Divine healing is one of the most significant factors for the YFGC's remarkable growth. Thousands of church members testify their experiences of healing through Cho's prayer.

Cho's experiences of extreme poverty and suffering from the disease became the soil for his pastoral and theological views. He developed the theology of the Fivefold Gospel and the Threefold Blessing, which have been the core growth theory of the YFGC. Cho's Fivefold Gospel are salvation, baptism in the Spirit, divine healing, the Second Coming, and blessing, which he began to teach from 1974. The Threefold Blessing has been the core pastoral doctrine of the YFGC from its tent-church era. Based on 3 John 2, Cho taught that blessings included salvation, prosperity in all things, and a healthy life. He proclaimed the hope for prosperity and health to his church members who were suffering from poverty and sickness. This theology is significant because the prosperity language has become an official doctrine of the church and has been successfully contextualized in the post-Korean-war society even though the mainstream Korean denominations accuse it of Christian shamanism.

Cho's other pastoral theology is the spirituality of the Fourth dimension. He employs an engineering terminology, "dimension," to explain how the spiritual world, which is the fourth dimension, takes control of the material world. According to Cho, as a higher dimension controls a lower dimension, faith can overcome all of life's problems and make dreams and visions come true.

Cho devoted himself to the growth of the church. The church membership reached up to 830,000 when he retired in 2011 and it was once the largest church not only in South Korea but also in the world.

Bibliography

Cho, Yonggi. 2015. *Fivefold Gospel and Threefold Blessing*. Seoul: Seoul Logos.

Cho, Yonggi. 1983. *The Fourth Dimension*, Second Edition. Plainfield, NJ: Bridge Publishing Inc.

Kennedy, Nell L. 1980. *Dream Your Way to Success: The Story of Dr. Yonggi Cho and Korea*. Plainfield, NJ: Logos International.

Lee, Sang Yun. 2018. *A Theology of Hope: Contextual Perspectives in Korean Pentecostalism*. Middletown, DE: APTS Press.

Ma, Wonsuk, William W. Menzies, and Hyeonsung Bae, eds. 2016. *David Yonggi Cho: A Close Look at His Theology & Ministry*. Eugene, OR: Wipf and Stock.

Sang Yun Lee

Choi, Jashil

Jashil Choi (1915–1989) was a prominent women in Korean Pentecostalism and Korean Christianity. She was the mother-in-law of Yonggi Cho and had a profound effect on the growth of Yoido Full Gospel Church (YFGC). She was born in Haeju City of Hwang-hae province in North Korea during the Japanese occupation. Her father passed away when she was a child. At the age of twelve, Choi attended a tent crusade led by Sung-Bong Lee with her mother. She heard about the gospel for the first time but did not convert to Christianity. She entered a nursing school to become a nurse because during that time, it was a socially respected profession with a high salary. She married an educated man who had with a good career. After moving to Seoul, she opened a new business and was successful within a short time. However, her business went bankrupt and her mother and oldest daughter died in a ten day period. Then her Buddhist husband abandoned her with three children. In 1956, she almost committed suicide as she felt that there was no hope in her life any more, but she found God and received Christ as the Savior. After being baptized by the Holy Spirit, she recognized her calling and studied in the Sunbogeum Theological Seminary where she met Yonggi Cho. Cho had a health crisis because his tuberculosis recurred. Choi took care of him and sincerely prayed for his healing. They became important ministry partners.

Choi's two major ministries remarkably contributed to Korean Christianity: the YFGC and Osanri Prayer Mountain (later re-named as Osanri Choi Jashil Memorial Prayer Mountain). Choi graduated from the Seminary in 1957 and planted a tent church with Cho on the outskirt of Seoul in 1958. Soon after the church was founded, she started a children's ministry, especially for orphans, and about seventy children came to the tent church in a year. Her ministry extended to adults. With the manifestations of spiritual gifts, such as speaking in tongues, exorcism, and divine healing, the tent church grew incredibly. It was moved to Sedaemoon in 1961 and the membership grew to 3,000 in 1964. It was then moved to Yoido in 1973.

While she was praying and fasting, she heard the voice of God asking her to establish a prayer mountain. She shared this vision with Cho, but he was negative about it. Nevertheless, she went to Osanri village and prayed for days and nights alone.

In 1978, a sanctuary and hostel for 5,000 people were completed on the prayer mountain. The sanctuary was expanded to 10,000 seats and 12 subsidiary chapels by 1993.

Choi started a mission for Korean migrants in Japan and the local, which was the beginning of her international ministry. Some Japanese church leaders invited her to lead evangelical meetings where various manifestations of the Holy Spirit occurred. Choi's anointed messages were fulfilled with the Spirit and had significant impacts on the growth of many Japanese churches. She emphasized repentance, praying, fasting, and being filled with the Holy Spirit. Through her spiritual influences, many Japanese Christians have constantly visited her prayer mountain. Her ministry reached to Thailand, Hong Kong, Germany, and the United States

Choi considered fasting and faithful prayer were the most important elements for spiritual growth ever since she became a Christian. She also developed intimate relationship with God. She was convinced that fasting was a quick way to receive an answer from God and was one of the indispensable initiatives in spiritual warfare. She also fast for evangelism, church growth, healing, preaching, problem-solving, and receiving spiritual gifts. Her emphasis on praying and fasting impacted many church members. Choi contributed to women's leadership in Korean Christianity, but it was not widely recognized because Korean Christians were still much influenced by Confucianism.

Choi's spiritual leadership and contributions for the growth of YFGC can never be neglected. She was not Cho's assistant pastor but his mentor and partner. He publicly acknowledged that without her, he could not have achieved such remarkable success in ministry.

Bibliography

Anderson, Allan Heaton. 2018. *An Introduction to Pentecostalism: Global Charismatic Christianity*. Cambridge: Cambridge University Press.

Choi, Jashil. 2009. *Hallelujah Lady*. Seoul: KIATS Press.

Choi, Jashil. 1978. *Nanun Halleluya Ajummayutta* [I Was Mrs. Hallelujah]. Seoul: Seoul Books.

Hurston, Karen 1995. *Growing the World's Largest Church*. Springfield: Gospel Publishing House.

Ma, Julie C. 2002. "Korean Pentecostal Spirituality: A Case Study of Jashil Choi." *Asian Journal of Pentecostal Studies* 5 (2): 235–254.

Sang Yun Lee

Christian Assemblies in Argentina

One of the earliest Pentecostal movements in Argentina, the Italian-Argentine Christian Assemblies (Asambleas Cristianas, AC) comprise several denominations and church networks.

The Pentecostalism among Italians in Argentina had two foundations. The first took place in 1909, when, Lucia Menna, Louis Francescon, and Giacomo Lombardi arrived in Buenos Aires. The country had one of the largest Italian migrant communities of the time. Family ties and believing in a divine revelation drew the Chicago missionaries to spread their message to their co-nationals. The missionaries went to the towns of Tres Arroyos, San Cayetano, Necochea, in the south of the province of Buenos Aires. Many of the Menna family converted and for a time attended the chapel of the Evangelical

Union in Tres Arroyos, an independent evangelical church founded by an alumnus of the Spurgeon College. After being arrested, Lombardi and Francescon left the country for Brazil. Lucia Menna would leave later. All the Menna family would re-emigrate to Chicago by 1913.

The second foundation of the Christian Assemblies happened in 1916. Again, Italian lay missionaries from Chicago (Narciso Natucci) and Gary, Indiana, (Francisco Anfuso), traveled guided by divine revelation to preach to their family and acquaintances. They began to hold services in the house of the Mingrino family in the Villa Devoto district in Buenos Aires. Soon, as the attendance increased, the new church acquired a storefront nearby for public worship.

In 1920, Giuseppe Petrelli came to ordain the first elders in Buenos Aires and in Mendoza. Despite this initial growth, the movement had the effects of internal divisions. In 1925, a split lead Natucci and some believers to open a church a few blocks near of Villa Devoto, at Calle Asunción. In 1932, Natucci's congregation would divide again, with the splitter group establishing a headquarters in Villa Lynch.

A pendulum migration trend also affected the Christian Assemblies. Immigrants from Calabria settled and founded a church in Rosario. From Buenos Aires, returning migrants founded churches in Corleone, Sicily, and in Selle River Valley, in Campania.

The development of the church into the inner parts of the country resulted from personal contacts through kin and ethnic networks. At this process, the role of Domingo Marino (1894–1974) was important. An Italian migrant, Marino had converted in Mendoza and moved to Buenos Aires, where he was a caretaker of the mother church in Villa Devoto. In 1941, he established himself in Santa Fe. In the city, he founded one of the largest Pentecostal congregations of Argentina before the mass-evangelist rallies of the 1960s.

A hesitant leadership fearing a centralized organization paired with the bureaucratic difficulties to register local churches made it difficult to develop a unified movement under the same legal framework. In 1942, the Villa Lynch church summoned and held the first convention of churches. In 1950, Marino did the same in Santa Fe. However, by 1955 it became clear that the leader's personal and doctrinal differences were deep enough to prevent unification. Thus, many church networks emerged. Often, they were identified after their headquarters, even though not all of them using a variation of the name "Christian Assembly".

The 1950s marked a transition in Argentine Pentecostalism. Until then, most churches were along ethnic lines, but the revivals from mass evangelism and migrant assimilation had changed aspects of the Pentecostal churches. Furthermore, the Pentecostal churches began to collaborate outside their denominational networks. The AC of Villa Devoto had an important role in organizing the Evangelical Pentecostal Confederation of Argentina. The Christian Biblical Church engaged in ecumenical activities related to the World Council of the Churches. The AC Villa Lynch became closer to the Christian Congregation in Brazil and in 1974 changed its denomination to Christian Congregation in the Republic of Argentina. Meanwhile, the Christian Church of North America (now the International Fellowship of Christian Assemblies) resumed contacts with the AC Villa Devoto and a smaller group. The AC Santa Fe worked to bring closer isolated churches and networks into their fellowship and began to spread to neighboring countries. Despite these efforts, the AC tends to live isolated within their networks of churches. Consequently, each group developed its ethos, practices, and theological nuances. Drawing from the records from the Ministry of Foreign Affairs and Worship, the main current groups are the following:

Asamblea Cristiana Evangelica, with headquarters in Villa Devoto, Buenos Aires. Incorporated as Asamblea Cristiana Cultural in 1927, most of its 150 churches are in the city and the province of Buenos Aires. Asamblea Cristiana "Dios es Amor", with headquarters in the city of Santa Fe, with over 1,000 congregations in the country and few affiliated churches abroad. Congregacion Cristiana en la Argentina, formerly Asamblea Cristiana reunida en el nombre de Jesus, with headquarters in Villa, Lynch, Buenos Aires. It has about 100 churches, with significant membership in the Misiones province. Iglesia Cristiana Vida Eterna, with headquarters in Rosario. It has 35 churches and is affiliated with the International Fellowship of Christian Assemblies. Iglesia Cristiana Biblica, with headquarters in Villa Devoto, Buenos Aires. This ecumenically oriented group began in 1970 with the founding AC Mingrino and Petrecca families. It counts with 30 churches. Iglesia Evangélica Cristiana Reunidos en el nombre de nuestro Señor Jesucristo, formerly the Asamblea Cristiana de Lomas del Mirador, with 5 churches.

Additionally, the Italian-Argentine Pentecostals have contributed for many other denominations, especially the Iglesia de Diós, the Unión de las Asambleas de Diós, and the Congregación Cristiana de Goya.

Doctrinally, theses churches have high regard for the Bible, believe in the doctrine of the Trinity, and salvation by faith. Although they welcome charismatic practices in worship, their performance is more moderate than other Pentecostals. Some middle class, urban groups adopts contemporary styles of worship and have seminar trained, salaried ministers. In smaller towns and among the working class, a more conservative outlook in worship style and lay ministry prevail. Despite the group differences, they share a concern with a diaconal work focused on poverty alleviation. Some middle-class congregations in major cities are more vocal in social justice, though keeping strong pro-family instances.

Bibliography

Aasmundsen, Hans Geir. 2016. *Pentecostals, Politics, and Religious Equality in Argentina*. Leiden: Brill.

Crimi, Ciro P. 2016. *Historia de Asamblea Cristiana de Villa Devoto*. Buenos Aires: Asamblea Cristiana Evangélica.

Köhrsen, Jens. 2016. *Middle Class Pentecostalism in Argentina: Inappropriate Spirits*. Leiden: Brill.

Sabatini, Angel. 2001. *80 años de la Asamblea Cristiana de Mendoza*. San Luiz, Argentina: the author.

Saracco, Norberto. 1989. "Argentine Pentecostalism: Its History and Theology." PhD thesis, University of Birmingham, UK.

Leonardo Marcondes Alves

Christian Congregation in Brazil

The Christian Congregation in Brazil (CCB) stands among the oldest and the largest Pentecostal denominations in that country. The church derives from the work of Italian-American Pentecostal missionaries, especially Louis Francescon.

In 1910, Francescon came from Chicago, via Argentina, to plant a church in a rural area in Santo Antonio da Platina, Parana state, and in São Paulo. For the first three decades, the church grew in São Paulo metropolitan area and at the agricultural frontier along the railroads in the country southeastern region, serving both Italians and Brazilians from different ethnicities. By the mid-1930s, the Vargas government's nationalist policies made the church acquire a more Brazilian outlook, switching the worship services to Portuguese. The initial ostracism by their fellow Protestants led to an increased isolationist policy, even applied to the similar Pentecostal denominations sharing the same milieu with the CCB, especially from the 1950s onwards.

Led by management-savvy lay ministers, the CCB increased to reach all Brazilian states and start foreign missions. The industrialist Miguel Spina and the accountant Victorio Angare traveled planting churches and establishing fellowship with churches of common Italian Pentecostal heritage in North America, Venezuela, Argentina, and Europe. Returning migrants also brought the church to Portugal, Spain, the Middle East, and Japan. Since the 1980s, migration of Brazilians towards the Global North and lay missionaries in the Global South resulted in many national churches.

Reflecting its worldwide scope, the CCB forged a framework of sister churches around the globe in 2003. Organizationally, each national movement in the fellowship is independent and on equal footing with each other, but the prominence of the Bras headquarters and the Senior Elder's Council, which assigns field representatives, is remarkable.

In theology, CCB expresses most of the finished work classical Pentecostalism doctrines. Its twelve-point articles of the faith hold the Bible as the infallible guide for doctrine and behavior, the belief in the triune God and Jesus' atoning work, the practice of water baptism by full immersion (from an age of accountability conventionally beginning at twelve) and the Lord's supper. Although the CCB believes in the existence of the Devil and anoints the sick with oil, there are no healing or exorcism performances during the public worship. Officially, it is premillennialist in its eschatology. The dualities of the Spirit and the body, the World and the Church, the divine and the human, lead to effective separation of the world while expecting the culmination of Christ's work in the afterlife. Thus, it results in less pressure to adapt to the novel forms of worship or involvement with affairs deemed too worldly for the Church, like secular politics. However, the increased access to education and the widespread internet information have challenged the CCB ministers to further reflections on doctrinal matters.

An avoidance of mass media and an isolationist policy have maintained the CCB apart from other Evangelicals in the country. Thus, the CCB has kept a distinctive liturgy, theological emphasis, and even its particular *mores*.

In smaller towns and agrarian locations, members often seek adherence to stricter holiness standards. In larger cities, two sets of networks are discernible. The discourse from congregations in poorer neighborhoods emphasizes separation from the world and the pursuit of a higher power to overcome everyday trials. Meanwhile, at middle-class congregations, the degree of involvement and the display of the religious practices pertain to a private sphere. For a time, this internal differentiation and the orality have enabled the CCB to absorb and adapt its theological discourse without major doctrinal controversies.

A uniform, though spontaneous, liturgy fosters a sense of denominational unity. A typical service consists of a "hymn sandwich" sung congregationally with the aid of an orchestra. Any person may call hymns, say the prayers, and give testimony, as felt led by the Holy Spirit. The sermon is also extemporaneous and theoretically, any (male) member could preach, but, in practice, it is reserved for the ministers. Female worshippers wear veils. The church observes a seating arrangement and greeting with a holy kiss according to each gender.

Without formal membership rolls (or tithing), the CCB has had considerable growth. By 2020, it had nearly 20,000 congregations listed on its directory and the past Brazilian census of 2010 reported 2.3 million adherents. Despite its growth and relative homogeneity, the CCB had a significant membership loss during the 2000s (Valente, 2015). The internal organization has shifted from kinship-like, anti-hierarchical congregationalism to an increasingly bureaucratic polity. It might reflect the difficulties of responding to social changes. Consequently, small though highly visible splits have occurred in the past decade.

The current polity resembles a Presbyterian model. The local congregations function under the administrative and ministry councils on regional, state, and national levels. The yearly meetings of elders appoint the ministers for ordination. The CCB has no seminaries or colleges (and many members still shun formal education) and the lay ministers serve without expecting salary. The diaconal Piety Work, funded by anonymous voluntary donations, diminishes social differences thorough basic welfare. The CCB avoids personalist leadership, valuing a collegiate decision-making process. A self-perpetuating Senior Elders' Council oversees the national (and international) structures. Admission to this council is by invitation and seniority is no longer a criterion for participating. Since 2010, the Senior Elders' Council has taken take some steps to minister to inmates, the deaf, children (through Bible instruction), and young people. In some regions, the ministers encourage regular home Bible studies. One reaction to the COVID-19 pandemic has been to broadcast online worship services publically. However, such measures are met with varied responses. While many members welcome them as progressive, others stand in opposition. Issues of gender (women do not participate in the decision processes, nor are ordained, or even play instruments other than the organ), formal biblical and theological education, and congregational participation in church government are still pressing. By being marginalized, dynamic, and old, the CCB remains an example of early Pentecostalism's vitality.

Bibliography

Foerster, Norbert Hans Christoph. 2010. *A Congregação Cristã no Brasil numa área de alta vulnerabilidade social no ABC paulista: aspectos de sua tradição e transmissão religiosa – a instituição e os sujeitos*. Doctoral diss., Methodist University of São Paulo.

Monteiro, Yara Nogueira. 2010. "Congregação Cristã no Brasil: da fundação ao centenário, a trajetória de uma igreja brasileira." *Estudos de Religião* 24 (9): 122–163.

St.Clair, George. 2017. "'God Even Blessed Me with Less Money': Disappointment, Pentecostalism and the Middle Classes in Brazil." *Journal of Latin American Studies* 49 (3): 609–632.

Valente, Rubia R. 2015. "Institutional explanations for the decline of the Congregação Cristã no Brasil." *Pentecostudies* 14 (1): 72–96.

Yuasa, Key. 2001. "Louis Francescon: A Theological Biography, 1866–1964." Doctoral diss., University of Geneve.

Leonardo Marcondes Alves

Church of God, Cleveland

The Church of God (COG) is an international denomination based in Cleveland, Tennessee. In September 2019, the denomination reported more than 7.6 million members and 39,696 churches in 185 nations and territories.

On August 19, 1886, Richard Green Spurling, with assistance from his father, Richard Spurling, established a congregation called Christian Union in Monroe County, Tennessee. Emphasizing the New Testament as their "only rule of faith and practice" along with loving God and neighbor, Spurling and the eight who joined him rejected the exclusivism of "men-made creeds and traditions" they experienced among Landmark Baptists. Subsequently, Spurling established other Christian Union congregations. In 1902, a group led by W.F. Bryant in nearby Camp Creek, North Carolina, called Spurling to organize and pastor a congregation named Holiness Church, reflecting their emphasis on sanctification as a second work of grace. This congregation was the fruit of an 1896 holiness revival in the community's Shearer Schoolhouse. From that revival, perhaps a hundred or more identified with the holiness movement and experienced spiritual manifestations including speaking in tongues and healings resulting in severe persecution from their Baptist neighbors.

Having observed the holiness revival in Camp Creek, A.J. Tomlinson joined the Holiness Church in 1903, and the congregation immediately selected him as pastor. A former Quaker from Indiana, Tomlinson had relocated to nearby Culberson, North Carolina, in 1899 to establish a school and orphanage for children, which he called Samson's Foxes. Under Tomlinson's leadership, five holiness congregations, including remnants of B.H. Irwin's Fire Baptized Holiness Association, came together in 1906 for what became an annual, now biennial, General Assembly. The second Assembly in 1907 adopted the name Church of God, which expresses a continuing commitment to restore God's church including embracing a biblical name.

Tomlinson relocated to Cleveland, Tennessee, in 1904, and immediately began efforts to plant a congregation there. He set in order the Cleveland Holiness Church, now North Cleveland COG, on October 10, 1906. For many years, the local congregation and the growing denomination shared leadership and influence.

Tomlinson was pastor of the local church; and, the General Assembly selected him as the first general moderator, now general overseer, in 1909. The Cleveland congregation hosted the annual General Assembly from 1908 to 1915 and from 1919 to 1920. The congregation remains at its original location, and as the oldest continuing COG, is considered the denomination's "mother" church.

Although some spoke in tongues, a lack of historical records makes it difficult to know the pneumatology of the Holiness Churches. The COG certainly had developed a classical Pentecostal theology of speaking in tongues as the Bible evidence of Spirit baptism by the time of Tomlinson's personal experience in 1908. Compelled by his experience, Tomlinson and the COG quickly began to expand. An evangelistic trip to Florida in spring 1909 brought many members, ministers, and congregations into the movement. Among those were Bahamian born Edmond Barr and his USA born wife, Rebecca, as well as R.M. and Ida Evans. In November 1909, the Barrs became the first COG ministers to reach outside the United States when they traveled to the Bahama Islands. Then in early January 1910, the Evans, along with Carl Padgett, joined them. R.M. Evans became overseer of the Bahamas in 1911.

International expansion accelerated with the ministry of J.H. Ingram who excelled at connecting already existed networks of congregations such as those established by Maria W. Atkinson in Mexico in the early 1930s. Ingram's tour of Central America in 1934 and global circumnavigation in 1936 were especially fruitful. Amalgamations with the Full Gospel Church of South Africa in 1951 and Geredja Bethel Indonesia in 1967 greatly expanded the COG's international ministry.

Prior to joining the Holiness Church, Tomlinson utilized media as a means of communication, networking, and evangelization. He published *Samson's Foxes* (1901–1902) and *The Way* (1904–1905) with M.S. Lemons. Following service as corresponding editor of *The Bridegroom's Messenger* (1908–1910), he began publishing *The Evening Light and Church of God Evangel*, now *Church of God Evangel*, in 1910. His Evangel Publishing Company became the Church of God Publishing House. Now Church of God Publications, this ministry includes Pathway Press and Editorial Evangélica. A subsidiary, Tennessee Music and Printing Company, began in the 1920s and was a major source of shape note music including the *Church Hymnal*, affectionately known as the "Red-Back Hymnal," which has sold millions of copies since its debut in 1951. The denomination's weekly radio broadcast Forward in Faith began in 1958.

Although the COG began as an anti-creedal movement, it views itself as a Wesleyan Pentecostal denomination. Leaders developed a list of doctrines in 1910, known as Church Teachings, as a study tool for ministerial candidates. Following controversy over sanctification, the General Assembly adopted a 14-item Declaration of Faith in 1948. Although not considered comprehensive, the document remains unchanged.

Under Tomlinson's leadership, a short-term Bible Training School began on January 1, 1918, in Cleveland. Now Lee University, it numbered 5,189 students in 2019 and announced the development of three doctoral programs in nursing, education, and counseling. Pentecostal Theological Seminary began in 1975 in Cleveland. Globally, the Division of Education coordinates 129 Bible colleges, universities, and seminaries along with another 100 Bible institutes.

COG organizational structure includes an International Executive Committee,

International Executive Council, and Divisions of Care, Discipleship, Education, Support Services, and World Evangelization along with state/regional offices. Structure outside the United States and Canada includes five fields with field directors, regional superintendents, and national overseers. Along with specific-purpose offerings, adherents are encouraged to tithe to local churches, which then send a tithe divided between international and state/regional ministries.

Bibliography

Conn, Charles W. 2008. *Like A Mighty Army: A History of the Church of God, 1886–1996*, Tribute Edition. Cleveland, TN: Pathway Press.

Phillips, Wade H. 2014. *Quest to Restore God's House: A Theological History of the Church of God (Cleveland, Tennessee).* Volume 1: *1886–1923: R.G. Spurling to A.J. Tomlinson, Formation-Transformation-Reformation.* Cleveland, TN: CPT Press.

Tomlinson, A.J. 2011. *The Last Great Conflict.* Cleveland, TN: White Wing Press.

David G. Roebuck

Church of God in Christ

The Church Of God In Christ (COGIC) belongs to the Holiness-Pentecostal branch of the Church. With congregations in nearly 100 countries on nearly every continent and reportedly 6 million globally, it is an international denomination with its global headquarters in Memphis, Tennessee. COGIC emerged as a holiness fellowship among black Baptist churches in Mississippi, Arkansas, and Tennessee in 1897 with leaders Charles Price Jones, Charles Harrison Mason, other Baptist clergy, and Baptist women as the leaders. Together, they launched a Black Baptist Holiness movement that accompanied the Wesleyan Holiness movement.

Charles Harrison Mason embraced the Pentecostal message and received the baptism of the Holy Spirit at the international Azusa Street Revival in February of 1907. Differing with Jones on whether an unknown language (tongues) could be a sign of the baptism of the Holy Spirit, Mason was dismissed from the fellowship of 110 congregations. In September of 1907, ten congregations joined Mason to form a Pentecostal denomination and electing him as the senior bishop of the denomination which he would lead from 1907 to until his death in 1961.

Under Mason's leadership, the denomination grew from ten congregations to 4,000 by 1961. During his early tenure, he presided over an interracial network of churches. These networks, led by E.N. Bell, Howard Adams and Leonard P. Adams, basically governed themselves. Beginning in 1914, these white-led networks began withdrawing from the COGIC. However, until Mason's death, there would be white clergy, white congregations, interracial congregations, and Latinx congregations within the Church of God in Christ.

Women leaders such as Lizzie Woods (later Robinson), Lillian Coffey, and Arena C. Mallory were instrumental in organizing the Women's Department into a vital ministry of the church. Along with Mason and other male leaders such as E.R. Driver (an attorney), Isaac Stafford (a physician), D.J. Young (a publisher), Ozro Thurston Jones, Sr., and Riley F. Williams, they built COGIC into a national and international denomination.

Music has been a hallmark of COGIC. As a scholar has noted, "the COGIC pianist and singer Arizona Dranes should be considered the Mother of Gospel Music." Dranes also was influential in crafting

Mason Temple, Church of God in Christ, Memphis, Tennessee, April 8, 2017.
Photo: Jim Roberts

a "sanctified church sound" within gospel music during the 1920s. This sound that would find its choral expression in the compositions of Anna Crockett Ford and Mattie Moss Clark during the 1950s. COGIC would be instrumental in the development of gospel music in other countries such as Canada, Great Britain, South Africa, and Japan. COGIC musical artists have been key to the development of the genres of contemporary gospel, gospel hip-hop, and praise and worship.

During the late 1910s and the 1920s, the denomination began to expand beyond the United States and established congregations in the Caribbean, including Cuba during the mid-1950s. In 1929, COGIC established the first Pentecostal congregation in Haiti and the first black Pentecostal congregation in Canada. During the 1930s and 1940s, COGIC entered Africa, particularly Liberia, South Africa, Botswana, and Ethiopia as well as sponsored ministries in Asia, especially in India and Thailand. COGIC entered Europe in 1948, establishing the first black Pentecostal congregation in Great Britain. From the 1960s to the present, COGIC entered other countries on the various continents.

In 1970, the C.H. Mason Theological Seminary was established as a member of the Interdenominational Theological Center in Atlanta, Georgia, becoming the first Pentecostal graduate level seminary in the United States. In Great Britain, Calvary Theological College was founded as a COGIC seminary, too. During the 1970s, the C.H. Mason System of Jurisdictional Institutes developed Bible schools across the United States. In 2001, All Saints Bible College was opened in Memphis, Tennessee.

COGIC has participated in various ecumenical activities on the local, state, national, and international levels. Locally, pastors have participated in interdenominational ministerial associations since the 1910s. Nationally, COGIC has been members of the National Fraternal Council of Negro Churches (1930s to 1950s), the Congress of National Black Churches (1970s to 1990s), the Pentecostal/Charismatic Churches of North America (1994 to the present). The denomination has also participated in the Faith and Order Commission of the National Council of Churches of Christ (1988 and the early 2000s). Internationally, it has been a member of Pentecostal World Fellowship since around 1950 and has periodically participated in the general assemblies convened by the World Council of Churches (WCC). COGIC has also been represented at the Global Christian Forum, consultations between Pentecostals and the World Council of Churches, international bilateral dialogues between Pentecostal and Reformed leaders, and the between Pentecostal and Baptist leaders.

COGIC clergy have been involved in national activist organizations of the United States such as the NAACP, the UNIA of Marcus Garvey, SCLC of Martin Luther King, Deacons for Defense and Justice, PUSH/Rainbow Coalition, Ten Point Coalition, and the Pan-African Charismatic Evangelical Congress.

The successors to Lizzie Woods Robinson in heading COGIC's women's department include Lillian Brooks Coffey (1945–1964), the founder of the Women's Convention; Annie L. Bailey (1964–1975); Mattie C. McGlothen (1975–1994); Emma Frances Crouch (1994–1997); and Willie Mae Rivers (1997–2017); and Barbara McCoo Lewis (2017–present).

The successors to Charles Harrison Mason as presiding bishop include Ozro Thurston Jones, Sr. (1961–1968); James Oglethorpe Patterson, Sr. (1968–1989); Henry Louis Ford (1990–1995); David Chandler Owens (1995–2000); Gilbert Earl Patterson (2000–2007); and Charles Edward Blake, Sr. (2007–present).

COGIC's legacy as a predominately African American-led church has exhibited vanguard ministries, social witness, and a global ministry. The vanguard ministries ranged from interracial, multicultural, white, Latinx, and First Peoples ministries during the era of legalized racial segregation in the United. During the same era, COGIC advocated pacifism, anti-segregation, anti-lynching, and pro-civil rights. Historically, the denomination also held official positions that pro-women voting, pro-union organizing, anti-capital punishment and ecological justice. It is among a limited cadre of Pentecostal denominations with congregations in over 100 countries. The Church of God in Christ is an international denomination within the progressive wing of the Pentecostal movement.

Bibliography

Alexander, Estrelda Y. 2011. *Black Fire: One Hundred Years of African American Pentecostalism*. Downers Grove, IL: Intervarsity Press.

Butler, Anthea. 2007. *Women in the Church of God in Christ: Making a Sanctified World*. Chapel Hill, NC: University of North Carolina Press.

Clemmons, Ithiel C. 2012. *Bishop C.H. Mason and the Roots of the Church of God in Christ*. Pneuma Life Publishing.

White, Calvin. 2012. *The Rise to Respectability: Race, Religion, and the Church of God in Christ*. Fayetteville, AR: The University of Arkansas Press.

David Daniels

Codreanu, Teodor

Teodor Codreanu (1928–2004) was born on August 20 in Avram Iancu, in the district of Bihor, Romania, as a second child in a family of four. Early on, at the age of 12, he moved to Timișoara for his studies and it was there that his ministry would take place for the rest of his life. On August 23, 1946 he was baptized by pastor Alexandru Izbașa in the church where he would minister later. In 1956 he married Aurica and they had three children: Estera, Ioan, and Marcel.

The ministry of Codreanu began in 1964 when he took the spiritual leadership of the Pentecostal Church on 18 Mangalia street in Timișoara and on March 15, 1970 he was ordained as the pastor of the church. By 1973 the church grew so much that they moved to a bigger location on 54 Romulus street. He served with total dedication with his special evangelistic gift which converted many to Christ, so the church numbers grew exponentially. People remember vividly how the various walls of the building were removed to accommodate the exceptionally-growing congregation. This happened during the communist regime so there were all kinds of pressures and restrictions. Yet Codreanu did not only continue the work, but also began to pray and search for a new location for the church since there was no space for so many people in the church and they were listening in the courtyard. After long conversations with the communist authorities, Codreanu was allowed to build a building in the new site. The church was called Elim and was officially opened in 1988. The congregation grew quickly in the next ten years, reaching almost 5,000.

Many people remarked Codreanu's bold preaching and his amazing evangelistic gift. He took a church from less than 200 people to many thousands in three decades while other evangelical churches in the city numbered mostly 1,000 people. Studies on this phenomenal development of Codreanu's church show that he had a clear mission strategy based on four key elements: prayer and fasting, high personal morality of believers, emphasis of evangelism, and charity and social involvement. Through this strategy he visioned to plant a Pentecostal church in every village in the Timiș district. He was able to see some 30 new churches planted by the Elim church in the surrounding villages.

Codreanu was also an outstanding poet and his many poems were eventually collected and published in two volumes. Even though he did not have any degrees of higher education, he had a great vision for theological education. In 1990, in partnership with several Pentecostal and evangelical pastors, he opened an extension of the Evangelical Theological Seminary originated from Osijek, Croatia in the Elim church, where hundreds of people received their very first theological training. Many students continue their theological training at various schools and some became the new leaders of Romanian Pentecostal theological institutions.

Being a man of great passion and dedication, Codreanu's sermons were very powerful and had a huge impact on the listeners regarding repentance and holy living. He also prayed for several hours every day and emphasized prayer in the church, which is continued to this day. His evangelistic preaching was greatly appreciated in Romania and among the diaspora community. He will be remembered as one of the most prominent evangelists of Romanian Pentecostalism in the last decades of the twentieth century and the pastor of the largest Pentecostal church in Romania.

Bibliography

Andreescu, Valeriu. 2012. *Istoria Penticostalismului Românesc*, Two Vols. Oradea: Casa Cărții.

"Biserica 'Elim' de-a lungul timpului." 2010. Accessed on November, 15 2019. http://www

.elim.ro/despre-biserica-penticostala-elim-timisoara/biserica-elim-de-a-lungul-timpului/.

Măcelaru, Marcel V. 2016. "Holistic Mission in Post-Communist Romania: A Case Study on the Growth of the 'Elim' Pentecostal Church of Timișoara (1990–1997)." In *Mission in Central and Eastern Europe: Realities, Perspectives, Trends*, edited by Corneliu Constantineanu, Marcel V. Măcelaru, Anne-Marie Kool, and Mihai Himcinschi, 327–44. Oxford: Regnum Books.

"Teodor Codreanu." 2004. *Cuvantul Adevărului*, anul XV, nr. 11, 23.

Corneliu Constantineanu

Colonialism

Colonialism, the political and economic rule by a foreign power of a people and their land, is essential for any accounting of the modern history of Christianity. Iberian nations colluded with the Catholic Church in their early campaigns of conquest and colonization, and the efforts of Protestant missionaries relied heavily on Europe's imperial presence throughout the world. As a result, academic studies of the connection between Christian expansion and colonial exploitation are numerous, especially up to the latter half of the twentieth century, by which time most nations of the world had gained independence. Precisely then, Pentecostalism took off in the global South, quickly displacing Protestantism and Catholicism as the driver of Christian growth. Pentecostalism is therefore less closely tied to colonialism than are its Christian predecessors, a fact reflected in the relative dearth of scholarship on the intersection of Pentecostalism and colonialism. Yet that intersection is of fundamental importance. For one, Pentecostal origins are (debatably) in the United States, a country that rose to the status of superpower – and colonizing power – in the late nineteenth and early twentieth centuries, just when Pentecostalism as an organized movement emerged. Additionally, Pentecostalism has grown most vibrantly over the past half century in the very countries that endured the brutalities of Western imperial rule, this despite Protestant and Catholic churches being remembered in such places as colonial churches. Finally, as a distinctly *post*colonial religion, but especially as one premised on the universal scope of the Holy Spirit, Pentecostalism has provided a means for formerly colonized people to negotiate and contest the legacies of the West's many centuries of global domination. For all these reasons, there is much to gain from considering the history of Pentecostalism in relation to the theme of colonialism.

Pentecostalism emerged in the early twentieth century at the height of modern imperialism. Although the United States, with which Pentecostalism's earliest history is most associated, was founded as an anti-colonial nation, it formally became a colonial power itself in the late nineteenth century and dominant sectors of its society shared in the bigoted and supremacist ideologies of the wider Euro-American world. It is therefore unsurprising that missionary reports and other historical sources show early Pentecostal evangelists to have carried with them to the global South perceptions of themselves as civilized and rational bearers of light, and of those they evangelized as backward and idolatrous (Anderson 2013). The spirit of expansionism and conquest, common to both evangelists and imperialists, pervaded Pentecostalism in the early twentieth century, as did an aloofness to worldly affairs that made early Pentecostal missionaries largely indifferent to the forms of colonial oppression they would have encountered. For the most part, the attitudes of early Pentecostal missionaries toward colonized peoples differed little from those of colonial-era Protestant and Catholic missionaries, lying somewhere on a spectrum between benevolent paternalism and overt racism.

Yet, of greatest importance to any counterhegemonic account of modern Pentecostalism is the recognition that Euro-American churches and missionaries were not the only, not even the most significant, actors in the story. Pentecostal movements never really took off in colonized parts of the world, only in *formerly* colonized parts of the world. It was in the post-independence period, from around the 1970s on, that Christianity began exploding in the global South, and it did so primarily because of indigenous, not Western, evangelists propagating, above all, the Pentecostal faith and theology. This postcolonial historical context corresponds with the rise of postcolonial critical theory. The implications of postcolonial thought on Pentecostal historiography are significant (Pulikottil 2002). In its attempt to recuperate the subjugated and silenced perspectives of marginalized peoples, postcolonialism offers scholars a framework through which to register the agency of non-Western, non-white Pentecostal missionaries. Historians today attribute the kind of Christianity spread – and spread widely – by African, Asian, and Latin American leaders to their own impulse and initiative, their ability creatively to meld global Pentecostal beliefs and practices with local concerns, commitments, and cultural conditions. Postcolonial historians also deconstruct what is until today the standard narrative of Pentecostalism's birth in the Topeka Revival and Azusa Street Revival, followed by its expansion outward to the ends of the earth. Allan Anderson in particular has argued forcefully for a polycentric, multinational account of Pentecostalism's origins (Anderson 2013). He locates Christian revival movements with distinctive Pentecostal characteristics and with no ties to the West in countries as diverse as Korea, India, and Chile. By shifting attention from a single narrative centered in the United States to a global network multiply constituted from the start, scholars have demonstrated both the pervasiveness of elitist thinking in discourses around Pentecostalism and the value of postcolonial perspectives in achieving a more fulsome understanding of Pentecostal diversity and dynamism.

Over recent decades, the kind of Pentecostalism that has spread especially powerfully throughout the world is that classified as neo-Pentecostalism. This is characterized by, among other things, its prosperity theologies, which regard wealth and capital accumulation as signs of God's favor. In denouncing "the prosperity gospel," critics of especially this kind of Pentecostalism repurpose the theme of colonialism: *neo*-Pentecostalism, they argue, is a form of *neo*colonialism. This perspective highlights the resonance of neo-Pentecostalism with US-based forms of capitalism, materialism, and individualism, and its dependence on US-based prosperity preachers and media technologies. At the same time that the United States has become a neocolonial force in economic and military terms, capable in even the post-independence period of subjugating other peoples and lands, it has also become one in religious and cultural terms. However, by presenting the embrace of prosperity theologies in the non-Western world as mere replicas of Western templates, charges of neocolonialism unwittingly end up reaffirming Western privilege and power, once again diminishing the agency of entire populations. It is important to see that preoccupations with health, security, and well-being – rarely just conspicuous opulence in and for itself – lie behind even indigenous spiritual practices and traditions precisely in places like Africa and Latin America where neo-Pentecostal ministries have recently flourished (Adogame 2013).

A final connection between Pentecostalism and colonialism lies in the specific aspects of Pentecostal theology that challenge hierarchical structures – whether racial, national, linguistic, cultural, or religious. Whereas the Pentecostal injunction to reject religious aspects of the past suggests something akin to cultural imperialism, the very process of demonizing non-Christian spirit worlds paradoxically affirms their reality. There is, thus, a cosmological continuity: a shared investment in an enchanted worldview that persists despite and even through Pentecostal discourses of denigration. Similarly, glossolalia subverts linguistic rules and expectations. It thus carries the potential to upend the hegemony of European languages, the dissemination of which was crucial in colonizers' efforts to control foreign populations (Tupamahu 2016). Above all, the biblical message that "the Spirit poured out on all flesh" lends Pentecostalism an egalitarian, democratizing aspect. This makes it, at least potentially, a radically inclusive religion within which Pentecostal theologians can write of non-Christian religions no less than non-Western cultures as sharing in the universal reach of the Holy Spirit (Yong and Richie 2010). This inclusiveness is also why marginalized people have been drawn to Pentecostalism, empowered and affirmed in the face of structural racism and colonial/neocolonial exploitation. Finally, it is to the Spirit's boundlessness that Pentecostals attribute the capacity of local, lay, and unlettered leaders to spring up so organically and so early, wresting ecclesiastic control from Western missionaries. The fact that Pentecostals from the global South are themselves creating and sustaining church organizations, spreading them not only in their homelands and to other former colonial territories, but also to the former metropoles of the global North, illustrates clearly the counter-imperialist potentialities of Pentecostalism itself.

Bibliography

Adogame, Afe. 2013. "Reconfiguring the Global Religious Economy: The Role of African Pentecostalism." In *Spirit and Power: The Growth and Global Impact of Pentecostalism*, edited by Donald E. Miller, Kimon H. Sargeant, and Richard Flory, 185–203. Oxford: Oxford University Press.

Anderson, Allan H. 2013. "The Emergence of a Multidimensional Global Missionary Movement: Trends, Patterns, and Expressions." In *Spirit and Power: The Growth and Global Impact of Pentecostalism*, edited by Donald E. Miller, Kimon H. Sargeant, and Richard Flory, 25–41. Oxford: Oxford University Press.

Pulikottil, Paulson. 2002. "As East and West Met in God's Own Country: Encounter of Western Pentecostalism with Native Pentecostalism in Kerala." *Asian Journal of Pentecostal Studies* 5 (1): 5–22.

Tupamahu, Ekaputra. 2016. "Tongues as a Site of Subversion: An Analysis from the Perspective of Postcolonial Politics of Language." *Pneuma* 38 (3): 293–311.

Yong, Amos, and Tony Richie. 2010. "Missiology and the Interreligious Encounter." In *Studying Global Pentecostalism: Theories and Methods*, edited by Allan Anderson, Michael Bergunder, André Droogers, and Cornelis van der Laan, 245–67. Berkeley: University of California Press.

Devaka Premawardhana

DR Congo

Before independence in 1960 the Congo Protestant Council (*Conseil Protestant du Congo, CPC*) was instituted as an advisory body for Protestant missionary agencies representing them to the predominantly Catholic Belgian colonial government. All Protestant churches, even Pentecostals, had to register by law. Church-names were standardised to *Communautés* (communities) and numbered to be identifiable. With 1970 CPC had to change its name to Church of Christ in the Congo (*Eglise du Christ au Congo, ECC*). This is the union of 64 largely independent Protestant churches or denominations. After 1991 there have been groups registered by the government without EEC-membership. Among the registered 64 churches, there are 25,504,220 church-members, in 320,101 congregations with 16,730 pastors and 1,265 missionaries. Nine Pentecostal churches are officially members of EEC (with numbers: 4; 7; 11; 30; 33; 37; 43; 59; 62).

The Congo Evangelistic Mission (CEM/CEPCO): British missionaries William Burton (1886–1971) and James Salter (1890–1972), educated with Pentecostal Missionary Union (PMU), commenced in 1909 in England) arrived in 1914 in South Africa: as it turned out the base for further work in the Congo. The Congo Evangelistic Mission (CEM) was established 1915 in the Katanga province at Mwanza by Burton, first unofficial under the covering of PMU, in 1922 officially. Mwanza was a Luba chiefdom, located west of the Congo River. In 1920 at Mwanza a "Luban Pentecost" happened while Burton taught on Mark 16:15–20 and that "these signs shall follow them that believe". Almost all of the 160 people went to receive the baptism in the Holy Spirit. These experiences of the first converts were soon to be given a normative authority of undreamt-of magnitude, which up to this day lays claim to almost all denominational formations of Christianity in Africa. It is unlikely that the Mission of CEM would have spread and consolidated without the role of a couple of former Angolan slaves among the first converts in 1916 who matured to "evangelists": Abraham Nyuki was the very first one. Ngoloma Ndela Bantu (+1939) and Shalumbo (+1937) contributed greatly to win many to the Christian faith. This Pentecostal mission CEM was the first and largest and has been immensely instrumental to the proliferation of Pentecostalism in the Congo through its members who proactively spread the mission across the country and beyond. The movement is since entangled with other parts of Africa, including Zambia, Angola, South Africa, and Ethiopia.

Mission libre Norvégienne (Communautés des Eglises Libres de Pentecôte en Afrique (CELPA): This missionary society goes back to Thomas B. Barratt (1862–1940). On his return journey from North America to Norway via Liverpool he was accompanied by some white missionaries who had also been baptised at the Azusa Street Revival and who, unlike him, were on the direct (return) journey to Africa: The Pentecostal Movement, contoured as a relationship movement, gains from its start on entanglements.

Mission libre Suedoise: The Swede Lewi Pethrus (1884–1974) founded the Svenska Fria Missions (SFM) in 1907. He was pastor of the Filadelfia parish in Stockholm and acted as chairman of the Mission Council (1926), which was to be responsible for Swedish-Pentecostal activities. From 1921 onwards several missionaries were sent out, reaching the Congo mostly on a route starting in East Africa and running overland. Between 1921 and 1970, 17 mission stations were founded in the southern Kivu. The most important one is that in the provincial capital of Goma (1960).

Jacques A. Vernaud (1932–2011), Independent Pentecostal Missionary: With few interruptions, he has lived in the area of today's DR Congo since 1965. After years as a missionary in the service of the French branch of the Assemblies of God (AG) in Gabon from 1955 and in the Republic of Congo from 1961, he moved to Kinshasa, working there ever since. In times of conflict and political turmoil, he seized the opportunity to establish a Pentecostal free church. Significantly, he made use of existing relationships with Congolese living in Kinshasa as he moved from the west bank of the Congo River (Brazzaville) to its east bank in the early 1960s. During times of his activity 16 churches were planted in Kinshasa and many more in the inland villages. The Congolese pastor Alphonse Futa worked together with him and they travelled widely holding Crusades and opening new Pentecostal churches. From 1984 on they built up the Centre Evangelique Francophone "La Borne", an independent church, which is the largest single congregation in Kinshasa with about 15,000 members.

FEPACO-Nzambe-Malamu and Alexandre Aidini Abala (1927–1997): FEPACO (Fraternité Evangélique Pentecôte en Afrique)-Nzambe-Malamu in Kinshasa dates back to 1967 with its entangled history back to 1957 (conversion of Abala at T.L. Osborn's first open-air healing campaign in Mombasa). A larger part of its approximately one million members live in the capital and other cities, but the church is also represented by rural congregations. Nzambe-Malamu is present through daughter congregations in several countries of central and southern Africa, Europe, and North America. It is basically one of many, rapidly growing Pentecostal formations in the DRC, but historically older and not to be classified as "neo-Pentecostal". Within the ECC it is assigned to the *Community of Assembles de Dieu au Congo* (CADC No. 37).

There were in the former ECZ other groups that continued to function even without membership well toward the end of the Mobutu regime, operating openly and missing any official government recognition. In some instances, they were even attended by government officials and ministers of the former MPR parliament. For this reason they were permitted to continue religious activities without harassment from the state, despite their lack of legal recognition.

Congolese Pentecostals engaged in social and development work: The Congolese Pentecostal movement is situated in one of the poorest countries of the world in terms of per-capita-income. Despite the excessive mineral wealth, the underground deposits of gold, diamonds, copper and cobalt as well as other precious minerals that the DR Congo possesses and which are coveted by many countries, the majority of the population is still destitute and lives in extreme poverty. While, the country itself prospered during the colonial period 1885–1960 and had become the second most industrialized state in Africa after South Africa. Since the DR Congo gained independence in 1960, it has not yet experienced development that benefits the entire population. The country faces pressing problems of poverty and human suffering, demanding social justice, human rights, liberation and holistic living in dignity. But these are secondary claims for the average Pentecostal understanding with its priority question being individual salvation. In addition, there is also the controversial gospel of prosperity in neo-charismatic communities that teaches that poverty is the result of personal sin and unfaithfulness to pay tithes. And there are Pentecostal communities involved in projects with education, health, and social aid.

Bibliography

Emmet, David Neil. 2016. "W.F.P. Burton (1886–1971) and Congolese Agency: A Biographical Study of a Pentecostal Mission." PhD thesis, University of Birmingham, UK.

Fischer, Moritz. 2020. "In and Uut of Africa: The Transnational Pentecostal Church Nzambe-Malamu, Its Migratory Entanglements and Its Missionary Strategy." *Missio Africanus: Journal of African Missiology* 5 (1).

Garrard, David John. 2003. "Art. Congo, Democratic Republic of." In *The New International Dictionary of Pentecostal and Charismatic Movements (NIDPCM)*, edited by Stanley M. Burgess and Eduard M. van der Maas, 67–74. Grand Rapids: Zondervan.

Pype, Katrien. 2012. *The Making of the Pentecostal Melodrama. Religion, Media, and Gender in Kinshasa*. New York/Oxford: Berghahn Books.

Moritz Fischer

Conversion

Though conversion is a common theme, there is not one unifying understanding of what signifies Pentecostal conversion. Recent scholarship has addressed Pentecostal conversion from a variety of theological, anthropological, and sociological perspectives, trying to define the phenomenon within a larger context of spirituality and religious conversion. Historically and theologically, Pentecostal conversion is linked to initiation-theologies of various waves of Pentecostalism with a key distinction between non-sacramental classical and neo-Pentecostals, and more sacramentally

Water baptism of a pentecostal pastor (Assemblies of God). Cancún, Quintana Roo. Photographer: Wikimedia, Rayttc (CC BY-SA)

oriented charismatic mainline, Catholic or Orthodox Christians. Recent research, however, reflects a need for even more nuanced and diversified categorizations of Pentecostalism with increasing sensitivity to contextual differences. As a social and cultural phenomenon, conversion represents a key dimension in order to understand the growth of global Pentecostalism by being the most important method through which Pentecostal beliefs and practices spread.

Embedded in their narrative hermeneutics, Pentecostals may draw from both Old and New Testament narratives for inspiration. In the New Testament, Luke-Acts represents a key model script for understanding Pentecostal conversion. With a literal, and yet experiential approach to reading and interpreting the Bible, Pentecostals often inscribe themselves into biblical conversion stories and view these as patterns to be followed in Christian everyday practices. For classical Pentecostals as well as neo-Pentecostals, Acts 2:38 and Paul's conversion experience on his way to Damascus are core texts. Oneness Pentecostals also see Acts as a prescriptive pattern for personal faith, but argues for the unity of the steps of repentance, water baptism, and Spirit-baptism for the constitution of salvation. Drawing upon an underlying understanding of a direct continuity between the early church and present day Christianity, conversion narratives from the Bible echo the experiential nature of Pentecostal faith and practice. By preaching and sharing contextualized versions of these narratives for one's own time and life situations, this larger conversion narrative continues to be spread transculturally in global Pentecostalism today.

From an anthropological perspective, Pentecostal conversion is often spoken of in terms of ritualized discontinuity (Robbins 2004), indicating a personal and cultural break with the past (Meyer 1998). This may involve a reorientation of worldview, social networks, spirituality, and ethics. Conversion does not remove the believer from spiritual or other life struggles, but rather empowers him or her for a victorious Christian life. Pentecostals also believe in societal transformation through conversion of individuals, and share with evangelicals an individualistic understanding of conversion in tradition of Puritan, revivalist and holiness ideas of personal religion and faith. Conversion usually entails a new/renewed commitment to a Pentecostal faith community. Pentecostals may speak of conversion as a transforming process and as a transforming event in terms of making a decisive and conscious decision to follow Christ. While there is no standardized pattern for conversion, there are some common key theological elements reflected in Pentecostal conversion narratives:

Pre-conversion conviction: The Spirit is active in the pre-conversion process of conviction (John 16:8), especially in contexts of preaching, evangelism, and prayer.

Repentance: Conviction leads to repentance, which essentially means to change one's mind, turn away from sin, and confess personal sins. Pentecostals often use sermons and outreach events as occasions for challenging people to respond to the 'call of salvation.'

Profession of faith: By asking people to come forward in a public altar call, or asking them to pray 'the sinner's prayer,' converts are invited to profess faith in Christ (Rom. 10:9) and thus be saved by accepting Christ as personal Lord and Savior.

Regeneration/new birth: On the basis of the salvific work of Christ and in response to the act of repentance, God brings about the divine supernatural work of regeneration and new birth. Many Pentecostals may here point to a specific date and time for having been 'born again' while others may point to a longer process of conversion.

Water baptism: Non-sacramental Pentecostals hold a baptistic view of water baptism. For most Pentecostals, baptism is practiced by full immersion and is a public personal symbolic act of faith and obedience, but which is not necessary for salvation.

A life of holiness: Through the new birth, the Spirit is given as indwelling agent of sanctification, leading the person into a life of holiness. Whereas the theme of victory over sin was an important theme in early and classical Pentecostalism, the theme of the victorious life is often referred to in global neo-Pentecostalism to emphasize victory and success also in material and social dimensions of life.

Recommitment: Pentecostals may call believers to recommit their lives to Christ if someone over time finds himself/herself on a notable distance from his/her faith commitment or church community.

For Pentecostals, conversion is a prerequisite for baptism of the Holy Spirit. Though Pentecostals at times speak of 'receiving the Spirit' in Spirit-baptism, Pentecostals believe they receive the indwelling Holy Spirit in the new birth. The baptism in the Holy Spirit is an experience subsequent to conversion but may potentially be experienced at any time after conversion as an empowering experience for Christian life and ministry. For most Pentecostals, Spirit-baptism is available to all converts, though interpretations of the normativity of Spirit-baptism differ in various strands of Pentecostalism, especially with regard to speaking in tongues. Following Acts 2 as an interpretive model, Pentecostals place themselves in a prophetic, eschatological and missiological era ushered in by the advent of the Spirit. By the coming of the Spirit upon "all flesh" (Acts 2: 14–17; Joel 2), many Pentecostals see themselves as part of an end time age of global evangelization, supernatural ministry and potential revival in which the conversion of many is possible. This connects Spirit-baptism with conversion both in terms of being a model and a focus for Pentecostal ministry.

Conversion is a strong mark of global Pentecostalism, highlighted in contemporary Pentecostal preaching, theologies and practices in the global south. Looking at the growth of neo-Pentecostal churches in Africa, Anderson (2015) ascribes much of the actual growth to the preaching of repentance and the need to be born again. Attending a Pentecostal crusade practically anywhere in the global south one will most likely witness hundreds of people running toward the alter when the invitation to accept Jesus as Lord and Savior is given. Large global Pentecostal denominations frequently hold up model conversion narratives of their founders or other leaders, and the number of recent converts are often used in order to boast the growth of a particular congregation. Due to a growing focus on the prosperity gospel within global Pentecostalism, conversion may represent a key to understand the appeal of the message, despite its radical consequences and focus on breaking with the past. The socioeconomic and spiritual experiences of many in the global south lead some scholars to see conversion as a path towards hope for improved material conditions, and a step towards mastery of one's personal and spiritual problems. Other scholars problematize an often seeming lack in lasting conversions after mass crusades, or that conversion becomes a public spectacle without root in existential realities of the individual. Some empirical studies, however, emphasize that the individual approach to conversion seems to empower the individual in terms of taking personal responsibility for his or her circumstances and destiny. By choosing to live for God (and break away from sin), the individual is committing her/himself to a new set of ideals and values which may help her/him to make strategic life choices.

Bibliography

Anderson, Allan Heaton. 2015. "'Stretching out Hands to God': Origins and Development of Pentecostalism in Africa." In *Pentecostalism in Africa: Presence and Impact of Pneumatic Christianity in Postcolonial Society*, edited by Martin Lindhardt, 54–74. Leiden: Brill.

Meyer, Birgit. 1998. "'Make a Complete Break with the Past.' Memory and Post-Colonial Modernity in Ghanaian Pentecostalist Discourse." *Journal of Religion in Africa* 28 (3): 316–349.

Milton, Grace. 2015. *Shalom, the Spirit and Pentecostal Conversion*. Leiden: Brill.

Robbins, Joel. 2004. "The Globalization of Pentecostal and Charismatic Christianity." *Annual Review of Anthropology* 33: 117–143.

Williams, J. Rodman. 1990. *Renewal Theology: Systematic Theology from a Charismatic Perspective. Salvation, the Holy Spirit, and Christian Living*. Grand Rapids, MI: Academy Books/Zondervan.

Young, Amos. 2005. *The Spirit Poured Out on All Flesh: Pentecostalism and the Possibility of Global Theology*. Grand Rapids, MI: Baker Academic.

Tomas Sundnes Drønen
Stian Sorlie Eriksen

Cook, Robert Felix

Robert Felix Cook (1880–1958) was one of the most effective North American Pentecostal missionaries in India. He was born in Los Angeles, California in 1879, to godly Christian parents who were Russian immigrants to the United States. His father was a lay preacher in a Baptist church and his mother was a praying woman. He came to a personal relationship with Christ at the age of twelve, and had received the call for ministry when he was fourteen.

From a young age Cook had a strong faith in healing and observed many healings as answers to prayer. His father was suffering from pneumonia to the point of death, but he was miraculously healed by the prayer of Cook. He and his wife Anna Cook were introduced to the Pentecostal experience in the Azusa Street Revival by his father. Their visit to the Mission in 1908 convinced them that speaking in tongues was a genuine experience. A few months later he received Spirit baptism while praying for his wife at his home. Then they were both convinced that the Lord had called them to serve overseas. They attended the first worldwide Pentecostal camp meeting in the spring of 1912. There they were motivated to go to India as missionaries after hearing the testimony of George Berg.

Robert and Anna Cook, with their two daughters, Blossom and Dorothy, traveled to India as independent missionaries. They reached Ootacamund, South India in October 1913. Then they moved to Bangalore and worked there for a few months. Their first prayer group was started among the Anglo-Indians and foreigners in 1914.

Motivated by Charles Cummine, an Anglo-Indian missionary and a native of Karnataka, Cook traveled to Tirunelveli (Tamil Nadu) in December 1913, and later in January 1914, he reached Kottarakkara, Kerala. Although he undertook a few evangelistic journeys to Kerala, he mainly lived in Bangalore, because of World War I. Meanwhile, Cook's wife died on August 31, 1917. He married another American Methodist missionary, Bertha Fox, in 1918, and continued his ministry. As the Pentecostal movement was taking momentum in Kerala, Cook decided to settle permanently in Kerala from 1921. He was traveling, preaching, and teaching the Pentecostal message in central Kerala, and subsequently a number of churches were formed. Although he came as an independent missionary, Cook joined the Assemblies of God (AG) in the USA in the 1920s when he met Mary Chapman, who was an AG missionary. However, he left the AG in 1929 at the insistence of indigenous leaders and later worked independently. Some indigenous Pentecostal churches formed the South India Full Gospel Church (SIFGC) under the leadership of Cook. The SIFGC later joined the newly formed indigenous church, the South Indian Pentecostal Church of God under K.E. Abraham, and formed the Malankara Full Gospel Church, with Cook as its president, and Abraham as vice-president. However, Abraham separated from Cook, and the SIFGC joined the Church of God (CoG, Cleveland, TN) in 1936, and was renamed as Church of God (Full Gospel) in India. CoG appointed him as the first Missionary Overseer of the Church of God (Full Gospel) in India, which he continued for the next 14 years, until he returned to the United States in 1950.

Cook's contribution to Indian Pentecostalism is important. First, his coming to India was one of the major reasons for the spreading of the Pentecostal message to South India, especially Kerala, which subsequently resulted the formation of many churches in central Kerala. Second, Cook became influential in the institutionalization of Pentecostalism in India. Some of the established Pentecostal churches, like the AG and CoG, began to take root in South India through the ministry of Cook. He also took initiative to purchase property for Pentecostal churches. Although through the work of Berg, the Thuvayur Church (Kerala) became the first Pentecostal church in India, Cook took effort to purchase a land and raised fund for constructing a church hall in 1920. He established Mt. Zion Bible Institute, one of the first Pentecostal Bible colleges in India. He started the Bible school at home to train local people to go to the mission field in Kottarakkara in 1922. Later, the school was moved to the newly built campus in Mount Zion, Mulakuzha, where a church and the headquarters of Cooks activities were located. Third, Cook played a crucial role of spreading the Pentecostal message among the Dalits, who responded actively when he began to work among them. While the indigenous Pentecostal ministers focused on the Syrian Christians, Cook concentrated on the Dalits. His work among the Dalits and their subsequent conversion was an essential factor behind the growth of Pentecostalism in Kerala in the early twentieth-century.

Bibliography

Bergunder, Michael. 2008. *The South Indian Pentecostal Movement in the Twentieth Century*. Grand Rapids: Eerdmans.

Cook, Robert F. 1955. *Half a Century of Divine Leading and 37 Years of Apostolic Achievements in South India*. Cleveland: Church of God Foreign Mission Department.

Cook, Robert F. 1938. *A Quarter Century of Divine Leading in India*. Chengannur, India: Church of God in India.

Morgan, L.F. 2002. "Cook Robert F." In *The New International Dictionary of Pentecostal and Charismatic Movements*, edited by Stanley M. Burgess and Eduard M. van der Maas, 305–306. Grand Rapids: Zondervan.

Philip, Mamman. 1997. *Robert F. Cook*. Vennukulam, India: Deepam Book Club.

Wessly Lukose

Cooper, Archibald

Archibald Cooper was a British sailor and soldier during the Anglo-Boer war (1899–1902). After the war he remained in South Africa as an agent in a shipping business (Anderson 2007). He was converted by Rodney Gipsy Smith (1860–1947), a British evangelist who came as a missionary to South Africa in 1905 (Hexham and Poewe-Hexham 2002). Upon his conversion he joined a Presbyterian church and congregated there for a while. During that time, he heard about William J. Seymour and the Azusa Street Revival through their publication, *Apostolic Faith* (Poewe 1988). He had a Pentecostal experience and received the baptism in the Holy Spirit in 1907 and started a church in Middlesbrough (George 2010).

Cooper heard about the arrival of John G. Lake and Thomas Hezmalhach who had come to South Africa in 1908 and founded the Apostolic Faith Mission (AFM). He immediately joined them and participated in their racially-integrated revival meetings which they had begun in Johannesburg. As Lake and Hezmalhach's services were similar to those in Azusa Street, Cooper was able to experience first-hand what he would have read in the *Apostolic Faith*. He was comfortable in these services because he was already familiar with the revival in Azusa Street (Hexham and Poewe-Hexham 2002). Cooper cooperated with Lake and Hezmalhalch for a while but after a year, he began to experience tensions with other leaders within AFM which led him to leave the church.

In 1909 the Bethel Pentecostal Assembly of Newark, New Jersey sent a missionary called George Bowie (a Scottish immigrant to the USA) to South Africa to start the Pentecostal Mission. Bowie had a colleague called Eleazer and in 1910 they both asked Cooper to join their ministry. At this point, the Pentecostal Mission was registered as a company in 1913 instead of a church. Unlike the mainline churches which had been recognized as religious bodies in South Africa for centuries, the Pentecostal phenomena was still new and the government was rather sceptical about it. Therefore, registering a church as a company was an easier way for some Pentecostal churches to have official recognition in South Africa. Unfortunately some congregants found this type of registration problematic and decided to break away. They formed their own church called Church of God. Cooper's church re-joined Bowie but split again in 1916 (Resane 1994). In 1921 Bowie and Cooper made amends but Cooper's church joined a conglomerate of churches called the Churche(s) of God. Before that, Cooper, held numerous tent meetings in Durban for nearly three decades (Poewe 1988). In 1921 the Pentecostal Mission and the Church of God reunited and called themselves Full Gospel Church (FGC). Over the years, numerous attempts were made to unite the AFM and the FGC. However, they clashed over differences regarding baptism and governance of their local churches. While the FGC practised single immersion, the AFM saw triple baptism as more biblical. Both were unwilling to compromise. Moreover, FGC local congregations were managed loosely and enjoyed more autonomy, in comparison to AFM congregations which were managed centrally and had less autonomy. The FGC is recognized as the largest Christian denomination among the Indian population in South Africa.

In March 1951 the Full Gospel Church (which was the largest Pentecostal group in South Africa at that time) and the Church of God in Cleveland, U.S. amalgamated to form the Full Gospel Church of God. Cooper is historically known to have been one of the pioneers of this activity with especially Afrikaner farmers in Middelburg (Anderson 2007). While it is said that this church did not grow quickly among black Africans as the legislative body was mainly white, Cooper was also recorded to have had an impact on the growth of the Pentecostal movement among the Zulu's of Natal and the Chinese in the Rand. Poewe argues that present day, some white Pentecostals and Neo-Pentecostals in South Africa also trace their historical links to Cooper (Poewe 1988).

Bibliography

Anderson, Allan. 2007. *Spreading Fires: The Missionary Nature of Early Pentecostalism*. London: SCM Press.

George, Bill. 2010. *Until All Have Heard: The Centennial History of Church of God World Missions*. Cleveland TN: Pathway Press.

Hexham, I., and Poewe-Hexham, K. 2002. "South Africa." In *International Dictionary of Pentecostal and Charismatic Movements*, edited by Stanley M. Burgess and Eduard M. Van der Maas, 227–238. Grand Rapids: Zondervan.

Poewe, Karla. 1988. "Links and Parallels Between Black and White Charismatic Churches in South Africa and the States: Potential for Cultural Transformation." *The Journal of the Society of Pentecostal Studies* 10 (2): 141–58.

Resane, Kelebogile T. 2018. "Pentecostals and Apartheid: Has the Wheel Turned around Since 1994?" *In die Skriflig* 52 (1): 1–8. https://dx.doi.org/10.4102/ids.v52i1.2324.

Naar M'fundisi-Holloway

Coote, Leonard Wren

Leonard Wren Coote (1891–1969) was born on April 22 in Enfield in North London, England to Ernest and Emma Elizabeth Coote. He was raised in the Methodist tradition. He studied at a private commercial school and worked for a few years as a stenographer. In October 1913, at the age of 22, Coote came to Kobe, Japan as a businessman working for Lever Brothers, a British soap manufacturer. Despite being a nominal Christian, he lived in a missionary home under the auspices of the Japan Evangelistic Band managed by J.B. Thornton.

Under the influence of Thornton and other Christians in Kobe, Coote decided to commit himself to Christ and was baptized on February 20, 1914. Mary Taylor, who had just come back to Japan as a missionary of the Pentecostal Missionary Union from the UK, was one of those who helped Coote become a born-again Christian. When Coote was seeking Spirit baptism, he regularly visited the Taylors.

Eventually Coote was baptized by the Spirit at the Taylors on November 19, 1917. He then felt called to ministry and resigned from his job on September 30, 1918. He had planned to do mission in the Belgian Congo, but his ship was cancelled due to the outbreak of World War I. Coote decided to wait for God's message and while praying at the Taylors', he heard God speaking to him, "Coote, Japan and Pentecost until Jesus comes." He thus remained in Japan.

Coote was invited to assist the Pentecostal missionaries in Japan. In the end of September 1918, he settled down in Tokyo to help Frank and May Gray, a missionary couple from the Upper Room Mission in Los Angeles.

Coote met Esther Inone Keene who was a member of W.H. Offiler's Bethel Temple in Seattle and assisted Mary Taylor in Kobe. Coote and Keene got married in 1920 and lived in Yokohama, where he was instrumental in one of the first strong Pentecostal outpourings recorded in Japan. However, his successful ministry there was destroyed by the Kanto Great Earthquake on September 1, 1923. He headed for Osaka with several of his followers.

Coote seemed indifferent to theological arguments and kept his relationships with both the Oneness and Trinitarian Pentecostal groups. Coote was regarded as part of the "Assembly of God" in Japan in 1919 and 1920. However, when a new generation of missionaries of American AG arrived in Japan in 1919 and founded the Japan District in the following year, Coote decided to work independently. He was affiliated with the Pentecostal Band in 1926 and Pentecostal Assemblies of the World from 1927 to 1929. In 1929, he started his own Japan Pentecostal Church (Nihon Pentekosute Kyokai) and the Japan Apostolic Mission.

Coote was introduced to the Apostolic Church in Britain in 1932 and connected with the Apostolic Church in New Zealand and Australia. They worked together for a period of time until the doctrinal issue arose about Coote's understanding of the Trinity and the name of Jesus at water baptism in 1938.

In 1924 Coote bought land in Nara and founded Ikoma Bible School (Ikoma Seisho Gakuin) in 1931. His ministry spread across Kyoto, Osaka, and Nara. A few Korean students studied at Coote's school and their work among Korean immigrants in Osaka grew significantly in the 1930s. Coote tried to establish the Korea Apostolic Full Gospel Bible School and a headquarters in Seoul in 1936 but failed.

From 1926, over 20 foreign Pentecostal missionaries who had known of his work from the widely circulated *Japan and Pentecost* visited him in Nara, including both independent and denominational Pentecostal missionaries from the U.S., New Zealand, Australia, Canada, and Britain. Many subsequently started their own ministries in Japan.

Coote went to the U.S. before the outbreak of World War II and arrived in Los Angeles on November 11, 1939. After a brief stay in Seattle, he moved to San Antonio, Texas, where he started the Emmanuel Church in 1941 and the International Bible College in 1942. He stayed in the U.S. during the War. His Bible School in Nara was closed during the war and the building was confiscated by the Japanese Army.

Several of his Korean students returned to Korea before the war, started ministries, and founded Chosŏn Pentecostal Church (Chosŏn Osunjŏl Kyohoe), a Oneness Pentecostal group. Their ministry grew and Oneness Pentecostals outnumbered the Trinitarian Pentecostals in the early post-war period. Coote restarted his ministry in Korea and opened the South Korean Central Bible School and Taejŏn Evangelist Tabernacle on the eastern outskirts of Taejŏn in April 1958.

Coote came back to Japan in 1950 as a United Pentecostal Church missionary and restarted the Bible School in Nara. Coote and Jun Murai of the Spirit of Jesus Church and Jun Nukida of the United Pentecostal Church worked together on the basis of their Oneness theology, but soon this coalition dissolved. Coote ran his Japan Apostolic Mission and Japan Pentecostal Church. He erected Osaka Tabernacle in 1951 and held meetings every day.

After the War many Pentecostal missionaries returned to Japan to work with Coote, but many of them subsequently started their own ministries. His students also established their own Pentecostal organizations after their graduation, such as Japan Evangelical Church, Next Towns Crusade, Total Christian Church Group, and the Flock of the Gospel of Jesus Christ.

Coote left Japan in 1967 and went back to San Antonio. Having lost his wife on July 19, 1962, Coote remarried a widow, Frances Mary Dodds on January 4, 1968. He died in San Antonio on February 22, 1969

Bibliography

Aoki, Yasunori. 2011. "Coote Family: The History of Oneness Pentecostalism 'United Pentecostal Church in Japan' and Pentecostal Mission Board 'Next Towns Crusade.'" Presented at the 40th Annual Meeting of the Society for Pentecostal Studies, Memphis, TN, March 10–12.

Choi, Jay Woong. 2017. "The Origins And Development Of Korean Classical Pentecostalism (1930–1962)." PhD diss., Fuller Theological Seminary.

Coote, Leonard W. 1991. *Impossibilities Become Challenges*, Fifth Edition. San Antonio, TX: Church Alive! Press.

Shew, Paul Tsuchido. 2004. "Leonard Coote and Early Pentecostal Missions in Japan." Presented at the 33rd Annual Meeting of the Society for Pentecostal Studies, Marquette University, Milwaukee, WI, March 11–13.

Suzuki, Masakazu. 2011. "The Origins and the Development of the Japan Assemblies of God: The Foreign and Japanese Workers and Their Ministries (1907 to 1975)." PhD diss., Bangor University.

Masakazu Suzuki

Copeland, Kenneth

Kenneth Copeland was born in Texas in 1936. He turned to Christianity in 1962 and attended Oral Roberts University in 1967. Within months, Copeland began Kenneth Copeland Ministries (KCM, originally the Kenneth Copeland Evangelistic Association). It was led by Copeland, his wife Gloria, and various family members and continues to flourish to this day. He describes its mission as "to minister the Word of Faith, by teaching believers who they are in Christ Jesus; taking them from the milk of the Word to the meat, and from religion to reality" (Kenneth Copeland Ministries, n.d.). KCM organizes regular conventions, offers daily television broadcasts, runs an academy, and publishes a free monthly magazine, *Believer's Voice of Victory*, since 1973.

Copeland's teaching is known for its focus on positive confession of faith in God's promises resulting in prosperity and health for those who believe. However, these are practical consequences of Copeland's underlying worldview evident in his theology, satanology, and anthropology. Copeland's theology is trinitarian, albeit in an implicit and unnuanced form. The creator God is personal, righteous, and all-powerful. God is both loving and just. In terms of Copeland's christology, he holds to an incarnationalism that is, in functional terms, highly kenotic. Copeland's

Kenneth and Gloria Copeland hosting the Believer's Voice of Victory television broadcast in 2011. Source: Eagle Mountain International Church Inc. aka Kenneth Copeland Ministries

markedly dualistic worldview is visible in his "high" satanology: he writes of satan with remarkable frequency, and ascribes surprising authority to satan, viewing this being as a fallen angel.

In turn, Copeland's anthropology is as follows: humans were created to share God's nature, and were thereby entitled to victory, prosperity, peace, and health. They were to rule over angels. It is also noteworthy that Copeland's trichotomous anthropology is compartmentalized and strictly pneumocentric ("you *are* a spirit, you *have* a soul, and you *live in* a body"). In Copeland's teaching, satan successfully stole humanity's legacy through the "fall," in which the first humans committed "high treason," plunging them into "spiritual death." Satan thus achieved rights of ownership over humans, which God had to win back. Starting with Abraham, God entered covenants with believing humans that provided God's and humanity's routes back to each other. The crux of this covenantal remedy was the substitutionary death and resurrection of Jesus. The death was primarily spiritual, while also physical. In this "spiritual death," which lasted the three days until his resurrection, Jesus was separated from God and was satan's prey, sharing the satanic nature (Atkinson 2009).

In his resurrection, however, Jesus won back from satan the rights to ownership of humans. By personal faith in Jesus and the declarations of the Bible, those who choose to follow Jesus and walk the path of victory are "born again" into life as God intended, partaking once again in God's nature, with access to physical health, prosperity in material and broader terms, sensitivity to the guidance of God's Spirit, and success in following God's "master plan" for one's life. While this life will be followed by eternal life thereafter, Copeland offers an unusually realized eschatology that focuses on this life's blessings, with little mention of the life to come.

Copeland's teaching will be recognizable to many as sitting firmly within the variously-called "Word of Faith," "Word-Faith," or simply "Faith" movement. Indeed, his stance deserves to be regarded as its epitome, and, since Kenneth Hagin's death in 2003, Copeland wears the informal mantle as the movement's leader. In common with much of Pentecostalism, the movement can be described accurately as fundamentalist with regard to its reading of the Christian scriptures and charismatic with regard to God's activity among people today. As its various names indicate, Word of Faith teaching such as that offered by Copeland also expresses a highly faith-filled attitude towards the accessibility of divine promises to those who believe and declare God's words.

On the surface, Copeland's teaching is derived from the Christian scriptures. However, he has written of the influence of Oral Roberts and Kenneth Hagin on his views. The voice of E.W. Kenyon, perhaps partly through that of Hagin, is also audible in his work. In turn, Copeland's "health and wealth" teaching is highly influential. It is to be found disseminated in Pentecostal and independent charismatic circles around the globe. In particular, observers note the pervasion of the Word of Faith teaching of Copeland and others in sub-Saharan Africa (Komolafe 2013). Copeland's ministry has proved highly controversial in various respects. Responses to his views have in turn often been highly polarized. In particular, some critics have labeled his views as "heretical," "cultic," and "occult" (Hanegraaff 1997, 33). On the other hand, some observers point out significant degrees of commonality between his teaching and broader aspects of Pentecostalism in particular, and Christianity in general (King 2008).

Bibliography

Atkinson, William P. 2009. *The "Spiritual Death" of Jesus: A Pentecostal Investigation.* Leiden: Brill.

Hanegraaff, Hank. 1993, 1997. *Christianity in Crisis.* Eugene, OR: Harvest House Publishers.

Kenneth Copeland Ministries. n.d. "Kenneth Copeland Ministries: About Us." Accessed March 29, 2019. https://www.kcm.org/about-us.

King, Paul L. 2008. *Only Believe: Examining the Origin and Development of Classic and Contemporary Word of Faith Theologies.* Tulsa, OK: Word & Spirit Press.

Komolafe, Sunday Jide. 2013. *The Transformation of African Christianity.* Carlisle: Langham Monographs.

William P. Atkinson

Cosmology

Cosmology, in its religious/philosophical sense, refers to an understanding of unseen or spiritual aspects of the universe. It is an aspect of worldview that deals with cosmic powers. A literalistic understanding of the spirit world is especially apparent in Pentecostalism, which affirms the reality of angels, demons, and the power of the Holy Spirit. In anthropological terms, Pentecostals could be characterized as having an enchanted worldview.

From its inception, Pentecostalism has emphasized tangible spiritual experience, including baptism in the Holy Spirit, glossolalia, divine healing, deliverance, and other signs and wonders. Oral testimony is a key feature, but claims detailing encounters with the spirit world are near-impossible to verify. Pentecostals revere the Bible and tend to interpret cosmological texts in a literal manner. Creation is suffused with spirit, and spiritual power can be accessed. Indeed, Spirit baptism increases awareness of the unseen world. The Church's mission is to proclaim Christ's triumph over evil powers. Cosmic dualism, in terms of "good and evil" and the "already-but-not-yet" kingdom of God, is sometimes exaggerated in Pentecostal piety, leading to beliefs and action with respect to a cosmic struggle, based on Eph. 6:10–20 and commonly termed spiritual warfare.

Literalistic cosmological views are especially prominent in the Global South. Traditional African religion, for example, affirms the reality of multiple spirits that influence all aspects of daily life. Pentecostal practices are therefore easily adopted in cultures that have a strong belief in nonmaterial realities. Troublesome spirits are reclassified as demons, and subsequently expelled when these cultures adopt Pentecostal Christianity.

There is little philosophical speculation on the problem of evil (although Pentecostals generally follow the Wesleyan emphasis on free will). Instead the approach is more existential, with a focus on overcoming evil through the power of the resurrected Christ. Because some sickness and suffering is seen as caused by evil spirits, spiritual sanctification and renewal is important. Prayer and deliverance are also proclaimed as solutions to evil.

Generally, Pentecostal cosmology includes the topics of heaven, hell, angels, demons, demonization, discernment and deliverance. In keeping with cosmic dualism (e.g. Lk 10:15), Pentecostals tend to view heaven as the dwelling place of God and his angels, and the eternal spiritual destination of the saved; hell is where the devil rules (and some demons are bound; 2 Pet 2:4) and is the destination of the damned. This is apparent in the North American evangelistic drama "Heaven's Gates and Hell's Flames," in which choice is presented between being with a literal Satan in a red-tinged hell or a white-robed Jesus in heaven surrounded by angels.

Although biblical terms are used fluidly, metaphorically, and sometimes ambiguously, Pentecostals emphasize heaven as an actual place (e.g. Mt 6:9, 20), and seldom consider the paradox of heaven as afterlife and heaven on earth. Hell is viewed as a literal place of eternal torment (e.g. Mt 13:42; Lk 16:23). Sometimes the heavenly realms are considered synonymously with the spirit world. Events here can parallel events on earth (dramatized in Frank Peretti's popular novels); prayer can affect spiritual realms (Riddell and Riddell 2007).

Pentecostals generally assign full ontological status to spiritual beings (Collins 2009). Biblically, angels function as messengers (e.g. Gen 16:7–11, Mt 28:2–7), worshipers (Ps 148:2; Heb 1:6), and judges (Mk 8:38; Acts 12:23). Pentecostals often emphasize their role in guidance and protection (e.g. Acts 8:26, 10:22, Heb 1:14). There are many anecdotal reports of angelic visitations (e.g. William Branham reported receiving powers of discernment from an angel). Glossolalia is sometimes referred to as the "tongues of angels," and speculations include angelic associations with UFOs, and "heavenly portals" through which angels descend.

Biblical terms for evil spirits are often ambiguous and polysemic: Satan/Beelzebul/devil/anti-Christ, demon/unclean spirit/evil spirit, and powers/principalities/spiritual forces are three such clusters, the last used primarily by Paul. They are enemies of God and his good creation (Mt 13:25–28) and appear to have superhuman strength (Mk 5:4; Lk 8:29) and abilities. They originated most likely from angelic rebellion (Rev 12:7) and their defeat is assured (Heb 2:14; Rev 20:10). Pentecostals often refer to an evil kingdom headed by Satan and composed of myriad demons (Kraft 1992). Some have also proposed cosmic-level principalities that rule over places and social structures (Wagner 1996). These powers of evil are in conflict with the kingdom of God, and seek to harm humans and disrupt God's plans. There are anecdotal reports of visualizing evil spirits as shadowy forms with green eyes, speculations such as an association between demons and rock concerts and complex categorizations of spirits, that may reflect specific contexts (e.g. ancestral spirits, nature spirits, and spirits of the occult, trauma, poverty, violence or sin).

The Gospels attest that evil spirits can "enter" people (Mk 1:23–26, 5:1–20; 9:14–29), causing physical and mental torment and disabilities (Mk 9:25, Lk 13:16). The term *daimonizomai*, literally "having a demon," is used. In Pentecostal Christianity there has been debate regarding terminology. Many argue that "demonization" is preferable to "possession," because the latter implies that Christians can be completely controlled or owned by an evil spirit, but the issue is not settled and tends to be contextually determined (e.g. some Africans believe ancestral spirits can possess people). Reports describe afflicted people as exhibiting bizarre behavior and extreme emotions (Riddell and Riddell 2007; Collins 2009). There is controversy regarding the prevalence of demonization and the degree of influence demons have. Many believe that people are susceptible to demonization as a result of sin, especially occult involvement and illicit sexual practices, which provides an "entry point" for evil spirits. Some suggest that demonization can be caused by generational sin and curses, spells and hexes are particularly prominent in some regions (such as parts of Africa), and some believe that inanimate objects, places, and geographical regions can be afflicted. This last has led to prayer marches and "strategic-level-spiritual-warfare" (Wagner 1996).

With respect to detection of demons, some suggest diagnostic lists (e.g. compulsive desires to curse God, revulsion against the Bible, suicidal or murderous thoughts, extreme moods, enslaving habits, compulsive temptations, and sensations like dizziness or choking). Many people claim to have discernment gifts (following 1 Cor 12:10), such as visualizing or smelling demons, testing air currents with fingers, or a mystical perception. Discernment is considered to be both natural and supernatural (e.g. a "word from the Lord"). Most note that it is important to distinguish between mental illness and demonization.

Jesus's earthly ministry included expelling demons from afflicted people (partly to demonstrate his messianic role and the arrival of God's kingdom). He gave his disciples authority to continue this mission (Mt 10:1, 8; Mk 16:17). The concepts of salvation, healing, and deliverance are closely related; for example, in the story of the Gerasene demoniac (Lk 8:26–39), the man is "healed," sits at Jesus's feet, then proclaims the Gospel. Multiple biblical terms are used to denote setting someone free from the influence of evil spirits. In Pentecostal ministry, deliverance is commonly practiced along with healing (especially when there is a belief that illness has demonic origin). Techniques have cultural variations but there are some common patterns (Kraft 1992; Collins 2009). In some contexts, such as the Global South, demons that are manifesting are expelled before any confession or counseling can occur. In the North American context, many practitioners encourage a team approach, with prayerful preparation, and professional counseling if available. Typically, demonized people are asked to affirm their faith, confess, repent, and forgive as needed. The minister then, through the authority of Christ, binds and expels the demons, often one by one. The session concludes with prayer, emphasizing being filled with the Holy Spirit. Liturgies often include an imperative such as, "In the name of Christ, I command you, spirit of (name) to leave." They may include laying on of hands and anointing with oil.

There are dramatic reports, not necessarily normative, of loud and long sessions, involving power encounters between the deliverance practitioner(s) and evil spirits, including demonic manifestations such as throwing objects, pseudo-seizures, and foaming at the mouth. There are some idiosyncratic theories (e.g. discovering the name and rank of each demon, encouraging coughing in case a demon is lodged in the throat), and group deliverance has been performed at large meetings. In Pentecostal mission, deliverance is often a route to conversion.

Although belief in the reality of the spirit world and the practice of deliverance is likely to remain, contemporary Pentecostal scholarship (including increasing contributions from the Global South) takes a more moderate, nuanced view of cosmology. There is recognition of the influence of politics, economics, gender oppression, and psychological factors in spiritual warfare. And there are alternate biblical interpretations being proposed that offer a *via media* between literalism and demythologization. For example, some use scientific models to suggest that spirits are emergent phenomena; as such, they have causal influence but are irreducible to the lower-level substrates from which they emerged (e.g. human minds) (Yong 2011). The increased use of audiovisual and social media is also likely to influence trends in Pentecostal Cosmology.

Bibliography

Collins, James M. 2009. *Exorcism and Deliverance Ministry in the Twentieth Century: An Analysis of the Practice and Theology of Exorcism in Modern Western Christianity.* Milton Keynes: Paternoster.

Kraft, Charles. 1992. *Defeating Dark Angels: Breaking Demonic Oppression in the Believer's Life.* Ann Arbor: Servant.

Riddell, Peter G., and Beverly Smith Riddell, eds. 2007. *Angels and Demons: Perspectives and Practice in Diverse Religious Traditions.* Nottingham: Apollos/IVP.

Wagner, C. Peter. 1996. *Confronting the Powers: How the New Testament Church Experienced the Power of Strategic-level Spiritual Warfare.* Ventura, CA: Regal,

Yong, Amos. 2011. *The Spirit of Creation: Modern Science and Divine Action in the Pentecostal-Charismatic Imagination.* Grand Rapids: Eerdmans.

E. Janet Warren

Côte d'Ivoire

The origins of Ivorian Pentecostal and Charismatic Christianity may be traced back to the Liberian Episcopalian evangelist William Wadé Harris (1860–1929), who toured the country with a gospel of modernity and prosperity in 1913–14, converting more than a hundred thousand Africans. Classic Pentecostal churches such as the Assemblies of God and the evangelical Christian and Missionary Alliance spread from the 1930s. The Harrist church was soon followed by other prophetic movements, which have held a prominent place in the Ivorian religious landscape throughout the last century. Prophets such as Papa Nouveau, Marie Lalou, Koudou Jeannot,

Kacou Séverin and Moïse Koré inspired and influenced the neo-Pentecostal and charismatic movement of the 1990s and 2000s (Dozon 1995). Ever since independence, Ivorian political leaders cultivated close links with Pentecostal and prophetic movements and in turn men and women of God embraced the doctrine of political leaders by tying their religious projects to a nationalist, developmental or anti-hegemonic agenda (Dozon 1995; Mary 2002). It is thus not surprising, that PCC played a major role during the Ivorian civil war (2002–11), which was imagined as an apocalyptic war of resurrection against (Muslim) evil and neo-colonialism. Laurent Gbagbo was hailed as the nation's first born-again president who would help Côte d'Ivoire to emerge as a nation baptized in Christ (Miran-Guyon 2015; N'Guessan 2015).

Today, the religious landscape in Côte d'Ivoire comprises of about 34 percent Christians, 43 percent Muslim, 4 percent "traditional" religion adherents and 19 percent "other" (according to the 2014 general census). The large majority of Ivorian Christians are Roman Catholic. Among the PCC churches active in Côte d'Ivoire are classical Pentecostal denominations such as the Assemblies of God, International Foursquare Church, and the Church of Pentecost, Ivorian branches of global neo-charismatic churches such as the Nigerian-founded Mountain of Fire & Miracles Ministries, the Brazilian-founded Universal Church of the Kingdom of God and the Shekina Glory Ministries (founded in Montréal, Canada), but also smaller Ivorian churches such as Kacou Sévérin's Ministry of the Power of the Gospel.

A rather recent development in the field of Pentecostal and charismatic spirituality arose since the 1990s, when a new generation of self-proclaimed prophets, bishops, evangelists, and apostles started to preach in markets and on street corners or in the backyards of their own houses and eventually founded their own church. In the context of the socio-economic crisis and the democratic and anti-establishment renewal in the realm of politics and religion, Pentecostal and Charismatic spirituality served as a stage upon which new forms of self-recognition, social relations and entrepreneurship were enacted. As elsewhere on the continent, the new wave focused on the prosperity gospel, healing and deliverance and prophecies that often alluded to the social and political day-to-day realities of a predominantly young, educated and urban audience (Guibléhon 2011; Newell 2007).

PCC churches are most active and visible in the urban centers of Côte d'Ivoire, where they dominate the visibility of Christianity in general and thus contribute to a Pentecostalization of the public sphere through popular media, political discourse, and "Pentecostalized" mainstream Christianity (Newell 2007). They can also be found in rural areas, where classical Pentecostal churches such as the Assemblies of God have large number of adherents, as well as prophetic movements and Pentecostal deliverance or prayer camps whose genealogy may be traced back to the "therapeutic villages" of healer-prophets such as Albert Atcho and Marie Lalou (Guibléhon 2011).

Bibliography

Dozon, Jean-Pierre. 1995. *La Cause des Prophètes: Politique et Religion en Afrique Contemporaine*. Paris: Editions du Seuil.

Guiblehon, Bony. 2011. *Le Pouvoir-Faire: Religion, Politique, Ethnicité et Guérison en Côte d'Ivoire*. Paris: L'Harmattan.

Miran-Guyon, Marie. 2015. *Guerres Mystiques en Côte d'Ivoire. Religion, Patriotisme, Violence (2002–2013)*. Paris, Karthala.

Newell, Sasha. 2007. "Pentecostal Witchcraft: Neoliberal Possession and Demonic Discourse in Ivoirian Pentecostal Churches." *Journal of Religion in Africa* 37: 461–490.

N'Guessan, Konstanze. 2015. "Pentecostalism, Politics and Performances of the Past in Côte d'Ivoire." *Nova Religio* 18 (3): 80–100.

Konstanze N'Guessan

Cuba

The original presence of Pentecostalism in Cuba can be traced back to the arrival of missionaries from Canada, Jamaica, Puerto Rico and the USA, although there were also autochthonous denominational groups. The historical development of Pentecostalism in Cuba can be divided into three key crucial moments: 1) its inception and subsequent explosion (1930s–1958), 2) during and after the Revolution (1959–1989), and 3) from the "special period" on (1990–present).

In the 1920s the Jamaican missionary Irene Tylor started a mission to form the Iglesia de Dios. Also, Anna Sanders (Canada), Harriet May Kelty (USA), and Francisco Rodríguez Agosto (Puerto Rico) were sent to Cuba, by the Assemblies of God, USA in 1930, with the intent of starting a mission on the island. This mission came to be called Iglesia Evangélica Pentecostal.

A number of groups and offshoots, both foreign and autochthonous, emerged during the following two decades. In the 1940s, Francisco Rodríguez decided to separate from the Iglesia Evangélica Pentecostal and founded his own denomination: the Primera Iglesia Pentecostal in Cuba. He was the first non-Anglo pastor to found a Pentecostal church in Cuba. Subsequently, Rodríguez established a relationship with Aimee Semple McPherson's Foursquare Church, but by 1951 he had returned to the Primera Iglesia Pentecostal. In 1956 Luis M. Ortíz split from the Iglesia Evangélica Pentecostal and joined Puerto Rican Avelino González, in an attempt to reject foreign leadership. Together they formed the Iglesia Cristiana Pentecostal.

As a result of two evangelistic campaigns in 1934, the Iglesia Evangélica Libre was born, though it did not adopt the Pentecostal confession until 1975. Almost at the same time, the Iglesia de la Fe Apostólica was also born. Soon thereafter, during the 1940s, the following churches emerged: the Iglesia Pentecostal in Cuba, the Iglesia de Dios el Evangelio Completo, the Iglesia de Dios de la Profecía, the Iglesia Biblia Abierta, the Iglesia Evangélica Monte Sinaí, and the Iglesia Evangélica Bethel. This last one was founded by Sixto López and Regla María Salmerón. And in the 1950s, the Iglesia Evangélica Santa Pentecostés, the Iglesia Liga Evangélica de Cuba, Iglesia Evangélica Getsemaní, the Hermandad Cristiana Agraria de Cuba, the Iglesia Misionera de Dios, the Iglesia Cristiana Evangélica Pentecostal, the Iglesia Evangélica Pentecostal Luz del Mundo (1957), the Iglesia de Dios en Cristo Jesús (1951), and Iglesia de Jesucristo Libre (1956) were formed.

After the Revolution of 1959, foreign missionaries were forced to leave (1961); many Cuban church leaders and pastors from all Christian denominations, including Pentecostals, followed suit. Foreign church leaders were quickly replaced by Cuban leaders. As a result, Cuba did not enjoy the rapid growth experienced by the rest of Latin America during the 1970s. Nevertheless, Pentecostal communities continued to populate the Cuban religious landscape. During the 1960–1970s, the

Iglesia Congregacional Pentecostal, the Iglesia de Dios Ortodoxa, and the Iglesia Misionera Amplias Mundiales were registered officially as Pentecostal denominations, and the Congregación Pentecostal was established. By the end of the 1960s, seven independent groups joined and formed La Iglesia Evangélica Pentecostal, Las Buenas Nuevas.

With the collapse of the Soviet Union, Cuba was plunged into what is commonly known as a "special period in time of peace," characterized by enormous basic needs, and which lasted a decade. Due to a variety of factors, including especially foreign aid, during the 1990s there was a revival in the entire Cuban religious landscape. Catholics, mainline Protestants, and other religious traditions saw an increase in followers. Pentecostals also grew exponentially, especially because of the formation of house churches. Today, out of the fifty-four denominational groups, twenty-five are registered as being Pentecostal.

There are some unique aspects to Cuban Pentecostalism. It is a young movement. Studies show that 60 percent of all Pentecostals are below the age of forty and that 78 percent are new converts; many of those are from another Christian tradition. Also, since the late 1960s, Pentecostal groups have been active members of the Cuban ecumenical movement. As a result, many Cuban Pentecostals have a strong involvement in issues of social justice. Often, some Pentecostals cite the example of Francisco Martínez Luis, an Afro-Cuban Pentecostal who joined the social struggle and enlisted in the Revolutionary Army.

Mainstream Protestants and Catholics have also been impacted by Pentecostalism. Since the house churches made Pentecostalism in Cuba, some Catholic communities across the country have adopted Pentecostal-charismatic practices. It is not uncommon to go to a Catholic mass, and Episcopalian and Presbyterian services and find liturgical styles and music which resemble Pentecostal expressions. Much like what Bernardo Campos calls the Pentecostalization of the church, Mainline and Catholic churches reflect this move toward charismatic worship.

Pentecostalism is undergoing a profound reconfiguration in Cuba. Women have started to reject their subordinate role and are reclaiming their role as agents and leaders in the church. As new and foreign doctrines are being imported (holy vomit, holy laughter, and prosperity gospel), Pentecostalism is being forced to reinvent itself on the Cuban soil. These new doctrines are raising key questions of what it means to be led by the Spirit.

Bibliography

Arce Martínez, Sergio. 1997. "Las iglesias pentecostales y los movimientos carismáticos en Cuba desde una perspectiva cubana." In *Carismatismo en Cuba*, edited by Reinerio Arce Valentín, and Manuel Quintero, compiled by Elizabeth Carrillo, 153–73. Cuba: Departamento de Comunicaciones del Consejo Latinoamericano de Iglesias.

Batista, Israel. 1997. "Del carismatismo revolucionario al carismatismo pentecostal." In *Carismatismo en Cuba*, edited by Reinerio Arce Valentín, and Manuel Quintero, compiled by Elizabeth Carrillo, 135–151. La Habana: Ediciones CLAI.

Berges Curbelo, Juana. 2008. *Pentecostalismo en Cuba: ¿Alienación o compromiso social?* Mexico DF: Publicaciones para el Estudio Científico de las Religiones.

Carrillo García, Elizabeth. 1997. "Renovación carismática en las iglesias protestantes históricas en Cuba." In *Carismatismo en Cuba*, edited by Reinerio Arce Valentín, and Manuele Quintero, compiled by Elizabeth Carrillo, 47–86. La Habana: Ediciones CLAI.

Cepeda Clemente, Rafael, Elizabeth Carrillo García, Rhode González Zorrilla, and Carlos Ham Stanard. 1995. "Causas y desafíos de las iglesias protestantes en Cuba: La influencia del movimiento pentecostal." In *En la fuerza del Espíritu: Los Pentecostales en América Latina: Un desafío a las iglesias históricas*, edited by Benjamín F. Gutiérrez, 141–74. Guatemala: Centro Evangélico Latinoamericano de Estudios Pastorales; Asociación de Iglesias Presbiterianas y Reformadas en América Latina.

Márquez Delgado, Luciano. 1997. "El Carismatismo: ¿Qué es y qué tenemos que ver con eso?" In *Carismatismo en Cuba*, edited by Reinerio Arce Valentín, and Manuele Quintero, compiled by Elizabeth Carrillo, 107–114. La Habana: Ediciones CLAI.

Medina, Néstor, and Ary Fernández-Albán. 2018. "Christianity in Cuba." In *Encyclopedia of Christianity in the Global South*, edited by Mark A. Lamport, with an introduction by Philip Jenkins, with a foreword by Katalina Tahaafe-Williams, with an afterword by Justin Welby, et al. Landham: Rowman & Littlefield Publishers.

Tabares Espinoza, Rodhe Esther. 2000. "Mujer y Pentecostalismo en Cuba." Unpublished Bachelor's thesis, Matanzas, Cuba, Seminario Evangélico de Teología.

Néstor Medina

Czech Republic

The Pentecostal movement first emerged in the region in 1910. The Association of Resolute Christians was founded by Jan Kajfosz in the region of Těšín (Czech Silesia), Nebory and Dolní Žukov. It originated from the Silesian Evangelical Church of the Augsburg Confession, where glossolalia and other gifts of the Holy Spirit appeared among the labourers and miners.

Another focus of the Pentecostal movement was in Prague in the Free Reformed Church (Svobodná církev reformovaná), now called Brethren Church (Církev bratrská), with some influence from Germany. This led to a tension in the churches, which eventually caused nineteen members to leave. Subsequently on 15 May 1908, they founded the 'Tábor Life-Saving Association' (Záchranný spolek Tábor) and another group formed in Úvaly, near Prague.

After WWI, attempts to reunite Pentecostal churches in Prague and Úvaly within the Unity of the Brethren Church (Jednota českobratrská) were thwarted due to the influence of Josef Novák, who came from Ukraine and who was in contact with German pastor Jonathan Paul known for his controversial teaching.

In the 1920s, Pentecostal churches emerged in other towns such as Kolín, Čáslav, Havlíčkův Brod, and Klatovy. The Pentecostal movement in the Czech Republic experienced some growth, with limits due to the political context. Newly founded Pentecostal churches, however, did not register during the interwar period, which turned out to be a fatal mistake in the subsequent Communist era (Brenkus 2000). Even though the Pentecostal movement was reinforced by repatriates, the October 1949 adoption of anti-church laws made all activity illegal. The Communist regime rejected the possibility of state church registration. Therefore, the Pentecostal believers tried to stay within the Czech Brethren Union. Still, many of their activities took place illegally in small, independent local groups. After the political situation eased in 1968, the movement was unable to pursue the possibility of state registration because of organizational fragmentation among Pentecostals. After a long struggle, including imprisonment of some representatives, the church was officially registered as the Apostolic Church in the Czech Republic (Apoštolská církev v ČR) on 25 January 1989. Later that year came the so-called Velvet Revolution and the fall of the Communist regime.

The focus of Pentecostal ministry was mostly in the eastern Silesia Region in the towns of Český Těšín and Třinec, with other congregations in Brno, České Budějovice, Kutná Hora, Prague, and Nýdek/Břeclav. The Revolution brought favourable conditions for extensive mission activity among Pentecostals. The newly formed Apostolic Church was the fastest-growing Christian church in the Czech Republic since 1989, particularly in the growing numbers of congregations. Concurrently, other Evangelical and Pentecostal influences came to the Czech Republic, which resulted in the creation of new independent congregations in other Czech towns. The number of people in the Apostolic Church grew from 180 in 1977 to 7327 in 2011. After 1989, more Pentecostal groups emerged, which were more theologically diverse and generally small in membership.

The beginnings of the Church of Christian Fellowship (CCF) are closely related to the Evangelical Church of Czech Brethren (ECCB). Due to the evangelizing efforts of the vicar of ECCB Dan Drápal, who had a pentecostal experience around 1978, one very small local church in Prague grew in number and exhibited characteristics of the charismatic movement. This resulted in the separation of the congregation from ECCB in 1990.

In 2002, the CCF became a state-registered church. The number of people identifying with the CCF grew from 4012 in 2001 to 9387 in 2011. The CCF consisted of forty-five congregations. The membership base is not large, but the number of sympathisers and occasional visitors has grown. The CCF represents a second wave of change and growth within Pentecostalism.

Following the influx of Pentecostal missionaries and the arrival of the Faith Movement after the Velvet Revolution, more Pentecostal groups emerged in the Czech Republic. These can be classified as the so-called Third Wave, or the Independent Pentecostals. Under the reign of the Communist Party, the ideas of the Faith Movement came into the region with some difficulty. The spread of the Faith Movement was largely through the West Berlin Fellowship "On The Way" (Společenství na cestě) and its pastor Wolfhardt Margies (1938), and his activities that included smuggling Bibles and brochures. In the second half of the 1980s, the Faith Movement spread through the efforts of foreign student Henry Kashweka. His activity laid a foundation for the church Water of Life (Voda života) currently known as Church of the Word of Life (Církev slovo života). This and other Third Wave groups are usually small independent congregations (about 30–100 members), more or less influenced by the Faith Movement and the Shepherding Movement.

The following independent churches have obtained state registration: Word of Life Church (Církev Slovo života), New Hope Church (Církev Nová naděje), Church of Living God (Církev živého Boha), Faith Church (Církev víry), New Life Church (Církev Nový život), and Oasis Church (Církev Oáza). The Faith Church formed after it separated from the Church of Christian Fellowship, because of its strong ties with Slovak congregations of the Faith Movement. In 2012, more than 700 people claimed to belong to this church.

New Hope Church was created from most of the ROFC congregations, which were founded by the Faith Movement missionary Steve Ryder. In the 2011 census, 430 people claimed to belong to this church. They have eight congregations in the Czech Republic. In order to obtain state registration, it is necessary for a church to have at least 300 members.

Bibliography

Brenkus, Jozef. 2011. "The Pentecostal Movement in the Czech Republic and Slovakia." In *European Pentecostalism*, edited by Andrew Davies and William K. Kay, 248–259. Leiden: Brill.

Brenkus, Josef. 2000. "A Historical and Theological Analysis of the Pentecostal Church in the Czech and Slovak Republics." *Journal of the European Pentecostal Theological Association*, 20 (1): 49–65.

Drápal, D. 2011. Zlom, *historie Křesťanského společenství Praha III*. Praha: Křesťanská společenství.

Drápal, D. 2009. *Léta růstu, historie Křesťanského společenství Praha II*. Praha: Křesťanská společenství.

Drápal, D. 2008. *Jak to všechno začalo, historie Křesťanského společenství Praha I*. Praha: Křesťanská společenství.

Halasová, Tereza. 2017. "Development of the Faith Movement in the Czech Republic." *Central European Journal of Contemporary Religion* 1: 3–16.

Nešpor, Z.R., and Z. Vojtíšek. 2015. *Encyklopedie menších křestanských církví v České republice*. Praha: Karolinum Publishers.

Schmidgall, Paul. 2013. *European Pentecostalism: Its Origins, Development, and Future*. Cleveland, Tennessee: CPT Press.

Tereza Halasová

Dallière, Émile

Émile-René Dallière (1900–1995) was born to a banker, Charles and Alma Dallière, in Nice, France. He married Marguerite Schmid and their son was Alain. He was baptized in the Église Réformée de France (ERF) and became a practicing lawyer. He was fluent in English and translated L.D. Weatherhead, *La maîtrise sexuelle* (*psychanalyse et religion*) (1930). He entered the ministry of the ERF but withdrew in 1934 after experiencing "baptism of the Holy Spirit" in Douglas Scott's meetings.

After leaving the ERF, Émile-René Dallière pastored Pentecostal congregations in Bernay and Évreux. He preached regularly in a network of congregations that included the ERF's Temple Protestant d'Enghien-les-Bains, near Paris, which was pastored by Jean Ameux (1891–1956) in 1929–1956.

He was recognized as one of the "Just Among the Nations" by Vad Yashem for protecting Jews during the Nazi occupation on December 14, 1994. A Jewish family of Phillipe A. lived in Paris. In June 1940 Phillipe's father disappeared and he as a child was sent to the grandparents who lived in Enghien-les-Bains, north of Paris. The grandparents made contact with Ameux who referred them to Émile Dallière, a frequent preacher at the Temple Protestant of Enghien-les-Bains. Dallière and his wife sheltered Phillipe from spring 1943 until spring 1944. When allied bombardment destroyed their house, a friend of Dallière, Marie Bailly and her daughter Otette accepted Philippe. The father died in the camps; his mother survived and was reunited with her son.

After the war, Dallière continued his pastoral work and preached widely in France and Switzerland in Protestant and Pentecostal churches as well as in public halls from the mid-1940s to the late 1960s. He took an active role in organizing and securing support for the World Pentecostal Conferences in Zurich (1947) and Paris (1948).

When the Charismatic Renewal began, Dallière immediately supported and organized ecumenical charismatic conventions with his brother Louis Dallière and Thomas Roberts. He also translated and published volumes to encourage the charismatic renewal in France, initially at his own expense. His translations helped establish the reputation of David du Plessis and the renewal in francophone Europe. These included: John Sherrill, *Ils parlent en d'autres langues* (Genève: Ed. Jura-Réveil); David du Plessis, *Commando de l'Esprit: récit d'un mouvement de réveil au sein des Eglises traditionnelles* (1972), which was re-issued as *Celui que l'on appelle Monsieur Pentecôte: David du Plessis* (1981); John Randall, *Providence: naissance d'une paroisse catholique charismatique* (1974); John and Elizabeth Sherrill, *Saga des Shakarian: ou les Gens les plus heureux sur terre – la vie de Demos Shakarian* (1986). All were reprinted multiple times.

Émile Dallière attended the 1971 Fountain Trust's international Charismatic conference in Guildford hosted by Michael Harper, where he was delighted by the ecumenical inclusiveness. In 1972, the Abbot, Dom Grammont, hosted a conference at the Abbey of Bec-Hellouin featuring Émile Dallière and David du Plessis. The event had an important influence on the development of the Charismatic renewal in the Catholic Church of France. As the Charismatic Renewal retreated into the ecclesiastical isolation, Émile Dallière and other non-Catholic activists were generally written out of the narratives of the revival in Protestant, Catholic and Pentecostal historiography.

Bibliography

Hébrard, Monique. 1987. *Les nouveaux disciples dix ans après: voyage à travers les communautés charismatiques: réflexions sur le renouveau spirituel*. Paris: Éditions du Centurion.

Landron, Olivier. 2004. *Les Communautés nouvelles: Nouveaux visages du catholicisme français*. Paris: Éditions du Cerf.

Veldhuizen, Evert. 1995. "Le Renouveau Charismatique Protestant en France (1968–1988)." PhD diss., University of Paris.

David Bundy

Dallière, Louis

Louis Dallière (1897–1976) was born in Chicago, son of a French banker, Charles and Alma Dallière. He was baptized in the Église Réformée de France (ERF) in Nice in 1901. He experienced conversion in 1910 before the family moved to Saint-Germain-en-Laye near Paris. He underwent a second conversion in 1915, accompanied by a call to ministry. He enrolled in the Faculté de théologie protestant in Paris in 1915–1921, taking time out for a year of military service. During 1921, Dalliere received the baccalauréat in theology and married Caroline Bœgner, becoming the brother-in-law of Gabriel Marcel. He began to study philosophy.

The academic year of 1922–1923 was spent at Harvard University studying with W.E. Hocking. Hocking became the subject of the licentiate thesis submitted to the Faculté de théologie protestant in Paris in 1924. It was partially published as *W.E. Hocking: La refonte de la nature humaine* (1929). On January 12, 1925, he became pastor of the ERF in Charmes-sur-Rhône where he spent his pastoral career. Being a protégé of Wilfred Monod, he sought to renew the ERF and was considered part of the Christianisme Social movement. He published extensively; the writings of the period were established in Bundy (1988a). Dallière was appointed to the Faculté de théologie protestant at Montpellier in 1931–1932, but later rejected the appointment because of the controversies over Pentecostalism, specifically baptism.

During that time, he hosted Donald Gee at Montpellier and translated his volume, *Gifts of the Spirit*, into French.

In January 1932, at a meeting conducted by British Pentecostal evangelist Douglas Scott, Dallière experienced baptism in the Holy Spirit. From 1932 to 1939, he served as advocate and apologist for Pentecostalism in France and Belgium. Dallière and Henri Théophile de Worm of Paturages, Belgium, co-edited a Pentecostal periodical, *Esprit et vie*. His writings during this period were established in Bundy (1988b). Most important were translation of Donald Gee's volume: *Gifts of the Spirit* and *D'aplomb sur la Parole de Dieu: Courte étude sur le Réveil de Pentecôte* (1932), an analysis and apologetic for Pentecostalism reflecting on a visit to churches in the UK. These were both advertized regularly in the Pentecostal periodical, *Viens et vois*. Later, he contributed *Le baptême en vue du retour de Jésus Christ* (1937) in which he argued for believer's baptism. Committed to the ERF, he was pressured by the Pentecostals to separate and by the ERF to reject Pentecostal ideas and practices. He was put on probation in 1932 by the ERF until 1951, remaining pastor only because of the loyalty of the congregation. Because of ERF strictures, he ceased both to speak outside his parish and to publish in 1939. But, because of his arguments for remaining in the ERF, numerous Pentecostal converts of the 1930s stayed in the ERF, becoming part of a loosely organized prayer and fellowship network led by Dallière.

During the decades on probation with the ERF, Dallière pastored, developed a school in Charmes-sur-Rhône, and organized an extensive ecumenical Pentecostal/Charismatic network, which was formalized as the Union de Prière de Charmes in 1946, based on the concept of Paul Couturier's invisible monastery. Even before WWII, Dallière sought a different approach to Judaism. Aiding Jewish persons during the genocide brought him recognition as one of the "Just among the Nations." An important essay was posthumously published, "La greffe judéo-chrétienne," in André Chouraqui, *Le Scandale d'Israël* (2011). His perspective on Judaism was analyzed by Boullion (2011). Bouillon has discussed the controversies and established the bibliography of unpublished documents in 2017.

Thomas Roberts (1902–1983), a Welsh Apostolic, then an independent ecumenist and a Pentecostal missionary became an important friend and ally of Dallière in 1932 and part of the Union de Prière de Charmes. When the Charismatic Renewal began in the U.S., and the student riots commenced in France in 1968, they began to organize ecumenical charismatic conventions. In 1973 the Union de Prière hosted the third interconfessional charismatic conference at Viviers. The important conference volume was edited by Thomas Roberts and A. and E. Schvartz, *Viviers 1973: Rencontre Charismatique Interconfessionelle, 31 octobre–4 novembre 1973* (1974). About 500 people attended, half of them Catholics. Thomas Roberts presided and Laurent Fabre, founder of the Chemin Neuf community, took responsibility for Catholic participation. For the rest of their lives, Roberts and Dallière, together with the support of Louis's younger brother, Émile Dallière who was a Pentecostal pastor, struggled to keep the Charismatic Renewal ecumenical, to develop it among Protestants, and to keep it as a renewal movement within the churches.

Bibliography

Bouillon, David. 2017. "Église – Baptême – Esprit-Saint: la théologie de Louis Dallière." PhD diss., Université de Strasbourg.

Bouillon, David. 2011. "Espérer d'Israël! Louis Dallière, un Pasteur face à la question juive." In *Le Scandale d'Israël*, edited by André Chouraqui. N.p.: Echoes d'Orient. 7–26.

Bundy, David. 1988a. "L'émergence d'un théologien pentecôtisant: Les écrits de Louis Dallière de 1922 à 1932." *Hokma* 38: 23–51.

Bundy, David. 1988b. "Louis Dallière: Apologist for Pentecostalism in France and Belgium, 1932–1939." *Pneuma* 10 (1): 85–115.

Thoorens, Jan. [1976]. *L'Union de Prière de Charmes s/Rhône: Mémoire, Maîtrise en théologie*. Institute Catholique de Paris.

David Bundy

Dallimore, A.H.

Arthur Henry Dallimore (1873–1970) was born in Kent, England raised as a Baptist and later became an Anglican. At age seven, he was healed of typhoid fever through his parent's prayers. This experience made an indelible mark on his life, and he would later claim to have been raised from the dead. He moved with his parents to New Zealand in 1886 where the family attended a Wesleyan Church in Opunake. Here, a Methodist missioner invited him to be involved in ministry. Dallimore declined and chose instead to leave for Alaska in 1902, then on to England where he married Ethel Ward in 1911. Together they settled in Canada where their three children were born. Dallimore tried his hand at farming then afterwards, went into business. However, the strain led to a nervous breakdown. He regained his health at divine healing services in Vancouver conducted by Charles S. Price. In 1920 he met prominent Pentecostal missionary John G. Lake while attending a British Israel conference in Vancouver. Encouraged by Lake to pursue ministry, Dallimore opened an independent healing mission in Vancouver which he led until his return to New Zealand in 1927. Shortly after his arrival, Dallimore commenced independent healing and evangelistic services in Auckland leading to the establishment of the Revival Fire Mission. Attendances were small for several years but then grew rapidly till over one thousand people met in Auckland's town hall on Sunday evenings in 1931. By 1935, Dallimore claimed to have baptized over 1,100 people during the seven years of his ministry in Auckland.

A description of Dallimore as being "no showman" (Guy 2005), contrasts with his charismatic and strong personality. Services were lively but reportedly lacking in drama; this point, Dallimore held, differentiated him from the mainstream Pentecostal healing movement that, in his view, deliberately "cooked up" emotionalism. At the height of his ministry, worship involved a band of more than twenty, regularly led by his wife who was an able musician. Utterances in tongues were common although Dallimore believed in order and did not allow more than three messages in tongues at one gathering. Services featured altar calls during which his wife Ethel joined him in anointing and praying for the sick. Most who came forward went "under the power" and the stage was often covered with prone bodies. Like Wigglesworth before him, Dallimore was well known for his use of "blessed handkerchiefs" anointed with oil as an aid to indirect healing. These were applied broadly to people, animals, and mechanical devices.

During 1932, meeting numbers rose to 2,000. Dallimore's ministry was popularized by the media who followed him closely through his *Revival Fire Monthly* (published for twenty years), and his books on healing (*Healing by Faith*) and British-Israelism (*Britain-Israel*). Dallimore achieved some notoriety as an advocate of

British-Israelite teaching when he erroneously predicted that Edward VIII, then heir to the throne, would not marry but would be a second Davidic messiah and usher in the reign of Christ in 1936. Dallimore's central themes, however, were that Jesus saves and heals. The latter emphasis proved the most attractive, and also the most divisive. Dallimore's healing ministry occurred during the worst of the Great Depression in New Zealand. Accordingly, Guy (2005) rightly describes Dallimore as "a bearer of hope in tough times." However, his literal reading of scripture led him to reject any form of medical intervention. God healed by faith alone, therefore, using modern healing drugs was akin to sorcery. This extreme stance became the focus of rising opposition leading to a formal Committee of Inquiry in 1932 made up of clergy, medical, and university professionals tasked with examining the results of Dallimore's faith-healing methods. Since Dallimore was opposed to medicine, he would not cooperate and advised his supporters to do the same resulting in the examination of only forty-six cases. The report, indicatively labelled *The Dallimore Campaign Exposed*, described Dallimore as a "sensation monger" whose cures by supernatural means were unsubstantiated. Although this did not deter Dallimore, he was soon barred from the Town Hall by the City Council, only to be re-admitted a few months later following the presentation of a petition of over 7,000 signatures. Following this incident, media interest waned, as did attendance at his meetings although he still drew 600 in 1939. Three congregations formed in Auckland, Hamilton, and Thames with two branch services in the Auckland suburbs of Onehunga and Avondale.

Although healing by faith was a key theme for Dallimore, he was also anti-trinitarian. Dallimore believed that Jehovah was the father of Jesus but stressed Jesus's humanity and denied his pre-existence. He also believed that the Holy Spirit was the "Breath" of God rather than a person. His anti-trinitarian views appear in the *Revival Fire Monthly* (1934–1953) and were publicly debated with Brethren leader, W.H. Pettit during 1957. In the latter years of his ministry, Dallimore drifted away from his earlier emphasis on Jesus as the key to healing to a view that believed healing occurred through natural (though God-given) laws by faith. As healings waned, and Dallimore moved further from orthodoxy, adherents began to drift to other churches. Few remained when Dallimore retired in 1957. The Revival Fire Mission closed its doors in 1968.

Bibliography

Guy, Laurie. 2005. "Miracles, Messiahs and the Media: The Ministry of A.H. Dallimore in Auckland in the 1930s." In *Signs, Wonders, Miracles: Representations of Divine Power in the Life of the Church*, edited by Kate Cooper and Jeremy Gregory, 453–463. Woodbridge: Ecclesiastical History Society.

Guy, Laurie. 2004. "One of a Kind? The Auckland Ministry of A.H. Dallimore." *Australasian Pentecostal Studies* 8: 125–45. Retrieved from https://aps-journal.com/index.php/APS/article/view/76.

Worsfold, James. E. 1974. *A History of the Charismatic Movements in New Zealand: Including a Pentecostal Perspective and a Breviate of the Catholic Apostolic Church in Great Britain*. Bradford: Julian Literature Trust.

Linda Flett

Davidson, Alexander Thomas

Alexander Thomas Davidson, 1902, Granville, NSW-18 Sep 1987, Mitcham, Victoria. The son of Alexander (auctioneer) and Eleanor Annie Davidson, 'Alec' or 'A.T.' Davidson was born in Granville, and grew up in Auburn, Sydney, New South Wales (NSW), Australia. Prior to his marriage in 1930, Davidson trained and worked as an accountant. The family were members of Auburn Baptist Church, where Alec became a lay preacher. In 1930, in the middle of the Depression, he married Olive Rita Kellaway (1903–1992). Due to lack of work, the young couple moved out of Sydney to Ettalong, on the NSW central coast, where Alec worked as an auctioneer, and they attended a Methodist church. Originally (like many Baptists) Davidson opposed pentecostalism ("as a young preacher I fought it tooth and nail"). Davidson was impressed, however, by "the simple folk with the shining faces" who were not phased by the surrounding Depression. His reading of the Scriptures brought him around, and after encountering pentecostal leader, Mary Tebay (who was running cottage meetings in the area), in about 1934 he was baptized in the Spirit. Another former Baptist who became a leading Australian pentecostal, Philip Duncan remembered "the delight of the Pentecostal people who were justified so wonderfully, when this honest antagonist bit the dust." Before long, the former Baptist/ethodist lay preacher took over as pastor of the Woy Woy Church, at the cost of losing almost every mainline church relationship that he had. "Other Christians declared me a fanatic, a heretic. Some have said I am of the Devil – quite a lot in fact.... Ministers' fraternals have excluded me, while at the same time welcoming into their midst modernists and ecclesiastical infidels. I have been publicly ignored and insulted – privately lied about and scandalised! All because I have dared to believe that God meant what He said!"

By 1937, Davidson was already a recognized element in NSW pentecostalism, being elected to the first National Presbytery of the Assemblies of God in Australia (AGA). Enthusiastic prayer meetings, "open air" work, and Sunday Schools built up his church, such that it needed its own building: a "little house" was built on Davis Street, near Webb Road, Booker Bay. With Newcastle a growing industrial area (to become even moreso during the war years) the NSW AGA committee appointed Davidson (still working to support himself as an auctioneer) as first pastor of the Hamilton church in 1937. From an initial group of twenty meeting in "an old dance hall," it grew rapidly to seventy members: here, too, Davidson again led the church building process.

The outbreak of war in 1939 made it difficult to obtain pastors: consequently, in 1941 the Davidsons were seconded to the state's oldest pentecostal church, in rural Parkes. Now in full time ministry Alec became an early pioneer of religous radio, by early 1942 running a "Radio Magazine," and every day at noon presenting "The Gospel in Song" on Radio 2PK. Following the common "radio club" format, Davidson also ran a "Junior Christian Fellowship Radio Sunday School" at 6.50 p.m. and the "Christian Fellowship of the Air" at 9:40 p.m., as well as a program called "World Review." From 1953 he extended the Australian version of Revivaltime to 12 country stations in NSW, Victoria, and Queensland. He was ahead of his time:

the much larger and better financed Assemblies of God in the USA would not organize a radio department until 1945.

His innovations raised Davidson's profile: he was appointed to roles such as Home Mission Secretary and being touted as a possible General Superintendent. His administration skills, irenic personality and emphasis on unity enabled him to work across the movement's state-based personality divides. Unlike the major city pastors, he was to have pastoral experience in all three eastern states (Parkes in NSW, Toowoomba in Queensland and Kyabram in Victoria), making him an "insider" in all the major pastoral cultures which combined to make up the Assemblies of God. In 1947, as State Superintendent, Davidson invited the Sturgeon Evangelistic team from Kansas City, USA, causing something of a sensation in pre-television, rural Australia. As one who had been out on the frontier of church planting, and had seen the costs of underprepared pastors leaving a "path ... strewn with the debris of mistakes and ignorance," he was among those who encouraged them to stay and to establish the first national AGA Bible College.

In 1951, Davidson was appointed General Superintendent (1951–1955; he would be Vice Chair to Bible College Principal James Wallace, 1957–1959; and Chairman again 1959–1969), his cool administrative head shepherding the movement through a difficult time of divisions over the perceived dominance of the Victorian church. In 1967 he travelled to the USA to look at governance and ministry models which would "further the cause of our ever increasing work." Supportive of younger men, Davidson "retired" to Mitcham, Victoria, in 1969 in order to make way for Ralph Read, only to find himself fulfilling AGA national functions left by the death in that year of C.L. Greenwood. W. George Forbes travelled with him when the position of "Director of Missions" was created for Davidson on his retirement from the superintendency: they visited Papua New Guinea repeatedly in 1969–1972. Forbes would be strongly influenced by Davidson's prayer life, seeing him rise at 2am and pray until 8am every day. His series of lectures on Prayer at Bethel House, Croydon, Victoria in 1980 remain in circulation today.

A heart attack in 1972 curtailed Davidson's activities, but did not stop his activities as a mentor and on ministry locums. Davidson was an innovator, a good administrator, and a movement man whose leadership style enabled the Assemblies of God in Australia to survive its own internal divisions long enough to take advantage of the upswing in charismatic, non-traditional Christianity which would mark the 1960s and 1970s. He died on 18 September 1987. Over 200 people, including many pastors, were in attendance at the Ringwood Assembly for the memorial service. He was survived by his wife, Olive, their only child (Ruth) having predeceased them due to cancer.

Bibliography

APSC, Assemblies of God in Australia, Commonwealth Conference Minutes, 1937–1969; and Forbes, George. 2010. "Interview with Mark Hutchinson 1 Sept. 2010." Archives, Australasian Pentecostal Studies Centre, Alphcrucis College.

Auburn Baptist Church. 1988. *Auburn Baptist Church, 1888–1988*, Auburn, NSW.: Auburn Baptist Church.

Australian Evangel, 1930–1970, 1987.

Blumhofer, Edith. 1993. *Restoring the Faith: The Assemblies of God, Pentecostalism and American Culture*, Urbana: University of Illinois Press.

Duncan, Phillip, *Pentecost in Australia*, nd. np.

Griffen-Foley, Bridget. 2008. "Radio ministries: Religion on Australian Commercial Radio from the 1920s to the 1960s." *Journal of Religious History* 32 (1): 31–54.

NSW Government Records: Electoral Rolls; NSW Births, Deaths and Marriages.

Mark Hutchinson

de Monléon, Albert

Albert Marie de Monléon (1937–) was born in Paris, son of a professor of philosophy at the Institut Catholique de Paris. Monléon studied at the Lycée Condorcet and Lycée Louis-le-Grand. He then enrolled in the Institut Catholique. Monléon received his licentiate in theology after completing studies at the Dominican School of Saulchoir at Étiolles. He joined the Dominican Order (1957) and was ordained priest on July 5, 1964.

Monléon became a member of the ecumenical Centre d'études en théologie Istina where he remained involved for twenty years (1968–1988). Being an early international interpreter of the French Charismatic renewal, at first pessimistically (November 1971), and then more optimistically (March 1972), Monléon was also part of the early charismatic Communauté de l'Emmanuel and participated in the early ecumenical charismatic conventions. The Community, officially established in 1976, grew from a prayer group founded in 1972 by Pierre Goursat and Martine Laffitte-Catta. During this period, a series of books established him as an important theologian of the church and the renewal, *perçus du Réveil charismatique* (1971); *L'Expérience des charismes: manifestations de l'Esprit en vue du bien commun* (1977); *Présence du Renouveau Charismatique: Enracinement et devenir* (1979); *Jésus Christ est Signeur* (1980); *Les Étapes de la vie spirituelle* (1984), and *Jésus doux et humble de coeur* (1988).

The Communauté was granted canonical statutes in 1981 by Cardinal Lustiger (Paris), supported by Cardinals Danneels (Mechelen/Brussels) and Etchegaray (Marseille). From 1983 to 1988, Monléon served the Communauté and the closely related Fraternité de Jésus with responsibility for the priests and seminarians of both bodies. From this community would come several bishops.

Monléon was bishop of Pamiers (1988–1999) and of Meaux (1999–2012). Exemplary of his work of renewal were his bringing 100 youth from his diocese to Paris in 1996 for Journées mondiales de la jeunesse, and his *Charte et guide pastoral des pôles missionnaires: des pôles missionnaires pour une mission renouvelée dans le diocèse de Meaux* (2008). An engaged participant in the Conference of the Bishops of France, he presided over the Commission on the Liturgy and Sacramental Pastoral Care. Under his leadership it produced guidelines enhancing eucharistic and funeral practices: *59 questions sur l'Eucharistie: repères pour les pratiques eucharistiques*; introduction de Albert-Marie de Monléon (2000); and, *Pastorale des funérailles: points de repère*; preface de Albert-Marie de Monléon (2003). Later he served on the Doctrinal Commission of the Conference of Bishops.

In addition to numerous books and articles, Monléon has a legacy as a popular speaker. Numerous sound recordings are preserved at the Bibliothèque National de France, including: *La Création nouvelle*; *Prière charismatique*; *Le Discernement des esprits* (three lectures); *Les Dons de l'Esprit-Saint: les vertus théologales et les charismes*; *L'Eucharistie*; and, *L'Espérance chrétienne*. These were delivered at the

Centre international Jean-Paul II Paris and circulated (1984) by Cahiers du Renouveau, a Catholic Charismatic Renewal organization. Two other addresses focused on Mary (1984) and *Marie figure et modèle de sainteté* (1988). Teachings given at international meetings of the Communauté de l'Emmanuel include: *Vous êtes la lumière du monde* (1992); *Pourquoi l'église chante* (1994); and, *L'art et le coeur du Christ* (1994). Numerous videos are on YouTube.

Since 2008 Monléon has been coordinator of the French Congrès nationale de la Miséricorde. The first congress held at Valpré (near Leon) attracted representatives of Charismatic communities Myriam Bethléem, Chemin Neuf, as well as of groups such as the Petites Soeurs des Pauvres and Secours Catholique. Subsequent congresses were held at Lisieux (2010), Notre Dame de Laus (2012), Lourdes (2015), Le Plan-Medoc (2017), Neuilly (2018), and Montligeon (2019). These are, since 2012, in solidarity with the call of Pope Francis to "live mercy." Two volumes published included contributions by Albert-Marie de Monléon: "Pastorale de la *miséricorde*," in *Miséricorde: approches pastorales et interreligieuses: actes du premier congrès national de la miséricorde, Lyon-Valpré, 4–5 octobre 2008* (2009) and "Oser le défi de la reconciliation dans les situations de soufrance," in *Oser le défi de la reconciliation, Congrès national de la miséricorde, 3–5 aôut 2012, sanctuaire de Notre-Dame du Laus* (2014).

Monléon retired as bishop (2012) and moved to the Dominican Monastery of La Clarté-Notre-Dame at Taulignan (Drôme). From there he has continued to lead the Congrès national de la miséricorde, the renewal, and to be involved in pastoral teaching.

Bibliography

Monléon, Albert Marie de. 2015. *Au coeur de la miséricorde*, Second Edition. Paris: Parole et silence.

Monléon, Albert Marie de. 2014. *Sur les pas du Christ*. Paris: Parole et silence.

Monléon, Albert Marie de. 1998. *Rendez témoignage: le renouveau charismatique catholique*. Paris: Mame.

Monléon, Albert Marie de. 1995. *Charismes et ministères dans l'Écriture et l'expérience de l'Église*. Collection Chemins ouverts; Paris: Éditions Desclée de Brouwer.

Monléon, Albert Marie de. 1995. *Jésus-Christ est Seigneur: il est toute nouveauté, le même hier, aujourd'hui et pour les siècles*. Preface by Robert Coffy, new edition. Paris: Éditions de l'Emmanuel.

David Bundy

Deeper Life Bible Church

Deeper Life Bible Church is one of the largest and oldest neo-Pentecostal denominations in Nigeria. Founded by William Folorunso Kumuyi (b. 1941), it has planted over 6,000 branches across Nigeria and has multiple branches in other African countries, Europe, Asia, Australia/Oceania, and the Americas. Its headquarters church in Lagos attracts around 150,000 attendees to its Sunday services, and its recently-completed 30,000-seater worship centre in Lagos is one of the largest church auditoriums in the world. Until the 1990s, Deeper Life was the leading Nigerian neo-Pentecostal church, exerting significant theological influence on the post-1970 Pentecostal revival in Nigeria. Kumuyi promoted strict holiness doctrines via a rigorous regime of Bible study and prayer

Deeper Life Bible Church headquarters, Gbagada, Lagos (Nigeria). Source: Center for the Study of Global Christianity

which helped to shape the early phase of the revival.

Kumuyi was brought up in an Anglican family but was converted in the Apostolic Faith Church, which was planted by missionaries from the United States during the 1950s. Like other early leaders of the revival, he was influenced by interdenominational groups such as Scripture Union and the university evangelical Christian unions. During secondary school, he joined a Scripture Union group. Subsequently, he studied mathematics at the University of Ibadan where he became involved in the Ibadan Varsity Christian Union, one of the main centres of the revival. In 1972, Kumuyi was employed as a lecturer at the University of Lagos, where he started a Bible study group in his home. Within a short time, he was being invited to other universities as a speaker. In 1975, Kumuyi was expelled from the Apostolic Faith Church for preaching without ordination credentials. The same year, the name Deeper Christian Life Ministry was first adopted by the group. Afterwards it spread beyond Lagos as Deeper Life Bible study groups were established in other cities and towns across Nigeria. Among the factors behind the early growth of the ministry was its interdenominational status, which enabled members to attend while maintaining allegiance to existing churches, and the establishment of its higher institution arm in 1979, later named the Deeper Life Campus Fellowship. Another factor was the establishment of Deeper Life camps and retreats, an idea borrowed from the Apostolic Faith Church. These events emphasized healing and miracles and living a 'holy life'. The first retreat was held in 1975, and the Easter 1976 retreat was attended by 2,500 people. Deeper Life's rapid church growth was also facilitated by evangelism and the distribution of free tracts.

The year 1982 marked the second phase of Deeper Life's history when it began to hold Sunday services in Lagos. This completed its transition to denominational status. In 1983, the church experienced significant growth through 'House Caring Fellowships', an idea borrowed from Yonggi Cho's Yoido Full Gospel Church in Seoul, South Korea, after a visit by some of Kumuyi's church leaders in 1982. By February 1983, 15,000 house fellowships were established across Nigeria. Other factors that strengthened Deeper Life's denominational status included the establishment of the International Bible Training Centre, the introduction of short-term ministerial courses to train pastors, and the church's expansion in and outside Nigeria. Another significant milestone occurred in 1990 when existing congregations in Nigeria were split into smaller branches, resulting in rapid multiplication.

Deeper Life Bible Church has branches in over 40 African nations. Its transnational expansion to Europe and the United States began during the 1980s. In 1985, it planted its first congregation in Britain and it now has around 65 congregations in Britain and the Republic of Ireland as well as branches in other European countries. The United States has over 90 Deeper Life branches.

Most of the doctrinal emphases and religious practices of Deeper Life are also found in other Pentecostal churches in Nigeria and elsewhere in the world. Many of its teachings echo doctrines held by the Apostolic Faith Church where Kumuyi was a member for 20 years. One of Deeper Life's distinctive doctrinal emphases is its teaching on restitution which is regarded as an essential part of repentance. Another distinctive emphasis, inherited from the Apostolic Faith Church, is its doctrine of sanctification as a second experience of the Holy Spirit subsequent to conversion whereby the believer is freed from sin. The church's teaching on sanctification is partly responsible for its separatist tendencies and its reputation in the 1980s for regarding only members of Deeper Life as Christians. Another important emphasis is divine healing, which is reinforced by Kumuyi's reputation as a 'miracle' worker and the testimonies of those healed through his ministry.

Recently, Deeper Life has embraced a more holistic approach to mission which includes social engagement activities. Deeper Life schools are operating in many of Nigeria's cities, and in 2016, the church's Anchor University in Lagos was accredited by the National Universities Commission (NUC). Deeper Life is also engaged in humanitarian projects such as prison and hospital visitation and disaster relief. Another significant development is Deeper Life's moderation of its exclusivist approach to other churches and its involvement in ecumenical organizations.

Bibliography

Akoda, Winifred. 2012. "May His Will Be Done: A History of the Deeper Life Bible Church, 1973–2006." *International Journal of Asian Social Science* 2 (4): 402–410.

Gaiya, Musa A.B. 2002. "The Pentecostal Revolution in Nigeria." Occasional Paper. Center of African Studies, University of Copenhagen.

Isaacson, Alan. 1990. *Deeper Life: The Extraordinary Growth of the Deeper Life Bible Church*. London: Hodder and Stoughton.

Ojo, Matthews A. 2006. *The End-time Army: Charismatic Movements in Nigeria*. Trenton, NJ: Africa World Press.

Ojo, Matthews A. 1988. "Deeper Christian Life Ministry: A Case Study of The Charismatic Movements in Western Nigeria." *Journal of Religion in Africa* 18 (2): 141–162.

Richard Burgess

Definitions

The question of how the Pentecostal movement is to be adequately defined and delimited has remained unresolved and contested (Anderson et al. 2010). The debate may have ebbed away somewhat in recent years, but increasing scholarly attention to global Pentecostalism makes the problem even more virulent. Current academic research on global Pentecostalism tends to favour a broad and vague understanding of its subject matter. At first glance, such an all-inclusive definition seems to be attractive to scholars as it avoids acrimonious battles about contested definitions. It also seems unproblematic because it not only corresponds to the received view in academia, but also prevails in certain Pentecostal circles. At second glance, it turns out, that such a broad understanding lacks theoretical justification and stands in unresolved tension with the narrower definitions that scholars also tend to apply. This problem of definition is not unique to Pentecostal studies, but characteristic for many fields in religious studies, and there is much to learn from these discussions (Bergunder 2014). Firstly, we need a theoretical and empirical justification of the widely accepted broad understanding – which we may call "Pentecostalism 2" – and secondly, we need to understand how this could lead to meaningful scholarly definitions of the subject matter – which we may call "Pentecostalism 1" (Maltese in Maltese et al. 2019).

The greatest problem lies with the justification of "Pentecostalism 2". It is certainly not enough to simply accept the existence of an extremely plural worldwide Pentecostal movement with many different currents, because this argument is circular: it only leads back to the question why one should understand such a global diversity as a single phenomenon at all. Accordingly, some anthropologists study global Pentecostalism without identifying it as a separate phenomenon, for example by conflating it with evangelicalism (Coleman and Hackett 2015). If "Pentecostalism 2" is to mean anything at all, it must refer to an existing Pentecostal identity "out there". Therefore, it has been suggested that "Pentecostalism 2" reflects an actual identity, formed and articulated within a global discourse (Bergunder in Anderson et al. 2010). As such it is a contested and contingent entity, and its present shape is the product of current discursive articulations, rather than something representing an entity behind these articulations. In fact, the very contentiousness of its boundaries is part of the Pentecostal identity discourse itself. In this discourse of "Pentecostalism 2", the power to represent is not uniformly distributed, and it includes scholarly as well as religious, cultural and political debates and practices. Researchers thus have to recognize these frontiers and reflect on conflicting claims of identity as well as on practices of inclusion or exclusion, for example with regard to Oneness Pentecostalism, Positive Confession movements, inter-/non-denominational churches, Charismatic movements, Hispanic Pentecostalism, or born-again Christians. The case of AICs should be noted as particularly complex in this regard (Anderson 2018).

In such a discursive understanding of Pentecostalism, no denomination, lay movement, or evangelistic ministry may be considered "Pentecostal" if it cannot be shown whether and how it is part of this "Pentecostalism 2", i.e. who demands or contests its inclusion. This understanding of Pentecostalism also takes seriously that there is no common dogmatic foundation or institutional framework that encompasses the entire cluster of churches, ministries, denominations, etc. that are commonly understood as Pentecostal (International umbrella organizations like the World Pentecostal Conference cover only comparatively small parts). Moreover, global Pentecostalism is constantly changing in character, scope and identity, and might even dissolve into other identities in the future.

"Pentecostalism 2" is the reference that justifies "Pentecostalism 1", i.e. any scholarly definition of global Pentecostalism. If scholars argue for a broad understanding, they can take the discursive nature of "Pentecostalism 2" as basis for their own definition, their "Pentecostalism 1". This would mean that they always need to contextualize their case studies within Pentecostal discourse, which means (re)constructing local settings and global entanglements of complex and contested articulations about Pentecostal identity. Recent studies have shown how this can be methodically implemented in an empirically grounded and productive way, opening up an innovative perspective for further research (Maltese et al. 2019). It is one of the strengths of this approach that it does not consider conflicting claims on Pentecostal identities to be a nuisance but rather a scholarly opportunity. The construction of scholarly definitions in the sense of "Pentecostalism 1" is therefore opened up to critical engagement and to different interpretations of the same source material.

There are several other approaches to a scholarly definition for global Pentecostalism in the sense of "Pentecostalism 1". A typological approach differentiates three, four or even more different types (e. g., Classical Pentecostals, Older Church Charismatics, Neo-Pentecostals, Neo-Charismatics, Older Independent or Spiritual Churches, or even a "Fourth Wave") (Anderson in Anderson et al. 2010). Some statistical overviews distinguish an almost endless number of types. The crucial weakness of the typological approach is its unexplained referentiality to "Pentecostalism 2". It does not explain why these different types should form a single Pentecostal movement and why the global Pentecostal discourse is not recognizably structured along this typology. Moreover, these typologies tend to imply a historiography that privileges US-American classical Pentecostal churches as a priori prototype of global Pentecostalism (see History).

Another type of definition in current scholarship relates to specific theological teachings or spiritual practices. It is certainly possible to identify doctrines and practices that occur in (much of) the global Pentecostal discourse ("Pentecostalism 2"), be it speaking in tongues, intuitive and experiential Spirit-centered devotion, oral liturgy, firm Biblical orientation, narrative theology and testimonies, strong lay participation, or healing, to name a few. However, these traits are entirely dependent on their articulation and mutual affirmation within the discourse itself, and this is subject to constant change, conflict, contestation and transformation. Thus, the importance of specific teachings and practices has to be read from concrete articulations in Pentecostal discourse itself, rather than be assumed a priori (or adopted from parts of the discourse) and then applied as universal criterion. Only then can they inform a scholarly definition, because "Pentecostalism 1" must always be justified through "Pentecostalism 2". It is certainly no adequate way to define a theological basis for global Pentecostalism in taking US-American churches which understand themselves as "classical Pentecostals" as a starting point. Even if formulated in very general terms, these definitions – as well as any other that privilege the theology of specific churches – will inevitably seek to appropriate the variety of global Pentecostalism for a specific theological cause.

Global Pentecostalism is a legitimate subject of scholarly research only as long as something like "Pentecostalism 2" can be empirically reconstructed. Any research on global Pentecostalism has to show that it addresses an actual discourse that produces a Pentecostal identity in the sense of "Pentecostalism 2". This is not a theoretical question as there have been dramatic changes in the respective articulation of religious identities in the recent past that could mean an end of Pentecostalism in favor of other identities.

Bibliography

Anderson, Allan. 2018. *Spirit-Filled World. Religious Dis/Continuity in African Pentecostalism.* Basingstoke: Palgrave Macmillan.

Anderson, Allan, Michael Bergunder, André Droogers, and Cornelis van der Laan, eds. 2010. *Studying Global Pentecostalism. Theories and Methods.* Berkeley: University of California Press.

Bergunder, Michael. 2014. "What is Religion? The Unexplained Subject Matter of Religious Studies." *Method and Theory in the Study of Religion* 26 (3): 246–286.

Colman, Simon, and Rosalind I.J. Hackett, eds. 2015. *The Anthropology of Global Pentecostalism and Evangelicalism.* New York: New York University Press.

Maltese, Giovanni, Judith Bachmann, and Katja Rakow. 2019. "Negotiating Evangelicalism and Pentecostalism: Global Entanglements, Identity Politics and the Future of Pentecostal Studies." *PentecoStudies* 18 (1): 7–19.

Michael Bergunder

Denmark

The Pentecostal movement entered Denmark in 1907 on the tails of popular Christian revival movements which had especially affected the Lutheran state church. It also coincided with the dawn of a new secular modern culture. The English-born Norwegian Methodist leader T.B. Barratt spent large parts of the first years of his Pentecostal ministry in Copenhagen. He saw the Danish capital as a potential bridgehead from which the movement could spread to the rest of the continent.

Though Barratt would have greater success elsewhere, the revival still made an impact that spanned all classes of society. The conversion of a famous actress, Anna Larssen (later Bjørner), led young socialists to physically assault Pentecostal meetings in 1909. They were also provoked by the movement's inroads among the working class. Pentecostalism was largely rejected by Evangelical and Holiness leaders within the state church. Since other Christian denominations were small, there was limited potential for the movement to recruit.

The most prominent Pentecostals in Copenhagen doubled down on the original vision of renewing the existing churches rather than forming a separate denomination. Many of their most dynamic leaders went into foreign mission fields. But elsewhere in Denmark, independent congregations were formed under influence from the neighboring countries, especially in the southern parts of the country. Those who left their previous churches often came from Baptist or Methodist backgrounds, where there was more active resistance to the movement. In the 1910s, these Pentecostals began to establish institutions such as magazines and conferences.

After disagreements over universalist eschatology, Pentecostal leaders finally agreed to enter into a nationwide network of formalized congregations in 1919. At the center of this was a new congregation in Copenhagen led by Anna and Sigurd Bjørner. The movement expanded to more towns and regions. In the capital a campaign by the English healing evangelist Smith Wigglesworth in 1921 was a great success. But lingering disagreements over authority and organization culminated in a schism in 1924. The Bjørners and a delegation of British leaders persuaded over half the Danish Pentecostals to join the more elaborately structured Apostolic Church.

The detractors, including nearly all the movement's foreign missionaries, retained a congregational polity under the influence of the Swedish Pentecostal movement. Around this time, a considerable number of Methodists became disillusioned by the corruption associated with their bishop, Anton Bast. Many chose to join the independent Pentecostal churches instead. Soon this denomination was larger than the Methodist Church as well as the Apostolic Church. But the Apostolic Church also grew, through its use of wide-ranging forms of evangelism and mission. Its hub was Kolding in southern Jutland, which became home to the International Apostolic Bible College, established in 1939.

The remaining Pentecostals also collaborated in publishing magazines and books and establishing several schools in the small town of Mariager in northeast Jutland. Both denominations still hold summer conferences at the site of their Bible schools. While the independent Pentecostal churches accepted some level of centralization in this way, the Apostolic Church began to decentralize from the 1930s. Thus, the two denominations have gradually met in the middle and ended the schism though they remain as separate denominations.

Adding to this plurality, the Charismatic Renewal arrived in Denmark around 1970, followed by the Jesus People Movement. Once again it was possible to encounter Pentecostal phenomena among Lutherans, Baptists, and others – and again the movement had a mixed reception from the key audience of traditional revivalists. The renewal also influenced classical Pentecostals, for example through the ministry of Alfred Lorenzen in Copenhagen. From here, Pentecostals would begin to use innovations in mission such as radio and TV.

In the 1980s, some Charismatics formed house churches and Vineyard churches. Prosperity teachings, represented by groups such as the Word of Faith, caused controversy across all strands of Pentecostalism. Among Lutheran Charismatics, this along with moral failures and outside criticisms led to a firmer organization as Dansk Oase in 1989. This was similar to what happened seven decades earlier in the early Pentecostal movement. However, this time it was not as a separate denomination but a formalized network within the institutions and limited freedoms of the established church.

Today, the entire span of Pentecostalism counts less than half of one percent of the Danish population among its adherents. Recently, the numbers have been bolstered by migrant churches. The most significant recent addition to the Pentecostal scene in Denmark is Hillsong Church which began services in Copenhagen in 2012. Among Lutherans, in later years Charismatics and traditional Evangelicals have in practice moved closed to one another. This has led to mutual revitalization, though on the institutional level they remain mostly separate.

In 2017, the main network of independent Pentecostal churches in Denmark changed its name to Mosaik to reflect the inclusion of local churches without roots in classical Pentecostalism. Furthermore, both Pentecostal and Apostolic churches joined together in a larger network known as FrikirkeNet in 2004. Up to a quarter of Danish foreign missionaries are

Pentecostals, reflecting the movement's global outlook. While early Pentecostals often went to China, more recently the most prominent focus has been Eastern Europe.

Secularization continues to be a challenge, but also an opportunity as other churches have been slower to adapt to the conditions of postmodernity. A few fringe groups have created bad press for the movement as a whole, whereas mainstream Pentecostals have sought to engage constructively with the surrounding culture.

Bibliography

Christensen, Nikolaj. Forthcoming. *Unorganized Religion: Pentecostalism and Secularization in Denmark, 1907–1924*. Leiden: Brill.

Jacobsen, T., and K.I. Tangen. 2017. "Pentecostal and Charismatic Movements in Denmark and Iceland." In *Global Renewal Christianity: Spirit Empowered Movements Past, Present, and Future*. Vol. 4, *Europe and North America*, edited by V. Synan and A. Yong, 215–27. Lake Mary: Charisma House.

Larsen, Kurt E. 2007. *Fra Christensen til Krarup: Dansk kirkeliv i det 20. århundrede*. Fredericia: Kolon.

Sørensen, Ib. 2010. "Leg med ilden: Pentekostale trosfællesskaber og problematiske omverdensrelationer." Ph.D. diss., University of Southern Denmark. https://www.sdu.dk/-/media/files/forskning/phd/phd_hum/afhandlinger/2010/ib_soerensen.pdf.

Tangen, Karl-Inge. 2012. *Ecclesial Identification Beyond Late Modern Individualism? A Case Study of Life Strategies in Growing Late Modern Churches*. Leiden: Brill.

Nikolaj Christensen

Dhinakaran, D.G.S.

Doraiswamy Geoffrey Samuel Dhinakaran, generally known as DGS Dhinakaran, was born on July 1, 1935, in a village named Surandai in the Tirunelveli district of Tamil Nadu, South India. His father Doraiswamy and mother Hepzibah acknowledged him as a gift from God after much prayer, and dedicated him to God's service. He was infected with polio that made his right leg disabled when he was eighteen months old, but was miraculously healed. His father was eager to get him the best education possible. He graduated with a bachelor's degree in mathematics from Madras University in 1955. His young life was characterized by pain, sickness, unemployment, and depression. He decided to commit suicide and was heading to a railway track near his home. On the way, he met his uncle Alex Rathanam who told him about the love of Jesus and asked him to commit his ways to the Lord. Dhinakaran believed that God forgave all his sins and instantaneously felt the warmth of his great love and comfort. He became a different person and believed that encountering with Christ led him to a wholesome life. He was baptized by S.P. Daniel then experienced the power of the Holy Spirit.

He started his career as a school teacher but later moved to banking. During his job, he travelled across South India, learning the culture and needs of the people which helped him identify with ordinary people during his ministry. Dhinakaran acknowledged three persons who contributed to his conversion and spiritual life: J.K. Rowlands, T.L. Osborn, and J.S. Lemiur. He experienced the baptism of the Holy Spirit on October, 10 1962, which led him to pursue the nine gifts of the Spirit. He started preaching in the streets and later on radio. He always believed that people could be miraculously healed from any type of sickness through prayers. His first public meeting was arranged in 1970 in Vellore, Tamil Nadu, India. Dhinakaran's evangelistic passion and the gift of healing propelled him to enter new arenas in his ministry. All his meetings were called "Jesus Calls" and later his organization became known with the same name. This is one of the leading free independent parachurch organizations in India.

Dhinakaran was well-known for his melodious singing and compassionate words that attracted mass crowd in his meetings. His crusades were attended by people of all faiths and denominations. His relationship with the Church of South India (CSI) continued until his death. Although he was recognized as a CSI member, his attention to other denominations offered him a wider platform for ministry. Thus, many remained in established churches rather than joining Pentecostal churches. He was a promoter of Pentecostal ministry in India. His association with G. Sundaram in the 1970s immensely influenced his approach to the poor and needy. Sundaram's care, concern, and holiness was seen as becoming exemplary in the ministry of Dhinakaran.

Dhinakaran was the first Indian link between global charismatic movements. His ministry had strong influence to likeminded healing ministers across the globe. He established a creative style to attract people. He distributed prayer oil that contained a label on the bottle, saying, "This is oil which Brother Dhinakaran has blessed with his prayer." Young partner club was another popular initiative with Jesus Calls ministry, in which children can register by paying a particular amount. Every year the child receives a prayer and birthday card. The child's family is also given opportunity to meet with a member of the leadership team during their meetings in different cities by paying a particular fee. In Indian Pentecostalism, Dhinakaran is identified as a healing evangelist, who influenced the wider public extending even to the media. In contrast to other healing ministers in India, Dhinakaran carefully chose praiseworthy testimonies to include in his sermons rather than allowing people share their testimonies in all his meetings. It was very common to hear him randomly call the names of people in a gathering of several thousands. Such naming practices could generate suspicion and result in criticism.

As an Indian Pentecostal preacher he raised financial support from Indians along with significant contributions from western countries. Although he is well-known preacher, his ministry also included social work, education, and development. In 2004 Dhinakaran established Karunya University which was the first-recognized Christian university in India. Jesus Calls prayer tower in Chennai operates around the clock and the prayer line helps many to trust God and find solutions to their problems. He was called to his eternal home on February 20, 2008.

Bibliography

Anderson, Allan Heaton. 2014. *An Introduction to Pentecostalism: Global Charismatic Christianity*. Cambridge: Cambridge University Press.

Bergunder, Michael. 2008. *The South Indian Pentecostal Movement in the Twentieth Century*. Grand Rapids, MI: William B. Eerdmans.

Dhinakaran, D.G.S. 1978. *Love So Amazing*. Madras: Christian Literature Society

Joy Samuel

Du Plessis, David

David du Plessis (1905–1987) was a major figure in the twentieth-century Charismatic Movement. As a Classical Pentecostal who came to embrace the ecumenical movement, du Plessis served as a helpful bridge for mainline Protestants and Roman Catholics seeking to understand and explore new experiences of the Holy Spirit. Du Plessis spent the first half of his life in his native South Africa. He converted to Pentecostalism together with his family during the First World War. Later, he joined the Apostolic Faith Mission (AFM), a group that had been founded by missionaries John G. Lake and Thomas Hezmalhalch. Embracing a call to ministry, du Plessis's involvement with the AFM involved a variety of responsibilities: evangelist, pastor, official denominational positions, and editor.

After the Second World War, du Plessis's ministry outside South Africa began in earnest. In 1947, he participated in the first conference of the Pentecostal World Fellowship. From around that time until 1958, he served – with some interruption – as its organizing secretary. In 1948, du Plessis began the process of immigrating to the United States with his family. His new residence there afforded increasing connections with American expressions of Pentecostalism, and in 1955 he adopted ministerial credentials with the Assemblies of God (AG).

Before long, du Plessis began to take the first steps towards that would mark the rest of his life: the ecumenical movement. In 1952, he met with leaders at the World Council of Churches (WCC) and National Council of Churches (NCC). Traveling to NCC offices in New York, he reported that they had significant curiosity about Pentecostalism. Continued conversations in this new arena led to attendance at International Missionary Conference meetings in the 1950s as well as the 1954 meeting of the WCC. Having both history and standing within Classical Pentecostalism, du Plessis was a central figure for ecumenical outsiders who were interested in an "official" insider's perspective. In 1959, various aspects of du Plessis's involvements came together as he delivered lectures at both Princeton Seminary and the Ecumenical Institute in Bossey, Switzerland.

While some mainline Protestants and ecumenical voices expressed interest in learning more about Pentecostalism, others known as "charismatics" wanted to go farther and embrace the gifts of the Spirit in their own ecclesial context. In the midst of this curiosity about Spirit-filled experience, David du Plessis's work in serving as a translator of the Pentecostal message and ethos marked him as an ideal consultant.

By the early 1960s, the AG became anxious about du Plessis's ecumenical activities, eliciting conversations at the highest levels of leadership. Tensions eventually came to a head when he was forced from the group in 1962. Many who have commented on this episode point to growing connections between the AG and American evangelicalism as the leading cause of du Plessis's ejection. Following his departure, he remained outside the official orbit of denominational Pentecostalism until the AG re-admitted him in 1980. Far from being hindered by his eighteen-year hiatus from the group, du Plessis took advantage of his newfound freedom from denominational strictures and continued to serve as a key resource for the burgeoning Charismatic Movement.

As the 1960s continued on, Roman Catholics also began to join the ranks of those interested in the Pentecostal message. The Roman Catholic Charismatic Renewal, growing out of meetings in 1967 at Duquesne and Notre Dame, grew to be a significant force within the broader Charismatic Movement. Du Plessis, who had been an invited observer at one of the sessions of the Second Vatican Council, was once again well positioned to serve as a resource for those exploring aspects of the revival movement. Overcoming historic theological and religious prejudices, du Plessis embraced this renewal and the opportunity it provided. Notably, du Plessis participated in both the 1972 founding and early years of an official Roman Catholic-Pentecostal Dialogue.

In his final years, du Plessis operated as an elder statesman of Pentecostalism and the Charismatic Movement. During this season, he published his autobiography entitled *A Man Called Mr. Pentecost* (1977) and another interview-style book on a variety of topics entitled *Simple and Profound* (1986). He died on February 2, 1987.

In 1985, du Plessis donated his papers to Fuller Theological Seminary. Seen together, these letters, sermons, writings, and other records demonstrate his unique role as a bridge to the Charismatic Movement. Du Plessis's ubiquitous presence and influence was significant in helping connect many to the Pentecostal ethos and experience while simultaneously offering an explanation and apologetic for a seemingly new work of the Spirit in his time. His legacy is that of a passionate and engaged Pentecostal figure who, though somewhat traditional, was nevertheless willing to adapt for the sake of his mission.

Bibliography

Blumhofer, Edith. 1993. *Restoring the Faith: The Assemblies of God, Pentecostalism, and American Culture*. Chicago: University of Illinois Press.

du Plessis, David J. 1986. *Simple and Profound*. Orleans, MA: Paraclete Press.

du Plessis, David J., and Bob Slosser. 1977. *A Man Called Mr. Pentecost*. Plainfield, NJ: Logos International.

du Plessis, David J. 1970. *The Spirit Bade Me Go*. Plainfield, NJ: Logos International.

Ziefle, Joshua R. 2012. *David du Plessis and the Assemblies of God: The Struggle for the Soul of a Movement*. Leiden: Brill.

Joshua Ziefle

Durham, William H.

William H. Durham (1873–1912) was born in Kentucky about fifty miles from Lexington. At the age of eighteen, Durham joined the Baptist church, but he did not experience conversion until 1898 while living in Minnesota. In 1901 he was sanctified though he would later re-interpret the experience as the reclaiming of the fullness of salvation (Jacobsen 2003). After

William Durham, 1873–1912. Image: http://www.zionchristianministry.com/

a year as an evangelist, Durham assumed the pastorate of Gospel Mission Church, an independent holiness mission on North Avenue, Chicago in 1903. Two years later he married Bessie Mae Whitmore. Their life together would end in tragedy, however. On August 8, 1909, Bessie died of complications two weeks after giving birth to their second child, who also passed away six months later. A few years later Durham married Gertrude Taylor, who was his daughter's caregiver. While preaching in Los Angeles, Durham developed a respiratory ailment and travelled back to Chicago with his new wife, where he died on July 7, 1912 at the age of thirty-nine.

When Durham first heard about the 1906 Azusa Street Revival in Los Angeles, he rejected the message that speaking in tongues was necessary evidence for the reception of Spirit baptism. However, after Mable and Jessie Smith brought news of the revival and members of his congregation experienced the baptism, Durham travelled to Los Angeles in February 1907 to attend the Azusa Street Mission. From February 26 to March 2, he experienced a feeling of mighty power and on the evening of March 2, he received the gift of tongues. William Seymour prophesied over Durham, claiming that wherever Durham preached the Spirit would fall. Durham then returned to Chicago and held revival meetings nightly, with people speaking in tongues and being slain in the Spirit. These meetings were crowded, and Chicago soon became a major Pentecostal center with connections to Los Angeles, Winnipeg, and Toronto (Faupel 1996).

In May 1910, Durham was invited to address the annual Pentecostal Convention at Stone Church, Chicago where he preached on "The Finished Work of Calvary." The message was controversial and forced a rift in the movement between Wesleyan holiness and Reformed-minded Pentecostals.

Durham preached that salvation and sanctification is found in identification with Christ, that perfection transpires in the acceptance of the historical reality of the cross where inbred sin is crucified with Christ and righteousness is imputed. Consequently, there is no need for a second definite work of grace for sanctification as advocated by holiness folk. Actual sin injures one's relationship with Jesus and the carnal nature resurfaces, but perfection is restored through faith in the power of the cross to redeem. Durham was in line with the holiness view that entire sanctification is a crucifixion of sinful nature, but he deviated from it by denying the need for a second act of grace distinct from justification, or that sin could be eradicated. For Durham, both justification and sanctification are applied by Christ through the act of faith. Sanctification is a consecration of service to God and the atoning work of Christ is realized through conversion, bringing one into Christ and making a person holy through the inward and outward cleansing from sin, giving a clean heart, and making one into a new creature (Faupel 1996).

Durham thus collapsed the three works of grace – justification, sanctification, and Spirit baptism – that was commonly accepted among Pentecostals prior to 1910 into two works of grace – justification and Spirit baptism. Spirit baptism was seen by Durham as an act of sanctification in that God empowered the Christian for service. Sanctification must also involve growth and maturation (Faupel 1996).

Richmann (2015) questions the standard historical reconstruction of Durham's role in the promulgating of finished work doctrine, however. Richmann proposes Durham's finished work sermon was preached in early 1911 and the finished work teaching was already being debated in Pentecostal circles at a camp meeting in Malvern, Arkansas in September 1910. Consequently, A.S. Copley is a co-architect of the doctrine and may have been the first to advocate the finished work message.

The origin of finished work theology notwithstanding, Durham was influential in the Pentecostal movement. Pentecostal figures such as E.N. Bell, A.H. Argue, Louis Francescon, Giacomo Lombardi, Peter Ottolini, Daniel Berg, Gunnar Vingren, F.A. Sandgren, William H. Piper, Robert and Aimee Semple, T.K. Leonard, Andrew Urshan, and Howard Goss were either brought into Pentecost, or influenced by Durham prior to 1910. After the breakout of the finished work controversy nearly 60 percent of the movement in the USA adopted the doctrine, except in the deep south where 75 percent retained the second work doctrine. If one includes Canada, then 80 percent of the Pentecostal movement adopted the finished work theory (Faupel 1996). Durham thus influenced a significant theological shift on the young Pentecostal movement, despite his untimely death.

Bibliography

Clayton, Allen L. 1979. "The Significance of William H. Durham for Pentecostal Historiography." *Pneuma* 1 (2): 27–42.

Faupel, D. William. 1996. *The Everlasting Gospel: The Significance of Eschatology in the Development of Pentecostal Thought.* Sheffield: Sheffield Academic Press.

Jacobsen, Douglas. 2003. *Thinking in the Spirit: Theologies of the Early Pentecostal Movement.* Bloomington, IN: Indiana University Press.

Richmann, Christopher J. 2015. "William H. Durham and Early Pentecostalism: A Multifaceted Reassessment." *Pneuma* 37 (2): 224–243.

Peter Althouse

Dzao, Timothy

Timothy Dzao (Zhao Shi-guang; 趙世光; 1908–1973) was born in Shanghai and was named as Zhao Yuan-chang (趙元昌). He was the only child in a family which adhered to folk religion. He was a descendant of the founder of Song Dynasty (AD 960–1279), Emperor Taizu of Song.

In 1921, Dzao's cousin brought him to Sunday School. He was baptized on Christmas day of 1924 at Moore Memorial Church in Shanghai by Dr. John Hawk of the Methodist Episcopal Church, South (Southern Methodist Church). In 1925, he experienced a spiritual rebirth at a revival led by an English missionary Rev. Paget Wilkes. He then changed his name to Shi-guang, which means "light of the world," and devoted his life to evangelism. He graduated from high school in 1926 and entered the Bible college of the Christian and Missionary Alliance (C&MA). In 1928, he began to minister Beulah Chapel (守真堂) of C&MA in Shanghai. He was ordained pastor in 1932 and was given the name Timothy. Dzao married his coworker Tang Ling-an in 1930 and had seven children.

In 1936 he was invited by a Canadian missionary Rev. Robert A. Jaffray of the Chinese Foreign Missionary Union (中華國外布道團). He conducted his first revival tour in southeast Asia for five and a half months. In 1938 he began his second revival tour in southeast Asia, which lasted for three and a half years.

When the Pacific War broke out in December 1941, Dzao was stuck in Shanghai. He started leading revival meetings there and publishing *Ling Liang* magazine (靈糧; Bread of Life) in March 1942. A Christian community was gradually developed and eventually became Ling Liang Church (靈糧堂; Bread of Life Church) in June 1942. During the mid-1940s, its branches were established in different parts of Shanghai, as well as in Nanjing, Hangzhou, and Suzhou. He also served Jewish refugees in Shanghai and the foreign missionaries who were kept in the Japanese concentration camp during the Sino-Japanese War.

In 1945, he founded Ling Liang Worldwide Evangelistic Mission, a non-denominational mission organization. He established orphanages, kindergartens, elementary and secondary schools, and elderly care centers. He also founded the Eastern China Seminary to train ministers and missionaries. In 1947, missionaries were ordained and sent to Calcutta in India and Jakarta in Indonesia.

When the political situation in China changed, Dzao fled to Hong Kong on October 1, 1949. He started holding Sunday services at the King's Theater in 1950. He built Kowloon Ling Liang Church in 1951 and held revival meetings for one hundred consecutive days since its dedication. He established Taipei Ling Liang Church in Taiwan in 1954. By 1966, Dzao had held six round-Taiwan evangelical tours. Between 1955 and 1956, he founded the Christian Cimoeiel University and a missionary college in Jakarta. On the first general meeting of the Ling Liang churches held in September 1957, Dzao was elected president. He was ordained bishop in July 1958. By 1967, Ling Liang churches had been founded in Africa, France, India, Japan, the Philippines, the UK, the U.S., and Vietnam.

Dzao was not only a church planter, but also a world-renowned evangelist and revivalist. Since 1949, he held a number of mission tours in the U.S., Japan, southeast Asia, and Europe. In 1965 he led over 200 evangelical meetings in South Korea. In 1966 Dzao spoke in the World Congress on Evangelism held in Berlin. He authored 35 volumes of Bible commentaries and several biographies and mission travelogues. He also edited *Ling Liang Gospel Songs*. Dzao was awarded honorary doctoral degrees by Taylor University, Boston University, and Baptist Theological Seminary in the U.S. in 1955 and 1956.

Bibliography

Dzao, Timothy. 1969. *A Missionary Pilgrimage*. Hong Kong: Ling Liang Publishing. 趙世光。《宣教歷程》。香港：靈糧出版社。

Dzao, Timothy. 1945. *A Memoir of Twenty Years*. Shanghai: Shanghai Ling Liang Publishing. 趙世光。《二十年回憶》。上海：上海靈糧刊社。

Jin, Li Zheng. "Timothy Dzao." In *Biographical Dictionary of Chinese Christianity*. Global China Centre. 金立正。〈趙世光〉。載《華典》。世華中國研究中心。http://bdccOnline.net/zh-hant/stories/zhao-shiguang.

Peng, Suk Man. 2014. "Timothy Dzao," in *Biography of Hong Kong Christianity*. Hong Kong: The Hong Kong Chinese Christian Churches Union. 彭淑敏。〈趙世光〉。載《香港教會人物傳》。香港：香港華人基督教聯會出版部。

Su, Edwin. "History of Ling Liang World-Wide Evangelistic Mission." Ling Liang World-wide Evangelistic Mission Association. http://www.llwwema.org/welcome.htm.

Shin Fung Hung

Ecclesiology

All across the globe, Pentecostalism has come to display the most diverse set of ecclesiastical forms. They stretch from highly independent local-community driven movements (Scandinavia), to Presbyterian and Congregationalist-type denominations (Assemblies of God, USA), and to episcopally, with the office of bishop led "high-church" models (Black Pentecostals in the USA and a number of traditions in various global contexts). Particularly in the Global South, this diversification further continues and deepens.

Factors such as passion for freedom, resistance to institutionalization, and an endless diversity of structures help explain the curious absence, or at least the dearth, of developed ecclesiological reflection (Kärkkäinen 2002, 2011; Green 2016). For example, the formative book written by the American Assemblies of God theologian M.L. Hodges, *A Theology of the Church and Its Mission: A Pentecostal Perspective* (1977) is instructive. While offering a number of helpful biblical and practical – in this case predominantly missiological – insights, it can hardly be regarded as a constructive theological reflection on the church. It is rather a practical approach to the topic of the church in the service of the mission. Indeed, mission plays such a central role that recent titles, such as *Network Church: A Pentecostal Ecclesiology Shaped by Mission* have been published (Lord 2012).

Amos Yong (2005) rightly remarks that Pentecostals' focus on experience rather than theological reflection led to "practical" and "realistic" perspectives on the church. Until recently, a major way most Pentecostals have approached the topic of ecclesiology is to reiterate some key biblical perspectives from the New Testament, often echoing more general evangelical viewpoints (e.g. Dusing 1994, and Duffield/Van Cleave 1983). Particularly the Book of Acts has served well the Pentecostal desire to continue the "apostolic" pattern of charismatically empowered missionary-focused life of their communities (Land 1992).

It is noteworthy that in some Pentecostal theological and doctrinal presentations a separate chapter on ecclesiology may even be missing despite extensive treatments of ministry, ordinances, and similar church-related themes (Clarke 2014; Warrington 1998). Even the recent massive collection of essays by leading Pentecostal scholars from various global contexts, *The Cambridge Companion to Pentecostalism*, devotes no chapter to ecclesiology (Robeck and Yong 2014). Furthermore, it is ironic – if not so illustrative of the endless desire among Pentecostals to borrow from other theological (re)sources – that the entry "Theology of the Church" in the *Dictionary of Pentecostal and Charismatic Movements* was authored by a Roman Catholic (charismatic) theologian (Hocken 2002).

Against the judgment of uninformed observers, there is a consensus among Pentecostal theologians that rather than primarily a "spirit-movement," Pentecostal spirituality and church life is a form of "Spirit-Christology," that is, a christologically founded experience of the Spirit and spiritual empowerment. This is conveniently named as the Pentecostal "Full Gospel" or the "Five-Fold Gospel." In other words, the Pentecostal understanding of Christian life and church ministry is embedded and anchored in a dynamic encounter with Christ depicted in his manifold role of Justifier, Sanctifier, Baptizer with the Spirit, Healer of the Body, and the Soon Coming King (Dayton 1987; for a constructive ecclesiological application of this framework, see Thomas 2010). When placed in the ecclesial framework, we can speak of Pentecostal *koinonia*, a distinctive form of communion ecclesiology.

With all their desire for healing and empowerment, Pentecostals have never lost sight of the first work of Christ as Savior. Yet in keeping with the contemporary ultra-individualistic cultural milieu as well as the Reformation insistence on the individual's access to God, Pentecostal soteriology too easily fails to envision Christ's soteriological presence in communitarian terms (Chan 2000). That said, while Pentecostals at times have lost sight of community in their understanding of the church, their view of salvation – and thus of the church – is holistic. Salvation for Pentecostals is not reduced to accepting a few doctrines; it is a lived experience that touches the whole being of the person.

Healing is a central hallmark of Pentecostalism since its inception. While Pentecostals came to the belief of healing by reading the book of Acts and comparing notes with their own experiences, unconsciously they also came to manifest and represent a leading contemporary motif in pneumatology and ecclesiology, namely holism. Nothing in human life, including the physical dimension, is to be excluded from God's care. An integral part of Pentecostal worship service and ministry therefore is prayer for healing and restoration.

While the roots of Pentecostalism reach in various directions, the Holiness Movements were the midwife of early Pentecostalism. With their belief in the possibility of and strong insistence on the need for sanctification and holiness, those movements reminded Pentecostals of the connection between character and charism. At its best, Pentecostal communal life, lived in the power of the Spirit and by the fruit of the Spirit, aims to cultivate and nourish Christians' lives.

Because of the centrality of the Christ-driven charismatic experience, it is understandable that empowerment for service and ministry, including the exercise of a wide variety of spiritual gifts (charisms) is an integral part of Pentecostal church life and ecclesiology. Indeed, the most distinctive Pentecostal experience, that of Spirit-Baptism, is deeply communal, and not only a personal experience. As the leading Pentecostal systematician Frank Macchia writes, "The Spirit is the Spirit of communion. Spirit baptism implies communion. This is why it leads to a shared love, a shared meal, a shared mission, and the proliferation/enhancement of an interactive charismatic life" (Macchia 2006, 205).

Unknowingly, early Pentecostals made the all-important theological connection between the pouring out of the Spirit, the end times, and church's mission. Notwithstanding excesses and at times overly enthusiastic expectation, the Pentecostal conviction of the urgency of mission to the world as a result of the "Latter Day Rain" leading up to the Second Coming of Christ is a legacy for all Christian communities. Eschatological urgency did not result in complacency but rather energized Pentecostal communities in service and mission.

What kinds of directions is the ecclesiological conversation taking among global Pentecostal families? No doubt, much work awaits Pentecostal theologians from various global settings to construct viable ecclesiologies which would be contextually sensitive to African, Asian, Latin-American, and other religio-cultural challenges and resources. Similarly, the rapidly growing Pentecostal constituencies in the USA deriving from Hispanic, Asian, and African contexts are calling for such ecclesiological reflections. Yet another urgent issue facing Pentecostal ecclesiology has to do with religious plurality and diversity (see Kärkkäinen in Robeck and Yong 2014, 294–312).

Bibliography

Chan, Simon. 2011. *Pentecostal Ecclesiology: An Essay on the Development of Doctrine*. Blandford Forum, UK: Deo Publishing.

Clarke, Clifton R., ed. 2014. *Pentecostal Theology in Africa*. Eugene, OR: Pickwick.

Dayton, Donald W. 1987. *Theological Roots of Pentecostalism*. Grand Rapids, MI: Zondervan.

Duffield, Guy P., and N.M. Van Cleave. 1983. *Foundations of Pentecostal Theology*. Los Angeles, CA: LIFE. Bible College.

Dusing, Michael. 1994. "The New Testament Church." In *Systematic Theology: A Pentecostal Perspective*, edited by Stanley M. Horton, 525–566. Springfield, MO: Gospel Publishing House.

Green, Chris E.W., ed. 2016. *Pentecostal Ecclesiology: A Reader*. Leiden: Brill.

Hocken, Peter. 2002. "Church, Theology of the." In *The New International Dictionary of Pentecostal and Charismatic Movements*, edited by Stanley M. Burgess and Eduard M. van der Maas, 544–554. Grand Rapids, MI: Zondervan.

Hodges, Melvin L. 1977. *A Theology of the Church and Its Mission: A Pentecostal Perspective*. Springfield, MO: Gospel Publishing House.

Kärkkäinen, Veli-Matti. 2002. *An Introduction to Ecclesiology: Ecumenical, Historical, and Contextual Perspectives*. Downers Grove, IL: InterVarsity Press.

Land, Steven J. 1992. *Pentecostal Spirituality: A Passion for the Kingdom*. Sheffield: Sheffield Academic.

Lord, Andy. 2012. *Network Church: A Pentecostal Ecclesiology Shaped by Mission*. Leiden: Brill.

Macchia, Frank. 2006. *Baptized in the Spirit: A Global Pentecostal Theology*. Grand Rapids, MI: Zondervan.

Robeck, Cecil M. Jr. and Amos Yong, eds. 2014. *The Cambridge Companion to Pentecostalism*. Cambridge: Cambridge University Press.

Thomas, John Christopher, ed. 2010. *Toward a Pentecostal Ecclesiology: The Church and the Fivefold Gospel*. Cleveland, TN: CPT Press.

Warrington, Keith, ed. 1998. *Pentecostal Perspectives*. Carlisle: Paternoster.

Yong, Amos. 2005. *The Spirit Poured Out on All Flesh: Pentecostalism and the Possibility of Global Theology*. Grand Rapids, MI: Baker Academic.

Veli-Matti Kärkkäinen

Ecology

Ecology examines the interconnected and interdependent created world (human and non-human) as ecosystem. Viewed from philosophical, religious or ethical perspectives, "ecosystems principally lead to notions that emphasize the intrinsic value and interdependence of all living things and nature" (Bauckham 2005, 469–470). The engagement of Christian communities with ecological awareness has given rise to ecological theologies.

"Ecotheologies" arose in the late twentieth century alongside a rising awareness for ecological crises. Christian ecotheology highlights the whole "household" of God's creation – especially the world of nature – as an inter-related system (Santmire 2003). As such, Christian ecotheologies aim at achieving ecological justice (Agbiji 2015). As a response to Lynn White's assertion that Judeo-Christian beliefs and teachings bore "a great burden of guilt" for ecological crises (cited in

Whitney 2005, 1736), biblical scholars and ecotheologians such as James Barr, Carl Braaten, John Cobb, and Joseph Sittler offered preliminary responses (Whitney 2005). Since, Christian responses to ecological realities have emerged – including global Pentecostals.

Pentecostals have often been caricatured as having reticence, indifference, and in some cases outright hostility to ecological issues (Rice 2014; Swoboda 2014 and Swoboda 2013). In response to this perceived ambivalence, scholars and Pentecostal thinkers such as Jean-Jacques Suurmond, Harold Hunter, Shane Clifton and Paul Yonggi Cho constructed preliminary responses (Rice 2014). Much of this was based on the social justice of Larry Christenson (Swoboda 2013) and the earth-care of John McConnell Jr. (Rodgers and Sparks in Swoboda 2014). It has been pointed out that primitive Pentecostalism had latent understanding of the environment as they sought to transform "immoral" or "dark" spaces – such as theatres, dance halls, saloons and tobacco warehouses – into houses of worship (Hubbard-Heitz in Swoboda 2014). Whilst Pentecostal ecotheology preliminarily developed in the Global North, African Pentecostals have also made salient contributions to Pentecostal ecotheologies under the auspices of African Independent Churches (AICs) through their creation spiritualities and Earth-keeping movements (Swoboda 2013).

Despite the lacuna of a formal global Pentecostal systematic theology, how can Pentecostal ecotheology be undertaken? Broadly speaking, Pentecostal ecotheology is situated within the broader context of Christian ecumenical ecotheologies in Roman Catholic, Orthodox, Protestant, and Ecofeminist traditions (Dalton & Simmons 2010). In that context, Pentecostal pneumatology has played this role. Tallman observes that the ecumenical turn to what Amos Yong has coined as "pneumatological imagination" (2009, 145) has opened the door for Pentecostals to enter the ecotheological conversation (Swoboda 2013; Clifton 2009). Ecological pneumatology (or ecopneumatology) has shown itself as a fruitful theological space for Pentecostals to do ecotheology (Swoboda 2013; Clifton 2009).

Ecopneumatology points to creation's emergence where the Spirit hovered over the waters of creation. The Spirit continues to hover over "the void" being caused by human sin that is destroying the creation. That same Spirit continues in the face of myriads of voids to inspire hope in God's salvation and healing for a glorious future (Clifton 2009).

The addition of soteriological and healing themes to Pentecostal ecotheology remains an increasingly critical area of examination. In our view, this has become inevitable, because the ecological crisis disproportionately affects the areas where the majority of Pentecostals live. With the majority of global wealth and political power held in developed nations, the effects of the global ecocrisis are most deeply felt and realized in places with the least wealth and food security. Healing of the environment is directly tied to the healing of the disadvantaged and the poor.

Imbach (1998) vividly connects Western greed and ecocide, the destruction of God's creation, drawing our attention to the "passion," or latent convictions, of the Western, industrial, developed mind, human greed and boundless selfishness. The attendant consequences of a rise in global temperatures, polar ice caps melting faster than ever, and a rise in cancer (Swoboda 2013) remain. God's creation continues to "groan" (Rom. 8:22). Yet there exists a resilient Pentecostal move towards creation care and ecological restoration in Africa (Tallman in Swoboda 2014), Latin American (Waldrop 2014), as well as among the grassroots Association of African Earthkeeping Churches (Daneel 1991).

A further, and equally important, intersection between Pentecostalism in the Majority World and the environment is found in the prosperity teachings commonly held among Pentecostal churches in such places (Swoboda 2015). Bowler identifies four distinct elements of prosperity teachings: 1) faith, 2) wealth, 3) health, and 4) victory. These theological dimensions are embedded in much of Pentecostalism's soteriology, eschatology and pneumatology. But scholars have argued that the wealth, health, and financial blessings promised by prosperity teachings – interpreted as signs of God's hand of blessing – offers a "gospel" which provides the theological, social, and practical vision which has great power to "fuel greed." (Wariboko 2012, 39). This kind of "anthropocentric prosperity" (Sarles 1986, 329) fails to take into account the planets well-being with its finite resources utilized for human consumption. Prosperity teachings offer a vision all too similar to the kind of Western consumerism that is destroying the planet in the first place, with its "vivid strains of American-style materialism and individualism" (Jong and Schieman 2012: 740).

Yet, at the same time, there remains one positive of prosperity gospels – it locates one dimension of salvation in the physical realm. Through renewed faith, positive thinking, and action in the power of the Holy Spirit, one can trust God to receive health, wealth, and victory in this temporal existence. As Bowler asserts: "The prosperity gospel is a widely popular Christian message of spiritual, physical, and financial mastery" (Bowler 2013, 3–7). Simply put, "God wants you to thrive" (Jong and Schieman 2012, 738). While this has yet to be fleshed out, what has great potential is a view of prosperity that includes the entire natural order – not only its human inhabitants.

Pentecostalism has long emphasized justice for the "least of these." Pentecostalism, historically, has been a movement of the poor, not merely a religion for the poor. What the ecocrisis has increasingly revealed is that the ramifications of the ecological crisis demands a re-examined approach to justice for the poor, who, as has been stated, are disproportionately affected by the ecocrisis. Through the Old and New Testaments, we are reminded that God goes to great pains to inspire an ethic for the needs of the poor to be cared for. The Psalmist writes, "I know that the Lord maintains the cause of the needy and executes justice for the poor" (Ps. 140:12). James chastised readers who had "dishonored the poor" (Jam. 2:5–6). And Jesus himself said, "[W]hen you give a banquet, invite the poor, the crippled, the lame, and the blind" (Lk. 14:13). On another occasion, Jesus spoke to his followers (and ultimately to the whole Christian community) about the eternal ramifications of what they did "to one of the least of these" – the hungry, the thirsty, the stranger, the naked, the sick, and the imprisoned (Matt. 25:31–46). Throughout his entire ministry, Jesus aligned himself with the Hebrew prophets who reprimanded those "that trample on the needy" and bring to ruin the poor of the land" (Amos 8:4). And with this compassion for the poor should arise a deeper sense of compassion for the natural order which is the space of the poor.

Without question, climate change, desertification, and water loss all have a disproportionate influence upon the poor.

Ironically, while the poor are disproportionately affected, the poor often live the most sustainable and environmentally simple lifestyles. In the twenty-first century, the Pentecostal community will need to re-examine ecological theology not merely as an effort to save the planet, but also to save the lives of the "least of these," particularly in the Majority World.

Bibliography

Agbiji, Obaji. 2015. "Religion and Ecological Justice in Africa: Engaging 'Value for Community' as Praxis for Ecological and Socio-economic Justice." *HTS Teologiese Studies/Theological Studies* 71 (2): 10 pages. doi:https://doi.org/10.4102/hts.v71i2.2663.

Bauckham, Richard. 2005. "Ecology." In *Encyclopedia of Christian Theology*, edited by J. Lacoste 1 (A–F), 469–471. London: Routledge.

Bowler, Kate. 2013. *Blessed: A History of the American Prosperity Gospel*. New York: Oxford University Press.

Clifton, Shane. 2009. "Preaching the 'Full Gospel' in the Context of Global Environmental Crisis." In *The Spirit Renews the Face of the Earth: Pentecostal Forays in Science and Theology of Creation*, edited by Amos Yong, 117–134. Eugene, OR: Wipf and Stock.

Dalton, Anne Marie, and Henry C. Simmons. 2010. *Ecotheology and the Practice of Hope*. Albany, NY: State University of New York Press.

Daneel, M.L. 1991. "Towards a Sacramental Theology of the Environment in African Independent Churches." *Theologia Evangelica* 24 (1): 2–26.

Imbach, Jeffrey. 1998. *The River Within: Loving God, Living Passionately*. Colorado Springs, CO: NavPress.

Jong, Hyun Jung, and Scott Schieman. 2012. "'Practical Divine Influence': Socioeconomic Status and Belief in the Prosperity Gospel." *Journal for the Scientific Study of Religion* 51 (4): 738–756.

Rice, Jonathan W. 2014. "Ecology and the future of Pentecostalism: Problems, Possibilities and Proposals." In *Pentecostal Mission and Global Christianity*, edited by Wonsuk Ma, Veli-Matti Karkkainen, and J. Kwabena Asamoah-Gyadu, 360–379. Oxford: Regnum Books International.

Santmire, H. Paul. 2003. "Ecotheology." In *Encyclopedia of Science and Religion* 1 (A–I), edited by N.H. Gregersen, W.J. Wildman, I. Barbour, and R. Valentine, 247–251. New York: Macmillan Reference USA (Gale).

Sarles, Ken L. 1986. "A Theological Evaluation of the Prosperity Gospel," *Bibliotheca Sacra* 143 (572): 329–352.

Swoboda, A.J. 2015. "Posterity or Prosperity? Critiquing and Refiguring Prosperity Theologies in an Ecological Age." *Pneuma* 37 (3): 394–411.

Swoboda, A.J., ed. 2014. *Blood Cries Out: Pentecostals, Ecology, and the Groans of Creation*. Eugene, OR: Wipf and Stock.

Swoboda, A.J. 2013. *Tongues and Trees: Toward a Pentecostal Ecological Theology*. Blandford Forum: Deo.

Tallman, Matthew. 2009. "Pentecostal Ecology: A Theological Paradigm for Pentecostal Environmentalism." In *The Spirit Renews the Face of the Earth: Pentecostal Forays in Science and Theology of Creation*, edited by Amos Yong, 135–172. Eugene, OR: Wipf and Stock.

Wariboko, Nimi. 2012. "Pentecostal Paradigms of National Economic Prosperity in Africa." In *Pentecostalism and Prosperity*, edited by Amos Yong and Katherine Attanasi, 35–62. New York: Palgrave MacMillan.

Whitney, E. 2005. "Thesis of Lynn White, (1907–1987)." In *Encyclopedia of Religion and Nature*, edited by B. Taylor, 1735–1737. London: Continuum.

Obaji Agbiji
A.J. Swoboda

Ecumenism

This article offers an overview of Pentecostal participation in ecumenism around the world. The term "ecumenism" derives from the Greek word *oikouméne*, which since antiquity has referred to "the whole, inhabited world", that is, the "household of creation". Its modern usage refers primarily to work done to restore unity and renew the Church, the "household of God" (Eph. 2:19). Ecumenism begins at the spiritual level for all who are "in Christ" but it involves more than interdenominational cooperation. It includes the resolution of issues that have divided the various Christian traditions through the centuries. It intends to bring healing and the visible restoration of unity to the whole Church. While dialogue with non-Christian religions, or interreligious dialogue, is very important, it should not be confused with Christian ecumenism.

Pentecostals have had a conflicted relationship with other Christian churches since they first appeared at the beginning of the twentieth century. Initially, other churches rejected them when they attempted to share their testimony of baptism in the Holy Spirit. At the same time, many early Pentecostals condemned the churches out of which they had emerged. Thus, people on both sides contributed to the separation between the historic churches and the new move of the Holy Spirit, now known as Pentecostalism. Thus, a dynamic form of spirituality available to all Christians became a separate movement. Following their denominational antecedents, Pentecostals also organized denominations, which older churches continued to marginalize.

In 1920, the Assemblies of God (AG) in the USA joined the Foreign Missionary Conference of North America, which in 1921, became part of the International Missionary Conference. While the World Christian Fundamentalist Association condemned Pentecostals in 1928, Pentecostals received some positive recognition when leaders founding the National Association of Evangelicals (NAE) in the USA invited them to join (1941). Despite significant historical and theological differences between Evangelicals and Pentecostals, this move made interdenominational cooperation possible. Pentecostals who were members of the NAE, soon formed the Pentecostal Fellowship of North America (PFNA), and in 1947, Pentecostals around the world, founded the Pentecostal World Conference (PWC), now the Pentecostal World Fellowship (PWF).

When the Charismatic Renewal broke out in the 1950s and 1960s, Pentecostals helped to facilitate its rise, through groups like Demos Shakarian's, *Full Gospel Businessmen's Fellowship International*, through books such as David Wilkerson's *The Cross and the Switchblade*, and through the work of individuals such as David du Plessis. Pentecostals often served as resources to many Christian leaders and churches, especially regarding baptism in the Spirit, and the use of charisms.

From the 1950s onward, David du Plessis, encouraged by the English Pentecostal, Donald Gee, editor of the PWC's magazine, *Pentecost*, became the leading Pentecostal voice for ecumenism. He frequented the halls of the World Council of Churches (WCC), and served officially on staff at the 1954 Evanston Assembly at the invitation of the WCC General Secretary, Willem Visser 't Hooft. During the 1960s, du Plessis rejoiced that several Pentecostal churches in Latin American had joined the WCC. At the same time, he followed closely, the Second Vatican Council (1961–1964), where he received Observer status during its third session.

Du Plessis' popularity and strong support for ecumenism led to conflict with his General Superintendent, Thomas F. Zimmerman, who was also Chair of the PWC, and President of the NAE, and who wanted to demonstrate AG loyalty to the NAE. As a result, Zimmerman condemned ecumenism at the 1961 PWC, defrocked du Plessis in 1964, and processed through the AG, an official position opposed to the Ecumenical Movement. The AG softened the statement in 2009.

While this position limited ecumenical participation among those affiliated with the AG, as early as 1960, Dutch Pentecostals held dialogues with Reformed Churches in the Netherlands, and Pentecostals in Scandinavia, especially in Finland and then in Norway and finally in Sweden, opened discussions with and then joined their respective National Councils of Churches. Later, Yoido Full Gospel Church (AG) joined the Korean National Council of Churches and the Apostolic Faith Mission of South Africa joined the South African Council of Churches. At least forty-five Pentecostal groups around the world now belong to their National Councils of Churches.

Following the end of the Second Vatican Council, du Plessis pursued the establishment of a dialogue between Rome and Pentecostals. The International Roman Catholic-Pentecostal Dialogue began in 1972, with du Plessis serving as Co-chair along with Fr. Kilian McDonnell, OSB. In 1984, Jerry L. Sandidge, an AG missionary in Belgium, joined as the Pentecostal Co-secretary. In 1985, Justus du Plessis succeeded his brother as the Pentecostal Co-chair, and Cecil M. Robeck, Jr. joined the steering committee. David du Plessis died in 1987. In 1992, Justus du Plessis retired and the Pentecostal members elected Robeck to begin service as the new Pentecostal Co-chair. He continues in that position.

To date, the Dialogue has completed six rounds, ranging from five to eight years each. It is currently in its seventh round of discussions. In spite of widespread appreciation for this dialogue in bringing greater understanding and cooperation between Catholics and Pentecostals, many Pentecostals, especially in Southern Europe and in much of Latin America remain strongly opposed to any Pentecostal contact with Catholics.

During the 1980s, Brother Jeffrey Gros, FSC, Director of the Commission on Faith and Order of the National Council of Churches in the USA (NCC) invited several Pentecostal scholars to join the Commission. Drawing upon these Pentecostals, the WCC invited Sandidge to serve as a Pentecostal Advisor to its Commission on Faith and Order meeting in Budapest, in 1989. He was unable to attend due to illness, and the WCC tapped Robeck to take his place. Subsequently, the WCC invited Robeck to participate in the Canberra Assembly, where he and Donald Dayton drafted recommendations that the Assembly adopted, encouraging the WCC to pursue Pentecostal contacts. Later that year, the WCC appointed Robeck to its Commission on Faith and Order, where he continues to serve.

Beginning in 1994, Huibert van Beek, who staffed the Ecumenical Relations office of the WCC, and Robeck brought together Pentecostal representatives from around the world to a series of ecumenical consultations in Latin America and Europe. They used these meetings to gauge potential Pentecostal interest in ecumenical initiatives and to build a list of participants for potential future work together. These consultations led eventually to the development of the Joint Consultative

Group, a dialogue between Pentecostals and the WCC, which the Harare Assembly of the WCC approved in 1998. It began its work in 2000 and in 2020 it completed its third round.

Due in part to these developing relationships, Konrad Raiser, General Secretary of the WCC convened a consultation in 1998 that led to the development of the Global Christian Forum (GCF). After testing the idea with Evangelicals and Pentecostals, the GCF held a meeting at Fuller Theological Seminary in 2002. It then convened regional meetings. Since 2007, it has also held three international meetings, Limuru, Kenya in 2007, Manado, Sulawesi, Indonesia in 2011, and Bogota, Colombia in 2018 that have succeeded in bringing a significant number of Pentecostal leaders into ecumenical contact. Several Pentecostal leaders now serve on the steering committee of the GCF.

The Secretaries of Christian World Communions hosts an annual meeting of General Secretaries, representing the full range of Church families. David du Plessis attended one such meeting in the late 1950s. The Secretaries sent many invitations to the General Secretary of the PWC, but failed to receive any response. In 1991 and 1992, Justus du Plessis attended their meetings. Upon his retirement, Justus du Plessis recommended that Robeck take his place as the Pentecostal voice. After consulting with Ray Hughes, then Chairman of the PWC, and with the General Superintendent of the AG, G. Raymond Carlson, Robeck has participated in this annual meeting since 1993.

The annual meeting of Secretaries proved to be fortuitous to further Pentecostal involvement in ecumenism. In 1994, Milan Opočenský, General Secretary of the World Alliance [now, Communion] of Reformed Churches, asked Robeck to consider opening up an international Reformed-Pentecostal dialogue. After an exploratory meeting in 1995 in Mattersey, England, the dialogue began. It completed its third round and report in 2020. At the same time, Gunnar Stålsett, the recently retired General Secretary of the Lutheran World Federation (LWF) asked Robeck to consider an international dialogue between Lutherans and Pentecostals. Due to the recent change in LWF Secretaries and the priority given the LWF gave to the completion of the Joint Declaration on Justification agreement with the Vatican, an exploratory meeting finally took place in Strasbourg, France in 2004, led by Theo Dieter, Director of the Ecumenical Institute there, and by Robeck. The following year, Robeck turned the leadership over to Jean-Daniel Plüss of the Swiss Pentecostal Mission, who continues to serve as chair. Following the completion of this six-year discussion, the LWF officially approved an international dialogue, which began in 2016. In 2020, it completed its first five-year report.

In 2014, a group of Pentecostal scholars representing several countries on four continents submitted a resolution to the PWF, calling for the establishment of a Commission on Relations with other Christian Communities. The Executive Committee rejected the proposal at that time. At its meeting in Calgary, Alberta, Canada in 2019, however, the Executive Committee revisited the request, revised it, and established such a Commission under the leadership of David Wells, General Superintendent of the Pentecostal Assemblies of Canada. Wells continues to encourage greater ecumenical participation by all PWF member churches. Reports from the various ecumenical dialogues including Pentecostals appear in the *Growth in Agreement* series published jointly by the World Council of Churches and the William B. Eerdmans Publishing Company since 2000.

Bibliography

Lutherans and Pentecostals in Dialogue. 2010. Strasbourg: Institute for Ecumenical Research.
Quebedeaux, Richard. 1983. *The New Charismatics II: How a Christian Renewal Movement Became Part of the American Religious Mainstream.* San Francisco: Harper & Row.
Robeck, Cecil M., Jr. 2019. "Can We Imagine an Ecumenical Future Together? A Pentecostal Perspective," *Gregorianum* 100 (1): 49–69.
Van Beek, Huibert, ed. 2009. *Revisioning Christian Unity: The Global Christian Forum.* Oxford: Regnum.
Vondey, Wolfgang, ed. 2013. *Pentecostalism and Christian Unity: Continuing and Building Relationships.* Eugene: Pickwick.
Vondey, Wolfgang, ed. 2010. *Pentecostalism and Christian Unity: Ecumenical Documents and Critical Assessments.* Eugene: Pickwick.
Ziefle, Joshua R. 2013. *David du Plessis and the Assemblies of God: The Struggle for the Soul of a Movement.* Leiden: Brill.

Cecil M. Robeck

Egypt

Situated in the northeast corner of the African continent, Egypt has undergone its fair share of geopolitical turmoil over the years. Despite the recent Arab Spring, its political and religious climate is still dominated by Islamic concerns and hegemony with little by way of actual freedom for dissidents.

According to *Christianity in North Africa-West Asia* (2018), Egypt has one of the largest number of Christians in the MENA region. With a total population of 91,508,000 people, Egypt is one of the largest Arab countries. 7,673,000 individuals identify as Christian. Of these, by far, the largest denomination is the Coptic Orthodox Church, with 95.2 percent of the Christian population. Renewalists, on the other hand, account for 7.4 percent or 567,802 individuals.

The earliest accounts tell of a recently Spirit-baptized Egyptian, Ghali Hana, carrying the Pentecostal experience to Assiyut, Egypt (Anderson 2007, 155). He had received Spirit baptism at the hands of Lucy Leatherman in 1906. Another missionary, Charles Leonard, joined the work in Assiyut in 1911 and Cairo in 1912. Other Pentecostal missionaries came as well: George and Lydia Brelsford, Sarah Smith, Frank Moll (1909), Ansel and Henrietta Post, Lillian Trasher (1910), and Herbert Randall (1912) (Anderson 2007, 155–7; Nagib 2016, 96). These Pentecostal missionaries linked up with the local networks of Pentecostal or sympathetic churches – networks that extend into the present era.

Without a doubt, the Renewalist movement in Egypt has been influenced by the Pentecostalization of Roman Catholicism, Pentecostal/Charismatic missions and conferences, as well as exchanges with the global Coptic diasporic and community. Beginning in the 1970s, many North American Egyptian Catholics accepted the Catholic Charismatic Renewal, held conferences that Coptic Orthodox leaders attended, and by 1982 established the Good News Ministry inside the Coptic Catholic Church. Further, through Francis MacNutt's work and the ongoing work of the Good News Ministry, the Renewal spread and flourished. Other non-denominational groups that attracted Coptic Orthodox believers sprang up in the 1980s such as Mohsen Nazem's Faith and Love Ministry that later became The Call of the Kingdom Movement. By 1989, it claimed 2,000 house churches. Additionally, former Coptic Orthodox priest, Father Daniel, launched Rivers of Life Ministry, which continues to minister to Copts and others throughout the Middle East (Nagib 2016, 98–101). Of significance, too, is American Mike Bickle's neo-Charismatic International House of Prayer's (Kansas City, MO) impact in the country. Beginning in 2009, IHOPKC has conducted large Onething Conferences outside of Cairo and established 400 houses of prayer. Its 2014 conference gathered 25,000 young people. Onething conferences are also regularly broadcasted on Arabic Christian TV, Sat-7 satellite, and streamed online (106). IHOPKC's millennial emphasis and concern for Israel echoes a return to early Pentecostal ideology. The ministry's success in Egypt also hints at a growing popularity for such ideas in the church.

Bibliography

Anderson, Allan H. 2007. *Spreading Fires: The Missionary Nature of Early Pentecostalism.* Maryknoll, NY: Orbis Books.

Nagib, Tharwat. 2016. "The Neo-Charismatic Movement in Egypt." In *Global Renewal Christianity Spirit-Empowered Movements: Past, Present and Future*, edited by Vinson Synan, Amos Yong, and J. Kwabena Asamoah-Gyadu, 93–108. Lake Mary, FL: Charisma House.

Ross, Kenneth R., Mariz Tadros, and Todd M. Johnson, eds. 2018. *Christianity in North Africa-West Asia.* Edinburgh: Edinburgh University Press.

Benjamin Crace

Ekman, Ulf

Ulf Ekman (1950–) was born into a working-class family in Gothenburg, Sweden, and grew up without any close contact with churches and the Christian faith, except for being baptized and confirmed in the Church of Sweden. In 1970 he was converted, shortly after his close friend became a Pentecostal after contacting some American Jesus People in Gothenburg. In the autumn of the same year, he began academic studies at Uppsala University and graduated in 1978 with two Bachelor degrees in History and Theology. While studying he was active in the Navigators, an American evangelical organization that specialized in evangelism and Bible studies among university students. Ekman was influenced by Reformed theology and also took part in Lutheran High-Church congregational life in Uppsala.

Ekman had more contact with the Swedish Charismatic renewal after marrying Birgitta Nilsson (1948–), the Daughter of Sten Nilsson (1915–2009), a Methodist minister and former missionary to India. Nilsson was a co-worker of E. Stanley Jones (1884–1973) and the leader of the European branch of the Ashram movement. The movement became a platform for Charismatic renewal in Sweden during the 1970s. Nilsson embraced Word of Faith teaching and introduced Ekman to different American Word of Faith ministries, especially Kenneth Copeland (1936–), Kenneth E. Hagin (1917–2003), and the Pentecostal missionary, Lester Sumrall (1913–96). Ekman was ordained a Lutheran minister in the Church of Sweden in 1979. For a few years he worked as a university chaplain in Uppsala.

In 1981–1982, Ekman studied at the Rhema Bible Training Center (RBTC) in Tulsa, Oklahoma and in the following year, he founded Word of Life, a non-denominational charismatic church and Bible school in Uppsala. The Bible school was partly modelled on RBTC, focusing on Word of Faith teaching combined with mainstream evangelical and Pentecostal theology. During those initial years, Ekman had important mentors including Bror Spetz (1926–2007), who was the pastor of Södermalmskyrkan. Södermalmskyrkan is a major Pentecostal congregation in Stockholm and became an early platform for the dissemination of Word of Faith teaching through Ekman. Sumrall also visited the Word of Life church regularly between 1985 and 1996 and influenced Ekman's support for mission work in Israel. The Word of Life church grew to a megachurch in the 1990s, having 3,300 members in 2009. The enrollment in the Bible school soared to around 1,000 students per year in the early 1990s, reaching about 10,000 students in total by 2009.

The Word of Life church also conducted mission work in the former Soviet Union in 1989 and developed several associations with neo-Pentecostal churches in the country through its efforts and its vast network of churches, organizations, and individuals in Scandinavia. Between 1989 and 1996, about 1,000 new local churches were planted and/or supported by the Word of Life church and its network through conferences, missionaries, short time volunteers, and Bible schools in different parts of Russia. Ekman's theology shaped the theology, practice, and social ethics of the Russian and Ukrainian churches that were founded and supported by his church.

The Word of Life Uppsala church was a controversial but also popular element in the religious landscape of Sweden. Through its strong emphasis on missions, the Word of Life church's international network comprises about 1,500 churches in Russia, East and Central Europe, Central Asia, and Scandinavia. Some of these churches have a formal organizational tie to the Word of Life Uppsala church, while others have more informal relationships.

Ekman became an important public figure in Sweden after assailing the Swedish brand of socialism in 1985 and the abortion law in the early 1990s. He also founded one of the largest private Christian schools in the country in 1985. He encouraged active Christian involvement in politics, which has resulted in the election of several members of parliament whose spiritual background and formation were developed from his Bible school and church.

In 1994 Ekman founded the Livets Ord University (LOU), which became a branch of the Oral Roberts University in 1997. The LOU provides theological education for pastors in Scandinavia, Central Europe, and Russia. In 2002, Ekman started a theological magazine, *Keryx*, containing articles with Lutheran, Catholic, and Pentecostal-Charismatic points of view.

Between 2004 and 2014, Ekman developed closer contacts with charismatics in the Roman Catholic Church, leading to his conversion to Catholicism in 2014. He resigned from the post of senior pastor of his church in 2013 and the ministry board in 2014. Ekman has continued his ministry as an author and speaker, while serving as a Catholic lay person.

Bibliography

Aronson, Torbjörn. 2012. "Continuity in Charismata: Swedish Mission and the Growth of Neo-Pentecostal Churches in Russia." *Religion in Eastern Europe* 31 (1): 33–40.

Aronson, Torbjörn. 2005. *Guds eld över Sverige. Svensk väckelsehistoria efter 1945.* Uppsala: Livets Ords Förlag.

Coleman, Simon. 2000. *The Globalisation of Charismatic Christianity: Spreading the Gospel of Prosperity*. Cambridge: Cambridge University Press.

Löfstedt, Torsten. 2018. "Ulf Ekman och auktoritetsfrågan." *Auktoritet*. Göteborg: Daidalos, 189–213.

Löfstedt, Torsten. 2017. "Pentecostals and Charismatics in Russia, Ukraine, and Other Post-Soviet States: History and Future Prospects." In *Global Renewal Christianity: Spirit-Empowered Movements Past, Present, and Future*. Vol. 4, *Europe and North America*, edited by Vinson Synan and Amos Yong, 19–32. Lake Mary, FL: Charisma House.

Torbjörn Aronson

El Salvador

The origin of Pentecostal Christianity in El Salvador corresponds with the global emergence of charismatic renewal movements during the twentieth century. The earliest documented Pentecostal missionary work there began after 1910 with the arrivals of the Canadian independent Pentecostal Frederic Mebius and a USA couple, Amos and Effie Bradley, who worked under the Pentecostal Holiness Church. Mebuis played a key role in establishing the first Pentecostal churches and what would become some of the largest Salvadoran Pentecostal denominations, including the Assemblies of God and the Church of God (Cleveland, TN), and the smaller fellowship of the Church of Apostles and Prophets.

Foreign Pentecostal missionaries working in El Salvador in the early twentieth century were limited to a few church planters who proselytized and organized meetings with coffee workers and indigenous groups in rural communities. Various scholars of Salvadoran Pentecostalism assert that a unique feature of the early movement was its relative independence from the control of U.S.-based denominations (Petersen 2012; Wadkins 2017). Their research offers persuasive evidence that from the outset it was Salvadorans who mainly directed, organized, and resourced this movement among neighbors in economically marginalized rural and urban communities. The number of Salvadorans identifying as Pentecostal Christians remained small for most of the twentieth century. The movement's rapid growth and urbanization, from the late 1960s onward, occurred even as everyday life for Salvadorans became increasingly engulfed in socioeconomic and political crisis. Today, approximately 35 percent of the Salvadoran population identifies as evangelical Christians, and the overwhelming majority of these attend churches affiliated with Pentecostalism (Wadkins 2017).

Like other local expressions of global Pentecostalism, the "social productivity" (Robbins 2009) of Salvadoran Pentecostals is notable and has generated numerous institutions in especially adverse contexts. Prior to El Salvador's civil war (1980–1992), urban churches were effective at attracting large numbers of households displaced by worsening economic conditions and increasing state repression in rural areas. Pentecostal radio programming also expanded considerably during this time. In the early 1960s, members of an Assemblies of God congregation in San Salvador, under the pastoral leadership of a U.S. missionary couple, John and Lois Bueno, founded the Liceo Cristiano private schools. Through local funding and U.S.-based child sponsorship programming, the system offered primary and secondary education and basic health care services to children from economically marginalized households in the capital. By 2010, Liceo enrolled over 17,000 students in thirty-five different schools located across El Salvador.

In the post-civil war era, the local expressions, organizational aspects, and global reach of the movement continue to diversify and expand. The country now has some of the largest Pentecostal megachurches in the region, including Misión Cristiana Elim, a church network of affiliate congregations across Central America and the USA with a membership of over 100,000 (Offutt 2015). Some affluent congregations manage robust foreign outreach budgets that support and send missionaries and short-term mission teams around the world (Offutt 2015, 120–3). Most Salvadoran Pentecostals, however, continue to meet in congregations of less than one hundred members in rural communities. A growing number of rural churches are expanding their social engagement activities to include participation in local community development arenas. ENLACE, a Pentecostal-affiliated non-government organization, currently partners with sixty Pentecostal churches and with community and government organizations to implement potable water and home garden projects, school, infrastructure, and health programs, and housing initiatives (Huff 2017).

Important empirical questions remain for scholars of the movement, including the relationship between religious change and socioeconomic and political conditions in a nation-state that struggles with economic inequality and chronic violence. Some see in Salvadoran Pentecostalism the production of a spirituality that is ready-made for everyday life in the contemporary, neoliberal order. The movement's emphasis on individual empowerment, its entrepreneurial ethos, and its deployment of diverse media to enable deterritorialized and personalized engagement with bible study and worship have been interpreted as cultural refractions of the larger processes of neoliberal change advanced by governing elites in the post war era. Others note that Pentecostals' increased public engagement, including their creation of ministries to gang members and community and economic development programs, suggests that adherents are looking to mobilize people to address the adverse effects of forces that are undermining their well-being (Huff 2017; Offutt 2015). Study of the dynamic formation of what has been aptly called Pentecostalisms in El Salvador should therefore continue to examine how local expressions intersect with, diverge from, and shape larger global processes of political, socioeconomic, and religious change.

Bibliography

Huff, James G. 2017. "Of Specters and Spirit: Neoliberal Entanglements of Faith-Based Development in El Salvador." *Urban Anthropology and Studies of Cultural Systems and World Economic Development. Special Issue: The Impact of State-Level and Global-Level Neoliberal Agendas on NGOs in Latin America* 46 (3/4): 173–220.

Offutt, Stephen. 2015. *New Centers of Global Evangelicalism in Latin America and Africa.* Cambridge: Cambridge University Press.

Petersen, Douglas. 2012. *Not by Might, Nor by Power: A Pentecostal Theology of Social Concern in Latin America.* Eugene, OR: Wipf and Stock.

Robbins, Joel. 2009. "Pentecostal Networks and the Spirit of Globalization: On the Social Productivity of Ritual Forms." *Social Analysis* 53 (1): 55–66. doi:10.3167/sa.2009.530104.

Wadkins, Timothy H. 2017. *The Rise of Modern Pentecostalism in El Salvador: From the Blood of the Martyrs to the Baptism of the Spirit.* Waco, TX: Baylor University Press.

James Huff

El Shaddai (Philippines)

El Shaddai DWXI Prayer Partners Foundation International is arguably the largest Catholic Pentecostal mass-movement in Asia. Based in Manila, it claims to number more than eight million followers gathering in chapters all over the Philippines and more than 62 other countries worldwide. It arose from a nondenominational Christian radio program started by a businessman turned radio evangelist Mariano "Mike" Velarde in the early 1980s, who was initially perceived as evangelical, due to his message of health and wealth that resembled that of North American Prosperity Gospel preachers. El Shaddai's emergence occurred in the context of the Cold War and the US-supported dictatorial regime of Ferdinand Marcos as well as in the context of a nationwide spiritual re-awakening and a mushrooming of Pentecostal-Charismatic groups. While the emphasis on lay-participation and Spirit-experience of these groups challenged the hegemony of the Roman Catholic hierarchy and its priest-centered spirituality, it represented a welcome counterweight to the Christian Left that cooperated with Communist groups and was gaining ground among Catholic clergy and nuns.

Velarde's outspoken critique of clerical Catholicism, which he perceived to be an intellectualist religion that kept people in bondage, proved to be highly appealing especially to the poorer segments of Philippine society. This is also the case with his decided rejection of the idea that suffering was a virtue, which is popular in traditional Catholicism. At the same time and unlike Evangelical Pentecostalism, his support for the mass and the sacraments enables El Shaddai adherents to remain part of the majority religion in the Philippines (more than 80 percent of the total population count as Catholic). Against this background, it proved to be a clever move by the Roman-Catholic hierarchy to co-opt El Shaddai into the Catholic Charismatic Renewal. Notwithstanding the embarrassment El Shaddai represented to the Catholic Bishops' Conference of the Philippines, in 1986 it was approved as a lay movement. In turn, Velarde had to cede some control by accepting Auxiliary Bishop of Manila Teodoro C. Bacani as spiritual advisor of the movement.

El Shaddai's rapid growth and development towards a class-heterogeneous movement, displayed in the weekly outdoor healing rallies that have attracted up to a million participants, has been accompanied by a steady rise of political influence. President Fidel V. Ramos (1992–1998) reached out to Velarde in an attempt to build an anti-hegemonic bloc against the traditional political elites backed by the Bishops' Conference. President Joseph Estrada (1998–2001) chose Velarde as spiritual advisor. During the so-called EDSA II-events, which eventually ousted Estrada, Velarde returned the favor, organizing a large pro-Estrada rally mainly attended by El Shaddai-members. In 2001, three years after the party-list system was introduced, intended to represent so-called underrepresented sectors with a maximum of three seats in the Lower House, Velarde founded Buhay Hayaan Yumabong Party-List (English: Let Life Prosper) with his son Rene Velarde as front man. This solicited the suspicion that BUHAY was El Shaddai's political arm. Since 2004, BUHAY has succeeded in gaining up to three seats in the House of Representatives running on a platform known primarily for its firm "pro-Life"-advocacy and for conservative positions on morality issues, which in the 2010s, at the peak of debates about new reproductive health policies, helped El Shaddai improve its relations towards the hierarchy. El Shaddai's parliamentary involvement has been accompanied by a stronger focus on organized civic engagement and the founding of the "College of Divine Wisdom," which offers professional training and higher education combined with "El Shaddai spirituality." Furthermore, in 2009, El Shaddai inaugurated the International House of Prayer, a cross-shaped building that can accommodate about 25,000 worshippers. It remains open whether this will lead to the institutionalization of the movement and whether it will result in a further rapprochement between El Shaddai and the Bishops' Conference. Velarde's recent political alignment seems to suggest the contrary, though. On the eve of the 2019 mid-term elections, all senators endorsed by El Shaddai were candidates connected to President Rodrigo Duterte who has repeatedly insulted the Catholic Church and whose gross human rights violations have been strongly criticized by the Bishops.

Scholars from the social sciences have described El Shaddai as religious populism centered on a charismatic leader whose Prosperity Gospel mystified neoliberal individualism distracting its adherents from structural causes of socio-economic insecurity and hindering a class-based struggle. Others, however, have suggested viewing El Shaddai's prosperity discourse as an intervention into the discourse on class and empowerment. From this perspective, El Shaddai's teachings and practices represent a protest against leftist discourses of struggle and poverty (and mainstream Catholic discourses of suffering) that define large parts of the Philippine population as victims, in contrast to the prosperity message that defines them as self-reliant and optimistic agents, offering new ways to reframe poverty and powerlessness.

Bibliography

Kessler, Christl, and Jürgen Rüland. 2008. *Give Jesus a Hand! Charismatic Christians: Populist Religion and Politics in the Philippines*. Quezon City: Ateneo de Manila University Press.

Maltese, Giovanni. 2019. "Reproductive Politics and Populism: Pentecostal Religion and Hegemony in the Philippines." *Journal of Law and Religion* 34 (1): 64–84.

Maltese, Giovanni. 2017. *Pentekostalismus, Politik Und Gesellschaft in den Philippinen*. Religion in der Gesellschaft 42. Baden-Baden: Ergon.

Wiegele, Katharine L. 2013. "Politics, Education and Civil Participation: Catholic Charismatic Modernities in the Philippines." In *Global Pentecostalism in the 21st Century*, edited by Robert W. Hefner, 223–250. Bloomington, IN: Indiana University Press.

Wiegele, Katharine L. 2005. *Investing in Miracles: El Shaddai and the Transformation of Popular Catholicism in the Philippines*. Honolulu: University of Hawai'i Press.

Giovanni Maltese

Elim Pentecostal Church, UK

The Elim Evangelistic Band was formed by the Welsh evangelist George Jeffreys and six others in Monaghan, Ireland, on January 7, 1915. The minutes of the instituting meeting indicate that the purpose of the new group was to reach "Ireland with the Full Gospel on Pentecostal lines."

Elim's *modus operandi* was to hold revival meetings for the purpose of preaching the Full Gospel with "signs following" (e.g. dramatic conversions, Spirit baptisms and divine healings), and to plant churches to disciple new converts and support evangelistic efforts. Indeed, the first Elim church was established in Belfast in the summer of 1915, the Elim Pentecostal Alliance was formed in 1918 to accommodate the needs of the growing movement, and in 1919 the *Elim Evangel* (now *Direction Magazine*) was first published to promulgate the emerging denomination's theology and activities. By the end of 1920 Elim had fifteen congregations, numerous ministers and various ministries in Ireland.

In the early 1920s Jeffreys shifted his focus from Ireland to Wales, England and Scotland. Evangelistic campaigning and church planting ensued in mainland Britain, and as the movement expanded increasing structure and central control were introduced in the 1922 constitution. In 1924 Elim opened its purpose-built printing press and in 1925 the Elim Bible College (now Regents Theological College) was established. In 1929 Elim changed its name to Elim Foursquare Gospel Alliance – which is still the denomination's official name today – and Jeffreys went on to define the four core beliefs of Jesus as (1) Saviour, (2) Healer, (3) Baptiser in the Holy Spirit and (4) soon coming King in his two-volume *The Miraculous Foursquare Gospel* (1929–30). The Foursquare Gospel in many ways is the explicit theological articulation of the main facets of the earlier "Full Gospel." The early formative years of Elim seem to have ended in 1934 when the Deed Poll cemented Elim's core convictions and transferred power from Jeffreys to the executive council approved by the ministerial conference, albeit Jeffreys remained as the main leader. By 1937 the alliance had around 230 churches.

The late 1930s and early 1940s were a turbulent time for Elim. During the mid-1930s Jeffreys began to argue that the movement should align itself with the controversial doctrine of British Israelism, but to his frustration the ministerial conference and executive council banned its teaching within Elim. Simultaneously Jeffreys changed his mind on church governance and sought to reform what he now saw as an overly centralized institution. Although many of Jeffreys's requests on governmental reform were accepted, the alliance stood firm in its rejection of British Israelism and Jeffreys resigned from Elim in December 1939. Jeffreys's resignation was naturally a blow to Elim, but it also forced the movement to revisit and realign its priorities and structures. Under the leadership of E.J. Phillips the governance of the alliance was transferred in 1942 from the executive council to the conference consisting of ministers and lay representatives. P.S. Brewster emerged as Elim's leading evangelist and by the early 1960s the alliance had up to 300 churches – some of these had been planted by Elim, whereas others were existing congregations which joined the denomination.

Up until the 1960s Elim with other classical Pentecostal denominations in the UK could claim uniqueness regarding their Pentecostal spirituality, but this changed when the Charismatic movement emerged. The Restoration and/or so-called House Church movement was particularly seen as a viable alternative to Elim as it was similar in its ethos, beliefs and practices, but more attuned to the British cultural mood of the 1970s and 1980s. This initiated a period of serious self-analysis within Elim with the Southport Conference of 1981 being especially significant. Elim sought yet again to renew its Pentecostal identity and practice, and it also reformed its governance by introducing regionalization and by giving greater autonomy to local churches in formulating their own leadership structures. In 1993 Elim adopted a revised Statement of Fundamental Truths which was more Evangelical and Charismatic in its theological outlook (e.g. pre-millennialism was removed as a Fundamental Truth), and in 1997 the Elim conference voted in favour of ordaining women ministers.

At the beginning of the twenty-first century a number of Elim departments were rebranded and relaunched (e.g. youth ministry, evangelism and overseas missions). In 2009 the Elim Headquarters and Regents Theological College (formerly Elim Bible College) moved to Malvern, Worcestershire, UK, forming the Elim International Centre. As things stand, in the UK and Ireland there are almost 650 Elim affiliated churches, an average total Sunday attendance of just over 50 thousand, and one thousand hold some form of ministerial credentials within the movement.

Bibliography

Cartwright, Desmond. 1986. *The Great Evangelists: The Remarkable Lives of George and Stephen Jeffreys*. Basingstoke: Marshall Morgan and Scott.

Frestadius, Simo. 2019. *Pentecostal Rationality: Epistemology and Theological Hermeneutics in the Foursquare Tradition*. London: Bloomsbury T&T Clark.

Frestadius, Simo. 2016. "The Elim Tradition: 'An Argument Extended through Time' (Alasdair MacIntyre)." *Journal of the European Pentecostal Theological Association* 36 (1): 57–68.

Hathaway, Malcolm R. 1998. "The Elim Pentecostal Church: Origins, Developments and Distinctives." In *Pentecostal Perspectives*, edited by Keith Warrington, 1–39. Carlisle: Paternoster.

Kay, William K. 2017. *George Jeffreys: Pentecostal Apostle and Revivalist*. Cleveland, TN: CPT Press.

Simo Frestadius

Embodiment, Body

Historically and comparatively, pentecostals have tended to move their bodies in creative ways. Critical outsiders decried early American pentecostals as "Holy Rollers," a comment focused on what from their perspective were the uncouth aspects of expressive pentecostal rituals. From a mainstream religious standpoint, the pentecostals stood for disorder incarnate. Indeed, radical evangelicals may have rejected Protestant traditions and rituals as lifeless and devoid of the Holy Spirit, but over time they cultivated their own implicit techniques of the body.

The body is the most visible instrument for pentecostal worship practices, yet it is an ambiguous, hybrid entity. The body is at once a self and collective, a singular and plural, an I and a we. To speak of a single pentecostal body is misleading. There are as many pentecostal bodies as there are pentecostalisms at work across the world. To study pentecostal bodies, one must study the vast cultural and ethnic complexes of Latino/a bodies, North Dakotan bodies, Afrikaner bodies, Chinese bodies, and Anglo-American bodies. Still another difficulty of studying embodiment is that as human persons who simultaneously are and have bodies in the world, when functioning efficiently, the objective presence of the body often disappears into the phenomenological background of everyday social life. In many situations, pentecostals do not always think about and theorize their bodies in objectified ways but put their physicality directly to use for various purposes. In other instances, pentecostals reflexively theologize the body, prescribe rules for best worship practices, and call for restraint and discipline regarding expressive worship, music, and other embodied considerations (Cooper 2017).

From an ethnographic and comparative perspective, kinaesthetic motion is arguably the defining characteristic of pentecostal embodiment. Sociologist Donald E. Miller (Miller and Yamamori 2007) did extensive international research to document the varieties of global pentecostalism. He recorded hours of video footage of Asian, African, and Latin American worshipers. Watching these segments of moving imagery, one is struck by the range and diversity of kinetic ritual expression. Wearing brightly colored saris, congregants from the Hyperbad region in India clap and sway as they move to the music. Ugandans beat at various percussion instruments; they clap their hands, sway at the waist, and shuffle back and forth on their feet. Brazilians jump up and down and sway side to side. Chileans close their eyes, in a state of concentrated focus, and raise hands high. Analogous worship rituals occur across the globe, including in North American communities. In the United States, worshipers engage in many of these embodied ritual forms, such as raising or lifting of the hands, kneeling, bowing, swaying, or other forms of motion. Worshipers create dense emotive environments for connecting the media of their bodies to transcendent domains (Brahinsky 2012). The social and cultural minutia of these expressions varies, but the primacy of the kinetic body remains. Pentecostals seek after healing for their bodies or in the opposite direction use their bodies as conduits, through physical contact, to convey the power of the Holy Spirit (Brown 2011). The body is one material-devotional media among others (Blanton 2015).

Not all the body's mediations are virtuous. Within pentecostal cosmologies, bodies tune in to all sorts of unseen wavelengths. The metaphysics of pentecostal embodiment have a dark side (Csordas 1997; Luhrmann 2012). Because pentecostal ontologies blur the categories of the material and the spiritual, bodies are susceptible to corruption by negative forces. Anthropologists studying Melanesian pentecostal spiritual warfare practices, for instance, have documented narratives of spiritual contagions empowering bodies in bizarre, unsettling ways, such as by causing onsets of vampirism or reconfiguring the afflicted body in animal-like ways (Eriksen/Rio in Rio et al. 2017). In the pentecostal lifeworld, bodies are conduits for efficacious non- or extra-human powers and presences, both sacred and profane, holy and evil. The paradox of the body, for pentecostals, is its ability to receive and convey divine healing and presence as well as transmit sickness and vice. Registering as a negative media, at times the body itself becomes contagion.

While social scientists have focused on ritual, practice, and experience, cultural historians have documented the centrality of pentecostal embodiment to global popular culture and the entertainment industry. Religious conservatives lambasted Elvis Presley's music for its sensuousness and denounced the singer's habit of swinging his hips and gyrating his body on stage. But Presley's performances drew implicitly on his background in the Assemblies of God, the largest white pentecostal denomination in the United States (Sánchez Walsh 2018). Consider also the Million Dollar Quartet, a collaborative jam session now identified as one of the key emerging moments for American Rock-and-Roll. This musical event combined the efforts of a young Elvis Presley, Jerry Lee Lewis, Johnny Cash, and Carl Perkins. Three out of four of these musicians, veritable forefathers of the Rock-and-Roll genre, had pentecostal backgrounds. Marvin Gaye, an iconic American musical figure with pentecostal roots, also cultivated a vivid sensuality in his musical oeuvre. Pop music, as an industry and cultural field, developed to no small extent out of expressive pentecostal cultures of the body across racial divides.

Connections between pentecostal embodiment, entertainment, and sexuality continue into the twenty-first century pop-cultural milieu. Singer-songwriter Katy Perry grew up pentecostal but in both her public career and the content of her music displays a complicated relationship with the religiosity of her past. Actor Megan Fox, like Katy Perry and Elvis, has been immortalized as a public celebrity for her sensuous physicality and visual charisma; Fox, too, has pentecostal roots. That she features as an icon of youthful sexuality in Michael Bay films and has gone on the record about speaking in tongues is a point of existential crisis for the actor's religious critics.

What is it about pentecostal habitudes, sensuousness, and expressivity that cause so much controversy for pentecostals in public discourse? The above critiques have origins in the archives of American popular culture but claims about pentecostal excessiveness are a global phenomenon. Non-pentecostal Christians and indeed pentecostals themselves levy their own criticisms against megachurch proponents of the international Prosperity Gospel. Often criticisms take to task luxurious lifestyle choices as theological critics police the manners by which wealthy megachurch pastors dress, adorn, transport, and house their bodies. Other times these issues carry over into moral issues of a sexual sort, ranging from the American televangelist scandals of the 1980s to the unregulated ritual creativities of the emerging South African neo-pentecostals.

Scholars have only recently begun to analyze the myriad forms of pentecostal embodiment in various global regions, dispelling caricatures about worship rituals as entirely unstructured and improvisational and focusing on how embodiment maps onto the registers of race, gender, power, globalization, and migration. Michael Wilkinson's and Peter Althouse's recent edited volume, *Pentecostals and the Body* (2017), certainly moves in these directions. Leah Payne's *Gender and Pentecostal Revivalism* (2015) examines the ideologies of gender and embodiment that structured early American pentecostalism and adds to scholarship on bodies, race, and dress (e.g., Butler 2007; Sánchez Walsh 2003). Anderson Blanton's *Hittin' the Prayer Bones* (2015) conceives of the pentecostal lifeworld as a ritual arena comprised of bodies, things, and practices. Future studies will do well to document developing pentecostal philosophies of the body and contribute even more sustained inquiries into the sensory hierarchies and semiotic ideologies at play in global pentecostal expressions.

Bibliography

Blanton, Anderson. 2015. *Hittin' the Prayer Bones: Materiality of Spirit in the Pentecostal South*. Chapel Hill: The University of North Carolina Press.

Brahinsky, Josh. 2012. "Pentecostal Body Logics: Cultivating a Modern Sensorium." *Cultural Anthropology* 27 (2): 215–238.

Brown, Candy Gunther, ed. 2011. *Global Pentecostal and Charismatic Healing*. New York: Oxford University Press.

Butler, Anthea D. 2007. *Women in the Church of God in Christ: Making a Sanctified World*. Chapel Hill: The University of North Carolina Press.

Cooper, Travis. 2017. "Worship Rituals, Discipline, and Pentecostal-Charismatic "Techniques du Corps" in the American Midwest." In *Pentecostals and the Body*, edited by Michael Wilkinson and Peter Althouse, 77–101. Lieden: Brill.

Csordas, Thomas J. 1997. *The Sacred Self: A Cultural Phenomenology of Charismatic Healing*. Berkeley: University of California Press.

Luhrmann, T.M. 2012. *When God Talks Back: Understanding the American Evangelical Relationship with God*. New York: First Vintage Books.

Miller, Donald E., and Tetsunao Yamamori. 2007. *Global Pentecostalism: The New Face of Christian Social Engagement*. Berkeley: University of California Press.

Payne, Leah. 2017. *Gender and Pentecostal Revivalism: Making a Female Ministry in the Early Twentieth Century*. New York: Palgrave Macmillan.

Rio, Knut, Michelle MacCarthy, and Ruy Blanes, eds. 2017. *Pentecostalism and Witchcraft: Spiritual Warfare in Africa and Melanesia*. New York: Palgrave Macmillan.

Sánchez Walsh, Arlene M. 2018. *Pentecostals in America*. New York: Columbia University Press.

Sánchez Walsh, Arlene M. 2003. *Latino Pentecostal Identity: Evangelical Faith, Self, and Society*. New York: Columbia University Press.

Wilkinson, Michael, and Peter Althouse, eds. 2017. *Pentecostals and the Body*. Leiden: Brill.

Travis Warren Cooper

Eritrea

The local Pentecostal movement originated in the 1960s in Ethiopia, and experienced significant growth in Eritrea in the 1970s and 1980s, despite the fact that the Derg, the ruling party in Ethiopia and Eritrea at that time, persecuted Evangelical and Pentecostal movements. At the end of the 1970s, some Ethiopian pastors moved to Asmara in order to carry out evangelization activities (Kileyesus 2006, 77), based in the Finnish Pentecostal Mission that had been working in Asmara since 1971 (Anderson 2013, 170). The *Finnish Pentecostal Mission* in Asmara ran a religious center (1971) and a School (1977), despite the expulsion of the missionaries by the Derg in 1978 (IVI, 171).

During the 1970s, Eritrea was engaged in a fight for independence from Ethiopia: a struggle that Eritreans considered to be an anti-colonialist and anti-imperialist one. Kileyesus points out that the success of Pentecostalism in Eritrea in the 1980s had to do with the open hostility of Pentecostal preachers towards the Ethiopian regime of institutionalized discrimination, which also provided spiritual support to members of opposition parties.

Following the independence of Eritrea in 1991, the Evangelical movement started operating out in the open: Pentecostals were able to adapt their speeches to the new situation: "it had created a form of community that spoke to the anxiety and uncertainty marking social relations in Asmara during the difficult times of the deportation from Ethiopia of thousands of Ethiopians of Eritrean origin, many of whom were Pentecostalists themselves, and the subsequent Eritrean-Ethiopian border war" (Kileyesus 2006, 78).

In the mid-1990s, the Pentecostal movement in Asmara counted about 10,000 believers (converted were both from Orthodox and Muslim background) and was starting to grow through the wide movements of the diaspora (IVI, 91, note n. 5). At that time, the six most important Pentecostal branches were the *Mulu Wengel* (Full Gospel, with about 3000 members), the *Qale Heywet Church* (baptist), *the Meseret Kristos* (Mennonite) the *Rhema*, the *Charisma* and the *Halleluya*. The first two churches are not officially Pentecostal, but their doctrines were subject of a pentecostalization process during the 1970s and 1980s in Ethiopia during the Dwerg persecution. The last three were new, while the rest had originated in Ethiopia in the 1960s. Kileyesus reported that people were attracted by the Prosperity Gospel, while Fantini (2012) and Haustein (2011) do not find that doctrine in the same denominations in Ethiopia.

In 2002 the Eritrean government decided to ban all religious groups except Catholic, Lutheran and Orthodox Christian ones, and Islamic, as these other groups also faced repressions anyway. As of the last census, 1 percent of the population adheres to Pentecostalism, one of the most persecuted groups, facing mass arrests, tortures, denial of administrative services, pressure to recant their faith (Immigration and Refugee Board of Canada 2014). Reports of clandestine Pentecostal political activity are abundant. As many sources point out, Pentecostals were considered a counter-revolutionary group with rumours of ties to the CIA already in the 1970's (Hepner 2014, 2003).

Pentecostalism was seen as difficult to manage by the state, in the first place because of its inherent fragmentation and congregationalism. It was considered a threat to national unity and sovereignty, because of the attitude of its adherents to consider themselves much more oriented towards a global identity rather than the local one. Moreover the works by Hepner and Conrad reported that conversion to Pentecostalism often led to the rejection of politics. Pentecostals saw the fight for independence, and the issues around post-independence, as the roots of evil in Eritrean society. Ethnographic studies carried out in Rome (Italy) among Eritrean Pentecostals (Costantini 2019; 2016), demonstrates how certain speeches and spiritual practices helped them reject their nationalistic past: they consider the time of the fight for independence and the post-independence era as being too "politicized", "indifferent to Jesus" and his doctrine. Pentecostalism promotes a Manichean view of the world in which "ignoring Jesus" leads to Satan. They "construct" the evil world they want to break with: thus the past is not about eating *injera* (bread) or dressing traditional clothes, but "politics": celebration for independence (by the ruling party as well as the opposition), flags exposition, political violence, military service. Rather than taking part in celebrations on May 24 (independence day), they go to the church to pray for the salvation of Eritrea, whose "illness" is identified with politics. Sometimes they tell short stories and prophecies about the dark times Eritrea experienced from 1991. These narratives represent a powerful critique of the "sacrality" of the Eritrean struggle (1991 is the year of the independence), that nobody else would do in the life outside of the church. At the same time they use to collaborate with Ethiopian believers in worship: the two national groups in fact tend to absorb through spiritual language the conflict between the two national groups. The two attitudes (being non-political and rejecting the conflict with Ethiopians) make Eritrean Pentecostalism akin to a counter-cultural movement.

Bibliography

Anderson, A.H. 2013. "Eritrean Pentecostals as Asylum Seekers in Britain." *Journal of Religion in Africa* 43 (2): 167–95.

Conrad, B. 2005. "From Revolution to Religion: The Politics of Religion in the Eritrean Diaspora in Germany." In *Religion in the Context of African Migration Studies*, edited by Afe Adogame and Cordula Weissköppel, Bayreuth African Studies Series, 217–241. Bayreuth: Eckhard Breitinger.

Costantini O. 2019. *La nostra identità è Gesù Cristo: Pentecostalismo e nazionalismo tra gli eritrei e gli etiopici a Roma*. Milano: Franco Angeli.

Costantini, O. 2016. "«ByesusSh'm». Breaking with the National Past in Eritrean and Ethiopian Pentecostal Churches in Rome." In *Witchcraft, Religion, Medicine: Power and belief in the human destiny*, edited by M. Pavanello, post faction by Birgit Meyer, 165–184. London: Routledge.

Cristofori, S. 2013. "Note sul movimento pentecostale in Africa." *Cristianesimo nella storia* 34(3): 823–878.

Fantini, E. 2015. "Go Pente! The Charismatic Renewal of the Evangelical Movement in Ethiopia." In *Understanding Contemporary Ethiopia*, edited by E. Fiquet, and G. Prunier, 123–146. London: Hurst.

Kileyesus, A. 2006. "Cosmologies in Collision: Pentecostal Conversion and Christian Cults in Asmara." *African Studies Review* 49 (1): 75–92.

Haustein, J. 2011 "Embodying the Spirit(s): Pentecostal Demonology and Deliverance Discourse in Ethiopia." *Ethnos* 76 (4): 534–552.

Hepner, T.R. 2014. "Religion, Repression, and Human Rights in Eritrea and the Diaspora." *Journal of Religion in Africa* 44 (2): 151–188.

Hepner, T.R. 2003. "Religion, Nationalism, and Transnational Civil Society in the Eritrean Diaspora." *Identities: Global Studies in Culture and Power* 10 (3): 269–293.

Immigration and Refugee Board of Canada. 2014. "Eritrea: Treatment of Evangelical and Pentecostal Christians by Authorities; including members of the Mulu Wongel [Full Gospel] Church; incidents of arrests and detention of Mulu Wongel Church members in Asmara (2002–October 2014)." Last accessed July 24th 2018. http://www.refworld.org/docid/55acc8e24.html.

Osvaldo Costantini

Eschatology

Eschatology is the theology of the last things. It deals with death, judgement, heaven and hell, the end of history, the end of the cosmos, and the coming kingdom of God. Eschatology can be oriented to the future or to the present. It can be otherworldly or this-worldly. In the United States, Pentecostal eschatology has passed through a variety of permutations rooted in historical and cultural factors though at the core is the belief in the second coming of Christ.

One view that was initially influential was the eschatology of the latter rain. Using the analogy of Palestine climate patterns for planting and harvest, many early Pentecostals saw the outpouring of the Spirit at Pentecost as the early rain of the church, followed by a drought and loss of the gifts of the Spirit in the post-apostolic era, but with the expectation of a latter rain outpouring that would immediately precede the second coming (Althouse 2013).

A second view followed the Wesleyan theology of John Fletcher, who divided the dispensations into three interlinked ages, the age of the Father, the age of the Son, and the age of the Spirit. Early Pentecostal writer Hattie Barth is representative of this view as she argues that the dispensational ages overlap like links in a chain. Charismatic signs following Pentecost are foretastes of age to come (McQueen 2012).

A third view was the premillennial dispensationalism articulated by John Nelson Darby, who argued for seven ages in which each dispensation followed a pattern of divine revelation, human testing, failure, and judgment. Darby added a novel and previously unheard doctrine of a secret rapture that would whisk away the church, followed by a seven-year tribulation and final battle between God and the antichrist. This speculative theology includes variations such as a mid-tribulation rapture and a post-tribulation rapture. Although latter rain and the three-fold dispensational pattern better fit the logic of Pentecostal pneumatology and ecclesiology, Darby's premillennialism took root in American religious culture and became the dominant view of Pentecostalism in the mid-twentieth century.

Since the 1980s, a growing cadre of Pentecostals have been dissatisfied with the millennial dispensationalism and the problems it creates for the inclusion of Pentecostal distinctives such as Spirit baptism and healing as well as ecclesiology and social justice. Some Pentecostals have attempted to modify millennial dispensationalism to make room for Pentecostal distinctives (McQueen 2012). Others have adopted a *proleptic* view of the already/not yet of the coming kingdom in order to interpret the distinctives of Spirit baptism, healing and the bestowal charismatic gifts as a fundamentally eschatological category (Althouse 2003).

The emergence of the charismatic renewal in the 1960s and neo-charismatics since the 1980s witnessed a proliferation of eschatologies. Both the charismatic renewal and neo-charismatic developments were influenced by latter rain theology as it was delineated through the Latter Rain Revival of 1948. Beliefs and practices included singing in the Spirit, the restoration of the fivefold ministries, and the laying on of hands to impart the anointing. As with latter rain eschatology, these practices were thought to be a sign of Jesus' soon return (Althouse 2003). John Wimber is a pivotal figure in reinterpreting Pentecostal eschatology. Following George Eldon Ladd, Wimber articulated a view of "signs and wonders" in which healing and other charismatic phenomena were rooted in the already/not yet existence of the kingdom of God. Wimber's eschatology has influenced the development of Catch the Fire, Global Awakening, Bethel Church in Redding, California, and other networked charismatics.

A global Pentecostal understanding of eschatology is difficult to assess due to ongoing developments in various sectors of the world. Kay (2013) notes that the pessimistic dispensational eschatology in global Pentecostalism has been replaced by an optimistic eschatology found in Pentecostal prosperity teaching that points to a better material future and the enjoyment of wealth in the present. According to Volf, the intersection of liberation theology and the prosperity gospel is centered on the materiality of salvation in which the present eschatological hope includes spiritual as well as socio-economic transformation (in Althouse 2003, 77). Pentecostalism in Latin America incorporates both prosperity and liberation. In Guatemala, Harold Caballeros, pastor of *Iglesia El Shaddai* articulates a view of socio-political engagement in which prayer, fasting, extensive capitation, and education is thought to bring not only personal transformation, but the transformation of family, community, and the nation as well (Garrard-Burnett 2016).

The prosperity gospel has had influence on the development of Pentecostal eschatology in Africa. Although prosperity is seen pejoratively in the Western world as it allies with consumer capitalism and materialism, prosperity takes on a liberative perspective in economies with abject poverty. Prosperity teaching took root in Africa in the 1980s with an emphasis on salvation as conversion, transformation, and empowerment. Salvation is viewed as liberation/deliverance from evil forces, recovery of happiness and joyous life in Christ, and transformation of material, physical, and psychic well-being. In other cases, African prosperity teaching is thought to bring a sense of inner peace, satisfaction, contentment, and social connections. However, the eschatological focus in African Pentecostal prosperity is not futuristic rewards after one has died, but immediate and this-worldly, bringing a better life in the present (Kalu 2008).

Turning to Asia, David Yonggi Cho is credited for the rise of Pentecostalism in South Korea and is influential in the region. Cho's message includes prosperity teaching with a concern to alleviate the suffering of *Han* (accumulated grief) located in illness, poverty, unemployment, spirit oppression, and sorcery. Specifically, Cho adds a theology of the three-fold blessing that addresses spiritual, physical, and circumstantial situations to the conventional four-fold gospel in Pentecostalism. Although Cho inherited premillennial eschatology from Assemblies of God missionaries, his emphasis on blessings points to this-worldly expectations of immediate spiritual, personal, and social effects of the kingdom impinging on the present (Anderson 2013; Kay 2013).

Global Pentecostal eschatology is diverse, but it anticipates the spiritual, material, and psychic blessings of Christian hope to be partially mediated in the present, while simultaneously looking to the coming of Christ in glory.

Bibliography

Althouse, Peter and Robby Waddel, eds. 2010. *Perspectives in Pentecostal Eschatology: World Without End*. Cambridge: James Clarke & Co.

Althouse, Peter. 2003. *Spirit of the Last Days: Pentecostal Eschatology in Conversation with Jürgen Moltmann*. London: T&T Clark International.

Anderson, Allan H. 2013. *To the Ends of the Earth: Pentecostalism and the Transformation of World Christianity*. Oxford: Oxford University Press.

Garrard-Burnett, Virginia. 2016. "Toward a Pentecostal Hermeneutics of Social Engagement in Central America? Bridging the Church and the World in El Salvador and Guatemala." In *New Ways of Being Pentecostal in Latin America*, edited by Martin Lindhardt, 187–208. Lanham: Lexington.

Kalu, Ogbu. 2008. *African Pentecostalism: An Introduction*. Oxford: Oxford University Press.

Kay, William K. 2013. "Gifts of the Spirit: Reflections on Pentecostalism and Its Growth in Asia." In *Spirit and Power: The Growth and Global Impact of Pentecostalism*," edited by Donald E. Miller, Kimon H. Sargeant and Richard Flory, 259–276. Oxford: Oxford University Press.

McQueen, Larry R. 2012. *Toward a Pentecostal Eschatology: Discerning the Way Forward*. Blandford Forum: Deo Publishing.

Peter Althouse

Ethics

Pentecostalism's extraordinary global diversity is reflected within the contextual nuancing of the movement's theological and social ethics. The first two decades of the twenty-first century marked a notable increase in Pentecostal theologico-ethical reflection, probing a broad spectrum of new and re-envisioning some of the old themes, engaged and/or anticipated within the works of their forerunners (Dempster 1987; Villafañe 1993). This development has produced noteworthy contributions in various subfields: theological ethics of social transformation and the pursuit of the common good; theologies of economics and globalization (including compelling reflections on finance, production, distribution, and consumption); political and public theologies of racial, ethnic, gender and socio-political justice; pneumatologies of peacebuilding and reconciliation; ecotheologies of planetary flourishing; as well as theology of disability. Throughout this thematic diversity, Pentecostal ethics continues to evidence the enduring gravity of theological inquiry's classical sources. Thus, Pentecostal experience prompts theologico-ethical reflections on the Holy Spirit's socio-transformative agency within living communities of faith and the broader cultural resonance of their social engagement (Augustine 2019, 212–228). These reflections are grounded within the sources of scripture (weaving together christological and pneumatological threads via the principle hermeneutical lens of the event of Pentecost), tradition (drawing from within the movement's own theological development, as well as exploring its complex, polyvalent historico-theological roots within the broader Christian tradition), and reason (contributing to the shaping of Pentecostal moral philosophy and motivating the interdisciplinary flair of theologico-ethical constructs).

Pentecostal social ethics often recaptures and nurtures the movement's living memory of the radically-egalitarian, racially- and ethnically-inclusive, strikingly pacifist community of Azusa Street and the prophetic challenge of its legacy (contained in the West mostly through the Black and Latin American Pentecostal liberation theologies) (Sanders 2020, 435–438). The relevance of Azusa's paradigmatic socio-ethical vision is uplifted as essential to the movement's identity and mission "in a nuclear age of extreme poverty" (Land 1993, 207; Castelo 2012, 1–2), deepened racial tensions, political disillusionment, systemic disenfranchisement and exclusion of ethnic, racial, political and cultural others.

Pentecostal ethics often highlight Classical Pentecostalism's theological roots within the Wesleyan holiness tradition and the formative significance of the doctrine of sanctification with its prominent "christological and pneumatological poles" (Coulter 2020, 239–245). Recognizing that Pentecostalism "is more Eastern than Western in its understanding of spirituality as perfection and participation in the divine life (theosis)" (and more "ascetic and mystical" than its Western antecedents), Pentecostal ethicists have mined constructively the treasures of Eastern Christianity, following "the line of Wesleyan continuity" (Land 1993, 30; Castelo 2017; Augustine 2019). In this theological trajectory, sanctification remains the key ethical motif of Pentecostal spirituality and practice. Reflecting its Wesleyan holiness roots, Pentecostal ethics articulates sanctification as an ontological renewal of humanity on the teleological journey toward Christoformation/

Christification through the Spirit's world-mending agency. The sanctified human life unfolds as perfect love for God and (both the anthropic and non-anthropic) neighbor. This love is experienced as nothing less than partaking of the divine life – the life of the proto-communal Trinity – as the life of the age to come embodied amidst the present age by the Spirit-filled faith community. Love is staged as the most potent creative force within the cosmos – the very substance of the divine creative act – revealing the world as 'love made matter.' In its reflectivity/mirroring of the divine life, the Spirit-saturated Christian life (as love for the other) creates the consecrated opening for shared flourishing in uncompromised commitment to the common good. Love is manifested and experienced as inclusion and empowerment – as making family out of strangers, creating space for them at the table, "empowering the voice of the other and securing their access to life, justice and flourishing" (Augustine 2019, 47). In all of these, love transfigures the community of faith into a living icon of the Spirit on earth (Coulter 2020, 243; Augustine 2012, 29).

In its theological constructs, Pentecostal ethics presents robust pneumatological engagements of social issues through its core hermeneutical lens – the biblical event of Pentecost. Marking the ontological renewal of the image of God within the human community, Pentecost offers a paradigmatic vision of God's radical hospitality to the other, manifested within the proclamation speech of the faith community. Embracing the language of the other in a gift of divine hospitality, the Spirit invites all humanity to make its habitat within the inter-sociality of the Trinity. This is an initiation of dialogue by re-spacing oneself and creating conditions for the conversational inclusion of the other – a powerful paradigmatic gesture "of welcoming all foreigners, aliens, strangers literally in their own terms" (Augustine 2012, 65). The Spirit's kenotic self-sharing with the other "produces the apocalyptic affection ... that binds people, even enemies, together and makes forgiveness possible" (Yong 2010, 343). Yet Pentecost is not only for societal but for cosmic renewal and reconciliation, for its communion in/of the Spirit is uplifted as "a fellowship of all flesh," providing a pneumatological justification for "a democracy of the commons," which circumscribes all of creation (Yong 2010, 345; Augustine 2019, 9–10). This ecotheological nuance enlarges the Pentecostal understanding of healing beyond its parochial grasp, in expression of compassion for and solidarity with all who suffer pain, disability, oppression, exploitation and marginalization (including the non-anthropic others) – an act of partaking in the Spirit's movement of cosmic world-mending through hallowed human lives.

Bibliography

Augustine, Daniela C. 2019. *The Spirit and the Common Good: Shared Flourishing in the Image of God*. Grand Rapids: Eerdmans.

Augustine, Daniela C. 2012. *Pentecost, Hospitality, and Transfiguration: Toward a Spirit-inspired Vision of Social Transformation*. Cleveland: CPT Press.

Castelo, Daniel. 2017. *Pentecostalism as a Christian Mystical Tradition*. Grand Rapids: Eerdmans.

Castelo, Daniel. 2012. *Revisioning Pentecostal Ethics: The Epicletic Community*. Cleveland: CPT Press.

Coulter, Dale M. 2020. "Sanctificaiton: Becoming an Icon of the Spirit through Holy Love." In *Routledge Handbook on Pentecostal*

Theology, edited by Wolfgang Vondey, 237–246. New York: Routledge.
Dempster, Murray W. 1987. "Pentecostal Social Concern and the Biblical Mandate of Social Justice." *Pneuma*: 9 (2): 129–153.
Land, Steven J. 1993. *Pentecostal Spirituality: A Passion for the Kingdom*. Sheffield: Sheffield Academic Press.
Sanders, Cheryl J. 2020. "Social Justice: Theology as Social Transformation." In *Routledge Handbook on Pentecostal Theology*, edited by Wolfgang Vondey, 432–442. New York: Routledge.
Villafañe, Eldin. 1993. *The Liberating Spirit: Toward an Hispanic American Pentecostal Social Ethic*. Grand Rapids: Eerdmans.
Yong, Amos. 2010. *In the Days of Caesar: Pentecostalism and Political Theology*. Grand Rapids: Eerdmans.

Daniela C. Augustine

Ethiopia

Pentecostals are known by the term *Pente* in Ethiopia. The term in the context of Ethiopia, is too confusing to be employed in any scholarly work without major qualification. The designation itself has now morphed into a generic label for all non-Orthodox and non-Catholic Christians in Ethiopia. The derogatory origin of *Pente* lends to the movement's negative image of being counter-cultural, alien and going against the national culture. Consequently, its adherents were depicted in the public sector as followers of a foreign faith. Though the term was employed as an allusion to the new "religious outsiders," over the years with rapid growth in a short span of time and its inclusion of diverse members of the society, particularly the educated younger youth, such public perceptions are gradually changing.

The term came into popular usage for the first time in the late 1960's, a formative phase of Pentecostalism, as an aftermath of an episode in Debre Zeit in August 1967. Soon the incident became an issue in the media that referred to the new expression of faith as *Pente* and an unknown religion (*Yaltaweke Addis. Haymanot*).

It was the media and other social forces that brought the term *Pente* into popular parlance. This is a phenomenon that has uniquely unfolded in Ethiopia and has no equivalence elsewhere in Africa. Members of the burgeoning new movement, mostly from an Ethiopian Orthodox Church background, popularized concepts such as *dageme ledet* (born again), *getan mekebel* (receiving Jesus) that were not as familiar in the theological and public discourse in the past. Coupled with their aggressive missionizing energy to draw many to their faith on convictional, decisional, and personal terms, they aroused the attention of the public at large.

Since most of those who launched the movement were young people from urban areas, mainly from colleges and high schools, they lent a national visibility to this new dimension of Christianity in Ethiopia, which was initially unfolding in the background, mainly in the rural parts of the country. The Christian faith that Western Protestant missionaries introduced in the rural regions of Ethiopia tended to be denominationally divided and ethnic based unlike the Pentecostals who inclined to be pan-Ethiopian. It was during the day of the *Derg* (the military regime) that the name *Pente* became lodged as generic tag to mark the various evangelical groups in Ethiopia. It should be noted that *Pente* is a shortened, albeit derogatory, reference to their theological Pentecostal faith experience, the most salient aspect of its expression being speaking with tongues as evidence of the "baptism of the Holy Spirit." Consequently, the lumping of all Protestant groups under the same category does not suggest that they share the same doctrinal convictions.

For most of their early history, Ethiopian Pentecostals maintained a narrow outlook of the gospel that did not encourage public engagement. Their exclusive stress on holiness, piety and purity that was meant to separate (*meleyet*) them from the world and discouraged them from having a sound theology of engagement in the socio-political sphere of the country. Engaging the world was feared to have a contaminating influence upon their religious lives. In their view, conversion required a "bridge-burning" process to live a sanctified life to demonstrate a transformed Christian identity. Until recently, the leaders of Mulu Wongel Church, the first independent Pentecostal Church in Ethiopia, kept socially conservative positions to avoid entanglement in the public square.

Pentecostals experienced severe persecution under the imperial rule as well as during the communist era, which did not stop the movement from growing. Pentecostals were key players in the expansion of Christianity through the underground church during the period of the revolution (1974–1990). It was during this time that singers proliferated with melodies that included crying, agony, and assurance of victory. Pentecostals held the conviction that the more their voices were muted, the more the spirit shouted. Hymns produced during the revolution by composers and singers stressed themes such as firmness, faithfulness, hope, courage, and the like. Songs became important vehicles for the spread of the faith in the absence of an open space. Pentecostals demonstrated dissent against the logic of dialectical materialism couched in religious terms and discursively interrogated hegemonic power. The Pentecostals waged a non-violent protest based on the logic of absolute faith in biblical truth.

The freedom that was obtained in the country following the deposition of the military rulers allowed for substantial growth of Pentecostalism in Ethiopia. New members were largely youth coming from urban areas who were being drawn to the movement for several reasons; the charismatic nature of the movement, preaching and worship styles, and the application of innovative forms of modern gospel music that stressed themes of praise, victory, and activism.

Contemporary Ethiopia has witnessed the rise of a variety of new Pentecostal movements that are becoming increasingly conspicuous and vocal in the public square. Some have dubbed the proliferation of these different strains of Pentecostalism with a heavy stress on power ministry and with a growing visibility and assertiveness as neo-Pentecostals or neo-Charismatics. It is hard to subsume the various expressions of the movement into one category and place them under a single phenomenological narrative. Most of the leaders of the new movement have television ministries that transmit their sermons and display healing practices. The new developments are unfolding at amazing speed and an alarming scale for those who oppose the new Pentecostals. They have flourished in Ethiopia relatively quickly and are already causing rifts between the new and older generations of Pentecostals.

A strong element within this new strain of Pentecostalism in Ethiopia is the desire to impact the society, attempting to transform it by making deep and strategic inroads in all sectors of the public square.

Bibliography

Eshete, Tibebe. 2009. *The Evangelical Movement in Ethiopia: Resistance and Resilience.* Waco: Baylor University Press.

Harrel, David E. 1975. *All Thing Are Possible.* Bloomington. Indiana University Press.

Haustein, Jörg. 2011. *Writing Religious History: The Historiography of Ethiopian Pentecostalism.* Studien Zur Aussereuropaischen Christentumsgeschichte (Asien/Afrika/Lateinamerika) 17. Wiesbaden: Harrassowitz Verlag.

Hollenweger, W.H. 1972. *The Pentecostals.* Minneapolis: Augsburg.

Wolde Kidan, Bekele. 2001/2. *Revival Ityopiyana Ye Mechereshaw Mecheresa.* Addis Ababa: Mulu Wongel Church.

Tibebe Eshete

Europe

The beginning of the Pentecostal movement in Europe occurred at the start of the twentieth century when vast areas of the continent had enjoyed a long period of peace, technological progress and prosperity. In northern Europe established churches were Lutheran or Anglican, and where they existed, religious tolerance extended to other forms of Protestantism.

After the 1906 revivalistic outpouring of the Spirit took place in Oslo under the ministry of T.B. Barratt (1862–1940) a Norwegian-British Methodist, there were similar scenes in Britain in the parish of Alexander Boddy (1854–1930), the Anglican vicar of Monkwearmouth in the northeast of England in 1907. Spirit-inspired prayer meetings included visions and speaking in tongues with the result that Boddy decided to hold an annual international conference in Sunderland, and this took place every year from 1908 to 1914. European Pentecostalism through the ministries of Barratt and Boddy reached out to the Netherlands and the larger Protestant community in Germany. From these ministries it spread to centres in the north and the south of Europe. During the seven years before the outbreak of the 1914–18 war, there was sufficient time for Pentecostal congregations to be started in territories that were to fall under communist control – in Russia, Estonia and Latvia.

Incipient Pentecostalism had to decide whether it wished to be a renewal movement within existing denominations or to strike out onto new terrain and become a series of free-standing denominations. Decisions were made both ways. In Germany the Mulheim Association was an example of the former. Norway and Britain were examples of the latter.

Across Europe as a whole, Pentecostals, like everyone else, were caught up in the post-war world. With the exception of neutral Scandinavia and Switzerland there was unemployment, bitterness, political extremism and all the uncertainties brought about by the creation of many new national boundaries following German and Austro-Hungarian surrender in 1918. Religion was brutally suppressed in the atheistic USSR and its satellite states. Elsewhere black-shirted fascism was ascendant and the Nazis perverted Christianity by forcing churches to preach an Aryan gospel. Nihilistic post-war culture was undergirded by fatalistic and hedonistic attitudes. Pentecostals pursued holiness and shunned such fashions. Women now outnumbered men since vast swathes of the male population had been killed in the trenches. There were many widows and spinsters, and some of these found themselves in Pentecostal revivalist meetings in the 1920s and 30s. In Germany, the dramatically converted Karl Fix (1897–1969) had been a socialist journalist, in England Smith Wigglesworth (1859–1947) had been a self-employed plumber and in France Douglas Scott (1900–67) had been a band leader. These were talented and energetic men who by prophetic utterances or other spiritual phenomena felt they were guided into full-time ministry by Christ. Fix was instrumental in the starting of the Volksmission and Scott helped to bring Assemblées de Dieu into being in the 1930s. Wigglesworth exercised an astonishing ministry of healing at first in Britain and then increasingly widely.

Several Pentecostal denominations or congregations were founded before the war, as in Norway in 1910, in Sweden in 1913 and in Germany through the Mulheim Association the same year. Others came into being in civilian areas far from the front line during the war itself: the Elim Pentecostal Church in Ireland in 1915 and the Apostolics in Wales in 1916. Others like Assemblies of God in the UK were formed soon afterwards in 1924. By 1929, when fascist registration was required, there were some 25 places of Pentecostal worship open to the public in Italy. In Russia in the 1920s there were congregations planted or influenced by Ivan Voronaev (1886–1937) but the number of them is unknown. In Romania there were about 130 places of worship established by 1931. Orthodoxy – whether Greek, Russian or Serbian – tends to be territorial and was therefore resistant to Pentecostalism with the result that Pentecostal penetration of those areas had to wait until later in the century. And in Spain the civil war of 1936–39 made the country inhospitable to any religious outreach. The 1930s were a miniature era of opportunity for Pentecostalism. In Britain huge evangelistic rallies were held all over the country, and especially in London, by George Jeffreys (1889–1962).

During the war itself the churches were badly disrupted. Not only were many men and women conscripted into the armed services but normal life was transformed by the difficulties of travel, the internal migration of people away from areas of intense bombing and the long weary hours required by factories making munitions. Some Pentecostal churches lost their offices and their records through bombing and others lost church buildings and finances as offerings dwindled. In Norway T.B. Barratt died in January 1940 two months before the Nazis invaded his country. In Germany, the 1930s meetings convened by Karl Fix could only take place under police surveillance and open air meetings were banned.

In Britain, conscientious objection was a legitimate moral stance and this created a dilemma for pastors. They had young people in their churches who put on uniform to fight and others who refused to do so. Wisely they supported both options and allowed freedom of conscience to their members. The war devastated the infrastructure of Europe. Roads, bridges, railways, electrical installations, factories, housing, industrial output, and mechanised farming all suffered. There was homelessness and there were stateless persons who became refugees. Countries invaded by the USSR like Estonia, Latvia and Lithuania lost their independence while those countries subjected to the Red Army like Poland, Bulgaria, Hungary, Czechoslovakia, Albania and East Germany now fell firmly within the Soviet sphere.

Pentecostal churches offered humanitarian aid with food, clothing and other resources paid for by their congregations. In Germany Karl Fix and the Volksmission were active and successful while, working from Britain, Fred Squire of the Full Gospel Testimony received aid from North

America and sent lorries loaded with goods to The Netherlands.

In 1947, European Pentecostals agreed to meet in Zürich. A pan-European Pentecostal conference had been held in Sweden in 1939 and there was now a grateful desire to re-assemble and, once numerous reports of hardship had been received, the conference began to make practical plans to distribute humanitarian aid, especially from the United States and Sweden. Nevertheless, they ran into an internal problem. The Scandinavian churches resolutely opposed any form of organisation beyond local congregations. Yet, the needs of the hour demanded inter-church corporation. Eventually a solution was found that satisfied all parties and the church in Basel became a depot for the collection and distribution of philanthropic aid.

At the end of the war, the map of Europe was redrawn. New national boundaries were put in place, new countries (e.g. East Germany) came into existence and new governments were elected or imposed. There was no trans-European political power stretching across the continent although visionary thinkers like Jean Monnet (1888–1979) and Robert Schuman (1886–1963) began to work for closer European integration to prevent future European wars: if European countries were inextricably connected, they would not be able to declare war on each other. Gradually, with industrial agreements between France and Germany in 1951 with the European Coal and Steel Community (Davies 1997, 1084), and then with the formation of the European Court (1952), the ground was laid first for the Common Market and later for the European Union.

As the post-war years passed, Western Europe prospered materially and the legal power and bureaucratic influence of the European Commission became more pronounced. Religious rights were legally safeguarded but the Christian history of Europe was not officially acknowledged despite objections from the Pope John Paul II in 2003 (Blunt 2003). Thus the 60 years after the end of World War II were a period of unbroken peace and prosperity accompanied by religious freedom but within a legal framework careful to give all religions an equal standing and not to prioritise Christianity. Such a framework, of course, did not apply to the oppressed peoples of Eastern Europe until the seemingly miraculous fall of the Berlin wall in 1989 and the liberalisation that followed.

The 1950s were a period of consolidation and recovery. Europe was split between the repressive and economically stagnant East and the liberal and economically successful West. Here the Pentecostal churches began to build, to move into larger premises, to engage in evangelism within their homelands and to consider overseas mission. The Pentecostals of Europe held their regular conferences and these were arranged to avoid clashing with the World Pentecostal Conferences in 1949, 1952, 1955 and 1964 which were all held in European cities. There was friendship between Pentecostal groups across Europe and although their doctrines might differ slightly, they agreed about the fundamental importance of baptism in the Spirit and charismatic gifts within the church today.

On the wrong side of the Iron Curtain Pentecostal Christians were deprived of educational opportunities, cultural support and financial power and many were imprisoned. Soviet propaganda treated religion as an irrational superstition and churches were controlled by a system of registration and constant bureaucratic interference in the hire and use of buildings, the timings of services, the number of baptisms allowed and in a range of other petty regulations designed to frustrate believers. Despite everything, the number of believers rose. It was sometimes asserted that persecution stimulated church growth while materialism choked it. It was certainly true that persecution removed the fringe of nominal Christianity that might still be found round the western churches.

The post-war era reopened travel routes. Commercial flights made international communication faster and easier. Pentecostal churches continue to send missionaries overseas into what was quickly becoming a post-colonial world. Although Alexander Boddy and T.B. Barratt had been ordained within the mainline churches of their day, there was no direct link between them and the charismatic movement that began in the late 1950s. This movement was essentially brought about by a fresh outpouring of the Holy Spirit upon many of the older churches with the result that Pentecostal phenomena like speaking in tongues, praying for the sick, visions and prophecies began to occur in the parishes and congregations of Methodist, Anglican, Lutheran, Presbyterian, and other streams of Christian churches.

The charismatic movement was essentially ecumenical in its capacity to draw churches together through a common experience of the Spirit and worship. By its association with the classical Pentecostal movement, it broadened the horizons of the older Pentecostals and gave the Pentecostal and charismatic streams an overlapping sense of purpose. As the charismatic movement rolled forward during the socially turbulent 1960s, it began to outgrow the classical Pentecostal churches. Classical Pentecostals began to look old-fashioned, which might have prevented charismatics from joining them.

Eventually the charismatic movement divided into at least two separate groupings: in the first, the emphasis was on renewal that entailed an inner spiritual revitalisation of church attendees through a fresh experience of the Holy Spirit. In the second, an emphasis on restoration was required which, in addition to inner personal renewal, sought an outer reform of the structures and practices associated with church governance. This second more radical group might go by the name of 'apostolic networks' and resisted the machinery of committees and conferences found in the old Pentecostal churches.

Once Europe was united under a free political system during the 1990s, the churches of Europe could exchange ideas and converge if they wished. Ideas and practices first found in the radical part of the charismatic movement began to appear in the older denominations and, conversely, liturgical ideas might surface in the new radical groups.

There was, across the world, a huge migratory flow from south to north, from poorer parts of African or Asian nations to the rich West. Within Britain the old Commonwealth countries had a political right to settle in the United Kingdom so that large numbers of West Africans began to plant their denominations into London and other major cities. The same occurred in the Netherlands and in Germany (at least 291 congregations by 2009) (Währisch-Oblau 2009, 47) with a result that African Christians found jobs in the West, learnt European languages and, within a generation, gave African modes of worship to major European cities. Booming megachurches were able to formulate worship styles that were part African, part derived from the music industry and part traditionally Pentecostal.

The same forces that brought Christians from the global south to Europe also brought other religions including Muslims. As a consequence Europe became multi-religious for the first time in its history. The presence of large non-Christian religious communities within European countries – as well as a rising number of ardent secularists (perhaps 15 percent of the population) – resulted in a legal climate that no longer favoured the church in the way that had been taken for granted by earlier generations, a change seen most clearly in the widespread redefinition of marriage.

As the new millennium broke, the largest number of Pentecostals in eastern Europe was found in Romania and this was followed by Russia and the Ukraine. In northern Europe Pentecostals and charismatics in Britain numbered perhaps half a million people or just under 1 percent of the population. As might be expected the larger countries had the larger Pentecostal movements and the fastest-growing Pentecostal groups appeared to be those that were starting from a very small base, as in Baltic states. In southern Europe the largest Pentecostal groups were found in Italy and Portugal, the former with something over 100,000 members.

Pentecostalism had first succeeded in countries with a tradition of Protestant variation (e.g. Scandinavia and Britain) and then penetrated south into the more Catholic and Orthodox parts of Europe (e.g. Portugal, Italy and Greece) once religious liberalisation arrived but, with liberalisation, came secularisation, plurality and a diminution in the default theism and Christian morality that had sustained previous generations. Along with these changes came extensive urbanisation associated with population growth.

While European Pentecostalism lacked the zeal and confidence of African or South American Pentecostalism, at its best it combined biblically grounded pastors, sustainable mission programs, imaginative evangelism, well established Bible Colleges and strategic plans for the twenty-first century, and it did so while retaining a balanced stance on charismatic gifts of all kinds. At its worst it sank to dreary conferences marked by fashion-driven leadership, hyperbolic preaching and factionalism.

Bibliography

Blunt, Liz. 2003. "Pope presses EU on Constitution." *BBC News*. Last modified June 29, 2003. http://news.bbc.co.uk/2/hi/europe/3029456.stm.

Davies, Norman. 1997. *Europe: A History*. London: Pimlico.

Gee, Donald. 1967. *Wind and Flame*. Pentecostal Pioneers Series 41. Nottingham: Assemblies of God Publishing House.

Hocken, Peter D. 2002. "Charismatic Movement." In *The New International Dictionary of Pentecostal and Charismatic Movements*, edited by Stanley M. Burgess, and Eduard M. van der Maas, 477–519. Grand Rapids, MI: Zondervan.

Kay, William K., and Anne E. Dyer, eds. 2011. *European Pentecostalism*. Leiden: Brill.

Judt, Tony. 2010. *Postwar: A History of Europe since 1945*. London: Vintage.

Röckle, Bernhard, and William K. Kay. 2003. "Born in Difficult Times: The Founding of the Volksmission and the Work of Karl Fix." *Journal of the European Pentecostal Theological Association* 23 (1): 72–101.

Synan, Vinson, and Amos Yong, eds. 2017. *Global Renewal Christianity: Spirit-Empowered Movements, Past, Present and Future*. Lake Mary, FL: Charisma Book Group.

Währisch-Oblau, Claudia. 2009. *The Missionary Self-Perception of Pentecostal/Charismatic Church Leaders from the Global South in Europe*. Leiden: Brill.

William K. Kay

European Pentecostal Theological Association

The European Pentecostal Theological Association represents and fosters Pentecostal and charismatic theological education and ministerial formation in Europe. It came into being in March 1979, first meeting in Vienna, Austria (Hocken 2003, 610). At the time, Pentecostals in Europe were gaining a greater appetite for serious theological education as part of ministerial training. With this context in mind, an early statement of purpose included "to promote excellence and effectiveness in Pentecostal scholarship, ministerial education and theological literature" and "to foster exchange, fellowship and cooperation between member institutions and individuals" (*JEPTA* until 2004, inside back cover). A more recent vision and purpose statement indicates that EPTA "promotes active fellowship and networking between Pentecostal educational institutions primarily in Europe and scholars from all over the world, and promotes research, education, and reflection in the broad area of Pentecostal theology ... It acts as a motivational forum for theology, pedagogy, history and leadership formation" (EPTA, n.d.). In order to facilitate these aims, EPTA has held conferences from its inception, and from 1981 has published a journal.

Ten years after EPTA's birth, the fall of Communism in eastern Europe affected the association. From 1989 until 2001, EPTA had an East-Europe Committee, aimed at spurring theological and ministerial education in these post-communist countries, both through short-term visits by teachers and through financial support. An example of its impact can be found in Jozef Brenkus' review of Pentecostalism in the Czech Republic, in which he describes as "an important milestone" the new "integration into European and global structures. This resulted in possibilities for its participation in the life and ministries of ..., e.g. EPTA" (Brenkus 2011, 253).

Unlike some academic groups that focus on research into Pentecostalism, EPTA is a confessional group. Its explicit confessional stance is maintained in two ways. First, all members "must subscribe to the Vision and Purpose statement of the Association" which includes the words: "EPTA seeks to further the work of God's kingdom, as expressed in Christ, on earth". Secondly, executive officers "shall affirm faith in Jesus Christ with the hope of eternal life in him, and belief in the continuing operation of gifts of the Spirit today including manifestations of the miraculous" (EPTA 2016). Given this confessional stance, EPTA conferences achieve a rare combination of both expressive Pentecostal worship and serious, considered scholarship.

Conferences are held annually. Each conference has a theme, reflected in the academic papers given and in other less formal meetings. The conference venue, typically a Pentecostal theological college, rotates around the continent so that, ideally, all corners of Europe have a conference within reach every few years. For example, in the first 20 years of the 21st century, conferences were held in a total of 11 different countries, from Portugal to Finland, and from the UK to Bulgaria. While maintaining a European focus, conferences attract scholars and research students from all over the world.

Many papers given at the conferences are considered worthy of publication, which typically occurs in the peer-reviewed *Journal of the European Pentecostal Theological Association* (*JEPTA*). This started as the *EPTA Bulletin*, changing its name in the mid-nineties (the 1996 edition carried both names). It has evolved over the years into a professionally produced journal, published twice-yearly by Routledge Taylor & Francis Group. Its editor is supported by a wide-ranging editorial board, while guest editors are occasionally commissioned to edit specific themed volumes. *JEPTA* is published in the English language, which is also the language of EPTA's conferences.

EPTA has a system of formal membership, both for individuals and for institutions. Individual membership is open to people operating anywhere in the world; institutional membership, conversely, is only open to Pentecostal theological colleges in Europe. Executive officers represent institutions across the continent, and the ten chairs between 1980 and 2020 have come from four nations. Office holders constitutionally occupy four-year terms. However, in practice, terms of office are often either extended or repeated. The longest-serving chair was David Petts, then principal of Mattersey Hall College, UK, who served from 1985 to 1990 and again from 1995 to 2000 (EPTA, n.d.).

EPTA has relations with the Pentecostal European Fellowship (PEF) and the World Alliance for Pentecostal Theological Education. Despite the activities and relationships in which EPTA engages, doubts are expressed about the capacity of it and other international organizations to create a "European agenda" in the face of other forces faced by European Pentecostalism. Thus, Pfister writes both that there is "little evidence that 'Europe' really matters for most of European Pentecostalism" and that, despite the work of EPTA, PEF, etc., there is "no clearly defined European agenda for most Pentecostal congregations in Europe" (Pfister 2011, 360–61). Such views indicate one challenge that EPTA continues to face.

Bibliography

Brenkus, Jozef. 2011. "Pentecostal Movement in the Czech Republic and Slovakia." In *European Pentecostalism*, edited by Anne E. Dyer and William K. Kay, 248–259. Leiden: Brill.

Hocken, Peter. 2002. "European Pentecostal Theological Association." In *The New International Dictionary of Pentecostal and Charismatic Movements*, edited by Stanley M. Burgess and Eduard M. Van der Maas, 610. Grand Rapids: Zondervan.

EPTA. n.d. "European Pentecostal Theological Association." Accessed October 23, 2019. http://www.eptaonline.com/.

Journal of the European Pentecostal Theological Association (JEPTA). 1996–2019 (previously published as *EPTA Bulletin*, 1981–1996).

Pfister, Raymond. 2011. "The Future(s) of Pentecostalism in Europe." In *European Pentecostalism*, edited by William Kay and Anne Dyer, 357–381. Leiden: Brill.

William P. Atkinson

Evangelicalism

The definitions of Pentecostalism and Evangelicalism are both problematic on a global scale. Many groups of persons who would be classified as Pentecostal or Charismatic by outside observers would not understand themselves in those categories. The meaning of Evangelical varies widely. It is contested and quite context dependent. For example, in Germany, Evangelisch means primarily Lutheran Protestant, while Evangelikal references conservative religious groups, many of which share the theology and values of the American and UK evangelicals. In Croatia, the term Evangelical refers to the older established churches while the twentieth century new churches, including Pentecostals, are called neo-evangelical.

In Latin America, evangélicos means primarily Protestant with no North American or European reference, but is sometimes used as the equivalent of Pentecostal. In Africa and Asia there is little agreement as to which groups are included within the terms Pentecostal and Evangelical. In most of Europe, the term is also used for the Evangelical Alliance (1846), now the World Evangelical Alliance (WEA) which has only had two non-USA or UK leaders, both from the Philippines. There have been no Pentecostal (by any definition) leaders of the WEA. In Asia, it generally refers to associations or denominations connected to the USA National Association of Evangelicals, related NGOs, or Billy Graham. The diverse and local significations of the term Evangelical make it impossible to define globally what Pentecostals and Evangelicals are or are not or how the two overlapping networks relate.

The focus of this entry are the USA-UK experiences of Pentecostalism and Evangelicalism because of their hegemonic status in World Christianity. In the USA the term Evangelical is used of a group that broke from Fundamentalism, primarily over issues of dispensationalism and ecumenism. The National Association of Evangelicals sought a middle way between Fundamentalism and Liberalism. In the United Kingdom, it developed, on the basis of already existing demarcations, primarily post WWII, as a theologically conservative network uniting persons in the older churches (often participants in the Keswick or related conventions) led by John R.W. Stott who wrote to distinguish Evangelicalism and Fundamentalism as well as to make the concept of Baptism with the Holy Spirit more usable outside Pentecostalism. These networks of individuals united with American and other like-minded leaders around the world in the Billy Graham Crusades and Lausanne Committee for World Evangelization (Lausanne Movement) which has also been dominated by the USA-UK Evangelicals. These defined themselves over against the World Council of Churches and the International Missionary Council. The USA-UK Evangelicals were determinately anti-Communist, anti-Socialist, and worked against systemic social reform around the world while supporting micro social support of individuals in a context of sharing the Gospel through NGOs such as World Vision.

A theological definition of this USA-UK Evangelicalism was proposed by David Bebbington, rooted in the Baptist and conservative religious experience of the UK and USA: conversionism, activism, biblicism, and crucicentrism. In addition, Pentecostals are also pneumatic or Holy Spirit focused, as well as committed to glossolalia, personal and social transformation, faith healing, and generally, to premillennialism. There are important differences in liturgy and expectations of religious experience between USA-UK Pentecostals and Evangelicals and their co-religionists around the world. Unlike Protestant, Evangelical and Catholic churches, most Pentecostal and Charismatic denominations and networks were not directly founded by the large USA or European mission agencies although early leaders and some laity may have initially been part of the older missions.

Some Pentecostals participate in USA-UK evangelical initiatives around the world, but those from outside the USA and UK have not achieved positions of power, nor have they had significant input into the theology or social programs of evangelical organizations. Most Pentecostal, Pentecostal-like, and

Charismatic denominations outside North America have not joined or participated. Importantly, most accrediting agencies for developing schools and universities in Asia, Latin America and Africa are dominated by the small, well-organized, and well-funded networks of USA evangelical education. This domination can be expected to increase because of the 2018 decision to merge the Association of Theological Schools (USA and Canada, primarily evangelical institutions) and the International Council of Evangelical Theological Education which is also dominated by USA leadership.

From the early days of the Azusa Street Revival, Pentecostals were attacked and then shunned by most of the older Holiness Movement denominations as well as conservative reformed Evangelicals. This was true in the USA, but also in Norway, Sweden, and especially Germany, where in 1909 conservative Lutherans of the Gemeinschaftsbewegung declared Pentecostals demonic, a classification that remained in place until the 1990s. In Chile, for example, missionaries of the Methodist Episcopal Church, the Reformed churches, and Catholics spoke out against Pentecostalism. In the UK, most Keswick, Holiness, Non-Conformist, and conservative reformed Anglicans opposed the Pentecostal movement. The impacts of these negative decisions were felt around the world through the missionary networks.

Racism was a defining element of the reception of Pentecostalism. In the USA, the Pentecostal revival quickly split along ethnic lines (white, black, Hispanic, German, Scandinavian, Italian, etc.). The newspapers reported on Pentecostals in racist ways. The quick growth and visibility of black Sanctified Pentecostal churches, socially embarrassed white Pentecostal churches and these were shunned by other Pentecostals. But it was a widespread problem. For example, in Norway and Denmark, racist cartoons tying Pentecostalism and Africa were widely published and this identification was often seen in popular and scholarly literature as a negative. In the USA and sometimes in Europe, this racism drove wedges between Evangelicals and the new movement. Conformity to racist norms and conservative political thought of Europe and North America, made Evangelicals and Pentecostals quite condescending toward Asian, African, and Latin American co-religionists. They generally resisted indigenous leadership as long as possible. Even then they have generally insisted on maintaining the missionaries' social and political perspectives in return for continued financial assistance. Missionaries from older churches and Evangelicals also objected to women in ministry, multiple stages of spirituality, pacifism, and the supernatural in personal religious experience and liturgy

During the first half of the twentieth century, increasing naïve higher criticism of the biblical texts and the equally naïve anti-critical defenses of biblical authority divided European and North American Christianity. These discussions influenced missionary decisions, social structures and education. The division of these versions of Christianity, into so-called Liberal and Fundamentalist branches, left Pentecostal churches caught in between, distrusted, despised and attacked by both sides. There were few ecumenical encounters at the local, national or international levels. Some individual Pentecostals were participants at the Edinburgh 1910 missionary conference; H.B. Garlock, an Assemblies of God (AG) USA missionary, represented the AG on the Missions Committee of the USA National Council of Churches until that became impossible after affiliation of the AG with the National Association of Evangelicals (NAE).

After World War II, the barriers between Pentecostals and groups definable as Evangelicals lowered. Important reasons were (1) Evangelicals and Pentecostals had endeavored to make their groups acceptable by the USA military to provide chaplains; (2) participation in NAE; (3) the diminishing (in USA and European Pentecostalism) of enthusiastic worship, public exercise of spiritual gifts including healing, and women in ministry. In the USA, there was a more defined separation of the races, and acceptance of elements of Fundamentalist theology. By the 1990s most AG clergy in the USA no longer believed in the initial evidence doctrine and otherwise downplayed the importance of speaking in tongues. This made relationships with Evangelicalism easier.

Thus, the global push of North American and British Evangelical organizations to correct the Pentecostals had an effect. By offering the reward of respectability and connections to them, North American Pentecostals were willing to change their theologies and social reform commitments. The large spectrum of what may be called Pentecostal churches outnumbers and out-evangelizes the traditional reformed Evangelicals in most countries. However, because of USA-UK financial power and leadership it is the reformed Evangelicals and their USA AG allies who are usually invited to represent Evangelicalism and Pentecostalism in the ecumenical forums of the world. Most accrediting agencies for higher education, that determine future directions of education in participating Evangelical and Pentecostal institutions, are dominated by the North American and UK Evangelicals, who often discourage participation in local or national educational structures. The same groups define needs, donate, and control most of the foreign funding available outside the USA and UK.

In the USA, the Pew Research Center polls have demonstrated that white Evangelicals and Pentecostals (along with Baptists, Churches of Christ, and Nazarenes), are among the most firmly supportive of right-wing conservative nationalism. They do not indicate concern over racism, white supremacist policies and language, anti-immigrant stances, return to segregated education and housing, or restriction of access to healthcare, food, and education. White Evangelicals and Pentecostals in the USA have made theological choices: they share the beliefs that the most important issue is personal salvation with heaven as the ultimate goal. Social comfort is equally important, which has led to efforts to use government to enforce their vision of public morality (pro-school prayer, anti-abortion, abstinence only sex-education, anti-LGBTQ). They believe they are living in an apocalyptic time during which the world is getting worse and believe that persecution of white evangelicals is happening and will become more intense.

The question of the political alignment of Pentecostals and Evangelicals with dictatorial regimes has been widely discussed. Within Europe, political party affiliations are less defined by religious affiliations including among Evangelicals and Pentecostals. There, and in most places, political allegiances are often complicated by a range of contextual factors. However, the tendency of Pentecostal and Evangelical leadership and most parishioners has been toward support for right-wing or left-wing authoritarian governments, as in Chile (Pinochet), Zimbabwe (Mugabe), Guatemala (Efrain Rios Montt who was a member of the Pentecostal Church of the Word/Iglesia Cristiana Verba), USA (Trump), and Brazil (Bolsonaro). In some places, such as Venezuela, most Pentecostals and Evangelicals have maintained a passive stance in the struggles related to the Chavez-Maduro governments, which essentially provides support for those governments. Usually Pentecostal and Evangelical leadership are more in solidarity with these governments than the laity. Pentecostal and Evangelical youth and minorities are more likely to suffer or be exiled in these situations. There were also, in each country, groups and individuals who did not support the authoritarian governments.

Pentecostal and Evangelical Christians from around the world have immigrated to USA and European cities, bringing their languages and faith traditions. The majority of these are Pentecostal. Detailed research on these groups in Paris has demonstrated their lack of relationship with each other and with the local Evangelical and Pentecostal churches. Exceptions can be seen in large Pentecostal and Evangelical churches in the UK and Scandinavia. Some USA, Dutch, and French churches, for example, rent space to co-religionist immigrants.

Bibliography

Alvarsson, Jan-Åke, and Rita Laura Segata, eds. 2003. *Religions in Transition: Mobility, Merging and Globalization in the Emergence of Contemporary Religious Adhesions*. Uppsala: Uppsala Universitet.

Anderson, Allan. 2004. *An Introduction to Pentecostalism: Global Charismatic Christianity*. Cambridge: Cambridge University Press.

Bebbington, David. 1989. *Evangelicalism in Modern Britain: A History from the 1730s to the 1980s*. London: Unwin Hyman.

Chiquete, Daniel. 2019. *Pentecostalismo, espacialidad y representaciones. Ensayos sobre algunas concepciones arquitectónicas, urbanas e iconoclásticas pentecostales*. Madrid: Editorial Académica Española.

Coleman, Simon, Rosalind I.J. Hackett, and Joel Robbins, eds. 2015. *The Anthropology of Global Pentecostalism and Evangelicalism*. New York: New York University Press.

Fer, Yannick, and Gwendoline Malogne-Fer, eds. 2017. *Le Protestantisme à Paris: Diversité et recompositions contemporaines*. Genève: Labor et Fides.

Freston, Paul. 2001. *Evangelicals and Politics in Asia, Africa and Latin America*. Cambridge: Cambridge University Press.

Hanciles, Jehu J. 2008. *Beyond Christendom: Globalization, African Migration, and the Transformation of the West*. Maryknoll: Orbis Books.

Jacobsen, Douglas. 2015. *Global Gospel: An Introduction to Christianity on Five Continents*. Grand Rapids: Baker Academics.

Ranger, Terrence O. 2006. *Evangelical Christianity and Democracy in Africa*. Oxford: Oxford University Press.

Stanley, Brian. 2013. *The Global Diffusion of Evangelicalism: The Age of Billy Graham and John Stott*. Downers Grove: IVP.

Stott, John R.W. 1964. *The Baptism and Fullness of the Holy Spirit*. Downers Grove: Inter Varsity Press.

Stott, John R.W. 1959. *Fundamentalism and Evangelicalism*. Grand Rapids: Eerdmans.

David Bundy

Exegesis

Exegesis refers broadly to the pursuit of an accurate interpretation of a religious text according to linguistic, historical, literary, and genre analysis. In a more restricted sense, exegesis belongs to employment of historical-grammatical criticism. The latter approach, championed in the twentieth century, typically marches through an array of critical methods (such as text, source, tradition, form, and redaction) and digs deep into grammatical and syntactical arrangement of a text (preferably in the original language). Upon successful arrival at the original author's intended meaning and purpose for the original audience, exegetes seek to apply the text for contemporary readers and communities. With the advent of the twenty-first century, attempts at definition become increasingly difficult due to the legion of emerging hermeneutical approaches. If pursuit of an exegetical methodology reveals the specific impulse of a movement, Pentecostals would be difficult to measure. Given its diversity, the quest for *the* Pentecostal approach must be deemed an impossibility. This impasse results from the diversity among those in pursuit of interpretation for and proclamation of a text. The location of the exegete, whether academician, pulpiteer, or devotional reader, will guide the questions brought to the biblical text.

Pentecostals emerge, both deliberately and unwittingly, in the twentieth century trajectory. Early Pentecostals found interpretative affinity alongside traditions that employed Scripture as the ultimate authority for belief (orthodoxy) and practice (orthopraxis). These Pentecostals employed an interpretative template marked by primitivist and pragmatic impulses in their attempt to recover first-century Christianity. They did so with a common-sense approach (plain reading), whereby they found little or no distance between themselves and biblical characters. With their enchanted worldview, these Pentecostals embraced a seamless defense of a biblical text ever-waiting to be performed (e.g., Acts 29). The Full-Gospel message led consistently to christocentric renderings and applications of the Scriptures mediated by intimate encounter with the Holy Spirit (orthopathos). Biblical interpretation moved steadily to four/fivefold experience of Jesus as Savior, Sanctifier, Spirit-baptizer, Healer, and Soon-coming King. For this reason, Bible reading and interpretation often migrates naturally toward emphasis upon salvation, holiness, Spirit-enablement, miracles, and spiritual gifts – all of these both realized and futuristic (eschatological).

By the mid-twentieth century, Pentecostals sought greater acceptance from Fundamentalists and burgeoning Evangelicals. This drive produced both enlivening and dulling effects on Pentecostal reading of Scripture. On the one side, the enchanted world of Pentecostals proved problematic for largely cessationist interpreters, who could not yet account for the growing pentecostalization of Christianity. Though Fundamentalists and the nascent Evangelicals sought a direct correlation (from "then" to "now"), their exegesis would be rigid, objective, formulaic, and modernistic; they focused often on historical reliability, authorial intent, intended audience, and transferability of these conclusions. These same readers would generally defend miracles, healing, prophecy, etc. – all hallmarks of Pentecostalism, yet they would generally reject modern equivalency. On the other hand, Pentecostals in their quest for acceptance gradually found themselves in Evangelical and Fundamentalist training centers. In these settings, Pentecostals found their enchanted and playful impulses challenged by the rigidity of modernist, formulaic, and scientific renderings, and they could not resist adopting Evangelical and Fundamentalist methods.

Given Pentecostal proclivities to historical narratives, particularly Acts, Pentecostal scholars made their grand move toward exegetical respectability alongside the advent of formalism, namely, the rise of narrative analysis in the humanities. Though Pentecostal scholar Gordon Fee secured the Pentecostal and Evangelical marriage, his reading of biblical narrative reflected more of the Evangelical movement than his fellow Pentecostals (Fee and Stuart 2003). For a more robust Pentecostal reading, the rise of literary critics ensured that Pentecostals found traction in the academy. Since biblical stories do not serve primarily as guides for biblical history or merely a backdrop for prescriptive teaching, Pentecostals capitalized on Luke's appeal to follow "all that Jesus began to do and teach" (Acts 1:1). Roger Stronstad (2012) stands as the foundational scholar for Pentecostal defense of an exegetical method. Modern interpreters, not unlike the earliest Pentecostals, must read narratives for didactic and normative value.

In a postmodern world now filtered through the turns defined by Ludwig Wittgenstein and Hans-Georg Gadamer, exegesis marked by rigidity come increasingly under duress. If Bible reading reflects the reader's *weltanschauung*, exegetical commitment to the historical critical domination of Evangelical and Fundamentalist methods cannot escape their positionality; indeed, their exegetes provide only one of many postmodern categories. Kenneth Archer (2005) argues that Pentecostal exegetes generally employ a triadic negotiation for meaning between biblical text, Spirit, and Pentecostal community; in so doing, the diversity of "communities" offers reasonable license for interpretation. The rapid growth of Global South Pentecostals and their subsequent rise in the academy contributes further to the diversity of interpretative "communities."

The diversity of Pentecostals makes moot any methodological uniformity among its participants. Instead, exegetical diversity among Pentecostals may reflect increasing maturation. Having said this, several threads and trends may be noted. First, in a world of ever-changing typologies, Pentecostals never cease to locate their lives in biblical stories and unashamedly place their experience upon the biblical template. In fact, though Pentecostals have been accused of "exegeting their experience," many would willingly embrace such criticism. Second, many Pentecostals share the cosmology of the ancient world. Pentecostals approach a text and assume the plausibility of a biblical worldview. Third, Pentecostal exegesis reflects the movable boundaries of a global phenomenon. They might be deemed exegetical ecumenists. Whether intentional or not, Pentecostals read and study Scripture widely and bring a multiplicity of methods and local worldviews into their interpretative process. Pentecostals might be broadly construed as opportunists willing to mine the rich resources of biblical interpreters, and ever-open to fresh and new readings of Scripture.

Bibliography

Archer, Kenneth J. 2005. *A Pentecostal Hermeneutic for the Twenty-First Century: Spirit, Scripture, and Community*. London: T&T Clark.

Fee, Gordon, and Douglas Stuart. 2003. *How to Read the Bible for All It's Worth*. Third Edition. Grand Rapids, MI: Zondervan.

Mittelstadt, Martin William. 2010. *Reading Luke-Acts in the Pentecostal Tradition*. Cleveland, TN: CPT Press.

Oliverio, L. William. 2012. *Theological Hermeneutics in the Classical Pentecostal Tradition: A Typological Account*. Leiden: Brill.

Stronstad, Roger. 2012. *The Charismatic Theology of St. Luke*. Second Edition. Grand Rapids, MI: Baker.

Martin W. Mittelstadt

Experience

The appeal to experience of God as a resource for theology became ubiquitous in Christian theology in the twentieth century, in forms varying from a broadly shared transcendent experience of God in human life or in particular social groups, to specific, individual mystical encounters. Pentecostals affirm an openness and an appeal to the experience of God, but the nature of this appeal is understood within a Pentecostal worldview and spirituality, distinguishing this perspective from other Christian traditions and theological approaches. In contrast to Christian traditions that emphasize doctrine or formal liturgy as their point of departure for spirituality and theology, Pentecostals begin with the assumption of (the possibility of) a direct or immediate experience of God.

The Pentecostal view of experience of God is embedded in a worldview that assumes the Holy Spirit to be present and active in human life and the world in perceptible and tangible ways. The Spirit is not merely a point of doctrine to be affirmed, but the personal presence of God to be encountered and felt, deeply transforming the affections and behaviour of the believer. In contrast also to appeals to a more immanent-transcendent experience of God, Pentecostal experience of God is best understood as an encounter with the God who is transcendent other. Such experience, then, is an interruptive in-breaking of the Spirit into the life of the believer and worshipping community.

This view shares some similarities with classical Christian mysticism, in that Pentecostals affirm the possibility of direct awareness or perception of God (as opposed to necessary mediation through physical perception or secondary sources, such as sermons, sacraments, nature, and such). But this also needs to be distinguished from mystical experience classically described in terms of the loss of one's conscious self in the divine. Pentecostal testimony affirms experiences with God as difficult to put into words, but the clear distinction between God and the worshipper is generally maintained. A better term to describe Pentecostal experience of God might be 'mystical encounter,' which conveys the idea of non-physical immediate experience of God, and yet preserves the distinction between the believer and God.

Openness to mystical encounter with God serves to enrich Pentecostal spiritual life more generally. Since experience of the Spirit is so personal, the believer may report feeling God's love, encouragement, strength, healing, and forgiveness, or perceive God as providing correction, direction in decision-making, and even new knowledge pertaining to circumstances or theological truth (through prophecy, words of wisdom or knowledge, dreams, and visions). Along with these, within the narrower tradition of classical Pentecostalism, a particular experience is pursued, commonly identified as "Spirit baptism." This experience is believed to result in the increased ability of the Christian believer to bear witness to Jesus and participate in God's mission in the world, and is often associated with the accompanying sign of speaking in unknown tongues (Acts 2:1–4).

Since Pentecostal mystical encounters are considered an immediate perception of God, by implication they are also are a means through which God is revealed something to the believer (affecting the way the believer responds to God, life circumstances, etc.). Put another way, there is an openness within the Pentecostal tradition to ongoing revelation by the Spirit, which means that experience of God holds some measure of authority for the individual and possibly the larger community. The fact that experience of God is to some degree authoritative makes it a significant theological resource within pentecostalism.

While enriching Pentecostal spiritual life, experience as an authority also comes with potential risks. The subjective nature of mystical encounters can lead, for example, to confusing one's psychological disposition or mood with God's revelatory activity and will. In short, experiences with God can be viewed as self-authenticating. Related here is the Pentecostal pragmatic impulse, which tends to equate experience-inspired new theological or ministry ideas as divinely sanctioned, if they reap immediate results. This has served as a cause of schisms among Pentecostals, since what serves as divinely authoritative for one may not be received by another.

Moderating this subjectivity and pragmatism, however, is the Pentecostal assumption that the Bible is the privileged theological authority and resource. Experience of God, then, is not free-floating, but anchored in the scriptural text, which identifies encounter with the Spirit as being the Spirit of Jesus Christ and God the Father, not a generic spirit. Any experience of God, to be considered authentic, must be framed by the biblical narrative; the Spirit will not contradict written revelation. When it comes to the interplay of experience and scriptural hermeneutics, there is current intramural debate among Pentecostals as to whether experience of God should serve merely to authenticate truth derived from rational interpretation of Scripture, or more as a dialectical resource helping believers discern God's voice in and through Scripture. In both cases, however, the privileged role of Scripture in Christian theology is affirmed.

Another qualification helps temper the subjectivity implicit in mystical encounter. There is growing acknowledgement within Pentecostal scholarship that experience of God occurs within and is strongly shaped or socialized by the cultural-linguistic theological community, or confessional framework, in which one is embedded. A tradition's worship and spirituality – sermons, testimonies, doctrinal articulation, songs, interpretations of Scripture, and so forth – provide a social-spiritual context in which experience of God is received and embodied. The cultural-linguistic (sub)tradition, then, encourages (or discourages) certain experiences of God, and both explicitly and tacitly vets what may be considered authentic mystical encounter (or not). This means that individual experience of God is mitigated by both Scripture and the tradition in which one worships. With this qualification, a more accurate way of understanding Pentecostal experience of God is as a "mediated immediacy." At the same time, Pentecostals would not want to limit experience of God to simply mirroring the corporate experience of the tradition; there must be room for the interruptive work of God. Pentecostal experience, then, should be understood as a dialectic involving God, the individual believer, Scripture, and the Christian community.

Bibliography

Cartledge, Mark J. 2015. *The Mediation of the Spirit: Interventions in Practical Theology*. Grand Rapids, MI: Eerdmans.

Neumann, Peter D. 2012. *Pentecostal Experience: An Ecumenical Encounter*. Eugene, OR: Pickwick.

Smith, James K.A. 2010. *Thinking in Tongues: Pentecostal Contributions to Christian Philosophy*. Grand Rapids, MI: Eerdmans.

Vondey, Wolfgang. 2013. *Pentecostalism: A Guide for the Perplexed*. London and New York: Bloomsbury T&T Clark.

Warrington, Keith. 2008. *Pentecostal Theology: A Theology of Encounter*. London; New York: T&T Clark.

Peter D. Neumann

Fangcheng Fellowship, China

Fangcheng Fellowship (方城团契), also known as the Chinese Conversion Fellowship or the Fangcheng Mother Church, was founded in Fengcheng County, Nanyang City, Henan province, China. It was established by Zhang Rongliang (张荣亮), one of its current leaders, in 1981. Zhang, ordained in the same year, used to tour and evangelize the rural areas of Nanyang with Rev. Li Tian-en (李天恩) during the latter half of the Cultural Revolution. Zhang and Li's testimonies were filled with numerous signs and wonders, healings, prophesies, and glossolalia, among which, the healings in particular, were a great attraction for the rural people. However, they were reluctant to be called charismatic, due to the conservative fundamental tradition in Chinese theology and the strict government policies on religious beliefs. Many people converted to Christianity as they found in Zhang's testimonies certain similarities between Christianity and Chinese folk religions that were almost eradicated during the Cultural Revolution.

In the 1980s and 1990s, with China's accelerating urbanization, more farmers went to work in the cities. This action was not approved by the leaders of the Fangcheng Fellowship at first. Influenced by their conservative theology, the leaders criticized believers who found jobs in the cities as slaves of money with a weak spirit. Hence, the believers in the fellowship always left their hometown quietly. However, the rural migrant Christian workers could not adapt to urban churches due to differences in theology, worship and lifestyle. They tried to build their own church to meet their own needs, but could not find satisfactory pastors, and therefore had no choice but to seek help from their mother church. By then, Fangcheng Fellowship was not only facing the crisis caused by losing young and middle-aged believers, but also the persistent pressure from the government on the its frequent crowded revival meetings. Considering this situation, the fellowship leaders changed their minds and started to send pastors to urban churches. By doing so, they gradually built their own church network and also maintained close connections with other family church networks, such as the Chinese Gospel Fellowship (中华福音团契), Lixin Fellowship (利辛团契), Yingshan Fellowship (颍上团契), and Wenzhou Yueqing Church (温州区会).

Western pastors also exerted a great influence on the revival of the Pentecostal-charismatic Movement in the Fangcheng Fellowship. In the 1980s, Dennis Balcombe (包德宁), an American pastor with a great passion for evangelizing China, found a chance to enter Guangzhou where he served a church in preparation for further evangelizing the rest of the China mainland. In Guangzhou, he found most of the mainland churches did not have Bibles. For this reason, Balcombe built a connection with the Fangcheng Fellowship through Guangzhou family churches. He was then invited by Zhang Rongliang to Fangcheng to deliver a sermon, after which, glossolalia (speaking in tongues) was evident. Inspired by this western pastor, many believers accepted glossolalia, except Zhang Rongliang, who believed glossolalia was just for personal benefits from his understanding of the Bible. Some believers who experienced glossolalia also regarded it as a holy gift sent by God directly, rather than brought to them by Balcombe.

At the beginning of the twenty-first century, several pastors and journalistic works attracted attention to Christianity in China. Two examples include David Akiman's book, *Jesus in Beijing: How Christianity is Transforming China and Changing the Global Balance of Power* (2006), and Pastor Yuan Zhiming's (远志明) documentary, *Cross in China*. As a result, more Chinese Christians, scholars, and officials have come to know about the Fangcheng Fellowship and their members, especially Lü Xiaomin (吕小敏), a Young female Christian who sang more than 5 thousand spirit songs and compiled them into the *Canaan Hymns*.

Fangcheng Fellowship also experienced some crisis in its development after Zhang Rongliang was put in prison for using a fake passport. Its network was divided and split into several factions. Even Zhang Rongliang could not bring the fellowship together when he was discharged from prison. The Fangcheng Fellowship was also facing questions about how most of its pastors did not have enough education and theological knowledge to meet the needs of urban Christians. As a result, the church sent potential candidates to overseas seminaries for further education and placing their hopes with the next generation to realize their dream of evangelizing the whole of China.

Bibliography

Akiman, David. 2006. *Jesus in Beijing: How Christianity is Transforming China and Changing the Global Balance of Power*. Washington, DC: Regnery.

Anderson, Allan, and E. Tong, eds. 2011. *Asian and Pentecostal: The Charismatic Face of Christianity in Asia*. Oxford, UK: Regnum Books.

Yang, Fenggang, Joy K.C. Tong, and Allan Anderson, eds. 2017. *Global Chinese Pentecostal and Charismatic Christianity*. Leiden, Brill.

Hui Li

Farrow, Lucy

Early Pentecostal pastor, evangelist, and missionary who played a key part in the birth of the Azusa Street Revival. Born in 1851 in Norfolk, Virginia, Lucy Farrow was allegedly a mulatto daughter of a white slave owner and slave woman, and was either born a slave or sold into it after her father died. Farrow is also claimed to be the niece of the famous abolitionist Frederick Douglass. By 1871 she had relocated to Mississippi, and by 1890 she had moved on to Houston, Texas. At this point she was widowed at least once and had borne seven children, only two of whom were still alive. While in Texas she lived with her son and pastored a Holiness mission church.

It was during this period that she met Charles Fox Parham, who arrived in Houston in the summer of 1905 to conduct evangelistic services. Farrow worked as a cook for Parham's organization while he was in the area. This close proximity exposed Farrow to Parham's ministry and message, which would eventually lead to her becoming a strong advocate for Spirit baptism with tongues. When Parham was ready to leave Houston and travel to Kansas he asked Farrow to come with him and work as a governess for his family. She agreed, and it was during her time in Kansas that Farrow had her Pentecostal experience. While Farrow was away, William Seymour – who had been attending her church – took over the pastorate in her absence. When Farrow returned she resumed her pastoral duties and shared about her new experience with Seymour. Farrow then introduced Seymour to Parham – who had also returned to Houston to set up a Bible training school – and asked Parham to allow Seymour to attend the classes at this new school. Parham agreed, though Seymour had to sit outside the classroom door due to Jim Crow laws.

In the spring of 1906 Farrow departed Texas and traveled to Los Angeles. The impetus behind the relocation was a summons from Seymour – who earlier in February had moved there to pursue another ministry opportunity – that was mailed to Parham to request more workers be sent to help in the work that God was doing. Farrow, along with Joseph Warren, arrived in Los Angeles in April and immediately began working alongside of Seymour. Her presence was beneficial, and she was described as "God's anointed handmaiden" who brought the full Gospel and whom God greatly used. Farrow is credited with laying hands on many to receive the experience of Spirit baptism with tongues. This includes Brother Lee, who is recognized as the first person among the small group of believers surrounding Seymour who had a glossolalic experience.

After a few months Farrow felt God calling her back to her childhood home in Virginia to engage in ministry there. She, thus, departed from Los Angeles to head east. On her journey she made stops in Texas and Louisiana, preaching and praying for others along the route. Once in Virginia she held church meetings, praying for persons to receive the experience of Spirit baptism with tongues, of which 150 did. By December she again felt God leading her somewhere else, this time overseas to Liberia – a destination that may have been a result of a Pentecostal version of the movement "back to Africa" which had arisen during this time in black denominations like the AME. Farrow set sail before the end of the year by way of England. She was accompanied by Mr. and Mrs. Bateman, and Mr. and Mrs. Hutchins and their niece. Once in Liberia she spent her time ministering to the people, many of whom were saved, sanctified, healed, and Spirit baptized, including some of them experiencing xenolalia and speaking in English. It is also said that twice Farrow herself received the gift of xenolalia and was able to preach a message in the native Kru language.

Farrow only remained in Liberia for seven months before she felt God calling her to return again to Los Angeles. On her return journey she first made stops in Virginia and other areas of the south. By May of 1908 she had made her way back to Los Angeles, supporting the work there and continuing her own ministry out of a "little faith cottage" attached to the back of the Mission. Here people came to her for prayer, healing, and to receive Spirit baptism. Farrow eventually returned to Houston and died in 1911 after she contracted intestinal tuberculosis.

Bibliography

Alexander, Estrelda. 2005. *The Women of Azusa Street*. Cleveland, OH: The Pilgrim Press.
Apostolic Faith, January 1908, no. 1.
Apostolic Faith, May 1908, no. 2.
Apostolic Faith, September 1906, no. 1.
Robeck, Cecil M., Jr. 2006. *The Azusa Street Mission and Revival*. Nashville: Nelson.

Lisa P. Stephenson

Finland

In the period 1809–1917, before its independence, Finland was the Autonomous Grand Duchy of Russia. Many important religious influences were mediated through Sweden, the former mother country, and by the Swedish speaking minority on the western coastal area, Ostrobothnia. This was the case also with Pentecostalism. The history of classical Pentecostalism in Finland goes back to the early twentieth century with some influences also from the Azusa Street Revival.

The Norwegian Methodist pastor Thomas B. Barratt was influenced by Pentecostalism in the USA in 1906. In Oslo, he started to arrange meetings that attracted people from neighbouring countries, Sweden and Finland. Barratt visited Finland in 1911 and again in the following year when the revival is said to have achieved its breakthrough. Nevertheless, even though Barratt's meetings have been regarded as the starting point of Finnish Pentecostalism, there were also other agents and facilitators paving the way for the new movement. For instance, returning migrants had spread the message, and as early as in 1907 Ostrobothnian newspapers reposted occurrences of baptism of the Holy Spirit and speaking in tongues in other revival movements. Namely, there were already some American originated churches such as Baptist, Methodist and Covenant Churches whose teachings were relatively close to Pentecostalism. Moreover, Pietistic movements had been advocating individualized spirituality already since the eighteenth century.

The first Pentecostal congregation was founded in Helsinki in 1915. Pentecostalism spread rapidly in its first years. The impact of women evangelists was important in planting new congregations throughout the country. However, during the organizing period, charisma was gradually interpreted as a gender specific characteristic, genuinely possessed by men, which excluded women from the leading positions in the Pentecostal churches.

In Finland, Neo-Pentecostalism (*uushelluntailaisuus*) is the label given to the short-term revival that centered on the evangelist Niilo Ylivainio in 1977–1981. His tent meetings gathered a lot of attention, especially in the media. Many people claimed to be healed through his prayers. The international charismatic renewal of the 1960–70s had an influence in the Evangelical-Lutheran Church of Finland (ELC). The association *Hengen uudistus kirkossamme ry* (The Spiritual Renewal within Our Church) was founded in order to introduce the biblical and theological principles, content, and functions of charismata within the ELC in co-operation with other ecclesiastical authorities. This association has been active since its inception.

Traditional Pentecostalism has been operating in Finland as a loose network of lay-based local congregations from the beginning. In fact, it started to divide already after 1910, into the supporters of organized congregations and into the Friends of Pentecost, who favoured informal community. The official arrangements for accomplishing the division took place in 2002 when the state-registered Pentecostal Church of Finland (PCF) was founded. Those congregations which were not willing to join the PCF remained independent and locally registered associations. Today, with over 40,000 members, Pentecostalism is the third largest religious group in the country including 238 Finnish speaking and twenty-six Swedish speaking congregations. At present, seventy-two of the Finnish speaking ones are organized under the umbrella organization PCF.

At the turn of the millennium, the impact of new charismatic movements gave rise to numerous new independent local congregations. The Toronto Blessing was the most influential of these revivals, and as a result, sixteen new congregations named City Churches were founded in different districts of the country. The worship in these congregations were characterized by the media as the "Laughing Revival" because of the ecstatic meetings with people laughing, crying and claiming to be healed miraculously. In addition to the City Churches, countless other independent local congregations were founded, mostly in the southern and western region of the country. The Faith Movement was introduced in Finland by a group of Finnish adherents and Bible School students of *Livets Ord* (Word of Faith) in Uppsala, Sweden. The Health and Wealth Gospel was strongly disapproved in the beginning not only by the representatives of the ELC, but also by older revival movements including Pentecostals.

In Finland, these movements and communities inspired by these recent developments are categorized as Neo-Charismatic (*uuskarismaattinen*). Most of these independent local congregations are communities of not more than a few dozen adherents. Only a few of them have hundreds of members, mainly in the capital area. However, occasional events featured with a popular evangelist may easily attract larger audiences. It is very difficult, if not impossible, to give accurate figures to the number of supporters. The independent small congregations do not register their members. Furthermore, the supporters are quite mobile. A rough estimation of the members of neo-Charismatic congregations is 3000–4000.

Many of the new congregations, however, disbanded within a few years, often over disagreements about issues like leadership and worship. There has been some convergence of resources among those congregations that continued operating, typically with a new name and leadership. One case is the Nokia Mission Church. It started as a charismatic group within the ELC in the 1990s, moved to a local Pentecostal congregation, and eventually, in 2008 organized as a church of its own with the goal of establishing a megachurch in Finland. However, following a scandal with its Pastor, the church reorganized in 2012 as the Congregation of New Hope.

In the twenty-first century, traditional Pentecostalism and independent charismatic churches, continue to converge and change, most notably with the influence of global forms of worship music like Hillsong and Jesus Culture and more progressive gender roles for women in leadership.

Bibliography

Helander, Eila. 1987. *Naiset eivät vaienneet: Naisevankelistainstituutio Suomen helluntailiikkeessä – Women Have not Remained Silent: A Study of the Institution of Female Evangelists in the Finnish Pentecostal Movement*. Helsinki: Suomen kirkkohistoriallinen seura.

Holm, Nils G. 2015. "Pentecostalism in Finland: The Precarious Beginning." *Approaching Religion: Pentecostalism around the Baltic Sea* 5 (1): 92–95.

Hovi, Tuija. 2014. "Servants and Agents: Gender Roles in Neo-charismatic Christianity." In *Finnish Women Making Religion: Between Ancestors and Angels*, edited by Terhi Utriainen and Päivi Salmesvuori, 177–196. Basinstoke: Palgrave Macmillan.

Teemu T. Mantsinen. 2018. "The Finnish Pentecostal Movement: An Analysis of Internal Struggle as a Process of Habitula Division." In *Charismatic Christianity in Finland,*

Norway and Sweden: Case Studies in Historical and Contemporary Developments, edited by Jessica Moberg and Jane Skjoldli, 109–136. Palgrave Macmillan.

Tuija Hovi

France

The first incidence of Pentecostalism in France was in October 1909, when Michel E. Mast was supported by a church in Sunderland to open a Pentecostal mission in Paris. The First World War forced him to become a chaplain for the army which interrupted the work of his mission. But his efforts were constant until 1935.

A second Pentecostal center was in the region of Le Havre in a restaurant, called "le Ruban Bleu", which was founded in 1896, not only as a restaurant but also a place of training, a Sunday school, a center of prayer, and a home for missionaries. It was Hélène Biolley who managed the "Ruban Bleu" and created an international network with the Pentecostal movement.

A third Pentecostal site in France began in 1925 which was influenced by the Welsh Revival. In a Pentecostal convention in Penygroes, in 1925, some prophesies challenged the audience on the spiritual needs in France. Two young men, Thomas Roberts and Robson, were sent as missionaries in 1925. In 1928, Thomas Roberts asked for help for France. The Apostolic Church sent him W. Gummer. In 1931, they were invited by Léon Seney, the lay leader of a small church in Sanvic, near Le Havre. Roberts taught Pentecostal theology and W. Gummer became the pastor of this little community. The Apostolic Churches have kept growing in France and have twenty-four churches today.

In January 1930, the English missionary Douglas Scott arrived with his spouse in Le Havre. He kept his promise to Mrs Biolley who asked him to come back because she saw in him someone who could lead a French revival when he first came in 1927. Born again and trained in the Elim Churches, he was sent by the Assemblies of God of Great Britain. Following a number of miracles and conversions, Scott quickly realized that he needed help and Felix Gallice, Christophe Domoustchief, and Ove Falg became his first colleagues (Stotts 1982).

After they saw what happened in Le Havre, two Baptist pastors from the North of France, Paul Pelcé and Pierre Nicolle, invited Scott for an evangelistic campaign. Paul Pelcé was at that time the president of the federation of the North Baptist Churches. These churches were favorable to the Pentecostal movement especially through the Irvingites and the Welsh Revival. Whereas normally Methodism was a precursor of Pentecostalism, it is the French Baptist movement which shaped the origins of French Pentecostalism. More than that, the French Baptist movement had a charismatic movement inside its own movement in the 1970s which took the name of Fédération des Églises et Communautés Baptistes Charismatiques (FECBC) that currently has twenty-seven churches.

The first French Pentecostal convention was held in Le Havre February 11–14, 1932. In March 1933, the first convention of the Assemblies of God in France was organized in Argenteuil. The French Assemblies of God was created at that convention. Most protestant and evangelical movements were indifferent or against the Pentecostal movement in France.

From 1933 to 1939, the Assemblies of God grew and planted churches particularly in Normandy, in the North and West of France, in the region of Paris and Lyon, and in the South of France. Pentecostalism also took root in the East of France with the ministry of Paul and Rosa Siefer. In addition to giving birth to different Assemblies of God congregations, there was the emergence in the 1990s of the Fédération des Églises du Plein Évangile (FEPEF) in which the most remarkable church is the Porte ouverte in Mulhouse. This federation currently has eighty-nine churches in France (Pfister 1995).

The French Assemblies of God was marked by the Second World War. More than the destruction and the local tragedies, the line between the occupied and the free zone split the Pentecostal movement. Currently, the North and South pastoral conventions are working together but have maintained their own internal logic.

The Assemblies of God continued to plant new congregations and structure the movement from 1940 to 1970 with a Foreign Mission Board, a committee for children's ministry, a publication called Viens et Vois, a Christian radio named Christ Vous Appelle, a Bible school, and a committee to help persecuted Christians. As noted by Jean-Paul Willaime (1999), we see an expansion marked by modernity and the willingness to use the latest technological advances serving the Pentecostal message.

A major turning point was in 1968 when pastor Clément Le Cossec decided with local pastors to focus on reaching out to the gypsy people. The Mission Vie et Lumière is the main Pentecostal denomination which joined the Fédération Protestante de France. Before launching a gypsy Pentecostal ministry, Clément Le Cossec encouraged charismatic Christianity among Roman Catholics in France with his friend Yvon Charles. After a trip in the United States of America, where they saw the impact of the second wave revival, the two French pastors came back with the conviction that the charismatic movement could touch the Roman Catholics and the historical Protestant churches. But in 1973, after different ecumenical meetings, they came to understand that every church would stay within their own theological and ecclessiastical frameworks, even if they embraced a charismatic experience, primarily among Roman Catholics. Currently, there are a range of charismatic groups that promote renewal in France: the Communauté du Chemin Neuf and Emmanuel among Roman Catholics and the Union of Charmes among Protestants.

In the 1970s and the 1980s, the French Assemblies of God sent missionaries to some of the French territories such as Réunion Island, the French Antilles, and French Polynesia where Pentecostalism was embraced (Stotts 1982). The French Assemblies of God associated with the Union Nationale des Assemblées de Dieu de France (UNADF) in 1983 (association by the law of 1905) and the Fédération Nationale des Assemblées de Dieu de France (FNADF) in 1996 (association by the law of 1901). In 2010, the Assemblies of God, with their 416 churches joined the Conseil National des Évangéliques de France (CNEF). The Conseil National des Évangéliques de France includes almost all of the charismatic and Pentecostal denominations together in addition to other Evangelical denominations.

Bibliography

Pfister, Raymond. 1995. *Soixante ans de pentecôtisme en Alsace (1930–1990): une approche socio-historique*. Frankfurt am Main: Lang.
Stotts, George Raymond. 1982. *Le pentecôtisme au pays de Voltaire*. Craponne: Viens et Vois.
Willaime, Jean-Paul. 1999. "Le pentecôtisme: contours et paradoxes d'un protestantisme

émotionnel." *Archives de Sciences Sociales des Religions* 105 (1): 5–28.

Alexandre Antoine

Francescon, Louis

As a pioneer in the Italian Pentecostal movement, Louis Francescon's (1866–1964) mission has transcended ethnic and national boundaries. Today, several denominations and local churches, especially the Christian Congregation in Brazil, the Assemblies of God in Italy, the International Fellowship of Christian Assemblies, the Christian Assemblies in Argentina, and the Canadian Assemblies of God trace their origins to his activities.

His parents Pietro and Maria Lovisa Francescon were peasants from Cavasso Nuovo, a village in the hesitant borderlands of Italy and the Austro-Hungarian Empire. They named him Luigi. With his brother, Luigi went to Budapest to learn the art of mosaic tiles. At the age of 23, Francescon moved to Chicago to carry out his mosaic profession. There, he was converted by the preaching of an independent Italian evangelist, Michele Nardi. Influenced by A.B. Simpson, Nardi gathered the newly converted Italians with some Waldensians and established the First Italian Presbyterian Church in 1893. At this congregation, Francescon held the offices of deacon, secretary, and elder. Around that time, he married Rosina Balzano, a Sunday school teacher. Later, she had a crucial role in the movement's teaching and missionary activities.

Francescon felt his Roman Catholic infant baptism did not fulfill his spiritual needs. After convincing a friend, Giuseppe Beretta, to undergo "believer's baptism" ministered by a Plymouth Brethren church, Francescon requested to be baptized by full immersion as an adult believer. Thus, on September 7, 1903, Beretta baptized Francescon and 18 Italian evangelicals in Lake Michigan. This group, some from the Italian Presbyterian Church and others from a home fellowship led by Beretta, organized an independent congregation styled after the American Holiness and the Italian Free Churches. They valued free forms of worship with active congregational participation in extemporaneous prayer, testimonies, and preaching led by unsalaried lay ministers. Francescon's fellowship with that group lasted for a short time. His and two other families withdrew because of their insistence on keeping the Sunday as the Sabbath.

In April 1907, Francescon learned that the North Avenue Mission was announcing the outpouring of the Holy Spirit. That mission's pastor, William H. Durham, had visited at the Azusa Street Revival in Los Angeles. After a while, the Francescon and the DiCicco families experienced speaking in tongues at North Avenue Full Gospel Mission.

By that time, Beretta's group had increased and rented a storefront at the Grand Avenue Mission. After Durham had prophesized a calling for the Italian people to organize, Francescon began to share his Pentecostal testimony with friends from that storefront church. On September 15, a revival broke out at the Grand Avenue and the leaders invited Francescon to come and meet them. The Francescon and DiCicco families then rejoined that church.

In the following months, the revival spread among the Italian community in Chicago. Soon, many lay missionaries departed from Chicago to other Italian communities in North America and around the world. Francescon and another recent convert, Giacomo Lombardi, began a series of missions in California, and later to South America, this time with Lucia Menna. They initially had limited success and experienced some persecution in Argentina and Brazil.

Most of Francescon's international ministry occured in Brazil. He travelled ten times to the country, totaling 125 months of stay there. Following his lay-led, personal evangelism, self-supporting missionary model, the Italian Pentecostal movement became the Christian Congregation in Brazil. By the time of his death, it had about 2,000 congregations and nearly 150,000 members.

Meanwhile, the North American Italian churches grew, though plagued by internal divisions. To safeguard a cooperative unity, the Unorganized Italian Christian Churches in North America held a convention in Niagara Falls, NY, in 1927. Although Francescon occupied a leadership position among that loose network of churches, he strongly opposed organization beyond the local churches. In 1939 Francescon withdrew from its yearly meetings, and after a temporary reconciliation, he left the network in 1948. For the remainder of his life, Francescon ministered at his local Christian Congregation, though maintaining correspondence and fellowship with individuals and churches in North America, Brazil, Argentina, and Italy. Before his death at the age of 98, he requested to donate any funeral contribution to the American Bible Society for the benefit of the blind.

Francescon's theology was typical of the classical finished work Pentecostals, though distinctively with a strong Trinitarian focus regarding soteriology and ecclesiology. He held that the Father calls, the Son's atoning work saves, while the Holy Spirit guides, transforms, heals, and progressively sanctifies believers. For him, Jesus was the head of the church, having the Holy Spirit to guide it. The divine love among believers should be the binding organizing force for the church. Thus, he mistrusted what he deemed human-led hierarchical church bureaucracies and mass evangelization methods. His staunch adherence to the Bible, read with a plain-sense hermeneutics, made him a man of a single book.

Bibliography

Fiorentino, Joseph R. 2015. "Luigi Francescon 1866–1964." Unpublished paper. Lakeland, FL: Southeastern University.

Francescon, Louis. 1952. *Faithfull Testimony*. Chicago: The Author.

Rebuffo, Ricardo. 1999. *Historia de las Asambleas Cristianas de la República Argentina: Correspondencia intercambiada entre los hermanos Louis Francescón y Ricardo Rebuffo entre los años 1943 y 1947*. Buenos Aires: The Author.

Toppi, Francesco. 2007. *Luigi Francescon: antesignano del Risveglio pentecostale Evangelico Italiano*. Rome: ADI-Media.

Yuaza, Key. 2001. "Louis Francescon: A Theological Biography, 1866–1964." PhD diss., University of Geneva.

Leonardo Marcondes Alves

Full Gospel

The phrase "full gospel" refers to a theological hermeneutic that takes account of Pentecostals' innate articulation of their own theological story. The most consistent framework for narrating the dominant set of Pentecostal experiences is known as the four- or five-fold gospel (Dayton 1987). The larger, five-fold pattern proclaims, usually in kerygmatic form, the good news that Jesus Christ brings (1) salvation, (2) sanctification, (3) baptism in the Spirit, (4) divine healing and (5) the impending arrival of the kingdom of God. This Christocentric pattern depends on a pneumatological narrative built around participation in foundational experiences associated with the day of Pentecost, so that the full gospel functions as both a biblical hermeneutic and a theological narrative of contemporary Pentecostal practices and experiences that reflect the biblical story (Archer 2010, 1–17). The dominant event where Pentecostals encounter the full gospel is the altar call. The full gospel is essentially a liturgical narrative aiming at participation in Pentecost through an experiential, hermeneutical, and theological move to and from the altar (Vondey 2017).

The order and content of the full gospel varies historically and geographically, the phrase "full gospel" is not always used directly, and Pentecostals sometimes adjust the theological pattern and combine or include other themes (Kärkkäinen 2007). The elements of the full gospel are never logically isolated or adhere to a strict theological sequence, since the experiences underlying the narrative have occurred worldwide in diverse fashion (Yong-gi Cho 1997). Although the full gospel possesses an inherent narrative plot which proceeds through each of the five motifs, the connections between the different elements are not just linear, and entrance to the altar, and participation in Pentecost, is possible in principle from any element of the full gospel.

The traditional full gospel narrative begins with a foundational concern for salvation. The soteriological scope of the full gospel extends towards complete salvation, which reaches the soul through a whole range of experiences marking the personal-spiritual, individual-physical, communal, socioeconomic, and ecological aspects of the Christian life. Pentecostal practices of salvation extend from Christ across individual, familial, ecclesial, social, material, cosmic and eschatological dimensions of life. In turn, the wide-ranging practices among Pentecostals suggest that all elements of the full gospel are possible steps to the altar and on the path of salvation (Vondey 2017, 37–58).

A second motif in the narrative of the full gospel is sanctification, typically seen as a distinct work of grace. Whereas salvation identifies the move of a person to the altar, the experience of sanctification is a remaining at the altar in anticipation of the coming Pentecost (Vondey 2017, 59–81). As part of a soteriological liturgy, sanctification is not a forward moving into new territory but a waiting and presentation of one's present circumstances, intentions, and convictions before God. This threshold practice keeps Pentecostals at the altar for the purpose of tarrying for the outpouring of the Holy Spirit.

A third, and typically central, element of the full gospel is Spirit baptism. The baptism in the Holy Spirit is most intimately tied to the altar as a metaphor for the encounter with Christ to which the other elements point and from which they receive their meaning. This transformative experience marks a turning point in the altar liturgy: after being baptized in the Spirit those who have come to the altar are transformed to leave the altar (Vondey 2017, 83–105). As a baptismal practice, this transformative experience is manifested in the change of the passive-receptive believer into an active agent of the Spirit: the person who has come to the altar is now equipped to leave the altar.

Divine healing signifies an important expansion of the baptism in the Spirit: while healing practices are often literal interpretations of biblical narratives, there are few restrictions on receiving and extending healing, and Pentecostal activities often connect with indigenous religious practices to form enculturated rituals departing from strict biblical or apostolic patterns. The liturgical contours of this theology remain thoroughly connected to the altar while diversifying rapidly through three intersecting dynamics: (1) those saved, sanctified, and filled with the Spirit come to the altar to find healing; (2) those who experience healing at the altar take the altar into the world; (3) and those in the world who receive healing come to the altar for salvation (Vondey 2017, 107–30).

The coming kingdom typically occupies a final place in the full gospel narrative, although eschatology does not mark the "end" of Pentecostal theology but returns the full gospel to its central concerns: Christ as the coming king not only draws Christians from the altar to the ends of the earth but urges them to return to the altar and the encounter with God. Eschatological practices are therefore, in principle, any altar practices acted out by the church for its mission to and transformation of the world: to be saved means eschatologically to be commissioned as agents of witness in the world; to be sanctified means a radical transformation from a life of the flesh to a life in the Spirit; the baptism in the Spirit seeks to equip and empower believers for eschatological witness to the lost and spiritual battle with the enemies of God; and divine healing points to a radical encounter with the coming kingdom already manifested in the life of believer (Vondey 2017, 131–51). A drive for the "fullness" of the kingdom of God sustains the entirety of the full gospel as a hospitable and critical theological liturgy that points to an eternal Pentecost already captured by the experiences of Christ as savior, sanctifier, Spirit baptizer, divine healer, and coming king.

Bibliography

Archer, Kenneth J. 2010. *The Gospel Revisited: Towards a Pentecostal Theology of Worship and Witness*. Eugene: Pickwick.

Dayton, Donald W. 1987. *Theological Roots of Pentecostalism*. Peabody: Hendrickson.

Kärkkäinen, Veli-Matti. 2007. "'Encountering Christ in the Full Gospel Way': An Incarnational Pentecostal Spirituality." *Journal of the European Pentecostal Theological Association* 27 (1): 5–19.

Vondey, Wolfgang. 2017. *Pentecostal Theology: Living the Full Gospel*. London and New York: Bloomsbury T&T Clark.

Yong-gi Cho, D. 1997. *The Five-Fold Gospel and The Three-fold Blessing*. Seoul: Logos.

Wolfgang Vondey

Garrigus, Alice Belle

Alice Belle Garrigus (1858–1949), born in Rockville, Connecticut, was the founder of Pentecostalism in Newfoundland and Labrador, Canada. Her sympathetic biographer, Burton K. Janes, based much of his work about her on the autobiography she published in serialized form in *Good Tidings*, the official publication of the Pentecostal Assemblies of Newfoundland and Labrador, in 1939–1940 (Janes 1982, 1983). Garrigus's life story is a familiar one in Newfoundland religious history. One popular publication with the subtitle "The Story of What One Little American Woman Helped Accomplish for God," confirms her central place in the history (Hammond 1982). Yet such diminutive references to

Alice Belle Garrigus, 1858–1949.
Source: Pentecostal Assemblies of Canada Archives

her are meant to emphasize how unlikely it was that a middle-aged woman of small stature, arriving from New England in the fall of 1910, could hope to successfully start mission work in Newfoundland. Garrigus herself admitted that she had expected to become a missionary to Asia, and when God told her that she would be going to Newfoundland instead, she had to consult a map. On Easter Sunday in 1911, Garrigus held her first service in a St. John's storefront building, which she called the "Bethesda Mission."

From those humble beginnings, the movement Garrigus introduced gained popularity until the 1935 Newfoundland census reflected that 3,721 people identified as Pentecostals. By 1945, 7,558 Newfoundlanders representing 2.3 percent of the total population, listed Pentecostal as their principal religious affiliation. Pentecostal schools became a recognized part of Newfoundland's publicly-funded denominational education system from 1954 to 1998. Those who identified as Pentecostals included the family of Joey Smallwood, the premier who led Newfoundland to join Canada as a province in 1949. After recruiting and training a series of leaders to manage both the administrative affairs and the expanding ministry in various communities across Newfoundland, Garrigus retired to Clarke's Beach, Conception Bay, Newfoundland, in 1942. She lived there until her death and was buried in the Pentecostal Cemetery in Clarke's Beach.

The familiar tale about Garrigus as "founder" of Newfoundland Pentecostalism has been called into question by scholarship that focused beyond the diminutive Miss Garrigus to point instead to the men whom she recruited into the movement. Pointing to them as the real reason for the success and growth of the Pentecostal message in this male-dominated region, the argument is that those male leaders, who pursued legal incorporation, paved the way twenty-five years after Garrigus's arrival, for Pentecostalism finally to gain momentum and status as a religion recognized by the state, for the first time in the 1935 census. Religious studies scholars observed that religious competition in Newfoundland meant that it was only after the indigenization of the movement through the efforts of several businessmen who converted, that the movement found firm footing and growth. In this view, Newfoundland Pentecostalism serves as a prime example of the institutionalization thesis that argues as new religious movements develop to the stage of being more like a church than a sect, women in leadership are inevitably pushed to the sidelines (Pinsent 1998). This scholarship leaves the distinct impression that it was not Garrigus, but rather the men she recruited, who eventually advanced the movement by adopting sound business practices and growth strategies.

A compelling feminist counter-narrative revisits the archival sources to hear Garrigus's own voice and emphasize how she clearly continued to exercise authority in the movement. For example, the verbal warnings that Garrigus commonly invoked as public disciplinary measures to silence men whom she deemed "out of order" in her meetings, reopens the question of how gendered authority operated in Newfoundland Pentecostalism. Focusing on the power dynamics of the movement, it becomes clear that while she did recruit men into leadership, Garrigus continued to exercise agency and power in unconventional ways even after male leaders expanded the movement, and despite her advanced age (Hattie-Longmire 2001).

On balance, beyond patriarchal readings of Newfoundland's Pentecostal history and also beyond the hagiographic accounts of Garrigus's calling and ministry, one sees that while she was the first to bring Pentecostalism to Newfoundland, it took the work of dozens of men and women together to establish and advance the movement. Just as Garrigus defied the gendered expectations of what a single, middle-aged woman might accomplish, the history of the movement she founded in Newfoundland is neither a feminist tale of one great founding woman, nor a patriarchal plot by a small group of business-minded men to displace the founding mother. Garrigus's initial work established a movement where people of both sexes occupied roles that, because of their setting and their Pentecostal convictions, were not as tightly defined by traditional gender boundaries as some versions of that story might suggest (Ambrose 2016). When Garrigus introduced Newfoundlanders to Pentecostalism, she seemed to be offering just one more option on an already crowded slate of religious expressions. Yet because Pentecostalism rose to such prominence in culture, education, and public life, the legacy of Alice Belle Garrigus has a central place in Newfoundland's religious and social history.

Bibliography

Ambrose, Linda M. 2016. "Gender History in Newfoundland Pentecostalism: Alice Belle Garrigus and Beyond." *PentecoStudies: An Interdisciplinary Journal for Research on the Pentecostal and Charismatic Movements* 15 (2): 172–199.

Hammond, John W. 1982. *The Joyful Sound: A History of the Pentecostal Assemblies of Newfoundland and Labrador*. St. Stephen, NB: Print'N Press Ltd.

Hattie-Longmire, Brenda. 2001. "'Sit Down Brother!': Alice Belle Garrigus and the Pentecostal Assemblies of Newfoundland." Master's thesis, Joint Women's Studies Program, Mount Saint Vincent University, Dalhousie University, and Saint Mary's University, Halifax, Nova Scotia.

Janes, Burton K. 1982. *The Lady Who Came: The Biography of Alice Belle Garrigus Newfoundland's First Pentecostal Pioneer, Volume One (1858–1908)*. St. John's, NL: Good Tidings Press.

Janes, Burton K. 1983. *The Lady Who Stayed: The Biography of Alice Belle Garrigus Newfoundland's First Pentecostal Pioneer Volume Two (1908–1949)*. St. John's, NL: Good Tidings Press.

Pinsent, William Paul. 1998. "The Institutionalization of Experiential Religion: A Study of Newfoundland Pentecostalism." Master's thesis, Memorial University of Newfoundland, St. John's, Newfoundland.

Linda M. Ambrose

Gee, Donald

Donald Henry Frere Gee (1891–1966) was a travelling preacher, writer, editor, musician, Chairman of British Assemblies of God (1945–1948), Bible College Principal and significant historian. His writings are the most varied and prolific of any of the early Pentecostals and his final book, *Wind and Flame* (1967), is the best early account of the movement's global reach and its affinity with emerging charismatic and ecumenical stirrings.

Gee won prizes at school but left in his mid-teens and never thereafter received any further formal education. He attended Finsbury Park Congregational Church where in 1905 he heard Seth Joshua, one of the evangelists who ignited the Welsh Revival, and received Christ as Saviour. His mother took him to early Pentecostal meetings in the home of Margaret Cantel as a result of which he spoke in tongues in 1913 and became aware of the mission field. He was prepared to take the dangerous and self-denying step of offering himself for missionary service. When compulsory military conscription was introduced in 1916, he went before a tribunal to assert his conscientious objection to warfare and was granted exemption from uniformed service on the condition he found approved work of national importance. He became a farm labourer working exhaustingly long hours. By now he was married and father to a young family. He endured vilification, as many conscientious objectors did, from other villagers but found support in a small Christian fellowship where he discovered his vocation to ministry.

After the war, he took on the pastorate of a small unruly Pentecostal assembly in Edinburgh (1920–1930) and, as a way of dealing with the situation, applied himself to a systematic study of charismatic and ministry gifts. Every morning he was in his office for prayer, study and devotion. He was one of the original leaders invited to the Birmingham meeting that led to the formation of British Assemblies of God in 1924; his rational and Scriptural approach to the challenges facing the young Pentecostal movement had been recognised early and his first articles were published in 1922. He defended – indeed helped to formulate – a classical Pentecostal position on tongues as the "initial evidence" of Spirit baptism (often pointing to Acts 10) and resisted the lure of a doctrine of universalism popular among those bereaved by the slaughter of World War I.

He had already attended an international Pentecostal conference in Amsterdam in 1921. In 1928 he was invited to Australia and money for the fare was cabled to him. On the voyage out he wrote his first book, *Concerning Spiritual Gifts*. Being well received there and in New Zealand he understood his ministry was primarily that of a teacher, someone who helped to steer the ship while others generated power in the engine room. He returned via the United States where he was received by leaders of American Assemblies of God. Many of his books were thereafter published by Gospel Publishing House (GPH), American AG's publishing arm. He was in Sweden in 1930, becoming friends with Lewi Pethrus, in Danzig in 1931 and in the Middle East and Palestine in 1932. He and his family moved to Louth in Lincolnshire where his wife, Ruth, became matron of the Women's Bible School. He was Vice-Chair of British AoG (1934 1944) and Chair (1945–1948), both elected offices.

In 1947 in Zürich, he participated in the European Pentecostal conference that coordinated humanitarian aid to still war-damaged cities and, at this meeting, was voted in as the editor of a new magazine, *Pentecost* (1947–1966), with a remit to be responsible only to God. This allowed him to speak without fear or favor on Pentecostal topics including the role of independent healing evangelists whose ministries were starting to overshadow less showy denominational activities. His wife died in 1950 and, after constant travel, he settled down as Principal of the British AoG Bible College in Kenley (1951–1964) where he oversaw the trebling of student enrolments and the payment of a debt on the building. Throughout his years as Principal he took no salary and lived from Sunday ministry. He continued to write for *Redemption Tidings*, the AoG magazine, and to preach. In 1960 his "Another Springtime" chairman's sermon to British AoG called for refreshment and renewal of British Pentecostal churches. He attended the World Council of Churches' Faith and Order meetings in Edinburgh but refused an invitation to the WCC assembly in New Delhi (1961) after pressure from American AG – though his friend David du Plessis did go. His editorials in *Pentecost* wrestle with Pentecostal identity as a movement or a revival. He remarried in 1964 but died in the summer of 1966. He published more than 500 articles which appeared in Pentecostal periodicals round the world and in many languages. He was a far-sighted statesman who, while defending Pentecostal distinctives, thought seriously and sometimes provocatively about Pentecostalism's role in the church as a whole.

Bibliography

Carter, John. 1975. *Donald Gee: Pentecostal Statesman*. Nottingham: Assemblies of God Publishing House.

Gee, Donald. 1967. *Wind and Flame*. Croydon: Assemblies of God Publishing House. (originally published under the title *The Pentecostal Movement* in 1941)

Kay, William K. 2007. "Donald Gee: An Important Voice of the Pentecostal Movement." *Journal of Pentecostal Theology* 16 (1): 133–153.

Massey, Richard. 1992. *Another Springtime: Donald Gee Pentecostal Pioneer, a Biography*. Guildford: Highland Books.

William K. Kay

Gender

Gender Studies holds great promise for Pentecostal scholarship because it pays attention to the roles that are assigned to men and women, to the power dynamics that result, and to the ways in which people order their lives within particular cultures. While cultural norms vary by region, gender studies can help to unlock these differences on both local and global stages. The binary consideration of male and female genders (a somewhat dated concept given recent attention to gender fluidity) still serves as a useful starting place to discuss how gender and Pentecostalism intersect.

Gender studies is by nature an interdisciplinary undertaking. For historians of gender, the field grew out of social history and women's studies in the last quarter of the twentieth century. With attention to how gender and power entwine, historians of North American Pentecostalism have noted that a common feature in the earliest chapters of the movement involved women taking lead roles as evangelists, pastors, and networkers (Ambrose and Payne 2014). That central role for women was in step with an urgent, pre-millennial eschatology and a literal reading of scriptures supporting the prophecy of Joel, cited in the book of Acts, that "in the last days, your sons AND daughters will prophesy." Pentecostals were frequently heard to cite those passages of scripture and proclaim with delight when preachers of both sexes proclaimed the Pentecostal message, "this is that" which the prophets foretold. While officially endorsing the full gifting of women and men, organizational culture often looked quite different (Poloma 1989; Stephenson 2011). In practice, classic Pentecostals came to resemble their evangelical cousins more and more, and the days of women assuming power in public roles by leading revival services and planting churches was increasingly relegated to commemoration rather than actual practice.

Sociological theory reminds us that the promise of egalitarianism held true in North American Pentecostalism, as it typically does with new religious movements, until institutionalization evolved to the point where women become marginalized (Barfoot and Sheppard 1980). Within the first decades of the Pentecostal movement business models came to dominate organizations in their evolution from revivalism to denominationalism, when elaborate management structures emerged. Patriarchal hierarchies shored up those emerging church subcultures. Following World War II, middle-class functionalist prescriptions about domesticity meant that binary male and female roles were established and reinforced. Men were designated as suitable for

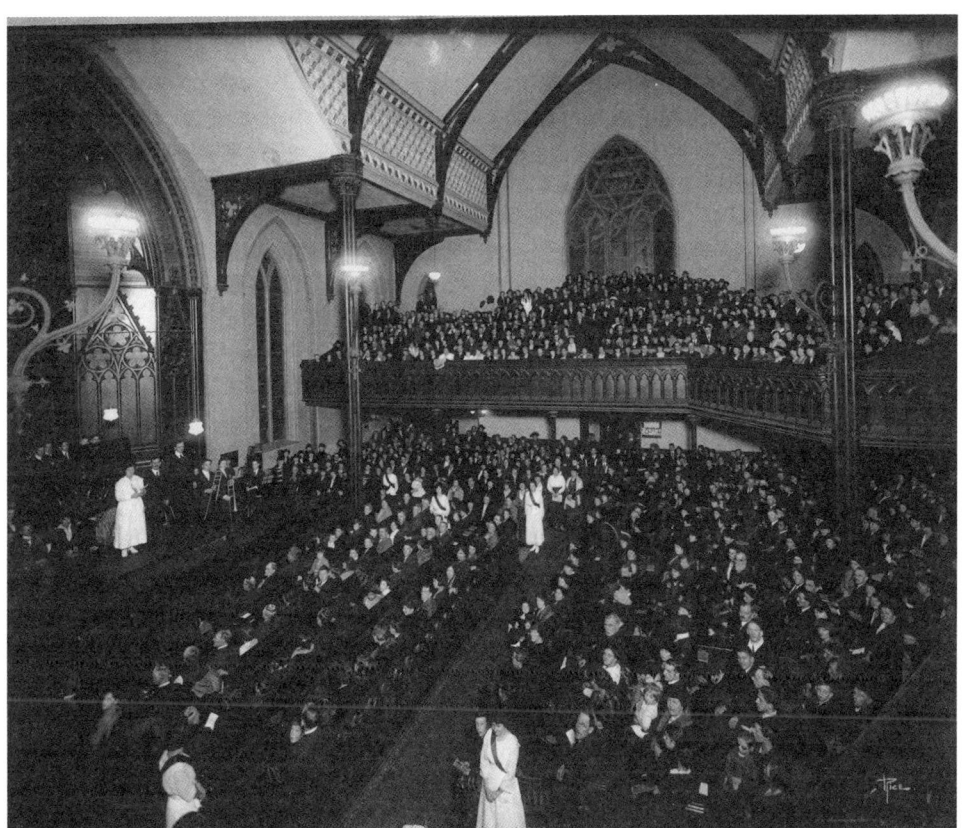

Aimee Semple McPherson at the Montreal Crusade 1920. Source: Pentecostal Assemblies of Canada Archives

roles in denominational leadership, local church governance, and as lead pastors. Women, who had previously led revivals and worked toward the establishment of local congregations, were pushed to the side, relegated to roles thought to be more culturally appropriate, namely in submission to male leaders where their ministry would be to women and children, or where no man was available, a situation frequently experienced in mission settings overseas. That mantra, "men lead, women follow" came to dominate the typical gender dynamics of Pentecostal organizations. The rationale behind this development can be variously explained, invoking sociological and feminist theories about power, institutionalization, gender performativity, embodiment, and routinization.

Debates by theologians and biblical studies scholars about acceptable gender roles centre around competing notions of how men and women are meant to interact in the church, the family, and the kingdom of God. Those competing views, expressed as "complementarianism" and "egalitarianism," define Pentecostal subcultures (Archer and Archer 2019). For complementarians, (the classic evangelical position) men are leaders and women are followers. Egalitarians counter that view with reference to biblical passages about equal giftings for both sexes and the blurring of roles for men and women, especially after Pentecost. Progressive Pentecostals tend toward the second view, but often remain committed to binary gender models. Given the socially conservative teachings of church subcultures, it is a quite leap to think of gender solely as a social construct and not a God-given characteristic. This leads some egalitarians to quickly concede that while they welcome the equal distribution of spiritual gifts and ministry roles, they still celebrate the differences between the sexes. In effect then, taking the egalitarian side in this debate does little to tear down the firm commitment to essentialist notions of male and female regardless of which "side" one takes in the interpretive/hermeneutical debates.

As gender studies moves away from attention to questions of power and into the realm of lived experiences, the focus for scholars of Pentecostalism shifts away from questions about the gendered nature of church leadership hierarchies toward the experiences of Pentecostal lay people. Here the attention shifts to how women and men in Pentecostal pews conduct themselves according to gendered expectations (Brusco 2010). Social scientific studies about global Pentecostalism complicate our understandings of gender by analysing other cultural institutions, especially the family. Here, the consequences of men adopting the Pentecostal faith is a key phenomenon. Exploring what happened to family life in Pentecostal homes, scholars have observed that men became more domestically oriented in their post-conversion lives, embracing family values and eschewing their former behaviours that revolved around excessive drinking, womanizing, and financial irresponsibility. The "reformation of machoism" (Brusco 1995) served to explain why women were so attracted to evangelicalism in general, and Pentecostalism specifically, in hopes that their men would come under the taming influence of new expectations for men in these churches. Women enjoyed tangible benefits when their domestic lives changed for the better because men's behaviours softened. But Pentecostalism also offered subversive opportunities for women to enjoy some public power within the church in lay ministry roles as bible teachers among their peers and with children. There are gendered paradoxes for Pentecostal women however, because while they experienced some power and agency in their ministry roles, at the same time there are heightened expectations that women would submit to husbands at home and to male pastors at church (Martin 2001).

Building on those well-established conclusions about gender and women's experiences, scholars of Pentecostalism followed the trend within gender studies to explore masculinity. While it was becoming clear why women were attracted to Pentecostalism, these scholars asserted that it was time to ask what was in it for the men. After conversion, as men abandoned more extreme expressions of toxic masculinity, they were typically perceived by their unchurched peers to have adopted a religion that emphasized emotional expressions, severed their ties with previous male friendships, and abandoned their pre-conversion leisure activities. Consequently, Pentecostal men seemed effeminate. Field work with Pentecostal men in Tanzania and Zambia, for example, reveals that men insisted their newfound faith made them stronger men because it gave them more self-control. They emphasized, for example, that unlike women, theirs was not a passive submission to authority (Lindhardt 2015; Van Klinken 2012). These men found ways to express their faith in more traditional "manly" ways. Taking on roles in lay ministry reinforced recognizable masculine traits of leadership, and not only in their homes. For example, when men engaged in loud and aggressive expressions of public prayer as part of their "spiritual warfare," they reinforced their association with militarism. Sometimes men who were new converts to Pentecostalism found ways to assert their masculinity through ministry roles including occupying pulpits in the role of evangelist, healer, or preacher; some of the most successful even came to enjoy celebrity status as their public reputations grew (Lindhardt 2015).

As these studies demonstrate, interrogating prescriptions about femininities and masculinities helps to unpack the historical, sociological, cultural, and theological developments that have contributed to Pentecostal practices. Understanding how gendered power dynamics operate among clergy and lay members, how those roles were first established, why they persist, and how they evolve, is a very rich field of inquiry for scholars of Pentecostalism. So too is attention to the experience of church members, whether they assume public ministry roles or not.

Pentecostal church cultures have been complicit in reinforcing cultural notions about appropriate gender roles. Recent revelations brought to light by the #metoo movement, might nudge churches to begin the task of deconstructing binary notions of gender. As those disturbing and ubiquitous stories of abuse make clear, toxic masculinities become particularly dangerous when exaggerated patriarchal power demands extreme female submission. Scholarship about gender holds great promise to interrogate systemic abuse culture. For example, if declarations about sons and daughters prophesying and the Pauline premise that in Christ there is "neither male nor female" were taken to their logical conclusions, then Pentecostals might actually lead the way to deconstructing binary categories of gender. However, there seems to be little appetite for that development while Pentecostalism continues to be characterized by adherence to conservative hermeneutics, patriarchal systems, and traditional cultural practices (both inside and outside the churches' own subcultures). To varying degrees, and with varying expressions globally, those realities serve to reinforce essentialist, binary understandings of gender roles even as they hold out the tantalizing possibility of rising above such prescriptions.

Bibliography

Ambrose, Linda M., and Leah Payne. 2014. "Reflections on the Potential of Gender Theory for North American Pentecostal History." *Pneuma* 36 (1): 45–63.

Archer, Kenneth, and Melissa Archer. 2019. "Complementarian and Egalitarian: Whose Side are you Leaning on? A Pentecostal reading of Ephesians 5:21–33." *Pneuma* 41 (1): 66–90.

Barfoot, Charles H., and Gerald T. Sheppard. 1980. "Prophetic vs. Priestly Religion: The Changing Role of Women Clergy in Classical Pentecostal Churches." *Review of Religious Research* 22 (1): 2–17.

Brusco, Elizabeth. 2010. "Gender and Power." In *Studying Global Pentecostalism: Theories and Methods*, edited by Allan Anderson, Michael Bergunder, Andre F. Droogers, and Cornelis van der Laan, 74–92. Berkeley: University of California Press.

Brusco, Elizabeth. 1995. *The Reformation of Machismo: Evangelical Conversion and Gender in Colombia*. Austin: University of Texas Press.

Lindhardt, Martin. 2015. "Men of God: Neo-Pentecostalism and Masculinities in Urban Tanzania." *Religion* 45 (2): 252–272.

Martin, Bernice. 2001. "The Pentecostal Gender Paradox: A Cautionary Tale for the Sociology of Religion." In *The Blackwell Companion to Sociology of Religion*, edited by Richard K. Fenn, 52–66. Oxford: Blackwell Publishing Ltd.

Poloma, Margaret M. 1989. *The Assemblies of God at the Crossroads: Charisma and Institutional Dilemmas*. Knoxville, TN: University of Tennessee Press.

Stephenson, Lisa. 2011. *Dismantling the Dualisms for American Pentecostal Women in Ministry: A Feminist-Pneumatological Approach*. Leiden: Brill.

Van Klinken, A.S. 2012. "Men in the Remaking: Conversion Narratives and Born-Again Masculinity in Zambia." *Journal of Religion in Africa* 42 (3): 215–239.

Linda M. Ambrose

Germany

Four external and four internal features characterized the beginning of German Pentecostalism at the turn of the nineteenth century. From abroad, reports of the revivals in Topeka, Kansas, USA (1901), Wales, UK (1904/5), Azusa Street, California, USA (1906), and Oslo, Norway (1906/7) sparked a desire within the believers to experience something similar in Germany. Internally, the four Holiness fundamentals (salvation, sanctification, healing, millenarianism), were already deeply engrained within the German *Gemeinschaftsbewegung* (Pietistic movement). As in many other countries of the world, so also in Germany, the Revival and Holiness branch of the *Gemeinschaftsbewegung*, served as cradle of German Pentecostalism. Revival broke out in 1905 in Mülheim (Ruhr), where Pastors Girkon and Modersohn were active. Evangelist Vetter joined them with a large tent, and during the Pentecost season of that year 3,000 people were saved. Eventually, the revival could not be contained and spread beyond Mülheim to the entire region of *Rhineland-Westphalia*. During the Week of Brieg, in the spring of 1907, the main issue was the reports of revivals that had sprung up all over the world and had been brought to Europe *via* Norway by T.B. Barratt. Heinrich Dallmeyer, a young evangelist, who had attended the meeting in Brieg for the first time, invited two Pentecostal Norwegian sisters, Dagmar Gregersen and Agnes Telle, to Kassel July 7 through August 1, 1907, in order to conduct revival meetings. *An Kassel kommt keiner vorbei!* – Nobody can ignore the events of Kassel! In 1909, the *Gemeinschaftsbewegung* accused the Pentecostal movement in the *Declaration of Berlin* of being responsible for the "enthusiasms" of Kassel. The Mülheim movement, however, rejected these accusations on the ground that the Pentecostals that had been involved in these meetings had requested moderation, and, when their admonitions were not heeded, had left the meetings. So, if there were no Pentecostals present at a meeting of the *Gemeinschaftsbewegung* when the disorder erupted, how could they be responsible for it? Fortunately, after almost a century of debates on this issue, important steps towards healing the breach among Evangelicals in Germany came about in the signing of the *Kassel Declaration* of 1996, when reconciliation and renewed cooperation between Pentecostals and Evangelicals was agreed upon.

Because of its international character, Pentecostalism in Germany is best summarized diachronically delineating five periods.

1. The years before World War I were characterized by international co-operation and mutual assistance. Annual conferences were held in Pentecostal centers like Sunderland, England; Mülheim, Germany; and Orebro, Sweden. Early Pentecostal leaders, such as T.B. Barratt (Norway), A.A. Boddy (England), G.R. Polman (Holland), and Jonathan Paul, father of German Pentecostalism, visited each other and spoke at each other's conventions. This international network was formalized in the International Pentecostal Consultative Council of Amsterdam in 1912.

2. Between the wars, cooperation became subsidiary in light of the fact that denominationalism and ideological concerns (e.g. congregationalism vs. episcopal structure) moved to the forefront. During this time and in the years right after World War II, most of the Pentecostal denominations were formed in Germany (year of beginning – number of members):
Mülheim Movement (1905/1914 – 4.000)
Bund Freikirchlicher Pfingstgemeinden (BFP) (1907/1947/1954 – 50.000)
Vereinigte Missionsfreunde (1931 – 1.000)
Volksmission entschiedener Christen (1934 – 4.000)
Gemeinde Gottes/Church of God (1936 – 4.000)
Freikirchliches Evangelisches Gemeindewerk/International Foursquare Church (1937 – 1.000)
Gemeinde der Christen Ecclesia (1944 – 4.000)
Apostolic Church (1946/53 – 1.000)
Jugend-, Missions-, und Sozialwerk Altensteig (1973 – 1.000)
Internationale Jesusgemeinde/Church of God of Prophecy (1974 – 1.000).

3. The influence of the Charismatic movement of the 1960s on Christendom in general and on the Pentecostal movement in particular cannot be overestimated. On the one hand, it changed the perception of Pentecostalism as a religion of the underprivileged and exerted influence on the form of worship, but on the other hand, it also tempered holiness convictions that Pentecostalism had taken over from the Holiness movement and redefined the understanding of the baptism in the Holy Spirit. Theological dialogue with the Charismatic movement increased appreciation for each other, and in 1979 brought Pentecostal churches closer together, when five Pentecostal churches formed the

Forum Freikirchlicher Pfingstgemeinden (*FFP*), which was later joined by most of the Pentecostal church bodies.

4. During the 1980s and early 1990s, the Third Wave movement (neo-pentecostalism), especially propagated among the Protestant free churches, emphasized once again the importance of the Holy Spirit for the church. The influence of the Third Wave challenged Pentecostalism with a renewed emphasis on healing, the metaphysical, and spiritual warfare. Theological dialogue increased the cooperation between the *FFP* and the *Kreis Charismatischer Leiter* (*KCL*). KCL was founded in 1993 and comprises about 40 leaders of the Charismatic movement (Catholic and Lutheran) the Third Wave movement (Baptist and Methodist) and leaders of independent Charismatic and Pentecostal bodies. Pentecostals and Charismatics also work together in the *Arbeitsgemeinschaft Pfingstlich-Charismatischer Missionen* (*APCM*), a Missions network founded in 1998, representing 500 missionaries and supporting 1,300 local mission workers.

5. Since the mid-1990s, Pentecostalism has been influenced by new revival movements like the Toronto Blessing and the Brownsville Revival as well as the increased growth of independent Pentecostal-Charismatic bodies, like the Gospel Forum Network, International Christian Fellowship (ICF), Hillsong Church, as well as ethnic and international churches. Even though it is not always possible to distinguish clearly between Pentecostal and Charismatic groups in the German context, an intelligent estimate would need to reckon with about 1,300 churches or fellowships for each branch representing about 150,000 adherents each. Many of these Pentecostal or Charismatic churches are also working together with other Evangelical denominations in the *Vereinigung Evangelischer Freikirchen* (*VEF*), on the level of the *Evangelical Alliance* (*DEA*), and the *Arbeitsgemeinschaft Christlicher Kirchen* (*ACK*).

Bibliography

Eisenlöffel, Ludwig David. 2006. *Freikirchliche Pfingstbewegung in Deutschland. Innenansichten 1945–1985*. Göttingen: V & R unipress.

Hampel, Dieter, Richard Krüger, and Gerhard Oertel, eds. 2009. *Der Auftrag bleibt. Der Bund Freikirchlicher Pfingstgemeinden auf dem Weg ins dritte Jahrtausend. Innenansichten 1980–2000*. Erzhausen: Bund Freikirchlicher Pfingstgemeinden.

Schmidgall, Paul. 2013. *European Pentecostalism. Its Origins, Development, and Future*. Cleveland, TN: CPT Press.

Schmidgall, Paul. 2008. *Hundert Jahre Deutsche Pfingstbewegung, 1907–2007*. Nordhausen: Bautz.

Simpson, Carl. 2012. *Revered and Reviled in a Quest for Pentecostal Holiness. Jonathan Paul and the German Pentecostal Movement*. Saarbrücken: LAP LAMBERT Academia Publishing.

Vetter, Ekkehart. 2009. *Jahrhundertbilanz – erweckungsfasziniert und durststreckenerprobt. 100 Jahre Mülheimer Verband Freikirchlich-Evangelischer Gemeinden*. Bremen: MV-Missionsverlag.

Paul Schmidgall

Ghana

Pentecostalism, as a movement associated with the experience and manifestation of the Holy Spirit, has been an important stream of Christianity in Ghana since the beginning of the twentieth century. At the turn of that century African Christians, having experienced mission activity through Western evangelization for nearly a century, started forming their own independent churches. Indigenous prophets beginning with William Wadé Harris who arrived in Ghana around 1914 spread his charismatic form of Christianity through healing and other acts of supernatural power in the western province of the country. The Harris revival led to the rise of the Ghanaian Spiritual or African independent/initiated/instituted Churches (AICs) as they are collectively called. The AICs did not refer to themselves as "Pentecostal". However, they are credited with the integration of charismatic renewal phenomena into Christianity in Ghana.

The rise of churches in Ghana, properly called "Pentecostal" started in the early 1920s. One Apostle Peter Newman Anim, once a Presbyterian, experienced the baptism of the Holy Spirit with speaking in tongues. He formed a prayer group that practiced "prevailing prayer" which meant, the solutions to all problems, particular those relating to ill-health were dealt with by prayer and not by medication. Anim invited the UK Apostolic Church to partner with him in the pastoral care of the prayer fellowship he had founded. The Apostolic Church sent Apostle James McKeown who then helped to give Anim prayer movement a decidedly Pentecostal orientation. The two – Anim and McKeown – worked together closely until a few years later when they fell out over whether Christians could use medicines to treat their ailments or not. This was a belief that Apostle Anim and his prayer fellowship had held on to prior to the arrival of the Pentecostal missionary McKeown and they would not give it up easily.

The relationship between Anim and McKeown and the fallout that followed is important for understanding the growth of the classical Pentecostalism tradition in Ghana. The relationship and its subsequent fallout produced three Pentecostal denominations: the Christ Apostolic Church, the Apostolic Church of Ghana, and the Ghana Apostolic Church. In 1962, the Ghana Apostolic Church changed its name to the Church of Pentecost. All three are still very active, but the McKeown led Church of Pentecost has grown to become the largest single Christian denomination in Ghana, at least in terms of church attendance, if not in registered membership. The other major classical Pentecostal denomination, the Assemblies of God, was established in Ghana by two American missionaries then working up in the Upper Volta, the country now known as Burkina Faso. These classical Pentecostal denominations – the Apostolic Churches, the Church of Pentecost, and the Assemblies of God – are the foundation members of the Ghana Pentecostal and Charismatic Council. This body started life as the Ghana Pentecostal Council but in the early 2000s, it started admitting into membership some of the urban-based contemporary Pentecostal denominations and hence the insertion of the word "charismatic" into its name.

Perhaps the most significant development within Ghanaian Christianity in the last thirty years has been the rise of the contemporary Pentecostal movement, or charismatic ministries as they are called in the country. A few of them have joined the Ghana Pentecostal and Charismatic Council but most of them belong to the newer National Association of Charismatic and Christian Churches. The key features of these new Pentecostals include their attraction for Africa's upwardly mobile youth, urban-based megachurch congregations, extensive and innovative uses of media technology in worship, broad international and transnational networks and a message of prosperity hinged on the positive confessions, and seed-sowing through the faithful discharge of tithing obligations. The charismatic ministries started in the late 1970s and although its leadership is almost entirely Ghanaian, they were very much inspired by North American televangelism. The pioneering founder of contemporary charismatic ministries in Ghana is Action Chapel International's Archbishop Nicholas Duncan-Williams, a protégé the late Archbishop Professor Benson Idahosa of Nigeria. The self-acquisition of these academic/ecclesial titles among charismatic figures in Ghana is inspired by Archbishop Benson Idahosa. Nicholas Duncan-Williams assumed the title "archbishop" as soon as his mentor, Benson Idahosa passed in the late 1990s.

Pentecostalism in Ghana, apart from the classical Pentecostals and neo-Pentecostal or charismatic ministries, has spawned quite a number of other groups. A number of these cast themselves as prophetic ministries and the stock-in-trade of their leaders is to "prophesy" over people's lives including making revelations regarding the supernatural sources of their existential problems. The prescribed solutions to these problems include the performance of healing and deliverance rituals and the anointing with olive oils. The Pentecostal prophets within their charismatic personalities and drive have become spiritual consultants within Ghanaian Christianity and their religious activities attract hundreds of thousands of patrons who consult them on any areas of life that pose particular problems understood as being "spiritual." In addition to these neo-Prophetic Pentecostal movements, the late 1970s saw the rise of other neo-Pentecostal trans-denominational fellowships like the Full Gospel Businessmen's Fellowship International (FGBMFI) and the Women Aglow. These are para-church Pentecostal/charismatic fellowships that bring together Christians who share their conversion testimonies over breakfast, lunch and dinner meetings. The trans-denominational charismatic groups have also attracted very high level political and public service personalities belonging especially to the mainline denominations. Thus, they constitute the source of charismatic renewal within these older denominations. Both the FGBMFI and Women Aglow have connections with their counterparts in other countries and Ghana has hosted international conventions of both organizations at one time or the other.

Pentecostalism is a very powerful religious movement and its influence on Ghanaian Christianity and within the public sphere is very palpable. This is particularly evident in their media presence. When Ghana adopted democratic governance in 1992 after years of military dictatorship, the media landscape was liberalized. It afforded Ghanaian Pentecostal/charismatic churches and movements the opportunity to purchase airtime to broadcast their programs and church services for the consumption of the wider public. The Pentecostal media presence has moved up a notch higher with the availability of digital satellite television. In Ghana, it is now impossible to talk about Pentecostalism without media and to talk about media without Pentecostalism. Thus, Pentecostal televangelism which originally consisted of preaching the word of God on television by particular preachers for example, has now taken different forms including live church services and sessions of exorcism and healing that are either pre-recorded for later transmission or even streamed live not only on television but also through the Internet and other social media outlets.

The classical Pentecostal denominations started off with a very eschatological message of new birth that leads to eternal life with God. This sort of message virtually demonized wealth as an obstacle to faithful Christianity and a hindrance for those aspiring to enter God's kingdom after death. With the rise of the contemporary Pentecostal movement and its prosperity theology, that message is now very subdued. Pentecostals still preach the traditional Born-again message, but on the whole, their religious orientation is now a bit more nuanced, existentially speaking. There is a strong emphasis on the acquisition of material things as important indicators of God's favor. In other words, contemporary Pentecostals now promote conspicuous consumption as part of prosperity preaching and that contributes to the appeal that this movement has for Ghana's youth and young professionals. It is a message that motivates people to look up in hope and to take advantage of opportunities in education and professional development to move higher on the social ladder and to dominate the public sphere. That, it is thought, is the way to establish the kingdom of God on earth.

In keeping with its strong existential message, Pentecostal/charismatic churches now participate in social developmental programs. In Ghana, this includes the establishment of higher education institutions. For example, one of the most popular and thriving private universities in Ghana, the Central University, is founded by Pastor Mensa Otabil's International Central Gospel Church. Archbishop Duncan-Williams' Action Chapel International also owns the Dominion University and the Lighthouse Chapel, whose founder Dr. Dag Heward-Mills is a trained medical doctor, has also established the Lighthouse Hospital in a suburb of the capital, Accra. The older classical Pentecostal denominations such as the Assemblies of God and the Christ Apostolic Church have all established their own universities and medical facilities too. With the numbers on their side, their strong media presence, their vibrant and dynamic churches and high-profile personalities, Pentecostal/charismatic Christianity is set to dominate the public sphere in Ghana for many years to come.

Bibliography

Asamoah-Gyadu, Kwabena J. 2005. *African Charismatics: Current Developments within Independent Indigenous Pentecostalism in Ghana.* Leiden: Brill.

Gifford, Paul. 2004. *Ghana's New Christianity: Pentecostalism in a Globalizing African Economy.* Bloomington: Indiana University Press.

Larbi, E. Kingsley. 2001. *Pentecostalism: The Eddies of Ghanaian Christianity.* Accra: CPCS.

Omenyo, Cephas N. 2002. *Pentecost outside Pentecostalism: A Study of the Development of CharismaticRenewal in the Mainline Churches.* Amsterdam: Boekencentrum.

Onyinah, Opoku. 2012. *Pentecostal Exorcism: Witchcraft and Demonology in Ghana.* Dorcet, UK: Deo Publishing.

Wyllie, Robert W. 1980. *Spiritism in Ghana: A Study of New Religious Movements.* Missoula: Scholars Press.

J. Kwabena Asamoah-Gyadu

Globalization

Globalization is a term that refers to worldwide social change that is widely discussed and debated across many disciplines. The focus of scholars revolves around a range of questions including the origins of the term, definitions, debates, social implications, social movements, anti-globalization, and the various ways globalization is used to understand politics, economics, and culture.

One way in which globalization is conceived focuses on the economic, political, and cultural features. Key developments have followed this observation although not all theories have given attention to religion. Economic explanations typically focus on the expansion and development of capitalism as a worldwide system of exchange that needs to be liberalized, reformed, or revolutionized. Political explanations make the nation-state central to their arguments and focus on international relations, the modernization of political systems, and the development of non-governmental forms. Cultural analyses of globalization examine how the entire world is shaped by a common culture that is local and particular where variation exists and whether or not a global culture is to be embraced or is inherently dangerous and to be rejected. Each of these developments, the economic, political, and cultural, have different implications for understanding religion generally, and Pentecostalism more particularly.

Scholars of Pentecostalism have employed globalization as a theoretical orientation for explaining the growth and spread of Pentecostalism, it's worldwide cultural qualities, migrant churches, social ministries, theological developments, missionary activities, political activities, and historical origins. There are numerous edited volumes that include perspectives from anthropology, history, religious studies, sociology, and theology on topics like healing, growth, politics, prayer, missionaries, gender, networks, etc. (e.g. Brown 2011; Wilkinson 2012; Hefner 2013; Miller, Sargeant, and Flory 2013; Coleman and Hacket 2015).

Some analyses of Pentecostalism and globalization include a range of case studies that reflect on the key debates about religion and globalization. For example, there is some important research on globalization and Pentecostalism that assumes Pentecostalism is a global culture that is not only "everywhere" but also universal in sharing a common history, spirituality, theology, and religious experience. For example, Harvey Cox's book *Fire from Heaven* (1995) focuses on the universal qualities of Pentecostalism as a key example of what he calls primal religion. The idea is that the success of Pentecostalism worldwide is also related to its ability to speak to the spiritual problems of modern life. This is accomplished through its ability to address those problems through primal spirituality and especially what he discusses as primal speech (glossolalia), primal piety (experience and healing), and primal hope (the promise of a better future, eschatology). The growth and spread of Pentecostalism is for Cox, "everywhere" because it represents a universal human quality that is recovered by the movement.

Several other scholars reflect the worldwide cultural qualities of Pentecostalism including Karla Poewe (1994) who writes about charismatic Christianity as a global culture that is unbound spatially, temporally, and institutionally. This global culture is transmitted throughout the world through media, conferences, networks, and megachurches. *The Globalization of Pentecostalism*, edited by Dempster, Klaus, and Petersen (1999) likewise maintains that the success and growth of Pentecostalism is largely rooted in its cultural qualities as a universal religion that easily travels the globe and is embraced by all people through the efforts of missionaries, denominations, media, and a theology that is not only experiential but one that pragmatically works. Coleman (2000) examines the spread of charismatic Christianity, most notably, prosperity theology, through its material culture of media, buildings, and products. Miller and Yamamori (2007) write about the progressive cultural qualities of Pentecostalism and its ability to meet the social needs of people throughout the world.

Allan Anderson's book *To the Ends of the Earth* (2013) is a critical historical examination of the movement. Anderson argues that the globalization of Pentecostalism must be understood from a more local perspective and one that does not privilege the role of Western Pentecostals. Pentecostalism for Anderson is multicultural and reflects important developments that are rooted in the local histories and activities of people, for example, in India, South Africa, and Korea. The impact of Pentecostalism rests on the local activities of women, independent churches, cultural flexibility, activism, evangelism, egalitarian community, and social programs.

A major contribution to the scholarly work on globalization and Pentecostalism is that of sociologist David Martin (2002) who attempts to explain the various ways in which Pentecostalism is a worldwide expression of Christianity that is rooted in local histories. Martin offers an explanation that is based in his work on secularization, differentiation, and the development of modern industrialized societies throughout the world. Modernization and secularization are not the end of religion as Pentecostalism reveals, says Martin. Rather, Pentecostalism represents a cultural revolution whereby new religious experiences, practices, and organizations adapt to the modernization of social life in unique ways around the world.

Studies on migration and migrant churches are quite a prominent theme in studies on globalization and Pentecostalism. For example, there is some research that explores how the arrival of Pentecostals from Africa, Asia, and Latin America are contributing to the de-Europeanization of Christianity in Canada and the transformation of existing denominations (Wilkinson 2006). There are studies that give attention to the role of migrant churches and how they attempt to re-Christianize disaffiliated European Christians through the planting of congregations and missionizing activities (Währisch-Oblau 2009). Studies in the United States and Mexico examine the transnational qualities of Pentecostalism and the development of border communities where Pentecostalism thrives as a religion that encompasses multiple sites and social space (Ramirez 2015).

Studies of globalization, Pentecostalism, and world Christianity need to further investigate several issues including how Pentecostalism is currently changing through a range of global and local expressions, experiences, organizations, and interactions with a variety of Pentecostal streams as well as other types of Christianity including evangelical Protestantism, Roman Catholicism, and Eastern Orthodoxy. Questions need to explore how Pentecostalism is constructed and defined as a global religion. More specifically, future studies should critically evaluate local histories of Pentecostalism by remapping the global flows that add complexity to those stories; reconsider key cultural qualities and how they are localized, thereby calling into question how Pentecostalism is a culturally cohesive expression of world Christianity; and finally, future studies should critically examine the role of Pentecostal organizations, media, and individuals and how they articulate and construct a global Pentecostal identity.

Bibliography

Anderson, Allan Heaton. 2013. *To the Ends of the Earth: Pentecostalism and the Transformation of World Christianity*. Oxford: Oxford University Press.

Brown, Candy Gunther, ed. 2011. *Global Pentecostal and Charismatic Healing*. Oxford: Oxford University Press.

Coleman, Simon. 2000. *The Globalisation of Charismatic Christianity: Spreading the Gospel of Prosperity*. Cambridge: Cambridge University Press.

Coleman, Simon and Rosalind I.J. Hackett, eds. 2015. *The Anthropology of Global Pentecostalism and Evangelicalism*. New York: New York University Press.

Cox, Harvey. 1995. *Fire From Heaven: The Rise of Pentecostal Spirituality and the Reshaping of Religion in the Twenty-first Century*. Reading, MA: Addison-Wesley.

Dempster, Murray W., Byrdon D. Klaus, and Douglas Petersen, eds. 1999. *The Globalization of Pentecostalism: A Religion made to Travel*. Oxford: Regnum Books.

Hefner, Robert W., ed. 2013. *Global Pentecostalism in the 21st Century*. Bloomington and Indianapolis, IN: Indiana University Press.

Martin, David. 2002. *Pentecostalism: The World Their Parish*. Oxford: Blackwell.

Miller, Donald E. and Tetsunao Yamamori. 2007. *Global Pentecostalism: The New Face of Christian Social Engagement*. Berkeley: University of California Press.

Miller, Donald E., Kimon H. Sargeant, and Richard Flory, eds. 2013. *Spirit and Power: The Growth and Global Impact of Pentecostalism*. Oxford: Oxford University Press.

Poewe, Karla, ed. 1994. *Charismatic Christianity as a Global Culture*. Columbia, South Carolina: University of South Carolina Press.

Ramírez, Daniel. 2015. *Migrating Faith: Pentecostalism in the United States and Mexico in the Twentieth Century*. Chapel Hill, NC: The University of North Carolina Press.

Währisch-Oblau, Claudia. *The Missionary Self-Perception of Pentecostal/Charismatic Church Leaders from the Global South in Europe: Bringing back the Gospel*. Leiden: Brill.

Wilkinson, Michael. 2006. *The Spirit Said Go: Pentecostal Immigrants in Canada*. New York: Peter Lang.

Wilkinson, Michael, ed. 2012. *Global Pentecostal Movements: Migration, Mission, and Public Religion*. Leiden: Brill.

Wilkinson, Michael. 2021. "Globalization." In *The Wiley Blackwell Companion to the Study of Religion*, Second Edition, edited by Robert A. Segal and Nickolas P. Roubekas, 277–288. Hoboken, NJ: John Wiley & Sons.

Michael Wilkinson

Glossolalia

Glossolalia, or "speaking in tongues," has long constituted a prominent feature of global Pentecostalism. Similar phenomenon occur in a number of ancient and modern non-Christian religions (e.g., Oracle of Delphi, African indigenous religions, Mormons), though the degree of commonality is debated. In Pentecostal and Charismatic circles, the experience usually signifies the "baptism in the Holy Spirit" – understood variously as a

Young pentecostals pray with hands up and speak in tongues at a meeting in Center of Faith Emanuel of Assemblies of God in Cancun (2012). Source: Wikimedia, Rayttc (CC BY-SA)

second or third work of grace subsequent to conversion. For some within the classical Pentecostal tradition, including (but not limited to) the Assemblies of God (AG), Congregational Holiness Church (CHC), the Church of God of Prophecy (COGOP), the International Pentecostal Holiness Church (IPHC), Pentecostal Church of God (PCG), glossolalia represents the "initial physical evidence" of Spirit baptism. This perspective though is less common outside the US, except where missionaries from these organizations have been involved in theological training and church planting.

The noun glossolalia is not found in the Bible, but rather the verbal phrase "to speak in tongues" (Gr. glōssais lalein).

References to the practice of glossolalia occur explicitly in three books of the New Testament, namely the longer ending of Mark (16:17), Acts 2:3–4, 11; 10:46; 19:6 and in Paul's discussion of spiritual gifts in 1 Cor. 12–14 (though some argue for implicit references elsewhere, especially, Luke 10:21; Rom 8:26–27; Eph 5:18–20; Col 3:16; and 1 Thess 5:19–20). Exegetical debates swirl around the nature of tongues speech in 1 Corinthians and Acts, while the longer ending of Mark 16 is sometimes considered evidence that glossolalia was valued among early to mid second-century Christians (Cartledge 2002, 62).

Paul in 1 Corinthians expounds on glossolalia as it relates to congregational worship and edification, while Luke in the book of Acts employs the term missiologically to emphasize the church's cross-cultural mandate accomplished in the Spirit's power (Keener 2007; Ireland 2019).

Although the Azusa Street Revival that began in 1906 in Los Angeles was instrumental in the modern proliferation of tongues speech, the broader history produces as many questions as answers. Even if the NT references to speaking in tongues are to be understood as Gordon Fee says, "normal but not normative" within early Christianity, questions arise regarding the long periods of silence within church history. Pentecostals have usually responded to questions about this silence by arguing for glossolalia among second century Montanists – a supposition based on a somewhat vague description by Eusebius – and thereby declaring that the heterodox nature of the sect cast a shadow over the practice, causing it to drop out of favour among orthodox believers until its nineteenth century revival. Pentecostals have occasionally drawn parallels to Luther's revival of the doctrine of salvation by grace (*sola gratia*).

What is more certain is that apart from the witness of the NT, there exist few clear references to glossolalia in church history. This absence may depend in part on the linguistic conflation of the gifts of tongues and prophecy (see Irenaeus, *Against Heresies*, 3.17.2; 5.6.1). Tertullian, who had joined the Montanists, comes closest to discussing tongues in an evidential way, arguing that the presence of the gift among Christians showed God was with the Christians but not the Marcionites (*ANF* 3, *Against Marcion*, 5:8). Origin, Chrysostom, and Augustine noted the disappearance of spiritual gifts in their day, Augustine most famously arguing they were no longer needed in the post-apostolic era. Augustine's argument appears to have been highly influential well beyond the Protestant Reformation. Glossolalia appeared rarely in the middle ages, one notable example being Christian mystics like Hildegard of Bingen (1098–1179) who reportedly sang in tongues. In the west, scholasticism related the gift to the demonic, though sporadic occurrences of xenolalia (speaking in unlearned known languages) were reported in or later attributed to the missionary work of Francis Xavier (1506–1552) and Louis Bertrand (1526–1581). Some have drawn a connection between glossolalia and persecution, as with a seventeenth century group of French Huguenots known as the "little prophets of the Cévennes." The Eastern Orthodox generally have neither elevated nor denounced the gift.

Contemporary Pentecostal understandings of tongues can be traced to nineteenth century movements such as the Irvingites in London, and healing movements led by John Alexander Dowie and Frank Sandford, who directly contributed to the burgeoning theology of Charles Parham. Parham is often credited with first articulating the doctrine of initial evidence. Parham's student, William Seymour led the Azusa Street revival but moved away from tongues as the only or primary evidence of Spirit Baptism, as did some missionaries that went out from Azusa Street, such as Alfred and Lillian Garr who served in India. This perspective has been even more common outside the US in places like Germany, Sweden, and the UK.

In contemporary constructive theologies, several scholars have shown interest in interpreting glossolalia sacramentally (for example, see Vondey 2018, 102). Others see in tongues speech scriptural demand for pluralistic social engagement (Wariboko 2012, 29–31), and the language of conversion needed for overcoming Christian nominalism (Poewe 1994, 12), to cite just a few examples. All of this points to contemporary Pentecostals stepping away from the very modern "evidential" language of the early movement and searching for a theological interpretation more at home among postmodern and/or non-western sensibilities. Indeed, some consider glossolalia in light of Wittgenstein's "linguistic turn" as an opportunity to move the church away from a hyper-rationalism and instead emphasize the inadequacy of language for describing God. Whereas in the early twentieth century, "evidence" may have been the most common term associated with glossolalia, in the early twenty-first century, the term "mystery" may be taking its place.

Beyond theology, different socio-scientific disciplines have contributed to the research on glossolalia. Neuroscientific studies have shown that glossolalia and language involve different parts of the brain, with decreased activity in the pre-frontal cortex of the speaker in ways consistent with the claims of glossolalics. Researchers have also shown that glossolalia cannot be linked to neuroticism or pathology, as was once believed (Ferguson 2011). Anthropologists have recorded the practice in various contexts and linked it to embodiment and aesthetics. Despite these advances in research, more studies are needed to document the variegated nature and contextual significance of the practice, particularly in non-Western contexts.

Bibliography

Cartledge, Mark, ed. 2006. *Speaking in Tongues: Multi-Disciplinary Perspectives*. Milton Keynes, UK: Paternoster.

Cartledge, Mark. 2002. *Charismatic Glossolalia: An Empirical-theological Study*. Burlington, VT: Ashgate.

Ferguson, Neil. 2011. "Separating Speaking in Tongues from Glossolalia using a Sacramental View," *Colloquium* 43 (1): 39–58.

Hovenden, Gerald. 2002. *Speaking in Tongues: The New Testament Evidence in Context*. Sheffield: Sheffield Academic.

Ireland, Jerry. 2019. "The Missionary Nature of Tongues in the Book of Acts." *PentecoStudies* 18 (2): 200–223.

Keener, Craig S. 2007. "Why Does Luke Use Tongues as a Sign of the Spirit's Empowerment?" *Journal of Pentecostal Theology* 15 (2): 177–184.

Menzies, Robert P. 2016. *Speaking in Tongues: Jesus and the Apostolic Church as Models for the Church Today*. Cleveland, TN: CPT.

Vondey, Wolfgang. 2018. *Pentecostal Theology: Living the Full Gospel*. London: T&T Clark.

Wariboko, Nimi. 2012. *The Pentecostal Principle*. Grand Rapids: Eerdmans.

Jerry M. Ireland

Greece

Very little is known about Greek Pentecostalism. Academic interest in Greek Pentecostal churches has always been limited, with very little scholarly research ever reaching publication. Whatever information we may possess, it originates with publications coming from the churches themselves, from important personalities of the movement, and from sources close to the Orthodox Church of Greece, which has been traditionally unfavorably disposed towards Pentecostalism. The most credible estimates talk about 15,000 members, which makes Greek Pentecostals the largest group among local Christians. Next to the Greek Pentecostal churches, a great number of Pentecostal churches among immigrants have emerged over the last decades, about which little is known.

The overwhelming majority of Greek Pentecostals belong to classical Pentecostal churches. The charismatic movement in Greek Orthodoxy met the vehement reaction of the Church of Greece and failed to attract much popularity. Equally limited within Greek Pentecostalism have remained neo-charismatic churches. Almost all Greek Pentecostal churches have adopted the Creed of Eastern Orthodox Christianity (without *filioque*).

The pioneers of Pentecostal movement in Greece were Greek immigrants who had experienced their spiritual revival in the USA. Many among them had been members of the Primitive Apostolic Church of Pentecost, a Los Angeles-based Greek Pentecostal body that was affiliated with the Assemblies of God. The oldest recorded arrival of a Greek Pentecostal from the USA in his native village was in 1924. The hostility of a large section of the population and of the Orthodox church itself, as well as a series of laws and administrative regulations designed to ensure the hegemony of the Church of Greece in the country posed insurmountable obstacles to the early Greek Pentecostals who, without exception, came from the lower strata of society, with few resources, and no adequate education. The first local church, affiliated with the Church of God of Prophecy, was founded in the Athenian district of Petralona. It was there that in 1927 it evidenced the first outpouring of the Holy Spirit in modern Greek history.

It was during the first post-war decades that the Pentecostal churches were consolidated in Greece. Although still small, the movement made some inroads into the middle classes. In the mid-1960s, the fifteen local churches numbering around 1,000 members were connected with five foreign missions, the Assemblies of God enjoying a lead vis-à-vis all other missions due to its long-established relationship with Greek Pentecostals in the USA. The churches affiliated with the Assemblies of God were united into a common Synod and adopted the name Apostolic Churches of Pentecost (the common term "Apostolic" in the name of Greek Pentecostal churches does not refer to the Oneness Movement). It was the Athens chapter of this church that eventually came to play a leading role in Greek Pentecostalism, not less because it gave birth to the Free Apostolic Church of Pentecost (FACP), which should give renewed impetus to the movement and decisively shape the Pentecostal landscape of the country.

The establishment of FACP in 1965 emerged as an act of institutional and doctrinal emancipation of the Apostolic Church of Pentecost in Athens from the Assemblies of God. The new church added to its old name the term "Free" indicating its autocephalous character. In the following years, FACP proved to be highly successful. As growing numbers of individual believers and even entire congregations entering its fold the church exhibited an astonishing 10 percent annual growth, making it the fastest-growing religious body in the country. In terms of church planting, FACP also achieved a remarkable success which remains unique in the history of "born-again" Christianity in Greece. Meanwhile, representing around three quarters of the Greek Pentecostals in more than 120 local churches, FACP has achieved a hegemonic position in the Pentecostal landscape of the country. Still, the first decades of the twenty-first century saw a leveling, if not decline, in the number of Pentecostals.

FACP's success may be seen as the result of the church's adaptation into what is widely perceived as Greek religious normality. Its autocephalous position as a national church; the rejection of a number of Protestant-Evangelical practices (first Sunday of the month communion, choirs and the use of musical instruments during the service, ordination of women, etc.); the adoption of proto-Christian elements (Mass every Sunday, women veiled in prayer); the ban on women preaching or even testifying in the church as well as on wearing of trousers; and a robust anti-western bias that tallies well with the traditional anti-western discourse of the Church of Greece, are among the most prominent factors that brought FACP closer to the Greek (Orthodox) realities, investing it with a *sui generis* character within global Pentecostalism. Moreover, FACP is characterized by a strong exclusivity claim which greatly constricts its relationship with other Pentecostal churches in Greece and abroad. Though this stance is occasionally justified by FACP personalities as a means to restore and safeguard the faith and way of life of the Apostolic era, something that FACP perceives as its ultimate goal, it has come under harsh criticism and has led to fissures even within the church itself, the most severe ones being the secession/expulsion of two prominent local churches in the Athens region.

The remaining classical Pentecostal churches combined in 1990 and created the Brotherhood of Greek Pentecostal Churches, a rather loose network of churches that allowed better co-ordination of their leaders. On the whole though, these churches never succeeded in acquiring dynamism comparable to that of FACP. Among the most important churches of the Brotherhood are the historical Apostolic Church of Pentecost and the Apostolic Church of Christ, which is associated with the International Church of the Foursquare Gospel and comprises in Athens the biggest local church in Greece. Being very active socially, in contradistinction to the FACP, the churches of the Brotherhood are also members of the Greek Evangelical Alliance, an umbrella organization, which promotes cooperation between Evangelical and Pentecostal churches, as well as the Pentecostal European Fellowship. Finally, a small group of autonomous churches in Athens and Thessaloniki with roots in churches of the Brotherhood but meanwhile distancing themselves from the designation "Pentecostal" formed the loose organization Greek Evangelical Charismatic Community which also became a member of the Pentecostal European Fellowship.

The Greek Pentecostal movement has not shown any particular interest in establishing educational structures. An Assemblies of God initiative to open a Pentecostal Biblical School in Athens in association with Global University found no positive response among Greek Pentecostals, turning the education of future Pentecostal leadership into a great challenge for the movement as a whole.

Bibliography

Chatzieleftheriou, Ilias. 2010. *The Development of Pentecostal Churches in Greece*. Master's diss., Mattersey Hall in association with Bangor University.

Karagiannis, Evangelos. 2020. "Pfingsten im Kontext: Zur Adaption des Pfingstglaubens in Griechenland." *Anthropos* 115 (1): 133–150.

Ελευθέρα Αποστολική Εκκλησία Πεντηκοστής. 2006. *Ελεύθερη Αποστολική Εκκλησία Πεντηκοστής: Η ιστορία της. Τί πιστεύει. Πως πολιτεύεται*. Αθήνα: Όρος.

Λίντερμαγερ, Ορέστης. 1998. "Φονταμεταλισμός και πνευματοληψία: Θεραπεία και μέθεξη στο πλαίσιο μιας πεντηκοστιανής κοινότητας στην Ελλάδα." *Εθνολογία*, no. 5 (1996–1997): 115–179.

Λίντερμαγερ, Ορέστης. 2009. "Η πεντηκοστιανή εκκλησία ως θρησκευτικό κίνημα στην Ελλάδα σήμερα." PhD diss., University of Crete.

Evangelos Karagiannis

Greenwood, Charles L.

Charles Louis Greenwood (1891–1969) was an Australian Pentecostal church planter, missional revivalist, healing evangelist and denominational leader. He pioneered and pastored Richmond Temple in Melbourne, one of the most significant churches within the Assemblies of God in Australia (AGA). Greenwood also served two terms as AGA general chairman.

Charles L. Greenwood, commonly known as C.L. Greenwood, was born in inner city Melbourne. He was one of the 12 children to Normington and Rebecca Greenwood. After his father died, C.L. Greenwood left primary school and entered the workforce. He attended church as a teenager but continued to struggle with heavy drinking and smoking. At the age of nineteen, Greenwood experienced healing after prayer.

After three years of seeking, Greenwood was filled with the Holy Spirit while waiting at a train station in 1913. He married Frances Ella Reed on August 19, 1915. They had five children – Hazel, Lois, Doreen, Leslie, and Elviss. The Greenwoods pioneered a church in their home for several years before the congregation of 30 people purchased land in the Melbourne suburb of Sunshine. Sunshine Gospel Hall opened in March 1925.

After American preacher Adolpho C. Valdez cancelled his tour with Sarah Jane Lancaster, owing to her anti-Trinitarian and annihilationist teachings, Greenwood invited Valdez to preach at Sunshine Gospel Hall. Revival broke out, hundreds were converted and services were described as being "bathed in glory" (Austin and Clifton 2019). The 500-strong congregation relocated to Prahran Town Hall, then into Richmond Theatre which they purchased and re-named Richmond Temple.

Greenwood also led revival meetings throughout regional New South Wales and attracted wide publicity. As a result, the Pentecostal Church of Australia was formed as a fellowship of autonomous churches in New South Wales, South Australia, and Western Australia. Richmond Temple was headquarters for the denomination which also distributed a national magazine entitled *Australian Evangel*.

Greenwood became senior pastor of Richmond Temple, in 1927, and served in that capacity for an outstanding 41 years. He hosted a radio program called "Harvest Gleanings" and published a magazine called *Harvest Grain*. The church purchased camp grounds and the annual Beulah Heights Christmas camp drew Pentecostals from across Australia. Richmond Temple also supported outreaches in various countries.

Only around 1.5m in height, Greenwood had famously taught himself to read and write from the Bible and a dictionary, yet was a powerful preacher, often prophetically exposing sins of congregation members from the pulpit. However, at one stage, Greenwood's "fire and brimstone" preaching and authoritarian leadership led to a mass exodus of people to the nearby Apostolic Church.

Needing to consolidate marginalized pockets of Pentecostals, in 1937, the

Pentecostal Church of Australia merged with the Assemblies of God in Queensland to form the Assemblies of God in Australia (AGA). Greenwood was elected as the first general chairman (1937–1941), overseeing around 1,000 people in 38 assemblies. He also served as state chairman for Victoria and chair of the AGA foreign missions committee.

Greenwood impacted many future AGA leaders, including: Philip B. Duncan, later state superintendent for New South Wales; John Lewis, later state superintendent for Queensland; his son, Elviss Greenwood, state chairman for South Australia; Andrew Evans, later AGA general superintendent; and Leo Harris who established Christian Revival Crusade.

Although many AGA leaders shared links to the Sunshine Revival, state rivalries surfaced when discussing where the national ministry training institute would be located. Greenwood even dramatically announced his resignation, only to withdraw it soon after. He was re-elected as AGA chairman (1943–1945) and Commonwealth Bible College (CBC) commenced at Richmond Temple in February 1948. While itinerating in the USA, Greenwood (1948) wrote, "When God's voice is heard deep within the soul, that man or woman is changed from that moment, for better or for worse according to their response in obedience or disobedience."

Possibly prematurely, Richmond Temple purchased a 22-room Missionary Rest Home for CBC. However, the 1949 AGA conference decided that CBC would relocate to an independent site in Brisbane. Greenwood attempted to keep running Victoria Bible College. However, low enrolments forced its closure at the end of 1951. Greenwood continued to serve on the CBC directorate until he was tragically killed in a car accident on January 5, 1969. He had served CBC for over 20 years.

C.L. Greenwood was a fiery preacher, dictatorial leader, and stalwart Victorian. Yet, his visionary and prophetic leadership saw the establishment of what became the largest and fastest growing denomination in Australia. He pastored one of the largest Pentecostal churches in Australia for over four decades. The generosity and foresight of Greenwood saw the founding of the AGA national training institute. His lifelong service to ministry and mission left an invaluable legacy.

Bibliography

Antcliff, Pat. 2003. "Charles Louis Greenwood." *Australasian Dictionary of Pentecostal and Charismatic Movements*. https://sites.google.com/view/adpcm/e-h-top-page/greenwood-charles-louis. Accessed May 23, 2019.

Austin, Denise A., and Shane Clifton. 2019. "Australian Pentecostalism: From Marginalised to Megachurches." In *Asia Pacific Pentecostalism*, edited by Denise A. Austin, Jacqueline Grey, and Paul W. Lewis, 372–399. Leiden: Brill.

Forbes, George. 2006. *The C.L. Greenwood Story*. Chirnside Park VIC: Mission Mobilisers International.

The Editor. 1948. "Harvest Gleanings." *Harvest Grain* 5 (3): 14.

Denise A. Austin

Guatemala

The presence of Pentecostalism in Guatemala was made possible by the entrance of mainline Protestantism, when President

Justo Rufino Barrios travelled to New York (1871) and requested the Presbyterian Missions to redirect one of their missionaries (John Clark Hill) to Guatemala. With the arrival of the Presbyterians, a number of other Protestant denominations also established missions in Guatemala, including the Nazarenes and the Primitive Methodist church. In 1901 the Nazarenes adopted the name the Pentecostal Mission of the Nazarenes, though by 1919 they had dropped "Pentecostal" from their title and came to be known as the Misión del Nazareno.

In 1916 Guatemala was visited by the Pentecostal missionaries Charles Furman, Carrie Smith, his wife and Thomas Pullin, who were affiliated with the Pennsylvania United Free Missionary Society. In their early missionary work, they collaborated with C. Albert Hines (an independent Pentecostal), and Charles F. Secord (a Plymouth Brethren missionary), who were working with several congregations in the province of Totonicapán. Due to conflicts with the Nazarenes, the Furmans were relieved from their missionary work only to return in 1921 under the auspices of the Primitive Methodist Church USA. They established a number of small churches in the towns in the regions of Quiché and Totonicapán. In 1934, the Furmans left the Methodist Church and affiliated themselves with the Church of God, Cleveland (Iglesia de Dios, Evangelio Completo). Fourteen pastors and communities from the Primitive Methodist Church left with them and together they began to expand among the Indigenous peoples in the highlands.

In 1932, a group of Pentecostal believers from El Salvador went into Guatemala in search of work. Identifying themselves as Lutheran Evangelicals, they also claimed to have received the baptism of the Spirit. They began to preach the gospel and established small local prayer groups, the first of which was in the village of Amatepeque, Jutiapa. Not too long after, a church was established in Atescatempa. The USA Assemblies of God missionary Rafael D. Williams together with the Salvadorans Francisco Arvizú and Pio Quinto Flores travelled to Guatemala from El Salvador to recognize and to support the evangelistic efforts at Atescatempa which became affiliated to the Assemblies of God. From Jutiapa, the evangelistic efforts spread and by 1975 the denomination had reached all of Guatemala. Today, Atescatempa is considered the site of the first organized local church and birthplace of the Assemblies of God in Guatemala.

The Assemblies of God went through a major schism at the beginning of the second half of the twentieth century when some pastors insisted upon the nationalization of the denomination and pushed for national leadership. One crucial figure was pastor José María Muñoz (Chema), who pastored the central church of the Assemblies of God in Guatemala City for 10 years, but was defrocked by the mission for his nationalistic stance. As he left the Assemblies of God, he, along with a number of other pastors, founded the church Principe de Paz in 1954. Other pentecostal groups, autochthonous to Guatemala, include La Iglesia Calvario (1961) and La Misión Cristiana Elim (1974).

As of 1970 Pentecostals and Protestants made up only a small percentage of the Guatemalan population. Key factors explain the "quiet" explosion of Pentecostalism (and Protestantism) that ensued during this decade. First, in the face of the devasting earthquake in 1976, Protestants and Pentecostals were able to effectively respond and provide relief to the population. Not having a centralized organization, they were able to respond better than the Catholics. Many Pentecostals offered relief in exchange for people listening to the gospel message. Many people converted to Pentecostalism because of the material help they received as a kind of lamina por anima (or "rice" Christians). Yet, when the foreign financial relief stopped, the increase in numbers continued. Pentecostal eschatology and preaching concerning the imminent second coming of Jesus, and reality of wars, earthquakes, famines, etc., reflected the experience of the people and influenced people to flock to the churches. Most importantly, the USA-financed and pushed for the adoption of anti-communist policies in Guatemala which contributed to the persecution of Catholic priests and lay people, so many Catholic believers switched to Pentecostalism fearing for their safety. By the end of the 1970s, Pentecostalism had become a national force without foreign involvement, but it would not be until the 1980s that it became conspicuously present in Guatemala's religious landscape.

But by the 1970s and 1980s it became strikingly evident that Protestant churches were also losing members to Pentecostalism through the renewal-Charismatic movement. Other mainline denominations lost entire churches when these communities adopted charismatism. Many of these groups organized and called themselves missions. For example, the Mission Lluvias de Gracia, which emerged around the middle of the 1980s, is an offshoot of the Guatemalan Presbyterian Church. The separation took place because the Presbyterian church was unwilling to accept charismatic expressions in their congregations. Edward Cleary reminds us that while Pentecostals go around recording record numbers of conversions, what remains unaccounted for are the growing numbers of Pentecostals who are returning to Catholicism, for example, via the Catholic Charismatic Movement (Cleary 1992).

The 1980s and 1990s saw the emergence of charismatic and Neopentecostal groups. Also, charismatic offshoots from mainline protestants began to appear. Such was the case with Misión Lluvias de Gracia (1985) which was organized from formerly Presbyterian churches. During the 1980s the neopentecostal Misión el Verbo also rose to prominence – though its presence in Guatemala can be traced back to 1951 – because the President Efraín Rios Montt was one of its members. Put in place by a military coup, Rios Montt staged a policy of genocide against the indigenous peoples in the name of God. During the early 1980s the now popular Hombres de Negocios del Evangelio Completo organization (Full Gospel Business Men's Fellowship International) was founded.

Neopentecostal churches have become hubs for people in the higher economic echelons to congregate. They reflect a more USA-Evangelical worship style and approach to doing church. Another neopentecostal group, El Shaddai, grew by drawing followers from other denominations particularly from El Verbo, after Jorge Serrano Elías was elected to president (1991–1993). The hype was short lived because Serrano Elías was marred with scandals of corruption, which forced him to resign the presidency and flee the country. Unlike the earlier (classical) expressions of Pentecostalism, neopentecostals have not remained disengaged from the social and political arena. Many aspire to hold public office as is exemplified by the

Viva Political Party, which was founded by Harold Caballeros, the former senior pastor of the El Shaddai church, who left the pastorate to become a presidential candidate in 2006.

Though space prevents a fuller discussion, several key themes represent the challenges and contradictions which confront Pentecostalism in Guatemala today. Many Indigenous communities are finding resonance between their Indigenous religious traditions and Pentecostalism. Many former pentecostal followers are finding their way back into Catholicism via charismatism. Prosperity gospel is promoted by many prominent preachers in the country. News of pastoral immorality and scandals of corruption have become common knowledge in the general population. Some pastors have been found to be involved with gang activity and organized drug trafficking. Nevertheless, the Pentecostal movement seems to be making enormous inroads by reinventing itself and becoming once again the movement of the disenfranchised. In many communities where the police are unable to get, Pentecostals are actively evangelizing gang members. It seems that the present social conditions of the country are forcing Pentecostals and charismatics to reclaim the social implications of the gospel.

Bibliography

Cleary, Edward L. 1992. "Evangelicals and Competition in Guatemala." In *Conflict and Competition: The Latin American Church in a Changing Environment*, edited by Edward L. Cleary and Hannah Stewart-Gambino, Chapter 9. Boulder, CO: Lynne Rienner Publishers.

Garrard-Burnett, Virginia. 1998. *Living in the New Jerusalem: Protestantism in Guatemala*. Austin: University of Texas Press.

Garrard-Burnett, Virginia. 2011. *Terror in the Land of the Holy Spirit: Guatemala Under General Efrain Rios Montt 1982–1983*. New York, NY: Oxford University Press.

"Investigación: 'Chamalé', condenado a dos décadas de prisión." *El Periódico*, Julio 27, 2015.

Medina, Néstor. 2016. "Renovación/Renewal and the Social Context in Guatemala: The Changing Theological Tides." In *Global Renewal Christianity: Spirit-Empowered Movements Past, Present, and Future, Vol. 2, Latin America*, edited by Vinson Synan, Miguel Álvarez, and Amos Yong, 25–37. Lake Mary, FL: Charisma House Publishers.

Medina, Néstor. 2011. "Pentecostal Eschatology in Guatemala." Paper presented at the Theology Symposium on Eschatology. Society of Pentecostal Studies: Receiving the Future: An Anointed Heritage. Memphis.

O'Neill, Kevin Lewis. 2010. *City of God: Christian Citizenship in Postwar Guatemala*. Berkeley: University of California Press.

Russell, John P. 2014. "Cash" Luna y el asesinato del pastor Claudio Martínez Morales. *Unidos contra la apostasía*. Accessed October 20, 2019. https://contralaapostasia.com/2014/08/15/cash-luna-y-el-asesinato-del-pastor-claudio-martinez-morales/.

Sanchíz Ochoa, Pilar. 1998. *Evangelismo y poder: Guatemala ante el nuevo milenio*. Sevilla, España: Universidad de Sevilla, Secratariado de publicaciones.

Wilson, Everett A. 1998. "Furman, Charles Truman." In *Biographical Dictionary of Christian Missions*, edited by Gerald H. Anderson, 231–232. New York: Macmillan.

Néstor Medina

Guneratnam, Prince

Prince Guneratnam is the senior pastor of the Malaysia-based Calvary Church, one of the largest churches in southeast Asia. He has been in the ministry since 1966. He and his wife, Petrina Guneratnam, became the senior pastors of Calvary Church in 1972. Under their leadership, the church has grown from a congregation of 120 to establishing over thirty-one daughter churches.

Guneratnam is a gifted speaker and evangelist. He served in several key leadership positions of national and international Christian bodies. He was the first Malaysian General Superintendent of the Assemblies of God of Malaysia (1974–2006), Chairman of the National Evangelical Christian Fellowship of Malaysia (1994–2006), Chairman of the Christian Federation of Malaysia (2001–2005), and vice Chairman of the World Assemblies of God Fellowship. Currently, he is the Chairman of the Pentecostal World Fellowship.

In recognition for his services, he received three honorary scholastic awards, "Doctor of Divinity" in 1980, "Doctor of Litterarium" in 1984, and "Doctor of Laws" in 2000. He was cited for leadership skills with Exceptional Leadership Award in 2008 and the Distinguished Global Leadership Award in 2012. Also, he was given national recognition by the King of Malaysia with two prestigious awards: the "Panglima Jasa Negara" (Order of Distinguished Service) award in 1999, which carries the title of "Datuk" and the "Panglima Setia Mahkota" (Commander of the Order of Loyalty to the Crown) award in 2008, which carries the title of "Tan Sri."

Calvary Church has the largest Christian facility in Malaysia. The Calvary Convention Center in Bukit Jalil is worth RM 200 million (about US$485,311). It boasts its 600,000-square foot, 5,000-seat auditorium, and its 6-storey multiplex, set with a multi-purpose hall, classrooms, lecture halls, a nursery and various other spaces. It intends to provide a world-class facility for services, conventions, banquets, seminars and even creative arts productions. The church has organized large prayer rallies, church growth conferences, and elaborate Easter and Christian events at the facility. For example, in one of its Easter musicals, Heaven & Earth Rejoice!, the facility hosted 10,000 attendants. It has hosted a highly acclaimed musical performed by Promise Ministries International, New York, with a 100-strong production cast and technical crew. Pop duo Air Supply also performed at the center. Besides its landmark building, the Calvary church is also known for its Calvaryland. It is an integrated social concern center which aims to serve the poor, homeless, orphans, and single mothers, regardless of religion, social or ethnic origin.

However, the Calvary Convention Center has been surrounded by controversy from the beginning. In 2009, a news report on *The Star* online exposed that a group of church members, who call themselves the Truth, Transparency and Good Governance Group, expressed concern over Guneratnam's financial mismanagement, unethical practices and abuse of power (Fernandez and Michael 2009). The allegation against him included laying a huge building project debt on the church, transferring substantial church funds into his personal Calvary International Ministry's account without members' knowledge, dictatorial conducts, and the sacking of church members for speaking out. A police report was filed against him by a member of the group on the Breach of Trust of Missions funds, but no action was taken. He was also investigated for personal Tax evasion during the church crisis period.

Bibliography

Anderson, Allan and Edmund Tang, eds. 2005. *Asian and Pentecostal.* Oxford: Regnum.

Austin, Denise A. and Lim Yeu Chuen. 2019. "Critical Reflections on the Growth of Pentecostalism in Malaysia." In *Asia Pacific Pentecostalism*, edited by Denise A. Austin, Jacqueline Grey, and Paul W. Lewis, 195–216. Leiden: Brill.

Eu Choong, Chong. 2018. "Pentecostalism in Klang Valley, Malaysia." In *Pentecostal Megachurches in Southeast Asia*, edited by Terence Chong. Singapore: ISEAS.

Fernandez, Charles, and Stuart Michael. 2009. "Crisis Rocks Calvary Church." *The Star* (November 18). Accessed November 21, 2019. https://www.thestar.com.my/news/community/2009/11/18/crisis-rocks-calvary-church/.

Kit Cheong, Weng and Joy K.C. Tong. "The Localization of Charismatic Christianity among the Chinese in Malaysia." In *Global Chinese Pentecostal and Charismatic Christianity*, edited by Fenggang Yang, Joy K.C. Tong, and Allan Anderson, 309–328. Leiden: Brill.

Yip, Jeaney. 2018. "Reaching the City of Kuala Lumpur and Beyond: Being a Pentecostal Megachurch in Malaysia." In *Pentecostal Megachurches in Southeast Asia*, edited by Terence Chong. Singapore: ISEAS.

Joy Tong

Ha, Young Jo

Ha, Young-jo (1946–2011) was an influential Korean pastor who dedicated his life to Christian mission worldwide. He served as a leader for Campus Crusade for Christ (CCC) in evangelism and Bible teaching for seven years. After studying at the Presbyterian University and Theological Seminary, Ha founded the Celebrity Church from which he had to resign because of hepatocirrhosis. While he was in the UK receiving treatment, Ha studied at London Bible College, Worldwide Evangelization for Christ (WEC), and at the London Institute of Contemporary Christianity (LICC) founded by John Stott.

Physical illness played a crucial role in Ha's ministry. Ha regarded his illness as the grace of God which drew him close to God in his life time. Through suffering physical illness and empowerment by the Holy Spirit, Ha's ministry and sermons embraced a strong sense of God's care, healing power, and hope that helped believers to focus on God who purifies, heals, restores, and brings hope. Moreover, Ha always claimed to receive a new vision from God while in the hospital during his illnesses. Sickness did not stop his passion for God, rather it rendered a personal renewal and turning point for Ha and his ministries. For example, a diagnosis of hepatocirrhosis brought Ha to the UK for treatment, during which he also began his preparation for the future Onnuri Community Church (OCC) that was founded in 1985. After serving in the OCC for six years, he joined Youth with A Mission (YWAM) in Hawaii. While he took a rest for his illness and health condition there, he believed God was calling him to turn his ministry into the "Holy Spirit Ministry." This transition in Ha's ministry brought about a new Holy Spirit movement and became a landmark for the church. OCC experienced explosive growth and became active in its mission through gathering Christians together for worship, Bible studies, conferences, and other social services from 1992 to 2011. OCC started with 12 family members in 1984 and grew to 2,571 members by 1991. However, the rapid growth of the church followed the start of "the Holy Spirit Ministry" when its members grew to 75,525 by 2010. In spite of his doctor's advice to stop preaching due to his health condition, Ha determined that he would live his life according to God's calling. Ha preached regularly until the day he passed away.

Ha's vision was a mission to save souls from all nations. The vision for the OCC was "the Church in Acts." Ha believed that church was empowered by the Holy Spirit and was to proclaim the gospel throughout the world. "Acts 29" (symbolic for the ongoing work of the church since the book of Acts ends at chapter 28) became the motto of the OCC. Ha taught that the nature of the church is one that is empowered by the Holy Spirit, where believers gather, pray, study the Bible, praise, and experience the Kingdom of God through healing, sanctification, and visions. The community is one where transcendent love and lively works are empowered by the Holy Spirit that attracts people to church for a life of sharing, serving, and worshipping; the life of this church is given from God. The empowerment of the Holy Spirit also leads Christians to be witnesses for Jesus Christ and the crucifixion and resurrection. There are eight branch churches called "Campus Church" in Korea, and twenty-four churches called "Vision Church" in other countries. Ha launched a satellite and created Christian Global Network Television (CGNTV) to provide inspirational Christian content, particularly in places where missionaries cannot reach or where Christians are isolated. In addition, Ha combined the ministry of OCC with a para-church organization known as Durano Seowon, which became a center for several key ministries: The Bible College, "1 on 1 Bible study," the Paternal School, the 2,000/10,000 Vision (which means sending 2,000 missionaries abroad and raising 10,000 ministers for the country), and a mission project to Japan called "Love Sonata."

Ha's pneumatology includes both Presbyterian and Pentecostal understandings of the baptism of the Holy Spirit. For Ha, the baptism of the Holy Spirit happens at salvation, where the Holy Spirit regenerates believers and includes justification, and sanctification. He emphasized regeneration and sanctification as the baptism of the Spirit. However, Ha also understood the empowerment by the Holy Spirit for mission described in Acts 1:8 as the baptism of the Holy Spirit from Pentecostal pneumatology, acknowledging that power in the verse does not point to salvation but power for mission from the Holy Spirit.

Bibliography

Anderson, Allan and Edmund Tang, eds. 2005. *Asian and Pentecostal*. Oxford: Regnum.
Ha, Yong-Jo. 2008. *I Put My Life for Mission*. Seoul: Durano.
Ha, Yong-Jo. 2007. *Dreaming of the Church in Acts*. Seoul: Durano.
Ha, Yong-Jo. 2003. *Like Wind and Like Fire*. Seoul: Durano.
Mun, Seong-Mo. 2010. *The Story of Pastor Ha Yong-Jo: With Onnuri Community Church and Its Vision 'Acts 29'*. Seoul: Durano.
Onnnri Community Church. 2019. Accessed April 5, 2019. http://www.onnuri.org/about-onnuri/church-introduction/onnuris-history/.

Eunhee Zoe Wang

Hagin, Kenneth

Kenneth Hagin (1917–2003) was perhaps the best known leader and teacher in the "Word of faith" or "positive confession" movement, which is closely associated throughout the world with the so-called prosperity gospel or prosperity theology. The prosperity emphasis in global Pentecostalism today has much to do with Hagin's nearly seventy-year-long preaching and teaching ministry. American religious historian Kate Bowler (2013) states that Hagin, while not alone in his views, was the most powerful theological influence of the prosperity gospel.

Hagin was primarily known as a teacher and author rather than as a healing evangelist, and his ministry reports that some 65 million copies of his books have been disseminated. In 1974 Hagin founded the Rhema Bible Training Center (RBTC) in Broken Arrow, a suburb of Tulsa, Oklahoma, USA. As of 2019, RBTC has more than 80,000 alumni, some of whom have established Word of Faith churches and/or parachurch evangelistic ministries. Rhema campuses exist today in 46 countries outside the US, including: Albania, Angola, Argentina, Australia, Austria, Bolivia, Brazil, Canada, Chile, China, Colombia, Costa Rica, Cuba, Egypt, Fiji, France, Germany, Ghana, Greece, Guatemala, Haiti, India, Indonesia, Ireland, Italy, Japan, Kenya, Mexico, Myanmar, Netherlands, Nicaragua, Nigeria, Norway, Papua New Guinea, Peru, Philippines, Portugal, Singapore, Samoa, Spain, Switzerland, Thailand, Ukraine, United Kingdom, Vanuatu, and Zambia. Still known among his followers as "Papa Hagin" or "Brother Hagin," he continues to influence the Pentecostal world.

By his own account, Hagin was born prematurely in 1917, with a deformed heart. Though not expected to survive, he managed to function for some 15 years before becoming a bed-ridden invalid. He was converted to faith in Christ on April 22, 1933, after having had three experiences of the horrors of hell, when, during a ten-minute period, his vital signs failed three times in a row. While en route to the hospital, his mind was fixed on a biblical text that soon became the center and leitmotiv of his teaching: "What things soever ye desire, when ye pray, believe that ye receive them, and ye shall have them" (Mark 11:24, Authorized Version). After Hagin repeatedly spoke God's word aloud over himself, he found that both his heart and an incurable blood disease were completely healed within eight months.

Hagin received no formal theological training, but he began to preach in 1934 in a small country church in Texas, attended primarily by Southern Baptists. By 1937 Hagin had undergone a Pentecostal baptism in the Holy Spirit. Joining himself to the Assemblies of God (USA), he pastored six churches in succession between 1937 and 1949 – all of them located in Texas. From 1949 to 1963 he was an itinerant Bible teacher and evangelist, and reportedly had eight visionary encounters with Jesus Christ. In the third vision, Hagin claims to have been granted a gift of discernment of spirits, enabling him to pray more effectively for the healing of the sick. He also reported that Jesus gave him a four-step guide to physical, spiritual, and financial health and prosperity: 1. Say it; 2. Do it; 3. Receive it; and 4. Tell it.

Hagin set up an office in his Garland, Texas home in 1963, and began distributing his audio tapes and books. Three years later he moved to Tulsa, Oklahoma. In 1979 he established a Prayer and Healing Center as a place where sick persons could come to build their faith and to receive healing. Hagin consistently taught and preached that God will bless his people in every area of their lives, if they will put full confidence in him and his promises. Hagin's protégés include Kenneth Hagin, Jr., Kenneth Copeland, Jerry Savelle, Fred Price, and Charles Capps. Also worth noting is Ulf Ekman, a RBTC graduate, and founder of *Livets Ord* ("Word of Life") – one of Europe's largest charismatic churches, located in Uppsala, Sweden. Eklund later left the church he founded to join the Roman Catholic charismatic renewal movement.

From the 1980s onward, Hagin's "health and wealth" message suffered relentless attacks from various detractors, including Hank Hanegraaff, John MacArthur, Jr., Gordon Fee, and Daniel McConnell. They pointed to obvious instances where Hagin in his books had plagiarized the writings of evangelist E.W. Kenyon (1867–1948), despite Hagin's claim that his ideas came to him directly from God. Critics have questioned Hagin for teaching that believers become "little gods," and that Jesus after his death and prior to his resurrection suffered the torments of hell within the realm of the dead. One key objection has been that – in borrowing ideas from Kenyon – Hagin taught not Christian "faith cure" but an esoteric "mind cure" doctrine of the kind associated with Mary Baker Eddy, founder of Christian Science. Geir Lie's book questioned whether Kenyon was in fact a "mind cure" or "new thought" author, and so whether Hagin erred in being influenced by Kenyon. Even the Vatican has weighed in on prosperity theology. In 2018 Pope Francis's close associate, and editor of *La Civiltà Cattolica*, Antonio Spadaro editorialized that this message is "dangerous and different" from the church's authentic teaching. Yet, in light of the global network of Rhema schools, and the availability of online teachings, Hagin may have more followers today than ever before.

Bibliography

Atkinson, William P. 2009. *The 'Spiritual Death' of Jesus: A Pentecostal Investigation*. Leiden: Brill.

Attanasi, Katherine, and Amos Yong, eds. 2012. *Pentecostalism and Prosperity: The Socio-Economics of the Global Charismatic Movement*. New York: Palgrave Macmillan.

Bowler, Kate. 2013. *Blessed: A History of the American Prosperity Gospel*. New York: Oxford University Press.

Chappell, Paul G. 1989. "Kenneth Hagin, Sr." In *Twentieth-Century Shapers of American Popular Religion*, edited by Charles H. Lippy, 186–193. New York: Greenwood Press.

Neuman, H. Terris. 1990. "Cultic Origins of Word-Faith Theology Within the Charismatic Movement." *Pneuma* 12 (1): 32–55.

Spadaro, Antonio, S.J. 2018. "The Prosperity Gospel: Dangerous and Different." *La Civiltà Cattolica*, 18 July. www.laciviltacatttolica.com.

Michael McClymond

Harper, Michael and Jeanne

Michael Claude and Jeanne Harper (1931–2010; ?–2017) were pioneers of the British Charismatic Renewal from the 1960s. Michael Claude was born to a business family and his father expected him to take over his business, but he decided to study law and theology at Emmanuel College in Cambridge. He was converted to Christianity during his first year of undergraduate study. He prepared for ordination at Ridley Hall, Cambridge and became a curate at St Barnabas' Church in Clapham Common, South London from 1955 to 1958. He then ministered at All Souls in Langham Place, London in 1958, which was the focal point of Anglican evangelicalism under its rector, John Stott. Michael was the chaplain for the shops in Oxford Street.

In September 1962, Claude spoke on the Epistle to the Ephesians at a weekend conference in Surrey. As he prepared his talk, he was "filled with all the fullness of the God" (Eph 3:19). He could not sleep and was filled with deep spiritual experiences for two weeks. He considered this being his Spirit baptism and in the following year, he also spoke in tongues. Jeanne also had a similar experience. This created tension between him and Stott, who would not allow Claude to preach about it. Eventually, Claude left All Souls in 1964 and became the General Secretary of the Fountain Trust (FT), an organization aiming to spread the Charismatic Renewal to different denominations, including the Roman Catholic Church. This ideal for the renewal actualized an alternative ecumenism grounded in lay people, a common experience of the Holy Spirit and affection.

Claude organized international ecumenical Charismatic conferences through the FT, especially the three conferences at Guildford (1971), Nottingham (1973) and Westminster (1975), which explored subjects related to the renewal, including Spirit baptism, charisms, worship, social concerns, and evangelism. In the evenings, Christians of all denominations worshipped together when healing, prophecy, and speaking in tongues happened. As a pianist and a graduate of the Royal Academy of Music, Jeanne Harper played a vital role in bringing the renewal alive through her musical talent, directing the worship in these conferences and meetings of the FT. She composed a song book with Betty Pulkingham in 1974, *Sound of Living Waters: A Charismatic Hymnal.* These conferences kindled the Charismatic Renewal in Sweden, Norway, Australia, New Zealand, and South Africa where local Charismatics established a Trust or held conferences in their own countries. Harper was invited to speak in the Charismatic events in most of these countries. Claude developed the Trust as a facilitator of the Charismatic Renewal in the UK and worldwide, reaching across cultures and denominations. Moreover, the Harpers' openness to the Roman Catholic Church led them to build up cordial relationship with officials like Cardinal Léon Joseph Suenens and Fr. Kilian McDonnell. Michael's talent in writing helped spread the renewal. He was the editor of *Renewal,* the Trust's magazine, and the author of 18 books. He resigned as director and editor in 1976 and was succeeded by Tom Smail. The Harpers settled in Hounslow, West London until 1981, then in Hayward Heath, Sussex.

Besides the FT, Harper founded the European Charismatic Consultation (ECC) with Larry Christenson in 1973 to connect leaders in European countries. In 1978, he convened a pre-Lambeth Charismatic Renewal conference in Canterbury. In 1981, he founded the Sharing of Ministries Abroad (SOMA) to bring the Charismatic Renewal overseas, an Anglican international organization connecting the western older churches with the younger ones in the non-western world with a particular focus on the Charismatic Renewal. It organized conferences, short-term missions, and international networking for Anglican ministers and laypeople to release indigenous gifts.

Another organization that Michael Claude founded was the International Charismatic Consultation on World Evangelism (ICCOWE). Its vision grew out of sharing between Claude, Fr. Tom Forrest (director of International Catholic

Charismatic Renewal Office), and Larry Christenson in Kenya in 1983. They discussed how Forrest's vision of "Decade of Evangelism" in the 1990s could be realized. These three gradually involved other Pentecostal and Charismatic leaders in the council and held a consultation in Singapore in 1987. As more and more leaders affirmed the vision of evangelization in the Charismatic Renewal, the ICCOWE held a much larger international conference in Brighton in 1991, gathering 3,100 delegates from 115 countries and 12 languages were used. Its theological articles were published in *All Together in One Place* (Sheffield, 1993). Subsequently, ICCOWE and ECC jointly held conferences in Prague in 1997 and 1999.

Michael Claude was Canon of Chichester Cathedral in 1984–1995. However, due to the issue of women's ordination and his desire to belong to a church that strongly honored the sacraments, the Scriptures and "Holy tradition" beginning with the Fathers, he and Jeanne left the Church of England that they had served for almost four decades and joined the Antiochian Greek Orthodox Church in 1995. In the final fifteen years of his life, he served as the Dean of the Antiochian Orthodox Deanery. He also developed the Orthodox Christian Studies' course, "The Way", and was founding priest of the English-speaking Orthodox parish in London, St Botolph's. After his death in 2010, Jeanne recorded his legacy by setting up Father Michael Harper Foundation and writing the biography, *Visited by God.* She passed away in 2017.

Bibliography

Au, Connie. 2011. *Grassroots Unity in the Charismatic Renewal.* Eugene: Wipf & Stock.

Harper, Jeanne. 2013. *Visited by God: The Story of Michael Harper's 48 Year-Long Ministry Told by Jeanne Harper.* Cambridge: Aquila Books.

Hocken, Peter. 1997. *Streams of Renewal: The Origins and Early Development of the Charismatic Movement in Great Britain.* Carlisle: Paternoster.

Connie Au

Harris, Leo Cecil

Leo Cecil Harris (1920–1977) was the founder of the CRC Churches International in Australia. He was the son of Cecil Harris, an Apostolic pastor who had been converted in Perth, Western Australia, under the ministry of flamboyant South African evangelist Frederick Van Eyk. As an eight-year-old, Leo Harris turned to the Lord through the preaching of Charles Greenwood. Immediately he became a fervent evangelist, writing out biblical texts with colored pencils and pasting them on local lamp posts.

In 1935, at the age of 15, Harris was baptized in water and the following year baptized in the Holy Spirit. He preached his first sermon at 19 and was soon shepherding a small Pentecostal congregation in Ipswich, Queensland. After three short pastorates, Leo joined his family in the Assemblies of God (AG). In 1941, in Ballarat, Victoria, he was convinced by Thomas Foster to accept British Israelism, which necessitated his leaving the AG. He launched a small magazine entitled *Echoes of Grace.*

In 1944, Harris visited New Zealand where in cooperation with a handful of independent churches, he launched a mission for revival in the nation which he called the National Revival Crusade.

Inspired by a strong prophecy and his own sense of call, he returned to Australia, where for several weeks, in Adelaide, South Australia, at the invitation of the British Israel World Federation, he conducted successful teaching rallies, out of which he established a new congregation. On November 2, 1945, he launched the National Revival Crusade in Australia. Over the next three years more than 100 people were baptized in the Holy Spirit. In 1948, he married Belle Davey of Ballarat, Victoria, whose support thereafter was devoted and unwavering.

Meanwhile, Foster was establishing the new movement in Melbourne while Cecil Harris and Leo's brother Alan, were active in Brisbane. The emphasis was on "the full kingdom gospel" which meant revival through the Pentecostal focus of the power of the Holy Spirit combined with the "Israel identity" and the need for national repentance and renewal. Additional congregations were raised up.

Originally, the Crusade was a fellowship of local churches whose "only constitution" was the word of God. By 1958, however, a national constitution was adopted by the majority. For three reasons, some Victorian assemblies dissented. First, they intended to maintain their independence. Second, it was because they had begun to teach the necessity of tongues not only for Spirit baptism but also for salvation, which Harris and the CRC churches absolutely rejected. Third, it was because Harris was also beginning to practise what they regarded as an excessive form of exorcism, an approach which he seriously modified in later years, partly as the result of input from several tertiary-educated young men who joined the movement.

In 1959 a part-time Bible School was established and a Papua New Guinea (PNG) missions program was initiated in co-operation with the International Church of the Foursquare Gospel. Church planting in Australia continued with 11 new assemblies being established in 1962.

In 1963, the name of the movement was changed to Christian Revival Crusade (CRC). Harris continued to exercise apostolic authority and leadership through his preaching, through his input to the growing number of pastors and his writings. By the 1970s, the Adelaide assembly, now approaching 1,000 congregants, was the largest Pentecostal church in Australia.

Towards the end of his life, Harris dropped British Israelism and it ceased to be a CRC tenet. Harris made important contributions to Australian Pentecostal theology in four areas. (1) He stressed the importance of the local church. He strongly resisted attempts to centralize denominational organization, although there is evidence that before his death he regretted that the fellowship ties within the CRC were not more strongly defined in its constitutional basis. (2) He taught the authority of Christ over sin, disease, and demonic power and the resultant authority of the believer. He stressed a message of grace, freedom, and spiritual victory in Christ. (3) He stressed the power of the Word of God to inspire faith. He regularly preached on divine healing and prayed for the sick. (4) He developed a ministry of deliverance from the power of Satan.

Harris died suddenly from a heart attack on September 24, 1977. His funeral service was one of the largest even seen in Adelaide with more than two thousand attendees and a procession over three kilometers in length.

By the time of his death, there were 65 CRC churches in Australia, eight in New Zealand and one in Papua New Guinea (PNG). 41 years later (2018), there were 119 in Australia, more than 350 in PNG, and many others in the South Pacific. There were 15,000 members in Australian churches.

Harris was generally conservative in methodology and distanced himself from emotionalism, extremism, and disorderly worship practices. He loved to relax on the tennis court. He dressed immaculately and acted with courtesy, dignity and grace. By the end of his life he was widely esteemed for his integrity, maturity, and apostolic status as a Christian leader.

Bibliography

Chant, Barry. 2015. *This Is Revival*. Miranda, NSW: Tabor.

Chant, Barry. 2011. *The Spirit of Pentecost: The Origins and Development of the Pentecostal Movement in Australia, 1870–1939*. Lexington, KY: Emeth Press.

Chant, Barry. 1997. *Heart of Fire*. Unley Park, SA: Tabor.

Cooper, Dudley. 1995. *Flames of Revival*. Endeavour Hills: CRC.

Turner, L., H. Adam, and N. Bettcher, eds. 2006. *Legacy: Timeless Truths for a New Generation: A Compendium of Works by Leo Harris*. Seaton, SA: CRC Churches Int.

Barry Chant

Hawtin, George

George Robert Hawtin (1909–1994) was a Pentecostal Assemblies of Canada minister who along with Percy Hunt and Herrick Holt was instrumental in launching the Latter Rain Revival in North Battleford Saskatchewan, Canada in 1948. Hawtin was born in Souris, Manitoba on February 27 to Eliza Harriet Roberts (1868–1957) and James William Hawtin (1875–1942). George was the fifth of six siblings: Hilda

George Hawtin and his family. Source: Pentecostal Assemblies of Canada Archives

Mae (1899–1985), James William (1900–1983), Lillian Edith (1901–2001), Philip Henry (1904–1984), and Ernest Harold (1911–2006). Philip and Ernest were also in ministry. The Hawtin family moved to Star City, Saskatchewan while he was young. George appears to have experienced the baptism of the Spirit with tongues at seventeen (Watt 2002). George attended Three Hills Bible Institute, Alberta for two years of training and he was ordained with The Pentecostal Assemblies of Canada in 1932. On October 4, 1933 George married Rhoda Isabel Mallory (1910–2007) of Macklin, Saskatchewan ("Wedding Bells" 1933).

In 1935, Hawtin pioneered the launch of Bethel Bible Institute in Star City, Saskatchewan with only eight students.

Two years later, he moved the Institute to Saskatoon with classes convening at Elim Tabernacle and in 1939 he purchased property on Avenue A North with the purchase of additional buildings in 1942 (Riss 1987). District officials asked Hawtin to resign in April 1947, but he requested that his resignation take place July 16 at the District Conference at the camp meeting in Watrous (Merryweather 1998). Hunt resigned a month later in protest. The PAOC took over the property. Hawtin was paid $3,800 and Hunt $2,200 over a ten-year period. They also took $1,500 that they claimed belonged to Global Missions, an organization they started (Riss 1987). Hawtin appears to have acted in a unilateral way in the operation of the school, without consultation or permission from district officials, which created conflict. Doctrinal differences did not appear to be the initial reason for the conflict (Merryweather 1998).

In the fall of 1947, Herrick Holt, a Foursquare pastor in North Battleford who operated an independent orphanage and wanted to start a vocational training school, asked Hunt to join him. Holt agreed if Hawtin could also be involved. The new school opened on October 21, 1947 with seventy students from Bethel Bible Institute transferring to Sharon. George's brother-in-law Milford Kirkpatrick and brother Ernest (Ern) Hawtin joined the ministry as well, with Kirkpatrick acting as secretary for Global Missions. In November George and others from Sharon travelled to Vancouver, B.C. to attend William Branham's healing campaign. Branham would cast out demons before performing a miraculous healing and would use the imposition or laying on of hands, innovations that were adopted by the Sharon brethren, but which proved controversial for older Pentecostals who practiced tarrying or waiting on the Spirit. On February 11, 1948 a prophecy was given that they were on the verge of revival, but they must open the door and enter in (Faupel 2010; Riss 1987). The revival broke out soon after and spread throughout Pentecostal circles in Saskatchewan, Western Canada, and the U.S. The Feast of Pentecost camp meeting from March 30 to April 4 and the Sharon camp meeting from July 7 to 18 were important events in the revival's development. At the latter meeting, James Watt mentioned while teaching that the third of Israel's great feasts, the Feast of Tabernacles, had not yet been fulfilled. George Warnock was present at the meeting and in 1951 published *The Feast of Tabernacles*, which became a major publication for the revival (Riss 1987). Invitations started arriving for Hawtin to preach throughout Canada and elsewhere.

George Hawtin and the Sharon group articulated doctrinal innovations that proved to be controversial for denominational Pentecostals. The restoration of the gifts of the Spirit and the fivefold ministry, especially apostles and prophets, the "manifested sons of God" or "overcomers" who would rise up in preparation for the end times and experience immortality, and the "restoration of all things" or "ultimate reconciliation" to their pre-fallen state in which the overcomers would reign with Christ proved to be too controversial (Faupel 2010). The last one was Hawtin's undoing with the Sharon group. It appears that Hawtin travelled to Europe to preach the new revival, but when he returned, he began proclaiming "ultimate reconciliation," which was too extreme. The leaders voted him out of the organization in 1957 (Watt 2002).

What happened to George Hawtin after leaving Sharon is not clear. According to James Watt (2002), Hawtin took the second rejection badly. George focused on his writing after the revival. Ern distanced himself from the Latter Rain and pastored Christian Assembly Church in Oakland, California (Kiteley 2019). The legacy of Hawtin and the Latter Rain Revival appears to reside in the charismatic movement, which adopted much of its theology and practices (Riss 1987).

Bibliography

Faupel, D. William. 2010. "The New Order of the Latter Rain: Restoration or Renewal?" In *Winds from the North: Canadian Contributions to the Pentecostal Movement*, edited by Michael Wilkinson and Peter Althouse, 239–263. Leiden: Brill.

Kiteley, David. 2019. Telephone Interview by Peter Althouse, August 6.

Merryweather, Frank. 1998. "Setting the Record Straight: A Reconstruction of the Rift that Developed between the PAOC and George R. Hawtin and his Supporters." Interview by Jim Craig. Pentecostal Assemblies of Canada Archives.

Riss, Richard M. 1987. *Latter Rain: The Latter Rain Movement of 1948 and the Mid-Twentieth Century Evangelical Awakening*. Etobicoke, ON: Honeycomb Visual Productions Ltd.

Watt, James. 2002. Interview by Jim Craig. Pentecostal Assemblies of Canada Archives, May 9.

"Wedding Bells." 1993. *The Pentecostal Testimony* (December): 7.

Wilkinson, Michael, and Linda M. Ambrose. 2020. *After the Revival: Pentecostalism and the Making of a Canadian Church*. Montreal & Kingston: McGill-Queen's University Press.

Peter Althouse

Haywood, G.T.

Early African-American Pentecostal theologian, author, leader and pastor. Garfield Thomas Haywood (1880–1931) was one of nine children born to Ben Haywood and Penny Ann Uzzle, July 15, 1880 in Greencastle, Indiana, to parents who had themselves been born into slavery. The family had moved from North Carolina in 1879, to the rural area around Greencastle, before relocating closer to Indianapolis when Garfield was just three years old. G.T. Haywood attended Shortridge High School, leaving in 1896 when he was sixteen, to help support his family. The family attended the St. Paul Baptist Church in Haughville about this time. G.T. Haywood and Ida Howard were married February 11, 1902 and their only child, Fannie Ann was born in 1903.

The same year he was married, Haywood went to work for *The Freeman*, a well-known African-American newspaper in Indianapolis, eventually becoming an accomplished illustrator and writer. His work at *The Freeman* gave Haywood considerable exposure to a wide variety of issues and current events both local and national. He drew cartoons that addressed the political and race issues that were of most importance to African-Americans. Haywood continued his work with *The Freeman* until at least sometime in 1909. He also did some work for a weekly paper called *The Recorder*. His work, and his talent as an artist, brought him into contact with some notable African-American figures, among whom was the world-renowned artist William Edouard Scott with whom Haywood developed a close friendship.

Haywood and his wife both received the baptism of the Holy Spirit in a downtown

G.T. Haywood and his wife Ida

Indianapolis mission in early 1908, within the first two years of the Azusa Street Revival in Los Angeles. They were then attending the small and recently established African-American Mission in Indianapolis pastored by Henry Prentiss. Haywood's quick grasp of the essentials of the new Pentecostal religion can be seen in that within four months of his conversion he became pastor of the church which became known as Christ Temple. In 1911, Haywood joined the Los Angeles based Pentecostal Assemblies of the World (PAW), one of the Pentecostal organizations in the earliest Azusa era. His views in accordance with the "Finished Work" theology of William Durham, and his later acceptance of the Oneness message probably influenced the PAW in embracing both of these doctrinal positions. A strong proponent of interracial church, Haywood was presiding bishop of the PAW from 1925 until his death in 1931.

Haywood was introduced to the idea of Jesus' name baptism by the Persian evangelist Andrew Urshan, in 1910 and was, in Urshan's words, "rather friendly about it."

However, it was not until March 1915 that Haywood was baptized in Jesus' name by Glen Cook at Oak Hill Tabernacle in Indianapolis. Several of his church leaders joined him in baptism that day and the remainder of Haywood's congregation of about 400 were baptized on April 4, which was Easter Sunday. Haywood spoke on behalf of the "New Issue" (baptism in Jesus' name and the Oneness of God) at the General Council of the Assemblies of God in 1915 and attended the historic meeting in 1916 which saw the fledgling organization split over this issue. Although Haywood was never a member of the Assemblies of God, he was respected among them. It is an indication, then, of the extreme feelings at this meeting over the New Issue, and of the importance of Haywood's involvement, that he was singled out for derision when one of the members, T.K. Leonard, referred to the Oneness doctrine as "hay, wood and stubble," (a re-ordering of 1 Cor. 3:12). Leonard also accused the Oneness believers of being "in the wilderness and they have a voice in the wilderness," an obvious reference to Haywood's periodical entitled *Voice in the Wilderness*.

G.T. Haywood is remembered as having "the most wide-ranging theological vision" of "any first-generation Pentecostal leader from either the Trinitarian or Oneness wings of the movement." He was a prolific writer, producing several books and many songs. His success as a pastor and preacher was witnessed by the steady growth of Christ Temple to a congregation of well over a thousand. Following a three-month visit to Jamaica, Haywood died of heart disease on April 12, 1931 at home in Indianapolis. Over 10,000 people came to pay their respects at his funeral. The city of Indianapolis renamed the street where

Christ Temple is located as Bishop Garfield T. Haywood Memorial Way.

Bibliography

French, Talmadge L. 2014. *Early Interracial Oneness Pentecostalism: G.T. Haywood and the Pentecostal Assemblies of the World 1901–1931*. Eugene, OR: Pickwick.

Jacobsen, Douglas. 2003. *Thinking in the Spirit: Theologies of the Early Pentecostal Movement*. Bloomington, IN: Indiana University Press.

King, Johnny L. 2020. "Spirit and Schism: A History of Oneness Pentecostalism in the Philippines." PhD thesis, University of Birmingham, UK.

Johnny King

Healing

Healing is a major theme in, and explanation for, the global expansion of Pentecostal and Charismatic Christianity (or "Pentecostalism") over the course of the twentieth century. During the famed Azusa Street Revival of 1906 that, in conjunction with similar revivals scattered across the world, spread Pentecostalism globally, claims of divine healing through prayer drew outsiders and inspired missionary zeal. Despite the emphasis that many observers of Pentecostalism give to glossolalia and financial prosperity, the Pew Research Center's 2006 ten-country survey identified divine healing as the central defining factor in setting apart Pentecostals as a distinct segment of Christianity. Indeed, the primary means by which Pentecostals, historically and today, have recruited and retained converts worldwide is their distinctive emphasis on expectant prayer for divine healing, coupled with widespread perception that such prayers are more effective than other available spiritual or medical approaches to healing.

When Pentecostals pray for divine healing, they often seek both physical cures and a more holistic sense of mental and spiritual wellbeing. Divine healings may not be instantaneous or evoke public wonder, and thus be classed as "miracles" (another of the nine gifts of the Holy Spirit enumerated in 1 Corinthians 12), but in order to denote a healing as "divine," Pentecostals generally require that it occur unusually rapidly or in circumstances in which recovery is unexpected through merely medical means or natural healing processes. For many Pentecostals, healing is not subsidiary to the gospel of salvation, but an important component of "full" salvation – which encompasses forgiveness from sin, deliverance from demonic oppression, and baptism with the Holy Spirit. Divine healing constitutes an aspect of God's ultimate redemptive purposes and demonstrates that the Kingdom of Heaven has come near (Matthew 10:7). Pentecostals here diverge from Christians who affirm that God often afflicts human bodies in order to sanctify their souls; in the theology of many Pentecostals, it is the devil who sends disease, whereas God's will for healing can be assumed.

Pentecostals cite a variety of passages in the Old and New Testaments to justify their expectation of divine healing. For many Pentecostals, the foundational text is Isaiah 53:5, commonly accepted by Christians as prophesying Jesus's atoning death. Pentecostals often emphasize that Isaiah uses similar language in describing the Messiah as having taken upon himself and carried away both sins and sicknesses. Thus, it is "by his wounds we are healed,"

Sick prayed for at Hicks Crusade Argentina 1954. Source: Pentecostal Assemblies of Canada Archives

an interpretation apparently confirmed by Matthew 8:16–17's explanation that Jesus cast out demons and healed the sick "to fulfill what was spoken through Isaiah the prophet: 'He himself took up our infirmities and carried away our diseases.'" One of the most frequently referenced New Testament verses is James 5:14–15, which instructs the sick to call upon elders of the church "to pray over them and anoint them with oil in the name of the Lord," promising that "the prayer offered in faith will make the sick person well." Pentecostals further emphasize that James 5 is addressed to the church – and that no subsequent biblical teaching indicates that gifts of healings have ceased or that Christians should cease to pray expectantly for healing. Despite biblical references, such as James 5, to "faith" being connected with healing, many Pentecostals object to the popularly used term "faith healing" as placing too much emphasis on human faith, as opposed to other factors important to healing, such as God's love and power or the anointing of the Holy Spirit. Pentecostals may also prefer the term "deliverance" to "exorcism" as a means of signaling the primary goal of liberating individuals from oppression as opposed to engaging in dramatic contests with demons.

In praying for divine healing, Pentecostals often ask God the Father to heal in the name of Jesus by the power of the Holy Spirit. They may also envision themselves as speaking and acting with the authority that Jesus delegated to his followers; consequently, prayers of command speak directly to diseases and demons, commanding them to leave in Jesus's name and authority, as well as commanding human bodies to be healed as they come in line with God's original design in creation and coming Kingdom order. Pentecostals often accompany their prayers with related

Healing "laying on of hands" ceremony in the Pentecostal Church of God. Lejunior, Harlan County, Kentucky, 09/15/1946. Item from Record Group 245: Records of the Solid Fuels Administration for War, 1937–1948. Photographer: Russell Lee.

practices – for each of which they claim biblical precedent – such as laying on of hands, confession of sins, anointing with oil, and distribution of anointed prayer cloths.

Pentecostals envision themselves as restoring healing and deliverance practices commonly exercised during the first several hundred years of church history, but that gradually eroded for a variety of historical reasons. For many Christians in Europe and North America, the legacy of the Protestant Reformation, Enlightenment, and scientific (including medical) discoveries diminished confidence that biblical miracles are relevant to the modern world. Some of these Christians have questioned the facticity of the Bible's miracle stories; many others accept the Bible's miracle claims, but argue that gifts of the Holy Spirit ceased (thus adopting a "cessationist" position) because they became unnecessary once people had the Bible to meet spiritual needs for salvation from sin – and modern medicine to address physical needs for healing from disease. Early twentieth-century Pentecostals in the global North embraced modern-day divine healing as what seemed to them a new discovery – sometimes rejecting medical means as apparently contrary to faith. Charismatics who emerged from mainline Protestant and Catholic churches in the 1960s–1970s self-consciously combined renewed emphasis on spiritual gifts with avoidance of seeming Pentecostal fanaticism, a stance that contributed to viewing spiritual and medical healing as complementary. Twenty-first-century Pentecostals in the global North who avow belief in divine healing nevertheless often seek medical attention as a first resort, turning to prayer as a supplement, or as a last resort when medical treatments prove inadequate.

Most Christians in the global South, including Latin America, Africa, and Asia, are "continuationists" who affirm that gifts of the Holy Spirit such as healings and miracles have continually been available from Bible times to the present – and they regularly report personal experiences of healing through prayer. Like their Northern co-religionists, Southern Christians frequently combine prayer with whatever traditional or modern medical resources are available and affordable, but these Christians typically rely more heavily on prayer – reflecting both more limited material resources and greater confidence in the relevance of biblical promises to their world. Southern Christians read the Bible as a textbook for daily life, so because the Bible teaches the power of intercessory prayer, Christians of nearly every denomination (Pentecostal or not) pray for healing. Opportunities to test the power of prayer abound because so many people in the two-thirds world live in crowded, unsanitary urban spaces and struggle daily to survive poverty and poverty-related sicknesses.

By contrast to the Enlightenment-oriented worldview that predominates in the global North, in the global South Christianity thrives in a world that many people perceive as populated by spiritual forces and agents actively at work for good or for evil. The question for many is not whether the supernatural exists or is relevant to life in the material world, but which source of supernatural aid is most powerful. Divine healing and deliverance are often viewed as two sides of the same coin. Christians envision a cosmic battle between the Kingdom of God and the kingdom of darkness and engage in spiritual warfare against sicknesses and evil spirits believed to cause physical infirmities and mental and spiritual torment.

As globalizing processes have accelerated, both the actual threat and the fear of disease have also increased, thereby fueling the growth of religious movements such as Pentecostalism for which healing is a central concern. Modernization has spread its benefits unevenly, sometimes causing more problems than it resolves. Contrary to the prognostications of secularization theorists, modern and postmodern peoples have continued to pray for healing even when they can readily access the most sophisticated medical resources. Pentecostals often appropriate technology to facilitate rather than replace divine healing practices: for instance, praying for healing over televisions, cell phones, or the internet. In the multidirectional flows of contemporary globalisation and migration, it is likely that healing may play an even more prominent role in twenty-first-century Christianity than ever before. People everywhere will likely continue to seek resources of practical daily help in confronting the unprecedented challenges of their rapidly changing world.

Bibliography

Alexander, Kimberly Ervin. 2006. *Pentecostal Healing: Models in Theology and Practice.* Leiden: Brill.

Brown, Candy Gunther. 2012. *Testing Prayer: Science and Healing.* Cambridge, MA: Harvard University Press.

Brown, Candy Gunther, ed. 2011. *Global Pentecostal and Charismatic Healing.* New York: Oxford University Press.

Espinosa, Gastón. 2014. *William J. Seymour and the Origins of Global Pentecostalism: A Biography and Documentary History.* Chapel Hill, NC: Duke University Press.

MacNutt, Francis. 2005. *The Healing Reawakening: Reclaiming Our Lost Inheritance.* Grand Rapids: Chosen.

Candy Gunther Brown

Hebden, Ellen

Ellen Wharton was born on January 15, 1865, in Gayton, Northamptonshire, England. She underwent an emotive conversion and sanctification experience at the age of fifteen, which contributed to her decision to move to London, England, to work under the tutelage of the renowned faith healer, Elizabeth Baxter, as well as her desire to establish a healing mission of her own.

After apprenticing with Baxter, Ellen met James Hebden – four years her senior, and, like Ellen, an aspiring missionary – who was raising his two children alone after the death of his first wife. Ellen and James were married on July 24, 1893, had four children together, and spent the next ten years living in Swinton, South Yorkshire, England. In 1903, after a hurricane had devastated the Caribbean island of Jamaica, Ellen, James, and their four youngest children, boarded a ship for Kingston, Jamaica, where they established a mission, however, it was short-lived, and in December 1904, the family relocated to Toronto, Canada, with the hope of beginning a more permanent ministry.

Once in Toronto, it took the Hebdens almost a year and a half to secure a former three-story bakery and tenement building at 651 Queen Street East where they established the East End Mission on May 20, 1906. On the evening of Saturday November 17, 1906, after claiming to have been prompted by God to get out of bed and pray for improved power to heal the sick, Ellen writes that she underwent a baptism of the Holy Spirit accompanied by speaking in tongues. Ellen then returned to bed, and when she awoke the next morning, explained to her husband what had happened to her the night before. Given that it was a Sunday, she also recounted her experience to those gathered at the mission's morning, afternoon,

East End Mission Toronto. Source: Pentecostal Assemblies of Canada Archives

and evening services. At these meetings, she again claimed to have exhibited supernatural manifestations. Within a month, James similarly claimed to have received the baptism of the Holy Spirit accompanied by speaking in tongues, and within five months, Ellen writes that between 70 and 80 others claimed to have shared the same experience. In time, Ellen would claim that God enabled her to both speak and write 22 different languages.

News of what had happened at the East End Mission quickly spread across Canada and the United States, prompting those seeking similar religious experiences to visit the mission. In time, early Pentecostal leaders such as Daniel Awrey, Frank Bartleman, William H. Durham, and Aimee Semple McPherson also visited the mission. In the wake of this new religious experience, the Hebdens transformed their mission from the healing home ministry paradigm learned from Baxter to a newly emerging Pentecostal ministry paradigm. In the new Pentecostal model, emphasis was not only placed on receiving the baptism of the Holy Spirit in a type of episodic, crisis event, but divine healing was also believed to be received instantaneously, rather than through a gradual processes of prayer and spiritual direction. No longer requiring a place for the sick to seek healing over an extended period of time, the Hebdens converted space in the mission to an "upper room," modelled after the experiences of the Apostles described in the Book of Acts, where visitors could seek the baptism of the Holy Spirit for the purpose of receiving divine empowerment for evangelism.

The Hebdens were responsible for many firsts within Canadian Pentecostalism. Ellen's experience in November 1906 makes her the first historically confirmed individual to have received the baptism of the Holy Spirit accompanied by speaking in tongues in Canada. Furthermore, the Hebdens not only began the first Pentecostal mission in Canada, but also founded the first Canadian Pentecostal periodical, held the first Canadian Pentecostal camp meeting, organized the first Canadian Pentecostal convention, sent the first Canadian Pentecostal missionary, Charles Chawner, to a foreign field, and were instrumental in establishing the first Pentecostal mission to Indigenous peoples in Canada. The most important contribution that the Hebdens made, however, was likely their role in training local evangelists in Ontario, Canada. One of these evangelists, Robert Semple, for instance, converted, and later married, Aimee Kennedy, who, as Aimee Semple McPherson, became the founder of the International Church of the Foursquare Gospel and one of the most important Pentecostal evangelists of the twentieth-century.

Despite these many achievements, the Hebdens experienced a number of challenges that contributed to their marginalization within the Canadian Pentecostal movement. First, the Hebdens strongly opposed the idea of consolidating the emerging network of Canadian Pentecostal missions into a formal religious organization, which served to alienate the Hebdens from many other early leaders who saw value in establishing a formal organizational structure. Second, the Hebdens left the country in the midst of a fundraising campaign for a new building during which time, they subsequently alleged, a group of dissenting members embezzled funds from the mission. Finally, there is evidence to suggest that the Hebdens were excluded from emerging patriarchal Canadian Pentecostal networks due to the fact Ellen, a woman, was the principal leader of the East End Mission. The Hebdens did eventually manage to build a new church in 1913 at 115 Broadway Avenue, Toronto, Ontario, where they ministered together until James's death in 1919. Ellen subsequently retired in 1921 and died just two years later in 1923 after a protracted illness.

Bibliography

Miller, Thomas William. 1986. "The Canadian 'Azusa': The Hebden Mission in Toronto." *Pneuma* 8 (1): 5–29.

Sloos, William. 2010. "The Story of James and Ellen Hebden: The First Family of Pentecost in Canada." *Pneuma* 32 (2): 181–202.

Stewart, Adam. 2014. "From Monogenesis to Polygenesis in Pentecostal Origins: A Survey of the Evidence from the Azusa Street, Hebden, and Mukti Missions." *PentecoStudies* 13 (2): 151–172.

Stewart, Adam. 2010. "A Canadian Azusa? The Implications of the Hebden Mission for Pentecostal Historiography." In *Winds from the North: Canadian Contributions to the Pentecostal Movement*, edited by Michael Wilkinson and Peter Althouse, 17–37. Leiden: Brill.

Wilkinson, Michael. 2010. "Charles Chawner and the Missionary Impulse of the Hebden Mission." In *Winds from the North: Canadian Contributions to the Pentecostal Movement*, edited by Michael Wilkinson and Peter Althouse, 39–54. Leiden: Brill.

Wilkinson, Michael, and Linda M. Ambrose. 2020. *After the Revival: Canadian Pentecostalism and the Making of a Canadian Church.* Montreal & Kingston: McGill-Queen's University Press.

Adam Stewart

Hermeneutics

Pentecostal biblical interpretation has a rich history, even though the movement is young. One reason is that early Pentecostals had to immediately defend their experience of Spirit Baptism signified primarily by tongues speech. Thus, from the beginning, spiritual experiences and interpretation of Scripture as a means to validate the experience were at the forefront of the movements' interaction with other Christian traditions. A more "developed" hermeneutic theologically and contextually speaking, would come into play in the contemporary discussions of Pentecostal biblical interpretation and theological method. In the end, a Pentecostal Hermeneutic is a theological hermeneutic that is concerned with understanding life and interpreting scripture.

A first approach to explaining Pentecostal hermeneutics was put forward by Archer (2004). Taking a historical approach, Archer argued that a Pentecostal hermeneutic developed over time and explained it by means of three phases, the early more pre-critical period (1900–1940's), the modern period (1940's–early 1980), and a contemporary period marked by a distinct literary and postmodern accent (1980's forward). Building on this work, but taking a more typological approach, Oliverio (2015) has constructed four main types of Pentecostal hermeneutics: "Early Evangelical-Pentecostal Hermeneutic", "Contemporary Evangelical-Pentecostal Hermeneutic", "Contextual-Pentecostal Hermeneutic" and an "Ecumenical-Pentecostal Hermeneutic".

Early Pentecostals utilized many of the same methods as other more radical evangelical holiness groups. This included the "Bible Reading Method" which was an inductive-deductive, "commonsense" approach used specifically to develop biblical doctrines. However, what distinguished Pentecostals from other Christian groups was the unique story of their identity which helped shaped their hermeneutical perspective. They identified as people of the Latter Rain outpouring of the Holy Spirit, proclaiming the Full Gospel message. This placed Acts 2 as the entrance point into the canon, which generated a pneumatic christological and soteriological framework, and created a community with a strong eschatological outlook.

Archer and Oliverio both identify that a shift happened when Pentecostals entered historically established academic evangelical seminaries. They adapted their early interpretive approach to the acceptable modernistic historical-critical methods while often trying to maintain their Pentecostal theological identity and spiritual experiences. Academic Pentecostals began contributing to important concerns associated with textual criticism (e.g. Gordon Fee), writing academically informed biblical commentaries and theological works. Their preferred exegetical method was the grammatical-historical method. When redaction criticism became popular, a few Pentecostals employed it successfully to show that the Lukan narrative has a distinct pneumatology, different, but not contradictory, to Paul's (e.g Roger Stronstad). Those who embraced this path would also identify with conservative academic Evangelicalism.

The ongoing interaction with Pentecostals in academic, educational institutions, encouraged a reexamination of Pentecostal identity. This led some to argue that Pentecostalism is a distinct tradition and does not fall easily into the North-American evangelical mold, even though Pentecostalism shared many similarities with other Christian traditions, including those traditions that make up north American Evangelicalism. During this period, Pentecostal scholars who made a postmodern and linguistic turn utilized literary, canonical, reader-response, and theological interpretative methods. As such, the interpretive communities became necessary. With Acts 15 providing the model, what emerged was a theological hermeneutic. This theological hermeneutic involved a close reading of Scripture including its social-cultural context, the socio-cultural and religious-experiential formation of the readers/hearers, and a priority to discern what the Spirit is saying in, through, and outside of Scripture. As such, the Spirit has more to say for today's audience than simply illuminating a past understanding of a text, or a scriptural principle, but forms a relationship between Scripture, interpretative community and its historical traditions. Thus a "trialouge" or a "tridactic negotiation" among the Spirit, Scripture and community became the heart of the contemporary/contextual-Pentecostal hermeneutic.

Oliverio also notes that during the later period, Pentecostals began creating a new type of Pentecostal hermeneutic – the "Ecumenical-Pentecostal Hermeneutic". Pentecostals engaged other traditions besides evangelicalism for helpful reflection on their hermeneutic. But they also offered helpful critiques of other methods, practices and theologies of interpretation. This type reflects the other methods noted above while intentionally being dialogical with other traditions.

There are eight elements which influence the Pentecostal Hermeneutic in varying degrees and transport the Pentecostal sensibilities in scripture interpretation:

First, Pentecostals claim that biblical readings should be *narrative* in nature, which moves Pentecostals beyond the modernistic tendency to try to find the "theological principal" by mining for authorial intent and locates Pentecostals more within a postmodern sensibility recognizing that meaning cannot be divorced not only from the story of the Bible, but it also cannot be estranged from the story of one's embodied life. This does not, then, divorce a Pentecostal reading from the metanarrative of the Gospel, but rather highlights the contextualized narratives found globally among Pentecostals.

Second, as the narrative element of the Pentecostal's Movement finds itself expressed *contextually and globally*, Pentecostals have had the opportunity to reflect on the colonialization that has been perpetuated by a Western interpretation of the text. Rather than accepting that one can be an unbiased and neutral reader of scripture that tends to dehumanize the hermeneutical process, a contextual hermeneutic allows for socio-rhetorical context to enlighten scripture through the Spirit in one's own tongue, highlighting the Spirit's work in Acts 2.

A third key element found within Pentecostal Hermeneutics is that it is not seen as a primarily individualist endeavor. As narrated in Acts 15, the movement of the Spirit in terms of understanding scripture is a *communal* dialogical effort. As such, interpretation of Scripture moves beyond a highly individualistic endeavor and seeks to understand the Spirit's moving within the community as it relates to interpretation.

Fourth, a narrative based reading that is contextual and communal also invites the hermeneut to recognize that interpretations are *dynamic* and never finalized. A Pentecostal hermeneutic recognizes that the text is not a dead text, but a growing story that each reader is invited to partake in. As such, the interpretation of a story will be nuanced within the context and community which engages with the scripture.

Fifth, given the Pentecostal's priority of experiencing the Spirit, as noted in Acts 2, Pentecostals start with their experiences with God as they approach scripture in seeking understanding of their experiences. The *experiential* nature of a Pentecostal hermeneutic has been criticized for its increased possibility for eisegetical input do to subjective experience, but also commended for its potential in bringing fresh insight into the text. In such ways, the social cultural and literary context of any verse(s) is important for a Pentecostal hermeneutic but not the loci or final word in the meaning that is found within the text through the Spirit's illumination/inspiration.

Sixth, Pentecostal reading of scripture has stressed that through the text one encounters the living God. These *encounters* are not to be contrived, and the encounter is not methodologically conjured, they are expected and experienced as the Spirit wills. It is the expectation to encounter the One who is nearer to the readers than the readers are to themselves.

Seventh, Encountering the Spirit through the text is not understood as a cathartic experience for Pentecostals, but rather reading to encounter the Spirit is a *pragmatic* experience that demands that one does not remain unchanged through the encounter. Thus, Pentecostals expect transformation through the text as they encounter the Spirit. Encountering the risen Christ through the Spirit is understood to call one to embody the eschatological kingdom in the now-but-not-yet.

Finally, given the elements purported above, a framework of being able to accept such dynamic interpretations has been proposed by arguing that interpretations are *sanctified* by the Spirit for the use of the community as a means to sanctify the community. Though humanity may be flawed in interpretative practices, the use of such interpretation can be sanctified in its usefulness for soteriological and spiritual development. Thus, a Pentecostal hermeneutic sees the primary function of Scripture as soteriological with epistemology as a secondary and subsumed function.

Moving forward, Pentecostals should be ecumenical and contextual with their hermeneutical practices. Thus ethnic/

racial identity, sex – gendered identity, as well as national identities not to mention hybridity will possibly generate fresh insights for consideration and even call for necessary re-vison to current hermeneutical procedures. As new interpretive methods emerge, Pentecostals should explore with discernment the applicability of such methods. Pentecostals should consider how their theological hermeneutic contributes to other disciplines. Pentecostals should continue to foster a hospitable charitable conversational hermeneutical attitude as they engage interpretation from their particular locations.

Bibliography

Archer, Kenneth J. 2004. *A Pentecostal Hermeneutic for the Twenty-First Century: Spirit, Scripture, and Community*. London: T&T Clark International.

Archer, Kenneth J., and L. William Oliverio, Jr., eds. 2016. *Constructive Pneumatic Hermeneutics in Pentecostal Christianity*. New York: Palgrave MacMillan.

Green, Chris E.W. 2015. *Sanctifying Interpretation: Vocation, Holiness, and Scripture*. Cleveland: CPT Press.

Grey, Jacqueline. 2011. *Three's a Crowd: Pentecostalism, Hermeneutics, and the Old Testament*. Eugene: Pickwick Publications.

Martin, Lee Roy, ed. 2013. *Pentecostal Hermeneutics: A Reader*. Leiden: Brill.

Oliverio, L. William, Jr. 2015. *Theological Hermeneutics in the Classical Pentecostal Tradition: A Typological Account*. Leiden: Brill.

Spawn, Kevin L., and Archie T. Wright, eds. 2012. *Spirit and Scripture: Exploring a Pneumatic Hermeneutic*. London: T&T Clark.

Yong, Amos. 2006. *Spirit-Word-Community: Theological Hermeneutics in Trinitarian Perspective*. Eugene: Wipf & Stock.

Kenneth J. Archer
Aaron Gabriel Ross

Hezmalhalch, Thomas

Thomas Hezmalhalch (1847–1934) is also known as Tom Hezmalhalch or "Brother Tom." He was an American missionary who together with John G. Lake founded the Apostolic Faith Mission (AFM) in South Africa with links to Azusa Street Revival (Kydd 2002). AFM went on to become the largest Classical denomination in South Africa to date (Kay 2011).

Hezmalhalch's parents were English born in New Jersey, U.S.. He went to Leeds in England after the civil war and served as a preacher in a Wesleyan Methodist Church. After his return to the U.S. in 1884, he joined the Holiness movement and was eventually baptized by the Holy Spirit at Azusa Street in the summer of 1906. He began to speak in tongues (Anderson 2013).

It is alleged that Hezmalhalch became a missionary after an adulterous affair with a fellow Pentecostal woman in Los Angeles. He was sent to Zion Illinois in 1907 by William J. Seymour to be rehabilitated. Charles Parham had established a Pentecostal community there but deserted the congregation. As soon as Hezmalhalch arrived he established his authority and led the congregation. John G. Lake and Fred Bosworth were part of Parham's congregation when Hezmalhalch joined them. Parham was arrested due to the deaths of three members who died from what were considered "botched exorcisms." This forced Parham's followers to flee Zion. Hezmalhalch, Lake, and Bosworth settled among local Pentecostals in Indianapolis where they continued to assume leadership in late 1907.

While in Indianapolis, Hezmalhalch and Lake stated that they had been called to be missionaries in Africa so they left Los Angeles. Thus with the help of Seymour, a fundraising event for their trip was done and enough funds were raised for them to go to South Africa in April 1908. By that time he was 60 years of age.

Hezmalhalch and Lake began their ministry in Doornfontein in Johannesburg on May 25, 1908 and thereafter called themselves AFM (Oosthuizen 1987; Kgatle 2016). Despite the racial segregation in South Africa at that time, these services were interracial just like those in the Azusa Street Revival (Farhim-Arp 2010). This only lasted for four months as the all-white AFM executive council, "with the influence of Lake, decided that baptisms and meetings would be racially segregated and that the native work would be overseen by the whites." (Kgatle 2016)

Most of the members of AFM at this point had been Zionists from John Alexander Dowie's Zion church. Hezmalhalch and Lake's connection to Dowie is believed to have paved the way for the expansion for the AFM because they saw the Apostolic Faith as "a logical extension of the message then being proclaimed by Zionists," (Robeck 2006) which was salvation, sanctification, divine healing, the imminent return of Christ, and triple baptism.

The first meeting of the AFM's executive council was held on May 27, 1909 when Hezmalhalch was elected president and chairperson and Lake as vice president (Nel 2016). Lake and Hezmalhalch had a falling out in 1910 as Hezmalhalch and other missionaries had accused Lake of financial misuse and abuse of power. After gaining support from other leaders and being vindicated by Lake's biggest financial supporter, The Upper Room in Los Angeles (Anderson 2007), Lake took over as president and dismissed Hezmalhalch by demoting him to remote provinces which led to his permanent return to the U.S. in 1913 (Anderson 2013). On his return to the U.S., he taught an adult class at Bethany Church, Alhambra (Kydd 2002).

Hezmalhalch was not considered a great preacher but still gained his reputation as one of the most influential pioneers of the Pentecostal movement in South Africa. He saw healing as an essential part of the gospel and also as a means of evangelism. He regarded the witness of healing of all manner of diseases as doing more for the spread of the gospel than what he considered "preaching and ecclesiastical machinery would do" (Anderson 2007). While history records that people like Hezmalhalch were key to the spread of the Pentecostal movement, Kgatle argues that it was the black pastors that played a significant role to give the Pentecostal movement in South Africa an African character which enabled it to spread among indigenous people (Kgatle 2016). Despite this, senior leadership was retained by the whites and Anderson argues that "although African pastors and evangelists were largely responsible for the growth of the Pentecostal movement in South Africa, they were written out of history with the exception of Nicholas Bhengu who contributed greatly to the South African Assemblies of God" (Anderson 2004).

Bibliography

Anderson, Allan H. 2013. *To The Ends of the Earth: Pentecostalism and the Transformation of World Christianity*. Oxford: Oxford University Press.

Anderson, Allan. 2007. *Spreading Fires: The Missionary Nature of Early Pentecostalism*. London: SCM Press.

Kgatle, Mookgo S. 2016. "Sociological and Theological Factors That Caused Schisms in the Apostolic Faith Mission of South Africa." *Studia Historae Ecclesiasticae* 42 (1): 1–15.

Kydd, R.A.N. 2002. "Healing in the Christian Church." In *International Dictionary of*

Pentecostal and Charismatic Movements, edited by Stanley M. Burgess and Eduard M. Van der Maas, 698–711. Grand Rapids: Zondervan.

Oosthuizen, G.C. 1987. *The Birth of Christian Zionism in South Africa*. Kwa Dlangezwa: University of Zululand.

Naar M'fundisi-Holloway

Hicks, Tommy

Tommy Hicks (1909–1973) developed a two-month ministry in Argentina (April– June, 1954) and produced one of the greatest spiritual impacts affecting the church and the nation.

Being the son of a Texas farmer in the Baptist tradition, he was ordained to the ministry in 1936 by the International Foursquare Church. A year earlier, 1935, he had graduated from Life Bible College, an evening theological school of the Foursquare Church, where he had Aimee Semple McPherson as one of his teachers. At this church he was a pastor, evangelist, and District Superintendent.

He had some painful experiences in his life that undoubtedly marked his ministry. In 1942 he lost a two-year-old son and in 1949 he suffered from a cerebral hemorrhage that left him paralyzed. According to Hicks, God healed him, and he came out of that painful experience with a deep conviction of the healing power of Jesus.

In his native country, Hicks was one of the countless post-war divine healing evangelists. For him, the possibility of developing his ministry in South America meant the materialization of an old dream. According to his own testimony, many years before, while praying intensely, he saw a large crowd and a map of South America. After more than two years of thinking and talking about this, he had the feeling that the time had come for that dream to be fulfilled. This was during a campaign in Tallahassee, Florida. He suddenly canceled all his commitments in the US and set out on a trip to South America.

Hicks's arrival in Argentina was surrounded by political and spiritual events. In the stories that try to explain those days, history is mixed with myth; facts with fantasies. The Tommy Hicks campaign took place in the context of the crisis of the Peronist government. On March 9, 1954 Hicks arrived in Buenos Aires. On the way he came up with the idea to talk to the Argentine president, although he did not even know his name. According to his own testimony, it was a stewardess who told him that Perón was the name of the president (Hicks 1956b). Zielicke has another version of these events and claims that according to Juan Carlos Ortiz, Hicks's personal assistant, the evangelist had met in Chile an Argentine senator who was a friend of Perón's, who had supposedly arranged an interview with the president (Zielicke 2012). In essence, Hicks wanted permission for his meetings and free access to the media.

On March 17, a week after his arrival, all the evangelicals were surprised to see Tommy Hicks' photo in the newspapers and the news that he had just had an interview with Perón. Here, too, the accounts differ. Some say that the interview was made possible because a doorman in the government house was healed; others attributed it to the healing of the Minister of Foreign Affairs. According to Hicks, he was received with honor and kindness (Hicks 1956b). The interview scheduled for 15 minutes but lasted 45 minutes and in it Hicks, as he told Ortiz, prayed for Perón, who was allegedly healed of a skin disease on his face. However, Enns states in his book that, according to a telephone interview that Hilton Merrit made to Hicks

Hicks at Argentina Crusade 1954. Source: Pentecostal Assemblies of Canada Archives

(May 22, 1967), Hicks denied having prayed for Perón's health (Enns 1960). The fact is that Perón agreed to Hicks's requests and made available to him everything he considered necessary for the crusade.

On April 14, 1954 the campaign began. The meetings originally scheduled for 15 days were extended until June 12. The Federal Police estimated that a total of six million people attended the 62-day crusade.

Tommy Hicks led a simple lifestyle. In Buenos Aires he stayed in a simple hotel. He did not sleep more than three or four hours a day and hardly ate. Sometimes, in private, he had violent reactions, which made personal relationships very difficult (Saracco 1989). The campaign ended when Hick's exhaustion made it impossible to continue.

Hicks returned to Buenos Aires the following year, and although he called this "the most historic trip of his life" (Hicks 1956a), the truth is that the results were discouraging. While he was warmly welcomed back to the US and tried to develop his ministry in eastern Europe, the experience in Argentina was unrepeatable.

Hicks's two months of ministry changed the history of the evangelical church in Argentina. He pioneered mass evangelistic meetings, opened the way for ministries such as Oswald Smith and Billy Graham, awakened the evangelistic fervor in the churches, hundreds received the call to ministry and produced pockets of revival throughout the Argentine territory.

Bibliography

Enns, Arno W. 1971. *Man, Milieu, and Mission in Argentina: A Close Look at Church Growth*. Grand Rapids, MI: Eerdmans.

Hicks, Tommy. 1956a. *Capturing the Nations in the Name of the Lord: The Miracle Revival of Russia*. Los Angeles, CA: International Headquarters of Tommy Hicks.

Hicks, Tommy. 1956b. *Millions Found Christ: History's Greatest Recorded Revival*. Los

Angeles, CA: International Headquarters of Tommy Hicks.

Saracco, Jose Norberto. 1989. "Argentine Pentecostalism: Its History and Theology." PhD thesis, University of Birmingham, UK.

Zielicke, Seth N. 2012. "The Role of American Evangelist Tommy Hicks in the Development of Argentine Pentecostalism." In *Global Pentecostal Movements: Migration, Mission and Public Religion*, edited by Michael Wilkinson, 135–152. Leiden: Brill.

Norberto Saracco

Higher Education

Pentecostalism is usually understood to have been initiated by a series of revivals at the start of the twentieth century. These revivals – although the outcomes varied in different parts of the world – quickly led to the formation of Pentecostal denominations and these denominations, with their newly formed or newly adopted congregations, required ministers who required training. The first Pentecostal educational institutions were Bible Institutes or colleges (the terminology varied) with a narrow curriculum focused on the Bible, Pentecostal doctrine, preaching and mission. Since, at the start of the twentieth century, secondary education was by no means universal, these new Pentecostal institutions often supplemented ministerial training with basic general education.

The quality of teaching offered by Bible colleges varied depending upon the size and socio-economic status of the Pentecostal movement in each country. North American Pentecostalism grew most rapidly and at a time when educational diversity in the United States was coming under forms of external validation to ensure comparability of standards. In Europe, Bible college training was valued as an entry qualification to denominational ministerial or missionary lists although, because there was a lingering tradition resisting education in the Pentecostal world, it was nearly always possible to obtain credentials without formal training. In the United States ministerial training became crucial to the preparation of Pentecostal military chaplains in World War II with the result that external accreditation of Pentecostal colleges became widely acceptable just prior to and after 1945.

In general, then, Pentecostal denominations might be configured as a group of several hundred churches, and each group might have its own missions department and training institution. In North America training institutions widened their curricula and faculty structures so that the largest of them became liberal arts colleges and eventually upgraded to become universities. In Europe where higher education was almost entirely tax-funded and government-controlled, Pentecostal colleges eventually sought validation through secular universities so that by the 1990s many of the main Pentecostal denominations were able to offer validated degree schemes of equal value to the equivalent schemes offered on secular campuses. Within the last several decades departments and programs have arisen in public universities of Europe specializing in topics related to Pentecostal and Charismatic interests and which are facilitated by Pentecostal academics and lead to doctoral degrees.

In other continents of the world, Pentecostal education frequently followed patterns derived from the sending countries of missionaries. Hong Kong, for instance, received missionaries from the USA and Canada with the result that two sets of churches were formed with different emphases that were able to share a common training institution. Assemblies of God (USA) was fortunate in its Director of Foreign Missions, J. Philip Hogan (1915-2002), who implemented a global strategy that anticipated handing over mission churches to indigenous leaders who would be prepared for this responsibility by training. In almost every part of the world where AG sent missionaries, it bought land and established ministerial training colleges, and this was especially so in the mid-twentieth century when the American economy was unchallenged and the dollar was strong.

Pentecostal higher education therefore followed two paths: one where it gained secular validation/accreditation and diversified into many branches of learning and so enabled its young people to climb the secondary system and transition out through Pentecostal universities into many types of skilled and professional employment (primarily in North America, Europe and Australia) and, the other, where Pentecostal education was unable to obtain validation by secular authorities and so supervised its quality primarily through faith-based agencies like the Asia Pacific Theological Association (APTA), the Association for Pentecostal Theological Education in Africa (APTEA), and the Asociación Teológica de América Latina (ATAL). These were further supplemented by the development (in connection with the Pentecostal World Fellowship) of the World Alliance for Pentecostal Theological Education (WAPTE) in 2009 to provide resources such as a journal specifically for Pentecostal theological educators – *The Pentecostal Educator* – and assessment documents as well as oversight to the aforementioned faith-based Pentecostal accrediting bodies.

A distinction may be made between training and education: training is the learning and performance of procedures without theoretical understanding; education requires political, historical and holistic understanding as well as mastery of procedure. Pentecostal higher education initially aimed merely to train ministers and later to educate them by providing them with the tools to grapple with biblical languages and engage with the wider perspectives of the academy and church. Whether training or educating, though, Pentecostal education was normally aware of the importance of character formation with the result that most Pentecostal institutions included collective worship on their campuses and encouraged personal prayer and spiritual discipline. The impartation of knowledge alongside spiritual experience might be held as an ideal.

In addition to the inclusion of heartfelt worship, Pentecostal institutions frequently gave a key or prime place to theology or biblical studies departments within the liberal arts or university setting. In some cases all students might be expected to undertake a Biblical Survey or Christian Worldview course at the outset of their studies and in others special lectures and the college ethos were expected to carry the student forward with a living faith alongside the growing capacity to engage with rational critique. This tension between critical intellectual development and active faith was difficult to hold but, in the best institutions, it was held and students emerged as rounded individuals fit to take a role in secular society and serve in the church.

Further, Pentecostal higher education has shown tendency toward the use of modules (i.e. short, self-contained, credit-bearing blocks of learning materials), intensives and the use of distance education to reduce costs and enrol practitioners. For instance, the majority of doctoral programs provided by Pentecostal institutions globally are offered in modules so that practitioners are not relocated to the institution for their studies. This has also occurred in many locations for undergraduate training of ministers where the students acquire their education via modules as they continue to serve in their respective places of ministry.

Bibliography

Blumhofer, Edith L. 1989. *The Assemblies of God: A Chapter in the Story of American Pentecostalism, since 1941*. Springfield, MO: GPH.

Hittenburger, Jeffrey S. 2006. "Education." In *Encyclopedia of Pentecostal and Charismatic Christianity*, edited by Stanley M. Burgess, 158–162. New York: Routledge.

Ma, Wonsuk, Daniel Chiquete, and Cephas N. Omenyo. 2010. "Theological Education in Pentecostal Churches." In *Handbook of Theological Education in World Christianity: Theological Perspectives – Regional Surveys – Ecumenical Trends*, edited by D. Werner, D. Esterline, N. Kang, and J. Raja, 729–749. Oxford, UK: Regnum.

Robeck, Cecil M. 2002. "Seminaries and Graduate Schools." In *The New International Dictionary of Pentecostal Charismatic Movements*, edited by Stanley M. Burgess and Eduard M. van der Maas, 1045–1050. Grand Rapids, MI: Zondervan.

Wilson, Lewis F. 2002. "Bible Institutes, Colleges, Universities." In *The New International Dictionary of Pentecostal Charismatic Movements*, edited by Stanley M. Burgess and Eduard M. van der Maas, 372–380. Grand Rapids, MI: Zondervan.

William K. Kay
Rick Wadholm

Hillsong

Hillsong is a contemporary church that originated in Sydney, Australia but is now comprised of congregations in twenty-two nations across the world. It was founded by Global Senior Pastors Brian (son of Frank Houston) and Bobbie Houston in 1983. At the time of writing, the church had a global attendance of over 130,000. Hillsong campuses are located mostly in urban centres including Sydney, London, New York, Los Angeles, Paris, Copenhagen, and Cape Town. However, the church is also streamed online into remote Australian outback locations via "Church of the Air." It is pentecostal/charismatic in its theology but socially progressive on many issues, and remains apolitical. The church's annual financial statements are made available via its website.

Hills Christian Life Centre initially met in a high school hall in suburban Baulkham Hills, Sydney, but quickly outgrew this venue. The church's reputation grew internationally due to its award-winning Christian congregational music, produced as a resource for worship teams. Due to its reputation, the church formally changed its name to "Hillsong," which was the name of its publishing house. In 1997, the Hills campus moved into its current location of Norwest Business Park, Sydney. In 1999, the church announced Hillsong London as its first overseas congregation, and in the year 2000, they merged with Sydney Christian Life Centre, acquiring its urban facilities in Waterloo, Sydney. Australia's Prime Minister John Howard was invited to open a new 3,500 seat Convention Centre at Norwest in 2002.

Hillsong music is extraordinarily popular. As well as dominating the Christian

Hillsong United Empire Tour 2016, Day 18. Source: Flickr, Michael Saechang.

congregational CCLI charts, the songs appear annually in Australia's mainstream ARIA Top 10, as well as the US Billboard Top 50. The song "Oceans" held the number 1 position on the US Billboard Hot Christian songs chart for 61 weeks. Hillsong's YouTube has over 700 million online streams. Worship pastor Geoff Bullock wrote the early music of the church. However, in the United States, Darlene Zschech rapidly became Hillsong's best-known songwriter and worship leader. Her song "Shout to the Lord" appeared on American Idol and is estimated to be sung in over thirty million churches each week. Numerous other worship leaders feature on the church's albums, including Joel Houston, Jad Gillies, Taya Gaukrodger (nee Smith), Dave Ware, and Reuben Morgan. Popular New Zealand singer/songwriter Brooke Ligertwood (nee Fraser)'s song co-written with Ben Fielding entitled "What a Beautiful Name" won a Grammy in 2018.

The church produces its music annually via Hillsong Music Australia (HMA). Initially distributed by Integrity USA, now the church has an arrangement with Capitol Records. To date, four generational music groups are associated with the Hillsong label, each with their distinct sound. Hillsong Worship is an annual collection of all the church's congregational songs, while Hillsong United is a Christian contemporary music band, led by Joel Houston. Young and Free (Y&F) is the youth band of the church, led by Laura Toggs. Also, Hillsong Kids albums are released periodically.

At its founding, Hillsong was affiliated with the Assemblies of God Australia (AGA) denomination (now Australian Christian Churches or ACC). In 2018, the church decided to credential its own pastors, retaining close association with its denomination, but forgoing member voting rights. Pastor Brian Houston served as the superintendent of this denomination from 1997 to 2009. During his time as superintendent, multiple accusations of child sexual abuse were lodged against Frank Houston, his father. The handling of this event resulted in a censure within a national Royal Commission due to a "potential or perceived" conflict of interest from his relationship.

The vision statement "The Church That I Now See" was revised by Brian Houston after twenty years, and includes various ministries of the church. CityCare offers various community services, including counselling, a health centre, a food bank, and youth mentoring. Volunteer "street teams" serve the community, particularly those who are alone or in need of assistance. The church hosts various conferences which begin in Sydney and tour the world. In March the global Colour Conference gathers women in six locations worldwide. Hillsong Conference, which is the largest annual Australian conference, was inaugurated in 1986 and is held each July annually. The Worship & Creative Conference (WCC) is held in October.

The Hillsong Channel was a joint venture started with Trinity Broadcasting Network (TBN) in the United States in 2016. That same year a documentary, Hillsong: Let Hope Rise, directed by Michael John Warren, was released to cinemas across the United States. The Hillsong College offers a range of courses in Australia's skill based vocational education training (VET) system, and also higher education degrees accredited via AlphaCrucis, Sydney.

Now a diverse organization, the church and ministries interrelate within the Hillsong brand. The Hillsong logo is one of the most recognizable symbols in the evangelical world. The church retains its original mission statement "to reach and influence the world by building a large Christ-centred, Bible-based church, changing mindsets and empowering people to lead and impact in every sphere of life." Within academic literature, the church is criticized for its "growth theology."

Notable associated figures include Christine Caine, one of Hillsong's former youth leaders, now one of the most widely known evangelical preachers in the United States. Other famous attendees include Justin Bieber and Hailey Baldwin, Selena Gomez and Nick Jonas. The Hillsong Network is a group of affiliated churches with which Hillsong shares resources.

Bibliography

Klaver, Miranda. 2015. "Media Technology Creating 'Sermonic Events.' The Hillsong Megachurch Network." *Crosscurrents* 65 (4): 422–433.

Riches, Tanya, and Tom Wagner, eds. 2017. *The Hillsong Movement Examined: You Call Me Out Upon the Waters*. New York: Palgrave McMillan.

Riches, Tanya, and Tom Wagner. 2012. "The Evolution of Hillsong Music: From Australian Pentecostal Congregation into Global Brand." *Australian Journal of Communication* 39 (1): 17–36.

Maddox, M. 2012. "'In the Goofy parking lot': Growth Churches as a Novel Religious Form for Late Capitalism." *Social Compass* 59 (2): 146–158.

Marti, Gerardo. 2017. "The Global Phenomenon of Hillsong Church: An Initial Assessment." *Sociology of Religion* 78 (4): 377–386.

Wade, Matthew, and Maria Hynes. 2013. "Worshipping Bodies: Affective Labour in the Hillsong Church." *Geographical Research* 51 (2): 173–179.

Tanya Riches

History

Writing Pentecostal history is no easy task, because historiographical narratives are inevitably linked to how Pentecostalism is defined (see Definition). In most of academic discourse, Pentecostalism tends to be seen as either the final outcome of a series of revivals in the beginning of the twentieth century, or as a global discourse in today's world with possibly more recent origins. The latter definition is becoming increasingly popular, as it avoids some of the historiographical problems associated with the former and is better adapted to local varieties in the articulation of Pentecostal identity.

For a long time, the predominant history of Pentecostalism understood the movement as the merger of several revivals, that first produced classical Pentecostals, then Charismatics and finally Neo-Pentecostals. This typological definition identified an "origin" of global Pentecostalism, typically located in the Azusa Street revival of 1906. Invested with the ideality of Pentecostal origin, the adequate interpretation of the Azusa Street Revival thus became a core issue in Pentecostal historiography. In a critical revision of sources and historical narratives, Walter Hollenweger and his school began in the 1970s to insist on the "black roots" of Azusa Street and argued that the origins of Pentecostalism were not to be found in white middle-class America but in the subaltern margins of society and their ability to transcend racial segregation (Hollenweger in Anderson and Hollenweger 1999).

Scholars who focused their research on the global Pentecostal movement, remained uneasy with this new critical narrative, inasmuch as it still implied a primary origin in the United States and explained the worldwide spread as the result of missionary work from there. Though he supported Hollenweger's emphasis on the black roots of Pentecostalism, Allan Anderson has pushed beyond this paradigm since the 2000s and sought to show that in other places of the world similar revivals had broken out independently from Azusa, and in some cases even predating it. According to Anderson, the joint global endeavors of people from all over world had brought about the Pentecostal movement. However, he still understood these early revivals, though now globally situated, as the formative, multipolar origin of today's Pentecostalism (Anderson 2007).

Newer approaches to Pentecostal historiography have criticized and moved away from the focus on early single "origins" and their normative character for the history of Pentecostalism (Bergunder in Anderson et al. 2010). They note that, firstly, these early events were part of a broader worldwide missionary revival and differed significantly in theology and practice from the "classical" Pentecostalism that arose years later in doctrinal statements and new denominations. Therefore their identification as "origin" of Pentecostalism disregards context and invites anachronisms. Secondly, and more importantly, a historiography that is fixated on "origins" tends to produce historical prototypes against which concurrent and later developments necessarily appear as deficient. This critical insight aligns global Pentecostal historiography more closely with post-colonial studies, where historians like Dipesh Chakrabarty have shown that the historical focus on origins easily leads to a structural Eurocentrism via the positing of European prototypes. All other non-European phenomena thus become deficient, since they are only read through the prototype of European history with which they then fail to correspond fully (Bergunder 2016). This criticism applies directly to any historiography of global Pentecostalism oriented toward discovering origins. Any posited singular origin, whether in the USA or in a specific set of revivals abroad will always posit a certain historical identity of today's Pentecostalism, against which its other historical influences become secondary developments.

Historiographical alternatives are necessary. Michel Foucault's concept of the genealogy provides a promising perspective (Bergunder in Anderson et al. 2010). Foucault sharply polemicized against the historical "pursuit of the origin" and advocated a genealogical approach which dispels "the chimeras of the origin" and detaches history from its metaphysics and teleology. From a genealogical point of view, history is always *pre*-history of the present and written from the present into a past. This means that historians need to gradually excavate the *pre*-history of the current global Pentecostal discourse rather than seek an entry point in purported "origins".

In this historical operation from the present to the past, the question is no longer one of "origins", but how far the current discourse can be meaningfully traced into the past. This is a question of continuity and discontinuity, which as of necessity remains controversial and points to the perspectivism of the genealogical operation. Inasmuch as continuity and discontinuity are both present in historical developments, scholarly analyses of historical lineages and ruptures are themselves hegemonic closures that are contingent. Yet they are not arbitrary nor purely subjective, because they have to relate directly to sources and adhere to the established methods of historical-critical inquiry.

This approach has at last two immediate practical implications. Firstly, there is ample evidence that the current global Pentecostal discourse came together only in the last three or four decades (Bergunder in Anderson et al. 2010). Statistics show that the remarkable growth of Pentecostalism did not take place before the 1970s and parallels its expansion into a broad global movement. This is in part due to the expansion of churches and movements that identified as Pentecostals or Charismatics, but also new statistical categories being generated to count them. Accordingly, the scholarly debate about a broad understanding of Pentecostalism also did not arise until the 1970s and should be seen in this context. Hence, the category of global Pentecostalism in our present understanding hardly pre-dates the 1970s and in this sense is only a few decades old.

Of course, it is possible to trace connections further back than the 1970s, but never to discover the "origin" of Pentecostalism. What emerges instead are historical precursors that stand in less and less continuity to the present Pentecostal discourse.

Secondly, the Pentecostal discourse about history and historical origins requires more attention in scholarly research, as it is an important arena for contemporary identity politics. Historians tend to use hagiographic Pentecostal histories only as a quarry for mining "real" historical data, whereas the complexities of identity production and representation contained in such accounts remain ignored. By contrast, Jörg Haustein's work on Ethiopian Pentecostalism offers a critical reading of the available historical sources, not only in order to reconstruct historical "facts", but to recover the intentionality and political thrust of current Pentecostal narratives about the past. In a similar vein, Yan Suarsana takes a fresh look at the Mukti Revival in India which is often regarded as one of the early "origins" of global Pentecostalism. He critically confronts the historical sources with the work of Pentecostal historians who have produced the story of a Pentecostal Mukti Revival by exclusion of other interpretations. As these and other works show, the genealogical approach is fully aware that the representation of the past is a powerful resource for identity debates in the present and as such takes seriously the contested character of Pentecostal historiography.

Bibliography

Anderson, Allan H. 2007. *Spreading Fires: The Missionary Nature of Early Pentecostalism.* London: SCM Press.

Anderson, Allan, Michael Bergunder, André Droogers, and Cornelis van der Laan, eds. 2010. *Studying Global Pentecostalism: Theories and Methods.* Berkeley: University of California Press.

Anderson, Allan H., and Walter J. Hollenweger, eds. 1999. *Pentecostals after a Century: Global Perspectives on a Movement in Transition.* Sheffield: Sheffield Academic Press.

Bergunder, Michael. 2016. "Comparison in the Maelstrom of Historicity: A Postcolonial Perspective on Comparative Religion." In *Interreligious Comparisons in Religious Studies and Theology*, edited by Perry Schmidt-Leukel and Andreas Nehring, 34–52. London: Bloomsbury.

Haustein, Jörg. 2011. *Writing Religious History: The Historiography of Ethiopian Pentecostalism.* Wiesbaden: Harrassowitz.

Suarsana, Yan. 2014. "Inventing Pentecostalism. Pandita Ramabai and the Mukti Revival from a Post-colonial Perspective." *PentecoStudies* 13 (2): 173–196.

Michael Bergunder

Hollenweger, Walter J.

Walter Jacob Hollenweger (June 1, 1927 – August 10, 2016) was a scholar of global Pentecostalism and interdisciplinary Reformed theologian. Growing up in a Pentecostal church in Zurich, Switzerland, he became well acquainted with the various facets of revivalist Christianity. He was active as youth leader, evangelist, author of articles, and interpreter at large events. He was ordained by the Swiss Pentecostal Mission and worked in that denomination until 1958. Personal tensions with the local church leadership and exaggerated accusations led to his abrupt resignation and Hollenweger joined the Swiss Reformed Church studying theology at the University of Zurich. There he received his Doctor in Theology degree in 1966 with a ten-volume dissertation on global Pentecostalism. For the rest of his life he would juggle his attention between the experiential and oral spirituality of Pentecostalism and the critical discipline of theology.

Based on Hollenweger's ecclesial experience and the research done on a worldwide scale, the World Council of Churches invited him to become Executive Secretary of the Department on Studies on Evangelism, a position he held from 1965 to 1971. At that time he began to champion the importance of non-western Christianity and called for inclusive approaches to dialogue between the church practices and theologies of the North and the Global South.

From 1971 to 1989 Walter Hollenweger was Professor of Missions at the University of Birmingham and Selly Oak Colleges in England. He published books and numerous articles on Pentecostalism and made this expression of Christianity accessible to a larger group of historians, sociologists, and theologians. At the same time he developed and propagated his insights on intercultural theology. The interdisciplinary nature of his method and publications necessitates a description of his work in four areas.

Narrative theology: drawing from the testimonial tradition in Pentecostalism, Hollenweger developed a narrative exegesis that could be understood by theologians and lay people alike. Perhaps his best known piece has been, Saints of Birmingham. He developed a hermeneutic that would be open to experience and contextual setting. He also wrote a book of prayers in which he related the existential situations of human beings to animals allowing for a fresh look at life.

Intercultural theology: As a Professor of Mission, Hollenweger was not interested in continuing the classical method that dealt with mission from a purely western point of view. He favored an approach that was open to the whole spectrum of world Christianity. He was convinced that theologians from the Global South had every right to question the claims of the specialists from the North. His theology was not exclusively religious, but also relevant with regard to the contextual realities of life such as the plight of the poor or the selfish interests of the powerful. For this reason he also focused for instance on the ethics of Dietrich Bonhoeffer and the social vision of the Reformer Ulrich Zwingli.

Participatory mission: Walter Hollenweger remained an evangelist at heart. However, instead of choosing a confrontational approach of a speaker to the audience, he was convinced that the gospel message could be better transmitted through plays and musicals. He wrote about two dozen theater pieces that drew from biblical stories and current situations. It was important to him that lay people and unchurched persons would be involved so that they could discover the gospel for themselves.

Ecumenical vision: working on his dissertation and his involvement with the World Council of Churches led to strong ecumenical convictions. It was clear to Hollenweger that the spirituality and theology of Pentecostals is most relevant to dialogue between churches. Using his intercultural approach he illustrated the need for different churches to work towards greater unity in Christ. The best testimony to the inspiring work of Walter Hollenweger is the great number of Master and PhD students from different churches and all parts of the world who continue to cherish the insights their professor gave them.

After retirement Walter bequeathed his library to the Hollenweger Center at the Vrije Universiteit Amsterdam, the Netherlands. Towards the end of his life, as he was suffering from dementia, the Swiss Pentecostal Mission met with his wife Erica and asked forgiveness for its misguided behavior towards them in the late 1950s. A part of his private book collection is now housed at the offices of the Swiss Pentecostal Mission.

Bibliography

Hollenweger, Walter J. 1997. *Pentecostalism: Origins and Developments Worldwide*. Peabody, MA: Hendrikson.

Hollenweger, Walter J. 1992 (1982). *Umgang mit Mythen: Interkulturelle Theologie 2*. Munich: Chr. Kaiser.

Hollenweger, Walter J. 1990 (1979). *Erfahrungen der Leibhaftigkeit: Interkulturelle Theologie 1*. Munich: Chr. Kaiser.

Hollenweger, Walter J. 1988. *Geist und Materie: Interkulturelle Theologie 3*. Munich: Chr. Kaiser.

Hollenweger, Walter J. 1988 (1972). *The Pentecostals*, Third Edition. Peabody, MA: Hendrikson.

Price, Lynne. 2002. *Theology Out of Place. A Theological Biography of Walter J. Hollenweger*. London: Sheffield Academic Press.

Jean Daniel Plüss

Holy Trinity Brompton Church in London. Photo: David Castor (Wikimedia)

Holy Trinity Brompton

At first glance, Holy Trinity Brompton (frequently known as HTB) is an inconspicuous-looking parish church positioned in Kensington, London. Yet HTB's external modest structure belies its national, indeed international, importance in evangelical circles. Its stated vision is "to play our part in the evangelisation of the nation, the revitalisation of the church and the transformation of society." The interior of the church contains elaborate furnishing, suggesting that it was of High Anglican tradition. The sparse space of the HTB is given over to the optimum use in the evangelizing initiative of the Alpha course, which was designed by HTB vicar, Nicky Gumbel. There are well-supplied conference rooms, a basement coffee shop, a bookshop offering a range of Christian literature and teaching material, and meeting facilities for Alpha spin-off programs (such as the Marriage and Parenting courses). However, even before Alpha became popular, HTB had grown to become a leading centre of the charismatic renewal movement and hub for revival under its previous vicar Sandy Millar.

HTB is the wealthiest Anglican church in England. Much of the income is derived from materials associated with Alpha. At the height of the popularity of Alpha in the early 2000s up to one thousand guests attended one of the weekly courses run at the church. HTB buildings, many in the form of at least half a dozen church plants accommodate some ten services each Sunday, with total Sunday service attendance at around 4,500. HTB offers a variety of services and ministries including those for youth and children. The formal services feature traditional Church of England liturgy and a conventional Anglican choir. The informal services are longer, incorporating contemporary worship with a lengthier sermon and reflective prayer.

Based in central London, HTB has a regular congregation comprised of a good number of wealthy parishioners. HTB is also a fairly transient congregation reflecting the demographics of the capital, with numerous visitors attracted to events at a high profile church. Many are young people of which a good number are students, while Alpha attracts people from other congregations who are visiting the home of the program. In an attempt to deal with the pastoral needs of large congregation, HTB uses the popular model of cells or pastorates which are small groups of 20–50 people who meet typically at least once a fortnight. Such arrangements attempt to forge congregational support and care, as well as developing individual spiritual gifts and ministries.

The Alpha course has been systematically exported across the world ensuring that HTB has an international network, exemplifying the fact that it is very much outward facing. HTB holds an annual church camp, named 'Focus', where typically 7,000 people attend, many from other churches, who are involved in seminars, workshops, recreational activities, and listening to prominent speakers addressing issues impacting the Christian Church and society. Since 1985, HTB has been actively involved in church plants, which often entails adopting declining churches in London and moving dozens of people from HTB to the identified church for at least a year. This also involves at least one member of HTB's clergy similarly moving to the new church to help lead worship, form pastorates, and run local Alpha courses, with some of these churches going on to make church plants of their own.

St. Paul's theological centre constitutes HTB's theological school which lasts for eight weeks. In 2005 HTB started providing talks given at the Sunday services through free downloads from its website and through such channels as YouTube. These downloads (called *HTB Podcasts*) have included answers to questions sent in by listeners (each month the total download count can reach over 40,000). In 2011, fulfilling its mission statement, HTB formed the William Wilberforce Trust that oversees social action projects linked with the church. These projects include work in deprived neighbourhoods, addressing homelessness, and providing practical support for people with addictions.

While the Alpha course has created international networks across the world, the reality is that HTB has long enjoyed evangelical networks of a Pentecostal/Charismatic persuasion. In the 1990s this had been enhanced with connections with the Association of Vineyard Churches, led by the late John Wimber in California, which had considerable impact on British evangelical churches, particularly Anglican. It is pertinent to note that HTB had been a major advocate and source of dissemination for the controversial so-called Toronto Blessing manifest originally in Vineyard churches – and its esoteric and ecstatic phenomena, much of which was associated with Pentecostal/Charismatic concerns such as prophecies, healing and speaking in tongues. It is such international connections and its historical role in renewal that will undoubtedly ensure that HTB will remain one of Britain's highly influential megachurches.

Bibliography

Hunt, Stephen. 2008. "'Packing Them in the Aisles': Is Alpha Working?" In *Evaluating Fresh Expressions: Explorations in Emerging Church*, edited by L. Nelstrop and M. Percy, 161–174. London: SPCK-Canterbury Press.

Hunt, Stephen. 2003. "The Alpha Programme: Some Tentative Observations." *Journal of Contemporary Religion* 18 (1): 77–93.

Hunt, Stephen. 1995. "The Anglican Wimberites." *Pnuema* 17 (1): 105–115.

Stephen J. Hunt

Homiletics

Homiletics, the act of preparing and preaching the intent of Scripture as the word of God, is a central feature of Pentecostal worship. In fact, according to Swiss theologian Walter Hollenweger, Pentecostal "oral homiletics" is "perhaps the most important contribution of Pentecostalism" even above its pneumatological contributions (2004, 219; echoed regarding the Filipino context, dela Cruz 2007, 193). However, Pentecostal preaching is not always conceived in light of homiletics by the Pentecostal preacher themselves (as homiletics tends to focus upon such things as, theory, methodology and style and is related to hermeneutics). Pentecostals consider the preaching of the word of God with expectation of the continuity with the experience of God found in Scripture. While Pentecostals have not often been as intentionally reflective upon their homiletical practice, the homiletics of Pentecostals is still characterized often by certain typical features: it is (1) Jesus centered, (2) pneumatic, (3) anointed, (4) storied, (5) eschatological, (6) participatory, and (7) pragmatic.

Pentecostal homiletics is Jesus centered. Preaching as an act is defined by the New Testament as the proclamation of the good news about Jesus. While many forms of speech may occur in the life of the Pentecostal community, it is this central act of preaching where Jesus is the focus. For Pentecostals the contents and focus are, thus, most often expressed within the Pentecostal "full gospel" message of Jesus: saving, (sanctifying), baptizing in the Holy Spirit, healing, and coming soon as king (for details on the role of this central message within Pentecostal practices, see Land 2001). However, there are times wherein within Pentecostal preaching the felt-needs of congregants or the desire of the preacher to demonstrate power and anointing take precedence even over the confessed "full gospel" message about Jesus.

Pentecostal homiletics is pneumatic. The Spirit is sought and believed to be the central actor in Pentecostal preaching. The Spirit is sought in the preparation of sermons and in the delivery. This has tended toward the idea of the preacher as background to the foregrounding of the work and voice of the Spirit. In the act of preaching, the Pentecostal preacher attempts to discern moment by moment the Spirit's leading both in light of sermon preparation and despite such (Leoh 2006, 41). Spirit empowerment for preaching becomes the empowerment of any and all to preach as equal proclaimers of the kingdom: majority and minority, young and old, rich and poor, female and male. This pneumatic element suggests an intentional spontaneity wherein the preacher might receive insights and words that are believed to supersede the preparation of the message and offer a prophetic insight for the moment.

Pentecostal homiletics is anointed. This "anointed" identification of Pentecostal preaching may refer to the animation and volume of a preacher, to the emotional impact of the message, to demonstrations of signs and wonders as part of the worship experience connected to the preaching, or any number of other experiences of preacher and/or congregants. While the language of "anointing" remains nebulous, it is still a primary term used to refer to the preaching in Pentecostal contexts both by preachers and congregants. Anointing in the act of preaching might be defined as an impassioned or moving message, but it will also be felt through signs of God's presence in the act of preaching. This might be through capturing the imagination of the hearers, inspiration to confess sins, or to act in the Spirit. In this fashion, the anointing appeals to the affections (the desire and will) of those hearing the message to be transformed by the indwelling Spirit. Sometimes this anointing is affirmed by verbalization from the congregants, sometimes by response to altar calls, but a testimony (through word and commitment to transformation via Spirit-filled action) of an "anointed" message is an intended outcome. The confession of a message as "anointed" becomes an endorsement of the preacher: their calling, empowerment, and nearness to God.

Pentecostal homiletics is storied. The storied nature of Pentecostal preaching entails such elements as testimony and a preference for narrativity (Holm 2003, 14). Testimonies inform the act of preaching and provide the congregants ways of considering application and response. The testimonies are both drawn from experiences of biblical texts and ideas or are offered as ways of participating in the Scriptures. This element is furthered by the tendency toward narrative texts of Scripture and/or narrative presentations of Scripture. It might be argued that the Luke-Acts canon-within-a-canon of Pentecostalism provides impetus for such self-understanding and expression through narrative forms of Scripture and narrative expression of the experience of Scripture. This storied aspect of Pentecostal preaching can also be demonstrated in the cadences of many preachers who make use of their distinctive orality deemed to be a preaching voice for the acts of preaching. This facilitates preaching that ebbs and flows in pitch, intensity, volume, rhythm, and movements that are embodied as well as vocalized.

Pentecostal homiletics is eschatological. Pentecostals consider the outpouring of the Spirit of Jesus to be the experience of eschatological expectation. Peter's interpretation on the day of Pentecost as "this is that" concerning Joel's prophecy of the outpoured Spirit becomes a regular feature of Pentecostal preaching. This interpretive understanding is in relation to the theological tension between the "already/not yet" understanding of the eschaton (the end of the age when the kingdom of God comes into its fullness). There is a tendency in Pentecostal preaching to give greater attention to the "this"-ness of the interpretation where the "already" is favored over the "not yet" of the fulfillment of Scripture. However, Pentecostal preaching is decidedly eschatological in what drives it (the soon coming of King Jesus) and its contents (the present evidential inbreaking of the kingdom) toward the fulfilment of its mission (to make Jesus known in fullness everywhere) (dela Cruz 2007, 196; Leoh 2007, 107–110).

Pentecostal homiletics is participatory. Many expressions of homiletics in other traditions expect a silent reception during a sermon. In Pentecostal contexts the expectation is response whether through exclamations of affirmation and praise, groans, confession of sins, prophetic gifts, conversions, healings, and experiences of the Spirit that invites admission of empowered witnesses (whether regarded as "prophets," "healers," or "preachers"), but also embodied responses (Chitando 2000). Pentecostal preaching calls for response whether formally or informally.

The expectation is that God is present by His Spirit moving upon the affections of those hearing the message to carry them into the joy of obedience to the message.

Pentecostal homiletics is pragmatic. The call to respond to the message is often framed by specific manners of responding (such as coming to an altar for prayer or confession) while remaining open to other responses (such as prophetic words or shouts of praise). Further, the pragmatic nature of Pentecostal homiletics has resulted in the wide use of media for dissemination by Pentecostals globally with mixed results and the expansion of the experience of the Pentecostal sermon. At times it appears driven by market concerns in various socio-cultural contexts (by example, with aims at franchising the preaching experience of Hillsong, see Klaver 2016, with more success in televised media by Pentecostal preachers in Brazil and far less in Guatemala, see Smith and Campos 2008, 49–64). This pragmatic approach to the use of media has also at times contributed to traditional constructions of perceived gender roles across Pentecostal fellowships despite Spirit-empowered gender inclusivity (Moore 2011, 254–270). Pentecostal preaching considers itself to call prophetically for specific responses in re-imagining how those hearing might walk in faithfulness to the Lord by the Spirit. This has at times been represented by preaching that drives at upward social mobility and advancement including through material prosperity, sense of life fulfilment, or positive confession (Leoh 2007, 110–112; Enyinnaya 2008, 146; Stevens 2006, 288, 293–94). While Pentecostal preaching appeals to the affections (the desires and will), this appeal is toward motivation to participate in practical ways in what God is doing in the world by the Spirit as those who have been saved, made holy, empowered for witness, healed, and work toward the culmination of the Day of the Lord.

Bibliography

Chitando, Ezra. 2000. "'Stop Suffering': An Examination of the Concepts of Knowledge and Power with Special Reference to Sacred Practitioners in Harare." *Religion & Theology* 7 (1): 56–68.

dela Cruz, Roli G. 2007. "A Historical-Doctrinal Perspective of Filipino Pentecostal Preaching." *Asian Journal of Pentecostal Studies* 10 (2): 192–217.

Enyinnaya, John O. 2008. "Pentecostal Hermeneutics and Preaching: An Appraisal." *Ogbomoso Journal of Theology* 13 (1): 144–153.

Hollenweger, Walter J. 2004. "An Irresponsible Silence." *Asian Journal of Pentecostal Studies* 7 (2): 219–224.

Holm, Randall. 2003. "Cadences of the Heart: A Walkabout in Search of Pentecostal Preaching." *Didaskalia* 7 (1): 13–27.

Klaver, Miranda. 2015. "Media Technology Creating 'Sermonic Events.' The Hillsong Megachurch Network." *Crosscurrents* 65 (4): 422–433.

Land, Steven J. 2001. *Pentecostal Spirituality: A Passion for the Kingdom*. Sheffield: Sheffield Academic Press.

Leoh, Vincent. 2007. "Eschatology and Pneumatic Preaching with a Case of David Yonggi Cho." *Asian Journal of Pentecostal Studies* 10 (1): 101–15.

Leoh, Vincent. 2006. "A Pentecostal Preacher as an Empowered Witness." *Asian Journal of Pentecostal Studies* 9 (1): 35–58.

Martin, Lee Roy, ed. 2015. *Toward a Pentecostal Theology of Preaching*. CPT Press.

Moore, Darnell L. 2011. "Constructing Gender: Old Wine in New Media(skins)." *Pneuma* 33 (2): 254–270.

Smith, Dennis A., and Leonildo Silveira Campos. 2008. "Christianity and Television in Guatemala and Brazil: The Pentecostal

Experience." *Studies in World Christianity* 24 (1): 49–64.

Stevens, Bruce. 2006. "'Up, Up and Away': Pentecostal Preaching and the Manic Defence." *Asian Journal of Pentecostal Studies* 9 (2): 284–294.

Rick Wadholm

Honduras

Pentecostalism has become a major religious force in Honduras. Pentecostalism did not arrive in Honduras until the years leading up to the Second World War. The earliest known Pentecostal missionary in Honduras was a Canadian man, Frederick Mebius, who crossed the border from El Salvador in 1931. He organized indigenous churches that came into contact with the Assemblies of God in the mid-1930s. In 1944 Fred and Lucille Litton established the first Church of God (Cleveland, TN) in the Bay Islands. Similarly, Josué and Vanette Rubio established the first Pentecostal Church in the nation's capital, Tegucigalpa, in 1951. The establishment and subsequent growth of Pentecostalism in Honduras is the result of sacrificial efforts by these and other church pioneers. A US Department of State survey in 2008 placed the number of Evangelicals in Honduras at 36 percent of the population. A large percentage of these are Pentecostal.

Many of the Pentecostals in Honduras report that they were raised as Roman Catholics, approximately 26 percent. Honduran Pentecostalism is characterized by expressive music and effusive worship. People will report singing, clapping, raising their hands, shouting, and jumping. Furthermore, they express a fervency for evangelism and sharing their faith. The Pew Center notes that 37 percent of those polled stated that they actively talked about their faith with someone at least once a week.

To give an idea of the growth of Pentecostalism, the Assemblies of God and the Church of God (Cleveland, TN) give impressive statistics over the exponential growth over the last half of the twentieth century. The Assemblies of God is the largest Pentecostal denomination in the country. In 2015, it reported approximately 160,000 members and 2,250 churches. These were served by 2,212 pastors. The Assemblies of God has three major Bible schools and 21 training programs with over 1000 students involved in one way or another.

The Church of God (Cleveland, TN) also reports impressive growth. The current statistical report includes 88,933 members and 1,164 churches. These are served by 1,720 credentialed ministers. The Church of God also has numerous educational initiatives. SETEPH, or the Seminario Teológico Pentecostal de Honduras attends to educational needs with students attending from different sectors of Honduras. The Church of God in Honduras also collaborates with other Central American nations and sends many of its students to Guatemala to study at SEBIPCA the Seminario Bíblico Pentecostal de Centro América.

The largest Pentecostal church in Honduras is Iglesia La Cosecha (Church of the Harvest). This church is the largest Foursquare church in the world and boasts over 20,000 attendees every Sunday. It is pastored by Misael Argeñal and is located in San Pedro Sula, the nation's main industrial city.

It appears that Honduran Pentecostalism has transitioned from being a mission field to becoming a mission force. COMIBAM, a major missionary agency, reported twenty-three independent Honduran missionary agencies. These were active in at least 20 different countries across the Americas, Europe, Africa, and Asia. Many Hondurans are actively planting churches in the United States. Some of them have established large ministries, such as Guillermo Maldonado of the El Rey Jesús Church in Miami, Florida. Others have planted churches in major urban centers, such as New York, Chicago, and Los Angeles. Honduras also has a well-known theological author, Dr. Miguel Álvarez (PhD Oxford Centre for Mission Studies), who is currently the President of the Asian Seminary of Christian Ministries in the Philippines.

Bibliography

Assemblies of God. 2009. "Honduras – Quick Facts." Springfield: Gospel Publishing House. Last Accessed May 22, 2018. http://agwebservices.org/Content/RSSResources/Honduras_Quick%20Facts.pdf.

Elridge, Joseph. 1991. "Pentecostalism and Social Change in Central America: a Honduran Case Study." *Towson State Journal of International Affairs* 25 (2): 10–12.

Holland, Clifton L. July 20, 2001. "An Historical Profile of Religion in Honduras." Accessed May 22, 2018. http://www.prolades.com/cra/regions/cam/hon/honduras.html.

Iglesia de Dios Honduras. December, 2017. "Estadística Oficina Nacional." Accessed May 22, 2018. http://www.iglesiadedioshn.org/estadistica-oficina-nacional/.

Pew Research Center. November 13, 2014. "Religion in Latin America: Widespread Change in a Historically Catholic Region."

US Department of State. 2008. "International Religious Freedom Report." Accessed May 22, 2018. https://www.state.gov/j/drl/rls/irf/2008/108530.htm.

Daniel Álvarez

Hong Kong

Hong Kong is a former British colony and has valued religious freedom even after its handover to China in 1997. It welcomes any foreign influences, be it missionary efforts or contemporary music and worship style. Therefore, classical Pentecostal and Charismatic churches as well as the Catholic Charismatic groups can all be found in HK. Most of them are small congregations with 100–200 people, but there are some megachurches with over 6,000 members.

Classical Pentecostalism in HK is predominantly constituted by four streams which are all trinitarian Pentecostals, but Oneness Pentecostal churches also exist, like True Jesus Church and United Pentecostal Church. The first stream is the Pentecostal Mission, founded in 1907 by Mok Lai Chi. Pentecostalism spread from Azusa Street through Alfred and Lillian Garr to Mok's Congregationalist church that year. The revived Congregationalists founded their own church with their own effort and it is probably the first Chinese indigenous Pentecostal church in Asia. Mok edited the Pentecostal periodical in Chinese and English entitled *Pentecostal Truths* to assist the preaching of the gospel to the Chinese in HK, China and overseas. Nowadays, it has two branches in HK and one in Vancouver.

The second stream is the Pentecostal Holiness Church (PHC) whose mission was first established in HK by Anna M. Deane in 1909. She came to the coasts to serve fishermen and worked with Mok to provide education for girls and women. The PHC had been rooted in HK until William Turner established a mission in Guangxi province in 1924. The Wing Kwong Pentecostal Holiness Church is the largest

PHC congregation outside the US, with approximately 6,000 members. The PHC in HK has one general council with three regional conferences: PHC Hong Kong Conference, PHC Chinese Conference and PHC Wing Kwong Conference.

The third stream is the Foursquare Gospel Church. In June 1910, Aimee Semple McPherson and her husband, Robert James Semple, arrived in HK. Unfortunately, Robert died of malaria after a few months. Aimee stayed in HK to give birth to a daughter, then returned back to the US where she founded the church in 1923. The church sent a Chinese pastor, Edwin Lee, and his wife to HK in 1936. He planted churches and launched the Semple Day School and an orphanage.

The fourth stream is composed of two sub-streams: Assemblies of God in Springfield, US and the Pentecostal Assemblies of Canada (PAOC). Before starting mission work in HK, their missionaries had been active in mainland China in the 1920s, but the American and Canadian missionaries applied different strategies. The Americans emphasized preaching the gospel, tongues and church planting. The Canadians focused on education and opened kindergartens and primary schools. Two female missionaries, Blanch Elizabeth Parto and Sadie Margaret McLeod, founded two primary schools for the children whose family homes were burnt in a disastrous fire in 1953.

The Canadian belief in education prompted Elmor Morrison, an early PAOC missionary, to build the first Pentecostal Bible school in China called Ming Tak Bible School in 1939. After the Second World War, he re-established the school in Guangzhou and renamed it Ecclesia Bible Institute in 1947. Due to the Communist regime, he restarted the Institute in HK in 1954. American and Canadian missionaries took turns to govern the Institute. Paul Greisen (American), succeeded Morrison to become the second president, then A. Walker Hall (American), followed by Paul Greisen, and Ray Austin (Canadian). Now it is called Ecclesia Theological Seminary with a Chinese president.

Since the 1950s, the partnership between missionaries and local Pentecostals became more frequent. In 1954, Morrison sent one of his students, Siu Hoi Lei, to plant a church called the Chuk Yuen Assemblies of God Church. This church has been active in social services and has opened elderly centres, rehabilitation centres and secondary schools. As the church grew bigger and its ministry extended to a larger area, the church became an independent council and Siu was the superintendent. In the 1960s, A. Walker Hall planted a church with some Chinese Christians and named it Wa Wai Assembly of God. It aimed to serve the poor and to establish schools.

Due to American and Canadian missionary efforts and numerous divisions, four AG councils have been founded: Ecclesia Ministries Ltd, General Council HK Assemblies of God, Pentecostal Church of HK and Asia Assembly Mission Council.

The charismatic renewal created controversy in HK since the 1960s and one of the controversial figures was Kong Duen Yee (Mui Yee). She had been an actress since the 1930s, but after being baptized by the Spirit in 1961, she was active in preaching the renewal message of blood, water and the Holy Spirit (1 John 5:6–8). She founded Grace of Jesus Christ Crusade and preached in Malaysia and Taiwan. She then founded the New Testament Church which were established in these regions. However, her radical teachings and actions left a stigma from the Charismatic renewal among Chinese evangelicals for decades.

Dennis Balcombe, an independent American Pentecostal missionary, founded the Revival Christian Church in 1969. For years, working for house churches in China was the ethos of his church and family, but in recent years, they also worked with the Three-Self Patriotic churches.

611 Bread of Life Christian Church is a megachurch with 8,000 members. It was planted by its mother church in Taipei in 2001 through Rev. Joshua Cheung and his wife. 611 stands for Isaiah 61:1. Its ministry does not only follow general Charismatic practices like healing and prophecy, but also adopts the narratives, feasts and teachings of the Old Testament. Members are divided into twelve tribes and celebrate the seven Old Testament feasts. They hold a Torah evening event and a Rosh Chodesh prayer meeting. It has successfully attracted students, young families, professionals, elderly and migrant workers to the church.

The CCR in HK started in the late 1970s through two streams: the Filipino and the Chinese Catholics. Since the 1970s, women's social mobility has increased through working full-time, including professional sectors. Consequently, the city has a high demand for Filipina workers to assist with household duties. The majority of the Filipina workers are Catholics and some of them transplanted the Charismatic prayer groups founded in the Philippines, like El Shaddai and the Loved Flock. However, there are also Chinese Catholic charismatic groups, such as Renewal in the Spirit Community founded in 2000 by a Catholic woman. It has about 30 prayer groups. Both Filipino and Chinese charismatics attend the Spirit in Life Seminar to prepare themselves for Spirit baptism. They absorb contemporary worship style of Chinese and English evangelical and charismatic churches, but they also seek to connect themselves with the Church's spiritual traditions like Jesuit spirituality. Members remain faithful to attend Mass every Sunday. All Catholic charismatic groups need to register with the Hong Kong Catholic Charismatic Service Committee which was founded in the 1980s. It is recognised by the Bishop of Hong Kong who has the authority to appoint a Diocesan Spiritual Coordinator.

Bibliography

Anderson, Allan and Edmond Tang, eds. 2011. *Asian and Pentecostal: The Charismatic Face of Christianity in Asia*. Revised Edition. Oxford: Regnum.

Au, Connie. 2018. "The Migrant Spirit: A Study of the Filipina Catholic Charismatics of the Loved Flock in Hong Kong." *Asian Journal of Theology* 3 (2): 119–140.

Au, Connie. 2017. "Elitism and Poverty: Early Pentecostalism in Hong Kong (1907–1945)." In *Global Chinese Pentecostal and Charismatic Christianiy*, edited by Fenggang Yang, Joy Tong, and Allan Anderson, 63–88. Leiden: Brill.

Connie Au

Hoover, Willis Collins

Willis Collins Hoover (1858–1936), originally a Methodist pastor during the early twentieth century, became a leading figure of a church revival that gave birth to the Chilean Pentecostal movement. Many contemporary Chilean Pentecostals consider Hoover to be a founding figure of their movement. In the history of Latin American and global Pentecostalism, he is often attributed an important role (Hollenweger 1997). The Methodist Pentecostal Church was founded in Chile in 1910 and Hoover became the first superintendent of the first Pentecostal denomination in Latin America, which was also financially and theologically independent as a Pentecostal denomination outside of Europe and Latin America.

Hoover was born in Freeport, Illinois and grew up in a Methodist family. He studied medicine in Chicago and graduated in 1884. However, in 1889 he felt a calling to serve God and decided to join the Methodist Mission of William Taylor in Chile, together with his wife Mary Anne Hilton Hoover. He first served as a teacher and later, from 1893 as a pastor in northern Chile. In 1902 he was transferred to the coastal city of Valparaíso in central Chile where he served as the pastor of the local Methodist church. Here he believed that that the congregants, although well organized, only had vague ideas of the meaning of sanctification.

Shortly after arriving in Valparaíso, Hoover started to conduct a series of studies of the Acts of the Apostles in the church. During a session in which chapter 2 was studied, a famous exchange of words occurred which many contemporary Chilean Pentecostals know by heart. A congregant asked, "What prevents us from being a church like that primitive church?" Hoover replied, "nothing prevents it, except something within ourselves." According to Hoover this conversation triggered a search for sanctification and a desire to become a church like the early church described in the Acts of the Apostles (Hoover 1977, 4).

In the following years, the revival movement gained force in the church in Valparaíso. Revival activities included late night meetings during which different spiritual manifestations occurred such as glossolalia, spontaneous laughing, weeping, shouting, visions, and other ecstasies. Although the Chilean revival had no direct relation to the Azusa Street Revival in the United States in 1906, the events in Valparaíso were not totally unconnected to the emergence of Pentecostal movements elsewhere in the world. During a visit to the USA in the 1890s, Hoover visited a "pre-Pentecostal" church in Chicago "which was living in a constant state of revival" (Hoover 1977, 25; Sepúlveda 1999, 114) and after 1907 he started corresponding with Pentecostal leaders in different parts of the world in order to learn more about the baptism of the Holy Spirit, a correspondence that strengthened his conviction that this experience was also meant for contemporary churches.

However, the Methodist authorities did not share this view and accused Hoover of teaching anti-Methodist doctrines. Hence, the revival in Valparaíso, which also spread to Methodist churches in Santiago, was a source of considerable tension, eventually culminating in an inevitable schism. In December 1909 revivalists from two Methodist churches in Santiago were formally expelled after they had started to organize revival meetings in private homes. In April 2010 Hoover formally resigned from the Methodist Episcopal Church and was followed by approximately 400 church members from Valparaíso. The dissidents in Santiago had already founded a new church with the name, the National Methodist Church, but when Hoover agreed to be the superintendent for a unified church of all the Methodist dissidents, he suggested that the name be changed to the Methodist Pentecostal Church. "Methodist" was preserved in the name of the new church as Hoover insisted that he was following the doctrines of John Wesley. "Pentecostal" was added to indicate that the church believed in the manifestations of the Holy Spirit as they occurred on the day of Pentecost. Finally, the word "national" was omitted as Hoover wished to make it clear that the division was not caused by nationalism (Hoover 1977, 66).

For the next two decades Pentecostalism only grew slowly with the total number of adherents reaching approximately 10,000 in 1929 (Kessler 1967, 322), compared to less than 2,000 in 1910. Hoover stayed in charge of the Methodist Pentecostal Church until 1932 when the church was divided in two almost equally sized fractions after an internal struggle between Hoover and Manuel Umaña, a pastor from Santiago. Umaña became the new leader of the Methodist Pentecostal Church whereas Hoover became the superintendent the newly founded Evangelical Pentecostal Church, a position he maintained until his death in 1936. Despite numerous subsequent schisms, these two churches are still two of the largest Pentecostal denominations in the country.

The schism was in part due to Hoover's authoritarian leadership. Although he greatly valued the freedom of expression in services, he also maintained a very strict discipline in the church in Valparaíso. For instance, he forbade church members to go to the cinema and participate in sports (Mario Hoover 2002, 237; Kessler 1967, 303), and he fiercely opposed the introduction of musical instruments into the church worship. He considered his Chilean brothers and sisters in Christ to be his spiritual equals, but he had little confidence in their capabilities to govern the church and he did not support an indigenous church. At one point he unsuccessfully tried to place his church under the authority of North American Pentecostalism and to find a North American Pentecostal leader. Even after growing old and becoming weakened, Hoover was unwilling to let go of power.

Although Hoover's status as a founding figure is more celebrated in the Evangelical Pentecostal Church than in the Methodist Pentecostal Church and other denominations, his historical legacy is widely acknowledged among Chilean Pentecostals and scholars. He is intrinsically connected with the original Pentecostal revival in the country, and he is in large part responsible for certain continuity with Methodism in many Chilean Pentecostal churches, which among other things is manifest in the practice of infant baptism and in an understanding of glossolalia as a spiritual gift, which should be placed on the same level as other spiritual gifts, but should not be seen as an indispensable sign of the baptism of the Holy Spirit. To this day, the Evangelical Pentecostal Church remains one of the most conservative and old-school Pentecostal denominations in Chile and it still does not allow the use of musical instruments, except from an organ, during services. Hence, there is little doubt that Hoover, although he was at times surrounded by controversies, has made a lasting impact on the Chilean Pentecostal movement, which is one of the largest in Latin America.

Bibliography

Hollenweger, Walther J. 1997. *Charismatisch-Pfingstlichs Christentum. Herkunft, Situation, Ökumenische Chancen.* Göttingen: Vandenhoeck & Ruprecht.

Hoover, Mario. 2002. *El Movimiento Pentecostal en Chile del siglo XX.* Santiago: Eben-Ezer.

Hoover, Willis Collins. 1977. *Historia Del Avivamiento Pentecostal En Chile.* Santiago: Eben-Ezer.

Kessler, J.B.A., Jr. 1967. *A Study of the Older Protestant Missions and Churches in Peru and Chile: With Special Reference to the Problems of Division, Nationalism and Native Ministry.* Goes: Oosterbaan & Le Cointre.

Sepúlveda, Juan. 1999. "Indigenous Pentecostalism and the Chilean Experience." In *Pentecostals after a Century: Global Perspectives on a Movement in Transition,* edited by Allan H. Anderson and Walter J. Hollenweger, 111–134. Sheffield: Sheffield Academic Press.

Martin Lindhardt

House Church Movement, UK

The growth of non-denominational and independent radical churches in the UK since the 1970s was originally termed the House Church Movement (HCM). These had their roots in the Pentecostal and charismatic movements of the 1950s and 1960s. During the 1970s and 1980s they were referred to as the New Churches or the Restorationist movement. More recently they have been referred to as Apostolic Networks of churches. Despite the variety and developments, these churches have continued to be rooted in the theological conviction that the church needs to be restored to its original glory as seen in the New Testament. The eschatological nature of the primitive church is seen as primary, giving a call to radical discipleship and kingdom living. Different eschatologies are followed, but post-millennial schemes were particularly influential in giving hope in the present. Crucially, this hope is to be enabled by a restoration of the five-fold ministry gifts of Ephesians 4:11 – apostles, prophets, evangelists, pastors and teachers. This represented a theological and structural challenge to existing churches and fed the call to leave such churches and start afresh.

Leadership of the church is crucial and it is not surprising that the HCM has been shaped by meetings of its leaders. Many trace the roots of the movement to a series of conferences organised by David Lillie and Arthur Wallis in the late 1950s and early 1960s, influenced by Brethren ecclesiology and the desire for revival. Different conferences spread these ideas across the UK, interacting with the charismatic movement of the time. In the early 1970s a group of seven and then fourteen leaders met and committed themselves to close cooperation, later linking with leaders in Fort Lauderdale. This close working did not last, with two broad streams emerging as articulated by Andrew Walker in his classic work, *Restoring the Kingdom* (1988). The first stream, R1, wanted more radical, exclusive and organised churches in clear opposition to existing denominations. Such churches often had well defined, Bible-based visions that were then worked out in practice. In contrast, the R2 stream were happier to work alongside existing denominations and sought more organic development in response to the work of the Holy Spirit. Such churches related more loosely but kept a focus on the kingdom of God. Arthur Wallis, David Lillie and Bryn Jones are examples of R1 with Gerald Coates, John Noble and Roger Forster are examples of R2.

The leaders in the HCM often see themselves as apostles, raised up by God to plant and build the church on the foundation of Christ. They carry authority and have the right to appoint elders and guide the churches they oversee. This is the pattern they see in the early church that was obscured by a growing emphasis on Bishops. The HCM saw a natural growth in networks of churches that related to a particular apostle or apostolic team. This is a relational approach to church life and decision making, with a flat church structure in which each congregation is freestanding but relates to an apostle. It challenges democratic approaches based on each person having a vote whilst encouraging collaborative leadership. To grow, these networks need to maintain an open and outgoing approach that seeks to plant churches (not just send missionaries) that continue to relate to the original apostle (rather than becoming gradually independent). These apostolic networks

(Kay 2007) continue to develop and present models adapted by churches beyond the HCM.

The HCM has both theological and sociological roots and attention needs to be paid to the wider changes in theology and culture over the last half century. In particular we might note the rise in importance of eschatology and the Trinity as well as the increased cultural diversity, mobility and connectedness through the internet. Theologically, the HCM presents an important challenge to existing ecclesiology with is emphasis on eschatology and the five-fold ministry. Sociologically, the HCM challenges a simple progression from charismatic sect to institutional church given its holding to elements of each. More complex descriptions of the HCM, ecclesiology and community need to be developed that combine theological and sociological elements. These will also recognise the overlaps between the HCM and the black churches that grew in the UK through immigration and church planting. There are also overlaps in Bible weeks, media and digital platforms that the HCM shares with other churches shaped by the charismatic and evangelical streams of church life in the UK. A challenge for the HCM in the future is how to hold to its radical distinctiveness whilst contributing and learning from the wider church.

Bibliography

Hocken, Peter. 2002. "House Church Movement." In *The New International Dictionary of Pentecostal and Charismatic Movements*, edited by Stanley M. Burgess and Eduard M. van der Maas, 773–774. Grand Rapids: Zondervan.

Kay, William K. 2007. *Apostolic Networks in Britain: New Ways of Being Church*. Milton Keynes: Paternoster.

Walker, Andrew. 1988. *Restoring the Kingdom: The Radical Christianity of the House Church Movement*, second edition. London: Hodder and Stoughton.

Wallis, Arthur. 1981. *The Radical Christian*. Eastbourne: Kingsway.

Andy Lord

House Churches, China

In China, the label "house church" is used symbolically, indicating all the churches which do not participate in the government-led Three-Self Patriotic Movement (TSPM). These churches are also called underground/unregistered/non-official churches in different contexts.

House churches started to emerge in the early 1950s when the communist government came into power and wanted to put Protestantism under control through the TSPM. Church leaders were asked to sign "The Christian Manifesto", attaching their churches to the TSPM. Some of those who refused to do so were arrested. In June 1955, Wang Mingdao published "We, Because of Faith", criticizing the modernists in the TSPM and expressing publicly his rejection to join this movement. The publication of this article symbolizes the beginning of the Chinese house church movement. However, it was not until 1958, when the unification of worship started, that a steady stream of Christians began to meet privately. Those who did not want to lose their denominational identities chose to leave the TSPM. The shutdown and the merger of churches, and the arrest of church leaders, made church life impractical for many Christians; therefore, they had to turn to house churches. Even the official churches were closed when the Cultural Revolution started in 1966, and it was not until 1979 that the first church was reopened in Ningbo. During these thirteen years, all the churches were by definition house churches.

The turmoil of the Cultural Revolution in effect gave house churches an opportunity to grow in the rural areas where the government organizations had broken down. It was also in the rural areas that house churches first experienced revival in the 1970s and the 1980s, because the fewer restrictions on personal mobility in the countryside made itinerant evangelism possible. The five largest Chinese house church networks, named after the places where they originated: Fangcheng (China for Christ), Tanghe (China Gospel Fellowship), Lixin (China is Blessed), Yingshang (Truth Network), and Wenzhou, were established and grew rapidly during this time. Because of the lack of institutionalized theological training, most of these churches were patriarchal, establishing their ecclesiastical authority on individual charisma.

The previous imprisoned church leaders were released in the 1970s and the early 1980s. Their experiences in prison became a spiritual asset for Chinese house churches. Most of these symbolic figures spent the rest of their lives in cities after being released; however, the revival of urban house churches started only in the 1990s. The centre of house churches began to transform from rural areas to cities since then. With urbanization, many peasants moved to cities for work, and this led to the decline of rural house churches and raised the demand for migrant workers' churches. The Tiananmen event in 1989 triggered religious seeking among young intellectuals, along with the work of foreign missionaries who came to China after the Open and Reform policy, resulting in a Christian revival on campuses in the 1990s and the 2000s. These activities contributed to the establishment of churches for intellectuals, also known as emerging urban churches.

In effect, house churches are not small gatherings which hide in someone's house any longer. Instead, many of them rent or purchase properties in public buildings as their sanctuaries. They seek to move from the underground and margins of society toward the public and central areas of China. However, new regulations on religious affairs were put into practice on 1 February 2018, which requires all house churches to register. These regulations will make the unregistered house churches that survived in the previous religious market illegal.

Bibliography

Aikman, David. 2006. *Jesus in Beijing: How Christianity Is Transforming China and Changing the Global Balance of Power.* Oxford: Monarch.

Bays, Daniel H. 2012. *A New History of Christianity in China.* Chichester: Wiley-Blackwell.

Fulton, Brent. 2015. *China's Urban Christians: A Light That Cannot Be Hidden.* Eugene, OR: Pickwick Publications.

Ma, Li, and Jin Li. 2017. *Surviving the State, Remaking the Church: A Sociological Portrait of Christians in Mainland China.* Eugene, OR: Pickwick Publications.

Xi, Lian. 2010. *Redeemed by Fire: The Rise of Popular Christianity in Modern China.* New Haven: Yale University Press.

Mary Zheng

Houston, William Francis (Frank)

William Francis (Frank) Houston. Born on 22 April 1922 at Wanganui, New Zealand, Frank Houston was the third of four children. Reportedly, in his initial weeks of life he contracted pneumonia and experiencing healing through prayer. The affliction would, however, be recurrent. A small boy teased at school about his stature, he carried the weight of expectation that he would "never amount to anything." When a friend was converted in a Salvation Army event, and then died young in an accident, Houston "was devastated" and felt he had to respond by converting. Entering training with the Salvation Army, Houston was influenced by William Booth's experiential theology, the many meetings, personal follow-up from "the captain," personal evangelistic work and regular 5 a.m. "knee drill" (prayer meetings). These instilled in him a discipline which he later carried over into his pentecostal evangelism.

Entering Bible College in July 1945, Houston met Hazel Rawson, who was to become his wife. After a posting to the Bramwell Booth Boys Home, Temuka, a "training farm for war orphans," they moved to Levin. There the Houstons encountered Salvationists that claimed to be "filled with the Spirit," and read Gordon Lindsay's biography of William Branham (*A Man Sent from God*). While prayer meetings and ministry prospered under the new influence, finances did not, and as was the case with others who left the Salvation Army for the new charismatic movements, the Houstons quit the ministry in a period of despondancy. Through Queen Street Assembly of God in Auckland he met and was influenced by David Batterham and Ray Bloomfield.

Houston, still suffering from bouts of pneumonia, was deeply impressed by the teaching of "healing in the atonement," and by Bloomfield's emphasis on healing, his personal love for people and ability to communicate. Houston joined Bloomfield's Ellerslie-Tamaki Faith Mission, and within six weeks was made assistant minister.

In 1955, Bloomfield unexpectedly accepted a call to minister in Canada, and Houston found himself leading a church again. Despite a sense of having received Bloomfield's mantle, within a month, attendance had dropped from 400 to 80 people. Houston followed Bloomfield's advice that, "The success of your work will not depend on how many you have lost or retained but rather on how many new ones you have added." Eventually the tide turned. New families started coming, and as miracles started happening again it was soon standing room only, and "the atmosphere in the meetings became electric." Much of the regional Pentecostal movement would later follow Houston's growth emphasis.

Frustrated with the Ellerslie eldership, which would make decisions without conferring with him, in December 1959 the Houstons moved to Lower Hutt. At the annual Assemblies of God (AGNZ) "Christmas camp," he was elected to the Executive Council, beginning a period of wider influence. In 1966, he was elected General Superintendent of the AGNZ, a position he retained until he left for Australia in 1977. Houston's influence was dynamic, as his crusades and example modelled a renewed interdenominational emphasis on power evangelism. Words of knowledge, a strong emphasis on speaking in tongues during ministry, and healing crusades in Māori villages, was the style adopted by others and spread throughout the movement. It was later claimed that "sixty five of the ninety something churches [comprising AGNZ at the time] were planted because of him and people that had come under his ministry." During a visit to New York in 1966, he felt strongly that he should return home and start a Bible College. The first class of thirteen students commenced in February 1967. It became a model for church based ministry training much adopted among later megachurch institutions. Organizationally, Houston replaced the congregational style of church government with a "pastor led" style, where the church was essentially a mechanism for preaching a gospel that was both contemporary in style (of worship music, architecture and dress) and supernatural in impact. By the early 1970s, Houston's ministry had (by attaching itself to the emerging charismatic movement) already extended around the world, including (through work with the Temple Trust) to Australia. His Australian ministry was powerful but – with its emphasis on deliverance ministry – controversial. In 1977, however, a younger executive organized by and around Andrew Evans took control of the AGA. Evans publicly welcomed the Houstons, who several months later moved permanently to Australia.

Houston planted Christian Life Centre (CLC) Sydney with a small team of eight adults and five children one Sunday morning in the "difficult" Eastern Suburbs. In the same year, he travelled to South Korea and was influenced by the church growth principles of Yonggi Cho's Yoido Full Gospel Church. Within six months over 150 attendees filled Double Bay's "Sherbrooke Hall." Houston adapted his approach to ministry, beginning to "pastor" and equip people: he developed a small group system and a ministry team. In order to overcome size and parking restrictions the Houstons planted a series of churches around the city. By the mid 1980s, CLC Sydney was exercising a significant influence on Australian (and international) charismatics and Pentecostals. It became "the church" to visit if you were in Sydney, and according to Cartledge it had an "incalculable impact." (D. Cartledge, interviews) Elected to the state and national executives, under his leadership the "Cinderella State" (as NSW had been known due to the AGA's lack of impact there) developed a strong churchplanting and leadership training culture.

At the peak of this success during the mid-1990s, Houston began to experience problems with short term memory. He resigned from his executive positions, and handed over leadership of CLC Sydney to his son Brian (founder of Hillsong Church) in May 2000. The next year, a letter regarding sexual misconduct was circulated to all ministers of the AGA, specifying "serious" and "repeated" misconduct some 30 years previously in New Zealand. His credentials with the AGA were withdrawn, but the process by which the AGA (now Australian Christian Churches, or ACC) dealt with these issues became a matter of intense speculation in the press, and criticism during the Royal Commission into Institutional Responses to Child Sexual Abuse (2015).

This very public fall raised questions about accountability, and the ACCs "pastor led" style of church government. It certainly dented the following generation's enthusiasm for individual pioneering. Despite this, there is no doubt that Houston was a significant figure in the rise of the Australian charismatic megachurch. His energetic and pragmatic leadership resulted in innovations aimed at making church a place of effective evangelism and, increasingly, discipleship; his open and inclusive attitude to others outside his denomination helped build – and heal divisions within – the church. Houston's faith and vision were contagious. In his latter years, Houston declined due to dementia, a situation aggravated by the earlier death of his wife, Hazel. On Sunday, 7 November 2004, he suffered a significant stroke, and died the next day.

Bibliography

Oral History Archives, Bridgewater M, Interview, 27 March 2002; Cartledge, D, Interviews, 8 May and 22nd May 2002, Australasian Pentecostal Studies Centre, Alphacrucis College.

Cartledge, D. 2000. *The Apostolic Revolution, The Restoration of Apostles and Prophets in the Assemblies of God in Australia.* Chester Hill, Sydney: Paraclete Institute.

Gibbs, Stephen. 2004. "Hillsong Farewells a Lost Sheep Pioneer." *Sydney Morning Herald* (November 13).

Houston, H. 1989. *Being Frank, The Frank Houston Story*, London: Marshall Pickering.

Knowles, B. 2000. *The History of a New Zealand Pentecostal Movement: The New Life Churches of New Zealand From 1946 to 1979.* Studies in Religion and Society 45. Queenston: Edwin Mellen Press.

"Findings released into Australian Christian Churches and affiliated Pentecostal churches." Royal Commission into Institutional Responses to Child Sexual Abuse. Accessed March 16, 2017. http://www.childabuseroyalcommission.gov.au/media-centre/media-releases/2015-11/findings-released-into-australian-christian-church.

1978. *Vision Magazine* 26 (March–April).

Mark Hutchinson

India

In a country shaped by many different religious traditions, Indian Christianity accounts for about 2 percent of the population. Nevertheless, in South India, where nearly two thirds of India's Christians live, Christianity represents a relatively strong minority. Here, the portion of Pentecostalism is also relatively high with a growing trend. Though reliable statistics are not available, pentecostal churches and ministries gained a visible presence within the south Indian church landscape by the beginning of the twenty-first century. Pentecostalism in India is very diverse and institutionally fragmented. It remains a theoretical and practical challenge to understand, describe, and define it properly as a joint movement. It started to take its current shape after the 1960s and 1970s when remarkable church growth started. The prehistory of many of the churches goes back further though, in some cases in the early twentieth century. It began with American, British, and Scandinavian missionary initiatives from classical Pentecostal churches, first in Kerala, and soon afterwards in other parts of South India. After World War II, global evangelistic campaigns associated with healing revivals had a deep impact. A strong Indian leadership arose in nearly all of the churches, not only those with an affiliation to institutions outside of India, like the Assemblies of God, but also independent churches and ministries that kept close ties to various British and American missionary and evangelistic organisations for material and spiritual support. At the same time, quite a number of them were financially self-supporting.

Close connections exist with Indian migrant pentecostal churches all over the globe, most notably with those in the Gulf States and in North America. India is tightly entangled in the global Pentecostal movement.

A special case makes Northeast Inda, a small but Christian dominated part of India, is of interest to scholars. After Independence, some Pentecostal churches made small inroads into the region, with a comparatively small presence of Pentecostalism. The Christians of northeast India have a tribal background. They are practicing a strong charismatic spirituality that might be influenced by Pentecostal examples but is also rooted in their own traditions. In recent years a growing presence of Pentecostal churches and ministries can be observed in Northeast India too.

Most of the Pentecostal congregations in North India are the result of missionary initiatives by South Indian Pentecostals, many of them from Kerala. A considerable Pentecostal presence has been reached among South Indian migrants, which is noticable in the big cities like Delhi and Bombay. Numerically, Pentecostalism in North India remains small like all other forms of Christianity. South Indian pentecostal missionaries also started to work successfully in tribal areas in North India. These tribal people who converted to Pentecosalism are socio-economically downtrodden, and they experienced a new Christian identity that they considered socially and spritually empowering. Though conversion to Pentecostalism among tribal groups in North India has happened in small numbers, it has increasingly become a nationwide and highly politicized issue in the wake of the ascendency of Hindu nationalist political parties since the beginning of the twenty-first century. Radical Hindu nationalist activists attribute these conversions, against all empirical evidence, to alleged "material inducements" and do not shy away from violent and discriminatory actions against these newly converted Christians, including forced reconversions.

Overall, the socio-economic context of Indian Pentecostalism is complicated. The Indian missionaries who brought Pentecostalism to the tribal groups were mostly from Kerala in South India. They belonged to the so-called Thomas Christians, who consider themselves an ethnically defined caste group of very high social status. As they dominated the Pentecostal churches and their leadership in Kerala, a perpetuation of an oppressive structure by the exclusion of subaltern groups from leadership positions took place. Similarly, in other places of South India, Pentecostal congregations and especially their leadership were dominated by people from the higher caste groups. As a result, internal conflicts in churches with membership from all strata of society occasionally took place and homogeneous Dalit congregations with Dalit leadership have formed. In recent years, such Dalit churches have made some inroads among South Indian slum dwellers. Though the leadership of these small Pentecostal slum churches was male, the converts were overwhelmingly female. Pentecostal spirituality helps women to cope with moral fault lines, existential stress, and interpersonal conflicts that make living in a slum for them especially challenging.

As in other parts of the world, religious healing is a central attraction to join pentecostal churches in India. Miraculous healing and exorcism play a prominent role in congregational practices. Many such healing practices exhibit phenomenological parallels to popular Hindu traditions, which shows pentecostals to represent a contextualized version of

Indian Christianity. Multi-contextuality must also be kept in mind, since in most cases, parallels to popular Hinduism are not one-to-one, but are simultaneously found in Indian Christian popular religiosity and elsewhere in the global pentecostal movement. However, most of the missionary activity takes place on a personal level in families, neighbourhoods, among workmates, and fellow students, usually without the direct intervention of pastors. For pastors too, the most important opportunities for mission occur during house visitations. The spectacular nature of healing and exorcism must not overshadow the fact that the missionary success of the pentecostal movement in India is mostly based on individual communication and intensive pastoral care.

There is also a Catholic Charismatic movement flourishing in India, but it currently acts separately to the Pentecostal churches. The Catholic Charismatic movement started in 1972 in Bombay, which long continued to be the center of the movement. In Kerala, since the end of the 1980s, Charismatic healing services experienced massive growth. Over a hundred thousand people have attended charismatic meetings and retreats, which is comparable to the large Pentecostal healing rallies. Another remarkable development of recent years is the charismatization of congregations from the mainline Protestant churches. There is a growing tendency to borrow elements of Pentecostal spirituality and it remains to be seen what this means for the future of Indian Protestantism.

Bibliography

Bergunder, Michael 2008. *The South Indian Pentecostal Movement in the Twentieth Century*. Grand Rapids, MI: Eerdmans.

Goh, Robbie B.H. 2018. *Protestant Christianity in the Indian Diaspora*. Albany, NY: State University of New York Press.

Roberts, Nathaniel. 2016. *To Be Cared For: The Power of Conversion and Foreignness of Belonging in an Indian Slum*. Berkeley, CA: University of California Press.

Sahoo, Sarbeswar. 2018. *Pentecostalism and Politics of Conversion in India*. Cambridge: Cambridge University Press.

Zeliang, Elungkiebe. 2014. *Charismatic Movements in the Baptist Churches in North East India: A Zeliangrong Perspective*. Delhi: ISPCK.

Michael Bergunder

Indonesia

The Pentecostal message had been received before the messengers arrived, since as early as 1909 when *Spade Regen*, a publication by Gerrit Polman, a prominent leader in Dutch Pentecostalism, had been distributed to Dutch speakers abroad including in the Dutch East Indies. The publication and subsequent contact with Polman seemed to have a significant influence on the Dutch speakers. Therefore, an ecumenical prayer group with a Pentecostal influence was started in 1911 in Temanggung, Central Java (van der Laan 2012).

In September 1920, Polman published a request to send missionaries to Java. The first people who responded to the request were Johan Thiessen, formerly a Dutch Mennonite missionary in Sumatera from 1902 to 1912, and Anna Gnirrep, Thiessen's wife, who both came back to Indonesia in early 1921 as Pentecostal missionaries. Missionaries from the USA also arrived in Indonesia in 1921, including Richard and Stien van Klaveren and Cornelis and Mies Groesbeek, all of whom were of Dutch descendants and were previously Salvation Army officers. The role of missionaries decreased after 1942, when Indonesian territory was under Japanese occupation. During 1942–1945, all foreign missionaries were interned by the Japanese. As a consequence, the name of *de Pinkstergemeente in Nederlandsch-Indië* also changed to its Indonesian name in 1942, known as: *Gereja Pantekosta di Indonesia/GPdI* (Indonesian Pentecostal Church).

Charismatic renewal entered Indonesia in the 1960s and it had close ties with some of the Indonesian classical Pentecostal denominations. The date can be traced to the arrival of Edwin Brownell Stube, an Episcopal priest, and Gerald Derstine, a Mennonite pastor, in October 1961. From July to August 1963, the Stubes ministered in more cities than on his first trip, and not only in Java but also on other islands of Indonesia. On some occasions local leaders spoke to Stube about an urgent need for a training centre for evangelists where the students could be trained with enthusiasm for spiritual ministry. This necessity would later become his main calling during his long-term ministry in Indonesia from 1965 to 1977. A number of prominent Charismatic evangelists, who were recognised as important leaders of the Charismatic movement during the 1970s and the 1980s in Indonesia, had direct or indirect connection with Edwin Stube. The Protestants accepted Stube and his ministry, possibly because of his theological education and identity as an Episcopal Priest, which was rare among the Indonesian Pentecostal leaders at that time.

In 1966, the Full Gospel Business Men's Fellowship International (FGBMFI) Indonesia was started in Bandung by Laksamana and Tanuwarta. In 1969, an evangelistic team from the FGBMFI America arrived to arrange a number of revival meetings in some cities of Java. Subsequently, the centre of FGBMFI Indonesia was moved to Jakarta. The significant growth of FGBMFI Indonesia and their influence on the Charismatic movement in Indonesia was not perceptible until the early 1980s. The strong ties between FGBMFI Indonesia and the growth of the Charismatic movement in Indonesia can clearly be observed during the second half of the 1980s. From the early 1980s, several chapters of FGBMFI Indonesia were started in various cities. A number of the chapter's leaders, such as Niko Njotorahardjo and Timotius Arifin Tedjakusuma, were recognised as influential leaders, not only within FGBMFI Indonesia but also among the broader network of the Charismatic movement in Indonesia.

In the 1970s the renewal resulted in many revival meetings and prayer groups which become characteristic of the Charismatic megachurches in Indonesia. A few of the megachurches also came from the classical Pentecostal tradition which emerged and developed from the 1930s to 1960s. There are roughly 40 Pentecostal megachurches with attenders ranging from 2,000 to 75,000 per week. Approximately three-quarters of them are located in Java, one of the main islands which only covers 6.8 percent of Indonesian, yet it is inhabited by 57.5 percent of 237,641,326 population.

The Charismatic renewal among the Roman Catholics in Indonesia started in May 1976. Bishop Leo Soekoto invited Father O'Brien from Bangkok and Father Schneider from Manila, both Jesuit, to conduct a Charismatic style retreat for a number of groups of priests and laypeople. This resulted in the first official Catholic Prayer Group in Jakarta in 1977. The prominent leader among the Catholic Charismatics is Yohanes Indrakusuma, a Carmelite priest. Indrakusuma started his

Carmelite Charismatic group in the late 1970s in East Java. The groups are known as The Daughters of Carmel, an order for women started in 1982, and as *Carmelitae Sancti Eliae*, an order for men started in 1986. There is also a group for laypeople which is known as The Holy Trinity Community, started in 1987. The majority of the Catholic Charismatics in Indonesia are mostly found in urban areas. More than half of them are Chinese-Indonesians (Prior 2007).

The most recent, and still the only national scale research conducted on Indonesian Charismatics, indicates that evangelistic fervour is considered essential by the vast majority of respondents (Gudorf, Bagir, Tahun 2014). While this growth is not primarily considered to be the results of conversion, 91.8 percent out of 3,748 respondents affirmed that they actively evangelise their families, friends, or neighbours. The in-depth interviews with many church leaders confirm that evangelism with religious conversion is believed to be an obligation. However, the research also shows that the percentage of conversions from other religions is quite low compared to the internal conversions from other churches, whether Protestant or Catholic. While conversion from Buddhism and Islam respectively were 6.45 percent and 3.9 percent of the total, conversion from other denominations made up 37.3 percent. Unfortunately, for the interviewed Muslim respondents, the growth of Pentecostal churches, indicated by the size of the building and the number of cars parking during Sunday services, were probably perceived as the result of "Christianisation" or converting Muslims to be Christians. Even though Muslim-Pentecostal relationships could be generally considered as peaceful, this is rather more of an indifferent tolerance. Any intentional initiatives between Muslims and Pentecostals is very rare among the leaders or members.

Bibliography

Anderson, Alan and Edmond Tang, eds. 2011. *Asian and Pentecostal: The Charismatic Face of Christianity in Asia*. Revised Edition. Oxford: Regnum.

Aritonang, Jan S., and Karel Steenbrink, eds. 2008. *The History of Christianity in Indonesia*. Leiden: Brill.

Laan, Cornelis van der. 2012. "Johan Thiessen, Margaretha Alt and The Birth of Pentecostalism in Indonesia." *PentecoStudies* 11 (2): 149–170.

Gudorf, Christine E., Zainal Abidin Bagir, and Marthen Tahun. 2014. *Aspirations for Modernity and Prosperity: Symbols and Sources Behind Pentecostal/Charismatic Growth in Indonesia*. Adelaide: ATF Press.

Prior, John Mansford. 2007. "The Challenge of the Pentecostals in Asia Part One: Pentecostal Movement in Asia." *Exchange* 36 (1): 6–40.

Robinson, Mark. 2008. "Pentecostalism in Urban Java: A Study of Religious Change, 1980–2006." PhD diss., University of Queensland.

Rony Chandra Kristanto

The Indonesian Pentecostal Fellowship of Churches (Persekutuan Gereja-gereja Pentakosta di Indonesia)

Persekutuan Gereja-gereja Pentakosta di Indonesia (PGPI) is an organization of Pentecostal denominations that cooperate to represent Pentecostal interests on public issues with the government. The development of the PGPI is largely related to the history of the Pentecostal movement in Indonesia. The beginnings of the pentecostal movement in Indonesia can be traced to the efforts of a number of people including Gerrit R. Polman, an early Pentecostal leader of Dutch origins in Indonesia around 1910. In 1911, prayer meetings were conducted by H.E. Horstman of the *Gereformeerde Kerk*, Weirs of the *Hervormde Kerk*, and Van Abkoude who later became important individuals in the early years of Pentecostalism in Indonesia (Cornelius van der Laan 1991). Another figure was Rev. J.G. Thiessen who actively planted a Pentecostal community in East Java. Two American pentecostal missionaries arrived in March 1921 after sailing to Jakarta (Batavia) with their families. Cornelius E. Groesbeek and Richard D. van Klaveren traveled overland through Mojokerto, Surabaya, and Banyuwangi, towards Singaraja (Bali) to begin their ministry in Indonesia.

The founding of the PGPI was largely in response to the increase in the number of Pentecostal denominations in Indonesia. But it also served to address issues of conflict among older Pentecostal denominations as well as the development of new Pentecostal denominations. The schisms were caused by some factors such as different theological beliefs and teachings, debates about the ordination of women, relations between local churches and centralized denominations, especially over financial matters, ministerial ethics, and financial assistance from overseas (Jan S. Aritonang 1995; Aritonang and Karel Steenbrink 2008). To this date, there are around 85 denominations that belong to the PGPI.

PGPI has its origins in earlier attempts of cooperation among Pentecostals. In 1955, Pentecostal pastors agreed to form PAPSI/Persatuan Antar Pendeta-pendeta Seluruh Indonesia (Association of Indonesian Pastors). This group agreed to create another organization named DKGKPSI/Dewan Kerjasama Gereja-gereja Kristus Pentakosta Indonesia (Collaborative Council of the Pentecostal Churches of Christ in Indonesia), and also the PPI/Persekutuan Pentakosta Indonesia (the Indonesian Pentecostal Fellowship). Pentecostal pastors also formed PUKRIP/Persekutuan Umat Kristen Pentakosta di Indonesia (Pentecostal Christian Fellowship in Indonesia). These early groups organized around internal needs for cooperation. However, the name was later changed to PUKP/Persekutuan Umat Kristen Pancasila (the Pancasila Christian Fellowship) to represent its views as Pentecostals on public issues, although this group did not last very long (Tapilatu 1982). Over time these groups became more interested in state and governmental issues.

Between August 28 and September 3, 1979 the DKGKPSI and PPI met and agreed to merge. The agreement was supported and approved by the Government of Indonesia in the Unified General Assembly on September 14, 1979. The new name of this organization was DPI/Dewan Pentakosta Indonesia (the Indonesian Pentecostal Council). On October 22, 1998, at the DPI General Assembly-IV in Cisarua, Bogor, the name was changed to the PGPI (the Indonesian Pentecostal Fellowship of Churches).

The PGPI is an umbrella organization that represents a fellowship of most Pentecostal denominations in Indonesia, although not all Pentecostal denominations have joined the organization. Some Pentecostals are members of the Communion of Churches in Indonesia (PGI), and/or the Indonesian Evangelical Churches and Foundations Fellowship (PGLII).

PGPI has had to adjust its policies over time on social and political matters, subject to approval of the government. The PGPI General Chairman is appointed as a member of the People's Consultative Assembly of the Republic of Indonesia (MPR-RI).

Those who have served as General Chairman of the DPI/PGPI include: Rev. Max D. Wakkary, DD (1988–2006); Rev. Soehandoko Wirhaspati, MA (2006–2010); Rev. Max D. Wakkary, DD with Rev. Robinson Nainggolan, MSc as the Acting Chairman (2010–2014); and Rev. Jacob Nahuway, DD (2014–2022). Before 1988 the leadership of the organization was somewhat unstable condition, although Rev. A.H. Mandey, DD was a prominent figure who gave guidance to the organization and facilitated its transition into its current form.

Bibliography

Aritonang, Jan S. 1995. *Berbagai Aliran Di dalam dan Di sekitar Gereja*. Jakarta: BPK Gunung Mulia.

Aritonang, Jan S., and Karel Steenbrink, eds. 2008. *The History of Christianity in Indonesia*. Leiden: Brill.

Laan, Cornelius van der. 1991. *Cornelis van der Laan, Sectarian Against His Will: Gerrit Roelof Polman and the Birth of Pentecostalism in the Netherlands*. Metuchen, NJ/London: The Scarecrow Press.

Tapilatu, M. 1982. "Gereja-gereja Pentakosta di Indonesia: Suatu Tinjauan tentang Sejarah, Organisasi. Ibadah, Kegiatan, Ajaran dan Sikap Terhadap Gereja-gereja Lain." ThM thesis, Jakarta Advanced School of Theology, Jakarta.

Junifrius Gultom

International Fellowship of Christian Assemblies

The International Fellowship of Christian Assemblies (IFCA) is a Finished Work or "Baptistic" Pentecostal association of churches with roots in the revival that began among Italian-Americans in Chicago in 1907. The IFCA has its headquarters in Transfer, Pennsylvania. Most of its nearly 80 US churches are located in the East and Northwest states, often using names like Christian Church, Full Gospel, and Christian Assembly.

The current name, adopted in 2006, reflects its worldwide scope since most of its affiliated churches are abroad. Its initial name was the Unorganized Italian Christian Churches of North America (1927). To express its institutionalization and accommodation to the US society, the peculiar adjective "Unorganized" and "Italian" were dropped within the next decades. When the movement was incorporated, the official designation was "The Missionary Society of the Christian Church of North America", later changed to "General Council". The different names for the CCNA/IFCA record the significant changes in this movement history.

The movement traces its origins to several roots, particularly the continental European revivals of the nineteenth century that had animated evangelism among Italians. Consequently, the Waldensian church, the Italian free churches, and British-American Evangelicalism (most of them from a Holiness or Higher Life background) had developed a considerable missionary work in Italy, and among the Italian migrant diaspora, especially in the United States. Most of the newly converted ranged from non-observant Roman Catholics to folk Catholicism.

In 1893, Michele Nardi, an independent evangelist associated with A.B. Simpson, began a missionary work, which later became the First Italian Presbyterian Church of Chicago. Meanwhile, in the same city, Giuseppe Beretta, who had converted among the Free Methodists, conducted cottage meetings for his co-nationals. In 1903, people from both groups came together for a time when they adopted the theological view of believer's baptism by immersion.

With the inception of a global Pentecostal revival, some charismatic manifestations took place among Italians in Italy and Los Angeles, but it would be in Chicago that a distinctive movement gained form. It happened when in 1907, Louis Francescon, a former Presbyterian baptized by Beretta, learned about William H. Durham's North Avenue Full Gospel Mission. At that storefront church, Francescon and his wife Rosina along Albert and Dora DiCicco had the experience of speaking in tongues. On September 15, 1907, a revival broke out at the nondenominational Free Church that gathered the people evangelized by Beretta. Francescon was invited to rejoin them as an elder.

In the following years, lay missionaries from this Chicago church, later named Assemblea Cristiana spread their message to other Italian communities in the United States, Canada, Argentina, and Brazil, as well as in Italy.

The movement followed much of Durham's theology (and controversies) about speaking in tongues as the initial evidence of the baptism in the Holy Spirit, salvation, and sanctification. Avoidance of "man-made" methods regarding church organization, Bible instruction, and missionary strategies also influenced the movement.

By 1936, about one hundred Italian congregations were located around the United States from Los Angeles to Boston. However, the growth was not without many internal disruptions. In the initial decades, the movement faced controversies about the need to speak in tongues for salvation, the name for the church, the abstinence of food with blood, and the degree of organizing the movement beyond the local congregation.

To ensure cooperation and dealing with the controversies, a council of congregations convened in Niagara Falls, NY, in 1927. At that gathering, the IFCA adopted twelve-point articles of the faith, a standard hymnal, and the practice to hold annual conferences. Local churches would be incorporated in each state, and in 1948, an umbrella missionary society was incorporated. Not all Italian-American congregations joined, with some networks remaining independent or affiliating with the Italian District of the Assemblies of God that existed between 1949 and 1991. In the 1960s, the IFCA sought to reach out to other ethnicities, and most of its churches made a generational transition with the worship services switching to English.

The IFCA has a combined presbyterian and congregational polity. The general authorities and the district overseers overlook the minister's ordination and coordinate cross-church activities. However, most of the church life occurs in the local assemblies. Being strongly oriented towards foreign mission, the fellowship counts for about 240 churches in Latin America, 1700 in Asia and Oceania, and 120 in Africa. In Europe, the affiliated Italian Assemblies of God (ADI) is the largest Evangelical denomination in Italy, and the Italian Christian Churches of North Europe (CCINE) works among the Italian diaspora. The Canadian Assemblies of God (CAG), formerly the Italian Pentecostal Church of Canada, is the sister denomination in that country.

Besides the IFCA, there are other churches from the Italian-American Pentecostal movement. Some remain independent, such as the historical congregations of Chicago, Philadelphia, and St. Louis. A few multi-sited megachurches developed into independent networks, like the Abundant Life Worship Center headquartered in Nutley, NJ; the Rochester Christian Church Ministries; the Faith Fellowship Ministries World Outreach Center in Sayreville, NJ; and the Waters Church in Norwood, MA. About 70 churches of Italian-American, Brazilian, and Hispanic origins constitute the Christian Congregation in the United States, with similar doctrine with the IFCA, but retaining pre-World War II practices of non-salaried ministers and the veiling for women. A dozen churches carry out the legacy of Giuseppe Petrelli. Finally, many congregations affiliated with the Assemblies of God, the Church of God (Cleveland, TN), and the Foursquare Gospel (like the historical Christian Assembly of Eagle Rock, CA) share their origins with the IFCA, but many of the newer members are not aware of this heritage.

The IFCA belongs and subscribes to the doctrines of the National Evangelical Association and the Pentecostal Fellowship of North America (now the Pentecostal Charismatic Churches of North America). It holds doctrinally to views of the infallibility of the Scriptures, beliefs in the Trinity and salvation by the atoning work of Christ, celebrates water baptism and the Lord's Supper, practices the anointing of the sick, abstinence as prescribed in Acts 15, and the premillennial return of Jesus.

Bibliography

DeCaro, Louis. 1977. *Our Heritage: The Christian Church of North America*. Sharon, PA: Christian Church of North America.

Galvano, Stephen, ed. 1977. *Fiftieth Anniversary: Christian Church of North America 1927–1977*. Sharon, PA: Christian Church of North America.

International Fellowship of Christian Assemblies. 2015. Articles of faith and core practices. Transfer PA: International Fellowship of Christian Assemblies. Available at http://ifcaministry.org/.

Martino, David. 1986. "The Emergence and Historical-Theological Development of the Christian Church of North America." Master's thesis, Ashland Theological Seminary.

Palma, Paul. 2019. *Italian American Pentecostalism and the Struggle for Religious Identity*. New York: Routledge.

Leonardo Marcondes Alves

International House of Prayer

The International House of Prayer (IHOP) was founded by Mike Bickle in 1999 in Kansas City, Missouri, USA, "to partner in the Great Commission by advancing 24/7 prayer and proclaiming the beauty of Jesus and His glorious return." IHOP views itself as "an evangelical missions organization that is committed to praying for the release of the fullness of God's power and purpose, as we actively win the lost, heal the sick, feed the poor, make disciples, and impact every sphere of society – family, education, government, economy, arts, media, religion, etc. ... [and] work in relationship with the wider Body of Christ" (https://www.ihopkc.org). Since 1999, prayer at IHOP has continued uninterruptedly twenty-four hours each day. Currently some two thousand Christian believers – called "intercessory missionaries" – serve full time by committing themselves to praying fifty hours per week. IHOP's so-called "harp and bowl" approach to prayer combines vocal and instrumental music with spoken prayers, and blends worship with intercession. Like participants in the Latter Rain Revival of 1948–50, and Charismatic teacher Derek Prince, IHOP stresses the need for extended fasting as well as prolonged prayer for the sake of spiritual breakthrough.

IHOP founder Bickle began as a youth pastor in St. Louis in 1979, and moved to Kansas City in 1982 to found Metro Christian Fellowship in 1982 – a megachurch congregation that grew to three-thousand members, and where Bickle led prayer six hours per day over seven years. Bickle came to believe that God intends to raise up a 24/7 prayer initiative to restore "the tabernacle of David" (Amos 9:11–12) – a movement that will prepare the way for worldwide revival prior to the glorious return of Christ. At the tenth anniversary in 2009, IHOP's leaders committed themselves to continuing in 24/7 prayer and yet added a new emphasis on works of justice, including on-site food distribution, provision of clothing, street clean-up, and inner city prayer initiatives. The IHOP's Children's Justice Initiative serves orphans and children at risk, Exodus Cry helps victims of human trafficking, while Women's Life Center assists women who reject abortion and choose life for their unborn children. For two decades IHOP has functioned globally as a model for innumerable networked Pentecostal-Charismatic "houses of prayer," many of which have no formal ties to IHOP, but nonetheless have been inspired by the Kansas City ministry.

During the 1980s Bickle became closely associated with the so-called Kansas City prophets – including Bob Jones, Paul Cain, and John Paul Jackson – who predicted the imminent arrival of apocalyptic events (e.g., nuclear war, famine, etc.) and the appearance of a "new breed" of youthful, wonder-working evangelists who will usher in a global, end-times Christian revival. The Kansas City prophets were then linked to John Wimber and the Association of Vineyard Churches, to which Bickle's congregation affiliated in 1990. Bickle's departure from this association in 1996 had much to do with Wimber's negative reaction to the Toronto Blessing. Controversy over the Kansas City Prophets commenced in the 1980s but increased markedly in 1990 after Ernie Gruen – a leading Pentecostal pastor in Kansas – issued a two-hundred-page critique. He accused the prophets, particularly Bob Jones, of wild speculation, false predictions, and bizarre visions. Gruen's report also argued that Bickle's fellowship manifested an elitist attitude, arising out of its teaching on a "new breed" of superior Christians. Bob Jones and Paul Cain were both later sanctioned on charges of sexual malfeasance. By 1993, Gruen and Bickle had reconciled their differences, and Bickle publicly admitted that his movement had formerly succumbed to a spirit of elitism.

Participants say that IHOP is not simply about extended times of praying and worship. It is instead about entering what Bickle calls "the beauty realm of God," which creates "lovesick worshipers." One of Bickle's closest associates is Lou Engle, co-founder with Ché Ahn of Harvest Rock Church in Pasadena, California, and leader since 2000 of The Call – a prayer initiative that brought 400,000 believers to the national mall in Washington, DC, to pray for the USA and the world. Bickle and Engle reveal subtle differences. While Bickle manifests a mystical emphasis on love for God, Engle is more political in stressing radical intercessory prayer to uproot social evils and to prepare for revival. Engle's recent *Ekballo* ("thrust forth") initiative is an attempt to mobilize young people who combine intercessory prayer with itinerant evangelism.

Bibliography

Ahn, Che, and Lou Engle. 2001. *The Call Revolution: A Radical Invitation to Turn the Heart of a Nation Back to God.* Colorado Springs, CO: Wagner Publications.

Bickle, Mike. 2006. *Encountering Jesus: Visitations, Revelations, and Angelic Activity; A Prophetic History and Perspective About the End-Times.* 12 CD Audio Album. Kansas City: Friends of the Bridegroom.

Bickle, Mike. 1994. "Filling Our Hearts With Holy Passion." *Charisma* (March): 31–34.

Engle, Lou, Catherine Paine. 1998. *Digging the Wells of Revival: Reclaiming Your Historic Inheritance Through Prophetic Intercession.* Shippensburg, PA: Destiny Image Publishers.

Gruen, Ernest, et al. 2020. "Documentation of the Aberrant Practices and Teachings of Kansas City Fellowship (Grace Ministries)." Accessed April 10th, 2020. http://www.banner.org.uk.

International House of Prayer. 2020. "About the International House of Prayer," and "Affirmations and Denials." Accessed April 10th, 2020. https://www.ihopkc.org/about/.

Jackson, Bill. 1999. *The Quest for the Radical Middle: A History of the Vineyard.* Cape Town, South Africa: Vineyard International Publishing.

Prince, Derek. 2002 (1973). *Shaping History Through Prayer and Fasting.* Foreword by Lou Engle. New Kensington, PA: Whittaker House.

Pytches, David. 1991. *Some Said It Thundered: A Personal Encounter with the Kansas City Prophets.* Nashville, TN: Oliver-Nelson.

Michael McClymond

International Pentecostal Holiness Church

Three streams flowed together in the second decade of the twentieth century to form the Pentecostal Holiness Church ("International" was added to the name in 1975). The Fire-Baptized Holiness Church and the Pentecostal Holiness of North Carolina merged at Falcon, North Carolina in 1911, and the Tabernacle Pentecostal Church (formerly the Brewerton Presbyterian Church) joined four years later at Canon, Georgia. Each group had formed in the closing years of the nineteenth century as part of the burgeoning Holiness movement, and then each embraced the Pentecostal message of the Azusa Street Revival that exploded from Los Angeles beginning in late 1906. Pentecostal Holiness evangelist G.B. Cashwell served as the catalyst for this revival in the southeastern United States. Almost overnight the preaching and demonstration of a "third blessing" called the Baptism of the Holy Spirit – accompanied by the "initial evidence" of speaking in tongues – became the primary marker of all three of these inchoate denominations.

Yet Holiness commitment to sanctification of heart and life was already entrenched at the core of each group. Their acceptance of Spirit baptism as a "third blessing" did not diminish in any way their belief in the necessity of experiencing Sanctification as a "definite second blessing." Rather it further empowered their preexisting commitment to personal evangelism and holy living. The name that survived the 1911 and 1915 merger – "Pentecostal Holiness Church" – well described their desire to see people "saved, sanctified, and filled with the Holy Ghost." Additionally, the early PHC stressed the availability of divine healing and the imminent return of Christ. Together these five commitments were preached to multiple generations as the church's "Five Cardinal Doctrines." To promote a consistency in the five-fold message, the PHC generated various types of publications and opportunities for training. Some of the most effective include a weekly paper titled *The Pentecostal Holiness Advocate*, a series of Sunday School quarterlies for all age groups, and a school eventually known as Emmanuel College. George Floyd Taylor, a precocious preacher-teacher who battled severe physical disabilities, played a leading role in launching all three of these establishing ministries.

While PHC leaders like J.H. King, G.F. Taylor, Paul Beacham, G.H. Montgomery, and Noel Brooks proved willing to defend each of their church's doctrinal positions with rigor – both in substantial books and in the pages of the *The Pentecostal Holiness Advocate* – they also displayed a humility about their own importance that led to consistent efforts throughout their history to minister with other groups. Sometimes they moved beyond cooperation to explore official affiliations and even mergers. In 1943 the PHC became one of a few Pentecostal denominations to become members of the new National Association of Evangelicals. And four years later, the PHC became founding members of the Pentecostal Fellowship of North America. Bishop J.A. Synan helped draw up the group's constitution, and evangelist Oral Roberts spoke at the opening rally. Following the formation of the PFNA, serious (but ultimately unsuccessful) merger negotiations were held with both the predominantly black United Holy Church and with the Church of God (Cleveland). In 1967, the PHC signed an affiliation with the Methodist Pentecostal Church of Chile, a substantial group that included the world's largest single congregation with over 60,000 members. In the early 1980s, the newly-renamed IPHC affiliated with several more denominations, including the United Holy Church and the Wesleyan Methodist Church of Brazil. For the past half-century, scholar-preacher Vinson Synan has been at the forefront of the dialogue between "classical Pentecostals" and the newer Charismatic Movement. In 2018, after more than half a century of affiliation, the IPHC fully merged with the Pentecostal Methodist Church, bringing the church's global membership to over two million.

Even before the Azusa Revival energized the emerging PHC, the founder of the Fire-Baptized Holiness Church, B.H. Irwin, placed in the movement a radical social vision that has continued to ferment, if unevenly, for more than a century. Before the end of the nineteenth century, Irwin demonstrated a compassion for the transient, isolated, and oppressed poor. He ordained women and African-Americans, placing both in the highest levels of leadership at the height of racism in the Jim Crow era. He spoke on behalf of single mothers and against abortion ("child murder," he called it). He worked for the creation of orphanages and schools for children with few opportunities in life. He treated new immigrants as potential brothers and sisters in endtime ministry. He encouraged tenant farmers and mill workers to envision themselves traveling abroad to preach in the poorest parts of the world, bringing both salvation and social mobility. Although Irwin's moral failures removed him from the church after only a few years, this vision resonated with many of those who would build the IPHC beyond the 1911 and 1915 mergers.

We can see ripples of Irwin's vision throughout the IPHC's history. We see it in the 1920s when Afro-Caribbean missionary

Kenneth Spooner's educational work with poor youth earned him a reputation as the "Booker T. Washington of South Africa." It was evident in the 1950s when Oral Roberts preached to racially-mixed crowds, bringing the hope of healing to many who had nowhere else to turn. The mission and values of the church were present in 1983 when IPHC Bishop Bernard Underwood spearheaded the dismantling of the segregated Pentecostal Fellowship of North America and its replacement by the inclusive Pentecostal/Charismatic Churches of North America. The worldwide ministry of evangelist-writer Lee Grady, who fights to expose the abuse of women, protect desperate people from hucksters dressed in Pentecostal trappings, and break down barriers inhibiting intergenerational worship and outreach, is also illustrative of the vision. The work of Falcon Children's Home, providing a surrogate family for at-risk children since 1909 – and more recently leading the effort to diminish the prevalence of abortion, is another expression of IPCH ministry values and beliefs.

While Irwin's vison of a Spirit-empowered Holiness church that challenges all oppressive social relationships has not always been consistently pursued over the past 120 years, the IPHC has never been able to shake these early radical impulses. Under the current leadership of Bishop A.D. Beacham, Jr., the church continues to work at coupling the twin imperatives of Pentecostal power and righteous living.

Bibliography

Harrell, David Edwin, Jr. 1985. *Oral Roberts: An American Life*. Bloomington: Indiana UP.

Moon, Tony G. 2017. *From Ploughboy to Pentecostal Pulpit: The Life of J.H. King*. Lexington KY: Emeth.

Synan, Vinson. 2019. *Where He Leads Me: The Vinson Synan Story*. Franklin Springs GA: LifeSprings.

Synan, Vinson. 1998. *Oldtime Power: A Centennial History of the International Pentecostal Holiness Church*. Franklin Springs GA: LifeSprings.

York, H. Stanley. 2013. *George Floyd Taylor: The Life of an Early Southern Pentecostal Leader*. Maitland FL, Xulon.

Daniel Woods

Inter-religious Relations

International globalization and the amazing growth of global Pentecostal movements frequently require Pentecostals today to engage with a wide variety of adherents of non-Christian religions. Such interaction is complex and multidimensional, including theological and relational dynamics between other Christians as well as with counterparts among non-Christian religious devotees. This article identifies significant terminology and trends, summarizes key features of the newly-developing discipline of Pentecostal theology of religions, and highlights a few pertinent observations drawn from experience in the field.

It is important to distinguish *intra*-Christian relations from *inter*-religious relations. The prefix "intra" signifies relations between Christian groups of differing persuasions while "inter" signifies Christian engagement with other world religions. Terms such as "inter-faith" or "multi-faith" are sometimes used instead of inter-religious but with varying degrees of emphasis. For some interfaith may suggest potential assimilation while multi-faith maintains clear distinctness. Intra-Christian relations, or ecumenism, do not include or necessarily lead to interreligious activities although the latter often involves overlapping partnerships. "Dialogue" describes intentional guided conversation while "cooperation" indicates joint efforts for the common good in the shared space of diverse communities.

Formal inter-religious engagements are usually bi-lateral (between two faiths) but are sometimes multi-lateral (involving three or more faiths). The latter is a much more complex process. Furthermore, inter-religious relations may occur outside formal platforms. The most common inter-religious relations are occasional and may be best described as "lived dialogue" – that is, when neighbors of diverse faiths get to know each other as human beings through informal encounters in their homes, on their jobs, or in their classrooms. Knowing one's own faith well coupled with willingness to listen guided by authenticity and humility are perhaps the best qualifications for spontaneous (or otherwise) inter-religious relations.

Religious pluralism can describe the factual reality of multiple religious faiths in the world today or political commitments to civil and legal liberties for constituents of different faiths. Neither of these two descriptions involve evaluative assessment of respective religions; rather, they focus on pragmatic societal considerations. However, the best known – and most controversial – perception of religious pluralism describes a formal ideology or philosophy affirming the equal validity of various religious faiths. Significantly, Pentecostal theology accepts the first two usages but unequivocally rejects the third as relativistic and unbiblical.

Christian theology of religions endeavors to establish appropriate theological parameters for understanding and assessing relational interaction between Christians and religious others. Obviously, Pentecostal theology of religions approaches this standardizing task from the perspective of established Pentecostal belief and practice. Central features of Pentecostal theology of religions include scriptural authority, high Christology, robust pneumatology, and ecclesial mission. As indicated above, formal theology of religions is a newly-developing discipline for Pentecostals. The broader tradition of Christian theology has not traveled much farther down the theology of religions path either. Nevertheless, clear conceptual categories are already emerging.

Although there are others, by far the most common typological classification of religious identities employs a threefold soteriological lens (Kärkkäinen 2003). *Exclusivism* asserts that only Christianity possesses divine revelation or salvific truth. It perceives all other religions as at best false or possibly demonic. *Inclusivism* recognizes some measure of goodness and truth in other religions but still asserts the superiority of Christianity. It distinguishes sharply between religious institutions and individual adherents. Non-Christian religious institutions are not vehicles of salvation. *Pluralism* asserts that all major religions point to the same ultimate reality but are expressed differently in particular contexts. In sum, exclusivism is closed to salvation outside of Christianity for the unevangelized or devout adherents of other faiths, inclusivism is more hopeful or optimistic regarding the redemptive reach of Christ for some individuals, and religious pluralism argues that all major religions are legitimate vehicles of salvation.

Where do Pentecostals fit in the preceding typology? It is often assumed that Pentecostals are predominantly exclusivists with a minority being inclusivists.

More likely many Pentecostals are a creative combination of both models. For example, Pentecostals adamantly insist on the necessity of Jesus Christ for salvation but also affirm the Holy Spirit's presence and activity beyond institutional churches or organized religions. Not surprisingly, Pentecostal missionaries often relate testimonies from previously unreached people groups recounting dreams and visions they have had of Jesus and/or of the message of salvation. Christological exclusivism is thus tempered with pneumatological inclusivism.

In sum, contemporary Pentecostal theology of religions turns on the concept of robust trinitarianism (Kärkkäinen 2004). An energetic doctrine of the Trinity provides long overdue attention to the too-oft neglected doctrine of the person and work of the Holy Spirit. Without diminishing full-orbed appreciation for God the Father and God the Son, correlate attention to God the Spirit inspires a pneumatological imagination accenting an active role for the Holy Spirit (Yong 2000). This orientation enables integration of Christological exclusivism with pneumatological inclusivism. Pentecostal theology of religions affirms both that Jesus Christ is the only Savior and Lord and that the Holy Spirit, who is, after all, the Spirit of God and of Christ, is at work in all the world – including the world of religions – in mysterious ways.

Taking its cue from Scripture, Pentecostal theology of religions approaches inter-religious relations via its firm commitment to exclusivist Christology and inclusivist pneumatology. However, ecclesiology and missiology, or ecclesial mission, profoundly influence and shape Pentecostal theology of religions as well (Richie 2013). Pentecostal churches comprise worshiping-witnessing communities in their missional identity. As such, they are fervently evangelistic in their missional activity and characterized by orality in their missional liturgy and spirituality. Just as Pentecostal preaching employs "call and response" methodology, so Pentecostal testimony easily becomes dialogical (Richie 2011). Testimonial dialogue does not approach inter-religious relations as a doctrinal debate. Its goal is not to produce a mutually agreed upon set of propositions for a position statement. Neither is it a veiled altar call. Rather, it seeks to discern interfaces between Christ's story and the human story. Then, it trusts the results to God. Is God's love shared? Is Christ declared? The rest is up to the Holy Spirit. Therefore, conversions are neither sought nor shunned.

A prudent approach to inter-religious relations emphasizing increased understanding and mutual enrichment can lead to respectful, cooperative partnerships formed for the benefit and peace of diverse communities. Accordingly, in the contemporary global religious context inter-religious relations have become a critical component of ministry for Pentecostal theologians.

Bibliography

Kärkkäinen, Veli-Matti. 2004. *Trinity and Religious Pluralism: The Doctrine of the Trinity in Christian Theology of Religions.* Burlington, VT: Ashgate.

Kärkkäinen, Veli-Matti. 2003. *An Introduction to the Theology of Religions: Biblical, Historical, & Contemporary Perspectives.* Downers Grove, IL: InterVarsity.

Richie, Tony. 2013. *Toward a Pentecostal Theology of Religions: Encountering Cornelius Today.* Cleveland, TN: CPT.

Richie, Tony. 2011. *Speaking by the Spirit: A Pentecostal Model for Interreligious Dialogue.* Lexington, KY: Emeth.

Yong, Amos. 2000. *Discerning the Spirit(s): A Pentecostal-Charismatic Contribution to Christian Theology of Religions.* Sheffield, UK: Sheffield Academic.

Tony Richie

Ireland

The Republic of Ireland is a relatively small country, both in geographical size and population. It has a rich Christian history that can be traced back to the fifth century and data from the most recent census of 2016 indicates the population of the Republic of Ireland stands at 4,761,865. The percentage of the population who identified as Roman Catholic on the 2016 census was 78.3 percent (CSO 2016). However, the influence of the Catholic Church has been eroded significantly since the 1980s. Religious language, symbols and rituals no longer frame Irish social life as they once did. The lives of many Irish Catholics are not lived within the framework of religious seasons, holy days, or liturgical calendars. The terms 'A la carte' or 'cultural' Catholic has been used to describe a substantial number of Catholics in today's society (Conway 2013). Ireland was once perceived as a socially conservative nation, but the passing of two referendums: one on same-sex marriage in 2015 and the second to legalise abortion in limited circumstances in 2018 indicate it has become a far more liberal society.

While this general erosion in the institutional church was occurring, the number of Pentecostal and Charismatic Christian communities was on the rise. The growth came from two main sources.

First, there was the rise and spread of the Charismatic Renewal Movement from the mid-1970s onwards. The Renewal spread across the country with several 'Life in the Spirit' seminars being organised in which the Spirit-filled Christian Gospel was explained to people. As a result, thousands of individuals came into a personal and vibrant relationship with God and many were filled with or baptised in the Spirit. Over time many people who had a deep experience of God now found their way into new charismatic groupings, thus a new situation emerged in Ireland in the 1980s.

Secondly, there were the beginnings of what was called the 'house church' movement that began to flourish in the late 1980s. These can be characterised as independent groups or fellowships that met in venues such as private houses, schools and hotels for prayer, worship, Bible studies and participative services. They could be described as accessible, informal, relational, and charismatic.

As a result, new independent congregations were being formed throughout the country, with some being established by overseas church planting mission agencies, like the Assemblies of God (AOG). Other Classical Pentecostal denominations such as the Elim Pentecostal Church and Apostolic church had a presence in the Republic of Ireland in the 1980s.

A steady and sustained growth of Pentecostal/Charismatic communities was evident in Ireland during the economic boom of the 1990s, aptly termed the 'Celtic tiger' years. Historic changes have taken place in Irish society over the past 30 years and Ireland has transformed from being a mono-cultural and mono-religious society to one that is multi-cultural and multi religious. 11.4 percent of the Irish population are now 'New Irish' (CSO 2016). The term

'New Irish' is used to describe the Ethnic diversity of individuals who have migrated to Ireland since the late 1980s.

One of the immediate consequences of the increased numbers of immigrants is the formation of new Christian communities. African-led Pentecostal churches are one of the key signifiers of the 'New Irish' presence in twenty-first century Ireland. Abel Ugba's book *Shades of Belonging*, 2009 was the first study of the religious life of African immigrants in Ireland and the research has contributed to our knowledge about Africans in Ireland.

The 2016 census offers a valuable insight into the numbers of individuals who describe themselves as Pentecostal, Apostolic, Born-again Christians, Christians and Evangelicals and the figure stands at 61,112 (CSO 2016). However, the census does not include the thousands of individuals from the mainline denominations who are Charismatic Christians. If one estimates that a further 1 percent of Roman Catholics and Church of Ireland are Charismatic, then approximately 40,000 individuals could be added to the census statistics.

One of the largest indigenous Pentecostal church networks in Ireland is Christian Churches Ireland (CCI), formerly (The Assemblies of God Ireland, AGI) and in 2018 it had 32 churches across the island of Ireland with another 70 associate churches. The name was formally changed in November 2016 and the CCI vision is to see more churches established, more people being reached with the gospel, more leaders being trained up and a desire to see Ireland having an impact in Europe with the Gospel (Garvey-Williams 2017, 17).

Another sizable network of Pentecostal churches is the Redeemed Christian Church of God which originated in Nigeria (RCCG). The first parish of the RCCG in the Republic of Ireland was planted in 1998 in Dublin. In 2018 it had no fewer than 200 communities in Ireland of various congregational sizes (Olajide Jatto 2017, 12–13).

A *Directory of Migrant-Led Churches* was published in 2009 and while there is a view that increasing secularization is forcing many church communities to close on the island, the directory offers a list of over 361 new local faith communities and charismatic congregations that are bringing new life and vitality to the Irish ecclesiological landscape. Migrant-Led may refer to churches with virtually one hundred percent migrant population being 'led' by a pastor and a board of officers who are also migrants. The term migrant-led also applies to congregations which, though established by Irish nationals and having Irish nationals in its leadership, organised or re-organised its ministry to cater for the inflow of migrants. The directory contributes to an ever-changing portrait of new Spirit-filled Christian communities coming to live in Ireland (Thompson 2010, 85–86).

It is to be expected that within the next decade relationships will have developed between the new and indigenous Pentecostal/Charismatic communities in the Republic of Ireland. The essential prerequisite in the twenty-first century is for the movement to stay informed, relevant and connected through the leading of the Holy Spirit. This can be achieved by encouraging men and women to participate in biblical/theological education in colleges such as the Irish Bible Institute. These individuals can in turn mentor the present and future generations of Spirit-filled and biblically conversant individuals to minister in Ireland in the spirit of unity, mutual respect and understanding.

Bibliography

All-Ireland Churches Consultative Committee on Racism. 2009. "Directory of Migrant-Led Churches." Belfast: AICCMR. Accessed December 12, 2019. https://www.irishchurches.org/cmsfiles/resources/Reports/DirectoryOfMigrantLedChurchesAndChaplaincies2009.pdf.

Carnduff, David. 2003. *Ireland's Lost Heritage*. Ireland: IPBC.

Central Statistics Office. 2016. Accessed May 5, 2018. http://www.cso.ie/en/media/csoie/newsevents/documents/census2016summaryresultspart1/Census2016SummaryPart1.pdf.

Conway, Brian. 2013. "Column: Is Ireland a Nation of á La Carte Catholics?" *TheJournal.ie*. April 26, 2013. http://www.thejournal.ie/readme/column-is-ireland-a-nation-of-a-la-carte-catholics-861758-Apr2013/.

Dunlop, Robert. ed. 2004. *Evangelicals in Ireland: An Introduction*. Dublin: The Columba Press.

Flynn, Thomas. 1974. *The Charismatic Renewal and the Irish Experience*. London: Hodder and Stoughton.

Garvey-Williams, Ruth. ed. 2017 "A New Name for a New Day." *Vox Magazine* 34 (April–June): 17. https://issuu.com/vox_ie/docs/vox_issue_34.

Ganiel, Gladys. 2016. *Transforming Post-Catholic Ireland: Religious Practice in Late Modernity*. Oxford: Oxford University Press.

Kelly, Miriam (Mimi) A. 2017. "The Origins and development of the Assemblies of God in the Republic of Ireland: Exploring the Opportunities and Challenges that Pentecostalism Faces in the Island of 'Saints and Scholars' in the Twenty-first Century." In *Global Renewal Christianity*, vol. 4, edited by Vinson Synan and Amos Yong, 254–258. Lake Mary, FL: Charisma House.

Olajide Jatto. 2017. "The Changing Face of Christianity in Ireland." *Vox Magazine* 34 (April–June): 12–13. http://www.vox.ie/oo1/2017/4/11/the-changing-face-of-christianity-in-ireland.

Robinson, James. 2005. *Pentecostal Origins: Early Pentecostalism in the Context of the British Isles*. Eugene: Wipf & Stock.

Thompson, Livingstone. 2010. "Pentecostal Migrants – A Challenge to the Churches." *Search* 33 (3): 185–193. https://www.academia.edu/8152663/Pentecostalism_in_Ireland.

Ugba, Abel. 2009. *Shades of Belonging: African Pentecostals in Twenty-First Century Ireland*. Trenton NJ: Africa World Press.

Mimi Kelly

Italian Transnational Pentecostal Movement

The Italian Transnational Pentecostal Movements (ITPM) refers to a variety of churches that trace their origins to the revival among Italian evangelicals of Chicago in 1907. The pioneer Louis Francescon and the International Fellowship of Christian Assemblies (IFCA) are central to its historical roots and its emergence as a worldwide Pentecostal movement.

The ITPM spread quickly through the migration and missionary networks built by other Evangelical predecessors in North America, Italy, Argentina, Canada, and Brazil. The ITPM has transcended ethnic and national boundaries, with its largest denominations founded outside Italy.

In Italy the IPM began with the lay missionary work of migrants from the United States. The initial social ostracism was met with harsh persecution, especially when the Buffarini-Guidi Circular prohibited Pentecostal worship between 1935 and 1955. After that, the number of churches doubled, but also suffered many schisms.

The majority joined the Assemblee di Dio in Italia (ADI), an autonomous denomination with dual affiliation with the World Assemblies of God Fellowship and the IFCA, being the country's largest Protestant denomination. Other denominations include the Zaccardiani, the Congregazioni Cristiane Pentecostali, the Congregazione Cristiana in Italia, the Chiese Cristiane Pentecostali in Italia, the churches from the Petrelli's legacy, and many independent churches. Other strands of Pentecostalism exist as well, such as the Elim and Apostolic churches hailing from the Welsh Revival. From the 1960s onwards, neo-Pentecostal and charismatic movements, namely John McTernan's Chiesa Evangelica Internationale and the Chiesa Evangelica della Riconciliazione, have changed the ITPM landscape. Migrants and minorities (like the Roma) have found a haven in the ITPM or established their own congregations.

Around World War II, in almost every "Little Italy" in the United States and Canada, there would be an ITPM church. The generational transition and diminishing migration changed their outlook. Mistrust against a bureaucratic organization and controversies over doctrine and maintenance of worship's practices standards contribute to the development of more loose networks of churches. Currently, the IFCA, the Canadian Assemblies of God, the Christian Congregation in the United States, and a handful of congregations are either independent or affiliated with other major Pentecostal denominations (mainly the Assemblies of God) as they continue the legacy of the ITPM.

In South America, the Christian Congregation in Brazil (CCB) and the Christian Assembly "God is Love" of Santa Fe, Argentina, are the largest groups of the ITPM. Both movements have significant foreign works and are more conservative in worship practices and in keeping "separated from the world." The IFCA affiliated churches and some Christian Assemblies (Villa Devoto, Iglesia Cristiana Biblica) are more similar to mainstream Pentecostalism in the region.

In Europe, there are ITPM migrant churches beyond Italy. Nearly a hundred assemblies belong to the Christian Congregation in Portugal, founded by returning migrants from Brazil in the late 1920s. Following in the World War II, the Portuguese and Italian diaspora in Western Europe funded churches like the Christian Congregation in France and the Chiese Cristiane Italiane del Nord Europa (with ties with the ADI and the IFCA). Additionally, this migratory wave helped plant churches in Australia. In the late 1990s, a migratory wave from Brazil added to those churches affiliated with the Christian Congregation in the continent, Japan, and the Middle East.

From the 1960s onwards, missionary endeavors from the ITPM had yielded national movements in places like Haiti (NEW Missions), Spain (Iglesias Cristianas Evangelicas Apostolicas), India (Manna Ministries), Philippines, South Africa, Angola and Mozambique (both countries with well-established churches from the Christian Congregation).

The ITPM shared the social marginality of other early Pentecostals, but the multiple minority status that included ethnicity set them apart. The initial movement and the more conservative groups of the ITPM espoused a view on sanctification that meant separation from the world. Rupture of former Roman Catholic religious practices and focusing on the life within the tightly-knit community have affected family and gender relations, placed a ban on smoking, gambling, and worldly amusement. Dietary regulation affected daily religious and social lives, especially questions about eating food containing animal blood and the ambiguous position on consuming wine and beer in family settings.

This sense of community has kept much of the ITPM apart from other Evangelicals and even other Pentecostals. No an event has gathered the leaders of the national denominations of the ITPM. The initial fellowship across nations only occurred on a personal level, but was sometimes problematic because of doctrinal controversies. Except for the more assimilated groups into mainstream Evangelicalism, like the IFCA or the Iglesia Cristiana Bíblica in Argentina, participation in interchurch dialogue is uncommon.

Theologically, the ITPM subscribes to the classical, Finish Work theology originated with William H. Durham. Distinctively, the ITPM has a Trinitarian theology that integrates with themes about pneumatology, soteriology, and ecclesiology. It shares with the Free Church tradition and with folk Catholicism the importance given to lived religion. High regard for the Bible, read by a variety of hermeneutical approaches, reflects a tension between anti-intellectualism and an articulated, Bible-based theology. Francescon supposedly burned his books before his baptism of the Holy Spirit, but there were also intellectuals like Giuseppe Petrelli. Nevertheless, some groups sponsored basic Bible and theological education. The Istituto Biblico Italiano (Rome), the IFCA Bible College (Cleveland, OH), the Facoltà Pentecostale di Scienze Religiose (Aversa), and Shepherd International University (Marchirolo) offer post-secondary education. Most of the ITPM theological publications remain within the movement, such as Petrelli, Roberto Bracco, Carmine Saginario, Alfred Palma, Guy Bongiovanni, and Francesco Toppi. A few academic-trained theologians connected to the ITPM have gained wider visibility, like Anthony Palma, Frank Macchia, and Juan Carlos Ortiz. Other authors include Daniel Delvecchio, Nicholas Cacciatore, John Lathrop, Carmine Napolitano, Domenico Barbera, Antonio Consorte, Giacinto Butindaro, and those under pseudonyms of FreeMinistry, Cedyl Ceu, and Theophilus.

The hesitation about women in ministry is reflected in scholarly publications. While theological reflection often is a male concern, many female social scientists (members or not) have conducted studies on the ITPM, like Ann Parsons, Miriam Castiglione, Maria Pia Di Bella, Yara Monteiro, Iranilde Miguel, Rubia Valente, Valéria Barros, Dayana Di Iorio, Patrizia Nicandro, Annalisa Butticci among others. By focusing on different aspects of church life, they make invaluable contributions to the understanding of its ecclesiology.

Only recent projects like that by Paul Palma (2019) and Mark Hutchinson's *Explorations in Italian Protestantism* have made a global assessment of the ITPM. Consequently, it remains a migrant, lay, missionary, and even marginal movement within the Pentecostal mainstreams and scholarship.

Bibliography

Colletti, Joseph. 1990. "Ethnic Pentecostalism in Chicago: 1890–1950." PhD thesis, University of Birmingham, UK.

Hutchinson, Mark P. 1999. *Pellegrini: An Italian Protestant Community in Sydney, 1958–1998*. Sydney: Australasian Pentecostal Studies.

Nicastro, Patrizia. 2015. "Origini delle storie del movimento pentecostale italiano: le Assemblee di Dio in Italia." Doctoral dissertation, Università degli Studi di Bergamo.

Palma, Paul. 2019. *Italian American Pentecostalism and the Struggle for Religious Identity*. New York: Routledge.

Yuaza, Key. 2001. "Louis Francescon: A Theological Biography, 1866–1964." Doctoral diss., University of Geneva.

Leonardo Marcondes Alves

Italy

Italy is a country with a large Catholic majority, even if the religious landscape is slowly changing due to the migratory flows affecting the peninsula. The situation of the relative monopoly of Catholicism is challenged by the levels of religious diversity that affect about 10 percent of the population. Although the presence of charismatic and Pentecostal churches marginally touches the Italian religious landscape, there are pastors who follow the flow of migrants from sub-Saharan Africa in the peninsula, which for many migrants represents the first landing on the European continent.

The presence of Pentecostal and charismatic churches in Italy has not been much studied. This is not only due to the small percentage of the population it affects but also to the difficulty of mapping the spread of churches and places of worship as the faithful move easily from one side of the country to another, causing the opening and closing of churches. There is no precise census data on their dissemination. Nevertheless, there are reliable estimates offered by the works of Enzo Pace (2018), Annalisa Butticci (2013, 2016), Paolo Naso (2013), and Massimo Introvigne (2009).

As noted by Naso (2013), the first Pentecostal missionaries in Italy were Italian emigrants who returned from Chicago to the country of origin to preach the Pentecostal message. Among these missionaries, there was Giacomo Lombardi who preached in Rome in 1908, even though his mission was not very successful. His pioneering work, however, continued from Rome, where there was the first Pentecostal church in Italy, to other centers of the peninsula. Pietro Ottolini, another Pentecostal missionary who worked in Italy from 1910 to 1914, founded some communities in Milan and the regions of Piedmont, Puglia, and Sicily. The fascist period blocked the spread of the Pentecostal communities which, by the end of the WWII, were about 250. They were centered in southern Italy, and especially in the Sicily region. The first denomination that succeeded in coordinating the Pentecostal churches at the national level was called the "Pentecostal Evangelical Church" which developed a very close relationship with the Assemblies of God, favored by the help of the United States for the allied countries after the war. In 1947, the Italian Pentecostals constituted the "Assemblies of God in Italy," which however, failed to put together the mosaic of small groups of Italian Pentecostal churches. In 2000, the Federation of Pentecostal Churches (FCP) was founded. It brings together networks of Pentecostal communities spread throughout the national territory (for example, the Elim Church, founded in 1993, which today has 90 churches; the Italian Pentecostal Christian Church, founded in 1997, with 42 churches; the New Pentecost Movement, founded in 2004, with 30 churches spread mainly in the Campania region). In Aversa, in the Campania Region, the Pentecostal Faculty of religious sciences was born, being connected to the Federation of Pentecostal churches. As Pace (2018) recently illustrated, Italy seems to be a fertile country for the spread of Pentecostalism: this is demonstrated by the growth of the Assemblies of God throughout the national territory, with almost 1200 congregations with a high concentration in the southern regions such as Sicily, Campania, Calabria and Puglia.

But beyond their historical presence, the strong push for the spread of Pentecostalism in Italy came from immigration, especially from sub-Saharan Africa, which made the picture of Pentecostal communities even more complex. According to estimates provided by Pace (2018), the African Pentecostal churches present in Italy account for about 858 places of worship and involve at least 150,000 faithful.

Annalisa Butticci (2013) has specifically studied the territorial distribution of the Ghanaian and Nigerian Pentecostal and charismatic churches in Italy, also deepening their missionary model. Following the request for workforce in the agricultural sector in southern Italy and the industrial sector in northern Italy, in the early 1990s, thousands of people from Nigeria and Ghana began to immigrate to Italy. Migration flows began in southern Italy, in the regions of Sicily and Campania, and then moved to the Lazio region and then north towards the regions of Veneto and Lombardy. If insertion into the economic world was relatively easy, cultural integration was more difficult, due to the difficulty in learning the Italian language and in adapting to a culture very different from that of the countries of origin. Many small Pentecostal communities have spread, led often by religious leaders, without specific theological preparation, but with a great communicative and relational capacity among migrants. Within these groups, usually small, the faithful pray in tongues and utilize other Pentecostal practices such as healing and prophesy. According to an estimate offered by Butticci (2013), the Nigerian Pentecostal churches could be about 500, while the Ghanaian churches around 350. As Butticci points out, these are very fragile and provisional estimates, because these small communities have a structure that is fluid where they formed very quickly and with the same rapidity, often disappear. Often they are communities that are born around the charism of a religious leader who, after a few months from forming the community, can decide to change cities or return to her country of origin, thus causing the closing of the community.

The mobility of the members, who move from one city to another according to the needs of the job market, must then be added to the economic difficulties in supporting the costs of renting buildings dedicated to worship. This institutional and logistical fragility must then come to terms with the ambitions of charismatic leaders who often prefer to open their own churches rather than join in more stable organizations.

As well as within the Protestant tradition, the charismatic movement in Italy has also found adherents within Catholicism, with the movement of the renewal of the Spirit, which involves about 250,000 faithful. While remaining within the Catholic tradition, it challenges the organizational construction that is based on the parishes, and follows a charismatic model, led by the laity, which is active in almost 1842 communities in all Italian regions.

Bibliography

Butticci, Annalisa. 2013. "Le chiese neopentecostali e carismatiche africane." In *Le religioni nell'Italia che cambia: Mappe e bussole*, edited by Enzo Pace, 85–96. Rome: Carocci.

Butticci, Annalisa. 2016. *African Pentecostals in Catholic Europe: The Politics of Presence in the Twenty-first Century*. Cambridge, MA: Harvard University Press.

Esposito, Salvatore. 2013. *Un secolo di pentecostalismo Italiano*. Milan: The Writer Edizioni.

Introvigne, Massimo. 2009. "Le minoranze pentecostali nelle comunità romane: Lo stato della ricerca e i principali problemi sociologici." *Religioni e sette nel mondo* 5: 73–78.

Naso, Paolo. 2013. "Protestanti, Evangelici, Testimoni e Santi." In *Le religioni nell'Italia che cambia: Mappe e bussole*, edited by Enzo Pace, 97–130. Rome: Carocci.

Pace, Enzo. 2018. "Religious Congregations in Italy: Mapping the New Pluralism." In *Congregations in Europe*, edited by Christophe Monnot and Joerg Stolz, 139–156. Cham: Springer.

Giuseppe Giordan

Jamaica

Pentecostal evangelism in the Caribbean and Jamaica, particularly, commenced in earnest in the second decade of the twentieth century. It followed in a sequence of similar initiatives involving Jamaicans and churches located on the east coast or in the mid-west of the United States. Around 1891, missionaries of the Adventist church were invited to Jamaica. There followed, in 1907, a similar invitation to a Holiness church based in Indiana to send missionaries following a destructive earthquake in Kingston. In 1917 a Pentecostal convert, J. Wilson Bell, wrote seeking affiliation to the Pentecostal Church of God in Cleveland, Tennessee. A.J. Tomlinson, the church's founder, sent one pastor and two evangelists to Kingston, the most prominent proving to be Nina Stapleton. One of her early converts was Rudolph Smith, the son of a prosperous small farmer who had come to Kingston in search of work. In 1922 he returned to Clarendon parish where he established numerous congregations. One of his disciples, Henry Hudson, continued independently to build further churches. By 1935, when there had been fission in the Church of God, Cleveland, Smith would become overseer in Jamaica for the Church of God of Prophecy and Hudson, overseer for the New Testament Church of God. Those who built each of these churches were mainly black Jamaicans, often described by the Americans as "native" evangelists. These two churches remain today among the largest Trinitarian Pentecostal churches in Jamaica.

In 1919, a Unitarian Pentecostal movement was begun by J.R. (later Mother) Russell in the parish of St. Ann. With the assistance of two American preachers and a young Jamaican couple, George and Melvina White, they established churches in rural parishes and in Kingston. Following a split in the Jamaican movement, the Whites became affiliated as minister and evangelist respectively with the black "oneness" organization, Pentecostal Assemblies of the World. Their major Kingston church was the Emmanuel Apostolic Tabernacle, an early centre for oneness or "Jesus-only" Pentecostalists. Mother Russell continued her association with the United States-based and predominantly white, United Pentecostal Church. Both became prominent churches open to all Jamaicans today.

The Pentecostal movement in Jamaica is comprised of some very large organisations, such as those cited here. There is, however, also a plethora of small, independent churches located both in urban areas and in the countryside. These dual aspects of the movement account for its dynamism. With some support from North America, the large congregations have systematically built their following in numerous congregations across the island while small churches proliferate often due to the inspiration of individuals. The dynamic of the movement is both organisational and charismatic. Four categories of the Jamaican Census bear on Pentecostalism which, in 2011, stood at almost thirty percent of those responding. The second largest category of census respondents was "No Religion," suggesting that the two marked developments in Jamaican religion through the twentieth century were the growth of Pentecostalism alongside secularism. Adventism, with 12 percent, is another prominent new religion in Jamaica. The entry of these new religions into Jamaica came as the United States began a period of major investment in the Caribbean region. Soon, these American sourced religions began to outstrip the often British-based colonial churches that had been prominent previously.

Bibliography

Austin-Broos, Diane. 2020. "Jamaican Pentecostalism: Its Growth and Significance." *Journal of Commonwealth and Comparative Politics* 58 (3): 285–300.

Austin-Broos, Diane. 2001. Churches and State: Aspects of Religious Ideology in Colonial and Post-colonial Jamaica. *Caribbean Quarterly* 47 (4): 1–32.

Austin-Broos, Diane. 1997. *Jamaica Genesis: Religion and the Politics of Moral Order*. Chicago: University of Chicago Press.

Austin-Broos, Diane. 1992. "Redefining the Moral Order: Interpretations of Christianity in Post-emancipation of Jamaica." In *The Meaning of Freedom*, edited by F. McGlynn and S. Drescher, 221–245. Pittsburgh: University of Pittsburgh Press.

Diane J. Austin-Broos

Jeffreys, George

George Jeffreys (1889–1962) healing evangelist, revivalist and founder of the Elim Pentecostal Church was born to a coal mining family in Maesteg, South Wales, in 1889. George and Stephen, his older brother (1876–1943), attended Siloh Independent Chapel. More dramatic and more formative than ordinary church-going was the Welsh Revival of 1904–05 during which Stephen and George were converted.

After leaving school at the age of 12 George worked, like Stephen, in the coal mines. At first the brothers were opposed to Pentecostalism but, when Edward, Stephen's son, spoke in tongues, their opposition melted and both experienced the Holy Spirit powerfully and were then later baptized by full immersion in a river in 1911. The Anglican Vicar, Alexander Boddy, asked George to speak at the Sunderland Convention in 1913. This international gathering of early Pentecostals launched the young preacher into his wider ministry.

George was invited to Ireland where, in January 1915 in Monaghan, he formed the Elim Evangelistic Band which established its first church in Belfast in 1916. The Band bought a tent for summer campaigns, held numerous gospel meetings in hired halls, farmhouses and private homes. The Band became the Elim Pentecostal Alliance in 1918 and was legally constituted as a property-holding body. By the end of 1920, it had 15 congregations in Ireland and by 1921 its first congregation was opened in England.

The next fifteen or so years witnessed extraordinary growth. The post-war population traumatised by war and high unemployment crowded into the meetings George held in the main cities in the British Isles. George was in Liverpool in 1926 and 3,000 attended the closing service, in Glasgow in 1927 where over 10,000 attended the closing weekend, in Leeds where 2,000 converts were claimed in the same year, and then in Birmingham and filling the Bingley Hall in 1930, but also with 15,000 in the Crystal Palace, London, in 1931 and then filling the 10,000 seats of the Royal Albert Hall, London, every year at Easter from 1926 to 1939. Donald Gee said, Jeffreys 'had a voice like music, with sufficient Welsh intonation to add inimitable charm ... he presented his message with a logical appeal and a note of authority that was compelling'. The national press from broadsheet to tabloid reported favourably in most instance and investigative journalists could follow up and verify cases of healing.

Behind the public success tensions arose. George and Stephen parted company in 1926 with bad feeling on both sides. George created the Elim Foursquare Gospel Alliance (EFGA) in 1929. The word 'foursquare' meant that Elim stood firmly on the Bible but also expressed four key beliefs (full gospel) about Jesus who was regarded as Savior, Healer, Baptizer in the Holy Spirit, and Coming King. Day-to-day control of the movement flowed through the administration in Clapham where E.J. Phillips (1893–1973) was in charge. In 1934 control was transferred to an Executive Council of nine men, of whom Jeffreys appointed three, two (Jeffreys and Phillips were *ex-officio*) and four were elected from the annual ministerial conference which became the final seat of authority. Jeffreys' majority on the Executive Council was not built-in and the ministerial conference, where decisions were reached after debate, might disagree with him and, on one crucial issue, it did.

British Israelism (BI) contended that the ten lost tribes of Israel were incorporated within the Anglo-Saxon population. Jeffreys had probably been persuaded of the doctrine while he was in Ireland and his acceptance of it complicated analysis of the power struggle that now followed. The ministerial conference of 1934 had debated the issue and only 17 out of 131 had accepted the teaching.

The disagreement between Jeffreys and Elim was framed in terms of the granting of local congregations ownership of their buildings, with Jeffreys thundering against the "Bablyonish bondage" that vested valuable trust deeds with the headquarters. After disagreements Jeffreys left Elim in 1940 and until his death in 1962 worked through the Bible-Pattern Church Fellowship (which he founded) and the World Revival Crusade. He continued to hold a punishing schedule of meetings though, because the Elim churches were now closed to him, he hired halls or used a big tent as he had done at the beginning. There were never more than about 60 Bible-Pattern congregations. Jeffreys himself had developed diabetes in the 1930s but this hardly slowed him down and, when the war ended, he was free to travel overseas. He was in Belfast in 1945 and 2,600 packed the Royal Hippodrome. Large crowds heard him in France (1946, 1948, 1950) and Switzerland (1947, 1948, 1950) and he preached in the USA, Canada, Belgium, and Palestine. He opposed the formation of the World Pentecostal Conference in 1947 and the World Council of Churches and he took comfort from the big Swedish Pentecostal Churches which, unlike Pentecostal churches almost everywhere else in the world, refused to organize themselves into denominations.

George never married and his close colleagues in the Revival Party were like a family to him. His main legacy is to be found in the Elim Pentecostal church, which he had founded in 1915. He wrote *Healing Rays* in 1932 and *Pentecostal Rays* in 1933 respectively setting out his teaching on divine healing and the Holy Spirit. He died quietly in his sleep in January 1962.

Bibliography

Boulton, E.C.W. 1928 (1999). *George Jeffreys: A Ministry of the Miraculous*. London: Elim Publishing Office.
Cartwright, Desmond. 1986. *The Great Evangelists*. Basingstoke: Marshall Pickering.
Gee, Donald. 1980. *These Men I Knew*. Nottingham: Assemblies of God Publishing House.
Kay, W.K. 2017. *George Jeffreys: Pentecostal Apostle and Revivalist*. Cleveland, TN: CPT Press.
Wilson, B.R. 1961. *Sects and Society*. London: Heinemann.

William K. Kay

Jesus Family Church, China

Jesus Family was an indigenous church founded by Jing Dianying (敬奠瀛; 1890–1957) in 1921 in Mazhung, Shandong province, China. He received traditional Confucian education from his father, then embraced Taoism as a teenager. He converted to Christianity in 1914 while attending a missionary school and teaching the Chinese language to a Methodist missionary, Nora Dillenbeck. Eventually, he became a Pentecostal.

Jing's idea to build up a novel Christian organization not only originated from religious reasons, but also from his concern with the rural problems of Mazhuang, where flood, drought, plague of insects and the corrupt local government, had caused the farmers' situation to worsen. In 1921, Jing established the Christian Trust and Saving Society. He argued that China was poor because people did not trust each other, and the only way to solve this problem was to organize the Christians, whom he considered had virtue and could be trusted to do business together. Nevertheless, Jing's practice was not successful. According to Daniel Bays (1988), Jing got illumination from a Pentecostal missionary called Anglin who belonged to the Assemblies of God and established the "Home of Onesiphorus" in Tai'an. Jing was attracted by its combination of secular life with the sacred, and particularly its religious experience that was much like the folk religion of Shandong. He began to transfer his economic activity from business to agriculture in 1924 and donated the land he had inherited. A chapel was built and farming commenced. He renamed his organization the "Jesus Home" or "Jesus Family" in 1927.

The Jesus Family developed gradually afterwards. In addition to the family in Mazhuang, which was called the "old family" (老家), Jing began to build "little families" (小家) along the lines of the old family. The total number of families reached 127 in 1952, spreading over the northwest, east, and south China. Most of them were in rural areas, while some of them were built in cities such as Nanjing, Wuhan, and Shanghai. The head of each family was called jiachang (家長). Members had to agree to donate their possessions and lead simple lives in the commune in submission to the jiachang. The total population of all the families grew from only around a dozen to about ten thousand in 1948. More than 3,000 Christians lived in Jesus Families, according to the Chinese government's statistics in 1952.

Jesus Family practiced the communitarian system and an egalitarian way of life. Adult members shared the same standards in food and clothing and lived in the same rooms except for babies and elders who had better treatment. Based on economic functionalism, Jesus Family relied on farming and industry, which made them self-sufficient. Production was efficient as a result of a planned division of labor. In the Mazhuang family, for example, the foundation was agriculture, and upon this were built various enterprises and departments. There were facilities provided for carpentry, boot-making, baking, smithy, and stone masonry. Machine shops and printing and book-binding houses were set up. Schools and a kindergarten were established. There were also electricity, finance, and external relations departments. The community-builders worked hard to maintain the Family's very modest standard of living in the chaotic years.

The Family was a total social and economic communal milieu. Life there was a formative experience that involved mutually-reinforcing elements such as prayer, work, and learning. Living in these communes not only involved a high degree of social, economic, and religious integration, but also profound social control that eliminated individuality. The pattern of their daily life was influenced by the theology of Jing Dianying, who was first known as jiazhang and later as the only laoren (Old Man), which exercised his sole authority over all the families.

After the People's Republic of China was founded, the Jesus Family cultivated a good relationship with the local government. During the Three-Self Patriotic Movement in the Protestant sector, the Family took the lead to show support. Jesus Family was regarded as a truly indigenous church without connection to western imperialism. However, the end of the Jesus Family did not come in the way as Jing had expected. Some attacked the churches because they overstressed the mystery of religious experiences, paid too much attention to religious activities, and ignored the responsibility to increase production that the people badly needed.

Some members were disillusioned by the oppressive organizational structure as well as the suspected corruption and licentiousness of some leaders. In other words, Jesus Family was deemed incompatible with the new system of the socialist country. After fierce criticism from the Family members, in the middle of 1952, the Family was "reformed" and renamed as the Beixin Zhuang (北新庄) church which is now an advanced Three-Self Patriotic church in Shandong province. Jing was jailed for a few years but released on medical parole later. Very few of the "little families" disappeared and most of them have become ordinary churches under the leadership of China Christian Council and China Three-Self-Patriotic Movement Committee.

Bibliography

Bays, Daniel H. 1988. "Christianity in China, A Case Study of Indigenous Christianity: The Jesus Family, 1927–1952." *Religion: Journal of the Kansas School of Religion* 26 (1): 1–3.

Gustavson, Helen I. "A Letter, 2086 Marshall Ave, St. Paul, Minn 55104, Dec. 22, 1971."

Rees, Delwyn Vaughan. 1959. *The 'Jesus Family' in Communist China: A Modern Miracle of New Testament Christianity*. Exeter: Paternoster Press.

Wang, Xipeng. 1950. *Documenting the Jesus Family*. Shanghai: The Rural Construction Committee of the National Christian Council of China. (汪锡鹏。《记耶稣家庭》。上海：上海中华基督教协进会上海乡村事业委员会。)

Xü, Jia Shu. 1952. *Thirty-one Year of the Jesus Family*. Shandong: Religious Affairs Department of the Culture and Education Committee of Shandong Province. (徐家枢。《耶稣家庭三十一年的历史》。山东：山东省文教委宗教事务处。)

Fei Ya Tao

Jesus is Lord Church Worldwide, Philippines

Celebration of the 39th anniversary of Jesus is Lord Church (2017). Wikimedia, UnangKarlito (CC BY-SA)

Jesus is Lord Church Worldwide, popularly known as Jesus is Lord Church (JIL), is one of the most visible Christian groups in the Philippines. JIL claims to have a constituency of more than four million both at home and in fifty-five other countries, including large branches in Hong Kong, Abu Dhabi, Qatar and Italy as well as North America and Australia. JIL-founder, Eduardo "Bro. Eddie" Cruz Villanueva, a member of the House of Representative since 2019, is arguably among the country's five most influential spiritual leaders.

As owner of a broadcasting network (Zoe TV) and a record label (Musikatha) JIL has a considerable media presence. In the Philippines, JIL draws its constituency mostly from the working and middle classes. Abroad, JIL adherents are mainly overseas workers. This corresponds with JIL's vision that aims at the spiritual and social uplifting of the Philippine people at large in order to reach out to the whole world; "Evangelizing and discipling Filipinos and all the peoples of the world through teaching, preaching and living-out the full-Gospel" and "bring all peoples to the kingdom of the living God regardless of race, status, belief and religious affiliations through the saving, healing, delivering, and transforming power of the Lord Jesus Christ" (JILW 2013). Unlike other megachurches and as a matter of policy, JIL conducts its services not in English but mainly in Philippine languages.

The beginnings of JIL go back to 1978 when Eduardo "Bro. Eddie" Cruz Villanueva, a former Marxist activist and professor of Political Economics at the Philippine College of Commerce (now Polytechnic University of the Philippines, Manila), formed a student bible group. Initially linked to the Church of the Foursquare Gospel the group soon grew into a megachurch, declared itself an independent charismatic fellowship and started branches all over the country eventually becoming a denomination in its own right. Yet, JIL has always kept ties to figures of the Pentecostal-Charismatic scene based in the United States, including exponents of the so-called New Apostolic Reformation network.

Although JIL's understanding of the "full-Gospel" comprises material prosperity and while Villanueva names Kenneth Hagin as one of his mentors, JIL distances itself from the Prosperity Gospel. Furthermore, it stresses the need for a nationwide "revolution of righteousness" that includes government-led structural changes as well as individual transformation. This parallels the political engagement of its founder, who in the heyday of the protests against the US-supported Ferdinand Marcos-regime had joined the youth-arm of the Philippine Communist Party, and organized rallies in close collaboration with leftist labor unions. Villanueva's "live-changing encounter," which in 1973 turned him from Marxist atheism to the "Full Gospel," did not diminish his concern for national politics. In 1983, he launched the Philippines for Jesus Movement (PJM), an umbrella organization for so-called independent Pentecostal-Charismatic ministries that represented a decidedly political counterpart to the Philippine Council of Evangelical Churches which counted most of the US-founded Evangelical and Pentecostal denominations as members and was criticized by Villanueva of being indifferent to social issues. In 1986, JIL supported the so-called EDSA I rallies that eventually ousted Marcos and established Intercessors for the Philippines, a teaching and mobilization arm, fashioned to raise awareness for the country's moral, economic and political issues. In 1992, Villanueva became spiritual advisor of President Fidel Ramos (1992–1998), the country's first Protestant president, who was interested in mobilizing JIL for an anti-hegemonic bloc against the political elites backed by the Catholic Bishops Conference. Interestingly, Ramos' initiative also included the Catholic Pentecostal mass-movement El Shaddai and resulted in a rapprochement between Villanueva and El Shaddai-leader Mike Velarde. In 1997, exponents of JIL formed Citizens Battle Against Corruption (CIBAC), a party-list for underrepresented community sectors. Initially criticized of being JIL's political arm and, thus, being unconstitutional, CIBAC was not admitted to the 1998 elections. Few years later, however, CIBAC and Villanueva found themselves at the center of the events leading to the ousting of President Estrada in 2001. Since then CIBAC has succeeded in gaining at least one of the three possible seats reserved for party-lists in the Lower House of Congress. Speculating on the increasing JIL-membership as potential voters, Villanueva aligned with other evangelical leaders to found Bagong Pilipinas Party and become its presidential candidate in 2004 and 2010. His rather social democratic platform stressed social justice and could be regarded as rather progressive compared to most other Catholic candidates (especially on issues concerning national economy, reproductive health and education), even if it espoused a morally conservative and pro-death penalty stance. While this helped Villanueva to draw support also from leftist circles and from the Muslim community (including exponents of the Moro National Liberation Front of the Moro Islamic Liberation Front Muslim), he lost both elections. His candidacy to the senate in 2013 was equally unsuccessful. In 2019, however, he became representative to the Lower House as CIBAC-nominee.

JIL-adherents, especially JIL-pastors, appear to be more politicized compared to other middle-class Christian groups. Yet, it turned out that they were less convinced that their top-leader would make a good president. This might be different with regard to his equally ambitious son Joel, who, after earning a solid reputation as CIBAC's first congressman, was appointed cabinet member by President Benigno Aquino III in 2010 and became senator in 2016. Recently, JIL has been criticized for being quietist with regard to President Rodrigo Duterte and his "war on drugs", tacitly supporting Duterte's autocratic government and his gross human rights violations in the same way as most megachurches and the majority of the Philippine population in general did. As evidence, critics have cited Eddie and Joel Villanueva's alignment with the pro-Duterte majority in Congress. Others, however, have pointed to various occasions in which Villanueva stated that "as a Christian" he did not accept the alleged drug-related killings and in which he reprehended the president for "insulting God." This, they argued, ought to be read as a careful move to distance JIL from Duterte without risking to lose the newly gained political influence. As JIL continues to expand (especially abroad), it remains open how it is going to live up to its vision of a "revolution of righteousness" and how JIL-adherents will respond to the political activities of their leaders, including Villanueva and his family members.

Bibliography

Cornelio, Jayeel S., and Ia Marañon. 2019. "A 'Righteous Intervention': Megachurch Christianity and Duterte's War on Drugs in the Philippines." *International Journal of Asian Christianity* 2 (2): 211–230.

Cornelio, Jayeel S. 2018. "Jesus Is Lord: The Indigenization of Megachurch Christianity in the Philippines." In *Pentecostal Megachurches in Southeast Asia: Negotiating Class, Consumption and the Nation*, edited by Terence Chong, 127–155. Singapore: ISEAS.

JILW, Jesus is Lord Church Worldwide. 2013. "Mission, Vision, Core Values." https://jilworldwide.org/church.

Kessler, Christl, and Jürgen Rüland. 2008. *Give Jesus a Hand! Charismatic Christians: Populist Religion and Politics in the Philippines*. Quezon City: Ateneo de Manila University Press.

Lim, David S. 2009. "Consolidating Democracy: Filipino Evangelicals between People Power Events, 1986–2001." In *Evangelical Christianity and Democracy in Asia*, edited by David Halloran Lumsdaine, 235–277. Oxford: Oxford University Press.

Maltese, Giovanni. 2019. "Reproductive Politics and Populism: Pentecostal Religion and Hegemony in the Philippines." *Journal of Law and Religion* 34 (1): 64–84.

Maltese, Giovanni. 2017. *Pentekostalismus, Politik und Gesellschaft in den Philippinen*. Religion in der Gesellschaft 42. Baden-Baden: Ergon.

Giovanni Maltese

Jesus People Movement

The Jesus People movment is a diverse and dynamic Christian phenomenon that arose in the late 1960s, attracting widespread attention across the United States. The Jesus People, also known as "Jesus freaks," never had a singular founder or place of origin, and were never centralized. Nonetheless, their earliest expressions were certainly located on the West Coast, especially in California: early examples include the Christian World Liberation Front, led by Jack Sparks in Berkeley, and Chuck Smith's Calvary Chapel in Santa Ana. Beginning in 1969, publications such as *Right On!* And the *Hollywood Free Paper* became voices for the movement, and they helped to popularize the "Jesus People" moniker. Buoyed by mainstream media coverage in the early 1970s, the movement was variously imitated across the country. As Enroth, Ericson, and Peters (1972) have demonstrated, those associations were sometimes partial and contrived; the movement was immensely popular, however, and many thousands identified with it.

In most cases, the Jesus People were young, in their late teens or early twenties, and they arose from the hippie counterculture of the 1960s. They were distinguished from "straight" Christianity by their profound dissatisfaction with a materialistic culture and with institutional spirituality. They were avid about rock music, they grew long hair, and they wore eccentric styles of clothing. Disillusioned with traditional political activism, they were rarely involved with matters of social policy and were remarkably silent about the Vietnam War. Indeed, for some contemporary critics (Streiker 1971), the Jesus freaks were simplistic and socially unproductive.

Just as importantly, however, they also viewed their movement as a radical alternative to the psychedelic hippie culture. They rejected casual sexuality and drug use, and they offered numerous testimonies about their deliverance from past addictions. Known for the Bibles they carried, their aggressive street preaching, and their evangelistic coffee houses, they became the proponents of an unconventional and unapologetic Christian faith. For many of their converts, the movement satisfied a deep desire for religious experimentation; in this regard, they frequently competed with Eastern spiritualities.

Theologically, the Jesus People held to traditional evangelical doctrines, with a heavy emphasis on personal conversion and the substitutionary atonement of Christ, who was explicitly named as the "One Way" to salvation. In keeping with Jesus' command to "go to all the world," a small number were commissioned as missionaries, and they enjoyed a modest level of success in the United Kingdom and Australia especially. They also took a literal approach to the Bible, showing little patience for ecclesiastical traditions or the insights of academic biblical scholarship. By contrast, many were intrigued with the bold dispensational interpretations of authors such as Hal Lindsey, in his *Late Great Planet Earth*. For them, the Second Coming of Christ was certain and imminent, a topic of frequent discussion.

Moreover, they frequently read the Bible through a restorationist lens. Many adopted communal lifestyles in accordance with the second chapter of Acts, where the earliest Christians were "together" and "had all things in common." That text proved pivotal in other ways, also, as most of the Jesus People embraced the practices of glossolalia and prophecy. In the research of Larry Eskridge (2013), a strong majority of former Jesus People recalled the baptism of the Holy Spirit, speaking in tongues, dramatic miracles, visions, personal revelations, and numerous answers to prayer. These recollections were not unanimous and the picture was always mixed; nonetheless, the overall center of gravity was unquestionably weighted toward Pentecostal and Charismatic convictions. Richard Bustraan (2014), likewise, has emphasized these particular features of the movement. David Wilkerson's overtly Pentecostal bestseller, *The Cross and the Switchblade*, became a favored book.

It is not possible to cite a specific endpoint to the Jesus People movement, but it was quickly filtered into numerous organizations and ministries. It was inevitable that a youth-oriented sensation would evolve as its participants grew older and began to start their own families; moreover, the hippie counterculture proved ephemeral also. The communal experiments were especially difficult to maintain on a long-term basis, and some, like David Berg's Children of God, were marginalized by their authoritarian and cultish reputations. The most explicit remnant of the original phenomenon might be the Jesus People USA, a community that operates on the North Side of Chicago. Nonetheless, the larger movement has taken residence, to an impressive degree, in many corners of mainstream Christian practice. Though the Jesus People lost their high-profile identity, Robert Ellwood (1975) correctly anticipated that they would be significant in "nonstatistical ways."

Since the 1970s, the movement's influence has been felt across the nexus of Fundamentalist, Evangelical, and Pentecostal traditions. It was a motley assortment from the beginning, and could never be classified in denominational categories. Significant leaders, like John Wimber and Lonnie Frisbee, became major players in the so-called "third wave" of Pentecostal and Charismatic growth, normally dated in the 1980s. Nonetheless, despite these kinds of doctrinal commitments (and their unconventional style), the movement was also endorsed by non-Pentecostal leaders such as Billy Graham and Bill Bright.

Most notably, this widespread influence has been exerted through their substantial musical legacy. While other Christian traditions attempted to resist the allure of rock music, Jesus People appropriated the genre for their own religious purposes. This creative impulse was typified by high-profile artists like Larry Norman, who sparred with traditionalist critics and asked why the devil should have "all the good music." Norman was joined by a rising tide of successful groups with names such as Love Song, Petra, Resurrection Band, and 2nd Chapter of Acts. Recorded and promoted by Christian labels such as Maranatha! Music and Myrrh Records, they paved the way for Keith Green, Amy Grant, and many other artists. Hence arose the juggernaut industry of Contemporary Christian Music, which has transformed hymnody and the very meaning of "worship" in churches around the world.

Beyond music, the Jesus People movement has inspired "seeker-sensitive" evangelism and specific ministries that are devoted to teenagers and young adults. Its story is crucial for understanding the current state of Christianity, especially conservative Protestantism in the United States.

Bibliography

Bustraan, Richard A. 2014. *The Jesus People Movement: A Story of Spiritual Revolution Among the Hippies.* Eugene, OR: Pickwick.

Ellwood, Robert S. 1975. *One Way: The Jesus Movement and Its Meaning.* Englewood Cliffs, NJ: Prentice-Hall.

Enroth, Ronald M., Edward E. Ericson, and C. Breckinridge Peters. 1972. *The Jesus People: Old-Time Religion in the Age of Aquarius.* Grand Rapids: William B. Eerdmans.

Eskridge, Larry. 2013. *God's Forever Family: The Jesus People Movement in America.* New York: Oxford University Press.

Streiker, Lowell D. 1971. *The Jesus Trip: Advent of the Jesus Freaks.* Nashville: Abingdon.

Keith Huey

Jing, Dianying

Jing Dianying (1890–1957) was born to a Confucian family in Mazhung village, Tai'an county, Shandong. He first received traditional education and became well versed in Confucian and Daoist classics. His hope to become a Confucian scholar-official ended with the abolishment of the civil service examination in 1905 and the fall of Qing Dynasty in 1911. In 1912, Jing began to study at the Cuiying Middle School of the Methodist Episcopal Church in Tai'an. Jing was baptized into the Methodist Church in 1914.

While serving as the Chinese language instructor of Nora Dillenbeck (1883–1938), a single woman missionary, Jing fell in love with her. Jing was tormented by guilt and divorced his wife in 1919. He eventually reconciled with her and she became a helper in his ministries until she passed away in 1940.

When the mission school was temporarily suspended in 1918, Jing moved to work as an evangelist in a mission hospital in Jinan. In 1921, he started the Saints' Credit and Savings Society (Shengtu She), a small Christian business cooperation, which was partly funded by Dillenbeck. During that time, he continued to work in the hospital and taught in Cuiying Middle School. In 1923, he sold his possessions and began to live by faith as a wandering preacher.

In 1924, Jing attended a revival meeting at an orphanage in Tai'an, the Home of Onesiphorus, run by Leslie M. Anglin (1882–1942) an American Baptist missionary who became a Pentecostal. Jing received his baptism of the Spirit and began to speak in tongues, see visions, fall into trances, practice spiritual singing and dancing. As Jing tried to spread the Pentecostal fire in the Methodist mission, he was expelled from both the church and the school.

After leaving the Methodist establishments, Jing worked at the Home of Onesiphorus for a few months. He learned how to organize a community with occupational departments such as carpentry, tailoring, and farming, which was useful for his establishing of the Jesus Family in China.

In 1926, Jing founded the Silkworm and Mulberry-Tree House for the Learning of the Way (Cansang Xuedao Fang) in Mazhuang, a Christian community for widows to make a living and to learn about Christianity. The Saints' Credit and Savings Society merged into it in the following year, and the community was renamed the Jesus Family. The Family was an egalitarian and communitarian group. To enter this utopian settlement, one needed to sell their possessions and give the proceeds to the poor or share with the group; no private ownership was allowed. Traditional familial blood relationships were replaced by new familial relationships as brothers and sisters in Christ. The group's religious beliefs and practices were Pentecostal, fundamental, and millenarian in nature. The Family was considered by the members the Ark in the end time.

An able leadership team was formed around Jing when Dong Hengxin (1907–1952), Zuo Shunzhen (1907–1987) and Chen Bixi (1904–1980) joined the Family in the 1930s. Dillenbeck left the Methodist Church in 1934 and subsequently joined the Family until she died in 1938. The Jesus Family grew under this gifted collective leadership. By the mid-1930s, sub-families were established in nearby provinces. Jing still retained certain power as a leader, including arranging marriages among members and executing disciplines.

The Jesus Family and Jing survived the Sino-Japanese War and the Chinese Civil War. Considering the Family as reactionary and politically subversive, the Communist regime disbanded it in 1952. Jing was denounced at mass reform meetings and imprisoned. He suffered from cancer and died in 1957.

Bibliography

Li, Yading. "Jing Dianying." *Biographical Dictionary of Chinese Christianity*. Accessed November 28, 2019. http://bdcconline.net/zh-hant/stories/jing-dianying.

Lian, Xi. 2010. *Redeemed by Fire: The Rise of Popular Christianity in Modern China*. New Heaven: Yale University Press.

Shin Fung Hung

Johnston, Barbara

Barbara Johnston (1879–1911) was a Canadian teacher, missionary to India, and Bible translator. She assisted Pandita Ramabai at the Mukti Mission in Kedgaon, where she worked to translate the New Testament from Greek to the Marathi language. She was the first Canadian Pentecostal missionary to India.

Barbara (née Johnston, sometimes misspelled Johnstone, married name Norton) was born on May 28, 1879, to a locally notable public school teacher and principal, John Johnston (1848–1928), and Alice Smith (1851–1926) in Sarnia, Ontario, Canada. She was the firstborn of the five children. Her father was a Presbyterian born in Scotland, while her mother attended a local Baptist church with the children.

At eight years old, Johnston heard about two young outgoing missionaries to India speaking at her Sunday school and hoped that one day she might travel to India to tell people about Jesus. In 1904, Johnston began the preparation for ministry at McMaster University in Toronto.

During her second year of study, she realized that despite achieving high grades she had lost her spiritual zeal. In April 1907, Johnston heard of the baptism of the Holy Ghost with the sign of speaking in new tongues at the Hebden Mission in Toronto since November 1906. In her biblical study of the phenomenon, she became convinced that speaking in tongues was the sign by which the apostles knew that the Holy Spirit had come. Johnston began to pray for this baptism. During this time of prayer and study, she experienced divine healing from an illness, and sanctification, which she described as freedom from the power of the old habits of sin.

Johnston graduated with a Bachelor of Arts degree on May 15, 1907, but was desiring something much greater. She went to the Hebden Mission, and after several consecutive days of waiting and praying in the mission's upper room, on Friday, May 31, 1907, Johnston received the baptism of the Holy Ghost and spoke in tongues. She returned to Sarnia, starting a Pentecostal mission, and worked as a public school teacher at a rural school.

In August 1908, James and Ellen Hebden visited Sarnia to conduct special meetings. During their visit, Johnston heard Ellen Hebden speaking in tongues and interpreting them in English, "they are calling to thee ... from over the sea [in] India." Johnston took this as a personal confirmation from God, and within three weeks found a replacement teacher for her school, and someone to take care of the Pentecostal mission. Johnston joined missionary Lillian Denney (who had recently visited the Hebden Mission) and approximately 30 other missionaries at Jersey City, New Jersey, embarking for India on November 7, 1908.

After one month of travel by boat and train, Johnston and the other missionaries arrived at Daund, Maharashtra, India, on December 9, 1908. They were welcomed with fireworks by John Norton, son of missionaries Albert and Mary Norton, who operated the Christian Boys' Home, an orphanage of about 135 boys. Like Johnston, nearly half of the boys there had received the baptism of the Holy Spirit with speaking in tongues, although the missionaries themselves had not. Two days after her arrival, they sent Johnston 30 km west to assist Pandita Ramabai at the Mukti Mission in Kedgaon, Maharashtra, India, where Johnston worked on translating the New Testament from Greek into the Marathi language.

Johnston married John Norton on June 23, 1909, in a ceremony hosted by Ramabai at the Mukti Mission. The newlyweds moved to Daund together, assuming full responsibility for the Christian Boys' Home. Johnston, a meticulous planner, also organized preaching tours for her husband and herself throughout remote villages.

During the last week of July 1911, Johnston became suddenly ill with kidney trouble.

On August 1, 1911, she died at the age of 32. Her husband was devastated, taking an immediate temporary leave from all missionary work.

Johnston's impact in her relatively short missionary life is evident in the posthumous comments of those who knew her best. Johnston's father-in-law Albert Norton wrote that she "worked hard, too hard, to care for the orphans and the Christian families at Daund, besides giving much help at Mukti." Pandita Ramabai eulogized, "Miss Barbara Johnston of Sarnia, Ontario … helped us in many ways, chiefly in the Greek work connected with the Bible translation. … At the Master's call she left all, and followed him to India, to live a Christ-like life among simple village men and women, devoting all her time and talents to the work of revealing Christ to them, that they might 'look and live.'"

Although Johnston was buried in India, on the Johnston family plot at Lakeview Cemetery in Sarnia, Ontario, there is a memorial marker that reads, "Barbara A. Johnston, wife of John E. Norton, died in India, 1879–1911."

Bibliography

Courtney, Caleb Howard. 2017. "Barbara Johnston of Sarnia, Ontario: The First Canadian Pentecostal Missionary to India." *Canadian Journal of Pentecostal-Charismatic Christianity* 8 (1): 1–18. https://journal.twu.ca/index.php/CJPC/article/view/189.

Norton, Barbara. 1909. "Testimony: Mrs. John Norton." *Jehovah-Jireh, A Witness to Christ's Faithfulness* 1, no. 4 (December).

Norton, J.E. 1912. "A Sketch of Mrs. Barbara Norton." *At The Roll Call* (April): 10–12.

Caleb Courtney

Jordan

The country of Jordan lies immediately west of Israel and Palestine, and its northern and north-eastern borders touch Syria and Iraq. Directly east and south, it shares the border with Saudi Arabia. Despite sharing a border with Saudi Arabia, overall, Jordanian culture has more in common with Syria and Palestine than the Arabian Gulf countries. This is partly due to its tourism and agriculturally-based economy rather than an oil-based one. Politically, Jordan is organized under a parliamentary monarchy with King Abdullah as its sovereign. Unlike the Gulf countries to the south, Jordan does not have as large a south/southeast Asian workforce. Its population is mostly native Jordanians with large groups of Palestinians and displaced Iraqis and Syrians.

Within an Islamic hegemony, Christians only make up a fraction of Jordan. Many of these Christians belong to the traditional churches, and some are involved in the maintenance and promotion of Christian tourist sites in the country, a growing industry. Evangelicals and Pentecostals, on the other hand, only comprise a small number of the nation's Christians. These congregations are generally in Amman, the capital, although there are other enclaves scattered about, often assisting in refugee work in the camps nearer to the Syrian and Iraqi borders. Evangelicals have two seminaries: Jordan Evangelical Theological Seminary and Biblical Theological Seminary. However, enrolment is quite small, with only a couple dozen graduates per year. Neither are explicitly Pentecostal or Renewalist in their curricula.

According to *Christianity in North Africa-West Asia* (Ross et al. 2018), in 2015 there were 7,595,000 people in Jordan with 127,000 or 1.7 percent identifying identifying as Christians. By far, the largest denominations are the Orthodox and Catholic at 61.4 percent and 23 percent respectively. Renewalists are 8.9 percent of the Christian population or roughly 10,680 people. Of the total Christian population, there were 3255 conversions to one form of Christianity or the other. However, 386 Christians defected from the faith and nearly 5000 emigrated, with a net, in-country growth of 580 or .46 percent.

With 50 percent of growth coming from conversions, Jordan is an active site for evangelism, and numerous mission agencies operate within the country. However, missionary work is not countenanced upon and missionaries in the country must keep a low profile. The same is true for Muslim background believers, who may face continued persecution from their families and communities. Given, too, many conversions occur due to miraculous interventions like dreams, visions, or healings, Renewalist and Pentecostal groups are well-positioned to build on seekers' previous spiritual experiences.

Like other countries in the region, the main Pentecostal denomination is the Assemblies of God, headed by Pastor Dirkan Salbashian. The Church of the Nazarene, Christian Mission Alliance, and a Oneness Pentecostal church also have an active presence in the country. Amman has also hosted large conferences that have attracted speakers like Cindy Jacobs and George Wood, general superintendent the USA Assemblies of God. Benny Hinn, too, has made several visits to the country.

Bibliography

Burton, Jeremy, and Carissa Bratschun. 2015. "Muslim Dominated Country Can't Stop the Holy Spirit." *Charisma News*. May 19, 2015. Accessed Oct. 3, 2019. https://www.charismanews.com/world/49701-muslim-dominated-country-can-t-stop-the-holy-spirit.

The Washington Times. 2001. "Islamic Country Promotes Tourism." *The Washington Times*. June 15, 2001. Accessed Oct. 3, 2019. https://www.washingtontimes.com/news/2001/jun/15/20010615-023756-3833r/.

Jacobs, Cindy. 2015. "The Third Pentecost: Jordan and Israel Trip Report." *Generales Internacionales*. May 28, 2015. Accessed Oct. 3, 2019. https://www.generals.org/es/articles/unico/the-third-pentecost-jordan-and-israel-trip-report/.

Ross, Kenneth R., Mariz Tadros, and Todd M. Johnson, eds. 2018. *Christianity in North Africa-West Asia*. Edinburgh: Edinburgh University Press.

Benjamin Crace

Juergensen, Carl Fredrick

Carl Fredrich Juergensen (1862–1940) and his wife Frederike Sophia Martin (1868–1961) came to Japan with their two little daughters on September 14, 1913. They were among the early independent Pentecostal missionaries to Japan. When they landed in Japan, Carl was 50 years old and Frederike was 45. Neither of them had any formal theological training nor a missionary organization to support them. They came to Japan believing that it was God's will.

Carl was born in Luckstad, Schleswig Holstein, Germany on December 4, 1862 and Frederike in Siciby, Schleswig Holstein on April 3, 1868. They got married on July 8, 1888. They moved to the U.S. with their son John (1893–1938) in 1897. There they had two daughters, Marie (1902–91) and Agnes (1905–92). Settling in Cleveland, Ohio, they were naturalized as U.S. citizens in 1906. Carl was a garment merchant and Frederike was a housewife.

The Pentecostal movement came to Cleveland by the end of 1906 and Charles F. Kelchner was one of the first Pentecostals in Cleveland. Although the Juergensens were Lutherans, the illness of their daughter Agnes spurred them to seek Kelchner for help. He visited the Juergensens and prayed for Agnes in 1909, which marked the Juergensens' first contact with the Pentecostal faith. Agnes's healing made them aware of God's power and after receiving the Pentecostal experience, they felt the call to be missionaries. They first thought that they should go to their native country, Germany, since they spoke the language and knew the culture, but God showed them that Japan should be their destination in visions.

The Juergensens left Cleveland and went to Los Angeles in 1912. They finally decided to go to Japan in January 1913. They left the U.S. leaving their son John behind on July 26, 1913 and landed on Yokohama on August 11, 1913. They had made no special arrangements before arrival, not even accommodation. However, a Korean Christian whom they met on board introduced them to Juji Nakada (1870–1939), a Holiness preacher in Japan, who helped them find their first house in Tokyo.

Looking for a place to launch their ministry, the Juergensens soon settled in a house in front of the University of Tokyo at the end of 1913, where they started their Full Gospel Mission (*Zenbi Fukuin Dendokan*). They held an evangelistic meeting almost every night, conducted street meetings, ministered to the sick, and ran a Sunday School. They taught Bible classes in English and German and attracted some students to their English classes, which helped their finances, but their student ministry through English classes was never successful.

The Juergensens were faith missionaries and from the beginning their finances were precarious. Carl had some savings from selling his business, but they mainly relied on the support from friends in the U.S., which was unstable and never sufficient. Because of WWI, being German even made it harder to raise funds. Carl was appointed by the American Assemblies of God (AG) to be missionary in Japan on May 23, 1918. However, unlike the mainline denominational missionaries, the Juergensens lived among the Japanese rather than in western houses, possibly because the Japanese lifestyle was cheaper.

Despite their lack of resources, the Juergensens tried to expand their work in Tokyo. They opened two other mission stations consecutively, in Koishikawa in 1915 and in Fujimae in 1917. Sunday Schools became one of their main ministries as it was easier to attract children to churches than adults. Having over a hundred children in a meeting was not unusual.

Since Carl did not speak Japanese, finding a good interpreter was crucial to his ministry. None of those he hired, however, were suitable, being either very irresponsible or unwilling to interpret what he said, especially concerning Spirit baptism. Therefore, when Marie, his oldest daughter, finished her Japanese studies, she became his first reliable interpreter.

Carl longed to see the blessing of Spirit baptism in his ministry, but it took six years. In 1919, at Fujimae Station he was able to see the first incident of Spirit baptism in Japan when he invited Leonard W. Coote, another Pentecostal missionary, for special meetings. The presence of the Holy Spirit was strong and many were baptized by the Spirit.

Juergensen's son John and his wife Esther (1898–1928), who were American AG missionaries, joined the team on November 17, 1919. When the American AG Japan District was founded in 1920, Carl became the first field representative. Since John and Esther were in Japan, the senior Juergensens were able to go back to America on furlough for the first time. They left Japan in April 1922, before the destruction of Tokyo caused by the Great Kanto Earthquake on September 1, 1923.

The Juergensens came back to Tokyo in April 1924 and now both Marie and Agnes had AG credentials. They held several evangelistic tent meetings for weeks in the Takinogawa District of Tokyo. Through collaborating with the AG missionaries, they were able to construct the building of Takinogawa Church on October 15, 1927, which was the first Pentecostal building in Japan. Takinogawa Church flourished under the leadership of Yumiyama Kiyoma, a Japanese Pentecostal minister, and Carl's daughter Marie. The Bible School was founded in 1931, and their ministry expanded through the graduates. Carl and Frederike retired from ministry in 1936 but remained in Japan.

Carl died of a stroke on August 29, 1940 in Karuizawa, Nagano at the age 77. Takinogawa Church (now Shinsho Church) survived during WWII, and it was where the Japan Assemblies of God was founded on March 15, 1949.

Bibliography

Juergensen, Marie. n.d. *Foundation Stones: Carl F. Juergensen*, Springfield, MO: Foreign Mission Department of Assemblies of God.

Shew, Paul Tsuchido. 2003. "History of the Early Pentecostal Movement in Japan: The Roots and Development of the Pre-War Pentecostal Movement in Japan (1907–1945)." PhD diss., Fuller Theological Seminary.

Suzuki, Masakazu. 2011. "The Origins and the Development of the Japan Assemblies of God: The Foreign and Japanese Workers and Their Ministries (1907 to 1975)." PhD diss., Bangor University.

Suzuki, Masakazu. 2005. "The Life and History of C.F. Juergensen and Takinogawa Mission in Japan." Presented at the 34th Annual Meeting of the Society for Pentecostal Studies, Regent University, Virginia Beach, VA, March 10–12.

Masakazu Suzuki

Kenya

Starting out as a religion for the poor who were largely excluded in the modernizing world, Pentecostalism was reared, for decades, as a religion in the margins of social and economic power. In the mid-1990s, African countries liberalized the media-scape, allowing market dynamics to drive the mass media industry. Up until the 1990s, Kenyan radio and television were dominated by a single national broadcaster, the Kenya Broadcasting Corporation (KBC), also the mouthpiece of the ruling party KANU, effectively a tool of political influence. After being pressured to expand democratic space, the Kenyan government licensed more media houses throughout the 1990s. As of 2020 the forces

Baptism, Kenya, 1930's. Photo: Otto Keller. Source: Pentecostal Assemblies of Canada Archives

of market competition have created more than a hundred ratio stations and sixty plus TV stations broadcasting over the Kenyan airwaves.

Pentecostalism, in all its expressions, harnessed the power of mass media more than any other denomination or religion. Already since the 1980s, Pentecostals had been adopting electronic media to evangelize the emergent urban culture (Kalu 2008). The proliferation of multiple modes of mass media cemented the relevance of religion in the public space (Meyers and Moors 1999). Pentecostalism, by making a home in the public space through media, has been at the fore front of this transformation of religion in the public sphere. It is a symbiotic relationship, where Pentecostalism is transformed as it spreads throughout the social landscape. In turn, Pentecostalism has engaged new publics and found affinities that are not necessarily religious. Before the liberalization of airwaves in the Kenyan sphere, social jurisdictions of leadership and authority were assigned to traditional positions of authority, particularly vested in political figures and older clergy. The expanded mediascape has evolved into a whole new class of social imaginaries, that of media-made influencers who include musicians and media celebrities, not the least of whom are of charismatic and Pentecostal persuasion. When mobilized in times of crises, they wield immense power over public opinion and action (Ntarangwi 2016; Gitau 2018). Pentecostal pastors whose careers have also been built ithrough these media forms are another such category.

Ever opportunistic, the political class discerned the opportunity early, and tapped into Pentecostalism's capacity to project a virtuous public persona, often to rehabilitate a damaged political career. For instance, President Moi, who ruled for 24 years, patronized Arthur Kitonga's Redeemed Gospel Church early in the push for more democratic space (Gifford 2010). That Pentecostal church lent him an extra aura of piety and appeal to the poor Pentecostals, which until then had remained apolitical. This acceptability buttressed

Moi's superficial call for peace in a nation that at the time was traumatized by ethnic clashes and struggles of his regime's making. Moi's spirituality worked like a charm and he was reelected twice while his political opponents, never having learnt the art of religious persuasion, struggled to gain substantial public legitimacy. The strategy of tapping into the Pentecostal brand for political gain would be perfected by Moi's young proteges, Uhuru Kenyatta and William Ruto when it was their turn to vie for a presidential and deputy presidential ticket. They appeared in churches and crusades, knelt for prayers, and had Christian musicians performing popular songs at campaign rallies. Harnessing a Pentecostal cosmology, they declared it was intercessory prayers that saved them from the International Criminal Court after being indicted for the 2008 post-election violence. After they were elected, they continued to make this argument while plundering the country through an opportunistic and dysfunctional governance system. Yet the salient point is that mainlines churches would never have given these politicians the kind of legitimacy that Pentecostalism enabled.

For all the opportunism, this alliance between Pentecostalism, the media and political posturing has contributed to the rehabilitation of religion as a strong discourse partner in contemporary society, albeit not in the expected way of influencing policy or even the public ethic of leaders. Rather, Pentecostalism projects symbolic power that politicians turn into social capital for votes when they need it. In a sense, this alliance is a way of creating a new category of what Jurgen Habermas referred to as the "public sphere" (Habermas 1989). The media plays a role as a facilitator of an emergent public sphere, enabling equal access to information and equal opportunities to participate in public debate, while Pentecostalism, by giving a space for its erstwhile patrons to have a public space, enables the emergence of a new spiritual or religious public sphere, quite separate from what the mainline churches or other religious traditions provided. While the politicians recognize Pentecostalism's power, it seems the religious have not seriously weighed the full potential of their own power and demanded better public good, and governance out of the leaders they helped to elect. To do so would require that the Pentecostal movement, in all its expressions, cultivate a sociological imagination.

The sociological imagination, according to C. Wright Mills (1959), connects the private, personal troubles, such as unemployment, homelessness, various kinds of exploitation, and personal anomie into public issues. For Pentecostal pastors, cultivating a sociological imagination would mean a disciplined exploration of how individuals and communities are actually shaped by social forces. These social forces include social institutions like education, governance structures and juridical arrangements, organization of capital and labor, and other bureaucratic processes that are controlled by politically elected officials that impact the daily lives of individuals. Pentecostals often tend to explain social problems in terms of individual choices and personal character. They work hard at preaching conversion and transformation, supposing that transformed individuals will also transform troubled societies. Contemporary social crises are showing that no matter how pious people become, or how larges churches grow, the needed social transformation is not happening. This is because the elite and political class structure is not accountable to the majority who elect them in the first place.

Mainline churches and their allies once led the charge for social change. Given the plateauing influence of denominational mainline churches, particularly in a social-media driven universe, it is necessary that the now numerically strong communities, Pentecostals and charismatics, move beyond an individualistic view of social reality and a theology of personal salvation. They need to see social problems as complex, networked social arrangements that produce the troubles of individuals who gather in the pews on Sunday. Cultivating a sociological imagination requires that pastors and scholars take seriously the trajectory of historical events, the agency of human beings, and the hermeneutics of social discourse, so as to generate a systems approach to resolving social problems that manifest as individual troubles. This is a much-needed turn in scholarship on Kenyan, African and perhaps global Pentecostalism as a whole. Despite the best intentions of pastors to form congregants who are moral, virtuous, ethical and committed to the common good, decades of bad leadership by an unscrupulous political class continue to generate the same problems that constantly plague human life. Pentecostalism has already created a public sphere for the poor and marginalized who now need to find a space for public representation. It can create, in its universe, a sociological imagination to engage social evils that stand in the way of the coming of the kingdom of God, on earth as in heaven.

Bibliography

Gifford, Paul. 2010. *Christianity, Politics and Public Life in Kenya*. Oxford: Oxford University Press.

Gitau, Wanjiru M. 2018. *Megachurch Christianity Reconsidered: Millennials and Social Change in African Perspective*. Downers Grove: Intervarsity Academic.

Habermas, Jürgen. 1991. *The Structural Transformation of the Public Sphere: An Inquiry into a Category of Bourgeois Society*. Translated by Thomas Burger. Cambridge: MIT Press.

Kalu, Ogbu. 2008. *Pentecostalism in Africa: An Introduction*. New York: Oxford University Press.

Meyer, Birgit, and Annelies Moors, eds. 1999. *Religion, Media and the Public Sphere*. Indianapolis: Indiana University Press.

Mills, C. Wright. 1959. *The Sociological Imagination*. New York: Oxford University Press.

Ntarangwi, Mwenda. 2016. *The Street is My Pulpit: Hip Hop and Christianity in Kenya*. Champaign: University of Illinois Press.

Wanjiru Gitau

Keswick Movement

The first Keswick Convention convened on June 29, 1875 in a scenic town nestled beneath Skiddaw mountain in northwest England. The convention became an annual event of week-long meetings consisting of Bible studies, addresses, prayer meetings, women's meetings, and a concern for practical holiness. The first conference was initiated by Canon Thomas Dundas Harford-Battersby (1823–1883), Robert Wilson (1824–1905), and Robert Pearsall Smith (1873–1898). Smith withdrew and Harford-Battersby took over as chairman. Several conferences predated Keswick but are generally included as part of the Keswick movement. William Edwin Boardman (1810–1896), R.P. Smith and his wife Hannah Whithall Smith (1832–1911)

Keswick Convention 1920. Image: courtesy of Keswick Ministries.

August 1874, Boardman and Smith were joined by Théodore Monod (1836–1921), Otto Stockmayer (1838–1917), Evan Henry Hopkins (1837–1918), and Oberlin President Asa Mahan (1799–1889) for a conference at Oxford. Smith, Hopkins, Monod, and Mahan conducted another convention in Brighton with the same goals. They along with Handley Carr Glyn Moule (1841–1920), Frederick Brotherson Meyer (1847–1929), Hanmer William Webb Peploe (1837–1923), Andrew Murray (1828–1917), and James Hudson Taylor (1832–1905) were key speakers at Keswick. Generally, the convention consisted of conservative evangelical Anglicans, Congregationalists, and Quakers, with Methodists underrepresented (Althouse 2005).

The Keswick movement was a hybrid of two theological developments: Wesleyanism and New School Calvinism. John Wesley (1703–1791) brought the life of holiness to the fore within Protestantism, arguing that Christian perfection is a separate and subsequent work to justification. The Holiness movement first articulated the idea when Phoebe Palmer (1807–1874) innovated the doctrine by arguing against older Wesleyans who believed the moment of sanctification occurred after many years, that entire sanctification was an instantaneous act of faith. Conversely, the Oberlin School of Charles Grandison Finney (1792–1875) and Asa Mahan advanced new measures for eliciting conversion, holiness through consecration in the fullness of Christ's love, and baptisms of the Holy Spirit for cleansing and enduement for service (Smith 1957).

Although Keswick had no official theology, advocates insisted the distinct experiences of new birth and the fullness of the Spirit as an experience of holiness (Anderson 2007). Generally, proponents agreed that while the penalty of sin was removed at conversion, the power of sin remained. Sin was not eradicated in the Wesleyan sense, nor gradually dying but not fully eliminated in the Reformed sense, but sin was countered (or suppressed) through the act of surrender. Surrender was both an initial crisis that instilled a new disposition for growth in holiness and a continual, daily surrender to the indwelling of the Holy Spirit (Russell 2014). By the end of the century, the language of baptism of the Spirit was used in a manner that shifted from holiness to empowerment for service (Anderson 2007).

Keswick theology was introduced into North America in the 1880s through Dwight Lyman Moody's (1837–1899) Northfield Conventions. Keswick speaker Arthur Tappan Pierson (1837–1911) was also a regular at Northfield as was William Henry Griffith Thomas (1861–1924), on whom Canadian Pentecostal educator James Eustace Purdie (1880–1977) claimed to have based his teaching materials.

Keswick leaders were also influential on the healing movement, many of whom participated in the London Healing Conference in 1885. Elizabeth Baxter (1837–1926), who conduct the ladies' meetings at Keswick from 1876–1883 joined the Boardmans and Charlette C. Murray to established Bethshan Healing Home. She was a key organizer of the healing conference, which was attended by notable healing advocates including keynote speaker, Albert Benjamin Simpson (1844–1919). Although Simpson did not appear to have participated in the Keswick meetings directly, he was prominent in the same networks and many early Pentecostal were connected to Simpson's ministry. Ellen Hebden, whose mission was responsible for the Pentecostal outpouring in Toronto in 1906, claimed to have lived with Baxter who was a tender mother to her (Althouse 2014). In 1894, Baxter travelled to India with C. Murray and the Stockmayers to meet Pandita Sarasvati Ramabai (1858–1922). Ramabai, whose faith mission in India experienced a Pentecostal revival in 1905, addressed the 1898 Keswick convention where she requested prayer for the outpouring of the Spirit on Indian Christians (Anderson 2007, 79).

The Welsh Revival (1904–1905), under the leadership of Evan Roberts (1878–1951), was also influenced by Keswick. Jessie Penn-Lewis (1861–1927), who came under the tutelage of Keswick teacher Evan Henry Hopkins (1837–1918) and spoke at the 1898 meeting, was approached by Welsh ministers at the 1902 meeting about starting a convention in Wales. She organized the Llandrindod Wells Convention in 1903 and provide spiritual guidance to Roberts throughout the revival (Baker-Johnson 2012). British Pentecostals Alexander Boddy, George Jeffreys, and Donald Gee participated in the Welsh Revival. Boddy, whose Bishop was H.G. Moule, distributed copies of *Pentecost for England* at the 1907 Keswick convention, where some attendees experienced glossolalia.

The advent of Pentecostal Christianity received mixed acceptance by Keswick participants. However, Keswick provided fertile ground for the development of Pentecostal theology and practice.

Bibliography

Althouse, Peter. 2014. "The Influences of Keswick and Healing Advocate Elizabeth Baxter on the Toronto Hebden Mission," Presented at the Annual Meeting of the Society for Pentecostal Studies, Springfield, MO, March 4–7.

Althouse, Peter. 2005. "Wesleyan and Reformed Impulses in the Keswick and Pentecostal Movements." *Pneuma Foundation* (Spring). http://www.pneumafoundation.org/article.jsp?article=/Keswick-PAlthouse.xml.

Anderson, Allan. 2007. *Spreading Fires: The Missionary Nature of Early Pentecostalism*. Maryknoll, NY: Orbis Books.

Baker-Johnson, Sharon. 2012. "The Life and Influence of Jessie Penn Lewis." *Priscilla Papers: The Academic Journal of CBE International*, April 30.

Russell, Andrew C. 2014. "Counteracting Classifications: Keswick Holiness Reconsidered." *Wesleyan Theological Journal* 49 (2): 86–121.

Smith, Timothy L. 1957. *Revivalism and Social Reform in Mid-Nineteenth Century America*. New York: Abingdon Press.

Peter Althouse

Kil, Seon Joo

Kil Seon Joo (1869–1935), the first pastor of the Presbyterian Seminary, led the Revival Movement of Korea from 1907 and formed the significant phenomena and traditions of Korean Christianity such as early morning prayer, revival conferences, and Bible studies. Before Kil became a Christian, he was deeply occupied by Seondo (an eastern mystical practice) with its spiritual enlightenment and concentration in prayer and meditation, held in the mountains for several months at a time. In 1897,

Kil read a copy of John Bunyan's *The Pilgrim's Progress* received from the missionary S.A. Moffet. He was deeply moved to tears and embraced the Christian gospel through reading the book. Meanwhile, during prayer, Kil heard God calling his name three times, "Kil Seon Joo, Kil Seon Joo, Kil Seon Joo." After this experience, Kil was filled with the Holy Spirit, and was baptized by Graham Lee in 1896. In 1907, the year of the Great Revival of Pyongyang, Kil was a senior pastor of the Jangdaehyeon Church, where the birth of the revival started. Kil began to confess his sin in public which brought the fire of the Holy Spirit to the whole congregation.

There are some unique features of the Great Revival movement led by Kil. First, the most predominant phenomenon was that it was a movement of repentance with tears, loud prayer and confession. Its atmosphere was full of joy, grace, praise, and prayer. It encouraged a desire to see miracles and healings in the Holy Spirit. Second, the Bible study called "Sa-Kyong" was based on Kil's revival movement. Third, this revival movement transformed both individuals and the community in terms of their regeneration, sanctification, and other spiritual gifts of the Holy Spirit. In particular, the revelation and transformation of one's inner being by the Holy Spirit reached other areas of life in society. Those who repented of their sins changed their behaviors and gave back voluntarily in their relationships with their neighbors and family, which had an impact in society. Fourth, the fire of the Holy Spirit fell upon all the people regardless of their social standing and race; missionaries, police, officers, and robbers equally received it. The barrier caused by the pride of the western missionaries and the sense of inferiority of the Korean people was narrowed. Within this manifestation of the Holy Spirit, the Korean churches grew rapidly, and 2,200 people became Christians in Pyongyang through Kil's preaching.

Kil's theology was influenced by Charles G. Finney and Dwight L. Moody in the late nineteenth century through the American missionaries who brought evangelical theology to Korea. Kil had a conservative background with its focus on holiness, repentance, and soul saving by being filled with the power of the Holy Spirit. Regardless of his conservative theology which stressed the separation between politics and religion, Kil was one of 33 signatories of Korea's Independence Declaration and was actively involved in the Korean Independence Movement against the violence of Japan in 1 March 1919. Kil's Holy Spirit Movement showed a holistic characteristics in terms of its Charismatic features and prophetic elements in his ministry. Its key source, and motivation, was Kil's inner faith manifested in his outer ministry both for the Charismatic and prophetic movements. Kil believed that it was God's calling to participate in the Independence Movement, yet he believed that extreme nationalism and evangelicalism could not be identical due to their different ultimate goals; one for glorifying the nation and the other glorifying God. Because of his faith, Kil had to endure not only the violence of Japanese colonialism but also the persecution of communists and socialists, who were in conflict with evangelicalism. Because of his involvement in the Independence Movement, Kil was arrested and in Japanese custody for two and a half years. During this critical time in jail, Kil read the Bible, particularly the book of Revelation more than 10,000 times and focused on his doctrine of eschatology, *Malsehak*, which stresses the Second Coming of Christ and God's intervention in history. After his release, Kill travelled across the country until his death due to a stroke in 1935. He focused on evangelism and the revival movement while preaching and teaching his eschatology to bring hope and comfort to the Korean people who suffered under the violence of Japanese colonialism. More than 60 churches were planted by Kil and because of the influence of the Great Revival Movement, most Korean churches share some Pentecostal and Charismatic forms of the Revival movement to some extent. His travels of 10,000 km over the Korean Peninsula to Manchuria showed that it was his passion motivated by his faith to strengthen the church and to give hope to the oppressed people rather than pessimism or ignorance of their present reality.

Bibliography

Gil, Jin-Kyung. 1980. *Yeongge Gil Seon-Ju*. Seoul: Jongro Books.

Huh, Ho-ik. 2009. *Pastor Gil Seon-Ju's Theology and Ministry*. Seoul: The Christian Literature Society of Korea.

Kim, Jaehyun. 2008. *Gil Seon-Ju: Essential Writing*. Translated by Hannah Kim. Seoul: KIATS Press.

Lee, Timothy S. 2010. *Born Again: Evangelicalism in Korea*. Hawaii: University of Hawaii Press.

Reu, Gum-Ju. 2002. "The Revival Movement of Korean Church Around 3.1 Independent Movement: With Special Reference to Gil Seon-Ju." *Theological Forum* 30: 297–318.

Eunhee Zoe Wang

Kim, Ik-du

Kim Ik-du (1874–1950) was a representative revivalist; a powerful praying person who performed miraculous healings; a passionate evangelical preacher with a ministry empowered by the Holy Spirit; and a martyr who had to endure the persecution of Japanese colonialism and the communists. After the Revival Movement led by Kil Seon-ju in 1907, Kim Ik-du became an outstanding revivalist who led the movement in the 1920s and 1930s, when people needed much comfort and hope in the oppressed and miserable time of Japanese oppression.

After his marriage at the age of eighteen, Kim squandered his family fortune due to his mistake to guarantee his friend's debt. In his early twenties, Kim lived his life as a gangster until he listened to the preaching of the missionary W. Swallen, which led him to repent and became a transformed Christian at age twenty-seven. Kim read the Bible more than a hundred times within ten months and was baptized by Swallen when he was aged twenty-eight. After forty days of fasting and praying, Kim received God's calling that "you will become a servant of the fire." Kim explained this experience as a fireball that came into his heart with his whole body feeling like fire. Kim responded with an "Amen" to God's calling.

Kim founded a church in Shincheon, a country village, where he had to endure persecution and curses. People in the village mocked him, that he was possessed by a Jesus goblin or western ghost. Nevertheless, Kim first prayed for three people to become Christians, which was answered, then thirty, and then three hundred believers, which gathered in the church in three years. During his ministry in Shincheon, Kim brought a great of revival movement there, including miraculous healings in the strong presence of the Holy Spirit like fire. Kim studied at Pyeongyang Presbyterian Seminary from 1906 to 1910. During Kim's life, he led the revival worship meetings more than 770 times, founded about

150 churches, miraculously healed more than 10,000 patients, and influenced more than 200 people to become pastors.

There are unique features in Kim's ministry. First, his revival worship attracted a great number of people so that conferences always became massive gatherings. For example, if there were several hundred people gathered for the first day of a gathering, by the last day several thousands gathered. Second, his ministry and worship conference always combined with miraculous healings. Because his miraculous healing ministry manifested all over the country, a group of 26 pastors and elders published a book called *A Testament of Miracles in the Joeson Jesus Church*, which investigated Kim's healing ministry from 1919 to 1921 and proved that miraculous healing still existed. Therefore, one of the provisions of the Presbyterian Church Constitution – "There are no miraculous signs and wonders at the present time" – was requested to be changed. Third, Kim's gatherings usually had a passionate revival atmosphere on the fire of the Holy Spirit. When Kim's preaching on the Cross of Jesus Christ pierced the hearts of people, with the fire of the Holy Spirit, the worship in the congregation was characterized as being on fire with tears, repentance, and praise of God. J.N. Milles, a missionary, reported in the *Missionary Review* that there was a breathtaking atmosphere during the meetings.

In the life of the Church, Kim tried to remove superstition, shamanism, and ancestor worship. He put his effort into reforming the system of the church and its structure. Kim's main focus of his ministry was on the poor and marginalized, with preaching, miraculous healing, hope, comfort, and courage to endure hard times, particularly after the failure of the Independent Movement in 1919. His main message was about the cross of Christ, the sacrifice of Jesus, the blood of Jesus, the resurrection, repentance, and judgment.

Despite the forced shrine worship by the Japanese powers, Kim refused shrine worship till the end. He endured torture and custody, and was forcibly dragged into a shrine in Sinuiju. However, because of this incident, Kim was misunderstood by other Christians as having worshipped the shrine. Because of his refusal of shrine worship, Kim was banned from his ministry and had to resign in 1938, following oppression from the Japanese police in 1938. After the Korean Liberation in 1945, Kim was able to return to his ministry at the age of 72 until he was killed by the communists after leading the morning prayer meeting at Shincheon church in October 1950. In his last years, Kim received various critiques for his relations with the CCF (Choson Christian Federation), which was created by the Communists to control and persecute all churches under their guards. There is controversy over how Kim became the president of the CCF not by his choice, but by claims of deception by Kang Yang-wook, a relative of Kim Il-seong and one of Kim's disciples.

Bibliography

Jin, Su-cheol. 1994. *The Biographies of Martyrdom*. Seoul: Yangmoon.

Kim, Ik-du, 2008. *Korean Leadership Preaching: Kim Ik Du*. Seoul: Hongseongsa

Milles, J.N. 1922. "The Cause of Changes in Korea." *The Missionary Review of the World* (February): 115–118.

Park, Yong-Kyu. 1991. *A Biography of Rev. Kim Ik-Doo*. Seoul: The Word of Life Press

Shin, Gwang-cheol. 1996. "Apostle of the Miracle Who Overcame the Ethnic Thread Rev. Kim, Ik-Du." *Ministry and Theology* 48 (June): 196–198.

Eunhee Zoe Wang

King, Joseph H.

Joseph Hillery King was born (1869–1946) in Anderson County, South Carolina, USA. The family had 11 children and he was the second. His father was an "extremely poor tenant farmer" (Muse 1946). When Joseph left home at the age of 20 (1889), he had only attended 18 months of public-school education.

King married Willie Irene King on August 10, 1890, but she left him and eventually got a divorce not wanting to be a pastor's spouse. He waited until her death and then married Blanche Leon Moore on June 1, 1920. They had 4 children, Easter Lily, Joseph, Virginia, and Mary Ann. None of them were married, and all returned to the King House in Franklin Springs to die.

The church of King's pre-teen years was the Prospect Baptist Church, but a family relocation got King to the Allens Methodist Episcopal Church South that was part of the Carnesville Circuit. Teenage King acknowledged a call to the ministry in June 1885 when he preached his first sermon while plowing cotton rows. He made a public conversion on August 11, 1885. On August 17, 1885, he joined the Bold Spring Methodist Episcopal Church South and applied for Exhorter's License in June 1887 when he was almost 18 years old, but was rejected. He then made another application to the Elberton District Quarterly Conference of the Methodist Episcopal Church South, North Georgia Conference. He was eventually granted the Exhorter's license in 1890. King joined the Marietta Street Methodist Episcopal Church North in Atlanta, Georgia. He was licensed to preach in March 1891, and by May became a junior pastor for the Methodist Episcopal Church North in Northeast Georgia. King pointed out that he was not a "circuit rider" but a "circuit walker." Since King had not completed all the courses to be ordained a deacon, he was admitted to Conference on Trial in January 1892 in Atlanta in the Methodist Episcopal Church North, Georgia Conference. By January 1894, he was ordained a deacon.

In 1892, King entered School of Theology of Ulysses S. Grant University in Chattanooga, Tennessee. He graduated with a diploma on May 11, 1897. His studies were in systematic, historical, biblical and practical theology with Hebrew and Greek. He was ordained an elder in January 1896 in Atlanta.

Benjamin Hardin Irwin's Fire-Baptised Holiness Movement attracted some of the members of the Trinity Methodist Episcopal Church in Franklin, Georgia where King ministered. In 1898, King was also involved in the movement and in February, he became firmly convinced that he was truly sanctified and received "fire baptism." When the Fire-Baptized Holiness Association (FBHA) convened its inaugural General Council in July-August 1898, King was counted as one of the charter members. The group advanced the Holiness notion of sanctification by identifying the subsequent fire baptism. The association expanded rapidly under Irwin, the general overseer, who appointed ruling elders across North America. In early 1899, King moved from Royston to Toronto. In the FBHA's General Council in 1899, Irwin appointed King as the ruling elder of the FBHA Ontario Association. Irwin's unceremonious exit from the position of general overseer came early in 1900. King was elected general overseer on July 2 when the FBHA met in Olmiz, Iowa.

When Pentecostal Holiness Church (PHC) minister G.B. Cashwell brought the Pentecostal message from the Azusa Street Revival in Los Angeles in 1906 to parts of the southeast USA, many of the early participants came from the PHC and the Fire Baptized Holiness Church (FBHC). With

FBHC members and ministers identifying themselves as Pentecostal, King spent time with the Greek text of the New Testament and the literature of various biblical commentators like Dean Alford, which led him to initially oppose the distinctive teaching of tongues as the initial evidence of Spirit baptism. He stated his opposition in *Live Coals*. However, when Cashwell came to King's FBHC in Toccoa, Georgia, King reversed course and claimed Spirit baptism with the initial sign of speaking in tongues on February 15, 1907.

The FBHC was racially integrated from the seminal national convention in 1898 until W.E. Fuller left in 1908 to organize what is now the Fire Baptized Holiness Church of God of the Americas, Inc. Irwin appointed female ruling elders including one woman of color and various men of color led by Fuller who became King's FBHC Assistant General Overseer. By contrast, King did not advance gender and race issues during his many years of leadership in the PHC.

King had served as the associate editor of FBHA's *Live Coals of Fire*, then editor of *Live Coals* followed by the *Apostolic Evangel*. While living in Falcon, North Carolina, he helped launch the 1909 orphanage that serves the IPHC to this day. During a brief stay in Memphis, Tennessee, he published the widely quoted *From Passover to Pentecost* in 1914. In 1925, he became editor of the *Pentecostal Holiness Advocate*.

The FBHC merged with the PHC on January 31, 1911. The church that King served is now known as the International Pentecostal Holiness Church (IPHC). During the consolidation, he was on a world tour and was elected assistant general superintendent. King travelled with a PHC minister, T.J. McIntosh, to China, and while in Hong Kong in October 1910, King ministered with the indigenous Pentecostal icon, Mok Lai Chi, in a ten-day Pentecostal convention. King then visited the legendary orphanage in Mukti, India in 1911 where he taught classes for one week and honored the founder, Pandita Ramabai. He also visited Palestine, and afterwards, Thomas B. Barratt, the apostolic European Pentecostal figure, managed the preaching stations for King throughout Europe in 1912. A reporter for the Finnish Lutheran church magazine, *Kotimma* (8 July 1912), praised King for being "open minded." During the launching of the International Pentecostal Council that convened in Sunderland, UK in May 1912, King was a keynote speaker and signed their public document. In 1917 King was elected as the general superintendent of the PHC. He remained at the helm of the church until 1941 when Bishop Dan T. Muse took the top spot, but King was returned to the top position in 1945, one year before his death. The "honorary" title, Bishop, was first conferred in 1937, but was not designated for life.

Bibliography

Alexander, David A. 1986. "Bishop J.H. King and the Emergence of Holiness Pentecostalism." *Pneuma* 8 (1): 159–183.

Boddy, Alexander. 1914. "Pastor King." *Confidence* 7, no. 9 (September): 173.

Moon, Tony. 2017. *From Plowboy to Pentecostal Bishop: The Life of J.H. King*. Lexington, KY: Emeth Press.

Muse, Dan T. 1946. "'I Have Fought A Good Fight,'" *Pentecostal Holiness Advocate* 30, no. 4 (May 23): 3.

Purinton, William. 2003. "Joseph Hillary King's View and Use of Scripture in the Holiness/Pentecostal Context." PhD diss., Trinity Evangelical Divinity Seminary.

Harold D. Hunter

Kong, Duen Yee (Mui Yee)

Kong Duen Yee (Mui Yee; 1923–1966) was a famous Hong Kong actress. She attracted many fans and curious audiences. Her messages were powerful. As a result, many accepted Christ, were filled with the Holy Spirit, and spoke in tongues. Many lives were transformed, revived, and renewed. Kong came to Singapore and Malaysia by the invitation and under the guarantee of Rev. Timothy Siu Wai Pun, conducting evangelistic rallies, preaching the gospel, and leading many people to Christ. However, Kong also caused some riots when she ministered in the Assembly of God Chapel, which today is called the First Assembly of God, Kuala Lumpur (AOGKL 1964; FAOGKL 2009). The riots were triggered by the conversion of a group of Taoist "Mao Shan" priests and a number of secret society members after Kong had successfully led them to Christ. These incidents were widely reported in local newspapers. Eventually, police forces and the Federal Reserve Unit had to intervene to prevent further commotion.

After this incident, Kong continued her journey to Singapore. She then returned to Malaysia and visited the First Assembly of God in Ipoh, the Penang First Assembly of God, and some churches in Sitiawan (Kong 1963a). In this series of evangelistic meetings, Kong led over 100 people to Christ. Many "backslidden" believers repented and re-dedicated themselves to the Lord. These evangelistic meetings were the most talked-about in the history of the Chinese churches in Singapore and Malaysia as many experienced the infilling of the Holy Spirit.

After these successful rallies, Kong planned and began to build new churches in Singapore and Malaysia which were later called the New Testament Church (NTC; Kong 1964). However, this violated the initial intention of the Assemblies of God, USA (AG) in bringing Kong and the Grace of Jesus Christ Crusade to this region. According to the account given by Rev. David Nyien, an American AG missionary to Asia, the purpose of inviting Kong to Singapore and Malaysia was to conduct evangelistic rallies that focused on preaching the gospel and not planting new churches. Unhappy with Kong's setting up of the NTC, the AG requested and sent Kong back to Hong Kong. Meanwhile, the AG cut off all ties and fellowship with the NTC. The stand enabled the AG to continue to preach and practice their Pentecostal beliefs; it also led to further conflict (David Nyien, reported to author, 1990).

After that, Kong announced that she had set up nine NTC congregations in over a month (Kong 1963b). However, she was criticized by many local churches, including those from the Methodist, Baptist, and Gospel Hall churches. These evangelical churches, together with AG churches, complained that Kong had invited some of their leaders and members to join the NTC. Furthermore, Kong continued to preach messages that were anti-denominational and distorted the messages preached by the denominational churches. Her action drew a huge backlash from the churches. Some traditional churches were upset by Kong's charismatic messages, including her extreme views on salvation, the Holy Spirit, the church, and the sacred-secular divide (Kong 1964; Kong 1963b). The Chinese churches of the Assemblies of God in Malaysia faced a major charismatic crisis from 1963 to 1966.

Consequently, many local churches, the Methodist Church, the Gospel Hall and the Baptist Church also gradually cut their ties with the NTC. Regrettably, this conflict led to further tensions and the subsequent opposition between the Pentecostal-Charismatic churches and the non-charismatic churches. Both parties stopped fellowshipping and communicating with each other. Many misunderstandings caused by the divisions turned into accusations and conflict. This resulted in a setback in the history of Chinese church relations in Singapore and Malaysia. It was not until the 1980s that the relationship started to change as both parties began to communicate and have fellowship with one another.

The NTC also experienced internal conflict with two major splits in 1966 and 1976 (Hong 1979). This conflict weakened the influence of the NTC in Singapore and Malaysia. Currently, there are only about 15 NTC churches in the region. The splits have affected church attendance as many members left the NTC. New independent charismatic churches, such as Philadelphia Church Kuala Lumpur, Full Gospel Church Johor Bahru, The Charismatic Church of Penang, Church of Sitiawan, and Sibu Full Gospel Church formed after the splits.

Bibliography

AOGKL (Assembly of God Kuala Lumpur). 1964. *Assembly of God Kuala Lumpur 1934–1964 – 30th Anniversary Magazine.*
FAOGKL (First Assembly of God Kuala Lumpur). 2009. *First Assembly of God Kuala Lumpur – 75th Anniversary Magazine.*
Hong, Elijah. 1979. *Elijah's Mantle.* Grace of Jesus Christ Crusade, Taipei.
Kong, Duen Yee. 1964. *Golden Lamp Stand.* Vol. 1. Hong Kong: Grace of Jesus Christ Crusade.
Kong, Duen Yee. 1963a. *Acts of the Holy Spirit.* Hong Kong: Grace of Jesus Christ Crusade.
Kong. Duen Yee. 1963b. "Acts of the Holy Spirit Part 1." *Living Testimony Compilation Chapter 1–50.* Hong Kong: Grace of Jesus Christ Crusade.

Paulus Wong

Kuhlman, Kathryn

Kathryn Johanna Kuhlman (1907–1976) was the single most significant female leader in mid-20th century charismatic Christianity in the United States. Born in Concordia, Missouri, she and American Pentecostalism grew up together. At age fourteen, she left home to tour the American west as a young evangelist under the guidance of her sister and brother-in-law, Myrtle and Everett Parrott. The Parrotts exposed Kuhlman to early Pentecostal teaching such as the sufficiency of Jesus' atonement for divine healing of the body and salvation of the soul, the soon return of Jesus to earth, and the present reality of the Holy Spirit. These Pentecostal emphases were handed down to the Parrotts and Kuhlman through the ministries of figures such as Aimee Semple McPherson, Charles S. Price, and A.B. Simpson.

In 1933, Kuhlman founded the Denver Revival Tabernacle in Colorado. With the able assistance of her pianist, Helen Gulliford, Kuhlman established herself as the sole pastor of a thriving ministry in Denver. The Tabernacle fell apart after a disastrous romance between Kuhlman and Burroughs Waltrip, a fellow evangelist who abandoned his wife and two children

I believe in miracles, Kathryn Kuhlman. Source: Archives of BG Center

to marry Kuhlman in 1938. Facing rejection by her former parishioners, Kuhlman quickly regretted the marriage. She spoke of her re-consecration to ministry during this time, stating that Kathryn Kuhlman "died" as the Holy Spirit claimed her life once again. She relocated to Pennsylvania in 1946, divorced Waltrip by 1947, and began a new phase of ministry marked by miracles of healing.

Kuhlman continued to preach a standard evangelical message of born-again Christianity, but increasingly she was known as a faith healer, a term she rejected for its association with Pentecostal healers such as William Branham and A.A. Allen. Kuhlman practiced healing through words of knowledge, a style similar to her predecessor Aimee Semple McPherson (although Kuhlman never acknowledged McPherson's influence). Kuhlman did not "lay on hands" to heal, or claim a "point of contact" for healing such as her contemporary Oral Roberts. Kuhlman would preach until she perceived the healing power of the Holy Spirit, then call out the healings taking place in the room or auditorium around her. According to Kuhlman, she was simply identifying what God was already doing in the bodies and lives of her audiences. Soon after what she called "the beginning of miracles," Kuhlman produced a short-lived television show in the 1950s called "Your Faith and Mine," where she drew miracle stories from her congregations in Pennsylvania and Ohio. Kuhlman collected these testimonies in a best-selling book entitled *I Believe in Miracles*, published in 1962, the first of several popular titles about Kuhlman's healing and salvation ministry.

Kuhlman led weekly services in Pittsburgh, which was now the center of her ministry and the site of her Kathryn Kuhlman Foundation offices. In 1965 she added monthly miracle services at the 7,000-seat Los Angeles Shrine Auditorium. In the following year, she launched her syndicated television talk show, *I Believe in Miracles*. Her popularity within the Catholic Charismatic Renewal was reinforced by her audience with Pope Paul VI in 1972. By 1974 Kuhlman was invited to *The Tonight Show* with Johnny Carson and in 1975 the *Dinah!* show starring Dinah Shore. As Kuhlman appeared on national television, her Foundation was operating a radio program, a television show, coordinating multiple worship services, and Bible studies in Pittsburgh, Ohio, and LA. The Foundation supported mission work in Nicaragua, Honduras, Costa Rica, India, Macau, Hong Kong, Benin (formerly Dahomey), Argentina, Taiwan, South Africa, Malaysia, Indonesia, Kenya, El Salvador, and Vietnam.

Kuhlman travelled to Vietnam in 1970 to visit a Foundation-supported hospital for the wounded. She travelled around the world at the height of her career, holding multiple miracle services in Sweden, Canada, and headlining at the 1974 and 1975 world conference on the Holy Spirit in Jerusalem. With the help of the director of World Vision, Dick Ross, Kuhlman decided to record a miracle service in full in 1975. *Dry Land ... Living Water* was filmed during Kuhlman's miracle service in Los Vegas, Nevada. The film captured on camera the striking style of Kuhlman as preacher, the manifestation of word of knowledge, and the phenomenon of audience members being "slain in the Spirit," or apparently swooning under the influence of the Holy Spirit. For the first time, outsiders were able to see what a Kuhlman service really looked like, for better or for worse.

Kuhlman's grueling schedule exacerbated an already serious heart condition, and Kuhlman became weaker as she approached the age of 70. She fell ill due to an enlarged heart and died after surgery on February 20, 1976. Controversy surrounded her will, which Kuhlman changed during her illness, leaving the Foundation nothing and transferring the bulk of the inheritance to a married couple of recent acquaintance. Kuhlman was buried in Forest Lawn Memorial Park in Glendale, California. Her tombstone carved with her trademark words, "I Believe in Miracles Because I Believe in God."

Bibliography

Artman, Amy. 2019. *The Miracle Lady: Kathryn Kuhlman and the Transformation of Charismatic Christianity*. Grand Rapids, MI: William B. Eerdmans.

De Alminana, Margaret and Lois E. Olena, eds. 2016. *Women in Pentecostal and Charismatic Ministry: Informing a Dialogue on Gender, Church, and Ministry*. Leiden: Brill.

Dry Land ... Living Water. 1975. Pittsburgh, PA: Kathryn Kuhlman Foundation. Videocassette (VHS), 85 min.

Warner, Wayne E. 1993. *Kathryn Kuhlman: The Woman Behind the Miracles*. Ann Arbor: Servant Publications.

Amy Artman

Kuwait

Kuwait is situated at the northeast corner of the Arabian Gulf, or, as more commonly known, the Persian Gulf. It is sandwiched between Saudi Arabia to the south and west and Iraq to its northern and eastern borders. Most of the four million inhabitants are situated in the main city, Kuwait City, and immediate outlying governorates. Its governmental structure consists of an *emir*, or chief ruler, a prime minister, parliament, and constitution. The constitution enshrines both freedom of religion tempered by the official religion of Sunni religion and an interpretation of *shari'a* law that follows what is known as Malaki jurisprudence. Culturally, it shares many similarities with Saudi Arabia, Qatar, the United Arab Emirates, Iran, and Bahrain.

Under Islamic hegemony, Christianity has managed to flourish on the margins. Like other countries in the Gulf, the local population is outnumbered by migrant workers who come from all over the world for higher wages inflated by the petrol industry. Although there are a few dozen local, Kuwaiti Christians, the majority of Christians in the country are migrant workers on some type of work visa. The greatest concentrations are Egyptians, Indians, and Filipinos. Of these, there are many Coptic Orthodox, Mar Thoma (a branch of Orthodoxy in South India), and Roman Catholic Christians. Protestant denominations also abound and generally congregate under the auspices of the National Evangelical Church of Kuwait. NECK, as it is locally called, has its own compound near the Roman Catholic Cathedral and hosts services with a wide variety of languages and spiritual orientations but all identifying as Protestant-Evangelical. Some of these congregations have a Renewalist/Pentecostal emphasis, while others, like the largely Western congregation, tend to have a nondenominational biblicism. Outside of the NECK compound, there are various and sundry churches that rent basements, villas, apartments, and other entertainment areas for their meetings. These non-NECK compound-based churches are not officially sanctioned by the government, and their leaders are usually bi-vocational, that is, not on a religious visa. Often, too, these "house" churches are branches of Pentecostal churches and denominations or carry a charismatic-renewalist flavor. Some are associated with or splits from the NECK.

According to *Christianity in North Africa-West Asia* (Johnson et al. 2018), as of 2015, there were 3,892,000 people living in Kuwait. Of these, 396,000 identified as Christians, constituting a 5.1 percent growth from 1970. Catholics make up 75.7 percent of the Christian population, followed by the Orthodox, both Eastern and Oriental, at 20.2 percent. Renewalists make up 21.3 percent of the Christian population, or roughly 84,000 individuals. 12,527 individuals converted to the faith in 2015 whereas 6,350 defected and another 2300 emigrated. Still, in 2015, Christianity in the country grew at a rate of 2.74 percent but that rate is expected to fall to 1.51 percent over the next 40 years. Pentecostalism, however, grew 37.29 percent over the five-year period from 2010–2015 and is the fastest growing form of Christianity in the country. On the whole, the statistics reflect non-Kuwaiti Christians living on visas rather than a growing, indigenous movement.

Bibliography

Olayan, Hamza. 2017. *Christians in Kuwait*, translated by Salama M. Issa. Kuwait: That Al-Salasil.

Ross, Kenneth R., Mariz Tadros, and Todd M. Johnson, eds. 2018. *Christianity in North Africa-West Asia*. Edinburgh: Edinburgh University Press.

Scudder, Lewis. 1998. *The Arabian Mission's Story: In Search of Abraham's Other Son*. Grand Rapids, MI: Wm. B. Eerdmans Publishing Co.

Benjamin Crace

Lake, John G.

John G. Lake (1870–1935) was a Canadian-born missionary to South Africa, traveling healing evangelist, Zionist Apostolic pastor, and co-founder with Thomas Hezmalhalch (1847–1934) of the Apostolic Faith Mission of South Africa denomination.

John Graham Lake was born in the community of Avonbank, Ontario, Canada, near the town of St. Marys on March 18, 1870. His father, James Lake (1841–1925), was a locally-born farmer, and his mother, Elizabeth Graham (1840–1913), had immigrated from Kilberry, Scotland. Family deaths became part of Lake's early life, as half of his parents' sixteen children had died before they reached adulthood. Lake attended St. Mary's High School, and then with his family moved to Sault Ste. Marie, Michigan in the late 1880s.

Lake met his wife Jennie Wallace Stephens (1867–1908) at the Methodist church in Sault Ste. Marie, Michigan, who was also Canadian (born in Bracebridge, Ontario). The two married on February 5, 1891, in Millington, Illinois, while Lake was living in nearby Chicago. They had seven children: Alexander James (1893–1961), Horace Houghton (1895–1970), Otto Bryan (1897–1960), Edna Jennie (1899–1982), Irene Margaret (1902–1992), John Graham Jr. (1904–1972), and Wallace Stephens (1907–1987). His wife was instantaneously healed of tuberculosis in meetings with John Alexander Dowie (1847–1907) of Chicago, Illinois, in 1898. Lake subsequently served as a deacon in Dowie's Zion Catholic Apostolic Church.

In 1896, Lake and his family moved back to Sault Ste. Marie. He held Dowie-like healing services in his home, occasionally referenced in the local newspaper and Dowie's periodical, *Leaves of Healing*.

Source: Oral Roberts University

In 1901, Lake moved his family to Zion, Illinois, Dowie's wholly-owned and theocratically-governed utopian city. Lake met Charles Parham (1873–1929) there during some tent meetings in 1907. Lake also visited the Apostolic Faith Mission in Azusa Street in Los Angeles, where he met William Seymour (1870–1922). In 1907, after nine months of seeking for it, Lake received the Pentecostal baptism in the Holy Spirit and spoke in tongues.

Shortly thereafter, in the wake of some questionable exorcisms that resulted in deaths, Lake moved to Indianapolis, Indiana. That same year, he felt God directing him to South Africa and the whole family arrived there in early 1908. Although he experienced some initial success, Lake quickly ran out of funds and his wife Jennie died within a year of their arrival. Lake referred this as "Satan's master blow."

Lake ministered in South Africa for five years, primarily in Johannesburg. He often wrote to Pentecostal periodicals back in North America and came home for speaking engagements, such as the 1910 Pentecostal Convention in Toronto with Ellen Hebden (1865–1923), James Hebden (1860–1919), William Durham (1873–1912), Aimee Semple McPherson (1890–1944) and her husband Robert Semple (1881–1910). He preached convincing accounts of dramatic healings and miracles, espousing a unique brand of Pentecostalism that was directly influenced by Dowie, Parham, and Seymour. Lake's many international connections with prominent Pentecostals helped validate his ministry.

Although Lake originally felt the camaraderie of several other missionaries in South Africa, his closest friends eventually withdrew their support from his endeavours there. Even Hezmalhalch, the man who founded the Apostolic Faith Mission of South Africa with Lake in 1908, abandoned him in 1912 in conflict.

Upon Lake's return to the United States in 1913 he married Florence Myrtle Switzer (1885–1964), a Canadian (born in Bellrock, Ontario), with whom he had five children: Livingstone Grier (1915–2001), Gertrude (1917–1983), Roderick Stuart (1919–1937), Elizabeth (1924–2018), and Esther (1927–2018). In the same year, the family moved to Spokane, Washington, where he opened "Lake's Divine Healing Rooms." Through this venue, Lake began to train "Divine Healing Technicians," who would carry out the ministry of healing to the sick. Lake traveled extensively during this time, particularly along the west coast of the US to California, establishing several "Healing Rooms" along the way. In 1920, the family moved to Portland, Oregon, where he continued to travel with a vision of building a national network of healing rooms. They moved back to Spokane, Washington, in 1931, where Lake died of a stroke on September 16, 1935.

Lake was largely accepted and admired during his missionary years, but he also faced criticism during his North American healing ministry. Newspapers were not always complimentary, sometimes medically disproving a healing. Some of Lake's incredible claims seemed exaggerated. There are also inconsistencies in his various autobiographical accounts, leading a few scholars to question their veracity.

Regardless of these controversies, Lake was an early influential figure in Pentecostal missions and in the faith healing movement. His brief five years in South Africa produced a Pentecostal denomination that still exists today. His work as a healing evangelist in the US prepared the way for the independent preaching and faith healing ministries of others. His legacy also remains in the ongoing work of healing rooms ministries.

Bibliography

Burpeau, Kemp Pendleton. 2004. *God's Showman: A Historical Study of John G. Lake and South African/American Pentecostalism*. Oslo: Refleks Publishing.

Lake, John Graham. 1991. *Adventures in God*. Tulsa: Harrison House.

Morton, Barry. 2017. "Yes, John G. Lake Was a Con Man: A Response to Marius Nel." *Studia Historiae Ecclesiasticae* 43 (2): 1–23. http://dx.doi.org/10.17159/2412–4265/2016/1821.

Nel, Marius. 2016. "'John G. Lake as a Fraud, Con Man and False Prophet': Critical Assessment of a Historical Evaluation of Lake's Ministry." *Studia Historiae Ecclesiasticae* 42 (1): 1–24. http://dx.doi.org/10.17159/2412-4265/2016/1134.

Caleb Courtney

Lancaster, Sarah Jane (Murrell)

Sarah Jane Lancaster (née Murrell), (1858–1935). Born in Williamstown, Victoria, Australia, Sarah Jane was the third child (of eight) of master mariner, William Lee Murrell and his wife Mary Anne (née Hume). In December 1879, Sarah Jane married railway "engineer" Alfred Henry Lancaster (31 Jan 1858, Manchester, England–4 Feb 1930). They lived with the Murrells for some years, until they had children (of whom there were seven). Their large family network of Catos, Murrells, Pyes and Buchanans, many of them Methodist or Salvationist, connected works in Tasmania, New Zealand, Melbourne, Ballarat, Bendigo, Sydney (especially around Mosman), and Brisbane (*The Mercury*, 29 Nov 1932, 8). Alfred and Sarah Jane were themselves active in the York St Methodist Mission in Ballarat, where Alfred sang and Sarah Jane preached at outdoor meetings, and were active Methodist "visitors." Sarah Jane also visited Salvation Army meetings (Chant 2011, 142).

In visiting the sick and housebound, Sarah Jane developed an interest in divine healing. There were various divine healing practitioners in Melbourne at the time, including such as Clara and Mary Ann Weare's "Divine healing and Full Gospel Mission on Russell Street" (*The Age*, 8 Jan 1900, 10) and a Divine Healing Association which had met regularly since at least Dowie's time in Melbourne. Lancaster also read Spurgeon, J.J. Wray, and others who presented a case for believing the miracles of the Bible to be true. (Spurgeon, "The Touch of Faith," *Leader*, 13 Jan 1900, 45; Wray, "All the Year Round," *Weekly Times*, 20 Jan 1900, 7.)

In 1906 she ordered a pamphlet from England entitled "Back to Pentecost" (possibly by James Pollock and his brother-in-law A.A. Boddy), (Robinson 2013, 171) and on 2 April 1908, Lancaster reported that she was baptized in the Spirit (BHS) and began speaking in tongues. In 1909 Lancaster and a number of others purchased an old Temperance Hall (Good News Hall) in North Melbourne, and founded "The Pentecostal Mission." Commencing with an all night prayer meeting, she and her core group were so overwhelmed that they never returned to the family home. Lancaster lived in the hall for the rest of her life. Services were held through the week, specializing in divine healing and the BHS. The congregation numbered about 100 on Sundays, but the Hall was always open for prayer, and was remodelled so visitors could stay, often for days or weeks. Other rooms held a Book and Tract Room and later a printing press on which the magazine *Good News* was printed (Chant 2011, 215–16). From 1910 Lancaster travelled around Australia preaching the "fourfold gospel": salvation, baptism in the Holy Spirit, divine healing and the Second Coming. Disciples such as Florrie Mortomore also went out from the Hall, establishing missions and works. In the first fifteen years, most of the early pentecostal works in Australia were established by women. Good News Hall remained Lancaster's base, and the place from which she issued what became a monthly publication, *Good News*. With a circulation of some 3000, the magazine reproduced articles from international Pentecostal and holiness publications, interspersed with reports of divine healing and articles by Lancaster interpreting world events in biblical terms.

Lancaster had first met Herbert Booth in Melbourne during his period as Commandant of the Salvation Army – during his 1923 campaign, he spent a week with Lancaster. His teaching on healing and pacifism were common themes in *Good News*. Booth's name became something of a touchstone of orthodoxy for Lancaster, his opinion that her "strange doctrines" were simply ahead of her time being used to fend off criticism from other pentecostals in Melbourne (such as Charles Greenwood, who was seeking to grow Sunshine Gospel Hall into the leading church in the city).

Lancaster eschewed personal publicity. In her teaching she asserted the equality of women and men before Christ and criticized the mainstream churches for not recognizing women's ministry, arguing that it was "the pride of man [that] forbids his acceptance of the grace of God toward those women upon whom He has poured His Spirit" (Chant 1999, 424). Her maternal approach to ministry (many of her followers referred to her as "Mother") was held within the bounds of respectability by acting under the putative headship of her husband Alfred, until his death on August 23, 1930.

In 1926 Lancaster helped gather the GNH network into a new organization entitled "the Apostolic Faith Mission of Australasia" (AFM) under the Presidency of J.A.D. Adams [q.v.] (she was Vice President). This transition from faith mission to church sparked disputes around doctrinal issues and the appropriate role for women in leadership. The movement splintered with two rival organizations forming and taking most of the membership. Lancaster rallied what was left of the AFM and in 1930 was elected its President (perhaps one of the reasons why she controversially remarried shortly afterwards) but the organisation folded soon after her death in North Melbourne on March 6, 1934. GNH thereafter declined, though Lancaster's influence continued to be felt through her many disciples, family members, and the pentecostal works that they founded. People influenced there included early Pentecostal leaders such as William Sloan, William Alexander Buchanan, Lloyd Averill, and the founders of such important pentecostal dynasties as the Mortomore and Enticknap families. From 1909 to 1930, Good News Hall supported missionaries in Asia, Africa, and Central Australia, and a range of social work.

While several of Lancaster's children had predeceased her, Henry Nelson (1886–1971) married into the Buchanan clan, and his brother in law William Alexander Buchanan would marry Leila Lancaster. The Buchanans, and Henry's son Fred, would become foundational leaders in the Assemblies of God in Australia, particularly in Queensland.

Bibliography

Chant, Barry. 1999. "The Spirit of Pentecost: Origins and Development of the Pentecostal Movement in Australia 1870–1939." PhD diss., Macquarie University.

Clifton, Shane. 2009. *Pentecostal Churches in Transition: Analysing the Developing Ecclesiology of the Assemblies of God in Australia.* Leiden: Brill.

"Lancaster, Sarah Jane." The Australian Women's Register, National Foundation for Australian Women. Accessed April 9, 2019. http://www.womenaustralia.info/biogs/AWE5177b.htm.

Robinson, James. 2013. *Divine Healing: The Holiness-Pentecostal Transition Years, 1890–1906: Theological Transpositions in the Transatlantic World.* Eugene, OR: Wipf and Stock Publishers.

Mark Hutchinson

Latin America

The history of Latin America is a long, diverse, and arduous account of mestizaje (miscegenation) and an experience of unbalanced development. Religion in the Americas obscures the visibility of the indigenous peoples, the vast population of African descent, and the millions of people who currently live in the United States. Latin American Christianity, in general, and Pentecostalism, in particular, are part of the ever evolving and shifting story, which is Latin America. In the five hundred years since the so-called "discovery of America," Christianity shifted from a regional religion to a multi-faceted global force, in some ways, similar to Africa and Asia. The recent spiritual surge of Pentecostalism did not suddenly happen overnight. It does, however, represent a continuation of a fragmented religious history that includes revitalization with a current increase of a pneumacentric option for the people of Latin America (Hatch 2014).

Latin America has become a centre for world Christianity with more Catholics and Pentecostals residing there than anywhere else on the planet. Latin American Pentecostalism, including the Catholic Charismatic Renewal (CCR), positioned as the epicenter of global Pentecostalism, is a significant example of religious globalization in terms of conversion growth in contrast to a diasporic establishment of Pentecostal churches. The astonishing development of Christianity in the Global South by virtue of its autonomous spiritual and social movement merits Latin America a contributing role in the discussion of global religion and politics. Within the countries, a pentecostalization has occurred – Pentecostal growth continues, Pentecostal influence on other religions, and Pentecostal impact on Latin American society ensues at different rates in these nations.

Latin Americanists observers above have described the phenomenon in terms of religious economies, pentecostalization, and a rebirth; but how are Pentecostals interpreting Latin American Pentecostalism? Bernardo Campos, a Peruvian Pentecostal theologian answers the question by acknowledging the existence of a plurality of Pentecostalisms – "Which Pentecostalism are we talking about when we speak of Pentecostalism?" (Campos 2016, 222). For Campos there are five trends of the movement: (1) classical Pentecostalism influenced by North America, (2) national Pentecostal movements, (3) neo-Pentecostals, (4) Iso-Pentecostalism (divine healing movements), and (5) post-Pentecostals. To identify theologically what is or is not Pentecostal, he espouses, "Pentecostality," a term he coined that "refers to the universal experience that qualifies the Pentecostal event in its mission to order the life of those who identify with the renewal initiated in the biblical Day of Pentecost" (Campos 2016, 224). Two other Pentecostal perspectives from Mexico and Chile are considered next.

Daniel Chiquete, an architect and Mexican Pentecostal theologian, studies the different forms of Pentecostalism in Latin America and their interactions with postmodernism to better understand their present and future role in society. In order to interpret the plethora of Pentecostal expressions, he prefers the term "Pentecostalisms" to appreciate the differences "... in doctrine, liturgy, the socio-cultural location of their communities, politics, [and] church organization" (Chiquete 2003, 30). Chiquete predicts a contracting and expanding relationship between Pentecostalisms and postmodernism as they develop within a context of distrust and fascination. Instead of utilizing the plural term, Chilean Pentecostal scholar Juan Sepulveda uses the singular form "Pentecostalism" with a broader interpretation. For him, Latin American Pentecostalism is a force of indigenization – "It is my own conviction that the central significance of modern Pentecostalism's emphasis on the work of the Holy Spirit ... lies in the affirmation of the legitimacy of understanding and experiencing Christian faith through cultural mediations other than Western rational and logo-centric culture" (Sepulveda 1988, 191, and Alfaro and Medina 2015,

17–33). Hence, Sepulveda's broadly defined Pentecostalism can incorporate other historic and confessional churches, which opting for the freedom of the Holy Spirit "become deeply indigenous in their way of being Christian" (Sepulveda 1998, 191).

The spread of Pentecostalism and religious conflict created a religious marketplace, which brought about transformation to the Catholic Church. Consequently, Latin American Pentecostalism acted as a catalyst to Catholic revitalization and its biggest competitor, the Charismatic Catholic Renewal. Pentecostalism and Charismatic Catholicism thoroughly transformed Latin America between 1970–2000 (Hartch 2014, 92). The Pew Research Center report found that there are more than twice as many Catholic Charismatics than Pentecostals, 170 million to 76 million, a fact less known and studied among students of religion in Latin America (Chestnut 2016, 2). The study found a median of 40 percent of Latin American Catholics who identify as "charismatic," which means "in nearly every country surveyed at least one-in-five Catholics describe themselves as charismatics" (Pew Research Center 2014, 15, 62). At least half of Catholics in Panama, Brazil, Honduras, the Dominican Republic, and El Salvador say they are Charismatic.

In October 1967 the CCR in Latin America began in Bogota, Colombia, nine months after but without direct connection to the North American Charismatic movement originating at Duquesne University in Pittsburg, Pennsylvania. While a group of Protestant Charismatics from the United States and Canada visited Colombia, "one of them, Samuel Ballesteros ... became friends with Padre Rafael Garcia-Herreros, the leader of Minuto de Dios [a low-cost housing cooperative], and carried on long conversations with him about the Charismatic understanding of the Holy Spirit and his gifts" (Clearly 2011, 56; Gooren 2012, 187). In the early 1970s, Padre Rafael received the baptism of the Holy Spirit and Minuto de Dios emerged as the first main center of the CCR in Colombia. The second renewal epicenter developed under Bishop Alfonso Uribe of Medellin at the peasant seminary he began in 1969. Both leaders established the strong presence of CCR in Colombia. The spread of Charismatic Catholicism in the early 1970s was also initiated by North American evangelists (Dominican and Jesuit priests) who brought the CCR to most of the major cities in Latin America. "Francis MacNutt played a pivotal role in establishing the CCR in several Latin American nations, including Mexico, Colombia, Peru, and Chile" (Chestnut 2003b, 63).

In 2016 Lindhardt and other social scientists considered the processes of religious transformation in Latin America and how these have led to different modes of being Pentecostal and explored the consequences of the shift. Changes occurring in Latin American Pentecostalism include a turning away from particular forms of institutionalized Pentecostalism and adjudicating for personal Pentecostal identities; emergent theological innovations from pentecostalized groups and Neo-Charismatics; the rise of new generations of Pentecostals (children of Pentecostal parents); the awareness of "el projimo" (the neighbor) has led Pentecostals to focus on social activity and involvement; a search for the meaning of Pentecostal citizenship; and revisions to the classic Pentecostal dualism of the Church and the world (Lindhardt 2016, x).

In the past forty years, the neoliberal era of "wholesale movement guided by capitalism with an ambiguous process of regulations, open trade, and free markets" failed to fulfill on its promise of stability, mobility, and development for most Latin Americans (Nolivos 2012, 90). Yet, neoliberalism has established an idiosyncratic perception of progress and consumerism, which some Pentecostals and Catholic Charismatics have become postmodern individualized consumers who are more often detached of churches and group affiliations. Chilean sociologist Miguel Mansilla Agüero depicts the development as "religious nomadism" and "supermarket religion," where such consumers are labeled by Pentecostal pastors as "spiritual tourists" or domingueros (Sunday-ers) in search of spiritual-emotional encounters but without commitment to any faith community (Lindhardt 2016, x–xi). It is becoming more common for Latin American religionists to shop around as they construct their particular way of being Pentecostal in a diverse free religious market.

Lindhardt's ethnographic study among Chilean Pentecostals demonstrates church shifting (switching) from traditional, conservative, and strict churches (e.g. Iglesia Evangélica Pentecostal) for a less strict and less restraining church home among neo-Pentecostal churches like Cristo Tu Única Esperanza. Another form of being Pentecostal among younger Chilean Pentecostals affirms the significance of congregational life, but accompanies it with extra-ecclesial ways of worship creating unique Pentecostal identities. For example, virtual forms of Evangelical Christianity, a youth phenomenon in contemporary Chile, and contemporary Evangelical ecumenical movements offering a postmodern view of Christianity, provide ways of being Pentecostal outside of church buildings (Fediakova 2016, 64–65). In addition to switching Pentecostal churches and being Pentecostal outside church edifices, the complex religious dynamic also includes the processes of apostasy. In rural Oaxaca, Mexico, the high social cost of becoming Pentecostal leads many to return to Catholicism (Groos 2016, 103).

Latin America's Pentecostal hermeneutic is one distinctive that has challenged and enhanced the Global Christian community. The new non-Western hermeneutical principles demonstrated in its methods and interpretations of "exegesis, contextualization, conscientization, social praxis, pneumatic emphasis and una misión integral (a holistic mission that addresses both the spiritual and social facets of life)" are part of a robust experiential spirituality among Pentecostals and Charismatics in the region (Nolivos 2011, 42).

The preferential option for the Holy Spirit by Catholic Charismatics in the twenty-first century has revitalized the Roman Catholic Church through this lay movement. The Pentecostal experience of the Baptism of the Holy Spirit among Catholic Charismatics is seen as a divine empowerment, transformation in an individual's life, and an initiation into the Charismatic group. Charismatic communities developed from the spontaneity of the prayer meeting, which provides the environment for experiences of the charismata where gifts of the Spirit like prophesy, glossolalia, and healing are manifest.

Although Charismatics and Pentecostals are pneumacentric, Charismatics are not as literal in their reading of the Bible or as ascetic as Pentecostals. The divergence between the two quickly emerges over devotion of the Pope and the Virgin; initially the CCR held Mary at a peripheral position but as it grew, Mariology became more central. Though both groups part on Marian doctrine and are inclined to live their pneumatic religiosity altogether independent of each other especially in Latin America, Catholic Charismatics and Pentecostals in practice reflect a shared affective-experiential hermeneutic of the Spirit.

In the twenty-first century, Latin American Christianity especially Pentecostal and Charismatic expressions represent a new force in Christian missions. Peripheral regions like Africa, Asia, and Latin America, which were once missional foci; however, today have become mission forces. Previously Latin America was regarded for centuries as a mission field in need of the Gospel and evangelization. For Latin American Protestants in general and Pentecostals in particular, the Church in terms of the universal priesthood of believers is the primary agent of God's mission on the continent and in the world. Pentecostals, Catholic Charismatics, and Neo-Charismatics have implemented the fundamental understanding of missio Dei as "evangelizing mission."

For the CCR and Catholic Charismatics, healing has been the most effective method of evangelization to attract nominal Catholics with the promise of restored health. Although not like Pentecostals, the CCR's evangelizing techniques have placed them as the leader for Catholic missionary efforts. In order to compete, Charismatics have emulated Pentecostal practices of home visits and mass media evangelization through television and radio (Chestnut 2016, 11). Mass media controls Catholic Church programming in numerous Latin American countries especially in Brazil and Guatemala. For example, Catholic Charismatic television is strongest in Brazil where Pentecostal broadcasting is deeply rooted. According to Chestnut, Father Edward Dougherty, known lovingly as "Padre Eduardo", can be credited as bringing the CCR to Brazil and also pioneering in Catholic TV.

Neo-Charismatics have been innovative and groundbreaking in the methods of evangelization and media but also controversial in their theologies of mission. In the case of the polemical Universal Church of the Kingdom of God (UCKG) in Brazil, their slogan "pare de sofrer" ("stop suffering") successfully attracts potential converts to consider the empowering message and Neo-Charismatic membership to overcome the demonic oppression, which keeps them poor (Chestnut 2016, 9). Edir Macedo founder of the UCKG like many Neo-Charismatic leaders see the restoration of the fivefold ministries to the Church especially of apostles and prophets. These leaders have become authoritative mediators and experts in spiritual warfare who view victory in this holy war as an occasion and precondition to expand God's mission (Campos 2015, 199). The evangelizing mission of the church for Neo-Charismatics is stringently understood in "apostolic terms"; these leaders are "apostles" to the nations intent on extending the Kingdom of God. The establishment of the kingdom is associated with the global mission of the church. For instance, the Apostle Denis Arana Cárdenas in Peru views the apostolic movement as God's final dispensation in the world.

Pentecostal and Charismatic Christianity's unprecedented expansion occurred as a result of the evangelistic practices of crusades, church planting, home visits, and TV and radio broadcasting. The evangelizing mission is part of the story that made the Pentecostal mission a missionary force in Latin America. Since the late 1960s, the emergent narrative of the maturation of the Church in Latin America and their appropriation of missio Dei from a Latin American perspective ensued. In addition to the "evangelizing mission," and as a result of the above development, the formulation of "holistic mission" or "misión integral" (integral mission) provided Latin Americans a broader missional worldview and a corrective to limited definitions of God's mission.

After a century of Pentecostal Christianity in the Americas, the subsequent diversification amongst Pentecostals,

Charismatics, and Neo-Charismatics lends to academic inquiries on current Spirit-centered praxis and spirituality. The transformations in the Latin American religious field especially the pentecostalization of the region are plentiful and have provided significant research opportunities for scholars to expand on earlier studies, which focused on the reasons and causes of Pentecostalism's growth and development. Central to the later qualitative findings are how Pentecostals and Charismatics live out their faith differently, in some instances, from first- or second-generation progenitors. Religious processes of pluralization, deinstitutionalization, individualized Pentecostal identities, theological renewals, and social engagement have transformed Pentecostalism. These developments have led to new ways of being Pentecostal in Latin America.

The preceding appraisal demonstrated alternative options to Catholicism that Latin Americans now have in the rising competitive religious markets throughout the continent. Within this economic framework, social scientists observe pneumatic consumers flourishing in countries like Guatemala, Honduras, Brazil, and Chile. This rapid and unprecedented escalation of Pentecostals and Catholic Charismatics, surpassing all other regions in the world, has made Latin America the epicenter of Global Pentecostalism. The increase, although numerical, is also a proliferation of expressions and practices of indigenous (homegrown) churches, an expanding-and-contracting tension of Pentecostal and Catholic Charismatic identities, the church-shifters who transfer allegiances between Pentecostals, Charismatics, or secular life, and the progressive Pentecostals who desire a less-strict kind of Pentecostal religiosity appeared in this study. In the end, Charismatic Christianity's worldview and praxis results from a hermeneutic of experience exemplified in the missionary strength (evangelizing mission) and integral (holistic) mission in and to the world. Latin American Pentecostalism is transforming the continent and at the same time is being transformed.

Bibliography

Alvarez, Miguel, ed. 2015. *The Reshaping of Mission in Latin America*. Oxford: Regnum International Books.

Chesnut, Andrew R. 2003. *Competitive Spirits: Latin America's New Religious Economy*. New York: Oxford University Press.

Hartch, Todd. 2014. *The Rebirth of Latin American Christianity*. Oxford: Oxford University Press.

Lindhardt, Martin, ed. 2016. *New Ways of Being Pentecostal in Latin America*. Lanham: Lexington Books.

Medina, Néstor, and Sammy Alfaro, eds. 2015. *Pentecostals and Charismatics in Latin America and Latino Communities*. New York: Palgrave Macmillan.

Nolivos, Eloy H. 2012. "Capitalism and Pentecostalism in Latin America: Trajectories of Prosperity and Development." In *Pentecostalism and Prosperity: The Socio-Economics of the Global Charismatic Movement*, edited by Katherine Attanasi and Amos Yong, 87–106. New York: Palgrave MacMillan.

Smith, Calvin, ed. 2011. *Pentecostal Power: Expressions, Impact and Faith of Latin American Pentecostalism*. Leiden: Brill.

Synan, Vinson, Amos Yong, and Miguel Alvarez, eds. 2016. *Global Renewal Christianity: Spirit-Empowered Movements Past, Present, and Future*. Volume 2: *Latin America*. Lake Mary, FL: Charisma House.

Eloy H. Nolivos

Latter Rain

The Latter Rain Movement (LRM) was a charismatic Christian revival of the 1940s that – though rejected by denominational pentecostal churches in Canada and the USA – exerted a lasting influence on the development of global charismatic Christianity. The revival broke out on 14 February 1948 (Valentine's Day) at the Sharon Orphanage and Bible College – a small pentecostal orphanage and school in the remote region of North Battleford, Saskatchewan, affiliated with the Pentecostal Assemblies of Canada. It had been preceded by months of prayer and fasting on the part of students, teachers, and staff at the college. Leaders at the college had read Franklin Hall's *Atomic Power Through Prayer and Fasting* (1946), which touted the benefits of prolonged fasting – including fasting on water alone for up to forty days at a time. For more than a decade prior to this, observers had described a spiritual dryness and deficient sense of God's presence in the North American pentecostal churches.

LRM leader George Hawtin wrote that "I can never begin to describe the things that happened that day. It seems that all Heaven broke loose upon our souls ... The power and the glory were indescribable" (Faupel 1989, 404). Hawtin became convinced that God was just about to pour out

H. Holt, P. Hunt and G. Hawtin (undated). Source: Pentecostal Assemblies of Canada Archives

the Holy Spirit on all nations to prepare for Christ's return, and to manifest new truths for the church. People soon came from around the world to camp meetings in North Battleford. The revival spread to various localities, including Glad Tidings Temple in Vancouver, Canada (pastored by Reg Layzell), Bethesda Missionary Temple in Detroit, Michigan (pastored by Myrtle D. Beall), Elim Bible Institute, at that time in Hornell, New York (founded by Ivan Q. Spencer), and Wings of Healing Temple in Portland, Oregon (pastored by Dr. Thomas Wyatt). By 1951 new leaders had emerged, and the North Battleford leaders became less central to the movement. Swedish pentecostal pastor Lewi Pethrus, of Filadelphia Church in Stockholm, Sweden came to investigate, and returned to commend the revival to European Pentecostals.

Like first-generation Pentecostals, LRM participants interpreted the words "latter rain" in Joel 2:28 in reference to an end-times outpouring. Leaders understood the movement not as a renewal but as a reestablishment of the church, requiring God's saints to break from existing denominations. Adherents believed that the church needed a manifestation of all nine gifts of the Spirit (including healing, prophecy, etc.; 1 Cor. 12:8–10), as well as the five-fold or "ascension gift ministries" (apostles, prophets, evangelists, pastors, and teachers; Eph. 4:10–12). The LRM was never a "tongues movement," since it broadly emphasized a range of spiritual gifts. The revival's message may be summarized in the word restoration. The LRM stressed the nature, mission, worship, and authority of the church, along with God-glorifying worship, according to the biblical principle that God "inhabits the praises" (Ps. 22:3) of his people. Reg Layzell said that he realized that "God actually lives in the praises of His people" – an idea that later propelled new forms of charismatic worship over the last several decades. Global mission became a focus at first National Latter Rain Convention, held in St. Louis, Missouri, in November 1950. Soon thereafter ministry teams went to Jamaica, India, Kenya, Ethiopia, Japan, Australia, New Zealand, Switzerland, France, Sweden, Ireland, Philippines. Like the earlier Pentecostal revival, the movement rapidly became internationalized. Today hundreds of independent charismatic congregations in North America, and many more thousands around the world, owe their origins to the work of LRM missionaries.

Typological interpretation of the Bible was integral to the LRM. The teaching was often not based directly on the New Testament but on a spiritual reading of the Old Testament. The Exodus of the Jews from Egypt, and the return of the Jews from Babylon to their homeland, were seen as types of the call for Christian believers to come out of the bondage of denominationalism. The LRM viewed its own worship as a restoration of the "tabernacle of David" (Amos 9:11). The Old Testament Feast of Tabernacles, for George Warnock, was the feast of "joy," "ingathering," "rest," "glory," "unity," and "restoration." In LRM theology, the Tabernacle or place of God's presence became an organizing motif, and congregations were often called Tabernacle or Temple (Faupel 1989, 457–458). A core conviction was that God himself is seeking a place where he may dwell (Darrrand and Shupe 1983, 102).

One controversial aspect of the revival was the practice of the laying on of hands. Earlier Pentecostals had "tarried for the Spirit" (Lk. 24:49), whereby they prayed and waited in the expectation that spiritual gifts would come directly from God, without human mediation. Yet having noted the biblical texts that link the conferral of spiritual gifts to "prophetic utterances" and the "laying on of hands" (1 Tim. 1:18, 4:14), LRM leaders began to lay on hands, pray, and prophesy for the impartation of new spiritual gifts to those who were already pentecostal believers. This aroused controversy, and was one key reason that both the Pentecostal Assemblies of Canada (PAOC) and the Assemblies of God (AG-USA) decided to disfellowship the LRM congregations.

Another contentious issue was the affirmation of present-day apostles and prophets – a teaching with nineteenth-century precedents among followers of Edward Irving and the Catholic Apostolic Church (Flegg 1992). Generally LRM teachers argued that "apostle" had more than one meaning, and they distinguished the "twelve apostles of the Lamb" from others. The apostle's work was missionary or missional in establishing new churches or imparting faith to newly founded churches. For the LRM, the prophet's ministry was second only to that of the apostle. When the prophet spoke, it was not the prophet's voice but God's voice that people heard. During 1948–49 George and Ernest Hawtin supported a congregationalist form of church governance. Yet, by late 1950, the Hawtins concluded that the New Testament church was not congregationalist but involved trans-local leadership of a hierarchical character. While elders and deacons ought to have charge of local affairs, they were nonetheless under the authority of itinerant ministers manifesting the "ascension gift ministries." George Hawtin announced that "God is raising up His church to be a glorious church without spot or wrinkle ... established on the foundation of the apostles and prophets" (Faupel 1989, 441).

The LRM stressed Christian unity. George Warnock wrote that "the foundational truth of this whole revival ... [is] that God would now at this time bring His people together to form one body." Reg Layzell exclaimed: "How we all rejoiced as we realized that God was moving to eliminate the competitive spirit ... It would be one church in one great building in each center. No longer would the church be called by its divisive names but The Church of Vancouver, The Church of Detroit or The Church of Portland" (Faupel 1989, 447). Yet the LRM insistence on church hierarchy, and the claim that their leaders had trans-local authority over Christians elsewhere, soured many on the movement. LRM ecclesiology was thus a paradoxical sort of sectarian ecumenism. The emphasis on submission to church leaders was also troubling to outsiders. Also alarming was the "manifest sons" doctrine that, starting around 1950, taught that LRM believers might advance so far spiritually in the present life as to become sinless, acquire foreign languages without study, transport themselves anywhere at will, and attain immortality. Spiritual elitism was evident in the LRM idea that not all Christians, but only some, were among the "overcomers," "eagle saints," or "many-membered Man-Child," whose spiritual maturity and ministry would prepare the world for Christ's return.

The long-term impact of the LRM has been many-sided. Despite its exile from pentecostal denominations (and perhaps because of this exile), the LRM became a catalyst for the mainline Charismatic Renewal of the 1960s and 1970s. Dominion theology – encouraging aggressive engagement with secular culture – emerged from the LRM teaching that God's supernatural power could transform whole societies. Prosperity teachers of the 1960s and 1970s had links not only to the post-World War II healing revival but also to the LRM. Mark

Hutchinson (2010) notes that Brian Houston's globally influential Hillsong Church grew out of the LRM in Australia. A kingdom-now emphasis on the felt presence and supernatural manifestation of God is apparent in Hillsong's music and worship style. Though "expelled from North America in the 1950s," the LRM "seep[ed] back through the search for cultural relevance and engagement with youth culture." Hutchinson adds: "While the [LRM] as such no longer continues, its influence has been very significant in fusing with charismatic, healing revival, corporate church and cultural relevance influences to produce some of the more dynamic charismatic movements in the world today" (280–81).

Bibliography

Darrand, Tom Craig and Anson Shupe. 1983. *Metaphors of Social Control in a Pentecostal Sect*. Lewiston, ME: Edwin Mellen Press.

Faupel, D. William. 2010. "The New Order of the Latter Rain: Restoration or Renewal?" In *Winds from the North: Canadian Contributions to the Pentecostal Movement*, edited by Michael Wilkinson and Peter Althouse, 239–263. Leiden: Brill.

Faupel, D. William. 1989. "The Everlasting Gospel: The Significance of Eschatology in the Development of Pentecostal Thought." PhD diss., University of Birmingham, UK.

Flegg, Graham. 1992. *'Gathered Under Apostles': A Study of the Catholic Apostolic Church*. Oxford, UK: Clarendon Press / New York: Oxford University Press.

Hutchinson, Mark. 2010. "The Latter Rain Movement and the Phenomenon of Global Return." In *Winds from the North: Canadian Contributions to the Pentecostal Movement*, edited by Michael Wilkinson and Peter Althouse, 265–284. Leiden: Brill.

Riss, Richard M. 1987. *Latter Rain*. Mississauga, ON: Honeycomb Visual Productions Ltd.

Wilkinson, Michael, and Linda M. Ambrose. 2020. *After the Revival: Pentecostalism and the Making of a Canadian Church*. Montreal & Kingston: McGill-Queen's University Press.

Michael McClymond

Le Roux, Pieter L.

Pieter Le Roux (1865–1943) was an Afrikaner missionary of the Dutch Reformed Church (DRC) in Wakkerstroom, South Africa. He was converted at 15 years old and trained as a school teacher in Cape Town. He went to a DRC theological seminary and became a school principal. It was then that he felt the calling to full-time ministry and was sent to Wakkerstroom in Eastern Transvaal with his wife. After two years, his congregation which was mainly Zulus grew to over 2,000 and he attributed this growth to "good earnest native preachers," who supported his ministry (Oosthuizen 1987).

Le Roux was influenced by Andrew Murray (1828–1917), a leading Dutch theologian, who wrote many books on holiness and divine healing and held revival campaigns (Sundkler 1976). Le Roux left the DRC and founded his own church after clashes over his preaching on divine healing. The DRC officials and ministers all agreed that divine healing was in the word of God, but deemed it "dangerous ground for public teaching," and asked him not to preach on it (Oosthuizen 1987). However, when his African friend prayed for the healing of his 15-month-old daughter, he openly declared his beliefs that healing was "at the very heart of the gospel" and resigned from the DRC in 1900 (Nel 2005;

Sundkler 1976). The DRC ostracized Le Roux leaving him homeless.

His new church was to be known as Zion Kerk (Zion Church) (Hexham and Poewa-Hexham 2002; Sundkler 1976; Nel 2005). His services integrated African beliefs, lively worship, and colorful clothing (Nel 2005). Le Roux heard about the Zionist movement through Dowies periodical, *Leaves of Healing*, which showcased testimonies of healing from Dowie's meetings and sent across the globe (Anderson 2007) and maintained correspondence with him. Dowie's movement emphasized "divine healing and triune baptism of adult believers by emersion," but not Pentecost. He and 400 African workers and converts then joined the Christian Catholic Apostolic Church (CCAC) of Dowie which was based in Zion City near Chicago in 1902 (Anderson 2004; Anderson and Hollenweger 1999). Le Roux is known to have played a pivotal role in the initial history of the CCAC in Zion among the blacks in particular Zulus in South Africa (Oosthuizen 1987). From 1890 he worked alongside a prominent Zulu leader called Nkonyane and Fred Lithuli (Kgatle 2016). His congregation in Wakkerstroom grew to 5,000 members by 1905, which led Dowie to send Daniel Bryant as a missionary to oversee their ministry. Initially, Bryant collaborated with Le Roux and his co-worker Johannes Bucher, who was a Swiss Pietist (Hexham and Poewe-Hexham 2002). By this time Le Roux had seven schools attended by 176 pupils (Oosthuizen 1987). Bryant returned to the U.S. in 1906. The "Zionists in the Wakerstroom area were the source out of which a whole series of African Zionist denominations emerged throughout southern Africa." (Anderson 2013)

In 1908 John G. Lake and Thomas Hezmalhalch came to South Africa as missionaries inspired by Dowie and William J. Seymour's Azusa Street Revival. They began to hold their services in a Zion building in Johannesburg. This was the beginning of the Apostolic Faith Mission (AFM). In 1909 "Le Roux together with 35 native preachers ministering to 5,000 people joined the AFM." According to Anderson, "a meeting between white representatives of the Zion church and the AFM executive in 1909 agreed that Le Roux would be in charge of the Zion mission work among Africans churches in the Transvaal region" (Anderson 2007). He further notes that Pentecostalism did not relinquish Dowie's Zionism but rather Zionism added to their beliefs the Pentecostal emphasis of the doctrine of the baptism of the Holy Spirit with the evidence of speaking in tongues and prophecy (Anderson 2004, 2007). It was decided by the executive council that since the natives held the name Zion as paramount to their roots and identity with Dowie's Zionism, that part of AFMs mission would be called the Zionist branch of the AFM (Anderson 2007). In 1910 Le Roux assumed leadership as part of the AFM executive as superintendent of missions (Nel 2015). Upon Lake's return to the USA, Le Roux became the first South African president for the AFM until his death in 1943.

Initially AFM services were racially integrated. Unfortunately the whites held all leadership positions and created racist laws against the blacks. This led to schisms within the movement and the exodus of many African Zionist leaders from the AFM. The earliest breakaway was in 1910 when Daniel Nkoyane, Le Roux's co-worker, left and formed the Christian Catholic Apostolic Holy Spirit Church in Zion (Anderson 2004).

Bibliography

Anderson, Allan. 2007. *Spreading Fires: The Missionary Nature of Early Pentecostalism*. London: SCM Press. Anderson, Allan. 2004. *An Introduction to Pentecostalism: Global Charismatic Christianity*. Cambridge: Cambridge University Press.

Hexham, I., and K. Poewe-Hexham. 2002. "South Africa." In *International Dictionary of Pentecostal and Charismatic Movements*, edited by Stanley M. Burgess, and Eduard M. Van der Maas, 227–238. Grand Rapids: Zondervan.

Nel, Marius. 2015. "Remembering and Commemorating the Theological Legacy of John G. Lake in South Africa After a Hundred Years." *Studia Historae Ecclesiasticae* 41 (2): 147–170.

Sundkler, Bengt. 1976. *Zulu Zion and Some Swazi Zionists*. Oxford: Oxford University Press.

Naar M'fundisi-Holloway

Leatherman, Lucy

One of the most remarkable of the first missionaries coming from the Azusa Street Revival was Lucy Leatherman (1870–1925), who was born near Greencastle, Indiana. She was probably also the most travelled of all the itinerant missionaries in early Pentecostalism. At the time she became a Pentecostal she was a doctor's widow and had been a student at A.B. Simpson's Missionary Training School in Nyack, New York. She received Spirit baptism when Lucy Farrow prayed for her in 1901 at Charles Parham's school in Topeka, Kansas. At Azusa Street in 1906, she believed she had spoken Arabic and was called to go to Palestinian Arabs. She was among the first group of missionaries who left Los Angeles for Jerusalem in August 1906. She first travelled to Oakland, California with Louise Condit and the Swedish missionary Andrew Johnson. From there they travelled to New York via Denver, Colorado. Once in New York Leatherman stayed at Alliance House and met T.B. Barratt from Norway. Leatherman and a Norwegian man prayed for Barratt to be baptized in the Spirit and he soon returned to Europe to pioneer Pentecostalism. Leatherman also wrote to Parham who at the time was trying to take over the Zion movement of J.A. Dowie in Zion, Illinois. She asked for missionaries to take over the Pentecostal mission in New York; and Parham sent Marie Burgess and Jessie Brown.

Leatherman was the first Pentecostal pioneer in the Middle East. On arrival in Jerusalem in late 1906 she reported that a "native minister" from Beirut and an Alliance missionary, Elisabeth Brown, had "received the baptism." She travelled from region to region sending back reports to several Pentecostal papers. Later she reported five others receiving Spirit baptism. The work seems to have had a boost, with report of a convention that Leatherman organized in Ramallah with about three hundred present. Leatherman herself was less optimistic, writing of "a few" who had received the Spirit. One was an Egyptian from Asyût, Ghali Hanna, and another a Syrian named Brother Zarub, who was "turned out" of his denomination when he started preaching about Spirit baptism. Leatherman undertook arduous lonely journeys, sometimes by mule in mountainous regions through Syria and Galilee. After meetings in Beirut, she proceeded to Asyût in Egypt in 1908 to see Ghali's work and reported a "great revival" there and that "multitudes" had been "saved, sanctified and baptized with the Holy Ghost and fire." Later she wrote of a hundred conversions in Asyût in two weeks. One of those baptized in the Spirit was leaving for Khartoum, Sudan to preach the Pentecostal message. Ghali Hanna also wrote of the effects of the visit of Leatherman. Asyût became the center for Pentecostal work in Egypt and was where Lillian Trasher later founded her famous orphanage.

Leatherman left Egypt in February 1909 and moved eastwards through Arabia to India, visiting the missions in the Pune area and meeting up with Carrie and George Montgomery on their round-the-world tour. She continued to Hong Kong and Shanghai, where she visited the missions of Antoinette Moomau and the Hansens, and then to Yokohama, Japan. Her ceaseless activity had taken its toll, for there she became ill and spent months resting. But by the end of that year she went to Manila in the Philippines and preached to American military personnel there. The report in *The Upper Room* in Los Angeles in January 1910 described her as "this brave woman whom God has made a pioneer in the Gospel." Leatherman visited the USA in 1910–1911 in poor health, where after her recovery she ministered in conventions before going to Pentecostal centers in Britain on her way back to Palestine. She wrote from Jerusalem in February 1912 where she encouraged the two women missionaries there. That July she was in Beirut, from where she intended to relocate permanently to the north of Syria and begin orphanage work. But in 1913 she was still in Beirut, as her health had again deteriorated. She wrote of the Balkan Wars and her own danger, as Christians (especially Armenians) were being killed throughout the Ottoman Empire. Late in 1913 Leatherman again visited Egypt and named two Egyptian workers who had become Pentecostals five years earlier during her ministry there, Ayub and Nashed Boulos. With the outbreak of war in 1914 she left for Philadelphia, but by 1917 she was a Church of God missionary travelling again, through Panama to Valparaiso, Chile and Argentina, until she returned to the USA in 1921 and was hospitalized with an unspecified serious illness. Although she planned to return to Jerusalem, her health deteriorated and she died in 1925.

Bibliography

Anderson, Allan. 2007. *Spreading Fires: The Missionary Nature of Early Pentecostalism*. London: SCM.

Newberg, Eric N. 2012. *The Pentecostal Mission in Palestine: The Legacy of Pentecostal Zionism*. Eugene, OR: Pickwick.

Allan H. Anderson

Lebanon

Positioned just north of Israel and Palestine and almost completely surrounded by Syria on its eastern borders, Lebanon has one of the largest and longest surviving Christian populations in the MENA region. Through the latter part of the twentieth century, Lebanon was ripped with sectarian violence that continues sporadically to this day. Its governmental system assiduously attempts to maintain a mixed representation of all the various groups and minorities. However, like other MENA countries with indigenous Christians, Lebanon faces emigration issues so that the larger Muslim population continues to grow and thus dominate the political and religious landscape.

According to *Spreading Fires* (Anderson 2007), Pentecostalism probably came to Lebanon in the 1900s through missionaries sent out by the Azusa Street Revival. The earliest of these was Lucy Leatherman, the first Pentecostal missionary in the Middle East, who started in Jerusalem and travelled to Syria, Lebanon, and other parts of the region. In 1906, she reported that "'a native minister' of Beirut and a missionary had 'received the baptism'" in Jerusalem. This establishes Lebanon's place as an early center of Pentecostalism in the Levant.

Christianity in North Africa-West Asia (Johnson, Ross, Tadros, eds. 2018) indicates that there were 5,851,000 people living in Lebanon in 2015. Of these, 2,004,000 identified as Christians. The largest denominations, like elsewhere in the region, were the Catholic or Maronite church with 80.5 percent and the Orthodox, typically Greek, with 17.1 percent. Only 3.2 percent identified as Renewalist or 64,128 individuals. In 2015, there were only 623 conversions to Christianity and 5,993 defections. Not all of these conversions are necessarily from Islam, either Sunni or Shi'a. The Druze faith is also a significant population in the country. And, secularism abounds in the postcolonial world, attractive to some and disaffecting to others. Another 19,000 Christians emigrated for an overall −.13 percent growth rate. However, reflecting a global trend, Pentecostalism grew 4.47 percent from 2010–2015.

Unlike its destabilized neighbor Syria or even nearby Jordan and Palestine, Christians in the country enjoy quite a degree of autonomy and freedom, establishing schools, building churches, monasteries, and seminaries, like the Arab Baptist Theological Seminary (ABTS). While not explicitly Pentecostal, ABTS welcomes students from all traditions and has a fairly broad faith statement with ecumenical dimensions. Unfortunately, the Church in Lebanon faces many internal conflicts between the Orthodox, Maronite, and the various Protestant communities. Age-old suspicions continue about the orthodoxy of the other and conversion/reversion constitutes a grave error; mixed marriages are not common.

Lebanese Christians have a significant presence in the public sphere. In 2017, downtown Beirut hosted a Hillsong praise and worship concert. In terms of media and publishing, Lebanon remains one of the major sources of Arabic Bible distributed around the region. Many Lebanese speak English, Arabic, and French, so translations of well-known Pentecostal and Evangelical teachers are also widely-produced; Joyce Meyer's material is a good example. Further, Lebanese Christians also maintain their own publications and satellite programming. Sat-7, the premier Christian satellite service in MENA, keeps a studio in Beirut and continues to broadcast around the area.

Bibliography

Anderson, Allan H. 2007. *Spreading Fires: The Missionary Nature of Early Pentecostalism*. Maryknoll, NY: Orbis Books.

Arab Baptist Theological Seminary. 2019. "Home." *Arab Baptist Theological Seminary*. Accessed Oct. 3, 2019. https://abtslebanon.org/.

Ross, Kenneth R., Mariz Tadros, and Todd M. Johnson, eds. 2018. *Christianity in North Africa-West Asia*. Edinburgh: Edinburgh University Press.

Sat-7 International. 2019. "About Us." *Sat-7 Arabic*. Accessed Oct. 3, 2019. https://sat7.org/our-channels/channel-overview/sat-7-arabic.

Benjamin Crace

Lee, Yong Do

Yong Do Lee (1901–1933) was the third son born to a poor family in Hwanghae province in the south of North Korea. He was unhealthy from his childhood and suffered from various diseases. His parents did not expect him to live long. His father was an alcoholic and abused his mother badly. She desperately prayed day and night. Lee's teachers favored him since he was dexterous and clever with great linguistic talent. The Declaration of Independence was announced on March 1, 1919. He was 19 years old at that time. He actively participated in protests, which caused him to be arrested and imprisoned. After being released, he attended Hyeop-seong Seminary in 1924, which was affiliated with the Methodist Church. He was imprisoned four times for approximately three years during his study period. Based on his Methodist background, his evangelism focused on personal and national repentance. There were also many miracles, signs and manifestations of the Holy Spirit in his revival meetings. He travelled around the whole country to conduct evangelical meetings.

On January 28, 1928, a day after graduating from the seminary, Lee went to Gangwon province, which is a mountainous area without many people residing. He began to pastor in a rural church called Dongcheon Church and found it difficult because he had not received the baptism in the Spirit. He climbed up to Geunggang Mountain and spent ten days to fast and pray. Eventually he was filled with the Holy Spirit. On Christmas' Eve in 1928, he had a mystical exprerience of fighting with the devil while praying throughout the night. After 11 days, in the morning of January 4, 1929, he had a similar mystical experience again. Despite his strict conservative Methodist background, these experiences transformed his ministry to become more charismatic. The mainstream denominations rejected the Pentecostal movements and referred to Lee's evangelism and mystical manifestations of the Spirit as heretical. However, as he began to work with two of his classmates at the seminary, Ho-bin Lee and Hwan-sin Lee, his revival movement extended to the nation. During the revival meetings, constant charismatic manifestations occurred such as speaking in tongues, and divine healing. People therefore called them "the three Lees." "Jesus-centered life and enthusiastic prayer" became the slogan of Lee's revival. He emphasized physical union with Christ and was convinced that faithful Christians could be united with God not only spiritually but also physically. He pursued mystical experiences and lived a pietistic life.

In the 1930s, Korean churches taught that the spiritual gifts ceased in the first century, but Lee emphasized the work of the Holy Spirit. He guided Korean Christians to focus on spiritual life in Christ and the spiritual experience of being filled with the Spirit. Through his efforts, Korean churches were more aware of spiritual awakenings. However, his ministries and theology of a "mystical union between Jesus and human beings" were often criticized as Christian mysticism. There are other negative reasons for his theology being considered as heretical. First, he proposed a dualistic understanding of flesh and spirit and taught that the body needed to be demolished for the spirit. Second, he over-emphasized the mystical union with Christ rather than salvation. He was defined as heretical by the Presbyterian Church in 1932 and his membership was terminated by the Methodist Church in 1933. Nevertheless, he still traveled around the Korean peninsula to spread the revival until his death in October 1933 due to tuberculosis. In 1999, 60 years after his death, the Korean Methodist Church recognized his ordination. With Lee's direct and indirect influences to the revival movement, Korean churches grew rapidly from 1929 to 1933.

Bibliography

Byun, Jong-ho, ed. 1993. *Biography of Yong-do Lee* [in Korean]. Seoul: Jang-Ahn.

Kim, Ig Jin. 2003. *History and Theology of Korean Pentecostalism*. Zoetermeer: Uitgeverij Boekencentrum.

Lee, Sang Yun. 2018. *A Theology of Hope: Contextual Perspectives in Korean Pentecostalism*. Middletown, DE: APTS Press.

Lee, Young-hoon. 2009. *The Holy Spirit Movement in Korea: Its Historical and Theological Development*. Oxford, UK: Regnum Books International.

Song, Gil-sup. 1982. *The Three Stars of the Methodist Church under Japanese Occupation* [in Korean]. Seoul: Sung-kwang.

Sang Yun Lee

Letwaba, Elias

Elias Letwaba (1870–1959) joined the John G. Lake revival in Doornfontein, Johannesburg, after a long search for intense spiritual meaning in various Protestant churches, including the Lutheran Church of the Berlin Missionary Society. Someone referred him to the "Zulu Mission" where Lake and his entourage of missionaries had just begun a powerful revival meeting. Immediately the two connected.

According to Lake there were at least two "Native" evangelists that impressed him the most; Edward "Lion" Motaung and Elias Letwaba. Motaung was the "uncultured" and "uneducated" evangelist anointed by God who healed 75 lepers in Lesotho. Letwaba was the more educated and spoke several languages including German (Lake 1908).

The white Pentecostals in the Apostolic Faith Mission (AFM) threatened to throw Letwaba out when Lake invited him onto the platform. Lake responded by saying, "If you throw him out then I will go too." Their friendship was confirmed by many sources (Morton 2016). On several occasions Letwaba invited Lake to come and preach in the Potgietersrus area where he had already made an impact in his evangelistic initiatives. Lake spoke fondly of Letwaba. He mentioned him to William Seymour on one occasion at least, telling a favourite story: "At Potgietersrus a dead child came back to life when our Native evangelist prayed seven hours after it died" (Lake 1909).

W.F. Dugmore, first secretary of the AFM after Lake's departure in 1913, mentioned him in a fleeting remark in an article in the *Word and Witness*, "Yesterday I heard the news that Bro. Letwaba was down with fever. We are praying for him" (Dugmore 1915). Reporting on Letwaba may have been because he was already known to the Americans, largely through positive reports by Lake. Morton (2016) notes with an element of repugnance that Letwaba was influenced by Lake's techniques of miracle working and ascribes it to what he calls "the placebo effect." Twelve years after Lake's departure in 1913 Letwaba was still active in the AFM. B. Fockler, a visiting American pastor, reported on him and his Patmos Bible School in Potgietersrus. He was effective as an evangelist, trained pastors and evangelists, and ran a Bible school with nominal resources. It was considered a great achievement in his time since not even the white Pentecostals in the AFM had a Bible school. Like the "Non-Pentecostal" mission churches, growth and expansion of the work among "Natives" was largely because of the "Native evangelists."

In 1913 when Lake returned to the USA, leadership in the AFM fell on Pieter le Roux. Some would argue that Letwaba should have been the candidate for leading the AFM. However, given the racial polarities and hostilities of the time, that was improbable. Le Roux became leader of the AFM from 1913 until his death in 1943. Le Roux was not only the leader of the AFM but also superintendent of the "Native" work, probably given his background with John Alexander Dowie Zionists in Wakkerstroom before joining the AFM.

Letwaba's undeniable impact in the AFM could only be determined within the confines and stipulations of le Roux and his "Missions Committee." While he was chosen as a "Native" superintendent, all funds from abroad were administered by the white "Missions Committee." However, it cannot be disputed that Letwaba's influence in the AFM was important and contributed enormously in the race relations between black and white people in the AFM. However, many other African leaders in the church left to form their own churches in what later became the rise of African Independent Churches (AICs) in South Africa. In the history of Pentecostalism in South Africa, Letwaba must rightfully be accorded his place as a pioneer of Pentecostalism in South Africa. He died in 1959 (Kgatle 2017).

Bibliography

Dugmore, W.F. 1915. "South Africa in Unity." *Word and Witness* (August): 6.
Kgatle, Mookgo Solomon. 2017. "African Pentecostalism: The Christianity of Elias Letwaba From Early Years Until his Death in 1959." *Scriptura* 116 (1): 1–9.
Lake, John G. 1909. "South Africa, Orange River Colony." *Confidence* (August): 185.
Lake, John G. 1908. "Missionaries for Africa." *The Pentecost* (August).
Morton, Barry. 2017. "Elias Letwaba, the Apostolic Faith Mission, and the Spread of Black Pentecostalism in South Africa." *Studia Historiae Ecclesiasticae* 43 (3): 1–17.

Steve Mochechane

Li, Changshou (Witness Lee)

Witness Lee (Li Changshou; 1905–1997) was a biblical commentator, revivalist, and church founder, who established a fellowship of churches and schools on all six inhabited continents over decades of ministerial labor. Lee's work developed from the legacy of his teacher, Watchman Nee. His followers are now some of the most numerous in congregations that consume Nee's publications, along with Lee's own prolific writings. The global reach of these churches has only increased in the years since Lee's death.

Lee was a third-generation Christian from his mother's side and was raised as a Southern Baptist in Penglai County, Shandong. His mother made sure that Lee and his siblings went to Sunday services. Lee was educated in a Baptist elementary school, but their Christian identity was nominal.

Although the family could not initially afford higher education, Lee showed an impressive aptitude for self-discipline and independent study. While working at a foreign firm, he aggressively studied Chinese and English on his own. Eventually, he won advanced standing at a local American Presbyterian college and graduated at the top of his class.

Lee experienced a dramatic conversion as a result of the preaching of the itinerant revivalist, Peace Wang. After his conversion, Lee immediately began to read the Bible and Christian literature voraciously. Persuaded by the biblical knowledge of the Plymouth Brethren, he joined their congregation.

Lee also discovered another even more impressive biblical interpretation from Watchman Nee, whom he revered as a mentor, though Nee was only two years his senior. Lee began to meet with a small group of Christians in the city of Yantai (then Chefoo) based on Nee's teachings. Soon afterwards, Lee resigned from his employment to live by faith as a minister. For almost two decades he worked closely with Nee, preaching and establishing churches throughout China.

On the eve of the Communist victory in 1949, Nee commissioned Lee to continue their work abroad. Lee came to Taiwan and led revival meetings and established churches, increasing the number of Christians under his care from a few hundred to about 40,000 within five years. For over a decade, Lee nurtured the Taiwanese churches and travelled abroad, holding conferences and supporting churches, primarily in Asia and Europe.

After repeated, short-term visits to the USA, Lee decided to immigrate in 1962. Southern California became his home and was his primary center of activity until his passing. The popularity of Nee's work in America gave Lee the opportunity to convert thousands, many from the evangelical subculture, who now, controversially, saw his teachings as more biblical than traditional Christianity.

Lee continued to refine Nee's teachings, including the latter's condemnation of denominations as unscriptural and divisive. Lee also adapted Nee's spirituality, making it more practical and accessible. At the same time, Lee added his own distinctive emphases, highlighting the importance of the divine life and its ability to transform Christians. He embarked on a decades-long project to interpret the entire Bible, book by book, according to these emphases. He eventually published almost 2,000 chapters in multiple volumes as *Life-Studies*.

Lee's biblical commentary was matched with other ministerial activity. In particular, he oversaw the spreading of churches in Europe, Latin America, and Australasia. He also promoted new church practices. These included a greater emphasis on evangelism, including meetings in homes and knocking on doors. They also included revised services, which set aside the Sunday morning sermon in favor of spontaneous short messages from members of the congregation.

All of these efforts were supported by Lee's Bible schools. Lee always emphasized the importance of training, or disciplined learning, practice, and service. In the 1980s, as he significantly reformed church practice, Lee also formalized his "full-time trainings" by founding two schools: one in Taipei in 1986 and one in Anaheim in 1989. Both were post-graduate institutions with two-year curricula. The Anaheim training program is now one of the largest graduate theological schools in the USA.

Beginning in 1994, Lee again significantly developed his teachings. In his final years, Lee intensified his emphasis on life, naming deification as the ultimate goal of the Christian life. His work paralleled long-standing mystical doctrines, which taught about the union of God and humanity.

Bolstered by such transcendent visions and vigorous practices, Lee's followers continue to spread and practice his teachings. There are now over a dozen full-time trainings internationally. Lee's trainings have also been institutionalized in regular international conferences, which give these congregations a fairly cohesive group identity, often known as the "Lord's Recovery" or "Local Churches" although they refuse these names for themselves.

Lee has also been unintentionally successful with splinter groups which divided themselves based on heterodox interpretations of his writings. Many of the most vibrant and controversial Christian groups in China today came across Lee's teachings at some point. Although he denounced their extreme interpretations, they continue to grow.

Bibliography

Chang, Paul H.B. 2016. "The Multiple Invisibilities of Witness Lee." *Journal of Asian/North American Theological Educators* 2 (1): 91–98.

Dunn, Emily. 2015. *Lightning from the East: Heterodoxy and Christianity in Contemporary China*. Leiden: Brill.

Zimmerman-Liu, Teresa. 2017. "From 'Children of the Devil' to 'Sons of God': The Reconfiguration of Guanxi in a Twentieth-Century Indigenous Chinese Protestant Group." *Review of Religion and Chinese Society* 4 (1): 59–86.

Zimmerman-Liu, Teresa, and Teresa Wright. 2015. "What Is in a Name? A Comparison of being branded a Religious Cult in the United States and the People's Republic of China: Witness Lee and the Local Churches." *Journal of Church and State* 60 (2): 187–207.

Zimmerman-Liu, Teresa. 2014. "The Divine and Mystical Realm: Removing Chinese Christianity from the Fixed Structures of Mission Church and Clergy." *Social Sciences and Missions* 27 (2/3): 239–266.

Paul Chang

Liberia

The theory that world Pentecostalism had its origins in the Azusa Street Revival of 1906 has been disproved by various studies. However, scholars are certain that missionaries from Azusa Street who travelled across the world to preach the gospel arrived in Liberia before 1920. If we consider that Pentecostalism is about the experience and ministry in the power of the Holy Spirit then one of its pioneering prophets as far as Liberia is concerned, would be Prophet William Wadé Harris. He was an indigenous man of the Kru tribe who was imprisoned for vandalizing the republican flag, preferring British rule and therefore hoisting in its place the Union Jack. It was during his incarceration that Harris claimed to have received an angelic visitation commissioning him to evangelize. In a trance-visitation, Harris claimed Angel Gabriel, called him to be a prophet, to preach a gospel of repentance, to destroy fetishes and to baptize those who obeyed. He started in his native Liberia and made an impact there before traveling along the West Africa coast to preach in other places.

Liberia has a long history of independent churches that focused on healing and other such charismatic phenomena associated with early twentieth century prophetic movements. One of the fruits of the evangelistic work of Prophet Harris was the formation of the Church of the Twelve Apostles in the then Gold Coast around 1914. Prophet Harris claimed the gift of speaking in tongues and those churches that trace their origins to his ministry functioned both in the speaking of tongues and belief in angelic beings. Fishermen from Ghana's coastal towns established branches of this and other independent church in Liberia where some of them settled. These were healing churches in which praying in tongues was central and blessed water was dispensed for therapeutic purposes as characterized the African independent church movement and as happens in some Pentecostal communities today. One of the most popular independent churches of Liberia is the Faith Healing Temple of Jesus Christ.

Liberia's classical Pentecostal churches included the traditional ones that came from the USA including the Apostolic churches and the Assemblies of God. Additionally, the Church of Pentecost, Ghana's largest classical Pentecostal church also has branches in Liberia. In other words, the Liberian Pentecostal terrain has a mixture of indigenous and Western mission Pentecostal churches. Liberia, Africa's oldest republic, was created in 1847 and until about 1980, was governed by politicians of largely African American origin and who pursued a mission of westernization of fellow Liberians of purely African ancestry. The historical relationship with the USA means Liberia is one of the contexts most influenced by North American televangelism. The Pentecostal Assemblies of the World, one of the biggest independent charismatic churches has its origins in America. The PTL Heritage Church for example was started in the 1980s with the direct inspiration and permission of the disgraced American apostle of the prosperity gospel, Jim Bakker. Liberia's economic collapse during the civil war era from 1989 led to the rise of many charismatic churches that came to depend on USA partners and branches for economic support.

The "Americanization" of Liberian independent Pentecostal churches is very evident in the Bible School culture of the movement. The Church of God based in Cleveland, Tennessee started a branch in Liberia in the mid 1970s with some of its teachers coming from the Oral Roberts University. The students came from other independent churches including the Burning Bush Tabernacle, and the Church of the Foursquare Gospel, all of which had some connection to the USA. Liberian Pentecostal churches have been particularly notorious for their failure to speak out against corruption and injustices and this, because of their propensity to patronize violent and disreputable regimes. The former warlord and President, Charles Taylor for example, declared himself a born-again Christian and the contemporary Pentecostals received as such, but this religious patronage simply helped to mask the atrocious human rights abuses and corruption that marked his reign as head of state.

The "health-and-wealth gospel" has had a very great influence on contemporary Liberian Pentecostalism. This influence came mainly through the media ministry of America's prosperity preachers. The main conduit of prosperity preaching in Liberia, however, were former students of Kenneth Hagin's Rhema Bible Training Center who in 1987 opened the Monrovia Bible Training Center (MBTC). This was in the late 1980s and by the early 1990s the MBTC was attracting close to one thousand students from almost two hundred churches scattered throughout Liberia. What makes the MBTC significant is that its theological orientation was the pure health-and-wealth gospel type propagated by names like Bakker, Hagin and Copeland. Virtually, apart from the Bible, all the books distributed to the students were authored by these prosperity-preaching American televangelists. For a country that has gone through such a difficult socio-political period leading to the collapse of its economy and lack of faith in a corrupted leadership, American style prosperity gospel has become the source of hope for many who dream about the material abundance that has come to be associated with America and how this reflects on its modern televangelists.

Bibliography

Clapham, Christopher. 1976. *Liberia and Sierra Leone: An Essay in Comparative Politics*. Cambridge: Cambridge University Press.

Ellis, Stephen, and Gerrie ter Haar. 2004. *Worlds of Power: Religious Thought and Political Practice in Africa*. London: Hurst and Company.

Gifford, Paul. 1998. *African Christianity: Its Public Role*. Bloomington and Indianapolis: Indiana University Press.

Gifford, Paul. 1993. *Christianity and Politics in Doe's Liberia*. Cambridge: Cambridge University Press.

Shank, David A. 1994. *Prophet Harris: The "Black Elijah" of West Africa*. Leiden: Brill.

Scheffers, Mark. 1987. "Schism in the Bassa Independent Churches of Liberia." In *Ministry of Missions in African Independent Churches*, edited by David A. Shank. Elkhart, IN: Mennonite Board of Missions.

Stakemann, Randolph. 1986. *The Cultural Politics of Religious Change: A Study of the Sanoyea Kpelle in Liberia*. Lewiston, NY: Edwin Mellen Press.

J. Kwabena Asamoah-Gyadu

Lindsay, Gordon

Gordon Lindsay (1906–1973) was a Pentecostal pastor, revivalist, and prolific writer who documented the Post-Second World War healing revival that was spearheaded by The Voice of Healing ministry. He is probably best known for his work with William Branham and as the co-founder of Christ for the Nations Institute in Dallas, TX.

The author of more than 200 books, Lindsay played a vital role in the ministry success of scores of healing evangelists during the 1940s and 1950s. He also helped to plant hundreds of churches in various countries. Over the years, he created international outreach programs for the distribution of Christian literature and support for foreign missions. He believed that it was in God's providence that "The Voice of Healing was used to spearhead apostolic ministry in many nations." (Lindsay 1992)

Lindsay was born on June 18, 1906, in Zion City, IL. His parents, Thomas and Effie (Ramsey) Lindsay, were devoted followers of John Alexander Dowie, the controversial faith healer who founded Zion City as a Christian community. When Zion City went into bankruptcy, Lindsay's family moved to Idaho, and later to California and then, Portland, OR.

Lindsay, while still a teenager, converted to Christ under the preaching of Charles Parham. The preaching occurred in a church pastored by John G. Lake, who was known as a famous healing evangelist and the founder of healing rooms in parts of the United States.

Lindsay attributed his spiritual experiences to his mother's prayers. Shortly after his conversion, he received the baptism in the Spirit with the evidence of speaking in tongues. When he surrendered his life to Christ, he felt a call to the ministry. He experienced a passionate interest in apostolic ministry with a longing to reach multitudes for Christ. After a period of time in prayer, he began preaching as an evangelist.

In the early 1930s, Lindsay was preaching in a revival meeting in Oregon when a young lady, Freda Schimpf, attended the service and surrendered her life to Christ.

Four years later, she and Lindsay began a casual friendship that led to their marriage on November 14, 1937. The couple spent a number of years ministering as evangelists. In July 1944, they received a call to pastor an Assemblies of God Church in Ashland, OR.

In the spring of 1947, Gordon received a letter from his friend, Jack Moore, telling him about the unusual ministry of William Branham. Moore invited Gordon and Freda to attend a Branham service in Sacramento, CA. It was during that service that Gordon and Branham felt led of the Lord to work together as a team. Gordon, who perceived Branham to be divinely gifted, but very simple and unassuming, agreed to manage his meetings. Gordon would use his networking skills, along with his writing and business acumen to introduce Branham to interdenominational audiences in citywide campaigns.

Gordon and Moore began publishing *The Voice of Healing Magazine* as the official organ of Branham's ministry. The first issue appeared in April 1948. However, in July of that year, Branham announced that he would be taking a break from the ministry because of issues related to his health. Gordon was shocked and disappointed, but after prayer, he decided to use the magazine as a promotional tool for other evangelists with healing ministries. The Voice of Healing evolved into a loose association of ministers with a set of ministry guidelines and regular conferences. As the circulation of the magazine grew, having up to 30,000 monthly subscribers in 1949, it featured many of the most prominent names in the movement, including Oral Roberts, Jack Coe, David Nunn, T.L. Osborn, W.V. Grant, A.A. Allen, and F.F. Bosworth.

By the late 1950s, the healing revival had started to wane, but that did not dampen Gordon's passion for writing. His literary output was nothing short of extraordinary. His book, *William Branham: A Man Sent from God*, was a popular title that helped to catapult Branham to international fame.

Gordon authored 250 books on various teachings of the Bible; he penned several biographies that included such figures as John Alexander Dowie and John G. Lake. In keeping with Gordon's new focus on global missions, the name of his magazine was changed to *World-Wide Revival*. The magazine later became *Christ for the Nations*, and The Voice of Healing ministry became known as Christ for the Nations Inc. In 1970, Gordon and Freda founded Christ for the Nations Institute as an interdenominational charismatic Bible college.

Gordon lived to see only the early years of his school. On a Sunday afternoon, on April 1, 1973, he died unexpectedly while sitting on the platform during a worship service at Christ for the Nations Institute. He was 66. The day after his funeral, the ministry's board voted unanimously to make Freda president of the ministry.

Bibliography

Harrell Jr., David Edwin. 1975. *All Things Are Possible: The Healing and Charismatic Revivals in Modern America*. Bloomington: Indiana University Press.

Lindsay, Gordon. 1992. *The Gordon Lindsay Story*. Dallas, TX: Christ For The Nations.

Lindsay, Gordon. n.d. *William Branham: A Man Sent From God*. Jeffersonville, IN: William Branham.

Lindsay, Mrs. Gordon. 1976. *My Diary Secrets*. Dallas, TX: Christ For The Nations.

Roscoe Barnes III

Liturgy

"Liturgy" comes from two Greek words that mean, in the strictest etymological sense, "work of the people." More broadly, various church traditions employ the term with different meanings. Relatively universal are the term's references to (1) all public worship of the church, as opposed to private prayers and other expressions of devotion and (2) worship surrounding celebration of the Eucharist in particular. Even these uses require qualification, however, for a couple of reasons. For example, one can pray the daily office, also called the liturgy of the hours, alone during the day throughout the church year. Also, church traditions that do not tend to script their worship or use "liturgy" to describe it – historically including the majority of pentecostals – still worship publicly. The latter point especially raises the question of whether or not all public worship is liturgy.

Two of the most characteristic elements of the worship in global pentecostalism are music and prayer. Pentecostal music is usually exuberant, emotional, embodied, and soulful, even as it takes the form of multiple genres (Ingalls and Yong 2015). Hymns, due in part to the heritage of evangelicalism and revivalism in the United States, were of utmost importance to the early years of pentecostal denominations. These songs connected seamlessly with the liturgical practice of giving testimony, or, sharing one's faith narrative during public worship, because the stanzas of

Members of the Pentecostal church praising the Lord. Chicago, Illinois. Library of Congress, Prints & Photographs Division, FSA/OWI Collection, LC-USF34-038774-D. Photographer: Russell Lee.

many of the hymns progressed in order from describing a state of sin and initial conversion to ultimate salvation and eternal reward. One of the most widely used English-language hymnals is *Church Hymnal* (1951) colloquially called "the red-back hymnal" and distributed by a pentecostal publishing house. It is famous for its shaped notes that allow persons who do not read music per se to distinguish the notes easily. In recent decades, singing hymns largely gave way to singing worship choruses and other music written and composed by professional musicians and performed through various international media outlets. The pentecostal traditions most dependent on this shift face a crisis over the role of music in public worship. Some of the changes are purely stylistic and are to be expected as times change. Others are more substantive, including theologically dubious song lyrics. Perhaps the most formidable challenge is that many congregants find the newest choruses, whatever their verbal content, to consist of largely monotone melodies that are difficult to remember and sing. This development, combined with the reality of the high volume at which instruments are broadcast through public address systems, undermines congregational singing. Many who have not learned the songs and who cannot hear the voices of other nearby worshippers respond by remaining silent during worship music. Another hallmark of pentecostal worship is prayer, which, like music, is often energetic and passionate. Worshippers praying aloud simultaneously, either in learned languages or in tongues, is common and is sometimes called "concert" prayer. Pentecostal prayer is also kinesthetic. Worshippers may raise or wave their hands while praying. They may lay their hands on others while interceding for them or commissioning them for a particular ministry.

They may also "pray over" an inanimate object like a cloth (cf. Acts 19:11–12), which is then given to someone in need. A more recent phenomenon in global pentecostalism is "soaking prayer," which sometimes involves worshippers publicly lying on the floor, at times with pillows and blankets, in order to bask or "soak" in God's presence (Wilkinson and Althouse 2014). Several of these prayer practices demonstrate at least formal, and maybe material, similarities with practices of more traditionally liturgical church traditions, including, for example, the Catholic practices of blessing religious objects, laying on of hands during the sacraments of confirmation and holy orders, and contemplative prayer.

Pentecostal scholars are beginning to recognize that their music, prayer, and other worship practices do indeed constitute liturgies (Albrecht 1999; Alexander 1997). Although the practices may not be scripted verbatim, they tend to occur in observable patterns, and when deviations from established patterns take place, the anomalies themselves are usually of a kind that are already-sanctioned, even if rarer, practices. Pentecostal theologians are also calling for normative liturgies of word and sacrament to supplant the more anemic facets of pentecostal worship and to complement the stronger facets. The hope is that pentecostals will become more conscious of the constitutive role that worship plays in making believers into the people of God. Such awareness may then lead to a more robust ecclesiology among pentecostals (Chan 2006). There is also potential for mutual exchange, with aspects of pentecostal worship revitalizing traditional liturgical structures (Vondey 2010).

Still, pentecostals are more likely to speak of a "theology of worship" – which may involve as little as theological reflections on worship practices – than a "liturgical theology" – which raises questions about relationships between theologies of worship and other sub-disciplines in theology. Pentecostal systematic theologians are just beginning to recognize the adage in the liturgical theologies of older church traditions that the "law of believing" is closely related to "the law of praying" (*lex orandi, lex credendi*). The majority of Anglophone liturgical theologians (and others) claim that the law of praying determines the law of believing, that worship – or at least the kernel of the traditional ordo of word and sacrament – informs theological formulations that come to expression outside the immediate context of worship. Such elements of worship are sometimes called "primary theology," and such theological formulations are sometimes called "secondary theology." Increased attention to *lex orandi, lex credendi* would increase the sophistication of pentecostal systematic theology by more intentionally tapping into the intuitions of pentecostal spirituality for academic theology. One of the prospects of this time-honored principle is greater coherence between pentecostal beliefs and practices. Pentecostals may also contribute to abiding concerns in liturgical theology by offering their own insights on the relationship between praying and believing, including whether worship and theology mutually inform each other to a greater degree than many imagine (Stephenson 2013).

Bibliography

Albrecht, Daniel E. 1999. *Rites in the Spirit: A Ritual Approach to Pentecostal/Charismatic Spirituality*. Sheffield: Sheffield Academic Press.

Alexander, Estrelda Y. 1997. "Liturgy in Non-Liturgical Holiness-Pentecostalism." *Wesleyan Theological Journal* 32 (2): 158–93.

Chan, Simon. 2006. *Liturgical Theology: The Church As Worshipping Community*. Downers Grove: InterVarsity.

Ingalls, Monique M. and Amos Yong. 2015. *The Spirit of Praise: Music and Worship in Global Pentecostal-Charismatic Christianity*. University Park: The Pennsylvania State University.

Stephenson, Christopher A. 2013. *Types of Pentecostal Theology: Method, System, Spirit*. Oxford: Oxford University Press.

Vondey, Wolfgang. 2010. *Beyond Pentecostalism: The Crisis of Global Christianity and the Renewal of the Theological Agenda*. Grand Rapids: Eerdmans.

Wilkinson, Michael, and Peter Althouse. 2014. *Catch the Fire: Soaking Prayer and Charismatic Renewal*. DeKalb: Northern Illinois University.

Christopher A. Stephenson

López, Abundio and Rosa

Abundio L. and Rosa López (ca. 1869–circa 1945?) were among the first Latinos in the Americas converted to Pentecostalism, to pastor a Spanish-language Pentecostal mission, and to write a bilingual testimony in William Seymour's *Apostolic Faith* newspaper, associated with the Azusa Street Revival. Abundio was born in Guadalajara, Mexico, around 1869. He traveled north to the U.S. settling in Los Angeles, where he and his wife Rosa were married by Rev. A. Moss Merwin, a Presbyterian minister, on July 18, 1902. He pastored the Gospel Detective Mission in Los Angeles. The López's began to attend the Azusa Street Revival on May 19, 1906, and on June 5 were reportedly baptized with the Holy Spirit. Abundio and Rosa ministered as lay workers at the Azusa Mission from 1906 to 1909 and possibly later. They published their conversion and reported on their ministry to the Spanish-speaking in Seymour's *Apostolic Faith*. They carried out street preaching in the Mexican Plaza District in downtown Los Angeles and throughout Mexican barrios and migrant labor camps from Los Angeles to San Diego. In 1909, in recognition of Abundio's service and calling, Seymour ordained him to the pastoral ministry. No reference is made to Rosa's ordination. In 1915, he was listed as a "Spanish minister" and he and his wife attended Maria Woodworth Etter's healing crusade in Los Angeles, where Rosa was reportedly healed of a tumor. Abundio continued to minister in the Latino community from 1906 to the 1920s. In 1920, he pastored a Spanish-speaking congregation in the larger Anglo-American Victoria Hall Pentecostal Mission in Los Angeles. Abundio briefly joined Francisco Olazábal's Latin American Council of Christian Churches, after which we know very little about his life and work.

Bibliography

Espinosa, Gastón. 2016. *Latino Pentecostals in America: Faith and Politics in Action.* Cambridge, MA: Harvard University Press.

Espinosa, Gastón. 2014. *William J. Seymour and the Origins of Global Pentecostalism.* Durham, NC: Duke University Press.

Robeck, Cecil M. 2006. *The Azusa Street Mission and Revival: The Birth of the Global Pentecostal Movement.* Nashville, TN: Thomas Nelson.

Gastón Espinosa

Luce, Alice Eveline

Alice Eveline Luce (1873–1955) was a missionary to India and church planting pioneer who entered the Pentecostal movement in 1910. Born in the home of an Anglican pastor in England, Luce studied nursing and theology at Cheltanham Ladies College and at age 22 she became a missionary with the Church Missionary Society (CMS), the Church of England's mission society. Her initial missions work sent her to India where she primarily focused on primary and secondary education, serving as the principle of Christian high school in Azimgarh, North India and Queen Victoria High school in Agra. While in India, word of the Pentecostal movement had reached her in 1910 and she sought out the baptism in the Spirit for herself. Not long after, she became ill and returned to England in 1912 to recover.

While working in India, Luce began to wrestle with contemporary missionary methods promoted by CMS, which was oriented toward social work such as schools and orphanages. The apostolic emphasis within Pentecostalism began to direct Luce to explore more "scriptural" principles of mission work. At the same time, Luce was reading Roland Allen's *Missionary Methods: St. Paul's or Ours?* (1912), which used Paul's missionary ministry as a model for indigenous missionary strategy. These two ideas convinced her that indigenous people made the best missionaries to their own cultures because they already understood the language, culture, and country, which were the greatest barriers to foreign missions. It was these principles that would shape the next phase of her missionary endeavors.

In 1914, while serving with the Bible and Medical Missionary Fellowship in Canada, she began to feel called to missions in Mexico. In 1915, Luce moved to Kingsville, Texas to become a missionary on the border of Mexico with H.C. Ball, who was a pioneer missionary to Mexico. It was there that she was officially ordained into the Assemblies of God (AG) by M.M. Pinson. After several years of effective work under Ball, in 1920 she moved to Los Angeles, California to begin her own work among migrant Mexicans along the border. In October 1926, Luce founded the Latin American Bible Institute of San Diego, California. It was there that Luce made her mark as a pioneer in missionary strategist and leader in Hispanic Bible school. Hispanic Bible School education was Luce's principles of self-supporting, self-governing, and self-propagating churches that shaped AG's missions strategy that continues to be utilized today.

Luce was also one of the earliest articulators of Pentecostal theology among early AG authors. She wrote three important early doctrinal books published by the Gospel Publishing House (GPH): *Pictures of Pentecost* (1920), a typological look at the Old Testament in light of the Pentecostal experience; *The Messenger and His Message* (1925), a handbook for expository preaching and ministerial development; and *The Little Flock and the Last Days* (1927), an eschatological book about the latter rain outpouring of the Spirit that was the first GPH book specifically on eschatology authored by a woman. Luce was also a regular contributor to the *Pentecostal Evangel* and *La Luz Apostolica* during the 1920s and 1930s, sharing articles on Pentecostal distinctives, ministry, and missions. She is probably best known for translating Pentecostal materials into Spanish, which were used by several Latin American Pentecostal Bible schools. Luce will always be remembered as an important woman who helped shape the message, ministry, and methods of the AG.

Bibliography

McGee, Gary B. 2014. *People of the Spirit.* Springfield, MI: Gospel Publishing House.
McGee, Gary B. 2002. "Luce, Alice Eveline." In *The New International Dictionary of Pentecostal and Charismatic Movements*, edited by Stanley M. Burgess, and Eduard M. van der Maas, 543–544. Grand Rapids: Zondervan.
Ruelas, Abraham. 2010. *Women and the Landscape of American Higher Education: Wesleyan Holiness and Pentecostal Founders.* Eugene: Pickwick.

Daniel D. Isgrigg

Lugo, Juan León

Juan León Lugo (1890–1987) was born in Yuaco, Puerto Rico, in 1890 to Juana Lugo. In 1900, she moved from there to Oahu with Juan and her daughter. She attended evangelistic meetings led by Rev. Francisco Ortiz, Sr., who had converted to Pentecostalism through the preaching of Azusa Street missionaries on their way to Asia. After spending months attending Pentecostal services with his mother and friends and reading John 5:24, Lugo converted on June 13, 1913. He joined Ortiz's church and was baptized on Waikiki beach. Lugo became an evangelist and sailed with Ortiz and his son, Panchito, to San Francisco on November 9, 1913, where they evangelized among the Puerto Rican diaspora.

In Los Angeles, he came into contact with Bethel Temple, one of the largest Assemblies of God (AG) churches in the city. Juan and Panchito attended the youth group meetings and Hulda Needham (the senior pastor's daughter) claimed that God had revealed to them through an interpretation of tongues that God wanted Lugo to go to Puerto Rico immediately. Lugo reportedly felt called to the city where he was born, Ponce. On August 17, 1916, he boarded a train for New York City and on his way, he stopped in St. Louis and met J. Roswell Flower, the General Secretary of the AG, who decided to sponsor Lugo's missionary work in Puerto Rico. Flower put Lugo in contact with Robert and Marie Brown, whose Glad Tidings Church in New York received Lugo warmly and allowed him to stay in their missionary rest home.

Bolstered by the support of Bethel Temple, the AG, and Glad Tidings Church, Lugo steamed for Puerto Rico and arrived on August 30, 1916 at the age of 26. He preached his first sermon there but he felt that it was "a stinging defeat." Not one person showed any interest in his message.

The first major turning point in Lugo's Pentecostal ministry took place a few nights later when he converted a group of eleven "Santomenan believers" to Pentecostalism. For the next 24 nights in a row, Lugo and his new allies conducted open-air evangelistic services on the street corners of Santurce with their testimonies.

The second major turning point came on November 3, 1916 when he traveled to Ponce, a city of approximately 80,000 and the major port-city on the south side of the island. He was surprised to find Solomon and Dionisia Feliciano, members of Ortizes' church in Hawaii and the San Francisco Bay Area, already ministering in the city. Lugo and the Felicianos conducted open-air evangelistic services. He claimed that their services attracted over 800 people a night. People flocked to his services, where he promised to transform the lives of "horrible sinners" into "joyful saints." Lugo and the Felicianos conducted nightly services for the next two months.

On July 29, 1917, Juan married Isabel from Guayanilla, who sought and received credentials from the AG in 1920. She worked with Lugo throughout his ministry. In 1922, Juan Lugo and Panchito Ortiz were elected president and secretary of the newly formed The Pentecostal Church of God (PCG). This church sent Tomás Alvarez to start a mission in New York, in 1928, but it grew slowly. In March 1931, Lugo took over Alvarez's work and the mission began to grow. In October 1932, Lugo opened up the second PCG congregation in the city and appointed Eleutero Paz, a Mexican Pentecostal evangelist to be the pastor. Paz suggested that Lugo move his burgeoning congregation to the empty Jewish Synagogue on 115 Street in Brooklyn. Shortly thereafter, La Sinagoga (the Synagogue) became the center of the PCG's work in New York where Lugo conducted revival and healing services. By 1933, over 250 people regularly attended La Sinagoga and thousands of people were converted in the following years.

In 1935, Lugo worked with Edmundo Jordán to establish the first preparatory school in La Synagoga to train Sunday school teachers. It was formally organized as a Bible school in January 1936 and was incorporated as the Hispanic American Bible Institute of the Eastern District of the Assemblies of God in 1939. This became the first Latino Pentecostal Bible School in New York City.

Lugo founded Mizpa Bible Institute in Bayamón in 1937 and Frank Finkenbinder took over the pastorate of La Synagoga. Lugo turned in his ministerial credentials in 1940 due to accusations about ministerial misconduct while serving on the island. He later served with Carlos Sepúlveda's Assembly of Christian Churches (AIC) for one year before becoming an independent evangelist and then entered retirement.

Lugo is recognized as one of the pioneers in Latino Pentecostalism in California, New York, and Puerto Rico. Despite the rise of new Pentecostal denominations in Puerto Rico, by 1945 Juan Lugo's PCG became the largest Protestant denomination on the island and grew from 4,100 members, 52 churches, and preaching points in 1930, to 7,100 members, 86 churches, and missions by 1941. Today, Pentecostals and charismatics make up 45 percent of Puerto Rican population, of 1,650,000 people. The Pentecostal movement that Lugo helped unleash has been one of the most important vehicles for the evangelization of Puerto Rico.

Bibliography

Díaz, Samuel. 1995. *La Nave Pentecostal: Crónica desde el inicio de las Asambleas de Dios y su Travesía por el noreste hispano de los Estados Unidos*. Grand Rapids, MI: Vida.

Espinosa, Gastón. 2016. *Latino Pentecostals in America: Faith and Politics in Action*. Cambridge, MA: Harvard University Press.

Torres, David Ramos. 1992. *Historia de la Iglesia de Dios Pentecostal, M.I.* Río Piedras, Puerto Rico: Editorial Pentecostal.

Torres, Rubén Pérez. 2004. *Poder desde lo Alto: Historia, Sociología y Contribuciones del Pentecostalismo en Puerto Rico, El Caribe y en Los Estados Unidos, 2nd Edición*. Terrassa (Barcelona) Clie.

Gastón Espinosa

Macedo, Edir

Edir Macedo Bezerra is the presiding bishop of the Igreja Universal do Reino de Deus (Universal Church of the Kingdom of God ; UCKG) and the CEO of the Universal Holding Companies.

When he was 32 years old, Macedo's father left his poor home in northeast Brazil, looking for a better life in the more prosperous south, where he met his wife, Eugênia Macedo Bezerra. Living in a small rural town, Macedo's parents were nominal Catholics with some Spiritualist incursions before they moved to Rio de Janeiro. Some years later, Macedo joined the New Life Pentecostal Church, a Rio de Janeiro upper-middle-class church, organized in the 1960s by the Canadian missionary Robert McAlister (Campos 1999). There, Macedo heard about the theology of prosperity, positive confession, spiritual warfare, and hereditary curses. Those ideas and experiences would support Macedo's emphasis on the relationship between exorcism and divine healing (a combination of spiritual warfare, deliverance, and health), and prosperity gospel – the famous "health and wealth" gospel (Mariano 1999).

In 1968, Romildo Ribeiro Soares, a former Baptist and future husband of Macedo's youngest sister, also joined McAlister's church. Macedo met Esther Eunice Rangel, his future wife, a daughter of a retired evangelical pastor. They married in 1971. Their first daughter Cristiane Cardoso (married to Renato Cardoso) was born in 1973 and the second daughter Viviane Freitas (married to Julio Freitas) was born in 1975. Moysés Macedo the adopted son was born in 1990.

Soares and Macedo left McAlister's church in 1975 and decided to establish their own church in 1979, the Universal Church of the Kingdom of God. However, two years later, amid a power struggle, Macedo took over the UCKG leadership and overthrew Soares in a kind of "coup d'état." With the objective to improve his plans for UCKG's global expansion, Macedo moved to New York in 1986. Since then, UCKG has been sending missionaries across the world and finding greater receptivity in Latin American countries, especially those of the Southern Cone, and among the lusophone Africans in Africa and Portugal (Castro and Dawson 2017). In 1989, UCKG international offices were transferred from Rio de Janeiro to São Paulo. Influenced by McAlister's extensive use of media like radio and TV, Macedo was convinced of the strategic role of mass communications for religious enterprises. Soon he began to acquire radios in different cities and increasingly rented timetables on different television open channels. In 1989, Macedo bought "Record Radio and TV Network". Today, UCKG has a wide network of communications that includes publishing houses, record companies, TV and Radio stations, magazines, and internet media. According to the 2010 Brazilian National Census, UCKG had over 6,000 temples, 12,000 pastors, and around 1.8 million adherents. The Temple of Solomon inaugurated in 2014 is the main temple of Macedo's UCKG and is the most extravagant of all his ideas. The sanctuary has the capacity for 10,000 people.

Macedo has also been involved in several scandals and conflicts. In 1992, Macedo spent 11 days in jail under suspicion of fraud, charlatanism, and embezzlement. Later, he was acquitted and released from prison without any formal accusation. It should be remembered that Macedo faced an unexpected turmoil in 1995 when one of his bishops kicked the image of Our Lady of Aparecida, during a program on Record TV. Following the police investigation into the crime of religious discrimination and intolerance due to the strong reaction of the Catholic Church, Macedo had to issue public apologies, and transferred his bishop to the USA.

Another problem that has brought continuous storms to Macedo has been the conflicts with his own colleagues of ministry resulting in the formation of several UCKG "clone denominations." After his 1980 divisive disagreements with Soares, perhaps the most dramatic and bitter rupture has been that with Valdemiro Santiago de Oliveira. He was one of Macedo's powerful bishop, who organized his own church in 1998, the World Church of the Power of God, adopting the self-designated title of "Apostle Valdemiro Santiago".

In his teachings, Macedo gives high priority to the satisfaction of human desires for health, happiness, and prosperity. Instead of the traditional blood sacrifices, believers are challenged to offer substantial and continuous money sacrifices – in sacrificial tithes and different sorts of offerings (Vasquez 2009; Premawardhana 2012).

Macedo's religious discourse has turned into a discourse of intolerance. During UCKG's deliverance rituals, the spiritual entities of Afro-Brazilian religions are exorcized and delegitimized, giving religious legitimacy to Macedo's church. Such legitimacy, however, is only possible by the assimilation of the practices that UCKG intends to delegitimate. This kind of religious syncretism facilitates the sowing and flourishing of the seeds of intolerance practiced by UCKG. In the last two decades, Brazilian courts have imposed high costs on Macedo's church for its practice of religious intolerance.

After the collapse of the civil-military dictatorship in 1985, the convocation of the National Constituent Assembly in 1986 brought a new era for political participation of Brazilian Evangelicals and Pentecostals. Members of Macedo's church have been elected to executive and legislative positions in all regions of Brazil. Its political influence in all levels of the Brazilian society has continuously grown up to now without any interruption since that year.

Bibliography

Campos, Leonildo Silveira. 1999. *Teatro, Templo e Mercado: Organização e Marketing de um Empreendimento Neopentecostal*. Petrópolis: Vozes.

Castro, C.M., and A. Dawson. 2017. *Religion, Migration, and Mobility*. New York: Routledge.

Mariano, Ricardo. 1999. *Neopentecostais: sociologia do novo pentecostalismo no Brasil*. São Paulo: Loyola.

Premawardhana, Devaka. 2012. "Transformational Tithing: Sacrifice and Reciprocity in a Neo-Pentecostal Church." *Nova Religio* 15 (4): 85–109. Van Wyk, Ilana. 2014. *The Universal Church of the Kingdom of God in South Africa: A Church of Strangers*. New York: Cambridge University Press. Vásquez, Manuel A. 2009. "The Global Portability of Pneumatic Christianity: Comparing African and Latin American Pentecostalism." *African Studies* 68 (2): 273–286.

Paulo Ayres Mattos

Malaysia

Malaysia sits between West and East Asia geographically, and straddles the region culturally and religiously. Unsurprisingly, denominational/institutional Pentecostalism and independent charismatic figures/movements have also come from both areas.

Institutionally, in West Malaysia, the Ceylon Pentecostal Mission (CPM) arrived first, missionizing Indian and Ceylonese migrants in the 1930s. American Assemblies of God (AG) missionaries later followed in 1934, evangelizing Chinese urban migrants. The AG's impact became more significant than the CPM due to the latter's Indianized form of Pentecostalism and stance on healing.

During World War II, many missionaries left Malaysia while many local congregations scattered and were left stranded. After the war, they returned to serve the church. As it grew, the English-speaking congregations were led by the missionaries while the Chinese-speaking ones were pastored by Chinese workers from Hong Kong.

Elsewhere, independent figures such as China's John Sung (in the 1930s) and Hong Kong's Kong Duen Yee (Mui Yee) in the 1960s, came and ministered. Sung's charismatic-like ministries of preaching, prayer, healing, deliverance and the word of knowledge led thousands of Chinese-speakers to Christ in Penang, Kuala Lumpur and Sibu while Mui Yee's healings and power encounters converted many, leading her followers to form the Church of Penang. However, Sung followers did not consolidate these gains into a denomination while Kong's calls for believers to leave their churches to form their own scandalized many and stunted her movement.

In East Malaysia, the Sidang Injil Borneo (SIB) is a key face of charismatic Christianity. Originating as the non-charismatic Borneo Evangelical Mission in 1927, it grew in Sarawak among the Lun Bawang and later in 1937, to British North Borneo (now Sabah). Charismatic features appeared in 1972 with a revival among members in Lawas and continued following the visit of an Indonesian minister to preach and exorcise demons. In 1973, the Kelabits underwent a revival in Bario when students and SIB members spoke in tongues, prophesied and experienced healing and deliverance. Around 1984, Ba Kelalan experienced spectacular signs and wonders under Pak Agung Bangau who exercised the charismatic gifts. SIB's charismatic marks remain today in some but not all congregations in East Malaysia.

After Malaya's independence in 1957 and Malaysia's formation 1963, it terminated all foreign missionary visas, depriving local churches of experienced leaders. Some remaining English-speaking missionaries helped the AG start the Bible Institute of Malaya in 1960 (later becoming the Bible

College of Malaya in 1967). In the proceeding decades, they graduated over 500 students to pastor mostly English-speaking Pentecostal churches.

Malaysia's charismatic movement begun in the late 1960s when Anglican priest Dennis Bennett visited nearby Singapore. Spill over effects of his visit and the popular readership of his book, *Nine O'Clock in the Morning* resulted in some Malaysians from the Anglican, Baptist, Brethren and Methodist churches becoming charismatic. Mainline church rejection of them led to the breakaway and establishment of newly independent charismatic churches such as Full Gospel Assembly, Tabernacle of God, and Full Gospel Tabernacle in the 1980s. Such rapid establishment of new charismatic churches risked theological laxity and unstable leadership and disciples. Subsequently, many gravitated towards the Shepherding Movement's strict principles of obedience and submission which produced tensions.

South Korean Pentecostalism came in the 1980s when David (originally Paul) Yonggi Cho conducted a church growth seminar and introduced the cell group model. Stressing massive prayer as a key to church growth, it became an emphasis of P/C churches as those who embraced his teachings later built many megachurches.

Another important influence is the Full Gospel Businessmen's Fellowship of Malaysia. Initiated in 1980, it attracted unbelievers, Catholics and mainline church members. These Catholics later returned to form charismatic services within Catholicism while some mainliners experienced rejection by their leaders and left to form new churches. In the corresponding decades, these newly independent charismatic churches grew by inviting Western speakers for evangelistic and healing rallies. The arrival of the Vineyard Church, Foursquare Gospel, and others expanded the diversity of charismatic churches in the following decades.

Sociologically, Malaysian Pentecostalism has grown as a minority faith under Islam. It sought assistance by adopting ministry emphases, musical forms and theological themes from the West, producing a non-contextualizing, Western style.

Two new developments in recent decades bear watching: indigenous P/C Christianity in East Malaysia and Chinese-speaking Pentecostalism. In the first, rapid urbanization in Kota Kinabalu, Sandakan and Kuching since the 1990s reproduced similar early rural-to-urban migrations in the peninsular that greatly helped Pentecostalism's growth there. Other influences include the availability of Indonesian translations of Western charismatic books, visiting Indonesian Pentecostal preachers, teachers and revivalists such as Daud Tony and Philip Mantofa. Somewhat related, the Anglicans, Basel Christian Church of Malaysia and the Protestant Church in Sabah have all experienced breakaways from their congregations or seen charismatic subgroups sprout within themselves. Emerging separately are the indigenous Pentecostal Church of Sabah and Gereja Baptist Pelita Cahaya Sabah.

For the second, Pentecostalism is currently experiencing rapid growth among Chinese-speakers through the True Jesus Church, increased visits of Taiwanese preacher-evangelists and Chinese translations of Western charismatic authors. If the TJC (i.e., Oneness Pentecostalism) is included, one can add 126 churches and about 13,000 members to Malaysia's P/C tally. Against decades of continued emigration of English-speaking Christians (including P/C believers) to other countries, Malaysian Pentecostalism's character and future will become increasingly Chinese and Malay-speaking but less English.

Bibliography

Cheong, Weng Kit, and Joy K.C. Tong. 2015. "The Localization of Charismatic Christianity among the Chinese in Malaysia: A study of Full Gospel Tabernacle." In *Global Chinese Pentecostal and Charismatic Christianity*, edited by Fenggang Yang, Joy K.C. Tong, and Allan H. Anderson, 309–328. Leiden: Brill.

Dahles, Heidi. 2007. "In Pursuit of Capital: The Charismatic Turn among the Chinese Managerial and Professional Class in Malaysia." *Asian Ethnicity* 8 (2): 89–109.

Lim, Yue Chuen. 2007. "An Analysis into the Growth Factors of the Chinese Churches in the Assemblies of God Malaysia." *Asian Journal of Pentecostal Studies* 10 (1): 78–90.

Tan, Derek. 2004. "Malaysia." In *International Dictionary of Pentecostal and Charismatic Movements*, edited by Stanley M. Burgess and Eduard M. van der Maas. Grand Rapids, MI: Zondervan.

Tan, Jin Huat. 2005. "Pentecostal and Charismatic Origins in Malaysia and Singapore." In *Asian and Pentecostal: The Charismatic Face of Christianity in Asia*, edited by Allan Anderson and Edmond Tang, 281–306. Oxford: Regnum.

Cheong Weng Kit

Mason, Charles Harrison

Charles Harrison Mason (1864–1961), an African American, was the founder and first senior bishop of the Church of God in Christ (COGIC), one of the largest Pentecostal denominations in the world. He was also a well-known Pentecostal evangelist, a supporter of world missions, an ally of education, a champion of pacifism, and an advocate of civil rights. During Mason's fifty-four year tenure as senior bishop, the COGIC grew from 10 congregations to 4,000 congregations, approximately two thousand members to 400,000 members, and churches within the U.S. and on five continents.

Born on September 8, 1864 in Bartlett, Tennessee, a village near Memphis, he was the son of an African American Union soldier, Jerry Mason and Eliza Mason. Since Memphis and some parts of Tennessee sided with Abraham Lincoln and the Union, Mason was born a free person in 1864 rather than enslaved as his parents and older siblings had been. A graduate of a Minister's Institute of Arkansas Baptist College, Mason was first ordained in the Baptist church. Between 1895 and 1907, he transitioned from being a Baptist to Holiness Baptist to a Pentecostal, becoming a leading pioneer within global Pentecostalism as an "alumnus" of the Azusa Street Revival, the founding event of the Pentecostal movement in the U.S. In 1897, he embraced the name Church of God in Christ as a biblical name for congregations, preferring this name over Baptist or Methodist which he deemed as unbiblical names for a church.

In September of 1907, he was elected as the head of COGIC as a Pentecostal body. Earlier in the summer of 1907, he was disfellowshipped from the holiness association to which he co-founded with Charles Price Jones, a leading African American Holiness pastor, author, and hymnist; his embrace of the Pentecostal message led to Mason's dismissal from the organization Jones headed.

During World War I, Bishop Mason preached against war. He sent representatives to Washington, D.C. to request conscientious objector status in order to exempt its draft-eligible men from drafted into the military. While the request was denied, he continued to protest the war, being jailed in Lexington and Jackson, Mississippi, as well as in Paris, Texas for obstructing the draft.

Mason was among a rare cadre of Pentecostal pioneers who built an African American-led international denomination that was multi-racial in its membership. Especially during the first few decades of his bishopric, the COGIC included black, white, and Latinx congregations. He led one of the oldest and largest continuous national interracial religious organizations in the U.S. There even existed interracial and multi-racial congregations in various states during his lifetime.

Mason's pastorate at Temple Church, Memphis, as well as the international headquarters complex, with its 5,000 plus auditorium and office building was used as sites for major civil rights rallies from the 1940s to the 1960s, often when other venues refused to open their facilities for these rallies. Civil Rights leaders like Martin Luther King Jr. would speak from the pulpit of Mason Temple in 1959 as well as later in 1968 and gospel artists like Mahalia Jackson would sing there during Mason's lifetime.

Mason's monthly newspaper, *The Whole Truth*, published by the COGIC also included occasionally anti-segregation articles. A supporter of labor unions, Mason issued a call for at least one economic boycott as a campaign to secure black jobs in new industries. In 1931, he issued a call in *The Whole Truth* to boycott interstate bus lines.

Mason was a "broad church" Pentecostal. Mason preached the infalliability of Scripture rather than inerrancy. He taught that "speaking in tongues" was a sign of the baptism of the Holy Spirit as opposed to the initial evidence. According to him, Spirit baptism was only given to those Christians who lived a sanctified life marked by love; consequently, to him it was impossible for a racist to be full of the Spirit. To Mason, Spirit baptism granted boldness to Christians to evangelize and confront racial hatred. In addition to being engaged in pacifism, racial justice, and labor union advocacy, he was also open to ecumenism and cooperated with other Christians. During the 1930s, the COGIC under Mason's leadership joined the Fraternal Council of Negro Churches, an ecumenical body of all the major African American Protestant denomination, including some black Pentecostal ones.

Mason was married three times, only remarrying after the death of each of his first two wives. He married Alice (Saxton) Mason in 1892; Leila (Washington) Mason in 1905; and Elsie (Washington Mason) in 1943. He and his wife, Leila, were the parents of his seven children. A world traveller, Mason traveled outside of the U.S., visiting Haiti, Jamaica, Great Britain, Holland, France, and Israel during the last two decades of his life. Mason died on November 8, 1961. His funeral was held in Memphis, Tennessee and was attended by thousands.

Bibliography

Clemmons, Ithiel. 1996. *Bishop C.H. Mason and the Roots of the Church of God in Christ.* Bakersfield, CA.

Daniels, David. 2002. "Charles Harrison Mason: The Interracial Impulse of Early Pentecostalism." In *Portraits of a Generation: Early Pentecostal Leaders*, edited by James Goff and Grant Wacker, 255–270. Fayetteville, NC: University of Arkansas Press.

Mason, Elsie. 1979. *The Man: Charles Harrison Mason (1866–1961).* Memphis, TN: Church of God in Christ International Publishing House.

Smith, Raynard D., ed. 2015. *With Signs Following: The Life and Ministry of Charles Harrison Mason.* St. Louis, MO: Chalice Press.

David Daniels

Mathews, Thomas

Thomas Mathews (1944–2005) was one of the most effective Indian Pentecostal leaders. He was a missionary, teacher, preacher, and writer. Due to his courage to take the Christian message to Rajasthan, the desert state of India, he is known as "the Apostle of the Desert." Mathews was born in Punaloor, Kerala to Pentecostal parents. As they considered him as an answer to their prayers for having children after four years of their marriage, they dedicated him to the service of the Lord. While doing his Bachelor degree in Physics in the University of Kerala, he had a miraculous escape from drowning, and he stopped his university education and transferred to Shalem Bible School, Kottayam for his studies. His passion to go to the hardest part in North India as a missionary was intensified by the visit of K.V. Philip, who was the first Kerala Pentecostal missionary to Rajasthan. Hearing the severe persecution which Philip had to face, Mathews was challenged and decided to go to Rajasthan.

In 1963 Mathews came as a faith missionary to Udaipur. In the early days he faced starvation and persecution. He baptized his first local convert in 1964, which was the beginning of Rajasthan Pentecostal Church (RPC), and it is currently the largest Pentecostal Church in Rajasthan. He married Mary, who shared the same vision with him. When he arrived in Rajasthan, only a few people were Pentecostals, and with his coming, Pentecostalism took a new turn in North India. Many non-Pentecostals comment that Mathews made Pentecostalism a movement in the state.

Over the years, Mathews realized that he had to transform himself into the particular North Indian context for an effective Christian mission. Consequently, he made necessary changes even to his food habits and language. He was one of the most effective Christian orators in Hindi. He advocated for worshipping, caring and witnessing churches in every village of North India. This emphasis on church planting is the chief reason for the growth of Filadelfia Fellowship Church of India (FFCI), which he formed. More than a thousand churches were established in 13 states during his 42 years of ministry. Donald McGavran wrote a note of appreciation about the fascinating growth of FFCI in Mathews's Bible, which he used when he attended McGavran's seminar.

He realized the importance of education. Along with his ministry, he completed his MA degree in English literature in the Mohanlal Sukhadia University. Due to his distinctive academic result, he was encouraged by the head of the English Department to do doctoral research. In his research, he analyzed John Milton's poems, *Paradise Lost* and *Paradise Regained*, from a biblical perspective. He was the first Indian Pentecostal pastor who earned a PhD from a secular university.

Mathews saw that theological education and church growth were inseparable in Christian mission. He believed that quality education would result in quality churches. It was his great ambition to produce capable young people in North India as preachers, teachers, church planters, and researchers. Therefore, in 1982 he selected five potential lay leaders and founded the Filadelfia Bible Institute to train them. Later it was upgraded as Filadelfia Bible College (FBC). Today FBC offers diploma, degree and masters programmes in Theology. To date it has produced over 1500 graduates.

Mathews recognized the importance of equipping Christians. Knowing that native missionaries are more effective, fruitful, and acceptable, he formed a missionary organization called Native Missionary

Movement (NMM) in 1981. He gave freedom to each church to function according to its own cultural and indigenous characteristics. He wanted churches to be self-governing, with the freedom to raise funds, train leaders, construct buildings, and use indigenous means to worship. He was influenced by the principles of "self-governing, self-supporting and self-propagating" churches.

In January 1981, Mathews and his coworkers planted churches beyond Rajasthan. They saw a vision of a particular geographical area touching Gujarat and Maharastra. Later in the same year Mathews and his team conducted a Christian meeting in the village called Karanjikhurdu in Navapur, Maharastra. Hardly 30 people attended the meeting, but it has grown to be the most famous Pentecostal convention in India, and is known as Navapur Convention with several hundreds in attendance.

Understanding the importance of media, Mathews began a Hindi periodical, *Angel*, for which he was a regular writer. His *Bhavishyavani ki Ruparekha* (An Outline of Prophecy) was his Hindi masterpiece. He also initiated an English periodical, *Cross and Crown*, which was one of the most prominent Pentecostal periodicals. He also published a commentary on the Book of Revelation entitled *Revelation Simplified*.

Community development was another important feature of his vision. Mathews established schools, orphanages, hostels, and vocational training centers in various places, and a printing press. Although his death on November 24, 2005 was unexpected, he made a lasting impact on Indian mission work.

Bibliography

Lukose, Wessly. 2013. *Pentecostalism in Rajasthan: Contextual Missiology of the Spirit.* Oxford: Regnum.

Lukose, Wessly. 2009. "Pentecostal Beginnings in Rajasthan, India: Part One." *Asian Journal of Pentecostal Studies* 12 (2): 231–256.

Lukose, Wessly. 2006. "Dr. Thomas Mathews and His Contribution to Indian Missions." *Cross and Crown* 36 (1): 24–27.

Simmons, Roger. 2008. *Vision Mission and a Movement: The Story of Dr. Thomas Mathews and the Native Missionary Movement.* Richardson, TX: Native Missionary Movement.

Thollander, John. 2000. *He Saw a Man Named Mathews: A Brief Testimony of Thomas and Mary Mathews, Pioneer Missionary to Rajasthan.* Udaipur, India: Cross and Crown.

Wessly Lukose

McAlister, R.E.

Robert Edward McAlister was born into a large Presbyterian farming family in Renfrew County, Ontario, in 1880. The family moved to Cobden, Ontario, in 1891, where McAlister had an important conversion experience in the holiness congregation led by Ralph Cecil Horner – an important Canadian radical holiness evangelist and founder of the Holiness Movement Church and the Standard Church of America. McAlister studied at God's Bible School in Cincinnati, Ohio, during 1900–1902, before returning home due to illness, where, in 1904, he married his first wife, Eliza. After hearing reports about the revival that was happening at William J. Seymour's Apostolic Faith Mission in Los Angeles, California, McAlister travelled there in December 1906 where he received the baptism of the Holy Spirit and subsequently returned to Canada as an enthusiastic evangelist for

Robert Edward McAlister and his family.
Source: Pentecostal Assemblies of Canada Archives

the new Pentecostal experience. For the next approximately three and a half years, the McAlisters appeared to have divided their time between Winnipeg, Manitoba, and the Ottawa Valley region of Ontario, until Eliza's untimely death in May 1910. McAlister was married two more times, to Lillie who also died prematurely in 1921, and then to Laura.

McAlister is most famous for the somewhat hagiographical role that he played in the development of the New Issue – the rejection of the Trinity among some Pentecostals and the resulting formation of the third major branch of Pentecostalism known as Oneness Pentecostalism. While preaching at a baptismal service at a Pentecostal camp meeting in Arroyo Seco, California, in the spring of 1913, McAlister observed that the Apostles had used the singular name of Jesus Christ rather than the triune name of Father, Son, and Holy Spirit, when baptizing new Christians. Despite McAlister's attempt to walk back his unintended repudiation of the traditional Trinitarian baptismal formula, his remark inspired the minister, John Schaepe, to publically declare that McAlister had been used by God to divinely reveal baptism in the name of Jesus only and the closely connected idea of the oneness of God. Although neither McAlister's comment nor the camp meeting as a whole appeared to have made any immediate impact within Pentecostal circles, at least one individual – McAlister's friend, the Australian evangelist, Frank Ewart – claimed that McAlister's sermon prompted Ewart's subsequent year-long effort to determine the correct biblical formula for water baptism. The result of Ewart's study was his firm conviction in the oneness of God, which led him and his assistant, Glen Cook, to re-baptize each other in the name of Jesus only at a tent meeting held in Belvedere, California, in April 1914. This event was an important catalyst for the dissemination of Oneness Pentecostalism around the world, McAlister himself soon joining the movement that he accidently helped to create.

McAlister also played a crucially important role in helping to unite Canadian Pentecostals through the formation of a national organization representing Pentecostals in all provinces and territories of Canada. What would eventually become the country's largest Pentecostal denomination – the Pentecostal Assemblies of Canada (PAOC) – was established on May 17, 1919, but, at that time, it only represented congregations in the eastern Canadian provinces of Ontario and Quebec. Also in 1919, Pentecostals in western Canada joined the American Pentecostal denomination, the Assemblies of God (AG), as the Western Canada District Council of the AG. The main reason for the existence of these two Canadian Pentecostal bodies, was the roughly geographical division of support for the New Issue that they represented. Eastern Canadian Pentecostals – such as McAlister – were more sympathetic to a non-Trinitarian position, while western Canadian Pentecostals – such as the important Winnipeg, Manitoba-based leader, Andrew Harvey Argue – tended to be more firmly Trinitarian in their views. Desiring to see the two groups unite, McAlister – one of the original framers of the initially oneness PAOC – publically retracted his oneness views, became a minister with the Trinitarian AG, and, in 1920, helped to successfully orchestrate a vote that saw the PAOC join the AG as the Eastern Canada District Council of the AG. In 1925 – after a period of theological, ritual, and organizational harmonization between the two Canadian districts – they amicably separated from the AG and merged as a single national organization under the corporate charter originally acquired by the PAOC in 1919.

The important roles that McAlister played in founding and uniting the PAOC, and subsequently as the denomination's Secretary-Treasurer, Missionary Secretary, and editor of its official magazine, *The Pentecostal Testimony*, resulted in him being remembered by denominational historians as an "architect" and "founding father" of Canadian Pentecostalism. Although undoubtedly an important figure who is certainly worthy of scholarly attention, the highly hagiographical and patriarchal tendencies of all existing official denominational histories of the PAOC, behooves future historians to carefully re-examine the denomination's history in order to recover the important contributions made by women and racialized men who are often marginalized or ignored within the official canon.

Bibliography

Craig, James. 1995. "'Out and Out for the Lord': James Eustace Purdie, an Early Anglican Pentecostal." Master's thesis, Wycliffe College.

Miller, Thomas William. 1994. *Canadian Pentecostals: A History of the Pentecostal Assemblies of Canada*. Mississauga: Full Gospel Publishing House.

Reed, David A. 2010. "Oneness Seeds on Canadian Soil: Early Developments of Oneness Pentecostalism." In *Winds From the North: Canadian Contributions to the Pentecostal Movement*, edited by Michael Wilkinson and Peter Althouse, 191–213. Leiden: Brill.

Reed, David A. 2008. *"In Jesus' Name": The History and Beliefs of Oneness Pentecostals*. Blandford Forum, UK: Deo Publishing.

Wilkinson, Michael, and Linda M. Ambrose. 2020. *After the Revival: Pentecostalism and the Making of a Canadian Church*. Montreal & Kingston: McGill-Queen's University Press.

Adam Stewart

McKeown, James and Sophia

James McKeown was the founder of the Church of Pentecost, which is the largest Protestant Church in Ghana. He was born on 12 September 1900 in Glenboig, near Glasgow. His parents were from Ballymena in Northern Ireland, but they lived temporarily in Scotland. His father, John William Mckeown, earned enough money to buy a farm in Tullynahinion, near Portglenone, County Antrim (Thomas 2016). James dropped out of school at the age of eleven to help his father in the farm. His parents were strict Presbyterians who became involved in the Pentecostal stirrings of the time. Some prominent Pentecostal preachers such as George Jeffreys and Smith Wigglesworth preached in the McKeowns' farm compound. They had profound impact on James' future ministry. His preaching style is said to resemble that of George Jeffreys' (Malcomson 2008).

In 1919, James was converted after hearing a sermon preached by Robert Mercer, a member of George Jeffreys' Elim Evangelistic Band (Thomas 2016). He was eventually baptized in the Holy Spirit. In 1925, he attended a convention of the Apostolic Church in Belfast where D.P. Williams accepted him as a member of the Apostolic Church (Thomas 2016). James's father was instrumental in the establishment of the Apostolic Assembly in Tullynahinion after a split occurred in the Elim group in Portglenone (Robinson 2005).

James married Sophia Kennock in 1927 and settled in Glasgow, where he worked as a tram conductor, and later a tram driver until 1937, when he accepted the call to go to the Gold Coast. Sophia was born in Ballymena in Northern Ireland in 1894. She was converted through the ministry of the Faith Mission Pilgrims and spent time with this group, hoping to become a pilgrim herself (Malcomson 2008). Sophia was drawn to the Pentecostal meetings where she received the baptism of the Holy Spirit. Being a pristine homemaker and splendid seamstress, Sophia was a pillar of strength for James and encouraged him to accept the call to Africa.

James arrived in the Gold Coast (now Ghana) on March 7, 1937, to work as the missionary of the Apostolic Church to Ghana with a group of believers, who were led by Peter Newman Anim. Sophia joined him six months later. James settled in Asamankese in the Eastern Region of Ghana until 1938 when he moved to another town called Winneba in the Central region. Through correspondence, the group of churches that James worked with had first been affiliated with the Faith Tabernacle Church of Philadelphia and later with the Apostolic Faith Mission of Portland, both in the USA. Afterwards, his group of churches became affiliated with the Apostolic Church of UK. He worked with the group until a misunderstanding on divine healing separated them in 1939 (Leonard 1989). The group held on to some beliefs of the Faith Tabernacle Church that forbade them from taking medication.

James intended to not plant English culture on African soil. He contextualized his message to meet the needs of Ghanaians. Unlike many other missionaries of that era, he taught his followers to respect their African culture while being a true Christian. He insisted on biblical Christianity and living a holy life. His four cardinal teachings were: radical evangelism for salvation of souls, effective prayer to overcome the strongholds of Satan, baptism in and empowerment of the Holy Spirit for spiritual growth, and holy living. Therefore, his converts were grounded appropriately in their own culture and his church gained respect among the people for the moral aptness of the members (Leonard 1989). Many people believed in the Lord and the church grew exponentially.

James appointed Ghanaians as leaders and respected them as his co-workers in a way that endeared him to them. As a result, in 1953, when James had to resign from the Apostolic Church over a constitutional amendment that James considered as separatist and racist, the Ghanaian leaders quickly seceded from the Apostolic Church and arranged for James to return from Britain to Ghana to lead them. James lived a very simple Christian life, full of faith and humility. He was bold and straightforward in his dealing with people, a strong personality who did not compromise (Opoku 2004). He understood his mission in Ghana as "setting the heart of the people on fire" for the love of Jesus Christ (Opoku 2004).

Sophia started the Women's Movement to promote neatness and helped women to be good homemakers and prayer partners (Opoku 2004). The McKeowns planted 3000 churches with 145,000 members, which now number about 3 million members, operating in 100 countries. Both Sophia and James retired in Northern Ireland. Sophia died on 27 January 1983 and James on 4 May 1989.

Bibliography

Leonard, Christine. 1989. *A Giant in Ghana: 3000 Churches in 50 Years, the Story of James McKeown and the Church of Pentecost.* Chester: New Wine Press.

Malcomson, Keith. 2008. *Pentecostal Pioneers Remembered: British and Irish Pioneers of Pentecost.* Maitland: Xulon Press.

Onyinah, Opoku, ed. 2004. *The Church of Pentecost: 50 Years of Sustainable Growth.* Accra: McKeon Memorial Lectures.

Robinson, James. 2005. *Pentecostal Origins: Early Pentecostalism in Ireland in the Context of the British Isles.* Milton Keynes: Paternoster.

Thomas, Marcus. 2016. *The God of Our Fathers: Belting the Globe with the Gospel.* Belfast: Ambassador International.

Lord Elorm Donkor

McPherson, Aimee Semple

Aimee Semple McPherson (1890–1944), founder of the International Church of the Foursquare Gospel, was born near Ingersoll, Ontario, Canada to Mildred (Minnie) Pearce, a Salvation Army worker, and James Kennedy, a Methodist farmer. As a precocious teenager, Aimee Kennedy grappled with difficult questions including the relationship between faith and science, but she also enjoyed popular culture and practiced her skills of performance and dramatic reading. In 1907 she attended a series of Pentecostal meetings conducted by evangelist Robert Semple, where she experienced the baptism of the Holy Spirit and promptly fell in love with the preacher (McPherson 1923). Following their marriage in 1908 Robert and Aimee Semple ministered across southern Ontario, partnered briefly with William Durham in Chicago, and left from the Toronto Hebden Mission to become missionaries in China. Sadly, Robert Semple contracted malaria and died in August 1910, just a few weeks before Aimee gave birth to their daughter Roberta. With no formal mission organization to turn to, nineteen-year-old Aimee made her own arrangements to return home, joining her mother in ministry in New York City. Her autobiography ascribes meanings to these formative events, explaining her deep encounters with the Holy Spirit (Ambrose 2017).

After her return, Aimee married Harold Stewart McPherson, giving birth to their son, Rolf, in March 1913. The marriage was unhappy and when Aimee determined that she must return to ministry, she embarked on a North American preaching tour. Harold joined her in some of those evangelistic travels, but by 1918 he had filed for separation on the grounds of abandonment, and they divorced in 1921. Meanwhile, Aimee's mother partnered in ministry with her and the two set out on an epic transcontinental automobile trip in 1918, driving their "gospel car," emblazoned with signs proclaiming "Jesus Is Coming Soon – Get Ready." McPherson's meetings drew crowds of curious spectators, with reports of conversions, Spirit baptisms, and miracles of physical healing.

Aimee, her mother, and the children, arrived in Los Angeles in December 1918 where McPherson founded the Interna-

Aimee Semple McPherson speaking in front of microphone at Angelus Temple, circa 1923. Source: Los Angeles Times Photographic Archive, UCLA Library. Copyright Regents of the University of California, UCLA Library.

tional Foursquare denomination, headquartered at the famous Angelus Temple, a domed church building with a seating capacity of 5,300, completed in 1923. The denomination has since expanded to more than 50,000 congregations worldwide with membership of more than six million people (Sutton 2007). The tenets of the "foursquare gospel" present Christ as savior, baptizer, healer, and coming king. Famous for incorporating theatrical production techniques into her illustrated sermons, McPherson continued to attract large crowds and media coverage, while she established her own radio network. During the 1930s, the Angelus Temple was well-known for generous provision of food and clothing to needy families in the area, a reminder that her Hollywood-style gospel presentations were paired with pragmatic social welfare initiatives.

Organizational accomplishments are only one part of McPherson's legacy. Having achieved celebrity status in North America, Aimee was subjected to relentless media coverage, and she had several controversial episodes that fueled the hype. In 1926, while on a beach outing, McPherson mysteriously disappeared. Presumed dead, her mother held a memorial service and her congregation mourned their loss. However, almost a month later, Aimee miraculously reappeared, reporting that she had been kidnapped and narrowly escaped. Adding intrigue to the story was the fact that McPherson's radio engineer, a married man named Kenneth G. Ormiston, had also disappeared at the same time. While titillating reports about sightings of the two at a secluded cottage swirled in the media, a grand jury was convened in July 1926 to consider the

Aimee Semple McPherson. Source: Pentecostal Assenblies of Canada Archives

case. Citing lack of evidence, the jury adjourned less than two weeks later, and the disappearance was left unsolved. Aimee married a third time in 1931 to actor David Hutton, but the couple separated two years later and divorced in 1934. Sadly, the final episode of McPherson's life echoes a familiar tragic trope of celebrity lives: McPherson died from an overdose of sleeping pills on September 26, 1944. Rumors about suicide circulated, but the coroner's report concluded the death was accidental, and the famous preacher was buried in the Forest Lawn Memorial Park Cemetery in Glendale, California.

Scholarship about Aimee Semple McPherson is rich. Gender studies provides a useful means of exploring her life because, as Leah Payne has argued, Aimee Semple McPherson leveraged her femininity to establish her authority in ministry, emphasizing her "sexy intimacy with Jesus" (Payne 2015). A master of the "performed self," one of McPherson's favorite motifs was to present herself as the embodied Bride of Christ, complete with a white wedding dress and a bridal bouquet of roses. Understanding McPherson in her historical context means considering her place in the larger field of media studies. Not only was she a media sensation reputationally, but she was a pioneer in the field of communications who used stage and sound very effectively and built a wide-ranging radio network (Blumhofer 1993). Historian Matthew Sutton argues that McPherson's engagement with American religious and popular culture is a prototype of how succeeding generations of evangelicals adopted her precedent to make forays into public life (Sutton 2007). Aimee Semple McPherson was North America's most widely known Pentecostal and her legacy is riddled with fascinating ambiguities.

Bibliography

Ambrose, Linda M. 2017. "Aimee Semple McPherson: Gender Theory, Worship, and the Arts." *Pneuma* 39 (1): 105–122.

Blumhofer, Edith L. 1993. *Aimee Semple McPherson and the Making of Modern Pentecostalism, 1890–1926*. London: Equinox.

McPherson, Aimee Semple. 1923. *This is That: Personal Experiences, Sermons, and Writings*. Los Angeles: Echo Park Evangelistic Association.

Payne, Leah. 2015. *Gender and Pentecostal Revivalism: Making a Female Ministry in the Early Twentieth Century*. New York: Palgrave Macmillan.

Sutton, Matthew Avery. 2007. *Aimee Semple McPherson and the Resurrection of Christian America*. Cambridge, MA: Harvard University Press.

Linda M. Ambrose

Mebius, Frederick E.

Although Frederick Mebius (1879–1944) is usually considered to be the founding missionary of the Pentecostal movement in El Salvador, his role cannot be fully understood apart from the history of Protestant evangelicalism in the area. Moreover, what is known about him is largely dependent on oral histories passed down in interviews with missionaries.

Among the earliest Protestants to enter El Salvador from the north were the missionaries from the fundamentalist and non-denominational Central American Mission (CAM), founded by C.I. Scofield in 1896. American Baptists came soon thereafter in 1911. Both denominations were welcomed by the Salvadoran government in an era of increasing anti-clericalism. Still, these early evangelicals found the thick and resistant Catholic ethos to be a major obstacle to growth. Mebius began his missionary work in the region in 1914 in association with these evangelical churches.

Mebius, who was from Victoria, Canada came to El Salvador in 1914. Previously he had spent time with the Salvation Army in Bolivia and later settled in the United States where he was baptized in the Holy Spirit and healed from tuberculosis. Commissioned by the Salvation Army, at the age of thirty-five he made his way south again, this time to El Salvador where he became an associate of Herbert Binder, an American missionary who, along with Samuel Purdie worked in the Central American Mission. Mebuis reportedly spoke very little Spanish but possessed a charismatic and authoritarian personality. He was placed in charge of a half dozen small congregations. Apparently in Binder's absence, Mebius persuaded several members of these congregations to embrace Pentecostal manifestations and soon several members began to speak in tongues. This group of very poor coffee pickers formed a congregation near the village of *Las Lomas de San Marcelino*, on the slopes of the volcano near *Santa Ana*, and additional churches began to grow as well. By 1927 there were twenty-four small and very poor congregations loosely associated with Mebius' Free Apostolic Church scattered throughout the coffee growing districts.

It was not long before some members of these churches became disgruntled with Mebius' leadership, and they formed separate congregations. One group was led by Fransisco Arbizu, a small scale land owner, former member of the National Guard, and the owner of a small leather factory. The small Salvadoran group concluded that they needed a leader and they began to focus on developing a relationship with the Assemblies of God. Arbizu eventually travelled to the Assemblies Bible Institute in San Antonio, and through his efforts, Ralph Williams, a Welsh Pentecostal working in Mexico City, eventually joined the work in El Salvador.

William's presence added to the rupture between Mebuis and Arbizu and as a result, Mebuis refused to allow his remaining churches to join the Assemblies of God. Nevertheless, under the leadership of Williams and Albizu, the Assemblies of God was organized in such a way to eventually become the largest Pentecostal denomination in El Salvador. In 1939, H.S. Syverson, an American missionary from the Church of God based in Cleveland, TN, was appointed overseer of the Central America region, and when he travelled to El Salvador he found Mebius living in a lean-to shack, mending shoes to support himself. By then Mebuis was old and ailing. Due to congregational splits, he had only five small churches. By the time Mebius died in 1944, all his churches had been absorbed into the Church of God (George 2010).

Bibliography

Conn, Charles W. 1959. *Where the Saints Have Trod.* Cleveland TN: Pathway Press.

George, Bill. 2010. *Until All Have heard: The Centennial History of the Church of God World Missions.* Cleveland TN: Pathway Press.

Knowles, James Purdie. 1908. *Samuel A. Purdie: His Life and Letters, His Work as a Missionary and Spanish Writer and Publisher in Mexico and Central America.* Plainfield, IN: Publishing Association of Friends.

Wadkins, Timothy. 2017. *The Rise of Pentecostalism in Modern El Salvador: From the Blood of the Martyrs to the Baptism of the Holy Spirit.* Waco: Baylor University Press.

Wilson, Everett A. 1983. "Sanguine Saints: Pentecostalism in El Salvador." *Church History* 52 (2): 186–198.

Timothy Wadkins

Media

Since its early beginnings, the spread of Pentecostal Christianity has depended to a great extent on the distribution of media forms such as booklets, radio tapes, flyers, but also music, dance and other performances that transport the Holy Spirit. "Media" here are understood to be carriers of divine messages and of spiritual energies.

Many of the Pentecostal media initially originated in the United States, which has ever since remained a global center of Christian media production. Gradually, throughout the twentieth century, Pentecostal media centers have been set up in various locations all over the world, the Global South included.

For scholars who look into the ways in which media contribute to community building, Pentecostal media are considered to create Pentecostal publics, that is communities that come together (physically or virtually) around a text, and reflect upon the content and form of a text. Pentecostal media texts incite their audiences/users to participate in public debates about "what is a good Christian?" and "how should a good Christian behave in society?" As such, Pentecostal media produce a discursive sphere that allows spectators/users to engage with religious content directly. One can write advice, or personal experiences online, call in on a radio show and have one's personal narrative discussed by the radio host and its audiences, as is the case in Cotonou, capital city of Bénin (Grätz 2014). Often, these Pentecostal media also deal with very intimate issues, such as "how to be a Christian while being married to a pagan?" Or, "how to raise my children in a Pentecostal fashion while the overall community is hostile to the religion?"

In various instances, Pentecostal media engage with urban and national politics, thus straddling the divide between the sacred and the secular. In Rio de Janeiro (Oosterbaan 2008, 125), for example, Pentecostals present "utopist visions of a better society, based on Christian values" and provide air time to "charismatic, trustworthy evangelical politicians (men of God) who answer to a 'Higher Authority' that man have created new political profiles for politicians in Brazil". Such is the public influence of Pentecostal media, that, also in Brazil, ex-bandidos (former gangsters/thugs) have become famous leaders after their testimonies were aired on multimedia (Machados 2014).

Yet, as Barber (2007) convincingly has argued, publics are historical, inherently instable, and dependent on technologies. In certain instances, these Pentecostal publics are almost invisible on the public stage, as is the case for Meru gospel singers in Kenya, who tackle in songs (circulating

100 Huntley Street Daily Telecast. Source: Pentecostal Assemblies of Canada Archives

via audio tapes and music videos) moral issues that churchgoers cannot raise within their congregations (Lamont 2010). The genre in which Meru Christians are singing does not operate on a national stage, mainly because their texts do not engage with national politics of belonging, identity, citizenship and human rights.

The easy adaptation to local cultures is one of the distinctive features of Pentecostal Christianity. Missionaries very quickly started publishing Pentecostal texts in local languages, where local media producers address Pentecostal themes from a local point of view, and communicate Pentecostal content in styles and forms that appeal to local audiences. In order to appeal to larger audiences, sometimes, Christian media producers need to borrow genres from non-religious contexts or even from other religions. An example of this process which Larkin (2008, 105) has called "promiscuity" in the public sphere, is the adoption of the Muslim music genre of *senwele* by Nigerian Charismatic Christians. *Senwele* draws on *waka* songs, which were developed to welcome returning Hajj pilgrims. In a Christian context, *senwele* reinforces the difference between Christian and Muslim publics in Nigeria (Brennan in Hackett and Soares 2014). The influence and traction of Pentecostal media are sometimes so significant that Pentecostal media styles also feed into media forms of other religions. In Accra, for example, Pentecostal media ministries have become so influential that Afrikania leaders, or so-called Traditionalists, are copying Pentecostal genres (De Witte 2005).

Further evidence of the localizing quality of Pentecostal and Charismatic media can also be seen in the different scripts for a successful life that Pentecostals propose to their audiences. Comparing television programs produced by the Universal Church of the Kingdom of God for Rio de Janeiro and New York City audiences,

Mora (2008) observed a similarity over the material and physical rewards that can be obtained through religious adherence. Yet, the main differences are related to the presented causality between religious practice and prosperity. The New York City television shows emphasized prayer, perseverance and struggle, while in Rio prayer, the ritualistic use of sacred objects, and miracles were said to bring prosperity.

Differences are also observed within sub-Saharan Africa. Pype (2012) noted a striking difference regarding the origins of "bad luck", when comparing Nigerian and Ghanaian evangelizing video films with Kinshasa's Pentecostal television serials. The former frequently locate the origins of human misfortune in a past reaching back several generations or even to a mythic "ancestral" time. Kinshasa's Pentecostal-charismatic leaders point to sorcerous practices enacted by persons in one's social environment. These are held responsible for determining daily life in the present (Pype 2012, 219–220).

One of the major analytical insights in Pentecostal media studies is the reinterpretation of religious "mediation", i.e. the management of the distance between religious subjects and the transcendental (Meyer and Moors 2005). Pentecostal television programs, chat rooms, and booklets are simply other kinds of media, literally "in-betweens", just like the Holy Book itself or the bodies of pastors that connect Christians with the spiritual world. While external observers might worry about the insertion of technological media in religious worship and spiritual work, most Pentecostals take it for granted that the mediating work that Pentecostal media perform are not that different from the mediating work done by classic leaders.

Pentecostal media producers indeed are not only eager to entertain their publics, and to contribute financially to their church via the sales of media, but first and foremost they want to establish proximity with the divine. The direct address to radio and television spectators, or to internet users, extends the presence of the church into the living room, the court yard, the bedroom and the taxi. Yet, proximity also reaches into the intimate bodily realm. Pentecostal media producers attempt to transfer Christian knowledge and powers by producing songs, melodramas, and radio shows that appeal to the senses, and that can transform audience's bodies. This kind of media has been called "haptic" media, as the goal is to "touch the spirits" of their audiences, and to trigger an immediacy or "live modality" (Pype 2015). From Accra over Kinshasa and Gabarone, to New York, Rio de Janeiro, and Vanimo, audiences hope to be visited by the Holy Spirit when they are listening to recorded songs on their MP3s, audiotapes or Pentecostal radio shows (Oosterbaan 2008; Togarasei 2012), or when watching video sermons (De Witte 2011), call-in shows, and evangelizing melodramas (Meyer 2015; Pype 2012).

In the recent two decades, a rich library of Pentecostal media studies has emerged. Major exciting lines for further analytical inquiry are (a) the decolonization of Pentecostal (media) studies; (b) the intertwinement of digitality and Pentecostalism; and, finally, (c) the insertion of media texts in Pentecostal colleges and universities that are being set up around the world.

Bibliography

Barber, Karin. 2007. *The Anthropology of Texts, Persons, and Publics*. Cambridge: Cambridge University Press.

De Witte, Marleen. 2005. "Afrikania's Dilemma: Reframing African Authenticity in a Christian Public Sphere." *Etnofoor* 17 (1/2): 133–155.

Grätz, Tilo. 2014. "Radio Call-In Shows on Intimate Issues in Benin: "Crossroads of Sentiments." *African Studies Review* 57 (1): 25–48.

Hackett, Rosalind, and Benjamin Soares, eds. 2014. *New Media and Religious Transformations in Africa*. Bloomington: Indiana University Press.

Larkin, Brian. 2008. "Ahmed Deedat and the Form of Islamic Evangelism." *Social Text* 26 (3): 101–121.

Lamont, Mark. 2010. "Lip-Synch Gospel: Christian Music and the Ethnopoetics of Identity in Kenya." *Africa: Journal of the International Africa Institute*, 80 (3): 473–496.

Machado, Carly Barboza. 2014. "Pentecostalismo e o sofrimento do (ex-)bandido: testemunhos, mediações, modos de subjetivação e projetos de cidadania nas periferias." *Horizontes Antropológicos* 20 (42): 153–180.

Meyer, Birgit. 2015. *Sensational Movies. Video, Vision, and Christianity in Ghana*. Berkeley, CA: University of California Press.

Meyer, Birgit, and Annelies Moors. 2008. *Religion, Media, and the Public Sphere*. Indianapolis, IN: Indiana University Press.

Mora, G. Cristina. 2008. "Marketing the 'Health and Wealth Gospel' Across National Borders: Evidence from Brazil and the United States" *Poetics* 36 (5/6): 404–420.

Oosterbaan, Martijn. 2008. "Spiritual Attunement: Pentecostal Radio in the Soundscape of a Favela in Rio de Janeiro." *Social Text* 26 (3): 123–145.

Pype, Katrien. 2015. "The Liveliness of Pentecostal-Charismatic Popular Culture in Africa." In *Pentecostalism in Africa: Presence and Impact of Pneumatic Christianity in Postcolonial Societies*, edited by M. Lindhardt, 345–378. Leiden: Brill.

Pype, Katrien. 2012. *The Making of the Pentecostal Melodrama: Religion, Media, and Gender in Kinshasa*. New York/Oxford: Berghahn Books.

Togarasei, Lovemore. 2012. "Mediating the gospel: Pentecostal Christianity and Media Technology in Botswana and Zimbabwe." *Journal of Contemporary Religion* 27 (2): 257–274.

Katrien Pype

Megachurches

Large churches have always existed in the history of the Christian church, from the early church in Antioch in the first century and its basilica, through the cathedrals of Europe, to Charles Spurgeon's Metropolitan Tabernacle in London (late 1800s) and Aimee Semple McPherson's Angelus Temple in Los Angeles (early twentieth century). But advancements in amplification technology, architecture, and the advent of the automobile and its accompanying asphalt infrastructure have led to the proliferation of megachurches and their development as a widespread religious form, alongside the development of megacities, megamalls, and electronic media. Typically, it is evangelicals who have taken advantage of these social and technological developments. While many see the megachurch as an American institution, some tracing its popularity to Robert Schuller's televised Crystal Cathedral (founded in 1955), David Yonggi Cho's Yoido Full Gospel Church, one of the largest megachurches in the world, began in 1958. Both churches took decades to develop into their megachurch form, but they underscore that the megachurch (generally taken to consist of attendance over 2,000 weekly) is best understood as a transnational, modern phenomenon.

When it is said that megachurches are a "global" social reality it does not mean that all countries have megachurches, that all traditions are equally predisposed to their development, or that they are monolithic

Culto in El Lugar de Su Presencia. Source: Wikimedia Commons, Photo: Cris12090823.

in their theological disposition. The United States, Korea, Brazil and Nigeria, for example, have more megachurches per capita than the global average. Warren Bird (2019), Research Director at Leadership Network, keeps the most up-to-date database on global megachurches, based on reports he receives from around the world. As of 2019 his list includes 119 in Africa (with 44 in Kenya, 37 in Nigeria, and 14 in South Africa), 145 in Asia (41 in China, 39 in Korea), 23 in Oceana (16 in Australia and 6 in New Zealand), 58 in Europe (18 in U.K., 13 in Netherlands), 49 in Latin America and Caribbean (18 in Brazil). Generally speaking, most megachurches are Protestant and conservative, and globally the Pentecostal-Charismatic stream appears to comprise the majority, with almost all led by male preachers (despite Pentecostalism's openness to female leadership).

Megachurches are transnational and maintain important networks throughout the world. While some megachurches have strong national and political ties, making them significant political forces and blending political identity with religion, most megachurches act like quasi-denominational bodies, forming alliances and partnerships across nation-state boundaries, and often with other megachurches and mission agencies that share their vision. For example, megachurches in South Korea have undergone rapid institutional expansion in part due to the charismatic attraction of the senior pastors as well as other socio-cultural factors, such as the economic rationalization of post-War Korea. More recently it has been argued that because South Korea is one of the most Internet-connected countries in the world the use of church web-sites played a key role in megachurch self-understanding, spiritual formation, outreach, and establishing pastoral authority (Kim 2007).

Reports of megachurches can also be found through mass media. Nigeria features prominently in the media, where articles highlight the large size of churches, the luxurious life of their pastors, and their transnational presence. Nigerian evangelists find themselves in large churches across the globe, such as the

12,000 member Kingsway International Christian Centre, London, which is led by Nigerian pastor Matthew Ashimolowo, or The Embassy of the Blessed Kingdom of God for All Nations, founded in 1994 in Kiev, Ukraine by Sunday Adelaja, also a Nigerian. The Nigeria-based Redeemed Christian Church of God (RCCG), led by the Pastor Enoch Adeboye, is home to several megachurches, which have fueled the church's expansion to now over 14,000 branches in 110 countries.

Megachurch leaders are public figures, and in some ways are in competition with each other for members, talent, and consumers of their books, podcasts, and music. Alliances and rivalries do develop and follow networks.

A majority of global megachurches are Pentecostal-Charismatic, meaning they have proclivities to a religiosity associated with the Azusa Street Revival in California in the early 1900s. This includes an emphasis on a personal experience of God, the work of the Holy Spirit, spiritual gifts, and especially healing. Outside of North America, megachurches can also be generally characterized as having some affinity with the prosperity gospel, or "health and wealth" theology, in which Christians are promised material rewards from God for their faithfulness and prayers. Similar to what Max Weber said about Calvinists, wealth becomes a symbol of one's piety, except one's health and healing are also included, and faith is understood as a protection against all negative events and a harbinger of all positive change in one's life.

While some critics see prosperity theology as a passive acceptance of neoliberalism and consumer capitalism, it can also be viewed as an active, selective sacralization of such a system in harmony with isolated themes in Scripture (eg. Mal 3:10; Phil. 4:19). This ethic helps with the upward mobility of its members and lends itself to a growing middle class in developing countries (Wanjiru 2018). Building on Weber and further delineating specific aspects of his notion of rationalization, studies framed by "McDonaldization" and commodification of religion extend across Asia to India, Singapore, Korea and Australia. Walmart and Disneyland have similarly been models to which the megachurch has been compared, and the best research here is wary of reducing all megachurch religiosity to economic calculus and consumerism (Schuurman 2019).

Prosperity theology offers a rationalization for larger budgets, larger staff, and larger church institutions with accompanying facilities – such as bookstores, restaurants, and recreation facilities. These churches mirror large corporations, with a large external campus and an internal focus on marketing, metrics, and management. Many have satellite campuses and are part of a transnational network of churches around the world that share their theology or even operate like franchises of an original church. One example is Hillsong Church in Sydney, Australia (est. 1983), which claims over 80 affiliated churches worldwide and suggests a vital importance of music in its global expansion. Since it began, it has produced over 40 albums, sold over 11 million copies, and in 2017 the churches income from its music totalled $14 million.

Further research is necessary to see where megachurches are located, with whom they are partnered and networked, and what form their theology and spirituality takes. While connections with political power and market forces are often first to be investigated, it is equally important to understand how megachurches use electronic media, foster religious identity and behaviour and contribute to civil society.

Bibliography

Bird, Warren. 2019. "World's Largest Megachurches," Leadership Network. https://leadnet.org/world/

Chong, Terence, ed. 2018. *Pentecostal Megachurches in Southeast Asia: Negotiating Class, Consumption and the Nation*. Singapore: ISEAS Publishing.

Coleman, Simon. 2007. *The Globalisation of Charismatic Christianity*. Cambridge: Cambridge University Press.

Hey, Sam. 2013. *Megachurches: Origins, Ministry, and Prospects*. Eugene, OR: Wipf & Stock.

James, Jonathan D., ed. 2015. *A Moving Faith: Mega Churches Go South*, Thousand Oaks, CA: SAGE Publications.

Kitiarsa, Pattana. 2008. *Religious Commodifications in Asia: Marketing Gods*. New York: Routledge.

O'Neill, Kevin Lewis. 2009. *City of God: Christian Citizenship in Postwar Guatemala*. Berkeley, CA: University of California Press.

Schuurman, Peter. 2019. *The Subversive Evangelical: The Ironic Charisma of an Irreligious Megachurch*. Montreal & Kingston: McGill-Queen's University Press.

Wanjiru, Gitau M. 2018. *Megachurch Christianity Reconsidered: Millennials and Social Change in African Perspective*. Downers Grove, IL: IVP.

Peter Schuurman

Mexico

The Pentecostal movement in Mexico traces its origins to the Azusa Street Revival in Los Angeles, 1906–1909. Genaro and Romana Carbajal de Valenzuela attended the Azusa Street Revival and brought Pentecostalism to Mexico between 1911 and 1915, around the same time that George and Carrie Judd Montgomery, Clarissa Nuzum, Francisca Blaisdell, Chonita Morgan Howard, and others did. It is also highly probable that other Mexicans from the Azusa Street revival like Abundio López, Juan Navarro Martinez, Brigido Perez, Luis Lopez, or a Mexican convert from Charles Fox Parham's Houston ministry brought Pentecostalism to Mexico between 1905–1915.

The largest Pentecostal denomination in Mexico is the Assemblies of God (AG). It traces its origins to the work of Henry C. Ball in South Texas in 1915, although work in Mexico did not begin in earnest until 1917. Alice E. Luce and Sunshine Marshall (who later married H.C. Ball) began work in Monterrey, Mexico. They conducted three months of house-to-house evangelism, preaching in prisons, and holding services in their home until the Mexican Revolution forced them back to the U.S. The Mexican work traces its roots to H.C. Ball, Miguel Guillén, Anna Sanders, George and Francisca Blaisdell, Rodolfo Orozco, David Ruesga, Cesáreo Buciaga, Modesto Escobedo, Ruben Arevalo, Manuel Bustamante, and Juan Orozco. David and Raquel Ruesga and Anna Sanders pioneered the work in Mexico City in 1921. A year later, Rodolfo C. Orozco traveled to Monterrey, Mexico, to establish a permanent AG church.

The AG in Mexico held its first national convention in 1926 and opened a Bible institute in Mexico City in 1928. By 2000, there were more than 1,400 students attending 30 Bible schools across the country. The Mexican work, which was under the supervision of the Latin District Council of the Assemblies of God in the U.S., severed its formal ties in 1929 when all religious bodies in Mexico tied to religious groups outside of Mexico were required to nationalize. David Ruesga was named the first superintendent of the AG in Mexico. In 1931, he left the AG and founded the Church of God in the Republic of Mexico

(Iglesia de Dios en la República Mexicana). In 1933, the Mexican AG began printing the periodical *Gavillas Doradas* (*Golden Sheaves*). By 1935 there were approximately 31 congregations and 2,800 adherents in Mexico. During the 1950s, the AG conducted large evangelistic campaigns throughout the country. By 1963 there were 5 Bible institutes, 647 ministers, 11 foreign missionaries, and approximately 13,500 adherents. In 1972, Gordon and Marilyn Marker opened the national office of the International Correspondence Institute (ICI) in Mexico City. By 1990, over one million people throughout Latin America had studied with ICI. By 1990, the work in Mexico had blossomed to an estimated 30 Bible institutes, 3,100 congregations, 3280 ministers and lay leaders, and more than 570,000 adherents. The AG in Mexico is one of the largest and most efficiently organized Pentecostal denominations.

The Apostolic Church of the Faith in Christ Jesus (Iglesia Apostólica de la Fe en Cristo Jesús) is the largest and oldest Oneness Pentecostal tradition in Mexico. The Apostolic Church was founded by Romana Carbajal de Valenzuela in 1914 after she converted twelve members of her family to Pentecostalism in Villa Aldama, Chihuahua, Mexico. Rubén Ortega and Miguel C. García served as the first two pastors of the small church. Around 1928, the Christian Spiritual Church (Iglesia Cristiana Espiritual) changed its name to the Apostolic Assembly of the Faith in Christ Jesus and in 1946, it replaced the word "Assembly" with "Church." In 1932, Felipe Rivas led the Apostolic Assembly in Mexico to sever its ties with the mother denomination in the U.S. That same year they also held their first general convention and counted 26 congregations and 800 members.

Notable growth took place after 1945 when the Apostolic Church grew from 111 churches and 5,000 members in 1946, to almost 330 churches and 13,000 members by 1956. The Apostolic Church sent missionaries to Guatemala, El Salvador, Nicaragua, Honduras, Costa Rica, Columbia, Argentina, Brazil, and the U.S. Like other Mexican Pentecostal denominations, it has gone through a number of major schisms (1930, 1965, 1974). Its organizational style is episcopal, with bishops as leaders. They operate Bible schools in Mexico City and Torreón. Theologically they are very similar to the Apostolic Assembly of Faith in Jesus Christ in the U.S. By 2000, the Apostolic Church numbered more than 1,500 congregations and 100,000 adherents throughout Mexico.

The Church of God in the Republic of Mexico (Iglesia de Dios en la República Mexicana) was founded by David Ruesga in 1931. Born in Michoacán, after studying for the priesthood in a Catholic Seminary, he participated in the Mexican Revolution. After the revolution, Ruesga and his wife Raquel immigrated to the U.S. to work in the film industry. After a near death experience, he became a Pentecostal and claimed that God had miraculously healed him. In 1920, the Ruesga's returned to Mexico where they began to preach throughout Mexico City. Three years later they organized an Assemblies of God church in the Plaza de la Concepción Tepisqueuca.

In 1925, Ruesga was ordained by H.C. Ball and the Latin American District Council of the AG (U.S.). After ordination he worked as a very successful AG evangelist and minister in Mexico City from 1925 to 1931. His church in Mexico City was one of the largest Pentecostal churches (over 1,000 members) at the time. His church established churches throughout Mexico and his strong and visionary leadership were the primary reasons why he was named the first leader of the AG in Mexico in 1929. Ruesga served in that capacity until 1931, when he and a number of followers left the AG and formed the Church of God in the Republic of Mexico. His decision to leave the AG split the work in Mexico and greatly weakened.

In 1940, Ruesga established formal ties with the U.S. based Church of God (Cleveland, TN). After Ruesga's death in 1960, the Church of God in the Republic of Mexico selected Gregorio Muñoz to be the bishop until his death in 1985. They adopted an episcopal form of government and operate a seminary in Mexico City. Theologically, they are influenced by dispensationalist pre-millennial theology and place a heavy emphasis on divine healing. They admonished women to wear head coverings in worship services and not to wear jewelry, cosmetics, or pants. They strongly oppose drinking of alcoholic beverages, smoking, dancing, and extra-marital sexual relations. The Church of God in the Republic of Mexico has experienced rapid growth throughout the twentieth century, growing from 17,000 adherents in 1961 to 80,000 adherents in 1970. By 1993, there were an estimated 625 congregations and 150,000 adherents throughout Mexico.

The Independent Evangelical Church (Iglesia Evangélica Independiente) was founded by Swedish Pentecostal missionaries Axel and Ester Andersson in San Luis Potosí in 1921. This church was supported by the Swedish Filadelfia Church in Stockholm, Sweden, until 1946. Today it is an indigenous Mexican Pentecostal denomination with its own authentic traditions. By 1965, there were an estimated 500 to 800 workers and 50,000 to 60,000 baptized members. The church has grown to an estimated 727 congregations and over 160,000 adherents in 1993.

The Independent Pentecostal Evangelical Church Movement (Movimiento Iglesia Evangélica Pentecostés Independiente – MIEPI) was founded by Valente Aponte González in the 1930s after leaving the Church of God in the Republic of Mexico. MIEPI believes that it is the one true church and are sectarian. They were openly critical of the Billy Graham evangelistic crusades in Mexico in the 1960s and in the past, have not participated in the Pentecostal Fraternal Association in Mexico (Asociación Fraternal de Iglesias Pentecostales en la República de México), an organization which includes many of the indigenous and foreign Pentecostal denominations in Mexico. Its sectarianism is characterized by an emphasis on personalismo (strong charismatic personalities) and leaders like Valente González exercised doctrinal uniformity, strict control over the denomination, and the practice of excommunication. Between 1961 and 1970, it grew from 70 ministers and 12,500 adherents to over 600 churches and 40,000 adherents. In the early 1990s, MIEPI reported an estimated 1,500 congregations and 85,500 adherents throughout Mexico.

The Light of the World Church (Iglesia La Luz del Mundo) was founded in Guadalajara, Mexico, by Eusebio (Aarón) Joaquín González in 1926. After serving in the military for eleven years (1915–1926), González was converted by José Perales and Antonio Muñoz of the Oneness Pentecostal Apostolic Church of Faith in Jesus Christ. Shortly after Eusebio was converted, he reportedly had a number of revelations from God which stated that his new name would be "Aarón" and that he would re-establish the New Testament Church on earth like in the book of Acts. Through these revelations, God also ordered him to leave Monterrey for Guadalajara where he would form the "Chosen People of God" as the new "Spiritual Israel" in the "Holy City." As he travelled to Guadalajara, Aarón reportedly performed miracles, converted people, and was persecuted and jailed.

On December 12, he arrived in Guadalajara and began preaching in front of the Catholic Cathedral near San Juan de Dios. In 1932, the Apostolic Church and Light of the World Church cut formal relations after a failed attempt to unite the two Oneness organizations. Shortly thereafter, Aarón opened up his first church building in 1934. In 1955, he purchased 35 acres of land to the east of the city in the Hermosa Provincia section of Guadalajara to build a new facility and to give followers an opportunity to buy land and build homes.

After Aarón's death in 1964, his apostolic leadership (God's living Apostle) was passed on to his son, Samuel Joaquín Flores. The Apostle has strong control over its members and in the past members of the church had to have the Apostle's authorization to leave Hermosa Provincia. Flores promoted foreign missions and by 2000 there were congregations in close to 30 countries. They began their work in the U.S. around the 1950s and by 2000 there were at least 50 congregations mostly in Texas and California. The biggest celebration in the Light of the World Church is the Holy Supper (Santa Cena). The Holy Supper is held every August 14 in Guadalajara, Mexico, and all members of the church from around the world are encouraged to attend. The week-long celebration attracts 60,000–100,000 people every year. In the 1980s, a new Cathedral-sized megachurch seating over 12,000 people was built in Guadalajara to accommodate the worshippers.

Although accurate figures are hard to come by, the church reports that they grew from 75,000 adherents in 1972 to over 1.5 million adherents and 1,200 congregations around the world in 2000. The Light of the World Church is important because it represents a unique, indigenous, and non-traditional form of charismatic Christianity. Despite its origins and ties with the Oneness movement in Mexico, it does not consider itself Pentecostal and believes it is the one true church of Jesus Christ in the world

Bibliography

de la Torre, Renée. 1995. *Los hijos de la luz: Discurso, identidad, y poder en La Luz del Mundo*. Universidad de Guadalajara, Departamento de Estudios en Comunicación Social.

de Walker, Luisa Jeter. 1990. *Siembra y Cosecha: Reseña histórica de Las Asambleas de Dios de México y Centroamérica*. Deerfield, FL: Editorial Vida.

Espinosa, Gastón. 2014. *Latino Pentecostals in America: Faith and Politics in Action*. Cambridge, MA: Harvard University Press.

Fortuny Loret de Mola, Patricia. 1995. "Origins, Development and Perspectives of La Luz del Mundo Church." *Religion* 25 (2): 147–162.

López Cortés, Eliseo. 1990. *Pentecostalismo y milenarismo: La Iglesia Apostólica de la Fe en Cristo Jesús*. Universidad Autonoma Metropolitana, Departamento de Filosofia.

Ramírez, Daniel. 2015. *Migrating Faith: Pentecostalism in the United States and Mexico in the Twentieth Century*. Chapel Hill, NC: The University of North Carolina Press.

Gastón Espinosa

Migration

Human migration is certainly not a new phenomenon. From the earliest times, humans have been on the move from different places of origin to wide-ranging destinations. The nature, causes, and processes of such movements have been explained by various migration theories stemming from different disciplines. The earliest known, the push-pull models and neo-classical perspectives, explain migration in terms economic, demographic, and environmental factors which 'push' people out of unfavorable conditions and 'pull' them into favorable locations. The historical-structural theories emphasize constraining factors such as historical colonial ties, unequal distribution of economic resources, and uneven geo-political power which influence migration decisions. The more recent migration system and transnational theories highlight the role of migrants' agency in the migration process. Here, migration is understood in terms of how migrants actively create and sustain social ties, networks, identities, and communities across borders, which tend to facilitate further migration (Castles, De Haas, and Miller 2014).

Since the end of the Second World War, international migration has witnessed significant changes in scale, direction, and character. Whereas for centuries Europeans were mostly moving outward to colonize and settle on foreign lands, Europe has, in recent times, been transformed into a global migration destination for migrants of formerly colonized lands. Today, the vast majority of international migration inflows to various destinations are from Asia, Africa, and Latin America. The changing direction in migratory movements has also coincided with a rising tide of irregular/illegal migration, refugee movements, undocumented migrant workers, and the displacement of populations worldwide. Migration is, thus, becoming increasingly politicized as politicians cleave to national sovereignty to regulate domestic borders. International organizations are simultaneously spurring governments to cooperate in the global governance of migration so as to balance the needs and interests of all stakeholders.

The growing politicization of migration has, unsurprisingly, contributed to a sustained logic of migration as an economic behavior or a forced movement – indeed, as a "problem" or "crisis" to be "managed". Migrants are also configured, rather problematically, as individuals whose mobility is exclusively based on cost-benefit analysis and utility maximization (Castles, De Haas, and Miller 2014, 29). Contrary to such dominant perceptions, human migration is never an isolated economic political phenomenon. When humans move, they draw along with them, other different social institutions and values, markedly, religion. Religious ideas, practices, experiences, and organizations are intricately connected to migratory movements. At the macro level, religion influences large scale institutional factors including state policies designed to "control" immigration, integration, religious diversity and multiculturalism. At the micro level, religion also influences how migrants themselves creatively navigate the tricky waters of migration through their individual religious expressions and their collective formation of immigrant religious communities and transnational religious networks. Most significantly, migration remains relevant in the global spread of world religions, notably, Pentecostalism.

Pentecostalism can be described as migratory religion. It is a religion that has, for over a century, traveled along the personal and collective networks of people on the move. Tracing their movement to the book of Acts, Pentecostals have always emphasized the conviction that adherents are being "sent by the Spirit" to spread the gospel message to the ends of the earth (Anderson 2014). This conviction has been the bedrock of Pentecostal mission and evangelism worldwide. Unlike the older Catholic and Protestant missions which were steered by institutional theology and state power, Pentecostal mission has historically been less institutionalized and predominantly catalyzed by individual and collective experiences of the working and gifting of the Holy Spirit. Grounded in the principle of priesthood of all believers, Pentecostals believe that the missionary spirit speaks equally to all practitioners, irrespective of their race, ethnicity, gender, nationality, and social status. This principle has contributed to the phenomenal expansion of the Pentecostal movement through various agents including immigrants.

Over the last three decades, a wealth of literature on Pentecostalism and migration has been published. This area of research has attracted diverse voices – theologians, religious studies scholars, missiologists, sociologists, ethnographers, even immigrants themselves. A fundamental question has been how to theoretically frame the relation between Pentecostalism and migration. Initial research in Europe and North America comprised case studies of individual Pentecostal-Charismatic churches started and attended largely by immigrants who were identified on the basis of their national and continental origins. Key questions included what significance Pentecostal immigrant churches hold for immigrants and their host societies; how Pentecostal churches and individual Pentecostal experiences undergo transformation in the context of migration; how Pentecostal immigrants' religious identities overlap with those of ethnicity, race, nationality, gender, and sexuality; and how Pentecostal immigrants actively create and sustain networks, identities, and communities across borders.

Following the changing direction of dominant migration flows, huge attention has been placed on Pentecostal immigrants from Africa, Asia, and Latin America, who are establishing so-called "migrant churches" in the supposedly secularizing European and North American landscapes. Here, scholars have debated whether they are experiencing the phenomenon of "reverse mission" or a north-south shift both in the direction of missionary sending and in the gravitational center of Global Christianity (Freston 2010). Overall, six analytical themes can be identified in how scholars have approached questions about Pentecostalism and Migration: reverse mission, transnationalism, globalization, immigrant integration, identity formation, and the public /social/civic engagement of Pentecostal immigrant communities.

Looking forward, future studies on Pentecostalism and migration can move beyond richly descriptive individual case studies to adopt frameworks that enable a more comprehensive, comparative, and theoretical synthesis. The reliance on congregational studies or Pentecostal "immigrant churches" as the main unit of analysis sometimes downplays the range of ways Pentecostalism emerges outside typical congregational settings, for example, in cities, families, workplaces, healthcare organizations, and educational institutions. The latter approach can expand the way Pentecostalism is conceptualized and measured and provide a more holistic picture of immigrants lived religious experiences. Additionally, scholars can also broaden analyses to include how Pentecostalism shapes public responses and policies toward migration at both domestic and international levels. Finally, research about Pentecostalism and migration will be more revealing if situated within broader geographic dimensions to encompass south-south and south-north migrations.

Bibliography

Adogame, Afe. 2013. *The African Christian Diaspora: New Currents and Emerging Trends in World Christianity*. London and New York: Bloomsbury.

Anderson, Allan H. 2014. *An Introduction to Pentecostalism: Global Charismatic Christianity*. Cambridge: Cambridge University Press.

Castles, Stephen, Hein de Haas and Mark J. Miller. 2014. *The Age of Migration: International Population Movements in the Modern World*. Fifth Edition. New York and London: Palgrave Macmillan.

Freston Paul. 2010. "Reverse Mission: A Discourse in Search of Reality?" *PentecoStudies* 9 (2): 153–74.

Wilkinson, Michael. 2006. *The Spirit Said Go: Pentecostal Immigrants in Canada*. New York: Peter Lang.

James Kwateng-Yeboah

Miracles, Signs, Wonders

Miracles, signs, and wonders are generally seen as evidence of God's immanence and divine care for humanity. The definition of miracle has changed over time. Prior to the Enlightenment, miracles were believed to be acts of God or an event caused by divine agency that invoked a sense of awe or wonder. After the Enlightenment, miracles were seen as violations of natural law that science could not explain yet.

The worldview assumptions and plausibility structures of the West provided some challenges for Pentecostals regarding miracles in the twentieth century. Pentecostals believe in an 'open' universe where divinely initiated activity such as miracles, signs, and wonders can occur vis-à-vis a 'closed' system determined by nature. The acceptance of an open universe runs contrary to pure scientific rationalism and provides an interpretive grid for Pentecostals to understand the contemporary world and biblical interpretation.

Globally, Pentecostals believe that miracles, signs, and wonders serve a missiological and evangelical purpose. Early Pentecostal missionaries saw their international efforts as empowered by the Holy Spirit, rife with signs, wonders, and miracles. In cultures and practices where post-Enlightenment skepticism is not the predominant influence, the Pentecostal belief in divine protection from evil forces, miraculous healing, and the activity of supernatural agents such as angels and demons, the holistic Pentecostal message addresses the felt need of individuals. In these contexts, Pentecostal Christianity readily adapts itself.

Signs, miracles, and wonders serve to confirm the truth of the gospel preaching. Pentecostals emphasize the preaching of the Word with signs following (Mark 16:20), meaning demonstrations of supernatural power are expected to accompany preaching. Pentecostal believers point to signs, miracles, and wonders to prove the veracity of their preaching or ministries. In some areas, competition between Pentecostal Christians and traditional healers may exist. In such situations, the miracles or signs serve as proof of ones esteemed status before God or divine favor along with affirming the message that is preached.

Along with the missional function of miracles, Pentecostals have interpreted signs, miracles, and wonders in an eschatological sense, especially during periods of revival. The signs and wonders experienced in the ministry of Maria Woodworth-Etter were interpreted as evidence of the imminent return of Christ. Similar interpretations and anticipations marked the Azusa Street Revival. This eschatological expectation fueled mission and evangelism efforts by Pentecostals.

The biblical foundation for the belief in the miraculous is grounded in a literal interpretation of the Bible. Pentecostals believe that the miracles of the Bible are not only historically tenable, but that similar events can and do occur today. Some common biblical evidence for the miraculous is often found in the commissioning of the twelve (Mark 6:7–13), seventy (two) (Luke 10:1) where Jesus instructs the disciples to perform miraculous deeds (heal the sick, raise the dead, and cast out demons) and in the gospel of John regarding the "greater works" followers of Jesus will do in his name (John 14:12). These passages and others are taken literally, providing an expectation that signs, miracles, and wonders should occur in the lives of believers.

Pentecostals view the gospel and salvation in holistic terms. Salvation (conversion) is not seen strictly in terms of eternal life, but participation in God's restorative efforts through signs, wonders, and miracles for this life. Miracles, signs, and wonders therefore extend to other areas of life and the felt needs of people such as provision of food or money, protection from evil, demons, or harm. In other circumstances, they function predominantly as signs for supernatural power through unusual manifestations such as gold dust clouds, feathers falling, gem stones, or oil flowing out of Bibles.

The belief in supernatural healing is especially prominent in the Pentecostal expectation of miracles, signs, and wonders. In areas where with little to no (Western) medical assistance as well as in some areas of the West, miraculous healing is often anticipated. Pentecostals inherited this belief from the Healing movement of the late nineteenth century. While the common assumption is that God executes the healing, it is mediated through a variety of thaumaturgical methods such as laying on of hands, prayer, anointing with holy water or oil, or a combination of both in accordance with James 5:14.

Pentecostalism in the early twentieth century emphasized the Christological aspects of signs, miracles, and wonders. During this time, many healings and miraculous signs were performed 'in the name of Jesus.' Miraculous healing was seen to come from the atonement as cited in Isaiah 53:5 and Matthew 8:17. Later on, especially after WWII up to the Faith Movement, Pentecostals emphasized the 'faith' aspect of miraculous events. Jesus' own commendation for certain individuals' faith, brought about the Pentecostal emphasis on the faith that an individual had. This has sometimes led to an overemphasis on the individuals will and a shaming of the individual for not having enough faith for the healing.

The charismatic movement of the late twentieth century brought about further emphasis on the Holy Spirit with respect to signs, wonders, and miracles. The ministries of Kathryn Kuhlman, Lonnie Frisbee, and John Wimber emphasized not only the spiritual gifts, but also a pneumatological understanding of signs and wonders. The "Third Wave" movement also emphasized a pneumatological understanding of healing. Along with the emphasis on the Holy Spirit, further emphasis on the sovereignty and personality of the Holy Spirit has also been emphasized. Some Pentecostal and charismatic ministers "make space" or time for the Holy Spirit to move, with varying results. The emphasis on the sovereignty of the Spirit shifted the expectation of healing away from the faith of the individual to the nature and character of God. The Third Wave presents God's goodness and the healing ministry of Jesus as evidence of God's desire to heal. This belief in God's goodness assumes that the lack of faith on part of the infirm should not be acknowledged or used against them as it was in the Faith Movement. While this provides an empathetic view of the infirm, it does provide a tension with Jesus' statements regarding faith and healing (Mark 2:5; Matt 9:2, 22).

While Pentecostals are not the only Christian population to believe in signs, wonders, and miracles, the emphasis on these events has been a distinguishing aspect of Pentecostalism. By addressing the felt needs of people, they play an important part of Christian experience.

Bibliography

Alexander, Kimberly. 2006. *Pentecostal Healing: Models in Theology and Practice.* Blandford Forum: Deo.

Anderson, Allan. 2013. *To the Ends of the Earth: Pentecostalism and the Transformation of World Christianity.* New York: Oxford University Press.

Dayton, Donald. 1987. *Theological Roots of Pentecostalism.* Metuchen, NJ: Scarecrow Press.

Hacking, Keith. 2006. *Signs and Wonders: Then and Now.* Leicester: Intervarsity Press.

Keener, Craig. 2011. *Miracles: The Credibility of the New Testament Accounts.* Grand Rapids, MI: Baker Academic Press.

McGee, Gary. 2010. *Miracles, Missions, and American Pentecostalism.* Maryknoll, NY: Orbis Books.

Brandon Walker

Missiology

Missiology, or mission studies, is the theological study of Christian mission worldwide. An outline of six features of Pentecostal and Charismatic mission describe their missiology.

Firstly, Pentecostalism places primary emphasis on being "sent by the Spirit". In comparison to the "Missio Dei" of older Catholic and Protestant missions and the "obedience to the Great Commission" of evangelical "Christocentric" missions, Pentecostal mission is grounded first and foremost in the conviction that the Holy Spirit is the motivating power behind all this activity. The Pentecostal movement from its commencement was a missionary movement, made possible by the Spirit's empowerment. Most Pentecostals also have a decidedly Christ-centred emphasis in their mission. The Spirit bears witness to the presence of Christ in the life of the missionary, and the message proclaimed by the power of the Spirit is of the crucified and resurrected Jesus Christ who sends gifts of ministry to people.

Secondly, Pentecostals believe that the coming of the Spirit brings an ability to do "signs and wonders" in the name of Jesus to accompany and authenticate the gospel message. The role of "signs and wonders," particularly that of healing and miracles, is prominent in Pentecostal mission praxis. Pentecostals see this as good news for the poor and afflicted. The central role given to healing is probably no longer a prominent feature of western Pentecostalism, but in the Majority World, the problems of disease and evil still affect the whole community and are not relegated to a private domain for individual pastoral care. Pentecostal movements went a long way towards meeting physical, emotional and spiritual needs of people, offering solutions to life's problems and ways to survive in an often hostile and insecure spiritual world. Unfortunately, a message of power has sometimes become an occasion for the exploitation of those who are at their weakest.

Thirdly, Pentecostals are notorious for aggressive forms of evangelism, as from its beginning, Pentecostalism was characterised by an emphasis on evangelistic outreach. All Pentecostal mission strategy places evangelism as its highest priority. For Pentecostals, evangelism meant to go out and reach the "lost" for Christ in the power of the Spirit. At first, missionaries were mostly untrained and inexperienced. Their only qualification was the baptism in the Spirit and a divine call; their motivation was to evangelize the world before the imminent coming of Christ. Despite the seeming naiveté of these missionaries, their evangelistic methods were flexible and pragmatic. Pentecostal evangelism was geared towards church planting, a central feature of all Pentecostal mission activity. The emphasis on self-propagation through evangelism and church growth through "signs and wonders" has sometimes resulted in Pentecostals being inward looking and seemingly unconcerned or oblivious to serious issues in the socio-political contexts, especially where there were oppressive governments. However, Pentecostals are again beginning to recognise the social implications of the gospel and this failure in their mission strategy.

Fourthly, one of the results of being "sent by the Spirit" was that there was a rapid transition from "foreign" to "indigenous" church. Pentecostal missions are quick to raise up national leaders who are financially self-supporting, and therefore the new churches are nationalized much quicker than older mission churches had been. Pentecostalism's religious creativity and spontaneously contextual character were characteristics held as ideals by mission strategists for over a century.

Fifthly, the remarkable growth of Pentecostal movements in the twentieth century cannot be isolated from the fact that these were often "people movements," a massive turning of different people to Christianity from other religions on an unprecedented scale, set in motion by a host of factors which older western missions were unprepared for. These movements did not proliferate because of the many secessions that occurred but because of mass conversions to Christianity through the tireless efforts of local missionaries, both men and women. The use of women with charismatic gifts was widespread throughout the Pentecostal movement. This resulted in a much higher proportion of women in Pentecostal ministry than in any other form of Christianity at the time.

Finally, the "freedom in the Spirit" that characterises Pentecostalism has contributed to the appeal of the movement in many different contexts. The emphasis on a direct experience of God through his Spirit, results in the possibility of ordinary people being lifted out of their mundane daily experiences into a new realm of ecstasy, aided by the emphases on speaking in tongues, loud and emotional, simultaneous prayer and joyful singing, clapping, raising hands and dancing in the presence of God – all common Pentecostal liturgical accompaniments. These practices made Pentecostal worship more easily assimilated into different contexts, especially where a sense of divine immediacy was taken for granted. They contrasted sharply with rationalistic and written liturgies presided over by a clergy that was the main feature of most other forms of Christianity. Pentecostals throughout the world proclaim a pragmatic gospel and seek to address practical needs like sickness, poverty, unemployment, loneliness, evil spirits and sorcery. In varying degrees, Pentecostals in their many and varied forms, and precisely because of their inherent flexibility, attain a contextual character which enables them to offer answers to some of the fundamental questions asked by people. This does not mean that Pentecostals provide all the right answers, a pattern to be emulated in all respects, but the enormous contribution made by Pentecostalism to alter the face of world Christianity irrevocably has enriched the universal church in its ongoing mission.

Bibliography

Anderson, Allan. 2014. *An Introduction to Pentecostalism: Global Charismatic Christianity*. Cambridge: Cambridge University Press.

Anderson, Allan. 2007. *Spreading Fires: The Missionary Nature of Early Pentecostalism*. London: SCM.

Dempster, M.A., B.D. Klaus, and D. Petersen, eds. 1991. *Called and Empowered: Global Mission in Pentecostal Perspective*. Peabody: Hendrickson.

Hodges, Melvin L. 1953. *The Indigenous Church*. Springfield: Gospel Publishing House.

Lord, Andrew. 2005. *Spirit-Shaped Mission: A Holistic Charismatic Missiology*. Milton Keynes: Authentic Media.

Ma, Wonsuk, V-M. Kärkkäinen, and J.K. Asamoah-Gyadu, eds. 2014. *Pentecostal Mission and Global Christianity*. Oxford: Regnum.

McClung, L. Grant, ed. 1986. *Azusa Street and Beyond: Pentecostal Missions and Church Growth in the Twentieth Century*. South Plainfield, NJ: Logos.

McGee, Gary. 2010. *Miracles, Missions, and American Pentecostalism*. Maryknoll, NY: Orbis Books.

Allan H. Anderson

Mok, Lai Chi

Mok Lai Chi, 1868–1926

Mok Lai Chi (1868–1926) was the founder of the Pentecostal Mission in Hong Kong (HK) in 1907, the first Chinese indigenous Pentecostal church in Asia. He had been a member of the Congregational Church established by the American Board of Commissioners for Foreign Mission, but on 8 October 1907, when A.G. and Lillian Garr came to his church to preach the revival message which they had received from the Azusa Street Revival, Mok was baptized by the Holy Spirit and spoke in tongues. He and other Congregationalists prayed out loud in the church and were accused of alluring people by hypnosis. The senior pastor, Charles Hager, requested them to move out and so they started their own church elsewhere. This church was first called Apostolic Faith Mission but changed to Pentecostal Mission in 1910. Mok stressed that it was "a Christian mission founded by Chinese themselves. It was not a branch of a foreign mission set up in my country."

Mok was one of the rare Chinese elites in the society of the British colonial period. Studying in the Government Central School, he was awarded a first class Morrison Scholarship and graduated with honors at the age of eighteen in 1886. After his graduation, he worked in the government as an assistant usher and a process server at the magistracy. From 1891, he worked as a clerk and interpreter at the Registrar General's office, the Royal Observatory and the Police Court. In his leisure time, he studied Isaac Pitman, chemistry and produced perfumes for sale. Despite such a privileged social and economic position, he felt spiritually discontent. In 1892, he founded the Morrison English School and educated 120 boys sponsored by the London Missionary Society. Besides education, he also dedicated himself to the ministry of the YMCA and his church. However, he could not find spiritual fulfilment in all his ministry until the Garrs brought the revival message.

To assist the spread of the revival gospel, he published *Pentecostal Truths* (*PT*), a Chinese Pentecostal newspaper from 1908 to 1917. Each issue contained three pages in Chinese and one in English. To enable millions of illiterates, especially women and children, to know the crucial revival message, he deliberately wrote in simple Chinese and made the newspaper free of charge. He simply relied on voluntary donations for printing and postage. This newspaper spread not just in HK, but to China, Australia, Canada, America, and Singapore. He frequently published the news of western Pentecostal periodicals *Confidence*, *Bridegroom's Messenger*, and *Apostolic Faith* in his newspaper to connect Chinese Christians with the global revival network. He also corresponded with the editors of these newspapers so that the West could also know the latest development of the revival in China.

Despite being a well-educated elite, Mok was not indifferent to the poverty in his society. He started a ministry among the poor laborers to preach the gospel and prayed for the sick. He also worked with the poor who had been converted through his ministry. He wrote the testimonies of the illiterate and women who were voiceless in the society and published them in the *PT*. He also travelled to villages and islands to reach the poor farmers and fishermen in HK and his own folks in South China. Mok and his Mission regularly organized Pentecostal Conventions in Heungshan (now Zhongshan) which brought the gospel and healing to the local people, especially Woo Tsz Ho and her relatives who founded two churches and one school for children and illiterate adults.

Although Mok primarily worked with the Chinese, he also collaborated with foreign missionaries. He opened a girls' school with Anna Deane, a missionary of the Pentecostal Holiness Church (PHC) and launched a Pentecostal Convention for ten days with J.H. King, the then general superintendent of the PHC, who travelled from the US to China in 1910. Mok also welcome missionaries who were en route to China to teach in the school and preach in his church for a short term.

Mok was very concerned about the high rent imposed on tenants by covetous businessmen in HK and was elected as the president of the Chinese Tenant Protective Association. He protested against the unjust system on behalf of several hundred thousand residents. Eventually, he successfully pushed the government to legalize the regulations of rent. Some members of the Association wanted to make a statue for him, but he declined as he simply wanted to "remove the pain of our people, not for the vague glory."

Mok had neither formal theological training nor a university degree, but he led the revival movement in HK and South China and founded a church, taught hundreds of children and founded several schools. What was more, he was committed to social justice. One of his sons recorded that his father taught at the school in the morning, solved the problems of the tenants in the afternoon and led a Bible study group in the evening. In his 58 years of life, he did not aim at personal wealth and prestige (although he had all the potentials to earn these), but he forsook these privileges for spiritual purposes, so that others might have a better life on earth and be ready for life in heaven.

Bibliography

Anderson, Allan. 2007. *Spreading Fires: The Missionary Nature of Early Pentecostalism*. London: SCM.

Au, Connie. 2019. "From Collaborations with Missionaries to Independence: A History of the Hong Kong Pentecostal Mission (1907–1930)." In *Asia Pacific Pentecostalism*, edited by Denis A. Austen, Jacqueline Grey, and Paul Lewis, 85–106. Leiden: Brill.

Au, Connie. 2017. "Elitism and Poverty: Early Pentecostalism in Hong Kong (1907–1945)." In *Global Chinese Pentecostal and Charismatic Christianity*, edited by Fenggang Yang, Joy Tong, and Allan Anderson, 63–88. Leiden: Brill.

Connie Au

Mongolia

When Mongolian socialism crumbled in 1990, there were around 20 Christians in the whole nation. Now, there are between 40,000 and 100,000 attendees in approximately 600 churches, as well as unregistered churches, preaching stations and home cell groups – comprising up to 10 percent of the voting constituency (Byambajav 2013; Jamsran 2012). Many attend Pentecostal or charismatic churches.

Pentecostalism came to Mongolia through American missionary Abigail Slager (1910–1912). William W. Simpson and his wife Otilia Ekvall arrived in 1912. Apostolic Faith ministers also conducted outreaches. Canadian Pentecostal missionaries Thomas and Louise Hindle served in Mongolia (1910–1917) when there were only 11 Protestant missionaries in the nation. The Hindles established Mongolia for Messiah Mission at Geshatu. Other pioneers included Clara Wyns, Grace Fordham, and Letta and Harold Hansen.

With the rise of socialism, Mongolia became a People's Republic in 1924. The Geshatu mission continued with reports of Chinese Pentecostal missionaries there as late as 1936. Carman Clare Scratch participated in government relief work in 1945. Swedish missionaries who received a Pentecostal experience in China, led similar meetings in Mongolia. However, brutal oppression eventually crushed the movement.

The reopening of Mongolia in 1990 saw an influx of missionaries. In 1993, International Christian Assembly, Hong Kong held a three-day outreach with over 800 people in attendance. As a result, Hope Church was founded in Ulaanbaatar with 500 members. The following year, the Mongolia Assemblies of God (MAOG) was established and a Bible school opened. In 1999, after completing studies at Asia Pacific Theological Seminary in the Philippines, Otgontsetseg Arslan became the first MAOG general superintendent – one of the few women of any nation to hold that position.

The Mongolian government banned ownership of church buildings in 1997, but Pentecostalism spread through cell churches that indigenized liturgy and worship. Brian and Louise Hogan of Youth With A Mission were involved in the 450-strong Jesus' Assembly cell movement in Erdenet. In fact, between 1990 and 2000, only 2 percent of churches were officially registered. Some international preachers, such as Yonggi Cho, also held mass meetings. By 2002, the ecumenical Mongolia Evangelical Alliance had begun to accept Pentecostal denominations.

To ensure a continuing Pentecostal presence, the not-for-profit Sunrise Educational Foundation was established in 1993 by the Assemblies of God, USA. This foundation provides humanitarian aid throughout Mongolia, including university scholarships, medical treatment and supplies, education, food programs, and building projects.

Prison ministry was promoted by New Zealand-born Pentecostal, Margaret Currie, executive director (1998–current) of Prison Fellowship Mongolia. It serves approximately 8000 prisoners across Mongolia's 25 prisons, providing vocational training, advocacy, food and medicine, and care for the families of inmates.

Pentecostal missionaries provided an early foundation in Mongolia. With the collapse of socialism, a successful outreach event was held and the first Pentecostal church was founded. An indigenized cell church model saw the movement expand rapidly. Pentecostals also serve local communities through much needed social welfare programs.

Bibliography

Austin, Denise A. 2017. "The 'Third Spreading': Origins and Development of Protestant Evangelical Christianity in Contemporary Mongolia." *Inner Asia* 19 (1): 64–90.

Byambajav, Dalaibuyan. March 2 3, 2013. "Christian in Mongolia after Socialism." The First SEFM International Workshop on Social Change and Religious Transformation in East Asia (Hokkaido University). Accessed September 4, 2018. http://www.slideshare.net/ByambajavDalaibuyan/christianity-in-mongolia.

Hogan, Brian. 2008. *There's a Sheep in my Bathtub: Birth of a Mongolian Church Planting Movement*. Bayside, CA: Asteroidea Books.

Jamsran, Purevdorj. 2012. "Developing Christianity in Mongolia during the Last Two Decades." In *Mongolians after Socialism: Politics, Economy and Religion*, edited by Bruce M. Knauft and Richard Taupier, 129–137. Ulaanbaatar: Admon Press, with Mongolian Academy of Sciences, National University of Mongolia and Open Society Forum, Mongolia.

Denise A. Austin

Montgomery, Carrie Judd

Carrie Judd Montgomery (1858–1946) was an American preacher and leader of the Divine Healing (Faith Cure) and Pentecostal movements. Through media forms like books, articles, and her journal, *Triumphs of Faith* (TOF), she influenced decades of readers. Her entrepreneurial efforts in the

Carrie Judd Montgomery, 1858–1946

establishment of healing homes on both coasts of the US, missionary enterprises, and a camp meeting in Oakland, California provided ministry opportunities for many in both the Healing and Pentecostal movements, as well as models for others to follow (Albrecht 1977). Following the trajectory of her own life and ministry, from Episcopalian proponent of divine healing, through the Christian and Missionary Alliance (CMA), to Pentecostal leader, her works provide valuable insight into significant segments of the American Pentecostal movement.

Incidents in Montgomery's first twenty years are critical to understanding her 66 years of ministry. On April 8, 1858, in Buffalo, New York, Carrie Frances Judd, the fourth of eight children, was born to Emily Sweetland and Orvan Kellogg Judd, devout Episcopalians (Miskov 2012). Her parents insisted on quality academic and religious training. Montgomery planned on a career in education. However, in January 1876, she slipped on the icy sidewalk while walking to school. There followed a long period in which she was an invalid. In February 1879, her father read about the ministry of Mrs. Edward (Sarah) Mix, an African-American itinerant healing evangelist. The Judds contacted Mix and received a letter instructing Carrie to "lay aside all medicine of every description", to "use no remedies of any kind for anything" as that would be "trusting in the 'arm of flesh.'" Mix appointed a time when her "female prayer-meeting" would pray for Carrie's healing and the Judd family were to pray at that same time. Carrie was then to "'*act faith*'" (Judd 1880; Montgomery 1936). According to Montgomery's account, she was able to raise up from her bed for the first time in two years. Within three weeks, she was walking and had gained twenty pounds. In six months, she reported that she was completely healed. The story was reported in newspapers in the northeastern US in October 1879.

Mix's three-step process, and Montgomery's appropriation of it are important theologically because they represent an adaptation of American Holiness leader Phoebe Palmer's "shorter way" to sanctification. This formulaic approach would have profound impact on healing theology and practice in Pentecostalism (Alexander 2006).

Montgomery became a sought-after speaker, beginning her itinerant preaching ministry shortly after the first publication of the healing miracle. She ministered with Mix and became especially influential in the circles around Dr. Charles Cullis and his publications and conferences. She was given a platform by noted evangelist and pastor A.B. Simpson, becoming the first recording secretary of Simpson's CMA (Alexander 2006; Miskov 2012).

In 1880, Montgomery published the account of her healing, *The Prayer of Faith*, later reprinted in four languages, reaching a circulation of 40,000 by 1893. In January 1881, she began publication of her journal, *TOF*; within five years, the journal had circulation of 2,200. She would edit this monthly periodical until her death in 1946 (Miskov 2012).

Following the model practiced by Cullis and others in the US, and based on the European models of Johann Blumhardt, Dorothea Trudel, and Samuel Zeller, Montgomery opened a room of her home in Buffalo as "Faith Sanctuary." This room, and later the healing homes which she would operate, provided space for the sick to learn about faith and receive prayer (Miskov 2012). In 1882, Montgomery opened a healing home, Faith Rest Cottage, in Buffalo (Alexander 2006; Miskov 2012).

In 1891, she married the wealthy George Montgomery, and in 1891, they moved to Oakland where they founded The People's

Mission, a rescue mission; Home of Peace, the first healing home on America's west coast; as well as the Beulah Heights community, a refuge for the needy, orphans and foreign missionaries in need of rest. Shalom Training School was established for the equipping of missionaries and a church, Beulah Chapel, was founded. The Cazadero Camp Meeting outside of Oakland was established by the Montgomerys. She continued her association with Simpson and the CMA, but also became an honorary Salvation Army officer and knew William Booth personally (Alexander 2006).

George Montgomery visited the revival at Azusa Street in 1906 and testified of the Pentecostal experience. Prior to this, Montgomery had been skeptical of the new movement, as is clear in *TOF* editorials published in 1906, where she labels the insistence on glossolalia and other phenomena as "false fire." By 1907, following her husband's experience and the commendations of the movement by others, her words are still cautious. It is noteworthy that she seems to attribute what she deemed "abnormal" there as associated with race and the African-American leadership and worshipers (Alexander 2006). By July 1908, Montgomery reported her own Pentecostal experience. Following this, she embraced Pentecostalism, testifying of her experience at CMA and other meetings in various parts of the world. A Tuesday afternoon "Pentecostal meeting" was held at Beulah Heights and it was reported that orphaned children were being baptized in the Holy Spirit with the evidence of speaking in other tongues. She became interested in foreign missions in 1908 and made several missionary trips to the Far East and Mexico. Montgomery became a minister in the Assemblies of God (AG) denomination in 1917. Beulah Chapel become an AG congregation, where she served as pastor. *TOF* became a vehicle for the spread of the Pentecostal message. Reports of Pentecostal outpourings all over the world were printed in its pages on a monthly basis and articles from *TOF* were often reprinted in other Pentecostal periodicals.

Ten years before her death, in 1936, Montgomery published her autobiography, *Under His Wings*, detailing her ministry over six decades. *TOF* was continued by her daughter Faith Montgomery Berry through the 1970s.

Bibliography

Albrecht, Daniel E. 1986. "Carrie Judd Montgomery: Pioneering Contributor to Three Religious Movements." *Pneuma* 8 (2): 101–119.

Alexander, Kimberly Ervin. 2006. *Pentecostal Healing: Models of Theology and Practice*. Leiden: Brill.

Judd, Carrie. 1880. *Prayer of Faith*. New York: Fleming H. Revell Company.

Miskov, Jennifer A. 2012. *Life on Wings: The Forgotten Life and Theology of Carrie Judd Montgomery (1858–1946)*. Cleveland, TN: CPT Press.

Montgomery, Carrie Judd. 1936. *Under His Wings: The Story of My Life*. Los Angeles, CA: Stationers Corporation.

Kimberly Ervin Alexander

Morrison, J. Elmor

J. Elmor Morrison (1896–1965) was born in Manitoba, Canada. He and his father, James Morrison, were farmers in Kingston, Ontario. His mother was a Pentecostal and Elmor was a member of the Pentecostal Assemblies of Canada (PAOC). He was called for duty in the Canadian army during WWI but was imprisoned in Kingston Penitentiary for being a conscientious objector at 21 years of age. He served part of his imprisonment in solitary confinement where he studied the Bible, which became his theological training. He was a pastor of Pentecostal Faith Mission in St Catherines, Ontario and felt called to be a missionary in South China where one of his cousins, Louella Morrison, had already been serving there.

He and his wife, Laura Mae Morrison (1896–?) arrived in China in 1923 without any financial support from the church, but still gave money to the poor and hungry in Guangzhou. They formed an evangelical band with three Chinese pastors and another Canadian missionary, Verent John Russell Mills. Elmor realized the necessity to train Chinese pastors and founded Ming Tak Bible Institute in Qingyuan.

Laura came to Hong Kong (HK) to give birth to their three youngest children in the Matilda International Hospital. She raised them in HK while Elmor worked in China. He visited them every one to two months. In 1939, when the Japanese invaded China in full scale, the British officials in HK and Red Cross sent his wife and four of his children initially to Manila and then to Australia. They lived in Sydney while the eldest son was in Canada. Elmor stayed in China as he believed he could not abandon the Chinese pastors. In 1940, the Japanese bombed Darwin which prompted the family to return to Canada.

They spent three months on ships from Australia to Canada. During the one and half years of separation, Elmor moved westward to Kwunming as the Japanese advanced towards inland. The British air force flew him to Canada via Burma and India. He pastored a church in Peterborough but resigned after one year because he was going back to China after WWII.

Elmor was appointed as the superintendent of the Assemblies of God South China District. He rebuilt the ruined churches in Qingyuan and founded the Ecclesia Bible Institute (EBI) in Guangzhou. By 1947, there were about 20 students, but the communists soon arrived. The institute was moved to HK to train local and southeast Asian Pentecostals. Canadian and American missionaries took turns to run EBI.

Elmor was also dedicated to church ministry. He founded the Chuk Yuen Assembly of God with a Chinese pastor in a poor area. This church opened kindergarten, primary, and secondary schools, centres for the intellectually disabled, and elderly homes. He also regularly traveled to AG churches in remote villages which had no ordained pastors to conduct baptisms and communion.

Elmor had a stroke in HK and lost his mobility on the right side. He was unconscious for seven days then gradually recovered. He returned to Canada and passed away in Ontario in 1965. Throughout his life he was a well-respected missionary among the Chinese. A number of schools and social facilities are named after him to commemorate his pioneering work for the PAOC and devotion to the HK people.

Bibliography

Interview with Keith and Eleanor Morrison, February 20, 2010.

Miller, Thomas William. 1994. *Canadian Pentecostals: A History of the Pentecostal Assemblies of Canada*. Mississauga, ON: Full Gospel Publishing House.

Wilkinson, Michael, ed. 2009. *Canadian Pentecostalism: Transition and Transformation*. Montreal & Kingston: McGill-Queen's University Press.

Wilkinson, Michael and Linda M. Ambrose. 2020. *After the Revival: Pentecostalism and the Making of a Canadian Church*. Montreal & Kingston: McGill-Queen's University Press.

Connie Au

Mukti Revival

The Holy Spirit revival that took place during 1905–1907 at Mukti, a Christian faith mission, at Kedgaon, near Pune, Maharashtra, is the most significant Indian revival that made a global impact. Despite its distinctiveness, the Mukti Revival was disregarded in popular Pentecostal historiographical accounts until recently. This was probably because it was later interpreted as an evangelical awakening, and the interpretation of tongues-speaking as initial evidence for Spirit baptism and a missionary tool for evangelism, was not emphasized as at the Azusa Street Revival. There was also a reluctance to report to the press in the initial days. Pandita Saraswati Ramabai, a highest caste Hindu Brahman widow and convert, and her daughter Manoramabai as well as Minnie F. Abrams, a North American woman missionary to India, were the spearheads of this revival.

Mukti was founded by Ramabai to care for the widows, orphans, and other dispossessed women and girls, irrespective of their socio-religious affinity. A large population was affected by the great famines and outbreaks of plagues in western and central India. This was in addition to the socio-religious and economic plight of Indian women because of the consequences of Hindu caste system. The firsthand receivers of the revival were those less privileged Indian women and young girls.

Hearing the reports of revivals in Australia (1903) and Wales (1904–05), Ramabai longed for a similar or greater revival in India and organized a system of prayer-circles among her friends far and near. She sent Manoramabai and Abrams to Australia to study and catch the revival fire. Realizing the role of prayer, Ramabai challenged the Mukti community to focus on intense times of prayer. Seventy volunteers came forward in January 1905 to join a special daily early-morning prayer for a revival in India. The number of praying girls, known as a "praying band," gradually increased to 550 by June 1905, and started praying twice daily.

Finally, the revival fell at Mukti in June 1905, as these girls and young women began to experience manifestations of the Spirit. Bible study and prayer were characterized in the revival. It is reported that one evening while Ramabai was teaching them from John 8, the Holy Spirit fell upon them powerfully, and the girls began to pray aloud that she had to stop teaching. They began to weep bitterly and confessed their sins, and a few had visions of Jesus. Waves of prayer went over the meetings and sometimes for hours. There was a report of an appearance of flames over the girls and they attempted to throw water to douse the fire out, claiming to not realize that it was the Spirit baptism by fire. Mukti residents had several Spirit experiences such as tongues, trembling, shaking, intense confession of sins, ecstasy, falling down, clapping, shouting of praises, and exorcism. A significant feature was the extreme feeling of repentance, as there was heart-searching, agony over sin, tears, crying for pardon and cleansing, and confession. Girls were stricken down under the conviction of sin while in school or at their work. They had to suspend the lessons in the school, and both the teachers and students had similar experiences of the Spirit. Ramabai did not allow the account of the revival to be published even a month after the revival broke out because of the fear that the work of the Spirit would be hindered. Later, Christian newspapers including *The Bombay Guardian* and *The Christian Patriot* reported on the revival.

The Mukti Revival made a unique contribution to Indian Pentecostalism. The "praying bands" of young women took the revival to various places as they went to hold special meetings and conferences at schools and mission stations in Maharashtra. The revival made a long-lasting impact in various denominations, such as the Christian and Missionary Alliance, Anglican, Baptist, Friends, Methodists and Presbyterians. The revival motivated several young women to engage in evangelism, which resulted in the conversion of many. Pentecostalism was introduced in the state of Rajasthan for the first time by a Mukti woman.

The Mukti Revival is an indispensable chapter in the origins of global Pentecostalism. The writers of *The Apostolic Faith*, including William Seymour, acknowledged that the Mukti Revival preceded and further motivated Azusa Street Revival. Unlike other revivals, women played a significant role in leadership and also taking the revival throughout India. Uniquely, the Mukti Revival resulted not only in the spiritual transformation of people but also in its holistic development as it created a self-sufficient community to include a rescue mission, a hospital, schools, vocational training units, printing press, and an oil-press. Mukti became the source of inspiration for revival in Latin America, and the development of Pentecostalism in the continent. In 1907 Abrams sent a copy of her book *Baptism of the Holy Ghost and Fire* to her friend Mary Hoover and her husband Willis Collins Hoover, who were missionaries in Chili. They prayed for a similar revival in Chili, and it finally arrived in 1907.

Bibliography

Anderson, Allan. 2006. "Pandita Ramabai, the Mukti Revival and Global Pentecostalism." *Transformation* 23 (1): 37–48.
Blumhofer, Edith L. 2008. "Consuming Fire: Pandita Ramabai and the Global Pentecostal Impulse." In *Interpreting Contemporary Christianity: Global Processes and Local Identities*, edited by Ogbu U. Kalu and Alaine Low, 207–237. Grand Rapids: Eerdmans.
Burgess, Stanley. 2006. "Pandita Ramabai: A Woman for all Seasons." *Asian Journal of Pentecostal Studes* 9 (2): 183–198.
Dyer, Helen S. 1907. *Revival in India*. New York: Gospel Publishing House.
Suarsana, Yan. 2014. "Inventing Pentecostalism: Pandita Ramabai and the Mukti Revival from a Postcolonial Perspective." *PentecoStudies* 13 (2): 173–196.

Wessly Lukose

Murai, Jun

Jun Murai (村井 純; 1897–1970) was born to a Methodist family in Kagoshima on June 27, 1897. His father Kisou Murai was a Methodist minister and Jun was baptized in April 1913. Murai attended the Theological Department of Aoyama Gakuin, a Methodist school, in Tokyo from 1914. In 1918, suffering from depression and attempting to commit suicide, Murai visited his cousin, Makoto Miyoshi, a Bible woman who was working with William and Mary Taylor. The Taylors were British missionaries in Japan who had been sent by the Pentecostal Missionary Union in 1913, but later transferred to the Assemblies of God, USA (AG) in 1917. While visiting Miyoshi, Murai experienced Spirit Baptism on September 8.

In 1919, Murai attended a tent meeting in Okayama organized by J.B. Thornton, an American missionary under the Japan Evangelistic Band with the recommendation of Miyoshi. Impressed by Thornton, Murai quitted Aoyama Gakuin and started working with him with his older brother Hajime. He married Suwa Yokota, another

Bible woman of Taylors on March 5, 1919. In 1920, Murai and Suwa were sent to minister an independent church in Okayama and he was ordained in March 1921. Leaving Okayama in the spring of 1921 Murai joined the faculty of Thornton's Japan Self-Help Bible School in Kaibara, Hyogo as Dean of Evangelism. With Thornton's return home in April 1926 and the school's merger with Seisho Gakusha in Mikage, Hyogo, Murai became an independent itinerant preacher.

In 1929, Murai was invited by C.F. Juergensen, an American AG missionary, to visit his Takinogawa Church, a branch of the Japan Bible Church (JBC) in Tokyo. After that, Murai was frequently invited to speak at JBC churches in the Tokyo vicinity such as Otsuka Church. After the sudden death of its pastor Mankichi Yamanaka on June 6, 1932, an American AG missionary N.H. Barth invited Murai to pastor Otsuka Church in October 1932.

Although Murai had experienced Spirit baptism, he did not stress it much in Otsuka Church. But on July 23, 1933, this Church experienced its first major outpouring of the Holy Spirit and several people were baptized by the Spirit. After that, Murai and his congregation decided to hold consecutive prayer meetings. Murai brought the spiritual blessing to different parts of Japan and became a well-known Holy Spirit evangelist. He emphasized speaking in tongues and divine healing. Through his ministry and the circulation of his newspaper, *Seirei* (Holy Spirit), non-Pentecostal pastors and lay people came to seek Spirit baptism.

JBC had been predominantly managed by American AG missionaries, but Murai was the first Japanese minister to take the leadership position in 1937. He was elected to be the denomination's kantoku (bishop) on June 1, 1940.

In June 1941, five ministers of JBC – Jun Murai, Tsuru Nagashima, Hajime Kawasaki, Fukuzo Ohta, and Otokuma Uwai – were invited by Japan True Jesus Church (Nihon Shin Yaso Kyokai) to visit Taiwan. It was a Japanese chapter of the True Jesus Church. Through this three-week trip Murai and Uwai were strongly influenced by the spiritual fervor and the doctrines of this church. They accepted the practice of water baptism "in the name of Jesus" and were re-baptized before they left Taiwan. On the way back to Tokyo, Murai stopped at Fukuoka in Kyushu and practiced what he had learned in Taiwan. He re-baptized some Christians and held services with foot washing and communion.

However, the other three other ministers strongly disagreed with Murai and Uwai. Upon their return to Japan, they took different directions which led to the dissolution of JBC. Only Murai's Otsuka Church and few other Christians accepted Murai's new teachings. The rest of the JBC joined the United Christ Church of Japan which was founded in June 1941.

After the trip, Murai started emphasizing Spirit baptism even more and had a new revelation: the true church will come from the East, namely, Japan. On November 16, 1941, Murai held a conference with his followers and decided to start a new church. They tried to register it at the Ministry of Education the following day but failed. After negotiating with the officials for several months, their new church was legally accepted as a religious association instead of a Christian church. It was called Toshima Spirit of Jesus Church (Toshima Iesu no Mitama Kyokai) on October 15, 1942.

Murai identified seven aspects of a true church and most of them were very similar to the practices of the Japan True Jesus Church to which he appealed: 1. baptism in the Holy Name of Jesus; 2. baptism of the Holy Spirit with speaking in tongues; 3. correct communion, 4. sacrament of foot washing; 5. keeping the Sabbath; 6. laying on of hands; 7. miracles and the works of the Holy Spirit as the proofs of the true church. The Spirit of Jesus Church started as a Japanese indigenous Pentecostal group with the emphases of these doctrines and preserving Japanese traditions, such as Sosen Sai (Festival of Ancestors). Murai explained that Sosen Sai was the time to go deeper into the understanding of the spiritual world. He also taught about the vicarious baptism for the dead found in 1 Cor. 15:29.

After World War II, in the early 1950s, Murai collaborated with L.W. Coote of the Japan Apostolic Mission and Jun Nukida of the United Pentecostal Church since they all shared a common Oneness theology. However, the coalition did not last long. The rapid growth of the Spirit of Jesus Church in the post-war period surprised other Japanese Christians. They were skeptical about the group's doctrines and mission reports. Murai passed away in Tokyo on March 26, 1970. His wife (Suwa), daughter (Mieko), and son (Sumimoto) consecutively became the kantoku of the denomination.

Bibliography

Mullins, Mark R. 1990. "Japan Pentecostalism and the World of the Dead: A Study of Cultural Adaptation in Iesu no Mitama Kyokai." *Japanese Journal of Religious Studies* 17 (4): 353–374.

Suzuki, Masakazu. 2011. "The Origins and the Development of the Japan Assemblies of God: The Foreign and Japanese Workers and Their Ministries (1907 to 1975)." PhD diss., Bangor University.

Masakazu Suzuki

Music

Music, particularly congregational singing, has long been central to Pentecostal-charismatic Christianity. Since the beginnings of the movement, collective music-making has provided a way for participants to create and maintain a distinct Pentecostal identity; to express, embody, and regularize emotion within the corporate worship ; to negotiate the boundaries between the church and the broader society; and to produce social harmony among participants of diverse backgrounds.

Pentecostal music-making has been characterized by global roots and routes. The songs and styles early North American Pentecostals used in worship drew from a number of intersecting streams that included African, European, and American oral traditions, evangelical revival hymns, and commercial popular music. As David D. Daniels III notes, the African American sanctified tradition's musical practices displayed sonic retentions from African spirituality, including an emphasis on polyrhythmic complexity, call-and-response, and improvisation (Daniels 2011). These characteristics that found their way into black holiness music became disseminated broadly across boundaries of race and class in the fervor of Azusa Street and other early revivals (Alexander 2011). Pentecostals have often been more willing than other Christian groups to adopt instruments with profane associations (for instance, the saxophone during the 1920s jazz era, or the electric guitar from 1960s rock 'n' roll) into their music for worship and outreach.

Music and media have a complex and generative relationship within global Pentecostalism. Pentecostal music has been transmitted via numerous forms of communications media, including radio, recordings, television, and the internet. However, music itself also acts as a medium, as listeners infer ideas through musical style, lyrics, and the extra-musical associations and practices that often accompany it. Pentecostal groups worldwide have been adept at using music as both an affective and communicative medium, often using the commercial popular music of the day – whether the styles are regional, national, or transnational – as a potent medium for spreading or opening hearts to the full gospel message.

Pentecostals have characteristically been willing to use music despite its "secular" or "profane" origins as a medium for worship and evangelism. This has had three interrelated effects. First, Pentecostal uses of new musical genres and forms of musical media have constantly troubled the boundaries between sacred and secular music. Secondly, a willingness to adopt or adapt secular music has allowed Pentecostal musicians a disproportionate influence on broader music culture in many societies in which Pentecostalism has taken root. In North America, this influence is demonstrated by the abundance of successful popular musicians with Pentecostal backgrounds and in the nearly century-long interplay between gospel music and mainstream popular music. In parts of West Africa beginning in the 1990s, the overlap between Christian and secular popular music scenes and audiences became considerable. In the 1980s and 1990s, Ghanaian Pentecostal megachurches not only promoted recorded music but also became important spaces for live performance of popular youth styles at a time when various oppressive government policies caused the near-death of highlife music (Collins 2012). In the East African context, Jean Kidula (in Ingalls and Yong 2015) argues that the gospel music promoted heavily by Pentecostal churches was the first truly "national" popular musical style of Kenya because it garnered an inter-ethnic, national audience. In the in the 2000s decade, gospel edged out hip hop as the best-selling commercial music genre in Kenya.

Finally, and significantly, Pentecostals have not only been early adopters of new musical media, but have also initiated new musical styles and liturgical "technologies." These generative elements include new liturgical structures formed in large part by music (Ingalls 2015; Marshall 2016), musical rituals that interweave local or indigenous elements with globalized Pentecostal practices (Lange 2003; Webb 2015; Kidula in Ingalls and Yong 2015), and song repertoires designed to help singers achieve intimacy with the divine (Percy 2013; Lim and Ruth 2017).

Revivals and recordings have long been the conduits for musical transmission within as well as outside Pentecostalism. The songs created by Pentecostal and charismatic groups have frequently served as the means through which non-Pentecostal congregations have adopted Pentecostal beliefs and practices. The growth of Pentecostalism is one of the most significant factors spurring the growth of regional and national Christian popular music industries worldwide (Ingalls 2014). In the early days of the commercial recording industry in the 1920s, black Pentecostal musical pioneers recorded albums incorporating the popular music of the day, including ragtime, jazz, and blues, and thereby introducing their Pentecostal musical culture to the African American Christian community more broadly (Daniels 2011). The Toronto Blessing revival inaugurated widespread changes in the evangelical Christian music industries of both North America and the United Kingdom. Pentecostals in South America and East Africa made widespread use of radio and recordings to spread their message. Pentecostal roots run deep within recording industries created to distribute popular worship music around the world.

In the North American context, the 1960s–70s charismatic youth revival in Southern California known as the "Jesus Movement" birthed both a new form of congregational music known as "praise and worship music" or "contemporary worship music," and alongside it, the evangelical Contemporary Christian Music (CCM) recording industry (Lim and Ruth 2017). North American charismatic recording companies such as Vineyard Music (est. 1982) and Integrity's Hosanna! Music (est. 1983) produced numerous worship music recordings that appealed to churches across the denominational spectrum. As non-charismatic evangelical and mainline Protestant churches began incorporating contemporary worship music in their services, scholarly observers began to describe a process of "pentecostalization," particularly within corporate worship practices (Gladwin in Ingalls and Yong 2015). Often riding in on the wings of song were marked shifts in liturgical structure, worship practices, and the theology of worship. But these musical adoptions also produced anxiety and a reification of boundaries in some quarters as non-charismatic churches struggled with what it meant for their churches to sing songs birthed in and for Pentecostal-charismatic worship.

Music is a powerful agent of the globalization of Pentecostalism, propelled by powerful media industries on national and transnational scales. Pentecostal-charismatic church networks form important channels for the worldwide spread of songs. Praise and worship music, a pop-rock-style congregational worship music repertoire that has become the musical lingua franca of Pentecostal and evangelical Christianity worldwide, is a useful lens for examining the globalization of Pentecostal ideas and practices. This repertoire originated within and is still often promulgated by powerful Pentecostal-charismatic churches and their affiliated media brands, the most influential of which are located in the Anglophone centers of economic and cultural power (North America, the UK, and Australia). One of the most well-known and widely studied exemplars of Pentecostal musical influence is Sydney-based charismatic megachurch Hillsong Church. Music is a crucial part of Hillsong's branding strategy, and musical recording and promotion concerns structure Hillsong's annual church calendar. Hillsong's music has been adopted across the world and has become a means whereby Christians collectively perform their membership in a global Christian community.

The globalization of Pentecostal music-making has driven widespread concerns for increasing homogeneity in musical worship, and many interpret it as an evidence of Western neo-colonial imposition. Yet global Pentecostal music-making also evidences the agency of local Pentecostals in navigating these processes. Along with rupture (Oosterbaan 2015; Marshall 2016), there is sometimes continuity with past cultural traditions or affinity with other Christian traditions (Johnson in Ingalls and Yong 2015; Lange 2001; Magowan 2007). Fiona Magowan (2007) writes that the music Aboriginal Australian Pentecostals encounter through transnational Pentecostal networks embodies a mindset that is simultaneously locally rooted yet cosmopolitan. Further, local agency in processes of Pentecostal musical globalization can result in unanticipated effects: for instance, Magowan recounts that viewing an America worship music video inspired her Aboriginal Australian Pentecostal friend to begin using an indigenous instrument in worship.

Within global Pentecostalism, music-making is an agent of change and continuity, of rupture and healing, of unity and division. Though musical styles may shift and songs may come and go, music will continue to be a central means by which Pentecostal-charismatic Christians locate themselves in relation to their home societies and to the global church.

Bibliography

Alexander, Estrelda. 2011. *Black Fire: One Hundred Years of African American Pentecostalism*. Downers Grove, IL: InterVarsity Press Academic.

Collins, John. 2012. "Contemporary Ghanaian Popular Music since the 1980s." In *Hip Hop Africa: New African Music in a Globalizing World*, edited by Eric Charry, 211–233. Bloomington, IN: Indiana University Press.

Daniels, David D. III. 2011. "Navigating the Territory: Early Afro-Pentecostalism as a Movement within Black Civil Society. In *Afro-Pentecostalism: Black Pentecostal and Charismatic Christianity in History and Culture*, edited by Amos Yong and Estrelda Y. Alexander, 43–62. New York: NYU Press.

Ingalls, Monique M., and Amos Yong, eds. 2015. *The Spirit of Praise: Music and Worship in Global Pentecostal-Charismatic Christianity*. University Park, PA: Pennsylvania State University Press.

Ingalls, Monique M. 2014. "International Gospel and Christian Music." Bloomsbury 333 Sound Blog: Sample Article for *The Continuum Encyclopedia of Popular Music of the World, Volume XII: International Genres*, edited by John Shepherd and David Horn. Accessed January 16, 2019. http://333sound.com/epmow-vol-9-gospel-and-christian-popular-music/.

Lange, Barbara Rose. 2003. *Holy Brotherhood: Romani Music in a Hungarian Pentecostal Church*. Oxford: Oxford University Press.

Lim, Swee Hong, and Lester Ruth. 2017. *Lovin' on Jesus: A Concise History of Contemporary Worship*. Nashville, TN: Abingdon.

Magowan, Fiona. 2007. "Globalisation and Indigenous Christianity: Translocal Sentiments in Australian Aboriginal Christian Songs." *Identities: Global Studies in Culture and Power* 14 (4): 459–483.

Marshall, Kimberly. 2016. *Upward, Not Sunwise: Resonant Rupture in Navajo Neo-Pentecostalism*. Lincoln, NB: University of Nebraska Press.

Oosterbaan, Martijn. 2017. *Transmitting the Spirit: Religious Conversion, Media, and Urban Violence in Brazil*. University Park, PA: Pennsylvania State University Press.

Riches, Tanya, and Tom Wagner, eds. 2017. *The Hillsong Movement Examined: You Call Me Out Upon the Waters*. Cham, Switzerland: Palgrave Macmillan.

Monique Ingalls

Mysticism

The language of "mysticism" is very difficult to define for Christian theological purposes. As a result, many – including most Pentecostals – sidestep it for a number of reasons. However, that need not be the case, and in fact, it should not be for this Spirt-filled movement, for it stands to benefit significantly from being characterized as a mystical movement.

One of the oft-cited reasons for avoiding the language of mysticism is that many established religions as well as newer, alternative spiritualities have mystical dimensions or branches; therefore, the language is not distinctively Christian and as such could contribute to religious relativism. Many Pentecostals and others fear that it represents a slippery slope. Another reason is that mysticism tends to defy the kind of reasoning that Westerners in particular are prone to emphasize; as such, the language is out of step with what is often deemed conventional thinking and so "traditional" Christian theology.

Here we have a tension as to what counts as significant and worthwhile knowledge. One final reason worth mentioning for mysticism's suspect-status is that many associate it with esoteric religious experiences that are defiant of evaluation. All these reasons have some merit, but they are not defeating for mysticism's prospects in Christian discourse, much less in Pentecostal identity negotiation.

A first point of order for addressing these concerns is definitional. Mysticism in a Christian sense highlights the transformative encounter Christians have with the God of their worship. This God is specific (YHWH-Trinity) and so is the end-goal (Christ-likeness); thereby, the slippery slope toward religious relativism need not be a concern when this kind of specificity is introduced and maintained. Pentecostals for their part emphasize transformational encounters with the God of their worship as a key element of their spirituality. Not only do they believe that these encounters are possible but these have the potential to change people's lives indelibly. As to the second point, mysticism has a way of defying and exposing the limits of regnant intellectual paradigms. This could be seen as a negative feature, but it could also be cast positively. After all, any regnant paradigm has its blind-spots, things that it cannot account for and so ignores. Therefore, the work of "critical thinking" is to show these limits, usually through a means that is unexpected and so alternative. For their part, Pentecostals stand in the wake of a properly "critical tradition" of their own that exposes the limits of the metaphysically deficient intellectual environment that was spawned by modernity and the European Enlightenment. Their alternative status within their environments helps them on this score. Finally, esoteric, reason-defying experiences can be dangerous, especially when individuals assume for themselves a species of knowledge that others cannot have. For their part, Pentecostals recognize those limits at least implicitly through the communal nature of their worship. A "good" worship service for Pentecostals is one in which many are gathered together to feel and sense the presence of God in their collective midst. On each of these points, then, Pentecostalism and Christian mysticism go hand in hand. In fact, one could make the argument that Pentecostalism is a relatively recent expression of the tradition of Christian mysticism.

Insiders and outsiders to Pentecostalism have noted this point. Harvey Cox (1995, 92–93) has opined that in some respects, this movement is "closer to the most sublime forms of mysticism than are the more respectable denominations that sometimes look down on it," adding later, "It is precisely this ragtag religion from across the tracks that is now bearing the mystical torch with most vigor." Simon Chan (2000, 12), has made a sustained case for the connection, as illustrated with this particular example: "The Pentecostal-charismatic penchant for dreams and visions ... could be fruitfully explored in the light of similar phenomena in late medieval mysticism." More recently, James K.A. Smith (2010, 77, n.70) has said that in terms of its affectivity, Pentecostalism is a kind of "mystical" tradition. Despite these observations and the aforementioned connections, many Pentecostals would still resist themselves being seen as "modern-day mystics," but doing so would provide them with a number of benefits.

First, the connection between mysticism and Pentecostalism would place the latter within a larger tradition of reflection. If Christian mysticism can be stressed to be part and parcel to Christianity itself stretching back to the "holy mysteries" of the faith (the Incarnation, the Resurrection, the practices of Baptism and Eucharist, and so on) and Pentecostalism can in turn be associated with that sensibility, then Pentecostalism can rid itself of the stereotype of being a twentieth century religious fad and more so a modern-day expression of a deeply entrenched Christian inclination that has a long-running pedigree. This association with a larger tradition of reflection can aid Pentecostalism with the catechizing and developmental challenges that naturally present themselves after a century of existence.

Second, the connection between mysticism and Pentecostalism can aid the latter as a way of resisting theological and intellectual currents that work against its ethos. Many have lamented that Pentecostalism's "evangelicalization" in certain parts of the world has made it lose significant features of its identity over time, including its racial-ethnic diversity, its tradition of pacifism, its missionary fervor, its biblical hermeneutic, and so on. By actively adopting an identity that is mystical in orientation, Pentecostals can preserve some key features of its ethos, including 1) a strong belief in the possibility and power associated with encountering the God of Christian confession, 2) the sense that miracles and the transformation of earthly realities can take place, 3) the awareness that vital knowledge is not simply empirical or rational but very much operative in registers that have to be awakened and honed by God's Spirit (including in what are sometimes called "the affections"), and 4) a deep desire for God and God's kingdom that is more than simply "love" but very much a kind of all-constituting, eschatologically shaped "passion." Smith (2010, 31–47) highlights variants of these as "elements of a pentecostal worldview," and the idea of a "worldview" or cosmology turns out to be quite helpful on this score. Pentecostals inhabit a specific religious-cultural orbit that is funded not only by particular values but also a detectable intellectual framework that does not easily fit within others. In some ways, it is "premodern," "modern," "paramodern," and even "postmodern." In other words, it requires a vibrant ethos so as to perpetuate its core identity in the face of challenges that would questionably change it. For Pentecostals who worry about matters of identity and generational change, the "mystical" label may be a way forward.

Bibliography

Castelo, Daniel. 2017. *Pentecostalism as a Christian Mystical Tradition*. Grand Rapids: Eerdmans.

Chan, Simon. 2000. *Pentecostal Theology and the Christian Spiritual Tradition*. Sheffield: Sheffield Academic Press.

Cox, Harvey. 1995. *Fire from Heaven*. Reading: Addison-Wesley.

Smith, James K.A. 2010. *Thinking in Tongues*. Grand Rapids: Eerdmans.

Hollenweger, Walter. 1992. "The Critical Tradition of Pentecostalism." *Journal of Pentecostal Theology* 1 (1): 1–7.

Daniel Castelo

Nee, Watchman (Ni, Tuosheng)

Watchman Nee (Ni Tuosheng; 1903–1972) was a writer, church founder, and independent minister who was one of the most influential Christian leaders in Chinese Christianity. Nee synthesized and reshaped key concepts in almost every area of Christian thought and practice, including the Bible, the Trinity, human nature, the church, ethics, and authority. He laid the foundation for Chinese theological discussion for generations. At the same time, Nee's accessible writings found significant worldwide reception. It is possible that among Chinese thinkers, only Confucius, Laozi (Daoism), and Mao Zedong have reached larger non-Chinese audiences.

Both Nee's paternal and maternal grandparents were Christians, and he was born and raised in the center of the sino-foreign Protestant establishment of Fuzhou. His family was educated in elite missionary schools and maintained connections with important foreign and domestic Christian figures. The family was politically active and Nee probably harbored political ambitions before he and his mother were converted by the itinerant revivalist, Dora Yu.

After his conversion, Nee and his mother were re-baptized by immersion by Margaret Barber, an English missionary living nearby. Mentored by Barber, Nee and a small group of fellow students at Trinity College (Fuzhou) led a revival where they converted hundreds. Most of the revival leaders wanted to focus on local evangelism. Nee, however, had a bigger vision that included churches throughout China and beyond, developed according to his understanding of the Bible. Nee thus left Fuzhou for Shanghai in 1924.

Once on his own, Nee focused on preaching, writing, and publishing. His intellectual capacity was quickly advanced through his deep engagement with the Bible and English Christian literature. His favored the dispensational system of the Plymouth Brethren and the self-denial spirituality found in devotional writers associated with the Keswick Convention. All these influenced Barber as well. He developed his teachings on promised spiritual victory which became the basis of tightly knitted communities.

In an atmosphere of anti-western sentiment, Nee implicitly believed that non-westerners could spearhead a return to apostolic truth and practice. Within a few years, his periodicals had thousands of regular readers, mostly within the Chinese-speaking world. During a life-threatening bout of tuberculosis, he wrote his longest work, *The Spiritual Man*, which systematically explained his view of spirituality and humanity as part of the consistent message of the entire Bible.

Upon his recovery, he published even more prolifically and held international conferences, joining disparate congregations that spanned in China and the Chinese diaspora together. These groups began to see themselves as a cohesive new fellowship, based on Nee's interpretation of Christianity, with the basic organizing principle of one church in each city. Notably, Witness Lee embraced Nee's ministry and energetically spread these teachings in north China.

In 1934, Nee married Charity Chang, a childhood friend. Nee's congregations also made contact with an international network of "closed" Plymouth Brethren who invited him to Europe and North America. In his travels, he impressed audiences and gave messages in English, which were later edited and printed. His international reputation began to develop.

Upon his return, China was in the middle of the Sino-Japanese War. Nee went into business to lend monetary support to his "co-workers" – travelling evangelists suffering extreme privation during the war. Probably because of this decision, Nee was excommunicated by the elders in Shanghai, who might have felt that Nee had contradicted his previous stance on living by faith, or, trusting God to take care of finances.

In 1948, after six years of sparse ministerial activity, Nee was restored to public leadership. Especially on the eve of Communist victory, Christian groups flocked to Nee as they thought that even though he was influenced by the West, he was relatively free of western influences. Nee, however, was targeted and arrested in 1952. He was imprisoned until his death in 1972. The truth of the politically-motivated charges remains hard to ascertain.

In China, the congregations that followed his ministry grew and shrank along with the general fortunes of Christianity under the harsh political climate. Still, Nee's followers stressed church practice more than other Chinese Christians. In the post-Reform and Opening-Up period, Nee's emphasis on local initiative has pushed grassroots mobilization and groups that follow him to maintain a tenuous autonomy, wavering between joining the Three-Self Patriotic Movement and forging more independent identities.

Outside China, Nee's well-edited and well-translated publications also spread rapidly. Especially during the Cold War, Nee had the paradoxical appeal of appearing to be both a Christian martyr and a departure from traditional western Christendom. A number of his followers, especially Lee, established churches globally and continued to adapt and spread Nee's legacy.

Nee's ability to write clearly and persuasively and his strict biblical grounding seemed to offer a comprehensive understanding of God's plan for the individual, the church, and the universe. He distilled and modernized the teachings of a significant group of Chinese Christians and adapted an Anglo-American evangelical and Pentecostal heritage for a wide variety of contemporary audiences.

Bibliography

Chow, Alexander. 2013. *Theosis, Sino-Christian Theology and the Second Chinese Enlightenment: Heaven and Humanity in Unity.* New York: Palgrave Macmillan.

Kinnear, Angus. 1978. *Against the Tide: The Story of Watchman Nee.* Wheaton, Ill.: Tyndale House Pub.

Lee, Joseph Tse-Hei. 2005. "Watchman Nee and the Little Flock Movement in Maoist China." *Church History* 74 (1): 68–96.

Lian, Xi. 2010. *Redeemed by Fire: The Rise of Popular Christianity in Modern China.* New Haven, CT: Yale University Press.

Xing, Fuzeng. 2005. *Fandi, aiguo, shuling ren: Ni Tuosheng yu Jidutu juhuichu yanjiu.* Hong Kong: Christian Study Centre on Chinese Religion and Culture.

Paul Chang

Neo-Pentecostalism

From a century's retrospect, the global Pentecostal-Charismatic movement displays a complex pattern, rendering it difficult to settle on an adequate taxonomy and terminology (Anderson 2010). Until recently, Pentecostal-Charismatic historiography was largely based on North American developments. The twentieth-century history was thought to fall into three phases – (1) a "Pentecostal" era (later called "classical Pentecostal"), beginning around 1901, expanding through the Azusa Street Revival in Los Angeles (1906–1909), and issuing in "classical Pentecostal" denominations (Assemblies of God USA, Church of God in Christ, etc.); (2) a "Charismatic" era, beginning around 1960, and affecting historic Protestant churches (Episcopal, Lutheran, Presbyterian, Methodist, Baptist, etc.) and the Roman Catholic Church, cresting in the 1970s, and then becoming less visible in the North American context (though arguably not elsewhere); and (3) a "Third Wave," beginning in the 1980s and including evangelical Christians who became "pentecostalized" (e.g., the Association of Vineyard Churches) as well as independent groups practicing spiritual gifts (e.g., the prosperity-oriented or Word-Faith churches).

Even in the North American context, this notion of defining Pentecostalism in "three waves" is highly debatable. The framework is much less plausible within other global regions. Complicating the terminological situation still further is that some of the literature published in the 1970s through 1980s used the term "neo-pentecostal" to refer to the mainline charismatic renewal or the so-called "second wave," as just noted. Moreover, certain contemporary authors use "neo-charismatic" in place of "neo-pentecostal." The standard, current nomenclature applies the term "neo-pentecostal" in diverse international contexts to charismatic churches and movements associated neither with the early 1900s Pentecostal revival movements, nor with the historic Catholic or Protestant churches in their pentecostalized manifestations. Anglo-European examples of neo-pentecostal megachurches would include Kingsway International Christian Centre in greater London (led by the Nigerian-born Matthew Ashimolowo), Embassy of the Blessed Kingdom of God for All Nations in Kiev, Ukraine (led by the Nigerian-born Sunday Adelaja), and *Livets Ord* (Word of Life Church) in Uppsala, Sweden (founded by Ulf Ekman, who was trained at Rhema Bible Institute in Tulsa, Oklahoma, USA; Coleman 2000).

Because of differing local adaptations, neo-pentecostalism is not one thing but many things. Even those charismatic groups that have come under the strong influence of North American megachurch pastors and televangelists have almost always adapted the message or training that they received, and so scholars today acknowledge North American influences yet generally reject the idea that neo-pentecostalism throughout the world is simply a North American or US export. In the phenomenon that some call "reverse globalization," developments originating in charismatic circles in Africa, Asia, Latin America, and Oceania are transmitted and adopted in North American or Anglo-European contexts, and so it is no longer possible to argue that any one global region functions as a preeminent, diffusive center for new ideas or practices throughout the entire, global, Spirit-filled movement.

In reference to neo-pentecostalism in sub-Saharan Africa, J. Kwabena Asamoah-Gyadu (2015) noted that a charismatization of the broader African Christian landscape led to the rise of independent congregations in the 1970s and 1980s as an alternative to the historic denominationalism of the mission churches. North American developments proved catalytic in Africa, including the trans-denominational fellowship known as the Full Gospel Businessmen's Fellowship International (FGBMFI), the Christian media culture of the USA, and the message of the prosperity gospel. Benson Idahosa of Nigeria, the German evangelist Reinhard Bonnke, and Nevers Mumba of Zambia encouraged the earlier spread of neo-pentecostalism in Africa. The neo-pentecostal churches interpret salvation holistically, as including not only eternal life, but also healing, employment, and human biological fruitfulness. They express an oral theology embodied in locally-composed choruses and testimonies of deliverance, and a gender ideology that acknowledges the leadership of women. Urban, megachurches appeal to an upwardly mobile youth, with worship styles that are exuberant and emotionally-laden, with innovative uses of modern media technologies, and an internationalist ethos that is evident in the names, symbolism, and travels of the congregational leaders, along with the establishment of their own transnational ministry networks.

Neo-pentecostal church leaders preach motivational messages that address the concerns of upwardly-mobile people, who seek to seize social, political, and economic opportunities, and apply social and biblical principles to realize success. Earlier, classical pentecostals focused on holy living, warned against the dangers of materialism, and preached Christ's imminent return to judge the world. Yet neo-pentecostals no longer focus chiefly on purity of belief, moral rigor, or separation from the world. Their understanding of salvation is highly experiential, and highlights God's ability to provide material things here and now. The preacher is often expected to serve as a model of the tangible, redemptive uplift. Asamoah-Gyadu notes that while "the prosperity gospel ... is often justifiably criticized for its materialistic orientation ... these newer pneumatic movements have also been keenly embraced because amidst the socio-economic challenges of modern Africa, many young people have found this message personally empowering and spiritually nourishing" (Asamoah-Gyadu, 111). This observation applies in other global regions as well.

Korean pastor David Yonggi Cho's idea of a "triple blessing" – including salvation, health, and prosperity – encapsulated a generalized neo-pentecostal message. Until a financial scandal struck in 2013–14, Cho's million-member Yoido Full Gospel Central Church in Seoul, South Korea, was something of a flagship congregation for global neo-pentecostalism. Regarding neo-pentecostalism in Latin America, Gerardo Corpeño comments that the movement is marked by "hierarchical organization with authority centered in the pastor ... [and] administration modeled on the business world, and megachurches that exploit television" (Corpeno 2011, 55). More perhaps than elsewhere, Latin American neo-pentecostalism emphasizes the centrality of the pastor. Some but not all neopentecostal congregations embrace a "five-fold" ministry concept based on Ephesians 4:11–12 – linked to the 1940s Latter Rain Revival in Canada – and affirm the ministry offices of apostles, prophets, evangelists, pastors, and teachers (while some combine pastors with teachers to yield a "four-fold" pattern). Congregations assigning an "apostolic" anointing, calling, or title to their leaders generally affirm a high level of authority for such persons – though there are significant variations (Kay 2007).

The evolution of Spirit-filled Christianity in Brazil has been especially complex. Pentecostalism arrived in Brazil in 1910, had only modest success initially, but then was followed by a second wave movement in the 1950s and 1960s, and a third wave in the 1970s and 1980s. Typifying the Brazilian third wave is the neo-pentecostal Universal Church of the Kingdom of God (*Igreja Universal do Reino de Deus*, or IURD), founded by Edir Macedo in 1977. Macedo lived in the USA from 1986 to 1989, where he selectively assimilated American religious models. Whille IURD reflects a pietistic emphasis on constant communion with God, it is nonetheless less legalistic and more liberal in regard to female clothing and adornment. IURD members reject the earlier Brazilian pentecostal reliance on a "clothing code" as gatekeeper for the community. Because of its open-ended cultural style, the IURD attracts a wider range of social types than the classical-penecostal Assemblies of God (AG) in Brazil.

IURD preaching stresses prosperity, health, the family, and liberation from demonic oppression. Some members undergo multiple exorcisms to gain full deliverance. Paul Freston comments: "The traditional AG ethic is that of primitive capitalism, a long and arduous struggle to reach modest respectability. The Universal's is a religious version of the yupple ethic, of rapid enrichment through daring risks" (Freston 1995, 131). Such daring risk-taking and an entrepreneurial ethos are evident in the expansionist policies of the IURD in different spheres of Brazilian society and beyond. This includes the acquisition of television and radio stations, a daily newspaper, printing press, construction company, furniture factory, small bank, and global church-planting enterprise. The basic principle of the IURD's prosperity teaching is the need to give generously to the church, so that God will return the investment with interest. The stress on financial giving with a view to future prosperity, and the reliance on deliverance or exorcistic practices to break free of hindrances and to attain one's full potential, are distinctive features of the IURD and of global neo-pentecostalism generally.

Bibliography

Anderson, Allan. 2010. "Varieties, Taxonomies, and Definitions." In *Studying Global Pentecostalism: Theories and Methods*, edited by Allan Anderson, 13–29. Berkeley, CA: University of California Press.

Anderson, Allan, and Edmond Tang, eds. 2005. *Asian and Pentecostal: The Charismatic Face of Christianity in Asia*. Oxford, UK: Regum Books International / Baguio, City, Philippines: APTS Press.

Asamoah-Gyadu, J. Kwabena. 2015. "Pentecostalism and the Transformation of the African Christian Landscape." In *Pentecostalism in Africa: Presence and Impact of Pneumatic Christianity in Postcolonial Societies*, edited by Martin Lindhardt, 100–114. Leiden: Brill.

Coleman, Simon. 2000. *The Globalisation of Charismatic Christianity: Spreading the Gospel of Prosperity*. Cambridge, UK: Cambridge University Press.

Corpeño, Gerardo. 2011. "Neopentecostalismo emergente: Pistas para el future de iglesias neopentecostales jóvenes." *Kairós* 48: 55–78.

Freston, Paul. 1995. "Pentecostalism in Brazil: A Brief History." *Religion* 25 (2): 119–133.

Kay, William K. 2007. *Apostolic Networks in Britain: New Ways of Being Church*. Milton Keynes, UK: Paternoster.

McClymond, Michael J. 2014. "Charismatic Renewal and Neo-Pentecostalism: From American Origins to Global Permutations." In *The Cambridge Companion to Pentecostalism*, edited by Cecil M. Robeck and Amos Yong, 31–51. Cambridge, UK: Cambridge University Press.

Michael McClymond

Netherlands

The history of Pentecostalism in the Netherlands displays the importance of transnational ties and influences from its early beginnings in 1907. The small Pentecostal movement until the 1950s, gained tremendous momentum after the visits of foreign healing evangelists like T.L. Osborn. Until the 1980s, Dutch Pentecostalism could be distinguished by three main groups: the 'classic' Pentecostals aligned with the

American Assemblies of God, the neo-Pentecostals, influenced by the faith movement and Indonesian Pentecostal churches as a result the independence of Indonesia from the Netherlands.

Influenced by the Pentecostal movement emerged the Dutch Charismatic Renewal movement (CWN) in the 1970s. In spite of its ecumenical character in the beginning, a catholic charismatic renewal movement has gone its own way. The CWN include mainline protestants and Old Catholics. It is a small but active movement which supports a special chair for charismatic theology at the Vrije Universiteit Amsterdam.

Since the 1980s, new Pentecostal denominations from abroad entered the Netherlands like the Foursquare Church, New Frontiers and Victory Outreach. The so-called 'Third Wave' movement, associated with John Wimber, was introduced in the early 1990s. This resulted in the establishment of several Dutch Vineyard churches.

In the year 2002 the classical and the new or neo Pentecostal denominations merged in the establishing of the VPE (United Pentecostal and Gospel Assemblies). This encouraged other churches to join the national body. The same year a special chair for Pentecostal Studies was established at the Vrije Universiteit Amsterdam.

A more recent trend is the increasing influence of Pentecostal megachurches from other parts of the world like the Hillsong church from Australia. Some churches seek renewal and innovation by reforming their liturgy according to formats of megachurches. Others join networks of international megachurches, based on an understanding of apostolic leadership and spiritual covering. At the same time, international Pentecostal megachurches have successfully established satellite churches in the Netherlands.

A second trend is the rise of apostolic networks. Through conferences, online media, courses and their music – Jesus Culture, Bethel from Redding California has become a prominent revivalist center not only for Pentecostals but also for an evangelical renewal movement within the Protestant church of the Netherlands (PKN). This points to a third trend namely the charismatization of the protestant tradition in the Netherlands. The decline of Protestant churches has led to a rapprochement between mainline churches and Pentecostal churches and an increased attention for the Holy Spirit, and practices like healing and prophecy. The charismatic theology developed by the charismatic renewal movement enhances the dialogue between the two denominations. A smaller protestant Calvinist denomination introduced the charismatic renewal movement New Wine from the UK after the turn of the century. This growing movement promotes John Wimber's legacy within the boundaries of Calvinistic Protestantism.

A fourth trend is the presence of Pentecostal megachurches from Africa and Latin America. In spite of their zeal for reverse mission they are mainly reaching a migrant audience. Next to these megachurches from the South, a variety of independent and networked Pentecostal migrant churches are present in the Netherlands, among many of Ghanaian and Nigerian descent.

Bibliography

Kay, William K., Kees Slijkerman, Raymond Pfister, and Cornelis van der Laan. 2011. "Pentecostal Theology and Catholic Europe." In *European Pentecostalism*, edited by William K. Kay and Anne E. Dyer, 313–331. Leiden: Brill.

Klaver, Miranda. 2019. "The Spirit of the Supernatural: The Rise of Apostolic Networks in the Netherlands." In *The Spirit is Moving: New Pathways in Pneumatology*, edited by Gijsbert van den Brink, Eveline van Staalduine-Sulman and Maarten Wisse, 346–362. Leiden: Brill.

Van der Laan, Cornelis. 2011. "The development of Pentecostalism in Dutch Speaking Countries." In *European Pentecostalism*, edited by William K. Kay and Anne E. Dyer, 85–112. Leiden: Brill.

Miranda Klaver

Networks

In the last three decades, the advent of digital communications technologies has created new ways for leaders of all types (religious, political, business) to organize people around a common goal. The ability of people and groups to communicate easily and quickly over great distances has increased the capacity of networks to mobilize people and resources outside of the structure of formal organizations. Thus, they retain their ability to adapt, experiment and innovate without the rules and constraints of formal bureaucracies (Castells 2000). The coordination of a large, decentralized global network of actors outside of formal organizations is now possible across the world and Pentecostalism is instructive for understanding this form of religion.

New Pentecostal and Charismatic leaders are taking advantage of this digital revolution to organize networks of like-minded leaders on a global scale. This led Christerson and Flory (2017) to document the emergence of what they call Independent Network Charismatic (INC) Christianity. They distinguish this networked form of Pentecostal/Charismatic Christianity from previous iterations with the following traits:

1) They do not seek to build a "movement" or franchise affiliated congregations using a particular name.

2) They are not primarily focused on building congregations in the traditional sense, but rather seek to influence the beliefs and practices of believers regardless of congregation or affiliation, including those who are not affiliated with any congregation or religious group.

3) They seek to transform society as a whole rather than saving individual souls and building up the church.

4) Instead of being formally organized into a "movement" or "denomination" the various leaders and ministries in this category are highly connected by networks of cooperation.

Most INC leaders are heavily invested in the idea that the role of apostle – meaning independent leaders with the kind of influence and authority that Weber called charismatic authority – continues to be a key element of the growth of Charismatic Christianity worldwide. In fact, many Charismatic Christians believe that the neglect of apostolic leadership has hindered the growth of Christianity in the past and that the rediscovery of the apostle's role is essential for a new global revival. The network form of governance allows apostles to collaborate together on specific projects, conferences, and events and multiply their followers and influence without the restrictions of forming formal organizations. Digital technology allows them to organize followers on a global scale while maintaining the ability to experiment with beliefs and practices, unhindered by the oversight of boards, presbyteries, denominations, and seminaries.

Miller and Yamamori (2007) in their analysis of global Pentecostalism observe that many of the fastest growing sectors of

Pentecostalism in the world are not part of a formal denomination. Instead they tend to associate with networks of like-minded independent charismatic leaders. William Kay (2007, 20) documents the emergence of apostolic networks in Britain, which he describes as "centered around the guiding ministry of an apostle" operating outside of traditional denominations. According to Kay (20), "There are no time honored procedures or traditions. Nor is there a bureaucratic or legal basis for the network; everything is vested in the apostle and the charismata of the apostle." Kay concludes that these networks will continue to grow while traditional denominations decline and speculates that these networks may ultimately replace institutions and alter the religious landscape, giving new life and an energized capacity for the expansion of Pentecostalism. Andrew Lord (2012) makes the case that network structures have always been particularly well suited to Pentecostal theology and practice, particularly where movements of leaders are led by the Spirit to connect and collaborate in a mission to expand their followers outside of formal organizations. Lord's theological – ecclesiastical work links the emergence of networks to the distinctive beliefs and practices of Pentecostalism.

A networked structure also allows charismatic leaders some freedom to do what they do best: inspire people through their heroic acts, innovative thinking, and ability to access supernatural forces to produce the miraculous. Independent charismatic leaders are using networks to solve the problem of sustaining a large movement. Instead of a single charismatic leader creating a bureaucratic-legal organization, groups of charismatic leaders are forming a decentralized network that is not dependent on any one leader. Thus when one leader dies or loses his or her following for some reason, his or her followers can simply migrate to another leader in the network – moving from one charismatic apostle to another. New apostles are regularly incorporated into the network, bringing new energy and followers of their own, so that, over time, one generation of apostles in the network is replaced by younger apostles.

In a network structure, the sources of funds are multiplied beyond individual church donations by regular members and includes other sources of revenue from podcasts, conferences, books, and music. The cost of maintaining the network is much lower than the expenses required for maintaining a formal congregation and/or denomination. This frees up resources to experiment with new projects and to pay high-profile individual leaders. In other words, more funding can go into activities that draw new followers, while much less is spent on staffing and running programs for local congregations.

Christerson and Flory (2017) conclude that the current structure of the religious economy rewards religious movements organized through networks of independent leaders rather than through formal congregations and denominations. They suggest that INC Christianity is poised to grow faster than other groups into the future, and that in general, religious groups that organize around networks will grow faster than those organized around formal denominations.

Bibliography

Castells, Manuel. 2000. *The Rise of the Network Society: The Information Age: Economy Society and Culture*. Second Edition. West Sussex, UK: Wiley.

Christerson, Brad and Richard Flory. 2017. *The Rise of Network Christianity: How Independent Leaders and Changing the Religious*

Landscape. New York: Oxford University Press.

Kay, William. 2007. *Apostolic Networks in Britain*. Milton Keynes, UK: Paternoster.

Lord, Andy. 2012. *Network Church: A Pentecostal Ecclesiology Shaped by Mission*. Leiden: Brill.

Miller, Donald and Tetsunao Yamamori. 2007. *Global Pentecostalism: The New Face of Christian Social Engagement*. Berkeley: University of California Press.

Wilkinson, Michael. 2016. "Charismatic Christianity and the Role of Networks: Catch the Fire and the Revival Alliance." *Pneuma* 38 (1/2): 33–49.

Brad Christerson

New Zealand

Pentecostalism in New Zealand is a diverse movement, shaped by both global processes and local particularities. Classical Pentecostalism in New Zealand is most often traced to the visits of British healing evangelist Smith Wigglesworth in 1922 and 1924, although the success of the Wigglesworth campaigns did not occur in a vacuum. Rather, there was a convergence of several factors including revivalist sentiments shaped by the Great Awakening, the influence of the Keswick movement and holiness tradition, and a growing fascination with divine healing. This interest in divine healing was further fuelled by a general uncertainty that had emerged after the significant loss of life during World War One and a widespread influenza epidemic in 1918. In this context, Wigglesworth's arrival in 1922 was enthusiastically received and his campaigns drew thousands of attendees resulting in more than 2,000 conversions to Christ and 800 baptized in the Spirit.

Although Wigglesworth himself had little interest in establishing a formal movement, efforts were made by local figures to coalesce various prayer groups and nascent pentecostal communities into a centralized movement. This resulted in the formation of the Wellington City Mission under Henry Roberts, which soon became the New Zealand Evangelical Mission, before being officially established as the Pentecostal Church of New Zealand (PCNZ) in 1924. Despite the enthusiasm of early pentecostal adherents in New Zealand, however, the fledgling movement struggled in the years to follow. Internal disagreements and divisions over several decades led to the formation of a number of different denominations including the Assemblies of God (AG), the Apostolic Church, Christian Revival Crusade and the Elim Church of New Zealand as well as some Latter Rain churches and various independent pentecostal congregations. The movement remained small and largely sectarian for several decades and by 1960 there were only 54 pentecostal churches in the entire country, almost all of which had less than 100 members.

It was in the early 1960s, however, that pentecostalism began to grow. The rising prominence of the evangelicalism in North America, as well as a resurgence of interest in healing in the years following World War Two fostered an environment receptive to revivalist and experiential spirituality. Moreover, the social upheaval of the 1960s, despite being associated with an apparent declining morality, emphasised experience and a growing distrust of institutional authority; these were conditions for which pentecostal spirituality was well-suited. Pentecostal evangelists, such as Rob Wheeler and Ron Coady – who had been shaped by the spirituality and theology of the Latter Rain movement that emerged in Saskatchewan, Canada in the 1940s and 1950s – began to hold revival and healing meetings throughout the country. Throughout the first half of the 1960s more than 60 Latter Rain churches were planted up and down New Zealand, emphasising healing, evangelism and Spirit baptism, along with particular Latter Rain characteristics such as singing in the Spirit, the laying on of hands, an intense restorationism and a resolute anti-denominationalism. For some years the Classical Pentecostal denominations looked upon the Latter Rain churches with distrust, but Frank Houston's appointment as the Superintendent of the AG movement in 1966 along with the more inclusive attitude of notable Latter Rain leader Peter Morrow led to an increasing openness between those two movements in particular.

The Latter Rain churches would eventually move beyond their fierce anti-denominationalism and become known as the New Life Churches of New Zealand in 1988; a movement that now has more than 80 churches nationwide. The AG had also begun to grow under Houston's leadership, and during his tenure (from 1966–1977) the movement grew from 26 churches to more than 80. It is this Latter Rain spirituality, albeit institutionalised over time, that is one of the notable features of New Zealand pentecostalism and its influence can still be felt through the profound impact of the globally influential pentecostal worship music that has emerged from Australasia. Altogether, the rapid change of landscape in the 1960s and 1970s saw Pentecostalism move from a fringe and sectarian movement to an important component of New Zealand Christianity. Along with this changing reality came a new sense of self-understanding, especially for Classical Pentecostals. No longer were they a small group on the margins awaiting Christ's return; they had come to see themselves as wielding the potential of religious, social, and political power.

During the same period of time as pentecostal and charismatic groups experienced this significant growth, New Zealand was also undergoing a notable demographic shift. In the 1960s and 1970s New Zealand had significant demand for low-skills labour in the larger cities and, as a small nation in the South Pacific, encouraged migration from the Pacific Islands. Additional changes to New Zealand's immigration law in 1987 would also open New Zealand to increased migration from Asia and other regions. The impact of these changes can be seen in the Assemblies of God denomination in particular. By 2014 there were more non-European churches in the movement then there were churches led by European pastors.

New Zealand pentecostalism has also been shaped in uniquely local ways through its relationship with Māori, the indigenous people of New Zealand. In the first half of the twentieth century Māori were often living in rural areas and many had rejected institutional Christianity after the rapid influx of settlers, the taking of Māori land and the deleterious impact of colonization. In contrast, the early years of the pentecostal movement were focused on the renewal of a largely non-Māori Christian constituency located in urban centres. This being the case, early pentecostal engagement with Māori was often minimal. Furthermore, when pentecostals did connect with Māori, they often failed to encourage indigenous leadership and were guilty of demonizing Māori culture and ethnicity. Of all the denominations, the Apostolic Church held the most attraction for Māori, likely due to both their empowerment of Māori leaders and their emphasis on prophets; a feature that appears to have resonated with aspects of the Māori prophetic tradition. Although the Māori constituency in the Apostolic Church has diminished since the 1990s, this is largely due to a Māori former Apostolic pastor, Brian Tamaki, leaving the denomination and starting the predominantly Māori network of Destiny Churches. These churches in particular, have expressed a unique fusion of African American pentecostalism and prosperity teaching, an emphasis on Māori culture and identity, and a nationally contentious political ambition.

In recent years, pentecostalism has continued to diversify. Many of the classical Pentecostal denominations have continued to grow, and a significant number of independent pentecostal churches have emerged since the 1980s. Of these, the church-growth influenced neo-pentecostal megachurches in New Zealand are the most notable and in many respects they exemplify a continuation and amplification of the earlier tendency to embrace local and transnational networks, rather than simply join local denominations. These churches are often connected to networks of 'like-minded' pentecostal churches and globalised expressions are localized into the particularities of the New Zealand context. In a different but related way, churches composed of migrants from countries such as South Korea are much more likely to attach to movements in their country of origin rather than to local denominational organisations on the ground in New Zealand. Thus, the present reality of pentecostalism(s) in New Zealand is rapid diversification and heterogeneity among pentecostal groups, even as the impact of globalizing forces influence pentecostal practices such as worship in similar ways.

Bibliography

Clark, Ian G. 2007. *Pentecost At the Ends of the Earth: the History of the Assemblies of God in New Zealand (1927–2003)*. Blenheim: Christian Road Ministries.

Frost, Michael J. 2018. *The Spirit, Indigenous Peoples and Social Change: Māori and a Pentecostal Theology of Social Engagement*. Leiden: Brill.

Knowles, Brett. 2014. *Transforming Pentecostalism: The Changing Face of New Zealand Pentecostalism, 1920–2010*. Lexington, KY: Emeth Press.

Morrison, Hugh, Lachy Paterson, Brett Knowle,s and Murray Rae, eds. 2012. *Mana Māori and Christianity*. Wellington: Huia Publishers.

Worsfold, James E. 1974. *A History of the Charismatic Movements in New Zealand: Including a Pentecostal Perspective and a Breviate of the Catholic Apostolic Church in Great Britain*. Bradford UK: Julian Literature Trust.

Michael Frost

Nicaragua

Nicaragua generally shares a similar history of Pentecostalism as its Central American neighbors. However, the 1979 Sandinista Revolution and subsequent current events have created a unique set of opportunities and challenges for Pentecostalism. Similar to the rest of Latin America, Nicaragua is historically Roman Catholic due to Spanish colonialism in the Western half of the country. The Atlantic Coast has a historical Protestant presence due to English colonialism, Moravian missions, and migration of freed slaves of African descent. Protestantism developed on the Pacific side following a military coup led by José Santos Zelaya who put an end to the Conservative government's pro-Catholic policies in 1893. Zelaya's liberal government implemented a new constitution with a lay state and freedom of religion for non-Catholic groups in 1894.

What followed is the development of denominations like the Central American Mission (1901), Assemblies of God (1912), Baptists (1917), Apostolics (1918), Church of Christ (1928), Nazarenes (1943), Church of God (1951), United Pentecostal Evangelical Mission (1954) and other evangelical denominations. Most were a relatively small sector of the general population until the latter half of the twentieth century. In 1900 Protestants represented 1.2 percent of the population, growing to 5.6 percent in 1970, and 8.4 percent in 1980 (Barrett 1982). Among evangelicals, Pentecostals are an increasingly higher percentage. In 1965 only 20 percent of evangelicals were Pentecostal, increasing to 73 percent in 1982 (Zub 1992, 40).

The Sandinista Revolution was a major socio-political event that provoked varying reactions from evangelicals generally, and Pentecostals particularly. A certain sector of evangelicals supported the Revolution, which not only toppled the 43-year Somoza dictatorship, but it also challenged the Roman Catholic oligarchy. Religion became part of the ideological battle ground in Nicaragua, and the larger Cold War conflict. Unlike the communist revolution in Cuba in 1959, the Second Vatican Council and the emergence of Latin American liberation theology opened the door for Christians to interpret scripture in light of the signs of the times and participate politically in the revolutionary process. "An interdenominational retreat of Pentecostal and Evangelical pastors immediately following the Revolution in October 1979 declared: "We give thanks to our Father God for the victory of the Nicaraguan people and its instrument of freedom, the Sandinista National Liberation Front" (Zub 1992, 40). The Council of Protestant Churches in Nicaragua (CEPAD), whose participation reflects the ecumenical spirit of many Nicaraguan Pentecostals, took a pro-government position in the years immediately following the triumph of the revolution.

On the other hand, evangelicals reacted against the leftist government through both apolitical and overt political opposition. The religious right in the United States led by figures such as Pat Robertson and the Christian Broadcasting Network supported evangelical opposition to the Sandinistas with ideological and financial contributions around $2 million per year to the *Contras* under the name of "Operation Blessing" (Diamond 2015). Phil Derstine of Gospel Crusade, Inc. delivered spiritual and humanitarian aid to the Contras in the 1980s with the support of Oliver North. Evangelist Jimmy Swaggart hosted three-day evangelistic crusade in the Plaza of the Revolution in 1988 and had an audience with Daniel Ortega. In the years following the Sandinista Revolution and the ensuing Contra war, there was tremendous religious fervor resulting in the growth of evangelicals from 8.4 percent in 1980 to 11.4 percent in 1990.

Following the defeat of the Sandinistas in the 1990 national elections a series of neo-liberal governments assumed power and attempted to reassert the central role of the Roman Catholic Church. Pentecostal worship style also influenced Catholics and the Pew Research Center reported in 2014 that 45 percent of Nicaraguan Catholics self-reported as "charismatic." Daniel Ortega was re-elected in 2006 and is presently in his third successive term becoming a very polarizing figure – especially among Pentecostals. Evangelicals have not been averse to politics and have formed many political parties, for instance the *Partido de Justicia Nacional* (National Justice Party) or *Camino Cristiano* (Christian Path), under the belief that the country could resolve its problems under an evangelical government.

While some Pentecostals were favorable toward the revolution, others opposed, and a third sector were apolitical and espoused a premillennial theology seeing the church as a refuge. In response to this growth the Catholic bishops accused evangelicals of being foreign. The Catholic-Evangelical divide became even more evident during the April 2018 uprising against a social security tax where Catholic priests supported the protesters and more than 300 people died. Among the dead were Pentecostal pastor, Óscar Velásquez Pavón, his wife and four children when his house was burned. Different reports estimate that between two-thirds and 85 percent of evangelicals are Pentecostal (Pew Research 2014). Six of the 10 largest non-Catholic churches in 2000 were Pentecostal. Especially strong among the poor, in some marginalized neighborhoods, Pentecostals make up as much as 50 percent of the population.

Around 2000 neo-Pentecostal groups began to form with a tendency toward the prosperity gospel, spiritual warfare, the apostolic movement, and contemporary prophets. Neo-Pentecostal churches, such as Comunidad Hosanna, Rios de Agua Viva and Centro Cristiano, using Brazillian style "cinema-churches" experienced rapid growth with social ministries, radio, and television programing. Their theology emphasized a liturgy of praise with contemporary music, adoration and dance. Music ministry is central as an evangelistic strategy transmitting the message through the songs for the conversion of non-believers. Images of spiritual warfare in the struggle between right and wrong are prominent throughout the service. The liturgy also promotes the prosperity gospel of material benefits for accepting Jesus Christ as savior.

In Nicaragua, evangelicalism is increasingly synonymous with Pentecostalism, but it is fragmented into 220 denominations and 133 independent churches. The Assemblies of God is the largest with 1,100 churches and over 500,000 members. The remaining portion are historical Protestant denominations such as the Central American Mission, Baptists, and Moravians. The percentage of Catholics self-reporting as Catholic has dropped to 50 percent with evangelicals growing to 40 percent.

Bibliography

Barrett, David B., Georgia T. Kurian, and Todd M. Johnson, eds. 2001. *World Christian Encyclopedia*, Second Edition, vol. 1. Oxford: Oxford University Press.

Gooren, Henri. 2003. "The Religious Market in Nicaragua: The Paradoxes of Catholicism and Protestantism." *Exchange* 32 (4): 340–360.

Peterson, Douglas P. 2016. "Pentecostals in Costa Rica and Nicaragua: A Historical/Theological Perspective." In *Global Renewal Christianity*, vol. 2, edited by Vinson Synan, Amos Yong and Miguel Álvarez, 75–98. Lake Mary, FL: Charisma House.

Pew Research Center. 2014. "Religion in Latin America: Widespread Change in a Historically Catholic Region." (November 13).

Zub, Roberto. 1992. "The Growth of Protestantism: From Religion to Politics?" *Envio* 137.

Philip Wingeier-Rayo

Nigeria

Owing to its large population and economy, Nigeria is often referred to as the "Giant of Africa". With 188 million inhabitants, Nigeria is the most populous country in Africa and the seventh most populous country in the world. Through the interactions of indigenous religions, Christianity and Islam, Nigeria has produced complex religious vivacities, which have attracted scholarly attention. Christianity in Nigeria is not only the second largest but the fastest growing religion. Central to the growth of Christianity in Nigeria is the power and persuasiveness of Pentecostalism. The message of health and wealth, makes Christianity a force to be reckoned with in Africa, especially in Nigeria.

In response to what was considered a 'cerebral' approach to Christianity in the early twentieth century, African Independent/Initiated churches (AICs) proliferated under the leadership of indigenous prophets and healers. In Nigeria these were called the Aladura (the praying people). These churches placed an emphasis on healing, prophecy, revelations through the prophets and prophetesses, ecstatic dances, use of local instruments, deliverance, testimonies and exuberant worship. Healing is usually effected through vibrant prayers, laying on of hands, loud shouts of Halleluiah and Amen, pouring of anointing oil, holy bathing, and drinking of holy water. Deliverance and healing remain key features of the AICs given that many Nigerians believe that mishaps, evil, bad luck, and some incurable diseases are often caused by evil forces like witches, demons, and unappeased ancestors. The preachers aimed at responding to contextual issues facing its members including the belief in malevolent spirits, witches and wizards, and interpretations of dreams and visions.

This new contextual expression of Christianity had implications for the mission churches. Many members of the 'mainline' historic mission churches left to join some of the AICs.

AICs offered Africans the freedom to exercise their gifts, of which they felt that the mission churches did not create enough room within their theology and worship. The translation of the Bible into the mother tongues of many African groups enabled the people to read the Bible in their own languages, thus they became more assertive in their understanding and interpretation of the Bible. The deadly influenza that spread through Nigeria in the early twentieth century to which medicine could not respond resulted in the emergence of prayer and healing groups. This scenario set the stage for a period of advocacy of warfare or powerful prayers conjoined with both an existential recognition of the spirit world as well as the conviction that prayer is a powerful weapon against the spiritual world. The AICs offered the spiritual resources from which many Pentecostal/Charismatic movements emerged in Africa.

Following on the AICs, both foreign and local Pentecostal/Charismatic churches were established from the middle of the twentieth century. Despite the seeming continuities of the theological emphasis within the AICs, many Pentecostal/Charismatic churches often assert themselves as a departure from the traditional religious-cultural context of the AICs.

The emphasis on salvation as a transformative experience carried out by the Holy Spirit, speaking in tongues, visions, healing, prophesies, miracles, revelations, signs and wonders are characteristics of the AICs but continue to have prominent features within many Pentecostal/Charismatic churches in Nigeria. The use of water and oil as means of healing have been incorporated within many Pentecostal/Charismatic churches as therapeutic substances. The payment of tithes and offerings is often seen a prerequisite for material prosperity and when that does not happen the popular interpretation is that the individual is 'under attack' by witches and wizards. Healing, deliverance and prayer with fasting are often prescribed as possible means for deliverance from such evil powers.

Some of these Pentecostal/Charismatic churches have continued to maximize mass media, internet and professionally designed websites within the global religious landscape. It is common to find on such websites, pages for submitting prayer requests, payment of tithes and live stream music and worship. The institutional capacity, demographic mobility, and public visibility of Pentecostal/Charismatic churches in Nigeria and throughout the world have placed them on the global religious map.

In addition, many of the Pentecostal/Charismatic churches constitute ministries that offer social services and development programs that state and local governments often fail to provide, including provision of schools, hospitals, and other welfare related services for members and communities. Within the public sphere these churches and their pastors exert influence on politics and are often seen as possessing the power to anoint future political office holders. Many politicians consult these pastors before, during and after elections for endorsement, prayer, anointing and spiritual protection from their political opponents.

Beyond partisan politics, Pentecostal/Charismatic churches in Nigeria have made an in-road into other sectors of public life. For example, Pentecostal/Charismatic churches operate television and radio stations, including Emmanuel TV, Mountain of Fire and Miracles (MFM) Ministries TV, ECWA TV, Deeper Christian Life Ministry TV, Redemption TV and LoveWorld TV. Others have established themselves as alternatives to the movie industry and have established and sponsored football clubs (for example the Mountain of Fire and Miracles, FC). Pentecostal/Charismatic churches have proved to be mobile, resilient and have dynamic strategies for expansion within the global religious market place.

Bibliography

Gifford, Paul. 1998. *African Christianity: Its Public Role*. London: Hurts & Company.

Mbiti, John. 1986. *Bible and Theology in African Christianity*. Nairobi: Oxford University Press.

Obadare, Ebenezer. 2018. *Pentecostal Republic: Religion and the Struggle for State Power in Nigeria*. London, UK: Zed Books.

Omenyo, Cephas. 2002. *Pentecost Outside Pentecostalism: A Study of the Development of Charismatic Renewal in the Mainline Churches in Ghana*. Amsterdam: Boekencentrum.

Stanley, Brian. 1990. *The Bible and the Flag: Protestant Missions and British Imperialism in the Nineteenth and Twentieth Centuries*. Leicester: Apollos.

Walls, Andrew. 2000. "Of Ivory Towers and Ashrams: Some Reflections on Theological Scholarship in Africa." *Journal of African Christian Thought* 3 (1): 1–5.

Elijah Obinna

Nikolov, Nicholas

Nicholas Nikolov (1900–1964) was born on March 15, 1900 in the small city of Karnobat, Bulgaria. His grandfather was an Eastern Orthodox priest and several of his relatives, including his mother and aunts, attended Missionary School in Samokov and Robert's College in Constantinople. Nikolov chose to study law in Sofia, but when the Bulgarian Pentecostal Movement began in 1920, he was influenced by his aunt Olga Popova Zaplishny.

While studying music in New York the following year, Nicholov was filled with the Holy Spirit on the night of Thanksgiving at Glad Tidings Tabernacle, as recorded in his Bible. Through the ministry of Pastor Robert and Marie Brown, Nikolov enrolled in Bethel Bible Training School where his aunt Olga had also studied. He graduated in 1924 and on Christmas day the same year, married Martha Nagel of New Jersey, a graduate of Elim Bible School in Rochester. Nikolov was invited by Principal Evans to teach at Bethel for two years while pastoring in New York and New Jersey. On May 7, 1926 Nikolov was ordained with the Assemblies of God in preparation to return to his native Bulgaria with his wife as missionaries under Noel Perkins and the Mission's Department.

The Nikolovs sailed from New York on the Majestic on September 18, 1926 and arrived in Bulgaria in early October only to find but a few of the 18 Pentecostal assemblies established by Voronaev and Zaplishny in 1921 still active. Nikolov renewed regular meetings in his mother's basement in Antim I 37 street in Bourgas and registered the churches with the government to establish unity among the Pentecostal. The congregation in Bourgas recovered quickly and moved into a 130-seat storefront at Tzar Ivan Shishman Street and later into a larger factory building. In the midst of this new revival, the Nikolovs' first son, Paul-Zachary, was born on November 9, 1927.

After preliminary meetings in Rouse, the Union of Evangelical Pentecostal Churches was established in Bourgas (March 28–31, 1928) with Nicholas Nikolov as the chairman/superintendent and first annual conference was held in October in Varna. The majority of Pentecostal churches in Bulgaria remained skeptical as the movement was divided over the subject of a centralized government. Although only four congregations joined initially, by 1930 when the Zaplishny family returned to Bulgaria to take charge of the work, the Union had 58 churches nationwide with thousands of attendance.

The Nikolovs' final year in Bulgaria was marked by heavy persecutions. They returned to the U.S. in 1931 for four years of education before joining the staff of the Bible School in Danzig, Poland on June 29, 1935 where Nikolov served as president. In 1938, they travelled back to Bulgaria to aid the work of the Pentecostal Union now with 224 assemblies and 8,000 members strong. Unfortunately, while there the Nikolovs lost their 20-month-old baby girl, Ruth-Marie, and forced by the Axis, left Bulgaria on the S.S. Saturnia October 10, 1939.

Back in America again, Nikolov served as president of the Metropolitan Bible Institute (1941–1950), while pastoring in North Bergen, New Jersey (1947–1950) before becoming president of the New England Bible Institute (1950–1952). He later joined the faculty of the Central Bible Institute of Springfield, Missouri and defended his dissertation on Bulgarian Bogomils at the Biblical Seminary in New York in 1956. He continued to teach until retiring in 1961 and after short sickness passed away November 6, 1964. His wife Martha visited Bulgaria in 1976 and then in 1978 for the 50th anniversary of the Pentecostal Union, where their legacy is remembered to this day.

Bibliography

Nikolov, Nicholas. *Ministry File and Periodical Mentions*. Flower Pentecostal Heritage Center.

Constitutions and By-Laws of the General Council of the Assemblies of God. 1931. (September 16–22, 1927; September 20–26, 1929; September 8–13).

Diulgerov, D.V. 1932. "Pentecostals (Part 1)." In *Annual Publication of the Theological Faculty at Sofia University*, vol. IX, *1931–1932*. Sofia: Gutenberg Press.

Dryanov, Yoncho. 2015. *History of the Evangelical Pentecostal Churches in Bulgaria (1920–1976)*. Sofia: Bulgarian Evangelical Theological Institute.

Minutes of the Executive Committee of the Evangelical Pentecostal Churches in Bulgaria (1928–1947).

Dony K. Donev

Njotorahardjo, Niko

Niko Njotorahardjo was born in Bondowoso, a city in the East Java province of Indonesia, on February 20, 1949. He is married to Hermien Herawati, and together they have one son, Billy Njotorahardjo, who is a pastor (Handoyo and Leenardo 2019). Niko Njotorahardjo was trained as an agricultural engineer.

Njotorahardjo began his ministry in 1985 as a lay worship leader in Gereja Bethel Indonesia (GBI) Bethany Surabaya (now Gereja Bethany Indonesia). In 1988, he was sent by the church to open GBI Bethany Jakarta and assigned as the overseer of GBI Bethany western region. Timotius Arifin was assigned the overseer of the eastern region and founding pastor Abraham Alex Tanuseputra as the coordinator of both regions (GBI Bogor n.d.).

Njotorahardjo was called to be a full-time minister due to two significant events. First, after he had finished leading worship at GBI Bethany in 1985, a pastor from the Netherlands, Rev. Schenk, prophesied to Njotorahardjo. He said, "I [that is, the Lord] had decided to use you as my tool to bring my people into my presence." The second time, in 1987, an evangelist, Stephanus Damaris, told Njotorahardjo that God had told him that it was time for Njotorahardjo to go into full-time ministry because God wanted to use him to restore the tabernacle of David (see Acts 15:15–18; Amos 9:11) (Handoyo and Leenardo 2019).

Njotorahardjo is the founding pastor of GBI Gatot Subroto, a Pentecostal church with over 250,000 members in Indonesia and around the world. The church is part of the GBI denomination and held its first service on September 4, 1988, which was attended by 400 people (PTS 2019; Healing Movement Ministry n.d.).

In 1997, the denomination decided that all GBI churches must adopt a name from the street where that church is located and let go of the unique name being used (for example Bethany, Tiberias, etc.). In 2002, Njotorahardjo changed the church's name to GBI Gatot Subroto, which is the name of the street where the church meets (GBI Bogor n.d.).

The GBI denomination is associated with the Church of God (Cleveland, Tennessee). Njotorahardjo is an ordained bishop of the Church of God and serves as a member in the denomination's International Council of Eighteen, which forms half of the International Executive Council of the Church of God that establishes and directs the polity and ministries of the denomination (Church of God 2018).

Njotorahardjo claims that focusing on the proclamation of prayer, praise, and worship is the catalyst for the growth of the church – a distinguishing feature of his ministry which he calls "The Restoration of the Tabernacle of David." It came from a vision that he claimed to be given by God over the years. The Tabernacle of David is a place where prayer, praise and worship take place day and night, fostering an intimate life with God, turning believers into God's soldiers. In the worship life of the church, this vision is manifested through three dynamics, namely, the presence of God, the anointing of the Holy Spirit, and speaking in tongues. Organizationally, the restoration brought vigorous church planting and the creation of 24-hour prayer towers called "The House of Prayer for All Nations" across Indonesia and other countries. It also motivated the construction of the Sentul International Convention Center and the organization of a revival crusade called "Healing Movement Ministry" that has conducted over 300 revival meetings since 2006 (Handoyo and Leenardo 2019).

Njotorahardjo holds two honorary degrees; first a Doctor of Divinity from the Pentecostal Theological Seminary in Cleveland, Tennessee awarded in 2001 and a second Honorary Doctorate from Hansei University in South Korea given in 2014. On April 28, 2016, The Pentecostal Theological Seminary (PTS) dedicated an academic chair called "The Niko Njotorahardjo Chair for the Restoration of the Tabernacle of David (Prayer, Praise and Worship)." His church donated US$1,000,000 for the endowment to establish the chair. The chair focuses on the study of prayer, praise and worship with French Arrington appointed as the chair's professor (Handoyo and Leenardo 2019). This is the fifth academic chair in PTS, and the first to be named after a non-American (CG World Mission 2019).

Njotorahardjo claimed that over the past ten years God has given him a vision about the outpouring of the Holy Spirit that would bring a third Pentecost movement around the world. On July 19, 2018 at an Empowered 21 event held in Jakarta, one of the speakers, Dr. Cindy Jacobs, prophesied over Njotorahardjo, saying "I [that is, the Lord] chose William Seymour. And this time, to be a messenger of the third Pentecost, I chose you!" It is believed that this third Pentecost will be bringing new ministry opportunities across Asia and the world. Within the Pentecostal/charismatic circle this prophecy was received with mixed receptions and it is too early to tell whether the outcome is consequential (Handoyo and Leenardo 2019; PTS 2019).

Bibliography

Church of God. 2018. "Church of God Council of Eighteen/ International Executive Council." Accessed July 15, 2019. http://www.churchofgod.org/leadership/international-executive-council.

Church of God World Mission. 2016. "Dedication of Niko Njotorahardjo Chair at Pentecostal Theological Seminary." *COG World Missions*. May 2, 2016. https://cogwm.org/uncategorized/dedication-of-niko-njotorahardjo-chair-at-pentecostal-theological-seminary/.

GBI Bogor. n.d. "GBI Jalan Gatot Subroto." Accessed July 9, 2019. https://dbr.gbi-bogor.org/wiki/GBI_Jalan_Gatot_Subroto.

Handoyo, Djohan, and Himawan Leenardo. 2019. *Messenger of the 3rd Pentecost: Pdt. DR. Ir. Niko Njotorahardjo*. Jakarta: WFC Production.

PTS. 2019. *Dr. Niko Njotorahardjo, Messenger of the 3rd Pentecost, Member of the Pentecostal Theological Seminary Board of Trustees.* https://vimeo.com/332504288.

Florian Simatupang

Norway

Building on undercurrents of holiness and revivalist forms of Christianity in the latter part of the nineteenth century, Pentecostalism was brought to Norway by the Methodist pastor Thomas Ball Barratt (1862–1940). Barratt had experienced a baptism in the Holy Spirit in New York in 1906 after having heard about the Azusa Street Revival in Los Angeles. Though there are additional accounts of Pentecostal type experiences before and in parallel to Barratt, in particular in the Free Friend Movement led by Erik Andersen Nordquelle, it was Barratt who became the key Pentecostal figure in Norway. The mainstream of Norwegian Pentecostalism, the Norwegian Pentecostal Movement, has the second largest church membership outside the majority Lutheran Church of Norway and the Catholic Church.

Through the twentieth century, there were also many renewal streams that both enriched and split the classical Pentecostal movement in terms of creating offshoots and new movements. One leading figure in what became the "Maranata" movement was the controversial Åge Samuelsen (1915–1887), a revival preacher, singer, and composer who emphasized divine healing inspired by the American healing revival in the early 1950s. Another leading charismatic figure with strong international ties was world evangelist Aril Edvardsen (1938–2008) who in 1965 started Troens Bevis (Evidence of Faith World Evangelism). In addition to initiating large-scale global evangelization through open-air campaigns, media, satellite television and support of indigenous evangelists, Edvardsen was also known for extending the charismatic message to the wider church. A key leader in what came to be known as the "faith movement" in Norway was Åge Åleskjær who founded Oslo Christian Center (OKS) in the mid-1980s after having attended Rhema Bible Training Center in Tulsa, Oklahoma.

Pentecostalism in Norway has from its inception been a movement with a global outlook and with strong transnational ties. Barratt soon became known as the European "apostle of Pentecost" and brought the Pentecostal message to a number of other European countries. Just weeks after the fire had fallen in Oslo (Kristiania), Dagmar Gregersen (l. Engstrøm) and Agnes Thelle were sent to Denmark, Germany, and Switzerland to spread the fire. Barratt was instrumental in bringing Pentecost to Great Britain through meetings in Sunderland in 1907. There have, in particular, been close relations among the Scandinavian Pentecostal movements (Alvarsson 2011). Lewi Pethrus accepted to re-baptize Barratt in water by full immersion ("believer's baptism") in 1913 and from that point, early Pentecostalism in Scandinavia drifted toward a baptistic ecclesiology. One of the distinctive features of Scandinavian Pentecostalism was the radical congregationalism that invested authority in self-governing local churches (rather than in denominational bodies) led a group of elders, with the pastor serving as the first among equals.

The global impact of Norwegian Pentecostalism has been noticeable despite its size and geographical location, especially through mission (Bundy 2009). The first missionaries were sent to India, China, and South Africa in 1910. Barratt was more cautious about sending missionaries to "heathen nations without relevant training." Telle and Gregersen, who traveled to India led by a specific prophecy, had received training at A.B Simpson's School of Mission in New York and they took time to learn about Indian culture in Mukti with Pandita Ramabai. Later in 1914, Gunnerius Tollefsen, who had received both theological and pharmaceutic training, initiated a missionary work in Congo. This work came to be the seed of the large Pentecostal movement there (CELPA). From the early 1930s and onwards the de-centralized congregational structures contributed to a massive mobilization for mission in Norwegian Pentecostal churches.

Currently, the most profiled and growing segments of Norwegian Pentecostalism are newer church planting networks within the Norwegian Pentecostal Movement aimed at attracting younger and unchurched generations with contemporary style music and communication and with strong emphases on relational structures. These (re-)brands of Pentecostalism are more mainstream and less eschatologically oriented than the pioneering and preceding generations. The most known of these have been the SALT network in Bergen, led by Øysteim Gjerme, and the Intro churches, led by Jostein Krogedal. In 2017, the Intro churches became Hillsong Norway. However, Barratt's old church, the Filadelfia church in Oslo, is still the largest Pentecostal church in Norway (in terms of attendance), having gone through a renewal from the late 1990s led by Egil Svartdahl.

A third key stream of Pentecostalism in Norway is the charismatic Lutheran renewal, the Oase (oasis) movement, which has sought to inspire the Norwegian church landscape from the 1970s. The annual Oase conferences often feature a wide range of Norwegian as well as internationally renowned speakers from various segments of the global charismatic landscape. One of the most profiled Lutheran congregations in Norway is IMI Church in Stavanger, which is known for nationally profiled youth events, worship and conferences on healing. Youth With a Mission (YWAM) has also been a key influence within the charismatic Lutheran renewal movement. The global scope of the Pentecostal landscape in Norway has in recent years been actualized by an emergence of a growing number of Pentecostal-type migrant churches initiated, led and congregated by migrants with origins in Africa, Asia and Latin America. While some of these have joined Norwegian church networks, many of these also are linked to their own transnational networks or global denominations.

Bibliography

Alvarsson, Jan Åke. 2011. "The Development Of Pentecostalism In Scandinavian Countries." In *European Pentecostalism*, edited by William Kay and Anne Dyer, 17–40. Leiden: Brill.

Bloch-Hoell, Nils. 1964. *The Pentecostal Movement: Its Origin, Development and Distinctive Character*. Oslo/London: Universitetsforlaget/Allen & Unwin.

Bundy, David. 2009. "Visions of Apostolic Mission: Scandinavian Pentecostal Mission to 1935." PhD diss., University of Uppsala.

Lie, Geir. 2000. "The Charismatic/Pentecostal Movement in Norway: The Last 30 Years." *Cyberjournal for Pentecostal-Charismatic Research*. Last modified February 22, 2016. http://www.pctii.org/cyberj/cyberj7/lie.pdf.

Tangen, Karl Inge. 2017. "Pentecostal Movements in Norway." In *Global Renewal*

Christianity. Spirit-Empowered Movements: Past, Present and Future. Vol. 4. Europe and North America, edited by Vinson Synan and Amos Yong, 198–214. Lake Mary, FL: Charisma House.

Stian Sorlie Eriksen
Karl Inge Tangen

Oceania

Oceania encompasses the continent of Australia (population 25 million in 2019), the large cluster of islands of New Zealand (4.5 million), and islands traditionally divided into three groups according to ethnic and cultural aspects: Polynesia (total population 680,000, many islands at 10,000 or less), including American Samoa (55,000), French Polynesia including Tahiti (280,000), Samoa (197,000), Tonga (104,000), the Cook Islands, Niue, the Tokelau Islands, Tuvalu and Wallis and Futuna Islands, each with 12,000 or less; Melanesia (total population 10.98 mi) including Fiji (890,000), New Caledonia (282,000), Papua New Guinea (8.77 mi), the Solomon Islands (669,000) and Vanuatu (300,000), and Micronesia (total population 545,000), including Guam (167,000), Kiribati (117,000), the Marshall Islands (59,000), Micronesia Islands (113,000), Northern Mariana Islands (57,000), and Palau and Nauru each with populations under 20,000. By convention Hawaii is excluded from the list.

In many parts of the Pacific world, the arrival of Christianity preceded the arrival of Pentecostalism by only fifty to one hundred years. Among indigenous populations, western forms of Christianity were often co-opted to support traditional power structures. Syncretic healing and prophetic movements emerged early in the history of Christianity and revivals sometimes flourished. There were revivalistic movements among the European settlers, and some proto-Pentecostal groups were also present in the nineteenth century, for example Irvingites and the ministry of John Alexander Dowie from Melbourne, who later founded Zion City in Illinois.

The first Pentecostal congregation in Australia, the Good News Hall, was founded by Sarah Jane (Jeannie) Lancaster in Melbourne in 1909. In 1926 this body joined the Apostolic Faith Mission. Then in 1922, the British Pentecostal evangelist, Smith Wigglesworth visited Australia and New Zealand, speaking in Melbourne, Sydney, and Wellington. Aimee Semple McPherson also visited Australia in 1922. A.C. Valdez (from McPherson's church), and Stephen Jeffreys of the Elim Pentecostal church also visited in the 1920s. By 1924 there were 18 Pentecostal congregations in Australia, and by 1939, some 80 congregations. In New Zealand by 1939 there were about 25 congregations.

Gradually the churches affiliated with international movements, notably the AG (1927 in New Zealand, 1937 in Australia), the Apostolic Church (1928 in New Zealand, 1930 in Australia), the Elim Church, and the Foursquare Gospel Movement. But there was also a strong separatist group in both countries that held British Israel beliefs including the Christian Revival Crusade in Australia and the Commonwealth Covenant Church in New Zealand. There were also independents including the Revival Fire Mission in New Zealand.

In Melanesia, the revivalist Queensland Kanaka Mission became the South Seas Evangelical Mission (SSEM) focusing on the Solomon Islands. In 1936 it experienced renewal, attracting Pentecostals to its mission force. A few American missionaries (mostly from the early AG) came to Polynesia, including the Pages who came to Fiji in 1913, then in 1926 the Heetebrys came to Fiji, and the Winkelmanns went to American Samoa. In Papua New Guinea (PNG), AG missionaries came from Australia in 1948 to the East Sepik Province.

In 1950 a Bible school was established in Fiji and the AG was formally established as a denomination in 1959. Preachers spread to Western Samoa in 1952. Revival movements in the islands of Melanesia and PNG also began to grow. After 1959 the missionary work of the AG included more Pentecostal features, and from the capital in Port Moresby, churches and Bible schools began to be planted throughout PNG. Most of the early congregations were hindered by their tendency to schism and churches did not penetrate into the villages.

American Pentecostal missionaries evacuated from Indonesia in 1942 planted a new Pentecostal movement in New Zealand and then Australia which adopted "latter rain" teachings. Out of this grew an unaffiliated revivalistic movement, which grew rapidly in New Zealand through evangelistic campaigns in parts of the South and North islands of New Zealand, founding New Life Centres. Its leaders reached out to people in traditional denominations both in Australia and New Zealand and the movement grew rapidly in the late 1960s. In 1970 the "Jesus People Movement" made a significant public impact and the traditional Pentecostal denominations also began to began to grow. Australians were slower to embrace the movement than New Zealanders.

From the 1980s some very large Pentecostal congregations emerged in the Australian cities, and some became global brands, notably Brian Houston's Hillsong. Third Wave churches have also flourished in Australia and New Zealand.

The indigenous Maori people of New Zealand had been nominally converted to Christianity in the nineteenth century but spiritual life was weak in these communities, except for independent prophet movements. Many Pentecostals felt a call to reach Maori. Destiny Church, which was led by a Maori couple, Brian and Hannah Tamaki, made a significant impact after 2000. There are few parallels in Australia apart from the Aboriginal Revival in Elcho Island in the Northern Territory, which spread to other parts of the north and west of Australia.

Large numbers of Pacific peoples came to Australia and New Zealand on temporary work permits. Some visited Pentecostal churches, and Samuelo Pulepule from Samoa planted AG churches for Samoans in New Zealand. These churches and parallels for other islanders, flourished in both countries, and their members encouraged parallel developments back in the Islands, and many split away from the mainstream AG. Other Pasifika people became very active in other Pentecostal churches, often deeply involved in the musical teams.

After World War II the South Seas Evangelical Church was formed by the SSEM in the Solomon Islands, but its spiritual life was subdued through involvement in politics. Then Muri Thompson, a Maori evangelist affected by the charismatic movement in New Zealand, held evangelistic meetings in PNG and the Solomons in 1970. A highly emotional revival developed which significantly touched Melanesian culture.

In the Polynesian states the Charismatic revival came through denominational and non-denominational youth organisations. In 1965 Senetuli Koloi established the evangelical Scripture Union movement in the schools of Tonga, and it developed a large following. In 1973 Youth for Christ began youth rallies in Apia in Western Samoa and their contemporary music appealed to young people from the very restrictive dominant Protestant churches.

The Youth With a Mission branch in New Zealand from 1967 began to reach out to Pacific peoples first in Fiji and Tonga. Then in 1974 Teen Challenge began work in both American and Western Samoa. "Island Breeze" became a key YWAM ministry from 1979. In 1991–92 YWAM was gifted a ship, the M.V. Pacific Ruby, which travelled across the South Pacific.

Another factor has been breakaways from these traditional Protestant churches. For example, the Rhema Family Church in the Solomons was founded by a pastor of the Anglican Church who was expelled, and the Bible Way Centre was founded by a former Minister of the SSEC. Similarly, in Samoa Pastor Viliame Mafoe, a former Methodist lay preacher, established the Worship Centre in 1997 and it grew rapidly, absorbing some other independent churches.

Pentecostal churches found outreach to the Pacific a relatively easy form of mission. The New Life Churches of New Zealand sent a tour to Samoa in 1983 and to Fiji in 1985. The Christian Outreach Centre of Brisbane planted branches in PNG and other parts of the Pacific.

Developments have been fostered by Islanders becoming missionaries to other Islands, as they did in the early planting of Christianity. In 1971 AG missionaries from Fiji began outreach in the Solomons and New Caledonia. Preachers from PNG brought the Christian Revival Crusade to the Solomons.

Another factor has been splits in existing Pentecostal churches. AG splits led to the formation of the hugely successful Peace Chapel in Western Samoa, the Bible Study Fellowship of Samoa, the Church on the Rock in Tonga and other groups. A group of Chinese founded the Polynesian Pentecostal Church in French Polynesia in 1968. Schisms often reflect family loyalties rather than theological issues, but they also reflect different attitudes towards accommodating culture, especially in the Melanesian context, where cargo cults retain some appeal.

Huge growth has taken place among the AG since the 1970s. In Samoa they are now the fifth largest denomination with 28,200 adherents (6.6 percent of the population in 2006) plus 12,000 in American Samoa. By 2010 there were some 925 congregations in PNG with a strong missionary focus.

From the 1980s the Assemblies of God began to penetrate into villages in Polynesia and Melanesia. By 2015 some 100,000 Samoans belonged to the Assemblies of God, and 8 percent of the population of Western Samoa. In Fiji the proportion is 4 percent.

The two strongest Pentecostal presences in Micronesia are in Guam and the Marshall Islands. In both cases they are replicas of American Pentecostalism. In Guam a variety of Pentecostal churches are now active, including the United Pentecostals, the Church of God (Anderson) and the Elim Church. Other organisations include Teen Challenge, YWAM and an AG bible school. The total nominal Pentecostal percentage is 5.4 percent. In the Marshall Islands, where the proportion is 35 percent, several new denominations have emerged, some of them breakaways from the AG, notably the Bukot Non Jesus

Church in Majuro, founded in 1985 and affiliated with the United Pentecostal Church. Further tensions led to the formation of another new church, the Light of Jesus Church and the Marshallese Pentecostal Church. Another Full Gospel Church was founded in the 1990s by Rev Ronald Edwards and this now has eleven congregations.

The high level of urbanisation and western influence in Micronesia has assisted the growth of Pentecostalism, and the issues of indigenous cultural adaptation have been less significant there. Moreover, Pentecostalism has assisted in the cultural assimilation of those Micronesians who have sought to relocate to the United States. There are Marshallese AG congregations in Hilo, Hawaii, Sacramento, California, and Springdale, Arkansas among other places.

The intensity of Protestant Christianity in the Pacific makes it an attractive place for Pentecostal ministry. International evangelists have begun to recognise the level of Christianisation of the islands and to hold crusades there, including Reinhard Bonnke and Benny Hinn.

Scholars have noted that Pentecostal values appeal strongly to Pacific cultures, with their traditions of dreams, signs and wonders, rituals and experiences, and some Pentecostal concerns with apocalyptic trends have resonated with the sense of crisis about climate change and poverty in Polynesia. On the other hand, Pentecostalism has over-ridden traditional recognition of the matai, village and social elders and social customs. Traditional island churches publicly announce and honour giving to denominational funds, and prosperity teaching is quite common within Pentecostal churches in the islands. Women find much greater freedom for public ministry in the Pentecostal setting, and young people are permitted to take much more initiative. The contemporary style of music is an important factor in the appeal of Pentecostal forms of faith, for the traditional singing in Pacific Islands churches is slow, unaccompanied and full of loud harmonies which do not resonate with contemporary trends.

Current Pentecostal numbers in the Pacific are at best conjectural. The World Christian database suggests that there are just over 1 million in Melanesia, about 11.5 percent of the population, and "the renewalists" as a group 20.9 percent of the total population. The Assemblies of God at more than 500,000 in PNG and 50,000 in Fiji and 58,000 in Vanuatu are the largest. The UPS is also very large in PNG (some 111,000).

In Polynesia, the same source has 14 percent of the population in renewalist groups including 31,500 or 4.8 percent in Pentecostal groups. The Assemblies of God have more than 10,000 members in both American Samoa and in Western Samoa, but they are much smaller proportions of the population.

In Micronesia Pentecostals account for 40,000 or 8 percent of the population according to the same source, which also has another 38,000 in Charismatic and Neo Charismatic groups. Assemblies of God had over 30,000 in the Marshall Islands.

Bibliography

Eriksen, Annelis, Ruy Llera Blanes, and Michelle MacCarthy. 2019. *Going to Pentecost: An Experimental Approach to Studies in Pentecostalism*. New York and Oxford: Berghahn Books.

Ernst, Manfred, ed. 2006. *Globalization and the Re-shaping of Christianity in the Pacific Islands*. Suva, Fiji: Pacific Theological College.

Ernst, Manfred. 1994. *Winds of Change: Rapidly Growing Religious Groups in the Pacific Islands*. Suva, Fiji: Pacific Conference of Churches.

Garrett, John. 1997. *Where Nets were Cast: Christianity in Oceania since World War II*. Suva & Geneva: Institute of Pacific Studies, University of the South Pacific & World Council of Churches.

Gore, Kellesi. 2019. "The Pentecostal Movement in the South Pacific Islands." In *Asia Pacific Pentecostalism*, edited by Denise A., Austin, Jacqueline Grey and Paul W. Lewis, 297–324. Leiden: Brill.

Fer, Yannic. 2015. "Charismatic Globalization, Morality and Culture in Polynesian Protestantism." In *The Anthropology of Global Pentecostalism and Evangelicalism*, edited by Simon Coleman, Rosalind I.J. Hackett and Joel Robbins, 228–242. New York: New York University Press.

Magowan, Fiona, and Carolyn Schwarz, eds. 2016. *Christianity, Conflict, and Renewal in Australia and the Pacific*. Leiden: Brill.

Peter Lineham

Olazábal, Francisco

Francisco Olazábal (1886–1937) was born in El Verano, Sinaloa, Mexico, on September 16, 1886. His parents were Catholic and his father served as major of El Verano. After his mother converted to Methodism, she brought her son to church and soon thereafter she became a traveling evangelist. His father abandoned the family because his mother became a Protestant. Together Francisco and her mother traveled the Sierra Madre Mountains selling thread and household supplies and spreading the Methodist message in villages throughout the region. Because they were Protestants, they often were not allowed to sleep in the town but on the outskirts, where they hunted rabbits and other game and slept by the campfire for survival. After many years of apprenticing for his mother's evangelistic ministry, he decided to visit his relatives in the San Francisco Bay area and sail the world as a merchant marine. There in Oakland, he met George Montgomery who gave him an evangelistic tract and led him to rededicate his life to Christ.

Francisco returned home and for three years attended the Wesleyan Methodist School of Theology in San Luis Potosi. During the summers, he and his companions would travel the region around the seminary and in the rugged mountains – sometimes barefoot – preaching the Gospel. He was ordained a Methodist minister in 1911 and pastored his first Methodist Church in El Paso, Texas, in 1912. There he met an American missionary and alumnus of Moody Bible Institute named Julia Ballinger, who helped raise funds for him to attend in 1913. He studied with R.A. Torrey and many other famous evangelical leaders. After six months, Torrey invited him to minister and head up the Mexican ministry at the Church of the Open Door in Los Angeles. After a short time, he parted company with Torrey over doctrinal concerns about the necessity of the baptism with the Holy Spirit (which Olazábal did not think at that time was necessary to live a fulfilled Christian life) and traveled to the San Francisco Bay area, where he served as an itinerant minister in several Methodist missions. Then he moved to Pasadena and became the senior pastor of a Mexican Methodist Church. In 1916, he married Macrina, who came from a Methodist family in Mazatlán, Mexico, and they went on to have eight children.

Shortly thereafter, he and Macrina traveled back to the San Francisco Bay area, where he met with George and Carrie Judd Montgomery. They spoke at length about the Pentecostal outpouring and after they prayed for his wife's healing, Francisco and Macrina both joined the Pentecostal movement. He was ordained in the Assemblies of God (AG) by Robert Craig in San Francisco in 1918. He served as an evangelist in California and Texas and pastored a mission in El Paso, where he founded the first AG Bible school in 1922 with the help of Julia Ballinger. The church he founded grew rapidly after he started praying for divine healing at his evangelistic services.

That same year the Anglo-American leaders at the AG headquarters in Springfield, Missouri, supported H.C. Ball to lead the church. Francisco resigned with 12 cents in his pocket. Many AG and independent churches in the Houston area asked him to create a new Mexican denomination completely run by and for Mexicans. In 1923, they created the Interdenominational Mexican Council of Christian Churches Pentecostal, today called the Latin American Council of Christian Churches (CLADIC or aka "Concilio"). This was the first legally-incorporated and completely Latino-led Protestant, evangelical, and pentecostal denomination in the U.S.

In 1924 after a powerful and widely publicized healing of a young girl named Guadalupe Gomez, his healing ministry took off and he began conducting evangelistic healing campaigns at missions and churches in his own denomination and in the AG throughout the Southwest. He was invited by a former colleague in the AG to conduct services in Chicago in 1929. Thousands attended the services and word spread rapidly to New York City, where another former colleague Francisco Paz invited him to Manhattan and Spanish Harlem to lead evangelistic healing services. He arrived in 1931 and held massive services with upwards of 1,500 people attending every night for several months. Reports indicated that over 100,000 Latinos (primarily Puerto Ricans) attended his services between 1931 and 1937. He founded Bethel Temple and this soon became the mother church that birthed a number of youth group ministries and the Damascus Christian Church founded by Leoncia Rosado Rosseau.

Word spread from the Puerto Rican diaspora in Spanish Harlem back to Puerto Rico about the massive healing services and Olazábal was invited by J.L. Rodríguez of the Defenders of the Faith to carry out an island-wide healing crusade in 1934. This crusade made history by breaking the monopoly that the AG's Pentecostal Church of God had on the island and over half a dozen Pentecostal denominations were birthed in the wake of his revivals, with upwards of 20,000 in attendance in services in the Hippodrome.

Due to jealousy and concerns about "sheep stealing", many of the Protestant and evangelical churches joined forces to successfully thwart his revival in 1936. The Catholic Church also published articles in the local newspapers warning people not to attend his services. He re-gained his spirit in 1936 when he attended the Church of God Convention in Cleveland, Tennessee, where he prayed for divine healing for over 1,500 white southerners. Ambrose and Homer Tomlinson had been grooming Olazábal for some time to join the Church of God, which he reluctantly did at the same convention. In an interview with the author, Olazábal's son stated that his father felt pressured by Tomlinson to join the Church of God and he did not have the legal authority to merge the CLADIC with the Church of God because it had to be decided on by the denomination and not just the president. Regardless, he did not see the merger consummated as he died of internal hemorrhaging in a car accident as he traveled from Texas to Mexico to carry out evangelistic healing services. He died on June 9, 1937. He was 51 years old and at the height of his ministry.

Olazábal founded El Mensajero Cristiano in 1923. He translated evangelical publications from English into Spanish and created his own hymnal with original scores. He sent missionaries throughout Latin America, largely from his Bethel Temple mother church in Spanish Harlem. At the time of his death, he claimed 150 churches and 50,000 adherents throughout the U.S., Mexico, and Puerto Rico. Olazábal's story is important because it challenges the traditional paradigm of American religious history as a story that moves from east to west. Instead, his story along with that of many of his followers shows that it also moves from south to north.

Bibliography

Espinosa, Gastón. 2016. *Latino Pentecostals in America: Faith and Politics in Action*. Cambridge, MA: Harvard University Press.

Espinosa, Gastón. 1999. "El Azteca: Francisco Olazábal and Latino Pentecostal Charisma, Power, and Faith Healing in the Borderlands." *Journal of the American Academy of Religion* 67 (3): 597–616.

Guillén, Miguel. 1992. *La historia del Concilio Latino Americano de Iglesias Cristianas*. Latin American Council of Christian Churches.

Olazábal Jr., Frank. Telephone Interview by Gastón Espinosa, May 1998.

Gastón Espinosa

Omahe, Chacha

Chacha Omahe was a Kenyan Pentecostal evangelist, church leader, and Bible translator, who pioneered evangelistic work among the Kuria and the Maasai in Kenya. He has also been credited with starting the Ethiopian Pentecostal movement.

Chacha belonged to the Kuria people, an ethnic group residing in the Kenya-Tanzania border region east of Lake Victoria. He was born in the Mara region of Tanzania in 1924 and moved to Kenya in the early 1930s. His father had passed away before he was born, and his mother died when he was young. Chacha attended a primary school in Bukuria (Migori county) run by Elim (Lima, NY) missionaries, but he was forced to drop out after fourth grade in order to work on his older brother's farm.

In 1946, Chacha joined the Elim Missionary Assemblies as an evangelist, and from 1952 to 1954 he studied for a diploma in theology at the Elim Bible school in Bukuria. He also took a correspondence course with Voice of Prophecy in South Africa and taught himself Greek and the New Testament. By 1961 he was ordained as a pastor with the Elim Missionary Assemblies, and after some months of studying creative writing, journalism, and linguistics in Zambia, he took a pastoral appointment in Nairobi in 1962.

At this time, Elim began to nationalize their work and had founded the Pentecostal Evangelistic Fellowship of Africa (PEFA) for this purpose. Chacha was appointed overseer of PEFA's Central and Eastern Kenya districts in 1963, and in 1965 he became the Regional Chairman for Nairobi. During this time, he pioneered PEFA's mission to the Maasai, working closely with the missionary Eva S. Butler, sister of Elim president Carlton Spencer. Chacha also took further linguistic courses and began to translate New Testament theology into the Kuria language, a work he had completed by his death in 1990.

In 1963, Chacha was invited to speak at the annual summer conference of the (Swedish) Philadelphia Church Mission in Awasa, Ethiopia. This invitation had come at the recommendation of Joseph Mattson-Boze, a Swedish-American evangelist who had met Chacha on one of his East Africa tours. Chacha's fiery preaching style and practical instructions to receiving the Holy Spirit baptism brought about a revival among the Ethiopian youths. Chacha was invited to preach at the Free Finnish Foreign Mission in Addis Ababa as well, where he clashed with the missionaries over his ministry style, while the Ethiopian youths took to him. When the Ethiopian students began to form their own national movement in the end of the 1960s, they attributed Chacha with having started Ethiopian Pentecostalism. Making him the one who "brought the Holy Spirit baptism" was an ideal articulation of missionary independence, while still connecting the Ethiopian movement to the worldwide Pentecostal revival. Chacha himself laid no claim to the movement, though he visited Ethiopia on two other occasions in 1964 and 1966.

During his 1963 Ethiopia visit, Chacha had met the Swedish Pentecostal missionary Bengt Sundh, who was looking to establish a work in Kenya. Chacha invited him to his home region of Kuria, where Sundh established a base in Komotobo in 1967 and subsequently grew a network of churches from there. This led to a conflict with PEFA, who considered the Kuria region as part of their missionary territory, and when they insisted that Chacha should apologize to the leadership of PEFA for inviting Sundh, he decided to leave PEFA instead. A number of Kenyan pastors followed him and together they established the International Fellowship for Christ (IFC) in 1972. This church is still present in Kenya and has a few international branches. Chacha continued to lead the work until his death in 1990. By now he had grown weary of western missionaries and did not accept foreign assistance. Chacha's ministry in Kenya thus came to resemble the kind of missionary independence that Ethiopian Pentecostals had attributed to him, even as they did not know about these later developments in his life.

Bibliography

Butler, Eva S. 2002. *In the Shadow of the Kilimanjaro: Pioneering the Pentecostal Testimony among the Maasai People.* Salisbury Center, NY: Pinecrest Publications.

Engelsviken, Tormod. 2014. "Mission, Pentecostalism, and Ethiopian Identity: The Beginnings of the Mulu Wongel Believers' Church." *Norsk Tidskrift for Misjonsvitenskap* 3: 195–215.

Haustein, Jörg. 2011. *Writing Religious History: The Historiography of Ethiopian Pentecostalism.* Wiesbaden: Harrassowitz.

Haustein, Jörg. 2013. "Historical Epistemology and Pentecostal Origins: History and Historiography in Ethiopian Pentecostalism." *Pneuma* 35 (3): 345–365.

Omahe, Chacha. 1970. "Life and Experience in the Lord's Ministry: From 1946–1970." Unpublished manuscript.

Jörg Haustein

Oneness Pentecostalism

Oneness Pentecostalism (OP) is the third stream – next to Holiness and Finished Work Pentecostalism – to emerge from the early-twentieth century Pentecostal revival, the consequence of a schism in 1916 within the newly formed Assemblies of God (AG). Initially called the "New Issue," the "Oneness" label emerged around 1930, and throughout its history OPs have shared the label "Apostolic" with various Trinitarian Pentecostal groups.

Theologically, OP rejected the doctrine of the Trinity and insisted upon water baptism in the name of the Lord Jesus Christ. In all other ways, it was traditionally Pentecostal. For more than a century OP has been an enigma to the wider church. Thus it presents a unique ecumenical challenge to understanding how its theologically controversial and often exclusive doctrines function within an otherwise common Pentecostal tradition.

The spiritual and theological impulses that gave rise to OP are rooted in the Christocentrism of both Evangelicalism and the early Pentecostal revival. Late nineteenth-century Evangelicals were engaged in a defense of the deity of Christ against the theological liberalism of their time. Their strategy was to engage in a biblical study of the Name of God to demonstrate that the names and titles of God in the Old Testament apply to Jesus. Although the name itself which Jesus bore varied from "Lord" to "Lord Jesus Christ," the preferred name for OPs was simply "Jesus." A further Christocentric shift occurred with the Revival's first schism led by William H. Durham (1873–1912), whose controversial teaching, "The Finished Work of Calvary," occasioned the formation of AG and eventual emergence within it of OP.

The seeds of the Oneness controversy, however, were planted in a baptismal sermon held during the 1913 Worldwide Camp Meeting in Arroyo Seco near Los Angeles. The preacher, a Canadian "Finished Work" evangelist by the name of Robert E. McAlister (1880–1953), was reflecting upon the apparent inconsistency between Jesus' commission to baptize in the triune name of "Father, Son and Holy Spirit" (Matt 28:19) and the Apostles' practice of baptizing in some combination of the name, "Lord Jesus Christ" (Acts 2:38). McAlister proposed that Jesus was speaking parabolically about himself, a statement which would be understood by only his disciples. What appeared novel and controversial in McAlister's sermon was in reality based on a slim volume published the same year by a Premillennial Evangelical, William Phillips Hall, *What Is "The Name?" OR "The Mystery of God" Revealed*.

Frank Ewart (1876–1947), Australian evangelist and McAlister's friend, having heard and reflected on the sermon, was finally persuaded. A year later, on April 15, 1914, he and co-worker Glenn Cook pitched a tent in nearby Belvedere, rented a tank, baptized each other and other candidates in the name of Jesus. From there the New Issue spread rapidly throughout the AG, into the Midwest, and north into Canada. By 1915 it had attracted such prominent leaders as Garfield T. Haywood (1880–1931), African-American pastor in Indianapolis, and Franklin Small (1873–1961) in Winnipeg, Canada. Andrew Urshan (1884–1967), popular Persian evangelist, embraced the movement in 1919 following expulsion from the AG.

The shape of Oneness theology emerged quickly. Ewart, its first doctrinal architect, became convinced that to be one, God's nature and name must be singular (Zech 14:9). From this he drew two conclusions that would be foundational to the oneness of God and God's Name. He reduced Hall's compound redemptive Name in baptism to the singular name, "Jesus." Deriving from this, God's being must be radically one. The effect was a fundamental rejection of the traditional doctrine of the Trinity in three "persons" in favour of a christocentric Modalism, which limits the triune nature of God to three "manifestations" in historical revelation.

By 1915, Oneness soteriology in particular was emerging in the writings of Haywood and Small; also later by Urshan. With Acts 2:38 as their paradigmatic Oneness text, Haywood and Urshan interpreted the threefold acts – repentance, baptism in the name of Jesus Christ, gift of the Holy Spirit – as constituting the new birth of water and the Spirit declared by Jesus in John 3:5. Ewart and Small, reflecting OP's Evangelical roots, believed that the new birth is accomplished in conversion, but that water and Spirit baptism are necessary for the believer's full provision for the Christian life. Small was unique among the four founding theologians for comprehending and teaching Durham's Finished Work of Calvary teaching throughout his ministry.

The Oneness apologists continued to advance their teaching throughout the AG, further exacerbating tensions. An attempt to achieve unity at the 1915 Third General Council failed, resulting in a confrontation at the Fourth Council meeting in 1916. The submission for vote on a strongly worded statement affirming the traditional doctrine of the Trinity was approved. The result was the disaffection of 156 of the 585 ministers, and the beginning of Pentecostalism's third stream.

The first OP organizational body was the Pentecostal Assemblies of the World (PAW), identifiably multi-cultural until 1924 when racial divisions resulted in schism. While the PAW retained its black members, the white members divided along regional lines. The two largest white groups merged in 1945 to form the United Pentecostal Church (UPCI). In 1971 the Apostolic World Christian Fellowship was formed as an alternative global alliance to promote fellowship and coordination of ministries. It currently numbers approximately 135 member organizations, which includes most Black and Hispanic groups.

Early US-based denominations such as the Pentecostal Assemblies of the World (PAW), the Apostolic Assembly of the Faith in Christ Jesus (AAFCJ), the Church of Our Lord Jesus Christ, and the United Pentecostal Church International (UPCI), have contributed to the global propagation of the commonly-called Jesus-name message. Most of the growth, however, can be attributed to the efforts by local organizations independent of the US. Within the orbits of Los Angeles in 1912, the Latino-majority AAFCJ claims that two of its founders were baptized in Jesus name. The movement spread to Mexico courtesy of the efforts of Romana Carbajal de Valenzuela in 1914. Her work later converged with that of the AAFCJ and Irish missionary Joseph Stewart. In 1932 they founded the nation's main OP denomination La Igelsia Apostólica de la Fe en Cristo Jesús.

Pentecostalism indigenized and reflected diverse theologies. For example, Eusebio Joaquín González, founder of the Guadalajara based La Luz de Mundo (LLDM), was baptized in Jesus name in 1925 and later proclaimed himself to be the living Apostle on the earth. LLDM baptizes in "Jesus name," but rejects fellowship with all others. The denomination affirms a view of the Godhead that is neither strictly trinitarian nor oneness. LLDM, now globalized, boasts of up to five million adherents across 50 countries. The most notable example of growth and independence in the Americas is the case in Colombia where Danish Canadian missionary Verner Larsen arrived in

1936 and was joined in 1949 by Canadian Bill Drost who implemented a program of evangelization by new converts. Today the United Pentecostal Church of Colombia (a nationalized body that emerged from a UPCI in 1967) is the largest Protestant denomination in the country and has members in the Americas and Europe. As for the rest of South America (particularly Brazil, Argentina, and Chile), the autochthonous growth has been complemented by US denominations.

OP missionaries arrived in China in 1915. But, as Melissa Wei-Tsing Inouye explains, in 1917 Paul Wei claimed that Jesus had appeared to him, personally baptized him, and mandated him to found the True Jesus Church (TJC) in Beijing. TJC teaches the two cardinal OP doctrines: a Modalist view of God and baptism in the name of the Lord Jesus Christ. If we were to qualify TJC as an OP movement, it would account for one of the largest worldwide with significant growth in Singapore, the Philippines, Australia, Europe, and the Americas. Nevertheless, the TJC would likely spurn such a classification. By 1949 the TJC was the largest indigenous Christian group in China, and in Japan it has spread alongside an even older OP movement which began in 1915 with PAW missionaries. The Spirit of Jesus church would coalesce with OP movements but later chart its own path, amassing over 400,000 followers. It maintains distinctive indigenized practices such as baptism by proxy for the dead. OP's most extensive growth in Asia Pacific has been in Indonesia, Australia, and especially in the Philippines where over two million followers are spread across nearly 120 organizations.

One of the largest OP movements in the world is found in the very grounds of Ancient Christianity. Jörg Haustein shows how the Apostolic Church of Ethiopia (ACE) began in the 1960s with the baptism of its leader Teklemariam Gezahagne through the evangelization of UPCI missionaries. The "divine flesh" doctrine which taught that Christ did not partake of the human flesh of Mary but instead embodied a glorified body, resulted in the ACE's break from the UPCI in 2003. Aside from ACE, various independent and UPCI churches have thrived in Zambia, South Africa, and Nigeria.

Reverse mission efforts, largely through the work of African and Afro-Caribbean churches in the UK, account for the majority of growth in Western Europe. Gordon Magee's Jesus name baptism in the 1950s and the Churches of God in Ireland's subsequent theological shift towards OP, however, emerged well before the demographic shifts. In addition, Russian Pentecostalism has shared OP characteristics since the late 1910s missionary work of the Persian-American Andrew Urshan. From there OP spread to Kazakhstan and Eastern European countries such as Yugoslavia and Bulgaria.

OP is complex and diverse. Its followers share a common Pentecostal heritage but hold teachings considered by many to be heterodox. They vary widely in their relations with Trinitarians, from strict exclusion to open fellowship. Their core doctrines of God and baptism occasionally inhabit groups which otherwise do not identify as OP, such as the Chinese indigenous TJC. All included, Talmadge French estimates their global number to be approximately 30 million, distributed with 40 percent Black, 30 percent Asian, 20 percent Hispanic, and 9 percent White.

Bibliography

Boyd, Gregory A. 1992. *Oneness Pentecostalism and the Trinity*. Grand Rapids, MI: Baker Book House.

French, Talmadge L. 1999. *Our God is One: The Story of the Oneness Pentecostals*. Indianapolis, IN: Voice & Vision Publications.

Fudge, Thomas A. 2003. *Christianity without the Cross: A History of Salvation in Oneness Pentecostalism*. Parkland, FL: Universal Publishers.

Haustein, Jörg. 2013. "Introduction: The Ethiopian Pentecostal Movement – History, Identity and Current Socio-Political Dynamics." *PentecoStudies* 12 (2): 150–161.

King, Johnny. 2017. "Spirit and Schism: A History of Oneness Pentecostalism in the Philippines." PhD diss., University of Birmingham, UK.

Norris, David S. 2009. *I AM: A Oneness Pentecostal Theology*. Hazelwood, MO: Word Aflame Press.

Ramírez, Daniel. 2015. *Migrating Faith: Pentecostalism in the United States and Mexico in the Twentieth Century*. Chapel Hill, NC: University of North Carolina Press.

Reed, David. 2014. "The Many Faces of Global Oneness Pentecostalism." In *The Cambridge Companion to Pentecostalism*, edited by Cecil M. Robeck Jr. and Amos Yong, 52–70. Cambridge: Cambridge University Press.

Reed, David A. 2008. *"In Jesus' Name": The History and Beliefs of Oneness Pentecostals*. Blandford, UK: Deo Publishing.

Wei-Tsing Inouye, Melissa. 2019. *China and the True Jesus: Charisma and Organization in a Chinese Christian Church*. New York: Oxford University Press.

David Reed
Lloyd Barba

Onyinah, Opoku

Opoku Onyinah (1954–) is a distinguished African missiologist and former Chairman of the Church of Pentecost, Ghana. He was born on July 22, 1954 in Kumasi, the capital city of the Ashanti Kingdom. His parents, Opanin Kwame Onyinah and Maame Akosua Addai, were peasant farmers. As Catholics, they sent their son to be baptized into the Catholic Church in Yamfo. Onyinah remained a staunch Catholic throughout his childhood. He attended a Presbyterian primary school and a Catholic Middle school in Yamfo. Then he studied carpentry and joinery at the Sunyani Technical Institute and the Tamale Technical Institute between 1970 and 1974. During his time at the Sunyani Technical Institute, he was converted to the Pentecostal faith, spoke in tongues and joined the Church of Pentecost. He eventually became popular among students for his ability to lead people to receive Spirit baptism with speaking in tongues.

He worked briefly as an estimator at the State Construction Corporation in Tamale until was called into full-time ministry of the Church of Pentecost in 1976. He married Grace in the same year. Onyinah's outstanding leadership potential ensured his rapid ministerial progression. He became a regional Apostle at an unusual age of 30. Whilst being a regional Apostle in 1986–1988, Onyinah attended the Elim Bible College. It was in Capel in Surrey when he started the diploma programme but it was moved to Nantwich in Cheshire when he completed.

Onyinah became the first International Missions Director of the Church of Pentecost in 1991–1995. During that period, the church was still steeped in Ghanaian culture and its services were held mainly in Akan and other local languages. There were a few English services, but the liturgy was culturally-conditioned, making it difficult for the church to attract non-Ghanaians. Onyinah initiated the establishment of the multi-cultural churches called Pentecost International Worship

Centre (PIWC). These churches cater to non-Ghanaians and the younger generation of Ghanaians who prefer worshipping in a multicultural environment with contemporary outlook. They use English or French in their services.

Onyinah enrolled in the MA programme of Applied Theology at the Regents Theological College in 1996 and the degree was granted by the University of Manchester in 1998. He obtained a doctoral degree at the University of Birmingham in 2002. His thesis addresses the traditional roots of the fear of witches and other malevolent spirits which is prevalent in African Christianity and other malevolent spirits. He also suggests that the gospel is a powerful resolution to the world of spirits. Onyinah developed a new area of research called "witchdemonology." He published *Pentecostal Exorcism* and *Spiritual Warfare* as well as several journal articles which offer direct insights regarding African religious anxieties.

Onyinah was the Principal of the Pentecost Bible College and initiated the upgrade of the College to a full-fledged university called the Pentecost University College in Accra for which he was the first Rector in 2004. He became the Chairman of the Church of Pentecost from 2008 to 2018. During this period the church experienced exceptional growth. Its missions reached 30 new countries for a total of 99 countries served, 7000 new local churches established growing to a total number of 20,865, and membership growth from 1.7 to 3 million.

Onyinah has made a significant impact on African Pentecostal thought and practice. He engages his scholarly and pastoral work with real life situations in the church and fosters a congenial relationship between the academy and the church. He stresses the need for the theological academy to serve the mission of the church. As the Chairman, he worked hard to move the church from being inward looking and separatist that discouraged certain people in society from accepting faith in Christ. One of the practices that he eradicated was the wearing of a headcovering by women. Most of the local churches insisted that all adult women must cover their heads during worship services. Visitors who did not know about this practice and arrived at any of those churches were given a scarf to cover their head. This was sent to the churches in a communique in 2010. He worked to change the image of the African Pentecostal pastorate from one of anti-intellectualism to one that is engaged in scholarship inspired by the Holy Spirit.

Onyinah's ecumenical activities were diverse. He was the co-chairman of Empowered 21 Africa, Advisory Board Member of *International Review of Mission*, member of the Catholic-Pentecostal International Dialogue (the sixth phase in 2011–2015 and the seventh phase in 2018), member of the Standing Committee of Health and Healing held by the World Council of Churches (WCC) and German Institute for Medical Mission (DIFÄM), member of the Commission on World Mission and Evangelism of the WCC, and member of the Editorial Board of the *Journal of Pentecostal Theology* since 2007. Throughout his ministry, he has distinguished himself as a theologian, ecumenist, missiologist, theological educator and Christian leader on both national and international platforms.

Bibliography

Annor-Antwi, Gibson. 2016. *Myth or Mystery: A Bio-autobiography of Apostle Professor Opoku Onyinah*. London: Inved.

Donkor, Lord Elorm, and Clifton Clarke. 2018. *African Pentecostal Missions maturing:*

Essays in Honor of Apostle Opoku Onyinah. Eugene, OR: Wipf and Stock.

Onyinah, Opoku. 2012. *Pentecostal and Exorcism: Witchcraft and Demonology in Ghana.* Blandford: Deo Publishing.

Onyinah, Opoku. 2012. *Spiritual Warfare: A Centre for Pentecostal Theology Short Introduction.* Cleveland: CTP Publishing LTD.

Onyinah, Opoku. 2002. "Akan Witchcraft and the Concept of Exorcism in the Church of Pentecost." PhD thesis, University of Birmingham, UK.

Lord Elorm Donkor

Osborn, T.L.

Tommy Lee Osborn (December 23, 1923–February 14, 2013) was an American independent itinerant Pentecostal evangelist. He held hundreds of open-air "mass-miracle-crusades" with healing ministry to millions for six decades, especially in the global south. He and his wife Daisy Washburn established the headquarters of Osborn Ministries International in Tulsa, Oklahoma in 1949. They were married for 53 years and engaged in evangelistic ministry together until Daisy passed away in 1995. Osborn continued to evangelise for another 15 years until he died in 2013. Since then the ministry has been succeeded by their daughter LaDonna Osborn.

After a disastrous experience as missionaries to India in 1945, the Osborns returned to the U.S. to pastor a church. In 1947, while witnessing successful healing of W.M. Branham in a campaign in Portland, Oregon, Osborn received his personal call to healing ministry. In 1948 the couple started to organize a ministry and had success in Jamaica in 1949. In 1951, he published his first book *Healing the Sick* as a manual for performing healing. It was translated into many languages and one million copies were sold. Osborn adhered to the theology of "Finished Work." He taught that healing was a completed work for everyone and emphasised that both the healing evangelist and the seekers should believe in "God's un-condemning, non-judgmental love in action." It is assumed that his theology of faith healing and prosperity was built upon the same views of faith and positive thinking that Kenneth E. Hagin borrowed from E.W. Kenyon, who in turn took the idea from the Unity School of Christianity.

In 1953 Osborn formed the Association for Native Evangelism. He was convinced that native workers should be trained to launch mass crusades. For this venture he partnered with many Pentecostal groups. He was one of the first missionaries who conducted evangelism and prayed for miracles in open fields in non-Christian nations. Today it has become a standard procedure. The Osborn National Missionary Assistance Program has sponsored over 30,000 national men and women as full-time missionaries to non-Christian tribes and villages. Over 150,000 new churches have been established and have become self-supporting through this evangelism program.

Osborn was influenced by and cooperated with independent Pentecostal healing evangelists such as William M. Branham, Oral Roberts, F.F. Bosworth, A.A. Allen, Gordon Lindsay, and Kenneth E. Hagin. He was affiliated with the Voice of Healing Organization. In 1958, he started a "co-evangelism" program which encouraged indigenous evangelists to use his films and to distribute his literature. He generally supported these missionaries for only one year. He trained them to

T.L. Osborn in The Hague during a revival meeting on 22 august 1958.
Source: Nationaal Archief. Photo: Herbert Behrens, Anefo.

build self-supporting congregations and provided them with vehicles, loudspeakers, etc. This was considered to be a viable project as western long-term missionaries in the mission field could be linked with Osborn's organization and the native evangelists. They were able to conduct evangelistic campaigns, provide training in Bible schools, and distribute teaching materials together.

In 1958, Gordon Lindsay discovered that Tommy was "unusually gifted" and offered him financial support. He was therefore able to launch an independent ministry in 1959. In 1961, Osborn used all kinds of media to evangelise inside and outside the U.S. In the late 1960s he focused on youth revivals in the U.S. It was a timely move as the Jesus People Movement had already begun to influence the youth. He adopted young people's language and even changed his hair style and wardrobe to identify himself with them. Osborn's missionary principle was considered to be innovative, grassroots, and intercultural. This was also reflected by the way that the Osborns adapted to the cultural customs of the countries of the southern hemisphere. The worship songs and the overall musical framework were decided by the local people.

In 1956, the Osborns' ministry employed 17 workers. The ministry published a magazine called *Faith Digest* and two years later it was printed in different languages with 250,000 copies distributed monthly. Osborn produced and circulated a movie dramatizing his work and started a radio ministry costing $10,000 every month. The films and videos of "Osborn Documentary Miracle" were produced in 67 languages and shown in thousands of villages and towns of 150 countries. Their books and tracts were published in 132 languages. The couple travelled to over 70 countries to hold large crusades by the 1980s.

Bibliography

Harrell, David Edwin Jr. 1975. *All Things Are Possible. The Healing & Charismatic Revivals in Modern America*. Bloomington: Indiana University Press.

Osborn, Tommy Lee. 1950. *Healing the Sick*. Tulsa: Harrison House Publishers.

Osborn, Tommy Lee and Daisy Osborn. 1985. *The Gospel according to T.L. & Daisy. Classic Documentary*. Tulsa: Osborn-Publishers.

Riss, Richard M. 2002. "Osborn, Tommy Lee." In *The New International Dictionary of Pentecostal and Charismatic Movement*, edited by Stanley M. Burgess and Eduard M. van der Maas, 950–951. Grand Rapids: Zondervan.

Moritz Fischer

Otabil, Mensa

Mensa Anamuah Otabil (August 31, 1959–) was an Anglican who made a personal commitment to Christ at the age of twelve. He then started attending an Assemblies of God church where he received the baptism of the Holy Spirit in 1975. In 1983, during a prayer meeting, Otabil announced his decision to start his own church called International Central Gospel Church (ICGC). From its beginning in February 1984 in Accra, Ghana the ICGC has grown to over 97,000 members, with 596 branches, of which 24 are in Europe and North America.

Otabil's messages are deeply connected with the liberation of the perceived African mindset of inferiority. He seeks to empower his audience, especially Africans, to "buy their future." Otabil focuses on African consciousness, liberation of the mind from defeatism and slavery mentality. He also talks about empowering for success in every sphere of life. Often using his personal success as a point of reference, Otabil seeks to empower his African audience to believe in their ability for success. For Otabil, the problem of Africa is not simply deliverance from demons and evil spirits, but transformation of thinking and life choices. His messages and theology are a mix of soteriology, liberation, success, and empowerment. With the Bible as a basis for his messages, Otabil stresses personal transformation as essential for success.

Otabil was voted as the most influential person by Ghanaians in 2015. He is widely known as the teacher of the nation. His radio and television programme, "Living Word," is listened and watched by millions in Ghana. He is noted for speaking about various national and political issues in Ghana. He is seen as one of the leading voices of Ghanaian pastors, African liberationists and progressive theologians. He speaks on many subjects nationally and internationally with the aim of impacting and motivating Africans to be proactive in establishing an African Christian identity. He has authored several books and devotionals. Known for his insatiable love for African fashion, Otabil is always seen in his traditional Ghanaian or African clothes. This has become a mark of his African consciousness and identity as a successful modern African Christian.

As an entrepreneur, Otabil has established and overseen the development of the training institute of the church from a ministerial institute in 1988 to Central University in 2016. It is now a leading university in Ghana and offers various undergraduate and postgraduate programmes. As a philanthropist, Mensa Otabil facilitates a programme which helps the poor and needy. In 1988, the church initiated an education grant programme which offers scholarships to pre-tertiary students, which is seen as one of the largest non-governmental scholarships in Ghana.

The church continues to make significant social and development contributions to hospitals, orphanages, and the needy in society.

Bibliography

Asamoah-Gyadu, J. Kwabena. 2005. *African Charismatics: Current Developments Within Independent Indigenous Pentecostalism in Ghana*. Leiden: Brill.

De Witte, Marlene. 2018. "'Buy the Future': Charismatic Pentecostalism and African Liberation in a Neoliberal World." In *Pentecostalism and Politics in Africa*, edited by Adeshina Afolayan, Olajumoke Yacob-Haliso, and Toyin Falola, 65–85. London: Palgrave Macmillan.

Gifford, Paul. 2004. *Ghana's New Christianity: Pentecostalism in a Globalizing African Economy*. Bloomington and Indianapolis: Indiana University Press.

Kalu, Ogbu. 2008. *African Pentecostalism: An Introduction*. Oxford: Oxford University Press.

Larbi, Kingsley E. 2001. *Pentecostalism: The Eddies of Ghanaian Christianity*. Accra: CPCP.

Caleb Nyanni

Page, Albert T. and Lou

Albert Page (1882–1918) was an Australian born evangelist and Love Lou Farrington (1886–1919) was an American school teacher. They met in the U.S. Love was her first name and by all accounts this was her nature. She was known by her middle name of Lou.

In 1905, Albert spent time in India working in the Government Service prior to coming to the U.S. where he encountered a Pentecostal mission and accepted Christ. Shortly after, he went to New York where he established a church and was later ordained as a Pentecostal Minister. Albert and Lou met through his ministry work and they married in 1911. Lou was baptized on July 4, 1911 and Albert was baptized on March 1, 1912.

Shortly after their wedding in the U.S., they travelled to Australia to see family. During a stop-over in Fiji they felt called to return to Fiji to minister to the people there, which they did after the birth of their first baby a few months later. With the assistance of Sister A. Ronnberg, they commenced their ministry in downtown Suva. Their first converts were Solomon Islanders living in a village in Matata. Albert developed strong relationships with members of the Fijian, Indian, and Solomon Islander communities where he saw many come to know Jesus. This was pioneering work because at that time in history, Indians were considered a subclass of laborers and Albert and Lou were among the first Christian missionaries in Fiji to reach out to them.

Without the support of a church behind them, it was incredibly difficult at times for the growing family who now had four children. With little income, they were living in leaking huts and surviving on meagre rations. Albert was known to walk or ride a bike between villages to preach, evangelize, and hand out gospel literature.

In 1916 the family moved inland to the Sigatoka River where Lou set up a school for the children of Indian shopkeepers in exchange for living supplies. By 1917, their school had 25 students and had become a ministry base for reaching out and ministering to the Indian community.

Albert felt called to extend his work into the Solomon Islands and commenced working towards this calling but unfortunately, he did not get the chance to fulfil this. In late 1917, the newly established

General Council of Assemblies of God in the United States of America (AGUSA) officially recognized the work being done in Fiji by the Pages and they were nominated as "Appointed Missionaries." This provided the Pages with additional spiritual support and a small financial contribution easing the burden on their family.

Albert was faithful in spending time with those who were sick, which is why in November 1918 he travelled to Suva with a newly converted Indian man to minister in temporary hospitals to those inflicted with the Spanish influenza. Sadly, both men fatally contracted the disease themselves and Albert passed away on December 9, 1918. His faith never left him, and even as the illness took hold, he was reportedly sharing his faith with others saying with a smile, "Don't worry about this old body, I shall soon have the glorified one in His Presence."

Upon Albert's death, Lou remained living in the interior with four children aged between 18 months and six years old. In February 1919, Lou wrote in the *Christian Evangel* that "the conflict has been great, but thus far I have had victory through the Blood. I intend to stay on here until I am sure of the Lord's leading and meanwhile, I shall do all I can for the spread of the gospel." She carried on with the ministry work she had started with Albert. For three months Lou continued to teach at the school, distribute Bibles and share her faith until she too succumbed to the same disease that took her husband's life. The four newly orphaned children spent time living in Fiji with a missionary until arrangements were made for them to move to Australia to live with family. Within months, the youngest daughter had passed away due to illness. The older three children, James, Olive, and Lloyd, moved to New York and went to live with separate relatives.

The work of Albert and Lou Page was instrumental in sowing the seeds for Pentecostal expansion across the islands of the southeast Pacific. After the Albert and Lou's passing, Adrian and Charlotte Heetebry continued their ministry which led to the founding of the first recognized and endorsed Assemblies of God Fiji (AGF) congregation in 1926. This church sent out missionaries who went and established Assemblies of God churches across the Melanesian region, including in Vanuatu, the Solomon Islands, and New Caledonia. The prevalence and strength of the Pentecostal church in the region is a legacy of the sacrificial and ground-breaking work of Albert and Lou Page.

Bibliography

Anderson, Allan. 2007. *Spreading Fires: The Missionary Nature of Early Pentecostalism*. London: SCM.

Dahler Kowalski, Rosemarie. 2014. "What Made Them Think They Could? Assemblies of God Female Missionaries." *Assemblies of God Heritage* 34: 70–71.

Larson, Lawrence R. 1997. *The Spirit in Paradise: History of the Assemblies of God of Fiji & Its Ministries to Other Countries of the South Pacific*. St. Louis, MO: Lawrence R. Larson.

Page, Lou. 1919. "In the Regions Beyond: Sister Lou Page writes ..." *The Christian Evangel: The Pentecostal Paper for the Home* 278 & 279 (March 8): 10.

Page, Lou. 1919. "In the Regions Beyond: Nadroga, Fiji." *The Christian Evangel: The Pentecostal Paper for the Home* 276 & 277 (February 22): 10.

Kellesi Gore

Palestine

In Palestine there are about 70,000 Christians in the West Bank and 1000 in Gaza out of a total population numbering approximately 4.5 million. Christians comprise approximately 2 percent of the population of the West Bank and less than 1 percent in Gaza. Christian groups in the West Bank and Gaza include Eastern Orthodoxy, Oriental Orthodoxy, Catholicism (Eastern and Western rites), Anglicanism, Protestantism, and Pentecostalism, concentrated mainly in East Jerusalem, Ramallah, Nablus, and Bethlehem (Sabella 2018, 141–42). Modern Pentecostalism was introduced to Palestine by missionaries associated with Classical Pentecostalism. As with other Western missionaries, Pentecostals in Palestine gained most of their converts by proselytizing Orthodox and Catholic Christian communities rather than by evangelizing non-Christians. Leaders of the historic indigenous churches of Palestine express resentment toward Pentecostals and Evangelicals for weakening their stance against Islam. At present there is no formal cooperation between the Middle East Council of Churches and any Pentecostal body in this region of the world (Robeck 2014, 206).

Pentecostalism emerged in Palestine during al-nakba, the War of 1948. About 715,000 Palestinian Arabs were caught in the crossfire between the armies of five Arab nations and the newly established State of Israel. Of these refugees, seven percent, or 50,000, were Christians (Sabella 1999, 84). It is estimated that 37 percent of the Christians in Jerusalem fled and became refugees (Dumper 1999, 60). In the crush of the Palestinian diaspora, many refugees resorted to living in tents, caves, and under trees out in the fields because there was no housing for them. The Suleiman family, formerly associated with Assemblies of God, fled from Jerusalem at the beginning of the war and settled in Bethlehem. They soon began holding services in their home. A Church of God (COG) missionary in the Middle East, D.B. Hatfield, held services in the Suleiman home. The political situation stabilized when jurisdiction over Bethlehem was transferred from the Egyptian army to the Hashemite Kingdom of Jordan. Hatfield came to Bethlehem and rented a building known as "the cave" where the Church of God established a work in Bethlehem. By the summer of 1950 the COG church in Bethlehem had grown to 100 in weekly attendance (Newberg 2012, 133–34).

In 1953, George M. Kuttab (1922–2006), a native of Jerusalem and former pastor of the Nazarene Church in Zarka, Jordan, affiliated with the COG and assumed leadership of the congregations in Bethlehem, Beit Jala and Beit Sahur (Conn 1977, 272–73). In 1962 the COG purchased land on the Mount of Olives and a church was built, including a residential facility. Kuttab assumed primary leadership of the newly established COG church on the Mount of Olives, which until 1967 was located outside of Israel in the territory of the Hashemite Kingdom of Jordan. Kuttab was well suited for the Arab population in East Jerusalem. He was known as a patriot of the Palestinian cause who would often speak out against the injustices suffered by the Palestinians (Newberg 2012, 135–36).

In 1964 Margaret Gaines (1931–2017), a graduate of Lee College, arrived in Israel after serving 10 years in Tunisia and two years in France as a COG missionary. Early on in her ministry Gaines started two churches. The first was in the village of Aboud, 33 miles northwest of Jerusalem. According to tradition, Aboud was the birthplace of the Old Testament prophet Obadiah (Gaines 1969, 7). Aboud had been an important Christian site with a population of 40,000 in the fifth century. Since then its population decreased to 3,000, of which half were Christian and half were Muslim. The second church planted by Gaines was in Amman, Jordan, where she rented an apartment so she could itinerate back and forth (Gaines 2000, 168–70).

Political events placed a damper on the COG mission and exposed Gaines to many ordeals. In 1964 the Palestinian Liberation Organization was founded by the Arab League with the purpose of waging an armed struggle for the liberation of Palestine. By July Jordan suspended its ties with the PLO, disavowing the PLO raids across Jordan into Israel, which nonetheless continued unabated. Provocations on both sides led to a war in 1967 in which Israel defeated the armies of Egypt, Jordan, and Syria and occupied the West Bank, East Jerusalem, Gaza, the Sinai Peninsula, and the Golan Heights. Since 1967 a total of about 300,000 Palestinians, including 18,000 Christians, have emigrated from the West Bank and Gaza in search of employment, reunification with family, education, and political stability (Sabella 1999, 92). However, according to Gaines (2000), after the 1967 war the Pentecostal mission benefited from a period of relative political stability in the West Bank. Work in Israel even at the minimum wage allowed families to enjoy a sense of prosperity and relief from hardship.

In March 1999 Gaines retired and left the field. She could take satisfaction in the fruit of the Pentecostal mission in Palestine. She had planned and secured funding for the construction of a Christian school and additions to the Church of God building in Aboud. The school's enrollment had increased from 32 to 121 between 1993 and 1999. The Department of Education held the principal and the teachers in high regard. Gaines was confident in the local Pentecostal leadership she had developed. In September 1999 her protégés Nihad and Salwa Salman established Immanuel Evangelical Church in Bethlehem, which grew to more 60 families and 250 congregants. Immanuel Church in turn planted churches in Ramleh and Haifa, and opened Christian book stores in Bethlehem and Haifa. With the sponsorship of World Vision and the Church of the Brethren in Germany, Immanuel Evangelical Church constructed an outreach center in Beit Jala with a vision for community outreach (Newberg 2012, 145).

Today a handful of Pentecostal congregations continue to operate in the West Bank, including Aboud Church and Elementary School, House of Bread Church and Immanuel Evangelical Church in Bethlehem, and New Life Evangelical Church of Ramallah. Virtually all of the congregants in these churches trace their roots to Orthodox and Catholic communities, as was generally the case with Protestants in Palestine since the eighteenth century. Palestinian Pentecostals are not exclusively anti-Israel, but this is by far the majority point of view (Sturm and Frantzman 2014, 2). In line with the strategy adumbrated in the Kairos Palestine document of 2009, Pentecostals in Palestine have appealed to their coreligionists in the West for greater awareness of the suffering of Palestinian Christians (Alexander 2012).

Bibliography

Alexander, Paul, ed. 2012. *Christ at the Checkpoint: Theology in the Service of Justice and Peace*. Eugene, OR: Wipf & Stock.

Conn, Charles W. 1977. *Where the Saints Have Trod: A History of the Church of God*. Cleveland, TN: Pathway, 1977.

Dumper, Michael. 1999. "Faith and Statecraft: Church-State Relations in Jerusalem after 1948." In *Palestinian Christians: Religion, Politics and Society in the Holy Land*, edited by Anthony O'Mahony, 56–81. London: Melisende.

Gaines, Margaret. 2000. *Of Like Passions: Missionary to the Arabs*. Cleveland, TN: Pathway.

Newberg, Eric Nelson. 2012. *Pentecostal Mission in Palestine: The Legacy of Pentecostal Zionism*. Eugene, OR: Pickwick.

Robeck, Jr., Cecil M. and Amos Yong, eds. 2014. *The Cambridge Companion to Pentecostalism*. Cambridge: Cambridge University Press.

Ross, Kenneth R., Mariz Tadros, and Todd Johnson, eds. 2018. *Christianity in North Africa and West Asia*. Edinburgh: Edinburgh University Press.

Sabella, Bernard. 1999. "Socio-economic Characteristics and Challenges to Palestinian Christians in the Holy Land." In *Palestinian Christians: Religion, Politics and Society in the Holy Land*, edited by Anthony O'Mahony, 82–95. London: Melisende.

Sturm, Tristan, and Seth Frantzman. 2014. "Religious Geopolitics of Palestinian Christianity: Palestinian Christian Zionists, Palestinian Liberation Theologians, and American Missions to Palestine." *Middle Eastern Studies* 20 (3): 1–19. https://doi.org/10.1080/00263206.2014.971768.

Eric Newberg

Paraguay

Paraguay is a land-locked country in South America of 7 million people (CIA 2019). The Philadelphia Evangelical Church arrived in 1938 and the Assemblies of God in 1945. The Church of God (Cleveland, TN) started in 1954. For many years, Pentecostal growth was limited. More successful was a unique local brand of Pentecostalism: *El Pueblo de Dios* (The People of God), founded in 1963. The last U.S. Pentecostal church arrived in 1985: the International Church of the Foursquare Gospel. That same year, Pastor Emilio Abreu founded the *Centro Familiar de Adoración* megachurch.

Brazilian neo-Pentecostal churches, emphasizing faith healing and prosperity, started using old cinemas in the mid-1990s. The Universal Church of the Kingdom of God and the God Is Love church attracted some Paraguayans (Barrett *et al.* 2001; Holland 2006). Protestants and Pentecostals numbered about 6 percent of the population in 2002. Mandryk (2010, 676) reported 10 percent Protestants, including 4.6 percent Pentecostals, in Paraguay.

The Catholic Charismatic Renewal (CCR) started in 1967 at Duquesne University and in Bogotá, Colombia (Cleary 2011), stressing the gifts of the Holy Spirit and personal discipline. In 1973, the CCR arrived in Paraguay with U.S. Redemptorist Father Andrew Carr at Perpetuo Socorro parish in Asunción. It had success among urban middle classes. A second growth period started in the 1990s under the central CCR organization in Asunción's Barrio Herrera, which organized mass meetings in soccer stadiums. The Catholic Charismatic Renewal reported 106,480 participants in 1995 – 5 percent of all Catholics, but 40 percent of active Catholics (Barrett *et al.* 2001, 588). In 2005, the Paraguayan bishops ended the central organization and the mass meetings. Like elsewhere in Latin America, the bishops encouraged priests and lay leaders to create new CCR prayer groups at parish level.

In 2010, Paraguay had the lowest CCR presence of all countries in Latin America: the total CCR community was estimated at 112,000 or only 2 percent of all Catholics. Even so, this number was highly inflated. There were 84 CCR parishes in the metropolitan area of Asunción, with a total participation of perhaps 3,000 adult participants. Ciudad del Este and Encarnación had much smaller groups, and the CCR did not have a strong presence elsewhere. This suggests a total national number of 5,000–8,000 participants. Adding children, relatives, ex-charismatics, and sympathizers yields a total CCR community in Paraguay of 15,000–25,000 (Gooren 2012, 200).

In 1945, a missionary of the U.S. Assemblies of God arrived in Encarnación to help war refugees (Duarte 1994: 106). In 1950, he organized the first congregation in Asunción. The first Assemblies of God Council was organized in 1958. By 1987, the *Concilio de las Asambleas de Dios del Paraguay* had 53 congregations and 35 daughter congregations, with a total of 5,550 baptized adults and a community of 12,200.

The total Assemblies of God membership in Paraguay grew from 2,000 in 1970 to 1,050 in 1980, 5,550 in 1987, 6,450 in 1993, 27,620 in 1995, and 12,454 in 2000 (Gooren 2013). In the 2002 national census, 9,879 people self-identified as members (79 percent of the membership).

A missionary of the *Iglesia de Dios del Paraguay* arrived in Asunción from Chile in April 1954, soon opening the first church (Núñez 2004: 27–28). He represented the Chilean branch of the classical Pentecostal Church of God from Cleveland, TN. By 1987, the *Iglesia de Dios del Paraguay* had only five congregations and six daughter congregations in Asunción, but 53 congregations and 80 daughter congregations in rural areas. It had 2,700 baptized adults and a wider community of 5,800 (Plett 1988, 114).

The *Iglesia de Dios del Paraguay* membership grew from 1,050 in 1970 to 820 in 1980, 2,700 in 1987, 3,471 in 1993, and 7,975 in 2000 (Gooren 2013). In the 2002 national census, only 1,550 people self-identified as Church of God members (19.4 percent of the membership).

In 1985, the *Centro Familiar de Adoración* (CFA) was founded by Pastor Emilio Abreu, born in Asunción in 1954 in a Brazilian business family. First the group met in hotels and members' houses, until in December 1987 they finished the building on Avenida España, which seated 2,000. In 2009, the new CFA temple was inaugurated in middle-class Barrio Herrera. It was 80 percent finished in 2010 and seated 10,000. In July-August 2010, average Sunday church attendance was 2,000–4,000. The huge building cost US $5 million and had a bookstore, a daycare center, meeting rooms, and offices. In 2010, the church had 17,000–20,000 members in Asunción and 20,000 elsewhere.

Multiple factors explained CFA's success. First, it maintained strong visibility in mass media and Asunción. Second, the CFA had a sophisticated system to track first-time visitors. They were asked to stand up during church meetings, come forward, and accompany pastors to record their information. The Mission department later contacted them, invited them to meetings, and connected them with cell group leaders. Third, it had 1,500 church cells in Asunción and 1,500 elsewhere. Fourth, the CFA had a pastoral corps of over a dozen married couples. Fifth, it was popular for the quality of its music and sermons. Sixth, the CFA combined multiple evangelization activities: Internet, books, a monthly magazine, special events (like a concert by Marcos Witt), training for pastors from other churches, Bible classes, leadership courses, and a prison ministry.

"More than Conquerors" started early 2001 as a prayer and Bible study group of Emilio Agüero and seven siblings and cousins, who recruited ever more friends and acquaintances. The group met in Agüero's parents' business, then an uncle's garage, their grandmother's patio, and finally in a friend's house; by 2002, it had 150 visitors.

Like the *Centro Familiar de Adoración*, MQV was very active in the mass media. In 2012, the *Más que Vencedores* website was among the most-visited of Paraguay. In 2006, Emilio Agüero started his TV program *Sálvese quien quiera* on Red Guaraní with interviews, preaching, and music. It drew 15,000–25,000 viewers in 2012, when Red Guaraní also started transmitting Agüero's sermons.

In 2009, MQV moved to a new building on Rodó 198, centrally-located east of downtown Asunción. That same year they started their glossy color magazine, *Libres*. In 2010, MQV started its radio program. Agüero sold his businesses in 2012 to become a fulltime pastor. Sunday attendance was 350–400. Agüero said 80 percent was 20 to 35; 10–15 percent was upper class and 60 percent middle class.

Bibliography

Barrett, David B., George T. Kurian, and Todd M. Johnson. 2001. *World Christian Encyclopedia*, Second Edition. Oxford: Oxford University Press.

Central Intelligence Agency (CIA). 2019. *The World Factbook: Paraguay*. Accessed June 19, 2019. https://www.cia.gov/library/publications/the-world-factbook/geos/pa.html.

Cleary, Edward L. 2011. *The Rise of Charismatic Catholicism in Latin America*. Gainesville, FL: University Press of Florida.

Duarte P., Rogelio. 1994. *El desafío protestante en el Paraguay*. Asunción: Centro Cristiano de Comunicación Creativa.

Gooren, Henri. 2013. "The Growth and Development of Non-Catholic Churches in Paraguay." In *Spirit and Power: The Growth and Global Impact of Pentecostalism*, edited by Donald E. Miller, Kimon H. Sargeant, and Richard Flory, 83–98. New York: Oxford University Press.

Gooren, Henri. 2012. "The Catholic Charismatic Renewal in Latin America." *Pneuma* 34 (2): 185–207.

Holland, Clifton L. 2006. "Paraguay." In *Worldmark Encyclopedia of Religious Practices*, edited by Andrew Riggs, *Volume 3, Countries M-Z*, 139–143. Detroit, MI: Thomson Gale.

Mandryk, Jason. 2010. *Operation World*. Seventh Edition. Colorado Springs, CO: Biblical Publishing.

Núñez, Miguel Atilio. 2004. *Historia de la Iglesia de Dios en el Paraguay*. Asunción: Iglesia de Dios del Paraguay.

Plett, Rodolfo. 1988. *El protestantismo en el Paraguay*. Asunción: FLET/IBA.

Henri Gooren

Parham, Charles

Born June 4, 1873 in Muscatine, Iowa, Charles Fox Parham was a holiness preacher, evangelist, and founder of the Bethel Healing Home and Bible school in Topeka, Kansas. He became the self-proclaimed Projector of the Apostolic Faith Movement, where he popularized the teaching that the "Bible evidence" of baptism in the Holy Spirit is speaking in other tongues. A small number of Apostolic Faith churches that he led, are located primarily in the south-central region of the United States.

As a young boy, Parham was quite ill. When he received healing through prayer, he determined that he would enter the ministry. He enrolled at Southwest Kansas College, but left soon thereafter, deciding that it was unnecessary for successful ministry. For a short time, he served as an interim Methodist pastor before engaging

Charles Parham, 1873–1929

more fully in the Holiness Movement and founding the Bethel Healing Home. He followed the teaching of John Alexander Dowie (Zion, Illinois), who encouraged his belief in divine healing. He adopted Frank Sandford's (Shiloh, Maine) teaching that God was restoring the church to its original New Testament purity and power, as well as his Anglo-Israel theory. The Anglo-Israel doctrine posited the superiority of the Anglo-Saxon race as the descendants of the lost tribes of Israel. The way that Parham applied this doctrine to the "Bride of Christ" was devastating to African Americans. Parham's interest in the fulfillment of biblical prophecy led him also to support the modern, secular Zionist Movement. Finally, David Baker, a Quaker and the grandfather of Sarah Thistlethwaite, Parham's future wife, introduced Parham to another provocative idea. The wicked would not experience eternal punishment, but would undergo annihilation.

In 1900, Parham founded a short-term Bible school in Topeka, Kansas. In late December 1900, Parham left his students to ponder the question, "What evidence does the Bible give that the disciples received the baptism with the Holy Spirit?" They responded that, according to Acts 2:4, the Apostles had spoken in other tongues. That New Year's Eve, the students prayed and a young woman, Agnes Ozman asked the rest to lay hands on her so that she might experience this baptism. That night the group allegedly ushered in the new century with Ozman speaking in other tongues as the Holy Spirit enabled her.

Local newspapers covered this incident in Topeka and for several months, Parham was in demand as a speaker. While many people soon lost interest, Parham continued to hold meetings in Kansas, Missouri, and Texas. Under the name Apostolic Faith Movement, Parham contended that he was simply restoring to the contemporary church the "Apostolic Faith," that is, the beliefs and practices of the original apostles. Following a highly publicized healing incident in Old Orchard, Texas in 1905, Parham, once again became a public figure. He focused attention on Houston, Texas. He dressed his students in Middle-Eastern costumes that he had purchased, and paraded them through the city's streets. He attracted attention by proclaiming his hope of locating Noah's Ark as well as the Ark of the Covenant, and he made the case for the restoration of Jews to their homeland in Israel.

In August 1905, Parham asked a local African American holiness pastor, Lucy Farrow, to accompany his family to Kansas while he held meetings there. She left a young African American minister, William J. Seymour, in charge of her congregation. When she returned to Houston in December, she reported that she had received the baptism in the Spirit and spoken in tongues. She encouraged Seymour to attend the new Bible school Parham established in Houston. Seymour studied there for about six weeks, before accepting a call to pastor a holiness church in Los Angeles. While he rejected many of Parham's idiosyncratic teachings, he accepted and preached the doctrine of baptism in the Spirit taught by Parham. The founder of the congregation accused him of preaching false doctrine and called for an inquiry. Seymour was forced to leave. He then began a Bible study that quickly developed into a global revival.

Seymour respected Charles Parham as his "father in the [Pentecostal] faith." In 1906, he invited Parham to hold meetings in Los Angeles. Parham initially promised to come by mid-September. Instead, he made a detour to Zion, Illinois. Dowie was now in trouble, and Parham, seeking to take advantage of the situation, spent nearly six weeks preaching in Zion before traveling to Los Angeles. When Parham arrived in Los Angeles at the end of October, he visited the Azusa Street Mission. He quickly rejected what he saw there. Seymour, he claimed, had let things get out of control. Parham characterized the revival as fanatical, and preached a sermon titled "God Is Sick at His Stomach." The congregation protested, claiming that they had prayed down their own revival. The elders insisted that Parham leave the Mission. For a short time, he opened meetings nearby.

Parham returned to Zion City in late December, where he preached to a crowd of 2,000 people on New Year's Eve. From there, Parham continued travelling to Cleveland, Toronto, Boston, Syracuse, back to Cleveland, Zion City and finally to Kansas and Texas. Rumors of sexual misconduct began circulating. In March 1907, a schism developed in his Apostolic Faith Mission over these rumors. W.F. Carothers, a Federal judge, who headed Parham's work in Texas, offered Parham the opportunity to explain. Parham refused, and continued his meetings among his "faithful." On July 19, he was arrested on charges of committing an "unnatural offence." Allegedly, he confessed to this act but argued that it was not intentional. The prosecutor ultimately dropped the charges. News of his arrest spread quickly, though Parham insisted on his innocence. In May 1908, Carothers again offered Parham the opportunity to clear his name. Again, Parham refused. Though there were many who continued to support him, his reputation was irreparably harmed, and he struggled to maintain leadership. He continued to lead a small following until his death in Baxter Springs, Kansas, January 29, 1929.

Bibliography

Goff, James R., Jr. 1988. *Fields White unto Harvest: Charles F. Parham and the Missionary Origins of Pentecostalism.* Fayetteville, AR: The University of Arkansas Press.

Martin, Larry. 1997. *The Topeka Outpouring of 1901: Eyewitness Accounts of the Revival that Birthed the 20th Century Pentecostal/Charismatic Movement.* Joplin, MO: Christian Life Books.

Parham, Charles F. 1910. *A Voice Crying in the Wilderness.* Rev. ed. Baxter Springs, KS: Apostolic Faith Bible College.

Parham, Charles F. 1902. *Kol Kare Bomidbar: A Voice Crying in the Wilderness.* Baxter Springs, KS: Apostolic Faith Bible College.

Parham, Sarah E., ed. 1985. *The Life of Charles F. Parham: Founder of the Apostolic Faith Movement.* New York, NY: Garland Publishing, Inc. Originally published in c.1930, Joplin, MO: Hunter Printing Co.

Cecil M. Robeck

Pentecostal Assemblies of Canada

The Pentecostal Assemblies of Canada (PAOC) was established on May 17, 1919. What would eventually become the country's largest Pentecostal denomination, however, initially represented fewer than thirty congregations in eastern Canada. Also in 1919, Pentecostals in western Canada joined the American Pentecostal denomination, the Assemblies of God, as the Western Canada District Council of the Assemblies of God. The existence of two separate Canadian Pentecostal organizations was a result of the roughly geographical division of support for the New Issue – or Oneness Pentecostalism – that they each represented. Eastern Canadian Pentecostals – such as the Ontario-based leader, Robert Edward McAlister – were more sympathetic to a non-Trinitarian position, while western Canadian Pentecostals – such as the Winnipeg, Manitoba-based leader, Andrew Harvey Argue – tended to be more Trinitarian in their views. Desiring to see the two groups unite, McAlister – one of the original framers of the initially oneness PAOC – publically retracted his oneness views, became a minister with the Trinitarian Assemblies of God, and, in 1920, helped to successfully orchestrate a vote that saw the PAOC join the Assemblies of God as the Eastern Canada District Council of the Assemblies of God. In 1925 – after a period of theological, ritual, and organizational harmonization between the two Canadian districts – they amicably separated from the Assemblies of God and merged as a single national organization under the charter originally acquired by the PAOC in 1919. It is important to note that until 1949, what is now

PAOC East and West Districts, Kitchener. Source: Pentecostal Assemblies of Canada Archives

known as the Province of Newfoundland and Labrador, was a self-governing British dominion and so Pentecostals there established their own denomination – currently the Pentecostal Assemblies of Newfoundland and Labrador – which was, and remains, independent of the PAOC.

Despite the frequent use of anti-institutional language by the first generation of PAOC leaders, they proved to be extremely effective at initiating the institutionalization of the PAOC from a sect into a denomination. They accomplished this through establishing a number of national programs and institutions that contributed to the development of a shared religious subculture that subsequently allowed the PAOC to carve out a successful niche in the broader Canadian religious marketplace. In 1920, for instance, the PAOC published the first issue of its official publication, *The Pentecostal Testimony*, which played an incredibly important role in constructing and disseminating the emerging Pentecostal religious subculture among its widely geographically dispersed network of congregations. In 1925, the PAOC opened its first clergy training school, Western Bible College, in Winnipeg, Manitoba – followed by the establishment of colleges in six other provinces over the next twenty years – which was vital in the common socialization and education of its clergy. In 1927, the PAOC adopted a *Statement of Fundamental and Essential Truths*, officially codifying the denomination's positions on matters of religious belief and practice. Also, through establishing groups such as the Women's Missionary Council in 1944, Pentecostal Crusaders in 1954, and the National Department of Men's Fellowship in 1955, the PAOC strategically developed a wide array of cradle-to-grave programs intended to socialize, educate, mobilize, and proselytize women, children, and men, which further solidified the PAOC as a full-fledged denomination capable of competing with more established evangelical and mainline Protestant denominations. By 2017, the PAOC had grown considerably, reporting 247,042 adherents, and in 2018, reported 1,071 congregations, 3,720 clergy, and 583 foreign and domestic missionaries.

Notwithstanding the early Pentecostal proclivity for racial and gender inclusiveness, if not full equality, the PAOC very quickly reverted to racist and patriarchal Canadian social norms after its establishment. Although Slavic, Finnish, German, and Francophone Pentecostals were permitted to join the PAOC through the establishment of arm's length, ethnically-homogenous, and semi-autonomous branches of the denomination, more stigmatized groups such as African-Canadian and Italian Pentecostals were largely excluded and instead either affiliated their congregations with existing ethnic denominations in the United States or founded their own denominations. The PAOC, unfortunately, uses a haphazard assortment of often synonymous terms to describe their congregations that conflate languages, ethnicities, nationalities, and continents, which makes accurately assessing the ethnic diversity of PAOC congregations very difficult. Nonetheless, in 2018, 88.8 percent of PAOC congregations were comprised of just six groups – English (700), French (82), Indigenous (77), Spanish (45), Filipino (27), and Korean (20) – and in 2014, approximately 89.1 percent of PAOC clergy self-identified as white, suggesting that a significant majority of congregations are predominated by white Anglophones. The practice of conceptualizing its congregations according to language, ethnicity, nationality, or continent can be understood as a vestige of early PAOC eschatology (requiring global proselytization to precede the Second Coming of Jesus Christ) and foreign missions imaginary (relying on early twentieth century concepts of race and the nation-state) that demands a mechanism to record and report progress on its *raison d'être* of world-wide evangelism.

Indigenous peoples are one of the main groups targeted for strategic proselytization by the PAOC's domestic missionary department known as Mission Canada, which provides direction to Indigenous congregations through its Aboriginal Ministries Guiding Group. The practice of conceptually subordinating Indigenous congregations under Mission Canada – in the same way they do Francophone congregations – reiterates colonialist, paternalistic, and racist constructions of Indigenous peoples as especially in need of proselytization and guidance from white Anglophones, despite the facts that Indigenous peoples are just about as likely as Canadians as a whole (63 percent compared with 67 percent, respectively) to identify as Christians and are fully capable of managing their own affairs. Fetishizing specific domestic groups – particularly Indigenous and Francophone Canadians – as comprising "mission fields" is not incidental, but, rather, is enabled by deeply entrenched – although frequently unconscious – Canadian social norms supporting white, Anglophone, Protestant superiority.

Even though important contributions were made by several early Canadian Pentecostal women such as Zelma Argue, Ellen Hebden, and Aimee Semple McPherson, the leadership of the PAOC has always been dominated by men. In 2018, only 26.8 percent of all PAOC clergy and 5.5 percent of PAOC senior pastors were women, and, in 2019, just three of the PAOC's twenty-five member General Executive were women. Although women are not formally prohibited from holding any position or office within the PAOC, they are informally excluded from accessing many of the higher-paying and influence-wielding positions within the denomination. How the PAOC addresses – or fails to address – this structural inequality will very likely play an important role in its future as a denomination considering that a majority of PAOC clergy are currently eligible for retirement and the number of men seeking careers as clergy is decreasing across North American evangelicalism.

Bibliography

Miller, Thomas William. 1994. *Canadian Pentecostals: A History of the Pentecostal Assemblies of Canada*. Mississauga: Full Gospel Publishing House.

Stewart, Adam. 2015. *The New Canadian Pentecostals*. Waterloo, ON: Wilfrid Laurier University Press.

Wilkinson, Michael, ed. 2009. *Canadian Pentecostalism: Transition and Transformation*. Montreal & Kingston: McGill-Queen's University Press.

Wilkinson, Michael, and Linda Ambrose. 2020. *After the Revival: Pentecostalism and the Making of a Canadian Church*. Montreal & Kingston: McGill-Queen's University Press.

Wilkinson, Michael, and Peter Althouse, eds. 2010. *Winds From the North: Canadian Contributions to the Pentecostal Movement*. Leiden: Brill.

Adam Stewart

Pentecostal Assemblies of Newfoundland and Labrador

The Pentecostal Assemblies of Newfoundland (PAON) had already firmly established roots by 1949 when the British Dominion of Newfoundland became part of the Canadian confederation. As in most of early North American Pentecostalism, there were core distinctives of the new movement. Tongues-speaking seen as evidence of having received Spirit baptism, pre-millennial dispensationalism, salvation as the ultimate spiritual crisis experience preached with urgency in view of the imminence of Christ's return, and the immediate reality of divine healing were foundational themes that characterized the spirituality of the Newfoundland revival.

Its beginnings are popularly traced to Alice Bell Garrigus, an American holiness-Pentecostal evangelist from Connecticut. Garrigus had been motivated by several revival occurrences including news of the 1904 Welsh Revival and the 1906 North Bonnie Brae and Azusa Street meetings in Los Angeles. While attending a 1907 Christian and Missionary Alliance camp-meeting in Old Orchard, Maine, she also came under the influence of Frank Bartleman, the Azusa revival journalist. Garrigus claimed that in October 1908, she had been the recipient of a tongues and interpretation message in which she distinctly heard the word 'Newfoundland'. Confident that the message was genuine, she recalled having to consult a map to determine the island's location.

Garrigus' Pentecostal piety sharply contrasted the rigid Catholic and Anglican religious culture of St. John's, the capital city, but answered the quest for spiritual transformation then prevalent among a sprinkling of holiness-type groups. Under her direction, Bethesda Mission opened its doors in St. John's on Easter Sunday, 1911 at 193 New Gower Street. Although in succeeding years leadership rapidly became male dominated, as late as 1918, she continued to refer to herself as "Evangelist in charge of Bethesda Mission" rather than its pastor. The same missional perspective of Pentecostalism continued to pervade its spread across the island. No corner was too remote or intimidating for the early spirit of adventure.

Bethesda Mission became a place of healings as Garrigus had envisioned as well as manifestations of the Spirit. In spite of an eventual waning of its original fervor and the inevitable conflicting of personalities following its first decade, the fledging Pentecostal movement survived. Meanwhile, it received impetus from an unexpected source – international evangelist Victoria Booth-Clibborn Demarest (1889–1982). The granddaughter of William and Catherine Booth conducted revival meetings in early 1919 at Gower Street Methodist Church. Maude Evans Whitt, a convert of the services later referred to it as "the greatest revival ever known in Newfoundland." Reports indicate that between 1000 and 2000 people experienced salvation with some of them joining Bethesda Mission. The most prominent of these was Robert C. English, a local jeweler, who from 1920 until 1927 co-led with Garrigus and became the president or overseer of the nascent Pentecostal church.

Nevertheless, the leading figure in the later Garrigus era and following was Eugene Vaters, a young Methodist minister and schoolteacher who became disillusioned with the perceived liberal drift of his denomination. He came into contact with Pentecostalism through a brief encounter with the Mission and subsequently enrolled for a brief period at Moody Bible Institute. After attending Rochester Bible Training School and then exposure to the ministry of Charles E. Baker's Evangel Tabernacle in Montreal, he returned to the island conducting independent meetings in his hometown and eventually merged his mission with Bethesda creating a distinct denomination called the Bethesda Pentecostal Assemblies of Newfoundland. Local historian Burton Janes argues that the merger was a turning point in the history of Pentecostalism on the island.

The late 1920s saw the spread of the movement into western Newfoundland spearheaded by lay people with direct or indirect contact with the Bethesda revival from which, in turn, other missions were established in scores of small communities. A relationship developed with the Pentecostal Assemblies of Canada (PAOC) that while fraternal never developed into official administrative oversight. The Depression years resulted in substantial gains for Newfoundland Pentecostalism such that by the end of the decade, it was clearly established as a denomination and in search of government recognition to operate its own schools along with the other churches – a goal realized in 1954 and officially recognized in 1988 by the Government of Canada in accordance with the 1949 Terms of Union.

By 1945, the number of PAON adherents had doubled since 1935 and then from 1951 to 1961 almost doubled again. The decades of the 1960s to 1970s and well into the next decade continued to see significant forward movement in the building of new churches and schools. Under succeeding superintendents A. Stanley Bursey (1962–1982) and Roy D. King (1982–1996), ministerial training and missions initiatives accelerated and expanded as the denomination sought to deploy extra missionaries and to enhance the training of its minsters, both in collaboration with the PAOC. During this period, the PAON continued to place high value on its day-school education system and the recruitment of Pentecostal teachers. The local church education program was reinforced through use of the US Assemblies of God Sunday School curriculum and its other resources. In 1960, the PAON introduced the AG campus ministry, Chi Alpha to Memorial University of Newfoundland. The denomination flourished as it increasingly emphasized ministry to youth and introduced the PAOC Crusader children's program, built a senior citizens residence and operated several bookstores across the island. Communication and fellowship were facilitated through the inception in 1935 of its official publication *Good Tidings* and its summer camp meeting, Camp Emmanuel begun in 1947, which relocated and expanded in 1977 to subsequently become a wider convention and retreat facility.

By 1980, the PAON was operating 52 schools with an enrollment of 6500. However, the publicly funded day school system was disbanded in 1995 as the result of a provincial referendum. The 1981 census recorded 37,450 Pentecostals or 6.6 percent of the province's population. In recent years, the PAON, now the Pentecostal Assemblies of Newfoundland and Labrador (PAONL), has experienced along with other denominations significant decline in the face of a demographic shift away from the province due to negative economic realities. Statistics Canada notes that from 2001 to 2011, the loss continued from 33,840 Pentecostals to 33,195. The original mandate and vision remain unchanged but the denomination has slowly found itself blending into the larger evangelical landscape of the rest of North America.

Bibliography

Ambrose, Linda M. 2016. "Gender History in Newfoundland Pentecostalism: Alice Belle Garrigus and Beyond." *PentecoStudies* 15 (2): 172–199.

Janes, Burton K. 1996. *History of the Pentecostal Assemblies of Newfoundland*. St. John's, NL: Good Tidings Press.

Janes, Burton K. 1983. *The Lady Who Stayed: The Biography of Alice Belle Garrigus: Newfoundland's First Pentecostal Pioneer*. Vol. 2: *1908–1949*. St. John's, NL: Good Tidings Press.

Janes, Burton K. 1982. *The Lady Who Came: The Biography of Alice Bell Garrigus Newfoundland's First Pentecostal Pioneer*. Vol. 1: *1858–1908*. St. John's, NL: Good Tidings Press.

Rideout, F. David. 1992. *History of Pentecostal Schools in Newfoundland and Labrador*. St. John's, NL: Good Tidings.

Ewen Butler

Pentecostal Assemblies of the World

The Pentecostal Assemblies of the World (PAW) is the oldest existing Oneness Pentecostal (OP) organization. It is also one of the first Pentecostal bodies, established as a ministerial association in 1907 in the same year the black Holiness Church of God in Christ (COGIC) reorganized as a Pentecostal body. The PAW was from its beginning an interracial church of the Azusa Street Revival.

The first General Secretary was J.J. Frazee (1851–1930), an obscure but effective organizational leader. Following his election in 1912, he moved both PAW headquarters and his family from Los Angeles to Portland, OR. When he resigned in 1918, the headquarters was moved to Indianapolis. Here the fledgling PAW would be deeply influenced by Garfield T. Haywood (1880–1931), an emerging black Pentecostal pastor, theologian, and by 1915 an emerging leader within the New Issue movement, as OP was initially called. He had joined PAW in 1911, and in 1919 was critical in bringing the Oneness dissidents into the PAW fold. As newly elected General Secretary in 1919, Haywood was instrumental in reconstructing the organization's dual but inseparable identity as both Oneness and interracial. That year the number of black ministers who joined quadrupled.

This interracial-Oneness Pentecostal experiment held together for five years. But racial tensions between black and white, north and south, soon surfaced, revealing three specific issues. First, the southern ministers were frustrated that, due to southern segregation laws, annual conventions were restricted to the north. Meetings were held in Indianapolis from 1919 to 1922. Resentment was sparked among the blacks when the southern ministers scheduled the 1923 convention in segregated St. Louis. Second, the whites complained their interracial identity hindered evangelizing efforts in the south. Finally, many white ministers requested their ministerial license be signed by a white official. In an attempt to hold the fellowship together a compromise was proposed: elect two secretaries for each race to sign their respective licenses. But when the ministers gathered in 1924 in Chicago, all issues resurfaced and the interracial experiment collapsed. The PAW ministerial roll was halved. The remaining leaders reorganized under an episcopal polity, electing Haywood as their first presiding bishop, an office he occupied until his death in 1931. The PAW experienced slow growth between 1924 and 1931.

The whites splintered into three groups which then resulted in a flurry of attempts to reunite. Not all were successful at the time, including a failed attempt in 1931 between the Apostolic Church of Jesus Christ (ACJC) and the Pentecostal Ministerial Alliance (PMA). The ACJC, however, almost immediately turned to the PAW. The proposed conditions for merger were generally agreeable, including the stipulation that there be only one secretary. The merger succeeded in November, 1931, resulting in a change of name to Pentecostal Assemblies of Jesus Christ (PAJC). But doubts lingered among some black PAW leaders: the haste with which the merger was consummated, lack of trust in the motives of ACJC leadership, change of name, and loss of episcopal polity. These leaders promptly reorganized under the original PAW charter, and most former PAW members returned home. Samuel Grimes of New York City was elected presiding bishop. A final crisis occurred in 1937 when the PAJC General Conference was set to meet in Tulsa, OK, a segregated city. Since the black ministers were not permitted to attend, the decision was interpreted as an offense, resulting in most former PAW members returning to their roots.

The PAW suffered only one further schism. Bishop Samuel N. Hancock of Detroit left to form the Pentecostal Churches of the Apostolic Faith (PCAF) in 1957. Hancock was converted under Haywood's ministry in Indianapolis, and soon rose to a position of leadership. He later moved to Detroit where his ministry thrived. Contention eventually emerged. He was criticized for deviating from the PAW's stated doctrine that Jesus was both God and man, taking an Adoptionist position that Jesus was only the human Son of God. Since no action was taken to discipline or remove him as bishop, it was speculated that he left the PAW due to resentment at being overlooked for the position of Presiding Bishop following Haywood's death.

As the first Oneness organization, the PAW adheres to the traditional OP doctrines of God and Christ, and follows Haywood's interpretation of water baptism and gift of the Spirit in Acts 2:38 as the "new birth." Distinctives include: intermarriage between races based on New Testament doctrine, divorce and remarriage in the case of adultery or separation of an unbelieving partner, liturgical practices of foot-washing and use of unleavened bread and wine in Communion, and episcopal polity in church government.

The PAW affirms its interracial identity as a doctrinal tenet, even though it has suffered loss of most white ministers and members since 1924. Its intention was to embody this principle by alternating the office of Presiding Bishop between black and white. However, of the 11 presiding bishops since 1924, the PAW was able to elect only two white leaders: Ross Paddock (1967–74) and Lawrence Brisbin (1980–86). Regarding gender equality, women in the PAW currently hold every office in the church except that of Presiding Bishop. Of 70 global Episcopal districts, two in Africa are led by women bishops, and two in the West include women Suffragan bishops.

Presently, the PAW is one of the largest Oneness organizations, its global strength estimated at approximately two million adherents in 4,000 congregations.

Its greatest concentration is in Africa, the Caribbean, and South America. Headquarters is in Indianapolis, IN.

Bibliography

French, Talmadge L. 2014. *Early Interracial Oneness Pentecostalism: G.T. Haywood (1901–1931)*. Eugene, OR: Pickwick Publications.
Golder, Morris E. 1973. *History of the Pentecostal Assemblies of the World*. Indianapolis, IN.N.p.
Reed, David A. 2008. *"In Jesus' Name": The History and Beliefs of Oneness Pentecostals*. Blandford, UK: Deo Publishing.
Tyson, James. 1992. *The Early Pentecostal Revival: History of Twentieth-Century Pentecostals and The Pentecostal Assemblies of the World, 1901–30*. Word Aflame Press.

David Reed

Pentecostal Charismatic Churches of North America

Formal cooperative relations between Pentecostal denominations in the United States and Canada remained informal through the first half-century of the movement but were catalyzed by the 1942 formation of the National Association of Evangelicals (NAE) and the initial post-World War II gathering of the Pentecostal World Conference. Following the 1948 NAE meeting in Chicago, representatives of eight Pentecostal denominations held a preliminary gathering, which was followed by a second meeting also in Chicago later that year when a name, Pentecostal Fellowship of North America (PFNA), was selected and a committee appointed to draw up articles of cooperation.

A formal gathering to establish the PFNA was held October 26–28, 1948, in Des Moines, Iowa, and the several groups initially constituting the organization accepted a statement pledging them to cooperate in matters of mutual interest in the missionary and evangelistic work and to manifest the unity of the movement to the world. The organization continued to exist through the next decades, but after the initial burst of enthusiasm in the 1950s, found that the implementation of cooperative work was difficult to carry out on both the local and national level. It was also never funded by the member churches to the extent that it could establish a permanent office. The PFNA did, however, keep the vision of unity before the movement and facilitated a growing respect between the leaders of the member churches.

The PFNA was from it beginning somewhat limited as it brought together only white Trinitarian denominations. The Oneness churches were excluded on doctrinal grounds and the Black churches due to the dominant racial mores that had permeated the movement almost from its beginning. Changes wrought by the Civil Rights Movement, and the many informal contacts between black and white Pentecostal leaders over the decades set the stage for change. Crucial to that change was the working relationship developed by Bishop Ithiel Clemmons of the Church of God in Christ and Bishop Bernard E. Underwood of the International Pentecostal Holiness Church while serving on the steering committee of the North American Renewal Service Committee to plan a charismatic rally in New Orleans in 1987.

Out of his experience, in 1991, Bishop Underwood, as president of the PFNA set plans in place to end the organization's segregated structure. Backed by the

PFNA's Board of Administration, Underwood facilitated three interracial gatherings through 1992 and 1993 in which white and black leaders met together. These encounters culminated in a fourth meeting in January 1994 in Memphis, Tennessee, at which 20 black leaders met with 20 white leaders sat down to formulate a plan for forward movement. Central to the plan was the disbanding of the PFNA and the creation of a new organization with neither racial nor ethnic boundaries.

A fourth meeting was planned for October 1994. Its plans called for daytime sessions at which scholarly papers analyzing Pentecostal racial history were presented, evening Pentecostal worship services, and smaller business sessions, at which the formalities of dissolving the PFNA and establishing a new organization were conducted. In true Pentecostal fashion, the proceedings were lively, emotional, and punctuated with unplanned spontaneous occurrences including a time of foot washing, a message in tongues interpreted by Jack Hayford, and a new name for the new organization. The service at which the foot washing occurred would later be dubbed the "Miracle of Memphis."

The sessions climaxed with the dissolving of the PFNA; the addition of the word "Charismatic" to the name of the new organization (a reflection of the changes wrought by the Charismatic movement through the 1980s); the adoption of a "Racial Reconciliation Manifesto" pledging future diligence in dealing with racial issues; and the formation of the new cooperative body – the Pentecostal/Charismatic Churches of North America. Somewhat lost amid the dominating concern for racial healing were commitments to deal with issues between the older Pentecostal and newer Charismatic church bodies as well as address the inequalities between men and women.

In the quarter of a century following formation of the Pentecostal Charismatic Churches of North America, the organization has overseen the development of cordial relations between black and white leadership in the various Pentecostal and Charismatic denominations. At the same time the overall Pentecostal/Charismatic movement has expanded and at the denominational and congregational level continues to manifest the strong segregated patterns in North American life. At the 25th anniversary gathering of the PCCNA (2019), COGIC's Presiding Bishop Charles E. Blake, Sr., noted, "Now twenty-five years after the Memphis Miracle, there is an undeniable resurgence of racial animosity ... As people of faith, it is imperative that we renew our commitment to reconciliation and that we aggressively shout the message of love and reconciliation in every venue from the local church pulpit to the places of power in the seat of our national government."

Bibliography

Daniels, David III. "North American Pentecostalism." In *The Cambridge Companion to Pentecostalism*, edited by Cecil M. Robeck, Jr. and Amos Yong, 73–92. Cambridge, UK: Cambridge.

PCCNA. n.d. "History". Accessed February 21st, 2020. http://www.pccna.org/about_history.aspx.

Macchia, Frank. 1996. "From Azusa to Memphis: Where Do We Go From Here? Roundtable Discussions on the Memphis Colloquy." *Pneuma* 1 (18): 113–140.

Macchia, Frank. 1995. "From Azusa to Memphis: Evaluating the Racial Reconciliation Dialogue Among Pentecostals." *Pnuema* 1 (17): 203–218.

Rosenior, Derrick. 2010. "The Rhetoric of Pentecostal Racial Reconciliation: Looking Back

To Move Forward." In *A Liberating Spirit: Pentecostals and Social Action in North America*, edited by Michael Wilkinson and Steven Studebaker, 53–84. Eugene, OR: Pickwick.

Warner, W.E. 2002. "Pentecostal Fellowship of North America." In *The International Dictionary of Pentecostal Charismatic Movements*, edited by Stanley E. Burgess and Eduard M. Van der Maas. Grand Rapids, MI: Zondervan.

John Gordon Melton

Pentecostal European Fellowship

The Pentecostal European Fellowship was formed in Lisbon in 1987 out of the European Pentecostal Fellowship (EPF) and the Pentecostal European Conference (PEC). It signifies a continuation of post-war efforts to coordinate Pentecostal mission, humanitarian outreach and educational work. PEF has 53 national denominations as members and represents about four million European Pentecostal believers. It functions through a central Presidium or committee and an annual conference designed to showcase preaching and teaching rather than as a decision-making body – though the conference certainly provides opportunities for feedback and networking. As an umbrella organisation for the Europe-facing parts of national Pentecostal denominations, PEF has contacts with the European Commission as well as other umbrella bodies to which Pentecostal churches in other parts of the world belong. While the loyalty of local churches is primarily to their own denomination they would support suitable PEF initiatives. For instance PEF organises annual summer impact events drawing together young people on mission and designed to assist the evangelisation of a particular city or area.

In 2005 Daniel Costanza was appointed as PEF's first full-time Co-ordinator and is based in Brussels. PEF has a branch for women, a forum for youth ministries, and a missions arm (PEM) which enhances cooperation between Pentecostal churches and mission agencies in Europe. It has links to the European Pentecostal Theological Association (qv) which publishes a journal of the same name. Its website (http://www.pef.eu) provides an overview of its aims, history, membership and activities. According to Dr Arto Hämäläinen, its past president, PEF exists for four reasons: as an inter-Pentecostal ecumenical expression that assists mission and global cooperation; as a vehicle for strengthening and coordinating mission departments among the 35 or so which have joined PEM; as a means of sharing and running humanitarian projects or of disseminating best practice on issues like migration, refugees, drug dependence and alcoholism; and for speaking with a united voice to political or governmental officers on legislation, Christian values and intergenerational issues.

Bibliography

Costanza, Daniel. 2016. *From Rome to Zagreb: 50 Years of Fraternal Cooperation for the Sake of Europe: A Brief History of the Pentecostal European Fellowship (PEF)*. Published privately by PEF.

William K. Kay

Pentecostal Mission, Hong Kong

Pentecostal Mission was founded in 1907 by a Chinese Congregationalist, Mok Lai Chi, and his fellow members who were baptized by the Holy Spirit during A.G. and Lillian Garr's revival ministry in Hong Kong (HK). These Congregationalists first worshipped in their church building but had to move out due to their pastor's complaint about their noise. They rented other places to worship and welcomed foreign missionaries. Mok edited the *Pentecostal Truths* in Chinese and English to report revival news in HK, China, and many places around the world. During Mok's pastorship, the church evangelized the poor in towns and villages. His members opened schools for girls and adult women with American missionaries like Anna Deane. They also went to the south of Guangdong Province to bring the message of revival and repentance to the people of their hometowns. Mok held two revival conventions in spring and summer for ten days in HK and China.

Mok died in 1926 and the church was ministered by Sung Teng Man (1883–1958) who was a top Chinese civil servant for 35 years. He and his wife, Wong Chit Kei (?–1954), were both baptized by the Spirit during Garr's ministry. Sung increased the number of Pentecostal conventions from two times to four times a year. He led the church to purchase two pieces of land in Hong Kong Island and Kowloon where they established two buildings. Both properties were paid by the members' free-will offerings. In the time of hardship and horror during the Japanese occupation from December 25, 1941 to August 15, 1945, the Japanese military forces attempted to occupy Pentecostal Mission's building for their garrison, but Sung boldly protected the building and the members. Services were able to continue despite curfew and the fleeing of most of the members to Macau and south China

Sung passed away in 1958 and his son Sung Sheung Hong (1917–2018) became the superintendent of the church. He studied mechanical engineering at the University of Hong Kong and mechanical metallurgy engineering at the Royal Technical College in Glasgow during the Second World War. After the war, he was employed by the British Oxygen Company, but a few years later he was involved in the business of the Union Metal Work Ltd in HK which manufactured appliances. Despite being a successful engineer and businessman, he was dedicated to the ministry of the church and supported the Bible Society. The church established a branch in Toronto, Canada and sponsored the re-building of the three churches in China in the 1980s. It also built two students' hostels for the Chinese University of Hong Kong.

Pentecostal Mission adheres to a classical Pentecostal worship style. Each service begins with 45-minutes of silent prayer when the congregation kneels down to pray by the pews. Some members speak in tongues and laugh in the Spirit briefly. They sing traditional Pentecostal hymns written in the early twentieth century. Sermons are given by the preachers who are trained by their own deacons and the superintendent instead of seminaries. The Chinese Bible that they use is a colloquial Cantonese version instead of the mandarin Union Version. The church remains faithful to the full gospel and emphasizes sanctification. They maintain strict spiritual and behavioural criteria for baptism; hence the baptismal service is held when there are acceptable candidates and numerical growth of membership is not their major concern.

Bibliography

Au, Connie. 2019. "From Collaborations with Missionaries to Independence: A History of the Hong Kong Pentecostal Mission (1907–1930)." In *Asia Pacific Pentecostalism*, edited by Denise A. Austen, Jacqueline Grey, and Paul Lewis, 85–106. Leiden: Brill.

Au, Connie. 2017. "Elitism and Poverty: Early Pentecostalism in Hong Kong (1907–1945)." In *Global Chinese Pentecostal and Charismatic Christianity*, edited by Fenggang Yang, Joy Tong, and Allan Anderson, 63–88. Leiden: Brill.

Au, Connie. 2013. "'Now Ye Are Clean': Sanctification as a Formative Doctrine of Early Pentecostalism in Hong Kong." *Australian Pentecostal Studies* 15 (January). Accessed December 12, 2019. http://aps-journal.com/aps/index.php/APS/article/view/124/121.

Connie Au

Pentecostal Missionary Union

The Pentecostal Missionary Union (PMU) was formed in January 1909 at a meeting between Alexander Boddy, a Spirit-filled Anglican vicar in Sunderland, UK, and Cecil Polhill, also an Anglican who had first spoken in tongues during the Azusa Street Revival. Polhill had gone out to China with the famous Cambridge Seven and worked with the China Inland Mission for 15 years, always with a heart for Tibetans. After returning to England and becoming a wealthy man by inheritance, Polhill set about forming a Pentecostal missionary organisation that would carry the gospel across the world but especially to Tibet. Boddy edited *Confidence*, a magazine which, in the early days of British Pentecostalism, disseminated widely sourced news and indirectly solicited donations for good missionary causes. Polhill had missionary experience, strategic know-how and wealth; Boddy was equally visionary, though more pastoral. Joined by others who comprised the PMU Council (varying in size between 4 and 10), a men's training home was established in London in 1909 and one for women a year later. Equipped with training facilities and able to publicise itself in *Confidence*, candidates were quickly processed. They completed an application form where they could indicate their evangelical convictions and their Pentecostal experience. Seven PMU missionaries were on their way to China by the end of 1910.

Eventually 36 of 60 PMU missionaries went to China (with many near the Yunnan-Tibetan border), 12 to India (none after 1915), 9 to Africa and 3 to South America. This was a "faith mission" without guaranteed income to the missionaries themselves although the PMU Council was diligent in propagating news of success and pressing personal or financial needs. Though voluntary offerings were made in Pentecostal churches, Polhill's generous donations were often needed to balance the books. Polhill himself led the first contingent of missionaries to western China and Tibet in September 1910 and visited again in 1914. Polhill was a member of the Council of the China Inland Mission until 1915 and sought collegial cooperation with CIM missionaries on the field, cooperation that was readily given until concerns were raised over "waiting meetings" and the propagation of tongues-speaking. The principles of the PMU followed many of those reached by CIM: no single mode of water baptism was stipulated and the type of church government in any congregation established by missionaries was not predetermined. Marriage between missionaries required permission from the Council and should not take place within two years of reaching the field. Language learning was expected and prayer for divine healing was practised. Premillennialism was widely held but not written into the PMU's tenets. Moreover, and in what turned out to be strategically important, after 1917 Polhill had pushed for evangelism to be conducted by indigenous workers and, in this sense, prepared for the eventual leadership of the overseas church by those native to their regions.

In 1921 a superintendent was appointed for China. The 1914–18 war, however, had changed the financial situation by devaluing sterling and raising the price of commodities. Polhill himself remained Anglican all his life and Boddy semi-retired in 1922. When the British Assemblies of God (AG) was formed in 1924, the PMU Council arranged an orderly transfer first by vacating half the council seats in favour of AG and then, in 1925, by giving over all the rest. This provided the British AG a ready-made missionary arm while entailing responsibility for its funding. The training homes remained independent for a while but eventually came into the orbit of British AG, especially as new entrants were accepted for pastoral work in Britain as well as for mission overseas. And for two generations the work in Yunnan continued to flourish, as Polhill would have hoped and prayed.

Bibliography

Anderson, Allan. 2007. *Spreading Fires: The Missionary Nature of Early Pentecostalism.* London: SCM.

Confidence, https://revival-books.com/products/confidence-magazine.

Gee, Donald. 1967. *Wind and Flame.* Croydon: Assemblies of God Publishing House. (originally published as *The Pentecostal Movement* in 1941)

Kay, Peter. 1995. "The Four-Fold Gospel in the Formation, Policy and Practice of the Pentecostal Missionary Union (PMU) (1909–1925)." Master's diss., Cheltenham & Gloucester College of Higher Education.

Minutes of the PMU, http://digitallibrary.usc.edu/cdm/compoundobject/collection/p15799coll14/id/38039/rec/7.

Usher, John. 2020. *Cecil Polhill: Missionary, Gentleman and Revivalist.* Leiden: Brill.

William K. Kay

Pentecostal World Fellowship

The Pentecostal World Fellowship (PWF) is a type of ecumenical organization of Pentecostals that first met in 1947 in Zurich, Switzerland at the Pentecostal World Conference. The PWF meets triennially with the most recent meeting held in Calgary, Canada in 2019. The PWF was initiated by Leonard Steiner, David Du Plessis, J. Roswell Flower, and Donald Gee to encourage cooperation among Pentecostal leaders. The first conference had approximately 3,000 in attendance. Early efforts at organizing Pentecostals worldwide were attempted as early as 1908 by Alexander A. Boddy in Europe at the Sunderland Conference. In 1911 Thomas B. Barratt proposed an international Pentecostal union that resulted in a series of meetings until WWI brought any effort to an end. In the 1920s and 1930s ongoing discussions were held in Europe and the US about unity and cooperation among Pentecostals with an International Pentecostal Convention held in Amsterdam in 1921 and world conferences held in London and Stockholm in 1939 and again in London in 1940. However, with WWII, efforts to organize an international conference for Pentecostal leaders was delayed until

Pentecostal World Fellowship meeting in 1958. Source: Pentecostal Assemblies of Canada Archives

1947. The PWF saw the organization as a place to offer a global perspective on what Pentecostals were doing around the world, to coordinate missionary efforts, and to cooperate together on a range of activities.

The PWF office is currently headquartered in Tulsa, Oklahoma in the US with William Wilson serving as chair. PWF objectives are the following:

1. To promote and encourage regional and continental alliances amongst Spirit-filled networks.
2. To promote and connect Spirit-filled leaders – shapers of communities and nations.
3. To speak to governments and nations when and where social justice and religious rights are compromised and/or violated for the sake of the gospel.
4. To foster world missions and to support humanitarian efforts and where possible to provide relief aid.
5. To serve as a cooperative fellowship for Pentecostal Theological institutions to promote the development of education and leadership training.
6. To change the global contour of Christianity by emphasizing coordinated worldwide prayer.
7. To organize a triennial celebration (Pentecostal World Conference) that will gather the global Spirit-filled family to advance the mission and purposes of the Pentecostal Fellowship.

Membership includes 65 denominations and ministries from 34 different countries (pwfellowship.org). Members subscribe to the PWF Statement of Faith, which can be substantiated through their organizations' theological positions and a statement of cooperation with PWF. The PWF Statement of Faith represents a Classical Pentecostal theological view with positions on the baptism of the Holy Spirit with the evidence of speaking in tongues and the gifts of the Holy Spirit. As a transnational Pentecostal organization it is similar to the World Assemblies of God Fellowship

(WAGF) but more broad in that its members are not solely those from Assemblies of God organizations. Organizations like PWF contribute to the construction of a global Pentecostal identity and cohesion among its members through a shared subculture. Members of PWF, however, also participate with other global evangelical organizations like World Evangelical Alliance. Some denominations like the Pentecostal Assemblies of Canada are members of multiple evangelical and Pentecostals groups like PWF and WAGF.

The PWF is criticized for a number of reasons including weak ties to the charismatic movement in the historic churches, lack of appeal with increased competition from a growing number of Pentecostal conferences and networks, a centralized office that is largely represented by Pentecostals in Europe and North America, and the lack of a unified voice to address ecumenical concerns such as those raised in the Roman Catholic-Pentecostal dialogue (Robeck 2002; 2020).

Bibliography

Barrett, David B., Todd M. Johnson, and Peter F. Crossing. 2009. "Christian World Communions: Five Overviews of Global Christianity, AD 1800–2025." *International Bulletin of Missionary Research* 33 (1): 25–32.

Jacobsen, Douglas. 2010. "The Ambivalent Ecumenical Impulses in Early Pentecostal Theology in North America." In *Pentecostalism and Christian Unity: Ecumenical Documents and Critical Assessments*, edited by Wolfgang Vondey, 3–19. Eugene, OR: Pickwick.

Pentecostal World Fellowship, https://www.pwfellowship.org/.

Robeck, Cecil M., Jr. 2002. "Pentecostal World Conference." In *The New International Dictionary of Pentecostal and Charismatic Movements*, edited by Stanley M. Burgess and Eduard M. van der Maas, 971–974. Grand Rapids, MI: Zondervan.

Robeck, Cecil M., Jr. 2020. "Pentecostal Ecclesiology." In *The T&T Clark Handbook of Ecclesiology*, edited by Kimlyn J. Bender and D. Stephen Long, 241–258. London: Bloomsbury.

Vondey, Wolfgang. 2011. "Pentecostals and Ecumenism: Becoming the Church as a Pursuit of Christian Unity." *International Journal for the Study of the Christian Church* 11 (4): 318–330.

Michael Wilkinson

Pethrus, Lewi

Lewi Pethrus (1884–1974), originally named Pethrus Lewi Johansson, was the prominent face of Swedish Pentecostalism for more than six decades. He was a controversial figure in his day, but also a man who instilled respect and admiration far beyond his own circles. His prolific writings, his vast national and international network, and his presence on key committees guaranteed his longevity.

Lewi Pethrus was born on the March 11, 1884 in Vargön, Sweden, to Johan and Kristina Johnson. At the age of 15, he moved to the neighboring town of Vänersborg where he found employment at a local shoe factory. He was also baptized in Vänersborg Baptist church. Pethrus found further employment in Oslo, Norway, in 1901, which was then a part of Sweden. His association with the Norwegian labor movement cemented social democratic values, but an opportunity to become an associate pastor of Arendal Baptist church in 1902, halted his political ambitions until the 1940s. Pethrus claimed to have experienced the baptism of the Holy Spirit with the evidence of speaking in tongues in 1902, but this was probably a theological reconstruction after he became a Pentecostal. Pethrus moved back to Sweden in 1903 and assumed a pastoral position at the Bengtsfors Baptist church. In 1904, he began theological studies at Betel seminary in Stockholm. Being introduced to liberal theology caused a profound personal crisis. Having encountered Jesus afresh, he assumed another pastoral position in Lidköping in 1906.

News of Thomas Ball Barratt's Pentecostal meetings in Oslo reached him the following year. Curious of the rumors, Pethrus attended the meetings and was personally challenged by Barratt to take a firm stance for Jesus, which he later regarded as his entrance into the Pentecostal movement. From 1907 to 1912, Pethrus imbibed Pentecostal influences from America, and would later give great emphasis on William Durham's non-denominational ecclesiology. In 1910 he received an invitation to pastor the "Pentecostal-friendly" Filadelfia church in Stockholm. The issue over Pentecostal theology and practices came to a boiling point in 1913. The Baptist Union decided to stem the influence by excommunicating Filadelfia on the basis of open communion practice. The decision backfired and caused other Baptist churches to break away from the denomination. Rather than creating a new Pentecostal denomination, Pethrus organized the movement around a number of joint ventures. By 1919, his industriousness had led to the establishment of a variety of media including a publishing house (*Förlaget Filadelfia*), a hymnal (*Segertoner*), the weekly magazine (*Evangelii Härold*), a Bible school, and two national conferences. Although local churches were theoretically independent, Pethrus became the *de facto* leader of the movement from this point onward. He managed, for instance, to remove competitors to his leadership, like missionary, A.P. Franklin, in 1929, by presenting mission organizations and the theological education of ministers as foreign to the New Testament ideal.

The 1930s was a decade of rapid growth. Pethrus oversaw the construction of Filadelfia's new church building, which had a seating capacity of 3,000 people. The toil of the ministry, and a brewing conflict with his closest co-worker, Sven Lidman, caused him to experience a burnout in the beginning of 1940. Having been granted a leave of absence, he left for Chicago. Experiencing an unfruitful time of ministry in America, Pethrus returned in 1941 with a deep conviction of stemming the tide of secularization and promoting Christian values in society. The conviction led to the establishment of the daily newspaper *Dagen* in 1945. Lidman opposed Pethrus' "politicization" of the movement and launched an all-out attack in secular media in 1948. The assault was multifaceted, but it was essentially an attack against Pethrus' dictatorial leadership style. Lidman lost, and to recover from the conflict, Pethrus refocused the Pentecostal movement's attention to its revivalist roots by promoting revivals, like the Latter Rain Revival. The conflict with Lidman did not change his conviction about the dire state of Swedish society. He therefore launched the Pentecostal bank, *Allmänna Spar-och Kreditkassan* in 1952, and in 1955, he formed the political lobbying group, *Kristet Samhällsansvar*. The same year he also broke the Swedish radio monopoly by having *IBRA Radio* broadcast Christian messages from Tangier, Morocco. His resignation as pastor of the Filadelfia church in 1958 opened up for the creation of the political party, *Kristen demokratisk samling* in 1964.

The last part of his life was also dedicated to promoting ecumenical efforts, and the Charismatic and Jesus People movements. Before his death on September 4, 1974, Pethrus achieved great recognition by being inducted as commander of the Vasa Order and receiving a personal invitation to attend Richard Nixon's presidential inauguration.

Bibliography

Alvarsson, Jan-Åke. 2007. "Pingstväckelsens etablering i Sverige: Från Azusa Street till Skövde på sju månader." In *Pingströrelsen: Händelser och utveckling under 1900-talet*, 11–43. Örebro: Libris förlag.

Carlsson, Carl-Gustav. 1990. *Människan, samhället och Gud: Grunddrag i Lewi Pethrus kristendomsuppfattning*. Lund: Lunds Universitet.

Davidsson, Tommy. 2015. *Lewi Pethrus' Ecclesiological Thought 1911–1974: A Transdenominational Pentecostal Ecclesiology*. Leiden: Brill.

Halldorf, Joel. 2017. *Biskop Lewi Pethrus*. Skellefteå: Artos förlag.

Halldorf, Joel. 2010. "Lewi Pethrus and the Creation of a Christian Counterculture." *Pneuma* 32 (3): 354–368.

Tommy Davidsson

Petrelli, Giuseppe

Giuseppe Petrelli (1876–1957) was born in 1876 Noepoli, Basilicata, Italy and died in Belleville, New Jersey, U.S.A. He was an early Italian-American Pentecostal missionary, journalist, prolific writer, theologian, and itinerant Bible expositor. Born to an affluent Roman Catholic family, Petrelli became a lay counsel in his late teens while studying Law and contributing to the Corriere di Napoli. Sometime after converting at a Baptist church, he had a crisis of conscience. He quit his legal practice and migrated to New York. Upon his ordination at the Mariners' Temple Baptist Church, he began to minister to the Italian population in the metropolitan area of New York. Petrelli occupied some leadership positions within the migrant community, being a lecturer at Colgate University and, for a time, moderator for the Italian Baptist Association of America (Londino 2012; Napolitano 2015).

By the mid-1910s, Petrelli had contact with Italian Pentecostals and following his Pentecostal experience, he left the Baptist church and never assumed again a pastoral charge, though remaining active on his preaching and writing ministries. In the early 1920s, credentialed by the Glad Tidings Tabernacle of New York, Petrelli traveled to South America as a missionary. During this trip he helped consolidate the Italian-Argentine Christian Assemblies, ordaining its first ministers. He travelled at least four times to Brazil where his brother lived. In the U.S., he settled in New Jersey while preaching among the Italian congregations across North America.

Around 1925 a controversy about consuming food with blood emerged among the Italian Pentecostal Movement. Petrelli sided with the "Liberty" party advocating that the injunction of Acts 15 was no longer applicable (Petrelli 1930). As the issue divided the movement, the leaders convened in a constitutive assembly in Niagara Falls in 1927, which adopted the articles of faith that favored the "Abstinence" party (Petrelli was in South America during that meeting). In the following years, nearly 30 churches of the "Liberty" party tried to set up parallel organizations, but Petrelli was not interested in leading them. His position reflected a strong emphasis on a pneumatological ecclesiology averse to any forms of visible church polity beyond the local congregation. Consequently, without his leadership, many would join the Assemblies of God and its Italian District of the Assemblies of God, the Italian Pentecostal Church of Canada, and the Christian Church of North America. In his last years, Petrelli conducted weekly Bible studies and lived in Belleville, NJ (Londino 2012).

Being a prolific writer, he authored many books and articles for periodicals, renouncing any revenue from his publications. His books included about 40 published titles in Italian, with some works in English, Spanish, and other European languages. The spiritual heirs of Petrelli in Italy – Aida Chauvie, Antonio Bernabei, and Caterina Londino – continued his publishing ministry. His published works covered christology, ecclesiology, and pneumatology, and exposition of biblical passages and characters (Napolitano 1999). Despite his voluminous writings, the reception of Petrelli's work remained restricted to a small niche of readers. His literature is still in print and circulates among individuals from different denominational backgrounds in Europe, North America, and Argentina.

After World War II, adherents of Petrelli's teachings in Italy resumed contact with their American counterparts. Missionaries, like Salvatore Garippa and Giovanni Ferrazzo, travelled to Italy to evangelize and plant churches, especially in Campania and Calabria. Currently, independent congregations in major cities in the north and in towns in the south (like the Selle Valley churches) reclaim his legacy. In the U.S. his work continues with a dozen churches named Christian Apostolic Church from two distinct networks of scattered congregations in the northeastern states. In Argentina, the Christian Assemblies "God is Love" with headquarters in Santa Fe, the largest denomination tracing to his mission in the country, keeps his teachings and memory alive.

Petrelli was an outlier in the early Italian Pentecostal movement. Erudite, polyglot, and from a higher social status, his message impressed his audience. However, his theology remained misunderstood (Toppi 1999). Detractors saw him as lenient on the food and blood controversy while some admirers tended to see his teachings under a mystical, allegorizing exegesis that supported an elitist view of themselves. Comfortable to quote the church fathers as well as contemporary authors, he combined critical and pneumatological hermeneutics of the scriptures, presenting his expositions in a quasi-legal reasoning. His christology highlighted a soteriology based on a relational faith. Devoid of sectarianism, he shunned many aspects of Pentecostalism, like the prevalent anti-intellectualism and the dogmatism resulting from the over-reliance on the authority of charismatic leaders. However, he insisted on the Holy Spirit's role in the church's life. Although he did not present his theology in a systematic way, he was a forerunner of a scholarly Pentecostal inquiry on the Bible and theology.

Bibliography

Londino Bernabei, Caterina. 2012. *Biografia del Servitore di Dio Giuseppe Petrelli*. Turin: the author.

Napolitano, Carmine. 1999. "Il pensiero di Giuseppe Petrelli: Per una storia del movimento pentecostale italiano". In *Movimenti popolari evangelici nei secoli XIX e XX*, edited by Domenico Maselli, 94–153. Prato: Fedeltà.

Napolitano, Carmine. 2015. *Giuseppe Petrelli: teologo pentecostale delle origini*. Aversa: Charisma.

Petrelli, Giuseppe. 1930. *Fra I due testamenti*. Bristol, PA: Merlo.

Toppi, Francesco. 1999. *E mi sarete testimoni: Il movimento pentecostale e le Assemblee di Dio in Italia*. Rome: ADI Media

Leonardo Marcondes Alves

Philippines

The Philippines has 87 million Christians, making it the fifth-largest population of Christians in the world. Situated between Taiwan and Malaysia, and between the Pacific and the South China Sea, with its 330 years of colonization by Catholic Spain overlaying a history of traditional religion, this nation of over 7,000 islands was singularly positioned in the region for a baptism of the Holy Spirit.

When the United States assumed control of the Philippines from Spain in 1898, the country was opened up to Protestantism. Pentecostalism in the Philippines was introduced but did not take hold during a three-month visit to Manila by Lucy Leatherman in 1909 (King 2016, 91–93). The first Pentecostal missionary was with the Church of God and arrived in 1918 (Suico 2011, 283).

Some of the earliest Filipino Pentecostals received their Spirit baptism in Hawaii and California, returning to their home country with an experience and a message. Thus, Pentecostalism in the Philippines could be considered to be a balikbayan (Filipinos who return from abroad) religion, brought home to share with their friends and family. Maximiano Somosierra is representative of these early missionaries, being converted in Hawaii by 1914 and returning to the Philippines in 1921. Somosierra lived in Santa Barbara, Iloilo, where he was listed as a member of the United States Assemblies of God General Council at least from 1921 through 1946. (King 2016, 95–96).

The total number of Pentecostals and Charismatics in the Philippines is difficult to ascertain. A 2016 study that focused on Oneness Pentecostals found there to be two million adherents, 4,724 local churches and at least 120 different organizations only among Oneness Pentecostals (King 2016, 211–214). The largest of these was the totally autochthonous Jesus Miracle Crusade International Ministry (JMCIM) claiming a membership of 1,500,000. JMCIM was founded by Evangelist Pastor Wilde Almeda and his wife, the late Lina C. Almeda, in Novaliches, Quezon City in 1975 as the Jesus Church. They took their current name in 1983 (King 2016, 206–211).

The Philippine Council of Evangelical Churches (PCEC) is an ecumenical umbrella organization that lists 298 various organizations, of which about three quarters are para-church organizations. There are only 18 organizations in the PCEC that are identifiably Pentecostal or Charismatic. According to the Pew Forum website, the Pew Survey in 2006 found fewer than five percent of Filipinos identify as Pentecostal, but forty percent, including Catholics, identify as Charismatic. Nearly seventy percent of Protestants claim to be Pentecostal or Charismatic. Including charismatics and independent churches, what have been termed "Renewalists" make up about 44 percent of the country. This number gives them a significant amount of influence in society and politics (Anderson 2013, 254). In Metro Manila, a recent study showed that eight out of the ten fastest growing congregations are Pentecostal or Charismatic (Yung 2011, 30–45).

One of the largest Pentecostal type organizations in the Philippines is the Jesus Is Lord (JIL) Church founded in 1978 by "Brother Eddie" Villanueva. The JIL is a significant religious and political force, claiming five million members worldwide. Another large religious group with roots in the Pentecostal movement is The Kingdom of Jesus Christ The Name Above Every Name with headquarters in Davao City. The Kingdom was started in 1985 when its founder, Pastor Apollo Quiboloy, left the United Pentecostal Church over some disagreements. Now claiming 6 million adherents worldwide, Quiboloy no longer identifies as Pentecostal although he maintains many Charismatic attributes such as lively worship, prayer and the belief in healing (King 2016, 193–195).

The largest Catholic Charismatic Renewal organization in the world is the seven million member El Shaddai movement in the Philippines. Mike Velarde, founder and leader of the politically powerful El Shaddai "has helped stem the tide of conversions from Catholicism to Pentecostal churches in his country" (Anderson 2013, 215). Even with the Catholic alternative to Pentecostalism, the movement continues to grow.

Pentecost, as defined in the second chapter of Acts, offers power. Power is something that most Filipinos can never approach. Pentecost becomes their path to power as they receive the baptism of the Holy Spirit. This offer of power, along with the obvious beliefs in healing, miracles, redemptive lift, divine provision and, of course, salvation, continues to make the Pentecostal experience desirable for the population of the Philippines.

Bibliography

Anderson, Allan Heaton. 2013. *To the Ends of the Earth: Pentecostalism and the Transformation of World Christianity*. New York: Oxford University Press.

King, Johnny Loye. 2017. "Spirit and Schism: A History of Oneness Pentecostalism in the Philippines." PhD thesis, University of Birmingham, UK.

Suico, Joseph. 2011. "Pentecostalism in the Philippines." In *Asian and Pentecostal: The Charismatic Face of Christianity in Asia*, edited by Allan Anderson and Edmond Tang, 279–293. Eugene, OR: Wipf and Stock.

Yung, Hwa. 2011. "Pentecostalism and the Asian Church." In *Asian and Pentecostal: The Charismatic Face of Christianity in Asia*, edited by Allan Anderson and Edmond Tang, 30–45. Eugene, OR: Wipf and Stock.

Johnny King

Planetshakers

Originally a youth movement and later a conference and global praise and worship label, Planetshakers is a large Pentecostal Church based in Melbourne Australia led by Pastors Russell and Samantha Evans. At the time of writing, Planetshakers has 6 campuses in the greater Melbourne area, four international campuses (Austin, Capetown, Geneva, Singapore) and a large number of like minded Planetshakers 'family' churches globally. Planetshakers has a simple vision, to "empower generations to win generations." Its 17,000 (Dec 2019) member Melbourne congregation is demographically representative of its diverse community with people from 150 nations in attendance and translation services available. And while the older generations are amply represented, Planetshakers is known throughout the world as a movement that reaches and mobilises young people. This strength is also represented in the congregation with around 30 percent under the age of 18 and 82 percent under the age of 40.

Founding pastor Russell Evans is the son of Andrew Evans who was the national superintendent of the Assemblies of God in Australia between 1977 and 1997 and the senior pastor of Klemzig AOG in Adelaide (then Paradise AOG, currently Influencers Church). Pastor Russell, as he is known, had been a youth pastor at Paradise AOG, and had seen remarkable growth during his tenure. In 1997, in response to a clear word from God – "Start a conference and call it Planetshakers" – Pastor Russell launched a conference in Adelaide with

Planetshakers 2005 conference in Melbourne, Australia. Photo: Wikimedia, Simon East (CC BY-SA)

300 full-time delegates and 700 in attendance at night meetings. The conference enjoyed rapid growth with between 8 thousand and 10 thousand in attendance by 2000, when Planetshakers released its first praise and worship album, "When the Planet Rocked." In 2001 a second Planetshakers conference was launched in Brisbane with 2,500 delegates, and in the following two years, venues were added in Perth and Sydney. By 2004 Planetshakers conferences across four venues were attended by 30,000 delegates. Despite the overwhelming success of the conferences, Pastor Russell followed the Holy Spirit's leading to scale them back and plant a church in Melbourne. From its beginnings in February 2004, Planetshakers Church grew to around 17,000 members in its first fifteen years making it one of the fastest growing Australian churches in its history. In addition to those in attendance weekly, over 100,000 people stream the services online every week via youtube and facebook live.

Pastor Russell Evans credits this growth to the 'new school, old school' approach that Planetshakers takes where the roots of Pentecostalism are cherished and practiced but packaged within a modern style and sound. This desire to (in Evans's own words) "speak the language of the day and embrace the fullness of Pentecost" has, in addition, to the main Planetshakers Band, inspired the creation of the Planetshakers youth Band "planetBoom". Testament to its popularity worldwide, the Planetshakers and planetBoom bands in 2019 played to an estimated 2 million people face to face in conferences and events in Europe, North America, Africa, the Middle East and Asia. As with many larger Pentecostal Churches Planetshakers has a significant social justice arm. Empower Australia feeds nearly 200 families weekly in the Melbourne area alone with a short term aspiration for ten times this amount. Its dedicated facility in South Melbourne has a warehouse where donated groceries are accepted and laid out on shelves similar to a supermarket. Those in need are given an opportunity to 'shop' for free before being served refreshments by Empower volunteers. Empower mobilises its volunteer base through street teams and supports refugee communities through English classes and other practical initiatives.

In 2016 Planetshakers commenced the 'Believe' initiative, a nation building and infrastructure project in the Pacific region which is seeing hundreds of volunteers travel to the Pacific in teams every year and the establishment of a network of community hubs in every district in Papua New Guinea, the region's most populous nation. As distinct from traditional missions the 'Believe' approach focuses on development and addressing key areas in society including healthcare, education, business, church and government.

In line with its motto of 'empowering generations', in 2006 Planetshakers College was established to equip and train future generations. Since that time it has grown to include an academic component with students enrolling to achieve awards including a Diploma of Leadership, an Associate Degree of Ministry and a Bachelor of Theology or Ministry. Training is conducted in an immersive environment with a discipleship ethos and every student volunteering a significant amount of time in the ministries of the Church.

As its name suggests, Planetshakers has fostered an audacious vision since its inception to impact the world. From its beginnings as a youth conference in Adelaide it has exceeded every expectation growing into a global movement that is catalysing revival and spreading its influence through conferences and concerts, social media and the annual Planetshakers conference in Melbourne. Its music is used in Pentecostal and other churches all over the world and it has achieved 200 million views on youtube.

Bibliography

Evans, Russell. 2019. The Planetshakers Story. Discussion with author, November 11.
Evans, Russell. 2014. *The Honor Key: Unlock a Limitless Life*. Springfield, Missouri: My Healthy Church.
Evans, Russell. 2004. *Profile of a Planetshaker*, edited by Dave Reardon. Adelaide, Australia: Planetshakers.
Rocha, Cristina, Mark P. Hutchinson, and Kathleen Openshaw, eds. 2020. *Australian Pentecos* eg. 2019. *God Is Good for You: A Defence of Christianity in Troubled Times*. Allen & Unwin.

Clayton Coombs
Scott Lim

Pneumatology

Pentecostals have always been Jesus-centered in their theological piety, but are best recognized for their strong pneumatological emphasis in their theology and spirituality. While other traditions might accent the role of Father or Son in the Godhead, Pentecostals stress the presence and activity of the Holy Spirit in Christian life and practice. The Pentecostal majority view of God falls firmly within traditional Trinitarian orthodoxy, although a minority (Oneness Pentecostalism) rejects conventional Trinitarian articulation concerning the Godhead. Concerning pneumatology, then, the standard Pentecostal confession is that the Spirit is both fully divine (equal to the Father and Son), and exhibits attributes of personality. Formally, Pentecostals affirm that the Spirit is not to be viewed as an impersonal force; however, in practice, their emphasis on the Spirit's power and subjective effect upon believers can make them susceptible at times to depersonalization of the Spirit.

Pentecostals assume and accentuate personal and communal experience with the Spirit in various dimensions. It is the Spirit who palpably convicts and draws unbelievers into the experience of salvation (i.e., conversion; the new birth), and then comes to indwell the convert. The Spirit then begins the work of sanctification, conforming the believer's character into the image of Christ. Some Pentecostal traditions identify sanctification as an identifiable crisis experience following conversion, but others view this aspect of the Spirit's work as an incremental process. In either case, Pentecostals take seriously the adjective "Holy" as descriptive of the Spirit, in that they accept that the Spirit-led life will be one of notable distinction from "worldly" activities and attitudes.

The primary experience of the Spirit celebrated by Pentecostals is the baptism in (with) the Holy Spirit (or Spirit baptism). Expectation of and encouragement to seek this crisis experience is grounded in the Acts 2 story of Pentecost, in which early disciples were "filled with the Holy Spirit and began to speak in other languages as the Spirit gave them ability" (Act 2:4, NRSV). Classical Pentecostals generally emphasize that Spirit baptism is an experience distinct from and occurring subsequent to conversion. It is a personal encounter with the Spirit, given to enable (empower) the believer to be a more effective witness for Jesus (Acts 1:5, 8). Speaking in other languages (tongues) is often viewed as the normative sign (or evidence) of this experience.

Pentecostal understanding of Spirit baptism has also generated a notable area of ongoing theological controversy. Debate continues between Pentecostals and other Christian traditions, and even within Pentecostalism itself, concerning the normativity of the Spirit baptism experience and the tongues requisite. Disagreement primarily centers on whether Spirit baptism should be considered a distinct crisis stage experience separate from conversion. A related critique has been that the Pentecostal view creates two tiers of Christians – those with and those without the Spirit (more precisely, Spirit-empowerment). Against the typical evangelical view that the entirety of the Spirit is received at conversion, Pentecostals maintain that there is more of the Spirit to be experienced post-conversion. Charismatics and Neo-Pentecostals share the Classical Pentecostal emphasis on empowering experiences with the Spirit, but are less likely to insist on the particular label of Spirit baptism and the crisis-stage conceptual framework used to identify this experience. Likewise, they would be far less apt to view tongues as the normative sign of Spirit baptism. Charismatics also tend to locate Spirit baptism within the theological framework of their particular ecclesial tradition. On this matter, Anthony C. Thiselton (2013) believes that this debate is not so much focused on the experience of the Spirit itself, but on diverse conceptualizations of the experience.

Related to the above is Pentecostals' assumption that the Spirit's activity will regularly be perceptible and tangible, with tongues serving as a primary example. In both prayer and worship, especially in corporate settings, Pentecostals expect to sense the presence of the Spirit, and to be used by the Spirit to minister to others. Pentecostals promote the working of the Spirit in the so-called spiritual gifts, and maintain that all the gifts listed in Scripture (e.g., Rom. 12:6–8, and 1 Cor. 12:4–11) continue to operate today; they reject the idea that any spiritual gifts have ceased to function within church history. Believers are encouraged to prayerfully seek to be used in the gifts, including through the more unusual gifts such as healing, revelational prophecy, and other miraculous demonstrations.

In recent decades, Pentecostal scholarship has expanded its scope of interest from explaining and defending its experiential pneumatology, to constructing theology that is able to contribute to substantial matters inside and outside the church. The Acts 2 story of the outpouring of the Spirit is often used as the point of departure for explicitly rooting theology in Pentecost. One noteworthy example of this approach is Frank D. Macchia's (2006) proposal of an ecumenical and expanded understanding of Spirit baptism, in which the Spirit's filling of creation can be understood as the divine eschatological goal, with Pentecost serving as an initiatory event in the realization of this plan. In this view, Spirit baptism serves as an all-encompassing metaphor, capable of explaining and shaping all aspects of Christian life and experience.

Other Pentecost-rooted theological developments are also worthy of note. Concerning biblical hermeneutics, while Pentecostals have always affirmed that the Spirit is the one who inspired and continues to illuminate scriptural interpretation, more recently, a number of Pentecostal theologians (e.g., Kenneth J. Archer [2004]) have encouraged Pentecostals to acknowledge and celebrate an explicit pneumatological influence involved in the interpretation and application of Scripture. Concerning ecclesiology, some scholars (e.g., Simon K.H. Chan [2010]; Daniela C. Augustine [2010]) are encouraging Pentecostals to rethink the Pentecost event as primarily a corporate, rather than individual, experience of the Spirit. Pentecost is thus viewed as a crucial event in Trinitarian history, in which the Spirit animates, energizes, and catches the ecclesial body up into God's own redemptive work. Some Pentecostal theologians believe Pentecost confirms a radical ubiquity of the Spirit's presence and activity in creation. Amos Yong (2005) and James K.A. Smith (2010), for example, have suggested a Spirit-infused metaphysics, and drawn out implications for scientific method in what must be a pneumatologically-open universe. Relatedly, Yong has also given significant attention to the complex issue of discerning the possibility of the Spirit's presence and activity in all cultures and religions.

These recent developments demonstrate that while Pentecostal pneumatology does accent personal experience of the Spirit, that reality does not exhaust the wider application of Pentecostal pneumatology in addressing many new and exciting questions.

Bibliography

Archer, Kenneth J. 2004. *A Pentecostal Hermeneutic for the Twenty-First Century: Spirit, Scripture and Community*. London: T&T Clark International.

Augustine, Daniela C. 2010. "The Empowered Church: Ecclesiological Dimensions of the Event of Pentecost." In *Toward a Pentecostal Ecclesiology: the Church and the Fivefold Gospel*, edited by John Christopher Thomas, 157–180. Cleveland, TN: CPT Press.

Castelo, Daniel. 2015. *Pneumatology: a Guide for the Perplexed*. London: Bloomsbury T&T Clark.

Chan, Simon K.H. 2010. "Jesus as Spirit-Baptizer: Its Significance for Pentecostal Ecclesiology." In *Toward a Pentecostal Ecclesiology: the Church and the Fivefold Gospel*, edited by John Christopher Thomas, 139–156. Cleveland, TN: CPT Press.

Kärkkäinen, Veli-Matti. 2018. *Pneumatology: the Holy Spirit in Ecumenical, International, and Contextual Perspective*. Second Edition. Grand Rapids: Baker.

Macchia, Frank D. 2006. *Baptized in the Spirit: a Global Pentecostal Theology*. Grand Rapids: Zondervan.

Smith, James K.A. 2010. *Thinking in Tongues: Pentecostal Contributions to Christian Philosophy*. Grand Rapids: Eerdmans.

Thiselton, Anthony C. 2013. *The Holy Spirit – in Biblical Teaching, Through the Centuries, and Today*. Grand Rapids: Eerdmans.

Yong, Amos. 2005. *The Spirit Poured Out on All Flesh: Pentecostalism and the Possibility of Global Theology*. Grand Rapids: Baker.

Peter D. Neumann

Poland

Pentecostalism reached Poland in a time of social and political change. The Polish state had not been on the European map for more than 100 years when after the World War I, it was established again. This meant a great deal of struggle with neighbouring countries in order to establish borders that could be protected for the national interest of the people. Pentecostalism emerges in this context.

Pentecostals activity was evident in the German Empire (before World War I) in 1907. Pentecostal meetings and conferences were taking place in parts of Germany, now in the Polish state, incuding Wrocław, Brzeg, Szczecin, Słupsk, and Ostróda.

The German Pentecostal leaders came into contact with Polish Christians who were members of the pietistic groups within the Lutheran church in the Cieszyn area. The region was a part of the Austrian-Hungarian empire, but many inhabitants spoke Polish. Some people were baptized in the Holy Spirit and started to organize house meetings. This coincided with the Berlin Declaration (Berliner Erklärung, 1909), which provoked a strong resistance against the Pentecostals. The Pentecostal responded with a written statement and managed to receive legislation to establish a religious society known as "Bund für entschiedenes Christentum" (Fellowship for Resolute Christianity). The first leaders of the society were Jan Kajfosz, Karol Kaleta, and Karol Śniegoń. The Fellowship was initially connected to the Lutheran Church and allowed the Pentecostals to cultivate their way of worship and secure their own buildings.

When the new Polish state was established and the Polish-Bolshevik war ended, there were a number of Polish immigrants in the United States who were impacted by the Pentecostal revival, were baptised in the Holy Spirit, and began to spread the news of the full gospel. They were ready to go back to their native country and bring the message of Christ the Saviour, and the Lord baptizing with the Holy Ghost. The preachers included Grzegorz Krasowski, Iwan Harris, Porfiry Ilczuk, Józef Antoniuk and others. Since 1920, Pentecostal preachers returned from the United States to their native land, their families and relatives, and their villages. There were converts and some being baptized in the Spirit. The congregations that started in the east of Poland were culturally different than those in the Cieszyn region. It was normal for their worship to be led in Polish, Ukrainian, Byelorussian and Russian. These churches established the Evangelical Faith Christians Assemblies Fellowship (later known as Church of Evangelical Faith Christians) in 1929, in Stara Czołnica. The denomination had Polish, Ukrainian and Byelorussian mixed congregations in Eastern and Central Poland. In East Poland the Pentecostals experienced revival and growth in the villages.

There was a need for young preachers to be trained in Central and Eastern Europe. The Eastern European Mission from the USA founded a Pentecostal theological school in the city of Gdańsk. The school was named the Gdańsk Bible Institute and opened in 1930. The students enrolled from across Central and Eastern Europe but it ceased to function in 1938 due to financial problems.

Poland is a multinational state with a large German minority that resulted in the establishing of a number of Pentecostal churches that worshipped in German. The year 1939, however, brought about a dramatic change in the Polish state that had an impact on the churches when German Nazis and Soviet communists invaded the country. Both groups were hostile to evangelical Christians and the Pentecostals, under German occupation, were forced to go under the protection of the Methodist Church. The churches lost many members during the war turmoil with many Pentecostal believers dedicated to helping the Jews.

When the war was over, there was another change in the borders of the Polish state. The Germans were to be moved to the German territory and the Poles were moved to the West and North of Poland. From 1945–1950, 3.5 millions Germans were relocated and over 2 million Poles during 1945–1948 and 1955–1958. For the Pentecostals it meant relocating whole congregations. For many years after the war some Pentecostal congregations in the West and North of Poland reflected the culture of the eastern farming communities, from "beyond Bug river".

Poland was under the political rule of the Soviet Union that installed the communist government during the parliamentary elections in 1947. Due to human loss caused by the war, small evangelical churches were even smaller that led to some attempts to consolodate their churches. Consolidation was discussed in some conferences organized in the Cieszyn area with the Fellowship for Resolute Christianity and the Free Brethren. The unification was a success only for a short time. The new communist regime was very reluctant to give any legal recognition to evangelicals and Pentecostals. In September of 1950 the secret police organized action against all evangelicals. Almost every leader was arrested and all worship was for a short time stopped. Under the secret services control, evangelicals formed into the United Evangelical Church with a large representation of Pentecostals from the Cieszyn area – the Fellowship for Resolute Christianity (they finally broke away from the Lutheran Church) and the Church of Evangelical Faith Christians. Some Pentecostals decided to stay unregistered and underground. In the following decades the communist regime was more relaxed towards the Pentecostals.

Full church freedom came in 1989 with the collapse of the communist regime. In the 1980s the state allowed some new Pentecostal denominations to be registered including the Church of God in Christ. In 1987 the United Evangelical Church decided that each denomination should become independent. The Pentecostal Church of Poland was established during this time and is the largest evangelical and Pentecostal denomination with 250 assemblies. The best known Pentecostal leaders of new democratic era are Michał Hydzik, Edward Czajko, Mieczysław Czajko, Kazimierz Sosulski, and Marek Kamiński.

In the 1970s and 1980s the Polish Catholic church experienced a charismatic renewal when many Charismatic Catholic fellowships were started. Charismatic activities took place within the Light & Life movement and the leader for many years was bishop Bronisław Dembowski who was well known for his political involvement.

In the 1990s some of the charismatic Catholic groups separated from the Catholic church and became independent churches, registered under the new democratic legislation. The present Government registry shows around 25 such groups. The Pentecostal movement in Poland is not numerically large. Pentecostal churches number about 40,000 worshippers. The charismatic movement in the Catholic church is larger. Pentecostals had some influence on the church culture of the country, establishing many institutions including schools, publishing houses, and media outlets that have had an influence beyond Pentecostal fellowships. The Pentecostal Church of Poland is one of 15 churches and religious organizations having a separate parliamentary bill that recognizes their legal right to exist.

Bibliography

Czajko, Edward. 2012. "Zielonoświątkowcy w Nowogródzkiem w latach 1919–1945." *Rocznik Teologiczny* 54 (1–2).

Gajewski, Wojciech. 2014. "Instytut Biblijny w Gdańsku. Dzieje i charakter seminarium pentekostalnego w okresie międzywojennym." *Studia Theologica Pentecostalia* 2.

Kamiński, Marek. 2012. *Kościół Zielonoświątkowy w Polsce w latach 1988–2008: Studium historyczno-ustrojowe*. Warszawa: Wydawnictwo Arka.

Edward Pawlowski

Polhill, Cecil

Cecil Henry Polhill (previously Polhill-Turner) was an Eton and Cambridge educated Anglican landowner, missionary and Pentecostal pioneer. He was born in Bedford on February 23, 1860 to Captain Frederick Polhill-Turner (former Conservative Minister of Parliament for Bedford) and Emily Frances née Barron (of the aristocratic Page-Turner Barron family). In 1885, Polhill along with his brother, Arthur, sailed to China with the China Inland Mission (CIM) as members of the "Cambridge Seven." After an initial period of probation,

Cecil Polhill, 1860–1938

Polhill developed an intense interest in the largely un-evangelized region of Tibet in the far west, north west and south west of China. In 1888, he and his wife, Eleanor Agnes, settled firstly in Xining, Qinghai (1888–1891); then in Songpan, Sichuan (May–July 1892); followed, after a short furlough in England, by Kalimpong, North India (1895–1897) and finally in Kangding (Chinese) or Dartsedo (Tibetan), west Sichuan (1897–1900), where he and Eleanor remained until the Boxer Uprising of 1900 when they returned to England again. The health of his family and the inheritance of a large estate prevented him from returning to full-time mission, and both Eleanor and his young son did indeed die within a matter of years.

From 1900, Polhill was an active promotor of mission to Tibet and a leading figure in the Tibet Prayer Union (a Moravian-led initiative designed to raise awareness of mission to Tibet). In 1903, he was elected to a position on the CIM Home Council, which he held until his resignation in 1915. Mission to Tibet was extremely difficult in the early twentieth century, and the diplomatically disastrous invasion of Lhasa by the British (1903–04) only worsened the situation. With effective mission in Tibet a remote possibility, Polhill developed a keen interest in revival, helping to fund the evangelistic campaign of Reuben Torrey and Charles Alexander in 1905, travelling to Wales to hear Evan Roberts in 1906 and following the Indian Revival with much interest. He was also interested in the *charismata*, having experimented with tongues as a young missionary and having had an experience of "uncontrollable laughter" after returning from Wales in 1906. These interests along with a premillennial eschatology tied to an imperative for mission predisposed Polhill to Pentecostalism.

In 1907, on a return journey from China, Polhill visited Los Angeles. He worshipped at the Apostolic Faith Mission (AFM) on Azusa Street and experienced a baptism in the Holy Spirit with tongues (although not at the mission hall itself). Shortly afterwards he cleared the mortgage on the AFM's hall amongst a number of other mainly mission-orientated donations. In 1908 he would return to England a convinced Pentecostal, just as the movement there was gathering momentum under Alexander A. Boddy. In June 1908 Polhill arranged to attend Boddy's first Whitsuntide (i.e. Feast of Pentecost) Convention in Sunderland. Here he started to build key networks in the fledgling British and pan-European Pentecostal movement, and his activity in the remaining months of 1908 illustrated the energy and resources that he had to give. For example, between the end of June and December he held Pentecostal meetings all over the country (in his native Bedford, St Andrews, and London) utilizing key Pentecostals in the process such as Boddy, Gerrit and Wilhelmina Polman, and Smith Wigglesworth. He rented a large property in London's West End to hold "drawing room meetings" and hired a room in the Cannon Street Hotel (formerly above Cannon Street Station, London) for midday "prayer meetings for business men." He contributed a quarter of the cost of the first purpose-built Pentecostal church in the country (in Bournemouth, in August 1908), then spoke at the hall's opening in November 1908 and proposed the formation of a Pentecostal mission in Hamburg, Germany in December 1908.

Polhill had many years of administrative and in-the-field experience with the largest Protestant mission in China (CIM). He utilized this experience and his financial resources to help forge the Pentecostal Missionary Union (PMU), arguably the most professionally organized Pentecostal mission in the world at that time. In his position as president of the PMU, he helped to establish, manage, and fund Pentecostal "training homes" (the ancestors of Pentecostal seminaries), providing at least some training and oversight to would-be Pentecostal missionaries. His moderate, evangelical background ensured that missionaries of the PMU were encouraged to acquire foreign languages via traditional pedagogical methods, but as an evangelical Anglican he had never envisaged establishing new Pentecostal denominations. When the PMU held a vote (found in favor) of merging with the Assemblies of God for Great Britain and Ireland (in 1924), he abstained and shortly afterwards tendered his resignation in 1925. It was a mild ideological reservation from a man who had helped establish many of the networks upon which modern British

Pentecostalism was built. He died at his home in Hampstead, North London in 1938.

Bibliography

Anderson, Allan Heaton. 2007. *Spreading Fires: The Missionary Nature of Early Pentecostalism*. London: SCM Press.

Polhill, Cecil Henry. 1980. "A China Missionary's Witness." Donald Gee Archive. Doncaster, UK: Donald Gee Archive, Mattersey Hall.

Usher, John Martin. 2020. *Cecil Polhill: Missionary, Gentleman and Revivalist Vol.1 (1860–1914)*. Leiden: Brill.

Usher, John Martin. 2012. "Cecil Henry Polhill: The Patron of the Pentecostals." *Pneuma* 34 (1): 37–56.

Usher, John Martin, ed. n.d. "The Polhill Collection Online" pconline.org.uk.

Venn, John Archibald. 1953. *Alumni Cantabrigiensis: A Biographical List of all Known Students, Graduates and Holders of Office at the University of Cambridge, from the Earliest Times to 1900*. Cambridge: Cambridge University Press, s.v. "Polhill-Turner (post Polhill), Cecil Henry."

John M. Usher

Politics

Pentecostalism is not only the fastest growing expression of global Christianity but one which continues to evolve. This is as true in respect of the movement's attitudes towards the political sphere as well as its theology and central beliefs. Largely such evolution is because, as an international movement, Pentecostalism is obliged to respond to the wider cultural and political environments in which it finds itself. Initially, emerging in the early twentieth century in the USA, Pentecostalism rejected the secular world as sinful and 'lost' and displayed a general disinterest in politics, dismissing it as a distraction from the mission of spreading the gospel message.

However, as the Pentecostal movement settled down, often growing into denominational forms, it began to engage with politics – holding the conviction that the evils of the world could be combatted through moral campaigns and political institutions, focusing in particular on issues such as homosexuality, abortion, divorce and family breakdown. It was not surprising then, that Pentecostalism came to have a reputation of being politically Right Wing in disposition. While this brought the movement into line with more conservative forms of Christianity, especially other evangelicals, over time Pentecostalism came to embrace selected aspects of social reform such as addressing economic inequalities, discrimination and women's issues which also enjoyed wide popular support. This fresh direction resulted from criticisms that the evangelical sector was selective in what sins it criticised, while social issues provided a further platform for seeking new means of winning converts.

It was during the 1970s that Pentecostal political activism took off in earnest. The USA, with seemingly a more religious culture than most Western nations, proved to be a fertile ground for Pentecostalism and its political activity as a significant part of the so-called Religious Right and the traditionalist evangelical lobby that supported the election of several Republic Presidents and constituted an elements of the 'cultural wars' – national divisions over moral values and lifestyles. The issues supported were not only familiar ones such as abortion but specifically USA controversies including Christian prayers in schools. By embracing these issues Pentecostalism was able to establish a greater unity with non-Pentecostal evangelicalism.

In Western Europe Pentecostal political involvement was far more muted. The United Kingdom was a case in point in that secularization largely meant the cultural decline of the Christian sector. While for several decades Pentecostalism marked a growth area, the movement only reluctantly entered into political activity and public moral campaigns. In doing so, the movement also attempted to combat liberalizing tendencies in the established denominations such as the endorsement of LGBT rights.

The picture was different in the Majority World, not least of all in Central and Latin America where Pentecostalism won political offices, often challenging the traditional political power of the Roman Catholic Church. Pentecostalism became a major political force in such countries as Brazil, Argentina and Guatemala. The former provides a good example. Here the Catholic Church has experienced a steep decline in popular loyalty and political power. Pentecostalism, in parallel, enjoyed significant growth and, while some Pentecostals remained aloof from politics, many of its church leaders gained political office at national and regional level. So powerful had the Pentecostal lobby become, that few Brazilian politicians aiming for high office would ignore its voting power. While Pentecostals, embraced the usual moral issues such opposing LGBT rights, in Brazil they were also able to endorse such social problems as poverty, urban deprivation, unemployment and land re-distribution.

Pentecostalism in Africa has in many countries came to be highly politicized, sometimes overcoming social divisions, sometimes forming the basis of social divides. In Nigeria, Pentecostals, along with other evangelical groupings, have opposed the spread of Islamic Sharia jurisdiction and the rule of a succession of military dictatorships led by Muslim rulers. At the same time, Pentecostal revivals in the country have managed to cut across traditional ethnic allegiances. From the 1990s, in particular, Pentecostals increased political participation at local, regional, and national level. Political activity was often viewed as combating evil spiritual forces perceived as dominating political office. As in other countries such as Uganda, Pentecostals in Nigeria have vehemently opposed homosexual rights on the grounds that it was a grievous sin and encroachment of Western degenerate culture.

Many of the developments discussed above are observable in countries where Christianity in one form or another has historically dominated. Elsewhere, in nations where non-Christian religions enjoy hegemony or Communist regimes rule, Pentecostals often constitute segments of a Christian minority, thus political activity remains muted – sometimes because of persecution. For example, in China Pentecostals have been at the forefront of revivals in underground 'house churches' but persecution has suppressed meaningful political activity.

In India Pentecostalism, along with other Christian sectors constituting a religious minority, has been subject to anti-Christian purges especially with the rise of Hindu nationalism and the dominance of the upper caste Hindu ideology. Nonetheless, Pentecostalism has come to appeal to lower castes and endorsed rights of marginalised social groups. This tendency for Pentecostalism to appeal to impoverished and marginalised peoples provides a reminder that the political dimension of the movement should not be limited to analysis of political institutions or moral campaigns. Rather, it can also be viewed more broadly as a religion offering a sense of community, providing opportunities for self-help and social advancement.

Bibliography

Frahm-Arp, Maria 2018. "Pentecostalism, Politics, and Prosperity in South Africa." *Religions* 9 (10): 1–16.

Freston, Paul. 2001. *Evangelicals and Politics in Asia, Africa and Latin America*. Cambridge: Cambridge University Press.

Guth, James. 1996. "The Politics of the Christian Right." In *Religion and the Culture Wars: Dispatches From the Front*, edited by J. Green, J. Guth, C. Smith, and L. Kellstedt. New York: Rowman.

Hunt, Stephen. 2016. "Glocalization and Protestant and Catholic Contestations in the Brazilian Religious Economy." In *New Ways of Being Pentecostal in Latin America*, edited by Martin Lindhardt, 15–38. New York: Lexington Books.

Marshall, Ruth. 2009. *Political Spiritualities. The Pentecostal Revolution in Nigeria*. Chicago: University of Chicago Press.

Obadare, Ebenezer. 2018. *Pentecostal Republic: Religion and the Struggle for State Power in Nigeria*. London: Zed Books.

Steigenga, Timothy J. 2001. *The Politics of the Spirit. The Political Implications of Pentecostalized Religion in Costa Rica and Guatemala*. Lanham, MD: Lexington Books.

Stephen J. Hunt

Portugal

Over the last number of centuries, Portugal has been marked by religious homogeneity, grounding its national identity on Catholicism. After the expulsion of Jews and Muslims in 1496, the first religious minorities emerged in the second half of the nineteenth century, with the arrival of foreign missionaries of Methodist, Baptist and Presbyterian background. In Portugal, Protestantism was therefore an imported movement, impelled by nineteenth century's Evangelical revivalism. In 1922, the majority of Protestant churches then present in the country founded the Portuguese Evangelical Alliance (Aliança Evangélica Portuguesa), which was officially recognized in 1935 and reconstituted in 1974. The establishment of democracy in 1974 was a turning point in Portuguese religious history, as it enhanced religious freedom. Furthermore, the entry into the European Union in 1986 boosted the economy, attracting increasing numbers of migrants from Africa, Latin America, Eastern Europe and Asia, who brought with them new spiritualities. These changes led to the gradual pluralisation of the Portuguese religious landscape, paving the way for the enlargement of pre-existing minorities and the proliferation of new religious movements. Today, the Evangelical community remains the largest minority alternative to Catholicism. In this context, the greatest growth has been experienced by Pentecostal and Neo-Pentecostal churches.

Pentecostalism arrived in Portugal at the beginning of the twentieth century, by means of two Portuguese emigrants, José Placido da Costa and Manuel José de Matos Caravela, who had joined the Assemblies of God (AG) in Brazil (Santos 2002). Both were converts of Gunner Vingren and Daniel Berg, founders of the AG in Brazil, and returned to their homeland as missionaries in 1913 and 1921, respectively. The first AG church was established by José de Matos Caravela in Portimão, Algarve, in 1924. Later, the AG took root with the support of Brazilian and Swedish missionaries – including Daniel Berg himself, who founded a congregation in Porto in 1934 – and Jack Härdstedt, who started a church in Lisbon in 1934. The first national convention took place in Lisbon in 1939. In the following years, AG congregations were established across the country, in the Azores and in the Portuguese diaspora. With a lively and participative liturgy, a decentralized structure and a strong penetration into local communities, in a few decades the AG became the largest Pentecostal denomination in Portugal in numbers of church buildings and believers. Today, the AG Convention in Portugal constitutes the majority in AEP, with 421 worship places. The Christian Congregation has also a significant number, especially in the north of the country, with 119 congregations (Prontuário Evangélico 2005). Other Pentecostal denominations are: Missionary Assembly of God, Universal Assembly of God, New Life, Apostolic Church, Church of God, Association of the Churches of Christ, Pentecostal Church of God, Churches of Deliverance, Wesleyan Methodist Church, Abundant Life, Maranata Evangelical Church, Filadélfia Evangelical Church. The latter, coming from Spain and legally recognized in Portugal in 1979, has had a remarkable success among Roma communities (Blanes 2008).

The most recent Pentecostal wave is constituted by Neo-Pentecostal churches, mostly of Brazilian origins, which emerged in the 1980s and have proliferated in the following decades (Mafra 2002; Rodrigues 2014; Swatowiski 2013). The main representatives of this stream are the Maná Christian Church and the Universal Church of the Kingdom of God (UCKG). The former was founded in 1984, in Lisbon, by the Portuguese-Mozambican pastor Jorge Tadeu, who converted in South Africa in the Apostolic Faith Mission. Despite its global reach, the Maná Church is an exception to the historical pattern of foreign implantation, being the first major Evangelical denomination of entirely Portuguese origin. The UCKG Brazilian megachurch arrived in Portugal in 1989, with the inauguration of the first church in Lisbon by Bishop Roberto Guimarães. It gained public visibility, quickly producing a strong social reaction, due to its aggressive proselytism, its success in attracting believers, its acquisition of secular buildings in central urban areas, and its use of media such as radio stations and TV channels as means of evangelization. In 1995, UCKG's attempt to buy the Coliseum of Porto, a famous theatre and concert venue, raised a vibrant protest in some sectors of the public opinion and among Catholic hierarchies. In response to these conflicts, UCKG reshaped its public posture, assuming a more discreet attitude and giving itself a new name – Centre for Spiritual Help. Concurrently, it maintained its doctrines and practices, as well as its Brazilian leadership. With more than 120 congregations, various bookshops and local radios, regular programs on UCKG's Record TV and extensive social work, the church has gained a rising number of members, not only among Brazilian and African migrants, but also among natives, becoming one of the largest UCKG's overseas branches. Furthermore, Portugal has been a strategic hub in UCKG's global expansion, turning it into a gateway to Europe and facilitating its spread in the Portuguese diaspora and in Portuguese-speaking African countries. Other Neo-Pentecostal denominations are the Pentecostal Church God is Love and the Worldwide Church of God's Power, both of Brazilian roots. This group of churches has been excluded from AEP, as some of their practices and ideas – including strong personal leadership, use of ritual objects and the controversial prosperity theology – were considered too distant from Evangelical principles.

The Catholic Charismatic Renewal movement (CCR) has limited expression in Portugal, both in membership and public visibility. Its two main groups are Pneumavita and New Song. The former is the first CCR community in the country. It was created in 1974 by the Portuguese Father

José da Lapa, Missionary of the Holy Spirit Congregation, who was introduced to CCR in Rome. The Brazilian New Song settled in Fatima in 1998, with the support of the local diocese. Its main instruments of evangelization are prayer meetings, retreats and media, including New Song's TV, radio and website. The sanctuary of Fatima, a Catholic site of pilgrimage on a global scale, is one of the hubs of New Song's international expansion (Gabriel 2009).

Bibliography

Blanes, Ruy Llera. 2008. *Os Alleluias: Ciganos Evengélicos e Música*. Lisboa: Imprensa de Ciências Sociais.

Gabriel, Eduardo. 2009. "A expansão internacional do catolicismo carismático brasileiro." *Análise Social* 44 (1): 189–207.

Mafra, Clara. 2002. *Na Posse da Palavra: Religião, Conversão e Liberdade Pessoal em dois Contextos Nacionais*. Lisboa: Imprensa de Ciências Sociais.

Rodrigues, Donizete. 2014. "Ethnic and Religious Diversities in Portugal: The Case of Brazilian Evangelical Immigrants." In *The Changing Soul of Europe: Religions and Migrations in Northern and Southern Europe*, edited by Helena Vilaça, Enzo Pace, Inger Furseth, and Per Pettersson, 133–148. London: Ashgate.

Santos, Luís Aguiar, 2002. "Pluralidade Religiosa: Correntes Cristãs e Não-Cristãs no Universo Religioso Português." In *História religiosa de Portugal* 3, edited by Carlos Moreira Azevedo, 399–501. Lisboa: Circulo dos leitores.

Swatowiski, Claudia Wolff. 2013. *Novos Cristãos em Lisboa: Reconhecendo Estigmas, Negociando Estereótipos*. Rio de Janeiro: Garamond.

Ambra Formenti

Prayer Mountain Movement, Korea

The beginning of the monastic movement of Protestants in Korea can be traced to the social context and religious fervor during the Japanese occupation (1910–1945). Individual Christians ran away from the extreme religious and political oppression into remote areas, such as mountains. Also, Buddhist tradition is often believed to have adopted shamanistic beliefs and valued mountains for their religious significance. Christians have on occasion secluded themselves from life's routines and submerged themselves in personal devotion, spiritual encounters, and religious piety. In this social and religious context, the Pyongyang Revival broke out at a church in Pyongyang City in 1907. The public confession of sins opened the floodgate of repentance and renewal during an overnight prayer meeting. In this week-long revival, which soon spread throughout the country, people experienced a strong move and power of the Holy Spirit, which made them seek a deeper spiritual realm through prayer in an isolated place. Several unique Korean prayer traditions such as daily dawn prayer and overnight prayer meetings began from this revival. This prayer movement influenced the churches in Korea. Some theologians attribute these prayer traditions to the widespread shamanistic influences, including early morning prayer, 40-day prayer, and the prayer mountains.

There are four different stages in the development of the prayer mountain movement (PMM). The first is the 1907 Great Pyongyang Revival. The Revival served as a watershed moment for Korean Christianity in general, and the prayer movement in particular. At the center was Rev. Sunjoo Gil of Jangdaehyun Church.

Prayer meeting in Pyongyang, 1907. Source: Wikimedia, Methodist Episcopal Church

The Revival was characterized by a deep sense of repentance, transformation in believers' lives, diligent study of the Bible, and the beginning of indigenous prayer patterns. Although the prayer mountain was not yet organized as an institution, the prayer movement provided a strong impetus to it.

The second period (1908–1950) of the prayer movement was led by Rev. Yongdo Lee and Rev. Sungbong Lee. Given the grave political and social environment as Japanese persecution increased, there was a strong emphasis on the internalization of Christian spirituality. The teaching of Y. Lee and S. Lee had a strong focus on praying based in the Bible, a clean heart through repentance, and praying for the nation. Upon his graduation from Bible college in 1930, Yongdo Lee spent ten days fasting and in prayer in Kumkang Mountain. In prayer, he saw a vision of God and heard a voice from heaven calling him "to cast out the demons." He spent much of his remaining life in prayer often in remote mountains.

The third period (the 1950s–1960s) marks the post-independence period when organized prayer mountains appeared. This movement was led by Bishop Woonmong Ra, who originally served as a Methodist elder. He regularly underscored spiritual piety as marks of a genuine believer. Ra placed a high emphasis on preparing for the second coming of Jesus.

The last period was from the 1970s–1980s with the proliferation of prayer mountains, both independent and church-related. Also, many spiritually gifted Christians opened prayer houses in urban areas. The most representative of this period is the massive prayer mountain established by David Yonggi Cho and Jashil Choi of Yoido Full Gospel Church, in South Korea, which added a formal focus on fasting and healing.

Currently, there are more than 5,000 prayer mountains and houses in South Korea and the following two examples offer further detail about their history. The Yongmoon Prayer Mountain was founded by Woonmong Ra (1914–2009) in October 1945, the year of liberation. He had been visiting and praying at the remote Yongmoon Mountain in North Gyeongsang Province, where he heard God's voice, "Clean your heart, and you will see me!" His prayer mountain also had two monastic communities for men and women and a Bible school.

In 1947, he held a camp meeting for revival at Yongmoon Prayer Mountain to celebrate the seventh anniversary of the visitation of the Holy Spirit during his prayer mountain experience. Thousands of people assembled in spite of treacherous road trips to reach this deep mountain community. Christians from different parts of the country and various church traditions came to experience God's presence and power. Soon the Yongmoon Prayer Mountain became known for God's intervention in resolving problems in daily life, healing sickness, casting out demons, and other experiences. At the 1954 anniversary camp at the Prayer Mountain, more than 10,000 people attended. Arguably Rah's Prayer Mountain was the bastion of the Holy Spirit movement, facilitating the spread of Pentecostal faith and spirituality across denominational boundaries. The Yongmoon Prayer Mountain has 57 daughter prayer mountains in different parts of Korea and three in the USA. In 1979, it became the Korean Pentecostal Holiness Church as an affiliate of the International Pentecostal Holiness Church in the USA. After Rah's death, the Prayer Mountain joined the Korean Methodist Church in 2012. In addition to its significant contribution to the development of Korean Pentecostalism, his popular weekly *Bokeum Newspaper* helped to spread the Pentecostal faith through its vast readership. It also experimented with the possibility of Protestant monasticism in Korea. Rah's strong emphasis on Christian mysticism and interpretation of the Bible raised various controversies among Christians.

The largest prayer mountain was established in 1973 by Rev. Jashil Choi, the associate pastor of Yoido Full Gospel Church. Choi is also the mother-in-law of Yonggi Cho, the founder of the church. Situated at Osanri, north of Seoul close to the Demilitarized Zone, this prayer mountain attracted large crowds with the ease of travel. Yoido Full Gospel Church facilitated a large number of visitors with the hourly shuttle services between the church and the prayer mountain. Soon, the prayer mountain added more chapels (13 in total), support facilities, and dormitories to accommodate the visitors. The main sanctuary has a seating capacity of 6,000.

The Osanri Prayer Mountain also became known for the practice of fasting as the accepted mode of prayer. However, more significant have been many testimonies of healing and miracles, widely disseminated through various media outlets, including the Church's monthly magazine and the weekly newspaper. The prayer mountain began to draw international Christians from nearby countries such as Japan and Taiwan.

The PMM in Korea was an institutional expression of the deep prayer tradition of Korean Christianity as well as a product of Korean history, traditional religiosity, and the Pyongyang Revival. Through the PMM, Pentecostal beliefs and practices spread widely, contributing to the Pentecostalization of Korean Christianity. The PMM is known for promoting a place where one can encounter God's presence, often through healing, miracles, blessing, and the baptism in the Holy Spirit while playing a significant role in shaping of Korean Christianity.

Currently, the larger centers for the PMM face a serious challenge as the number of visitors has steadily declined with more local churches opening their own prayer retreat centres. However, the decline is also linked to the general decline of Christianity and further social change leaving the future of the PMM uncertain.

Bibliography

Cho, SungGeun Cho. 2005. "The Impact of Carmel Fasting Prayer Mountain Revival upon Believers." DMin thesis, Oral Robert University.

Eim, Yeol Soo. 2003. "South Korea." In *International Dictionary of Pentecostal Charismatic Movement*, edited by Stanly M. Burgess, 239–246. Grand Rapids, MI: Zondervan.

Jung, YongKwon. 2002. "Korean Prayers: Evaluating the Prayer Phenomena at the Prayer Mountain Centers in Korea." PhD thesis, Asbury Theological Seminary.

Ma, Julie. 2019. "Influence of Pentecostal Spirituality to Asian Christianity." Paper Presented at an Annual International Ecumenical Summer Seminar, Strasburg France, July 3–10.

Yoido Full Gospel Church. "Osanri Cho Jashil Memorial Fasting Prayer Mountain."

Julie Ma

Price, Charles S.

Charles S. Price (1887–1947) was a traveling evangelist whose evangelistic and divine healing meetings drew thousands and earned headlines in local newspapers, particularly in the U.S. and Canada. He was born on May 7, 1887, in Sheffield, England to Charles Henry Price and Mary Hannah Bee. According to his autobiography, he studied law at Oxford University for two years (Price 1944). Although he was never granted a degree, he would later adopt the honorary title "Dr. Price."

In September 1906, Price left for a fresh start in Canada. He arrived in Quebec and eventually gained employment with the Canadian Pacific Railroad Company in Medicine Hat, Alberta, and then at a logging camp in Nelson, British Columbia. In March 1907, he moved to Spokane, Washington. There he attended a meeting at the Free Methodist "Life Line Mission" where he responded to an altar call for salvation. The following night he gave a public testimony of his conversion and was later invited to preach there. He met Bessie Rae Osborn (1889–1956) at the mission, and they were married on August 23, 1907. Price had four children: Ethel Mae (1907–1997), born in England from a previous non-marital relationship, and three more with his wife, Marjorie Evangeline (1908–1994), Charles Vernon (1910–2001), and Lucile Bessie (1912–1996).

Price heard about the Azusa Street Revival and some of his mission co-workers had received Spirit baptism and had spoken in tongues. Being eager to receive this baptism himself, he set out to pray for it with a few friends. On his way to meet them, another minister convinced him against it, and he never made it to the meeting. Price later looked on this decision as a major turning point of his life in the wrong direction (Price 1944).

Ordained by the Methodist Episcopal Church, Price pastored several congregations in the states of Washington and Idaho. Embracing modernism, he severed ties with Methodism, and from 1913 to 1917 pastored several Congregational churches along the west coast of the U.S. from Valdez, Alaska to Oakland, California, quickly gaining prominent social standing in the cities of his pastorates. Price involved himself in service clubs, fraternal associations, and Freemasonry (Price 1944). While in Oakland, he convinced his church to build a large maple dance floor with a capacity for 1,500 people, along with several smoking lounges (Enloe 2008).

During WWI, Price sold war bonds for the government, and in 1920, he left pastoring to give lectures for Chautauqua, a social movement that promoted the education of adults. In 1921, he re-entered pastoral ministry at the First Congregational Church in Lodi, California, while maintaining a part-time lecture schedule with Chautauqua (Price 1944).

In August 1921, Aimee Semple McPherson was holding tent meetings in San Jose, California, where people were reportedly being saved, healed, and were receiving the baptism in the Holy Spirit. Price attended the meetings intending to collect evidence to "blow the whole thing to pieces" (Price 1944). Instead, on his second night of attendance, he responded to McPherson's invitation for salvation, to the surprise of his ministerial peers. The next day, McPherson had Price give his testimony and lead the song service (Enloe 2008). He later received Spirit baptism at a tarrying meeting and began to hold similar prayer meetings at his own church, where 500 of his church members were baptized in the Holy Spirit (Enloe 2008). This prompted the Congregational church authorities to step in, forcing Price to organize his own independent Pentecostal church, Lodi Bethel Temple (Price 1944).

In 1922, Price joined McPherson for an evangelistic tour to Ohio and New York. He subsequently accepted an invitation to Ashland, Oregon, where in September 1922, he held nearly a month of evangelistic meetings that drew over 3,000 nightly in a town with a population of 5,000. By the end of the month, the local newspapers were proclaiming that few sinners were left in the city and people were testifying to being healed (Enloe 2008). The news traveled as far as Victoria, British Columbia, Canada, where Price was invited for his next meetings. These were his most successful yet, but would be surpassed by his next meetings in Vancouver, British Columbia. There, Price held a three-week campaign where 250,000 people attended the meetings, and on the final day alone 23,000 people attended over three separate meetings (Price 1944; Opp 2005). Local newspapers carried stories of healing, descriptions of the huge crowds, and photos of people lying with their backs on the floor, having fallen there as they were anointed with oil for healing.

The Vancouver campaign was also met with great controversy. After Price left the city, a committee of medical practitioners and clergy in Vancouver undertook an investigation, examining 350 cases of the approximately 6,000 people who had been anointed for healing (Opp 2005). The report disputed several of the purported healings and was made public. A dissenting minority report, arguing for the validity of several healings, was released by two of the committee members. In Canada, Price held his largest campaign in Edmonton, followed by others in Calgary, Regina, Brandon, Winnipeg, and at Massey Hall in Toronto. In America, Price held campaigns in Minneapolis, Duluth, St. Louis, Dallas, Seattle, Oklahoma City, Kansas City, Pittsburgh, and Los Angeles, among others (Enloe 2008).

In 1925, Price began producing a monthly periodical, the *Golden Grain*, which contained his sermons and regularly documented cases of people who had received salvation, physical healing, and deliverance from tobacco, alcohol, and drugs. Accompanying photos further legitimized such testimonies. By 1927, Price's emphasis on speaking in tongues had strengthened his informal relationship with Pentecostal denominations and networks, particularly the Assemblies of God (USA). In 1934, Price held meetings with Lewi Pethrus in Stockholm, Sweden, and with T.B. Barratt in Oslo, Norway (Price 1944).

Price's marriage was fraught with complications. By 1930, Price and his wife had separated, and they later divorced. Price retired to Pasadena, California, in 1945, and died there on May 8, 1947. He published over 21 books in addition to his monthly newsletter, which continued to be published for a decade posthumously by his longtime assistant, Evelyn Carvell. Part of Price's legacy can be found in the list of prominent evangelists who cite him as a primary influence in their life, including Demos Shakarian (founder of Full Gospel Business Men International), healing evangelist Kathryn Kuhlman, evangelist Lorne Fox, and D.N. Buntain (denominational leader of the Pentecostal Assemblies of Canada, and father of famed missionary to India, Mark Buntain). His evangelistic campaigns bolstered the growing Pentecostal movement in North America, and especially gave prominence to the doctrine of divine healing.

Bibliography

Enloe, Tim. 2008. "Dr. Charles S. Price: His Life, Ministry and Influence." *Assemblies of God Heritage*: 4–13.

Opp, James. 2005. *The Lord for the Body: Religion, Medicine, and Protestant Faith Healing in Canada, 1880–1930*. Montreal & Kingston: McGill-Queen's University Press.

Price, Charles S. 1944. *The Story of My Life*. Pasadena: Charles S. Price Publishing Company.

Caleb Courtney

Prosperity Gospel

Prosperity Gospel (PG) has come to be regarded as the fastest growing strand of global Christianity. Referred to also as "health and wealth," "name it, claim it" and "Faith Gospel," PG is said to be crucial to the expansion of Pentecostalism in the Global South and to have extended even into secular as well as non-Christian milieus, such as Islam (Heuser in Heuser 2015). At the same time, PG is said to represent one of the most controversial movements of contemporary Christianity. This is especially the case if PG is read through the lenses of wealthy preachers known for tax fraud charges and for displaying affluence and lavishness.

Many researchers define PG as a set of beliefs and practices that are typical for newer Pentecostal groups (e.g. Neo-Pentecostalism) and draw from the assumption that Christ's atonement is not solely about otherworldly redemption but also includes believers' socio-economic prosperity as well as health and success. From this view, the key ideas of PG are that believers ought to claim this-worldly abundance through the power of the spoken word (positive confession) and by giving tithes and offerings to ministries and ministers while expecting God to generously reward their monetary investment in the kingdom of God (seed faith). The popularization of PG is usually seen in connection to US-American preachers, such as Kenneth E. Hagin, Oral Roberts, Kenneth and Gloria Copeland, Frederick K.C. Price, Benny Hinn and others, who became popular in the 1970s and 1980s primarily but not solely through their media and television ministries. On the basis of this understanding, some researchers have criticized PG while others have emphasized its empowering aspects.

Initially, scholarly works on PG were driven by theological interests and church politics. The focus was on the above-mentioned US-American preachers (or figures connected to them) whose teachings and display of affluence seemed to threaten Evangelical and Pentecostal denominations. As early as 1979, Pentecostal theologians polemicized against the "faith-formula" propagated by evangelists who taught believers to call things into existence. By the 1980s, "The 'Gospel' of Prosperity" (Fee 1984) had become a name by which theologians distinguished themselves from evangelists who were said to teach that poverty and sickness indicated a lack of faith and a sinful life. Such prosperity teachings, it was argued, represented a deification of wealth and consumption and a sell-out of the theology of the cross (Sharpe 2013). Although the main reference of these theological works were American televangelists, they also condemned South African and Korean ministers like Yonggi Cho, whose notion of blessing included material prosperity. This understanding was criticized by theological studies that suggested understanding theologies of health and prosperity that were popular in the Global South as contextual theologies (Anderson 2003). In this view, PG represents a critique of self-complacent theologies that are rooted in Eurocentric body/soul-dichotomies that deny the material and this-worldly dimension of the gospel.

Studies concerned with the history of PG have mainly focused on North America. An early analysis of Hagin's sermons and publications, arguably driven by the theological interests of its time, contended that PG had its roots in the New Thought movement and, hence, in "suspicious" early twentieth-century American Esotericism and Occultism (McConnell 1988; Lie 2003). MacGregor (2007) even argued that some of PG's roots can be found in The Nation of Islam and Mormonism.

According to MacGregor, PG should be understood in the context of American New Religious Movements offering personal empowerment to people outside the socio-economic mainstream. Studies of PG in African American churches tended to agree with this latter aspect (Harrison 2005). By contrast, other scholars argue that historical investigations should take the mainstream-character of PG as point of departure – proved by secular talk shows where phrases, such as "as name it, claim it" have become a staple (Bowler 2013). PG, they argue, was an offspring of the 1950s Healing revival, which fused New Thought ideas with American post-World War II optimism sustained by a transnational network of preachers and conferences. Against this rather parochial focus on North America, studies focusing on Latin America, Africa and Asia offered a different picture. They pointed to differences of emphasis within PG practices (such as spiritual warfare or entrepreneurship) and argue that, as in the case of Latin America, practitioners are influenced by South Korean or African innovations, while influencing the practices of believers in the global North (Garrard-Burnett 2013). This raises the question of how to define PG in a way that takes its heterogeneity and fluidity into account.

Socio-scientific treatises on PG have largely been dominated by the broader question of whether or not Pentecostalism fostered political empowerment and socio-economic mobility, especially in the Global South. Drawing on Max Weber, some accounts suggest that the moral conservativism (abstinence from alcohol, smoking and extramarital affairs) championed by PG in combination with a financial discipline (deferred gratification, budgeting, tithing) promoted entrepreneurialism and eventually translated in socio-economic advancement (Drønen in Heuser 2015). This account is contrasted by researchers who view PG as an export product of US-ideology cementing neo-imperial structures and stabilizing global asymmetries (Brouwer et al 1996). PG therefore, represents a mystification of global neoliberalism and individualism that conceals structural and systemic causes for poverty and socio-economic insecurity. PG fostered a magical worldview by which preachers enriched themselves at the costs of their followers. Even if this understanding is said to presuppose PG to be a stable set of teachings and to deny PG adherents any kind of agency (which revealed a colonial bias on the side of the researchers), PG's role in promoting social mobility and empowerment remains inconclusive. Coleman (2011, 23) distinguishes between "an initial phase [of scholarship] where economic factors are given strong causal explanatory force" in accounting for the upsurge of PG in the Global South, and a more recent one that dismisses the presupposition that religion and economy could be studied as two different spheres and which complicates common "understandings of the relationships between religious and economic action." From this perspective, PG should not be perceived as a mere reaction to economic circumstances, but as being entangled with it in such a way as to produce new economic (and political) subjects. Thus, the researcher's focus should be on how PG is understood in concrete contexts and locally sedimented practices. Accordingly, studies on PG in Africa have operationalized Marcel Mauss' notion of the gift to show how PG teachings and practices foster networks of exchange based on ambition and obligation and reactivate local practices of responsibility and sociality. Thus, they contest both the conceptualization of PG as a mere superstructure to economic (base) conditions and of PG as ideology that reinforces a mystified individualism. Others have focused on how (visual) media constitute, rather than just transmit, PG in specific contexts, reframing poverty and producing new political and economic subjects (Attanasi and Yong 2012; Heuser 2015).

The main challenge to current study of PG remains the question of definition. There is an increasing consensus to dismiss the idea that PG represents a specific canon of ideas, ethics, or practices and to view it as a transformative global network of ministries and individuals. Another option is to conceptualize PG "as a name" which scholars and believers refer to and by which they position themselves in hegemonic discourses on religion, Pentecostalism, economy, politics, and asymmetries that are local and global at the same time (Maltese in Heuser 2015).

Bibliography

Anderson, Allan. 2004. "The Contextual Pentecostal Theology of David Yonggi Cho." *Asian Journal of Pentecostal Studies* 7 (1): 101–123.

Attanasi, Katherine, and Amos Yong, eds. 2012. *Pentecostalism and Prosperity: The Socio-Economics of the Global Charismatic Movement*. New York: Palgrave Macmillan.

Bowler, Kate. 2013. *Blessed: A History of the American Prosperity Gospel*. New York: Oxford University Press.

Brouwer, Steve, Paul Gifford, and Susan D. Rose. 1996. *Exporting the American Gospel: Global Christian Fundamentalism*. New York: Routledge.

Coleman, Simon. 2011. "Prosperity Unbound? Debating the 'Sacrificial Economy.'" In *Economics of Religion: Anthropological Approaches*, edited by Lionel Obadia and Donald C. Wood, 23–45. Bingley: Emerald.

Fee, Gordon D. 1984. "The 'Gospel' of Prosperity – an Alien Gospel." *Reformation Today*, 39–43.

Garrard-Burnett, Virginia. 2013. "Neopentecostalism and Prosperity Theology in Latin America: A Religion for Late Capitalist Society." *Iberoamericana* 42 (1/2): 21–34.

Harrison, Milmon F. 2005. *Righteous Riches: The Word of Faith Movement in Contemporary African American Religion*. Oxford: Oxford University Press.

Heuser, Andreas, ed. 2015. *Pastures of Plenty: Tracing Religio-Scapes of Prosperity Gospel in Africa and Beyond*. New York: Peter Lang.

Lie, Geir. 2003. *E.W. Kenyon: Cult Founder or Evangelical Minister? An Historical Analysis of Kenyon's Theology with Particular Emphasis on Roots and Influences*. Oslo: Refleks Publishing.

MacGregor, Kirk R. 2007. "The Word-Faith Movement: A Theological Conflation of the Nation of Islam and Mormonism?" *Journal of the American Academy of Religion* 75 (1): 87–120.

McConnell, Dan R. 1988. *A Different Gospel: A Historical and Biblical Analysis of the Modern Faith Movement*. Peabody, MA: Hendrickson Publishers.

Sharpe, Matthew. 2013. "Name It and Claim It: Prosperity Gospel and the Global Pentecostal Reformation." In *Handbook of Research on Development and Religion*, edited by Matthew Clarke, 164–79. Cheltenham, UK: Edward Elgar.

Giovanni Maltese

Psychology

The psychological study of Pentecostals is a subfield of the Psychology of Religion within social psychology. A major additional subfield is clinical psychology, which requires doctors to consider a patient's spirituality in the diagnosis and treatment of mental health conditions. Leading theorists such as Raymond Paloutzian and Crystal Park (2013) view religion and spirituality as a coherent system consisting of beliefs, behavioral practices, experiences, and symbols that enable people to meet their need for a meaningful life, though unfortunately only five of nearly 700 pages contain references to Pentecostalism in this otherwise comprehensive handbook. Stefan and Odilo Huber (2010) provide a more detailed review of Pentecostal studies. Consistent with previous investigators, they identify a historic period of "hostility" toward Pentecostal behavior between 1910 and the 1960s, which has been followed by the current "friendly" period. Early hostility was often associated with perceptions linking Pentecostal spirituality such as glossolalia with psychotic disorders, whereas more recent studies described Pentecostals as emotionally stable, extraverted, self-controlled, and highly submissive to spiritual leaders. In addition, Pentecostals did not have significant problems with anxiety, depression, or hostility, but were lower in self-esteem.

As part of his foray into a field called neurotheology, Andrew Newberg and his colleagues (2006) studied brain scans (SPECT: Single Photon Emission Computed Tomography) of five Pentecostal women during glossolalia and singing. The observed differences in the imaging revealed less blood flow (representing less brain activity) in the frontal lobes during glossolalia compared to when they were singing. Newberg interpreted the findings as supporting the participants' reported experience as less intentional control over the activity of glossolalia. At this point, the limited association found in a small sample is insufficient to draw any conclusions about possible links between supernatural experiences and biopsychological processes.

Unlike the phenomenon of glossolalia commonly identified with Pentecostals, miracles of healing have been reported throughout the history of the church, though arguably, Pentecostals have made healing prayer a significant focus of worship in the past century. Using several research methods such as surveys, reviews of medical records, and medical tests, Candy Gunther Brown (2012) provides scientific evidence of the value of healing prayer by Pentecostals. Positive effects for those who did not recover in response to prayer included some improvement in symptoms as well as feeling love and support.

Because Pentecostals have roots in the holiness traditions, they place a significant emphasis on moral purity. Though not unique to Pentecostals, their clergy have made national news for their preaching about sexual purity as well as for moral failures by highly visible televangelists. Studies of Pentecostal morality based on moral foundations theory reveal that Pentecostals, like other evangelicals, more strongly endorse moral arguments that rely on principles of authority, loyalty, and purity and less on principles of harm and equality, which are more typically argued by progressive Christians.

Psychologists have generally viewed Pentecostals as fundamentalists based on their historic use of scripture to justify various beliefs and practices including glossolalia and other spiritual gifts as well as miracles. Not surprisingly, high levels of fundamentalism predict high levels of moral purity and authority concerns. This concept of fundamentalism comes from the theory of intra-textual fundamentalism developed by Ralph Hood, Peter Hill, and Paul Williamson (2005). In this theory, fundamentalists interpret their sacred texts within the context of other texts rather than drawing upon external sources like tradition or reason to adduce a moral response. The Intra-textual Fundamentalism Scale, derived from the theory, has reasonable psychometric properties in research explaining Pentecostals' general approach to traditional values of prohibitions against sex outside of heterosexual marriage. Ralph Hood has also applied intra-textual fundamentalism theory to explain why some American Pentecostals in Appalachia engage in the risky practice of handling venomous snakes. That is, they rely on the text of Mark 16: 17–18 (KJV) to support their beliefs in "signs and wonders" and interpret "They shall take up serpents …" as a command.

Regarding the Psychology of Gender, intra-textual fundamentalism and experience combine to explain support for women holding positions as pastors and missionaries in some Pentecostal traditions. That is, since the early 1900s, women spoke in tongues and demonstrated spiritual gifts, and Pentecostals considered this consistent with biblical texts describing God's Spirit at work in both women and men (e.g., Joel 2:28, 29; Acts 2:16–18).

In the past two decades, a plethora of forgiveness studies, some including Pentecostals, have documented the benefits of forgiveness (for a general review see, Rasmussen et al., 2019). An experimental study by Geoffrey Sutton and Eloise Thomas (2005) revealed a tendency for Pentecostals to be more forgiving toward, and willing to restore to ministry, younger rather than older male clergy who were guilty of a moral failure. Another study by Geoffrey Sutton and his colleagues (2007) revealed a cross-gender effect in which men were more forgiving toward female clergy and women were more forgiving toward male clergy.

Psychologists study religion and other aspects of behavior using tests and questionnaires, though instruments for studying Pentecostals are still in their infancy. Most researchers rely on participants to identify their faith tradition often by checking a category such as "Pentecostal/ Charismatic" or entering text in an "other" option. In addition to asking about Christian beliefs (e.g., "I have had a born-again experience.") and practices (e.g., "I pray each day."), researchers at Evangel University in Springfield Missouri, USA have published three sets of items titled Christian Service (e.g., "I am an effective witness for my faith."), Spiritual Gifting (e.g., "I speak in tongues."), and Healing (e.g., "I have prayed for the sick and they've been healed."). All three scales were significantly associated with a strong sense of attachment to God characterized by feeling close to God and non-anxious in his presence. The scales were also linked to a strong sense of faith as an internalized experience (intrinsic religious orientation) rather than a faith derived from social or personal benefits (extrinsic religious orientation).

Few published studies have examined the practice of psychotherapy with Pentecostal patients. Researchers at Evangel University have published two studies of mostly Pentecostal psychotherapists and patients. As expected, psychotherapists generally hold the traditional Pentecostal values of sexual purity and intolerance of substance abuse. What sets Pentecostal psychotherapists apart is their willingness to pray in tongues with their Pentecostal clients and encourage the use of glossolalia (referred to as prayer language) as part of a patient's intersession treatment activities (Sutton et al., 2016). A study of patients who identified as Pentecostal or Charismatic did not indicate any obvious differences compared to those who identified as evangelicals (Sutton et al., 2018). Other questionnaires have been developed to measure aspects of Pentecostal ministry, but these have not yet appeared in the peer-reviewed psychology literature.

Bibliography

Brown, Candy Gunther. 2012. *Testing Prayer*. Cambridge: Harvard University Press.

Hood, Ralph W., Peter C. Hill, and W. Paul Williamson. 2005. *The Psychology of Religious Fundamentalism*. New York: Guilford Press.

Huber, Stefan, and Odilo W. Huber. 2010. "Psychology of Religion." In *Studying Global Pentecostalism: Theories and Methods*, edited by Allan Anderson, Michael Bergunder, André Droogers, and Cornelis Van Der Laan, 133–55. Berkeley, CA:University of California Press.

Newberg, Andrew B., Nancy A. Wintering, Donna Morgan, and Mark R. Waldman. 2006. "The Measurement of Regional Cerebral Blood Flow During Glossolalia: A Preliminary SPECT Study." *Psychiatry Research: Neuroimaging* 148 (1): 67–71. doi:10.1016/j.pscychresns.2006.07.001.

Paloutzian, Raymond F., and Crystal L. Park. 2013. *Handbook of the Psychology of Religion and Spirituality*, Second Edition. New York: Guilford Press.

Rasmussen, Kyler R., Madelynn Stackhouse, Susan D. Boon, Karly Comstock, and Rachel Ross. 2019. "Meta-analytic Connections Between Forgiveness and Health: The Moderating Effects of Forgiveness-related Distinctions." *Psychology & Health* 34 (5): 515–534 doi:10.1080/08870446.2018.1545906.

Sutton, Geoffrey W., Christine Arnzen, and Heather L. Kelly. 2016. "Christian Counseling and Psychotherapy: Components of Clinician Spirituality that Predict Type of Christian Intervention. *Journal of Psychology and Christianity* 35: 204–214.

Sutton, Geoffrey W., Heather L. Kelly, Everett L. Worthington, Jr., Brandon J. Griffin, and Chris Dinwiddie. 2018. "Satisfaction with Christian Psychotherapy and Well-being: Contributions of Hope, Personality, and Spirituality." *Spirituality in Clinical Practice* 5 (1): 8–24, doi: 10.1037/scp0000145

Sutton, Geoffrey W., Kelly C. McLeland, Katie K. Weaks, Patricia E. Cogswell, and Renee N. Miphouvieng. 2007. "Does Gender Matter? An Exploration of Gender, Spirituality, Forgiveness and Restoration Following Pastor Transgressions." *Pastoral Psychology* 55: 645–663. doi 10.1007/ s11089-007-0072-3.

Sutton, Geoffrey W., and Eloise K. Thomas. 2005. "Can Derailed Pastors be Restored? Effects of Offense and Age on Restoration." *Pastoral Psychology* 53: 583–599.

Geoffrey Sutton

Purnomo, Petrus Agung

Petrus Agung Purnomo (1962–2016) was the founder and senior pastor of *JKI Injil Kerajaan* (The Gospel of the Kingdom Church/GKC) in Semarang, Central Java, Indonesia. The GKC was one of the largest megachurches in Indonesia with approximately 16,000 weekly attendants on its peak. The Holy Stadium, the main venue of the megachurch, was built between 2004 and 2007 and is probably the second largest Indonesian megachurch site with 12,000 seats.

The GKC was well known for its extensive public engagement with more than 30 department of ministries serving the impoverished through free education, medication, meals, cheap groceries, charity markets and various regular engagements. Interestingly such an extensive public engagement was triggered by a vision that he saw on January 1, 2007. Purnomo felt that God's presence could not be sensed during the megachurch's New Year celebration. This led him to ask the pastoral team to join in prayer on the first day of 2007. While walking in front of the megachurch building he confessed that he saw a vision of so many people outside the megachurch site. They were Muslims and the poor. And soon after he said

Image: courtesy of the staff of the late Rev Petrus Agung

that he heard a clear voice saying, 'Reap them, or they will rot and end as waste if you are late'.

Purnomo was born in Semarang as Lie Tjong Hian. He was growing in a modest Chinese-Indonesian family. His childhood was quite often re-told as a phase where he grew as a shy boy who was always accompanied by his father during his elementary schooldays. He struggled with his inferiority complex until his late thirties.

Purnomo had a "born-again" experience at a student evangelistic service called Ecumenical Night in 1979. This was explicitly one of his major epiphanies which significantly influenced his later life journey. In 1980, he received an offer to study at Perth Bible College in Australia. However, it was his father who rejected his plan to be a minister. Purnomo himself felt that God asked him to stay in the city and take his favourite field to study. He accordingly studied at a state university and took history as his major.

During his university life Purnomo actively served as a lay preacher in various prayer groups in the countryside of Semarang. In this period his struggle with his humble family background brought him to search for a faith-based answer to resolve his financial problems. He acknowledged that Kenneth Hagin's teaching had laid a firm foundation on his understanding of the role and mechanism of faith, frequently taught as "believing and speaking" or the Prosperity Gospel. But it was his reading of Yonggi Cho's *The Fourth Dimension* that answered his struggle in understanding and experiencing the power of faith.

The influence of Adi Sutanto was significant during Purnomo's university years. Purnomo most frequently mentioned his previous personal conversation or experience with Sutanto as a relevant insight for his ministry. Sutanto's most observable influence on Purnomo was on his evangelistic zeal.

Purnomo became an itinerant evangelist after his graduation and started to preach in a number of small prayer groups in Jakarta and Surabaya. At the same time, he served with Sangkakala and became one of its preachers. It was in the heyday of his ministry that Agung believed that God had called him to start a church and became a pastor. During the early years of his pastorate he was frustrated with the slow growth of the church. This situation brought him to question the calling that he had supposed to be the voice of God.

From 1992 to 1994 Purnomo frequently attended Benny Hinn's services in the U.S. and Canada. It seems that Agung's pneumatology and his worship style would later be influenced by that of Hinn. While Agung quite frequently attended Hinn's services as an ordinary visitor, he never had a direct and personal contact with Hinn. It seems to be Agung's personal experience of the Holy Spirit, while he was waiting for five hours for one of Hinn's services in 1992, that shaped his later pneumatology.

The megachurch founded a Bible school called The School of Acts (TSOA) affiliated with Raymond Mooi's TSOA in Malaysia. Mooi was the Asian director for Morris Cerullo Ministries which gave him a broad connection with global Charismatic networks. It seems that the founding of TSOA Indonesia also brought Mooi's network to the megachurch, which seemingly broadened Agung's network of the teachers, including some well-known leaders in the Charismatic circles who came from various countries, but mostly from the U.S. While most of them have a loose network with the megachurch, a closer network was made with Morris Cerullo and his ministries since Agung was one of Cerullo's interpreters in Indonesia. Agung was also frequently invited as a speaker in Cerullo's annual conference in the U.S., Israel, Russia, and the Netherlands during the first half of the 2010s.

In 2005, Purnomo founded a network of ministry called Bahtera (the Ark) with five evangelists from West Java and a pastor from Central Java. This network had an exceptional influence on his later approach and style of ministry. Although visions, prophecies, and hearing the voice of God were quite common for Purnomo, it was not until his involvement in Bahtera that he began to experience and refer to them more frequently.

Bibliography

Anderson, Allan, and Edmond Tang, eds. 2005. *Asian and Pentecostal*. Oxford: Regnum Books.

Kristanto, Rony Chandra. 2018. "Evangelism as Public Theology: The Public Engagement of the Gospel of the Kingdom Church in

Semarang, Indonesia." PhD thesis, University of Birmingham, UK.

Steenbrink, Karel, and Jan Aritonang, eds. 2008. *A History of Christianity in Indonesia*. Leiden: Brill.

Wiyono, Gani. 2019. "Pentecostalism in Indonesia." In *Asia Pacific Pentecostalism*, edited by Denise A. Austin, Jacqueline Grey, and Paul W. Lewis, 243–270. Leiden: Brill.

Rony Chandra Kristanto

Pyongyang Revival

Pyongyang (or P'yŏngyang) Revival refers to the charismatic Protestant movement that originated in Changdaehyŏn Presbyterian church at Pyongyang in January, 1907, the current capital of the Democratic People's Republic of Korea (DPRK), and spread throughout the Korean Peninsula. During its Bible classes and revivals, members of Pyongyang's Presbyterian and Methodist churches repeatedly repented of all their wrongs while praying aloud, and openly confessed their own awakenings. Such Pentecostal experiences have become the prototypical ground that actuated Protestant churches to grow fast in twentieth century Korea. A crucial event that defined the nature of Korean Protestantism, Pyongyang Revival is of the most controversial religious phenomenon that is simultaneously praised and also criticized inside and outside Korean Christian circles.

Around the time when Protestantism was introduced into Korea in 1894, there was unrest in Korean society. While the established China-center worldview was being collapsed, as well as Chosŏn dynasty (1392–1910) was falling, a good number of Koreans took Protestantism as a civilized religion that might help the Korean nation in crisis. After its victory in the Russo-Japanese War (1904–05), Japan forced Korea to sign the Protectorate Treaty in 1905 and eventually annexed it in 1910. Against this backdrop of political upheaval, Pyongyang Revival started with Bible training classes, in which about four hundred Presbyterian churches of South Pyŏngan Province participated in from January 2–15, 1907. It did not come from nowhere, but was related to a series of predecessors that inspired it, such as the great revival in Wonsan in August 1903, revivals in Pyongyang and Ch'ilsan in January, 1906, revivals in Chinnampo and Chaeryŏng,

American Presbyterian Mission Annual Meeting in Pyongyang, 1910s. Source: American pyongyang.com.

and prayer meetings of Western missionaries in Pyongyang. For example, Robert A. Hardie (1865–1949), the Canadian medical missionary, led Bible studies and was a leader at the Wŏnsan Revival of 1903. Dr. Hardie, who was concerned for the spiritual situation of the Korean churches, confessed his fault in disdaining Koreans in the meeting, realizing that what God wanted was not a Korean awakening, but his own awakening. This touched many Korean believers so much so that they too confessed their wrongdoings that eventually caused a great religious awakening among the Korean populace.

On January 14, Pyongyang Revival erupted when about 1,500 Protestant believers were having an evening revival service in Changdaehyŏn Presbyterian church. Bible training classes started on January 6 but on January 14, Graham Lee (1861–1916) led a prayer service and William Hunt (1869–1939) delivered a sermon. In the course of the service, Graham Lee and Kil Sŏn-ju (1869–1935) exerted their charismatic characteristics. Lee described a scene of the meeting as follows: "after prayer, when asked if anyone would want to confess, it looked like the Spirit of God came to the congregation. One by one people stood up and confessed their own sins, and burst out crying or fell over the floor and writhe in a guilty of conscience, smacking up the floor.... All the congregation prayed verbally, and this scene of hundreds of men praying aloud was beyond words.... Like that, the meeting continued with prayers, confessions and tears until 2 am" (Lee 1907, 34). On January 15, the last day of the Bible training class, there continued to be the evening service in which Kil Sŏn-ju delivered a sermon. As Kil, the Korean elder, preached a fiery sermon and confessed his wrongdoings, hundreds of Koreans confessed their hidden vices and crimes openly. Like the previous day, they prayed aloud and lamented collectively, and many of them writhed in agony of sin.

Even after the Bible training class in Chandaehyŏn Presbyterian church was over, a "flame of revival" continued across Pyongyang. The venues in which the historic revivals continued in the current DPRK capital were Pyongyang Girls high school, Boy's primary school of Chandaehyŏn Presbyterian church, missionaries midday prayer meeting, Wednesday evening prayer meeting of Chandaehyŏn Presbyterian church, Methodist churches, mission schools and so forth. Beyond Pyongyang, the revival movement spread to other parts of Pyŏngan Province, in which Pyongyang is included, such as Sŏnch'ŏn, Haeju, Yangtŏk, Chŭngsan, Yongpyŏn and Chaekyŏng. Beyond Pyŏngan Province, it continued to spread to Seoul, Incheon, Kongju, Taegu and even Manchuria (Park 2005, 205–345). In the wake of Pyongyang Revival, Western missionaries and Korean laypeople continued to repent and confess sins or guilt to one another. Campaigns for evangelism became so active nationwide that the Million Soul Movement was launched.

Pyongyang Revival marks a milestone in the history of Korean Protestantism, which has become one of the most controversial events in the modern history of religion in Korea. Liberal and/or progressive Christians and thinkers have often criticized it as a "defining event that turned Korean Protestantism, which had had very participatory and reforming characteristics, into a depoliticized, other-worldly oriented and even anti-intellectual religion." On the other hand, Pyongyang Revival may be interpreted as a "conversion to modernities" in which modern imaginaries of subjectivity were expressed in that it crucially contributed to a shift from a communitarian and ritualistically-oriented religiosity of the feudalistic society to a more individualistic, confessional and self-transforming form of contemporary religion.

Bibliography

Blair, William N., and Bruce Hunt. 1977. *The Korean Pentecost and the Suffering Which Followed*. Edinburgh: Banner of Truth
Park, Yong Kyu. 2005. *The Great Revivalism in Korea: Its History, Character, and Impact. 1901–1910* [P'yŏngyang taepuhŭng untong]. Seoul: Word of Life Books.
Park, Myung Soo. 2003. *Study on the Church Revival Movement in Korea*. [Hankukkyohoe taepuhŭnguntong yŏnku]. Seoul: Institute of the History of Christianity in Korea.
Lee, Chang Ki. 2003. *The Early Revival Movement in Korea (1903–1907): A Historical and Systemic Study*. Mission 34. Zoetermeer: Boekencentrum.
Oak, Sung-Deuk. 2012. "Major Protestant Revivals in Korea, 1903–35." *Studies in World Christianity* 18 (3): 269–290.

Kyuhoon Cho

Ra, Woonmong

Woonmong Ra (1914–2009) is one of prominent leaders of prayer mountain movement. He was born in Pakcheon, North Pyongan province of North Korea during the Japanese occupation. He attended the Osan School which was founded by Protestant nationalists, including Seung Hun Lee. In his young age, he suffered from depression and attempted to commit suicide. To overcome depression, he devoted himself to Buddhism. He later went to Yongmunsan (Yongmun Mountain) in Yecheon-gun, Gyeongbuk Province, where he had spiritual experiences that changed his entire life. He then decided to attend a Presbyterian church and became a leader. When he moved to Seoul, he attended Soopo Bridge Methodist Church and was ordained as elder. His inter-denominational experience became the soil of his non-denominational spiritual movement.

The Yongmun Prayer Movement was developed out of the "Ae Hyang Sook" (house of loving country) movement in 1940, which was started as a group to actively enlighten the nation. It taught young students with three slogans: love of God, love of the earth, and love of the nation. Since the 1950s, it was transformed into a prayer movement focusing on revivalism with speaking in tongues, fasting, divine healing, and other manifestations of the Spirit. As the Japanese government defined it as a group to stimulate the liberation of Korea, it was almost disbanded. Woonmong Ra tried to re-kindle it after Korean independence in 1945. However, as the Korean War broke out in 1950, he was unable to accomplish his plan.

In 1954, a year after the end of the Korean War (1950–1953), a revival meeting was held on Yongmun Prayer Mountain. It was attended by more than 10,000 people and became the decisive beginning of the prayer mountain movement. In 1955, Yongmun Mountain Bible School was established and in the following year, it was extended and re-named as Gidon High Bible School. By that time, Ra founded the Gideon Monastery for the revival of the nation and established another Bible school called Gideon Theological Seminary in 1956. These seminaries became the growth engines of the prayer mountain movement. More than half of the leaders who carried out the prayer mountain movement graduated from these seminaries. The students were taught the Bible systematically and prayed enthusiatically. They fast for up to 40 days and preached the gospel with the power of the Spirit. The graduates established various churches and prayer mountains throughout the country. Ever since Yongmun Prayer Mountain was established on October 5, 1945, the number of prayer mountains grew from 207 (1975), 239 (1978), 462 (1988), to 500 (1994) due to the effort of the graduates. Some of them were affiliated with the mainstream denominations, such as Presbyterian, Baptist, and Methodist, but many of them evangelized without any denominational background. As a result, Yongmun mountain was called the "faith village."

Ra focused on the "three-fold evangelism movement": enthusiastic evangelism, evangelism with publication, and intercessory prayer. His Yongmunsan Prayer House published a monthly periodical, *Nongminsungbo* (*The Voice of the Farmer*), and the weekly newspaper, *Kidok Gongbo*, in 1946. A monthly magazine, *World of Faith*, and the newspaper, *The Gospel Times*, were published in 1960. Ra also wrote more than 50 books on revival movement and Christian doctrines based on his belief and evangelism.

Pentecostal/Charismatic movement were not welcomed by the major denominations in Korea. Due to the influence of cessationism, most Korean churches believed that spiritual gifts such as tongues, prophecy, and divine healing ceased after the apostolic age. They did not practise spiritual gifts and considered the Christian groups which emphasized these aspects as heretical until the 1980s. However, Ra made a great impact on the development of Pentecostalism in Korea. His Yongmun Prayer Mountain movement especially played a significant role for the expansion of the Pentecostal movement in Korea. He contributed to the spiritual awakening of Korean churches and the spreading of the Holy Spirit movement through numerous Christian books, magazines, and newspapers, whose influences cannot be under-estimated. Many Korean Christians and churches changed their negative views on spiritual gifts and the manifestations of the Spirit because of the Prayer Mountain Movement. Nonetheless, Ra and the Yongmun Prayer Mountain movement are not yet free from the "heretical debate" among conservative Korean denominations.

Bibliography

Anderson, Allan. 2018. *An Introduction to Pentecostalism: Global Charismatic Christianity*. Cambridge: Cambridge University Press.

Eim, Yeol Soo. "South Korea." In *The New International Dictionary of Pentecostal and Charismatic Movements*, edited by Burgess, Stanley M., and Eduard M. Van Der Maas, 240. Grand Rapids, Michigan: Zondervan.

Kim, Ig Jin. 2003. *History and Theology of Korean Pentecostalism*. Zoetermeer: Uitgeverij Boekencentrum.

Yongmunsan Evangelism, ed. 1980. *The 40 Years History of Yongmunsan Movement*. Seoul: Aehyangsook Press.

Yongmunsan Evangelism, ed. 1969. *The Track of Yongmunsan Movement*. Seoul: Aehyangsook Press.

Sang Yun Lee

Race, Racism

Race and racism are key terms employed in the study of Pentecostalism with questions such as: How did race structure nascent Pentecostalism in the United States, Chile, South Africa, and other countries? Did "interracial unity" ever exist during the Azusa Street Revival ? Where did Pentecostalism defy racial norms and offer an interracial or multi-racial alternative to racism? How has Pentecostalism been racialized throughout its over one hundred years of existence?

Two famous quotes on American racism frame the Pentecostal engagement of race by W.E.B. DuBois, an early twentieth-century Harvard-trained African American scholar, and Frank Bartleman, a Euro-American Pentecostal pioneer. DuBois is often quoted in saying that "the problem of the twentieth century is the color-line – the relation of the darker to the lighter races of men in Asia and Africa, in America and the islands of the sea" (1903, 13). Bartleman (1871–1936), in a way, responds to DuBois by surmising that "The color-line has been washed away in the blood [of Jesus]" (1970, 55).

In Pentecostal studies, racism is often defined as racial prejudice. Yet, according to major theorists of race, such as William J. Wilson (1973, 3–4, 8–9), racism is more complex than merely a form of prejudice. For Wilson, racism is the combination of racial privilege, prejudice and power. Racism requires that one racial group – white people in the modern era – possess the power to impose its racial prejudices on another group; that it can subordinate another racial group. Racial privilege exists in two forms: unearned entitlement and conferred dominance. Privilege is exclusionary by allotting certain opportunities – economic, political, social, religious – to one group and denying these opportunities to another. Racial power, prejudice, and privilege operate according to specific racial regimes that kept whites as a race at the apex of the hierarchy of race.

There is a need for Pentecostal studies to employ race within a broader framework such as Wilson's that includes prejudice as a topic but refuses to let the topic of prejudice exhaust the discussion of race. Prejudice is merely one type of racism, a psychological form of racism. Racial prejudice as an emotional disdain, fear, and hatred of a particular race along with negative attitudes and feelings toward particular races that can define interpersonal or group relations. In addition to prejudice, racism can be defined sociologically, ideologically, and intersectionally.

First, institutional racism (Phillips 2011; Wilson 1973) as a sociological phenomenon focuses on the social and political structures of racism. Sociologically, racism focuses on how race structures an organization, religion or nation as well as how it operates as a system. It highlights how religions and societies are organized around race, granting or limiting rights, privileges, status, authority, and opportunities according to a group's racial designation. Sociologically, theorizing about race ranges from analyses based on racial formation, racial hierarchies, and the reproduction of racial inequality in outcomes related to income, health, education, governance, and lifespan. Another sociological trajectory is racialization or racial formation. Interpreting race under the rubric of racialization, we would critically inquire about the historicity and specificity of race. The focus is on how race changes over time, and how race-making as a process receives scrutiny. Such a move offers a more dynamic approach to race as well as a theological understanding of race that takes history and context seriously (Omi and Winant 1994, 55–56).

Second, ideological theorizing about race focuses on racial scales that plot different races along a spectrum from superior to inferior peoples. These racial scales include theories ranging from the eighteenth-century ideas of Carolus Linnaeus to nineteenth century theories of the Darwinists and the twentieth century theories of Richard Herrnstein and Charles Murray. The ideology of white supremacy coupled with its Eurocentric universalism contended that a Eurocentric view of reality is universal, silencing all other "race-particular" perspectives of realities (Copeland 2004, 503).

Third, intersectionality as a theory argues that race is on an axis and should be interpreted in conjunction with other variables such as gender, class, or ability, for instance. Without an intersectional analysis, the experiences of black women, for instance, are often rendered invisible because discussions of race often highlight the plight of black men, and discussions of gender analyses privilege the experience of white woman. Intersectional analysis aims at overcoming the limits of classic race and gender methodologies with its dual or multiple axes approach (Casselberry 2017).

With a more complex concept of racism, Pentecostal studies could pursue how power and authority was or was not shared between different races within early Pentecostal organizations. In predominately white denominations with segregated polities in which African American, Latinx, indigenous African, or First People members were subordinated, there could be more studies of whether these structures were justified by Bible-based theories of white supremacy and the inferiority of non-Europeans such as those espoused by Charles Parham.

Conversely, there is a debate in Pentecostal studies about whether "interracial unity" existed during the Azusa Street Revival. While this debate deserves more attention, a more important question might be what happened after the revival? How did any interracial or all-white congregations within denominations such as the Church of God in Christ led by Charles Harrison Mason and the Pentecostal Assemblies of the World led by Garfield Haywood actually emerge when they were not present in Baptist, Methodist, Presbyterian, and other Protestant denominations in the United States during the first three decades of early Pentecostalism? How did these limited but significant interracial sectors within early Pentecostalism deploy race differently?

Since race is a social construct, can post-racialism as either color blindness or the abolition of racism occur? Color blindness, the idea that race can be unrecognized, is contested in many quarters. However, some critics view race as akin to other social constructs like gender. For some critics, post-racialism is best framed as post-racist; polities or interpersonal relations undefined by racism. Building on Courtney Jung (2009, 367), post-racist structures reject the racial use of differences to craft practices of racial inclusion, exclusion, allocation, and outcomes.

In contrast to these broader and more systemic questions, race and racism have mostly been studied within Pentecostal studies on questions of racial exclusion and inclusion. The practices of racial exclusion were examined from wider social theories about white purity, superiority, and domination and concepts of anti-miscegenation. Calls for white purity rejected "race-mixing" or interracial relations. White superiority assumed the subordination of minoritized races since Europeans were the master race deemed to rule or dominate other all races. During the first ten years of the Pentecostal movement in the United States and South Africa, racial division and subordination of minoritized races became quickly visible (MacRoberts 1988, 60–76).

Racial inclusion has been explored mainly with the ecclesial realities of interracial and multiracial Pentecostal congregations and denominations. Practices and polities of racial inclusion emerged at the genesis of classical Pentecostalism during the Azusa Street Revival. They both engaged race within the black-white binary and beyond that binary. Studies have focused on the constructive black-white racial exchanges with Pentecostal interracialism. They have also explored how race across different axes structures Pentecostalism: black-white-Latina/o-Asian; black-Latina/o-white; Asian-white-Latina/o. (Daniels 2014)

Race as a term still retains currency within Pentecostal studies. Scholarship on race and Pentecostalism includes the work of ethicists such as Leonard Lovett, theologians such as Estrelda Alexander and David Michel, and historians such as Joe Newman and David Daniels. The challenge is to engage race as a concept with more critical acumen than merely prejudice in order for scholars to analyze how race functions within Pentecostalism as well as to theorize about race from Pentecostal data. In that way, the study of race can be advanced through the study of Pentecostalism and Pentecostal studies.

Bibliography

Bartleman, Frank. 1970. *Another Wave Rolls In! What Really Happened at Azusa Street*, Revised Edition. Monroeville: Whitaker House.

Casselberry, Judith. 2017. *The Labor of Faith: Gender and Power in Black Apostolic Pentecostalism*. Durham: Duke University Press.

Copeland, M. Shawn. 2004. "Race." In *The Blackwell Companion to Modern Theology*, edited by Gareth Jones, 499–511. Oxford: Blackwell.

Daniels III, David D. 2014. "North American Pentecostalism." In *The Cambridge Companion to Pentecostalism*, edited by Cecil M. Robeck, Jr. and Amos Yong, 73–92. New York: Cambridge University Press.

DuBois, W.E.B. 1903. *The Souls of Black Folk: Essays and Sketches*. Chicago: A.C. McClurg & Co.

Jung, Courtney. 2009. "Race, Ethnicity, Religion." In *The Oxford Handbook of Contextual Political Analysis*, edited by Robert E. Goodin and Charles Tilly, 360–375. Oxford: Oxford University Press.

Lovett, Leonard. 2007. *Kingdom Beyond Color: Re-examining the Phenomenon of Racism*. Higher Standard Publishers.

MacRobert, Iain. 1988. *The Black Roots and White Racism of Early Pentecostalism in the USA*. London: MacMillan.

Michel, David. 2019. "Toward an Ecclesiology of Racial Reconciliation: A Pentecostal Perspective." PhD diss., Chicago Theological Seminary.

Newman, Joe. 2005. *Race and the Assemblies of God: The Journey from Azusa Street to the "Miracle Memphis."* Youngstown, NY: Cambria Press.

Omi, M., and H. Winant. 1994. *Racial Formation in the United States from the 1960s to the 1990s*. Second Edition. New York: Routledge.

Phillips, Coretta. 2011. "Institutional Racism and Ethnic Inequalities: An Expanded Multilevel Framework." *Journal of Social Policy* 40 (1): 173–192.

Wilson, William J. 1973. *Power, Racism, and Privilege: Race Relations in Theoretical and Sociohistorical Perspectives*. New York: MacMillan Press.

David Daniels

Ramabai, Pandita Saraswati

Pandita Saraswati Ramabai (1858–1922) was the most prominent Indian Christian woman in the twentieth century. She was a social reformer, educator, and Pentecostal pioneer. She was born as a Brahman (the highest caste in Hinduism), but her family went on a permanent pilgrimage

Pandita Ramabai Sarasvati, 1858–1922

because of financial crisis. They moved constantly, and lived on the alms received from the reading of the Puranas in public. Her parents taught her Sanskrit, Puranas, and the Gita, which was against the orthodox Hindu culture that denied girls' education. She learned many languages, including Sanskrit, Hindi, Marathi, Kannada, and English. She lost her parents and elder sister when she was only 16. She and her brother traveled various parts of India, mostly on foot for over 2,000 miles. She was left alone when her brother died in 1880, and so married Bipin Behari Das, a friend of her brother. The marriage caused a furor as he was from a lower caste, but he died soon, leaving Ramabai with her baby daughter, Manoramabai.

Soon after his death, Ramabai went to Pune and founded an organization, Arya Mahila Samaj, for the advancement of women. In 1883 she came to England with her daughter to study medicine. She became a Christian and was baptized in the Church of England in 1883. She also studied Greek and Hebrew. At the invitation of the American Episcopal Church, she traveled to the U.S. in 1886. Meanwhile, she published a book, *The High Caste Hindu Women*, explaining the plight of Hindu women and the need to provide educational institutions for them. Subsequently, she formed Ramabai Association in the U.S. for the advancement of women in India, which later supported her school for child widows. Observing the free democracy in the U.S., she wrote a book, *The Peoples of the United States*, in her mother tongue, Marathi.

At her return to India in 1889, she started Sharada Sadan, a home for widows near Bombay (now Mumbai), and it was moved to Pune in one year. In 1895 she established a school, Mukti Sadan, in Kedgaon near Pune. As there were great famines and outbreaks of plagues, it was expanded to become a huge mission to accommodate the dispossessed women and girls, irrespective of their caste affinity. Many of these women later became Christians and began to engage in evangelistic activities. As Mukti gradually became an evangelical Christian organization, many who initially supported Mukti financially stopped doing so. However, Ramabai continued her mission and by 1905 it became an internationally well-known faith mission.

One of the greatest impacts of the Mukti Revival is related to the history of Pentecostalism. After her second trip to England, Ramabai began to emphasize the need to pray for an outpouring of the Holy Spirit. Inspired by the revivals in Australia (1903) and Wales (1904–1905), Ramabai commenced special prayer meetings for revival every morning from the beginning of 1905. The number of praying girls gradually increased from 70 to 500. From mid-1905, these girls began to experience the manifestations of the Spirit. Ramabai formed "Praying Bands" of young women praying in groups and being trained for evangelism.

Contribution of Ramabai and her Mukti Mission is beyond any parallel. First, Mukti revival is a significant center of the origin of Pentecostalism. The writers of *The Apostolic Faith*, including William Seymour, acknowledged that the Mukti revial began before the Azusa Street Revival. Second, Mukti played a pivotal role in the conversion of many people to Christianity. Ramabai was so passionate for the evangelization of India. While she attended the Keswick Convention in 1898, she asked the delegates to pray for an outpouring of the Holy Spirit on all Indian Christians, and also for 100,000 men and women to preach the gospel. The young women who had experienced the power of Pentecost during the revival went to nearby villages, towns, and states. Third, Ramabai showed a great zeal for the social transformation of the community. Aiming to make a holistic impact, Ramabai created a self-sufficient community at Mukti that included a rescue mission, hospital, school, printing press, and an oil-press. In recognition of her remarkable contribution to the advancement of Indian women, the Indian government issued a commemorative stamp in 1989 with her image and a caption, "Pandita Ramabai – Social worker," printed on. Fourth, Ramabai translated the Bible into her mother tongue, Marathi. Fifth, women's position was highly established at Mukti as they were given prominent leadership role in revival and evangelism. Sixth, Ramabai generated an earnest desire for prayer among Indian Christians as she strongly emphasized on fasting and prayer. She circulated a letter to more than 3,500 Christian workers all over India to request the names of Christians so that the Mukti members might pray for them by name. The girls of her praying band prayed for many hundreds of people like this every day. On April 5, 1922, Ramabai died of septic bronchitis at Mukti.

Bibliography

Adhav, Shamsundar Manohar. 1979. *Pandita Ramabai*. Madras: Christian Literature Society.

Anderson, Allan. 2007. *Spreading Fires: The Missionary Nature of Early Pentecostalism*. London: SCM Press.

Blumhofer, Edith L. 2008. "Consuming Fire: Pandita Ramabai and the Global Pentecostal Impulse." In *Interpreting Contemporary Christianity: Global Processes and Local Identities*, edited by Ogbu U. Kalu and Alaine Low, 207–237. Grand Rapids: Eerdmans.

Burgess, Stanley. 2006. "Pandita Ramabai: A Woman for all Seasons." *Asian Journal of Pentecostal Studies* 9 (2): 183–198.

Dyer, Helen S. 1900. *Pandita Ramabai: The Story of Her Life*. New York: Fleming H. Revell.

Wessly Lukose

Ranaghan, Kevin and Dorothy

Kevin Ranaghan was born in 1940 in New York to devout Irish Catholic parents and Dorothy was born in 1942. Kevin married Dorothy in 1966 and they have six children. Both the Ranaghans have degrees in theology from Notre Dame University. Kevin taught theology at St. Mary's College, Indiana, while his wife taught at a Catholic High School. They have been associated with the Catholic Charismatic Renewal (CCR) since its beginning in 1967 at Duquesne University, Pennsylvania (Rahaghan 1969). Initially, both Kevin and Dorothy Ranaghan were skeptical about the Charismatics; however, they knew that the people involved in Charismatic movement were professors, scholars and theology students. Moreover, they noticed that something dramatically changed the lives of these people and so they too longed to have a similar experience. Kevin devoted himself to a six-week course on the Bible to learn more about the baptism in the Holy Spirit. Later he asked his Charismatic colleagues to pray for him for baptism in the Holy Spirit. As he received it, he had a profound experience of the power of God, which changed his life. He experienced the presence of Jesus in him. He got a renewed interest in reading the Bible and relished it as the Word of the living God. He also experienced a thorough renewal in his faith. His wife too experienced the same after she received the baptism in the Holy Spirit. Even though the Ranaghans were faithful Catholics, they did not hesitate to contact Pentecostals belonging to the Full Gospel Business Men's fellowship, in order to learn more about the roots of Pentecostalism and the use of charisms. In the coming years, this ecumenical encounter helped the Ranaghans to lead Charismatic prayer sessions and conferences welcoming all people irrespective of their denominations. They travelled all over the USA and other parts of the world to spread the fire of the Holy Spirit through CCR.

The Ranaghans note in their book, *Catholic Pentecostalism*, that Charismatic worship is not only a place to seek the extraordinary charisms of the Holy Spirit, but also a place to seek genuine renewal and transformation of life in the Holy Spirit. Moreover, for them renewal primarily means to have a real experience of Jesus as the Lord, which leads a person to repent and rediscover the beauty of the Christian faith. Even though the Ranaghans freely worshipped with the Pentecostals, they always sought to remain faithful to the teachings of the Catholic Church. They did not see the CCR as an independent entity outside the Church life. Rather they looked upon the CCR as an intrinsic part of the Church. The Ranaghans always respected the liturgy, the sacraments and various spiritual traditions of the Catholic Church.

In order to promote the Charismatic spirituality, Kevin became one of the founders of the People of Praise, an ecumenical Pentecostal/Charismatic community in South Bend, Indiana. He organized several Charismatic conferences in the USA, which attracted thousands of people. Kevin served as an executive of the National Service Committee (NSC) of the U.S. from 1970 to 1985. In 1977, he also served as a member of the International Communications Office (ICO) situated in Ann Arbor, Michigan. Later in 1978, Cardinal Suenens shifted ICO to Brussels and renamed it as International Catholic Charismatic Renewal Office (ICCRO). Kevin served as a councillor of ICCRO from 1978 to 1985 and again from 1990 to 1993. In 1993, the Holy See renamed ICCRO as International Catholic Charismatic Renewal Services (ICCRS). Kevin served as a councillor of ICCRS again from 1993 to 1999. Pope Francis recommended ICCRS to merge with another private association of the faithful, Catholic Fraternity of Covenant Communities and Fellowships. After this merger in 2018, ICCRS is named as Catholic Charismatic Renewal International Service (CHARIS).

Apart from his association with the CCR, Kevin also wanted to serve the Church and therefore became a permanent deacon in 1973. He also pursued theological studies and received a doctorate in theology in 1974. He and his wife have written many articles in journals and magazines to introduce Charismatic spirituality, the theology of the baptism in the

Holy Spirit and the need for spiritual unity among Christians. They continue to work for the renewal of the Church and spread the Kingdom of God. They are convinced that the CCR is a genuine work of the Holy Spirit to bring new life and vigor in the Church.

Bibliography

Anderson, Allan Heaton. 2013. *To the Ends of the Earth: Pentecostalism and the Transformation of World Christianity*. Oxford: Oxford University Press.

Hayford, Jack, and David Moore. 2009. *The Charismatic Century: The Enduring Impact of the Azusa Street Revival*. New York: Warner Faith, Hachette Book Group.

Ranaghan, Dorothy Garrity. 2018. *Blind Spot: War & Christian Identity*. Second Edition. New York: New City Press.

Ranaghan, Kevin. 1981. "The Church, the Spirit, and the Charismatic Renewal." *New Covenant* 11 (2): 10.

Ranaghan, Kevin, and Dorothy Ranaghan. 1969. *Catholic Pentecostals*. New York: Paulist Press.

Reginald Alva

Redeemed Christian Church of God

The Redeemed Christian Church of God (RCCG) is a Pentecostal denomination with its headquarters in Lagos, Nigeria. It is one of the largest transnational Pentecostal churches in the world, with over 14,000 branches in Nigeria and branches in over 178 nations. The RCCG was founded by Josiah Akindayomi (b. 1909), a semi-illiterate Yoruba man who was converted by the Anglican Church Missionary Society. He later became a prophet in the Cherubim and Seraphim (C&S) Church, one of the earliest Aladura churches in Nigeria. In 1952, Akindayomi left the C&S and founded a new church, called the Church of the Glory of God, which was largely made up of uneducated women and artisans. Initially, the church became affiliated to the Apostolic Faith Mission (AFM) in South Africa, but the link with the AFM was later terminated following Nigeria's independence in 1960. The adoption of the name "Redeemed Christian Church of God" marked a significant landmark in the church's history. Coupled with the new name was the "covenant" which God is said to have made with the founder regarding the establishment and sustenance of the church: as long as the conditions of the covenant were met, the success of the church was guaranteed. One of the promises given to Akindayomi was that the church would spread to the ends of the earth before the Second Coming of Christ. This covenant, widely known in RCCG circles, is considered to be one of the driving forces behind its global expansion.

The subsequent history of the RCCG can be divided into two phases. Between 1952 and 1980, Akindayomi laid the foundation of the church by planting other branches in southwestern Nigeria. RCCG culture under Akindayomi was characterized by a strict holiness ethic and worship services mostly conducted in Yoruba. When he died in 1980, the RCCG had 39 branches with a membership largely drawn from the poorer sector of Yoruba society. The second phase (1981 to today) began with the accession of Enoch Adejare Adeboye (b. 1942) as head of the church. This leadership transition is regarded as the major event in RCCG's history, propelling the church into a period of rapid expansion. It was a time when Nigeria was undergoing a fresh phase of revival, focused around the university campuses. As a former university lecturer, Adeboye knew how to appeal to these people. Furthermore, although never letting go of the holiness doctrine, he started to emphasize prosperity and miracles. In this, he was influenced by Kenneth Hagin, widely regarded as the 'father' of the Word of Faith movement.

Adeboye has been largely responsible for transforming the image and constituency of the church by his implementation of a series of innovative initiatives. The most important was the model parish system, initiated to stimulate the growth of the RCCG by attracting young, urban professionals. The most significant goal of the church, as expressed in its four-fold mission statement, is to "plant churches within five minutes walking distance in every city and town of developing countries and within five minutes driving distance in every city and town of developed countries." This has generated a proliferation of parishes around the world. The countries with the most RCCG churches outside Nigeria are Britain and the United States.

RCCG has a holistic understanding of mission that combines evangelism with belief in divine healing and miracles.

The emphasis on healing and miracles is reflected in the popularity of RCCG's monthly Holy Ghost services, Annual Convention and Holy Ghost Congress, which attract huge crowds, largely due to the expectation of miracles associated with the ministry of Adeboye. Civic engagement is increasingly regarded as an integral component of the RCCG's missionary vision. The church's social initiatives include feeding programmes for the poor, rehabilitation centres for street children and drug addicts, prison ministries, reproductive and maternal health care, and HIV/AIDS programmes. The RCCG is also heavily involved in education. Its educational institutions include Christ the Redeemer's Schools Movement, Redeemed Christian Bible College, Redeemed Christian School of Missions, the School of Disciples, and Redeemer's University (RUN). The church is also recognized as a significant political player. Since Nigeria's return to civilian rule in 1999, successive presidents have solicited Adeboye's support for their electoral campaigns, and in 2015, RCCG pastor, Yemi Osinbajo, became the vice-President of Nigeria under the Muslim President Muhammadu Buhari.

RCCG is famous for its 850-acre Redemption Camp (or City), located along the Lagos-Ibadan expressway. At the centre of the camp is the Congress Arena with a seating capacity of three million people. To accommodate the crowds attending conferences at the campground, RCCG provides various facilities including offices, guest houses, electricity and water supplies, a post office, a health clinic, several banks, supermarkets, and restaurants. The camp is home to the RCCG's international headquarters. It also features residential housing estates where members can either build their own houses or purchase pre-built houses constructed by a developer.

Bibliography

Adeboye, Olufunke. 2007. "'Arrowhead' of Nigerian Pentecostalism: The Redeemed Christian Church of God, 1952–2005." *Pneuma* 29 (1): 24–58.

Adogame, Afe. 2004. "Contesting the Ambivalences of Modernity in a Global Context: The Redeemed Christian Church of God, North America." *Studies in World Christianity* 10 (1): 25–48.

Burgess, Richard, Kim Knibbe, and Anna Quaas. 2010. "Nigerian-Initiated Pentecostal Churches as a Social Force in Europe: The Case of The Redeemed Christian Church of God." *PentecoStudies* 9 (1): 97–121.

Marshall, Ruth. 2009. *Political Spiritualities: The Pentecostal Revolution in Nigeria*. Chicago: The University of Chicago Press.

Ukah, Asonzeh. 2008. *A New Paradigm of Pentecostal Power: A Study of the Redeemed Christian Church of God in Nigeria*. Trenton, NJ: Africa World Press.

Richard Burgess

Revival

Writers use the terms "revival" and "revivalism" in various ways. *Webster's Third New International Dictionary* defines the term "revival" as "a period of religious awakening: renewed interest in religion" with "meetings often characterized by emotional excitement...." "Revivalism" is "the spirit or kind of religion or the methods characteristic of religious revivals." Some authors, and especially Calvinists, define revival as an unplanned event that reflects God's initiative, and revivalism as a humanly orchestrated effort to stir up religious interest. Yet in practice it is often difficult to draw this distinction. What is common to all accounts of revivals is an *intensification* of spiritual experience. Participants in revivals speak of their vivid sense of spiritual things, great joy and faith, deep sorrow over sin, passionate desire to evangelize others, and heightened feelings of love for God and fellow humanity. A revival is a communal event, in which groups of people share these sorts of experiences. Often it is used synonymously with renewal.

Revivals can best be understood through first-hand accounts, such as the following from Sixto Lopez, a participant in a 1949 Pentecostal revival in Detroit: "I opened my heart to the Lord, and felt as though I was giving myself as an offering to Him. Every Scripture and every message took on a new meaning to me. The most outstanding thing I felt in those meetings was a desire to pray – just to stay before the Lord. I have always found it difficult to spend long periods in prayer, but there I felt a great desire to stay before the Lord in prayer. Many of the people there have lost their appetite for food and go days without food. I had a big appetite for food but came to the place that I did not care to eat." Thousands of such accounts document the Pentecostal and charismatic revivals of the last century.

In times of revival, people often crowd into available buildings for religious services, and fill them beyond capacity. The services may last from morning until midnight or later. News of a revival usually travels rapidly, and sometimes the reports of revival – in person, print, or broadcast media – touch off new revivals in distant localities. During a revival, clergy and other Christian workers may receive many requests for their services, and find themselves harried by inquirers. Sometimes people openly confess their sins in public settings. Another mark of revivals is generosity – individuals willing to give their time, money, or resources to support the work of the revival. Revivals are usually controversial, with opponents and proponents who vehemently criticize one another. Often there are bodily manifestations as well, such as falling down, rolling on the ground, involuntary muscle movements, and spiritual dancing.

Many of the above phenomena appeared in Protestant evangelical revivals prior to the birth of modern pentecostalism around 1900. Yet a distinguishing feature of Pentecostal and charismatic revivals is a stress on the gifts of the Holy Spirit, including speaking in tongues, visions and prophecies, the healing of the sick, and the casting out of demons.

Of all the gifts, speaking in tongues is the most characteristic feature of Pentecostal-charismatic revivals in distinction from evangelical revivals. Yet today the boundaries between evangelicalism and the Pentecostal-charismatic movement are probably more blurry than ever before. During the last two centuries, the gifts of the Spirit that first appeared in isolation have tended to flow together. In North America, a stress on divine healing first emerged in the mid-1800s, tongues-speaking began on a large scale just before and after 1900, and prophecy became increasingly important in the 1946–50 revival and subsequently. Exorcism and spiritual warfare (with demons through prayer) is a distinctive of the 1980s and 1990s. Twenty-first century Christians are heirs to all these preceding movements. Tongues-speaking, prophecy, healing, and exorcism occur in varied combinations today in Pentecostal, charismatic, and some evangelical groups.

Among the many revivals and renewal movements worldwide, some of the key revivals for Pentecostalism, historically and theologically, include: Welsh Revival, Keswick Conventions, Pyongyang Revival, Mukti Mission, Hebden Mission, Azusa Street Revival, Latter Rain Revival, African Indigenous Churches, Catholic Charismatic Revival, Anglican Renewal, Chinese House Churches, Weepers, Shouters, Indonesian Revival, Jesus People Movement, John Wimber and the Vineyard Churches, and the Toronto Blessing.

Bibliography

McClymond, Michael J. 2016. "Charismatic Gifts: Healing, Tongue-Speaking, Prophecy, and Exorcism." In *Wiley-Blackwell Companion to World Christianity*, edited by Lamin Sanneh and Michael J. McClymond, 399–418. Oxford: Wiley-Blackwell.

McClymond, Michael J. 2016. "Christian Revival and Renewal Movements," In *Wiley-Blackwell Companion to World Christianity*, edited by Lamin Sanneh and Michael J. McClymond, 244–262. Oxford: Wiley-Blackwell.

McClymond, Michael J. 2014. "Charismatic Renewal and Neo-Pentecostalism: From American Origins to Global Permutations." In *The Cambridge Companion to Pentecostalism*, edited by Cecil M. Robeck and Amos Yong, 31–51. Cambridge, UK: Cambridge University Press.

McClymond, Michael J., ed. 2007. *Encyclopedia of Religious Revivals in America*. 2 vols. Westport, CT: Greenwood Press.

Riss, Richard M. 1988. *A Survey of 20th-Century Revival Movements in North America*. Peabody, MA: Hendrickson Publishers.

Synan, Vinson, ed. 2001. *The Century of the Holy Spirit: 100 Years of Pentecostal and Charismatic Renewal, 1901–2001*. Nashville, TN: Thomas Nelson.

Michael McClymond

Roberts, Oral

Oral Roberts (1918–2009) was a preacher, revivalist, healer, radio and television evangelist, and university founder. He is one of the most consequential figures in the development of Pentecostal-Charismatic Christianity. His story is emblematic of changes that occurred from the 1930s to the early 2000s. Roberts was part of a post-World War II generation of American Christians that no longer wanted to perpetuate the small, sectarian congregations they had been raised in. Through accommodating his message to mainstream Christians, Roberts transmitted Pentecostal beliefs and practices beyond the narrow bounds of the existing denominations, and "no one [did] more to bring the Pentecostal message to respectability and visibility in America" (Harrell 1985, 494). Roberts was a crucial link in the USA between "Pentecostals" and "Charismatics."

Granville Oral Roberts was born near Ada, Oklahoma, into a poor family. His father was a farmer and active in Pentecostal Holiness churches, while his mother (who was of Cherokee and Choctaw Indian descent) prayed for the sick and shared the gospel. Despite a stuttering problem in Roberts's youth, his mother believed that he would speak to multitudes. On turning sixteen, Roberts moved away from home, seeking a better life, only to contract tuberculosis. A traveling evangelist came to Ada and Robert's brother brought him to a meeting where he was prayed for and received physical healing. Robert's healing was also a commissioning, as he reported that God spoke to him: "Son, I am going to heal you and you are going to take My healing power to your generation" (Harrell 1985, 5). Roberts experienced in early life a dramatic healing from life-threatening illness, and went on to preach a message of salvation and healing.

Oral Roberts, 1918-2009. Source: Oral Roberts University

Roberts began his pastoral and evangelistic ministry in 1936 in the Pentecostal Holiness Church, and in the same year married a preacher's daughter, Evelyn Lutman Fahnestock, to whom he was married for sixty-six years. After several years in ministry, he enrolled in classes at Oklahoma Baptist University in 1942, but did not complete a degree. He resigned his pastorate in Shawnee, Oklahoma in 1945, began publication of the magazine *Healing Waters* in 1947, founded the Oral Roberts Evangelistic Association in 1948, and began traveling across the USA. His gospel tent held 3000 persons, and was later replaced with one that held 12,000 and was said to be the world's largest. In his earlier years, Roberts "laid on hands" to pray individually for thousands. Through half a century, he conducted more than 300 crusades on six continents, and personally prayed for some 1.5 to 2 million persons.

Roberts began broadcasting by radio in 1947, and by television in 1954, making him a pioneer in Pentecostal media ministry. During the 1950s his public ministry was racially integrated, despite the severe opposition that he faced for seating blacks and whites together. Not only healing but prosperity was an element in Roberts's message. Because of his impoverished upbringing, he had no misconceptions about the supposed benefits of poverty. To the poor and the sick, he preached that God had better things in store. Roberts was among the first to teach the "seed faith" principle, that a generous financial donation could function as an expression of faith, and bring greater financial blessing in the future.

Roberts cultivated relationships with mainline Protestants, evangelical Protestants, and Romans Catholics. When Demos Shakarian founded the Full Gospel Businessmen's Fellowship International in Los Angeles in 1951, Roberts was the first speaker. In 1966 he addressed the World Evangelism Congress in Berlin, sponsored by the USA-based evangelical periodical *Christianity Today*. In 1968 Roberts joined the United Methodist Church and because of this change of affiliation, Roberts lost some of his initial Pentecostal support. Yet, when an expanded television ministry soon commenced in the 1970s, almost 20,000 letters per day came into his ministry office. *Time* magazine reported that "Oral Roberts and You" was then the leading religious television program in the USA.

An educational initiative took shape after Roberts responded to what he took to be God's call. Oral Roberts University (ORU) was founded in 1963 and dedicated in 1967 with Billy Graham as keynote speaker. By 1971 the university was accredited. As of 2020 it has about 4000 students enrolled. However, not all of Roberts's initiatives succeeded. The effort to establish an ORU law school failed. A medical and research center – City of Faith – opened in 1981. In 1987 Roberts made a controversial public statement that he believed the Lord would "take him home" if he failed to raise $8 million for his medical center. The centre closed in 1989. Despite its brief existence, its focus on treating the whole person – spirit, mind, and body – had continuing influence on Christian medical professionals. While Roberts never completed a degree, his founding of a Charismatic university with a global profile is part of his legacy.

A series of tragedies and scandals impacted the Roberts family. Roberts's daughter Rebecca died with her husband in a plane crash in 1977, his son Richard was divorced in 1979, and his eldest son, Ronnie – who had lost a job, and come out as gay – killed himself in 1982. 1987 was a year of sex-and-money scandals, involving the televangelists Jimmy Swaggart and Jim and Tammy Faye Bakker. In Roberts's case, there was no credible evidence of financial malfeasance during the period in which he led his ministry and the university. In 1993 Roberts and his wife semi-retired to California, and Richard Roberts succeeded him as president of ORU. In 2007 Richard Roberts resigned from the presidency amid questions regarding his leadership and ORU's serious financial situation. Mart Green (son of the founder of Hobby Lobby) donated a total of $70 million to keep the university afloat.

One important legacy lay in Roberts's pioneering effort to merge modern medicine with healing prayer that is also linked with his view of prosperity. Believing that illness generally involves emotional or psychosomatic components, he favored holistic healing. This expanded notion of healing appealed to prosperous non-Pentecostals for whom inner malaise and broken relationships were of greater moment than untreated or unresponsive physical illnesses. Roberts's version of prosperity – stressing emotional as well as physical wellness, higher education, and ecumenical openness – was never as narrowly focused on money as the preaching of most televangelists. Roberts may have been second only to Billy Graham (also born in 1918) as a popular Christian leader in the USA. As compared with Graham's evangelism, though, Roberts's healing-and-prosperity evangelism offered a more encompassing message regarding God's blessing and wellness in one's soul, body, emotions, relations, and finances. Roberts thus exemplified an enduring Pentecostal ideal of "full gospel" ministry.

Oral Roberts's life and impact were multidimensional. His story followed a classical American narrative of rags-to-riches and obscurity-to-fame. For some impoverished followers, the man was the message, signifying that they too could rise above their limitations. By reputation, Roberts was a hard-driving man who expected much of himself as well as of others. Roberts authored more than 50 books, including three autobiographies (in 1952, 1972, and 1995) that reveal his shifting self-perception over the decades.

Bibliography

Harrell, David Edwin, Jr. 1985. *Oral Roberts: An American Life*. Bloomington, IN: Indiana University Press.
Ma, Wonsuk, et al. 2018. "Oral Roberts Centennial." *Spiritus: ORU Journal of Theology* 3 (2): 157–388.
McCoy, Michael R. 1989. "Oral Roberts." In *Twentieth-Century Shapers of American Popular Religion*, edited by Chareles Lippy, 342–349. New York: Greenwood Press.
Roberts, Oral. 1995. *Expect a Miracle: My Life and Ministry*. Nashville, TN: Thomas Nelson.
Roberts, Oral. 1972. *The Call: An Autobiography*. Garden City, NY: Doubleday.
Roberts, Oral. 1952. *Oral Roberts' Life Story, As Told By Himself*. Tulsa, OK.

Michael McClymond

Roman Catholic-Pentecostal Dialogue

The international dialogue between the Roman Catholic Church and representatives of Pentecostal churches has taken place through usually annual meetings, in which theological and ecclesial representatives from the two traditions conduct focused discussions on topics of mutual faith as well as differences, producing final summative reports at the end of each dialogue phase. The dialogue began in 1969 through the partnership of the Pentecostal ecumenist David du Plessis and Fr. Kilian McDonnell, OSB, who directed a Catholic ecumenical institute in Minnesota, USA. Initial exploratory meetings began in 1970 and continued into 1971 to discover what was possible for a "serious theological discussion" between Catholics and Pentecostals. The question of structural and organic unity, prominent in other official dialogues for the Catholic Church, was set aside in favor of the following tasks: "'to explore the life and spiritual experience of Christians and the Churches', 'to give special attention to the meaning for the Church of fullness of life in the Holy Spirit', attending to 'both the experiential and theological dimensions' of that life. 'Through such dialogue' those who participate 'hope to share in the reality of the mystery of Christ and the Church, to build a united testimony, to indicate in what manner the sharing of truth makes it possible… to grow together'" ("First Final Report" 5). With small modifications to these articulations found in the "First Final Report", the dialogue has continued along the lines of these stated purposes. In 1972, the first dialogue began between official representatives from the Roman Catholic Church's Secretariat for Promoting Christian Unity and, given initial resistance to the dialogue from Pentecostal churches and fellowships, the first participants included "some Pentecostal churches and participants in the charismatic movement within Protestant and Anglican churches" ("First Final Report" 4).

The dialogue has continued through six completed phases with a seventh in process at the time of the publication of this encyclopedia (2020). David du Plessis was succeeded as the Pentecostal chair of the dialogue by his brother Justus du Plessis in 1987. Since 1992, Cecil M. (Mel) Robeck, Jr. has served in this role. Succeeding McDonnell during the Fifth Phase of the dialogue, Monsignor John Radano became the Catholic chair in 2001. Bishop Michael Burbidge (Raleigh, North Carolina, USA) served as the Catholic chair during the Sixth Phase and into the beginning of the Seventh. The dialogue has seen development in participation on the Pentecostal side. In the initial period stand-in work from Protestant charismatics provided time for growing official representation by Pentecostals, which first begun in the Third Phase (then called a Quinquennium, 1985–1989), when Pentecostal bodies joined in participation with the dialogue. By the Sixth Phase (2011–2015), official representatives from a variety of Pentecostal church fellowships fully participated, including those from several of the largest Pentecostal bodies.

The dialogue reports do not have the status of official statements by the Roman Catholic Church nor any of the involved Pentecostal bodies. They are the work of the dialogue teams themselves. The teams have sought to faithfully represent Catholic and Pentecostal teaching, respectively, while finding insights for developing mutual understanding between the approximately 1.2 billion Catholics and 600 million charismatic-Pentecostals worldwide, including their overlap. The dialogue reports are co-written by the Catholic and Pentecostal participants after the end of each phase. Typically, these reports characterize historical and contemporary Catholic and Pentecostal positions on issues which the dialogue teams have investigated, and then include evaluative statements which assess places of agreement and disagreement between official Catholic teaching and Catholic practices, on the one hand, and generalizable Pentecostal teaching and Pentecostal practices, in so far such is possible, on the other hand. While conciliatory between these two traditions, the reports honestly identify problems, criticisms, and differences between Catholics and Pentecostals.

The First Phase (1972–1976) of the dialogue centered on Spirit baptism in relation to salvation and sanctification with a focus on biblical exegesis, relating the more historic rights of Christian initiation to their counterparts in younger charismatic and Pentecostal movements; additional attention was given to discernment of spirits, and then connections between prayer and praise. The Second Phase (1977–1982) accounted for commonalities and differences in interpretations of post-Vatican II Catholicism and Classical Pentecostal theologies on topics including speaking in tongues, biblical and experiential resources for theology, tradition, divine healing, and religious rites prior to addressing beliefs concerning Mary the mother of Jesus, ministry and ordination, and apostolic succession. The Third Phase took on the theme "Perspectives on *koinonia*," as the Christian sense of *koinonia* had proven fruitful in other ecumenical dialogues; this topic allowed for conceptual and practical dialogue that merged into ecclesiological issues placing the emphasis on the Spirit as the source of communion rather than focusing on firmer ecclesiological differences between Catholics and Pentecostals. The Fourth Phase (1990–1997) addressed a point of tension among expanding Pentecostal communities in traditionally Catholic contexts with the theme of "Evangelism, Proselytism and Common Witness," as this dialogue reflected on the Christian call to mission and evangelization, its biblical and systematic theological bases, related cultural issues, the role of social justice in Christian witness, the tense issue of proselytization, religious freedom, and the common witness of Catholics and Pentecostals together. The Fifth Phase (1998–2006) "On Becoming a Christian" drew on biblical and patristic resources in order to inform Pentecostal and Catholic theologies and practices regarding conversion, discipleship, and Spirit baptism. The Sixth Phase (2011–2015) "'Do Not Quench the Spirit'" considered the bestowal of divine gifts on the Church in the form of charismatic manifesting manifestations, while reflecting on their genuine use, again drawing on biblical and historical sources while also attending to contemporary theologies and practices of prophecy, healing, discernment of spirits, and the oversight of charisms in the Church. The Seventh Phase began in 2018 with an agenda concerning the Christian life; it has been put on pause for 2019 as the appointment for an appropriate successor for the Catholic chair had not yet been made and plans for the 2020 meeting in Italy have been postponed, and future plans are on hold, due to the COVID-19 pandemic.

The dialogue has provided a significant set of forays into ecumenical understanding that has moved ahead of the ecclesial bodies and fellowships represented. The dialogue thus offers a model of how the two largest Christian traditions might engage one another, although whether those they represent will seek to understand, recognize, and join together in common faith as the dialogue does is continually determined by Catholic and Pentecostal ecclesial leaders and adherents.

Bibliography

Creemers, Jelle. 2009. "Time Will Teach Us … Reflections on Thirty-five Years of Pentecostal-Roman Catholic Dialogue." *Ecclesiology* 5 (3): 322–344.

Hollenweger, Walter J. 1999. "Roman Catholics and Pentecostals in Dialogue." *Pneuma* 21 (1): 135–153.

Kärkkäinen, Veli-Matti. 1999. *Ad Ultimum Terrae: Evangelization, Proselytism, and Common Witness in the Roman Catholic-Pentecostal Dialogue, 1990–1997*. Frankfurt am Main: Peter Lang.

Murphy, Karen. 2018. *Pentecostals and Roman Catholics on Becoming a Christian: Spirit-Baptism, Faith, Conversion, Experience, and Discipleship in Ecumenical Perspective*. Leiden: Brill.

Robeck, Jr., Cecil M. 2012. "The Achievements of the Pentecostal-Catholic International Dialogue." In *Celebrating a Century of Ecumenism: Exploring the Achievements of International Dialogue*, edited by John A. Radano, 163–194. Grand Rapids, MI: Eerdmans.

Sandidge, Jerry L. 1987. *Roman Catholic/Pentecostal Dialogue (1977–1982): A Study in Developing Ecumenism*, 2 volumes. Frankfurt am Main: Peter Lang.

L. William Oliverio

Romania

Pentecostalism in Romania is a dynamically growing religious movement. The first community of the movement was founded in Păuliş (Arad county) with a handful of members in 1922 by a returnee Romanian who converted in America. During the past century Pentecostalism has developed into a home-grown movement within Romania with significant international connections.

The most recent population census (2011) registered 367,938 Pentecostals in the country. Today Pentecostals make up about 2 percent of the total population of Romania. The church is legally recognized as: "Cultul Penticostal Biserica lui Dumnezeu Apostolică", the Pentecostal Union. Its most important international affiliation is with the Church of God based in Cleveland (Tennessee) in the United States of America. The church is organized in more than 2,500 local assemblies being the largest neo-Protestant denomination in Romania. The membership of the church is unevenly spread geographically, most members are clustered in the western counties (Arad, Bihor, Timiş, and Cluj) and in Northern Moldova (Suceava and Botoşani Counties); however, there are important Pentecostal communities throughout Romania.

During their history, Pentecostals' relationship with the state and the dominant historical churches of Romania was often marked by tensions. Different political regimes suppressed, persecuted, or even banned Pentecostalism. Historical churches also looked at the Pentecostal conversions as threatening their long established positions.

The period after World War One when Romanian Pentecostalism emerged, was characterized by government attempts to deal with a rather high degree of ethno-religious diversity within the country. Part of these attempts were oriented to (1) reinforce the dominance of the Orthodox Christian and Greek Catholic Churches, which were seen as national churches, (2) to offer legal frames of the 'minority denominations' like Roman Catholics, Calvinists, Lutherans, and Unitarians (most of these being Hungarians or Germans), as well as to the non-Christians, like Muslims Turkish and Tatar population and the Jewish communities, and (3) to control and suppress the 'sects' as movements which subvert the hegemony of the national culture. Pentecostals were seen as part of this later category. Persecution of these smaller denominations culminated during the fascist regime of Ion Antonescu (1940–44).

After World War Two, the Communist Party had a different approach trying to infiltrate and control religious organizations. The Greek Catholic Church was banned and 'merged into' the Romanian Orthodox Church, and minority denominations and smaller churches were brought under closer state control. As part of these attempts, the central office of the Pentecostals was moved from Arad to Bucharest in 1954 and the church leadership gradually was replaced with people loyal to the regime and the values promoted by it. In order to reduce the role of religion in public life, the socialist state systematically tried to regulate the internal workings of churches. Most of these interventions were suppressive for the Pentecostals. Nevertheless the movement succeeded in slowly increasing the number of followers in particular during the late period of Romanian socialism (1970s and 80s).

A particular aspect of living under the socialist regime was the development of informal strategies for survival and accommodation to the regime. For example, when the building of churches was restricted Pentecostals organized services at private houses or renovated and built private prayer houses that were later donated to the community. In this way, Pentecostals could organize their community life in relative autonomy from the state even if closely watched by the secret service.

Following the regime change in 1989, Pentecostals were able to practice freely their faith and nurture their international links. The movement expanded and new Romanian Pentecostal assemblies were opened not only within Romania but, following the large scale westward migration of the Romanians, in different European cities.

Pentecostalism is remarkably successful in attracting followers from different demographic and cultural backgrounds. After the initial period of rural expansion among peasants of the early twentieth century, the appeal of the movement included members of newly urbanized strata from the socialist cities that diversified the social composition of the church after the fall of socialism (Fosztó and Kiss 2012).

Compared to the traditional churches, Pentecostalism relies less on ethnic and linguistic boundaries. While traditional churches in most cases tend to form mono-ethnic assemblies that may signify ethno-national allegiance, Pentecostals approach social divisions and culture rather differently. On the one hand, belonging to an ethnic group is rarely a precondition for recruitment while, on the other, nurturing cultural or ethno-national belonging is never a central focus of religious mobilization, unlike the case of the minority churches (Fosztó 2006).

Among the different ethnic groups, the success of Pentecostalism among the large population of Romanian Roma is worth some consideration. Roma started to convert to Pentecostalism already during the socialist regime and they joined the church in increasing number after its collapse (Fosztó 2009). Recent studies observe that migrant Roma use the institutional frame offered by the church in order to reinforce their community and ideas about belonging while living abroad as a consequence of their mobility within the European Union (Lipan 2017). The social scientific interpretation of this success has focussed on the relationship between recent neoliberal forms of capitalism and the role of Pentecostalism (Rubiolo 2016; Voiculescu 2017).

A recent development has occurred between the historical churches and Pentecostals who joined with the "Coaliția pentru Familie" ('Coalition for the Family'), a trans-denominational movement with a clear conservative and pro-life agenda. This movement in 2016 collected about 3 million signatures to support the changing of the Romanian Constitution in order to make it more restrictive regarding the definition of the family as the union of "a man and a woman." The initiative provoked protest by supporters of the LGBTQ community and the liberal civil society, which advocate for keeping the present inclusive definition (allowing single parents and non-married couples to be defined as families). This move signals that Pentecostalism has been slowly transformed from a persecuted religious movement into one of the mainstream actors in the public debates of the present day Romania.

Bibliography

Fosztó, László. 2009. *Ritual Revitalisation after Socialism: Community, Personhood, and*

Conversion among Roma in a Transylvanian Village. Halle Studies in the Anthropology of Eurasia 21. Münster: Lit Verlang.

Foszto, László. 2006. "Mono-Ethnic Churches, the 'Undertaker Parish', and Rural Civility in Postsocialist Romania." In *The Postsocialist Religious Question: Faith and Power in Central Asia and East-Central Europe*, edited by Chris Hann, 269–92. Münster: Lit Verlang.

Foszto, László, and Dénes Kiss. 2012. "Pentecostalism in Romania. The Impact of Pentecostal Communities on the Life-Style of the Members." *La Ricerca Folklorica* 65: 51–64.

Lipan, Ștefan. 2017. "The Interplay between Ethnic and Religious Frontiers: The Case of Repented Roma Migrants Living in a Belgian City." *The Romanian Journal of Society and Politics* 12 (1): 53–78.

Rubiolo, Cecilia. 2016. "The Ambivalent Autonomy of Mobile 'Pocăiți' between Vicovu de Sus, Romania and Turin, Italy after 1989." *Studia Universitatis Babes-Bolyai Sociologia* 61 (2): 71–97. doi:10.1515/subbs-2016-0011.

Voiculescu, Cerasela. 2017. "Nomad Self-Governance and Disaffected Power versus Semiological State Apparatus of Capture: The Case of Roma Pentecostalism." *Critical Research on Religion* 5 (2): 188–208. doi:10.1177/2050303217690894.

László Foszto

Ruibal, Julio Cesar

Julio Cesar Ruibal, named the "Apostle of the Andes," was a prominent Pentecostal preacher, evangelist, and founder of Ekklesia, the largest Pentecostal denomination in Bolivia. Ruibal was born on 15 May 1953 in Sucre Bolivia to a Catholic family, although he lived in La Paz for most of his childhood. Since a young age, he had an affinity for spirituality that led him to experiment with different new age practices and to abandon his Catholic upbringing. In 1969, Ruibal immigrated to the United States at the age of 16 to study medicine and by 1971 he started his medical degree with the intention of becoming a surgeon. However, in 1972 while attending a healing service of preeminent Pentecostal evangelist Kathryn Kuhlman, Ruibal converted to Pentecostalism. In his own words: "Immediately, I was touched by the Holy Spirit, but more importantly … I was saved." Feeling the call to preach, Ruibal returned to Bolivia and shortly after was preaching, healing and gathering a large following.

It was during the following years that the secular press called him the "Apostle of the Andes," as some of his crusades gathered up to 80,000 people. It was reported that sometimes he had to climb on to the roof of stadiums to address the crowd that could not fit inside. Ruibal's popularity did not go unnoticed, and after the miraculous healing of a government official, President Hugo Banzer Suarez requested a meeting with him. In his biography, Ruibal recounts that the President asked how he could help and Ruibal answered with the following: "First, Give me the authority to use all the football stadiums in the country.… Second: that the national television and radio stations transmit these messages, and Third: a plane to take me from city to city" (Ruibal 1999, 28).

Following his success in Bolivia, including the founding of Ekklesia, the largest non-Catholic Church at the time, Ruibal was invited to preach in most South American countries, including Colombia where he met his future wife Ruth Johnson. After marriage in 1976, and the births of their daughters Abigail (1977) and Sarah (1979), Ruibal and his family immigrated to Colombia with the intention of ministering there. During the 1980s, Ruibal founded Ekklesia Christian Centre in Cali, as well as several Christian educational institutions, including the first Latin American Christian University (UCLA, Colombia). Ruibal's ministry did not go unnoticed and he was targeted by the Cali Cartel for assassination. Ruibal was martyred on 13 December 1995 when leaving a pastors' meeting.

Ruibal's lasting influence on Bolivian and Latin American Pentecostalism cannot be underestimated. His ministry was the catalyst for the explosion of Pentecostal growth in the 1980s and 1990s. Some unique features of his influence were: 1) he preached using a simple message that was based around the phrase *"Jesus te ama"* (Jesus loves you); 2) he spearheaded the use of media technology (television and radio) as means of communication leading later to the use of the internet; 3) he established Ekklesia, the largest Pentecostal denomination in Bolivia; 4) he modeled a successful partnership between preachers and government which was often replicated; 5) he valued education as a necessity in spreading the gospel; and, 6) he promoted cooperation between different denominations and churches.

Bibliography

Anon. n.d. "Biografía Fundador: Dr. Julio Cesar Ruibal." *Colegio Ekklesia* (blog), 1. Accessed July 28, 2019. http://www.colegioekklesia.edu.co/fundador-julio-cesar-ruibal/.

Anon. 1996. "Prominent Bolivian Evangelist Murdered." *ChristianityToday.Com*, February 5, 1996, 1. Accessed July 28, 2019. https://www.christianitytoday.com/ct/1996/february5/6t2099.html.

Peñaloza, C. 2011. *La Otra Cara de La Victoria: Un Impactante Testimonio de Fe Construido En Medio de La Muerte Del Sufrimiento.* Virginia, Estados Unidos: Ekklesia.

Ruibal, J.C. 1999. *Ungido para la cosecha del tiempo final.* Mami: Editorial Vida.

Daniel Ortiz

Russia

Russia's huge territory embraced Christianity more than 1,000 years ago. Russian Orthodoxy is known for a beautiful sung liturgy and a theology that identifies the will of God with the will of the Czar, the anointed ruler. Consequently the Orthodox Church supported the Czarist government so that when, in 1917, a political revolution occurred the Church was persecuted by the atheistic Bolsheviks who seized power. However, at first smaller churches, like the Baptists, were spared since it was thought their growth would undermine Orthodoxy.

Ivan Voronaev, born in central Russia in 1886, was converted in 1908 and served with the Baptists until persecution by the Orthodox drove him to the United States where he pastored until soon after receiving Spirit baptism in New York. Bravely he returned to Russia (the Odessa area on the Black Sea) in 1920 and ministered among Baptists and evangelicals and some Jewish people until he had built up a congregation approaching 1,000. He then made lengthy preaching tours and in six years founded 350 Pentecostal congregations with 17,000 members joined, in 1924, in a Union of Christians of Evangelical Faith. By 1928 he had launched a magazine, *Evangelist*. But in April 1929 state persecution of all Christians began and churches were denied legal existence. Voronaev was arrested and died in a prison camp in the 1930s. Aggressive atheism confiscated buildings from Christians forcing them to worship in secret until, in a drive to stimulate patriotism in what he called the Great Patriotic War against Germany, Stalin restored some religious freedoms. In 1944 Baptists and evangelicals were combined in a single Union, buildings were permitted but registered, tongues speaking and testimony were forbidden and any form of ministerial training severely restricted. Thus the freedom given to Christians was partial and controlling. Inevitably some Pentecostals refused these conditions and broke away from the Union but, in doing so, they put themselves on the wrong side of the law and gave the communists excuses for discrimination and further imprisonments.

Soviet persecution including vile anti-religious propaganda fluctuated in the period after 1945. In 1990, with the fall of the USSR, freedom of conscience was restored and Pentecostals were at last able to receive preachers, funds and teaching from abroad. Imprisoned leaders with powerful spiritual gifts and uncompromising standards of holiness were released. Disagreements occurred between modernising charismatics and classical Pentecostals whose doctrines were similar to Assemblies of God and the Church of God. After an initial period when churches revived and flourished and numbers of Christians emigrated, President Putin promoted Orthodoxy at the expense of other charismatic and free churches. The current position is that Pentecostals are said by several sociologists to number about 1.5m although others give figures of around 300,000. Accuracy is obscured by the presence of unregistered congregations and unknown numbers of unaffiliated Christians. The great majority of Russians are Orthodox (between 43–75 percent) and therefore patriotic. Further barriers to understanding spring from the Russian annexation of Crimea in 2014 and the competing political identities of Orthodox Russians and Ukrainian Pentecostals.

Bibliography

Löfstedt, Torsten. 2017. "Pentecostals and Charismatics in Russia, Ukraine, and other Post-Soviet States: History and Future." In *Global Renewal Christianity*, vol. 4, edited by Vinson Synan and Amos Yong, 19–32. Lake Mary, FL: Charisma House.

Mozer, Pavel, and Oleg Bornovolokov. 2011. "The Development of Pentecostalism in Russia and the Ukraine." In *European Pentecostalism*, edited by William K. Kay and Anne E. Dyer, 261–289. Leiden: Brill.

William K. Kay

Rwanda

Pentecostalism in Rwanda is primarily located within the "Association des eglises de Pentecote au Rwanda (ADEPR)" also known as the Pentecostal church of Rwanda, and second, among the several non-traditional denominations. The Pentecostals are characterized by speaking in tongues, ecstatic worship and preaching. In recent times though, some nontraditional churches, especially those led by theologically trained pastors do not like to be associated with some excesses attributed to some Pentecostal churches, and as such, some have refused the Pentecostal label but still embrace the gifts of the spirit.

Pentecostalism in Rwanda is associated with the outbreak of revival in the 1930s in the eastern part of the country at Gahini.

The revival spread to Uganda, Kenya and Tanzania. The Pentecostal movement emanated from the preaching and conviction of a young Cambridge medical doctor, Joe Church who had located to Rwanda to lead a hospital. In May 1936, ecstatic signs started to appear in Gahini, as people publicly confessed sins, were falling down, shaking, seeing visions and dreams and other phenomena. The critics of the Pentecostal revival alleged that it lacked doctrine, was dispensational in its theology, and typological in its preaching. Christianity in Rwanda is polarized between Pentecostals, Roman Catholics, and the historic Protestant churches, although there have been some forums for dialogue between the groups.

The "association dentraide des eglises de pentecotes du Rwanda" (ADEPR) started as a free Swedish mission. In January 1984 it changed its name to "association des eglise de pentecotes du Rwanda" (ADEPR) and is the second largest denomination in Rwanda after the Roman Catholic Church. It tends to emphasize outward disassociation with worldliness, forbidding women from braiding their hair and adorning themselves with earrings and other ornaments. Their worship is associated with prophecy and ecstatic bodily expressions.

There are other growing churches that are labelled Pentecostal mainly because they embrace the gifts of the holy spirit such as speaking in tongues and miracles. The Evangelical Restoration church led by Bishop Joshua Masasu popularly referred to as Papa or Daddy, is characterized by fasting including an annual forty day fast. It has 80 local churches with a membership of 25,000. Zion Temple led by apostle Gitwaza, organizes regular conferences referred to as "Africa Haguka" meaning Africa arise. It has 60 local churches and a membership of 14,000. The Assemblies of God has 153 local churches and a membership of 15,000 while the Miracle Center has a membership of 13,000. New Life Bible Church, another growing church, annually organizes Refresh Rwanda with an emphasis on experiencing God's manifest presence. The conference has had a great impact with people being slain in the spirit (falling) and visions with claims of being covered by gold dust. Christian Life Assembly also holds revival services akin to those of New Life Bible Church often sharing the same speakers.

There appears to be a movement of people from the traditional historic Protestant churches and the Roman Catholic Church towards Pentecostalism that still requires some analysis, along with the social impact of the growth of Pentecostalism in Rwanda.

Bibliography

Clarke, Clifton R. 2014. *Pentecostal Theology in Africa*. Eugene, OR: Pickwick.

Ogbu, Kalu. 2008. *African Pentecostalism: An Introduction*. Oxford: Oxford University Press.

Osborn, H.H. 2000. *Pioneers in the East African Revival*. Apologia Publications.

Ward, Kevin, and Emma Wild-Wood. 2010. *The East African Revival: History and Legacies*. Kampala: Fountain Publishers.

Eugene Mugisha

Ryan, Martin Lawrence

Martin Lawrence Ryan (1869–1963) was born to Milton and Elizabeth Ryan in Vevay, Michigan on May 17. His father was a magistrate. Ryan married Rowena E. in 1893 and they had five children. After becoming a minister of the Apostolic Holiness Mission in the 1890s, Ryan became the superintendent of the Pentecostal Mission and

Pacific Holiness College in Salem, Oregon in 1905. He published a newspaper called *Apostolic Light* in Salem.

He was an avid reader of *Apostolic Faith* and was greatly interested in the work of the Azusa Street Mission. He visited there in the fall of 1906 and went up to the second floor to pray for Spirit baptism for several hours, which he received. He returned to Salem and started a Pentecostal ministry with his family, but the town people were skeptical of them by calling them "Tonguers."

By the end of 1906, Ryan moved to Portland, Oregon, and in the spring of 1907 to Spokane, Washington, where his ministry was successful. About one hundred people received Spirit baptism in the Spokane area in 1907, while Ryan formed the Apostolic Assembly of Spokane, Washington, which was strongly missionary-oriented. The 1907 yearbook of his group listed about 35 missionaries.

After a farewell party on August 27, 1907, Ryan and his Apostolic Light missionaries sailed for Japan from Seattle on September 12. They arrived in Yokohama on September 27 then travelled to Tokyo. They were the first Pentecostal missionaries who landed in Japan. The group was composed of Martin L. and Rowena E. Ryan with their four sons, William A. and Edith M. Colyar and their two sons, Homer L. and Emma B. Lawler and their daughter and son, Archibald W. and Vinnie M. McDonald, Edward Riley, and five single ladies (Rosa Pittman, Cora Fritsch, Lillian Callahan, Bertha Milligan, and May Law). The oldest adult was the 53-year-old Riley and the youngest was the 19-year-old Fritsch.

None of these missionaries had any theological education except Ryan. They responded the calling from God and left their families, believing that the second coming of Jesus Christ was very near and God would supply all their needs. Moreover, they believed in the gift of speaking in foreign languages (xenolalia). Entrusting everything to God, they headed to Asia. While some of the members soon continued their journey to China, the Ryans, the MacDonalds, the Colyars, and Cora Fritsch, and Bertha Milligan remained in the Tokyo area.

Juji Nakada (1870–1939) was a former Methodist minister who introduced the Holiness Movement to Japan. Soon after their arrival, Nakada warned the Christians in Japan that the Pentecostals were "a kind of neurotics or the work of the Satan" in his *Hono-o no Shita* (Tongues of Fire). As Nakada held negative views about the Pentecostal movement until his death, many of his Holiness colleagues and their disciples were convinced by it.

Realizing right away that their tongues were not communicative, Ryan and his group started learning Japanese. Their main ministry was teaching English and giving Bible study classes. From the beginning, the Ryans and his group faced financial difficulties and for that reason, the Ryans left Tokyo and moved to Yokohama in 1908. They bought a small ship and named it "The Pentecost." They ministered to the coastal areas of Tokyo Bay. The Ryans returned to Tokyo in 1909 and worked with university students, some of whom were Chinese and Korean. Among them was S. Ito, who became the first Japanese person to receive Spirit baptism in September 1909.

Ryan thought of making their Tokyo base the hub of their ministry in Asia. They published a few issues of *Apostolic Light* in English, Japanese, and Korean. Many Pentecostal missionaries came to Japan and joined them for a short period before moving onto their next destination, such as A.G. Garr, Lucy Leatherman, and I.G. Hitch and Thomas Hindle who were missionaries of the Hebden Mission in Toronto.

Cora Fritsch and Bertha Milligan assisted William and Mary Taylor, who were missionaries of the Japan Evangelistic Band, in the spring of 1908. The Taylors sought Spirit baptism and received it during their furlough. In 1913, the Taylors were sent back to Japan by the Pentecostal Missionary Union, becoming the first Pentecostal missionaries sent by a Pentecostal missionary organization.

The members of the Apostolic Light left Japan one by one. Ryan was the last to leave Japan on November 19, 1910. In January 1911, after returning to Spokane, Ryan was sued by his wife on the grounds of harsh treatment and neglect of his family in Japan, and their divorce was granted in March 1911.

Sometime after the divorce, Ryan went to China alone and ministered to the Japanese. He remained there until 1915. Several of his former Apostolic Light members became lifetime American Assemblies of God missionaries, but Ryan kept on his own way. Moving to South Pasadena, California, he started a group called Ecclesia of California and became the editor of the *New Age Herald*. He left for missionary work in Europe and the Near East in 1922. He arrived in Glasgow on March 5, 1922 and stayed abroad for more than 20 years. He returned to the U.S. on December 15, 1946 via Beirut at the age of 77. Ryan died in Calaveras, California on October 3, 1963.

Bibliography

Fritsch, Homer and Alice. eds. 1987. *Letters From Cora: Cora Fritsch, 1907–1912*: Self-published.

Shew, Paul Tsuchido. 2003. "History of the Early Pentecostal Movement in Japan: The Roots and Development of the Pre-War Pentecostal Movement in Japan (1907–1945)." PhD diss., Fuller Theological Seminary.

Suzuki, Masakazu. 2011. "The Origins and the Development of the Japan Assemblies of God: The Foreign and Japanese Workers and Their Ministries (1907 to 1975)." PhD diss., Bangor University.

Masakazu Suzuki

Salt & Light

The Salt & Light family of churches is one of the apostolic networks that came into being in Britain in the late 1960s and 1970s, most of them with a radical Restorationist emphasis (Walker 1998, 38–41, 51–64, 129–171; Trudinger 1982: 38–41, 51–64, 129–171). The charismatic movement had started to impact the historic denominations, including a small Baptist church in Basingstoke, England, led by former London police officer Barney Coombs. Meanwhile, 50 miles north in the Oxfordshire town of Witney, a youth group in a Methodist church left to start a house church and one of its leaders, Dave Richards, began to seek oversight from Coombs. Another young Baptist pastor, Oxford-educated Steve Thomas, then connected with Richards and Coombs and their friendship culminated in them becoming the founders of the Salt & Light network in the late 1970s (Whitchurch 2002, 13–25; Rolles 2019, 9–15). William Kay summarizes the process thus: "… the charismatic movement, with all its energies, innovations, activities, and dreams, eventuated in the house churches and these, in many cases, rapidly became apostolic networks" (Kay 2007, 344–345).

In the UK the Salt & Light network grew over the following 40 years to around 75 churches, mainly by the planting of new churches. It expanded much more significantly elsewhere primarily by forming relationships with other church networks in Canada, USA, Kenya, Zimbabwe, Uganda, India, New Zealand, France, Belgium, Switzerland, and Scandinavia. Salt & Light did not require its name to be adopted by these other networks but encouraged them to continue with their own identities. The several hundred churches across four continents which are now part of the Salt & Light family are connected by strong relationships between the various apostolic leaders who bring oversight and direction to the related networks. They share a conservative evangelical ethos, are committed to a complementarian position and their worship services are strongly charismatic. Salt & Light has also established a Bible College, many medical, educational and poverty-relief projects in Africa and India, and a number of Christian schools and pregnancy crisis centers in the UK and Canada (Whitchurch 2002, 25–39).

The founding apostle of an apostolic network often nominates his successor and this happened smoothly for Salt & Light as Coombs passed its leadership to Thomas in 2010. Kay quotes this transition as "apostolic ministry reproducing itself," evidence that the apostolic networks have "… against the odds, found a way to solve the problem of charismatic succession" (Kay 2007, 350–351). Following the death of Coombs in 2018, the question of leadership transition to the next generation is one that Thomas and Richards both say that they are giving considerable thought. A number of other factors also raise questions about Salt & Light's future: its weak brand identity, competition from newer networks, and challenges from some of its younger leaders about biblical interpretation and the nature of apostolic authority (Rolles 2019, 23–30).

Bibliography

Kay, William. 2007. *Apostolic Networks in Britain: New Ways of Being Church*. Milton Keynes: Paternoster.

Rolles, David. 2019. "A Fifty-year Perspective of the Origins, Development and Identity of the Salt & Light Church Network." Master's diss., University of Birmingham, UK.

Trudinger, Ron. 1982. *Built to Last: Biblical Principles for Church Restoration*. Eastbourne: Kingsway Publications.

Walker, Andrew. 1998. *Restoring the Kingdom: The Radical Christianity of the House Church Movement*. Guildford: Inter Publishing Service Ltd.

Whitchurch, Bob. 2002. *The Journey*. Oxford: Salt & Light Publishing.

David Rolles

Sandru, Trandafir

Trandafir Sandru (1924–1998) was born on April 13, 1924 in Secaș, Arad, Romania, and he learned of Pentecostal faith from his childhood. He was baptized at the age of 17 (1941) and began his lay ministry at 21 when he was already elected as the general secretary of the Romanian Pentecostal church (1945). Upon completion of his secondary studies in Arad, Sandru went to study ancient history at the University of Bucharest (1951–1956). He was ordained as pastor in 1953 in Bucharest and worked until 1998 in the "Philadelphia" church (43 Sebastian street), one of the largest Pentecostal churches in Bucharest.

Despite being young, Sandru was a very gifted, dynamic, bold, and influential leader in the Pentecostal denomination. The Communists saw him as a threat and therefore revoked his pastoral credentials twice (between 1958–63 and 1965–68) and limited his influence among the Pentecostal constituency. However, Sandru was not discouraged and remined determined to strengthen and equip the Pentecostal churches. In fact he committed most of his time, knowledge, and energy to train Pentecostal ministers by launching his own training courses. Like all leaders in his time, he had to sign an "agreement of cooperation" with the communist regime. In 1976, Sandru was the key person to establish the very first undergraduate Pentecostal theological school called Seminarul Teologic Penticostal in Bucharest where the first generation of Pentecostal pastors were trained in Romania. Since during the communist times all the religious life was controlled by the state, the seminary only accepted 15 students for the first cohort (1976–1080), five in the second period (1980–84), then ten students (1984–1988) and only three students every year. All students who were accepted by the seminary had to be "approved" by the communist regime. With the collapse of communism, the school was renamed as Institutul Teologic Penticostal, București and became a university-level institution in 1992. Sandru was the founding president of the school from 1976 till 1997. It is one of the strongest Pentecostal theological institutions in Europe.

Sandru also served in some important positions within the Romanian Pentecostal Church including the vice-president (1948) and the general secretary (1945–46, 1949–56, 1986–94). He was also the editor of the denominational magazine, *Vestitorul Evangheliei* [The Gospel Herald], in 1945–1948 and *Buletinul Cultului Penticostal* [Pentecostal Bulletin] in 1968–1986. He has contributed substantially to the elaboration of the Romanian Pentecostal statement of faith, which has been in use ever since. Internationally, Sandru served in the European Pentecostal Committee (1978–1990) and in the Consultative Committee of the Global Pentecostal Conference (1980–1990). Sandru's greatest influence on Romanian Pentecostalism was exercised through his writings and publications. With 12 books and many articles in the Pentecostal magazines, Sandru is probably still considered to be a prolific writer on Pentecostal identity, theology, and spirituality. This is especially significant since his writings were for many years the only theological resources for Pentecostal students and ministers in Romania, including (in English) Pastor's manual (1976); Pneumatology: The Person and the Work of the Holy Spirit (1979); The Pentecostal Apostolic Church of God in Romania (1982); The Pentecostal Revival in Romania (1997).

In 1992, Cleveland Theological Seminary, TN, awarded him a Doctor Honoris Causa, a clear recognition of his significant leadership and theological writings. Sandru made a significant contribution to Romanian Pentecostalism as the founding president of the first Pentecostal Theological Institute in Bucharest and through his theological writing.

Bibliography

Andreescu, Valeriu. 2012 *Istoria Penticostalismului Românesc*, Two Vols. Oradea: Casa Cărții.

Bălăban, Ciprian. 2016. *Istoria Bisericii Penticostale din România (1922–1989): Institutie și Harisme*. Oradea: Scriptum.

Croitor, Vasilică. 2010. *Răscumpărarea memoriei*. Medgidia: Succeed Publishing.

Sandru, Trandafir. 1997. *Trezirea spirituală penticostală din România*. București: Institutul Teologic Penticostal.

Corneliu Constantineanu

Sanford, Agnes

Agnes Mary Sanford (1897–1982) was an author, teacher, and speaker pivotal in the expansion of many aspects of Pentecostalism into the mainline and historic churches in the mid twentieth century. Her book *The Healing Light* was first published in 1947 and became the foundation of the Charismatic Movement's theology of healing; it has gone through multiple printings and is still in print today. As one of the main speakers for Camps Farthest Out, she had a profound influence on many who became renewal leaders in their own denominations, including Larry Christenson and Francis MacNutt. Agnes is perhaps best known for developing a scientific and interdisciplinary approach to healing prayer, combatting Cessationism, and founding the inner healing movement. She authored at least 21 publications: 5 books on healing, 7 novels, an autobiography, a book of meditations, an apologetic on a Christian responsibility to the environment, 5 articles and excerpts on healing, and an academic booklet.

Agnes was the first child of Hugh and Augusta White, Southern Presbyterian missionaries in China. She loved growing up in China, and she attributed some of her insights on prayer and healing to having a worldview that drew from both eastern and western cultures. Nevertheless, cessationist teachings within the denomination, splits between families at the mission station, and her baby sister's death from dysentery resulted in depression and cynicism toward Christianity that continued for many years. Agnes traveled to the US when she was 16 to obtain a teaching degree at Peace College in North Carolina, then returned to China, eventually teaching at an Episcopal school for boys. There, she met and married Edgar (Ted) Sanford, a priest teaching at another nearby Episcopal school. A few years later, they relocated to the US where Ted eventually became the rector of a small church in New Jersey.

Agnes found life in the US difficult, and her depression continued until suicide seemed inevitable. It was then that she met Hollis Colwell, an Episcopal priest who worked with Ted. Colwell prayed for her youngest child, who was instantly healed from a chronic ear infection. Agnes was astonished, having been taught miracles had ceased. A year later, she asked Colwell to pray for her depression; the change was both profound and immediate. At his direction, she began writing and learning how to pray for herself, and over a period of months, she was completely healed of depression. These two experiences led Agnes to re-evaluate many of the doctrines she had been taught, and she committed to spending a year reading nothing except the gospels. This began her journey to understand how to effectively pray for the sick.

As well as promoting a physical healing model emphasizing observation and allowing for repeated prayer, Agnes also developed an inner healing model addressing emotional and psychological needs.

She coined the term "healing of memories" to describe a practical way to apply forgiveness and salvation on the heart level. Based upon developments in the field of psychology, Agnes believed that the subconscious significantly affected a person's experiences not only of the world but also of God. Throughout her work, she details how the subconscious mind often took precedence over the conscious mind for both healing and faith.

Agnes affirmed a decidedly orthodox Christian theology and the nature of the Trinity, often describing the Father as Creator, the Son as Redeemer, and the Holy Spirit as Sanctifier and Empowerer. She affirmed the necessity for the redemptive power of Jesus Christ for salvation. Additionally, she believed scripture was the uniquely inspired word of God. However, some of her works were written for nonbelievers, using language and terminology more metaphysical than theological. She also leaned toward some beliefs controversial in many conservative traditions, such as theistic evolution, bodily transformation, and a post-millenialism where God waits for the church to transform the world.

For Agnes, creation displaying God's glory meant that discoveries in non-theological disciplines often revealed truths about God and the world. She embraced the scientific method as the optimal vehicle for evaluating the effectiveness of healing prayer, believing it emulated humility, and *The Healing Light* describes her healing model in terms of hypothesis, experimentation, observation, and adjustment. She accepted many of the discoveries in physics, psychology, astronomy, and biology as valid and incorporated them into her worldview. A significant difference between Agnes and Pentecostal healing theologies of her time was her affirmation of medicine, physicians, and psychology. Her membership in the Episcopal church, her interdisciplinary approach to prayer, and her defense of medical science were the primary reasons for her teachings being accepted by many churches that would have been less inclined to accept a more traditional Pentecostal message. Through her message, many churches in the US and Europe became open to the baptism of the Holy Spirit and the gifts of the Spirit.

Bibliography

DeArteaga, William L. 2015. *Agnes Sanford and Her Companions: The Assault on Cessationism and the Coming of the Charismatic Renewal*. Eugene, OR: Wipf & Stock.

Dignard, Martin L. 2018. *Revealed Orders: Agnes Sanford's Theological Journey*. Emeth: Lexington.

Dignard, Martin L. 2014. "God's Faithful Freedom: Healing as an Outflow of God's Presence." *Journal of Pentecostal Theology* 23 (1): 68–84.

Hocken, Peter D. 2002. "Sanford, Agnes Mary." In *The New International Dictionary of Pentecostal and Charismatic Movements*, edited by Stanley M. Burgess and Eduard M. van der Maas, 1039. Grand Rapids: Zondervan.

Sanford, Agnes. 1947. *The Healing Light: On the Art and Method of Spiritual Healing from the Christian Viewpoint and in the Christian Tradition*. St. Paul: Macalester Park.

Martin Dignard

Science

Science is one of the most significant intellectual achievements of human history that has important implications for Pentecostalism. Broadly speaking, contemporary science is identified by its systematic methodology for studying the physical world, with the aim of producing reliable explanations of material phenomena. This typically involves experimentation and observations of nature, deductive hypothesizing, and the formulation of general principles from discovered patterns. Importantly, these exercises occur in the social and historical contexts of scientific communities. Science is also frequently identified by its research foci. For instance, biology, chemistry and physics are considered core natural sciences because of their empirical observations of natural events, while the study of literature or philosophy would not be constituted sciences because of their humanities-centered subject matter. Science is also distinguished from other pursuits by its commitment to methodological naturalism. This is an epistemological tenet that limits scientific reports to natural systems and materialistic explanations, which eschews non-natural descriptions of the physical world.

In relation to Pentecostalism, science's imbued naturalism could be interpreted as placing it in direct opposition with the enchanted worldview that typifies Pentecostalism's pneumatological theology. Indeed, Pentecostalism has at times been perceived by some to be anti-intellectual, as well as a premodern and even counter-modernizing Christian movement (Smith and Yong 2010). Many Pentecostals have simply not engaged directly with the sciences, and Pentecostal theology often reflects a disregard for scientific concerns (Wacker 1998; Yong 2008). Yet Pentecostals have proven to be technological pragmatists, quick to accept leading-edge technologies borne from modern science when it is of use. In fact, delineating the associations between science and Pentecostalism is more complicated than it may at first appear; reflecting historical complexities and contemporary aspirations. The vicissitudes of these interactions are underscored when considering Pentecostal responses to medicine, biological evolution and views of an ancient earth, as well as climate change and the naturalistic premises of modern science.

From Pentecostalism's early days forward, theologies of divine healing have remained an important characteristic of the movement. Miraculous cures have been taken as being demonstrative of Jesus' divine healer role, while illnesses are sometimes ascribed to satanic activity and a consequence of the Fall of Man. Through these spiritual interpretations of health and sickness, many early twentieth century Pentecostal leaders exhibited hostility towards physicians and pharmaceutical dispensers. The applied science of medicine was interpreted to be an inferior method of healing when contrasted with God's faithful provision of wellbeing. Pharmaceutical medicines were sometimes understood to be demonic, unnatural remedies, as they often contained alcoholic or narcotic ingredients contravening early Pentecostalism's renunciative cultures. It has been postulated that aversions to seeking medical treatment lead to the deaths of hundreds of Pentecostal adherents in the first three decades of the twentieth century, as doctors were spurned as agents of a secular world. Nevertheless, the latter half of the 1900s witnessed not only the active acceptance of leading medical practices, but also the development of Pentecostal-led medical institutions; which have held fast to both pneumatological theology and the medical sciences in tandem (Wacker 1998).

With regard to biological evolution, the Darwin-skeptic messages of Young Earth Creationism's mid-twentieth century renaissance initially found little traction among Pentecostal audiences. This was because creationism was associated with Christian fundamentalists, who tended to dismiss emphases on pneumatology and divine healings as nonbiblical falsehoods. In fact, Pentecostals had largely ignored the topic of evolution in the early 1900s, though a spate of antievolutionist Pentecostal writings were published in the 1920s and 1930s. Even as a revitalized Young Earth Creationism spread throughout North America during the 1960s onwards, several notable and often scientifically trained Pentecostal leaders warned fellow charismatic Christians against accepting the claims of Young Earth Creationists. Instead, Pentecostals were frequently devoted to the Gap Theory of creation, which posits an ancient universe with a considerable temporal interlude between Genesis 1:1 and 1:2. This allowed Pentecostals to accede to the preponderance of scientific data signaling that the earth is much older than Young Earth Creationists insist, by assuming a pre-Adamic creation before the second verse of Genesis. Nevertheless, as Young Earth Creationism took root more broadly amid conservative Christianity in the 1970s and 1980s, it also started receiving significant backing from lay Pentecostals. This support was then reflected by Pentecostal frontrunners, who made counter-evolutionary perspectives commonplace in preaching and teaching. Despite this development, many Pentecostals remain committed to ancient earth and Evolutionary Creationist perspectives, calling for an openness to a breadth of views on evolutionary science, human origins, and interpretations of scripture (Smith and Yong 2010).

Along with these considerations, research has demonstrated that in some regions Pentecostals are less concerned about climate change, and are among the most skeptical toward scientific data that reveals it to be human caused (Pepper, Leonard, and Powell 2013). This may be due to political affiliations, as well as theological views about God's authority in nature. Pentecostal theology also tends to perceive humanity as possessing divinely appointed dominion over the earth. In short, humans have been given rulership over the natural world that God lovingly created, and only God has supreme control over such variables as the world's climate.

In addition to this, an important question for Pentecostal theologians has been how charismatic Christianity's Holy Spirit-infused worldview, with its focus on the miraculous and what has been described as hyper-supernaturalism, may coincide with the naturalism of science. In particular, questions have been raised as to whether a pneumatological ontology fundamentally conflicts with science's methodological naturalism. How can the scientific dictum stipulating that science needs to operate under the assumption that the universe functions purely by natural processes be reconciled with Pentecostalism? Moreover, can a Pentecostal who maintains an enchanted, pneumatological worldview coherently engage in scientific practice? In answer to such questions it has been proposed that Pentecostals can adhere to an *enchanted naturalism*, which assumes that the world functions through law-like, naturalistic mechanisms, though it is the Holy Spirit that provides this regularity in nature (Smith 2008). With this supposition in mind, it has been contended that no inconsistencies exist for Pentecostals observing methodological naturalism in science. Altogether then, when it comes to conceptualizations of scientific practice, or the reception of scientific theories and medical science, Pentecostalism has had complex associations ranging from rejection to approval.

Bibliography

Brown, Candy Gunther. 2012. *Testing Prayer: Science and Healing*. Cambridge, MA: Harvard University Press.

Pepper, Miriam, Rosemary Leonard, and Ruth Powell. 2013. "Denominational Identification, Church Participation, and Concern about Climate Change in Australia." In *Climate Change Cultural Change: Religious Responses and Responsibilities*, edited by Anne F. Elvey and David Gormley O'Brien, 35–47. Preston: Mosaic Press.

Smith, James K.A. 2008. "Is the Universe Open for Surprise? Pentecostal Ontology and the Spirit of Naturalism." *Zygon* 43 (4): 879–96. doi: 10.1111/j.1467-9744.2008.00966.x.

Smith, James K.A., and Amos Yong, eds. 2010. *Science and the Spirit: A Pentecostal Engagement with the Sciences*. Bloomington: Indiana University Press.

Wacker, Grant. 1998. "The Pentecostal Tradition." In *Caring and Curing: Health and Medicine in the Western Religious Traditions*, edited by Ronald L. Numbers and Darrel W. Amundsen, 514–38. Baltimore: Johns Hopkins University Press.

Yong, Amos. 2008. "Pentecostalism, Science, and Creation: New Voices in the Theology-Science Conversation." *Zygon* 43 (4): 875–77. doi: 10.1111/j.1467-9744.2008.00965.x.

Tom Aechtner

Secularization

There are two broad issues linking Pentecostalism with secularization which will be discussed in turn. The first is the argument that the growth of the Pentecostal movement worldwide from the 1960s onwards disproves the once widely accepted 'unilinear' theory among social scientists that secularization is a universal and inevitable consequence of modernity.

In the 1960s it was widely accepted by social scientists that secularization was a universal consequence of modernity. The theory was an extrapolation from the evolutionary arguments underpinning the founding texts of sociology, notably by Comte, Durkheim, Marx and, to a lesser extent and with more nuance, by Weber. It was assumed that modernity must inevitably undermine religion both at the cognitive level, where scientific and rational knowledge would disprove and displace religious and mythic modes of thought; and at the societal level, where religious institutions would progressively lose social functions in complex and differentiated modern societies – social control and socialization, education, welfare, leisure activity, and patronage of the arts – as each of these functions was hived off into an autonomous secular sphere, a process sometimes termed 'functional differentiation'. Some sociologists envisaged that this would (and/or should) render religious belief and practice a purely private activity with no involvement in the politics of 'the public sphere'; or that religious institutions and attendance at worship would automatically atrophy and eventually disappear altogether.

This theory was based on the history of Western Europe and from the 1960s began to encounter criticism on several grounds. First, some sociologists argued that even within the West there was no uniform pattern of religious decline. Ideological, secularist elements in the evolutionary assumptions were also challenged. Postcolonial theorists also disputed the concept of 'religion' itself as a colonial construction imposed on subaltern peoples whose social arrangements and cosmologies were quite differently constituted. This, it was claimed, misrepresented the colonial and post-colonial reality, thus rendering western theories of secularization inapplicable.

From the late 1970s, empirical observation showed a burgeoning of faith traditions outside the developed world, notably an Islamic revival and the growth and global spread of the Pentecostal movement, initially in Latin America from the 1960s and subsequently in Asia and sub-Saharan Africa. Some scholars saw these developments as a clear refutation of the theory of inevitable secularization (Martin 1990; Berger 1999). Others continued to defend the 'classical' theory arguing that these movements were themselves evidence that these societies were not 'modern', (implying a circular definition of secularization not testable by empirical evidence, and of Pentecostalism and Islam as intrinsically 'pre-modern'); and/or that their growth demonstrated the 'transitional' state of societies which had not yet arrived at the 'stage' of rational rather than metaphysical and religious knowledge even if their economies and state structures had modern features (Bruce 2011).

The migrations from the global South to the developed North Atlantic and European countries have accelerated in recent decades, particularly since 1990. One result is that the most flourishing Christian congregations in the cities of the Global North tend to be either diaspora migrant churches or non-denominational megachurches. Both types are likely to be Pentecostal or evangelical with strong Pentecostal elements. Observers who argue that the growth of such churches reverses the acknowledged secularization trends in the developed North (Goodhew 2012) are challenged by those who see these flourishing Pentecostal congregations as essentially a phenomenon of migration from the Global South rather than indigenous or indigenizing in the Global North (Okyerefo 2014). The 'Pentecostalization' of many mainstream churches, including the Roman Catholic Church, particularly through the 'charismatic' movement, also tends to make 'Pentecostalized' local churches growth points, contrasting with the secularizing trends apparent elsewhere (Gooren 2010).

The second set of arguments about Pentecostalism and secularization concerns the extent to which Pentecostalism itself is subject to secularization as it matures over time. Some observers regard Pentecostalism itself as displaying a process of secularization (Togaresei 2015). Successive waves of Pentecostal growth are sometimes thought to show organizational and theological developments which make greater accommodation to the values of the wider society than did the 'classical', 'world-denying' Pentecostal churches from the early decades of the twentieth century (Robbins 2018). The neo-Pentecostal churches of the third wave of Pentecostal growth, particularly from the 1990s, which developed a Prosperity Gospel, (also associated with a sector of American conservative Evangelicalism), saw material prosperity and personal well-being as prominent among the gifts of the Spirit. To critical observers this could appear 'secularizing' or even as specific accommodation to neo-liberal capitalist values (Gifford 2004). To others it was evidence of the 'Christianization' and integration of indigenous cosmologies into local variants of Pentecostalism in many parts of the Global South (Kalu 2008).

The increasing evidence of educated middle-class and business class membership of Pentecostal churches might also be regarded as a mark of secularization in the sense of accommodating to a business ethic or developing more intellectually sophisticated theologies and modes of social presentation. Until the 1960s Pentecostal churches were largely the churches of the poor and took pride in valuing the spiritual above the material. 'Classical' Pentecostalism enforced a rigorous code of sexual behavior which involved strict dress and behavioral codes and insulated members from involvement in all forms of popular and commercial culture. This has been progressively relaxed over the last few decades especially as significant sectors of the younger generations of Pentecostals became educationally and socially mobile. The distinctive 'look' and manners of the older Pentecostal generations was often experienced as stigmatizing in no longer reflecting the rising status of mobile younger Pentecostals (Lindhardt 2016). In some places, particularly the large cities of Asia, including China, and Africa, the middle classes among Pentecostal congregations also include new converts from other faiths (or none) rather than being solely the result of social mobility within established Pentecostal congregations. In many places there are now churches designed to meet the requirements of these new middle classes, including in China (Cao 2011). There is cumulative evidence that the boundaries separating the Pentecostal congregation from the wider world which once confined acts of charity and mutual support to the group, have become more porous. This includes the development of social and welfare initiatives which reach out to the wider society (Miller and Yamamori 2007) and even co-operation with international aid programs run by NGOs, for instance initiatives to control the spread of AIDS (van Dijk et al. 2014).

Some observers see any relaxation of the strict perfectionism of early Pentecostalism not so much as 'inner secularization' as evidence of movement from sect towards denomination, (as applied to Pentecostalism in the 1960s and 1970s by Bryan Wilson); while others regard Pentecostalism, like its holiness and Methodist antecedents, as denominational *ab initio* (Martin 1990).

Bibliography

Berger, Peter L., ed. 1999. *The Desecularization of the World: The Resurgence of Religion in World Politics*. Grand Rapids, MI: Eerdmans.

Bruce, Steve. 2011. *Secularization: In Defence of an Unfashionable Theory*. Oxford: Oxford University Press.

Cao, Nanlai. 2011. *Constructing China's Jerusalem: Christians, Power and Place in Contemporary Wenzhou*. Stanford, CA: Stanford University Press.

Gifford, Paul. 2004. *Ghana's New Christianity: Pentecostalism in a Globalising African Economy*. London: Hurst.

Goodhew, David, ed. 2012. *Church Growth in Britain 1980 to the Present*. Farnham: Ashgate.

Gooren, Henri. 2010. "The Pentecostalization of Religion and Society." *Exchange* 39 (4): 355–376.

Kalu, Ogbu. 2008. *African Pentecostalism: An Introduction*. Oxford: Oxford University Press.

Lindhardt, Martin, ed. 2016. *New Ways of Being Pentecostal in Latin America*. Lanham MD: Lexington.

Martin, David. 1990. *Tongues of Fire: The Explosion of Protestantism in Latin America*. Oxford: Blackwell.

Miller, Donald, and Tatsunao Yamamori. 2007. *Global Pentecostalism: The New Face of*

Christian Social Engagement. Berkeley, CA: University of California Press.

Okyerefo, Michael Perry Kweku. 2014. "African Churches in Europe." *Journal of Africana Religions* 2 (1): 95–124.

Robbins, Roger G., ed. 2018. "Special Issue: Global Trajectories in Global Pentecostalism: Culture, Social Engagement and Change." *Religion* 9: 368 et seq.

Togarasei, Lovemore. 2007. "Modern/Charismatic Pentecostalism as a Form of 'Religious' Secularisation in Africa." *Studia Historiae Ecclesiasticae* 41 (1): 55–66.

Dijk, Rijk van, et al., eds. 2014. *Religion and AIDS Treatment in Africa: Saving Souls, Prolonging Lives*. London: Routledge.

Bernice Martin

Sexuality

As a global phenomenon, with no centralised ecclesiastical government, Pentecostalism has no single, unified position or theology of sexuality. This entry focuses on the majority view of Pentecostals on sexuality.

Pentecostal views on sexuality are grounded in two connected concepts: a restorationist orientation, and a spirit-body dualism. Early twentieth-century Pentecostals regarded their movement as a restoration of first-century Christianity. Grounded in a common-sense realist biblical hermeneutic, and holding the belief that doctrine and the Holy Spirit would always confirm the 'plain meaning of Scripture', Pentecostals tend to regard biblical narratives of glossolalia, healing, and exorcism as not only historical, but also normative today (Wacker 2001, 70–76). Similarly, many Pentecostals have uncritically assumed a continuity between the moral norms and mores of the writers of the New Testament and the modern world.

Based in part on this restorationist orientation, Pentecostals tend to hold a spirit-body dualism, with a strong theological priority on the spirit. Demonic spiritual forces can infiltrate and control the human body, and thus the body is often perceived as the physical site for a battle between the spiritual forces of good and evil (Wilkinson 2017, 26). Human sinfulness, as well as demonic forces, may be regarded as the cause of physical ailments or psychological issues, rectifiable through supernatural healing. Pentecostals generally advocate the disciplining of sexual desire, requiring strict celibacy prior to marriage.

Within monogamous, heterosexual marriage, however, Pentecostals celebrate the exuberant enjoyment of healthy sexual union. What counts as "healthy" (that is, not sinful) sexual enjoyment would in many cases exclude practices deemed perverse, such as role-playing, anal sex (either heterosexual or homosexual – see below) or bondage, discipline, and sadomasochist (BDSM) sexuality. Pentecostals generally permit the use of birth control within marital relations, but almost universally condemn abortion. In some contexts, Pentecostal teaching on heteronormative marital sexuality may reinforce gender-based distinctions, wherein women are encouraged to please husbands in order to prevent infidelity, while men are simply urged to practice self-control (Quiroz 2016). However, this is certainly not an issue unique to Pentecostal teaching.

Beyond monogamous, heterosexual marriage, Pentecostals tend to align with conservative societal and religious norms. Pornography is generally condemned as sinful, based on a common sense literal interpretation of Matthew 5:28.

Historically, Pentecostals have taken the view that masturbation is likewise sinful and immoral, although attitudes in some modern contexts are shifting toward a regard of lustful thoughts and fantasy as sinful, rather than simply the act itself. Similarly, and ostensibly grounded upon a literal reading of texts such as Romans 1:24–32 (where Paul refers to same-sex intercourse as "unnatural" and "shameless"), Pentecostals have generally regarded non-heteronormative sexuality as immoral and prohibited. In the past, it was not uncommon for same-sex desire and viewing of pornography to be attributed to demons, as some early Pentecostals took the view that sinful human sexuality itself is a battleground for spiritual warfare, in need of divine intervention and healing.

Pentecostal beliefs regarding the availability of healing today, coupled with the view that same-sex attraction can be a manifestation of spiritual malaise, has meant in the past that Pentecostals have regarded praying for the healing or exorcism of LGBTQ people as an inclusive and compassionate act. This is particularly accurate if coupled with the belief that someone engaging in same-sex intercourse may not only be risking God's displeasure in present existence, but may experience damnation in the afterlife. This may help explain why many LGBTQ Pentecostals continue to seek out "conversion therapy" or "SOCE" (Sexual Orientation Change Efforts) – a form of quasi-psychological intervention designed to 'convert' same-sex attracted people to heteronormativity – despite the fact that its harmful effects are well documented. While SOCE is not a uniquely Pentecostal practice, specific features of Pentecostal SOCE have often included prayer ministry and exorcism (Barton 2012; Jennings 2018).

More recently, many modern Pentecostals (also known as neo-Pentecostals) have moved beyond the absolute rejection of non-heteronormative sexuality held in previous generations. While some modern neo-Pentecostals may continue to hold that same-sex attraction can be 'healed,' many now adopt a position emerging from Evangelical Christianity, usually referred to as "welcoming but not affirming." In practice, this means that LGBTQ people are welcome to attend Pentecostal churches, but their sexuality cannot be 'affirmed.' LGBTQ people who are "welcome but not affirmed" may report spiritual experiences within their congregations, but unless they commit to celibacy from any same-sex relations, they generally cannot hold ministry positions. While some LGBTQ neo-Pentecostals have reported thriving in non-affirming churches, many experience exclusion and rejection. Bernadette Barton's research indicates that LGBTQ Christians may experience the "toxic closet" in such churches, longing to be fully known and accepted but fearing being exposed and shunned (Barton 2012).

A minority of neo-Pentecostal churches would identify as "affirming," wherein LGBTQ people are invited to participate fully in the ministry, volunteering, and other aspects of the life and community of church, whether they are in same-sex relationships or not. Within many of these churches, monogamous sexual relationships, preferably within marriage, would still be regarded as mandatory. Pentecostals tend to condemn mutually consensual multiple-partner relationships (i.e. 'polyamory'), once again citing Scripture as morally binding today (for example, 1 Timothy 3:2), and in some contexts Pentecostal sexuality represents the monogamous alternative in which polygamy (particularly polygyny) is the cultural norm (Quiroz 2016).

Bibliography

Barton, Bernadette. 2012. *Pray the Gay Away: The Extraordinary Life of Bible Belt Gays*. New York: New York University Press.

Jennings, Mark A.C. 2018. "Impossible Subjects: LGBTIQ Experiences in Australian Pentecostal-Charismatic Churches." *Religions* 9 (2): 53. https://doi.org/10.3390/rel9020053.

Quiroz, Sitna. 2016. "The Dilemmas of Monogamy: Pleasure, Discipline and the Pentecostal Moral Self in the Republic of Benin." *Religions* 7 (8): 102. https://doi.org/10.3390/rel7080102.

Wacker, Grant. 2001. *Heaven Below: Early Pentecostals and American Culture*. Cambridge, MA: Harvard University Press.

Wilkinson, Michael. 2017. "Pentecostalism, the Body, and Embodiment." In *Pentecostals and the Body*, edited by Michael Wilkinson and Peter Althouse, 17–35. Leiden: Brill.

Mark Jennings

Seymour, William

William J. Seymour (1870–1922) was born to former slaves Simon and Phyllis Salabar in Centerville, Louisiana, on May 2. He and his seven brothers and sisters attended the Catholic Church of the Assumption in Franklin before attending New Providence Baptist Church in Centerville. In the 1890s, like thousands of other southern Blacks, he traveled north along the routes of the former Underground Railroad and lived variously in Memphis, TN, St. Louis, MO, Indianapolis, IN, Cincinnati, OH, and elsewhere. He attended the all-Black Simpson Chapel Methodist Episcopal

William Joseph Seymour, 1870–1922.
Source: Pentecostal Assemblies of Canada Archives

Church in Indianapolis, where he became a born-again Christian. During that time, Seymour was influenced by Daniel S. Warner's Evening Lights Saints, later called the Church of God Reformation Movement. This radical Holiness group promoted racial equality and reconciliation at the height of Jim Crow Segregation and regularly evangelized and served in the Black community. After a bout with small pox that left Seymour blind in one eye and pox marks on his face that he covered with a light beard, he responded to God's calling and was ordained an evangelist by the

Evening Lights Saints. In 1904–1905, he visited Holiness leader Charles Price Jones in Louisiana before moving to Houston in 1905, where he hoped to reconnect with family members lost during slavery. In Houston he was introduced by Lucy Farrow to Charles Fox Parham, and attended his Houston Bible School for two to six weeks, where he was asked to respect Texas segregation laws by sitting in the hallway or an adjacent room. After soaking up Parham's teachings that speaking in tongues was the initial physical evidence of Spirit baptism, Seymour and Parham jointly carried out evangelistic work in the Black community for a short period of time.

However, as Seymour became increasingly aware of Parham's unique racial, social, and theological views (annihilationism, 8th Day Creation, and British Israelism), he decided to accept an invitation to pastor a Black Holiness mission in Los Angeles. Seymour arrived on February 22, 1906 and preached about Spirit baptism, a belief that the interim pastor Julia Hutchins found unbiblical. She therefore expelled him from the mission on March 4. On April 6, Seymour started a ten-day fast for revival at Richard and Ruth Asberry's home at 214 Bonnie Brae Street. On April 9, Seymour prayed for Ed Lee to receive the Spirit baptism and Lee began to speak in tongues. A few days later, Seymour, Jennie Evans Moore (pianist), and others received the Spirit baptism on April 12. Within just a few days the prayer meeting erupted into a revival that outgrew the Neely's home and they moved to the former St. Steven's African Methodist Episcopal Church at 312 Azusa Street, in the Black section of Los Angeles. On April 14, several Black women from the prayer group prayed for a Mexican in the mission to receive the Holy Spirit, which was the first supernatural manifestation of the Spirit at the Azusa Mission. Seymour led the first service at the mission in the following day. The revival started off as a prayer meeting and grew rapidly, attracting upwards of 1,200 people per night. The services ran three times per day for three years straight from April 15, 1906 to 1909, though the exact ending date that year is unknown. Later in April, a Mexican man with club foot was the first person reportedly healed of his ailment at the Azusa Mission.

Thousands of people attended from across the U.S. and around the world, especially missionaries on furlough. Some 20 nationalities participated, with white, Black, and Mexican immigrants/Americans being the most prominent. "Hundreds" of Catholics attended, "many" of whom were Latinos. According to eyewitness Arthur Osterberg, they were among the first to receive the Holy Spirit. Latinos like Abundio and Rosa López, Susie Villa Valdez and her son A.C., and many other Latinos helped transform a largely biracial, national, and English-language prayer meeting on Bonnie Brae Street into a multiracial, international, and multilinguistic revival on Azusa Street. Seymour ordained at least three Latinos to the ministry, including Abundio López. Susie Villa Valdez and Emma Osterberg along with many others also carried out evangelistic social work in the slums of Los Angeles and in Mexican migrant farm labor camps in Riverside and San Bernardino.

The revival attracted many clergy, pastors, evangelists, and Christian workers seeking spiritual renewal. This helps to explain why by 1915, Azusa missionaries had spread the Pentecostal revival to over 50 countries and almost every town over 3,000 in population in the U.S. In 1906,

Seymour sent missionaries to Sweden, Liberia, South Africa, China, and India and countless others thereafter until his death in 1922. The stories of the revival and Seymour's theological teachings were spread through the 405,000 copies of the *Apostolic Faith* newspaper between 1906 and 1908.

The most distinctive qualities of Seymour's revival were its emphases on having a personal conversion experience with Jesus Christ, being baptized with the Holy Spirit, the practice of most of the spiritual gifts listed in I Corinthians 12 and 14 except apostleship, a focus on spiritual renewal, divine healing, spiritual warfare and exorcisms, powerful enthusiastic worship, music, lengthy services, times of prayer and meditation, and evangelism, missions, and evangelistic social work. The revival attracted women, immigrants, the poor, the handicapped, and the working class and even some from upper class backgrounds. Seymour created a Christian transgressive social space wherein people could cross hitherto prescribed religious, racial, class, educational, and other social boundaries. To nurture and disciple followers, he also provided regular spiritual guidance and mentorship through letter writing, personal visits, his newspaper, and preaching tours across the U.S.

William married Jennie Evans Moore on May 13, 1908 in a private wedding for immediate family only. Seymour never had any biological children, but reportedly had an adopted daughter, though nothing is known about her. Charles Mason later wrote that this led to a rift with Clara Lum (Seymour's newspaper editor and right-hand person) because she reportedly had feelings for him. Shortly thereafter, Lum took the newspaper mailing lists and production effort from Azusa to join Florence Crawford's Apostolic Faith Mission in Portland, Oregon, where she continued the paper under her leadership. After a failed attempt to publish another paper, Seymour gave up on the venture, something which undermined his ability to guide and influence the movement in the U.S. and the world.

After purchasing the mission and for other reasons, tensions arose with some white leaders like Charles Parham, Florence Crawford, Clara Lum, a Mr. Carpenter, and William Durham. In 1911, Durham led a second Azusa revival and attempted a take-over while Seymour was on a speaking tour back east. Durham was expelled and died from tuberculosis not long thereafter.

In 1913, the Oneness controversy divided the Pentecostal movement in Los Angeles. In 1914, because of the attempted take overs by white Pentecostals, Seymour decided to revise the Azusa Mission Constitution and Articles of Incorporation to state that only people of color could hold the top three leadership posts at the Azusa Mission and in his new Azusa Street Apostolic Faith Mission of Los Angeles denomination. In 1915, he published his Doctrines and Disciplines minister's manual, which lays out his theology and ministerial advice. After several attempts to promote racial reconciliation and unity between 1916 and 1919, he organized a fourteenth Azusa anniversary, though only a handful of people attended. Seymour's star and influence had waned because new leaders, churches, and denominations sprung up and because he transformed his Azusa Mission renewal center into its own denomination. Despite his marginalization within the burgeoning Pentecostal movement, he still kept a very active discipleship and mentorship ministry going through letter writing and guest speaking across the U.S.

While dictating a letter to one of his many followers, Seymour died from a heart attack on September 28, 1922. About 200 people attended his funeral. Jennie became the new leader and pastor of the Azusa Mission, but refused the title of Bishop out of honor to her husband and because she did not believe women should serve as bishop. After an attempted takeover by another white man named Griffiths (who claimed to be a Coptic bishop), the Mission suffered financially and went into receivership and was torn down in 1931. Jennie died several years later in 1936 and was buried next to her husband in Evergreen Cemetery in East Los Angeles.

The history of the Pentecostal and Charismatic movement that Seymour helped to create and shape in its earliest years has since blossomed over the past 100 years into denominational, non-denominational, and independent churches. It has grown from 58 million in 1970 to 644 million people, 19,300 denominations, and 1,336,000 congregations around the world in 2020. By 2050, scholars project that there will be 1 billion Pentecostal/Charismatic Christians.

Bibliography

Blumhofer, Edith L. 1989. *The Assemblies of God: A Chapter in the Story of American Pentecostalism, Volume I-To 1941*. Springfield, MO: Gospel Publishing House.

Espinosa, Gastón. 2014. *William J. Seymour and the Origins of Global Pentecostalism*. Durham, NC: Duke University Press.

Goff, James R. Jr. 1988. *Fields White unto Harvest: Charles F. Parham and the Missionary Origins of Pentecostalism*. Fayetteville: University of Arkansas Press.

Robeck, Cecil M. 2006. *The Azusa Street Mission and Revival*. Nashville, TN: Thomas Nelson.

Wacker, Grant. 2001. *Heaven Below: Early Pentecostals and American Culture*. Cambridge, MA: Harvard University Press.

Gastón Espinosa

Shandong Revival, China

The culminating example of Protestant revivalism in early twentieth century China, which began in the early 1930s in Shandong (Shantung) province, spread quickly across parts of North and Central China, and waned around the time of the Japanese invasion in 1937. It demonstrated evident Pentecostal characteristics. Prepared with intensive prayer and preaching meetings, the participants exhibited outbursts of extraordinary religious fervor, often with tearful confession of sins, holy laughter, glossolalia, miraculous healings, and other "gifts of the Holy Spirit."

The movement has two identifiable strings of influence. The originating stream of revivalism came from the mission churches, which gradually gave way to the indigenous leadership. The former stemmed from the work of the Norwegian missionary, Marie Monsen. Having labored in Central China with the Southern Baptists since 1901, Monsen witnessed the lethargy in the church – due to anti-Christian instigations, continual bandit attacks, and the Great Depression turned into an opportunity for revivals. By the end of 1929, Monsen was holding revival meetings for large and mixed groups, focusing on public confessions of sins and

China 1935, Goodwill Center Hartwell

sensational calls for spiritual renewal. At the end of each session, she reportedly stood by the attendants, pressing everyone with the convicting question, "Have you been born again?" As a result, many received Spirit baptism and began their own revival campaigns.

The indigenous influence in the Shandong revival came from the Spiritual Gifts Society (Ling'en hui), a revival movement minimally organized in southern Shandong. It began in 1930, with two members of a local Presbyterian church, Yang Rulin and Sun Zhanyao, who, upon receiving the spiritual gifts, left to start the Independent Chinese Christian Spiritual Gifts Society. By the end of the following year, the movement swept across the extensive parts of Shandong and a host of denominations, with an enthusiastic response from Baptist congregations. In this regard, the Pentecostal revival helped facilitate greater collaborations across denominational lines in Shandong. Most of the revival meetings centered on dramatic public confessions of sins and apocalyptic messages emphasizing the speedy return of the Lord in a violence-torn world. Together with hymns, prayers, healings, and testimonies, they were often packed into a nerve-racking schedule that ran from a few days to two weeks.

Other indigenous factors, though fragmentary in terms of historical records, also contributed to the impressive church growth in Shandong since the early 1930s. For example, Feixian reportedly experienced a revival brought by a Pentecostal pastor Ma Zhaorui as early as 1928. Many Christians were "filled by the Holy Spirit" and organized a dozen of evangelistic bands. However, they met opposition both within and outside of the ecclesiastic community. This halting setback was not overcome by the local rural Christians until six years later, who were then riding on the burgeoning Shandong revival. Other itinerant evangelists were also attracted to the revival. The Bethel Band, headed by Ji Zhiwen (Andrew Gih) and Song Shangjie (John Sung), held successful revival meetings in Jining and Huangxian in the early 1930s. Song himself, having left the Bethel Band, went back to Shandong for more evangelistic meetings in the mid-1930s. While converging with local revivalism on public confessions and long prayers, these nationally-minded revivalists, often invited by urban congregations, focus less on the emotional aspects but the homiletic call to repentance.

In general, the missionary community was divided on the Shandong revival, especially concerning its strong Pentecostal expressions. An early report published in the *China Christian Year Book of 1932–1933* described the emotional meetings as "pandemonium." Later missionary accounts also criticized the revival as "primitive, individualistic, and on the margins of superstition." However, many missionaries also had definite experiences in the revival, documenting how "the Spirit came in mighty power." Rare personal accounts on internal spiritual experience as such came mostly from the missionaries.

While scholars differ on the relationship between the Western Pentecostal force and the Shandong revivals, they tend to recognize the indigenous nature of this Christian movement, as being advanced with autonomous lay leadership and little direct organizational planning. This indigenizing tendency points to the empowering effect of Pentecostalism – since anyone could receive the gifts, ordained pastors or missionaries were no longer deemed indispensable. Also, for this reason, the Shandong revival had a profound impact on future Chinese Christian leaders like Yu Ligong (Moses Yu), who then dedicated himself to the ministry of evangelism at the age of eleven. As Shandong lay in the shadow of the Japanese invasion in the late 1930s, Yu and his fellow evangelists carried the message of healing and repentance to western China. There he would lead a significant student revival in Chongqing, 1945.

Bibliography

Bays, H. Daniel. 1993. "Christian Revival in China, 1900–1937." In *Modern Christian Revivals*, edited by Edith Waldvogel Blumhofer and Randall Herbert Balmer, 161–179. Urbana: University of Illinois Press.

Crawford, K. Mary. 1933. *The Shantung Revival*. Shanghai: China Baptist Publication Society.

Gao, Fude. 1934. *Shandong Fuxing* [The Shandong Revival]. Shanghai: China Baptist Publication Society.

Lian, Xi. 2010. *Redeemed by Fire: The Rise of Popular Christianity in Modern China*. New Haven: Yale University Press.

Tiedemann, R.G. 2012. "Protestant Revivals in China with Particular Reference to Shandong Province." *Studies in World Christianity* 18 (3): 213–236.

Zexi (Jesse) Sun

Shepherding Movement

In the 1970s and early 1980s, the burgeoning Charismatic Renewal in the United States experienced a significant controversy over the teachings and practices of the Shepherding movement. The movement grew out of the association of five popular Bible teachers in the Renewal: Don Basham (Disciples of Christ), Ern Baxter (Canadian Pentecostal), Bob Mumford (Assemblies of God), Derek Prince (British Pentecostal), and Charles Simpson (Southern Baptist Convention). In 1970, the leader of the Ft Lauderdale, Florida based Holy Spirit Teaching Mission (HSTM), publisher of the *New Wine Magazine*, was forced to resign because of charges of immorality. Although the teachers maintained their own independent ministries, Basham, Mumford, Prince, and Simpson had close ties to the HSTM and *New Wine* and were asked to assume leadership as a team. The four, joined by Baxter in 1974, were concerned about the public scandal caused by the leader's alleged failure. They were also concerned about what they believed was the extreme independence of many leaders in the Charismatic Renewal. Chastened by the crisis at the HSTM, the men joined together in mutual submission to one another hoping to assure some measure of accountability for their own ministries. In 1972 the HSTM's name was changed to Christian Growth Ministries.

Soon the teachers began emphasizing the importance of discipleship, submission, and spiritual authority. These teachings were popularized in various media forms and specifically through the growing circulation of *New Wine Magazine* (circulation by the late 1970s was over 100,000) and through the teachers' popularity and influence on the Charismatic speakers circuit. Thousands of independent charismatic leaders/pastors began submitting to Mumford and the others seeing them as their spiritual leaders. Through a series of annual "shepherds" conferences from 1973 to 1975, the five men emphasized the need for accountability for all believers and argued that every Christian needed a personal pastor, or "shepherd," using their term. By 1976 they found themselves leading a growing movement that numbered nearly 50,000 adherents.

The teachings of the movement provoked heated debate as critics charged that the men sought to take over the independent sector of the Charismatic movement and start a new denomination, a charge they adamantly denied. Fueling the debate were allegations and charges that some pastor/shepherds were abusing their spiritual authority and controlling the lives of followers. M.G. "Pat" Robertson banned the five teachers from appearing on his Christian Broadcasting Network, calling the Shepherding teachings outright heresy. Charismatic leaders like David du Plessis, Dennis Bennett, and Demos Shakarian joined Robertson in criticizing the movement's teachings. Conversely, a number of charismatic leaders including Larry Christenson, Kevin Ranaghan, Ralph Martin and others sought to be mediating voices and stood by the five teachers and what they represented.

A number of gatherings of significant leaders in 1975 and 1976 tried without success to resolve the issues surrounding the controversy. Opposition to the movement would continue but became less public during the late 1970s and early 1980s. The Shepherding Movement created tensions that dimmed the ecumenical hopes many had for the Charismatic Renewal and some leaders never participated again in the annual Charismatic leaders conferences. Some leaders chose to start their own unity groups but the subsequent gatherings seldom reflected the diverse character of the Renewal and often were without Catholic participation. Derek Prince quietly left the Shepherding Movement in 1983; the other four ended their relational association in 1986 and ceased publishing *New Wine Magazine*.

Bibliography

McNair Scott, Benjamin G. 2017. *Apostles Today: Making Sense of Contemporary Charismatic Apostolates: A Historical and Theological Appraisal*. Eugene, OR: Wipf & Stock.

Moore, S. David. 2012. "'Discerning the Times': The Victorious Eschatology of the Shepherding Movement." In *Perspectives in Pentecostal Eschatology*, edited by Peter Althouse and Robby Waddel, 273–292. Cambridge: James Clarke & Co.

Moore, S. David. 2003. *The Shepherding Movement: Controversy and Charismatic Ecclesiology*. London: T&T Clark.

S. David Moore

Shouters, China

The "Shouters" or the "Yellers" refers to the ministry initiated by Watchman Nee (Ni Tuosheng, 1903–1972) and Witness Lee (Li Changshou, 1905–1997), which is also called "the Assembly Hall," "the Little Flock," or "Local Church" in different contexts. It also became a label for the "house churches" in China, during the political campaign of the 1980s.

The ministry started from Fuzhou in 1922, with a symbolic ritual of breaking bread. Nee personally was influenced by some evangelists such as Margaret E. Barber (1866–1930) and Dora Yu (Yu Cidu, 1873–1931). Later, he also read broadly the works of the inner life group. Nee developed his ministry in Shanghai through the 1930s, and built a strong friendship with T. Austin-Sparks (1888–1971), founder of the Christian Fellowship Center in London. However, his ministry was influenced by the Plymouth Brethren and in particular, the principle of one church in one city.

As other Chinese independent churches starting in early twentieth century, "the Shouters" is connected with Pentecostalism, partly due to its indigenous or popular characteristics with traditional Chinese religions, such as healing. Watchman Nee's personal spiritual experience as well his classic, *The Spiritual Man*, strengthened this link. In the 1930s, during the Shandong Spiritual Revival, Nee did have some contacts with the Pentecostal movement, but he de-emphasized the gift of speaking in tongues among his followers. Later, he even thought it was a distraction to his ministry.

In the 1950s, when Nee was put into prison, Witness Lee continued and developed his ministry overseas first in Taiwan and later in California. In California he started Living Stream Ministry, which became the headquarters for a global network. When compared with other co-workers of Watchman Nee, Lee distinguished his ministry with some creative practices, such as calling on the Lord's name, prayer-reading the Bible, and prophesying. His work corresponded to the Jesus People Movement in California and was highly successful. But, he was also involved in controversies, both in China and abroad where he was said to be the leader of a cult.

Lee's ministry had a strong egalitarian character featured by the use of terms like brotherhood and sisterhood. His practice of calling on the Lord's name and prayer-reading the Bible was effective in creating an emotional and passionate atmosphere. Like Nee, Lee also highlighted spiritual experiences. With a strong Christian network and a Chinese origin, Lee's ministry shocked the Chinese administration with images of shouting and yelling, hence the references to the Shouters or the Yellers. Followers were accused of calling on Witness Lee's name during meetings. They were also thought to be connected with a later cult, the Eastern Lightening. Lee's co-workers totally denied such accusations.

In short, the ministry of Watchman Nee and Witness Lee may not be solely categorized as Pentecostal, though it shares some characteristics of Pentecostalism such as healing. In particular, they de-emphasized and even denied the practice of speaking in tongues. As other Chinese indigenous churches, they could be defined as "spiritual" or charismatic.

Bibliography

Hu, Jiayin. 2017. "Spirituality and Spiritual Practice: Is the Local Church Pentecostal?" In *Global Chinese Pentecostal and Charismatic Christianity*, edited by Fenggang Yang, Joy K.C. Tong, and Allan H. Anderson, 161–180. Leiden: Brill.

Kinnear, Angus. 1998. *The Story of Watchman Nee: Against the Tide*. Fort Washington, PA: Christian Literature Crusade.

Liu, Yi. 2016. "Globalization of Chinese Christianity: A Study of Watchman Nee and Witness Lee's Ministry." *Asia Journal of Theology* 30 (1): 96–114.

Reetzke, James. 2004. *Recollections with Thanksgiving: A Brief History of the Beginnings of the Lord's Recovery in the United States*. Chicago: Chicago Bibles and Books.

Tang, Edmond. 2011. "'Yellers' and Healers: Pentecostalism and the Study of Grassroots Christianity in China." In *Asian and Pentecostal: The Charismatic Face of Christianity in Asia*, edited by Allan Anderson and Edmond Tang, 379–394. Eugene, OR: Wipf & Stock.

Yi Liu

Sierra Leone

Although contemporary African Pentecostalism only emerged in the 1970s, Sierra Leone's position as the first Protestant mission field where Christianity was reintroduced to tropical Africa is well documented in African church historiography (Olson 1969). This article reviews the liberated Africans's profound impact on West African Christianity and examines the role of para-church agencies and key players in the foundation and development of Pentecostalism in Sierra Leone.

Nestled along the picturesque and leonine mountainous peninsula overlooking the Atlantic coastline in West Africa, Sierra Leone has an established place in Christian history (Land and Shocket 2008). Founded in 1792 by Evangelical British abolitionists, the country played a pivotal role in the emancipation of liberated African slaves and the incarnation of early African Christianity (Ryan 2013). It was to Sierra Leone that the Black Poor, Nova Scotians, Maroons and Re-captive former slaves were resettled and given western education at Fourah Bay College (the first university in Africa founded in 1827), before being dispersed to serve West Africa as clergy, school masters and civil servants in the British colonies (Paracka and Jr 2015). Soon, these liberated slaves whose growing experience in indigenous Christian leadership was gallantly displayed in the Rt. Revd. Dr. Samuel Adjai Crowther (the first black bishop in the Anglican Communion), pioneered the diffusion of Christianity and preservation of the infant church in tropical Africa (Sanneh 2009). The native pastorate, first implemented in Sierra Leone between 1860 and 1890, transformed liberated former slave churches into organized parishes and assemblies (Hanciles 2001), and led to the founding of the Council of Churches in Sierra Leone (CCSL 1924) and the Evangelical Fellowship of Sierra Leone (EFSL, 1959). Collaboration between foreign missionaries and indigenous agents facilitated the initiation of para-church ministries at schools and colleges which inspired the later formation of Pentecostal and Charismatic movements.

The climate of ecumenical cooperation provided exigencies that were suitable for the formation of Pentecostalism. This development began with EFSL's New Life for All evangelistic campaigns which held national crusades in the 1950s and 1960s, preaching the gospel and inviting young people to faith in Christ. Their efforts were bolstered by the Scripture Union of Sierra Leone which was revived by Bill Roberts, a charismatic British missionary. Roberts's reassignment to Sierra Leone in 1970 following a troubled career in Biafra war-stricken Nigeria, saw the reintroduction of vibrant Bible study, prayer, fellowship and national youth camps that attracted scores of students. Other initiatives such as the Sierra Leone Fellowship of Evangelical Students (1982), Youth With a Mission (1987) and the Freetown Bible Training Centre (founded by American Charismatic Evangelist, Russ Tatro in 1990), built on those gains and emphasized the need for believers to be born again, to have a new experience with the Holy Spirit, to engage in spiritual warfare and to attain material and spiritual prosperity. This novel pneumatic emphasis attracted an even wider array of youthful followers and aroused disgust for the failure of existing Protestant missionary and Evangelical churches to deal effectively with spiritual pathologies that blight the profession of faith by African converts. Some of these young people broke ranks with their churches and founded Bible study and prayer fellowships which eventually developed into independent churches that have become major players in the Pentecostal and Charismatic movements. The most prominent of which include: Pastor Francis Mambu's Faith Healing Bible Church (1987), Bishop Abu Koroma's Flaming Evangelical Ministries International (1987), Bishop Akintayo Sam-Jolly's Living Word of Faith Outreach Ministries International (1988), Apostle Mrs Dora Dumbuya's Jesus is Lord Ministries International (1989), Bishop Julius Laggah's Bethel World Outreach Ministries International (1992) and Bishop J.A. Cole's New Life Ministries International (1993) (Bangura 2013). Thus, Pentecostalism in Sierra Leone projects seriousness about Holy Scripture and desires to relate its pristine message to the obfuscating cultural and traditional challenges confronting the Christian life (Bangura 2016b). As such, this new form of Pentecostalism speaks to issues of evil spirits, witchcraft, diminution of life as well as promising prosperity, good health, wealth and spiritual power to those who profess it (Bangura 2016a).

Indigenous African Pentecostalism inspired two developments that transformed Sierra Leone's church scene. First, soon after Pentecostal/Charismatic churches were constituted, they attracted the young, highly educated urban élites who felt that this form of Christianity made sense and addressed spiritual needs. Their skilful integration of the African quest for power, wealth and health in the proclamation of the gospel enhanced their stature as a viable stream which made Pentecostalism a contextually convergent faith. The second was the formation of the Pentecostal Fellowship of Sierra Leone (PFSL) in 2002 whose aim is to coordinate activities and serve the interests of all Pentecostals. Presided over by Bishop J.A. Cole, PFSL sought to promote ecclesiastical networking as well as offer a Pentecostal perspective on important national issues (Bangura 2017; Shaw 2007). Together, these factors opened up Pentecostalism to global missions, where churches have been planted among Sierra Leone's diaspora in the

UK, US, Canada, Germany and Australia, among others.

Bibliography

Bangura, Joseph Bosco. 2017. "Charismatic Movements, State Relations and Public Governance in Sierra Leone." *Studies in World Christianity* 23 (3): 237–256.

Bangura, Joseph Bosco. 2016a. "Hope in the Midst of Death: Charismatic Spirituality, Healing Evangelists and the Ebola Crisis in Sierra Leone." *Mission Missionalia* 44 (1): 2–18.

Bangura, Joseph Bosco. 2016b. "The Gospel in Context: Hiebert's Critical Contextualisation and Charismatic Movements in Sierra Leone: Original Research." *In Die Skriflig* 50 (1): 1–7.

Bangura, Joseph Bosco. 2013. *The Charismatic Movement in Sierra Leone (1980–2010): A Missio-Historical Analysis in View of African Culture, Prosperity Gospel and Power Theology*. Amsterdam: VU University Amsterdam.

Hanciles, Jehu J. 2001. "Anatomy of an Experiment: The Sierra Leone Native Pastorate." *Missiology: An International Review* 29 (1): 63–82.

Land, Isaac, and Andrew M. Shocket. 2008. "New Approaches to the Founding of the Sierra Leone Colony, 1786–1808." *Journal of Colonialism and Colonial History* 9 (3).

Olson, Gilbert W. 1969. *Church Growth in Sierra Leone: A Study of Church Growth in Africa's Oldest Protestant Mission Field*. Grand Rapids, MI: William B. Eerdmans.

Paracka, Daniel J., Jr. 2015. *Athens of West Africa: A History of International Education at Fourah Bay College*. Freetown, Sierra Leone: Routledge.

Ryan, Maeve. 2013. "'A Most Promising Field for Future Usefulness': The Church Missionary Society and the Liberated Africans of Sierra Leone." In *A Global History of Anti-slavery Politics in the Nineteenth Century*, edited by William Mulligan and Maurice Bric, 37–58. London: Palgrave Macmillan.

Sanneh, Lamin. 2009. *Abolitionists Abroad American Blacks and the Making of Modern West Africa*. London: Harvard University Press.

Shaw, Rosalind. 2007. "Displacing Violence: Making Pentecostal Memory in Postwar Sierra Leone." *CUAN Cultural Anthropology* 22 (1): 66–93.

Bosco Bangura

Simpson, William Wallace

William W. Simpson (1869–1961) arrived in China as a Christian and Missionary Alliance (CMA) missionary in 1892 and spent most of the next 57 years there. He was no relation to the CMA founder A.B. Simpson. When Pentecostal phenomena broke out in north-west China at a CMA convention in Taozhou, Gansu in 1912, Simpson and his wife Otilia were baptized in the Spirit. They passed on their Pentecostal experience to many CMA churches in Gansu and their testimony was published in the official CMA's *Alliance Weekly*. Their Tibetan Border district was greatly affected by this Pentecostal revival. The Simpsons' annual report at the end of 1912 stated that there had been "many cases of instantaneous and remarkable healings" and that "more than thirty have received the Holy Spirit accompanied by speaking in tongues and prophesying."

This was the time of controversy within the CMA over Pentecostal experience, and Simpson's dogmatism caused his relations with the CMA to sour. He resigned in 1914 "because they required us to subscribe to unscriptural teaching about the Baptism in Holy Spirit." He applied to join the British Pentecostal Missionary Union (PMU) led by Cecil Polhill. The PMU Council expressed support for his Pentecostal position but were cautious over his dealings with his former mission and the China Inland Mission, whose Board Polhill was still a member of. Simpson travelled about CMA stations praying for missionaries and Chinese pastors to be baptized with the Spirit, later claiming that "nearly all" the Chinese leaders had received Spirit baptism "according to Acts 2." Simpson wrote to Polhill that several Chinese workers in Gansu (including three pastors) would leave the CMA and asked Polhill if the PMU could take on the entire work. The PMU realized the sensitivity of this and did not do so, and by 1915 Simpson had joined the new American Assemblies of God. In a printed circular distributed to various missionaries, Simpson wrote that he hoped "to carry the Pentecostal Baptism and the faith once for all delivered to the saints all over Northern and Central China, to every part of Mandarin speaking China where Pentecost has not fallen." This circular provoked CIM director D.E. Hoste to write to Polhill in January 1915 to complain about Simpson's "propaganda", as Simpson had named Polhill and other prominent Pentecostals as character references. Polhill had a serious dilemma, as several other missionaries in China had already left the CIM and the CMA to become Pentecostals. But he defended Simpson and distanced himself from the recent anti-Pentecostal stance of the CIM.

After he left the CMA Simpson travelled to Shanghai for a while and visited the Door of Hope rescue mission for prostitutes in Shanghai, where Pentecostal pioneer Antoinette Moomau had meetings. He helped open a new work in Nanjing where Chinese preacher Nathan C.S. Ma and his wife were working, a year later running a girls' school. One of the missionary couples Simpson recruited was Leslie and Ava Anglin, Free Baptists who established a community called the House of Onesiphorus, with workshops, schools and orphanage, eventually affiliating with the Assemblies of God. Simpson returned to the USA in 1915 and for two years led the newly-established Bethel Bible School in Newark, New Jersey. He returned to China in 1918 after the death of his wife Otilia and made his base in Minzhou, Gansu. He travelled throughout China and became one of the best-known Pentecostal missionaries. His letters brimmed with confidence in the progress of his work. By January 1920 he reported that there were ten "Assemblies" with about three hundred members spread over three counties, and had 24 students in his Bible school. Two Chinese preachers, Wei Chen-mo and Feng Tsi-hsin had started a new congregation to the south of Minzhou. Other early full-time preachers in Simpson's mission were Chow Feng Ling, pastor of a congregation in Taozhou (Simpson's former CMA mission base), Meng Mingshi at Minzhou, and Mei Paochen at a congregation in Titao. These preachers came from other churches, as Simpson stated that they had been Christians for between 12 and 16 years. Later in 1920 Simpson reported four hundred baptized in the Spirit and a total of a thousand people connected with the Assemblies of God in the province of Gansu. He was committed to training and encouraging Chinese leaders, which became his life's work. He married Martha (another missionary) in 1925 and remained working in China until the Communist takeover in 1949, when he returned to the USA at the age of eighty. Much of his itinerant preaching and teaching all over China was done on foot, and he assisted in the training of many Chinese ministers, especially at the

Truth Bible Institute established in Beijing in 1936.

Bibliography

Anderson, Allan. 2007. *Spreading Fires: The Missionary Nature of Early Pentecostalism.* London: SCM Press.

Allan H. Anderson

Singapore

Pentecostalism in Singapore has been shaped by the forces of colonialism, nationalism, industrialization, and material affluence, all within a span of a few decades. This compression of economic development, coupled with openness to global theological influences, has injected local Pentecostalism with both transnational and indigenising characteristics. Indeed, Pentecostalism's ability to harness local cultures and energies with a global spirituality has allowed it to navigate transnational boundaries and vernacular languages with relative ease. Approximately 18 percent of Singapore's population profess to be Christian (Department of Statistics 2010). Out of this, an estimated 220,000 are Catholics and 350,000 are Protestants. The exact number of Pentecostals is difficult to ascertain because Pentecostalism does vary and exists as distinct churches or as fringe congregations in mainline denominations. Nevertheless, the conventional definition of Pentecostalism is the emphasis on the deeply personal spiritual experience of God, baptism of the Holy Spirit, expressive worship, belief in signs and miracles, and the speaking of tongues or glossolalia (Anderson 2004). Nonetheless, according to some estimates, there are about 150,000 Charismatic Pentecostals in Singapore (Johnson and Zurlo 2010).

As an island open to the flows of people, capital and ideas, Singapore has seen its fair share of Pentecostal revivals. Early revivals at the turn of the twentieth century include the visit of Chinese itinerant evangelist John Sung to the colonial entrepot in 1935. Sung preached 40 times in 14 days at the Telok Ayer Methodist Church located in the Chinese quarter. Sung's ability to blend his Mandarin sermons with the vivid dramatization of parables and songs to reach out to the downtrodden masses, many of whom were giving up hope of ever returning to China, was instrumental in converting many Chinese residents. This Pentecostal revival was a working class one that swept through the community of indentured immigrants, a world away from the Anglican and Methodist churches of British colonials.

For the next few decades as the country experienced merger with Malaysia and independence shortly after, local Pentecostalism was shaped by the spiritual reverberations from larger revivals in greater Asia (Chong and Goh 2014). A more locally distinct Pentecostal Charismatic revival made itself felt in the 1970s and 1980s. By this time Singapore was an industrialising country that was already seeing the fruits of economic progress. Key events in this local revival were the Billy Graham Crusade (1978) and Reinhard Bonnke Mission (1987) in which thousands of Singaporeans were converted. These two events were coordinated by churches from several different denominations on a national scale and were instrumental in entrenching Pentecostal practices deeper in local churches.

The 1990s saw rapid Pentecostal growth in Singapore. There are several reasons for this. Firstly, the Pentecostal Charismatic revival of the 1970s and 1980s not only served to renew the faith and introduce Pentecostal beliefs to many older mainline Singaporean Christians, but also saw the conversion of young dynamic well-educated Singaporeans who would become more active in the 1990s. Secondly, Pentecostalism, with greater emphasis on a personal relationship with God and the individualistic religious-ecstatic experience, was ideal in filling the gap left behind by the decline of liberal and socially activistic Christianity due to state suppression and restrictions (Goh 2010). Thirdly, strong economic growth in much of Asia and the expansion of the middle class saw the rise of the megachurch, which served as an important vehicle for the growth of Pentecostalism.

Beyond its size, the megachurch is usually non-denominational or loosely tied to a mainline denomination, practices Pentecostal or charismatic beliefs such as the baptism of the Holy Spirit, gifts of the Spirit including the speaking of tongues, as well as emphasis on the religious-ecstatic experience. Pentecostal megachurches also exhibit ease with popular culture, music, media, and mass consumption. They are "not only very large churches that experiment with tradition, liturgy and doctrine, but also draw on popular culture and a consumerist logic in order to attract an audience more familiar with rock and roll, shopping malls, and self-help culture than with traditional church liturgies, hymns, or symbols" (Ellingson 2010: 247). The biggest megachurches in Singapore are City Harvest Church, New Creation Church, Lighthouse Evangelism, and Faith Community Baptist Church. They share characteristics such as youthful congregations, charismatic leadership, Pentecostal beliefs, experiential worship, and denominational independence.

The growth of Pentecostalism in Singapore should come as no surprise. It has demonstrated the dual ability to be transnational in crossing cultural boundaries while indigenising itself with local traditions and practices. Whether in the form of itinerant preachers reaching out to Chinese immigrants in the early twentieth century to the adroit use of popular culture in megachurches, Pentecostalism is successful because it has relied on adaptive innovations and the zeal of local believers to grow. This has resulted in the retention of a broad global identity that is coupled with deep local relevance.

Bibliography

Anderson, Allan. 2004. *An Introduction to Pentecostalism*. Oxford: Oxford University Press.

Chong, Terence, and Goh, Daniel P.S. 2014. "Asian Pentecostalism: Renewals, Megachurches, and Social Engagement." In *Handbook of Religions in Asia*, edited by Bryan Turner and Oscar Salemink, 402–417. London: Routledge.

Ellingson, Stephen. 2010. "New Research on Megachurches: Non-denominationalism and Sectarianism." In *The New Blackwell Companion to the Sociology of Religion*, edited by Bryan S. Turner, 245–266. Oxford: Wiley-Blackwell.

Goh, Daniel P.S. 2010. "The State and Social Christianity in Postcolonial Singapore." *SOJOURN* 25 (1): 54–89.

Johnson, Todd M., and Gina A. Zurlo, eds. 2010. *World Christian Database*. Leiden: Brill.

Singapore Department of Statistics. 2010. *Singapore Census of Population 2010: Advance Census Release*. Singapore: Department of Statistics.

Terence Chong

Slovakia

The beginnings of the Pentecostal movement in Slovakia are related to Juraj Zelman, who participated in the Pentecostal movement in the USA. He helped to spread Pentecostal teachings through Apostolic Faith Mission literature. Similarly, Jan Balca took part in Norway's pentecostal movement and later assisted with a visit of Pentecostal missionaries from Sweden in Bratislava. Juraj Zelman gained his pentacostal experience through Jan Gaj, who settled in the USA and was active in the Church of God. Many small Pentecostal groups were created that eventually gradually grew and spread throughout the country.

The first Pentecostal fellowship was founded in 1924 in Lapaské Darmoty (renamed to Golianovo). Another fellowship was established in 1928 in the town of Uhrovec. Every region in Slovakia had a Pentecostal congregation or a mission group prior to WWII. Generally, Pentecostal Missions were more successful in Slovakia than in the Czech Republic (both as separate countries and as regions of former Czechoslovakia, from 1918 to 1992, with a break during WWII).

With the beginning of the Communist era shortly after WWII, anti-church laws were adopted and all activities of the movement became illegal. After a series of protests, Pentecostal churches in Slovak were forced to join the New Apostolic Church (Novoapoštolská cirkev) which was registered in Czechoslovakia, even though there was no link – the New Apostolic Church was founded by Edward Irving. The Communist regime generally refused to grant registration to any new churches and did not distinguish between the diverse and various origins of churches.

With the easing of the political situation in 1968, the Czechoslovak Republic became a federation, which meant a certain independence for both republics. The Pentecostal Church in Slovakia then consolidated under the name of the Apostolic Church and were more or less tolerated (unlike the church in the Czech Republic). After 1977, with a new leadership under Milan Bednar, the situation improved. The Church was lead by Josef Brenkus from 1988 until he died in 1999. In 2000, the new bishop was Ján Lacho.

The Revolution of 1989 made extensive mission activity possible. The Apostolic Church continued growing and presently has over 36 local churches and more than 20 mission stations. Altogether, it has about 5831 members (Brenkus 2011). Moreover, the inflow of foreign missionaries resulted in a creation of many small independent Pentecostal churches, such as Unitas Fratrum in Slovakia (Jednota bratská na Slovensku), Vineyard Christian Fellowship (Kresťanské spoločenstvo Vinica), Faith Church – Christian Fellowship Humenné (Cirkev viery – Kresťanské spoločenstvo Humenné), Manna Church (Cirkev Manna), Christian Fellowship Joyful Heart (Spoločenstvo kresťanov Radostné srdce), Blue Cross (Modrý kríž), and others. The largest independent Pentecostals, numbering about several thousand adherents, are the Christian Fellowships (Kresťanská spoločenstvá) and the Word of Life (Slovo života).

All of these church bodies are registered as Civic Associations. This is because on 1 January 1993, Czechoslovakia peacefully divided into two independent republics. While the largely secularized Czech Republic has allowed state registration for comparatively small churches, in Slovakia there was a strong opposition from the Catholic Church, which negotiated a profitable financial settlement between the State and the registered churches. In addition, in 2007 Slovakia adopted a restrictive amendment to the Law of State Registration of Churches and Religious Institutions that required 20,000 members to obtain state registration. This practically eliminated the registration of any new churches. Another restriction came with the March 2017 amendment, which increased the registration minimum to 50,000 members. Small church fellowships could not take advantage of state church registration and had to be registered as Civic Associations.

The Word of Life church, initally pastored by Ulf Ekman in Uppsala, Sweden, and other new Pentecostal leaders like Pastor Sándor Németh, from the Fellowship of Faith (Hit Gyülekezete) in Budapest, Hungary have had a significant influence on the Christian Fellowships. Two important figures to influence these churches are Kenneth Hagin and Derek Prince. After Ulf Ekman's conversion to Roman Catholocism (viewed as a failure in these circles), Sándor Németh became a key leader of the Faith Movement in Europe. The Christian Fellowships are now led by Pastor Jaroslav Kříž from Banská Bystrica. This fellowship is known for its long-term legal struggle to obtain state registration for social recognition and the financial benefits that go with it. However, this remains impossible not only because of the inability to meet the conditions for state registration, but also due to the controversies surrounding the Faith Movement.

Bibliography

Brenkus, Jozef. 2011. "The Pentecostal Movement in the Czech Republic and Slovakia." In *European Pentecostalism, Global Pentecostal and Charismatic Studies*, edited by Andrew Davies and William K. Kay, 248–259. Leiden: Brill.

Brenkus, Josef. 2000. "A Historical and Theological Analysis of the Pentecostal Church in the Czech and Slovak Republics." *Journal of the European Pentecostal Theological Association* 20 (1): 49–65.

Halasová, Tereza. 2015. "Divergence české a slovenské konfesněprávní úpravy: Vývoj od roku 2007." [Divergence of religious law in the Czech Republic and Slovakia: Development from 2007]. Studie a texty Evangelické teologické fakulty, Teologická východiska evropské kulturní identity 26 (2): 133–151.

Moďoroši, Ivan. 2012. Book Reviews. *Ľubomír Martin Ondrášek, Neocharizmatické hnutie na Slovensku: Analýza základných aspektov teológie a praxe Kresťanských spoločenstiev* [The Neocharismatic Movement in Slovakia: an Analysis of the Fundamental Aspects of Theology and Practice of the Christian Fellowship]. (Bratislava, Slovakia: Institute for State-Church Relations, 2011), 267 pp. Pneuma 34 (3): 431–432. DOI: 10.1163/15700747-12341240.

Moravčíková, Michaela, and Eleonóra Valová, eds. 2010. *Financing Churches and Religious Societies in the 21st Century*. Institute for State-Church Relations, Bratislava: SVK.

Ondrasek, Ľubomir Martin. 2011. *Neocharizmatické hnutie na Slovensku: Analýza základných apektov teológie a praxe Kresťanských spoločenstiev*. Bratislava: Ústav pre vzťahy štátu a cirkví.

Ondrasek, Ľubomir Martin. 2009. "On Religious Freedom in the Slovak Republic." *Occasional Papers on Religion in Eastern Europe (OPREE)* 29 (3): 1–9.

Schmidgall, Paul. 2013. *European Pentecostalism: Its Origins, Development, and Future*. Cleveland, TN: CPT Press.

Tereza Halasová

Socialization

Socialization is a theory found in the social sciences, especially sociology and social psychology, that seeks to explain how people become members of social groups and move from the outside to the inside. In terms of religion, it explains the ways in which people become members of a group and adopt the beliefs, values, and practices of the group, eventually becoming advocates for the religious beliefs themselves (Berger 1969). Very often there is a differentiation made between primary and secondary socialization. Primary socialization refers to the basic processes that children experience as they are born into a family and learn how to be a family member as well as a member of the larger society. Parents are the mediators of the familial and cultural norms; and children learn these norms from parents and other family members. Secondary socialization processes often refer to wider social institutions, such as schools, social and sports clubs, as well as religious groups that also socialize children into membership and participation. Essentially, socialization refers to the process whereby individuals become members of groups and these include religious groups as well as broader cultural identities because very often these affiliations and identities are intertwined.

There are various factors that influence the process of socialization. These include significant others, which initially would be parents or guardians, and then teachers and leaders to whom the individuals look for guidance and inspiration. These people embody the norms and values of the group and show how to be a member. In other words, they are exemplary. In religious groups, these people can be placed in formal roles like priests and pastors, but they can also be significant lay leaders exercising considerable informal authority. Provided that they mediate authority and influence to would-be members they could qualify as significant others. There are also peer groups and they form an immediate social reference cluster that supports the assimilation of beliefs and values, norms and practices by the individual as he or she takes on the life of the group for themselves (McGuire 2002, 37–39, 195–201). Peers are especially important for specific groups of people, for example, teenagers are especially indebted to peers for approval and acceptance by groups.

There are also wider influences that are mediated through the cultural practices and artefacts of the group. These can be through the symbolic worlds of texts, such as books and magazines, or through music and events, as well as buildings such as churches that display messages through their architecture and furnishings (White 1977). Very often these artefacts and cultural practices illuminate particular ways in which beliefs and values are embodied, presented and articulated within religious cultures. They facilitate membership and are used to draw boundary lines between who is an insider and who is an outsider, for example through rites of initiation.

In all of the many aspects of the socialization process, there is individual agency. Sometimes this agency can be compromised and strong socialization pressure can minimize agency as individuals seeks to conform to the expectations of the group. In so doing, they put aside or minimize their personal preferences and interests to fit in with the group. At other times, they place themselves at the margins of the group because when one is closer to the periphery there is greater freedom, even if such a location means that there is always the temptation by the powers to consider the individual as not fully assimilated or a rebel of some kind (Danzinger 1971).

There are basically two scholars who are known for having considered the theory of socialization and Pentecostalism. The first is William J. Samarin, who, through his work on the nature of glossolalia (speaking in tongues) in the late 1960s and early 1970s, argued that tongues speech was in fact a learned behavior (Samarin 1972). This learned speech was explained in sociological terms as a means of assisting a person to become a member of the Pentecostal group. On this account, tongues speech is considered to be a 'badge' of membership. For outsiders to be considered insiders this symbolic form of speech is required, but since it is a human activity with a religious meaning, it could be learned through imitation and practice. While the religious meaning construed it to be supernatural and evidence of Spirit Baptism, the sociological meaning framed it as a human activity in the process of transitioning from the outside to the inside of Pentecostalism.

The second scholar to use this theory extensively is Mark J. Cartledge. He used Samarin's work as a starting point (1999), but developed the idea considerably over a number of studies. First, he applied it to the study of glossolalia in which he explored it with qualitative data and then subsequently he operationalized specific measures (questions) focusing on key factors and tested them quantitatively (2002). Second, he applied it to a group of students that were comprised of ecumenical, evangelical and pentecostal contexts and was able to explain the socialization factors that contributed to specific beliefs in God, in particular empirical-theological models of the Trinity (2017). Third, he applied it to the concept of Godly Love (2017). This idea suggests that religious people act benevolently based on energy that emerges from an interaction with others that is motivated by their perception of both giving and receiving love from and to God. In the final area of study, Cartledge developed his quantitative instrument to measure socialization in a more up-to-date way and this measure is regarded as both valid and reliable, thus able to be used in future studies (2017).

The significance of this theory for Pentecostal and Charismatic Christianity lies beyond the acquisition of glossolalia, beliefs in God and benevolent action. Of course, these are all important, but, in terms of the empirical study of Pentecostalism as a form of religion, it allows researchers to appreciate just how external and internal forces shape individuals in their religiosity. It is a theory that can be used more extensively in future research and could address important issues, such as gender relations, boundary keeping within and among different groups, the role that doctrine plays in boundary keeping, as well as a host of ethical postures and their acquisition.

Bibliography

Berger, Peter. 1969. *The Social Reality of Religion.* London: Faber and Faber.

Cartledge, Mark J. 2017. *Narratives and Numbers: Empirical Studies of Pentecostal and Charismatic Christianity.* Leiden: Brill.

Cartledge, Mark J. 2002. *Charismatic Glossolalia: An Empirical-Theological Study.* Aldershot: Ashgate.

Cartledge, Mark J. 1999. "The Socialization of Glossolalia." In *Sociology, Theology and the Curriculum,* edited by Leslie J. Francis, 125–134. London: Cassell.

Danzinger, Kurt. 1971. *Socialization*. Harmondsworth: Penguin.

McGuire, Meredith B. 2002. *Religion: The Social Context*. Fifth Edition. Belmont, CA: Wadsworth Thomson.

Samarin, William J. 1972. *Tongues of Men and of Angels*. New York: Macmillan.

White, Graham. 1977. *Socialization*. London: Longman.

Mark J. Cartledge

Society for Pentecostal Studies

The founding meeting of the Society for Pentecostal Studies (SPS) took place November 6, 1970 in Dallas, TX during the Pentecostal World Conference. Of the 139 attendees, SPS formed with 108 charter members. Three Pentecostal scholars envisioned the Society: Dr. Vinson Synan of the Pentecostal Holiness Church; Dr. Horace Ward of the Church of God, Cleveland, TN; and Dr. William Menzies of the Assemblies of God. Synan had visited Pentecostal archives in 1969 and encountered scholars desiring an academic society where diverse Spirit-filled believers could reflect on Pentecostalism theologically and historically. Menzies was elected president; Hollis Gause (Church of God, Cleveland) VP; Synan, Secretary; and Edward Wood of Eugene Bible College, treasurer. The group planned for annual meetings to present scholarly papers and for an academic journal on the Pentecostal movement. The first annual meeting occurred November 1971 at Open Bible College in Des Moines, Iowa.

Though initially associated with the Pentecostal Fellowship of North America (PFNA), SPS soon distanced itself from the whites only PFNA over purpose statement issues and to be more racially and denominationally inclusive. In 1979 SPS adopted the statement of faith of the Pentecostal World Conference (Robeck 2002) as the basis for membership. In 2014, after several years of debate, the SPS revised its purpose statement as one not associated with any outside institutional body (SPS-usa.org 2019). Formed initially "to serve the churches by providing an authoritative interpretation of the Pentecostal movement," (Faupel and McGinn 2010), the SPS mission has morphed over time to a more exploratory "forum of discussion for all academic disciplines as a spiritual service to the kingdom of God. ... To stimulate, encourage, recognize, and publicize the work of Pentecostal scholars and scholars of Pentecostalism ..." (SPS-usa.org 2019). The Society is a collegial, stimulating environment that seeks to reflect diverse global Pentecostalism and steward the tension between Church and Academy; as such it will continue to provide a venue for lively and meaningful scholarship that serves the churches for many decades to come.

SPS leadership consists of six Executive Committee members – President, First Vice President, Second Vice President, and Immediate Past President, Executive Director, and Secretary/Treasurer. *Pneuma* editors serve on the Executive Committee with voice but no vote. Interest Group Leaders, Committee Chairs, and full voting members also provide key influence in the direction of the Society. The Society has enjoyed many "firsts" in its nearly fifty-year history, such as Father Kilian McDonnell, a Roman Catholic scholar and one of the charter members of the Society addressing the group at its inaugural meeting (Faupel and McGinn 2005); its first African American president, Dr. Leonard Lovett (1975); its first female president, Dr. Edith Blumhofer (1987); and its first female Executive Director, Dr. Lois Olena (2011). Additionally, a Charismatic Presbyterian, J. Rodman Williams; a Wesleyan non-Pentecostal, Donald Dayton; a Oneness Pentecostal, Manuel Gaxiola-Gaxiola (from Mexico); and two Roman Catholic Charismatics, Peter Hocken and Ralph Del Colle (Synan 2005) served as president.

The first issue of *Pneuma: The Journal of the Society for Pentecostal Studies* was published in 1979 to promote the study of Pentecostalism in the academy. Topics have reflected the maturation of the Society and its ongoing relevance to current issues. As with the annual conference, the journal reflects interdisciplinary contributions both national and international in scope, from a variety of Christian traditions. From its beginnings, SPS was ecumenical in flavor, serving as a place where previously estranged Trinitarian and Oneness persons could dialogue and worship together (Yong 2012). SPS also provided a venue for interaction with its Wesleyan cousins, and through the Roman Catholic-Pentecostal dialogue (Faupel and McGinn 2010).

Annual SPS conferences convened in autumn through 1994 but shifted to spring in 1996, after no 1995 meeting, to avoid schedule conflicts with the annual AAR/SBL meeting and the COGIC annual Convocation. It was hoped that adjusting for the latter would encourage inclusion of more racial diversity in the SPS. Meetings have convened across the USA, twice in Canada, and once in Mexico. In 1991, SPS expanded its breadth of scholarship through the establishment of Interest Groups, which now include Biblical Studies, Christian Ethics, Ecumenical Studies, History, Missions and Intercultural Studies, Philosophy, Practical Theology/Christian Formation, Religion and Culture, and Theology. The SPS Diversity Committee was established in 1999 to foster diversity in the Society and to address issues of inclusion; concurrently, the Bishop Ithiel Clemmons Scholarship began, to defray costs of racial and ethnic minorities attending and contributing to SPS. In 2009 the SPS Women's Caucus was established to foster fellowship and professional networking among female scholars and to address issues of importance relative to Pentecostal women globally. The Student Caucus was launched in 2014 for the purpose of building next generation scholarship through an annual Caucus gathering and the Young Scholars "Best Student Paper" Award. The 2018 #pentecostalsisterstoo meeting at SPS and the 2020 conference theme, "This is My Body: Addressing the Global Violence against Women," represent key developments in addressing urgent contemporary issues. Other SPS affiliations include the Canadian Pentecostal Research Network, the Roman Catholic-Pentecostal Dialogue, SPS sessions at the Society of Biblical Literature, and SPS Liaisons to the National Council of Churches (NCCCUSA).

As of 2019, SPS has 520 members representing nearly every continent. Annual conferences average 350 registrants and include symposia, a worship service, parallel sessions, networking receptions, a business meeting, and a final banquet that includes presentations of the *Pneuma* Book Award and Lifetime Achievement Award.

Bibliography

Blumhofer, Edith. 2002. "Pentecostal Fellowship of North America (PFNA)." In *The New International Dictionary of Pentecostal and Charismatic Movements*, edited by Stanley M. Burgess and Eduard M. van der Maas, 968–969. Grand Rapids, MI: Zondervan.

Blumhofer, Edith, Russell P. Spittler, and Grant A. Wacker, eds. 1999. *Pentecostal Currents in American Protestantism*. Urbana, IL: University of Illinois Press.

"Dr. Vinson Synan Elected Secretary of Society for Pentecostal Studies." *Pentecostal Holiness Advocate* 54 (January 2, 1971): 15.

Faupel, William, and Kane McGinn, eds. 2010. "Commemorating Thirty Years of Annual Meetings." *Society for Pentecostal Studies*. Accessed December 7, 2019. http://storage.cloversites.com/societyforpentecostalstudies/documents/sps_30_anniversary_monograph.pdf.

Hocken, Peter. 2016. *Azusa, Rome, and Zion: Pentecostal Faith, Catholic Reform, and Jewish Roots*. Eugene, OR: Pickwick.

Isgrigg, Daniel. 2019. "Where the Spirit Leads Me: An Oral History of the Life and Ministry of Vinson Synan, Ph.D." Oral Roberts University Digital Showcase (Holy Spirit Research Center, AV Collection), accessed December 3, 2019. https://digitalshowcase.oru.edu/synan/.

Robeck, Cecil M. 2002. "Pentecostal World Conference (PWC)." In *The New International Dictionary of Pentecostal and Charismatic Movements*, edited by Stanley M. Burgess and Eduard M. van der Maas, 971–974. Grand Rapids, MI: Zondervan.

Robeck, Cecil M. 1985. "The Society for Pentecostal Studies." *Ecumenical Trends* 14 (2): 28–30.

Spittler, Russ P. 2002. "Society for Pentecostal Studies." In *The New International Dictionary of Pentecostal and Charismatic Movements*, edited by Stanley M. Burgess and Eduard M. van der Maas, 1079–1080. Grand Rapids, MI: Zondervan.

Synan, Vinson. 2005. "The Beginnings of the Society for Pentecostal Studies." A plenary session presented at the 34th Annual Meeting of the Society for Pentecostal Studies. Virginia Beach, VA: Regent University. http://sps-usa.org/home/bylaws-and-history; direct link: http://storage.cloversites.com/societyforpentecostalstudies/documents/synan_sps_beginnings.pdf.

Synan, Vinson. 1997. *The Holiness-Pentecostal Tradition: Charismatic Movements in the Twentieth Century*. Second Edition. Grand Rapids, MI: Eerdmans.

Synan, Vinson. 1985. "Fifteen Years of the Society for Pentecostal Studies." A paper presented to the Society for Pentecostal Studies. Gaithersburg, Maryland, The Mother of God Community.

Society for Pentecostal Studies. 2019. "Who We Are," "Bylaws and History," "Interest Groups," Executive Committee." Accessed December 3, 2019. http://sps-usa.org.

Yong, Amos. 2012. "Pentecostal Scholarship and Scholarship on Pentecostalism: The Next Generation." *Pneuma* 34 (2): 161–165.

Lois E. Olena

Sociology

Sociology is the study of society, and more specifically, the study of human social interaction, socialization, the development of structures, culture, stratification, institutions, and social change. The emergence of sociology is historically located alongside the modernization of Europe, with rapid urbanization, industrialization, and a series of economic and political revolutions. Early sociological thinkers like Max Weber and Emile Durkheim, focused on the implications of social change for society and the various problems associated with modernization. Important analyses revolved around the development of a capitalist economic system, the shift to urban life, power and authority, the rationalization of social life including religion and its relationship to the state and other spheres like the economy, and as a cultural form that provided a moral order for the society. For example, Durkheim examined religious beliefs and rituals associated with the sacred that functioned as a moral order while Weber explored the rationalization of society and the relationship between modernization and religious beliefs and practices. The longstanding view in sociology, and still prominent among many sociologists, is that with modernization there is secularization at a range of levels from the differentiation of social institutions separating the religious from the political for example, to the decline of participation in religious organizations, and lower levels of personal beliefs and practices (Bruce 2011). Secularization, however, is not without its opponents, most notably, Rodney Stark and Roger Finke (1992, 2000) who employ a market model of religious activity rooted in rational choice theory.

Stark and Finke (1992) argue that an open religious market where religious providers are able to freely compete demonstrates how some groups grow while others decline. In America, the decline of churches is related to their inability to meet the demand which is in contrast with those who are growing. A free market of religion that operates without any single religion monopolizing the market, allows for innovation and growth. In Europe, state monopoly and state churches were unable to meet the demand for religion with the result being lower participation rates and declining church attendance. Hence, secularization refers to the inability of some churches to meet the demand and the loss of market share in a market without choice. However, Stark (1999) and Stark and Finke (2000) have become some of the most critical voices of secularization, including their earlier view of secularization as the decline and loss of some providers, to the view that secularization is a myth (1999, 2000). While secularization and religious market theories illustrate one important debate in the sociology of religion, there are other theoretical options.

Sociological studies of Pentecostalism are framed within the various theoretical debates in the sociology of religion and a range of studies reflect those broader concerns (Hunt 2010; Wilkinson 2014). For example, scholarly work on Pentecostalism and the assumptions about modernization, secularization, differentiation, and institutionalization have been conducted by Margaret Poloma (1989) and David Martin (2002). Conversely, studies of Pentecostalism that gravitate towards market model explanations include those by R. Andrew Chesnut (2003) and Donald Miller and Tetsunao Yamamori (2007). Cultural analyses of religion focus on religious subcultures, lived religion, and the cultural interactions between religions and the broader society (Edgell 2012). Studies on Pentecostalism that take a cultural approach include those that explore Pentecostalism as a lived religion, Pentecostal identity, how Pentecostalism is embodied, and the culture of Pentecostal denominations and congregations (Wilkinson and Ambrose 2020).

Globalization and religion is another substantive area of research where Pentecostalism is explored by sociologists. The various interpretations of Pentecostalism are related to the different assumptions about globalization (Wilkinson 2021). Researchers studying the economic dynamics of globalization, for example, tend to view religions like Pentecostalism as movements that facilitate a shift towards capitalism or as protest groups that push back against the inequalities and relations of dependency with high income countries. Research on religion and the view that globalization is the expansion of modern social institutions like democracy, science, and education, view Pentecostalism, especially in so-called traditional societies, as primarily a type of fundamentalism that is yet to embrace modernity. Scholars who focus on the cultural aspects of globalization, tend to explore a range of issues such as migration and the transplanting of culture and religion from one region to another, the localization of religious practice, the expansion of Pentecostalism through the work of missionaries and media, and issues around hybridization and identity. Related to globalization is the study of social networks where some study of Pentecostalism has offered insight into the role of networks (Christerson and Flory 2017).

Areas of future research among sociologists that may find some resonance with Pentecostal studies include queer theory, posthumanism, postsociality, and prosumption theory. These emerging theories are exploring a range of issues around human sexuality and identity; science, technology and intelligence as active agents; the interaction between human bodies and the natural environment; and finally, the impact of production and consumption and new technologies on knowledge and human interaction.

Bibliography

Bruce, Steve. 2011. *Secularization: In Defence of an Unfashionable Theory*. Oxford: Oxford University Press.

Chesnut, R. Andrew. 2003. *Competitive Spirits: Latin America's New Religious Economy*. Oxford: Oxford University Press.

Christerson, Brad, and Richard Flory. 2017. *The Rise of Network Christianity: How Independent Leaders Are Changing the Religious Landscape*. New York: Oxford University Press.

Edgell, Penny. 2012. "A Cultural Sociology of Religion: New Directions." *Annual Review of Sociology* 38 (1): 247–265.

Finke, Roger, and Rodney Stark. 1992. *The Churching of America: Winners and Losers in our Religious Economy*. New Brunswick, NJ: Rutgers University Press.

Hunt, Stephen. 2010. "Sociology of Religion." In *Studying Global Pentecostalism*, edited by Allan Anderson, Michael Bergunder, André F. Droogers and Cornelis van der Laan, 179–201. Berkeley, CA: University of California Press.

Martin, David. 2002. *Pentecostalism: The World their Parish*. Oxford, UK: Blackwell.

Miller, Donald E., and Tetsunao Yamamori. 2007. *Global Pentecostalism: The New Face of Christian Social Engagement*. Berkeley, CA: University of California Press.

Poloma, Margaret. 1989. T*he Assemblies of God at the Crossroads: Charisma and Institutional Dilemmas*. Knoxville, TN: The University of Tennessee Press.

Stark, Rodney. 1999. "Secularization, R.I.P." *Sociology of Religion* 60 (3): 249–273.

Stark, Rodney and Roger Finke. 2000. *Acts of Faith: Explaining the Human Side of Religion*. Berkeley, CA: University of California Press.

Wilkinson, Michael. 2014. "Sociological Narratives and the Sociology of Pentecostalism." In *The Cambridge Companion for Pentecostal Studies*, edited by Amos Yong and Mel Robuck, 215–234. Cambridge, UK: Cambridge University Press.

Wilkinson, Michael. 2021. "Globalization." In *The Wiley Blackwell Companion to the Study of Religion*, Second Edition, edited by Robert A. Segal and Nickolas P. Roubekas, 277–288. Hoboken, NJ: John Wiley & Sons.

Wilkinson, Michael, and Linda M. Ambrose. 2020. *After the Revival: Pentecostalism and the Making of a Canadian Church*. Montreal & Kingston: McGill-Queen's University Press.

Michael Wilkinson

Soteriology

Classical Pentecostals, especially western ones (e.g., North American) and global movements influenced by them, experience salvation in two-stages. The first stage is conversion and Christocentric. The second is Spirit-based charismatic experience. Classical Pentecostals (Wesleyan and Finished Work) sharply distinguish conversion and the subsequent experience of Spirit baptism; indeed, this distinction is the foundation of their doctrinal identity. Classical Pentecostals understand this two-stage soteriology within the structure of the Full Gospel, according to which Christ is savior, sanctifier, baptizer in the Spirit, healer, and soon coming King. As such, the Full Gospel fuses the traditional ordo salutis and the history of redemption. Christ's death on the cross saves by giving justifying grace through faith. Sanctification, Spirit baptism, and healing are part of the subjective application of grace. Christ, as soon coming king, indicates the Pentecostal perspective of their eschatological place in redemptive history as part of an end-time revival that heralded the second coming of Christ. That synthesis of personal salvation and eschatological history is essential to the Pentecostal vision of salvation. Pentecostals believe that they are saved, sanctified, and baptized in the Spirit in order to take part in the latter day outpouring of the Holy Spirit and return of Christ. The Charismatic movement that spread among the mainline Protestant and Catholic churches retained their traditional views of salvation (e.g., sacramental grace for Lutheran and Catholic Charismatics) and saw Spirit baptism as an organic development from conversion. Charismatic experience, nevertheless, usually manifested in a person's life after conversion. So, on a functional level, they retained the two-stage soteriology of conversion and subsequent charismatic experience.

Classical Pentecostal theology ironically relied on evangelical categories of justification and sanctification to articulate its experience of salvation. This yielded two results. Pentecostal theology (although not Pentecostal experience) marginalized the holistic and material experience of grace and separated the works of Christ and the Spirit. As North American Pentecostals became increasingly middle and upper-middle class, the radical transformational experiences of grace were replaced with domesticated and spiritualized experiences of grace. Toward the end of the twentieth century, Pentecostal theology had become evangelical theology *plus* the doctrine of Spirit baptism. The Signs and Wonders renewal that emerged in the 1970s as well as the popularity of the prosperity gospel in Pentecostal groups worldwide, however, attest to the enduring transformational and holistic praxis of Pentecostal soteriology.

The turn of the twenty-first century inaugurated a period of constructive Pentecostal theology. More recent Pentecostal theology recognizes the tension between the Pentecostal experience of redemption and the borrowed evangelical categories employed to understand it. A growing appreciation of global Pentecostalism also contributes to the expanding vision of Pentecostal soteriology, three of which are highlighted below.

Frank D. Macchia proposes a trinitarian account of Spirit baptism (2006) and justification (2010). These key works in Pentecostal pneumatology endeavor to recover the central place of the classical doctrine of Spirit baptism for the movement. Against the popular trend to portray Pentecostalism in terms of charismatic experience and doctrinal diversity, Macchia argues that Spirit baptism is the key biblical and theological metaphor that captures the essence of the Pentecostal experience of God's grace. His understanding of Spirit baptism is more expansive than the Classical Pentecostal view. His holistic theology of Spirit baptism inspires a Pentecostal revision of the doctrine of justification. He proposes a Pentecostal theology of justification that moves beyond the traditional Catholic view of moral and spiritual transformation and the Protestant emphasis on a forensic declaration of righteousness. The result is a trinitarian interpretation of justification. The Spirit justifies people through Spirit baptism and includes them in the koinonia of God. Justification consists in Spirit baptism that brings a renewal of life and inclusion in the divine koinonia.

Amos Yong (2012) argues that salvation is a holistic and multidimensional process that transforms people in all areas of their lives from personal and spiritual to ecclesial and social. The experience of the Holy Spirit as divine love grounds Pentecostal experience and ministry. Salvation and the transformation of life are manifestations of the human encounter with God's love. Pentecostal experiences, such as Spirit baptism and signs and gifts of the Spirit, arise from the presence of the Holy Spirit and are the concrete articulations of the encounter with God's love. Pentecostal worship and prayer is the relational and reciprocal expression of gratitude for God's loving presence. The Spirit of Pentecost, therefore, is fundamentally the presence of God's love. But that love is active. It gives and renews life. A loving presence that heals, cares, and leads Pentecostals into a renewed life of God's Spirit. Being baptized by the Spirit of Pentecost is, thus, the gift of gifts – the dynamic and active presence of a loving God.

Using the traditional Pentecostal Full Gospel paradigm, Wolfgang Vondey (2017) also contributes to the revision of Pentecostal soteriology. He maintains that Pentecostal spirituality (salvation) consists in participating personally and ecclesially in the redemptive work of God in Christ through the presence and power of the Holy Spirit. The structure of that Spirit-engendered experience of Christ is the Full Gospel. Accordingly, salvation is Spirit-enabled experience of the elements of the Full Gospel centered on Christ. Vondey thus resources the historical Full Gospel paradigm for the Pentecostal experience of salvation, but transcends the

Classical Pentecostal two-stage construct, which invariably dislodges the Spirit from and subordinates the Spirit to Christ.

A perennial critique of Pentecostal theology is that its emphasis on the Holy Spirit and charismatic experience displaces Christ. Macchia, Yong, and Vondey affirm that the Spirit is central, and not an adjunct to Christian salvation. They do not displace Christology however. They make the Spirit an equal partner in the work of redemption. Christ and the Holy Spirit contribute to the substance of salvation.

Pentecostal soteriology should continue in the direction advocated by Macchia, Yong, Vondey, and others, because they better capture the place of the Spirit in the biblical narrative of redemption and in the Pentecostal holistic experience of grace. They also free Pentecostal theology from the evangelical categories that too often constrained its historical formulations. In doing so, they also make Pentecostal theology more inclusive of the diversity of global Pentecostal movements. Finally, this direction promises a richer contribution to ecumenical theology on account of the trinitarian stimulus it offers to established soteriologies.

Bibliography

Hollis Gause, R. 2009 (1980). *Living in the Spirit: The Way of Salvation*. Revised and Expanded Edition. Cleveland, TN: CPT.

Machia, Frank D. 2010. *Justified in the Spirit: Creation, Redemption, and the Triune God*. Grand Rapids: Eerdmans.

Macchia, Frank D. 2006. *Baptized in the Spirit: A Global Pentecostal Theology*. Grand Rapids: Zondervan.

Vondey, Wolfgang. 2017. *Pentecostal Theology: Living the Full Gospel*. London: Bloomsbury.

Yong, Amos. 2012. *Spirit of Love: A Trinitarian Theology of Grace*. Waco: Baylor University Press.

Steven Studebaker

South Africa

African Pentecostalisms (rather than African Pentecostalism) consist of complexities and diversities of categorizations and serve as a genre of Christianity distinctive because of its emphasis on the experience of repentance, a personal relationship with God through Christ, baptism in the Spirit, and the resultant transformation of lives through the power of the Holy Spirit.

Available estimates indicate Pentecostals in Africa to number about 202.9 million in 2015, or 35.3 percent of the continent's Christian population of 574.5 million and 17 percent of the continent's population of 1.19 billion. In South Africa, Pentecostal churches consisting of more than 5,000 independent Christian denominations grew from 2.2 million members in 1996 (with a total South African population of 40.58 million) to 3.4 million in 2001 (of a total population of 44.82 million), a growth of 55 percent. In South Africa, Pentecostalism is not limited to a denomination or a creed, but rather represents a movement or cluster of religious practices and attitudes that transcends ecclesiastical boundaries. Although they are phenomenologically pentecostal because their worship exhibits the features of pentecostal spirituality and they were influenced by the high impact spread of the American Pentecostal movement, African Pentecostals have developed in a unique manner and display distinctive features (Cox 1995).

In trying to typify South African Pentecostalism, one needs to take into consideration various historical and theological categories. The oldest type of classical Pentecostal movements goes back to the missionary work that originated mainly from William Seymour's Azusa Street Revival (1906). By far the largest number of missionaries from the Azusa Street Mission went to Africa. Already by May 1908, Thomas Hezmalhalch and John G. Lake had established the Apostolic Faith Mission of South Africa, with the Full Gospel Church of God, the Assemblies of God Church and others originating in the next decade (Burger and Nel 2008). Other movements started through African initiatives, although they were mostly not carefully documented. Due to the classical Pentecostal influence they were established within the African Initiated (Instituted, Indigenous, Independent) Churches (AIC), that originally resulted from the work of African prophets in reaction to mistrust in the mission churches and their version of the biblical message. They represent the earliest form of authentic expression of Christianity in the African milieu. The Spirit churches form a major part of AIC. Since the 1960s, charismatic renewal groups within established churches changed the face of many mainline churches, mainly English-speaking churches. Since the 1980s, many established churches followed pentecostalizing trends in order to reach the African market more effectively. At the same time, independent churches originated with pentecostal sentiments in their spirituality and teaching, in some instances growing into megachurches led by apostles and prophets who became prominent public figures due to their successful media exposure. A last trend is neo-prophetism, which is an amalgamation of forms of ministries of the AIC and neo-Pentecostals (Omenyo 2014). Since 2017, several of these last groups made headlines in South Africa with leaders' financial and psychological abuses of their members, like forcing them to eat grass and drink petrol, spraying them with insecticide and even staging a mock resurrection.

The popularity of Pentecostalism can be ascribed to its affinity with African traditional religion. Primal spirituality constitutes the substructure of pentecostal religion in Africa and gives it a distinctive quality. It assimilates a wide variety of indigenous religious practices into the fabric of pentecostal prayer and praise, providing a thoroughly Africanized version of Christianity. Although African Pentecostalism may have the same theological foundations as Western Pentecostalism, in its non-Western context it acquired characteristics influenced by traditional religious worldviews and modes of spirituality. The primal imagination encapsulated a certain culturally innate sense of the world of transcendence and involves belief in a sacramental, enchanted universe in which the physical world is indicative of spiritual realities. In the primal worldview, all events have spiritual causes and the holy is perceived as non-rational that can only be experienced, not cognitively understood or contained in human language. Sacred and secular realities are inseparable. The forces of evil are seen as real and the weapons of the Spirit are needed to fight their manifestations in disease and discord.

Pentecostalism functions (unintentionally, for the most part) with a worldview that resonates strongly with familiar ways of being religious, resulting in South African Pentecostalism contributing decisively to the current process of reshaping spirituality. Pentecostalism's traditional prerequisite of Spirit baptism also takes spirit possession seriously, a phenomenon that Africans have been experiencing traditionally for a long time. For this reason, most South African initiatives in Christianity have had a pneumatic orientation; pneumatic Christianity is closer to the grain of African culture and its worldview resonates closely with the indigenous worldview (Cox 1995). In Africa, healing is most probably the main motivation why people go to worship (Anderson 2014). Healing is interpreted in Africa in the holistic sense; it includes the total wellbeing of the individual, including material prosperity. The typical disciple comes to church for the first time in search of healing, usually for a malady that traditional and modern medicine was unsuccessful in treating. In many instances, the Pentecostal prophets' primary function is to be healers.

Bibliography

Anderson, Allan Heaton. 2018. *Spirit-filled World: Religious Dis/Continuity in African Pentecostalism*. Cham, Switzerland: Palgrave Macmillan.

Anderson, Allan H. 2014. *An Introduction to Pentecostalism*. Cambridge: Cambridge University Press.

Burger, Isak, and Marius Nel. 2008. *The Fire Falls in Africa: A History of the Apostolic Faith Mission of South Africa*. Vereeniging: Christian Art.

Cox, Harvey. 1995. *Fire from Heaven: The Rise of Pentecostal Spirituality and the Reshaping of Religion in the Twenty-First Century*. Cambridge, MA: Addison-Wesley.

Omenyo, Cephas N. 2014. "African Pentecostalism." In *The Cambridge Companion to Pentecostalism*, edited by Cecil M. Robeck and Amos Yong, 132–151. New York: Cambridge University Press.

Synan, Vinson, Amos Yong, and J. Kwabena Asamoah-Gyadu, eds. 2016. *Global Renewal Christianity: Spirit-Empowered Movements Past, Present and Future*. Vol. 3: *Africa*. Lake Mary, FL: Charisma House.

Marius Nel

South Korea

The origins of the Korean Pentecostal Church can be found in the revival events of 1906 in Wonsan and 1907 in Pyung Yang (today in North Korea). From a Korean Pentecostal perspective, these revivals were orchestrated by the power of the Holy Spirit and became the cradle of a great awakening in the churches. A few years later, invasion by Japan moved Koreans toward personal repentance – many felt their bad behavior caused Japanese colonialism. The Church offered a place for spiritual and physical protection and comfort where conventional religions could not provide any impetus for social and cultural transformation. Christianity was generally accepted quickly among ordinary people and transformed old habits and customs at both the personal and social level. Given Korean traditional beliefs in God as a heavenly being it was understandable for Koreans to accept God as creator and sustainer of life. In addition, the Holy Spirit fit into traditional understandings of spiritual beings.

Korean Protestantism can be best divided into three main types of Korean Churches: first, those who focus on God as Father; second, those who see Jesus Christ as a socio-political reformer; and third, those who experience the Holy Spirit as the spring of prosperity. The first type represents the largest portion among Protestants. All three types are strongly affected by Confucianism and Taoism with strong patriarchal and conservative outlooks. The second type, the smallest of the three, highlights socio-political engagement, as they experience Jesus not only as personal saviour, but also as social reformer. The first type is impacted by Confucian structure and literality, while the third type is connected to Shamanistic flexibility and orality. In addition, the third type focuses on healing and material blessing through the Holy Spirit – based on the theology of prosperity and Three-Fold Blessing (the blessing of the spirit, soul, and body).

In 1928, American missionary Mary C. Rumsey, who experienced the Azusa Street Revival, arrived in Korea. In the same year, Yong Do Lee (1901–1933) established a prayer place and contributed to the growth of the Pentecostal movement. In the 1930s, the first Pentecostal congregation was established in Seoul by Hong Hoeh, a former Salvation Army secretary. Gradually, North American missionaries and Korean preachers established together six more Pentecostal churches which grew slowly during the Japanese occupation. In the 1940s, Woonmong Ra (1914–2009) preached on Spirit baptism and initiated a healing ministry at the "Yong Mun prayer mountain," a seminal movement in Pentecostalism in South Korea.

Female missionaries, supporting themselves, did more than is commonly recognized. Mary C. Rumsey worked with other Western women doing evangelism through educational activities. Indigenous leaders, such as Hong Heoh, Seong-San Park, and Bu-Geun Bae were active in the development of Korean Pentecostalism in Seoul. Evangelist Gui-Im Park founded the Suncheon Pentecostal Congregation. Under Japanese colonialism in the late 1930s Western missionaries were banished and Pentecostal congregations were oppressed and scattered like other denominations.

After the Korean War, through the help of a US Army chaplain, Assemblies of God missionaries were invited to Korea. Abner Chesnut arrived in 1952 as the first missionary and one year later the Korean Assembly of God was officially organized. They opened their own theological seminary and Hong Heoh was later elected as the first Korean chairperson.

After the war, anti-communist sentiments increased and Pentecostalism grew rapidly. While South Korea focused on Western modernization and economic growth, Pentecostalism was established among marginalized people. Yoido Full Gospel Church was founded in this context. The founders were David Yong-Gi Cho (1936) and his mother-in-law, Ja-Shil Choi (1915–1989). They studied at the same Bible school, began a team ministry for a small congregation at Choi's apartment and shortly after that expanded to a tent ministry.

In the early 1980s, The Yoido Full Gospel Church became the world's largest congregation with more than half a million members. The church was located on an island in the Han River, in central Seoul, along with media and financial companies and the South Korean National Assembly building. The church offered seven worship services on Sunday and several others during the week. They also offered intensive prayer on the prayer mountain nearby in Seoul. Pastor Cho divided Seoul into zones and introduced cell groups in each zone for worship and Bible study in homes on weekdays with trained "cell leaders." This methodology of "cell multiplication" was quite successful. As a result, many mainline Protestant churches, and even Catholics and Buddhists, incorporated components of Pentecostal worship style. They also encouraged the poor with the optimistic approach of the threefold blessing contextualized to economic growth in the 1970s and 1980s, while political matters of democracy and social justice were generally neglected.

Pentecostal churches, like other denominations, battle corruption, sexual abuse, lack of financial transparency and other scandals. At the same time, they have suffered a number of schisms based on personality, as well as theological and political differences. Some of the churches began with mystical experiences and sect-like fanaticism in the 1970s and 1980s but gradually became more orthodox through theological education and contact with other churches. Some did not, such as the Unification church, Shincheonji, Dalagbang, Guwonpa and the World Mission Society Church of God. Each of these highlights the founder as a kind of personal saviour. Even though they focus on diaconal work for marginalized people, their exclusivism as sectarian movements causes many kinds of problems. A combination of Confucianism and Calvinism reinforces the personality cult and authoritarian hierarchical leadership.

While contributions of female missionaries and indigenous women were not properly recognized, women in ministry today are not fully represented in decision making bodies and are not allowed to preach. Their domain is defined as diaconal work. Many women work as cell leaders in small groups and homes where they help to strengthen lay leadership.

The strength of Pentecostalism is found in its inclusivity and flexibility. Their ongoing efforts to provide spiritual and humanitarian help to marginalized people, and praying for the sick should be evaluated positively. Diaconal work for marginalized people could be marshalled to engage the causes of social problems. However, the prosperity gospel, found in so many of the churches, can work against helping the poor. In addition, God's femininity manifested in the Holy Spirit is a special gift of Pentecostalism to Korean theology. In these and other ways, Pentecostalism offered a fresh and engaging faith to Koreans during the social upheaval of the twentieth century and now, in the twenty-first century.

Bibliography

Cho, Yonggi. 1984. *Prayer: Key to Revival.* Dallas: Word.

Chung, Meehyun. 2018. "Inquiry of Pentecostalism Regarding Pneumatology: A Theological Suggestion of a Feminist Perspective." *International Review of Mission* 107 (1): 49–63.

Chung, Meehyun. 2015. "Korean Pentecostalism and the Preaching of Prosperity." *Zeitschrift für Missionswissenschaft und Religionswissenschaft* 99 (3/4): 276–296.

Lee, Hong-Jung. 1999. "Minjung and Pentecostal Movements in Korea." In *Pentecostals After a Century: Global Perspectives on a Movement in Transition*, edited by Allan H. Anderson and Walter J. Hollenweger, 141–150. London: Sheffield Academic Press.

Lee, Young-hoon. 2009. *The Holy Spirit Movement in Korea: Its Historical and Doctrinal Development.* Oxford: Regnum Books.

Lee, Young-hoon. 2004. "Life and Ministry of David Yonggi Cho and the Youido Full Gospel Church." In *David Yonggi Cho*, edited by Wonsuk Ma. Baguio, Philippines: APTS Press.

Lee, Young-hoon. 2001. "Korean Pentecost: The Great Revival of 1907." *Asian Journal of Pentecostal Studies* 4 (1): 73–83.

Myung sung-Hoon, and Young-Gi Hong, eds. 2003. *Charis and Charisma: David Yonggi Cho and the Growth of Yoido Full Gospel Church.* Oxford: Regnum.

Meehyun Chung

South Sudan

Out of South Sudan's population of over 12 million there are an estimated 7,462,064 Christians, 728,178 of whom are adherents to Pentecostal/Charismatic (P/C) churches. However, as even the best statistics about South Sudan are approximations from very limited data, attempts at the P/C population have limited usefulness: even before the death and displacement from the present war (2013 onward), not only is there a dearth of literature on P/C in South Sudan, but there is no reliable estimate for South Sudan's population more generally.

Nonetheless, Christianity can certainly claim between 70–95 percent of the South Sudanese population, of whom Pentecostal, Evangelical, and Charismatic (PEC) churches are the fastest growing. Such growth is not uniform, however, and the explosion of P/Cs in the capital of Juba is not necessarily replicated in rural areas. Moreover, knowledge of contemporary South Sudanese religious life results from an uneven spread of scholarly attention, with more being known about religious life among the politically and numerically dominant Dinka and Nuer populations than other South Sudanese peoples. In fact, discrepancies in P/C adherence often reproduce localised patterns of conflict, displacement, and resettlement as well as origin.

The first Christian encounters in South Sudan took place in the late nineteenth century. The dynamics of South Sudan's contemporary Christian landscape suggests a critical distinction between early conversions connected to mainline churches and later ones of an American-influenced, biblical literalist, and Evangelical form. Early Christian influence was limited and largely restricted to an urban, educated elite by the time foreign missionaries were expelled in 1964. Since then two major changes have taken place: firstly, a significant number of people have become self-professing Christians; secondly, many of these have joined P/Cs.

Christianity in 'modern' South Sudan has three distinct phases, each connected to a moment in regional history. These are: one, the coming of colonial-linked missions in the late nineteenth and early twentieth centuries; next, "the Second Wave of Christianisation" (O'Byrne 2016) of the 1960–70s, which saw not only the expulsion of foreign missionaries but largescale south-north labour migration and a general indigenisation of protestant churches; lastly, refugee-based entanglements with American-influenced Protestantism from the late 1980s onwards, an ongoing process O'Byrne (2016) terms "the Third Wave of Christianisation", probably the most important process in the current growth of P/Cs in South Sudan.

Indeed, many South Sudanese first experienced P/C Christianity during the Second Sudanese War (1983–2005). Until this time, Christianity had generally not spread far beyond urban centres. Displacement changed this, however, with huge numbers of South Sudanese converted to multiple denominations. In the refugee camps, the churches that gathered the most converts were international – primarily American – in origin and distinctly biblical literalist in orientation. Alternatively, among the approximately 1.5 million South Sudanese in greater Khartoum, indigenous PEC churches gained such widespread following that they were once called the 'fastest growing movements of Christian conversion in the world' (Hutchinson 1996, 337).

With the signing of the Comprehensive Peace Agreement (CPA) in 2005, decades of civil war led to South Sudan's July 2011 independence. When the new state granted access to foreign missionaries a huge growth in the numbers of P/C churches followed. Moreover, the resettlement of refugees in countries like Australia and the USA saw many South Sudanese join new churches. Such resettlements re-focused spiritual orientations towards international or diasporic congregations and, when resettled pastors returned, they brought new doctrines with them. Consequently, many "First" and "Second Wave" churches have begun (re)producing forms of Christianity reminiscent of "Third Wave" churches.

Bibliography

Brown, Elijah M. 2008. "The Road to Peace: The Role of the Southern Sudanese Church in Communal Stabilisation and National Resolution." PhD thesis, The University of Edinburgh.

Brown, Timothy 2011. "Building Social Capital in South Sudan: How Local Churches Worked to Unite a Nation in the Lead up to the 2005 Comprehensive Peace Agreement." Master's thesis, University of Ottawa.

Hutchinson, Sharon Elaine. 1996. *Nuer Dilemmas: Coping with Money, War, and the State.* Berkeley: University of California Press.

O'Byrne, Ryan Joseph. 2016. "Becoming Christian: Personhood and Moral Cosmology in Acholi South Sudan." PhD thesis, University College London.

Zillinger, Martin. 2014. "Modernisations chrétiennes: Pratiques circulantes des media le long du Nil." [Christian Modernizations: Circulating Media Practices of the Mission along the Nile.] *L'Année du Maghreb* 11: 17–34.

Ryan Joseph O'Byrne

Spain

In the 1920s, Swedish missionaries arrived in Spain, bringing the first Pentecostal experiences to the Iberian Peninsula. Pastors Julia and Martin Wahlsten, founded the first Pentecostal church in the city of Gijon. Other Swedish missionary families such as the Johansson's, Stahlberg's, Armstrong's, and Forsberg's helped to found congregations throughout the country (Martín-Arroyo and Branco 2011). However, by 1936, Pentecostals were forced out by the Civil War (1936–1939) and anti-evangelical sentiments grew afterwards, further hampering the evangelical efforts of a small number of missionaries struggling to withstand the atmosphere of repression and uncontested Catholic hegemony.

In 1950, Cuban Pentecostal ministers, Roman and Carmen Perruc, discovered a group of Pentecostal believers in the city of Ronda (Andalusia) who had survived decades of Protestant persecutions. This group founded an Assemblies of God church that, later in 1963, became the national organization of the Assemblies of God in Spain. During this period, the first Pentecostal denominations, leaders, and converted individuals, started articulating their own liturgical perspectives and integrating experiential facets of the Pentecost into their worship. These nuances reshaped their religious practices without necessarily leaving aside their original religious traditions.

Between the 1950s and early 1960s, the arrival of French and Spanish evangelists mostly from the Roma ethnic people based in France, strongly shaped the movement in Spain. Evangelists such as Emiliano Jiménez Escudero had the goal of converting the Spanish Roma people (*gitanos*, or gypsies, being the preferred term amongst scholars and the Roma poeple). The group belonged to the Gypsy Evangelical Movement (in French, *Mission Evangelique des Tziganes*) founded in the 1950s by former Assemblies of Gods pastor Clément Le Cossec (1921–2001).

The mission landed in the Iberian Peninsula, home of one of the largest settlements of Roma people in Europe, finding a territory ruled by military dictatorship and a strong cultural and political influence of the Catholic Church. Nevertheless, early evangelists from the movement promptly trained and raised *gitano* religious leaders successfully (Montañes 2016).

In May 1956, a Commission for the Defense of Evangelicals was constituted. The commission was held as the early custodians of the Protestant community gained rights in the country and carried out its work until 1982. Usage of the term *evangélicos* (in English, evangelicals) was born out of a consensus amongst Pentecostals and other Protestant denominations that shared a similar approach of Christian revival.

The 1970s and 1980s marked a period of mass conversions amongst the gypsy people, making Pentecostalism the largest Protestant group in Spain. Following this trend, a national church lead by Spanish gypsies was created in 1969 under the name of *Iglesia Evangelica de Filadelfia* (IEF). The organization was formed as a national association with branches all over the country (Cantón 2001). At that point, most activities developed by gypsy Pentecostals in Spain were carried out within and by the IEF, though other denominations were also in place.

The arrival of democracy in the Spanish State (1978) brought an unprecedented series of constitutional innovations such as the Act of Religious Freedom of 1980 allowing Spanish citizens freedom of religion and worship. In 1982 the Commission for the Defense of Evangelicals initiated conversations for the signing of a cooperation agreement between the State and the Protestant confessions. The Commission demanded the creation of a legal mechanism that would be able to mediate the relationship between Protestant entities and the government. The response came in November 1986 with the foundation of the Federation of Evangelical Religious Entities of Spain (FEREDE). In 1992, the FEREDE signed the *Acuerdo de Cooperación del Estado con la FEREDE* Ley 25/1992, de 10 de noviembre (in English, Agreement of Cooperation between the State and FEREDE). The agreement governed the relationships between Evangelical churches and the public administration while recognizing FEREDE as representative of Evangelical entities in Spain.

The growing presence of Latin American migrants during the Spanish economic boom of the late 1990s and mid 2000s led the way for the more recent expansion of Pentecostalism (García 2010) in major cities like Madrid, Valencia, Barcelona and Seville. By 2016 Spain had 3,921 Evangelical places of worship registered at the Directory of Religious Institutions, which constitutes 55 percent of all registered institutions, excluding Catholic churches. The majority (20 percent) located in the Autonomous Community of Catalonia followed by the Community of Madrid (17 percent), Andalusia (15 percent) and Valencia (10 percent) (Observatorio Del Pluralismo Religioso En España 2016).

Ecuadorians, Colombians, Bolivians, Peruvians and Argentineans are the major nationalities among foreign citizens

(Instituto Nacional de Estadística 2018) notably, countries with a strong Pentecostal background. Although in smaller numbers, migrants from sub-Saharan Africa significantly contributed to fostering the new wave of Pentecostals. Nigerians, Congolese, Ghanaians, and Guineans (Bissau and Equatorial) are often found leading and attending Pentecostal congregations across the country. In the migratory trend of the last decade, Pentecostal-Charismatic churches, also called Neo-Pentecostals, became the forefront of Christianity in Spain.

In addition to that, a Catholic movement called The Neocatechumenal Way (in Spanish, Camino Neocatecumenal) has an important role in this Christian renewalist wave in the country. Also known as "the Neocatechumenate" and often referred as "the Catholic Pentecostals", this charismatic movement was founded by Francisco Argüello (Kiko), Carmen Hernández, and Italian priest Mario Pezzi, in 1964. They started the movement evangelizing in small prayer groups mostly formed by gypsy communities in the area of Palomeras Altas, a shanty town in the outskirts of Madrid (Vázquez 1999). The group's core mission was to bring back the basic premises of a Christian life and encourage its modernization by looking at three key areas of Catholicism: the liturgy, the Church and the Bible. Today this organization is present in more than two thousand parishes across all continents, with 5,118 communities, each one of them having an average of 25 to 30 members (Blazquez 1988, 13). Due to the nickname of its founder, Kiko, the members of this movement in Spain are popularly known as "the Kikos".

Bibliography

Blazquez, Ricardo. 1988. Las Comunidades Neocatecumenales. Discernimiento Teologico. Bilbao: Desclée de Bower. https://pt.scribd.com/document/345067812/BLAZQUEZ-R-Las-Comunidades-Neocatecumenales-Discernimiento-Teologico-DDB-3-Ed-1988.

Cantón, Manuela. 2001. "Gitanos Protestantes. El Movimiento Religioso de Las Iglesias 'Filadelfia' En Andalucía, España." Julio-Diciembre 11 (22): 69–74.

García, Paola. 2010. "Integración y migración: las Iglesias pentecostales en España." Amérique Latine Histoire et Mémoire. Les Cahiers ALHIM, 20 (November). http://journals.openedition.org/alhim/3691.

Martín-Arroyo, Manuel, and Paulo Branco. 2011. "The Development Of The Pentecostal Movement In Iberia (Spain & Portugal)." In European Pentecostalism, edited by William Kay and Anne Dyer, 165–188. Leiden: Brill.

Montañes, Antonio. 2016. "Etnicidad e identidad gitana en los cultos pentecostales de la ciudad de Madrid. El caso de la 'Iglesia Evangélica de Filadelfia' y el 'Centro Cristiano Vino Nuevo el Rey Jesús.'" Papeles del CEIC. International Journal on Collective Identity Research 2016 (2): 1–26.

Vázquez, Carmen Castilla. 1999. "De neófitos a iniciados. El movimiento neocatecumenal y sus ritos de admisión." Gazeta de Antropología 15 (febrero). http://www.gazeta-antropologia.es/?p=3443.

Rafael Cazarin

Spiritual Gifts

The New Testament bears witness to a church that pulsated with a diversity of spiritual gifts. The term most often used to depict these gifts is charisma (pl. charismata). This term can have a more generalized meaning, referring to the gift of salvation or its universally accessible benefits (Romans 5:15–16; 6:23; 11:29). But this term is more often used in the New Testament of the diversely gifted congregation through which the Holy Spirit is present and active to build up its members in the love of Christ and to guide its mission. 1 Corinthians 12–14 represents the most thorough reflection on their purpose and function, though Romans 12:4–8 and Ephesians 4:8–16 are also worthy of note (the latter uses domata in 4:8 for "gifts" rather than charismata, perhaps due to the fact that it quotes the Greek translation of Psalm 68:18). The term charismata is almost exclusively used in the New Testament by Paul and takes its place among a number of words used by him to depict the rich variety of ways in which grace (charis) is experienced among the people of God: joy (chara), rejoicing (chairō), and thanksgiving (eucharisteō or eucharistia).

Paul's preference for this "grace" language when describing spiritual gifts was particularly poignant, since indications are that the Corinthians were prone to want credit for participating in some of the more obviously "spiritual" gifts, like speaking in tongues (1 Cor. 14:23). Paul's own ministry was accompanied by "the Spirit and power" but it was even more fundamentally focused on "Jesus Christ, and him crucified" (1 Cor. 2:2–4). The implication here is that the Spirit and the Spirit's gifts come to us by grace, poured forth from the Father through Christ own self-giving to us (Eph. 4:7–11). Self-giving love for the benefit of others must therefore orchestrate the gifted life of the congregation (1 Cor. 13), for the spiritually gifted church is constantly "building itself up in love" (Eph. 4:16).

Paul does not otherwise seem to rank the gifts. The "greater gifts" appear to refer to love and whatever gift clearly serves to call the congregation to obedience in given circumstances, like prophecy (1 Cor. 12:31; 14:1). In the church, prophecy thus takes precedence over speaking in tongues, because prophecy edifies others. Though self-edification in private is also valuable, in the assembly the common good takes precedence. In that context, tongues must be interpreted for the edification of others in order to approximate the effectiveness of prophecy (1 Cor. 14:2–3, 13–19). Yet, Paul is careful to avoid all cause for boasting. Those members whose giftings might appear less honorable (perhaps less prominent or less obviously "spiritual") are to be granted more honor (1 Cor. 12:22–24). All are to exercise great care for one another (1 Cor. 12:25). "If one member suffers, all suffer together with it; if one member is honored, all rejoice together with it" (12:26).

The essential role of divine love (agapē) in governing the spiritual gifts of the congregation makes sense, for "God's love has been poured into our hearts through the Holy Spirit that has been given to us" (Rom. 5:5). Love does not just fulfill the spiritually gifted life of the church, that life loses its meaning entirely without it (13:1–3). All of the gifts will no longer be needed once we see Christ face to face, but divine love is forever (13:8–13). All of this means that the sanctification of the mind and will is indispensable to the flourishing and proper functioning of the spiritually gifted life of the church. It is indeed possible to be spiritually gifted while lagging behind in the sanctified life (1 Cor. 3:1). The Spirit can work through a flawed vessel. Yet, the discernment of God's will in these gifts and their proper exercise still depend on the sanctification process through which we conform to love (Rom. 12:1–8, esp. v. 2).

That the spiritual gifts of a congregation is distributed by the Spirit's will (1 Cor. 12:11) would seem to indicate that they were distributed to meet uniquely contextual needs. Yet, the presence throughout Acts of the list given in 1 Corinthians 12:8–10 would also indicate that the uniquely Corinthian gifts were fairly widespread among the churches. Note in Acts the exercise of the word of wisdom (6:10), the word of knowledge (5:3–4), special faith (14:9), gifts of healing (3:6–7), working of miracles (20:9–12), forms of assistance (6:1–3), prophecy (21:9), discernment of spirits (13:8–12), various kinds of tongues and interpretation of tongues (2:4–12), teaching (2:42), and administration (14:23). For Pentecostals, this raises the question as to why all of these gifts are no longer widely practiced, especially since Paul indicates that the church is to come behind in no gift while awaiting Christ's return (1 Cor. 1:7). Only then will the gifts pass away, when we see Christ face to face and fully know him as he knows us (1 Cor. 13:12).

The lists of gifts given in 1 Corinthians and elsewhere seem ad hoc, with no systematic organization in evidence. In the mix one can find permanent ministries involving tasks that utilize natural abilities and disciplined learning (apostles, forms of serving, forms of leadership, teaching and preaching: Eph. 4:11; 1 Corinthians 12:28). Paul tells Timothy to practice his preaching more often, "so that all may see your progress" (1 Tim. 4:15). But one can also find more dramatically spiritual or supernatural activities that were perhaps less typical of select persons and less dependent on natural abilities or training (word of wisdom, word of knowledge, special faith, gifts of healing, working of miracles, prophecy, discernment of spirits, speaking in tongues, and interpretation of tongues: 1 Cor. 12:8–10). Perhaps the difference between the two above-mentioned kinds of gifts is indicated in Paul's distinction between "ministries" (diakoniōn) and "operations" (energematōn) evident among the charismata (1 Cor. 12:4–6).

It is indeed possible to overemphasize the more extraordinary or obviously spiritual operations of the Spirit (like prophecy, speaking in tongues, or miracles) out of a sensationalistic supernaturalism, but it is also possible to de-emphasize them out of a lack of faith that such operations of the Spirit can still be evident in the churches today. As a result, those gifted in these ways can become marginalized within a congregation and valuable signs of the coming Kingdom eclipsed in the process.

The importance of spiritual gifts accented by the Pentecostal movement has helped to awaken the larger church to the valuable ministry of all the people of God, overturning the "clericalization" of the ministry and the passivity of the so-called laity. In the light of the charismatic structure of the church, those ordained to exercise oversight are properly to be viewed as ministers of ministers. There has also been a growing awareness among Pentecostals that all Christians are charismatic. Those who believe a special endowment of the Spirit is the gateway to these gifts as a whole fail to realize that even the disciples prior to Pentecost exercised spiritual gifts like preaching and healing (e.g., Luke 10:9).

Though all believers share the same call to discipleship, all serve uniquely and diversely in the gifted ministries and operations of the Spirit in the church. These gifts are determined by the Spirit (1 Cor. 12:11) and not by social privilege.

Rich and poor, sons and daughters, prophesy; the old dream dreams and the young have visions (Acts 2:17–18). All have been baptized into Christ and bear his Spirit; all have put on Christ, whether Jew or Greek, bond or free, male or female (Gal. 3:27–28; 1 Cor. 12:13). Thus, Pentecostal theology attests that all may serve in any capacity willed by the Spirit of Christ for the common good.

Bibliography

Fee, Gordon. 1980. "Tongues-Least of the Gifts: Some Exegetical Observations on 1 Corinthians 12–14." *Pneuma* 2 (2): 2–14.
Koenig, John. 1978. *Charismata: God's Gifts for God's People*. Philadephia: Westminster Press.
Lim, David. 2016. *Spiritual Gifts: A Fresh Look*. Springfield, MO: Gospel Publishing House.
Michaels, J.M. 1988. "Gifts of the Spirit." In *Dictionary of Pentecostal and Charismatic Movements*, edited by Stanley M. Burgess and Gary B. McGee, 332–334. Grand Rapids, MI: Zondervan.
Schatzmann, Sigfried. 1987. *A Pauline Theology of Charismata*. Peabody, MA: Hendrickson.

Frank Macchia

Spirituality

Spirituality, the study of how people live in response to God, is related to theology, which concerns what people think about God. Their complementary relationship is widely recognized in Pentecostal studies, for its cardinal doctrines often define intense experiences, as is the case with Spirit baptism. With the emergence over the last quarter century of spirituality as a primary category for Pentecostal research, the nature of the relationship is under review. Castelo (2020, 29–31) proposes that Pentecostal theology is a feature of Pentecostal spirituality that includes four models: integrationist, philosophical, liberationist, and mystical.

The salient characteristic of Pentecostalism is the emphasis on an encounter with God/the Spirit as life transformation. Consequently, the trinitarian starting point for Pentecostals is the Holy Spirit who mediates the life-giving work of God in Christ (Land 2001, 23). The ubiquitous terminology in various Christian traditions of the "Spirit-filled life" or "life in the Spirit" is particularly apt for Pentecostals, encapsulating the conviction that newness of life is available through the power of the Spirit.

Given the complexities of global Pentecostalism, the search for descriptive categories has proven elusive. As the movement continues to evolve, old categories are adjusted and new ones added. The traditional American-centric history of Pentecostal origins based in the Azusa Street Revival and tripartite periodization of Pentecostal development in three "waves" – classical Pentecostals, 1900s; Charismatic renewalists, 1960s; and neo-Charismatics (or, neo-Pentecostals), 1980s – is being re-assessed as regional histories of Pentecostal origins continue to be published. This model is losing some of its currency as *the* explanation of origins and as *the* definition of Pentecostalism, which presumes that classical Pentecostal theology and spirituality are the qualitative measuring stick for all subsequent variants.

The significance of American classical Pentecostalism for Pentecostal spirituality is best seen in Steven Land's *Pentecostal Spirituality: A Passion for the Kingdom*, first published in 1993 (2001). Drawing on two primary matrices, the Wesleyan/Holiness tradition, and following Swiss theologian Walter Hollenweger's emphasis on the role of the African-American tradition, Land (2001, 47) formulates an early Pentecostal spirituality with a focus on its "oral-narrative theology" as expressed in songs, testimonies and newsletters. His typology of Pentecostal spirituality not only includes the affections along with beliefs and practices, but he also positions orthopathy (right affections) as the integrating factor for orthodoxy (right belief) and orthopraxy (right practice). As the subtitle suggests, these three are interpreted within the apocalyptic framework common to classical Pentecostals – a framework that caused them to both celebrate the Kingdom as revealed but also to act as a missionary fellowship towards its imminent fulfilment.

Connie Au (2020) engages the two phases of Pentecostal revival and Charismatic renewal in a constructive manner that acknowledges their distinctive contributions to global Pentecostalism while reinterpreting them as the heritage for all Pentecostals, even at the level of personal experience. With three Pentecostal churches in Hong Kong used as examples, Pentecostal spirituality is defined according to three categories. 1) "Beliefs" are the tenets of the five-fold/full gospel of classical Pentecostalism, which are foundational for the entire movement, and a base that charismatics engage with to meet their needs. 2) "Ethos" (fundamental values or character) is constituted by revival, renewal, restoration, and triumph. The import of experience for Pentecostalism is subsumed under this rubric, for it is within this ethos that the nature of Pentecostal experience is made plain. Citing Peter Hocken, revival is a process that refers to new beginnings and discontinuity. As such, they may be incorporated into a personal spiritual trajectory: from revival as beginning, to continual renewal, to restoration (where elements of the past are reclaimed, and healing is emphasized), and then to triumph. 3) "Practice" focuses on the worship event as the arena where beliefs and ethos are actualized.

In *African Pentecostalism*, Ogbu Kalu (2008) argues that the roots of African Pentecostalism are to be found in Africa, and that the highpoint of American influence on African Pentecostalism would not come until the 1980s. The success of the Pentecostal and charismatic influences that cycled through the continent is attributable to the fact that they found root as they interacted with African sensibilities. The appeal of Pentecostalism's emphasis on power for life and transformation reinforced the African understanding of soteriology as "transformation of material, physical and psychic well-being" (261). Consonant with the cosmology of the New Testament and sectors of Pentecostalism (especially classical Pentecostals and some neo-charismatics), African Pentecostalism understands that the power of the Spirit confronts the ubiquitous presence of the demonic, liberating the individual and society from bondage and propelling them toward the shalom of health and prosperity.

The worship service is viewed as a microcosm of Pentecostal spirituality, which highlights Pentecostal spirituality as a collective embodied spirituality: it is within the gathered worshipping community that individual encounters are generated and interpreted (Wilkinson 2020). For example, whether healing is seen as physical, or something more psychological, relational, or even societal, or whether glossolalia is seen as the sign of Spirit Baptism and power for evangelism, or as personal edification through prayer language, the interpretation of these and other manifestations of the Spirit are socialized according to the ethos of the congregation.

Albrecht's *Rites in the Spirit* (1999) analyzes the constituent elements of the worship service with insights gleaned from ritual studies. Pentecostal rituals mediate experience, not only symbolically, but for how they effect the transformations they symbolize. He identifies a common liturgical progression through three primary rites – worship in praise, pastoral message, and altar service wherein time and space is created for the "microrites" for which Pentecostals are known, such as glossolalia, prophecy, and healing (152–153). The exuberance and physicality of Pentecostal spirituality is on full display in the worship event: "According to traditional Pentecostal ritual logic, God is expected to move, but so are God's worshipers" (148). With the altar service, movement is directed outwards toward home and society. Kalu (2008, 268) states: "Answering the altar call is like a degradation ritual that ensures that the respondents can now act differently and perceive the world in a different way." The "different way" varies as the elements of Pentecostalism are combined within any given setting, serving to socialize participants about a Pentecostal spirituality.

This overview shows how Pentecostal spirituality is understood in various ways including as encounter, as apocalyptic or eschatological in practice, as a process of renewal and revival, as personal and social transformation, and as an experience of religious socialization for the participants.

Bibliography

Albrecht, Daniel. 1999. *Rites in the Spirit: A Ritual Approach to Pentecostal/Charismatic Spirituality*. Sheffield: Sheffield Academic Press.

Au, Connie. 2020. "Pentecostal Spirituality." In *Protestant Spiritual Traditions*, vol. 2, edited by Frank Senn, 148–175. Eugene: Cascade Books.

Castelo, Daniel. 2020. "Pentecostal Theology as Spirituality: Explorations in Theological Method." In *The Routledge Handbook of Pentecostal Theology*, edited by Wolfgang Vondey, 29–39. New York: Routledge.

Kalu, Ogbu. 2008. *African Pentecostalism: An Introduction*. Oxford: Oxford University Press.

Land, Steven. 2001. *Pentecostal Spirituality: A Passion for the Kingdom*. Sheffield: Sheffield Academic Press.

Wilkinson, Michael. 2020. "Worship: Embodying the Encounter with God." In *The Routledge Handbook of Pentecostal Theology*, edited by Wolfgang Vondey, 117–128. New York: Routledge.

Van Johnson

Statistics

Until recently, it was almost mandatory for authors writing a book about Pentecostalism to begin by emphasizing its significant growth – especially in Africa and Latin America – since the time of its origination in the first decade of the twentieth century (Stewart 2012). This authorial ritual was motivated by an either real or perceived need for scholars interested in the study of Pentecostalism to legitimate their work among their disciplinary peers who largely understood Pentecostalism as either a social compensatory mechanism for the poor, uneducated, and oppressed or – from the opposite perspective – an oppressive form of cultural imperialism that homogenizes vulnerable poor and uneducated global populations. From both perspectives, Pentecostalism was understood as a distasteful religious tradition not meriting serious academic examination. This practice was further facilitated by the proliferation of global Pentecostal population estimates generated by, most notably, David Barrett, and his closest intellectual successor, Todd Johnson (Barrett 1988; Johnson and Zurlo 2019). These basic population estimates – usually organized according to some combination of geography or nationality, denomination or organizational type, and theology or practice – are what usually pass for "statistics" within the academic study of Pentecostalism.

There exist two major problems with this common understanding of statistics within Pentecostal studies. First – within the social sciences – the term statistics specifically refers to the *collection, analysis,* and *interpretation* of numerical data relating to social phenomena. Statistics can be used to summarize the characteristics of a sample of a population (descriptive statistics), generalize about a population based on an analysis of a sample of this same population (inferential statistics), or visualize data representing a sample in order to better understand the underlying social structure that this analysis reveals (exploratory data analysis). It was acknowledged at least as early as the time of Émile Durkheim's pioneering sociological work, *On Suicide* ([1897] 2006), that in order to be considered more than simply an exercise in mathematics, statistics requires that the collection and analysis of numerical data relating to social phenomena are interpreted using social theory in order to reveal their greater social significance for, primarily, *explaining* the significance of these social phenomena, *generalizing* these social phenomena to other contexts, or *predicting* how these social phenomena might effect, or be effected by, other social phenomena. Simply counting a social phenomenon such as, for instance, the number of Pentecostals around the world and organizing this data into categories, then, is not, strictly speaking, the statistical study of Pentecostalism. A complete statistical research design requires that data relating to, for instance, the increasing global prevalence of Pentecostals is additionally interpreted in order to generate a theoretical explanation for why this is happening, which could be accomplished in this particular case by describing the demographic implications of the higher-than-average fertility rates of Pentecostal women. Without some kind of theoretical interpretation demonstrating the greater social significance of the numerical data relating to social phenomena that was initially collected and analyzed, statistics – again, as traditionally understood within the social sciences – has not occurred (Berger 1963).

While this first major problem with the common understanding of statistics within Pentecostal studies can be rather easily remedied by adding an additional interpretive step to one's research design, the second problem requires a more complex intervention. The fact that Pentecostal adherents, information classification systems, and even the world's leading scholars of Pentecostalism, cannot agree on what Pentecostalism is or how it is defined (Stewart 2107, 2019), points to the reality that Pentecostalism – like all forms of religion – exists as an abstract object rather than a concrete object (Zinov'ev 1973). It is helpful to conceptualize Pentecostalism as a complex of culturally prescribed practices, such as prayer, worship, and the gifts of the Spirit, based on a belief in the imminence of God and the power of God's Spirit, which are intended to help practitioners gain access to this divine power in the hope of renewing Christianity towards the purpose of evangelizing the world (Anderson 2010; Smith 2017; Anderson 2018; Kyrios and Stewart 2020). The fact that Pentecostalism does not describe a real thing *per se*, does not by any means imply that it cannot – at least indirectly – be empirically studied. Conceptualizing Pentecostalism as an *abstractum* rather than a *concretum*, simply means that scholars are restricted to studying the *values*, *beliefs*, *attitudes*, *actions*, and *behaviours* in which Pentecostalism is encoded. Put another way, Pentecostalism does not exist in such a way that it can be directly observed, but, rather, only indirectly observed through those values, beliefs, attitudes, actions, and behaviours that it engenders.

This empirical understanding of Pentecostalism poses a problem for the popular practice of counting Pentecostals *qua* Pentecostal, which commonly passes for the statistical study of Pentecostalism. Since Pentecostalism can only be empirically studied through the lens of the values, beliefs, attitudes, actions, and behaviours that it generates, measures of affiliation or attendance will not always accurately identify those who are Pentecostal. In other words, relying primarily on affiliation or attendance to measure Pentecostalism can result in either overestimating, or underestimating, the global Pentecostal population. As my colleagues and I have demonstrated elsewhere (Stewart 2015; Stewart, Gabriel, and Shanahan 2017), sometimes a person will self-identify as Pentecostal, attend a Pentecostal congregation, formally join a Pentecostal congregation, or even become a Pentecostal clergyperson, without demonstrating any affinity with, or knowledge of, Pentecostal values, beliefs, attitudes, actions, and behaviours as they are commonly understood, namely, those relating to some aspect of Spirit baptism, speaking in tongues, and divine healing. Alternatively, sometimes a person will demonstrate Pentecostal values, beliefs, attitudes, actions, and behaviours without demonstrating any corresponding self-identification as Pentecostal or attendance at a Pentecostal congregation that affiliation or attendance measures exclusively rely on. This second major problem with the common understanding of statistics within Pentecostal studies can be remedied – although, admittedly, not without great effort – by shifting the methodological focus from simply counting those people who either self-identify as Pentecostals or attend Pentecostal congregations, to measuring those people who display the values, beliefs, attitudes, actions, and behaviours generated by Pentecostalism understood as an abstract object. This shift would require prioritizing the measurement of, first, religious practices (actions and behaviours), and, second, the religious premises (values, beliefs, and attitudes) that these practices are based on, which share a family resemblance with Pentecostalism's historical emphasis on immanence, power, conversion, and renewal.

In order for the statistical study of Pentecostalism to move out of its infancy, scholars need to develop more rigorous research designs, research methodologies, and interpretive frameworks, which are capable of explaining, generalizing, and predicting the social significance of the abundance of data that is continually generated regarding global Pentecostalism. The focus needs to move from simply counting Pentecostals in order to demonstrate the distribution and growth of Pentecostalism, to interpreting Pentecostal social phenomena so that we might better understand how they both influence, and are influenced by, other important social phenomena such as ageing, cities, class, crime, culture, deviance, disability, economics, environmentalism, education, emotions, the body, ethnicity, family, gender, globalization, health, inequality, leisure, media, migration, politics, racialization, sexuality, social movements, social networks, status, technology, violence, and work.

Bibliography

Anderson, Allan. 2018. *Spirit-Filled World: Religious Dis/Continuity in African Pentecostalism*. Cham: Palgrave Macmillan.

Anderson, Allan. 2010. "Varieties, Taxonomies, and Definitions." In *Studying Global Pentecostalism: Theories and Methods*, edited by Allan Anderson, Michael Bergunder, André Droogers and Cornelis van der Laan, 13–29. Berkeley: University of California Press.

Barrett, David B. 1988. "The Twentieth-Century Pentecostal/Charismatic Renewal in the Holy Spirit, with Its Goal of World Evangelization." *International Bulletin of Missionary Research* 12 (3): 119–129.

Berger, Peter L. 1963. *Invitation to Sociology: A Humanistic Perspective*. New York: Doubleday.

Durkheim, Émile. [1897] 2006. *On Suicide*. Translated by Robin Buss. London: Penguin.

Johnson, Todd M., and Gina A. Zurlo. 2019. eds. *World Christian Database*. Leiden: Brill.

Kyrios, Alex, and Adam Stewart. 2020. "EPC Exhibit 143-S28.1: Pentecostalism." Report for the Dewey Decimal Classification Editorial Policy Committee, OCLC, The Library of Congress, Washington, DC.

Smith, Christian. 2017. *Religion: What It Is, How It Works, and Why It Matters*. Princeton: Princeton University Press.

Stewart, Adam. 2019. "Sociohistorical Recommendations for the Reclassification of Pentecostalism in the Dewey Decimal Classification System." *o-bib: Das offene Bibliotheksjournal* 6 (1): 42–59.

Stewart, Adam. 2017. "A Subject Analysis of Pentecostalism in the Dewey Decimal Classification System." *Biblioteka* 21: 243–250.

Stewart, Adam. 2015. *The New Canadian Pentecostals*. Waterloo, ON: Wilfrid Laurier University Press.

Stewart, Adam. 2012. "A Brief Introduction." In *Handbook of Pentecostal Christianity*, edited by Adam Stewart, 3–8. DeKalb: Northern Illinois University Press.

Stewart, Adam, Andrew Gabriel, and Kevin Shanahan. 2017. "Changes in Clergy Belief and Practice in Canada's Largest Pentecostal Denomination." *Pneuma* 39 (4): 457–481.

Zinov'ev, Alexander Alexandrovich. 1973. *Foundations of the Logical Theory of Scientific Knowledge (Complex Knowledge)*. Dordrecht: D. Reidel Publishing Company.

Adam Stewart

Suenens, Leo Jozef

Léon Jozef Suenens was born in Ixelles, Belgium in 1904. He was ordained as a priest in 1927 and later as a bishop in 1945. In 1961, Pope John XXIII appointed him as the Archbishop of Mechelen-Brussels and in the following year as a Cardinal. He was an astute progressive person who championed for the overall renewal of the Catholic Church at the Second Vatican Council. Pope Paul VI appointed him as one of the four moderators of the Council. As a moderator, he was actively involved in drafting one of the key documents of the Council, Dogmatic Constitution on the Church (*Lumen Gentium*). He also influenced the drafting of another important document of the Council, Pastoral Constitution on the Church in the Modern World (*Gaudium et Spes*). During the Council debates, he urged the Council Fathers to deliberate on vital issues like the active role of the laity in the life of the Church, the Church's proactive role in social action and the spreading of peace in the world. His impressive opposition to Cardinal Ernesto Ruffini during the debate on the cessation of the charisms of the Holy Spirit in the modern world influenced the Council Fathers to vote in favor of his resolution, which noted that the Holy Spirit continued to bestow charisms, both ordinary and extraordinary in the present times to renew and build up the Church (see *Lumen Gentium* no.12). Thus, his timely intervention proved to be prophetic, especially with the birth of various New Ecclesial Movements, which claim their work as charisms of the Holy Spirit. In the post-conciliar period, Suenens worked tirelessly to implement the various reformations in the Catholic Church as envisaged by the Second Vatican Council. He wished the Church to be humble in serving the people of God and keep away from worldly power.

He was a man who was always open to the promptings and workings of the Holy Spirit. He welcomed the Charismatic Renewal in the Catholic Church. He encountered the CCR in 1972–1973. He attended various charismatic conventions held in the U.S. and was convinced that the CCR was the genuine work of the Holy Spirit and a gift to the Church. He did not hesitate to ask Francis Martin, a Catholic priest to pray for him for the baptism in the Holy Spirit. He supported the newly formed charismatic prayers groups and communities in the USA. He wanted the charismatic type of worship to spread in Europe and so he spoke about the work of the CCR to the Pope and the Curia in Rome. Initially, not many in the Curia took it seriously. However, Pope Paul VI supported Suenens in his efforts to spread the CCR in the Catholic Church and asked him to serve as a spiritual assistant to the worldwide renewal services. Because of his close contact with the Curia in Rome, Suenens also acted as a liaison of the CCR with the Vatican.

Suenens maintained that the Church needed the CCR, however he wanted the CCR to avoid superficiality and remain faithful to the teachings of the Catholic Church. Thus, he invited a group of theologians and leaders associated with the CCR to reflect on the work of the Holy Spirit in the CCR and draft theological documents. This group published six documents, also known as Malines Documents, which examine the various aspects and potentials of the CCR from a theological perspective. Following are the 6 Malines Documents published between 1974 to 1987. 1. *Theological and Pastoral Orientations on the Catholic Charismatic Renewal* (1974). 2. *Ecumenism and Charismatic Renewal* (1978). 3. *Charismatic Renewal and Social Action*, written in collaboration with Cardinal Suenens' associate, Dom Helder Camara of Brazil (1979). 4. *Renewal and the Powers of Darkness*, Foreword written by Cardinal Joseph Ratzinger (1982). 5. *Le Culte du Moi et Foi Chretienne* (1985). 6. *Resting in the Spirit*, also known as *A Controversial Phenomenon: Slaying in the Spirit* (1987).

Suenens was convinced that the CCR was a grace not only for the Church but also for the whole humanity. He strongly believed in the dynamic presence of the Holy Spirit and saw the CCR as an instrument of the Holy Spirit to rekindle faith in the lives of Christians. Even though he supported the CCR, he did not hesitate to criticize excess emotionalism in some charismatic worship meetings. For him, charismatic worship meetings were not for merely enjoying lively music but primarily for forming a personal relationship with Jesus and accept Him, as the Lord. He noted that friendship with Jesus led a person to true repentance and interior transformation in the power of the Holy Spirit. He believed the Holy Spirit bestows charisms, which Christians need for the growth of the community and the common good.

Suenens was one of the first Catholic Church's high-ranking official to recognize the potential of the CCR in promoting spiritual ecumenism. He looked upon the CCR to bring together all Spirit-filled Christians and worship the Lord as believers united in love. Cardinal Suenens also wished the charismatics not to insulate themselves from world but to channelize their goodness to bring transformation to the society.

Suenens devoted all his energies until his death on May 6, 1996 to implement the Second Vatican Council's reforms in the Catholic Church and promote the Marian Spirituality of complete submission to the will of God.

Bibliography

Alva, Reginald. 2014. *The Spirituality of the Catholic Charismatic Renewal Movement*. New Delhi: Christian World Imprints.

Congar, Yves. 2012. *My Journal of the Council*. Translated by Mary John Ronayne & Mary Cecily Boulding. English Translation edited by Denis Minns. Collegeville: The Liturgical Press.

Donnelly, Doris. ed. 1999. *Retrieving Charisms for the Twenty-First Century*. Collegeville: The Liturgical Press.

Suenens, Léon Joseph. 1980. *Open the Frontiers: A Spiritual Testimony from Cardinal Suenens in Conversation with Karl-Heinz Fleckenstein*. London: Darton, Longman and Todd.

Reginald Alva

Sung, John (Song Shangjie)

One of the best-known Chinese healing evangelists of the twentieth century, John Sung (Song Shangjie) (1901–1944), was an independent itinerant preacher in the 1930s. He lived during a turbulent time in China; but this was also the time of the Shandong Revival, when spiritual gifts were accepted in many Protestant churches. Song drew thousands to his meetings and regularly prayed for the sick, anointing them with oil. Startling results were reported. Born in the home of a Methodist preacher in Xinghua, Fujian, in southeast China, Song went to Ohio State University, graduating with a PhD in chemistry in 1926. One eventful year in the USA included a semester at Union Theological Seminary, New York, when he burned all his theological books and renounced theological education. After a breakdown (which he always claimed was a mistaken diagnosis for a spiritual experience) and six months in a mental hospital, he returned home in early 1927.

For the next 13 years he devoted himself exclusively to evangelism and healing, bringing at least 100,000 to conversion and revival to hundreds of churches. His preaching schedule took him throughout China and Southeast Asia as far as Burma.

Wherever he went, his diary recorded hundreds of conversions and healings from all kinds of afflictions. His hundreds of meetings were characterized by drama and emotion, including vivid illustrations on the platform, vigorous clapping, spontaneous prayer in unison, and free-flowing tears. Song dressed in an informal long Chinese shirt and often appeared disheveled. His stern revivalist preaching appealed to common people, demanded repentance from moral vices, and was accompanied by revival songs, emotional scenes of people repenting with loud cries, and exorcizing demons. Overwhelming numbers of people lined up for prayer for healing and exorcism in his meetings. He set up hundreds of evangelistic teams to continue his work throughout China and Southeast Asia. He became an international figure, but his many critics charged him with fanaticism, emotionalism, and even insanity.

Although Song cautioned against what he saw as Pentecostal excesses, his ministry certainly was characterized by Pentecostal phenomena and he preached in Pentecostal churches. He was baptized by immersion in 1932 in Hong Kong, he regularly prayed in tongues (a gift he first received in March 1934), and prayed for the sick during every campaign, but he also exercised a gift of knowledge and prophecy in the course of his preaching. He would speak out personal details of people in his audience without knowledge beforehand. He was also reported to use predictive prophecy and his diary records his occasional visions. His view on tongues was that it was the least of the gifts, but that every Christian should be filled with the Spirit. He saw this as an experience subsequent to conversion, prayed for people to receive the experience, and taught that it should be accompanied by receiving love and at least one of the nine gifts of the Holy Spirit in 1 Corinthians. He was also a conservative fundamentalist who sometimes used questionable exegesis and allegory, an outspoken critic of "liberal" theology, and one who believed that western missionary control was a hindrance to the Chinese church. He wrote in his diary that only after the missionaries had left and western funds stopped would the Chinese church really grow. He declared: "I feel that most of the [church] organizations set up by Westerners do not last long. The churches that God blesses are those built by Holy Spirit-inspired Chinese." He held annual Bible Conferences for church leaders; the one in Beijing in 1937 was attended by 1,600 delegates. Song prophesied that there would be a great revival in China after the missionaries had left and after the Chinese church had suffered greatly.

In spite of his often searing outbursts against western missionaries, Song was welcomed in western-founded evangelical churches and occasionally he was invited by the missionaries themselves. His effective ministry was regarded by many as preparing the Chinese church for the rigors of the impending Japanese war and the repression under Communism that was to follow. Song suffered from recurring tuberculosis and in 1940 was forced to give up his heavy travelling and preaching schedule when diagnosed with cancer. He died in 1944 at the age of 43 after several major operations. His funeral service was conducted by his friend and well-known Beijing pastor Wang Mingdao. Song's impact on Chinese Christianity was enormous. Not only was he spiritual father to many thousands of Chinese Christians, but his style of integrating emotional prayer with fundamentalist evangelism, is a prominent form of Chinese Protestantism.

Bibliography

Lyall, Leslie T. 2004. *John Sung*. Singapore: Armour Publishing.

Sung, John. 1995. *The Diaries of John Sung*. Translated by Stephen L. Sheng. Brighton, Michigan: L.H. Sheng, S.L. Sheng.

Xi, Lian. 2010. *Redeemed by Fire: The Rise of Popular Christianity in Modern China*. New Haven, Connecticut: Yale University Press.

Allan H. Anderson

Sutanto, Adi

Adi Sutanto (1948–) is the founder of *Sangkakala* (Trumpet) Foundation, a mission foundation which was started on 27 May 1977. The foundation was established as the result of a longing from some young people from Bangsri, a small town in the north coast of Central Java. The youth experienced the Charismatic renewal in the Mennonite churches in Java during the 1960s, where Sutanto himself experienced it. The renewal began among the Javanese Mennonite Churches (GITJ) and later spread to the Chinese-Indonesian Mennonite Churches (GKMI).

Sutanto was acquainted with the charismatic renewal through Edwin Stube's ministry in Semarang from 1965 to 1966. He experienced Spirit baptism while he was an undergraduate student at Jakarta Theological Seminary. He was impressed by Kathryn Kuhlman's ministry during his study in the United States, a type of power ministry that he would later emphasize in his own ministry along with evangelism.

After finishing his graduate degree in 1976, Sutanto was assigned to conduct research on the mission and history of the GKMI with Lawrence Yoder. However, he realized that his passion was on practical evangelism rather than theological research. His emphasis on evangelism apparently was not only influenced by the individualistic approach to interpreting the Great Commission proposed by Peter Wagner, who was his masters and doctoral supervisor, but also fundamentally influential for his personal calling to enter ministry.

Sutanto often testified that he heard a clear crying voice of somebody who longed for salvation while he prayed for a confirmation of his calling to study theology and leave his medical education. He believed

Adi Sutanto. Image: courtesy of the daughter of Rev Sutanto

that God challenged him to answer the crying of many more lost souls through a personal involvement which until recently marked his ministry. While Wagner in the last decade of his life revised his "saving souls" emphasis which formed his church growth theory and leaned toward social transformation that resulted in what he called dominion theology, Sutanto consistently accentuated quantitative growth as the result of zealous evangelism.

Sutanto started a prayer group as the initial ministry of the foundation. It started with eight people and reached its peak of three hundred people gathered each week in the second half of 1980, and was known as *Kebaktian Kharismatik* (Charismatic Service). It was moved several times to different houses and at its peak rented a city hall called *Gedung Pemuda*.

The Foundation also pioneered a number of prayer groups in Semarang and seven groups had been established by the end of 1979. The number of prayer groups under *Sangkakala* grew to 35 in 1981, and in following years saw 46 prayer groups with approximately 1,600 people. A few of the prayer groups grew rapidly and they were registered as a religious organization under the Indonesian legal system. The groups already used *Jemaat Kristen Indonesia/JKI* (Indonesia Christian Fellowship) as their groups' name, but it was not registered as a church institution at that time.

The JKI was legally established in 1985 as the solution to this situation, that was also related to the renunciation of Sutanto's former Mennonite denomination to accommodate the results of his ministry. At that time the leaders of his former denomination required these groups to give up their Charismatic features in worship, including enthusiastic worship style and speaking in tongues, as the prerequisite of integration. Currently the denomination is more accommodating towards Charismatic experience and some of the pastors are known as healing evangelists as well.

Sutanto moved to the U.S. to earned his doctorate in 1984 and served the JKI in the U.S. since 1986. The JKI currently has more than 300 local churches and a theological seminary. Some of the churches under JKI are among the largest megachurches in Indonesia, including Jakarta Praise Community Church (JPCC) in Jakarta and Gospel of the Kingdom Church (GKC) in Semarang.

Bibliography

Aritonang, Jan S., and Karel Steenbrink, eds. 2008. *The History of Christianity in Indonesia*. Leiden: Brill.

Kristanto, Rony Chandra. 2018. "Evangelism as Public Theology: The Public Engagement of the Gospel of the Kingdom Church in Semarang, Indonesia." PhD thesis, University of Birmingham, UK.

Sutanto, Adi. 1986. "A Strategy for Planting Churches in Java through The Sangkakala Mission with Special Emphasis on Javanese and Chinese People." DMiss diss., Fuller Theological Seminary.

Rony Chandra Kristanto

Sweden

Revival movements in the second half of the nineteenth century (including the Holiness movement and Örebro Baptists) paved the way for Pentecostalism in Sweden. At the same time, in both Sweden and Finland, the Laestadians from the Lutheran church experienced charismatic phenomena. The Baptist pastor Lewi

Pethrus visited T.B. Barratt soon after his return from the USA, and became convinced about the new Pentecostal experience. The Örebro Baptists were active in spreading the new message between 1907–1912. Not all Baptists were happy about the new movement, and the Filadelfia church in Stockholm was expelled from the Baptist Union in 1913. This was the beginning of the Swedish Pentecostal movement with Pethrus as a leading figure.

The new movement grew rapidly. In the difficult economic circumstances in the 1920s and 1930s, Pethrus' church was socially active and won the trust of many ordinary people. Soon a large megachurch building with 3000 seats was constructed in Stockholm. Pethrus was the initiator of several new activities including the Pentecostal daily newspaper *Dagen*, the weekly evangelistic magazine *Evangelii Härold*, publishing house, worldwide radio network (IBRA), Pentecostal bank (Samspar), and social ministry among alcohol and drug addicts (LP-Stiftelsen). He also believed in the need for political influence by Christians and founded the Christian Democratic party in Sweden. Pethrus understood the value of training young people and was instrumental in starting Pentecostal Folk High Schools. Pethrus was active in international relations and promoted the idea of the Pentecostal European Conferences (PEC). The first one was held in Nyhem in 1969. He was also an active member in the Pentecostal World Fellowship and the World Pentecostal Conference that was held in Sweden twice, in 1955 and in 2010.

The early Nordic Pentecostals were wary of theological training with many Pentecostal preachers emphasizing God's calling and the empowerment by the Holy Spirit. At a leaders' conference in Sweden in 1919 a decision was made that only short Bible courses would be recommended for ministry training. That decision affected all Nordic countries for almost a century. In Finland graduate Bible education started in the 1990s, and later other Nordic countries followed. In 2011 the Swedish Pentecostal Movement started an academic education program for future pastors called ALT, Academy for Leadership and Theology, and it is operated with two other free church denominations, EFK and Alliansmissionen. There are five student centers in five different cities and the students combine academic studies with pastoral work alongside pastors in local churches. It takes four years to graduate as a pastor.

The Pentecostal movement in Sweden is the largest among the Nordic countries and in the mid-1980s claimed to have over 100 000 baptised members and almost 500 local churches. Its missionary work has been the largest of all European Pentecostals. At its high point, over 900 Swedish missionaries worked abroad. The development work and humanitarian assistance program (PMU Interlife) started in 1965 and has been supported by SIDA (funded by the Swedish government). It is regarded highly and works with Swedish local churches and partners in countries around the world. In 2018 Dr. Denis Mukwege from the Democratic Republic of Kongo, was awarded the Nobel Peace Prize. He is known all over the world for his devoted work on sexual violence among women. He has received numerous international awards over the years and the Panzi hospital in Bukavu that was built by the Swedish Pentecostal Mission. Dr. Mukwege also pastors a large Pentecostal Church in Bukavu, which is a sister church to the Swedish Pentecostal movement and a partner in the missionary work still going on in DR Congo.

The Swedish Pentecostal church changed its structure at the beginning of the new millennium and became Pingst (Pentecost), The Swedish Alliance of Independent Churches. It consists of nearly 440 local churches, and about 88,000 members. The first leader of the new organization was Sten-Gunnar Hedin. He was followed by Pelle Hörnmark and, since 2016, Daniel Alm is the General Superintendent. The yearly conference, Pingst Rådslag, takes place annually in May.

Bibliography

Anderson, Allan. 2004. *An Introduction to Pentecostalism*. Cambridge: Cambridge University Press.

Coleman, Simon. 2000. *The Globalisation of Charismatic Christianity*. Cambridge: Cambridge University Press.

Moberg, Jessica, and Jane Skjoldli, eds. 2018. *Charismatic Christianity in Finland, Norway, and Sweden: Case Studies in Historical and Contemporary Developments*. Cham, Switzerland: Palgrave Macmillan.

Schmidgall, Paul. 2013. *European Pentecostalism: Its Origins, Development, and Future*. Cleveland, TN: CPT Press.

Waern, Claes, ed. 2007a. *Pingströrelsen Händelser och utveckling under 1900-talet*. Örebro: Libris Förlag.

Waern, Claes, ed. 2007b. *Pingströrelsen Verksamheter och särdrag under 1900-talet*. Örebro: Libris Förlag.

Wahlström, Magnus, ed. 2010. *Pingströrelsens årsbok 2010*. Örebro: Libris Förlag.

Arto Hämäläinen
Ulrika Ramstrand

Taiwan

No Pentecostal/Charismatic missionary works had been established in Taiwan prior to the end of the Japanese colonial era (1895–1945), with the exception of the Japan Apostolic Mission (although no detailed records remain about it). In 1948, China Assemblies of God (中國神召會) initiated a missionary enterprise in Taiwan. This AG body was organized in Wuhan, China, in 1948. It was a constellation of Pentecostal churches planted by missionaries from various countries that were scattered throughout China in the pre-1949 era, and has a strong American Assemblies of God connection. Taiwan Assemblies of God (台灣神召會) is another AG body launched in 1949, along with the retreat and resettlement of the Kuomingtang (KMT, 國民黨) regime to Taiwan, by missionaries of the Finnish Free Foreign Mission (FFFM, currently FIDA International) from China. This was a mission society organized by, and stemmed from, the Pentecostal churches in Finland. Three remaining AG groups must be mentioned. The first is the Assemblies of God Mountain District Council (神召會山地區議會), an aboriginal body that became independent from the China Assemblies of God in 1972. In 1954, the Pentecostal Assemblies of Canada arrived in Taiwan, and named itself the Pentecostal Assemblies of China (PAOC, 中華聖召會). The Taiwan Full Gospel Church (TFGC, 台灣純福音教會) was initiated by the Yoido Full Gospel Church in Korea, in 1979. The AG groups, the Foursquare Church, United Pentecostal Church, Church of God (Cleveland), and the Zion Church, could be included in the category of Classical Pentecostals as well. Generally, the Classical Pentecostal community is marginalized in Taiwan's Protestantism, since it is considered weak in terms of number of adherents and churches.

During the 1960s, mainline Protestant churches in Taiwan did not experience the parallel massive Charismatic Renewals, as it only occurred in certain areas such as North America. Although there were Protestants from mainline churches involved in Pentecostal/Charismatic movements, only a few stayed within their own denomination or traditions. On the other hand, some missionaries in the Catholic Church managed to import and promote Charismatic Renewal Movement to Taiwan since 1969, and local prayer groups were organized in response to this trend. However, in general, Charismatic Renewals are marginalized in the Taiwan Catholic community.

The 1980s could be a watershed for the Pentecostal/Charismatic movement in Taiwan. Two significant phenomena should be mentioned here. Firstly, the Independent renewal churches such as the Taipei Truth Church and the Worship Center have mushroomed. Secondly, the "ecclesiastical apartheid" between Pentecostals and non-Pentecostals has decreased. The Elim Christian Center (以琳基督徒中心) was established by Ukraine Canadian missionary Nicholas Krushnisky (柯希能, 1932–2016) and its related organization Elim Bookstore (which were indirectly connected with the Canadian Latter Rain movement), as well as the Chinese Christian Prayer Mountain (CCPM, 中華基督徒祈禱院), a Korea-inspired ministry directed by a Baptist Daniel Dai (戴義勳, 1930–) which had played an important role in promoting renewal movements. The Former party translated and published select Pentecostal/charismatic writings on a large scale, which made charismatic Christianity more acceptable among Taiwanese Christians; while the latter served as a bridge between Pentecostal/Charismatic and non-Pentecostal/Charismatic churches by promoting fasting and prayer based spirituality.

Since the 1990s, Taiwanese evangelical churches have been more open to renewal movements. Among those churches, the Bread of Life Christian Church (BOL, 靈糧堂) could be the most influential one. This church was founded as an independent church in Shanghai by evangelist Timothy S.K. Dzao (趙世光, 1908–73), in 1943. Though practicing healing, Dzao's ministry was not within the synchronous network of Chinese Pentecostals in the 1940s. The shifting of the practice and belief of traditional evangelical to renewal could be attributed to Nathaniel Chow (周神助), who became the senior pastor of the Taipei BOL Church in 1977. Chow encouraged empirical faith, imported Pentecostal/Charismatic spirituality, and managed to change the core foundation of this church. BOL has also built connections with churches sharing similar values on a global scale, gradually growing into the "BOL Global Apostolic Network." In addition, the Agape Renewal Ministry (愛修更新會, ARM), established by Ernst Chan (陳仲輝) in 1987, might be another prominent force of renewal movements among evangelicals. ARM is based on diasporic Chinese/Taiwanese Christian communities in North America, and also developed its ministry and planted churches and training institutions in Taiwan. Briefly, both of BOL and ARM tend to be neo-charismatic theologically.

Defining Pentecostalism in Taiwan and investigating taxonomies of which could be as complicated as doing it in global context, independent or indigenous churches such as the True Jesus Church (真耶穌教會) and the New Testament Church (新約教會) have been defined as Pentecostal (the TJC in particular) by western scholars, primarily due to their Pentecostal characteristics. Nevertheless, they are not only lacking of synchronous networks with those who identify themselves as Pentecostals, but also strongly decline to be classified as Pentecostal. Furthermore, plenty of Protestant churches have been influenced by renewal movements to varying degrees. They utilize Pentecostalism as a certain type of method for growth in their congregations, and claim networks with Pentecostal/Charismatic churches. These churches might be categorized as neo-charismatic. However, some of them are reluctant to identify their churches as Pentecostal/Charismatic. Moreover, many of the churches have mainline Protestant backgrounds, including Presbyterians, Lutherans, and Methodists, but it might be inappropriate to classify them into the category of "Second Wave" or Charismatic Renewal. They show no continuity with the Charismatic Movement that started in the 1960s. Theologically, without pursuing accommodation or harmonization of charismatic spirituality and their own tradition as what Charismatic Renewals have done, they incline to discard the tradition. This could be a challenge to the American-centric "Three Waves" model of taxonomy, not only locally, but globally as well. To sum up, the boundary between Pentecostals/Charismatics and non-Pentecostal/Charismatics is blurred and imprecise in Taiwan. Meanwhile, Charismatic spirituality has become highly influential in current local Protestantism.

Bibliography

Au, Connie. 2012. "Justice and Peace for Global Commercial Sex Workers: The Plight of Aboriginal Migrant Women in Taiwan." *The Ecumenical Review* 64 (3): 267–280.

Iap, Sian-Chin and Maurie Sween. 2016. "Pentecostal and Charismatic Christianity in Protestant Taiwan." In *Global Renewal Christianity: Spirit-Empowered Movements Past, Present, and Future*, edited by Vinson Synan and Amos Yong, 127–41. Lake Mary: Charisma House.

Li, Jieren. 1999. "A History of the Finnish Free Foreign Mission in Taiwan (1949–1998)." Master's thesis, ICI University.

Rubinstein, Murray A. 1996. "Holy Spirit Taiwan: Pentecostal and Charismatic Christianity in the Republic of China." In *Christianity in China: From the Eighteenth Century to the Present*, edited by Daniel H. Bays, 353–366. Stanford: Stanford University Press.

Shih, Shu-ying. 2013. "Apocalyptic Eschatology: A Case Study of the Charismatic Movement among the East Paiwan Tribes of the Presbyterian Church in Taiwan from the 1960s to 1980s." *Taiwan Journal of Religious Studies* 12 (1/2): 123–146.

Iáp Sian-chîn

Tanzania

Tanzania, the East African country that was born from the union on Tanganyika and Zanzibar in 1964, has a Pentecostal history that parallels that of other Sub-Saharan countries insofar as it is characterized by a slow and rocky start, followed by more massive growth in the last quarter of the twentieth century. The first foreign Pentecostal missionaries in Tanganyika whose history is known were Karl and Marian Wittick and Clarence Grothaus. They left Canada as independent missionaries in 1913 and were originally headed for Kenya, but due to opposition against mission of British governors they instead arrived in (what was then German) Tanganyika where they were permitted to settle at Utigi near present day Dodoma. However, their evangelization efforts were short-lived as both Karl Wittick and Clarence Grothaus died within a few months of their arrival. Marian Wittick stayed, but with the outbreak of World War I all links with her Canadian support base were cut, and after being briefly incarcerated by German authorities she eventually left for Kenya (Fisher 2011, 101; Garrard 2002, 264).

It was not until the 1930s that foreign Pentecostal missionaries started arriving in larger numbers in (what had by then become British) Tanganyika. Among the first to arrive were the Scandinavian Mission societies, the Swedish Free Mission and the Finish Free Foreign Mission, both of which had a holistic approach to mission, combining evangelization with the creation of schools and clinics (Hasu 2012, 70–71). Other European and North American missions followed during the late 1930s, 1940s and 1950s, in large part arriving from the neighboring British colonial territories of Kenya and Zambia. The Pentecostal Holiness Association Mission was planted in the southern highlands of Tanganyika in 1938 by members of the Pentecostal Holiness Church from Malawi and Zambia. Missionaries from the British Elim Pentecostal Church planted the Elim Pentecostal Church Tanzania in the late 1940s, opening mission stations at Morogoro, Kikilo, Kinoko, Tanga and Arusha.

The work of the Pentecostal Assemblies of God was started in the 1940s when the Kenyan preacher Renata Siemans travelled to Tanganyika to hold services among Kenyan migrants living near the border. The foundation of a national church, the Pentecostal Assemblies of God Tanzania, was aided by missionaries from the Pentecostal Assemblies of Canada. Other missionary churches that were established early on include the Tanzanian Assemblies of God that cooperated closely with the American Assemblies of God, the Church of God World Mission and the Pentecostal Evangelistic Fellowship of Africa (PEFA) (Garrard 2002).

For the first three quarters of the twentieth century missionary Pentecostal churches represented no real competition to the Catholic and the historical mainline churches. Besides, the African Initiated Churches which scholars often see as members of a larger Pentecostal family (Anderson 2014) have only had a marginal presence in Tanzania, much unlike Kenya, where these churches have been quite influential (Mwaura 2004). A historical phenomenon that was probably no less important in terms of introducing Tanzanians to a spirit-filled revivalist version of Christianity than the influx of Pentecostal missionaries in the mid-twentieth century was the East African Revival, a spiritual revival movement that originated within the Anglican Church in Rwanda and Uganda in the mid-1930s and then spread to Kenya and north-eastern Tanganyika, where it took root in the Anglican and, mainly, the Lutheran Church. The movement brought several classical revivalist phenomena into these historical Protestant churches such as seizure by the Holy Spirit, ecstatic experiences, speaking in tongues, restrictions on the behavior of revivalists and a theological emphasis on sin, repentance and sanctification. Such phenomena were highly controversial and viewed with considerable skepticism by church authorities and non-revivalist Lutherans as were the revivalists' practice of putting their private lives on display through public confessions of sin (Peterson 2012, 184–85). Nevertheless, the revival movement was by and large contained within mainline Protestant churches although a schism did occur in 1952 when Lutheran revivalists in the Kagera region were expelled and eventually formed their own church, The Church of the Holy Spirit, which was at the time the largest African-run church in Tanganyika.

While the East African revival left a lasting impact on the Lutheran church, especially in the North-Eastern parts of the country, it was not until the 1980s that Pentecostal/charismatic Christianity started spreading rapidly and became a major force on Tanzania's religious scene. Not only did the overall number of Pentecostal/charismatic Christians grow but a reduction of government restrictions and supervision also facilitated the proliferation of endless new movements and denominations, some of which have very few followers (Fisher 2011, 103). Whereas early missionary churches were mostly so-called first-wave classical Pentecostals, many newer Pentecostal churches that arrived or, in most cases, have been founded after schisms within existing churches, are better categorized as third-wave neo-Pentecostals. Besides, revival movements within historical Protestant churches and the Catholic Church, often referred to as a second wave of Pentecostal/charismatic Christianity, have grown, in large part due to Pentecostal competition and sheep stealing.

Neo-Pentecostal denominations of foreign origin include the Full Gospel Bible Fellowship which was introduced to Tanzania from Nigeria in the 1980s and is headed by Bishop Zacharia Kakobe, one of the most charismatic and famous Pentecostal preachers in the country. Kakobe is the pastor in charge of a mega-church in Dar es Salaam, he travels frequently and is well known, not only for inviting 'big shots' to founding ceremonies when officially opening new church buildings (Fisher 2011, 102–103) but also for his criticism of the government and his support of opposition politicians, resulting in the ministry of Home Affairs threatening to de-register his church in 2017. Parallel to the arrival and foundation of new churches, some of the older churches have experienced significant growth with the Tanzanian Assemblies of God claiming 250,000 baptized adult members and an aggregate attendance of 400,000 in 1997, figures that if correct would have made it the largest Pentecostal denomination in the country at the time (Garrard 2002, 267).

Finding exact figures is indeed a challenge for scholars on Pentecostalism in Tanzania, as statistics on religious affiliation are few and unreliable. But a study from the beginning of the twentieth century reports numbers that seem rather realistic: 1.5 million classical Pentecostals, 1.4 million charismatics and 0.7 million neo-Pentecostals in Tanzania out of a population of approximately 35 million people (Garrard 2002). I would expect a more updated study to show not only some overall growth but also a tipping of the balance towards an increased dominance of neo-Pentecostalism. In any case, decades of cross-fertilization and inter-denominational cooperation have made sharp categorical distinctions increasingly difficult to maintain. For instance, the themes of health and economic wealth and the strong emphasis on offerings as a prerequisite for receiving blessings, all of which are generally associated with third wave neo-Pentecostalism, are also prevalent within older (first wave) churches and within charismatic movements in mainline churches. In fact one of the most famous prosperity preachers in the country, Christopher Mwakasege has a Lutheran background and while he works as an interdenominational preacher, attracting multi-denominational crowds to his seminaries and open-air meetings in Tanzanian cities he still cooperates closely with the Lutheran Church (Hasu 2006).

This is not say that Tanzanian Pentecostals/Charismatics now constitute a homogenous group, only that historical distinctions between first, second and thirds waves may not provide the most useful framework for understanding contemporary Pentecostal/charismatic diversity. Churches and movements certainly differ, for instance in the extent to which they are centered around particular charismatic leaders, in the theological emphasis they place on themes such as spiritual warfare, economic prosperity and offerings, miracles and self-development and in the behavioral requirements that are imposed on members. Research has demonstrated how theological differences in some cases follow social class, with the strong emphasis on spiritual warfare being more appealing more to lower class Pentecostals and the message of self-development appealing to middle classes (Hasu 2012).

A little more than a century after the arrival of the first missionaries, Pentecostalism has become a force to be reckoned with in Tanzanian society, due to the numerical growth of Pentecostals but also to a certain Pentecostalization of mainline Christianity. Besides, Pentecostalism has become an increasingly public religion in Tanzania. Most larger and many smaller cities host open-air revival meetings every year, and since the 1990s international evangelists such as Reinhard Bonnke have held crusades in the country. Pentecostal and other evangelical ministries run Christian weekly newspapers and radio stations, and there is an industry of taped sermons, music videos, and gospel music, which is not only played in private homes but also in busses, bus stations, markets and other public places. Furthermore Nigerian movies that explore Pentecostal themes such as spiritual warfare have found a large, Pentecostal and non-Pentecostal, audience in Tanzania. Hence Pentecostalism has established itself as a significant religious and cultural force whose influence extends far beyond the confines of church buildings.

Bibliography

Anderson, Allan H. 2014. "Origins and Developments of Pentecostalism in Africa." In *Pentecostalism in Africa*, edited by M. Lindhardt, 54–74. Leiden: Brill.

Fischer, M. 2011. "'The Spirit Helps Us in Our Weakness': Charismatization of Worldwide Christianity and the Quest for an Appropriate Pneumatology with Focus on the Evangelical Lutheran Church in Tanzania." *Journal of Pentecostal Theology* 20 (1): 95–121.

Garrard, D.J. 2002. "Tanzania." In *The New International Dictionary of Pentecostal and Charismatic Movements*, edited by Stanley M. Burgess, and Eduard M. van der Maas, 264–269. Grand Rapids, MI: Zondervan.

Hasu, P. 2012. "Prosperity Gospel and Enchanted World Views: Two Responses to Socio-Economic Transformations in Tanzanian Pentecostal Christianity." In *Pentecostalism and Development: Churches, NGOs and Social Change in Africa*, edited by D. Freeman, 67–86. New York: Palgrave Macmillan.

Hasu, P. 2006. "World Bank and Heavenly Bank in Poverty and Prosperity: The Case of Tanzanian Faith Gospel." *Review of African Political Economy* 33 (110): 679–692.

Mwaura, P.N. 2004. "African Instituted Churches in East Africa." *Studies in Third World Christianity* 10 (2): 160–184.

Peterson D.R. 2012. *Ethnic Patriotism and the East African Revival*. Cambridge: Cambridge University Press.

Martin Lindhardt

Taylor, George Floyd

George Floyd Taylor (1881–1934) was born in Dumpling County near Magnolia, North Carolina. Bishop J.H. King of the Pentecostal Holiness Church (PHC) wrote the following after the passing of Taylor, "When George Floyd Taylor came into the home of his father, it required three days of vigorous effort on the part of the attending physician and others to keep his soul from departing to the Great Beyond. His mother did not see him until the third day after his advent" (King 1935). He suffered "specific significant neurological deficits" so that he stuttered when speaking, suffered from hand tremors while writing, and had trouble with his balance when walking (York 2013). These physical limitations kept him from getting a minister's license with the Methodist Episcopal Church South. However, this did not deter him from evolving into a "Father" of the International Pentecostal Holiness Church.

The first churches known to Taylor in Magnolia were the Universalist, Freewill Baptist, and Methodist Episcopal Church South. In 1897, Taylor attended the first Holiness Convention in Magnolia that led to the 1901 formation of the PHC there that he would join in 1903. In 1907, Taylor moved to Falcon, North Carolina, to become principal of what was known as the Falcon Holiness School, he previously being the founding principal of Bethel Holiness School near Rose Hill, North Carolina.

Taylor had been critical to the 1911 merger of the PHC with the Fire Baptized Holiness Church and had distinguished himself for taking the PHC beyond the USA. Among the most demanding challenges Taylor addressed was the Gift Movement of 1916 in Virginia and West Virginia. Those caught up in this movement surrendered to prophetic utterances that directed them to marry persons unknown to them, remove photos of dead family members, burn books, and start for China with no preparation or funding (Woods 1997). A.E. Robinson wrote, "At a period in our church history, when we were passing through a severe struggle, Mr. Taylor was elected General Superintendent, of the Pentecostal Holiness Church, and for four years, 1913 till 1917, capably filled that office" (Robinson 1935).

In 1917, at the General Conference in Abbeville, South Carolina, where Taylor gladly relinquished the position of general superintendent, he advocated the publication of an official PHC periodical. The Conference accepted his suggestion, elected him editor and business manager, and gave him authority to begin the publication of a church paper named the *Pentecostal Holiness Advocate* (*PHA*), which he did in May of the same year.

That same year (1917), the PHC acquired the property at Franklin Springs, Georgia, and Taylor moved there. Soon the first section of the publishing house was erected, and suitable machinery installed to publish the paper in addition to Sunday

School and other literature. Taylor was the first writer and publisher of Pentecostal Holiness Sunday School literature. Taylor continued to serve for some years (e.g. 1917–1926) as the manager of the publishing house (now known as LifeSprings Resources), and his editorship of the Sunday School literature was continuous from its beginning in 1913 until his untimely death. He was also the editor of the *PHA* all the while, apart from one term of four years, which he spent out of the office continuing his preparation for better service of his academic ministry. The time was well utilized, completing the college work which he had been compelled to give up some years before and obtaining the degrees of Bachelor of Arts and Master of Arts (MA) from the University of North Carolina. Taylor was 50 years old when he earned his MA.

Taylor's *The Spirit and the Bride*, which originated in 1907, was the first of its kind for North American Pentecostalism. He published several other books including a catechism. Travel to Palestine in 1929 led to a book entitled *My Tour of the Bible Lands*. He also pioneered religious dramas for the PHC, including "The Prodigal Son" and "The Tragedy of Saul: First King of Israel." The Franklin Springs Institute – now Emmanuel College – was opened under Taylor's superintendence in 1919 with him serving as the first president. In 1921, he was appointed archivist of the PHC. Taylor was serving on the faculty of Emmanuel College when he died on November 16, 1934.

For Taylor, the tenets of Pentecostalism were so important that their defence was worth dividing the Holiness Movement. The "most pious and deeply spiritual people of the land" were seeking their Pentecost, while Holiness preachers who were jealous of their loss of prestige fought against it. Taylor considered religious criticism of Pentecostalism misguided and based on an erroneous interpretation of the Bible. He denounced and dismissed such critics as being unwitting allies of the devil. He wrote, "God, in His mercy, has enabled me to see the unscriptural teachings … appearing in prominent holiness papers and … pulpits," and he proceeded to refute them point by scriptural point. Taylor was so committed to initial-evidence Spirit baptism that he insisted deaf-mutes must speak in tongues to be certifiably baptized in the Spirit (Taylor 1908). Robinson put it well when he wrote, "George Floyd Taylor was the outstanding character among us in so many respects that it is unlikely we shall see his equal" (Robinson 1934).

Bibliography

King, J.H. 1935. "'He Being Dead Yet Speaketh': Hebrews 11:4." *Pentecostal Holiness Advocate* 18, no. 36 (January 10): 8.

Robinson, A.E. 1934. "'In Labors More Abundant.'" *Pentecostal Holiness Advocate* 18, no. 36 (January 10): 9–10.

Taylor, G.F. 1907. *The Spirit and the Bride*. Falcon, NC: 1–9, 40–49, 90–99.

Woods, Daniel Glenn. 1997. "Living in the Presence of God: Enthusiasm, Authority, and Negotiation in the Practice of Pentecostal Holiness." PhD diss., University of Mississippi.

York, H. Stanley. 2013. George *Floyd Taylor: The Life of an Early Southern Pentecostal Leader*. Maitland, FL: Xulon Press.

Harold D. Hunter

Theology

Pentecostal theology emerged at the beginning of the twentieth century as a revivalist ideology focused on a transformative experience of Jesus Christ through a personal encounter with the Holy Spirit and has since then developed toward doctrinal and systematic formulations with attention to a wide range of theological, spiritual, ethical, sociocultural, philosophical, economic, and political concerns (Yong 2005). The debate on the character of Pentecostal theology shows a number of critical concerns surrounding the identity of Pentecostalism in distinction from other theological traditions (Cross 2000; Dabney 2001). The focus of Pentecostal theology during the first decades can be seen in its recourse to the scriptures and the organization of biblical themes around diverse Pentecostal experiences (Stephenson 2012). Association with evangelicalism since the 1950s, the rise of charismatic theology in the mainline churches since the 1960s, the prominence of ecumenical conversations since the 1970s, the birth of Pentecostal theological scholarship since the 1990s, and the broadening of theological interests among Pentecostals today have further shaped the definition, content, and methodology of Pentecostal theology. This debate has involved concerns for the relationship of theology and spirituality, the role of experience, the importance of the affections, the emergence of distinctive theological practices and themes, the embodiment of such themes in Pentecostal life and worship, and the emergence of a genuine Pentecostal theological narrative.

Pentecostal spirituality is widely seen as the expression of a personal participation of the individual and the community in the biblical story of God. Pentecostals seek recourse in scripture, particularly Luke-Acts, to interpret their own experiences, and the move to interpretation and theological reflection always passes through a personal encounter with Christ through the Holy Spirit. Theological articulation among Pentecostals can be speculative and systematic albeit only if that means an integration of spirituality in terms of the cognitive, affective, and behavioral dimensions of participating in the biblical story (Stephenson 2012, 28–58, 114–19).

The heartbeat of Pentecostal spirituality is the experience of the Holy Spirit exemplified on the day of Pentecost (Vondey 2017, 14–20). A dominant perception of this spirituality emerging from Pentecost is its pneumatic character (as the experience resulting from the encounter with the Spirit) and pneumatological orientation (as reflection on that experience). On the level of contemplation, Pentecostal theology begins with the Spirit and from there submits to the current of spirituality: oral narrative and testimony, proclamation, prayer, song and dance, prophecy and speaking with tongues are some of the native expressions at the core of this theology. Scripture contains these expressions in a normative but second-order fashion that allows Pentecostals to reflect on and discern their own experiences (Cross 2000). Doctrine is in this process a third-order moment of an implicit theological method that emerges from and aims at returning to the original experience.

Debate about the native expression of Pentecostal spirituality has centered on Pentecostals' articulation of their own theological story (Dabney 2001). External emphasis is often placed on particular moments, therefore isolating prominent experiences (e.g., speaking with tongues) as exemplary of Pentecostal theology. A more inclusive framework used consistently for narrating the set of Pentecostal experiences is the full gospel, which emerged historically as a four- or five-fold pattern: Jesus Christ is savior, sanctifier, Spirit baptizer, healer, and coming king (Vondey 2017). This narrative has emerged as a liturgical hermeneutic of Pentecostal theology in consistent, dynamic, and even playful ways.

The playfulness of Pentecostal theology is attributed to the variety of experiences narrated by the Pentecostal story and their communication and interpretation through the affections (Suurmond 1995, 27–98), so that theology proceeds on the premise of abiding individual and communal dispositions, not mere spontaneous emotional states, but transformative manifestations of the encounter with God. The affections bring Pentecostal theology to the limits of speech, concepts, theory, and systematization: image, symbol, song, poetry, prophecy, vision, dreams, and testimony are the media of the imagination carried by the affections towards theological articulation (Vondey 2017, 24–27). The goal of this articulation is worship and a theology that is always doxology.

Doxology expresses the affective spirituality of Pentecostal theology that is both praxis-oriented and demands the continuous association of doctrine with the original experience. Pentecostal theology relies on the wonder of experience so that it can be embodied and lived, sometimes in pre-cognitive or irrational ways (Stephenson 2012, 82–110). Embedded in the experiences of Pentecost is the unbounded presence of God in the world, so that Pentecostal theology exists more in the realm of expectation, possibility, and wonder than in the realm of already actualized and objectified propositions (Suurmond 1995, 52–58). Dogmatic and philosophical considerations have to be brought into the embodied world of Pentecostal liturgies, rituals, and practices where they can expand into a constructive and systematic framework (Vondey 2017, 153–280).

Pentecostals are divided whether their embodied experiences can or should be articulated systematically amidst criticisms concerning borrowed or artificial doctrinal expressions of Pentecostal identity and character that jeopardize the integrity of the original experiences. Other concerns are that theology as a discipline is dominated by western ideas and constructs that are not always readily shared by global Pentecostal sensitivities. A systematic account of Pentecostal theology may threaten to institutionalize and theorize the human encounter with God. The continuing challenge of Pentecostalism as an emerging theological tradition is the reduction of the Pentecostal story to isolated doctrines at the cost of losing the dynamic of the experience, reflection, practice, and transformation which stand at the core of Pentecostal theology.

Bibliography

Cross, Terry. 2000. "The Rich Feast of Theology: Can Pentecostals Bring the Main Course or Only the Relish?" *Journal of Pentecostal Theology* 8 (16): 27–47.

Dabney, D. Lyle. 2001. "Saul's Armor: The Problem and Promise of Pentecostal Theology Today." *Pneuma* 23 (1): 115–146.

Suurmond, Jean-Jacques. 1995. *Word and Spirit at Play: Towards a Charismatic Theology*. Grand Rapids: Eerdmans.

Stephenson, Christopher A. 2012. *Types of Pentecostal Theology: Method, System, Spirit*. Oxford: Oxford University Press.

Vondey, Wolfgang. 2017. *Pentecostal Theology: Living the Full Gospel*. London: Bloomsbury.

Yong, Amos. 2005. *The Spirit Poured Out on All Flesh: Pentecostal Theology and the Possibility of Global Theology*. Grand Rapids: Baker.

Wolfgang Vondey

Toronto Blessing (Catch the Fire)

The Toronto Blessing refers to a revival which took place at the Toronto Airport Vineyard (TAV) in the mid-1990s. John Arnott (1995), pastor of the revival, preferred to call it "The Father's Blessing" because it came from the Father and was not confined to Toronto, Canada. The revival began on January 20, 1994 when approximately 120 people gathered at the TAV for a series of four scheduled meetings with American Vineyard Pastor Randy Clark. Days turned into weeks as the revival gathered momentum and news spread around the world.

The TAV hosted revival meetings six days per week, taking only Mondays off. A typical evening service consisted of praise and worship music, testimonies from people impacted by the revival, preaching, and a lengthy ministry time. Charismatic phenomena occurred during the meetings. While the call for salvation was regularly offered, the revival focused on the renewal of believers. Respondents to a 1995 survey indicated that 95 percent of attendees were charismatic or Pentecostal Christians (Poloma 2003, 67, 88). This has led people to question whether the revival would better be called a renewal among Christians (as opposed to a revival characterized by evangelism and conversion), language Arnott used more frequently.

The Toronto Blessing was marked by an intense presence of the Holy Spirit accompanied by physical charismatic phenomena including laughter, 'drunkenness' in the Spirit, weeping, falling to the floor, physical convulsions, jumping up and down, shouting and roaring (Arnott 1995; Beverley 1995; Chevreau 1994). Divine healing and prophecy were also hallmarks of the movement (Poloma 2003). Significant controversy surrounded the phenomena of animal sounds. The practice of people barking like dogs, roaring like lions, and even clucking like chickens was a major factor which led Vineyard leader, John Wimber, to sever ties with the TAV in December 1995 (Poloma 2013). The mimicking of animals was explained in methaphorical and symbolic language often in reference to biblical themes. TAV then changed its name to the Toronto Airport Christian Fellowship (TACF) before renaming itself Catch the Fire (CTF) in 2010.

The motto of the Toronto Blessing became its theme: "To Walk in God's Love and Then Give It Away" (Poloma 2013; Wilkinson and Althouse 2014). Arnott emphasized this theme through his speaking and writing. For Arnott, the revelation of the Father's love "needs to reach deep into our inner beings" where we are transformed into the type of people that love others in the same way God loves (Arnott 1995, 25). Arnott used quasi-erotic language to explain the Father's love, urging people that "Jesus wants a love affair with you" (Arnott 1995, 20). The overall teaching of the Toronto Blessing differs from other revivals in its laid-back therapeutic style that emphasized love and mercy over judgment (Poloma 2003).

The Toronto Blessing did not arrive *ex nihilo* – a number of antecedents can be identified which facilitated the renewal. The denominational context of the Association of Vineyard Churches (AVC) provided a plausibility structure for the variety of charismatic phenomena experienced during the revival. Most of the phenomena had been seen before in more limited fashion in other Vineyard churches. The AVC also provided the soundtrack with intimate music about the Father's love. The transference of anointing is also important in understanding the Toronto Blessing. Arnott travelled to Argentina in November of 1993 where he was singled out and anointed by Assemblies of God evangelist Claudio Freidzon. Arnott reported bringing this anointing home to Toronto. An American AVC pastor, Randy Clark, attended a Rodney Howard-Browne meeting in August 1993 where he was anointed. Howard-Browne's meetings in Lakeland, Florida became known as the "Laughing Revival" due the prominence of uncontrollable laughter. Arnott heard about Clark's anointing and invited him to lead a series of meetings which launched the Toronto Blessing.

Theologians and church leaders have evaluated the Toronto Blessing both positively and negatively. Guy Chevreau (1994) and Clark Pinnock (1996) have written positively about the movement. Chevreau places the Toronto Blessing in the lineage of Jonathan Edwards's meetings. Clark Pinnock was known to attend the Toronto Blessing and his theological views are sympathetic to charismatic Christianity. On the other hand, reformed theologians like Hank Hanegraaff and John McArthur have dismissed the revival as unorthodox.

Sociologists have used a variety of approaches to understand the Toronto Blessing. For example, Margaret Poloma (2003) viewed the Toronto Blessing through the lens of institutionalization where the Toronto Blessing is understood as a movement that served to revitalize Pentecostalism. What began as spontaneous charismata in the emergence stage moved quickly into a coalescence stage when the church was cut off from its parent organization. The movement is now firmly in the bureaucratization stage having created a new denominational structure. Stephen Hunt (2009) explored the role of globalization for the transporting of Pentecostal phenomena around the world and the various ways in which it is local and global. Hunt, however, questioned some of the assumptions of globalization and examined how a market model might offer another way to interpret the growth of the Toronto church in relation to a longer history of Pentecostalism and its competitors. Michael Wilkinson and Peter Althouse (2014) argue that specific embodied practices such as soaking prayer keep the emotional energy of the revival alive as CTF develops its brand and plants satellite churches throughout the world.

Cartledge's (2014) analysis highlights one final feature of the Toronto Blessing: its portability. Pilgrims attended Toronto not to stay, but to return to their own congregations refreshed by the Spirit. Many congregations reported phenomena similar to the Toronto Blessing when their people returned. During the first two years, it was estimated that over 600,000 attended the nightly meetings making it Toronto's most notable tourist attraction. Now that the flood of pilgrims has turned into a trickle, the ongoing work of revitalized congregations around the world carries its legacy, most notably the many independent congregations that have some affiliation through apostolic networks with CTF but also through the planting of new congregations by CTF in cities like London, Houston, and Montreal.

Bibliography

Arnott, John. 1995. *The Father's Blessing*. Orlando, FL: Creation House.

Beverley, James A. 1995. *Holy Laughter and The Toronto Blessing: An Investigative Report*. Grand Rapids, MI: Zondervan.

Cartledge, Mark J. 2014. "'Catch the Fire': Revivalist Spirituality from Toronto to Beyond." *PentecoStudies* 13 (2): 217–238.

Chevreau, Guy. 1994. *Catch the Fire: The Toronto Blessing: An Experience of Renewal and Revival.* London, UK: Marshall Pickering.

Hunt, Stephen. 2009. "The Toronto Blessing, A Lesson in Globalized Religion?" In *Canadian Pentecostalism*, edited by Michael Wilkinson, 233–248. Montreal & Kingston: McGill-Queen's University Press.

Pinnock, Clark H. 1996. *Flame of Love: A Theology of the Holy Spirit.* Downers Grove, IL: Inter Varsity Press.

Poloma, Margaret M. 2003. *Main Street Mystics: The Toronto Blessing & Reviving Pentecostalism.* Walnut Creek, CA: AltaMira.

Wilkinson, Michael and Peter Althouse. 2014. *Catch the Fire: Soaking Prayer and Charismatic Renewal.* DeKalb, IL: Northern Illinois University Press.

Stephen Barkley

True Jesus Church

Founded in 1917, the True Jesus Church 真耶穌教會 is one of the oldest Pentecostal churches in China. Early church leaders were Chinese Pentecostals who first encountered Pentecostal doctrines and practices in fledgling mission churches established by foreign veterans of the 1906 Azusa Street Revival in Los Angeles.

True Jesus Church, Taiwan. Source: Center for the Study of Global Christianity

Often, members of this first generation of Chinese Pentecostals also had experience within older, more established mission organizations that had operated in China since the nineteenth century. Early Chinese Pentecostal churches like the True Jesus Church, therefore, drew on diverse organizational and ritual resources from transplanted Western Christian and native Chinese religious traditions while maintaining very close genealogical ties to the classical Pentecostal movement overseas.

The founding history of the True Jesus Church exemplifies these complex institutional and interpersonal connections. The church's charismatic founder Wei Enbo 魏恩波 was born and raised in rural north China and had initially joined the London Missionary Society in 1903. In 1915 Wei joined the Pentecostal congregation run by Bernt Berntsen, a Norwegian American missionary who had become a Pentecostal at the Azusa Street Revival in 1907 and subsequently established "Apostolic Faith Churches" in north China. Many of Wei's early associates in the leadership of the True Jesus Church had been leaders in other churches, including not only the churches of the mission establishment and international Pentecostalism but also denominations such as Seventh-day Adventism.

The success of the True Jesus Church in attracting members was due to many factors including a culture of charismatic practice, emphasis on independence from foreign church institutions, a flexible locally oriented organizational structure, savvy utilization of mass media and printing, and a theological emphasis on strict adherence to the Chinese text of the Bible. Throughout the 1920s and 1930s, evangelists of the True Jesus Church carried its message and distinctive practices throughout North and South China and overseas to Chinese diaspora communities in locales such as southeast Asia,

Japan, Hawai'i, California, and the United Kingdom. Despite various schisms, up until the mid-1950s there existed a major centralized international network of True Jesus Churches administered by a general headquarters in China. Maoist era political persecutions drove the church in China underground from approximately 1958 to 1974, during which time regional practice diversified and overseas centers such as Taiwan took on new prominence. By the turn of the twenty-first century, large regional networks of the True Jesus Church in the People's Republic of China had been reestablished, some of which developed connections to international networks of the True Jesus Church with major institutional hubs in Taiwan, the United States, and Canada. Today the international organization of the True Jesus Church maintains a global mission network that includes congregations in Africa and South America. Altogether the True Jesus Church claims about 1.5 million members worldwide, with the majority of members in the People's Republic of China.

Theologically, the True Jesus Church belongs to the Oneness Pentecostal tradition. The church teaches that baptism should be by immersion, face-down, in a natural body of water, with ritual language invoking the name of Jesus. Baptism of water should be accompanied by the baptism of fire, that is, the baptism of the Holy Spirit. Glossolalia is thought to be the sign of this baptism by the Holy Spirit. In a session of prayer, believers begin speaking in tongues almost immediately, in the form of repeated syllables, often accompanied by physical movement, and cease when the person leading the prayer rings a bell. Another core rite within the True Jesus Church is footwashing, performed by elders, deacons, and deaconesses following the rite of baptism, in emulation of Christ at the Last Supper. The sacrament of the Last Supper is performed periodically during the course of a year with unleavened bread and grape juice. Local congregations are led by elders (male), deacons (male), deaconesses (female), and preachers (who may be male or female). In many chapels around the world, the speaker's podium is equipped with double microphones so that sermons may be given in two languages, usually Mandarin Chinese and a local language. The main weekly worship service is on Saturday morning, a Sabbatarian tradition that seems to have come from the influence of Seventh-day Adventism on early church founders.

Although members of the True Jesus Church represent only a small percentage of the hundreds of millions of Christians in the People's Republic of China, the influence of the True Jesus Church and other Pentecostal churches is apparent in Chinese Christian culture's strong emphasis on charismatic experience, both historically and in the present, within both unofficial and officially registered churches. In diaspora, the True Jesus Church is a center of Chinese ethnic identity, language, and culture, as well as an outpost of global Pentecostal and restorationist teaching.

Bibliography

Bays, Daniel. 1995. "Indigenous Protestant Churches in China, 1900–1937: A Pentecostal Case Study." In *Indigenous Responses to Western Christianity*, edited by Steven Kaplan, 124–143. New York: New York University Press.

Huang, Ke-Hsien. 2016. "Sect-to-Church Movement in Globalization: Transforming Pentecostalism and Coastal Intermediaries in Contemporary China." *Journal for the Scientific Study of Religion* 55 (2): 407–416.

Inouye, Melissa Wei-Tsing. 2019. *China and the True Jesus: Charisma and Organization in a Chinese Christian Church*. New York: Oxford.

Lian, Xi. 2010. *Redeemed by Fire: The Rise of Popular Christianity in Modern China*. New Haven, CT: Yale University Press.
Reed, David. 2008. *In Jesus' Name: The History and Beliefs of Oneness Pentecostals*. Dorset, UK: Deo Publishing.
Yang, Fenggang, Joy K.C. Tong, and Allan H. Anderson, eds. 2017. *Global Chinese Pentecostal and Charismatic Christianity*. Leiden: Brill.

Melissa Wei-Tsing Inouye

Turner, William H.

William Henry (Bill) Turner (1895–1971) was born on May 24, 1895 in the mountains of Western North Carolina. It is reported that he became a Christian at the age of six, having been led to an altar of prayer by an elderly lady. At the age of fifteen, he made this commitment anew under the influence of the fiery assistant general overseer of the Fire-Baptized Holiness Church, F.M. Britton. His public-school education was limited due to demands of mountain farm duties. After the death of his mother, their home was broken up, and he went to work with a Christian family for board and $12 a month.

In June 1912, Turner entered Altamont Bible and Mission Institute (now Holmes Bible College in Greenville, SC) on Paris Mountain, South Carolina. Feeling like he was foreign to formal education, he started low and thrived earning a diploma in 1915. In 1916, he studied one year at the Falcon Holiness School in Falcon, North Carolina where he graduated with a diploma. In 1918, he studied at Emory University in Atlanta, Georgia. He received his Bachelor of Arts degree from Oskaloosa College in 1921 and his Bachelor of Divinity in 1923. At the age of fifty-three, he earned a Master of Arts in journalism from the University of Georgia.

In 1915 while teaching school in Raleigh, North Carolina, Turner was ordained by the North Carolina Conference of the Pentecostal Holiness Church (PHC). He initially served as pastor of three PHC congregations. In August 1917, Turner received a letter from G.F. Taylor, general treasurer of the PHC, preparing him to go to China as a PHC missionary. That same year he married his wife, Orine Entrekin, whom he had known from their days at the Altamont Bible and Mission Institute as one also "called" to China.

The Turners sailed from San Francisco on Oct 20, 1919, landing in Hong Kong on November 15, 1919. The Turners spent part of the first four years of their 24 years in China learning Cantonese. W.H. Turner would later learn Mandarin good enough for preaching. In 1922, with the help of several colporteurs, Turner sold around 12,000 gospels, and distributed other literature to make a total of 56,750 pieces.

In 1923, Turner was notified of his election by the PHC General Board as superintendent of the South China PHC work. Turner's initial footing in mainland China was Pakhoi, a British Treaty port in Gaungxi province. He was able to buy a compound owned by Joseph Smale who had abandoned active ministry there. Julie Payne would emerge as a leading figure here for the PHC.

Connie Au (2011) details how Turner's vision for China ran into the harsh reality of severe political and social chaos between 1920 and 1930 and particularly from 1924 to 1928 when the radicalized Anti-Christian Movement became violent. During these years, the Turners dealt with boycotts, isolation, and authentic threats to their lives. Turner's account of these years was published in 1928 under the title, *Pioneering in China*.

W.H. Turner had envisioned thousands of followers led by their own people. Turner would aid and abet the work through a publishing house and a Bible school. According to William Purinton, Turner continued to support the faith missionary model he learned at the Altamont Bible and Missionary Institute. However, he saw firsthand the ruins of various eschatologically driven missionaries in places like Pakhoi, China. Turner could look to J.H. King who observed some of the same during his 1910–1911 tour of Asia. Building on Daniel Bays's views, Purinton points to Turner's belief in miracles for the "latter rain" as his mission engine (Purinton 2003).

The Turners were sent to Shanghai in 1936 where they organized five churches. While still in Shanghai Turner wrote in *Building for God in Blood, War, and Death*, "God gave us capable Chinese men to place in key positions and in that war-torn city that was taken over by the Japanese, the work of the Lord moved on." Their children were sent back to the USA and after Pearl Harbor, the Turners were interned for 18 months (1941–1943) at what was once the Great China University. During the Japanese occupation, it became the Chapei Concentration Camp.

The Turners suffered at the hands of their Japanese captors, but as non-combatants they were spared the horrors known to other parts of the Pacific theater. Alex Mayfield marks Turner as given to theocentric motivated acts of resistance, that meant Turner "… burns documents, refuses to repatriate, launders money, violates Japanese regulations, runs shadow distribution networks, refuses to give up food stocks, bribes officials, and hands over authority to Chinese ministers" (Mayfield 2017).

The Turners were exchanged for Japanese prisoners and returned to the USA in 1943. They set sail in September 1943 on a Japanese ship that was fraught with danger, then over to a European cruise ship which got them to New York City on December 1, 1943.

Turner served as director of PHC World Missions for 12 years before his retirement in 1965 due to failing health. His ministry landmarks included reading the Bible through more than sixty times, countless all-night prayer meetings, and always an evangelist. He was a prodigious author having written over 20 books. He passed away on September 24, 1971.

Bibliography

Au, Connie. 2012. "Resisting Globalization: The Pentecostal Holiness Church's Mission and the 'Anti-Globalization Movement' in China (1920–30)." In *Global Pentecostal Movements: Migration, Mission, and Public Religion*, edited by Michael Wilkinson, 117–134. Leiden: Brill.

Mayfield, Alex. 2017. "'A Gloriously Free Work': Pentecostal POWs and Spirit-Filled Resistance." Unpublished paper read to the American Academy of Religion, Boston, MA.

Purinton, William T. 2003. "W.H. Turner and the Chinese Pentecost." *Wesleyan Theological Journal* 38 (1): 226–241.

Harold D. Hunter

United Kingdom

Pentecostal and charismatic churches in the UK are diverse. They vary in their history, to some extent in their doctrine, ecclesiology, practice and social attitudes, and in their resources. Their congregations range from small and struggling start-ups to powerful megachurches.

Three classical indigenous Pentecostal denominations can date their beginnings to the years of, or just after, the 1914–18 war.

Essentially, they came out of the Welsh Revival of 1904–05. The first Pentecostal denomination to be formed was the Apostolic Faith Church in Bournemouth in 1908 and this included a number of Welsh congregations which, in January 1916, broke free from the parent body to form their own Apostolic Church which continues until this day. They fully embraced the Pentecostal and charismatic gifts of the Spirit but also believed that the government of local churches should be by apostles and prophets.

George Jeffreys founded the Elim Pentecostal Church in Ireland in 1915. Jeffreys had been converted during the Welsh revival and had had dealings with the Apostolic Faith Church at a very early stage in his ministry but he came to reject its doctrines and practices and so established his own denomination with pastors in charge of congregations and his own ministry of evangelism and church planting. The Elim church transferred to England in 1921.

Independently and separately of both these denominations, a collection of independent congregations of various types and origins came together in 1924 as the Assemblies of God. Assemblies of God was, from the beginning, democratic in outlook and governed through an annual conference.

The Apostolics and Elim were largely founded by recognised and dominant individuals, the Williams brothers (Apostolics) and George Jeffreys (1889–1962, Elim), whereas Assemblies of God had no such founder. During the 1920s and 1930s Assemblies of God and Elim grew remarkably by holding campaigns and crusades and other outward-looking evangelistic events. The Jeffreys crusades were the most stunning and regularly reported in the national and local press and attracted huge crowds including, each year from 1926 until 1939, one that filled the Royal Albert Hall. While they were zealously evangelistic, these Pentecostal groupings were also critical of other churches and therefore effectively sectarian.

So determined were the Pentecostal churches to grow that they rarely paid attention to social, political, and economic circumstances. Revival was the cure to all ills and the churches had no interest in a "social gospel." As a second war loomed on the European horizon, the Pentecostal churches felt eschatological forebodings. From 1939–45, evangelism was almost impossible due to petrol shortages and blackout, and Sunday school was hampered by the evacuation of many children from the cities.

In 1952 the World Pentecostal Conference came to London. This coincided with the beginnings of post-war immigration from the Caribbean to Britain. Oliver Lyseight (1920–2006) arrived from Jamaica in 1951 and established the New Testament Church of God by 1957. Consequently, the scene was set for the main classical Pentecostal denominations to coexist amicably side-by-side. None was prepared for what happened next.

During the 1960s the mainline denominations began to experience charismatic or Pentecostal phenomena. From the 1970s, a radical group within the charismatic movement was unsatisfied at the failure to reform the ecclesiology and governance systems of the mainline churches. This radical group of as many as 15 new networks eventually struck out on a restorationist path. One example is the Salt & Light network of churches.

Some networks were ecumenical and others sectarian; some accepted female leadership and others did not. All accepted apostolic leadership. The acquisition of property, especially outside London, followed. Theologically the networks remained committed to charismatic gifts and a direct personal encounter with God through the Spirit was always desired, and high quality and newly written music in worship was directed to precisely this end.

Huge shifts in the world's population occurred after 1945. Migratory flows, charted by the United Nations, were predominantly from the global south to the global north. As far as Britain was concerned, its Commonwealth fostered links between countries that had originally been within the British Empire. Without any government plan or conscious international strategy, people movements of high significance to the religious life of Britain occurred: many migrating Africans saw themselves as travelling to the "prodigal continent" on a journey of "reverse mission." The consequence was visible to all: black majority churches began to burgeon.

Although the Cherubim and Seraphim Church had started in Britain in 1965, many others date from the 1970s: the Aladura International Church (1970), the Celestial Church of Christ (1974), Christ Apostolic Church Mount Bethel (1974), Church of Jesus Christ Apostolic (1975) and Christ Apostolic Church of Great Britain (1976). The surge of activity was sustained in the 1980s with the planting of the Church of Pentecost's first UK congregation in 1988, the same year as the Redeemed Christian Church of God (RCCG). Others also arrived including Deeper Life Bible Church (1985), Foursquare Gospel Church (1985) and New Covenant Church (1986); and Universal Prayer Group Ministries (UPG) opened its first church in 1988. The 1990s saw the trend continue. Matthew Ashimolowo left Foursquare to start Kingsway International Christian Centre (KICC) in 1992, at a time when Nigerian immigration was on the increase: statistics show 47,201 migrants in 1991 and 88,380 in 2001 and about 80 percent were resident in London. By 2017 the Church of Pentecost had 132 congregations in the UK, the RCCG an astonishing 864 and Kingsway International, pursuing a strategy through its new 24 acre site in Dartford, attracts 10,000 people in just two congregations.

While restorationists left their churches in the 1970s to set up new congregations outside existing denominational parameters, many others remained and worked from within their home denominations. The New Wine network now comprises over 2,000 congregations and offers a range of advice, ministry, help and inspiration through its regional conferences and summer events.

Holy Trinity Brompton (HTB) is an Anglican church strongly affected by the charismatic movement in a fashionable part of London. The church launched the Alpha course, a program of teaching based around key questions and with a specific introduction to charismatic Christianity, a marriage course (designed to prepare people for marriage or enrich existing marriages) and started planting congregations in dying parishes. Nicky Gumbel, who organised and wrote much of the Alpha course, took over in 2005 and the church has continued to expand as a charismatic centre seeking to contribute to evangelisation of the nations and the transformation of society. Its Alpha course has been adapted for use with young people, in prisons, and in many countries while its church planting activities, unusual in Anglicanism, have continued to revitalise evangelical Christianity in London and beyond.

Hillsong, now in several UK cities, originally grew in the ecosystem of Australian Assemblies of God which passed through renewalist transformations in the 1970s and 1980s. Fresh Streams, the

Baptist charismatic network, runs conferences and provides leadership to some 350 connected congregations, some of which are also members of New Wine. Operating in their own sphere Roman Catholic charismatics are a vital group within the 5 million people in the UK describing themselves as Catholics. Of these about 1 million are regular church attenders.

The turbulent and exciting events taking place in Britain after 1970 impacted the older classical Pentecostals. Assemblies of God attempted to reform itself in the 1970s and again after 2008 by concentrating power into fewer hands but the effects were disappointing and led to a reduction in the size of the denomination by about 20 percent. There was also doctrinal revision of Elim in 1993. In eschatology the pre-millennial framework in which belief in the Second Coming was set was stripped away and Elim simply asserted its belief in "the personal, physical and visible return of the Lord Jesus Christ to reign in power and glory." The New Testament Church of God (NTCoG) having been established in the 1950s and grown steadily now plans to become more cosmopolitan so as to reflect more closely the locations where its congregation are set. Multiplication of congregations has continued at about 5 percent per year to reach 138 in 2017.

No study of Pentecostal and charismatic churches within the UK would be complete without reference to megachurches. These are usually defined as congregations comprising 2,000 or more. Of these there are 12 in the UK of which only one (All Souls, Langham Place) is unequivocally un-Pentecostal. In some instances the congregation is a denominational flagship but others are independent or at the centre of their own ring of satellite congregations, and sometimes both.

Bibliography

Brierley, Peter, ed. 2017. *UK Church Statistics no 3: 2018 edition.* Tonbridge: ADBC.

Burgess, Richard. 2012. "African Pentecostal Growth: the Redeemed Christian Church of God in Britain." In *Church Growth in Britain: 1980 to the present*, edited by D. Goodhew, 129. Aldershot: Ashgate.

Kay, William K. 2017. *George Jeffreys: Pentecostal Apostle and Revivalist.* Cleveland, TN: CPT Press.

Kay, William K. 2007. *Apostolic Networks in Britain.* Milton Keynes: Paternoster.

William K. Kay

United States of America

The modern Pentecostal movement can be traced to 1900 in Topeka, Kansas, at the assignment given students at a small Holiness Bible school led by Charles Fox Parham. Asked to examine the biblical text to find the evidence of the baptism of the Holy Spirit, the students discovered speaking in tongues. At a worship service on January 1, 1901, one student, Agnes Ozman, became the first modern person to speak in tongues as a result of her search for the baptism of the Holy Spirit. In the months following, Parham offered the Pentecostal baptism evidenced by speaking in tongues at gatherings in Kansas and Missouri, with speaking in tongues highlighted as one of the gifts of the Spirit (Corinthians 12) along with prophecy, miracles, and healing.

In 1905, Anna Hall, one of Parham's coworkers, brought the Pentecostal message to Texas, where Parham soon relocated. Successful meetings over the summer in Houston attracted the first African Americans and Mexican Americans to what was being termed the Apostolic Faith Movement. From Houston the movement would spread to surrounding states, northward to Illinois, westward to California, and southwestward along the Gulf Coast into Mexico.

Toward the end of 1905, Black minister Lucy Farrow (1851–1911) urged a colleague, William J. Seymour (1870–1922), to attend classes being organized by Parham for his co-workers. Early in 1906 Seymour accepted the invitation to pastor a Black church in Los Angeles. Though he had yet to experience tongues, he preached the Apostolic Faith message and on April 9, the first members of the group initially spoke in tongues. As a movement emerged and the group expanded, they relocated to a building on Azusa Street. Over the next three years, hundreds from across the United States visited Azusa and carried the movement across the continent. One such visitor, Black Holiness minister Charles H. Mason founded the Church of God in Christ, later to become the largest Pentecostal church in America, after experiencing the baptism at Azusa.

Evangelist G.B. Cashwell carried the message to Georgia, the Carolinas, and Tennessee where he introduced the message to several pre-existing Holiness groups, which later emerged as the Church of God (Cleveland, Tennessee), the Pentecostal Fire-Baptized Holiness Church, the Pentecostal Holiness Church, the Congregational Holiness Church, and Pentecostal Church of Christ.

Founded within the Holiness movement, Pentecostalism emphasized a second experience of grace subsequent to salvation termed sanctification, a cleansing of the heart from sin. Holiness Pentecostals saw the Pentecostal baptism as a third experience in which the sanctified believer was filled with the Spirit. Baptist minister William Durham challenged the Holiness position and suggested that the Pentecostal experience was immediately available to all believers. His approach, termed the Finished Work perspective, split the movement. In 1914, the widely scattered Finished Work proponents would come together to form the Assemblies of God, joined within a few years by other Finished Work groups such as the Pentecostal Church of God and the Church of the Foursquare Gospel. The Assemblies also facilitated the development of structures serving the Mexican American community.

The Assemblies of God formed just as a new issue arose among Finished Work Pentecostals. Proponents advocated baptizing believers in the "name of Jesus" only (replacing the more tradition formula, "Father, Son, and Holy Spirit"). This questioning of the baptismal formula led to the replacing of the Trinity with an affirmation of the Oneness of God. When the Assemblies of God adopted a statement affirming the Trinity, a large minority withdrew and affiliated with the Pentecostal Assemblies of the World.

The Pentecostal Assemblies of the World included a large contingent of African Americans. The movement had already separated along racial lines, especially in the South where Black Pentecostals had formed not only the Church of God in Christ, but a host of additional new denominations. In 1924, the Pentecostal Assemblies of the World split along racial lines with three new predominantly White groups emerging. These groups reunited in 1945 as the United Pentecostal Church, currently the largest Oneness group in the United States.

While the older Pentecostal denominations continued on a growth trajectory through the twentieth century, significant Pentecostal increase resulted from a series of movements that swept Pentecostalism in the decades after World War II. In the later 1940s, a new emphasis on healing developed around the ministry of independent evangelist William M. Branham. As dozens of evangelists initiated healing ministries, a national movement developed around a periodical, *The Voice of Healing*. A young evangelist Oral Roberts took the movement to the new medium of television and emerged as the most well-known Pentecostal minister in the country.

Simultaneously, another new movement swept across the United States from Canada. The Latter Rain Movement emphasized the re-organization of the church around the five offices of apostle, prophets, evangelists, pastors, and teachers (Ephesians 4:11) with a particular emphasis on restoring the offices of apostle and prophet. Like the healing movement, as the Latter Rain Movement ran its course, its core following formed additional new Pentecostal denominations.

In the 1970s, a movement appropriating the gifts of the Spirit permeated the older non-Pentecostal denominations. This new Charismatic movement created fellowship groups within the older Protestant churches, but in the long run proponents realized that Charismatics would remain at best a tolerated minority, causing many to withdraw and found independent Charismatic denominations further adding to the spectrum of the larger Pentecostal community.

Growing out of themes initially articulated in the healing movement of the 1950s, in the 1970s evangelist Kenneth E. Hagin urged Christians to exercise their faith by claiming the promise of God to give to believers whatever they asked of Him (Mark 11: 23–24). This promise includes financial support. The Faith movement he launched became popularly known as the Prosperity Gospel movement as those influenced by him rose to prominence as leaders of megachurches and affiliated congregational associations.

In the 1990s, a new generation of Pentecostal/Charismatic leaders emerged who advocated the Latter Rain's five-fold ministry and led associations of congregations bound together by their apostolic and prophetic leadership. These apostles and prophets formed the New Apostolic Reformation movement through the efforts of Professor C. Peter Wagner and created a set of new organizational networks including the US Coalition of Apostolic Leaders, the Federation of Ministers and Churches International, and the International Coalition of Prophetic Leaders.

As the twenty-first century begins, the Pentecostal-Charismatic movement has taken its place as an equal partner among America's denominational families. Since the late twentieth century it has formed part of the growing edge of American Christianity with several denominations reaching a million members and a half dozen more claiming more than a hundred thousand members. While growth has been spectacular, exact figures have been difficult to estimate as the movement is divided into several hundred denominational associations and with a significantly large segment still found within the membership of the Catholic Charismatic fellowship.

Bibliography

Alexander, Estrelda Y. 2011. *Black Fire: One Hundred Years of African American Pentecostalism*. Downers Grove, IL: IVP Academic.

Bowler, Kate. 2013. *Blessed: A History of the American Prosperity Gospel*. New York: Oxford University Press.

French, Talmage L. 1999. *Our God Is One: The Story of the Oneness Pentecostals*. Indianapolis, IN: Voice & Vision.

Goff, James R., Jr. 1988. *Fields White unto Harvest: Charles F. Parham and the Missionary Origins of Pentecostalism*. Fayetteville, AR: Univ. of Arkansas Press.

McGee, Gary B. 2010. *Miracles, Missions, and American Pentecostalism*. Maryknoll, NY: Orbis Books.

McGee, Gary B. 2004. *People of the Spirit: The Assemblies of God*. Springfield, MO: Gospel Publishing House.

Wacker, Grant. 2001. *Heaven Below: Early Pentecostals and American Culture*. Cambridge, MA: Harvard University Press.

John Gordon Melton

Universal Church of the Kingdom of God

God (Universal Church/UCKG), or Igreja Universal do Reino de Deus (IURD) as it is known in its country of origin Brazil, is a Neo-Pentecostal church considered to be part of the "third wave" of Brazilian Pentecostalism. This wave is often characterised by miraculous healing, "Prosperity Gospel" and "spiritual battles" – all of which are prominent in the global theology and spiritual practices of this megachurch.

Formally established in 1977, the UCKG traces its beginnings to a humble bandstand in a poor neighborhood of Rio de Janeiro where one of its founders, and now head of the church, Edir Macedo would preach to passersby. During the late 1970s and early 1980s, the UCKG became prominent in the Brazilian religious landscape, while also becoming socially and politically powerful. Indeed, the church remains politically influential enough to play a significant role in securing the election of Brazil's current president Jair Bolsonaro. In the 1980s and 1990s, it expanded abroad. Today it has an extensive global network of branches ranging from cathedrals and temples (such as the opulent replica of the biblical Temple of Solomon in São Paulo) that seats thousands, to church-like "HelpCentres", local shop-front churches and "Special Works" (usually a community space rented for services). Church planting runs through centralized UCKG channels ensuring that Macedo maintains decision-making power even at a global level. Across its world-wide networks the Bishops and senior pastors are almost exclusively Brazilian or Portuguese, while church assistants and junior pastors tend to come from the local congregation. The UCKG is well known for its extensive proselytizing through street preaching and regular "miracle" events aimed at attracting newcomers as well as across multiple media avenues including print, radio, television and online platforms. It also strives to be readily available on-site with most of its global branches having four services a day, and pastors on-hand between services for "walk-ins."

The UCKG's congregation in Brazil and across its global branches tends to attract people on the socio-economic margins of society with adherents being disproportionately poor and ill-educated. Its popular slogan *Pare de sofrer!* ("Stop suffering!") is translated across its transnational branches, and by offering a "totally transformation" focus in the lives of those who are suffering, the UCKG is often successful in recruiting those who experience structural marginality. The UCKG provides its congregants spiritual technologies to overcome their everyday adversities, converting victims to warriors. The church's neoliberal ethos of individual responsibility encourages its congregants to be industrious pioneers using an "active faith" (comprised of earthly and spiritual labor) to overcome their plight. This globally consistent message is balanced with a localized presence, thereby addressing local problems and glocalizing evil.

The UCKG is autochthonous to Brazil's diverse and syncretic religious sphere, blending elements of Afro-Brazilian religions and folk Catholicism into its own practices. This is evident in its daily use of religious objects as both pedagogical tools and within spiritual practices: profane objects such as money, olive oil or even bed sheets become sacred things. Through the practice of spiritual warfare, the UCKG also continuously blurs the boundaries between the supernatural and earthly realms. This is observable in three interwoven practices for which it is well known: miraculous healing, deliverance, and sacrifice.

Narratives of miraculous healing are ubiquitous in the UCKG. Testimonies of seemingly impossible resolution of ailments in all facets of adherents' lives (from persistent physical and psychological illnesses, to love life woes and visa complications) are commonplace. As the process of holistic healing in the UCKG is entwined with spiritual warfare, evil entities are blamed for interfering in the lives of adherents and blocking the blessings of God. Sacred things, such as blessed oil or consecrated water, believed to be imbued with spiritual powers from God are applied or ingested by adherents as panaceas for all ills. These things act to purge evil from the lives of congregants, and are often incorporated into the church's infamous deliverance services.

These dramatic services form part of the congregants' weekly spiritual therapy where they are liberated from evil – curses are broken and demons are (often aggressively) cast out of congregants. Indeed, evil in the UCKG is as diverse as its global congregation and is manifested through the cultural lenses of local congregants (from juju and witchcraft to curses and demonic possessions). Congregants may also invoke change in their lives through the practice of sacrifice facilitated by the church.

Much has been written in the media and academia about the UCKG's emphasis on financial sacrifice. Certainly, the UCKG places significance on a contractual relationship with God. In addition to their Christian obligation to tithe, sacrifice is a mechanism through which congregants call God's attention to situations they consider impossible to change without divine intervention. In the UCKG's practice of spiritual war, sacrifices are believed to have persuasive potential and can be spiritually and materially transformational. For adherents of the church, sacrifice (of all kinds, not just financial) is one of the ways they actively appeal to God to build a serious spiritual relationship and to better their circumstances.

The UCKG has also not always found popularity or a warm reception during its global expansion, nor indeed at home in Brazil, often gaining a reputation for disrupting the lives of adherents, pressuring congregants into making large financial sacrifices to the church and being devoid of Christian fellowship. The UCKG has been marred by very public controversies across the world including financial scandals, bad press regarding its spiritual practices, relationships with other religions and an anti-ecumenical attitude towards fellow Christian denominations, as well as accusations of questionable (and sometimes illegal) conduct across the church's hierarchy from local pastors to head bishops and

Edir Macedo himself. However, regardless of such negative attention the UCKG has continued to expand while increasing its numbers and presence worldwide, through various ways including migration.

Bibliography

Birman, Patricia, and David Lehmann. 1999. "Religion and the Media in a Battle for Ideological Hegemony: The Universal Church of the Kingdom of God and TV Globo in Brazil." *Journal of Latin American Studies* 18 (2): 145–164.

Chesnut, R. Andrew. 1997. *Born Again in Brazil: The Pentecostal Boom and the Pathogens of Poverty*. New Brunswick, N.J.: Rutgers University Press.

Freston, Paul. 2001. "The Transnationalisation of Brazilian Pentecostalism: The Universal Church of the Kingdom of God." In *Between Babel and Pentecost: Transnational Pentecostalism in Africa and Latin America*, edited by Andre Corten and Ruth Marshall-Fratani, 196–213. Bloomington: Indiana University Press.

Freston, Paul. 2005. "The Universal Church of the Kingdom of God: a Brazilian Church finds Success in Southern Africa." *Journal of Religion in Africa* 35 (1): 33–65.

Furre, Berge. 2006. "Crossing Boundaries: the 'Universal Church' and the Spirit of Globalization." In *Spirits of Globalization: Growth of Pentecostalism and Experiential Spiritualities in a Global Age*, edited by Sturla Stålsett, 39–51. London: SCM Press.

Kramer, Eric W. 2002. "Making Global Faith Universal: Media and a Brazilian Prosperity Movement." *Culture and Religion: An Interdisciplinary Journal* 3 (1): 21–47.

Mafra, Clara, Claudia Swatowiski, and Camila Sampaio. 2013. "Edir Macedo's Pastoral Project: A Globally Integrated Pentecostal Network." In *The Diaspora of Brazilian Religions*, edited by Cristina Rocha, and Manuel Vásquez, 45–67. Leiden: Brill.

Oro, A Pedro, and Pablo Semán. 2001. "Brazilian Pentecostalism Crosses National Borders." In *Between Babel and Pentecost: Transnational Pentecostalism in Africa and Latin America*, edited by Andre Corten and Ruth Marshall-Fratani, 181–195. Bloomington: Indiana University Press.

Premawardhana, Devaka. 2018. *Faith in Flux: Pentecostalism and Mobility in Rural Mozambique*. Philadelphia: University of Pennsylvania Press.

van de Kamp, Linda. 2016. *Violent Conversion: Brazilian Pentecostalism and Urban Women in Mozambique*. Rochester, NY: Boydell & Brewer.

van Wyk, Ilana. 2014. *The Universal Church of the Kingdom of God in South Africa: A Church of Strangers*. Cambridge: Cambridge University Press.

Kathleen Openshaw

Velarde, Mariano

Mariano Zuniega Velarde, popularly known as Brother Mike was born on August 20, 1939 in Caramoran Catanduanes, Philippines. Velarde is a geodetic engineer, who runs a real estate business in the Philippines. He is married to Avelina Belen del Monte and they have four children. In February 1978, the doctors at the Philippine Heart Center for Asia Hospital scheduled a major surgery for Velarde as he suffered severe cardiac ailments. Velarde claims that one night, an angel disguised as a nurse visited him in the hospital and asked him to meditate on a biblical passage (1 Cor. 10:13). He further claims that in the following morning, he experienced a tremendous peace within him and felt he had regained strength. The doctors too were surprised to see him healthy and thus ordered a thorough medical examination of his cardiac parameters. All the medical reports showed that his heart was stable and he had no need of any surgical intervention. However, Velarde decided to have further examination of his cardiac conditions in a hospital in Los Angeles. This hospital's report too showed he had no cardiac ailments. Velarde was convinced that God had healed him miraculously for a purpose. This life transforming experience led him to participate in Charismatic prayer meetings to study the Word of God and experience baptism in the Spirit. Even though his real estate business was in doldrums and his bank debts had crossed over 200 million pesos, he decided to donate 50,000 pesos, which was his remaining bank balance, to a Charismatic prayer group. After his donation, Velarde believed that God would bless him with a financial miracle. In the following week, a group of business people bought a part of his real estate holdings for 60 million pesos. This event led him to believe that tithes and offerings for religious purposes have a direct connection with prosperity.

In 1981, Velarde bought a radio station, DWXI to transmit Christian programs and messages. The high maintenance charges of DWXI were hurting Velarde's business interests and savings. However, he firmly kept the radio station running as it helped many people to strengthen their faith lives. He further instructed his treasurer to donate 10 percent of all his profits for the support of the radio ministry. He claims that his firm faith and decision to tithe reaped him more financial blessings.

In 1984, Velarde invited DWXI's audience for Holy Eucharist and healing services in the radio station premises. More than a thousand people participated in this event. Furthermore, many people testified that they had experienced the power of the Spirit, which transformed their lives. These testimonies encouraged Velarde to plan monthly Holy Eucharist celebration with healing prayer services, which later became weekly because of their huge demand. Velarde also decided to air his programs three times a week. He wanted to give a title to his series of programs and came across a Hebrew word, *El Shaddai*, which appeared on the cover of a magazine. He checked for the translation of the word and found that it means "God Almighty" in the Good News Bible. Velarde claims that God revealed to him this name and so he decided to name the weekly fellowship program at the DWXI radio station premises as El Shaddai DWXI-PPFI (Prayer Partners Foundation International). As the crowds started gradually swelling in the weekly Holy Eucharist and healing prayer services at the DWXI premises, Velarde decided to spread the El Shaddai ministry, both in the Philippines and abroad with the help of migrant Filipina/os. El Shaddai prayer groups are in Australia, Austria, Bahrain, Belgium, Brunei Darussalam, Canada, Cyprus, France, Germany, Greece, Hong Kong, India, Israel, Italy, Japan, Korea, Kuwait, Lebanon, Libya, Malaysia, Netherlands, New Zealand, Oman, Singapore, Spain, Switzerland, Taiwan, U.A.E., U.K., and U.S. Even though the practices of the Pentecostal churches greatly influenced Velarde's preaching and healing services, he did not break away from the Catholic Church. Thus, El Shaddai continues to be part of the Catholic Charismatic movement in the Philippines with Bishop Emeritus of Novaliches, Teodoro Bacani, as its spiritual director. Velarde and his team are actively involved in training lay people for evangelization and counseling. They also distribute free Bibles and Christian literature to people seeking renewal of their spiritual lives. They also work for the social welfare of the society by providing free education, medicine, and legal services (Wiegele 2005).

Velarde's preaching on tithing to seek miracles, the use of handkerchiefs and umbrellas to seek God's miraculous blessings are controversial. Moreover, his political affiliations also created controversies and dissent, especially among the Bishops and the priests (Wiegele 2005). Nevertheless, Velarde continues to be a popular Charismatic preacher and an astute businessman in the Philippines.

Bibliography

Wiegele, Katharine L. 2013. "Politics, Education and Civic Participation: Catholic Charismatic Modernities in the Philippines." In *Global Pentecostalism in the 21st Century*, edited by Robert W. Hefner, 224–250. Bloomington and Indianapolis, IN. Indiana University Press.

Wiegele, Katharine L. 2012. "The Prosperity Gospel among Filipino Catholic Charismatics." In *Pentecostalism and Prosperity: The Socio-Economics of the Global Charismatic Movement*, edited by Katherine Attanasi, and Amos Yong, 171–188. New York. Palgrave Macmillan.

Wiegele, Katharine L. 2005. *Investing in Miracles: El Shaddai and the Transformation of Popular Catholicism in the Philippines*. Honolulu, HI. University of Hawai'i Press.

Reginald Alva

Venezuela

The origins of Pentecostalism in Venezuela can be traced back to the following initiatives: The pioneer efforts of G.F. Bender and his wife Christine from 1919 to 1942 and secondly, the 1946 establishment of three national districts within the Assemblies of God with a National Convention in 1947.

The first Pentecostal missionary in Barquisimeto in the state of Lara was G.F. Bender, a German American pastor. While still living in New York, Bender was converted in a Holiness congregation of the Evangelical United Brethren in 1902, was baptized in the Holy Spirit at a Christian and Missionary Alliance congregation in 1907, and studied at the Nyack Bible Institute. According to the official missionary profile of G.F. Bender, Bender was born in Germany August 25, 1877, and became "American by naturalization." He was ordained on December 1, 1912, at Newark Pentecostal Assembly and appointed officially as missionary of the Assemblies of God on May 20, 1937. According to Luisa Jeter de Walker the Convention of the Assemblies of God was organized in August 14–17, 1947 in Caracas, Venezuela.

Bender was a person of prayer, deep conviction, and a sense of calling into missionary work. One day while praying he had a vision in which a world map showed Venezuela as the only country, and he took it as a sign. He was very reluctant at the beginning about this calling to Venezuela. However, on February 24, 1914, his Nyack Bible Institute friend Federico Bullen, who later worked in Venezuela with the American Bible Society, put Bender in contact with Rev. Geraldo Bially, director of the Christian and Missionary Alliance in Venezuela. Bender subsequently departed for Caracas, Venezuela, where he was trained as a missionary at the Hebrón Bible Institute and learned Spanish. Hans Waldvogel, pastor of an independent Assemblies of God church in Brooklyn, New York, was another friend and collaborator with

Bender during his initial incursions in Venezuela.

After Bullen's death, Bender continued to discern his role and future in Venezuela. He returned to the United States and married Christine Schwager Kopittke in 1918, then returned to Venezuela to begin a mission in Barquisimeto, in the Lara district of northern Venezuela. This time Bender did not have the support of friends at the Christian and Missionary Alliance, but he felt that God would direct the way into Barquisimeto. On September 21, 1922, Bender, his wife Christine, inaugurated Bethel Chapel as the first Pentecostal mission in Barquisimeto.

Bender was interested in educating the people and caring for their needs. In 1924 he inaugurated the Instituto Evangélico, an elementary school during the day and a Bible institute to prepare pastors and leaders in the evenings. Bender hoped for a revival in Barquisimeto. During a worship service August 9, 1924, a revival did erupt, and it became the initial impulse for the expansion of Pentecostalism in Venezuela. Expanding from Lara to Falcón and on to other districts of Venezuela, the Pentecostal experience reached many lives. By 1926 Bender was convinced that this growing movement was a missionary initiative of the Holy Spirit to bless the Venezuelan people. The next two decades were a complete success both in establishing educational institutions and orphanages and in starting new congregations.

The Pentecostal movement in Venezuela grew fast, and soon a desperate need for financial resources and missionary personnel became apparent. Bender and the "Barquisimeto movement" decided to join the Assemblies of God, which had been founded in 1947 with Rafael Alvarado, Juan Bautista Alfaro, Segundo Gil, Prisciliano Rodríguez, Martín Chirinos, Sacramento Cobos, and Edmundo Jordán as the key leaders in the different states of Venezuela According to Luisa Jeter de Walker, the Convention of the Assemblies of God was organized in August 14–17, 1947, in Caracas, Venezuela.

In 1948 the Assemblies of God established the "Instituto Bíblico Central" in Barquisimeto. This Institute became the training center for national pastors. Ingve Olson, the first Assemblies of God missionary from the United States to Venezuela, was named the first Superintendent of the Assemblies of God in Venezuela. Later, Pastor Exeario Sosa became the first native Venezuelan named to the post of Superintendent in 1952. Sosa was very attentive to the establishment of the missionary training school.

G.F. Bender came to Venezuela with a dream and a vision that bore fruit. For years he and his wife Christine prayed for a revival. When it finally came in 1924, their congregation, Bethel in Barquisimeto, became the harbinger of a revival that spread to many states in Venezuela. Bender's wisdom and capacity to teach, counsel, administrate, and relate to people provided a place at Bethel Chapel in Barquisimeto for Scandinavian independent missionaries, independent evangelists, and a new generation of Venezuelan pastors to find unity and support while hosting national conventions and retreats, preaching, and leading Bible studies.

When it was time to complete his term as missionary in 1947, Bender praised the Venezuelan people who had joined with him and his wife Christine in an adventure of faith. After leaving, he continued in communication with Venezuelan Pentecostals, particularly those at the Bethel congregation. Christine returned to Barquisimeto in 1964, three years after his death, and received the love and admiration of many sisters and brothers from different parts of the country. All over

Venezuela the Benders are recognized to this day as pioneer missionaries of the Pentecostal movement in the country.

The pioneer Pentecostal missionaries to Venezuela are Gerardo A. Bially and his wife Carrie, although they came initially as missionaries of the Christian and Missionary Alliance. They arrived in Caracas in February 1897. Bially was a representative of the American Bible Society. Federico Bullen joined the Biallys in 1909 and founded the Bible Institute Hebron in Caracas, becoming its first director. Federico Bullen, then invited his friend Gottfried (Godofredo) Bender who joined them in February 1914.

By 1914 Bially received the Baptism in the Holy Spirit. Leaders of the Christian and Missionary Alliance were not sympathetic with these tendencies and Bially decided to form a "Confraternidad Pentecostal" (a Pentecostal Fellowship) with the congregations he established already in La Guaria, Los Teques, and Caracas. Bially left the Christian and Missionary Alliance. Bender and the Eddings joined Bially. The new church was named the Missionary and Apostolic Church of Venezuela. Adah Winger, an Assemblies of God missionary, arrived in Caracas and directed a primary school and orphanage in Caracas. The Benders went to Barquisimeto in 1919 and the Eddings went to Isla Margarita in 1917. Bender was an independent missionary for more than two decades (1914–1937), even though he was an ordained pastor in the Assemblies of God in the United States in 1937. Today the Pentecostal movement is present in all states of Venezuela, with a consistent and constant growth.

Bibliography

Álvarez, Carmelo. 2006. "Sharing in God's Mission: The Evangelical Pentecostal Union of Venezuela and the Christian Church (Disciples of Christ) in the United States." PhD diss., Amsterdam Free University.

Lindhardt, Martin, ed. 2016. *New Ways of Being Pentecostal in Latin America.* Lanham: Lexington Books.

Medina, Néstor, and Sammy Alfaro, eds. 2015. *Pentecostals and Charismatics in Latin America and Latino Communities.* New York: Palgrave Macmillan.

Smith, Calvin, ed. 2011. *Pentecostal Power: Expressions, Impact and Faith of Latin American Pentecostalism.* Leiden: Brill.

Synan, Vinson, Amos Yong, and Miguel Alvarez, eds. 2016. *Global Renewal Christianity: Spirit-Empowered Movements Past, Present, and Future.* Volume 2, *Latin America.* Lake Mary, FL: Charisma House.

Carmelo Alvarez

Villanueva, Eddie

Eduardo "Eddie" Cruz Villanueva was born on October 6, 1946 in Bocaue, Bulacan, the Philippines. His parents were Joaquin Villanueva and Maria Cruz. He is married to Adoracion Jose Villanueva. They have four children: Eduardo, Joni, Joel, and Jovi.

Villanueva graduated from the Philippine College of Commerce (now Polytechnic University of the Philippines) with a Bachelor's degree in commerce. He describes himself as a former "communist-atheist," "radical activist," and "street parliamentarian" and now "one of the most powerful preachers of God's Word in the world today." He was converted through the influence of his older sister, Leonor Buan, and had a "life changing encounter with the Lord in 1973 while at the forefront of a leftist movement fighting against ... social injustice." He never attended a Bible college but was influenced by the ministries of Morris Cerullo, T.L. Osborn,

Oral Roberts, Kenneth Hagin, and Ralph Mahoney. He was ordained in 1979 by Michael McKinney of Victory in Christ Church and International Ministries (now known as World for Jesus International Christian Center and Ministries) based in Covina, California.

Villanueva is most widely known as Brother Eddie, the founder and head of the Jesus Is Lord Church (JIL) headquartered in the Philippines. He founded JIL in 1978 and built it into a Filipino religious and political force. Joseph Suico stated that "JIL church has 106 Sunday services in Metro Manila, 25 in Bulacan, 275 in other provinces ... and 72 worldwide in 27 countries ... claiming altogether two million members" (Anderson and Tang 2011). As of 2017 the JIL website claimed five million members in 60 countries, if accurate, an increase of 150 percent in six years. JIL had its beginnings at the Polytechnic University of the Philippines where Villanueva had returned to teach. From the Bible studies he taught to a small group of 15 students, it has reached its current status as probably the largest Pentecostal organization in the Philippines. Brother Eddie's vision includes education, media, and politics. He founded and owns Jesus Is Lord Colleges Foundation (JILCF), offering preschool, elementary, high school, and college courses at its main branch in Bocaue, Bulacan, and 25 branches throughout the Philippines. He started a weekly television program, "Jesus The Healer," in 1982. After years of negotiation, Channel 11 (ZOE TV-11, now ZOE Broadcasting Network) was acquired in 1998 as an important media outlet.

His immediate family is heavily involved in local and national politics. His eldest son, Eduardo Jr., is the former mayor of the family home-town of Bocaue, Bulacan. His daughter Joni Villanueva-Tugna is the current mayor of the same town. His other son, Emmanuel Joel, was the youngest member of the House of Representatives, serving three terms before being elected to the Senate in 2016. Eddie Villanueva himself was a presidential candidate in the 2004 Philippine presidential elections, polling last in a field of five candidates but with a respectable 6 percent of the total votes cast. He also ran for president in the 2010 Philippine elections, polling fourth out of nine candidates with just over 3 percetn of the vote. He also ran unsuccessfully as a senatorial candidate in the 2013 Philippine elections. He is president and chairman of Bangon Pilipinas Party (BPP, literally "Rise Up Philippines Party") founded in 2004. In 2019, Eddie Villanueva was appointed to the Philippine House of Representatives as one of the two congressmen of a political party known as CIBAC (the Citizen's Battle Against Corruption) in the two seats won during the election of May 13, 2019.

Bibliography

Anderson, Allan Heaton. 2013. *To the Ends of the Earth: Pentecostalism and the Transformation of World Christianity.* Oxford: Oxford University Press.

Austin, Denise, Jacqueline Grey, and Paul W. Lewis, eds. 2019. *Asia Pacific Pentecostalism.* Leiden: Brill.

Chong, Terence, ed. 2018. *Pentecostal Megachurches in Southeast Asia.* Singapore: ISEAS.

Suico, Joseph. 2011. "Pentecostalism in the Philippines." In *Asian and Pentecostal: The Charismatic Face of Christianity in Asia*, edited by Allan Anderson and Edmond Tang, 279–293. Oxford: Regnum.

Johnny King

Voronaev, Ivan Efimovich

Ivan Efimovich Voronaev (1886–1943?), the most prominent Pentecostal pioneer in Eastern Europe and communist Russia, began his life under the name Nikita Petrovich Cherkasov. His birthplace was the Cossack train station (then a military base) of Nepluevskaia in the Orenburg province of the Ural Mountains. Voronaev was converted on April 23, 1907 while serving in the Russian military and his new Christian convictions soon conflicted with his military career for the Tsar. Court-martialed in January, 1908 as a Baptist minister, he was forced to change his name and flee the country. In 1912, he immigrated to the United States via Japan. His wife Ekaterina Bahskirova, with their children Vera and Paul, followed him to San Francisco shortly. Attending Berkeley Baptist Divinity School, Voronaev joined the Baptist Convention and pastored in California (1913), Washington (1914), and New York (1917). After being filled with the Holy Spirit at Glad Tidings Tabernacle in June of 1919, Voronaev pioneered a small Russian Pentecostal congregation at the Emmanuel Presbyterian Church on 735 6th Street, before returning to Bulgaria as an ordained Assemblies of God missionary.

With the support of E.N. Bell, chairman of the Assemblies of God, on July 13, 1920, Voronaev began the difficult journey across the Atlantic via Constantinople and landed in Bourgas, Bulgaria along with Dionissy Zaplishny, V.R. Koltovich, V. Klikibik, and N. Kardanov. Before reaching Odessa on August 12, 1921, Voronaev started 18 Pentecostal congregations across Bulgaria, establishing the foundation of the Bulgarian Pentecostal Union.

During the first three months in Odessa, his Pentecostal work grew the movement to almost 1,000. Encouraged by the success, Voronaev and his team traveled extensively through the USSR reaching communist strongholds like Leningrad and Moscow with the Pentecostal message. In 1924 the Union of Evangelical Christians (Pentecostal) was organized and by 1926 it grew into the General-Ukrainian Union of Christians of Evangelical Faith. The organization united 350 Pentecostal assemblies with 17,000 believers in the Odessa region alone, and by 1928 reached membership of 80,000 across the USSR.

When the Soviet government launched its anti-religion campaign in 1930 with the arrest of some 800 Russian pastors, Voronaev and Koltovich were taken by the secret militia on July 6th, convicted for espionage and sentenced to life in the Siberian Gulag. Voronaev's wife Ekaterina was arrested in March 1933 and sentenced to 24 years in prison for her faith. Their six children were left alone in the famine haunted streets of Odessa. Their three sons born in America (Alexander, Peter and John) were soon brought back stateside by the Red Cross. With the tireless efforts of the oldest son Paul, the rest of the children joined them in 1934.

A quarter of a century later, they received the surprising news that their mother was still alive and finally released from prison. Paul personally interceded before the Russian Secretary General Khrushchev during his 1959 visit to Washington, DC and with the help of Presidents Eisenhower and Nixon, Ekaterina, now 73, was brought back to the United States in July 1960, where she lived with her family until her death.

Ivan Voronaev remained imprisoned for his faith in Siberia until his death, except for a brief release in 1936 when he was again arrested in Kaluga. In order to demean his heroic impact among Pentecostal believers, the secret Russian NKVD faked documents of his recanting from the faith and even the time of his death. But neither the hard labor camp nor the communist propaganda were able to destroy the legacy and martyrdom of the Father of Slavic Pentecostalism.

Bibliography

Donev, Dony. 2011. *The Life and Ministry of Rev. Ivan Voronaev*. Sofia: Spasen Publishers.

Ministry File and Periodical Mentions of Ivan E. Voronaeff (Flower Pentecostal Heritage Center).

Minutes of Baptist Conventions (Northern California, 1912–1914; Western Washington, 1916–1917; Southern New York, 1918–1920). Graduate Theological Union of Berkeley.

Koltovich, Vassily. 1927. *Minutes of the Jubilee Meeting*.

Spiritual Heritage of the Ascetics in the Russian Lands, 2015. (Case 5629 Odessa Reg., Case 9552 54–10 SudTroiku, SpetsOtdel #1 (Feb., 1 1858), Case 18 Marinsky Prison (GUGB/NKVD/USSR)). Typescript (unpublished).

Dony K. Donev

Wagner, Charles Peter

Charles Peter Wagner (August 15, 1930–October 21, 2016) was an American missionary, educator, a founder of multiple organizations, a promoter of the "third wave" of the charismatic movement and of the New Apostolic Reformation (with both movements having had their name coined by Wagner himself). He was also himself an apostle, at least as measured by his own standards.

After being awarded a Th.M. from Princeton Theological Seminary, Wagner began his career as a missionary in Bolivia. From 1956 to 1971, he worked with two missionary organizations, the South American Mission and the Andes Evangelical Mission. He also served for a period as the head of Bolivian Theological Educational Association and the General Director of the Bolivian Indian Missions. Even by his own measurements, his evangelistic efforts garnered little success, certainly not the level of success enjoyed by Bolivian Pentecostals.

In 1971, Wagner left Bolivia to become an instructor at Fuller School of World Missions (now known as the School of Intercultural Studies), an organization affiliated with Fuller Seminary, a leading evangelical institution at the time. Wagner's specialty was "Church Growth" as founded and taught by Donald McGavran. The Church Growth movement developed a social-science approach for the study of missionary activity to understand why some churches were growing and how churches could learn from them by replicating programs and strategies. Wagner would later become McGavran's intellectual heir, and after McGavran's death, co-authored new editions of the book *Understanding Church Growth*, McGavran's landmark textbook in this field. Wagner wrote the influential book *Look out! The Pentecostals are Coming!* (1973). In this book, he assessed South American Pentecostal practices suggesting that many of them could be adopted by evangelical missionaries to increase conversion rates as well as retention.

The interest in Pentecostal growth rates led to an investigation of spiritual gifts, and eventually, to a partnership with John Wimber, a Vineyard Pastor and Fuller Theological Seminary church growth consultant, who became a specialist in the American application of church growth techniques. Wimber would go on to become an influential leader and shaping force of the Vineyard church and charismatic meetings like the Toronto Blessing (Catch the Fire). Wagner became the teacher of record in a Fuller School of World Missions course in the early 1980s entitled "MC510: Signs, Wonders, and Church Growth" where a lab or clinic component included the practice of spiritual gifts taught by Wimber. Students would have hands-on practice in healing and deliverance from demons that was shaped by teaching on signs and wonders. This course received a great deal of both positive and negative attention in American Christian media, and eventually became so controversial that it was canceled, ending Wimber's teaching at Fuller. Despite what was read by some as a public repudiation of Wagner by Fuller, Wagner would continue to hold a position and teach there until his retirement in 2001.

Wagner would use that position to promote what he called the "third wave." The third wave included of a variety of independent, neo-Pentecostal, charismatic, and evangelical churches and networks, all of which shared a tendency to view spiritual gifts as primarily serving an evangelistic purpose that was also critical of the anti-charismatic evangelicalism they encountered. The third wave often built on the tradition of contemporary music and the Jesus People Movement of the 1970s. This new form of worship music songs were expressions of popular rock music, but that were also designed to lead to highly affective collective worship experiences. Wagner presented these churches and church networks as a new wave of the Holy Spirit, contrasting it with the earlier historical periods that included Classical Pentecostals from the Azusa Street Revival and the charismatic groups from the Roman Catholic and historical Protestant churches of the 1960s and 1970s. While this framing of Pentecostal history as three waves of the Holy Spirit is historically questionable, the concept of a third wave became an important thematic in both many neo-Pentecostal churches' self-understanding and the historiography of these churches and movements.

Popularizing charismatic practices as the third wave of the Holy Spirit was not only Wagner's contribution. He worked to integrate charismatic religious techniques on prayer, worship, and ecclesiology into McGavran's Church Growth Movement. Wagner was also a proponent of "spiritual mapping" as a form of spiritual warfare waged against territorialized spirits that were believed to have some spiritual authority over a building, neighborhood, city, or even a nation. Wagner imported this technique from Argentina (although it is not clear how widespread it was among evangelicals and Pentecostals there), and his popularization helped it become a globally common practice in charismatic and neo-pentecostal circles. Wagner founded both the World Prayer Center, which was presented as a high-technology hub to assist in the practice of spiritual warfare, and Global Harvest Ministries, which was intended to promulgate Wagner's spiritual warfare techniques. The building and the organization, which were jointly located in Colorado Springs, Colorado, were closely affiliated with Ted Haggard and New Life Church. Wagner's affiliation with Global Harvest Ministries ended in 2011. Subsequently, he directed his energies into the Wagner Leadership Institution (now Wagner University), a parachurch organization with goals similar to those of Global Harvest Ministries.

Wagner was also a key player in the establishment of the New Apostolic Reformation (NAR), a group characterized by a wide set of beliefs that included the restoration of the five Ephesian church offices (pastor, teacher, evangelist, prophet, and apostle), the teaching of dominion theology, and the promotion of the charismatic "Seven Mountains" theology that included cultural control and influence over and within a broad range of social spheres in society including government and media. Wagner played an organizing and popularizing role in the NAR that included the "National Symposium on the Postdenominational Church," a convention that played an important role in the NAR in the 1990s.

Wagner was a prodigious author, who by his own account, had written over seventy books. He was also an important figure in introducing North Americans and Europeans to forms of worship and charismatic practice from the Global South. Along with Charles Kraft, another Fuller Theological Seminary professor, he introduced evangelicals to the idea of using spiritual gifts as part of a rationalized missiological program. However, his desire for religious innovation often caused disruption to the movements that he affiliated himself with and has led some to temper their assessment of his accomplishments by a perceived tendency towards opportunistic self-promotion.

Bibliography

Bialecki, Jon. 2015. "The Third Wave and the Third World: C. Peter Wagner, John Wimber, and the Pedagogy of Global Renewal in the Late Twentieth Century." *Pneuma* 37 (1): 177–200.

Wagner, C. Peter. 1973. *Look out! The Pentecostals Are Coming!* Carol Stream, Il: Creation House.

Wagner, C. Peter. 1988. *The Third Wave of the Holy Spirit: Encountering the Power of Signs and Wonders Today*. Ann Arbor, MI: Servant Publications, Vine Books.

Wilkinson, Michael. 2016. "Charismatic Christianity and the Role of Networks: Catch the Fire and the Revival Alliance." *Pneuma* 38 (1/2): 33–49.

Jon Bialecki

Wang, Zai (Leland Wang)

Zai Wang (Leland Wang, 1898–1975) was born to a non-Christian family in Fuzhou. He received education in Nanyang College in Shanghai and Chefoo Navel College. He became a naval officer after graduation.

Wang was led to Christ by his wife Pan Xiao Rong. They married in 1916 in a Protestant church. Wang started going to church with her on the first Sunday after their wedding. After studying the Bible, Wang came to Christ and was baptized by immersion in Xiamen in 1920. In 1921, Wang responded to the growing call into ministry; he was particularly moved by Isaiah 52:11: "Depart, depart, go out thence ... purify yourselves." He left the navy as the first mate on his ship and returned to Fuzhou. He never received theological education and was not supported by any western mission. He started with outdoor evangelism by ringing a handbell, singing hymns, reading the scripture, distributing tracts, and telling Gospel stories and personal testimonies to draw crowds.

In the same year, Wang met Watchman Nee (1903–1972). The Wangs and Nee held the first bread-breaking gathering in Wang's home. The gathering later developed into the Christian Assemblies (also known as the Little Flock or Local Church), an indigenous church without denominational affiliation. They were soon joined by some other students from the Anglican Trinity College in Fuzhou. They were involved in roadside evangelism and held revival meetings in the area. In 1924, Wang and Nee had an irreconcilable disagreement over whether Wang should accept ordination as a pastor. As a result, Nee was expelled from the work in Fuzhou.

By 1924, Wang started leading evangelical and revival meetings across China, including Shanghai, Guangzhou, provinces along Yangtze River, North China, Northeast China, Mongolia, and Hong Kong. In

1928, at the request and with the help of Rev. R.A. Jaffray (1873–1945), Chairman of the Christian & Missionary Alliance in South China, Wang embarked on a mission trip to Southeast Asia, including Vietnam, Singapore, Malaya, Indonesia, Borneo, and the Philippines. During the trip he saw the needs of the people, especially that of the Chinese diaspora. In 1929, with Jaffray and other mission-minded Christians, they established the Chinese Foreign Missionary Union (CFMU), the first Chinese mission society founded for foreign mission and Wang became the first chairman. Apart from holding evangelical meetings, CFMU started bread-breaking gatherings for new believers. Leaders of the Christian Assemblies were sent to supervise work in newly established congregations.

Wang later extended his mission endeavor to other parts of the world. From the 1930s to 1960s, he visited over 30 countries in Asia, Oceania, America, Middle East, and Europe. By 1955, CFMU had over 30 co-workers serving over 5,000 people in different nations. Wang therefore received worldwide recognition and some referred him as Moody of China. He was invited to speak at the Keswick Convention and received the Doctor of Divinity degree from Wheaton College. Wang died in California on December 13, 1975 at age 77.

Bibliography

Li, Shaoming. 2006. "A Study of Issues Related to the Christian Assemblies." *Religious Studies* 2: 96–102. 李少明，〈對基督徒聚會處若干問題的考證和考察〉，《宗教學研究》，第二期（2006年）。

Li, Yading. 2019. "Wang Zai." *Biographical Dictionary of Chinese Christianity*. Accessed November 28, 2019. http://bdcconline.net/zh-hans/stories/wang-zai.

Lian, Xi. 2010. *Redeemed by Fire: The Rise of Popular Christianity in Modern China*. New Haven; London: Yale University Press.

Wong, Hoover. "Wang Zai." *Biographical Dictionary of Chinese Christianity*. Accessed November 28, 2019. https://bdcconline.net/en/stories/wang-zai.

Shin Fung Hung

Weepers, China

The "Weepers" refers to the Word of Life Movement or Born-again Movement under the leadership of Peter Xu Yongze, which is one of the largest "house church" networks of China since the 1980s. It is said that the believers always cried out loud during prayer and even considered it as a sign of salvation. To some extent, the Weepers are a counterpart of the "Shouters" as a twin brother of Chinese "house churches."

Its origin can be traced back to 1982, when Peter Xu Yongze called the first general conference of "house churches" in Henan Province. They also sent the first group of 17 "Messengers of the Gospel" to other provinces. Later, "the Seven Principles" were drafted by Xu as a guideline for his co-workers and followers, including salvation through the cross, the way of the cross, discerning the adulteress, building the church, providing for life, fellowship, and evangelism. In 1988, Xu bravely went to meet the American evangelist Billy Graham (1918–2018) during the latter's Beijing trip, and was captured by the police before he could see Graham. In 2002, after another prison experience, Xu moved with his family to the USA as religious refugees.

"Salvation through the Cross" and the "Way of the Cross" represents the core theological ideas of this "house church" network. It reflects the suffering experienced by Chinese Christians during that time, as well as the legacy of the first generation of Chinese evangelical/conservative leaders, such as Wang Mingdao (1900–1991), Jia Yuming (1880–1964), and Ni Tuosheng (Watchman Nee, 1903–1972). From the very beginning, it had a strong criticism of the Three-self Patriotic Committee, the official representative of Chinese churches.

In particular, Xu was influenced by the Norwegian evangelist Marie Monsen (1878–1962), who had been working in Henan for many years with a strong emphasis on the born-again experience. New life after salvation and a life relationship with the Lord became another hallmark of the movement. Followers also preferred to call themselves "the Word of Life Movement" and they highlighted the "Word and the Spirit" in their theology and practice. Crying or weeping during prayers was more a common among the "house churches" in Henan.

This movement is actually the newest of several other "house church" networks. Xu was also involved in the unity initiative of Chinese "house churches." Xu also became one of the leaders for the "Great Commission of Back to Jerusalem," especially after he moved to US. The Weepers were similar to the "Shouters" and the role of home meetings, new life, fellowship, and preaching. The Word of Life Movement or Born-again Movement is an evangelical, conservative movement, with charismatic characteristics.

Bibliography

Hattaway, Paul. 2009. *Henan: The Galilee of China*. Carlisle, UK: Piquant Editions Ltd.

Lambert, Tony. 2006. *China's Christian Millions*. Oxford: Monarch Books.

Liu, Yi. 2014. "Pentecostal-Style Christians in the 'Galilee of China'." *Review of Religion and Chinese Society* 1 (2): 156–172.

Wesley, Luke. 2004. *The Church in China: Persecuted, Pentecostal, and Powerful*. Baguio, Philippines: AJPS Books.

Xin, Yalin. 2009. *Inside China's House Church Network: The Word of Life Movement and Its Renewing Dynamic*. Lexington, KY: Emeth Press.

Yi Liu

Wei, Paul (Wei, Enbo)

Paul Wei (1876–1919) was the leading figure in the founding of the indigenous Chinese True Jesus Church (TJC). Following his Christian conversion, Wei's beliefs were shaped in part by Western missionaries, especially Oneness Pentecostals (OP) and Seventh-Day Adventists. OP taught that baptism should be invocated in the name of Jesus Christ, and the Trinity belong to only the economy of salvation. Before his death, however, Wei broke fellowship with missionaries, and claimed the authority of divine revelation for his foundational beliefs. He spent his last days evangelizing and building the groundwork for a new and indigenous church.

Wei was brought up in a rural village in Hebei Province, south of Beijing. He married and in 1901 moved to Beijing where he hoped to succeed in the textile trade. Following an invitation, he visited a congregation of the London Missionary Society, and was eventually baptized. He soon opened a cloth shop which he called "Grace, Faith, Eternity."

The next decade was for Wei a time to develop his leadership skills in the Christian community. This, however, was abruptly halted in 1913 when he married a second wife. An otherwise common

Chinese custom resulted in his removal from the church, which led to a downward spiral of depression. The turning point came two years later when Wei reported hearing a voice calling him back to serve God. With renewed involvement, in December, 1915, he attended a meeting at the Apostolic Faith Church, a local Pentecostal mission. It was there that he received the Baptism of the Spirit. A year later, he was miraculously healed of tuberculosis.

Wei's future changed in 1916 when he met Bernt Berntsen (1863–1933), the Norwegian American Pentecostal missionary and overseer of the Apostolic Faith Church. Berntsen introduced Wei to the controversial Oneness Pentecostal teaching, which would become a fundamental doctrine of the TJC. In 1917, however, anti-missionary sentiment by Wei and Zhang Zhongsan, a friend and fellow-member, began to mount. During a 39-day fast, Wei met and counseled visitors, and began writing a diary account of his spiritual encounters, *The True Testimony of the Holy Spirit*. On May 22, 1917, Wei and a small band of followers made their way to a nearby river, and proceeded to baptize themselves. Wei claimed that Jesus baptized him and instructed him to baptize face-forward, a ritual unknown to Berntsen but permanently embedded in the TJC teaching and practice.

This baptismal moment symbolically marked the separation of Wei's future from the Apostolic Faith Mission and all future missionary movements. He first called the new church, "The Corrected Church," but later changed it to "True Jesus Church." Following his death, the church grew rapidly through the evangelistic efforts of his fellow-workers, Zhang Zhongsan and Zhang Lingsheng.

Bibliography

Huang, Ke-hsien. 2018. "Emergence and Development of Indigenous Christianity in China: A Class-Culture Approach." In *Transfiguration of Chinese Christianity: Localization and Globalization*, edited by Cheng-tian Kuo, Fu-Chu Chou, and Sian-chin Iap, 153–193. Taipei: Chengchi University Press

Inouye, Melissa Wei-Tsing. 2018. *China and the True Jesus: Charisma and Organization in a Chinese Christian Church*. New York: Oxford University Press.

Melton, J. Gordon. 2017. "Pentecostalism Comes to China: Laying the Foundations for a Chinese Version of Christianity." In *Global Chinese Pentecostal and Charismatic Christianity*, edited by Fenggang Tang, Joy K.C. Tong, and Allan H. Anderson, 43–62. Leiden: Brill.

David Reed

Welsh Revival

The principality of Wales has for centuries been part of United Kingdom. It retains its own ancient language although the vast majority of speakers are bilingual in English and Welsh. Its population is concentrated on the south and north coasts with only farming villages and small towns in the mountainous and hilly interior. Late Victorian railways, coal mines and quarries brought prosperity to the region. Religiously, the monoglot English tended to be landowners worshipping in the Anglican church while the native Welsh tended to be nonconformists worshipping in an array of Calvinistic Methodist, Baptist, Presbyterian, Congregationalist, Wesleyan and Independent chapels. The revival that swept through Wales in the

Evan Roberts. Source: Oral Roberts University

years 1904–1905 was largely based in these Welsh-speaking chapels.

Because the 1859 revival remained in living memory there was a widespread desire for a new revival at the start of the twentieth century. Preaching by Seth Joshua (1858–1925) in January 1904 stirred the young people of New Quay in west Wales. Others were stimulated by the 'Welsh Keswick' in Llandrindod Wells and by preaching in the north but it was Joshua's preaching at Blaenannerch that triggered a memorable reaction. There the young Evan Roberts (1878–1951), in training for Calvinist Methodist ministry, responded and soon afterwards began his public preaching.

Roberts was a religious young man who had worked as a miner and was apprenticed as a blacksmith. He had read the Welsh version of A.A. Hodges' *Systematic Theology* and spent hours in prayer and reported seeing 14 visions between September and October 1904. Returning to his home chapel on 31 October 1904, he preached in Welsh to the young people, successfully urging them to surrender to Christ. Moving nightly from chapel to chapel in an easterly direction he formulated four conditions for revival: 1. To confess sin openly, 2. To remove anything doubtful, 3. To obey the promptings of the Holy Spirit and 4. To confess Christ openly. He was not an expository preacher or a classical evangelist but his exhortations and the open and free format of his meetings encouraged nominal Christians and unbelievers to embrace conversion, often with tears. He occasionally used the phrase 'baptism in the Spirit' and saw himself as guided by the Spirit both with regard to the invitations he accepted and during his meetings. Women and children took a prominent part in his gatherings and occasionaly would lead the stirring Welsh hymns sung late into the night.

The popular press, including the *London Times* but especially the *Western Mail*, fanned the revival by printing regular sympathetic and detailed reports: 'he walked up and down the aisles, open Bible in one hand, exhorting one, encouraging another, and keeling with a third to implore a blessing from the Throne of God. A young woman rose to give out a hymn, which was sung with deep earnestness …' However after Christmas a letter in the *Western Mail* criticised Roberts for propagating an emotional and sham version of the real revival. Turning norward Roberts preached in Liverpool and then in Bangor but his behaviour occasionally became erratic and judgmental when the crowds failed to respond to his pleadings. Examined by doctors he was found to be normal but overworked and in need of rest. By the autumn of 1905 he was starting to withdraw from preaching and public life and come under the influence of Jessie

Penn-Lewis and her dualistic theology. Reporting to students in Bala he found it hard to distinguish between the voice of God and the devil and he began to repudiate many aspects of the revival during which, in an amazing year, it is estimated 100,000 people had been brought into a relationship with Christ.

Figures show membership of the chapels as well as confirmations in the Anglican church increased dramatically. Many of those converted turned their moral earnestness towards Welsh political parties, campaigning for better education in Wales and the temperance movement. Figures also show how arrests for drunkenness declined and there is evidence of better relationships between management and unions in the industrial sector. There is also evidence for the international impact of the revival among Welsh-speaking congregations in different parts of the world as well as among English-speaking congregations that were inspired by what they read. There is a direct link between the Azusa Street Revival (1906–1912) and the Welsh Revival both because of correspondence between Frank Bartleman and Evan Roberts in 1905, and because Joseph Smale visited the revival in Wales before resuming his influential ministry in Los Angeles in May 1905. Equally, there is a direct link between the revival and British Pentecostalism since the founders of the Welsh Apostolic Church were converted in the revival as were the Jeffreys brothers, Stephen and George. Stephen evangelised powerfully for British Assemblies of God and George founded the still-thriving Elim Pentecostal Church and conducted large meetings in the 1920s and 1930s. Whether, however, speaking in tongues occurred during the revival meetings is unknown and contested.

Bibliography

Evans, Eifion. 2000. *The Welsh Revival of 1904*. Bridgend: Bryntirion Press.

Kay, William K. 2009. "Why Did the Welsh Revival Stop?" In *Revival, Renewal and the Holy Spirit*, edited by Dyfed Wyn Roberts, 169–184. Milton Keynes: Paternoster.

Pope, Robert. 2006. "Demythologising the Evan Roberts Revival, 1904–1905." *Journal of Ecclesiastical History* 57 (3): 515–534.

Tudur Jones, R. 2004. *Faith and the Crisis of a Nation: Wales 1890–1914*. Cardiff: University of Wales Press.

William K. Kay

Wigglesworth, Smith

Smith Wigglesworth (1859–1947) has been seen as the archetypal preacher of early Pentecostalism: brusque, uneducated, unconventional, biblical, tongues-speaking and with a compassionate evangelistic and healing ministry. Born

Smith Wigglesworth, 1859–1947

into a poor rural working-class family in the north of England he never seems to have gone to school. His grandmother was Methodist but he was confirmed in the Church of England and later underwent believer's baptism.

Becoming a plumber he started to prosper while continuing to be fervent and denominationally eclectic. He worshipped for a while with the Salvation Army where he met his wife, Mary Jane Featherstone (or Polly as she was known), a fiery and effective speaker whom he married in 1882. The young couple made contact with Alexander Dowie's Zion City healing meetings in London and Leeds, and Polly was baptized in water by Dowie in 1900. They led and served at the Bowland Street Mission in Bradford (where healings were known to occur) but it was in Sunderland in 1907, after the outpouring of the Spirit in the Anglican parish, that Wigglesworth made his way to the Vicarage where Mary Boddy, the vicar's wife (Alexander Boddy), laid hands on him and he received a vision of Christ "in a reigning position" and spoke in tongues.

The experience of Spirit-baptism transformed him. Already a man who believed in divine healing and prayed for the sick, he now found confidence to preach – something that until then he had left to Polly. She had taught him to read when he was 23 (though never to spell or punctuate) and he now started to expound Scripture while interweaving his sermons with stories of dramatic healings and occasional messages in tongues which he immediately interpreted. Wigglesworth was always "on duty" as a soul-winner and would pray aloud or testify to Christ anywhere he happened to be. In services he would use the leaders of meetings to illustrate his sermons, which kept everyone on their toes, and would pray for the sick after or during his preaching, laying hands on them or asking them to lay hands on themselves if the crowds were too great.

His theology was simple, but not as simple as is sometimes made out. He undoubtedly believed sickness comes from the devil and would therefore fight it and command it to leave bodies as if every ailment had a spiritual cause. He would lay hands on those who were ill and sometimes hit a tumor or rupture in his spiritual combat with suffering. He also had an almost mystical appreciation of what it was to be "in Christ" and for Christ's new life to be powerfully at work in him. He held a nuanced concept of sanctification believing inbred sin must be rooted out but without embracing complete perfectionism. He felt his own body to be "quickened" by the Spirit and his prayers to reach into heaven to manifest Christ on earth. His understanding of the range of charismatic gifts in 1 Corinthians 12 grew from the biblical text as well as practical experience and, while he was not a man who engaged in long days of prayer, he said that, while he scarcely ever prayed for more than half an hour, he rarely went half an hour without praying. "Only believe" (Mk 5: 36) was his signature text and faith the hallmark of his ministry.

In 1913 Polly died and he never remarried. He was a member of the Council of the Pentecostal Missionary Union (for which he had raised large sums of money) but resigned in 1920 over a misunderstanding with a young woman and then, after briefly holding credentials with American Assemblies of God, remained as an independent for the rest of his life. Polly's death released him to travel. He was in North America in 1914 for a series of campaigns and camp meetings but back in Bradford for 1915. Two years later he was in Ireland and Scotland. He visited Switzerland, France, Denmark, and Sweden in 1920–1921 and Australia and New

Zealand in 1923–1924. Crowds attended his meetings which were reported in the secular press. On at least one occasion in Sweden he was briefly imprisoned for praying for the sick without a medical licence. His visits to Australia and New Zealand helped establish the Pentecostal churches there and his sermons were taken down in shorthand on this tour and led to the publication of *Ever Increasing Faith* (1924) which sold rapidly, spread his fame and is still in print. Throughout the 1920s he preached wherever he was invited including in Sri Lanka (Ceylon) and India in 1926. He spoke for Amy Semple McPherson in California. Between 1930–1933 he suffered from kidney stones which caused him great pain. Refusing surgery and passing the stones, he mellowed for the last 15 years of his life while continuing to pray and preach. He held meetings in South Africa in 1936 and delivered a prophecy to the young David du Plessis about the coming charismatic renewal. He remained committed to mission, often raising large sums of money. He was active in big and small meetings till the very end of his life and died in his 88th year on a snowy day in the north of England while attending the funeral of an old friend.

Bibliography

Carp, Sandra Ann. 2015. "A Pentecostal 'Legend': A Reinterpetation of the Life and Legacy of Smith Wigglesworth." Master's diss., University of Birmingham, UK.

Cartwright, Desmond. 2000. *The Real Wigglesworth*. Tonbridge, Kent: Sovereign World.

Frodsham, Stanley Howard. 1965. *Smith Wigglesworth: Apostle of Faith*. London: Assemblies of God Publishing House.

Robinson, James. 2014. *Diving Healing: The Years of Expansion, 1906–1930*. Eugene, OR: Pickwick.

Wigglesworth, Smith. 1924. *Ever Increasing Faith*. Various editions including Kindle.

William K. Kay

Wimber, John

John Wimber (1934–1997) was a musician, adult convert, pastor, teacher, author, and church founder. He was associated with the "signs and wonders" movement, contemporary Christian worship music, and the Association of Vineyard Churches. Born in Kirksville, Missouri, USA, into a working-class family, he showed musical talent early in life, and in 1962 organized and played keyboard with The Righteous Brothers. Wimber was converted in 1963 and abandoned his musical career just when it was poised to take off.

Ordained by the California Yearly Meeting of Friends (Quaker) in 1970, Wimber pastored in Yorba Linda, California. In 1974 he began to work with the Institute of Evangelism and Church Growth at Fuller Seminary. When a portion of the Yorba Linda congregation had become charismatic in 1977, he was asked to leave. Some left with him to affiliate with the Calvary Chapel in Costa Mesa, under Pastor Chuck Smith. A friendship with Kenn Gulliksen – who had formed a new church called The Vineyard – led Wimber to merge their two congregations. The combined church in Anaheim grew to 5,000 and dozens of new congregations affiliated with the Vineyard.

A Mother's Day service in 1979 or 1980 (the date is uncertain) proved pivotal, when Wimber witnessed hundreds of young people falling to the floor, overcome by the Spirit with Lonnie Frisbee as the speaker. Wimber left his affiliation with Calvary Chapel in 1982 and pioneered a worship style with lively, soft-rock music, followed by quieter songs, practical biblical instruction, personal testimonies, and a "ministry time" in which people came forward to receive prayer. Today's global contemporary Christian worship style evolved in part from these 1980s experiments. Wimber stressed intimacy with God, believing that heartfelt worship led into deeper surrender, and that "it is our first priority to give God's love back to him in worship" (Williams 2005).

Wimber was associated with a series of controversies during the 1980s and 1990s, including his teaching on "signs and wonders," and ties to the Kansas City Prophets, and the Toronto Blessing revival. At Fuller Seminary Wimber co-taught a course with C. Peter Wagner on "Signs, Wonders, and Church Growth." Wimber's practice of directing students to pray in the classroom for healing did not find favor and he was charged with excessive emotionalism, credulity toward miracle stories, fixation on physical manifestations, unwillingness to accept suffering, irreverent worship and dress, and harsh words for Christians outside their group. A few evangelical scholars, such as Jack Deere and Wayne Grudem, supported Wimber. Wimber's "power evangelism" reflected the influence of students from Africa, Latin America, and Asia whom he met at Fuller Seminary, who had much more open attitudes toward supernatural phenomena. In *Power Evangelism* (1986) and *Power Healing* (1991), Wimber argued that Western Christians were skeptical of the supernatural because they had unwittingly accepted the naturalistic worldview of the Enlightenment. Non-Western Christians, by contrast, held a worldview closer to that of scripture, acknowledging that God's miraculous power is available today.

Subsequent events tested the limits of Wimber's supernaturalism. After encountering the Kansas City prophets around 1988 and Vineyard Pastor, Mike Bickle, Wimber was initially impressed by their work. One of the prophets, Paul Cain, publicly announced the speedy arrival of a massive revival at Wimber's meeting in London. When nothing materialized as predicted by 1990, this led to disappointment, especially among British charismatics. Wimber dialed back the prophetic emphasis, and Mike Bickle took his congregation out of the Vineyard, establishing what became the International House of Prayer. Another controversy erupted over the revival that began in 1994 at the Toronto Airport Vineyard/Toronto Blessing through the preaching of Randy Clark, a Vineyard pastor from St. Louis. Observers reported spiritual drunkenness, uncontrolled laughter, and animal sounds, though many participants said they had experienced God's love in a new way. By late 1995 Wimber concluded that the Toronto revival was imbalanced, and he disfellowshipped the Toronto congregation. Wimber was then in ill health, suffering from heart problems, and died of a brain aneurysm in 1997.

Wimber's theology was charismatic but not pentecostal, in that he did not accept the "initial evidence" doctrine of tongues as the initial, physical, and definitive, outward sign of Spirit baptism. For Pentecostal critics, Wimber's biblical teaching was more Pauline than Lukan, seeing charismatic expressions as "spiritual gifts" for edification, whereas Classical Pentecostals understood them as "power" for witness, received through a distinct, Spirit-baptism event. C. Peter Wagner called Wimber's movement the "Third Wave" of the Spirit, broadly influencing evangelicalism. Bill Jackson proposed a "radical middle" between Evangelicalism and Pentecostalism, allowing people to be "Word-plus-Spirit" Christians.

Wimber's teaching was Jesus-centered and kingdom-focused. It suggested that Jesus came to evangelize the poor, heal the sick, drive out demons, liberate the oppressed, and establish his lordship. Wimber rejected the intellectualistic notion that spiritual gifts existed simply to corroborate doctrines. Instead, he saw healing ministry as an expression of compassion, and wanted the entire church to become kingdom-minded in its eschatology. The "already-but-not-yet" kingdom – that Wimber had learned from George Ladd at Fuller Seminary – implied that the "already" could explain why healing would now occur, and the "not yet" why healing might not occur (or occur in the future). Wimber attributed his understanding of healing to the Catholic charismatic leader, Francis MacNutt.

Wimber's evangelical outlook was evident in his scriptural emphasis. When an alarmed observer, on seeing physical manifestations, asked – "how far is this going to go?" – Wimber held up a Bible and said – "no farther than this." Most Vineyard congregations today feature in-depth biblical preaching – often for thirty minutes or more – as an integral part of worship. Yet Wimber's ministry was not rigidly by-the-book and it made room for the unpredictable. He was slow to intervene when something new transpired. He said that he would let a bush grow first, and test its fruit, before trimming it back. Wimber anticipated the Spirit's moment-by-moment guidance, commencing prayer for someone and awaiting God's leading as he prayed. This aspect of Wimber's ministry may have something to do with his Quaker roots.

From his early days as a church consultant, Wimber loved the Christian church in its various branches and expressions. He felt that the diversity of churches was a good thing, since they occupied different niches and met different needs. His ministry had a two-fold focus on renewing existing churches and planting new churches, which sometimes led to misunderstandings. Wimber's renewal work bore much fruit in Britain, where it is estimated that his ministry affected some 15 percent of Anglican parishes by the 1990s (Williams 2005). Wimber was skeptical of centralized church governance. At a 1988 Vineyard conference, he deflected an initiative to create a centralized administration, since he thought that too much structure would dampen the Spirit's work. Wimber's ministry to the poor was not widely advertised, and yet the Anaheim congregation regularly distributed one million meals per year. More than half of all Vineyard churches today are involved in ministry to the poor.

Wimber blended a business-like practicality with a mystic's attunement to the Spirit's mysterious workings. His ministry was something of a high-wire act, as he balanced openness to supernatural manifestations with the need to reject extreme or disruptive behavior. It is notable that Wimber separated twice from church bodies in his early days (Quakers and Calvary Chapel), and yet, as he led the Vineyard, the roles were reversed, and he twice separated his church association from exuberant charismatic expressions (Kansas City Prophets and Toronto Blessing).

Because of Wimber's multifarious ministry, one can see several trajectories emerging from his life work. His kingdom-values and his passion for evangelism are evident in Vineyard congregations today, and yet his church-growth philosophy is apparent in parts of the Vineyard that are "seeker-sensitive" and that downplay charismatic gifts. His supernaturalism is manifest in the revivalistic hopefulness and fervent prayer of the International House of Prayer. Beginning in the college towns of Cambridge, Massachusetts, and Ann Arbor, Michigan, a small splinter of breakaway Vineyard congregations – renamed as Blue Ocean Faith – embrace progressive politics, LGBT affirmation, and outreach to highly educated nonbelievers. That one personality could incorporate such divergent tendencies is remarkable. Wimber's largest legacy may lie in the diverse possibilities that he created for charismatic Christianity to find faithful, fervent, and relevant expression in varied cultures and subcultures.

Bibliography

Coggins, James R., and Paul G. Hiebert, eds. 1989. *Wonders and the Word: An Examination of Issues Raised by John Wimber and the Vineyard Movement*. Winnipeg, Canada: Kindred Press.

Jackson, Bill. 1999. *The Quest for the Radical Middle: A History of the Vineyard*. Cape Town, South Africa: Vineyard International Publishing.

Lewis, David. 1989. *Healing: Fiction, Fantasy or Fact?* London: Hodder and Stoughton.

Pytches, David, ed. 1998. *John Wimber: A Tribute*. Guildford, UK: Eagle.

Smedes, Lewis B., ed. 1987. *Ministry and the Miraculous: A Case Study at Fuller Theological Seminary*. Pasadena, CA: Fuller Seminary Press.

Williams, Don. 2005. "Theological Perspective and Reflection on the Vineyard Christian Fellowship." In *Church, Identity, and Change: Theology and Denominational Structures in Unsettled Times*, edited by David Roozen and James Neiman, 163–187. Grand Rapids, MI: Eerdmans.

Wimber, John, and Kevin Springer. 1987. *Power Healing*. San Francisco: Harper & Row.

Wimber, John, and Kevin Springer. 1986. *Power Evangelism*. San Francisco: Harper & Row.

Michael McClymond

Winners Chapel

Living Faith Church Worldwide, popularly known as Winners Chapel, is a transnational Nigerian megachurch, with multiple branches in Nigeria and congregations in 147 countries in Africa, Asia, Europe, Canada, and the USA. Its founder and leader, David Oyedepo, is a former member of the Aladura Cherubim and Seraphim church which emerged from the Anglican Church in the 1920s. He trained as an architect and holds a PhD in human development from Honolulu University. In 1983, Oyedepo launched Faith Liberation Hour Ministries in Ilorin, after he claimed that God spoke to him to "liberate the world from all oppressions of the devil, through the preaching of the Word of faith". On the same day, he was ordained by Enoch Adeboye, who had recently become the General Overseer of the Redeemed Christian Church of God. In 1985, Oyedepo moved to Kaduna, northern Nigeria, where

he established the first branch of Winners Chapel, after a successful crusade in the city. By the late 1980s, there were at least six branches of Winners Chapel in Nigeria. In 1988, a group of Pentecostal leaders, led by Archbishop Benson Idahosa, ordained him the Pentecostal Bishop of northern Nigeria in recognition of his success. Soon after, Oyedepo moved his base to Lagos, the commercial centre of Nigeria, due to increasing Muslim-Christian conflict in Kaduna. Winners Chapel is well-known for its message of faith and prosperity, and Oyedepo is regarded as one of the foremost prosperity teachers in Africa. As a significant religious figure in Nigeria, he is regularly courted by prominent politicians. However, he has also attracted criticisms in the media for his flamboyant lifestyle, his ownership of several private jets, and for some of his more controversial practices.

In 1995, Oyedepo began a period of expansion, planting new branches in towns and cities across Nigeria as well as in other African countries. By 2000, Winners Chapel had planted 400 branches in Nigeria and was present in the capital cities of 38 African countries. Nigerian pastors were posted to lead these churches. Oyedepo's strategy was to have only one large congregation in any one city or town. However, this changed in 2009, when he claimed a mandate from God to plant multiple branches in urban and rural areas. By 2013, Winners Chapel had established 6,000 branches in Nigeria, 700 branches in other African countries, and thirty in Europe and the USA. In 2019, Oyedepo announced plans to plant 5,000 new branches in Nigeria by the end of the year. Within six months, Winners Chapel reported that 3,000 new churches had been established. Currently, it boasts the largest single congregation in East Africa (Nairobi). It has also planted 26 branches in Britain, 18 in other European nations, and 13 in the USA.

Oyedepo's theology is influenced by the Word of Faith movement in the USA, and especially the teaching of Kenneth Hagin and Kenneth Copeland. In 1986, he travelled to Tulsa, USA, to learn from Hagin. In 1987, he received a revelation from God while visiting the USA: "Arise, get back home, and make my people rich". Winners Chapel encourages members to pray for and appropriate the "covenant blessings" of health and wealth through faith. Related to this is its teaching on "sowing and reaping", lifted directly from American Word of Faith teaching, which encourages Christians to expect financial returns from their giving. Another theological strand is the prophetic anointing. In order to prosper, people are encouraged to seek out those who are sent with the message of prosperity. Associated with the message are rituals such as anointing with oil, feet-washing, the mantle (a handkerchief that has touched Oyedepo), impartation of the anointing, and Holy Communion. It is through the medium of these rituals that blessings are imparted to believers by the pastor's anointing. A third theological strand is an emphasis on miracles, a prominent feature of Oyedepo's ministry as well as the ministries of other pastors in Winners Chapel.

Winners Chapel is not just a church but a large multinational enterprise. Under the auspices of the David Oyedepo Ministries International, Oyedepo runs two private universities – Covenant University and Landmark University; and a third is nearing completion in Abuja. Other educational institutions owned by Winners Chapel include Kingdom Heritage Model nursery and primary schools, Faith Academy secondary schools, and the Word of

Faith Bible Institute. The Gilead Medical Centre provides subsidized medical services for church members. Oyedepo's businesses include a bakery, a pure water factory, and Dominion Publishing House, a media outlet, which has published over four million copies of his books. In 2011, Oyedepo was listed in Forbes magazine as Nigeria's richest pastor. However, he is also a philanthropist who has donated large amounts of money to fund development initiatives. The David Oyedepo Foundation, which he founded, is a non-profit organization focusing on four main areas: educational support, social welfare for disadvantaged children, youth leadership development, and health intervention. Winners Chapel's campground, called Canaan Land, is situated in the town of Ota, adjacent to Lagos. It is home to the international headquarters of Winners' Chapel, the 50,000-capacity church auditorium known as Faith Tabernacle, and Covenant University. The Canaan Land complex also has schools, restaurants, stores, banks, and residential estates that cater for church employees and university students.

Bibliography

Burgess, Richard. 2012. "Pentecostals and Political Culture in Sub-Saharan Africa: Nigeria, Zambia, and Kenya as Case Studies." In *Global Pentecostal Movements: Migration, Mission, and Public Religion*, edited by Michael Wilkinson, 17–42. Leiden: Brill.

Gaiya, Musa. 2015. "Charismatic and Pentecostal Social Orientations in Nigeria." *Nova Religio: The Journal of Alternative and Emergent Religions* 19 (3): 63–79.

Gifford, Paul. 2015. "The Prosperity Theology of David Oyedepo, Founder of Winners' Chapel." In *Pastures of Plenty: Tracing Religio-Scapes of Prosperity Gospel in Africa and Beyond*, edited by Andreas Heuser, 83–100. New York: Peter Lang.

Gifford, Paul. 2015. *Christianity, Development and Modernity in Africa*. London: Hurst & Co.

Kuponu, Selome I. 2007. "The Living Faith Church (Winners Chapel), Nigeria: Pentecostalism, Prosperity Gospel and Social Change in Nigeria." PhD diss., University of Bayreuth, Germany.

Ojo, Matthews A. 2006. *The End-time Army: Charismatic Movements in Nigeria*. Trenton, NJ: Africa World Press.

Richard Burgess

Woodworth-Etter, Maria

Maria Woodworth-Etter was an evangelist of the late nineteenth and early twentieth centuries who bridged the spaces between the Holiness and Healing movements and Pentecostalism. By the time she embraced

Maria Woodworth-Etter, 1844–1924

Pentecostalism, she had been preaching for over 30 years. Her revivals and mass meetings held in churches, auditoriums, and a tent with a capacity for 8,000 people, were marked by physical manifestations including trances, visions, dreams, and healing miracles. By 1885 she had gained national attention and her meetings were widely covered in the press, but also, later, in Pentecostal periodicals.

Born Maria Beulah Underwood on July 22, 1844 in Lisbon, Ohio, she was raised in a farming family who were not particularly religious or pious. Her father was abusive and an alcoholic, resulting in the family's poverty. Upon his death when she was 12 years old, she and her siblings were forced to begin working on the family's farm. Woodworth-Etter never had the advantage of formal education (McMullen 2010; Payne 2015). Shortly after her father's death, when she was 13, Woodworth-Etter attended a revival service at a Disciples of Christ church and responded to the altar call. She was baptized the next day and reported that from that time she had dreams of being the wife of a minister or missionary.

Woodworth-Etter married Philo (P.H.) Woodworth, a Civil War veteran, while still a teenager; five of six of their children died while still in their childhood. Along with a number of illnesses, the grief over the loss of her children would mark her life until, at the age of 35, in 1889, she began an itinerant preaching ministry. Having reported another conversion-type experience she became associated with the Winebrenner Churches of God (until 1904 when she was dismissed). She was accompanied throughout the midwestern US by a reluctant and ill-equipped P.H. Woodworth. Rumors of his inappropriate language, propositions of women, and profiteering from his wife's ministry followed them. Eventually, he left her and they divorced, on grounds of adultery, that was finalized in 1891 (McMullen 2010; Payne 2015). She married Samuel Etter in 1902.

Following her divorce, Woodworth-Etter, now unencumbered, began traveling widely throughout the US. Already, by 1885 she was preaching to crowds, in at least one case estimated at 25,000. Some meetings lasted for up to five months (Warner 1986). She planted churches and appointing pastors as she itinerated. Additionally, she published autobiographies including *Trials and Triumphs of the Evangelical Mrs. M.B. Woodworth, Written by Herself* (1885), and *Life and Experience of Maria B. Woodworth, Written by Herself* (1894).

Physical manifestations continually marked her meetings. Her critics, including medical professionals, attributed the healings and trances to hypnotism. While these kinds of manifestations had accompanied revivals in Wesleyan and Holiness meetings in both the US and England, and were understood as enthusiasm, Woodworth-Etter saw them as essential to spiritual renewal (McMullen, 2010). As a result, her transition into the Pentecostal movement was predictable.

Though Woodworth-Etter's own embrace of Pentecostalism is somewhat ambivalent, by 1912, Woodworth-Etter was a much sought-after evangelist in Pentecostal circles. Assemblies of God (AG) pastor, F.F. Bosworth invited her to preach at his church in Dallas, Texas. The meeting ran for six months. E.N. Bell's Pentecostal periodical *Word and Witness* began reporting on the revival as early as August. Bosworth's account, titled "The Wonders of God in Dallas," reported that thousands were in attendance and that deaf-mutes, paralytics, and invalids were being healed. Explicit and descriptive accounts of Woodworth-Etter's meetings are found consistently throughout the Pentecostal literature from 1912 onward and, in the earlier issues, are often front-page news (Alexander 2006).

Woodworth-Etter employed various healing practices including anointed handkerchiefs, verbal command, stretching her hands out over crowds, rebuking the spirit of infirmity, and imposition of hands. Trances, or being slain in the Spirit, continued to be a hallmark of her meetings, often accompanied by visions and healing miracles (Alexander 2006). Many of these miracles and manifestations are described in her 1920 publication, *Acts of the Holy Ghost; or, the Life, Work, and Experience of Mrs. M.B. Woodworth-Etter, Evangelist.*

Woodworth-Etter is noted for her influence on Pentecostal women ministers, such as Aimee Semple-McPherson. From the time of her own beginnings she had defended her ministry as a female evangelist, offering confirmation based on both a visionary call and miraculous signs (McMullen 2010). She also found warrant in scripture, identifying with Deborah, a Mother in Israel (Payne 2015).

On May 19, 1919 Woodworth-Etter invited the *The Weekly Evangel* (AG) readers to attend the opening and dedication of the Woodworth Etter Tabernacle in Indianapolis [now Lakeview Church (AG)], a church she had planted the year before. Though she was pastor of the church, she continued to travel and preach until her death on September 16, 1924.

Bibliography

Alexander, Kimberly Ervin. 2006. *Pentecostal Healing: Models of Theology and Practice.* Leiden: Brill

McMullen, Joshua J. 2010. "Maria B. Woodworth-Etter: Bridging the Wesleyan-Pentecostal Divide." In *Aldersgate to Azusa:* *Wesleyan, Holiness, and Pentecostal Visions of the New Creation*, edited by Henry H. Knight, III, 185–193. Eugene, OR: Pickwick.

Payne, Leah. 2015. *Gender and Pentecostal Revivalism: Making a Female Ministry in the Early Twentieth Century.* New York: Palgrave MacMillan.

Warner, Wayne. 1986. *The Woman Evangelist: The Life and Times of Charismatic Evangelist Maria B. Woodworth-Etter.* Metuchen, NJ: Scarecrow Press.

Kimberly Ervin Alexander

World Assemblies of God Fellowship

The World Assemblies of God Fellowship (WAGF) is a cooperative body of Classical Pentecostal churches closely aligned with the Assemblies of God, USA from around the world. There are 141 denominational organizations and Pentecostal bodies affiliated with WAGF representing approximately 63 million adherents in 2009 (Molenaar 2011). According to WAGF, "The nature of this Fellowship is a cooperative body of worldwide Assemblies of God (AG) national councils of equal standing. It is not a legislative organ to any national entity, but it is rather a coalition of commitment for the furtherance of the Gospel to the ends of the world and thus shall function as a service agent" (worldagfellowship.org). The WAGF promotes the following objectives:

1. To support and encourage one another in the task of missions and evangelism.
2. To promote Christian fellowship and cooperation among Pentecostal and Assemblies of God people throughout the world.

3. To affirm commitment to the Bible as God's complete and authoritative written revelation to humanity.
4. To bear testimony to the distinctive truths of the full gospel of Jesus Christ.
5. To provide non-legislative means of consultation and cooperation among the member churches, regional councils, and related agencies.
6. To share mutual concerns and insights relating to the various crucial, spiritual, and temporal issues of the Church.
7. To promote ministerial and missionary education with special emphasis on world evangelization.
8. To uphold one another in prayer and administer relief in times of crises.
9. To advance biblical, theological, and moral standards among the members.
10. To promote exchange of personnel in special areas of ministry.

Historically, the formation of an international group of AG churches and denominations was proposed in 1957 as an initiative of the General Council. The Foreign Missions Department was given the responsibility to begin discussions. However, the initiative was not well recieved by those AG churches outside of the US where there were some questions about its leadership and the role of the American AG (McGee 1989; Jacobsen 2010). It was not until 1989 that the World Pentecostal Assemblies of God Fellowship came into being at the Decade of Harvest Conference held in Indianapolis. Ongoing discussions have revolved around organizational polity and the financing of its shared mission and relief activities (Molenaar 2011).

WAGF is constituionally a cooperative body of Pentecostals that share a common statement of faith. Membership is subject to the approval of the Executive Council of the Assemblies of God, US. The current general superintendent of the AG is Rev. George O. Wood, who also acts as the chair of WAGF. Nationally delegated leaders from the membership gather at least every three years with the Executive Council meeting annually to discuss business matters. Sources of income for WAGF come from the member organizations as well as voluntary gifts. WAGF is organized regionally with representatives from Africa, Asia Pacific, Eurasia, Europe, Latin America/Caribbean, North America, Northern Asia, and Southern Asia.

WAGF is a transnational Pentecostal organization although it is limited in scope to churches in the Classical Pentecostal tradition. Theologically, WAGF retains a Classical Pentecostal theological statement with an emphasis on traditional statements such as the baptism of the Holy Spirit and tongues as initial evidence as well as other statements on divine healing, sanctification, the gifts of the Holy Spirit, and eschatology (Yong 2014). Organizations like WAGF contribute to the construction of a shared global Pentecostal identity among a group of Pentecostals that can be in tension with other Christian groups such as the World Council of Churches or they may be more cooperative with groups like the Pentecostal World Fellowship and evangelical organizations such as the World Evangelical Alliance (Barrett, Johnson, Crossing 2009; Robeck 2020).

Bibliography

Barrett, David B., Todd M. Johnson, and Peter F. Crossing. 2009. "Christian World Communions: Five Overviews of Global Christianity, AD 1800–2025." *International Bulletin of Missionary Research* 33 (1): 25–32.

Jacobsen, Douglas. 2010. "The Ambivalent Ecumenical Impulses in Early Pentecostal Theology in North America." In *Pentecostalism and Christian Unity: Ecumenical Documents and Critical Assessments*, edited by Wolfgang Vondey, 3–19. Eugene, OR: Pickwick.

McGee, Gary B. 1989. *This Gospel Shall Be Preached: A History and Theology of Assemblies of God Foreign Missions*, volume 2. Springfield, MO: Gospel Publishing House.

Molenaar, William. 2011. "The World Assemblies of God Fellowship: United in the Missionary Spirit," *Assemblies of God Heritage* (March): 40–47.

Robeck, Cecil M., Jr. 2020. "Pentecostal Ecclesiology." In *The T&T Clark Handbook of Ecclesiology*, edited by Kimlyn J. Bender and D. Stephen Long, 241–58. London: Bloomsbury.

World Assemblies of God Fellowship, https://worldagfellowship.org.

Yong, Amos. 2014. *Renewing Christian Theology: Systematics for a Global Christianity*. Waco, TX: Baylor University Press.

Michael Wilkinson

Yoido Full Gospel Church, Korea

Yoido Full Gospel Church (YFGC) is one of the world's largest Pentecostal congregations, located in Yŏŭido in Seoul, South Korea, which belongs to the Assemblies of God of Korea. As of 2020, the number of its registered members is estimated at about 560,000. The YFGC is a prime example of Korean Protestantism and global Christianity, and the evidence of de-secularization of contemporary society. After Yonggi Cho (b.1936) had founded it on the outskirts of Seoul on May 18, 1958 in the aftermath of the Korean War (1950–1953), the YFGC experienced rapid growth in the 1960s–1980s. Among key factors that fueled its growth are Cho's charismatic leadership, the so-called prosperity theology, and the shamanic spirituality of Korea. Civil society of today's South Korea questions the public values of its materialist orientation and anti-communist political ideology. In the aftermath of the post-Cold War and democratization, the YFGC has pursued rationalization, universalization and transnationalization. Since Cho retired in 2008, Young-hoon Lee (b.1954) has served as the head pastor of the YFGC.

The majority of the YFGC consists of urban migrants who left the country to find a better life in Seoul during the 1960s–1980s. The YFGC offered those who were uprooted with a redemptive message of hope and positivity, a new local community to help them survive in the unfamiliar urban environment and formulaic techniques to raise them up by utilizing transcendence in the secular world. The

Service at Yoido Full Gospel Church Seoul (South Korea). Source: Center for the Study of Global Christianity

fundamentals of the YFGC's faith formation are made up of the "fivefold gospel", "threefold blessings" and "spirituality of the four dimensions". Cho explains the core principle of the Bible as the fivefold gospel, namely, salvation, the fullness of Holy Spirit, divine healing, blessing and the second coming of Christ. If one understands and fulfills it, he or she receives the threefold blessings – salvation of soul, health of body and prosperity of wealth. If you want to change your life toward receiving the blessings, according Cho, you should practice the spirituality of the four dimensions, by transforming your own thought, belief, dream and language. This massive congregation is sustained by and also divided into the basic units of "home cells", each of which consists of 15 persons. Like the leading role of the female shaman in Korean Shamanism under the traditional patriarchal-hierarchical society, this cell-group institution extensively allows the leadership of women in everyday and micro-collective religious lives of its members. The YFGS appealed very much to the marginalized by providing a sense of belonging as well as healing for the vulnerable such as the poor, the disabled and/or the sick who were hurt and needed medical services in the capitalist urban circumstances.

Like the Protestant ethic informed by Max Weber (1864–1920), the YFGC afforded a new moral view to Koreans, many of whom were close to losing the meaning of life due to the rise of the secular capitalist urban environment. The 1945 liberation from colonial Japan brought about secularization, a transition from colonial society in which everyone had to participate in State Shinto to a postcolonial context, in which religion was mainly considered as matter of individual choice. The compressed modernization that transferred Korean society from a rural community to an industrialized society in the 1960s–1980s came as shock to many Koreans. However, members of the YFGS confessed that they felt a surge of energy to rise up whenever listening to sermons at the YFGS even if they went bankrupt or lost their jobs. The desired model of the modern person presented at the YFGS is one who considers growth sacred while feeling positive about her or himself. It is a moral imperative that being in the fullness of the Holy Spirit, they should be healthy and successful. Traditional cultural elements are included in efforts to reintegrate them into this new society. Divine healing, prayers to expunge the evil spirits and fervent and mystical rituals keep in step with the Shamanic tradition in Korea. The YFGS believers commonly hold to the idea that in the fullness of the Holy Spirit the faithful can overcome or find solutions when being disturbed or having a hard times by fasting and praying all night.

Along with these individual or cultural elements, the rapid growth is also attributed to its institutional response to socio-religious needs through its active utilization of mass media such as broadcasting, newspaper and magazines. The YFGC started Kukmin ilbo (Kukmin Daily), a nation-wide daily newspaper in 1988 and FGTV, an Internet broadcaster in 1998, and also utilized magazines and other radio or television programs to exercise its influence in Korea and the world. Calling into question the YFGC's theology, the Presbyterian Church of Korea (T'onghap), the mainstream Protestant denomination in Korea, labelled the YFGC as a heresy from 1983 to 1993. Liberal or progressive Koreans have joined in the criticism, arguing that the YFGC is cultic, materialist and/or selfish, and has chosen to focus on individual salvation, neglecting the structural problems of Korean society. Being mindful of these social and religious criticisms, in recent decades the YFGC has strengthened its missionary and public service activities at the national, regional and global levels. For example, the YFGC established "Elim Welfare Town" in 1988 especially for unemployed youths and elderly persons and also "Good People" in 1999, a faith-based NGO affiliated with the United Nations which is focused on international development programs. In 2007, it began constructing "Yonggi Cho Cardiology Hospital" in Pyongyang, North Korea, the completion of which has been delayed due to inter-Korean tension. The internationalization of the YFGC's propagation and humanitarian activities has facilitated the de-centralization and de-Westernization of Christianity, which in turn contributes to its multiple glocalizations.

Bibliography

Cho, David Yonggi. 1987. *Salvation, Health and Prosperity: Our Threefold Blessings in Christ.* Altamonte Springs, Fl: Creating House.
Cho, David Yonggi. 1979. *The Fourth Dimension.* Seoul: Seoul Logos Co.
Kim, Ig-Jin. 2003. *History and Theology of Korean Pentecostalism: Sunbogeum (Pure Gospel) Pentecostalism.* Zoetermeer, Netherlands: Uitgeverij Boekencentrum.
Kim, Hui-yeon. 2018. "Yŏŭido Sunbogŭm Kyoheo", in *Handbook of East Asian New Religious Movements,* edited by Lukas Pokorny and Franz Winter, 343–359. Leiden: Brill.
Myung, Sung-hoon, and Yong-gi Hong, eds. 2003. *Charis and Charisma: David Yonggi Cho and the Growth of Yoido Full Gospel Church.* Oxford: Regnum Books.

Kyuhoon Cho

Yu, Cidu (Dora Yu)

Dora Yu (Yu Cidu; 1873–1931) was a medical doctor, revivalist, and Bible school founder who gained an international reputation and inspired a generation of Chinese Christians. Yu was among the first Chinese women trained in modern western medicine. She also travelled throughout China to preach to thousands of people and founded two Bible training institutions to teach hundreds of students. She had a lasting effect on a generation of Chinese Christians, for whom she was a model of biblical knowledge, profound spirituality, and Christian ministry financially supported by the faith principle.

Yu was born to in a Christian family in an American Presbyterian mission compound in Hangzhou, Zhejiang. Her father was trained as a physician by an American missionary doctor and was later employed by the Presbyterian mission as a preacher. Dora Yu also studied medicine and was one of the first two women to graduate from Suzhou Medical College (founded by the Methodist Episcopal Church, South) in 1896. After spending years as a doctor and a teacher in the Methodist mission to Korea, Yu was promoted from a Bible woman to a missionary in 1901.

However, in 1903, Yu returned to China and began to develop her independent ministry. She became one of the first Christians in China to practice the faith principle, meaning supporting Christian work through prayer and trust in God, rather than a fixed income or institutional commitment. According to Yu's understanding, the faith principle was not an end in itself, nor primarily a means of proving God's faithfulness, but part of a larger spirituality focussing on total submission to God and constantly abiding in God's presence. This mode of spirituality drew from the Holiness currents, especially the Keswick Convention, which promoted constant prayer and obedience as a means of defeating sin, which was understood as any contradiction against God's will, especially as revealed through God's personal inner guidance.

Yu's independent preaching increasingly attracted large audiences and invitations to speak, especially from central and south China. Her background as an educated woman allowed her to reach cultural elites and popular audiences alike. Her particular style of revival preaching was assisted with her self-published revival hymnal, rigorous prayer and confession of sins beforehand. Her preaching provoked parallel responses in her audiences: public confessions, weeping, and restitutions in response to sins.

Besides her itinerant revivalism, Yu established two institutions in the metropolitan area of Shanghai, including a Bible Study and Prayer House in 1908 and a Summer Bible School in 1910. The former primarily trained women and gradually more facilities and a chapel were developed. The latter attracted attendants from many denominations and Yu developed herself as a teacher of spiritual revival and prophecy. Both continued until Yu's health decline in the late 1920s, and she donated them to the China Women's Theological Seminary.

For a period of time, Yu was one of the most famous Chinese Christians. Reports of her success spread throughout China and missionary networks publicized her work in international circles. As a result, Yu was honored as a major speaker for the International Missionary Meeting at the 1927 Keswick Convention in the UK. She denied that she was a representative of China, but rather of Jesus Christ and a "Heavenly City." She took the opportunity to denounce theological modernism as confusing the gospel and supporting anti-Christian sentiment in China.

Probably Yu's most significant legacy was found in the Chinese Christians whom she inspired. She was directly involved in influencing the conversion and Christian ministries of a number of key figures, including Andrew Gih (Ji Zhiwen), Ruth Li (Li Yuanru), Lin Heping, Watchman Nee (Ni Tuosheng), Leland Wang (Wang Zai), and Peace Wang (Wang Peizhen). She provided an important example of Christian work that was not directed by missionaries, when the Chinese society at large and the Chinese Christian world in particular were shaken by native attempts to establish independence from foreign powers.

Bibliography

Wu, Silas H. 2002. *Dora Yu and Christian Revival in 20th Century China*. Boston, MA: Pishon River Publications.

Robert, Dana. 2009. *Christian Mission: How Christianity Became a World Religion*. Malden, MA: Wiley-Blackwell.

Paul Chang

Yumiyama, Kiyoma

Kiyoma Yumiyama (弓山喜代馬; 1900–2002) was one of the charter members of *Nihon Assenbuliizu obu Goddo Kyodan* (Japan Assemblies of God/JAG), its first general superintendent, and the first president of JAG Bible School in Tokyo. He mentored other Pentecostal ministers in Japan as well.

Yumiyama was born in a rural village of Ehime on Shikoku Island on August 10, 1900. His family was one of the distinguished clans of the village with a traditional Japanese Buddhist-Shintoist background. He was the third son of the family and had five siblings. After graduating from a junior high school, Yumiyama studied at *Okayama Igaku Senmon Gakko* (Okayama Medical College) in Okayama. However, Yumiyama was very depressed at the college and tried to find the meaning of his life. The desperate Yumiyama ran to a church nearby alone on June 10, 1920 and became a Christian.

When he studied at the medical college, he met Fui, his wife to be. A year after accepting Christ, he quit his medical studies and came to Tokyo to marry her. They had two daughters and a son. In the end of 1922, Yumiyama met an American Assemblies of God (AG) missionary John W. Juergensen and was baptized by the Spirit through him. He then worked with Juergensen from the beginning of 1923 and assisted him with the publishing work, distributing tracts, and leading evangelical services.

Carl F. Juergensen (1862–1940) was another American AG missionary. He returned from the U.S. to Japan with his wife and two daughters in April 1924 after their furlough. Since then Yumiyama started working with Carl in the Takinogawa District of Tokyo, but Yumiyama was considering whether he should pursue medical studies or be committed to ministry. After attending a retreat in around 1926 hosted by Fujito Tsuge (1873–1927), a Holiness minister, he decided to dedicate himself to ministry even though his wife seemed to oppose the decision.

Yumiyama became the pastor of Takinogawa Church in November 1927 and was ordained in March 1928, which did not make his life more stable. Because of family issues, he quit his position at Takinogawa Church and left Tokyo sometime in 1928, asking his relatives in the countryside to raise his daughters. He went to Korea for several months and during that time his son died. Then he returned to Tokyo alone in January 1930. The Juergensens welcomed him and he was reinstalled as pastor of Takinogawa Church in May 1930.

In December 1930, a spiritual revival in Takinogawa Church prompted Yumiyama to start a Bible School called *Takinogawa Seirei Shingakuin* (Takinogawa Holy Spirit Bible School) in January 1931. Yumiyama did not receive any formal biblical or ministerial training, but his proficiency in both English and German seemed to enable him to self-study the Bible. In 1936, with Carl F. Juergensen and his wife officially retired, Yumiyama and the Juergensen's daughter Marie were to lead the church.

The American AG missionaries founded the Japan District and formed the Japan Pentecostal Church in 1920. In April 1929, they reconstructed the organization and started the Japan Bible Church (JBC). Takinogawa Church became the headquarters of JBC in 1930. In 1937, JBC appointed a reconstruction committee to launch a reform, inviting Jun Murai (1897–1970), pastor of Otsuka Church, and Yumiyama to join the committee. Although the historical sources have been lost, seemingly the reconstruction resulted in Yumiyama and Marie Juergensen leaving the JBC and forming *Takingawa Seirei Kyokai* (Takinogawa Holy Spirit Church) and their branch churches in 1938.

When the United Christ Church of Japan was founded under the enforcement of *Shukyo Dantai Ho* (Religious Organization Law) in June 1941, Yumiyama joined this new organization and changed the name of his church to Shinsho Church. On August 29, 1940, Carl F. Juergensen passed away in Karuizawa, Nagano; then on October 20, 1941, Marie and her mother Frederike left Japan on the last ship to cross the Pacific before the outbreak of the war. Yumiyama was left to maintain the ministry.

Yumiyama managed to avoid the draft and served as the pastor of the Shinsho Church throughout the war. Like all other Japanese churches, Shinsho Church faced many difficulties and the attendance was below ten people sometimes. But the church building escaped destruction even though much of Tokyo was burned by air raids.

After the war, Pentecostal ministers sought a way to rebuild their fellowship. In March 1949, the American AG helped them to organize the JAG. At the founding meeting of the JAG at Shinsho Church, 7 missionaries and 12 Japanese ministers gathered together. Yumiyama was chosen to be the first superintendent of the denomination and would remain in that position until 1973. In April 1950, *Chuo Seisho Gakko* (Central Bible Institute) was founded and Yumiyama was elected to be the principal, a position which he would hold until 1992. Under his leadership, both JAG and Central Bible Institute flourished.

After the war, Yumiyama had the vision to establish an independent Pentecostal church in Japan. He strongly felt that Japan needed a centralized denominational body rather than a loose fellowship. He also wanted the Japanese to have major control over the denomination with the assistance of the missionaries. The Japan District and the Foreign Division of American AG supported Yumiyama and his JAG to realize this idea. He was then given extensive authority as the general superintendent. In 1951, Yumiyama destined three mottoes for JAG: *Jishu Keizai* (self-financed), *Jishu Dendo* (self-evangelism), and *Jishu Seiji* (self-governing). He accomplished all of them eventually. He lived in the compound of JAG's headquarters from 1953 until he passed away at the age of 101 on February 10, 2002.

Bibliography

Shew, Paul Tsuchido. 2003. "History of the Early Pentecostal Movement in Japan: The Roots and Development of the Pre-War Pentecostal Movement in Japan (1907–1945)." PhD diss., Fuller Theological Seminary.

Suzuki, Masakazu. 2011. "The Origins and the Development of the Japan Assemblies of God: The Foreign and Japanese Workers and Their Ministries (1907 to 1975)." PhD diss., Bangor University.

Suzuki, Masakazu. 2006. "The Life and Ministry of Kiyoma Yumiyama and the Foundation of Japan Assemblies of God." *Asia Journal of the Pentecostal Studies* 9 (2): 220–243.

Masakazu Suzuki

Zambia

Zambian Pentecostalism is a contribution from Pentecostalism as well as Pentecostal missions and independent ministries from North America and Europe. It existed since early 1950s, if not earlier, but people began to experience its presence beginning from the late 1980s (Kaunda 2016). Various Zambian para-church organizations such as Scripture Union, the Zambia Fellowship of Evangelical Students, Campus Crusade and the Navigators that served as a platform where young students encountered this expression of the Christian faith, played a significant role of indirectly influencing the spread of Pentecostalism in the country (Sakupapa 2016). It was the youth who were quickly attracted to the emphasis on miracles, signs and wonders, and the acknowledgement of the impact of the spiritual realm on the physical world away from what could be described as the lethargic spiritual state of various denominations. Pentecostalism in Zambia at the time was characterized by overt renewal fervor among the youth who were reacting either to cultural, social, spiritual or perhaps ecclesiastical situation they deemed weak or inadequate. But, President Fredrick Chiluba's declaration of Zambia as Christian Nation toward the end of 1991 is what functioned as a catalyst is and an important defining moment in the acceleration of the explosion of Pentecostalism in the country. A proliferation of new Pentecostal churches that had no direct link with classical Pentecostalism soon followed especially during the 1990s. The success of Pentecostalism in Zambia has been undoubtedly evident especially among the urban population, and that most of those who joined came from mainline and other evangelical denominations. Although Pentecostalism is strong in the urban areas, it has shown itself more adaptable to the rural areas than most post-classical churches. Very quickly, in its many forms and expressions, Pentecostalism, became the face of Christianity in Zambia.

The growth of Pentecostalism in Zambia struck a chord with existential issues of daily life. The primary concerns were about success and failure and the knowledge needed to control one's life and be victorious. Many people were pragmatic and as a result many Zambians were attracted to Pentecostalism as they went about "shopping", as it were, for healing, prosperity and solutions to their daily problems. Pentecostal churches publicly claimed to be able to heal through the power and work of the Holy Spirit. Sickness and disease were attributed to the work of the devil. Many became Christians to acquire more power, which is the ability to make things work for their good and glory. In many cases it was argued that this view distorted the biblical view of power that directed the followers of Christ to be stewards and managers and not owners, urgeing them to be faithful in using the power God gives them for his glory (Hiebert 1999).

Pentecostalism has greatly influenced ecclesiastical and theological transformations within Zambia, with many churches being influenced by their doctrines. The Pentecostalization of non-Pentecostal churches has occured through renewal groups and activities such as Bible studies, youth, women, and men's prayer groups, overnight prayer meetings, fasting and prayer days, etc. Many churches experienced remarkable growth as a result of adopting some elements of Pentecostalism and incorporating them into their beliefs and practices. Nevertheless, Pentecostalism also negatively impacted some churches. It created some strain and clashes which led to the formation of other churches. The experiences of spiritual encounters, visions, revelations, signs and wonders and other manifestations of the Holy Spirit's presence and power have been the source for Pentecostal missiology. The emphasis on the renewing and reviving work of the Holy Spirit is the very dynamism that created new organizations, new faith communities and new ways of worshipping God.

While nationalist movements were the major players in the decolonization process, mainline church leaders were deeply involved in the democratization efforts since many people identified with the Christian faith, which gave the churches legitimacy in their advocacy role (Longwe 2017). As their numbers grew, soon the Pentecostals became important political actors. They spoke of praying for and electing Christians into power so that government and society would be transformed into a 'Christian nation'. Pentecostalism influenced President Frederick Chiluba after taking office and he invited a group of Pentecostal ministers to 'cleanse' the presidential palace of evil spirits and publicly dedicate Zambia and its government to 'the Lordship of Jesus Christ'. Chiluba's declaration of Zambia as a 'Christian nation' was not only anti-democratic but was soon discredited (Chiyeka 2008). Although there has rarely been any real friction between Christians and Muslims in Zambia, Pentecostals oftne organized public evangelistic campaigns to counter Islam and to contain Muslims in the eastern part of the country (Longwe 2017).

While early Pentecostals in Zambia stayed away from politics, contemporary Pentecostals chose to engage in politics, a relationship that has sent different signals to society and the government. Pentecostalism in Zambia has revolutionized church liturgy with a fervent style of worship that has affected other Christian denominations. It has revived the existing churches and influenced people to become dedicated followers of Jesus. As a result, it has moved from the fringes to the centre of Christian experience. However, Pentecostalism in Zambia has not replaced the mainline churches or other forms of Christian expression.

Bibliography

Cheyeka, Austin. 2008. *Church, State and Political Ethics in a Post-Colonial State: The Case of Zambia*. Zomba: Kachere.

Hiebert, Paul G., Daniel R. Shaw, and Tite Tienou. 1999. *Understanding Folk Religion: A Christian Response to Popular Beliefs and Practices*. Grand Rapids: Baker.

Kaunda, Chammah J. 2016. "The Making of Pentecostal Zambia: A Brief History of Pneumatic Spirituality." *Oral History Journal of South Africa* 4 (1): 15–45.

Longwe, Hany. 2017. "Zimbabwe, Zambia and Malawi." In *Edinburgh Companion to Global Christianity: Christianity in Sub-Sahara Africa*, edited by Kenneth R. Ross, J. Kwabena Asamoah-Gyadu, and Todd M. Johnson. Edinburgh: Edinburgh University Press.

Sakupapa, Teddy Chalwe. 2016. "Christianity in Zambia." In *Anthology of African Christianity*, edited by Isabel Apawo Phiri, Dietrich Werner, Chammah Kaunda and Kennedy Owino, 758–765. Oxford: Regnum.

Hany Longwe

Zaplishny, Dionissy Michailovitch

Dionissy Michailovitch Zaplishny was born on October 3 (September 10?), 1888 in the village of Pogachevka near Kiev, Ukraine. He immigrated to the United States in 1913 along with his two brothers. Zaplishny was converted in the Russian Baptist church of Waterbury, CT in 1918 and entered the Baptist Bible Teachers' Training School in New York. He also attended Glad Tidings Tabernacle with pastor Robert Brown and received Spirit baptism on October 10, 1919. This new experience forced him to leave school to minister in Stanford, CT where six families experienced Pentecostalism in seven months. They founded a church in Greyrock Place on February 2, 1920 and a week later joined the Slavic Pentecostal Union.

Dionissy married a Bulgarian immigrant Olga Popova Kalkandjieva (b. May 31, 1887) who came to the United States in 1914 with her first daughter Vassilka. Having attended the Missionary School in Samokov and Roberts College, Olga enrolled in Gramercy Park Bible College around 1915 and later Bethel Bible Institute in Newark.

On June 18, 1920 the Zaplishny family undertook a mission trip to Russia with Ivan Voronaev and his coworkers. After 21 days travelling by sea, they stopped at Istanbul and ministered among Russian immigrants. But with Olga being pregnant, the Zaplishny's left for her hometown Bourgas. They first brought the Pentecostal message to her home Congregationalist church in the fall of 1920.

Soon Voronaev and his team joined them in Bulgaria and starting in the spring of 1921, 14 Pentecostal assemblies and four small groups were established across the country. Zaplishny's first child John Dionisii was born on May 24, 1921 and shortly afterwards Voroanev and his coworkers moved to Varna. After working for several months there, they were finally able to board a ship and arrived in Odessa in August 1921.

Zaplishny continued the Pentecostal work in Bulgaria during 1922–1923 and set forth seven Bulgarian presbyters who became foundational for the development of the national movement. After enduring severe persecution and Olga pregnant with their second child Mary (October 23, 1924), the Zaplishnys were forced to leave Bulgaria and arrived in Ellis Island on May 21, 1924. Zaplishny resumed ministry with the Slavic Union as an evangelist, a secretary, and a chairman. He was ordained by the Assemblies of God (February 18, 1926). Meanwhile they had two more children: Martha (1926) and Joseph (1929).

The Pentecostal movement in Bulgaria slowly recovered from a major division when the Assemblies of God sent Olga's nephew Nicholas Nikolov to organize the Union of the Evangelical Pentecostal Churches in 1928. On July 6, 1929 Zaplishny was also assigned as pastor/evangelist for the work in Bulgaria. In September, 1930 the whole family returned to Bourgas sponsored by the Russian and Eastern European Mission (REEM). After Nikolov left Bulgaria in 1931, Zaplishny assumed pastorship of the Bourgas church and was elected chairmen of the Pentecostal Union, which had some 60 congregations nationwide. However, most presbyters whom Zaplishny ordained during his first visit strongly opposed the new organization under the Assemblies of God and remained unregistered.

In just a few short years in Bulgaria, Zaplishny's health quickly declined as a result of endured persecutions and he died of leukemia on January 12, 1935. After his burial in Bourgas, the oldest son John attended school in the United States while Olga remained in Bulgaria with the other three children for the next decade. When the Communist regime took over the country in 1944, persecution against evangelical churches resumed, forcing the children to return to the United States in 1946. Still a Bulgarian citizen, Olga was not allowed to leave Bulgaria until John and Mary petitioned the U.S. Department of State allowing the family to be re-united the following year. They joined the Gospel Tabernacle in North Bergen, New Jersey. Olga continued communication with believers in her home country, but was never able to return. She died on January 10, 1982 in Attleboro, Massachusetts, leaving the Zaplishny family legacy as the first Pentecostal missionaries to Bulgaria.

Bibliography

Family archive with detailed postscript, travel diary (1946), correspondence, Mary and Martha Zaplishny.

Koltovich, Vassily. 1927. *Minutes of the Jubilee Meeting.*

Minutes of the Executive Committee of the Evangelical Pentecostal Churches in Bulgaria, 1928–1947.

Ministry File and Periodical Mentions of Dionissy M. Zaplishny.

Zaplishny, Dionissy M. 1930. "Bulgaria Again Calls the Gospel Call of Russia."

Dony K. Donev

Zhang, Rongliang

Zhang Rongliang (1951–) was born in Sunlu village, Henan Province. Zhang first encountered the church when he was four years old. His younger sister, who had taken ill, was brought to the local church by their older sister, as they had no money to pay for a doctor. It was widely believed that Jesus could heal the sick, and his older sister was already a practising Christian. It was not until Zhang was 12 years old that he converted to Christianity. A village elder explained to Zhang about the evangelistic notions of eternal life, friendship in Christ, sin, Christ's atonement and resurrection, and final judgement. After hearing the gospel, Zhang accepted Christ, and the village elder witnessed the Holy Spirit entering his heart. Zhang was encouraged to insert his own name into the text while reading Isaiah 53:2–6. With such a personalized reading, Zhang was convicted of the heaviness of his own sin, which led to an outpouring of weeping when he experienced the removal of sin by Christ. This experience remains with Zhang as the foundation and certainty of his faith.

In 1967, during the height of the Cultural Revolution, Zhang started conducting his own services. The meetings initially were held in his own home and later moved to a local cave, which became a powerful symbol for his network. Zhang attracted many members who later became ministers of the network. In 1971, Zhang was arrested for the first time, and for the following nine years experienced different lengths of imprisonment in study camps, labor camps, and jails, while still developing his fledging network until 1980.

On the seventh day of the Chinese New Year in 1980, being moved by the Spirit, Zhang and another elder, Yao Wangmin, conducted a week's training programme for young ministers to instruct them on prayer, bible reading, and preaching. In the first four days, the programme focused on preaching and prayer and was attended by 20–30 people. By the fifth day, 60 people attended. As Zhang was preaching from Ezekiel 34:4–6, suddenly, the Spirit poured out powerfully, which was described by many as a "waterfall." The outpouring was like a strong wind that shook the building and filled the entire house with a fragrant aroma. All ministers began to weep and cry out to God for their sins, weaknesses, and sorrows without control. They also earnestly prayed for a simple and passionate desire to love and serve the Lord. Those who experienced all these reflected on what had happened, focussing on the spontaneous works of the Spirit and attributed these as a renewed "baptism" and call for mission. Many ministers connected the incidents of that day to the passage of Ezekiel, and they were convinced that they should be stronger and more protective shepherds for their flocks. This in turn initiated a renewed mission drive, marked by passion, love, faith, power, and courage to share the gospel.

Despite the strong presence and influence of the Spirit among many of the leaders working with Zhang, there also developed a cautious scepticism regarding the spreading of work of the Spirit, given the concern of how to discern which S/

spirit(s) was actually operating. Even after the formal establishment of the *Fangcheng* Network in 1981, there was still little formal pneumatological teaching in the network, other than that ministers should seek to speak and preach in the power of the Spirit and not rely on their own words. In 1984, Zhang met Dennis Balcombe in Guangzhou with other leaders of the Network as they had heard that Balcombe was a Spirit-filled man. As the leaders were concerned about spiritual attack, they met Balcombe for three years to determine the nature of Zhang's Spirit filling. The leaders and Balcombe developed a trusting relationship and invited him to Henan Province to teach more about the filling of the Spirit. Balcombe taught about Acts 2 and provided a theological framework for the experiences witnessed in churches. These teachings were quickly adopted by house churches, and since Zhang introduced them to other networks, they became quite common. The *Fangcheng* Network developed in China and worldwide. In 1994, it was re-named as Zhonghua Guizhu Tuandui (China for Christ Network). Zhang was totally arrested six times and spent 16 years in prison throughout his life. During his last imprisonment from 2004 to 2011, his eldest son gradually assumed the leadership of the network due to his deteriorating health. He remains active in ministry.

Bibliography

Aikman, David. 2003. *Jesus in Beijing: How Christianity Is Transforming China and Changing the Global Balance of Power*. Washington, DC: Regnery Publishing.

Su, Selena Y.Z., and Allan H. Anderson. 2017. "'Christianity Fever' and Unregistered Churches in China." In *Global Chinese Pentecostal and Charismatic Christianity*, edited by Fenggang Yang, Joy Tong, and Allan H. Anderson, 219–239. Leiden: Brill.

Su, Selena Y.Z., and Dik Allan. 2019. "Self-Narration and Theological Formation of Contemporary Chinese House Church Networks." In *Asia Pacific Pentecostalism*, edited by Denise A. Austin, Jacqueline Grey, and Paul Lewis, 61–84. Leiden: Brill.

Zhang, Rongliang. 2015. *The Apostle of Fire: The Acts of Modern China* (火煉的使徒：現代中國使徒行傳). Hong Kong: Kingdom Ministries.

Zhang, Rongliang, and Eugene Bach. 2015. *I Stand with Christ: The Courageous Life of a Chinese Christian*. New Kensington: Whitaker House.

Selena Su Dik Allan

Zimbabwe

Any discussion on Pentecostalism in Zimbabwe progresses towards a binary contestation between those who are for and against it. The first school of thought speaks to the development of Pentecostalism with much suspicion and focuses its critique on how the gospel of prosperity has been manipulated by charismatic preachers who have used it to amass great personal wealth (Bishau 2013). The second school of thought traces Pentecostalism's history in Zimbabwe arguing that the contemporary prophetic phase is a continuation of a longer deep rooted movement geared towards the spread of the gospel in Zimbabwe (Mpofu 2013). The period between 2007 and 2008 is an era of renewal that saw the emergence of megachurches run and controlled by Zimbabwean leaders. This binary debate however has consumed academia around Pentecostal churches in Zimbabwe at the expense of unpacking the historical and cultural evolution of the movement in post-colonial contexts. Ganiel (2009) adds another emergent theme in Pentecostal research that examines how the movement leads to congregants' withdrawal from politics and thus leads to apathy. This article provides a brief alternative view of Pentecostalism in Zimbabwe beyond the debates around the prosperity gospel.

Within the literature there is a distinct narrative that casts suspicion on the emergence of prophetic movements in post-2000 Zimbabwe (Marongwe and Maposa 2015). Such narratives argue that the upsurge in Pentecostal churches and prophets and prophetesses leading these movements cannot be separated from the socio-economic and political crises that have characterized post-2000 Zimbabwe (Chitando 2013). With increased poverty and suffering, various entrepreneurial individuals have innovated biblical movements based on a specific gospel of prosperity as a means to amass wealth and social status (Mangena and Mhizha 2013). Some of the scholars within this school of thought describe people who follow such movements variously as desperate and delusional (Togarasei 2011). Bishau (2013) notes how the gospel is geared towards seeding (give and you shall receive), naming and claiming things. Related to this discussion is the issue of miracles associated prophets and prophetesses, which proponents of this school tend to label as false. These miracles include raising the dead, making barren woman to conceive and deliver within three days, having miracle money appear in congregant's bank accounts and instant weight loss among other things (Mapangura, Chitando and Gunda 2013). Madzokere and Machingura (2015, 66) argue that prophets/prophetesses in Zimbabwe often use miracles to push the message that God has finally remembered Zimbabwe after decades of economic malaise and they conclude that "... Zimbabwean Christians have been divided when it comes to contemporary prophets/esses, where most of them preach peace where there is violence. They preach prosperity where there is hunger, poverty, disease and unemployment although the elite rich enjoy themselves." Related to miracles and accumulation is the rise of spiritual merchandising which includes the selling of anointing oil, water, bangles, wrist bands, t shirts and various other anointed goods. This branding is tied to a sophisticated marketing scheme which utilises new media technologies to enhance sells and profits (Togarasei 2012).

Scholars such as Mpofu (2013) and Mukwakwama (2010) provide a historical analysis of Christianity in Zimbabwe. They theorise that this contemporary period of Pentecostalism should be viewed as the Third Wave Religious Right Movement albeit with differing characteristics than earlier waves. Other scholars have argued that the negative descriptions of Pentecostal churches in Zimbabwe is driven mainly by mainstream churches who are jealous of the rise and success of these churches. Such jealousy, Gifford (1998) concludes, is based on the decline in numbers in mainline denominations because these churches are failing to meet the spiritual needs of congregants. The work of Ganiel (2008; 2009) and Togarasei (2011) attempts to provide a material explanation related to positive aspects of Pentecostal Christianity such as the churches contribution to sustainable development, poverty reduction and how they use religious resources to develop a vision for reconstruction and reconciliation.

Machingura (2011) focuses on an important and also controversial part of Pentecostalism: speaking in tongues. Speaking in tongues is an important characteristic of Pentecostal churches as it signifies the baptism by the Holy Spirit. Using the example of the Apostolic Faith Mission church, he highlights how for Pentecostal churches, glossolalia is based on biblical texts. Yet, some mainstream churches such as Anglican and Roman Catholic also use the bible to argue that tongues are meaningless. Chitando (2007) on the other hand focuses on how Pentecostalism in Zimbabwe is nurturing soft masculinities in the wake of the HIV epidemic. Other studies have focused on the biographical analyses of church founders such as Togarasei's (2005) study of the Family of God ministry. Maxwell (2000) provides an analysis of how Pentecostal churches relate to post-colonial politics using the case of Zimbabwe Assembly of God church's relationship with the ruling ZANU PF.

Bibliography

Bishau, D. 2013. "The Prosperity Gospel: An Investigation into Its Pros and Cons with Examples Drawn from Zimbabwe." *International Open & Distance Learning Journal* 1 (1): 1–11.

Chitando, E. 2013. "Prophets, Profits and Protests Prosperity Theology and Zimbabwean Gospel Music." In *Prophets, Profits and the Bible in Zimbabwe*, edited by E. Chitando, R.M. Gunda, and J. Kugler, 95–112. Bamberg: University of Bamberg Press.

Chitando, E. 2007. "A New Man for a New Era? Zimbabwean Pentecostalism, Masculinities, and the HIV Epidemic." *Missionalia: Southern African Journal of Mission Studies* 35 (3): 112–127.

Ganiel, G. 2008. "Beyond Pietism and Prosperity: Religious Resources for Reconstruction and Reconciliation in Zimbabwe." Africa Peace and Conflict Network Occasional Paper 1.

Ganiel, G. 2010. "Pentecostal and Charismatic Christianity in South Africa and Zimbabwe: A Review." *Religion Compass* 4 (3): 130–143.

Ganiel, G. 2009. "Spiritual Capital and Democratization in Zimbabwe: a Case Study of a Progressive Charismatic Congregation." *Democratization* 16 (6): 1172–1193.

Gifford, P. 1998. *African Christianity: Its Public Role*. London: Hurst.

Machingura, F. 2011. "The Significance of Glossolalia in the Apostolic Faith Mission, Zimbabwe." *Studies in World Christianity* 17 (1): 12–29.

Madzokere, N., and F. Machingura. 2015. "True and False Prophets/esses in the Light of Prophets/esses and Wonders in Zimbabwe." *Journal of Critical Southern Studies* 3: 53–71.

Mangena, F. and Mhizha, S. 2013. "The Rise of White Collar Prophecy in Zimbabwe: A Psycho-Ethical Statement." In *Prophets, Profits and the Bible in Zimbabwe*, edited by E. Chitando, R.M. Gunda, and J. Kugler, 133–150. Bamberg: University of Bamberg Press.

Mapuranga, T., E. Chitando, and R.M. Gunda. 2013. "Studying the United Family International Church in Zimbabwe: The Case for Applying Multiple Approaches to the Study of Religion and Religious Phenomena." In *Prophets, profits and the Bible in Zimbabwe*, edited by E. Chitando, R.M. Gunda, and J. Kugler, 290–321. Bamberg: University of Bamberg Press.

Marongwe, N., and Maposa, R.S. 2015. "PHDs, Gospreneurship, Globalisation, and the Pentecostal 'New Wave' in Zimbabwe." *Afro-Asian Journal of Social Sciences* 4 (1): 1–22.

Maxwell, David. 2000. 'Catch the Cockerel before Dawn': Pentecostalism and Politics in Post-Colonial Zimbabwe. *Africa: Journal of the International African Institute*, 70 (2): 249-277.

Mpofu, S. 2013. "The 'Third Wave' Religious Right Movement and the Growth of Zimbabwean Christianity: Faith or Economic Response?" PhD thesis, University of Pretoria, South Africa.

Mukwakwama, L. 2010. *Our Subtle Christianity*. West-Lake: Book Surge.

Togarasei, L. 2018. *Aspects of Pentecostal Christianity in Zimbabwe*. New York: Springer.

Togarasei, L. 2012. "Mediating the Gospel: Pentecostal Christianity and Media Technology in Botswana and Zimbabwe." *Journal of Contemporary Religion* 27 (2): 257–274.

Togarasei, L. 2011. "The Pentecostal Gospel of Prosperity in African Contexts of Poverty: An Appraisal." *Exchange* 40 (4): 336–350.

Togarasei, L. 2005. "Modern Pentecostalism as an Urban Phenomenon: The Case of the Family of God Church in Zimbabwe." *Exchange* 40 (4): 336–350.

Manase Kudzai Chiweshe

Zschech, Darlene

Darlene Joyce Zschech (1965–) is a world renowned composer, worship leader, author and conference speaker. She is an ordained minister of Australian Christian Churches (formerly Assemblies of God in Australia) and has been credited as one of the leading pioneers of the contemporary worship and music movement worldwide.

Darlene Zschech (née Steinhardt) was born on September 8, 1965 in Brisbane, Australia. She is the eldest of four children to Des and Joan Steinhardt. From ten years old she sang, danced and hosted a weekly children's television show. Converted to Christianity as a teenager, she fronted various local gospel bands and wrote jingles for prominent commercial brands. She met Mark Zschech when he auditioned to be her drummer and they were married one week after her nineteenth birthday.

The couple moved to Sydney and, in 1985, joined Hills Christian Life Centre (HCLC), which was founded by Brian and Bobbie Houston in 1983. There were around 180 congregants and Darlene Zschech was part of the worship team while raising her daughters, Zoe, Amy and Chloe. HCLC praise and worship was emerging as a new sensation, under the leadership of worship pastor, Geoff Bullock. Its first live worship album, "The Power of Your Love," was released, in 1992, to international acclaim.

In February 1994, Zschech's song "Shout to the Lord" was included on the album "People Just Like Us". In October 1995, Zschech was the worship leader for the live album "Shout to the Lord" released by Integrity Music under the Hosanna! Music label. It became the first Christian album in Australia to go gold and platinum in the US. The album reached No. 13 on the Billboard Top Contemporary Christian Albums Chart. "Shout to the Lord" was nominated for Album of the Year at the 1997 Dove Awards and Song of the Year at the 1998 Dove Awards. It is now sung by around 30 million people each week, and has been covered by at least 20 other prominent Christian artists.

HCLC was renamed Hillsong Church in 1999 and Zschech served as worship pastor for 11 years (1996–2007), leading the worship and creative arts department. She wrote over 60 songs and produced numerous albums for Hillsong Music Australia, many of which achieved gold status. Mark Zschech became media manager of Hillsong Church and director of the television ministry which now reaches over 125 different countries.

Darlene Zschech was nominated for Songwriter of the Year at the 2000 Dove Awards and received an International Award for influence in praise and worship. In 2004, "For All You've Done" debuted on the ARIA Top 50 Albums chart at No. 1. Diana Bagnall (2004) claims, "She is the poster girl for extravagant worship." Mark Evans (2006) argues that Zschech became the "face and sound" of Hillsong. He adds (2017) that she was "responsible for spreading this music globally." Demonstrating broad appeal, "Shout to the Lord" was performed by contestants on American Idol.

Active in social welfare projects, Mark and Darlene Zschech were involved in Mercy Ministries for at risk women. They also pioneered Hope: Rwanda in 2004, providing practical solutions for communities devastated by war, genocide, and poverty. Later renamed HOPE: Global, this organization expanded into other parts of Africa, Cambodia, Sri Lanka, Vietnam, and India.

Darlene Zschech has promoted ecumenical dialogue, performing at the Roman Catholic Church's World Youth Day in Sydney July 15–20, 2008 and contributing to the Compassion art worship album for charity. At the 2015 "Voices of Prayer" organized by Catholic charismatic group "Renewal in the Spirit", Zschech sang "Shout to the Lord" for Pope Francis in St Peter's Square. Zschech has written several books which have been translated into over 20 different languages.

After serving in Hillsong Church for 25 years, in 2011, Mark and Darlene Zschech moved on to become the co-senior pastors of Hope Unlimited Church (HopeUC) on the New South Wales Central Coast. The church grew rapidly and also added campuses in India and the US. During this time, Darlene Zschech also recorded further worship albums, including "Here I Am, Send Me" and "The Table."

In 2013, Zschech was diagnosed with breast cancer and appeared on an episode of Joyce Meyer's "Everyday Answers" to discuss her long journey through the illness. She notes that maintaining an attitude of worship strengthened her during treatment. The Zschechs continue to pastor HopeUC and travel extensively for ministry while also remaining close with their children and grandchildren.

Award winning song writer and singer, Darlene Zschech was the global face of Hillsong Church for over two decades. Her songs have become integral to contemporary church worship across the world. She and her husband continue to make a significant social contribution through their global ministry and welfare projects.

Bibliography

Austin, Denise A., and Shane Clifton. 2019. "Australian Pentecostalism: From Marginalised to Megachurches." In *Asia Pacific Pentecostalism*, edited by Denise A. Austin, Jacqueline Grey and Paul W. Lewis, 372–399. Leiden: Brill.

Bagnall, Diana. 2004. "Jesus Christ's Superstar." *Bulletin with Newsweek* 122 (6441): 30–34.

Evans, Mark. 2006. *Open Up the Doors: Music in the Modern Church*. London: Equinox Publishing.

Evans, Mark. 2017. "Creating the Hillsong Sound: How One Church Changed Australian Christian Music." In *The Hillsong Movement Examined: You Call Me Out Upon the Waters*, edited by Tanya Riches and Tom Wagner, 63–84. Cham, Switzerland: Palgrave Macmillan.

Hutchinson, Mark. 2009. "The Contribution of Women to Pentecostalism." In *Raising Women Leaders: Perspectives on Liberating Women in Pentecostal and Charismatic Contexts*, edited by Shane Clifton and Jacqueline Grey, 191–220. Sydney: Australasian Pentecostal Studies.

Denise A. Austin

Combined Bibliography

Aasmundsen, Hans Geir. 2016. *Pentecostals, Politics, and Religious Equality in Argentina*. Leiden: Brill.

Abrams, Minnie F. 1906. *The Baptism of the Holy Ghost and Fire*. Kedgaon, India: Mukti Mission Press.

Abrams, Minnie F. 1908. "A Message from Mukti." *Confidence* (September 15).

Abrams, Minnie R. 1989. *The Baptism of the Holy Ghost & Fire*. Bombay: GLS Press.

Adeboye, Olufunke. 2007. "'Arrowhead' of Nigerian Pentecostalism: The Redeemed Christian Church of God, 1952–2005." *Pneuma* 29 (1): 24–58.

Adhav, Shamsundar Manohar. 1979. *Pandita Ramabai*. Madras: Christian Literature Society.

Adogame, Afe. 2004. "Contesting the Ambivalences of Modernity in a Global Context: The Redeemed Christian Church of God, North America." *Studies in World Christianity* 10 (1): 25–48.

Adogame, Afe. 2013. "Reconfiguring the Global Religious Economy: The Role of African Pentecostalism." In *Spirit and Power: The Growth and Global Impact of Pentecostalism*, edited by Donald E. Miller, Kimon H. Sargeant, and Richard Flory, 185–203. Oxford: Oxford University Press.

Adogame, Afe. 2013. *The African Christian Diaspora: New Currents and Emerging Trends in World Christianity*. London and New York: Bloomsbury.

Agbiji, Obaji. 2015. "Religion and Ecological Justice in Africa: Engaging 'Value for Community' as Praxis for Ecological and Socio-economic Justice." *HTS Teologiese Studies / Theological Studies* 71 (2): 10 pages. doi:https://doi.org/10.4102/hts.v71i2.2663.

Agosto Cintrón, Nélida. 1996. *Religión y Cambio Social En Puerto Rico, 1898–1940*. Río Piedras, P.R: Ediciones Huracán: Ateneo Puertorriqueño.

Ahlstrom, Sydney E. 2004. *A Religious History of the American People*. New Haven: Yale University Press.

Ahn, Che, and Lou Engle. 2001. *The Call Revolution: A Radical Invitation to Turn the Heart of a Nation Back to God*. Colorado Springs, CO: Wagner Publications.

Akiman, David. 2006. *Jesus in Beijing: How Christianity is Transforming China and Changing the Global Balance of Power*. Washington, DC: Regnery.

Akoda, Winifred. 2012. "May His Will Be Done: A History of the Deeper Life Bible Church, 1973–2006." *International Journal of Asian Social Science* 2 (4): 402–410.

Akoko, Robert Mbe. 2007. "'Ask and You Shall be Given.' Pentecostalism and the Economic Crises in Cameroon." PhD thesis, Leiden, African Studies Centre.

Albrecht, Daniel E. 1986. "Carrie Judd Montgomery: Pioneering Contributor to Three Religious Movements." *Pneuma* 8 (2): 101–119.

Albrecht, Daniel E. 1999. *Rites in the Spirit: A Ritual Approach to Pentecostal/Charismatic Spirituality*. Sheffield: Sheffield Academic Press.

Alegre, Rakel Ystebø. 2019. "The Pentecostal Apologetics of T.B. Barratt: Defending and Defining the Faith 1906–1909." PhD. diss, Regent University.

Alexander, David A. 1986. "Bishop J.H. King and the Emergence of Holiness Pentecostalism." *Pneuma* 8 (1): 159–183.

Alexander, Estrelda Y. 1997. "Liturgy in Non-Liturgical Holiness-Pentecostalism." *Wesleyan Theological Journal* 32 (2): 158–93.

Alexander, Estrelda Y. 2011. *Black Fire: One Hundred Years of African American Pentecostalism*. Downers Grove, IL: Intervarsity Press.

Alexander, Estrelda. 2005. *The Women of Azusa Street*. Cleveland, OH: The Pilgrim Press.

Alexander, Estrelda. 2010. "Women as Leaders in Pentecostal/Charismatic Religions." In

Gender and Women's Leadership: A Reference Handbook, edited by Karen O'Conner, 533–543. Thousand Oaks, CA: Sage Publications.

Alexander, Kimberly Ervin. 2006. *Pentecostal Healing: Models in Theology and Practice.* Leiden: Brill.

Alexander, Paul, ed. 2012. *Christ at the Checkpoint: Theology in the Service of Justice and Peace.* Eugene, OR: Wipf & Stock.

Allen, Lexie E. 1954. *God's Man of Faith and Power: The Life Story of A.A. Allen.* Dallas: A.A. Allen.

All-Ireland Churches Consultative Committee on Racism. 2009. "Directory of Migrant-Led Churches." Belfast: AICCMR. Accessed December 12, 2019. https://www.irishchurches.org/cmsfiles/resources/Reports/DirectoryOfMigrantLedChurchesAndChaplaincies2009.pdf.

Althouse, Peter. 2003. *Spirit of the Last Days: Pentecostal Eschatology in Conversation with Jürgen Moltmann.* London: T&T Clark International.

Althouse, Peter. 2005. "Wesleyan and Reformed Impulses in the Keswick and Pentecostal Movements." *Pneuma Foundation* (Spring). http://www.pneumafoundation.org/article.jsp?article=/Keswick-PAlthouse.xml.

Althouse, Peter. 2014. "The Influences of Keswick and Healing Advocate Elizabeth Baxter on the Toronto Hebden Mission," Presented at the Annual Meeting of the Society for Pentecostal Studies, Springfield, MO, March 4–7.

Althouse, Peter and Robby Waddel, eds. 2010. *Perspectives in Pentecostal Eschatology: World Without End.* Cambridge: James Clarke & Co.

Alva, Reginald. 2014. *The Spirituality of the Catholic Charismatic Renewal Movement.* New Delhi: Christian World Imprints.

Álvarez, Carmelo. 2006. "Sharing in God's Mission: The Evangelical Pentecostal Union of Venezuela and the Christian Church (Disciples of Christ) in the United States." PhD diss., Amsterdam Free University.

Alvarez, Miguel, ed. 2015. *The Reshaping of Mission in Latin America.* Oxford: Regnum International Books.

Alvarsson, Jan-Åke. 2007. "Pingstväckelsens etablering i Sverige: Från Azusa Street till Skövde på sju månader." In *Pingströrelsen: Händelser och utveckling under 1900-talet*, 11–43. Örebro: Libris förlag.

Alvarsson, Jan Åke. 2011. "The Development Of Pentecostalism In Scandinavian Countries." In *European Pentecostalism*, edited by William Kay and Anne Dyer, 17–40. Leiden: Brill.

Alvarsson, Jan-Åke, and Rita Laura Segata, eds. 2003. *Religions in Transition: Mobility, Merging and Globalization in the Emergence of Contemporary Religious Adhesions.* Uppsala: Uppsala Universitet.

Amanze, J.N., and T. Shanduka. 2015. "Glossolalia: Divine Speech or Man-made Language? A Psychological Analysis of the Gift of Speaking in Tongues in the Pentecostal Churches in Botswana." *Studia Historiae Ecclesiasticae* 41 (1): 3–19.

Ambrose, Linda M. 2009. "Establishing a Gendered Authority through Pentecostal Publications: The Writings of Zelma Argue, 1920–1969," in *Historical Papers: Journal of the Canadian Society of Church History*, 69–80.

Ambrose, Linda M. 2010. "Zelma and Beulah Argue: Sisters in the Canadian Pentecostal Movement." In *Winds from the North: Canadian Contributions to the Pentecostal Movement*, edited by Michael Wilkinson and Peter Althouse, 99–127. Leiden: Brill Academic Publishers.

Ambrose, Linda M. 2016. "Gender History in Newfoundland Pentecostalism: Alice Belle Garrigus and Beyond." *PentecoStudies: An Interdisciplinary Journal for Research on the Pentecostal and Charismatic Movements* 15 (2): 172–199.

Ambrose, Linda M. 2017. "Aimee Semple McPherson: Gender Theory, Worship, and the Arts." *Pneuma* 39 (1): 105–122.

Ambrose, Linda M., and Leah Payne. 2014. "Reflections on the Potential of Gender Theory for North American Pentecostal History." *Pneuma* 36 (1): 45–63.

Amos, Ashish. 2011. *Pentecostal Churches in Kerala and Indigenous Leadership*. Delhi: ISPCK.

Amouzouvi, Hippolyte D.A. 2005. *Le Marché de la Religion au Bénin*. Berlin: Verlag Dr. Koster.

Anderson, Allan. 2004. "The Contextual Pentecostal Theology of David Yonggi Cho." *Asian Journal of Pentecostal Studies* 7 (1): 101–123.

Anderson, A. 2006. "The Pentecostal and Charismatic movements." In *Christianity: World Christianities c.1914–c.2000*, edited by H. McCleod, 89–106. Cambridge: Cambridge University Press.

Anderson, Allan. 2006. "Pandita Ramabai, the Mukti Revival and Global Pentecostalism." *Transformation* 23 (1): 37–48.

Anderson, Allan H. 2007. *Spreading Fires: The Missionary Nature of Early Pentecostalism*. London: SCM Press.

Anderson, Allan. 2010. "Varieties, Taxonomies, and Definitions." In *Studying Global Pentecostalism: Theories and Methods*, edited by Allan Anderson, 13–29. Berkeley, CA: University of California Press.

Anderson, A.H. 2013. "Eritrean Pentecostals as Asylum Seekers in Britain." *Journal of Religion in Africa* 43 (2): 167–95.

Anderson, Allan H. 2013. "The Emergence of a Multidimensional Global Missionary Movement: Trends, Patterns, and Expressions." In *Spirit and Power: The Growth and Global Impact of Pentecostalism*, edited by Donald E. Miller, Kimon H. Sargeant, and Richard Flory, 25–41. Oxford: Oxford University Press.

Anderson, Allan H. 2013. *To the Ends of the Earth: Pentecostalism and the Transformation of World Christianity*. Oxford: Oxford University Press.

Anderson, Allan H. 2014. *An Introduction to Pentecostalism*. Cambridge: Cambridge University Press.

Anderson, Allan H. 2014. "Origins and Developments of Pentecostalism in Africa." In *Pentecostalism in Africa*, edited by M. Lindhardt, 54–74. Leiden: Brill.

Anderson, Allan Heaton. 2015. "'Stretching out Hands to God': Origins and Development of Pentecostalism in Africa." In *Pentecostalism in Africa: Presence and Impact of Pneumatic Christianity in Postcolonial Society*, edited by Martin Lindhardt, 54–74. Leiden: Brill.

Anderson, Allan H. 2018. *Spirit-filled World: Religious Dis/Continuity in African Pentecostalism*. Cham, Switzerland: Palgrave Macmillan.

Anderson, Allan, Michael Bergunder, André Droogers, and Cornelis van der Laan, eds. 2010. *Studying Global Pentecostalism. Theories and Methods*. Berkeley: University of California Press.

Anderson, Allan H., and Walter J. Hollenweger, eds. 1999. *Pentecostals after a Century: Global Perspectives on a Movement in Transition*. Sheffield: Sheffield Academic Press.

Anderson, Allan and Edmond Tang, eds. 2005. *Asian and Pentecostal: The Charismatic Face of Christianity in Asia*. Oxford: Regnum.

Anderson, Allan and Edmond Tang, eds. 2011. *Asian and Pentecostal: The Charismatic Face of Christianity in Asia*. Revised Edition. Oxford: Regnum.

Andreescu, Valeriu. 2012 *Istoria Penticostalismului Românesc*, Two Vols. Oradea: Casa Cărții.

Annor-Antwi, Gibson. 2016. *Myth or Mystery: A Bio-autobiography of Apostle Professor Opoku Onyinah*. London: Inved.

Annual Report of the American Bible Society, 1891ff.

Anon. 1996. "Prominent Bolivian Evangelist Murdered." *ChristianityToday.Com*, February 5, 1996, 1. Accessed July 28, 2019. https://www.christianitytoday.com/ct/1996/february5/6t2099.html.

Anon. n.d. "Biografía Fundador: Dr. Julio Cesar Ruibal." *Colegio Ekklesia* (blog), 1. Accessed

July 28, 2019. http://www.colegioekklesia.edu.co/fundador-julio-cesar-ruibal/.

Antcliff, Pat. 2003. "Charles Louis Greenwood." *Australasian Dictionary of Pentecostal and Charismatic Movements*. https://sites.google.com/view/adpcm/e-h-top-page/greenwood-charles-louis. Accessed May 23, 2019.

AOGKL (Assembly of God Kuala Lumpur). 1964. *Assembly of God Kuala Lumpur 1934–1964 – 30th Anniversary Magazine*.

Aoki, Yasunori. 2011. "Coote Family: The History of Oneness Pentecostalism 'United Pentecostal Church in Japan' and Pentecostal Mission Board 'Next Towns Crusade.'" Presented at the 40th Annual Meeting of the Society for Pentecostal Studies, Memphis, TN, March 10–12.

Apostolic Faith, September 1906, no. 1.

Apostolic Faith, January 1908, no. 1.

Apostolic Faith, May 1908, no. 2.

APSC, Assemblies of God in Australia, Commonwealth Conference Minutes, 1937–1969; and Forbes, George. 2010. "Interview with Mark Hutchinson 1 Sept. 2010." Archives, Australasian Pentecostal Studies Centre, Alphcrucis College.

Arab Baptist Theological Seminary. 2019. "Home." *Arab Baptist Theological Seminary*. Accessed Oct. 3, 2019. https://abtslebanon.org/.

Arce Martínez, Sergio. 1997. "Las iglesias pentecostales y los movimientos carismáticos en Cuba desde una perspectiva cubana." In *Carismatismo en Cuba*, edited by Reinerio Arce Valentín, and Manuel Quintero, compiled by Elizabeth Carrillo, 153–73. Cuba: Departamento de Comunicaciones del Consejo Latinoamericano de Iglesias.

Archer, Kenneth J. 2004. *A Pentecostal Hermeneutic for the Twenty-First Century: Spirit, Scripture, and Community*. London: T&T Clark International.

Archer, Kenneth J. 2010. *The Gospel Revisited: Towards a Pentecostal Theology of Worship and Witness*. Eugene: Pickwick.

Archer, Kenneth J., and L. William Oliverio, Jr., eds. 2016. *Constructive Pneumatic Hermeneutics in Pentecostal Christianity*. New York: Palgrave MacMillan.

Archer, Kenneth, and Melissa Archer. 2019. "Complementarian and Egalitarian: Whose Side are you Leaning on? A Pentecostal reading of Ephesians 5:21–33." *Pneuma* 41 (1): 66–90.

Aritonang, Jan S. 1995. *Berbagai Aliran Di dalam dan Di sekitar Gereja*. Jakarta: BPK Gunung Mulia.

Aritonang, Jan S., and Karel Steenbrink, eds. 2008. *The History of Christianity in Indonesia*. Leiden: Brill.

Arnott, John. 1995. *The Father's Blessing*. Orlando, FL: Creation House.

Aronson, Torbjörn. 2005. *Guds eld över Sverige. Svensk väckelsehistoria efter 1945*. Uppsala: Livets Ords Förlag.

Aronson, Torbjörn. 2012. "Continuity in Charismata: Swedish Mission and the Growth of Neo-Pentecostal Churches in Russia." *Religion in Eastern Europe* 31 (1): 33–40.

Artman, Amy. 2019. *The Miracle Lady: Kathryn Kuhlman and the Transformation of Charismatic Christianity*. Grand Rapids, MI: William B. Eerdmans.

Asamoah-Gyadu, Kwabena. 1997. "'Missionaries Without Robes': Lay Charismatic Fellowships and the Evangelization of Ghana." *Pneuma* 19 (1): 167–188.

Asamoah-Gyadu, J. Kwabena. 2005. *African Charismatics: Current Developments Within Independent Indigenous Pentecostalism in Ghana*. Leiden: Brill.

Asamoah-Gbadu, J. Kwabena. 2013. *Contemporary Pentecostal Christianity: Interpretations from an African Context*. Eugene: Wipf and Stock.

Asamoah-Gyadu, J. Kwabena. 2015. "Pentecostalism and the Transformation of the African Christian Landscape." In *Pentecostalism in Africa: Presence and Impact of Pneumatic*

Christianity in Postcolonial Societies, edited by Martin Lindhardt, 100–114. Leiden: Brill.

Assemblies of God. 2009. "Honduras – Quick Facts." Springfield: Gospel Publishing House. Last Accessed May 22, 2018. http://agwebservices.org/Content/RSSResources/Honduras_Quick%20Facts.pdf.

Atkinson, William P. 2009. *The 'Spiritual Death' of Jesus: A Pentecostal Investigation*. Leiden: Brill.

Attanasi, Katherine, and Amos Yong, eds. 2012. *Pentecostalism and Prosperity: The Socio-Economics of the Global Charismatic Movement*. New York: Palgrave Macmillan.

Atter, G.F. 1963. *The Student's Handbook: Cults and Heresies*. Peterborough: College Press.

Campbell, F. 1974. *Stanley Frodsham: Prophet With a Pen*. Radiant Books. Springfield, MO: Gospel Publishing House.

Au, Connie. 2011. *Grassroots Unity in the Charismatic Renewal*. Eugene: Wipf & Stock.

Au, Connie. 2012. "Justice and Peace for Global Commercial Sex Workers: The Plight of Aboriginal Migrant Women in Taiwan." *The Ecumenical Review* 64 (3): 267–280.

Au, Connie. 2012. "Resisting Globalization: The Pentecostal Holiness Church's Mission and the 'Anti-Globalization Movement' in China (1920–30)." In *Global Pentecostal Movements: Migration, Mission, and Public Religion*, edited by Michael Wilkinson, 117–134. Leiden: Brill.

Au, Connie. 2013. "'Now Ye Are Clean': Sanctification as a Formative Doctrine of Early Pentecostalism in Hong Kong." *Australian Pentecostal Studies* 15 (January). Accessed December 12, 2019. http://aps-journal.com/aps/index.php/APS/article/view/124/121.

Au, Connie. 2017. "Elitism and Poverty: Early Pentecostalism in Hong Kong (1907–1945)." In *Global Chinese Pentecostal and Charismatic Christianiy*, edited by Fenggang Yang, Joy Tong, and Allan Anderson, 63–88. Leiden: Brill.

Au, Connie. 2018. "The Migrant Spirit: A Study of the Filipina Catholic Charismatics of the Loved Flock in Hong Kong." *Asian Journal of Theology* 3 (2): 119–140.

Au, Connie. 2019. "From Collaborations with Missionaries to Independence: A History of the Hong Kong Pentecostal Mission (1907–1930)." In *Asia Pacific Pentecostalism*, edited by Denis A. Austen, Jacqueline Grey, and Paul Lewis, 85–106. Leiden: Brill.

Au, Connie. 2020. "Pentecostal Spirituality." In *Protestant Spiritual Traditions*, vol. 2, edited by Frank Senn, 148–175. Eugene: Cascade Books.

Auburn Baptist Church. 1988. *Auburn Baptist Church, 1888–1988*, Auburn, NSW.: Auburn Baptist Church.

Augustine, Daniela C. 2010. "The Empowered Church: Ecclesiological Dimensions of the Event of Pentecost." In *Toward a Pentecostal Ecclesiology: the Church and the Fivefold Gospel*, edited by John Christopher Thomas, 157–180. Cleveland, TN: CPT Press.

Augustine, Daniela C. 2012. *Pentecost, Hospitality, and Transfiguration: Toward a Spirit-inspired Vision of Social Transformation*. Cleveland: CPT Press.

Augustine, Daniela C. 2019. *The Spirit and the Common Good: Shared Flourishing in the Image of God*. Grand Rapids: Eerdmans.

Austin, Denise A. 2017. "The 'Third Spreading': Origins and Development of Protestant Evangelical Christianity in Contemporary Mongolia." *Inner Asia* 19 (1): 64–90.

Austin, Denise A. and Lim Yeu Chuen. 2019. "Critical Reflections on the Growth of Pentecostalism in Malaysia." In *Asia Pacific Pentecostalism*, edited by Denise A. Austin, Jacqueline Grey, and Paul W. Lewis, 195–216. Leiden: Brill.

Austin, Denise A., and Shane Clifton. 2019. "Australian Pentecostalism: From Marginalised to Megachurches." In *Asia Pacific Pentecostalism*, edited by Denise A. Austin,

Jacqueline Grey and Paul W. Lewis, 372–399. Leiden: Brill.

Austin, Denise, Jacqueline Grey, and Paul W. Lewis, eds. 2019. *Asia Pacific Pentecostalism*. Leiden: Brill.

Austin-Broos, Diane. 1992. "Redefining the Moral Order: Interpretations of Christianity in Post-emancipation of Jamaica." In *The Meaning of Freedom*, edited by F. McGlynn and S. Drescher, 221–245. Pittsburgh: University of Pittsburgh Press.

Austin-Broos, Diane. 1997. *Jamaica Genesis: Religion and the Politics of Moral Order*. Chicago: University of Chicago Press.

Austin-Broos, Diane. 2001. Churches and State: Aspects of Religious Ideology in Colonial and Post-colonial Jamaica. *Caribbean Quarterly* 47 (4): 1–32.

Austin-Broos, Diane. 2020. "Jamaican Pentecostalism: Its Growth and Significance." *Journal of Commonwealth and Comparative Politics* 58 (3): 285–300.

Australian Evangel, 1930–1970, 1987.

Autero, Esa J. 2016. *Reading the Bible Across Contexts: Luke's Gospel, Socio-Economic Marginality, and Latin American Biblical Hermeneutics*. Leiden: Brill Academic.

Bagnall, Diana. 2004. "Jesus Christ's Superstar." *Bulletin with Newsweek* 122 (6441): 30–34.

Bahu, Helder Pedro Alicerces. 2017. "A Aldeia de oração do Lubango." In *Paisagens e Memórias Religiosas em Angola. Um Itinerário*. Vol. 1, *Currents of Faith, Places of History*, edited by Ramon Sarró and Ruy Llera Blanes, 33–37.

Baker-Johnson, Sharon. 2012. "The Life and Influence of Jessie Penn Lewis." *Priscilla Papers: The Academic Journal of CBE International*, April 30.

Bălăban, Ciprian. 2016. *Istoria Bisericii Penticostale din România (1922–1989): Institutie și Harisme*. Oradea: Scriptum.

Balcombe, Dennis. 2011. *One Journey, One Nation: Autobiography of Dennis Balcombe, Missionary to China*. Chambersburg: eGenCo. LLC.

Balcombe, Dennis. 2014. *China's Opening Door: Incredible Stories of the Holy Spirit at Work in One of the Greatest Revivals in Christianity*. Lake Mary, FL: Charisma House.

Bangura, Joseph Bosco. 2013. *The Charismatic Movement in Sierra Leone (1980–2010): A Missio-Historical Analysis in View of African Culture, Prosperity Gospel and Power Theology*. Amsterdam: VU University Amsterdam.

Bangura, Joseph Bosco. 2016. "Hope in the Midst of Death: Charismatic Spirituality, Healing Evangelists and the Ebola Crisis in Sierra Leone." *Mission Missionalia* 44 (1): 2–18.

Bangura, Joseph Bosco. 2016. "The Gospel in Context: Hiebert's Critical Contextualisation and Charismatic Movements in Sierra Leone: Original Research." *In Die Skriflig* 50 (1): 1–7.

Bangura, Joseph Bosco. 2017. "Charismatic Movements, State Relations and Public Governance in Sierra Leone." *Studies in World Christianity* 23 (3): 237–256.

Bangura, Bosco. 2018. "Holding My Anchor in Turbulent Waters: God, Pentecostalism and the African Diaspora in Belgium." *Pneuma: The Journal of the Society for Pentecostal Studies* 40 (4): 498–516.

Bankov, Stefan. 2001. *Dossier: On Both Sides of the Iron Curtain*. Bourgas: self-published.

Barber, Karin. 2007. *The Anthropology of Texts, Persons, and Publics*. Cambridge: Cambridge University Press.

Barfoot, Charles H., and Gerald T. Sheppard. 1980. "Prophetic vs. Priestly Religion: The Changing Role of Women Clergy in Classical Pentecostal Churches." *Review of Religious Research* 22 (1): 2–17.

Barnes III, Roscoe. 2009. *F.F. Bosworth: The Man Behind 'Christ the Healer.'* Newcastle upon Tyne: Cambridge Scholars Publishing.

Barratt, Thomas Ball. 1927. *When the Fire Fell, and an Outline of My Life*. Oslo: Alfons Hansen & Sønner.

Barrett, David B. 1968. *Schism and Renewal in Africa: An Analysis of Six Thousand Contemporary Religious Movements*. Oxford: Oxford University Press.

Barrett, David B. 1970. "AD 2000: 350 million Christians in Africa." *International Review of Mission* LIX:233 (January): 39–54.

Barrett, David B. 1982. *World Christian Encyclopedia*. Nairobi: Oxford University Press.

Barrett, David B. 1988. "Global Statistics." In *Dictionary of Pentecostal and Charismatic Movements*, edited by Stan Burgess and Gary McGee, 810-830. Grand Rapids, MI: Zondervan.

Barrett, David B. 1988. "The 20th Century Pentecostal/Charismatic Renewal of the Holy Spirit, with its Goal of World Evangelization." *International Bulletin of Missionary Research* 12 (3): 119–29.

Barrett, David B., and Todd M. Johnson, eds. 2001. *World Christian Trends*. Pasadena, CA: William Carey Library.

Barrett, David B., George T. Kurian, and Todd Johnson. 2001. *World Christian Encyclopedia. A Comparative Survey of Churches and Religions in the Modern World*. Second Edition. Oxford: Oxford University Press.

Barrett, David B., Todd M. Johnson, and Peter F. Crossing. 2009. "Christian World Communions: Five Overviews of Global Christianity, AD 1800–2025." *International Bulletin of Missionary Research* 33 (1): 25–32.

Bartleman, Frank. *c.*1925. *How Pentecost Came to Los Angeles: As It Was in the Beginning*. Los Angeles, CA: F. Bartleman.

Bartleman, Frank. 1970. *Another Wave Rolls In! What Really Happened at Azusa Street*, Revised Edition. Monroeville: Whitaker House.

Barton, Bernadette. 2012. *Pray the Gay Away: The Extraordinary Life of Bible Belt Gays*. New York: New York University Press.

Batista, Israel. 1997. "Del carismatismo revolucionario al carismatismo pentecostal." In *Carismatismo en Cuba*, edited by Reinerio Arce Valentín, and Manuel Quintero, compiled by Elizabeth Carrillo, 135–151. La Habana: Ediciones CLAI.

Bauckham, Richard. 2005. "Ecology." In *Encyclopedia of Christian Theology*, edited by J. Lacoste 1 (A–F), 469–471. London: Routledge.

Bays, Daniel H. 1988. "Christianity in China, A Case Study of Indigenous Christianity: The Jesus Family, 1927–1952." *Religion: Journal of the Kansas School of Religion* 26 (1): 1–3.

Bays, H. Daniel. 1993. "Christian Revival in China, 1900–1937." In *Modern Christian Revivals*, edited by Edith Waldvogel Blumhofer and Randall Herbert Balmer, 161–179. Urbana: University of Illinois Press.

Bays, Daniel. 1995. "Indigenous Protestant Churches in China, 1900–1937: A Pentecostal Case Study." In *Indigenous Responses to Western Christianity*, edited by Steven Kaplan, 124–143. New York: New York University Press.

Bays, Daniel H. 2012. *A New History of Christianity in China*. Chichester: Wiley-Blackwell.

Beatty, Don. "ARM – The Early Years." *Anglicans for Renewal Canada*. Issues: Oct 2002, Feb 2003, Sept 2003, Feb 2004, Aug 2004, May 2005.

Bebbington, David. 1989. *Evangelicalism in Modern Britain: A History from the 1730s to the 1980s*. London: Unwin Hyman.

Begbie, Jeremy. 2000. *Voicing Creations Praise: Towards a Theology of the Arts*. London: T&T Clark.

Bennett, Dennis. 1970. *Nine O'clock in the Morning*. Alachua, FL: Bridge-Logos.

Berger, Peter L. 1963. *Invitation to Sociology: A Humanistic Perspective*. New York: Doubleday.

Berger, Peter. 1969. *The Social Reality of Religion*. London: Faber and Faber.

Berger, Peter L., ed. 1999. *The Desecularization of the World: The Resurgence of*

Religion in World Politics. Grand Rapids, MI: Eerdmans.

Berges Curbelo, Juana. 2008. *Pentecostalismo en Cuba: ¿Alienación o compromiso social?* Mexico DF: Publicaciones para el Estudio Científico de las Religiones.

Bergunder, Michael 2008. *The South Indian Pentecostal Movement in the Twentieth Century.* Grand Rapids, MI: Eerdmans.

Bergunder, Michael. 2014. "What is Religion? The Unexplained Subject Matter of Religious Studies." *Method and Theory in the Study of Religion* 26 (3): 246–286.

Bergunder, Michael. 2016. "Comparison in the Maelstrom of Historicity: A Postcolonial Perspective on Comparative Religion." In *Interreligious Comparisons in Religious Studies and Theology,* edited by Perry Schmidt-Leukel and Andreas Nehring, 34–52. London: Bloomsbury.

Bethel Church. 2020. "You are Made for Revival." Accessed April 10, 2020. http://bssm.net/school/introduction/.

Beverley, James A. 1995. *Holy Laughter and The Toronto Blessing: An Investigative Report.* Grand Rapids, MI: Zondervan.

Beyer, Peter. 2006. *Religions in Global Society.* New York: Routledge.

Bialecki, Jon. 2015. "The Third Wave and the Third World: C. Peter Wagner, John Wimber, and the Pedagogy of Global Renewal in the Late Twentieth Century." *Pneuma* 37 (1): 177–200.

Bialecki, Jon. 2017. *A Diagram for Fire Miracles and Variation in an American Charismatic Movement.* Berkeley, CA: University of California Press.

Bickle, Mike. 1994. "Filling Our Hearts With Holy Passion." *Charisma* (March): 31–34.

Bickle, Mike. 2006. *Encountering Jesus: Visitations, Revelations, and Angelic Activity; A Prophetic History and Perspective About the End-Times.* 12 CD Audio Album. Kansas City: Friends of the Bridegroom.

Bird, Warren. 2019. "World's Largest Megachurches," Leadership Network. https://leadnet.org/world/

Birman, Patricia, and David Lehmann. 1999. "Religion and the Media in a Battle for Ideological Hegemony: The Universal Church of the Kingdom of God and TV Globo in Brazil." *Journal of Latin American Studies* 18 (2): 145–164.

"Biserica 'Elim' de-a lungul timpului." 2010. Accessed on November, 15 2019. http://www.elim.ro/despre-biserica-penticostala-elim-timisoara/biserica-elim-de-a-lungul-timpului/.

Bishau, D. 2013. "The Prosperity Gospel: An Investigation into Its Pros and Cons with Examples Drawn from Zimbabwe." *International Open & Distance Learning Journal* 1 (1): 1–11.

"Bishop William J. Seymour," 312 Azusa Street, accessed January 17, 2017. http://www.azusastreet.org/WilliamJSeymour.htm.

Bjørner, Anna Larssen. 1954. *Hørt, tænkt og talt.* Copenhagen: Facula.

Blair, William N., and Bruce Hunt. 1977. *The Korean Pentecost and the Suffering Which Followed.* Edinburgh: Banner of Truth

Blanes, Ruy Llera. 2008. *Os Alleluias: Ciganos Evangélicos e Música.* Lisboa: Imprensa de Ciências Sociais.

Blanes, Ruy Llera. 2015. "Politics of Sovereignty: Evangelical and Pentecostal Christianity and Politics in Angola." In *The Anthropology of Global Pentecostalism and Evangelicalism,* edited by Simon Coleman and Rosalind I.J. Hackett, 197–213. New York: New York University Press.

Blanton, Anderson. 2015. *Hittin' the Prayer Bones: Materiality of Spirit in the Pentecostal South.* Chapel Hill: The University of North Carolina Press.

Blazquez, Ricardo. 1988. Las Comunidades Neocatecumenales. Discernimiento Teologico. Bilbao: Desclée de Bower. https://pt.scribd

.com/document/345067812/BLAZQUEZ-R-Las-Comunidades-Neocatecumenales-Discernimiento-Teologico-DDB-3-Ed-1988.

Bloch-Hoell, Nils. 1956. *Pinsebevegelsen: en undersøkelse av pinsebevegelsens tilblivelse, utvikling og særpreg med særlig henblikk på bevegelsens utforming i Norge*. Oslo: Universitetsforlaget.

Bloch-Hoell, Nils. 1964. *The Pentecostal Movement: Its Origin, Development and Distinctive Character*. Oslo/London: Universitetsforlaget/Allen & Unwin.

Blumhofer, Edith L. 1989. *The Assemblies of God: A Chapter in the Story of American Pentecostalism*. Vols. 1–2. Springfield, MO: Gospel Publishing House.

Blumhofer, Edith L. 1993. *Aimee Semple McPherson and the Making of Modern Pentecostalism, 1890–1926*. London: Equinox.

Blumhofer, Edith L. 1993. *Restoring the Faith: The Assemblies of God, Pentecostalism, and American Culture*. Urbana and Chicago: University of Chicago Press.

Blumhofer, Edith. 2002. "Pentecostal Fellowship of North America (PFNA)." In *The New International Dictionary of Pentecostal and Charismatic Movements*, edited by Stanley M. Burgess and Eduard M. van der Maas, 968–969. Grand Rapids, MI: Zondervan.

Blumhofer, Edith L. 2008. "Consuming Fire: Pandita Ramabai and the Global Pentecostal Impulse." In *Interpreting Contemporary Christianity: Global Processes and Local Identities*, edited by Ogbu U. Kalu and Alaine Low, 207–237. Grand Rapids: Eerdmans.

Blumhofer, Edith, Russell P. Spittler, and Grant A. Wacker, eds. 1999. *Pentecostal Currents in American Protestantism*. Urbana, IL: University of Illinois Press.

Blunt, Liz. 2003. "Pope presses EU on Constitution." *BBC News*. Last modified June 29, 2003. http://news.bbc.co.uk/2/hi/europe/3029456.stm.

Bochian, Pavel. 1979. "Calitatea de cetățean al patriei." *Cuvântul Adevărului* 27 (2): 9–12.

Bochian, Pavel. 1997. *The Life of a Romanian Pastor*. București: Editura Privilegiu.

Boddy, Alexander. 1914. "Pastor King." *Confidence* 7, no. 9 (September): 173.

Bonnke, Reinhard. 1994. *Evangelism by Fire*. Eastbourne, UK: Kingsway.

Bonnke, Reinhard. 2009. *Living a Life of Fire: An Autobiography*. Orlando, FL: E-R Productions.

Borlase, Craig. 2006. *William Seymour: A Biography*. Lake Mary, FL: Creation House.

Bosworth, F.F. 2008. *Christ the Healer*. Grand Rapids, MI: Revell.

Bouillon, David. 2011. "Espérer d'Israël! Louis Dallière, un Pasteur face à la question juive." In *Le Scandale d'Israël*, edited by André Chouraqui. N.p.: Echoes d'Orient. 7–26.

Bouillon, David. 2017. "Église – Baptême – Esprit-Saint: la théologie de Louis Dallière." PhD diss., Université de Strasbourg.

Boulton, E.C.W. 1928 (1999). *George Jeffreys: A Ministry of the Miraculous*. London: Elim Publishing Office.

Bowler, Kate. 2013. *Blessed: A History of the American Prosperity Gospel*. New York: Oxford University Press.

Boyd, Gregory A. 1992. *Oneness Pentecostalism and the Trinity*. Grand Rapids, MI: Baker Book House.

Bradin, Gheorghe. 2010. "Autobiografie" (excerpt). *Cuvantul Adevarului*. 21 (1): 17–18.

Brahinsky, Josh. 2012. "Pentecostal Body Logics: Cultivating a Modern Sensorium." *Cultural Anthropology* 27 (2): 215–238.

Brand, Chad, ed. *Perspectives on Spirit Baptism*. Nashville: B&H Publishing Group.

Brandt Bessire, Daniel. 1987. "Considérations historiques, théologiques et bibliographiques concernant directement ou indirectement le mouvement de Pentecôte Francophone Belge (1928–1982)." Master's thesis, Brussels: Faculté Universitaire de Theologie Protestante de Bruxclles.

Brawner, Mina Ross. 1975. *Woman in the Word*. Dallas TX: Christ for the Nations.

Breed, Sarah. 2014. "Mercy in Calcutta." *Charisma* (April): 20–25.

Brenkus, Josef. 2000. "A Historical and Theological Analysis of the Pentecostal Church in the Czech and Slovak Republics." *Journal of the European Pentecostal Theological Association* 20 (1): 49–65.

Brenkus, Jozef. 2011. "Pentecostal Movement in the Czech Republic and Slovakia." In *European Pentecostalism*, edited by Anne E. Dyer and William K. Kay, 248–259. Leiden: Brill.

Bridges, Lynn. 2006. *The American Religious Experience: A Concise History*. New York: Rowman and Littlefield.

Brierley, Peter, ed. 2017. *UK Church Statistics no 3: 2018 edition*. Tonbridge: ADBC.

Brookes, A. ed. 2007. *The Alpha Phenomenon*. N.p.: Churches Together in Britain and Ireland.

Brouwer, Steve, Paul Gifford, and Susan D. Rose. 1996. *Exporting the American Gospel: Global Christian Fundamentalism*. New York: Routledge.

Brown, Candy Gunther, ed. 2011. *Global Pentecostal and Charismatic Healing*. New York: Oxford University Press.

Brown, Candy Gunther. 2012. *Testing Prayer*. Cambridge: Harvard University Press.

Brown, Elijah M. 2008. "The Road to Peace: The Role of the Southern Sudanese Church in Communal Stabilisation and National Resolution." PhD thesis, The University of Edinburgh.

Brown, Timothy 2011. "Building Social Capital in South Sudan: How Local Churches Worked to Unite a Nation in the Lead up to the 2005 Comprehensive Peace Agreement." Master's thesis, University of Ottawa.

Bruce, Steve. 2011. *Secularization: In Defence of an Unfashionable Theory*. Oxford: Oxford University Press.

Brusco, Elizabeth. 1995. *The Reformation of Machismo: Evangelical Conversion and Gender in Colombia*. Austin: University of Texas Press.

Brusco, Elizabeth. 2010. "Gender and Power." In *Studying Global Pentecostalism: Theories and Methods*, edited by Allan Anderson, Michael Bergunder, Andre F. Droogers, and Cornelis van der Laan, 74–92. Berkeley: University of California Press.

Bülhmann, Walbert. 1976. *The Coming of the Third Church*. Maryknoll, NY: Orbis Books.

Bundy, David. 1988. "L'émergence d'un théologien pentecôtisant: Les écrits de Louis Dallière de 1922 à 1932." *Hokma* 38: 23–51.

Bundy, David. 1988. "Louis Dallière: Apologist for Pentecostalism in France and Belgium, 1932–1939." *Pneuma* 10 (1): 85–115.

Bundy, David. 2009. "Visions of Apostolic Mission: Scandinavian Pentecostal Mission to 1935." PhD diss., University of Uppsala.

Bundy, David. 2009. *Visions of Apostolic Mission: Scandinavian Pentecostal Mission to 1935*. Uppsala: Uppsala Universitet.

Burdick, John. 1998. *Blessed Anastacia: Women, Race, and Popular Christianity in Brazil*. New York: Routledge.

Burger, Isak, and Marius Nel. 2008. *The Fire Falls in Africa: A History of the Apostolic Faith Mission of South Africa*. Vereeniging: Christian Art.

Burgess, Richard. 2012. "African Pentecostal Growth: the Redeemed Christian Church of God in Britain." In *Church Growth in Britain: 1980 to the present*, edited by D. Goodhew, 129. Aldershot: Ashgate.

Burgess, Richard. 2012. "Pentecostals and Political Culture in Sub-Saharan Africa: Nigeria, Zambia, and Kenya as Case Studies." In *Global Pentecostal Movements: Migration, Mission, and Public Religion*, edited by Michael Wilkinson, 17–42. Leiden: Brill.

Burgess, Richard, Kim Knibbe, and Anna Quaas. 2010. "Nigerian-Initiated Pentecostal Churches as a Social Force in Europe: The Case of The Redeemed Christian Church of God." *PentecoStudies* 9 (1): 97–121.

Burgess, Stanley, ed. 2002. *The New International Dictionary of Pentecostal and Charismatic Movements*. Grand Rapids, MI: Zondervan.

Burgess, Stanley. 2006. "Pandita Ramabai: A Woman for all Seasons." *Asian Journal of Pentecostal Studes* 9 (2): 183–198.

Burpeau, Kemp Pendleton. 2004. *God's Showman: A Historical Study of John G. Lake and South African/American Pentecostalism.* Oslo: Refleks Publishing.

Burton, Jeremy, and Carissa Bratschun. 2015. "Muslim Dominated Country Can't Stop the Holy Spirit." *Charisma News.* May 19, 2015. Accessed Oct. 3, 2019. https://www.charismanews.com/world/49701-muslim-dominated-country-can-t-stop-the-holy-spirit.

Burton, W.F.P. 1933. *God Working with Them: Being Eighteen Years of Congo Evangelistic Mission History.* London: Victory Press.

Bustraan, Richard A. 2014. *The Jesus People Movement: A Story of Spiritual Revolution Among the Hippies.* Eugene, OR: Pickwick.

Butler, Anthea D. 2007. *Women in the Church of God in Christ: Making a Sanctified World.* Chapel Hill: The University of North Carolina Press.

Butler, Eva S. 2002. *In the Shadow of the Kilimanjaro: Pioneering the Pentecostal Testimony among the Maasai People.* Salisbury Center, NY: Pinecrest Publications.

Butticci, Annalisa. 2013. "Le chiese neopentecostali e carismatiche africane." In *Le religioni nell'Italia che cambia: Mappe e bussole,* edited by Enzo Pace, 85–96. Rome: Carocci.

Butticci, Annalisa. 2016. *African Pentecostals in Catholic Europe: The Politics of Presence in the Twenty-First Century.* Cambridge, MA: Harvard University Press.

Byambajav, Dalaibuyan. March 2–3, 2013. "Christian in Mongolia after Socialism." The First SEFM International Workshop on Social Change and Religious Transformation in East Asia (Hokkaido University). Accessed September 4, 2018. http://www.slideshare.net/ByambajavDalaibuyan/christianity-in-mongolia.

Byun, Jong-ho, ed. 1993. *Biography of Yong-do Lee* [in Korean]. Seoul: Jang Ahn.

California Census, 1920, 1936, 1940. https://californiacensus.org/.

Campos, Bernardo. 2017. *¿Apóstoles Hoy? Historia y Teología del Movimiento Apostólico-Profetico.* Salem, Oregon: Publicaciones Kerigma.

Campos, Leonildo Silveira. 1999. *Teatro, Templo e Mercado: Organização e Marketing de um Empreendimento Neopentecostal.* Petrópolis: Vozes.

Campos, Leonildo Silveira. 2016. "Traditional Pentecostalism." In *Handbook of Contemporary Religions in Brazil,* edited by Bettina Schmidt and Steven Engler, 95–116. Leiden: Brill.

Cannell, Fenella, ed. 2006. *The Anthropology of Christianity.* Durham, NC: Duke University Press.

Cantalamessa, Raniero. 2008. *Come, Creator Spirit: Meditations on the Veni Creator.* Translated by Dennis and Marlene Barrett. Collegeville: Liturgical Press.

Cantalamessa, Raniero. 2012. *Sober Intoxication of the Spirit: Born Again of Water and the Spirit.* Part Two. Translated by Marsha Daigle-Williamson. Cincinnati: Servant.

Cantalamessa, Raniero. 2018. *Jesus Christ: The Holy One of God.* Translated by Alan Neame. Eugene: Wipf & Stock.

Cantalamessa, Raniero and Aldo Maria Valli. 2015. *Serving the Word: My Life.* Translated by Marsha Daigle-Williamson. Cincinnati: Servant.

Cantón, Manuela. 2001. "Gitanos Protestantes. El Movimiento Religioso de Las Iglesias 'Filadelfia' En Andalucía, España." *Julio–Diciembre* 11 (22): 69–74.

Cao, Nanlai. 2010. *Constructing China's Jerusalem: Christians, Power, and Place in Contemporary Wenzhou.* Redwood City, CA: Stanford University Press.

Carlsson, Carl-Gustav. 1990. *Människan, samhället och Gud: Grunddrag i Lewi Pethrus kristendomsuppfattning.* Lund: Lunds Universitet.

Carnduff, David. 2003. *Ireland's Lost Heritage.* Ireland: IPBC.

Carp, Sandra Ann. 2015. "A Pentecostal 'Legend': A Reinterptetation of the Life and Legacy of Smith Wigglesworth." Master's diss., University of Birmingham, UK.

Carrillo García, Elizabeth. 1997. "Renovación carismática en las iglesias protestantes históricas en Cuba." In *Carismatismo en Cuba*, edited by Reinerio Arce Valentín, and Manuele Quintero, compiled by Elizabeth Carrillo, 47–86. La Habana: Ediciones CLAI.

Carter, John. 1975. *Donald Gee: Pentecostal Statesman*. Nottingham: Assemblies of God Publishing House.

Cartledge, D. 2000. *The Apostolic Revolution, The Restoration of Apostles and Prophets in the Assemblies of God in Australia*. Chester Hill, Sydney: Paraclete Institute.

Cartledge, Mark J. 1999. "The Socialization of Glossolalia." In *Sociology, Theology and the Curriculum*, edited by Leslie J. Francis, 125–134. London: Cassell.

Cartledge, Mark J. 2002. *Charismatic Glossolalia: An Empirical-Theological Study*. Aldershot: Ashgate.

Cartledge, Mark J. 2014. "'Catch the Fire': Revivalist Spirituality from Toronto to Beyond." *PentecoStudies* 13 (2): 217–238.

Cartledge, Mark J. 2015. *The Mediation of the Spirit: Interventions in Practical Theology*. Grand Rapids, MI: Eerdmans.

Cartledge, Mark J. 2017. *Narratives and Numbers: Empirical Studies of Pentecostal and Charismatic Christianity*. Leiden: Brill.

Cartledge, Mark, ed. 2006. *Speaking in Tongues: Multi-Disciplinary Perspectives*. Milton Keynes, UK: Paternoster.

Cartwright, Desmond. 1986. *The Great Evangelists: The Remarkable Lives of George and Stephen Jeffreys*. Basingstoke: Marshall Morgan and Scott.

Cartwright, Desmond. 2000. *The Real Wigglesworth*. Tonbridge, Kent: Sovereign World.

Casselberry, Judith. 2017. *The Labor of Faith: Gender and Power in Black Apostolic Pentecostalism*. Durham: Duke University Press.

Castells, Manuel. 2000. *The Rise of the Network Society: The Information Age: Economy Society and Culture*. Second Edition. West Sussex, UK: Wiley.

Castelo, Daniel. 2012. *Revisioning Pentecostal Ethics: The Epicletic Community*. Cleveland: CPT Press.

Castelo, Daniel. 2015. *Pneumatology: a Guide for the Perplexed*. London: Bloomsbury T&T Clark.

Castelo, Daniel. 2017. *Pentecostalism as a Christian Mystical Tradition*. Grand Rapids: Eerdmans.

Castelo, Daniel. 2017. *Pentecostalism as a Christian Mystical Tradition*. Grand Rapids: Eerdmans.

Castelo, Daniel. 2020. "Pentecostal Theology as Spirituality: Explorations in Theological Method." In *The Routledge Handbook of Pentecostal Theology*, edited by Wolfgang Vondey, 29–39. New York: Routledge.

Castles, Stephen, Hein de Haas and Mark J. Miller. 2014. *The Age of Migration: International Population Movements in the Modern World*. Fifth Edition. New York and London: Palgrave Macmillan.

Castro, C.M., and A. Dawson. 2017. *Religion, Migration, and Mobility*. New York: Routledge.

Cathcart, W., and Marian S. Cathcart. 1976. *The Faith Life-Story of a Pioneer Servant of God: from Gloom to Glory*. Dallas, TX: Christian Communications Trust.

Central Intelligence Agency (CIA). 2019. *The World Factbook: Paraguay*. Accessed June 19, 2019. https://www.cia.gov/library/publications/the-world-factbook/geos/pa.html.

Central Statistics Office. 2016. Accessed May 5, 2018. http://www.cso.ie/en/media/csoie/newsevents/documents/census2016summaryresultspart1/Census2016SummaryPart1.pdf.

Cepeda Clemente, Rafael, Elizabeth Carrillo García, Rhode González Zorrilla, and Carlos Ham Stanard. 1995. "Causas y desafíos de las iglesias protestantes en Cuba: La influencia del movimiento pentecostal." In *En la fuerza del Espíritu: Los Pentecostales en América Latina: Un desafío a las iglesias históricas*, edited by Benjamín F. Gutiérrez, 141–74. Guatemala: Centro Evangélico Latinoamericano de Estudios Pastorales; Asociación de Iglesias Presbiterianas y Reformadas en América Latina.

Chambe, Juan J. 2011. *Teologia pentecostal Popular. La fe en comunidades periurbanas y andinas*. Colección Teología y Filosofía Andinas, no. 6. La Paz, Bolivia: ISEAT.

Chan, Simon K.H. 2010. "Jesus as Spirit-Baptizer: Its Significance for Pentecostal Ecclesiology." In *Toward a Pentecostal Ecclesiology: the Church and the Fivefold Gospel*, edited by John Christopher Thomas, 139–156. Cleveland, TN: CPT Press.

Chan, Simon. 2000. *Pentecostal Theology and the Christian Spiritual Tradition*. Sheffield: Sheffield Academic Press.

Chan, Simon. 2006. *Liturgical Theology: The Church As Worshipping Community*. Downers Grove: InterVarsity.

Chan, Simon. 2011. *Pentecostal Ecclesiology: An Essay on the Development of Doctrine*. Blandford Forum, UK: Deo Publishing.

Chang, Paul H.B. 2016. "The Multiple Invisibilities of Witness Lee." *Journal of Asian/North American Theological Educators* 2 (1): 91–98.

Chant, Barry. 1997. *Heart of Fire*. Unley Park, SA: Tabor.

Chant, Barry. 1999. "The Spirit of Pentecost: Origins and Development of the Pentecostal Movement in Australia 1870–1939." PhD diss., Macquarie University.

Chant, Barry. 2011. *The spirit of Pentecost: the origins and development of the Pentecostal Movement in Australia, 1870–1939*. Lexington, KY: Emeth Press.

Chant, Barry. 2015. *This Is Revival*. Miranda, NSW: Tabor.

Chappell, Paul G. 1989. "Kenneth Hagin, Sr." In *Twentieth-Century Shapers of American Popular Religion*, edited by Charles H. Lippy, 186–193. New York: Greenwood Press.

Chatzieleftheriou, Ilias. 2010. *The Development of Pentecostal Churches in Greece*. Master's diss., Mattersey Hall in association with Bangor University.

Cheong, Weng Kit, and Joy K.C. Tong. 2015. "The Localization of Charismatic Christianity among the Chinese in Malaysia: A study of Full Gospel Tabernacle." In *Global Chinese Pentecostal and Charismatic Christianity*, edited by Fenggang Yang, Joy K.C. Tong, and Allan H. Anderson, 309–328. Leiden: Brill.

Chesnut, R. Andrew. 1997. *Born Again in Brazil: The Pentecostal Boom and the Pathogens of Poverty*. New Brunswick, N.J.: Rutgers University Press.

Chesnut, R. Andrew. 2003. *Competitive Spirits: Latin America's New Religious Economy*. Oxford: Oxford University Press.

Chevreau, Guy. 1994. *Catch the Fire: The Toronto Blessing, An Experience of Renewal and Revival*. Toronto: HarperCollins Publishers.

Chewachong, Amos Bongadu. 2017. "Intra-African Pentecostalism and the Dynamics of Power: the Living Faith Church worldwide (Winners' Chapel) in Cameroon, 1996–2016." PhD thesis, University of Edinburgh.

Cheyeka, Austin. 2008. *Church, State and Political Ethics in a Post-Colonial State: The Case of Zambia*. Zomba: Kachere.

Chikane, F. 1977. "Christianity and Black Consciousness." Unpublished.

Chikane, F. 1985. "Contextualisation and Indigenisation." Grahamstown: Unpublished.

Chikane, F. 1988. *No Life of My Own*. Maryknoll, NY: Orbis Books.

Chikane, F. 2012. *Eight Days in September: The Removal of Thabo Mbeki*. Johannesburg: Picador.

Chiquete, Daniel. 2019. *Pentecostalismo, espacialidad y representaciones. Ensayos sobre algunas concepciones arquitectónicas, urbanas e iconoclásticas pentecostales*. Madrid: Editorial Académica Española.

Chit, Myo. 1980. "Even the Buddhist Monks Are Listening." *Pentecostal Evangel* (10 February): 18.

Chit, Myo. 1981. "The Youth Camp That Became a Bible School." *The Pentecostal Evangel* (29 November): 20–21.

Chitando, E. 2007. "A New Man for a New Era? Zimbabwean Pentecostalism, Masculinities, and the HIV Epidemic." *Missionalia:*

Southern African Journal of Mission Studies 35 (3): 112–127.

Chitando, E. 2013. "Prophets, Profits and Protests Prosperity Theology and Zimbabwean Gospel Music." In *Prophets, Profits and the Bible in Zimbabwe*, edited by E. Chitando, R.M. Gunda, and J. Kugler, 95–112. Bamberg: University of Bamberg Press.

Chitando, Ezra. 2000. "'Stop Suffering': An Examination of the Concepts of Knowledge and Power with Special Reference to Sacred Practitioners in Harare." *Religion & Theology* 7 (1): 56–68.

Cho, David Yonggi. 1979. *The Fourth Dimension*. Seoul: Seoul Logos Co.

Cho, David Yonggi. 1987. *Salvation, Health and Prosperity: Our Threefold Blessings in Christ*. Altamonte Springs, Fl: Creating House.

Cho, Kyu-Hyung. 2009. "The Move to Independence from Anglican Leadership: An Examination of the Relationship between Alexander Alfred Boddy and the Early Leaders of the British Pentecostal Denominations (1907–1930)." PhD thesis, University of Birmingham, UK.

Cho, SungGeun Cho. 2005. "The Impact of Carmel Fasting Prayer Mountain Revival upon Believers." DMin thesis, Oral Robert University.

Cho, Yonggi. 1983. *The Fourth Dimension*, Second Edition. Plainfield, NJ: Bridge Publishing Inc.

Cho, Yonggi. 1984. *Prayer: Key to Revival*. Dallas: Word.

Cho, Yonggi. 2015. *Fivefold Gospel and Threefold Blessing*. Seoul: Seoul Logos.

Choi, Jashil. 1978. *Nanun Halleluya Ajummayutta* [I Was Mrs. Hallelujah]. Seoul: Seoul Books.

Choi, Jashil. 2009. *Hallelujah Lady*. Seoul: KIATS Press.

Choi, Jay Woong. 2017. "The Origins And Development Of Korean Classical Pentecostalism (1930–1962)." PhD diss., Fuller Theological Seminary.

Chong, Terence, and Goh, Daniel P.S. 2014. "Asian Pentecostalism: Renewals, Megachurches, and Social Engagement." In *Handbook of Religions in Asia*, edited by Bryan Turner and Oscar Salemink, 402–417. London: Routledge.

Chong, Terence, ed. 2018. *Pentecostal Megachurches in Southeast Asia: Negotiating Class, Consumption and the Nation*. Singapore: ISEAS Publishing.

Chow, Alexander. 2013. *Theosis, Sino-Christian Theology and the Second Chinese Enlightenment: Heaven and Humanity in Unity*. New York: Palgrave Macmillan.

Christensen, Nikolaj. 2017. "Flickering Flames: The Early Pentecostal Movement in Denmark, 1907–1924." PhD thesis, University of Birmingham, UK.

Christensen, Nikolaj. Forthcoming. *Unorganized Religion: Pentecostalism and Secularization in Denmark, 1907–1924*. Leiden: Brill.

Christerson, Brad, and Richard Flory. 2017. *The Rise of Network Christianity: How Independent Leaders Are Changing the Religious Landscape*. New York: Oxford University Press.

Chung, Meehyun. 2015. "Korean Pentecostalism and the Preaching of Prosperity." *Zeitschrift für Missionswissenschaft und Religionswissenschaft* 99 (3/4): 276–296.

Chung, Meehyun. 2018. "Inquiry of Pentecostalism Regarding Pneumatology: A Theological Suggestion of a Feminist Perspective." *International Review of Mission* 107 (1): 49–63.

Church of God World Mission. 2016. "Dedication of Niko Njotorahardjo Chair at Pentecostal Theological Seminary." *COG World Missions*. May 2, 2016. https://cogwm.org/uncategorized/dedication-of-niko-njotorahardjo-chair-at-pentecostal-theological-seminary/.

Church of God. 2018. "Church of God Council of Eighteen/ International Executive Council." Accessed July 15, 2019. http://www.churchofgod.org/leadership/international-executive-council.

Claffey, Patrick. 2007. *Christian Churches in Dahomey-Benin. A Study of their Socio-Political Role.* Leiden: Brill.

Clapham, Christopher. 1976. *Liberia and Sierra Leone: An Essay in Comparative Politics.* Cambridge: Cambridge University Press.

Clark, Ian G. 2007. *Pentecost At the Ends of the Earth: the History of the Assemblies of God in New Zealand (1927–2003).* Blenheim: Christian Road Ministries.

Clarke, Clifton R. 2014. *Pentecostal Theology in Africa.* Eugene, OR: Pickwick.

Clayton, Allen L. 1979. "The Significance of William H. Durham for Pentecostal Historiography." *Pneuma* 1 (2): 27–42.

Cleary, Edward L. 1992. "Evangelicals and Competition in Guatemala." In *Conflict and Competition: The Latin American Church in a Changing Environment*, edited by Edward L. Cleary and Hannah Stewart-Gambino, Chapter 9. Boulder, CO: Lynne Rienner Publishers.

Cleary, Edward L. 2011. *The Rise of Charismatic Catholicism in Latin America.* Gainesville, FL: University Press of Florida.

Clemmons, Ithiel. 1996. *Bishop C.H. Mason and the Roots of the Church of God in Christ.* Bakersfield, CA.

Clifton, Shane. 2007. "The Spirit and Doctrinal Development: A Functional Analysis of the Traditional Pentecostal Doctrine of the Baptism in the Holy Spirit." *Pneuma: The Journal of the Society for Pentecostal Studies* 29 (1): 5–23.

Clifton, Shane. 2009. "Preaching the 'Full Gospel' in the Context of Global Environmental Crisis." In *The Spirit Renews the Face of the Earth: Pentecostal Forays in Science and Theology of Creation*, edited by Amos Yong, 117–134. Eugene, OR: Wipf and Stock.

Clifton, Shane. 2009. *Pentecostal Churches in Transition: Analysing the Developing Ecclesiology of the Assemblies of God in Australia.* Leiden: Brill.

Clifton, Shane. 2009. *Pentecostal Churches in Transition: Analysing the Developing Ecclesiology of the Assemblies of God in Australia.* Leiden: Brill.

Cocker, J., and J. Malton Murray, eds. 1930. *Temperance and Prohibition in New Zealand.* London: Epworth Press.

Coggins, James R., and Paul G. Hiebert, eds. 1989. *Wonders and the Word: An Examination of Issues Raised by John Wimber and the Vineyard Movement.* Winnipeg, Canada: Kindred Press.

Coleman, Simon. 2000. *The Globalisation of Charismatic Christianity: Spreading the Gospel of Prosperity.* Cambridge: Cambridge University Press.

Coleman, Simon. 2011. "Prosperity Unbound? Debating the 'Sacrificial Economy.'" In *Economics of Religion: Anthropological Approaches*, edited by Lionel Obadia and Donald C. Wood, 23–45. Bingley: Emerald.

Coleman, Simon and Rosalind I.J. Hackett, eds. 2015. *The Anthropology of Global Pentecostalism and Evangelicalism.* New York: New York University Press.

Colletti, Joseph. 1990. "Ethnic Pentecostalism in Chicago: 1890–1950." PhD thesis, University of Birmingham, UK.

Collins, James M. 2009. *Exorcism and Deliverance Ministry in the Twentieth Century: An Analysis of the Practice and Theology of Exorcism in Modern Western Christianity.* Milton Keynes: Paternoster.

Collins, John. 2012. "Contemporary Ghanaian Popular Music since the 1980s." In *Hip Hop Africa: New African Music in a Globalizing World*, edited by Eric Charry, 211–233. Bloomington, IN: Indiana University Press.

Confidence, https://revival-books.com/products/confidence-magazine.

Congar, Yves. 2012. *My Journal of the Council.* Translated by Mary John Ronayne & Mary Cecily Boulding. English Translation edited by Denis Minns. Collegeville: The Liturgical Press.

CONICET. 2019. *Segunda encuesta nacional sobre creencias y actitudes religiosas en Argentina.* Buenos Aires: CONICET.

Conn, Charles W. 1959. *Where the Saints Have Trod.* Cleveland TN: Pathway Press.

Conn, Charles W. 1977. *Where the Saints Have Trod: A History of the Church of God.* Cleveland, TN: Pathway, 1977.

Conn, Charles W. 2008. *Like A Mighty Army: A History of the Church of God, 1886–1996, Tribute Edition.* Cleveland, TN: Pathway Press.

Conrad, B. 2005. "From Revolution to Religion: The Politics of Religion in the Eritrean Diaspora in Germany." In *Religion in the Context of African Migration Studies*, edited by Afe Adogame and Cordula Weissköppel, Bayreuth African Studies Series, 217–241. Bayreuth: Eckhard Breitinger.

Constitutions and By-Laws of the General Council of the Assemblies of God. 1931. (September 16–22, 1927; September 20–26, 1929; September 8–13).

Contreras-Flores, Jenniffer. 2015. "The Social Impact of the 1916 Pentecostal Revival in Puerto Rico." In *Pentecostals and Charismatics in Latin America and Latino Communities*, edited by Néstor Medina and Sammy Alfaro, 157–165. New York, NY: Palgrave Macmillan.

Conway, Brian. 2013. "Column: Is Ireland a Nation of á La Carte Catholics?" *TheJournal.ie.* April 26, 2013. http://www.thejournal.ie/readme/column-is-ireland-a-nation-of-a-la-carte-catholics-861758-Apr2013/.

Cook, Robert F. 1938. *A Quarter Century of Divine Leading in India.* Chengannur, India: Church of God in India.

Cook, Robert F. 1955. *Half a Century of Divine Leading and 37 Years of Apostolic Achievements in South India.* Cleveland: Church of God Foreign Mission Department.

Cooper, Dudley. 1995. *Flames of Revival.* Endeavour Hills, Vic: CRC.

Cooper, Travis. 2017. "Worship Rituals, Discipline, and Pentecostal-Charismatic "Techniques du Corps" in the American Midwest." In *Pentecostals and the Body*, edited by Michael Wilkinson and Peter Althouse, 77–101. Lieden: Brill.

Coote, Leonard W. 1991. *Impossibilities Become Challenges*, Fifth Edition. San Antonio, TX: Church Alive! Press.

Copeland, M. Shawn. 2004. "Race." In *The Blackwell Companion to Modern Theology*, edited by Gareth Jones, 499–511. Oxford: Blackwell.

Cornelio, Jayeel S. 2018. "Jesus Is Lord: The Indigenization of Megachurch Christianity in the Philippines." In *Pentecostal Megachurches in Southeast Asia: Negotiating Class, Consumption and the Nation*, edited by Terence Chong, 127–155. Singapore: ISEAS.

Cornelio, Jayeel S., and Ia Marañon. 2019. "A 'Righteous Intervention': Megachurch Christianity and Duterte's War on Drugs in the Philippines." *International Journal of Asian Christianity* 2 (2): 211–230.

Corpeño, Gerardo. 2011. "Neopentecostalismo emergente: Pistas para el future de iglesias neopentecostales jóvenes." *Kairós* 48: 55–78.

Corten, Andre, and Ruth Marshall-Fratani, eds. 2001. *Between Babel and Pentecost: Transnational Pentecostalism in Africa and Latin America.* Bloomington IN: Indiana University Press.

Corum, Fred T. 1981. *Like As of Fire: A Reprint of the Old Azusa Street Papers.* Wilmington, MA: Fred T. Corum.

Costantini, O. 2016. "«ByesusSh'm»". Breaking with the National Past in Eritrean and Ethiopian Pentecostal Churches in Rome." In *Witchcraft, Religion, Medicine: Power and belief in the human destiny*, edited by M. Pavanello, post faction by Birgit Meyer, 165–184. London: Routledge.

Costantini O. 2019. *La nostra identità è Gesù Cristo: Pentecostalismo e nazionalismo tra gli eritrei e gli etiopici a Roma.* Milano: Franco Angeli.

Costanza, Daniel. 2016. *From Rome to Zagreb: 50 Years of Fraternal Cooperation for the Sake of Europe: A Brief History of the Pentecostal European Fellowship (PEF).* Published privately by PEF.

Coulter, Dale M. 2020. "Sanctificaiton: Becoming an Icon of the Spirit through Holy Love."

In *Routledge Handbook on Pentecostal Theology*, edited by Wolfgang Vondey, 237–246. New York: Routledge.

Courtney, Caleb Howard. 2017. "Barbara Johnston of Sarnia, Ontario: The First Canadian Pentecostal Missionary to India." *Canadian Journal of Pentecostal-Charismatic Christianity* 8 (1): 1–18. https://journal.twu.ca/index.php/CJPC/article/view/189.

Cox, Harvey. 1995. *Fire From Heaven: The Rise of Pentecostal Spirituality and the Reshaping of Religion in the Twenty-first Century*. Reading, MA: Addison-Wesley.

Craig, James. 1995. "'Out and Out for the Lord': James Eustace Purdie, an Early Anglican Pentecostal." Master's thesis, Wycliffe College.

Crawford, K. Mary. 1933. *The Shantung Revival*. Shanghai: China Baptist Publication Society.

Creemers, Jelle. 2009. "Time Will Teach Us ... Reflections on Thirty-five Years of Pentecostal-Roman Catholic Dialogue." *Ecclesiology* 5 (3): 322–344.

Creemers, Jelle. 2017. "All Together in One Synod? The Genesis of the Federal Synod of Protestant and Evangelical Churches in Belgium (1985–1998)." *Trajecta. Religie, cultuur en samenleving in de Nederlanden* 26: 275–302.

Crimi, Ciro P. 2016. *Historia de Asamblea Cristiana de Villa Devoto*. Buenos Aires: Asamblea Cristiana Evangélica.

Cristofori, S. 2013. "Note sul movimento pentecostale in Africa." *Cristianesimo nella storia* 34(3): 823–878.

Croitor, Vasilică. 2010. *Răscumpărarea Memoriei*. Medgidia: Succeed Publishing.

Cross, Terry. 2000. "The Rich Feast of Theology: Can Pentecostals Bring the Main Course or Only the Relish?" *Journal of Pentecostal Theology* 8 (16): 27–47.

Csordas, Thomas J. 1997. *The Sacred Self: A Cultural Phenomenology of Charismatic Healing*. Berkeley: University of California Press.

Cumbo, Enrico C. 2000. "Your Old Men Will Dream Dreams: The Italian Pentecostal Experience in Canada, 1912–1945." *Journal of American Ethnic History* 19: 35–81.

Cunha, Cristina Vidal. 2018. "Pentecostal Cultures in Urban Peripheries: A Socio-anthropological Analysis of Pentecostalism in Arts, Grammars, Crime, and Morality." *Vibrant: Virtual Brazilian Anthropology* 15 (1): e151401. Epub October 22.

Czajko, Edward. 2012. "Zielonoświątkowcy w Nowogródzkiem w latach 1919–1945." *Rocznik Teologiczny* 54 (1–2).

Dabney, D. Lyle. 2001. "Saul's Armor: The Problem and Promise of Pentecostal Theology Today." *Pneuma* 23 (1): 115–146.

Dahler Kowalski, Rosemarie. 2014. "What Made Them Think They Could? Assemblies of God Female Missionaries." *Assemblies of God Heritage* 34: 70–71.

Dahles, Heidi. 2007. "In Pursuit of Capital: The Charismatic Turn among the Chinese Managerial and Professional Class in Malaysia." *Asian Ethnicity* 8 (2): 89–109.

Dalton, Anne Marie, and Henry C. Simmons. 2010. *Ecotheology and the Practice of Hope*. Albany, NY: State University of New York Press.

Daneel, M.L. 1991. "Towards a Sacramental Theology of the Environment in African Independent Churches." *Theologia Evangelica* 24 (1): 2–26.

Daniels, David. 2002. "Charles Harrison Mason: The Interracial Impulse of Early Pentecostalism." In *Portraits of a Generation: Early Pentecostal Leaders*, edited by James Goff and Grant Wacker, 255–270. Fayetteville, NC: University of Arkansas Press.

Daniels, David D. III. 2011. "Navigating the Territory: Early Afro-Pentecostalism as a Movement within Black Civil Society. In *Afro-Pentecostalism: Black Pentecostal and Charismatic Christianity in History and Culture*, edited by Amos Yong and Estrelda Y. Alexander, 43–62. New York: NYU Press.

Daniels III, David D. 2014. "North American Pentecostalism." In *The Cambridge Companion to Pentecostalism*, edited by Cecil M.

Robeck, Jr. and Amos Yong, 73–92. New York: Cambridge University Press.

Danzinger, Kurt. 1971. *Socialization*. Harmondsworth: Penguin.

Darrand, Tom Craig and Anson Shupe. 1983. *Metaphors of Social Control in a Pentecostal Sect*. Lewiston, ME: Edwin Mellen Press.

Davidsson, Tommy. 2015. *Lewi Pethrus' Ecclesiological Thought 1911–1974: A Transdenominational Pentecostal Ecclesiology*. Leiden: Brill.

Davies, Norman. 1997. *Europe: A History*. London: Pimlico.

Dayton, Donald W. 1987. *Theological Roots of Pentecostalism*. Peabody: Hendrickson.

Dayton, Donald. 1987. *Theological Roots of Pentecostalism*. Metuchen, NJ: Scarecrow Press.

De Alminana, Margaret and Lois E. Olena, eds. 2016. *Women in Pentecostal and Charismatic Ministry: Informing a Dialogue on Gender, Church, and Ministry*. Leiden: Brill.

de la Torre, Renée. 1995. *Los hijos de la luz: Discurso, identidad, y poder en La Luz del Mundo*. Universidad de Guadalajara, Departamento de Estudios en Comunicación Social.

de Surgy, Albert. 2001. *Le Phénomène Pentecôtiste en Afrique Noire. Le Cas Béninois*. Paris: L'Harmattan.

de Walker, Luisa Jeter. 1990. *Siembra y Cosecha: Reseña histórica de Las Asambleas de Dios de México y Centroamérica*. Deerfield, FL: Editorial Vida.

De Witte, Marleen. 2005. "Afrikania's Dilemma: Reframing African Authenticity in a Christian Public Sphere." *Etnofoor* 17 (1/2): 133–155.

De Witte, Marlene. 2018. "'Buy the Future': Charismatic Pentecostalism and African Liberation in a Neoliberal World." In *Pentecostalism and Politics in Africa*, edited by Adeshina Afolayan, Olajumoke Yacob-Haliso, and Toyin Falola, 65–85. London: Palgrave Macmillan.

DeArteaga, William L. 2015. *Agnes Sanford and Her Companions: The Assault on Cessationism and the Coming of the Charismatic Renewal*. Eugene, OR: Wipf & Stock.

DeCaro, Louis. 1977. *Our Heritage: The Christian Church of North America*. Sharon, PA: Christian Church of North America.

dela Cruz, Roli G. 2007. "A Historical-Doctrinal Perspective of Filipino Pentecostal Preaching." *Asian Journal of Pentecostal Studies* 10 (2): 192–217.

Demaerel, Ignace. 1990. "Tachtig jaar pinksterbeweging in Vlaanderen (1909–1989): een historisch onderzoek met korte theologische en sociologische analyse." Master's thesis, Brussels: Universitaire Faculteit voor Protestantse Godgeleerdheid te Brussel.

Dempster, M.A., B.D. Klaus, and D. Petersen, eds. 1991. *Called and Empowered: Global Mission in Pentecostal Perspective*. Peabody: Hendrickson.

Dempster, Murray W. 1987. "Pentecostal Social Concern and the Biblical Mandate of Social Justice." *Pneuma*: 9 (2): 129–153.

Dempster, Murray W., Byrdon D. Klaus, and Douglas Petersen, eds. 1999. *The Globalization of Pentecostalism: A Religion made to Travel*. Oxford: Regnum Books.

Denis, Philippe. 2015. "Bulletin d'Histoire du Christianisme en Afrique." *Revue d'Histoire Ecclésiastique* 110 (1/2): 288–301.

Dhinakaran, D.G.S. 1978. *Love So Amazing*. Madras: Christian Literature Society

Di Giacomo, Michael. 2009. "Pentecostal and Charismatic Christianity in Canada: Its Origins, Development, and Distinct Culture." In *Canadian Pentecostalism: Transition and Transformation*, edited by Michael Wilkinson, 15–38. Montreal and Kingston: McGill-Queen's University Press.

Di Giacomo, Michael. 2011. "Identity and Change: The Story of the Italian-Canadian Pentecostal Community." *Canadian Journal of Pentecostal-Charismatic Christianity* 2: 83–130.

Díaz, Samuel. 1995. *La Nave Pentecostal: Crónica desde el inicio de las Asambleas de Dios y su Travesía por el noreste hispano de los Estados Unidos*. Grand Rapids, MI: Vida.

Dignard, Martin L. 2014. "God's Faithful Freedom: Healing as an Outflow of God's Presence." *Journal of Pentecostal Theology* 23 (1): 68–84.

Dignard, Martin L. 2018. *Revealed Orders: Agnes Sanford's Theological Journey*. Emeth: Lexington.

Dijk, Rijk van, et al., eds. 2014. *Religion and AIDS Treatment in Africa: Saving Souls, Prolonging Lives*. London: Routledge.

Diulgerov, D.V. 1932. "Pentecostals (Part 1)." In *Annual Publication of the Theological Faculty at Sofia University*. Vol. 9, *1931–1932*. Sofia: Gutenberg Press.

Donaldson, Hal, and Kenneth M. Dobson. 2012. *Huldah Buntain: Woman of Courage*. Calcutta, India: Devtech Publishers and Printers Pvt. Ltd.

Donev, Dony. 2011. *The Life and Ministry of Rev. Ivan Voronaev*. Sofia: Spasen Publishers.

Donkor, Lord Elorm, and Clifton Clarke. 2018. *African Pentecostal Missions maturing: Essays in Honor of Apostle Opoku Onyinah*. Eugene, OR: Wipf and Stock.

Donnelly, Doris. ed. 1999. *Retrieving Charisms for the Twenty-First Century*. Collegeville: The Liturgical Press.

Dowie, J. 1904. "Satan the Defiler." *Leaves of Healing* (14 May): 99.

Dozon, Jean-Pierre. 1995. *La Cause des Prophètes: Politique et Religion en Afrique Contemporaine*. Paris: Editions du Seuil.

"Dr. Vinson Synan Elected Secretary of Society for Pentecostal Studies." *Pentecostal Holiness Advocate* 54 (January 2, 1971): 15.

Drápal, D. 2008. *Jak to všechno začalo, historie Křesťanského společenství Praha I*. Praha: Křesťanská společenství.

Drápal, D. 2009. *Léta růstu, historie Křesťanského společenství Praha II*. Praha: Křesťanská společenství.

Drápal, D. 2011. *Zlom, historie Křesťanského společenství Praha III*. Praha: Křesťanská společenství.

Drønen, Tomas. 2013. *Pentecostalism, Globalisation, and Islam in Northern Cameroon. Megachurches in the Making?* Leiden: Brill.

Dry Land...Living Water. 1975. Pittsburgh, PA: Kathryn Kuhlman Foundation. Videocassette (VHS), 85 min.

Dryanov, Yoncho. 1977. *History of the Evangelical Pentecostal Churches in Bulgaria (1920–1976)*. Unpublished manuscript, Varna.

Dryanov, Yoncho. 2015. *History of the Evangelical Pentecostal Churches in Bulgaria (1920–1976)*. Sofia: Bulgarian Evangelical Theological Institute.

du Plessis, David J. 1970. *The Spirit Bade Me Go*. Plainfield, NJ: Logos International.

du Plessis, David J. 1986. *Simple and Profound*. Orleans, MA: Paraclete Press.

du Plessis, David J., and Bob Slosser. 1977. *A Man Called Mr. Pentecost*. Plainfield, NJ: Logos International.

Duarte P., Rogelio. 1994. *El desafío protestante en el Paraguay*. Asunción: Centro Cristiano de Comunicación Creativa.

DuBois, W.E.B. 1903. *The Souls of Black Folk: Essays and Sketches*. Chicago: A.C. McClurg & Co.

Dueck, Lorna. 2014. "The Enduring Revival" *Christianity Today* (March 7), accessed on February 17, 2017. http://www.christianitytoday.com/ct/2014/march-web-only/enduring-revival.html

Duffield, Guy P., and N.M. Van Cleave. 1983. *Foundations of Pentecostal Theology*. Los Angeles, CA: LIFE. Bible College.

Dugmore, W.F. 1915. "South Africa in Unity." *Word and Witness* (August): 6.

Dumper, Michael. 1999. "Faith and Statecraft: Church-State Relations in Jerusalem after 1948." In *Palestinian Christians: Religion, Politics and Society in the Holy Land*, edited by Anthony O'Mahony, 56–81. London: Mclisende.

Duncan, Phillip, *Pentecost in Australia*, nd. np.

Dunlop, Robert. ed. 2004. *Evangelicals in Ireland: An Introduction*. Dublin: The Columba Press.

Dunn, Emily. 2015. *Lightning from the East: Heterodoxy and Christianity in Contemporary China*. Leiden: Brill.

Durkheim, Émile. [1897] 2006. *On Suicide*. Translated by Robin Buss. London: Penguin.

Dusing, Michael. 1994. "The New Testament Church." In *Systematic Theology: A Pentecostal Perspective*, edited by Stanley M. Horton, 525–566. Springfield, MO: Gospel Publishing House.

Dyer, Helen S. 1900. *Pandita Ramabai: The Story of Her Life*. New York: Fleming H Revell.

Dyer, Helen S. 1907. *Revival in India*. New York: Gospel Publishing House.

Dzao, Timothy. 1945. *A Memoir of Twenty Years*. Shanghai: Shanghai Ling Liang Publishing. 趙世光。《二十年回憶》。上海：上海靈糧刊社。

Dzao, Timothy. 1969. *A Missionary Pilgrimage*. Hong Kong: Ling Liang Publishing. 趙世光。《宣教歷程》。香港：靈糧出版社。

Eby, J.P. 1976. "The Battle of Armageddon, Part IV." *Kingdom Bible Studies* (September): 10.

Edgell, Penny. 2012. "A Cultural Sociology of Religion: New Directions." *Annual Review of Sociology* 38 (1): 247–265.

Eido Research. 2020. "The Story of Bethel School of Ministry Alumni." Accessed April 10, 2020. https://www.eidoresearch.com/report-bethel-school-of-supernatural-ministry-alumni/.

Eim, Yeol Soo. 2003. "South Korea." In *International Dictionary of Pentecostal Charismatic Movement*, edited by Stanly M. Burgess, 239–246. Grand Rapids, MI: Zondervan.

Eisenlöffel, Ludwig David. 2006. *Freikirchliche Pfingstbewegung in Deutschland. Innenansichten 1945–1985*. Göttingen: V & R unipress.

Ελευθέρα Αποστολική Εκκλησία Πεντηκοστής. 2006. *Ελεύθερη Αποστολική Εκκλησία Πεντηκοστής: Η ιστορία της. Τί πιστεύει. Πως πολιτεύεται*. Αθήνα: Όρος.

Ellingson, Stephen. 2010. "New Research on Megachurches: Non-denominationalism and Sectarianism." In *The New Blackwell Companion to the Sociology of Religion*, edited by Bryan S. Turner, 245–266. Oxford: Wiley-Blackwell.

Elliott, Peter. 2018. "Four Decades of 'Discreet' Charismata: The Catholic Apostolic Church in Australia 1863–1900." *Journal of Religious History* 42 (1): 72–83.

Ellis, Stephen, and Gerrie ter Haar. 2004. *Worlds of Power: Religious Thought and Political Practice in Africa*. London: Hurst and Company.

Ellwood, Robert S. 1975. *One Way: The Jesus Movement and Its Meaning*. Englewood Cliffs, NJ: Prentice-Hall.

Elridge, Joseph. 1991. "Pentecostalism and Social Change in Central America: a Honduran Case Study." *Towson State Journal of International Affairs* 25 (2): 10–12.

Emmett, David. 2017. "W.F.P. Burton (1886–1971) and Congolese Agency: A Biographical Study of a Pentecostal Mission." PhD thesis., University of Birmingham, UK.

Engelke, Matthew. 2007. *A Problem of Presence: Beyond Scripture in an African Church*. Berkeley CA: University of California Press.

Engelsviken, Tormod. 2014. "Mission, Pentecostalism, and Ethiopian Identity: The Beginnings of the Mulu Wongel Believers' Church." *Norsk Tidskrift for Misjonsvitenskap* 3: 195–215.

Engle, Lou, Catherine Paine. 1998. *Digging the Wells of Revival: Reclaiming Your Historic Inheritance Through Prophetic Intercession*. Shippensburg, PA: Destiny Image Publishers.

Enloe, Tim. 2008. "Dr. Charles S. Price: His Life, Ministry and Influence." *Assemblies of God Heritage*: 4–13.

Enns, Arno W. 1971. *Man, Milieu, and Mission in Argentina: A Close Look at Church Growth*. Grand Rapids, MI: Eerdmans.

Enroth, Ronald M., Edward E. Ericson, and C. Breckinridge Peters. 1972. *The Jesus People: Old-Time Religion in the Age of Aquarius*. Grand Rapids: William B. Eerdmans.

Enyinnaya, John O. 2008. "Pentecostal Hermeneutics and Preaching: An Appraisal." *Ogbomoso Journal of Theology* 13 (1): 144–153.

EPTA. n.d. "European Pentecostal Theological Association." Accessed October 23, 2019. http://www.eptaonline.com/.

Eriksen, Annelis, Ruy Llera Blanes, and Michelle MacCarthy. 2019. *Going to Pentecost: An Experimental Approach to Studies in Pentecostalism*. New York and Oxford: Berghahn Books.

Ernst, Manfred. 1994. *Winds of Change: Rapidly Growing Religious Groups in the Pacific Islands*. Suva, Fiji: Pacific Conference of Churches.

Ernst, Manfred, ed. 2006. *Globalization and the Re-shaping of Christianity in the Pacific Islands*. Suva, Fiji: Pacific Theological College.

Eshete, Tibebe. 2009. *The Evangelical Movement in Ethiopia: Resistance and Resilience*. Waco: Baylor University Press.

Eskridge, Larry. 2013. *God's Forever Family: The Jesus People Movement in America*. New York: Oxford University Press.

Espinosa, Gastón. 1999. "El Azteca: Francisco Olazábal and Latino Pentecostal Charisma, Power, and Faith Healing in the Borderlands." *Journal of the American Academy of Religion* 67 (3): 597–616.

Espinosa, Gastón. 2014. *William J. Seymour and the Origins of Global Pentecostalism: A Biography and Documentary History*. Durham, NC: Duke University Press.

Espinosa, Gastón. 2016. *Latino Pentecostals in America: Faith and Politics in Action*. Cambridge, MA: Harvard University Press.

Esposito, Salvatore. 2013. *Un secolo di pentecostalismo Italiano*. Milan: The Writer Edizioni.

Estermann, Josef. 2006. *Filosofía Andina: Un Visión para un Mundo Nuevo*. La Paz: ISEAT.

Estrada Adorno, Wilfredo. 2016. *El Fuego Está Encendido: Infancia Del Pentecostalismo Puertorriqueño Y Su Impacto En La Sociedad*. Cleveland, TN: CEL Publicaciones.

Estrada-Carrasquillo, Wilmer. 2018. "Entre El Templo Y La Ciudad: Constructing a Pentecostal Lived Ecclesiology." PhD diss., Asbury Theological Seminary.

Eu Choong, Chong. 2018. "Pentecostalism in Klang Valley, Malaysia." In *Pentecostal Megachurches in Southeast Asia*, edited by Terence Chong. Singapore: ISEAS.

Evans, Eifion. 2000. *The Welsh Revival of 1904*. Bridgend: Bryntirion Press.

Evans, Mark. 2006. *Open Up the Doors: Music in the Modern Church*. London: Equinox Publishing.

Evans, Mark. 2017. "Creating the Hillsong Sound: How One Church Changed Australian Christian Music." In *The Hillsong Movement Examined: You Call Me Out Upon the Waters*, edited by Tanya Riches and Tom Wagner, 63–84. Cham, Switzerland: Palgrave Macmillan.

Evans, Russell. 2004. *Profile of a Planetshaker*, edited by Dave Reardon. Adelaide, Australia: Planetshakers.

Evans, Russell. 2014. *The Honor Key: Unlock a Limitless Life*. Springfield, Missouri: My Healthy Church.

Evans, Russell. 2019. The Planetshakers Story. Discussion with author, November 11.

Fantini, E. 2015. "Go Pente! The Charismatic Renewal of the Evangelical Movement in Ethiopia." In *Understanding Contemporary Ethiopia*, edited by E. Fiquet, and G. Prunier, 123–146. London: Hurst.

FAOGKL (First Assembly of God Kuala Lumpur). 2009. *First Assembly of God Kuala Lumpur – 75th Anniversary Magazine*.

Farrant, Edgar D. 1949. *The Taieri Plain: tales of the years that are gone*. Christchurch, N.Z.: Whitcombe & Tombs.

Faupel, D. William. 1989. "The Everlasting Gospel: The Significance of Eschatology in the Development of Pentecostal Thought." PhD diss., University of Birmingham, UK.

Faupel, D. William. 1996. *The Everlasting Gospel: The Significance of Eschatology in the*

Development of Pentecostal Thought. Sheffield: Sheffield Academic Press.

Faupel, D. William. 2010. "The New Order of the Latter Rain: Restoration or Renewal?" In *Winds from the North: Canadian Contributions to the Pentecostal Movement*, edited by Michael Wilkinson and Peter Althouse, 239–263. Leiden: Brill.

Faupel, William, and Kane McGinn, eds. 2010. "Commemorating Thirty Years of Annual Meetings." *Society for Pentecostal Studies*. Accessed December 7, 2019. http://storage.cloversites.com/societyforpentecostalstudies/documents/sps_30_anniversary_monograph.pdf.

Fediakova, Evguenia. 2016. "To serve or to Save: The Social Commitment of Chilean Evangelicals (1990–2014)." In *New Ways of Being Pentecostal in Latin America*, edited by Martin Lindhardt, 151–164. Lanham: Lexington Books.

Fee, Gordon. 1980. "Tongues-Least of the Gifts: Some Exegetical Observations on 1 Corinthians 12–14." *Pneuma* 2 (2): 2–14.

Fee, Gordon D. 1984. "The 'Gospel' of Prosperity – an Alien Gospel." *Reformation Today*, 39–43.

Fee, Gordon D. 1985. "Baptism in the Holy Spirit: The Issue of Separability and Subsequence." *Pneuma: The Journal of the Society for Pentecostal Studies* 7 (2): 87–99.

Fee, Gordon, and Douglas Stuart. 2003. *How to Read the Bible for All It's Worth*. Third Edition. Grand Rapids, MI: Zondervan.

Félix-Jäger, Steven. 2015. *Pentecostal Aesthetics: Theological Reflections in a Pentecostal Philosophy of Art and Aesthetics*. Leiden: Brill.

Fer, Yannic. 2015. "Charismatic Globalization, Morality and Culture in Polynesian Protestantism." In *The Anthropology of Global Pentecostalism and Evangelicalism*, edited by Simon Coleman, Rosalind I.J. Hackett and Joel Robbins, 228–242. New York: New York University Press.

Fer, Yannick, and Gwendoline Malogne-Fer, eds. 2017. *Le Protestantisme à Paris: Diversité et recompositions contemporaines*. Genève: Labor et Fides.

Ferguson, Neil. 2011. "Separating Speaking in Tongues from Glossolalia using a Sacramental View," *Colloquium* 43 (1): 39–58.

Fernandez, Charles, and Stuart Michael. 2009. "Crisis Rocks Calvary Church." *The Star* (November 18). Accessed November 21, 2019. https://www.thestar.com.my/news/community/2009/11/18/crisis-rocks-calvary-church/.

"Findings released into Australian Christian Churches and affiliated Pentecostal churches." Royal Commission into Institutional Responses to Child Sexual Abuse. Accessed March 16, 2017. http://www.childabuseroyalcommission.gov.au/media-centre/media-releases/2015-11/findings-released-into-australian-christian-church.

Finke, Roger, and Rodney Stark. 1992. *The Churching of America: Winners and Losers in our Religious Economy*. New Brunswick, NJ: Rutgers University Press.

Finto, D. 2001. *Your People Will be My People*. Minneapolis: Chosen.

Fiorentino, Joseph R. 2015. "Luigi Francescon 1866–1964." Unpublished paper. Lakeland, FL: Southeastern University.

Fischer, M. 2011. "'The Spirit Helps Us in Our Weakness': Charismatization of Worldwide Christianity and the Quest for an Appropriate Pneumatology with Focus on the Evangelical Lutheran Church in Tanzania." *Journal of Pentecostal Theology* 20 (1): 95–121.

Fischer, Moritz. 2020. "In and Uut of Africa: The Transnational Pentecostal Church Nzambe-Malamu, Its Migratory Entanglements and Its Missionary Strategy." *Missio Africanus: Journal of African Missiology* 5 (1).

Flegg, Columba Graham. 1992. *"Gathered Under Apostles": A Study of the Catholic Apostolic Church*. Oxford, UK: Clarendon Press.

Flegg, Graham. 1992. *'Gathered Under Apostles': A Study of the Catholic Apostolic Church*. Oxford, UK: Clarendon Press / New York: Oxford University Press.

Flynn, Thomas. 1974. *The Charismatic Renewal and the Irish Experience.* London: Hodder and Stoughton.

Foerster, Norbert Hans Christoph. 2010. *A Congregação Cristã no Brasil numa área de alta vulnerabilidade social no ABC paulista: aspectos de sua tradição e transmissão religiosa – a instituição e os sujeitos.* Doctoral diss., Methodist University of São Paulo.

Forbes, George. 2006. *The C.L. Greenwood Story.* Chirnside Park VIC: Mission Mobilisers International.

Fortuny Loret de Mola, Patricia. 1995. "Origins, Development and Perspectives of La Luz del Mundo Church." *Religion* 25 (2): 147–162.

Fosztó, László. 2006. "Mono-Ethnic Churches, the 'Undertaker Parish', and Rural Civility in Postsocialist Romania." In *The Postsocialist Religious Question: Faith and Power in Central Asia and East-Central Europe*, edited by Chris Hann, 269–92. Münster: Lit Verlang.

Fosztó, László. 2009. *Ritual Revitalisation after Socialism: Community, Personhood, and Conversion among Roma in a Transylvanian Village.* Halle Studies in the Anthropology of Eurasia 21. Münster: Lit Verlang.

Fosztó, László, and Dénes Kiss. 2012. "Pentecostalism in Romania. The Impact of Pentecostal Communities on the Life-Style of the Members." *La Ricerca Folklorica* 65: 51–64.

Frahm-Arp, Maria 2018. "Pentecostalism, Politics, and Prosperity in South Africa." *Religions* 9 (10): 1–16.

Francescon, Louis. 1952. *Faithfull Testimony.* Chicago: The Author.

Frank Bartleman. 1925. *How Pentecost Came to Los Angeles As It Was in the Beginning.* Los Angeles: self published.

Franklin, Judy, and Ellyn Davis. 2012. *The Physics of Heaven: Exploring God's Mysteries of Sound, Light, Energy, Vibrations, and Quantum Physics.* Shippensburg, PA: Destiny Image Publishers.

French, Talmadge L. 1999. *Our God is One: The Story of the Oneness Pentecostals.* Indianapolis, IN: Voice & Vision Publications.

French, Talmadge L. 2014. *Early Interracial Oneness Pentecostalism: G.T. Haywood (1901–1931).* Eugene, OR: Pickwick Publications.

Frestadius, Simo. 2016. "The Elim Tradition: 'An Argument Extended through Time' (Alasdair MacIntyre)." *Journal of the European Pentecostal Theological Association* 36 (1): 57–68.

Frestadius, Simo. 2019. *Pentecostal Rationality: Epistemology and Theological Hermeneutics in the Foursquare Tradition.* London: Bloomsbury T&T Clark.

Freston Paul. 2010. "Reverse Mission: A Discourse in Search of Reality?" *PentecoStudies* 9 (2): 153–74.

Freston, Paul. 1995. "Pentecostalism in Brazil: A Brief History." *Religion* 25 (2): 119–133.

Freston, Paul. 2001. "The Transnationalisation of Brazilian Pentecostalism: The Universal Church of the Kingdom of God." In *Between Babel and Pentecost: Transnational Pentecostalism in Africa and Latin America*, edited by Andre Corten and Ruth Marshall-Fratani, 196–213. Bloomington: Indiana University Press.

Freston, Paul. 2001. *Evangelicals and Politics in Asia, Africa and Latin America.* Cambridge: Cambridge University Press.

Freston, Paul. 2005. "The Universal Church of the Kingdom of God: a Brazilian Church finds Success in Southern Africa." *Journal of Religion in Africa* 35 (1): 33–65.

Friesen, Aaron T. 2013. *Norming the Abnormal: The Development and Function of the Doctrine of Initial Evidence in Classical Pentecostalism.* Eugene: Pickwick.

Fritsch, Homer and Alice. eds. 1987. *Letters From Cora: Cora Fritsch, 1907–1912*: Self-published.

Frodsham, Stanley Howard. 1965. *Smith Wigglesworth: Apostle of Faith.* London: Assemblies of God Publishing House.

Frost, Michael J. 2018. *The Spirit, Indigenous Peoples and Social Change: Māori and a Pentecostal Theology of Social Engagement.* Leiden: Brill.

Frykenberg, Robert E. 2003. *Pandita Ramabai's America.* Grand Rapids, MI: Eerdmans Publishing.

Fudge, Thomas A. 2003. *Christianity without the Cross: A History of Salvation in Oneness Pentecostalism.* Parkland, FL: Universal Publishers.

Fulton, Brent. 2015. *China's Urban Christians: A Light That Cannot Be Hidden.* Eugene, OR: Pickwick Publications.

Furre, Berge. 2006. "Crossing Boundaries: the 'Universal Church' and the Spirit of Globalization." In *Spirits of Globalization: Growth of Pentecostalism and Experiential Spiritualities in a Global Age,* edited by Sturla Stålsett, 39–51. London: SCM Press.

Gabriel, Eduardo. 2009. "A expansão internacional do catolicismo carismático brasileiro." *Análise Social* 44 (1): 189–207.

Gaglardi, B. Maureen. 1965. *The Pastor's Pen, Early Revival Writings of Pastor Reg Layzell.* Vancouver, BC: New West Press.

Gaines, Margaret. 2000. *Of Like Passions: Missionary to the Arabs.* Cleveland, TN: Pathway.

Gaiya, Musa A.B. 2002. "The Pentecostal Revolution in Nigeria." Occasional Paper. Center of African Studies, University of Copenhagen.

Gaiya, Musa. 2015. "Charismatic and Pentecostal Social Orientations in Nigeria." *Nova Religio: The Journal of Alternative and Emergent Religions* 19 (3): 63–79.

Gajewski, Wojciech. 2014. "Instytut Biblijny w Gdańsku. Dzieje i charakter seminarium pentekostalnego w okresie międzywojennym." *Studia Theologica Pentecostalia* 2.

Galvano, Stephen, ed. 1977. *Fiftieth Anniversary: Christian Church of North America 1927–1977.* Sharon, PA: Christian Church of North America.

Ganiel, G. 2008. "Beyond Pietism and Prosperity: Religious Resources for Reconstruction and Reconciliation in Zimbabwe." Africa Peace and Conflict Network Occasional Paper 1.

Ganiel, G. 2009. "Spiritual Capital and Democratization in Zimbabwe: a Case Study of a Progressive Charismatic Congregation." *Democratization* 16 (6): 1172–1193.

Ganiel, G. 2010. "Pentecostal and Charismatic Christianity in South Africa and Zimbabwe: A Review." *Religion Compass* 4 (3): 130–143.

Ganiel, Gladys. 2016. *Transforming Post-Catholic Ireland: Religious Practice in Late Modernity.* Oxford: Oxford University Press.

Gao, Fude. 1934. *Shandong Fuxing* [The Shandong Revival]. Shanghai: China Baptist Publication Society.

García, Paola. 2010. "Integración y migración: las Iglesias pentecostales en España." *Amérique Latine Histoire et Mémoire. Les Cahiers ALHIM,* 20 (November). http://journals.openedition.org/alhim/3691.

Garrard, David. 1983. "History of the Congo Evangelistic Mission/ Communauté Pentecôtiste au Zaïre from 1915 to 1982." PhD diss., University of Aberdeen.

Garrard, D.J. 2002. "Tanzania." In *The New International Dictionary of Pentecostal and Charismatic Movements,* edited by Stanley M. Burgess, and Eduard M. van der Maas, 264–269. Grand Rapids, MI: Zondervan.

Garrard, David John. 2003. "Art. Congo, Democratic Republic of." In *The New International Dictionary of Pentecostal and Charismatic Movements (NIDPCM),* edited by Stanley M. Burgess and Eduard M. van der Maas, 67–74. Grand Rapids: Zondervan.

Garrard, David. 2015. "William F.P. Burton and the Birth of Congolese Pentecostalism." In *Pentecostalism in Africa: Presence and Impact of Pneumatic Christianity in Postcolonial Societies,* edited by Martin Lindhardt, 75–99. Leiden: Brill.

Garrard-Burnett, Virginia. 1998. *Living in the New Jerusalem: Protestantism in Guatemala.* Austin: University of Texas Press.

Garrard-Burnett, Virginia. 2011. *Terror in the Land of the Holy Spirit: Guatemala Under General Efrain Rios Montt 1982–1983.* New York, NY: Oxford University Press.

Garrard-Burnett, Virginia. 2013. "Neopentecostalism and Prosperity Theology in Latin America: A Religion for Late Capitalist Society." *Iberoamericana* 42 (1/2): 21–34.

Garrard-Burnett, Virginia. 2016. "Toward a Pentecostal Hermeneutics of Social Engagement in Central America? Bridging the Church and the World in El Salvador and Guatemala." In *New Ways of Being Pentecostal in Latin America*, edited by Martin Lindhardt, 187–208. Lanham: Lexington.

Garrett, John. 1997. *Where Nets were Cast: Christianity in Oceania since World War II*. Suva & Geneva: Institute of Pacific Studies, University of the South Pacific & World Council of Churches.

Garvey-Williams, Ruth. ed. 2017 "A New Name for a New Day." *Vox Magazine* 34 (April–June): 17. https://issuu.com/vox_ie/docs/vox_issue_34.

GBI Bogor. n.d. "GBI Jalan Gatot Subroto." Accessed July 9, 2019. https://dbr.gbi-bogor.org/wiki/GBI_Jalan_Gatot_Subroto.

Gee, Donald. 1967. *Wind and Flame*. Pentecostal Pioneers Series 41. Nottingham: Assemblies of God Publishing House.

Gee, Donald. 1980. *These Men I Knew*. Nottingham: Assemblies of God Publishing House.

Geivett, R. Douglas, and Holly Pivec. 2014. *God's Super-Apostles: Encountering the Worldwide Prophets and Apostles Movement*. Wooster, OH: Weaver Book Company.

George, Bill. 2010. *Until All Have Heard: The Centennial History of Church of God World Missions*. Cleveland TN: Pathway Press.

Gibbs, Stephen. 2004. "Hillsong Farewells a Lost Sheep Pioneer." *Sydney Morning Herald* (November 13).

Gifford, Paul. 1987. "'Africa Shall Be Saved': An Appraisal of Reinhard Bonnkes Pan-African Crusade." *Journal of Religion in Africa* 17 (1): 63–92.

Gifford, Paul. 1993. *Christianity and Politics in Doe's Liberia*. Cambridge: Cambridge University Press.

Gifford, Paul. 1998. *African Christianity: Its Public Role*. London: Hurst.

Gifford, Paul. 1998. *African Christianity: Its Public Role*. Bloomington and Indianapolis: Indiana University Press.

Gifford, Paul. 2004. *Ghana's New Christianity: Pentecostalism in a Globalizing African Economy*. Bloomington and Indianapolis: Indiana University Press.

Gifford, Paul. 2010. *Christianity, Politics and Public Life in Kenya*. Oxford: Oxford University Press.

Gifford, Paul. 2015. "The Prosperity Theology of David Oyedepo, Founder of Winners' Chapel." In *Pastures of Plenty: Tracing Religio-Scapes of Prosperity Gospel in Africa and Beyond*, edited by Andreas Heuser, 83–100. New York: Peter Lang.

Gifford, Paul. 2015. *Christianity, Development and Modernity in Africa*. London: Hurst & Co.

Gil, Jin-Kyung. 1980. *Yeongge Gil Seon-Ju*. Seoul: Jongro Books.

Gitau, Wanjiru M. 2018. *Megachurch Christianity Reconsidered: Millennials and Social Change in African Perspective*. Downers Grove: Intervarsity Academic.

Goff, James R. Jr. 1988. *Fields White unto Harvest: Charles F. Parham and the Missionary Origins of Pentecostalism*. Fayetteville: University of Arkansas Press.

Goh, Daniel P.S. 2010. "The State and Social Christianity in Postcolonial Singapore." *SOJOURN* 25 (1): 54–89.

Goh, Robbie B.H. 2018. *Protestant Christianity in the Indian Diaspora*. Albany, NY: State University of New York Press.

Golder, Morris E. 1973. *History of the Pentecostal Assemblies of the World*. Indianapolis, IN.N.p.

González, Justo L., and Ondina E. González. 2007. *Christianity in Latin America: A History*. New York, NY: Cambridge University Press.

Goodhew, David, ed. 2012. *Church Growth in Britain 1980 to the Present*. Farnham: Ashgate.

Gooren, Henri. 2003. "The Religious Market in Nicaragua: The Paradoxes of Catholicism and Protestantism." *Exchange* 32 (4): 340–360.

Gooren, Henri. 2010. "The Pentecostalization of Religion and Society." *Exchange* 39 (4): 355–376.

Gooren, Henri. 2012. "The Catholic Charismatic Renewal in Latin America." *Pneuma* 34 (2): 185–207.

Gooren, Henri. 2013. "The Growth and Development of Non-Catholic Churches in Paraguay." In *Spirit and Power: The Growth and Global Impact of Pentecostalism*, edited by Donald E. Miller, Kimon H. Sargeant, and Richard Flory, 83–98. New York: Oxford University Press.

Gooren, Henri. 2015. "The Growth and Development of Non-Catholic Churches in Chile." *Review of Relgious Research* 57 (2): 191–218.

Gooren, Henri. 2016. "Pentecostal Conversion Careers, Generational Effects, and Political Involvement in Latin America." In *New Ways of Being Pentecostal in Latin America*, edited by Martin Lindhardt, 165–186. Lanham: Lexington Books.

Gore, Kellesi. 2019. "The Pentecostal Movement in the South Pacific Islands." In *Asia Pacific Pentecostalism*, edited by Denise A., Austin, Jacqueline Grey and Paul W. Lewis, 297–324. Leiden: Brill.

Grätz, Tilo. 2014. "Radio Call-In Shows on Intimate Issues in Benin: "Crossroads of Sentiments." *African Studies Review* 57 (1): 25–48.

Green, Chris E.W. 2015. *Sanctifying Interpretation: Vocation, Holiness, and Scripture*. Cleveland: CPT Press.

Green, Chris E.W., ed. 2016. *Pentecostal Ecclesiology: A Reader*. Leiden: Brill.

Greenaway, Richtard L.N. 2002. *Waimari Cemetery transcriptions*. library.christchurch.org.nz/Heritage/Cemeteries/Waimairi/WaimairiCemeteryWalk.pdf.

Grey, Jacqueline. 2011. *Three's a Crowd: Pentecostalism, Hermeneutics, and the Old Testament*. Eugene: Pickwick Publications.

Griffen-Foley, Bridget. 2008. "Radio ministries: Religion on Australian Commercial Radio from the 1920s to the 1960s." *Journal of Religious History* 32 (1): 31–54.

Griffith, R. Marie. 1997. *God's Daughters: Evangelical Women and the Power of Submission*. Berkely, CA: University of California Press.

Griffith, R. Marie. 1999. "A Network of Praying Women: Women's Aglow Fellowship and Mainline American Protestantism." In *Pentecostal Currents in American Protestantism*, edited by Edith L. Blumhofer, Russell P. Spittler, and Grant A. Wacker, 131–151. Urbana: University of Illinois Press.

Grubb, Kenneth. 1968. *World Christian Handbook*. London: World Dominion Press.

Gruen, Ernest, et al. 2020. "Documentation of the Aberrant Practices and Teachings of Kansas City Fellowship (Grace Ministries)." Accessed April 10th, 2020. http://www.banner.org.uk.

Gudorf, Christine E., Zainal Abidin Bagir, and Marthen Tahun. 2014. *Aspirations for Modernity and Prosperity: Symbols and Sources Behind Pentecostal/Charismatic Growth in Indonesia*. Adelaide: ATF Press.

Guiblehon, Bony. 2011. *Le Pouvoir-Faire: Religion, Politique, Ethnicité et Guérison en Côte d'Ivoire*. Paris: L'Harmattan.

Guillén, Miguel. 1992. *La historia del Concilio Latino Americano de Iglesias Cristianas*. Latin American Council of Christian Churches.

Gustavson, Helen I. "A Letter, 2086 Marshall Ave, St. Paul, Minn 55104, Dec. 22, 1971."

Guth, James. 1996. "The Politics of the Christian Right." In *Religion and the Culture Wars: Dispatches From the Front*, edited by J. Green, J. Guth, C. Smith, and L. Kellstedt. New York: Rowman.

Guthrie, Steven. 2011. *Creator Spirit: The Holy Spirit and the Art of Becoming Human*. Grand Rapids, MI: Baker Academic.

Guy, Laurie. 2004. "One of a Kind? The Auckland Ministry of A.H. Dallimore." *Australasian Pentecostal Studies* 8: 125–45. Retrieved from https://aps-journal.com/index.php/APS/article/view/76.

Guy, Laurie. 2005. "Miracles, Messiahs and the Media: The Ministry of A.H. Dallimore in Auckland in the 1930s." In *Signs, Wonders, Miracles: Representations of Divine Power in the Life of the Church*, edited by Kate Cooper and Jeremy Gregory, 453–463. Woodbridge: Ecclesiastical History Society.

Ha, Yong-Jo. 2003. *Like Wind and Like Fire*. Seoul: Durano.

Ha, Yong-Jo. 2007. *Dreaming of the Church in Acts*. Seoul: Durano.

Ha, Yong-Jo. 2008. *I Put My Life for Mission*. Seoul: Durano.

Habermas, Jürgen. 1991. *The Structural Transformation of the Public Sphere: An Inquiry into a Category of Bourgeois Society*. Translated by Thomas Burger. Cambridge: MIT Press.

Hackett, Rosalind, and Benjamin Soares, eds. 2014. *New Media and Religious Transformations in Africa*. Bloomington: Indiana University Press.

Hacking, Keith. 2006. *Signs and Wonders: Then and Now*. Leicester: Intervarsity Press.

Hagin, Kenneth. 1983. *Understanding the Anointing*. Tulsa, OK: K. Hagin Ministries.

Halasová, Tereza. 2015. "Divergence české a slovenské konfesněprávní úpravy: Vývoj od roku 2007." [Divergence of religious law in the Czech Republic and Slovakia: Development from 2007]. Studie a texty Evangelické teologické fakulty, Teologická východiska evropské kulturní identity 26 (2): 133–151.

Halasová, Tereza. 2017. "Development of the Faith Movement in the Czech Republic." *Central European Journal of Contemporary Religion* 1: 3–16.

Hall, Geoffrey G. 2006. "Hanlon, Alfred Charles 1866–1944." *Dictionary of New Zealand Biography*. http://www.dnzb.govt.nz/.

Halldorf, Joel. 2010. "Lewi Pethrus and the Creation of a Christian Counterculture." *Pneuma* 32 (3): 354–368.

Halldorf, Joel. 2017. *Biskop Lewi Pethrus*. Skellefteå: Artos förlag.

Hammond, John W. 1982. *The Joyful Sound: A History of the Pentecostal Assemblies of Newfoundland and Labrador*. St. Stephen, NB: Print'N Press Ltd.

Hamon, Bill. 1997. *Apostles, Prophets, and the Coming Moves of God*. Santa Rosa Beach, FL: Christian International.

Hampel, Dieter, Richard Krüger, and Gerhard Oertel, eds. 2009. *Der Auftrag bleibt. Der Bund Freikirchlicher Pfingstgemeinden auf dem Weg ins dritte Jahrtausend. Innenansichten 1980–2000*. Erzhausen: Bund Freikirchlicher Pfingstgemeinden.

Hanciles, Jehu J. 2001. "Anatomy of an Experiment: The Sierra Leone Native Pastorate." *Missiology: An International Review* 29 (1): 63–82.

Hanciles, Jehu J. 2008. *Beyond Christendom: Globalization, African Migration, and the Transformation of the West*. Maryknoll: Orbis Books.

Handoyo, Djohan, and Himawan Leonardo. 2019. *Messenger of the 3rd Pentecost: Pdt. DR. Ir. Niko Njotorahardjo*. Jakarta: WFC Production.

Hanegraaff, Hank. 1993, 1997. *Christianity in Crisis*. Eugene, OR: Harvest House Publishers.

Harding, Susan F. 1991. "Representing Fundamentalism: The Problem of the Repugnant Other. *Social Research* 58 (2): 373–393.

Harding, Susan F. 2000. *The Book of Jerry Falwell: Fundamentalist Language and Politics*. Princeton NJ: Princeton University Press.

Harper, Jeanne. 2013. *Visited by God: The Story of Michael Harper's 48 Year-Long Ministry Told by Jeanne Harper*. Cambridge: Aquila Books.

Harper, Michael. 1974. *As at the Beginning*. London: Hodder & Stoughton.

Harper, Michael. 1980. *Charismatic Crisis: The Charismatic Renewal – Past, Present, and Future*. London: Hodder & Stoughton.

Harrell, David E. 1975. *All Things Are Possible*. Bloomington. Indiana University Press.

Harrell, David Edwin, Jr. 1985. *Oral Roberts: An American Life*. Bloomington, IN: Indiana University Press.

Harrison, Milmon F. 2005. *Righteous Riches: The Word of Faith Movement in Contemporary African American Religion*. Oxford: Oxford University Press.

Hartch, Todd. 2014. *The Rebirth of Latin American Christianity*. Oxford: Oxford University Press.

Harvey, John. 1997. "Image of God: Artistic Inspiration and Pentecostal Theology (A Case Study)." *Journal of Pentecostal Theology* 5 (10): 111–124.

Hassing, Arne. 1980. *Religion and Power: The Case of Methodism in Norway*. Lake Junaluska, NC: General Commission on Archives and History, The United Methodist Church.

Hasu, P. 2006. "World Bank and Heavenly Bank in Poverty and Prosperity: The Case of Tanzanian Faith Gospel." *Review of African Political Economy* 33 (110): 679–692.

Hasu, P. 2012. "Prosperity Gospel and Enchanted World Views: Two Responses to Socio-Economic Transformations in Tanzanian Pentecostal Christianity." In *Pentecostalism and Development: Churches, NGOs and Social Change in Africa*, edited by D. Freeman, 67–86. New York: Palgrave Macmillan.

Hathaway, Malcolm R. 1998. "The Elim Pentecostal Church: Origins, Developments and Distinctives." In *Pentecostal Perspectives*, edited by Keith Warrington, 1–39. Carlisle: Paternoster.

Hattaway, Paul. 2009. *Henan: The Galilee of China*. Carlisle, UK: Piquant Editions Ltd.

Hattie-Longmire, Brenda. 2001. "'Sit Down Brother!': Alice Belle Garrigus and the Pentecostal Assemblies of Newfoundland." Master's thesis, Joint Women's Studies Program, Mount Saint Vincent University, Dalhousie University, and Saint Mary's University, Halifax, Nova Scotia.

Haugen, Heidi Østbø. 2013. "African Pentecostal Migrants in China: Marginalisation and the Alternative Geography of a Mission Theology." *African Studies Review* 56 (1): 81–102.

Haustein, J. 2011 "Embodying the Spirit(s): Pentecostal Demonology and Deliverance Discourse in Ethiopia." *Ethnos* 76 (4): 534–552.

Haustein, Jörg. 2011. *Writing Religious History: The Historiography of Ethiopian Pentecostalism*. Wiesbaden: Harrassowitz.

Haustein, Jörg. 2013. "Historical Epistemology and Pentecostal Origins: History and Historiography in Ethiopian Pentecostalism." *Pneuma* 35 (3): 345–365.

Haustein, Jörg. 2013. "Introduction: The Ethiopian Pentecostal Movement – History, Identity and Current Socio-Political Dynamics." *PentecoStudies* 12 (2): 150–161.

Hawtin, E. 1949. "How This Revival Began." *The Sharon Star* (August 1): 3.

Hawtin, G. 1950. "The Church – Which Is His Body." *The Sharon Star* (March 1): 2.

Hayes, Alan. 2004. *Anglicans in Canada: Controversies and Identity in Historical Perspective*. Urbana and Chicago: University of Illinois Press.

Hayford, Jack, and David Moore. 2009. *The Charismatic Century: The Enduring Impact of the Azusa Street Revival*. New York: Warner Faith, Hachette Book Group.

Haynes, Naomi. 2017. *Moving by the Spirit: Pentecostal Social Life on the Zambian Copperbelt*. Berkeley: University of California Press.

Hébrard, Monique. 1987. *Les nouveaux disciples dix ans après: voyage à travers les communautés charismatiques: réflexions sur le renouveau spirituel*. Paris: Éditions du Centurion.

Hefner, Robert W., ed. 2013. *Global Pentecostalism in the 21st Century*. Bloomington and Indianapolis, IN: Indiana University Press.

Helander, Eila. 1987. *Naiset eivät vaienneet: Naisevankelistainstituutio Suomen helluntailiikkeessä – Women Have not Remained Silent: A Study of the Institution of Female Evangelists in the Finnish Pentecostal Movement*. Helsinki: Suomen kirkkohistoriallinen seura.

Hembree, Ron. 1983. *The Mark Buntain Story.* Minneapolis, MN: Bethany House.

Henderson, Lawrence W. 1990. *A igreja em Angola. Um rio com várias correntes.* Lisbon: Editorial Além Mar.

Hepner, T.R. 2003. "Religion, Nationalism, and Transnational Civil Society in the Eritrean Diaspora." *Identities: Global Studies in Culture and Power* 10 (3): 269–293.

Hepner, T.R. 2014. "Religion, Repression, and Human Rights in Eritrea and the Diaspora." *Journal of Religion in Africa* 44 (2): 151–188.

Heuser, Andreas, ed. 2015. *Pastures of Plenty: Tracing Religio-Scapes of Prosperity Gospel in Africa and Beyond.* New York: Peter Lang.

Hexham, I., and K. Poewe-Hexham. 2002. "South Africa." In *International Dictionary of Pentecostal and Charismatic Movements*, edited by Stanley M. Burgess, and Eduard M. Van der Maas, 227–238. Grand Rapids: Zondervan.

Hey, Sam. 2013. *Megachurches: Origins, Ministry, and Prospects.* Eugene, OR: Wipf & Stock.

Hicks, Tommy. 1956. *Capturing the Nations in the Name of the Lord: The Miracle Revival of Russia.* Los Angeles, CA: International Headquarters of Tommy Hicks.

Hicks, Tommy. 1956. *Millions Found Christ: History's Greatest Recorded Revival.* Los Angeles, CA: International Headquarters of Tommy Hicks.

Hiebert, Paul G., Daniel R. Shaw, and Tite Tienou. 1999. *Understanding Folk Religion: A Christian Response to Popular Beliefs and Practices.* Grand Rapids: Baker.

Hittenburger, Jeffrey S. 2006. "Education." In *Encyclopedia of Pentecostal and Charismatic Christianity*, edited by Stanley M. Burgess, 158–162. New York: Routledge.

Hocken, Peter. 1997. *Streams of Renewal: The Origins and Early Development of the Charismatic Movement in Great Britain.* Carlisle: Paternoster.

Hocken, P.D. 2002. "Alpha Course."In *The New International Dictionary of Pentecostal and Charismatic Movements*, edited by Stanley M. Burgess. Grand Rapids, MI: Zondervan.

Hocken, Peter D. 2002. "Charismatic Movement." In *The New International Dictionary of Pentecostal and Charismatic Movements*, edited by Stanley M. Burgess, and Eduard M. van der Maas, 477–519. Grand Rapids, MI: Zondervan.

Hocken, Peter D. 2002. "Sanford, Agnes Mary." In *The New International Dictionary of Pentecostal and Charismatic Movements*, edited by Stanley M. Burgess and Eduard M. van der Maas, 1039. Grand Rapids: Zondervan.

Hocken, Peter. 2002. "Church, Theology of the." In *The New International Dictionary of Pentecostal and Charismatic Movements*, edited by Stanley M. Burgess and Eduard M. van der Maas, 544–554. Grand Rapids, MI: Zondervan.

Hocken, Peter. 2002. "European Pentecostal Theological Association." In *The New International Dictionary of Pentecostal and Charismatic Movements*, edited by Stanley M. Burgess and Eduard M. Van der Maas, 610. Grand Rapids: Zondervan.

Hocken, Peter. 2002. "House Church Movement." In *The New International Dictionary of Pentecostal and Charismatic Movements*, edited by Stanley M. Burgess and Eduard M. van der Maas, 773–774. Grand Rapids: Zondervan.

Hocken, Peter. 2013. *Pentecost and Parousia.* Eugene, OR: Wipf and Stock.

Hocken, Peter. 2016. *Azuza, Rome and Zion: Pentecostal Faith, Catholic Reform and Jewish Roots.* Eugene, OR: Pickwick Publications.

Hodges, Melvin L. 1953. *The Indigenous Church.* Springfield: Gospel Publishing House.

Hodges, Melvin L. 1977. *A Theology of the Church and Its Mission: A Pentecostal Perspective.* Springfield, MO: Gospel Publishing House.

Hogan, Brian. 2008. *There's a Sheep in my Bathtub: Birth of a Mongolian Church Planting Movement.* Bayside, CA: Asteroidea Books.

Holdcroft, T. 1980. "The New Order of the Latter Rain." *Pneuma* 2 (Fall): 46–60.

Holland, Clifton L. July 20, 2001. "An Historical Profile of Religion in Honduras." Accessed May 22, 2018. http://www.prolades.com/cra/regions/cam/hon/honduras.html.

Holland, Clifton L. 2006. "Paraguay." In *Worldmark Encyclopedia of Religious Practices*, edited by Andrew Riggs, Volume 3, Countries M-Z, 139–143. Detroit, MI: Thomson Gale.

Hollenweger, W.J. 1965–67. *Handbuch der Pfingstbewegung*, vols. 1–10. Zürich: Genf.

Hollenweger, Walter J. 1972. *The Pentecostals*. London: SCM Press.

Hollenweger, Walter J. 1986. "After Twenty Years' Research on Pentecostalism." *International Review of Mission* 75 (297): 3–12.

Hollenweger, Walter J. 1988. *Geist und Materie: Interkulturelle Theologie 3*. Munich: Chr. Kaiser.

Hollenweger, Walter J. 1990 (1979). *Erfahrungen der Leibhaftigkeit: Interkulturelle Theologie 1*. Munich: Chr. Kaiser.

Hollenweger, Walter. 1992. "The Critical Tradition of Pentecostalism." *Journal of Pentecostal Theology* 1 (1): 1–7.

Hollenweger, Walter J. 1992 (1982). *Umgang mit Mythen: Interkulturelle Theologie 2*. Munich: Chr. Kaiser.

Hollenweger, Walther J. 1997. *Charismatisch-Pfingstlichs Christentum. Herkunft, Situation, Ökumenische Chancen*. Göttingen: Vandenhoeck & Ruprecht.

Hollenweger, Walter J. 1997. *Pentecostalism: Origins and Developments Worldwide*. Peabody, MA: Hendrickson.

Hollenweger, Walter J. 1999. "Roman Catholics and Pentecostals in Dialogue." *Pneuma* 21 (1): 135–153.

Hollenweger, Walter J. 2004. "An Irresponsible Silence." *Asian Journal of Pentecostal Studies* 7 (2): 219–224.

Hollis Gause, R. 2009 (1980). *Living in the Spirit: The Way of Salvation*. Revised and Expanded Edition. Cleveland, TN: CPT.

Holm, Nils G. 2015. "Pentecostalism in Finland: The Precarious Beginning." *Approaching Religion: Pentecostalism around the Baltic Sea* 5 (1): 92–95.

Holm, Randall. 2003. "Cadences of the Heart: A Walkabout in Search of Pentecostal Preaching." *Didaskalia* 7 (1): 13–27.

Holmes, Pamela M.S. 2010. "Zelma Argue's Contribution to Early Pentecostalism." In *Winds from the North: Canadian Contributions to the Pentecostal Movement*, edited by Michael Wilkinson and Peter Althouse, 129–150. Leiden: Brill Academic Publishers.

Hong, Elijah. 1979. *Elijah's Mantle*. Grace of Jesus Christ Crusade, Taipei.

Hood, Ralph W., Peter C. Hill, and W. Paul Williamson. 2005. *The Psychology of Religious Fundamentalism*. New York: Guilford Press.

Hoover, Mario. 2002. *El Movimiento Pentecostal en Chile del siglo XX*. Santiago: Eben-Ezer.

Hoover, Willis Collins. 1977. *Historia Del Avivamiento Pentecostal En Chile*. Santiago: Eben-Ezer.

Houston, H. 1989. *Being Frank, The Frank Houston Story*, London: Marshall Pickering.

Houston, Hazel. 1989. *Being Frank*. London: Marshall Pickering.

Hovenden, Gerald. 2002. *Speaking in Tongues: The New Testament Evidence in Context*. Sheffield: Sheffield Academic.

Hovi, Tuija. 2014. "Servants and Agents: Gender Roles in Neo-charismatic Christianity." In *Finnish Women Making Religion: Between Ancestors and Angels*, edited by Terhi Utriainen and Päivi Salmesvuori, 177–196. Basinstoke: Palgrave Macmillan.

Hu, Jiayin. 2017. "Spirituality and Spiritual Practice: Is the Local Church Pentecostal?" In *Global Chinese Pentecostal and Charismatic Christianity*, edited by Fenggang Yang, Joy K.C. Tong, and Allan H. Anderson, 161–180. Leiden: Brill.

Huang, Ke-Hsien. 2016. "Sect-to-Church Movement in Globalization: Transforming Pentecostalism and Coastal Intermediaries in

Contemporary China." *Journal for the Scientific Study of Religion* 55 (2): 407–416.

Huang, Ke-hsien. 2018. "Emergence and Development of Indigenous Christianity in China: A Class-Culture Approach." In *Transfiguration of Chinese Christianity: Localization and Globalization*, edited by Cheng-tian Kuo, Fu-chu Chou, and Sian-chin Iap, 153–193. Taipei: Chengchi University Press.

Huber, Stefan, and Odilo W. Huber. 2010. "Psychology of Religion." In *Studying Global Pentecostalism: Theories and Methods*, edited by Allan Anderson, Michael Bergunder, André Droogers, and Cornelis Van Der Laan, 133–55. Berkeley, CA:University of California Press.

Huff, James G. 2017. "Of Specters and Spirit: Neoliberal Entanglements of Faith-Based Development in El Salvador." *Urban Anthropology and Studies of Cultural Systems and World Economic Development. Special Issue: The Impact of State-Level and Global-Level Neoliberal Agendas on NGOs in Latin America* 46 (3/4): 173–220.

Huh, Ho-ik. 2009. *Pastor Gil Seon-Ju's Theology and Ministry*. Seoul: The Christian Literature Society of Korea.

Hunt, Stephen. 1995. "The Anglican Wimberites." *Pnuema* 17 (1): 105–115.

Hunt, Stephen. 2003. "The Alpha Programme: Some Tentative Observations." *Journal of Contemporary Religion* 18 (1): 77–93.

Hunt, S. 2004. *The Alpha Enterprise: Evangelism in a Post-Christian Era*. Aldershot: Ashgate.

Hunt, S. 2005. "Alpha: The Theological Debate." *Pentecostudies*. asnws.scw.vu.nl/Pentecostudies.

Hunt, S. 2005. "The *Alpha* Programme: Charismatic Evangelism for the Contemporary Age." *Pneuma* 17 (1): 105–118.

Hunt, Stephen. 2008. "'Packing Them in the Aisles': Is Alpha Working?" In *Evaluating Fresh Expressions: Explorations in Emerging Church*, edited by L. Nelstrop and M. Percy, 161–174. London: SPCK-Canterbury Press.

Hunt, Stephen. 2009. "The Toronto Blessing, A Lesson in Globalized Religion?" In *Canadian Pentecostalism*, edited by Michael Wilkinson, 233–248. Montreal & Kingston: McGill-Queen's University Press.

Hunt, Stephen. 2010. "Sociology of Religion." In *Studying Global Pentecostalism*, edited by Allan Anderson, Michael Bergunder, André F. Droogers and Cornelis van der Laan, 179–201. Berkeley, CA: University of California Press.

Hunt, Stephen. 2016. "Glocalization and Protestant and Catholic Contestations in the Brazilian Religious Economy." In *New Ways of Being Pentecostal in Latin America*, edited by Martin Lindhardt, 15–38. New York: Lexington Books.

Hurston, Karen 1995. *Growing the World's Largest Church*. Springfield: Gospel Publishing House.

Hutchinson, Mark P. 1999. *Pellegrini: An Italian Protestant Community in Sydney, 1958–1998*. Sydney: Australasian Pentecostal Studies.

Hutchinson, Mark. 2009. "The Contribution of Women to Pentecostalism." In *Raising Women Leaders: Perspectives on Liberating Women in Pentecostal and Charismatic Contexts*, edited by Shane Clifton and Jacqueline Grey, 191–220. Sydney: Australasian Pentecostal Studies.

Hutchinson, Mark. 2010. "The Latter Rain Movement and the Phenomenon of Global Return." In *Winds from the North: Canadian Contributions to the Pentecostal Movement*, edited by Michael Wilkinson and Peter Althouse, 265–284. Leiden: Brill.

Hutchinson, Mark. 2017. "Framing Australasia's Charismatic Past: Australian charismatic movements as a space of flows." *Pentecostal and Charismatic Christianities in Australia*, Conference Paper, University of Western Sydney, 11 August.

Hutchinson, Mark P. 2018. "Dissenting Preaching in the Twentieth-Century Anglophone

World." In *The Oxford History of Protestant Dissenting Traditions Volume V: The Twentieth Century: Themes and Variations in a Global Context*, edited by Mark P. Hutchinson, 170–198. Oxford: Oxford University Press.

Hutchinson, Mark P. "Mina Conrod Ross Brawner." *Australasian Dictionary of Pentecostal and Charismatic Movements*. Accessed February 26, 2019. https://sites.google.com/view/adpcm/a-d-top-page/brawner-mina-conrod-ross.

Hutchinson, Sharon Elaine. 1996. *Nuer Dilemmas: Coping with Money, War, and the State*. Berkeley: University of California Press.

Iap, Sian-Chin and Maurie Sween. 2016. "Pentecostal and Charismatic Christianity in Protestant Taiwan." In *Global Renewal Christianity: Spirit-Empowered Movements Past, Present, and Future*, edited by Vinson Synan and Amos Yong, 127–41. Lake Mary: Charisma House.

Iglesia de Dios Honduras. December, 2017. "Estadística Oficina Nacional." Accessed May 22, 2018. http://www.iglesiadedioshn.org/estadistica-oficina-nacional/.

Ignatov, Pavel. 2004. *The Bloodless Persecution of the Church*. Sofia: Lik.

Imbach, Jeffrey. 1998. *The River Within: Loving God, Living Passionately*. Colorado Springs, CO: NavPress.

Immigration and Refugee Board of Canada. 2014. "Eritrea: Treatment of Evangelical and Pentecostal Christians by Authorities; including members of the Mulu Wongel [Full Gospel] Church; incidents of arrests and detention of Mulu Wongel Church members in Asmara (2002 – October 2014)." Last accessed July 24th 2018. http://www.refworld.org/docid/55acc8e24.html.

Ingalls, Monique M. 2014. "International Gospel and Christian Music." Bloomsbury 333 Sound Blog: Sample Article for *The Continuum Encyclopedia of Popular Music of the World, Volume XII: International Genres*, edited by John Shepherd and David Horn. Accessed January 16, 2019. http://333sound.com/epmow-vol-9-gospel-and-christian-popular-music/.

Ingalls, Monique M. and Amos Yong. 2015. *The Spirit of Praise: Music and Worship in Global Pentecostal-Charismatic Christianity*. University Park: The Pennsylvania State University.

Ingle, Venu. 1999. *Pandita Ramabai Mukti Mission, Mukti Kiran, 1899–1999. Church Centenary Edition*. Mumbai: Ebenezer Printing House.

Inouye, Melissa Wei-Tsing. 2018. *China and the True Jesus: Charisma and Organization in a Chinese Christian Church*. New York: Oxford University Press.

Institute of Contextual Theology. 1988. *The Kairos Document: A Theological Comment on the Political Crisis in South Africa*. Grand Rapids, MI: Eerdmans.

International Catholic Charismatic Renewal Service. 2000. David B. Barrett, and Todd M. Johnson, eds., *"Then Peter Stood Up ...": Collections of the Popes' addresses to the CCR from its origin to the year 2000*. Vatican: International Catholic Charismatic Renewal Service.

International Fellowship of Christian Assemblies. 2015. Articles of faith and core practices. Transfer PA: International Fellowship of Christian Assemblies. Available at http://ifcaministry.org/.

International House of Prayer. 2020. "About the International House of Prayer," and "Affirmations and Denials." Accessed April 10th, 2020. https://www.ihopkc.org/about/.

Introvigne, Massimo. 2009. "Le minoranze pentecostali nelle comunità romane: Lo stato della ricerca e i principali problemi sociologici." *Religioni e sette nel mondo* 5: 73–78.

"Investigación: 'Chamalé', condenado a dos décadas de prisión." *El Periódico*, Julio 27, 2015.

Ippolito, Daniel. 2009. *Identity-Heritage-Destiny: A History of the Canadian Assemblies of God, Formerly the Italian Pentecostal Church of Canada*. Montreal: Canadian Assemblies of God.

Ireland, Jerry. 2019. "The Missionary Nature of Tongues in the Book of Acts." *PentecoStudies* 18 (2): 200–223.

Isaacson, Alan. 1990. *Deeper Life: The Extraordinary Growth of the Deeper Life Bible Church*. London: Hodder and Stoughton.

Isgrigg, Daniel. 2019. "Where the Spirit Leads Me: An Oral History of the Life and Ministry of Vinson Synan, Ph.D." Oral Roberts University Digital Showcase (Holy Spirit Research Center, AV Collection), accessed December 3, 2019. https://digitalshowcase.oru.edu/synan/.

Jackson, Bill. 1999. *The Quest for the Radical Middle: A History of the Vineyard*. Cape Town, South Africa: Vineyard International Publishing.

Jacobs, Cindy. 2015. "The Third Pentecost: Jordan and Israel Trip Report." *Generales Internacionales*. May 28, 2015. Accessed Oct. 3, 2019. https://www.generals.org/es/articles/unico/the-third-pentecost-jordan-and-israel-trip-report/.

Jacobsen, Douglas. 2003. *Thinking in the Spirit: Theologies of the Early Pentecostal Movement*. Bloomington, IN: Indiana University Press.

Jacobsen, Douglas. 2010. "The Ambivalent Ecumenical Impulses in Early Pentecostal Theology in North America." In *Pentecostalism and Christian Unity: Ecumenical Documents and Critical Assessments*, edited by Wolfgang Vondey, 3–19. Eugene, OR: Pickwick.

Jacobsen, Douglas. 2015. *Global Gospel: An Introduction to Christianity on Five Continents*. Grand Rapids: Baker Academics.

Jacobsen, T., and K.I. Tangen. 2017. "Pentecostal and Charismatic Movements in Denmark and Iceland." In *Global Renewal Christianity: Spirit Empowered Movements Past, Present, and Future*. Vol. 4, *Europe and North America*, edited by V. Synan and A. Yong, 215–27. Lake Mary: Charisma House.

James F. Clarke. 1885. *Missionary News from Bulgaria*, Issues 1–55. Harvard University.

James, Jonathan D., ed. 2015. *A Moving Faith: Mega Churches Go South*, Thousand Oaks, CA: SAGE Publications.

Jamsran, Purevdorj. 2012. "Developing Christianity in Mongolia during the Last Two Decades." In *Mongolians after Socialism: Politics, Economy and Religion*, edited by Bruce M. Knauft and Richard Taupier, 129–137. Ulaanbaatar: Admon Press, with Mongolian Academy of Sciences, National University of Mongolia and Open Society Forum, Mongolia.

Janes, Burton K. 1982. *The Lady Who Came: The Biography of Alice Bell Garrigus Newfoundland's First Pentecostal Pioneer*. Vol. 1: *1858–1908*. St. John's, NL: Good Tidings Press.

Janes, Burton K. 1983. *The Lady Who Stayed: The Biography of Alice Belle Garrigus Newfoundland's First Pentecostal Pioneer Volume Two (1908–1949)*. St. John's, NL: Good Tidings Press.

Janes, Burton K. 1996. *History of the Pentecostal Assemblies of Newfoundland*. St. John's, NL: Good Tidings Press.

Jennings, Mark A.C. 2018. "Impossible Subjects: LGBTIQ Experiences in Australian Pentecostal-Charismatic Churches." *Religions* 9 (2): 53. https://doi.org/10.3390/rel9020053.

Jensen, Kristian. 1954. *Mindeskrift: Sigurd Bjørner*. Copenhagen: Vanløse Evangelieforsamlings Forlag.

Jesus Culture. 2020. "About Jesus Culture Music." Last accessed April 10, 2020. https://jesusculture.com/music/.

JILW, Jesus is Lord Church Worldwide. 2013. "Mission, Vision, Core Values." https://jilworldwide.org/church.

Jin, Li Zheng. "Timothy Dzao." In *Biographical Dictionary of Chinese Christianity*. Global China Centre. 金立正。〈趙世光〉。載《華典》。世華中國研究中心。http://bdccoline.net/zh-hant/stories/zhao-shiguang.

Jin, Su-cheol. 1994. *The Biographies of Martyrdom*. Seoul: Yangmoon.

Johansson, Göran. 1992. *More Blessed to Give: A Pentecostal Mission to Bolivia in*

Anthropological Perspective. Stockholm Studies in Social Anthropology 30. Stockholm: Gotab.

Johnson, Bill. 2003. *When Heaven Invades Earth.* Shippensburg, PA: Destiny Image.

Johnson, Bill. 2018. "Bethel and the Assemblies of God." Accessed April 10, 2020. https://web.archive.org/web/20110701134709/http://www.ibethel.org/bethel-and-the-assemblies-of-god.

Johnson, Todd M. 2009. "The Global Demographics of the Pentecostal and Charismatic Renewal." *Social Science and Modern Society* 46 (6): 479–483.

Johnson, Todd M. 2014. "Counting Pentecostals Worldwide." *Pneuma* 36: 265–288.

Johnson, Todd M., and Brian J. Grim. 2013. *The World's Religions in Figures: An Introduction to International Religious Demography.* Oxford: Wiley-Blackwell.

Johnson, Todd M., and Brian J. Grim, eds. 2019. *World Religion Database.* Leiden: Brill.

Johnson, Todd M., and Gina A. Zurlo. 2019. eds. *World Christian Database.* Leiden: Brill.

Johnson, Todd M., and Kenneth R. Ross, eds. 2009. *Atlas of Global Christianity, 1910–2010.* Edinburgh: Edinburgh University Press.

Johnson, Todd M., and Gina A. Zurlo. 2019. *World Christian Encyclopedia*, Third Edition. Edinburgh: Edinburgh University Press.

Jong, Hyun Jung, and Scott Schieman. 2012. "'Practical Divine Influence': Socioeconomic Status and Belief in the Prosperity Gospel." *Journal for the Scientific Study of Religion* 51 (4): 738–756.

Journal of the European Pentecostal Theological Association (JEPTA). 1996–2019 (previously published as *EPTA Bulletin*, 1981–1996).

Judd, Carrie. 1880. *Prayer of Faith.* New York: Fleming H. Revell Company.

Judt, Tony. 2010. *Postwar: A History of Europe since 1945.* London: Vintage.

Juergensen, Marie. n.d. *Foundation Stones: Carl F. Juergensen*, Springfield, MO: Foreign Mission Department of Assemblies of God.

Jung, Courtney. 2009. "Race, Ethnicity, Religion." In *The Oxford Handbook of Contextual Political Analysis*, edited by Robert E. Goodin and Charles Tilly, 360–375. Oxford: Oxford University Press.

Jung, YongKwon. 2002. "Korean Prayers: Evaluating the Prayer Phenomena at the Prayer Mountain Centers in Korea." PhD thesis, Asbury Theological Seminary.

Kalu, Ogbu. 2008. *Pentecostalism in Africa: An Introduction.* New York: Oxford University Press.

Kamiński, Marek. 2012. *Kościół Zielonoświątkowy w Polsce w latach 1988–2008: Studium historyczno-ustrojowe.* Warszawa: Wydawnictwo Arka.

Karagiannis, Evangelos. 2020. "Pfingsten im Kontext: Zur Adaption des Pfingstglaubens in Griechenland." *Anthropos* 115 (1): 133–150.

Kärkkäinen, Veli-Matti. 1999. *Ad Ultimum Terrae: Evangelization, Proselytism, and Common Witness in the Roman Catholic-Pentecostal Dialogue, 1990–1997.* Frankfurt am Main: Peter Lang.

Kärkkäinen, Veli-Matti. 2002. *An Introduction to Ecclesiology: Ecumenical, Historical, and Contextual Perspectives.* Downers Grove, IL: InterVarsity Press.

Kärkkäinen, Veli-Matti. 2003. *An Introduction to the Theology of Religions: Biblical, Historical, & Contemporary Perspectives.* Downers Grove, IL: InterVarsity.

Kärkkäinen, Veli-Matti. 2004. *Trinity and Religious Pluralism: The Doctrine of the Trinity in Christian Theology of Religions.* Burlington, VT: Ashgate.

Kärkkäinen, Veli-Matti. 2007. "'Encountering Christ in the Full Gospel Way': An Incarnational Pentecostal Spirituality." *Journal of the European Pentecostal Theological Association* 27 (1): 5–19.

Kärkkäinen, Veli-Matti. 2018. *Pneumatology: the Holy Spirit in Ecumenical, International, and Contextual Perspective*. Second Edition. Grand Rapids: Baker.

Kaunda, Chammah J. 2016. "The Making of Pentecostal Zambia: A Brief History of Pneumatic Spirituality." *Oral History Journal of South Africa* 4 (1): 15–45.

Kay, Peter. 1995. "The Four-Fold Gospel in the Formation, Policy and Practice of the Pentecostal Missionary Union (PMU) (1909–1925)." Master's diss., Cheltenham & Gloucester College of Higher Education.

Kay, William K. 2007. "Donald Gee: An Important Voice of the Pentecostal Movement." *Journal of Pentecostal Theology* 16 (1): 133–153.

Kay, William K. 2007. *Apostolic Networks in Britain*. Milton Keynes: Paternoster.

Kay, William K. 2009. "Why Did the Welsh Revival Stop?" In *Revival, Renewal and the Holy Spirit*, edited by Dyfed Wyn Roberts, 169–184. Milton Keynes: Paternoster.

Kay, William K. 2013. "Gifts of the Spirit: Reflections on Pentecostalism and Its Growth in Asia." In *Spirit and Power: The Growth and Global Impact of Pentecostalism,*" edited by Donald E. Miller, Kimon H. Sargeant and Richard Flory, 259–276. Oxford: Oxford University Press.

Kay, William K. 2017. *George Jeffreys: Pentecostal Apostle and Revivalist*. Cleveland, TN: CPT Press.

Kay, William K., and Anne E. Dyer, eds. 2011. *European Pentecostalism*. Leiden: Brill.

Kay, William K., Kees Slijkerman, Raymond Pfister, and Cornelis van der Laan. 2011. "Pentecostal Theology and Catholic Europe." In *European Pentecostalism*, edited by William K. Kay and Anne E. Dyer, 313–331. Leiden: Brill.

Keane, Webb. 2007. *Christian Moderns: Freedom and Fetish in the Mission Encounter*. Berkeley CA: University of California Press.

Keener, Craig S. 2007. "Why Does Luke Use Tongues as a Sign of the Spirit's Empowerment?" *Journal of Pentecostal Theology* 15 (2): 177–184.

Keener, Craig. 2011. *Miracles: The Credibility of the New Testament Accounts*. Grand Rapids, MI: Baker Academic Press.

Kelly, Miriam (Mimi) A. 2017. "The Origins and development of the Assemblies of God in the Republic of Ireland: Exploring the Opportunities and Challenges that Pentecostalism Faces in the Island of 'Saints and Scholars' in the Twenty-first Century." In *Global Renewal Christianity*, vol. 4, edited by Vinson Synan and Amos Yong, 254–258. Lake Mary, FL: Charisma House.

Kennedy, Nell L. 1980. *Dream Your Way to Success: The Story of Dr. Yonggi Cho and Korea*. Plainfield, NJ: Logos International.

Kenneth Copeland Ministries. n.d. "Kenneth Copeland Ministries: About Us." Accessed March 29, 2019. https://www.kcm.org/about-us.

Kessler, Christl, and Jürgen Rüland. 2008. *Give Jesus a Hand! Charismatic Christians: Populist Religion and Politics in the Philippines*. Quezon City: Ateneo de Manila University Press.

Kessler, J.B.A., Jr. 1967. *A Study of the Older Protestant Missions and Churches in Peru and Chile: With Special Reference to the Problems of Division, Nationalism and Native Ministry*. Goes: Oosterbaan & Le Cointre.

Kgatle, Mookgo S. 2016. "Sociological and Theological Factors That Caused Schisms in the Apostolic Faith Mission of South Africa." *Studia Historae Ecclesiasticae* 42 (1): 1–15.

Kgatle, Mookgo Solomon. 2017. "African Pentecostalism: The Christianity of Elias Letwaba From Early Years Until his Death in 1959." *Scriptura* 116 (1): 1–9.

Khai, Chin Khua. 2003. *The Cross Among Pagodas: A History of the Assemblies of God in Myanmar*. Baguio: APTS.

Kileyesus, A. 2006. "Cosmologies in Collision: Pentecostal Conversion and Christian Cults in Asmara." *African Studies Review* 49 (1): 75–92.

Kim, Hui-yeon. 2018. "Yŏuido Sunbogŭm Kyoheo", in *Handbook of East Asian New Religious Movements*, edited by Lukas Pokorny and Franz Winter, 343–359. Leiden: Brill.

Kim, Ig Jin. 2003. *History and Theology of Korean Pentecostalism*. Zoetermeer: Uitgeverij Boekencentrum.

Kim, Ik-du, 2008. *Korean Leadership Preaching: Kim Ik Du*. Seoul: Hongseongsa

Kim, Jaehyun. 2008. *Gil Seon-Ju: Essential Writing*. Translated by Hannah Kim. Seoul: KIATS Press.

King, J.H. 1935. "'He Being Dead Yet Speaketh': Hebrews 11:4." *Pentecostal Holiness Advocate* 18, no. 36 (January 10): 8.

King, Johnny. 2017. "Spirit and Schism: A History of Oneness Pentecostalism in the Philippines." PhD diss., University of Birmingham, UK.

King, Paul L. 2006. *Genuine Gold: The Cautiously Charismatic Story of the Early Christian and Missionary Alliance*. Tulsa, OK: Word & Spirit Press.

King, Paul L. 2008. *Only Believe: Examining the Origin and Development of Classic and Contemporary Word of Faith Theologies*. Tulsa, OK: Word & Spirit Press.

Kinnear, Angus. 1978. *Against the Tide: The Story of Watchman Nee*. Wheaton, Ill.: Tyndale House Pub.

Kinnear, Angus. 1998. *The Story of Watchman Nee: Against the Tide*. Fort Washington, PA: Christian Literature Crusade.

Kirkpatrick, M.E. "The 1948 Revival & Now." Accessed February 17, 2017. http://oklord.sperryruss.com/48revival/part1/48intro.html.

Kit Cheong, Weng and Joy K.C. Tong. "The Localization of Charismatic Christianity among the Chinese in Malaysia." In *Global Chinese Pentecostal and Charismatic Christianity*, edited by Fenggang Yang, Joy K.C. Tong, and Allan Anderson, 309–328. Leiden: Brill.

Kiteley, David. 2019. Telephone Interview by Peter Althouse, August 6.

Kitiarsa, Pattana. 2008. *Religious Commodifications in Asia: Marketing Gods*. New York: Routledge.

Klaver, Miranda. 2015. "Media Technology Creating 'Sermonic Events.' The Hillsong Megachurch Network." *Crosscurrents* 65 (4): 422–433.

Klaver, Miranda. 2019. "The Spirit of the Supernatural: The Rise of Apostolic Networks in the Netherlands." In *The Spirit is Moving: New Pathways in Pneumatology*, edited by Gijsbert van den Brink, Eveline van Staalduine-Sulman and Maarten Wisse, 346–362. Leiden: Brill.

Klein, Herbert S. 2003. *A Concise History of Bolivia*. Cambridge: Cambridge University Press.

Knowles, B. 2000. *The History of a New Zealand Pentecostal Movement: The New Life Churches of New Zealand From 1946 to 1979*. Studies in Religion and Society 45. Queenston: Edwin Mellen Press.

Knowles, Brett. 2002. "Adams, J.A.D." In *New International Dictionary of Pentecostal and Charismatic Movements*, edited by S. Burgess and E. Van Der Maas. Grand Rapids: Zondervan.

Knowles, Brett. 2014. *Transforming Pentecostalism: The Changing Face of New Zealand Pentecostalism, 1920–2010*. Lexington, KY: Emeth Press.

Knowles, James Purdie. 1908. *Samuel A. Purdie: His Life and Letters, His Work as a Missionary and Spanish Writer and Publisher in Mexico and Central America*. Plainfield, IN: Publishing Association of Friends.

Koenig, John. 1978. *Charismata: God's Gifts for God's People*. Philadephia: Westminster Press.

Koesel, Karrie J. 2017. "China's Patriotic Pentecostals." In *Global Chinese Pentecostal and Charismatic Christianity*, edited by Fenggang Yang, Joy Tong, and Allan Anderson, 240–263. Leiden: Brill.

Köhrsen, Jens. 2016. *Middle Class Pentecostalism in Argentina: Inappropriate Spirits*. Leiden: Brill.

Komolafe, Sunday Jide. 2013. *The Transformation of African Christianity*. Carlisle: Langham Monographs.

Kong, Duen Yee. 1963. *Acts of the Holy Spirit*. Hong Kong: Grace of Jesus Christ Crusade.

Kong. Duen Yee. 1963. "Acts of the Holy Spirit Part 1." *Living Testimony Compilation Chapter 1–50*. Hong Kong: Grace of Jesus Christ Crusade.

Kong, Duen Yee. 1964. *Golden Lamp Stand*. Vol. 1. Hong Kong: Grace of Jesus Christ Crusade.

Kosambi, Meera. 2000. *Pandita Ramabai: Through Her Own Words*. Oxford: Oxford University Press.

Kraft, Charles. 1992. *Defeating Dark Angels: Breaking Demonic Oppression in the Believer's Life*. Ann Arbor: Servant.

Kramer, Eric W. 2002. "Making Global Faith Universal: Media and a Brazilian Prosperity Movement." *Culture and Religion: An Interdisciplinary Journal* 3 (1): 21–47.

Kristanto, Rony Chandra. 2018. "Evangelism as Public Theology: The Public Engagement of the Gospel of the Kingdom Church in Semarang, Indonesia." PhD thesis, University of Birmingham, UK.

Kuponu, Selome I. 2007. "The Living Faith Church (Winners Chapel), Nigeria: Pentecostalism, Prosperity Gospel and Social Change in Nigeria." PhD diss., University of Bayreuth, Germany.

Kürschner-Pelkmann, Frank. 2004. *Reinhard Bonnkes Theology: A Pentecostal Preacher and His Mission, a Critical Analysis*. Nairobi: All Africa Conference of Churches.

Kydd, Ronald A.N. 1996. "The Impact of the Charismatic Renewal on Classical Pentecostalism in Canada." *Pneuma* 18 (1): 55–67.

Kydd, R.A.N. 2002. "Healing in the Christian Church." In *International Dictionary of Pentecostal and Charismatic Movements*, edited by Stanley M. Burgess and Eduard M. Van der Maas, 698–711. Grand Rapids: Zondervan.

Kyrios, Alex, and Adam Stewart. 2020. "EPC Exhibit 143-S28.1: Pentecostalism." Report for the Dewey Decimal Classification Editorial Policy Committee, OCLC, The Library of Congress, Washington, DC.

Laan, Cornelius van der. 1991. *Cornelis van der Laan, Sectarian Against His Will: Gerrit Roelof Polman and the Birth of Pentecostalism in the Netherlands*. Metuchen, NJ/London: The Scarecrow Press.

Laan, Cornelis van der. 2012. "Johan Thiessen, Margaretha Alt and The Birth of Pentecostalism in Indonesia." *PentecoStudies* 11 (2): 149–170.

Lado, Ludovic. 2009. *Catholic Pentecostalism and the Paradoxes of Africanisation: Processes of Localisation in a Catholic Charismatic Movement in Cameroon*. Leiden: Brill.

Lake, John G. 1908. "Missionaries for Africa." *The Pentecost* (August).

Lake, John G. 1909. "South Africa, Orange River Colony." *Confidence* (August): 185.

Lake, John Graham. 1991. *Adventures in God*. Tulsa: Harrison House.

Lalive d'epinay, Christian. 1969. *Haven of the Masses: A Study of the Pentecostal Movement in Chile*. London: Lutterworth.

Lambert, Tony. 2006. *China's Christian Millions*. Oxford: Monarch Books.

Lamont, Mark. 2010. "Lip-Synch Gospel: Christian Music and the Ethnopoetics of Identity in Kenya." *Africa: Journal of the International Africa Institute*, 80 (3): 473–496.

"Lancaster, Sarah Jane." The Australian Women's Register, National Foundation for Australian Women. Accessed April 9, 2019. http://www.womenaustralia.info/biogs/AWE5177b.htm.

Land, Isaac, and Andrew M. Shocket. 2008. "New Approaches to the Founding of the Sierra Leone Colony, 1786–1808." *Journal of Colonialism and Colonial History* 9 (3).

Land, Steven J. 1992. *Pentecostal Spirituality: A Passion for the Kingdom*. Sheffield: Sheffield Academic.

Landron, Olivier. 2004. *Les Communautés nouvelles: Nouveaux visages du catholicisme français*. Paris: Éditions du Cerf.

Lange, Barbara Rose. 2003. *Holy Brotherhood: Romani Music in a Hungarian Pentecostal Church*. Oxford: Oxford University Press.

Larbi, E. Kingsley. 2001. *Pentecostalism: The Eddies of Ghanaian Christianity*. Accra: CPCS.

Larbi, Kingsley. 2001. *Pentecostals: The Eddies of Ghanaian Christianity*. Accra: Centre for Pentecostal and Charismatic Studies.

Larkin, Brian. 2008. "Ahmed Deedat and the Form of Islamic Evangelism." *Social Text* 26 (3): 101–121.

Larsen, Kurt E. 2007. *Fra Christensen til Krarup: Dansk kirkeliv i det 20. århundrede*. Fredericia: Kolon.

Larson, Lawrence R. 1997. *The Spirit in Paradise: History of the Assemblies of God of Fiji & Its Ministries to Other Countries of the South Pacific*. St. Louis, MO: Lawrence R. Larson.

Laurent, Pierre-Joseph, and Furtado, Cláudio. 2008. "Le pentecôtisme brésilien au Cap-Vert: L'Église Universelle du Royaume de Dieu." *Archives de sciences sociales des religions* 141: 113–131.

Lawrence, B.F. 1916. *The Apostolic Faith Restored*. St. Louis, MO: Gospel Publishing House.

Lee, Chang Ki. 2003. *The Early Revival Movement in Korea (1903–1907)*. Zoetermeer: Uitgeverij Boekencentrum.

Lee, Hong-Jung. 1999. "Minjung and Pentecostal Movements in Korea." In *Pentecostals After a Century: Global Perspectives on a Movement in Transition*, edited by Allan H. Anderson and Walter J. Hollenweger, 141–150. London: Sheffield Academic Press.

Lee, Joseph Tse-Hei. 2005. "Watchman Nee and the Little Flock Movement in Maoist China." *Church History* 74 (1): 68–96.

Lee, Sang Yun. 2018. *A Theology of Hope: Contextual Perspectives in Korean Pentecostalism*. Middletown, DE: APTS Press.

Lee, Timothy S. 2010. *Born Again: Evangelicalism in Korea*. Hawaii: University of Hawaii Press.

Lee, Young-hoon. 2001. "Korean Pentecost: The Great Revival of 1907." *Asian Journal of Pentecostal Studies* 4 (1): 73–83.

Lee, Young-hoon. 2004. "Life and Ministry of David Yonggi Cho and the Youido Full Gospel Church." In *David Yonggi Cho*, edited by Wonsuk Ma. Baguio, Philippines: APTS Press.

Lee, Young-hoon. 2009. *The Holy Spirit Movement in Korea: Its Historical and Theological Development*. Oxford, UK: Regnum Books International.

Leoh, Vincent. 2006. "A Pentecostal Preacher as an Empowered Witness." *Asian Journal of Pentecostal Studies* 9 (1): 35–58.

Leoh, Vincent. 2007. "Eschatology and Pneumatic Preaching with a Case of David Yonggi Cho." *Asian Journal of Pentecostal Studies* 10 (1): 101–15.

Leonard, Christine. 1989. *A Giant in Ghana: 3000 Churches in 50 years, the Story of James McKeown and the Church of Pentecost*. Chester: New Wine Press.

Lephoko, Daniel Simon Billy. 2010. *Nicholas Bhekinkosi Hepworth Bhengu's Lasting Legacy: A Study of the Life and Work of one of Africa's Greatest Pioneers*. Accessed July 15, 2019. https://repository.up.ac.za/handle/2263/27505.

Lewis, David. 1989. *Healing: Fiction, Fantasy or Fact?* London: Hodder and Stoughton.

Lewis, Paul W., ed. 2014. *All the Gospel to All the World: 100 Years of Assemblies of God Missiology*. Springfield, MO: Assemblies of God Theological Seminary.

Li, Jieren. 1999. "A History of the Finnish Free Foreign Mission in Taiwan (1949–1998)." Master's thesis, ICI University.

Li, Shaoming. 2006. "A Study of Issues Related to the Christian Assemblies." *Religious Studies* 2: 96–102. 李少明，〈對基督徒聚會處

若干問題的考證和考察〉，《宗教學研究》，第二期（2006年）。

Li, Yading. 2019. "Wang Zai." *Biographical Dictionary of Chinese Christianity*. Accessed November 28, 2019. http://bdcconline.net/zh-hans/stories/wang-zai.

Lian, Xi. 2010. *Redeemed by Fire: The Rise of Popular Christianity in Modern China*. New Haven: Yale University.

Liardon, Roberts. 2003. "William Branham: A Man of Notable Signs and Wonders." In *God's Generals: Why They Succeeded and Why Some Failed*. New Kensington, PA: Whitaker House.

Lie, Geir. 2000. "The Charismatic/Pentecostal Movement in Norway: The Last 30 Years." *Cyberjournal for Pentecostal-Charismatic Research*. Last modified February 22, 2016. http://www.pctii.org/cyberj/cyberj7/lie.pdf.

Lie, Geir. 2003. *E.W. Kenyon: Cult Founder or Evangelical Minister? An Historical Analysis of Kenyon's Theology with Particular Emphasis on Roots and Influences*. Oslo: Refleks Publishing.

Lim, David S. 2009. "Consolidating Democracy: Filipino Evangelicals between People Power Events, 1986–2001." In *Evangelical Christianity and Democracy in Asia*, edited by David Halloran Lumsdaine, 235–277. Oxford: Oxford University Press.

Lim, David. 2016. S*piritual Gifts: A Fresh Look*. Springfield, MO: Gospel Publishing House.

Lim, Swee Hong, and Lester Ruth. 2017. *Lovin' on Jesus: A Concise History of Contemporary Worship*. Nashville, TN: Abingdon.

Lim, Yue Chuen. 2007. "An Analysis into the Growth Factors of the Chinese Churches in the Assemblies of God Malaysia." *Asian Journal of Pentecostal Studies* 10 (1): 78–90.

Lincoln, C. Eric, and Lawrence H. Mamiya. 1990. *The Black Church in the African American Experience*. Durham, NC: Duke University Press.

Lindhardt, Martin. 2012. *Power in Powerlessness: A Study of Pentecostal Life Worlds in Urban Chile*. Leiden: Brill.

Lindhardt, Martin. 2015. "Men of God: Neo-Pentecostalism and Masculinities in Urban Tanzania." *Religion* 45 (2): 252–272.

Lindhardt, Martin. 2016. "'We, the Youth, Need to be Effusive': Pentecostal Youth Culture in Contemporary Chile." In *New Ways of Being Pentecostal in Latin America*, edited by Martin Lindhardt, 135–150. Lanham: Lexington Books.

Lindhardt, Martin, ed. 2016. *New Ways of Being Pentecostal in Latin America*. Lanham: Lexington Books.

Lindhardt, Martin. 2019. "Chilean Pentecostalism. Methodism Renewed." In *The Oxford History of Protestant Dissenting Traditions* vol. 4, edited by Jehu Hanciles. Oxford: Oxford University Press.

Lindsay, Gordon. 1950. *William Branham: A Man Sent from God*. Jeffersonville, IN: W. Branham.

Lindsay, Gordon. 1992. *The Gordon Lindsay Story*. Dallas, TX: Christ For The Nations.

Lindsay, Mrs. Gordon. 1976. *My Diary Secrets*. Dallas, TX: Christ For The Nations.

Lipan, Ştefan. 2017. "The Interplay between Ethnic and Religious Frontiers: The Case of Repented Roma Migrants Living in a Belgian City." *The Romanian Journal of Society and Politics* 12 (1): 53–78.

Λίντερμαγερ, Ορέστης. 1998. "Φονταμεταλισμός και πνευματοληψία: Θεραπεία και μέθεξη στο πλαίσιο μιας πεντηκοστιανής κοινότητας στην Ελλάδα." *Εθνολογία*, no. 5 (1996–1997): 115–179.

Λίντερμαγερ, Ορέστης. 2009. "Η πεντηκοστιανή εκκλησία ως θρησκευτικό κίνημα στην Ελλάδα σήμερα." PhD diss., University of Crete.

Liu, Yi. 2014. "Pentecostal-Style Christians in the 'Galilee of China.'" *Review of Religion and Chinese Society* 1 (2): 156–172.

Liu, Yi. 2016. "Globalization of Chinese Christianity: A Study of Watchman Nee and Witness Lee's Ministry." *Asia Journal of Theology* 30 (1): 96–114.

Löfstedt, Torsten. 2017. "Pentecostals and Charismatics in Russia, Ukraine, and Other Post-Soviet States: History and Future Prospects." In *Global Renewal Christianity: Spirit-Empowered Movements Past, Present, and Future*. Vol. 4, *Europe and North America*, edited by Vinson Synan and Amos Yong, 19–32. Lake Mary, FL: Charisma House.

Löfstedt, Torsten. 2018. "Ulf Ekman och auktoritetsfrågan." *Auktoritet*. Göteborg: Daidalos, 189–213.

Londino Bernabei, Caterina. 2012. *Biografia del Servitore di Dio Giuseppe Petrelli*. Turin: the author.

Longwe, Hany. 2017. "Zimbabwe, Zambia and Malawi." In *Edinburgh Companion to Global Christianity: Christianity in Sub-Sahara Africa*, edited by Kenneth R. Ross, J. Kwabena Asamoah-Gyadu, and Todd M. Johnson. Edinburgh: Edinburgh University Press.

López Cortés, Eliseo. 1990. *Pentecostalismo y milenarismo: La Iglesia Apostólica de la Fe en Cristo Jesús*. Universidad Autonoma Metropolitana, Departamento de Filosofia.

Lord, Andrew. 2005. *Spirit-Shaped Mission: A Holistic Charismatic Missiology*. Milton Keynes: Authentic Media.

Lord, Andy. 2012. *Network Church: A Pentecostal Ecclesiology Shaped by Mission*. Leiden: Brill.

Lovett, Leonard. 2007. *Kingdom Beyond Color: Re-examining the Phenomenon of Racism*. Higher Standard Publishers.

Ludwig, Frieder, and J. Kwabena Asamoah-Gyadu. 2011. *African Christian Presence in the West: New Immigrant Congregations and Transnational Networks in North America and Europe*. Trenton, NJ: Africa World Press.

Luhrmann, Tanya M. 2012. *When God Talks Back: Understanding the American Evangelical Relationship with God*. New York: Alfred A. Knopf.

Lukose, Wessly. 2006. "Dr. Thomas Mathews and His Contribution to Indian Missions." *Cross and Crown* 36 (1): 24–27.

Lukose, Wessly. 2009. "Pentecostal Beginnings in Rajasthan, India: Part One." *Asian Journal of Pentecostal Studies* 12 (2): 231–256.

Lukose, Wessly. 2013. *Pentecostalism in Rajasthan: Contextual Missiology of the Spirit*. Oxford: Regnum.

Lutherans and Pentecostals in Dialogue. 2010. Strasbourg: Institute for Ecumenical Research.

Luvis Núñez, Agustina. 2009. "Sewing a New Cloth: A Proposal for a Pentecostal Ecclesiology Fashioned as a Community Gifted by the Spirit with the Marks of the Church from a Latina Perspective." Dissertation, Lutheran School of Theology.

Lyall, Leslie T. 2004. *John Sung*. Singapore: Armour Publishing.

Ma, Julie C. 2002. "Korean Pentecostal Spirituality: A Case Study of Jashil Choi." *Asian Journal of Pentecostal Studies* 5 (2): 235–254.

Ma, Julie. 2019. "Influence of Pentecostal Spirituality to Asian Christianity." Paper Presented at an Annual International Ecumenical Summer Seminar, Strasburg France, July 3–10.

Ma, Li, and Jin Li. 2017. *Surviving the State, Remaking the Church: A Sociological Portrait of Christians in Mainland China*. Eugene, OR: Pickwick Publications.

Ma, Wonsuk, Daniel Chiquete, and Cephas N. Omenyo. 2010. "Theological Education in Pentecostal Churches." In *Handbook of Theological Education in World Christianity: Theological Perspectives – Regional Surveys – Ecumenical Trends*, edited by D. Werner, D. Esterline, N. Kang, and J. Raja, 729–749. Oxford, UK: Regnum.

Ma, Wonsuk, V-M. Kärkkäinen, and J.K. Asamoah-Gyadu, eds. 2014. *Pentecostal Mission and Global Christianity*. Oxford: Regnum.

Ma, Wonsuk, William W. Menzies, and Hyeonsung Bae, eds. 2016. *David Yonggi Cho: A Close Look at His Theology & Ministry*. Eugene, OR: Wipf and Stock.

Ma, Wonsuk, et al. 2018. "Oral Roberts Centennial." *Spiritus: ORU Journal of Theology* 3 (2): 157–388.

Macchia, Frank D. 1998. "Groans too Deep for Words: Towards a Theology of Tongues as

Initial Evidence." *Asian Journal of Pentecostal Studies* 1 (2): 149–73.

Macchia, Frank D. 2006. *Baptized in the Spirit: A Global Pentecostal Theology*. Grand Rapids: Zondervan.

Macchia, Frank. 1995. "From Azusa to Memphis: Evaluating the Racial Reconciliation Dialogue Among Pentecostals." *Pnuema* 1 (17): 203–218.

Macchia, Frank. 1996. "From Azusa to Memphis: Where Do We Go From Here? Roundtable Discussions on the Memphis Colloquy." *Pneuma* 1 (18): 113–140.

Măcelaru, Marcel V. 2016. "Holistic Mission in Post-Communist Romania: A Case Study on the Growth of the 'Elim' Pentecostal Church of Timișoara (1990–1997)." In *Mission in Central and Eastern Europe: Realities, Perspectives, Trends*, edited by Corneliu Constantineanu, Marcel V. Măcelaru, Anne-Marie Kool, and Mihai Himcinschi, 327–44. Oxford: Regnum Books.

MacGregor, Kirk R. 2007. "The Word-Faith Movement: A Theological Conflation of the Nation of Islam and Mormonism?" *Journal of the American Academy of Religion* 75 (1): 87–120.

Machado Jr., Celso. 2018. "Market as Religion: The Dynamics of Business Network of Megachurches." *Brazilian Business Review* 15 (3): 262–283.

Machado, Carly Barboza. 2014. "Pentecostalismo e o sofrimento do (ex-)bandido: testemunhos, mediações, modos de subjetivação e projetos de cidadania nas periferias." *Horizontes Antropológicos* 20 (42): 153–180.

Machia, Frank D. 2010. *Justified in the Spirit: Creation, Redemption, and the Triune God*. Grand Rapids: Eerdmans.

Machingura, F. 2011. "The Significance of Glossolalia in the Apostolic Faith Mission, Zimbabwe." *Studies in World Christianity* 17 (1): 12–29.

MacNicol, Nicol, and Vishal Mangalwadi. 1996. *What Liberates a Woman?* New Delhi: Pritha Offsets Pvt. Ltd.

MacNutt, Francis. 2005. *The Healing Reawakening: Reclaiming Our Lost Inheritance*. Grand Rapids: Chosen.

MacRobert, Iain. 1988. *The Black Roots and White Racism of Early Pentecostalism in the USA*. London: MacMillan.

Maddox, M. 2012. "'In the Goofy parking lot': Growth Churches as a Novel Religious Form for Late Capitalism." *Social Compass* 59 (2): 146–158.

Madzokere, N., and F. Machingura. 2015. "True and False Prophets/esses in the Light of Prophets/esses and Wonders in Zimbabwe." *Journal of Critical Southern Studies* 3: 53–71.

Mafra, Clara. 2002. *Na Posse da Palavra: Religião, Conversão e Liberdade Pessoal em dois Contextos Nacionais*. Lisboa: Imprensa de Ciências Sociais.

Mafra, Clara, Claudia Swatowiski, and Camila Sampaio. 2013. "Edir Macedo's Pastoral Project: A Globally Integrated Pentecostal Network." In *The Diaspora of Brazilian Religions*, edited by Cristina Rocha, and Manuel Vásquez, 45–67. Leiden: Brill.

Mager, Anne and Gary Minkley. 1990. "Reaping the Whirlwind: The Easter London Riots of 1952." Presented at History Workshop on February 6–10, 1990, available at the Wits Africana Library.

Magowan, Fiona, and Carolyn Schwarz, eds. 2016. *Christianity, Conflict, and Renewal in Australia and the Pacific*. Leiden: Brill.

Magowan, Fiona. 2007. "Globalisation and Indigenous Christianity: Translocal Sentiments in Australian Aboriginal Christian Songs." *Identities: Global Studies in Culture and Power* 14 (4): 459–483.

Malcomson, Keith. 2008. *Pentecostal Pioneers Remembered: British and Irish Pioneers of Pentecost*. Maitland: Xulon Press.

Maltese, Giovanni. 2017. *Pentekostalismus, Politik Und Gesellschaft in den Philippinen*. Religion in der Gesellschaft 42. Baden-Baden: Ergon.

Maltese, Giovanni. 2019. "Reproductive Politics and Populism: Pentecostal Religion and

Hegemony in the Philippines." *Journal of Law and Religion* 34 (1): 64–84.

Maltese, Giovanni, Judith Bachmann, and Katja Rakow. 2019. "Negotiating Evangelicalism and Pentecostalism: Global Entanglements, Identity Politics and the Future of Pentecostal Studies." *PentecoStudies* 18 (1): 7–19.

Mandryk, Jason. 2010. *Operation World*, Seventh edition. Colorado Springs, CO: Biblica Publishing.

Mangena, F. and Mhizha, S. 2013. "The Rise of White Collar Prophecy in Zimbabwe: A Psycho-Ethical Statement." In *Prophets, Profits and the Bible in Zimbabwe*, edited by E. Chitando, R.M. Gunda, and J. Kugler, 133–150. Bamberg: University of Bamberg Press.

Mansilla, Miguel, A. 2011. "El pentecostalismo clasico y el neopentecostalismo en America Latina." In *fe y pueblo. Nada es imposible para Dios. Una ventana a la fe neopentecostal*, no. 18, 6–22. La Paz, Bolivia: ISEAT.

Mapuranga, T., E. Chitando, and R.M. Gunda. 2013. "Studying the United Family International Church in Zimbabwe: The Case for Applying Multiple Approaches to the Study of Religion and Religious Phenomena." In *Prophets, profits and the Bible in Zimbabwe*, edited by E. Chitando, R.M. Gunda, and J. Kugler, 290–321. Bamberg: University of Bamberg Press.

Mariano, Ricardo. 1999. *Neopentecostais: sociologia do novo pentecostalismo no Brasil*. São Paulo: Loyola.

Marina, Peter. 2016. *Chasing Religion in the Caribbean*. New York, NY: Palgrave.

Marongwe, N., and Maposa, R.S. 2015. "PHDs, Gospreneurship, Globalisation, and the Pentecostal 'New Wave' in Zimbabwe." *Afro-Asian Journal of Social Sciences* 4 (1): 1–22.

Márquez Delgado, Luciano. 1997. "El Carismatismo: ¿Qué es y qué tenemos que ver con eso?" In *Carismatismo en Cuba*, edited by Reinerio Arce Valentín, and Manuele Quintero, compiled by Elizabeth Carrillo, 107–114. La Habana: Ediciones CLAI.

Marshall, Kimberly. 2016. *Upward, Not Sunwise: Resonant Rupture in Navajo Neo-Pentecostalism*. Lincoln, NB: University of Nebraska Press.

Marshall, Ruth. 2009. *Political Spiritualities. The Pentecostal Revolution in Nigeria*. Chicago: University of Chicago Press.

Marti, Gerardo. 2017. "The Global Phenomenon of Hillsong Church: An Initial Assessment." *Sociology of Religion* 78 (4): 377–386.

Martin, Bernice. 2001. "The Pentecostal Gender Paradox: A Cautionary Tale for the Sociology of Religion." In *The Blackwell Companion to Sociology of Religion*, edited by Richard K. Fenn, 52–66. Oxford: Blackwell Publishing Ltd.

Martin, David. 1990. *Tongues of Fire: The Explosion of Protestantism in Latin America*. Oxford: Blackwell.

Martin, David. 2002. *Pentecostalism: The World Their Parish*. Oxford: Blackwell.

Martin, Larry. 1997. *The Topeka Outpouring of 1901: Eyewitness Accounts of the Revival that Birthed the 20th Century Pentecostal/Charismatic Movement*. Joplin, MO: Christian Life Books.

Martin, Larry. 1999. *The Life and Ministry of William J. Seymour and a History of the Azusa Street Revival*. Joplin, MO: Christian Life Books.

Martin, Lee Roy, ed. 2013. *Pentecostal Hermeneutics: A Reader*. Leiden: Brill.

Martin, Lee Roy, ed. 2015. *Toward a Pentecostal Theology of Preaching*. CPT Press.

Martín-Arroyo, Manuel, and Paulo Branco. 2011. "The Development Of The Pentecostal Movement In Iberia (Spain & Portugal)." In *European Pentecostalism*, edited by William Kay and Anne Dyer, 165–188. Leiden: Brill.

Martino, David. 1986. "The Emergence and Historical-Theological Development of the Christian Church of North America."

Master's thesis, Ashland Theological Seminary.

Maskens, Maïte and Joël Noret. 2007. "La Nouvelle Jérusalem. Éléments d'histoire et de sociologie d'une Église pentecôtiste en Belgique." *Le Figueur* 1: 117–37.

Mason, Elsie. 1979. *The Man: Charles Harrison Mason (1866–1961)*. Memphis, TN: Church of God in Christ International Publishing House.

Massey, Richard. 1992. *Another Springtime: Donald Gee Pentecostal Pioneer, a Biography*. Guildford: Highland Books.

Mayfield, Alex. 2017. "'A Gloriously Free Work': Pentecostal POWs and Spirit-Filled Resistance." Unpublished paper read to the American Academy of Religion, Boston, MA.

Mayrargue, Cédric. 2002. *Dynamiques Religieuses et Démocratisation au Bénin. Pentecôtisme et Formation d'un Espace Public*. Thèse de Doctorat en Science Politique, Bordeaux: CEAN, Université de Bordeaux.

Mayrargue, Cédric. 2005. "Dynamiques Transnationales et Mobilisations Pentecôtistes dans l'Espace Publique Béninois." In *Entreprises Religieuses Transnationales en Afrique de l'Ouest*, edited by Laurent Fouchard, André Mary and René Otayek, 243–265. Ibadan, Paris: IFRA, Karthala.

Mbiti, John. 1986. *Bible and Theology in African Christianity*. Nairobi: Oxford University Press.

McClung, L. Grant, ed. 1986. *Azusa Street and Beyond: Pentecostal Missions and Church Growth in the Twentieth Century*. South Plainfield, NJ: Logos.

McClymond, Michael J. 2014. "Charismatic Renewal and Neo-Pentecostalism: From American Origins to Global Permutations." In *The Cambridge Companion to Pentecostalism*, edited by Cecil M. Robeck and Amos Yong, 31–51. Cambridge, UK: Cambridge University Press.

McClymond, Michael J. 2016. "Charismatic Gifts: Healing, Tongue-Speaking, Prophecy, and Exorcism." In *Wiley-Blackwell Companion to World Christianity*, edited by Lamin Sanneh and Michael J. McClymond, 399–418. Oxford: Wiley-Blackwell.

McClymond, Michael J. 2016. "Christian Revival and Renewal Movements," In *Wiley-Blackwell Companion to World Christianity*, edited by Lamin Sanneh and Michael J. McClymond, 244–262. Oxford: Wiley-Blackwell.

McClymond, Michael J., ed. 2007. *Encyclopedia of Religious Revivals in America*. 2 vols. Westport, CT: Greenwood Press.

McConnell, Dan R. 1988. *A Different Gospel: A Historical and Biblical Analysis of the Modern Faith Movement*. Peabody, MA: Hendrickson Publishers.

McCoy, Michael R. 1989. "Oral Roberts." In *Twentieth-Century Shapers of American Popular Religion*, edited by Chareles Lippy, 342–349. New York: Greenwood Press.

McGee, Gary B. 1989. *This Gospel Shall Be Preached: A History and Theology of Assemblies of God Foreign Missions*, volume 2. Springfield, MO: Gospel Publishing House.

McGee, Gary B., ed. 1991. *Initial Evidence: Historical and Biblical Perspectives on the Pentecostal Doctrine of Spirit Baptism*. Peabody: Hendrickson.

McGee, Gary B. 1999. "Baptism of the Holy Ghost and Fire: The Mission Legacy of Minnie F Abrams." *Missiology* 27 (4): 515–522.

McGee, Gary B. 2002. "Luce, Alice Eveline." In *The New International Dictionary of Pentecostal and Charismatic Movements*, edited by Stanley M. Burgess, and Eduard M. van der Maas, 543–544. Grand Rapids: Zondervan.

McGee, Gary B. 2004. *People of the Spirit: The Assemblies of God*. Springfield, MO: Gospel Publishing House.

McGee, Gary B. 2010. *Miracles, Missions, and American Pentecostalism*. Maryknoll, NY: Orbis Books.

McGee, Gary B. 2014. *People of the Spirit*. Springfield, MI: Gospel Publishing House.

McGuire, Meredith B. 2002. *Religion: The Social Context*. Fifth Edition. Belmont, CA: Wadsworth Thomson.

McMullen, Joshua J. 2010. "Maria B. Woodworth-Etter: Bridging the Wesleyan-Pentecostal Divide." In *Aldersgate to Azusa: Wesleyan, Holiness, and Pentecostal Visions of the New Creation*, edited by Henry H. Knight, III, 185–193. Eugene, OR: Pickwick.

McNair Scott, Benjamin G. 2017. *Apostles Today: Making Sense of Contemporary Charismatic Apostolates: A Historical and Theological Appraisal*. Eugene, OR: Wipf & Stock.

McPherson, Aimee Semple. 1923. *This is That: Personal Experiences, Sermons, and Writings*. Los Angeles: Echo Park Evangelistic Association.

McQueen, Larry R. 2012. *Toward a Pentecostal Eschatology: Discerning the Way Forward*. Blandford Forum: Deo Publishing.

Medina, Néstor. 2011. "Pentecostal Eschatology in Guatemala." Paper presented at the Theology Symposium on Eschatology. Society of Pentecostal Studies: Receiving the Future: An Anointed Heritage. Memphis.

Medina, Néstor. 2016. "Renovación / Renewal and the Social Context in Guatemala: The Changing Theological Tides." In *Global Renewal Christianity: Spirit-Empowered Movements Past, Present, and Future, Vol. 2, Latin America*, edited by Vinson Synan, Miguel Álvarez, and Amos Yong, 25–37. Lake Mary, FL: Charisma House Publishers.

Medina, Néstor, and Ary Fernández-Albán. 2018. "Christianity in Cuba." In *Encyclopedia of Christianity in the Global South*, edited by Mark A. Lamport, with an introduction by Philip Jenkins, with a foreword by Katalina Tahaafe-Williams, with an afterword by Justin Welby, et al. Landham: Rowman & Littlefield Publishers.

Medina, Néstor, and Sammy Alfaro, eds. 2015. *Pentecostals and Charismatics in Latin America and Latino Communities*. New York: Palgrave Macmillan.

Medina, Néstor, and Sammy Alfaro, eds. 2015. *Pentecostals and Charismatics in Latin America and Latino Communities*. New York: Palgrave Macmillan.

Mehta, Rama. 1970. *The Western Educated Hindu Woman*. Bombay: Asia Publishing House.

Meloon, M. 1974. *Ivan Spencer: Willow in the Wind*. Plainfield, NJ: Logos International.

Melton, J. Gordon. 2017. "Pentecostalism Comes to China: Laying the Foundations for a Chinese Version of Christianity." In *Global Chinese Pentecostal and Charismatic Christianity*, edited by Fenggang Yang, Joy K.C. Tong, and Allan H. Anderson, 43–62. Leiden: Brill.

Menzies, Robert P. 2016. *Speaking in Tongues: Jesus and the Apostolic Church as Models for the Church Today*. Cleveland, TN: CPT.

Menzies, W.W. 1971. *Anointed to Serve: The Story of the Assemblies of God*. Springfield, MO: Gospel Publishing House.

Mercado, Moisés M. 2002. *Denominaciones cristianas no católicas en Bolivia: Una aproximación tipológica desde las divisiones del cristianismo del siglo XVI*. La Paz: Presencia.

Merryweather, Frank. 1998. "Setting the Record Straight: A Reconstruction of the Rift that Developed between the PAOC and George R. Hawtin and his Supporters." Interview by Jim Craig. Pentecostal Assemblies of Canada Archives.

Meyer, Birgit. 1998. "'Make a Complete Break with the Past.' Memory and Post-Colonial Modernity in Ghanaian Pentecostalist Discourse." *Journal of Religion in Africa* 28 (3): 316–349.

Meyer, Birgit. 1999. *Translating the Devil: Religion and Modernity among the Ewe in Ghana*. Edinburgh: Edinburgh University Press.

Meyer, Birgit, ed. 2009. *Aesthetic Formations: Media, Religion, and the Senses*. London: Palgrave Macmillan.

Meyer, Birgit. 2015. *Sensational Movies. Video, Vision, and Christianity in Ghana*. Berkeley, CA: University of California Press.

Meyer, Birgit, and Annelies Moors, eds. 1999. *Religion, Media and the Public Sphere*. Indianapolis: Indiana University Press.

Michaels, J.M. 1988. "Gifts of the Spirit." In *Dictionary of Pentecostal and Charismatic Movements*, edited by Stanley M. Burgess and Gary B. McGee, 332–334. Grand Rapids, MI: Zondervan.

Michel, David. 2019. "Toward an Ecclesiology of Racial Reconciliation: A Pentecostal Perspective." PhD diss., Chicago Theological Seminary.

Miller, Donald and Tetsunao Yamamori. 2007. *Global Pentecostalism: The New Face of Christian Social Engagement*. Berkeley: University of California Press.

Miller, Donald E., Kimon H. Sargeant, and Richard Flory, eds. 2013. *Spirit and Power: The Growth and Global Impact of Pentecostalism*. Oxford: Oxford University Press.

Miller, Eric, and Ronald J. Morgan. 2019. *Brazilian Evangelicalism in the Twenty-First Century: An Inside and Outside Look*. Cham, Switzerland: Palgrave Macmillan.

Miller, Thomas William. 1986. "The Canadian 'Azusa': The Hebden Mission in Toronto." *Pneuma* 8 (1): 5–29.

Miller, Thomas William. 1994. *Canadian Pentecostals: A History of the Pentecostal Assemblies of Canada*. Mississauga: Full Gospel Publishing House.

Milles, J.N. 1922. "The Cause of Changes in Korea." *The Missionary Review of the World* (February): 115–118.

Mills, C. Wright. 1959. *The Sociological Imagination*. New York: Oxford University Press.

Milton, Grace. 2015. *Shalom, the Spirit and Pentecostal Conversion*. Leiden: Brill.

Miran-Guyon, Marie. 2015. *Guerres Mystiques en Côte d'Ivoire. Religion, Patriotisme, Violence (2002–2013)*. Paris, Karthala.

Miskov, Jennifer A. 2012. *Life on Wings: The Forgotten Life and Theology of Carrie Judd Montgomery (1858–1946)*. Cleveland, TN: CPT Press.

Mittelstadt, Martin William. 2010. *Reading Luke-Acts in the Pentecostal Tradition*. Cleveland, TN: CPT Press.

Moberg, Jessica, and Jane Skjoldli, eds. 2018. *Charismatic Christianity in Finland, Norway, and Sweden: Case Studies in Historical and Contemporary Developments*. Cham, Switzerland: Palgrave Macmillan.

Mod'oroši, Ivan. 2012. Book Reviews. *Ľubomír Martin Ondrášek, Neocharizmatické hnutie na Slovensku: Analýza základných aspektov teológie a praxe Kresťanských spoločenstiev* [The Neocharismatic Movement in Slovakia: an Analysis of the Fundamental Aspects of Theology and Practice of the Christian Fellowship]. (Bratislava, Slovakia: Institute for State-Church Relations, 2011), 267 pp. *Pneuma* 34 (3): 431–432. DOI: 10.1163/15700747-12341240.

Molenaar, William. 2011. "The World Assemblies of God Fellowship: United in the Missionary Spirit," *Assemblies of God Heritage* (March): 40–47.

Monléon, Albert Marie de. 1995. *Charismes et ministères dans l'Écriture et l'expérience de l'Église*. Collection Chemins ouverts; Paris: Éditions Desclée de Brouwer.

Monléon, Albert Marie de. 1995. *Jésus-Christ est Seigneur: il est toute nouveauté, le même hier, aujourd'hui et pour les siècles*. Preface by Robert Coffy, new edition. Paris: Éditions de l'Emmanuel.

Monléon, Albert Marie de. 1998. *Rendez témoignage: le renouveau charismatique catholique*. Paris: Mame.

Monléon, Albert Marie de. 2014. *Sur les pas du Christ*. Paris: Parole et silence.

Monléon, Albert Marie de. 2015. *Au coeur de la miséricorde*, Second Edition. Paris: Parole et silence.

Montañes, Antonio. 2016. "Etnicidad e identidad gitana en los cultos pentecostales de la ciudad de Madrid. El caso de la 'Iglesia Evangélica de Filadelfia' y el 'Centro Cristiano Vino Nuevo el Rey Jesús.'" *Papeles del*

CEIC. *International Journal on Collective Identity Research* 2016 (2): 1–26.

Monteiro, João Mateus. 1997. "The Church of the Nazarene in Cape Verde: a Religious Import in a Creole Society." PhD thesis, New Jersey, Drew University.

Monteiro, Yara Nogueira. 2010. "Congregação Cristã no Brasil: da fundação ao centenário, a trajetória de uma igreja brasileira." *Estudos de Religião* 24 (9): 122–163.

Montgomery, Carrie Judd. 1936. *Under His Wings: The Story of My Life.* Los Angeles, CA: Stationers Corporation.

Moon, Tony G. 2017. *From Ploughboy to Pentecostal Pulpit: The Life of J.H. King.* Lexington KY: Emeth.

Moore, Darnell L. 2011. "Constructing Gender: Old Wine in New Media(skins)." *Pneuma* 33 (2): 254–270.

Moore, S. David. 2003. *The Shepherding Movement: Controversy and Charismatic Ecclesiology.* London: T&T Clark.

Moore, S. David. 2012. "'Discerning the Times': The Victorious Eschatology of the Shepherding Movement." In *Perspectives in Pentecostal Eschatology*, edited by Peter Althouse and Robby Waddel, 273–292. Cambridge: James Clarke & Co.

Mora, G. Cristina. 2008. "Marketing the 'Health and Wealth Gospel' Across National Borders: Evidence from Brazil and the United States" *Poetics* 36 (5/6): 404–420.

Moravčíková, Michaela, and Eleonóra Valová, eds. 2010. *Financing Churches and Religious Societies in the 21st Century.* Institute for State-Church Relations, Bratislava: SVK.

Morgan, L.F. 2002. "Cook Robert F." In *The New International Dictionary of Pentecostal and Charismatic Movements*, edited by Stanley M. Burgess and Eduard M. van der Maas, 305–306. Grand Rapids: Zondervan.

Morrison, Hugh, Lachy Paterson, Brett Knowle,s and Murray Rae, eds. 2012. *Mana Māori and Christianity.* Wellington: Huia Publishers.

Morton, Barry. 2017. "Elias Letwaba, the Apostolic Faith Mission, and the Spread of Black Pentecostalism in South Africa." *Studia Historiae Ecclesiasticae* 43 (3): 1–17.

Morton, Barry. 2017. "Yes, John G. Lake Was a Con Man: A Response to Marius Nel." *Studia Historiae Ecclesiasticae* 43 (2): 1–23. http://dx.doi.org/10.17159/2412-4265/2016/1821.

Mozer, Pavel, and Oleg Bornovolokov. 2011. "The Development of Pentecostalism in Russia and the Ukraine." In *European Pentecostalism*, edited by William K. Kay and Anne E. Dyer, 261–289. Leiden: Brill.

Mpofu, S. 2013. "The 'Third Wave' Religious Right Movement and the Growth of Zimbabwean Christianity: Faith or Economic Response?" PhD thesis, University of Pretoria, South Africa.

Mukwakwama, L. 2010. *Our Subtle Christianity.* West-Lake: Book Surge.

Mullins, Mark R. 1990. "Japan Pentecostalism and the World of the Dead: A Study of Cultural Adaptation in Iesu no Mitama Kyokai." *Japanese Journal of Religious Studies* 17 (4): 353–374.

Mun, Seong-Mo. 2010. *The Story of Pastor Ha Yong-Jo: With Onnuri Community Church and Its Vision 'Acts 29'.* Seoul: Durano.

Murphy, Karen. 2018. *Pentecostals and Roman Catholics on Becoming a Christian: Spirit-Baptism, Faith, Conversion, Experience, and Discipleship in Ecumenical Perspective.* Leiden: Brill.

Muse, Dan T. 1946. "'I Have Fought A Good Fight,'" *Pentecostal Holiness Advocate* 30, no. 4 (May 23): 3.

Mwaura, P.N. 2004. "African Instituted Churches in East Africa." *Studies in Third World Christianity* 10 (2): 160–184.

Myung sung-Hoon, and Young-Gi Hong, eds. 2003. *Charis and Charisma: David Yonggi Cho and the Growth of Yoido Full Gospel Church.* Oxford: Regnum.

N.a. *fe y pueblo. Nada es imposible para Dios. Una ventana a la fe neopentecostal.* 2011. No 18. La Paz, Bolivia: ISEAT.

N'Guessan, Konstanze. 2015. "Pentecostalism, Politics and Performances of the Past in Côte d'Ivoire." *Nova Religio* 18 (3): 80–100.

Nagib, Tharwat. 2016. "The Neo-Charismatic Movement in Egypt." In *Global Renewal Christianity Spirit-Empowered Movements: Past, Present and Future*, edited by Vinson Synan, Amos Yong, and J. Kwabena Asamoah-Gyadu, 93–108. Lake Mary, FL: Charisma House.

Napolitano, Carmine. 1999. "Il pensiero di Giuseppe Petrelli: Per una storia del movimento pentecostale italiano". In *Movimenti popolari evangelici nei secoli XIX e XX*, edited by Domenico Maselli, 94–153. Prato: Fedeltà.

Napolitano, Carmine. 2015. *Giuseppe Petrelli: teologo pentecostale delle origini*. Aversa: Charisma.

Naso, Paolo. 2013. "Protestanti, Evangelici, Testimoni e Santi." In *Le religioni nell'Italia che cambia: Mappe e bussole*, edited by Enzo Pace, 97–130. Rome: Carocci.

Nel, Marius. 2015. "Remembering and Commemorating the Theological Legacy of John G. Lake in South Africa After a Hundred Years." *Studia Historae Ecclesiasticae* 41 (2): 147–170.

Nel, Marius. 2016. "'John G. Lake as a Fraud, Con Man and False Prophet': Critical Assessment of a Historical Evaluation of Lake's Ministry." *Studia Historiae Ecclesiasticae* 42 (1): 1–24. http://dx.doi.org/10.17159/2412-4265/2016/1134.

Nešpor, Z.R., and Z. Vojtíšek. 2015. *Encyklopedie menších křestanských církví v České republice*. Praha: Karolinum Publishers.

Neuman, H. Terris. 1990. "Cultic Origins of Word-Faith Theology Within the Charismatic Movement." *Pneuma* 12 (1): 32–55.

Neumann, Peter D. 2012. *Pentecostal Experience: An Ecumenical Encounter*. Eugene, OR: Pickwick.

Newberg, Andrew B., Nancy A. Wintering, Donna Morgan, and Mark R. Waldman. 2006. "The Measurement of Regional Cerebral Blood Flow During Glossolalia: A Preliminary SPECT Study." *Psychiatry Research: Neuroimaging* 148 (1): 67–71. doi:10.1016/j.pscychresns.2006.07.001.

Newberg, Eric N. 2012. *The Pentecostal Mission in Palestine: The Legacy of Pentecostal Zionism*. Eugene, OR: Pickwick.

Newell, Sasha. 2007. "Pentecostal Witchcraft: Neoliberal Possession and Demonic Discourse in Ivoirian Pentecostal Churches." *Journal of Religion in Africa* 37: 461–490.

Newman, Joe. 2005. *Race and the Assemblies of God: The Journey from Azusa Street to the "Miracle Memphis"*. Youngstown, NY: Cambria Press.

Ngarsouledé, Abel. 2016. *Enjeux sociologiques et théologiques de la sécularisation: Une étude de cas à N'Djaména en République du Tchad*. Langham Monographs.

Nicastro, Patrizia. 2015. "Origini delle storie del movimento pentecostale italiano: le Assemblee di Dio in Italia." Doctoral dissertation, Università degli Studi di Bergamo.

Nikolov, Nicholas. *Ministry File and Periodical Mentions*. Flower Pentecostal Heritage Center.

Nolivos, Eloy H. 2012. "Capitalism and Pentecostalism in Latin America: Trajectories of Prosperity and Development." In *Pentecostalism and Prosperity: The Socio-Economics of the Global Charismatic Movement*, edited by Katherine Attanasi and Amos Yong, 87–106. New York: Palgrave MacMillan.

Nonini, Rogelio. 1985. *Conclusiones sobre la campaña en San Justo*. Zona Oeste Jesús te ama, No1 (Mazo, 1985).

Norris, David S. 2009. *I AM: A Oneness Pentecostal Theology*. Hazelwood, MO: Word Aflame Press.

Norton, Barbara. 1909. "Testimony: Mrs. John Norton." *Jehovah-Jireh, A Witness to Christ's Faithfulness* 1, no. 4 (December).

Norton, J.E. 1912. "A Sketch of Mrs. Barbara Norton." *At The Roll Call* (April): 10–12.

Ntarangwi, Mwenda. 2016. *The Street is My Pulpit: Hip Hop and Christianity in Kenya*. Champaign: University of Illinois Press.

Núñez, Miguel Atilio. 2004. *Historia de la Iglesia de Dios en el Paraguay*. Asunción: Iglesia de Dios del Paraguay.

O'Byrne, Ryan Joseph. 2016. "Becoming Christian: Personhood and Moral Cosmology in Acholi South Sudan." PhD thesis, University College London.

O'Connor, E. 1971. *The Pentecostal Movement in the Catholic Church*. Notre Dame: Ava Maria Press.

O'Neill, Kevin Lewis. 2009. *City of God: Christian Citizenship in Postwar Guatemala*. Berkeley, CA: University of California Press.

O'Neill, Kevin Lewis. 2010. *City of God: Christian Citizenship in Postwar Guatemala*. Berkeley: University of California Press.

Oak, Sung-Deuk. 2012. "Major Protestant Revivals in Korea, 1903–35." *Studies in World Christianity* 18 (3): 269–290.

Obadare, Ebenezer. 2018. *Pentecostal Republic: Religion and the Struggle for State Power in Nigeria*. London, UK: Zed Books.

Offutt, Stephen. 2015. *New Centers of Global Evangelicalism in Latin America and Africa*. Cambridge: Cambridge University Press.

Ogbu, Kalu. 2008. *African Pentecostalism: An Introduction*. Oxford: Oxford University Press.

Ogouby, Laurent O.A.G. 2011. *Le Développement du Protestantisme Évangélique et Pentecôtiste au Benin de 1990 a nos Jours*. Thèse de doctorat en Sciences Religieuses. Paris: EPHE.

Ojo, Matthews A. 1988. "Deeper Christian Life Ministry: A Case Study of The Charismatic Movements in Western Nigeria." *Journal of Religion in Africa* 18 (2): 141–162.

Ojo, Matthews A. 2006. *The End-time Army: Charismatic Movements in Nigeria*. Trenton, NJ: Africa World Press.

Okyerefo, Michael Perry Kweku. 2014. "African Churches in Europe." *Journal of Africana Religions* 2 (1): 95–124.

Olajide Jatto. 2017. "The Changing Face of Christianity in Ireland." *Vox Magazine* 34 (April–June): 12–13. http://www.vox.ie/001/2017/4/11/the-changing-face-of-christianity-in-ireland.

Olayan, Hamza. 2017. *Christians in Kuwait*, translated by Salama M. Issa. Kuwait: That Al-Salasil.

Olazábal Jr., Frank. Telephone Interview by Gastón Espinosa, May 1998.

Oliverio, L. William. 2012. *Theological Hermeneutics in the Classical Pentecostal Tradition: A Typological Account*. Leiden: Brill.

Olson, Gilbert W. 1969. *Church Growth in Sierra Leone: A Study of Church Growth in Africa's Oldest Protestant Mission Field*. Grand Rapids, MI: William B. Eerdmans.

Omahe, Chacha. 1970. "Life and Experience in the Lord's Ministry: From 1946–1970." Unpublished manuscript.

Omenyo, Cephas N. 2014. "African Pentecostalism." In *The Cambridge Companion to Pentecostalism*, edited by Cecil M. Robeck and Amos Yong, 132–151. New York: Cambridge University Press.

Omenyo, Cephas. 1994. "The Charismatic Renewal Movement in Ghana." *Pneuma* 15 (2): 169–185.

Omenyo, Cephas. 2002. *Pentecost Outside Pentecostalism: A Study of the Development of Charismatic Renewal in the Mainline Churches in Ghana*. Amsterdam: Boekencentrum.

Omi, M., and H. Winant. 1994. *Racial Formation in the United States from the 1960s to the 1990s*. Second Edition. New York: Routledge.

Ondrasek, Ľubomir Martin. 2009. "On Religious Freedom in the Slovak Republic." *Occasional Papers on Religion in Eastern Europe (OPREE)* 29 (3): 1–9.

Ondrasek, Ľubomir Martin. 2011. *Neocharizmatické hnutie na Slovensku: Analýza základných apektov teológie a praxe Kresťanských spoločenstiev*. Bratislava: Ústav pre vzťahy štátu a cirkví.

Onnnri Community Church. 2019. Accessed April 5, 2019. http://www.onnuri.org/about-onnuri/church-introduction/onnuris-history/.

Ono, Akiko. 2012. "You gotta throw away culture once you become Christian: How 'culture' is Redefined among Aboriginal Pentecostal

Christians in Rural New South Wales." *Oceania* 82 (1): 74–85.

Onyinah, Opoku, ed. 2004. *The Church of Pentecost: 50 Years of Sustainable Growth*. Accra: McKeon Memorial Lectures.

Onyinah, Opoku. 2002. "Akan Witchcraft and the Concept of Exorcism in the Church of Pentecost." PhD thesis, University of Birmingham, UK.

Onyinah, Opoku. 2012. *Pentecostal and Exorcism: Witchcraft and Demonology in Ghana*. Blandford: Deo Publishing.

Onyinah, Opoku. 2012. *Pentecostal Exorcism: Witchcraft and Demonology in Ghana*. Dorcet, UK: Deo Publishing.

Onyinah, Opoku. 2012. *Spiritual Warfare: A Centre for Pentecostal Theology Short Introduction*. Cleveland: CTP Publishing LTD.

Oosterbaan, Martijn. 2008. "Spiritual Attunement: Pentecostal Radio in the Soundscape of a Favela in Rio de Janeiro." *Social Text* 26 (3): 123–145.

Oosterbaan, Martijn. 2017. *Transmitting the Spirit: Religious Conversion, Media, and Urban Violence in Brazil*. University Park, PA: Pennsylvania State University Press.

Oosthuizen, G.C. 1987. *The Birth of Christian Zionism in South Africa*. Kwa Dlangezwa: University of Zululand.

Opp, James. 2005. *The Lord for the Body: Religion, Medicine, and Protestant Faith Healing in Canada, 1880–1930*. Montreal & Kingston: McGill-Queen's University Press.

Oro, A Pedro, and Pablo Semán. 2001. "Brazilian Pentecostalism Crosses National Borders." In *Between Babel and Pentecost: Transnational Pentecostalism in Africa and Latin America*, edited by Andre Corten and Ruth Marshall-Fratani, 181–195. Bloomington: Indiana University Press.

Osborn, H.H. 2000. *Pioneers in the East African Revival*. Apologia Publications.

Osborn, Tommy Lee. 1950. *Healing the Sick*. Tulsa: Harrison House Publishers.

Osborn, Tommy Lee and Daisy Osborn. 1985. *The Gospel according to T.L. & Daisy. Classic Documentary*. Tulsa: Osborn-Publishers.

Owens, Robert R. 2005. *The Azusa Street Revival: Its Roots and Its Message*. Maitland, FL: Xulon Press.

Pace, Enzo. 2018. "Religious Congregations in Italy: Mapping the New Pluralism." In *Congregations in Europe*, edited by Christophe Monnot and Joerg Stolz, 139–156. Cham: Springer.

Page, Lou. 1919. "In the Regions Beyond: Nadroga, Fiji." *The Christian Evangel: The Pentecostal Paper for the Home* 276 & 277 (February 22): 10.

Page, Lou. 1919. "In the Regions Beyond: Sister Lou Page writes..." *The Christian Evangel: The Pentecostal Paper for the Home* 278 & 279 (March 8): 10.

Palma, Paul. 2019. *Italian American Pentecostalism and the Struggle for Religious Identity*. New York: Routledge.

Paloutzian, Raymond F., and Crystal L. Park. 2013. *Handbook of the Psychology of Religion and Spirituality*, Second Edition. New York: Guilford Press.

Paracka, Daniel J., Jr. 2015. *Athens of West Africa: A History of International Education at Fourah Bay College*. Freetown, Sierra Leone: Routledge.

Parham, Charles F. 1902. *Kol Kare Bomidbar: A Voice Crying in the Wilderness*. Baxter Springs, KS: Apostolic Faith Bible College.

Parham, Charles F. 1910. *A Voice Crying in the Wilderness*. Rev. ed. Baxter Springs, KS: Apostolic Faith Bible College.

Parham, Sarah E., ed. 1985. *The Life of Charles F. Parham: Founder of the Apostolic Faith Movement*. New York, NY: Garland Publishing, Inc. Originally published in c.1930, Joplin, MO: Hunter Printing Co.

Park, Myung Soo. 2003. *Study on the Church Revival Movement in Korea*. [Hankukkyohoe taepuhŭnguntong yŏnku]. Seoul: Institute of the History of Christianity in Korea.

Park, Yong-Kyu. 1991. *A Biography of Rev. Kim Ik-Doo*. Seoul: The Word of Life Press

Park, Yong Kyu. 2005. *The Great Revivalism in Korea: Its History, Character, and Impact*.

1901–1910 [P'yŏngyang taepuhŭng untong]. Seoul: Word of Life Books.

Payne, Leah. 2015. *Gender and Pentecostal Revivalism: Making a Female Ministry in the Early Twentieth Century*. New York: Palgrave Macmillan.

PCCNA. n.d. "History". Accessed February 21st, 2020. http://www.pccna.org/about_history.aspx.

Peñaloza, C. 2011. *La Otra Cara de La Victoria: Un Impactante Testimonio de Fe Construido En Medio de La Muerte Del Sufrimiento*. Virginia, Estados Unidos: Ekklesia.

Peng, Suk Man. 2014. "Timothy Dzao," in *Biography of Hong Kong Christianity*. Hong Kong: The Hong Kong Chinese Christian Churches Union. 彭淑敏。〈趙世光〉。載《香港教會人物傳》。香港：香港華人基督教聯會出版部。

Pentecostal World Fellowship, https://www.pwfellowship.org/.

Pepper, Miriam, Rosemary Leonard, and Ruth Powell. 2013. "Denominational Identification, Church Participation, and Concern about Climate Change in Australia." In *Climate Change Cultural Change: Religious Responses and Responsibilities*, edited by Anne F. Elvey and David Gormley O'Brien, 35–47. Preston: Mosaic Press.

Perkins, Eunice M. 1921. *Joybringer Bosworth: His Life Story*. Detroit, MI: John J. Scruby.

Perrot, Etienne. 2008. "Les enjeux du Pentecôtisme africain." *Revue de Culture Contemporaine* 409 (7): 61–71.

Perry, David. 2017. *Spirit Baptism: The Pentecostal Experience in Theological Focus*. Leiden: Brill.

Petersen, Douglas. 2012. *Not by Might, Nor by Power: A Pentecostal Theology of Social Concern in Latin America*. Eugene, OR: Wipf and Stock.

Peterson D.R. 2012. *Ethnic Patriotism and the East African Revival*. Cambridge: Cambridge University Press.

Peterson, Douglas P. 2016. "Pentecostals in Costa Rica and Nicaragua: A Historical/Theological Perspective." In *Global Renewal Christianity*, vol. 2, edited by Vinson Synan, Amos Yong and Miguel Álvarez, 75–98. Lake Mary, FL: Charisma House.

Petrelli, Giuseppe. 1930. *Fra I due testamenti*. Bristol, PA: Merlo.

Petts, David. 1998. "The Baptism in the Holy Spirit: The Theological Distinctive." In *Pentecostal Perspectives*, edited by Keith Warrington, 98–119. Carlisle: Paternoster.

Pew Forum on Religion and Public Life. 2006. "Spirit and Power: A 10-Country Survey of Pentecostals," www.pewforum.org.

Pew Forum on Religion and Public Life. 2011. *Global Christianity: A Report on the Size and Distribution of the World Christian Population*, www.pewforum.org.

Pew Hispanic Center. 2007. *Changing Faiths: Latinos and the Transformation of American Religion*. Washington, D.C.: Pew Research Center.

Pew Research Center. 2014. "Religion in Latin America: Widespread Change in a Historically Catholic Region." (November 13).

Pfister, Raymond. 1995. *Soixante ans de pentecôtisme en Alsace (1930–1990): une approche socio-historique*. Frankfurt am Main: Lang.

Pfister, Raymond. 2011. "The Future(s) of Pentecostalism in Europe." In *European Pentecostalism*, edited by William Kay and Anne Dyer, 357–381. Leiden: Brill.

Philip, Mamman. 1997. *Robert F. Cook*. Vennukulam, India: Deepam Book Club.

Phillips, Coretta. 2011. "Institutional Racism and Ethnic Inequalities: An Expanded Multilevel Framework." *Journal of Social Policy* 40 (1): 173–192.

Phillips, Ron. 2011. *An Essential Guide to Speaking in Tongues*. Vol. 2, *Foundations of the Holy Spirit*. Lake Mary, FL: Charisma House.

Phillips, Wade H. 2014. *Quest to Restore God's House: A Theological History of the Church of God (Cleveland, Tennessee). Volume 1: 1886–1923: R.G. Spurling to A.J. Tomlinson,*

Formation-Transformation-Reformation. Cleveland, TN: CPT Press.

Pinn, Anthony. 2001. *Fortress Introduction to the Black Church*. Minneapolis, MN: Fortress Press.

Pinnock, Clark H. 1996. *Flame of Love: A Theology of the Holy Spirit*. Downers Grove, IL: Inter Varsity Press.

Pinsent, William Paul. 1998. "The Institutionalization of Experiential Religion: A Study of Newfoundland Pentecostalism." Master's thesis, Memorial University of Newfoundland, St. John's, Newfoundland.

Plett, Rodolfo. 1988. *El protestantismo en el Paraguay*. Asunción: FLET/IBA.

Poewe, Karla, ed. 1994. *Charismatic Christianity as a Global Culture*. Columbia, SC: University of South Carolina Press.

Poewe, Karla. 1988. "Links and Parallels Between Black and White Charismatic Churches in South Africa and the States: Potential for Cultural Transformation." *The Journal of the Society of Pentecostal Studies* 10 (2): 141–58.

Polhill, Cecil Henry. 1980. "A China Missionary's Witness." Donald Gee Archive. Doncaster, UK: Donald Gee Archive, Mattersey Hall.

Poloma, Margaret M. 1989. *The Assemblies of God at the Crossroads: Charisma and Institutional Dilemmas*. Knoxville, TN: The University of Tennessee Press.

Poloma, Margaret M. 2003. *Main Street Mystics: The Toronto Blessing & Reviving Pentecostalism*. Walnut Creek, CA: AltaMira.

Pope, Robert. 2006. "Demythologising the Evan Roberts Revival, 1904–1905." *Journal of Ecclesiastical History* 57 (3): 515–534.

Premawardhana, Devaka. 2012. "Transformational Tithing: Sacrifice and Reciprocity in a Neo-Pentecostal Church." *Nova Religio* 15 (4): 85–109.

Premawardhana, Devaka. 2018. *Faith in Flux: Pentecostalism and Mobility in Rural Mozambique*. Philadelphia, PA: University of Pennsylvania Press.

Price, Charles S. 1944. *The Story of My Life*. Pasadena: Charles S. Price Publishing Company.

Price, Lynne. 2002. *Theology Out of Place. A Theological Biography of Walter J. Hollenweger*. London: Sheffield Academic Press.

Prince, Derek. 2002 (1973). *Shaping History Through Prayer and Fasting*. Foreword by Lou Engle. New Kensington, PA: Whittaker House.

Prior, John Mansford. 2007. "The Challenge of the Pentecostals in Asia Part One: Pentecostal Movement in Asia." *Exchange* 36 (1): 6–40.

PTS. 2019. *Dr. Niko Njotorahardjo, Messenger of the 3rd Pentecost, Member of the Pentecostal Theological Seminary Board of Trustees*. https://vimeo.com/332504288.

Pulikottil, Paulson. 2002. "As East and West Met in God's Own Country: Encounter of Western Pentecostalism with Native Pentecostalism in Kerala." *Asian Journal of Pentecostal Studies* 5 (1): 5–22.

Purinton, William T. 2003. "W.H. Turner and the Chinese Pentecost." *Wesleyan Theological Journal* 38 (1): 226–241.

Purinton, William. 2003. "Joseph Hillary King's View and Use of Scripture in the Holiness/Pentecostal Context." PhD diss., Trinity Evangelical Divinity Seminary.

Pype, Katrien. 2012. *The Making of the Pentecostal Melodrama. Religion, Media, and Gender in Kinshasa*. New York / Oxford: Berghahn Books.

Pype, Katrien. 2015. "The Liveliness of Pentecostal-Charismatic Popular Culture in Africa." In *Pentecostalism in Africa: Presence and Impact of Pneumatic Christianity in Postcolonial Societies*, edited by M. Lindhardt, 345–378. Leiden: Brill.

Pytches, David. 1991. *Some Said It Thundered: A Personal Encounter with the Kansas City Prophets*. Nashville, TN: Oliver-Nelson.

Pytches, David, ed. 1998. *John Wimber: A Tribute*. Guildford, UK: Eagle.

Quebedeaux, Richard. 1983. *The New Charismatics II: How a Christian Renewal Movement*

Became Part of the American Religious Mainstream. San Francisco: Harper & Row.

Quiroz, Sitna. 2013. *Relating as Children of God: Ruptures and Continuities in Kinship among Pentecostal Christians in the South-East of the Republic of Benin.* PhD thesis, Social Anthropology, The London School of Economics and Political Science.

Quiroz, Sitna. 2016. "The Dilemmas of Monogamy: Pleasure, Discipline and the Pentecostal Moral Self in the Republic of Benin." *Religions* 7 (8): 102. https://doi.org/10.3390/rel7080102.

Quiroz, Sitna. 2016. "Seeking God's Blessings: Pentecostal Religious Discourses, Pyramidal Schemes and Money Scams in the Southeast of Benin Republic." In *Neoliberalism and the Moral Economy of Fraud*, edited by David Whyte, and Jörg Wiegratz, 170–183. Abingdon, Oxon: Routledge.

Ramabai, Pandita. 1887. *The High Caste Hindu Woman.* Philadelphia, PA: J.B. Rogers Printing Co.

Ramabai, Pandita. 1992. *A Testimony of Our Inexhaustible Tresure*, 11th ed. Bombay: G.L.S. Press.

Ramírez, Daniel. 2015. *Migrating Faith: Pentecostalism in the United States and Mexico in the Twentieth Century.* Chapel Hill, NC: The University of North Carolina Press.

Ramos, Max Ruben. 2015. "Missionários do Sul: evangelização, globalização e mobilidades dos pastores cabo-verdianos da Igreja do Nazareno." PhD thesis, Lisbon, Institute of Social Sciences, University of Lisbon.

Ramos, Max Ruben. 2016. "Cape Verde." In *Anthology of African Christianity*, edited by Phiri, Isabel Apawo, and Werner, Dietrich. Oxford: Regnum Books.

Ramos, Max Ruben 2018. "Cape Verde." In *Encyclopedia of Christianity in the Global South*, edited by Mark A. Lamport. Lanham: Rowman & Littlefield Publishers.

Ranaghan, Dorothy Garrity. 2018. *Blind Spot: War & Christian Identity.* Second Edition. New York: New City Press.

Ranaghan, Kevin. 1981. "The Church, the Spirit, and the Charismatic Renewal." *New Covenant* 11 (2): 10.

Ranaghan, Kevin, and Dorothy Ranaghan. 1969. *Catholic Pentecostals.* New York: Paulist Press.

Ranger, Terrence O. 2006. *Evangelical Christianity and Democracy in Africa.* Oxford: Oxford University Press.

Rasmussen, A.W. 1973. *The Last Chapter.* Monroeville, PA: Whitaker House.

Rasmussen, Kyler R., Madelynn Stackhouse, Susan D. Boon, Karly Comstock, and Rachel Ross. 2019. "Meta-analytic Connections Between Forgiveness and Health: The Moderating Effects of Forgiveness-related Distinctions." *Psychology & Health* 34 (5): 515–534 doi:10.1080/08870446.2018.1545906.

Rebuffo, Ricardo. 1999. *Historia de las Asambleas Cristianas de la República Argentina: Correspondencia intercambiada entre los hermanos Louis Francescón y Ricardo Rebuffo entre los años 1943 y 1947.* Buenos Aires: The Author.

Reed, David A. 2008. *"In Jesus' Name": The History and Beliefs of Oneness Pentecostals.* Blandford Forum, UK: Deo Publishing.

Reed, David A. 2009. "Denominational Charismatics – Where Have They All Gone? A Canadian Anglican Case Study." In *Canadian Pentecostalism: Transition and Transformation*, edited by Michael Wilkinson, 197–213. Montreal and Kingston: McGill-Queen's University Press.

Reed, David A. 2010. "Oneness Seeds on Canadian Soil: Early Developments of Oneness Pentecostalism." In *Winds From the North: Canadian Contributions to the Pentecostal Movement*, edited by Michael Wilkinson and Peter Althouse, 191–213. Leiden: Brill.

Reed, David. 2014. "The Many Faces of Global Oneness Pentecostalism." In *The Cambridge Companion to Pentecostalism*, edited by Cecil M. Robeck Jr. and Amos Yong, 52–70. Cambridge: Cambridge University Press.

Rees, Delwyn Vaughan. 1959. *The 'Jesus Family' in Communist China: A Modern Miracle of New Testament Christianity*. Exeter: Paternoster Press.

Reetzke, James. 2004. *Recollections with Thanksgiving: A Brief History of the Beginnings of the Lord's Recovery in the United States*. Chicago: Chicago Bibles and Books.

Resane, Kelebogile T. 2018. "Pentecostals and Apartheid: Has the Wheel Turned around Since 1994?" *In die Skriflig* 52 (1): 1–8. https://dx.doi.org/10.4102/ids.v52i1.2324.

Reu, Gum-Ju. 2002. "The Revival Movement of Korean Church Around 3.1 Independent Movement: With Special Reference to Gil Seon-Ju." *Theological Forum* 30: 297–318.

Ribay, Jean-Marie, and Rebecca Redon. 2007. *'Toi, vas-y !': Albert Burkhardt, missionnaire, homme de Dieu*. Dijon: EMF.

Rice, Jonathan W. 2014. "Ecology and the future of Pentecostalism: Problems, Possibilities and Proposals." In *Pentecostal Mission and Global Christianity*, edited by Wonsuk Ma, Veli-Matti Karkkainen, and J. Kwabena Asamoah-Gyadu, 360–379. Oxford: Regnum Books International.

Riches, Tanya. 2017. "(Re)imagining identity in the Spirit: Worship and Social Engagement in Urban Aboriginal-led Pentecostal Congregations." PhD thesis, Fuller Theological Seminary.

Riches, Tanya, and Tom Wagner. 2012. "The Evolution of Hillsong Music: From Australian Pentecostal Congregation into Global Brand." *Australian Journal of Communication* 39 (1): 17–36.

Riches, Tanya, and Tom Wagner, eds. 2017. *The Hillsong Movement Examined: You Call Me Out Upon the Waters*. New York: Palgrave McMillan.

Richie, Tony. 2011. *Speaking by the Spirit: A Pentecostal Model for Interreligious Dialogue*. Lexington, KY: Emeth.

Richie, Tony. 2013. *Toward a Pentecostal Theology of Religions: Encountering Cornelius Today*. Cleveland, TN: CPT.

Richmann, Christopher J. 2015. "William H. Durham and Early Pentecostalism: A Multifaceted Reassessment." *Pneuma* 37 (2): 224–243.

Riddell, Peter G., and Beverly Smith Riddell, eds. 2007. *Angels and Demons: Perspectives and Practice in Diverse Religious Traditions*. Nottingham: Apollos/IVP.

Rideout, F. David. 1992. *History of Pentecostal Schools in Newfoundland and Labrador*. St. John's, NL: Good Tidings.

Rio, Knut, Michelle MacCarthy, and Ruy Blanes, eds. 2017. *Pentecostalism and Witchcraft: Spiritual Warfare in Africa and Melanesia*. New York: Palgrave Macmillan.

Riss, R.M. 1982. "The Latter Rain Movement of 1948." *Pneuma* 4 (Spring): 32–45.

Riss, R.M. 1987. *Latter Rain: the Latter Rain Movement of 1948 and the mid-twentieth century evangelical awakening*. Mississauga: Honeycomb Visual Productions.

Riss, Richard M. 1987. *Latter Rain: The Latter Rain Movement of 1948 and the Mid-Twentieth Century Evangelical Awakening*. Etobicoke, ON: Honeycomb Visual Productions Ltd.

Riss, Richard M. 1988. *A Survey of 20th-Century Revival Movements in North America*. Peabody, MA: Hendrickson Publishers.

Riss, Richard M. 2002. "Osborn, Tommy Lee." In *The New International Dictionary of Pentecostal and Charismatic Movement*, edited by Stanley M. Burgess and Eduard M. van der Maas, 950–951. Grand Rapids: Zondervan.

Riubal, J.C. 1999. *Ungido para la cosecha del tiempo final*. Mami: Editorial Vida.

Rivera, Paulo Barrera. 2016. "Pentecostalism in Brazil." In *Handbook of Contemporary Religions in Brazil*, edited by Bettina Schmidt and Steven Engler, 117–131. Leiden: Brill.

Rivière, Gilles. 2005. "Cambios sociales y pentecostalismo en una comunidad aymara." In *De indio a hermano. Pentecostalismo indígena en américa latina*, edited by B. Jiménez, 329–354. Iquique, Chile: Ediciones Campus Universidad Arturo Prat.

Rivière, Gilles. 2007. "Bolivia: el pentecostalismo en la sociedad aimara del Altiplano". *Nuevo Mundo Mundos Nuevos*. Accessed May 8, 2019. https://journals.openedition.org/nuevomundo/6661.

Robbins, Joel. 2004. "The Globalization of Pentecostal and Charismatic Christianity." *Annual Review of Anthropology* 33: 117–143.

Robbins, Joel. 2004. *Becoming Sinners: Christianity and Moral Torment in a Papua New Guinea Society*. Berkeley CA: University of California Press.

Robbins, Joel. 2009. "Pentecostal Networks and the Spirit of Globalization: On the Social Productivity of Ritual Forms." *Social Analysis* 53 (1): 55–66. doi:10.3167/sa.2009.530104.

Robbins, Roger G., ed. 2018. "Special Issue: Global Trajectories in Global Pentecostalism: Culture, Social Engagement and Change." *Religion* 9: 368 et seq.

Robeck, Cecil M. 1985. "The Society for Pentecostal Studies." *Ecumenical Trends* 14 (2): 28–30.

Robeck, C.M. 2002. "Azusa Street Revival." In *New International Dictionary of Pentecostal and Charismatic Movements*, edited by S. Burgess and E. Van Der Maas. Grand Rapids: Zondervan.

Robeck, Cecil M. 2002. "Pentecostal World Conference (PWC)." In *The New International Dictionary of Pentecostal and Charismatic Movements*, edited by Stanley M. Burgess and Eduard M. van der Maas, 971–974. Grand Rapids, MI: Zondervan.

Robeck, Cecil M. 2002. "Seminaries and Graduate Schools." In *The New International Dictionary of Pentecostal Charismatic Movements*, edited by Stanley M. Burgess and Eduard M. van der Maas, 1045–1050. Grand Rapids, MI: Zondervan.

Robeck, Cecil M., Jr. 2002. "Pentecostal World Conference." In *The New International Dictionary of Pentecostal and Charismatic Movements*, edited by Stanley M. Burgess and Eduard M. van der Maas, 971–974. Grand Rapids, MI: Zondervan.

Robeck, Cecil M. 2006. *The Azusa Street Mission and Revival*. Nashville, TN: Thomas Nelson.

Robeck, Jr., Cecil M. 2012. "The Achievements of the Pentecostal-Catholic International Dialogue." In *Celebrating a Century of Ecumenism: Exploring the Achievements of International Dialogue*, edited by John A. Radano, 163–194. Grand Rapids, MI: Eerdmans.

Robeck, Jr., Cecil M. 2013."Launching a Global Movement: The Role of Azusa Street in Pentecostalism's Growth and Expansion." In *Spirit and Power: The Growth and Global Impact of Pentecostalism*, edited by Donald E. Miller, Kimon H. Sargeant, and Richard Flory, 42–64. New York: Oxford University Press.

Robeck, Cecil M., Jr. 2019. "Can We Imagine an Ecumenical Future Together? A Pentecostal Perspective," *Gregorianum* 100 (1): 49–69.

Robeck, Cecil M., Jr. 2020. "Pentecostal Ecclesiology." In *The T&T Clark Handbook of Ecclesiology*, edited by Kimlyn J. Bender and D. Stephen Long, 241–258. London: Bloomsbury.

Robeck, Jr., Cecil M. and Amos Yong, eds. 2014. *The Cambridge Companion to Pentecostalism*. Cambridge: Cambridge University Press.

Robert, Dana. 2009. *Christian Mission: How Christianity Became a World Religion*. Malden, MA: Wiley-Blackwell.

Roberts, Dave. 1994. *The Toronto Blessing*. Eastbourne: Kingsway Publications.

Roberts, Nathaniel. 2016. *To Be Cared For: The Power of Conversion and Foreigness of Belonging in an Indian Slum*. Berkeley, CA: University of California Press.

Roberts, Oral. 1952. *Oral Roberts' Life Story, As Told By Himself*. Tulsa, OK.

Roberts, Oral. 1972. *The Call: An Autobiography*. Garden City, NY: Doubleday.

Roberts, Oral. 1995. *Expect a Miracle: My Life and Ministry*. Nashville, TN: Thomas Nelson.

Robinson, A.E. 1934. "'In Labors More Abundant.'" *Pentecostal Holiness Advocate* 18, no. 36 (January 10): 9–10.

Robinson, James. 2005. *Pentecostal Origins: Early Pentecostalism in Ireland in the Context of the British Isles.* Milton Keynes: Paternoster.

Robinson, James. 2013. *Divine Healing: The Holiness-Pentecostal Transition Years, 1890–1906: Theological Transpositions in the Transatlantic World.* Eugene, OR: Wipf and Stock Publishers.

Robinson, Mark. 2008. "Pentecostalism in Urban Java: A Study of Religious Change, 1980–2006." PhD diss., University of Queensland.

Rocha, Cristina, Mark P. Hutchinson, and Kathleen Openshaw, eds. 2020. *Australian Pentecostal and Charismatic Movements.* Leiden: Brill.

Röckle, Bernhard, and William K. Kay. 2003. "Born in Difficult Times: The Founding of the Volksmission and the Work of Karl Fix." *Journal of the European Pentecostal Theological Association* 23 (1): 72–101.

Rodrigues, Donizete. 2014. "Ethnic and Religious Diversities in Portugal: The Case of Brazilian Evangelical Immigrants." In *The Changing Soul of Europe: Religions and Migrations in Northern and Southern Europe*, edited by Helena Vilaça, Enzo Pace, Inger Furseth, and Per Pettersson, 133–148. London: Ashgate.

Roger Bastide. 2007. *The African Religions of Brazil: Toward a Sociology of the Interpenetration of Civilizations.* Baltimore: The John Hopkins University Press.

Rolles, David. 2019. "A Fifty-year Perspective of the Origins, Development and Identity of the Salt & Light Church Network." Master's diss., University of Birmingham, UK.

Rosas, Yolanda. 2011. "Textos bíblicos en la celebración y teología neopentecostales." In *fe y pueblo. Nada es imposible para Dios. Una ventana a la fe neopentecostal*, no. 18, 43–51. La Paz, Bolivia: ISEAT.

Rosenior, Derrick. 2010. "The Rhetoric of Pentecostal Racial Reconciliation: Looking Back To Move Forward." In *A Liberating Spirit: Pentecostals and Social Action in North America*, edited by Michael Wilkinson and Steven Studebaker, 53–84. Eugene, OR: Pickwick.

Ross, Kenneth R., Mariz Tadros, and Todd Johnson, eds. 2018. *Christianity in North Africa and West Asia.* Edinburgh: Edinburgh University Press.

Rowe, W.A.C., n.d. *One Lord, One Faith.* Bradford: Puritan Press.

Rubinstein, Murray A. 1996. "Holy Spirit Taiwan: Pentecostal and Charismatic Christianity in the Republic of China." In *Christianity in China: From the Eighteenth Century to the Present*, edited by Daniel H. Bays, 353–366. Stanford: Stanford University Press.

Rubiolo, Cecilia. 2016. "The Ambivalent Autonomy of Mobile 'Pocăiți' between Vicovu de Sus, Romania and Turin, Italy after 1989." *Studia Universitatis Babes-Bolyai Sociologia* 61 (2): 71–97. doi:10.1515/subbs-2016-0011.

Rudolph, D. 2013. "Messianic Judaism in Antiquity and in the Modern Era." In *Introduction to Messianic Judaism*, edited by D. Rudolph and J. Willitts, 21–36. Grand Rapids, MI: Zondervan.

Ruelas, Abraham. 2010. *Women and the Landscape of American Higher Education: Wesleyan Holiness and Pentecostal Founders.* Eugene: Pickwick.

Russell, Andrew C. 2014. "Counteracting Classifications: Keswick Holiness Reconsidered." *Wesleyan Theological Journal* 49 (2): 86–121.

Russell, John P. 2014. "Cash" Luna y el asesinato del pastor Claudio Martínez Morales. *Unidos contra la apostasía.* Accessed October 20, 2019. https://contralaapostasia.com/2014/08/15/cash-luna-y-el-asesinato-del-pastor-claudio-martinez-morales/.

Ryan, Maeve. 2013. "'A Most Promising Field for Future Usefulness': The Church Missionary Society and the Liberated Africans of Sierra Leone." In *A Global History of Anti-slavery Politics in the Nineteenth Century*, edited by William Mulligan and Maurice Bric, 37–58. London: Palgrave Macmillan.

Rybarczyk, Edmund. 2012. "Pentecostalism, Human Nature, and Aesthetics: Twenty-First Century Engagement." *Journal of Pentecostal Theology* 21 (2): 240–259.

Sabatini, Angel. 2001. *80 años de la Asamblea Cristiana de Mendoza*. San Luiz, Argentina: the author.

Sabella, Bernard. 1999. "Socio-economic Characteristics and Challenges to Palestinian Christians in the Holy Land." In *Palestinian Christians: Religion, Politics and Society in the Holy Land*, edited by Anthony O'Mahony, 82–95. London: Melisende.

Sahoo, Sarbeswar. 2018. *Pentecostalism and Politics of Conversion in India*. Cambridge: Cambridge University Press.

Saju. 2011. *Kerala Pentecosthu Charithram* [The History of Kerala Pentecost in Malayalam]. Kochi: Sanctuary Media.

Sakupapa, Teddy Chalwe. 2016. "Christianity in Zambia." In *Anthology of African Christianity*, edited by Isabel Apawo Phiri, Dietrich Werner, Chammah Kaunda and Kennedy Owino, 758–765. Oxford: Regnum.

Samarin, William J. 1972. *Tongues of Men and of Angels*. New York: Macmillan.

Sánchez Walsh, Arlene M. 2003. *Latino Pentecostal Identity: Evangelical Faith, Self, and Society*. New York: Columbia University Press.

Sánchez Walsh, Arlene M. 2018. *Pentecostals in America*. New York: Columbia University Press.

Sanchíz Ochoa, Pilar. 1998. *Evangelismo y poder: Guatemala ante el nuevo milenio*. Sevilla, España: Universidad de Sevilla, Secratariado de publicaciones.

Sanders, Cheryl J. 2020. "Social Justice: Theology as Social Transformation." In *Routledge Handbook on Pentecostal Theology*, edited by Wolfgang Vondey, 432–442. New York: Routledge.

Sandidge, Jerry L. 1987. *Roman Catholic/Pentecostal Dialogue (1977–1982): A Study in Developing Ecumenism*, 2 volumes. Frankfurt am Main: Peter Lang.

Sandru, Trandafir. 1997. *Trezirea Spirituală Penticostală din România*. Bucureşti: Institutul Teologic Penticostal.

Sanford, Agnes. 1947. *The Healing Light: On the Art and Method of Spiritual Healing from the Christian Viewpoint and in the Christian Tradition*. St. Paul: Macalester Park.

Sanford, Agnes Mary White. 1983. *The Healing Light*. New York: Ballantine Books.

Sann Oo, Saw Tint. 2014. "The History of the Assemblies of God Theological Education in Myanmar: Development of the Assemblies of God Bible School." *Asian Journal of Pentecostal Studies* 17 (2): 187–206.

Sanneh, Lamin. 2009. *Abolitionists Abroad American Blacks and the Making of Modern West Africa*. London: Harvard University Press.

Santmire, H. Paul. 2003. "Ecotheology." In *Encyclopedia of Science and Religion* 1 (A–I), edited by N.H. Gregersen, W.J. Wildman, I. Barbour, and R. Valentine, 247–251. New York: Macmillan Reference USA (Gale).

Santos, Luís Aguiar, 2002. "Pluralidade Religiosa: Correntes Cristãs e Não-Cristãs no Universo Religioso Português." In *História religiosa de Portugal* 3, edited by Carlos Moreira Azevedo, 399–501. Lisboa: Circulo dos leitores.

Saracco, Jose Norberto. 1989. "Argentine Pentecostalism: Its History and Theology." PhD diss., University of Birmingham, UK.

Saracco, José Norberto. 2014. *Pentecostalismo argentino, origen, teología y misión (1909–1990)*. Buenos Aires: ASIT.

Sarles, Ken L. 1986. "A Theological Evaluation of the Prosperity Gospel," *Bibliotheca Sacra* 143 (572): 329–352.

Sat-7 International. 2019. "About Us." *Sat-7 Arabic*. Accessed Oct. 3, 2019. https://sat7.org/our-channels/channel-overview/sat-7-arabic.

Schatzmann, Sigfried. 1987. *A Pauline Theology of Charismata*. Peabody, MA: Hendrickson.

Scheffers, Mark. 1987. "Schism in the Bassa Independent Churches of Liberia." In

Ministry of Missions in African Independent Churches, edited by David A. Shank. Elkhart, IN: Mennonite Board of Missions.

Schmidgall, Paul. 2008. *Hundert Jahre Deutsche Pfingstbewegung, 1907–2007*. Nordhausen: Bautz.

Schmidgall, Paul. 2013. *European Pentecostalism. Its Origins, Development, and Future*. Cleveland, TN: CPT Press.

Schuurman, Peter. 2019. *The Subversive Evangelical: The Ironic Charisma of an Irreligious Megachurch*. Montreal & Kingston: McGill-Queen's University Press.

Scudder, Lewis. 1998. *The Arabian Mission's Story: In Search of Abraham's Other Son*. Grand Rapids, MI: Wm. B. Eerdmans Publishing Co.

Sébastien, Fath. 2002. "Réveil, and Petites-Églises." *Bulletin de la Société de l'Histoire du Protestantisme Français*, t. CILVIII (Oct.–Dec): 1101.

Sepúlveda, Juan. 1999. "Indigenous Pentecostalism and the Chilean Experience." In *Pentecostals after a Century: Global Perspectives on a Movement in Transition*, edited by Allan H. Anderson and Walter J. Hollenweger, 111–134. Sheffield: Sheffield Academic Press.

Setta, Susan M. 1986. "Healing in Suburbia: The Women's Aglow Fellowship." *Journal of Religious Studies* 12 (2): 46–56.

Seymour, W.J. 1915. *The Doctrines and Discipline of the Azusa Street Apostolic Faith Mission of Los Angeles, California*. Los Angeles: no publisher.

Shah, A.B., ed. 1977. *The Letters and Correspondence of Pandita Ramabai*. Bombay: Maharashtra State Board for Literature and Culture.

Shank, David A. 1994. *Prophet Harris: The "Black Elijah" of West Africa*. Leiden: Brill.

Sharpe, Matthew. 2013. "Name It and Claim It: Prosperity Gospel and the Global Pentecostal Reformation." In *Handbook of Research on Development and Religion*, edited by Matthew Clarke, 164–79. Cheltenham, UK: Edward Elgar.

Shaw, Rosalind. 2007. "Displacing Violence: Making Pentecostal Memory in Postwar Sierra Leone." *CUAN Cultural Anthropology* 22 (1): 66–93.

Shearer, Sheryl. 2002. "Zelma Argue: Handmaiden of the Lord." *A/G Heritage* (Spring): 18–23.

Sheridan, Greg. 2019. *God Is Good for You: A Defence of Christianity in Troubled Times*. Allen & Unwin.

Sherry, Patrick. 2002. *Spirit and Beauty: An Introduction to Theological Aesthetics*, Second Edition. London: SCM Press.

Shew, Paul Tsuchido. 2003. "History of the Early Pentecostal Movement in Japan: The Roots and Development of the Pre-War Pentecostal Movement in Japan (1907–1945)." PhD diss., Fuller Theological Seminary.

Shew, Paul Tsuchido. 2004. "Leonard Coote and Early Pentecostal Missions in Japan." Presented at the 33rd Annual Meeting of the Society for Pentecostal Studies, Marquette University, Milwaukee, WI, March 11–13.

Shih, Shu-ying. 2013. "Apocalyptic Eschatology: A Case Study of the Charismatic Movement among the East Paiwan Tribes of the Presbyterian Church in Taiwan from the 1960s to 1980s." *Taiwan Journal of Religious Studies* 12 (1/2): 123–146.

Shin, Gwang-cheol. 1996. "Apostle of the Miracle Who Overcame the Ethnic Thread Rev. Kim, Ik-Du." *Ministry and Theology* 48 (June): 196–198.

Shuttleworth, Abigail D. 2015. "'On Earth as It is in Heaven': A Critical Discussion of the Theology of Bill Johnson." *Journal of the European Pentecostal Theological Association* 35 (2): 10–14.

Simmons, Roger. 2008. *Vision Mission and a Movement: The Story of Dr. Thomas Mathews and the Native Missionary Movement*. Richardson, TX: Native Missionary Movement.

Simpson, Carl. 2012. *Revered and Reviled in a Quest for Pentecostal Holiness. Jonathan Paul and the German Pentecostal Movement*.

Saarbrücken: LAP LAMBERT Academia Publishing.

Singapore Department of Statistics. 2010. *Singapore Census of Population 2010: Advance Census Release*. Singapore: Department of Statistics.

Singleton, Andrew. 2017. "Strong Church or Niche Market? The Demography of the Pentecostal Church in Australia." *Pentecostal and Charismatic Christianities in Australia*, Conference Paper, University of Western Sydney, 11 August.

Sloos, William. 2010. "The Story of James and Ellen Hebden: The First Family of Pentecost in Canada." *Pneuma* 32 (2): 181–202.

Smedes, Lewis B., ed. 1987. *Ministry and the Miraculous: A Case Study at Fuller Theological Seminary*. Pasadena, CA: Fuller Seminary Press.

Smith, Calvin, ed. 2011. *Pentecostal Power: Expressions, Impact and Faith of Latin American Pentecostalism*. Leiden: Brill.

Smith, Christian. 2017. *Religion: What It Is, How It Works, and Why It Matters*. Princeton: Princeton University Press.

Smith, Dennis A., and Leonildo Silveira Campos. 2008. "Christianity and Television in Guatemala and Brazil: The Pentecostal Experience." *Studies in World Christianity* 24 (1): 49–64.

Smith, James K.A. 2008. "Is the Universe Open for Surprise? Pentecostal Ontology and the Spirit of Naturalism." *Zygon* 43 (4): 879–96. doi: 10.1111/j.1467-9744.2008.00966.x.

Smith, James K.A. 2010. *Thinking in Tongues: Pentecostal Contributions to Christian Philosophy*. Grand Rapids: Eerdmans.

Smith, James K.A., and Amos Yong, eds. 2010. *Science and the Spirit: A Pentecostal Engagement with the Sciences*. Bloomington: Indiana University Press.

Smith, Raynard D., ed. 2015. *With Signs Following: The Life and Ministry of Charles Harrison Mason*. St. Louis, MO: Chalice Press.

Smith, Timothy L. 1957. *Revivalism and Social Reform in Mid-Nineteenth Century America*. New York: Abingdon Press.

Society for Pentecostal Studies. 2019. "Who We Are," "Bylaws and History," "Interest Groups," Executive Committee." Accessed December 3, 2019. http://sps-usa.org.

Song, Gil-sup. 1982. *The Three Stars of the Methodist Church under Japanese Occupation* [in Korean]. Seoul: Sung-kwang.

Sørensen, Ib. 2010. "Leg med ilden: Pentekostale trosfællesskaber og problematiske omverdensrelationer." Ph.D. diss., University of Southern Denmark. https://www.sdu.dk/-/media/files/forskning/phd/phd_hum/afhandlinger/2010/ib_soerensen.pdf.

Spadaro, Antonio, S.J. 2018. "The Prosperity Gospel: Dangerous and Different." *La Civiltà Cattolica*, 18 July. www.laciviltacatttolica.com.

Spawn, Kevin L., and Archie T. Wright, eds. 2012. *Spirit and Scripture: Exploring a Pneumatic Hermeneutic*. London: T&T Clark.

Spiritual Heritage of the Ascetics in the Russian Lands, 2015. (Case 5629 Odessa Reg., Case 9552 54–10 SudTroiku, SpetsOtdel #1 (Feb., 1 1858), Case 18 Marinsky Prison (GUGB/NKVD/USSR)). Typescript (unpublished).

Spittler, Russ P. 2002. "Society for Pentecostal Studies." In *The New International Dictionary of Pentecostal and Charismatic Movements*, edited by Stanley M. Burgess and Eduard M. van der Maas, 1079–1080. Grand Rapids, MI: Zondervan.

St.Clair, George. 2017. "'God Even Blessed Me with Less Money': Disappointment, Pentecostalism and the Middle Classes in Brazil." *Journal of Latin American Studies* 49 (3): 609–632.

Stakemann, Randolph. 1986. *The Cultural Politics of Religious Change: A Study of the Sanoyea Kpelle in Liberia*. Lewiston, NY: Edwin Mellen Press.

Stanley, Brian. 1990. *The Bible and the Flag: Protestant Missions and British Imperialism in the Nineteenth and Twentieth Centuries.* Leicester: Apollos.

Stanley, Brian. 2013. *The Global Diffusion of Evangelicalism: The Age of Billy Graham and John Stott.* Downers Grove: IVP.

Stark, Rodney and Roger Finke. 2000. *Acts of Faith: Explaining the Human Side of Religion.* Berkeley, CA: University of California Press.

Stark, Rodney. 1999. "Secularization, R.I.P." *Sociology of Religion* 60 (3): 249–273.

Statistics Canada. 2011. *National Household Survey.* Statistics Canada Catalogue no. 99-010-X2011037. Ottawa: Statistics Canada.

Steele, Ron. 1987. *Plundering Hell to Populate Heaven: The Reinhard Bonnke Story.* Melbourne, FL: DOVE Christian Books

Steenbrink, Karel, and Jan Aritonang, eds. 2008. *A History of Christianity in Indonesia.* Leiden: Brill.

Steigenga, Timothy J. 2001. *The Politics of the Spirit. The Political Implications of Pentecostalized Religion in Costa Rica and Guatemala.* Lanham, MD: Lexington Books.

Stephenson, Christopher A. 2012. *Types of Pentecostal Theology: Method, System, Spirit.* Oxford: Oxford University Press.

Stephenson, Lisa. 2011. *Dismantling the Dualisms for American Pentecostal Women in Ministry: A Feminist-Pneumatological Approach.* Leiden: Brill.

Stevens, Bruce. 2006. "'Up, Up and Away': Pentecostal Preaching and the Manic Defence." *Asian Journal of Pentecostal Studies* 9 (2): 284–294.

Stewart, Adam. 2010. "A Canadian Azusa? The Implications of the Hebden Mission for Pentecostal Historiography." In *Winds from the North: Canadian Contributions to the Pentecostal Movement*, edited by Michael Wilkinson and Peter Althouse, 17–37. Leiden: Brill.

Stewart, Adam. 2012. "A Brief Introduction." In *Handbook of Pentecostal Christianity*, edited by Adam Stewart, 3–8. DeKalb: Northern Illinois University Press.

Stewart, Adam. 2014. "From Monogenesis to Polygenesis in Pentecostal Origins: A Survey of the Evidence from the Azusa Street, Hebden, and Mukti Missions." *PentecoStudies* 13 (2): 151–172.

Stewart, Adam. 2015. *The New Canadian Pentecostals.* Waterloo, ON: Wilfrid Laurier University Press.

Stewart, Adam. 2017. "A Subject Analysis of Pentecostalism in the Dewey Decimal Classification System." *Biblioteka* 21: 243–250.

Stewart, Adam. 2019. "Sociohistorical Recommendations for the Reclassification of Pentecostalism in the Dewey Decimal Classification System." *o-bib: Das offene Bibliotheksjournal* 6 (1): 42–59.

Stewart, Adam, Andrew Gabriel, and Kevin Shanahan. 2017. "Changes in Clergy Belief and Practice in Canada's Largest Pentecostal Denomination." *Pneuma* 39 (4): 457–481.

Stoll, David. 1990. *Is Latin America Turning Protestant?: The Politics of Evangelical Growth.* Berkeley: University of California Press.

Stott, John R.W. 1959. *Fundamentalism and Evangelicalism.* Grand Rapids: Eerdmans.

Stott, John R.W. 1964. *The Baptism and Fullness of the Holy Spirit.* Downers Grove: Inter Varsity Press.

Stotts, George Raymond. 1982. *Le pentecôtisme au pays de Voltaire.* Craponne: Viens et Vois.

Strandsbjerg, Camille. 2015. *Religions et Transformations Politiques au Benin: Les Spectres du Pouvoir.* Paris: Karthala.

Streiker, Lowell D. 1971. *The Jesus Trip: Advent of the Jesus Freaks.* Nashville: Abingdon.

Stronstad, Roger. 2012. *The Charismatic Theology of St. Luke.* Second Edition. Grand Rapids, MI: Baker.

Sturm, Tristan, and Seth Frantzman. 2014. "Religious Geopolitics of Palestinian Christianity: Palestinian Christian Zionists, Palestinian Liberation Theologists, and American Missions to Palestine." *Middle Eastern Studies* 20 (3): 1–19. https://doi.org/10.1080/00263206.2014.971768.

Su, Edwin. "History of Ling Liang World-Wide Evangelistic Mission." Ling Liang World-wide

Evangelistic Mission Association. http://www.llwwema.org/welcome.htm.

Su, Selena Y.Z., and Allan H. Anderson. 2017. "'Christianity Fever' and Unregistered Churches in China." In *Global Chinese Pentecostal and Charismatic Christianity*, edited by Fenggang Yang, Joy Tong, and Allan H. Anderson, 219–239. Leiden: Brill.

Su, Selena Y.Z., and Dik Allan. 2019. "Self-Narration and Theological Formation of Contemporary Chinese House Church Networks." In *Asia Pacific Pentecostalism*, edited by Denise A. Austin, Jacqueline Grey, and Paul Lewis, 61–84. Leiden: Brill.

Suarsana, Yan. 2014. "Inventing Pentecostalism. Pandita Ramabai and the Mukti Revival from a Post-colonial Perspective." *PentecoStudies* 13 (2): 173–196.

Suenens, Léon Joseph. 1980. *Open the Frontiers: A Spiritual Testimony from Cardinal Suenens in Conversation with Karl-Heinz Fleckenstein*. London: Darton, Longman and Todd.

Suico, Joseph. 2011. "Pentecostalism in the Philippines." In *Asian and Pentecostal: The Charismatic Face of Christianity in Asia*, edited by Allan Anderson and Edmond Tang, 279–293. Eugene, OR: Wipf and Stock.

Sundkler, Bengt. 1976. *Zulu Zion and Some Swazi Zionists*. Oxford: Oxford University Press.

Sung, John. 1995. *The Diaries of John Sung*. Translated by Stephen L. Sheng. Brighton, Michigan: L.H. Sheng, S.L. Sheng.

Sutanto, Adi. 1986. "A Strategy for Planting Churches in Java through The Sangkakala Mission with Special Emphasis on Javanese and Chinese People." DMiss diss., Fuller Theological Seminary.

Sutton, Geoffrey W., and Eloise K. Thomas. 2005. "Can Derailed Pastors be Restored? Effects of Offense and Age on Restoration." *Pastoral Psychology* 53: 583–599.

Sutton, Geoffrey W., Christine Arnzen, and Heather L. Kelly. 2016. "Christian Counseling and Psychotherapy: Components of Clinician Spirituality that Predict Type of Christian Intervention. *Journal of Psychology and Christianity* 35: 204–214.

Sutton, Geoffrey W., Heather L. Kelly, Everett L. Worthington, Jr., Brandon J. Griffin, and Chris Dinwiddie. 2018. "Satisfaction with Christian Psychotherapy and Well-being: Contributions of Hope, Personality, and Spirituality." *Spirituality in Clinical Practice* 5 (1): 8–24, doi: 10.1037/scp0000145

Sutton, Geoffrey W., Kelly C. McLeland, Katie K. Weaks, Patricia E. Cogswell, and Renee N. Miphouvieng. 2007. "Does Gender Matter? An Exploration of Gender, Spirituality, Forgiveness and Restoration Following Pastor Transgressions." *Pastoral Psychology* 55: 645–663. doi 10.1007/ s11089-007-0072-3.

Sutton, Matthew Avery. 2007. *Aimee Semple McPherson and the Resurrection of Christian America*. Cambridge, MA: Harvard University Press.

Suurmond, Jean-Jacques. 1995. *Word and Spirit at Play: Towards a Charismatic Theology*. Grand Rapids: Eerdmans.

Suzuki, Masakazu. 2005. "The Life and History of C.F. Juergensen and Takinogawa Mission in Japan." Presented at the 34th Annual Meeting of the Society for Pentecostal Studies, Regent University, Virginia Beach, VA, March 10–12.

Suzuki, Masakazu. 2006. "The Life and Ministry of Kiyoma Yumiyama and the Foundation of Japan Assemblies of God." *Asia Journal of the Pentecostal Studies* 9 (2): 220–243.

Suzuki, Masakazu. 2011. "The Origins and the Development of the Japan Assemblies of God: The Foreign and Japanese Workers and Their Ministries (1907 to 1975)." PhD diss., Bangor University.

Swatowiski, Claudia Wolff. 2013. *Novos Cristãos em Lisboa: Reconhecendo Estigmas, Negociando Estereótipos*. Rio de Janeiro: Garamond.

Swenson, Donald S. 1972. The Charismatic Movement within Denominational Christianity. Master's thesis: Calgary Alberta, The University of Calgary.

Swenson, Donald S. 2009. *Society, Spirituality, and the Sacred. A Social Scientific Introduction*. Toronto: The University of Toronto Press.

Swenson, Donald S. 2009. "The Canadian Catholic Charismatic Renewal." In *Canadian Pentecostalism*, edited by Michael Wilkinson, 214–232. Montreal & Kingston: McGill-Queen's University Press.

Swenson, Donald S. 2018. *Alleluia: An Ethnographic Study*. Lanham, MD: Lexington Books.

Swindoll, Orville. 2017. *Tiempos de restauración*. Buenos Aires: Logos.

Swoboda, A.J. 2013. *Tongues and Trees: Toward a Pentecostal Ecological Theology*. Blandford Forum: Deo.

Swoboda, A.J. 2015. "Posterity or Prosperity? Critiquing and Refiguring Prosperity Theologies in an Ecological Age." *Pneuma* 37 (3): 394–411.

Swoboda, A.J., ed. 2014. *Blood Cries Out: Pentecostals, Ecology, and the Groans of Creation*. Eugene, OR: Wipf and Stock.

Synan, Vinson. 1972. *The Holiness-Pentecostal Movement in the United States*. Grand Rapids, MI: Eerdmans.

Synan, Vinson. 1985. "Fifteen Years of the Society for Pentecostal Studies." A paper presented to the Society for Pentecostal Studies. Gaithersburg, Maryland, The Mother of God Community.

Synan, Vinson. 1997. *The Holiness-Pentecostal Tradition: Charismatic Movements in the Twentieth Century*. Grand Rapids, MI: Eerdmans.

Synan, Vinson. 1998. *Oldtime Power: A Centennial History of the International Pentecostal Holiness Church*. Franklin Springs GA: LifeSprings.

Synan, Vinson, ed. 2001. *The Century of the Holy Spirit: 100 Years of Pentecostal and Charismatic Renewal, 1901–2001*. Nashville, TN: Thomas Nelson.

Synan, Vinson. 2005. "The Beginnings of the Society for Pentecostal Studies." A plenary session presented at the 34th Annual Meeting of the Society for Pentecostal Studies. Virginia Beach, VA: Regent University. http://sps-usa.org/home/bylaws-and-his tory; direct link: http://storage.cloversites .com/societyforpentecostalstudies/docu ments/synan_sps_beginnings.pdf.

Synan, Vinson. 2019. *Where He Leads Me: The Vinson Synan Story*. Franklin Springs GA: LifeSprings.

Synan, Vinson, and Charles R. Fox, Jr. 2012. *William J. Seymour: Pioneer of the Azusa Street Revival*. Alachua, FL: Bridge-Logos.

Synan, Vinson, Amos Yong, and J. Kwabena Asamoah-Gyadu, eds. 2016. *Global Renewal Christianity: Spirit-Empowered Movements Past, Present and Future*. Vol. 3: *Africa*. Lake Mary, FL: Charisma House.

Synan, Vinson, Amos Yong, and Miguel Alvarez, eds. 2016. *Global Renewal Christianity: Spirit-Empowered Movements Past, Present, and Future*. Volume 2: *Latin America*. Lake Mary, FL: Charisma House.

Tabalaka, A., and F. Nkomazana. 2009. "Aspects of Healing Practices and Methods among Pentecostals in Botswana –Part 1." *Boleswa Journal of Theology, Religion and Philosophy* 2 (3): 137–159.

Tabalaka, A., and F. Nkomazana. 2009. "Faith Healing and Reasoning: Aspects of Healing and Methods among Pentecostals in Botswana –Part 2." *Boleswa Journal of Theology, Religion and Philosophy* 2 (3): 160–169.

Tabares Espinoza, Rodhe Esther. 2000. "Mujer y Pentecostalismo en Cuba." Unpublished Bachelor's thesis, Matanzas, Cuba, Seminario Evangélico de Teología.

Tallman, Matthew. 2009. "Pentecostal Ecology: A Theological Paradigm for Pentecostal Environmentalism." In *The Spirit Renews the Face of the Earth: Pentecostal Forays in Science and Theology of Creation*, edited by Amos Yong, 135–172. Eugene, OR: Wipf and Stock.

Tan, Derek. 2004. "Malaysia." In *International Dictionary of Pentecostal and Charismatic*

Movements, edited by Stanley M. Burgess and Eduard M. van der Maas. Grand Rapids, MI: Zondervan.

Tan, Jin Huat. 2005. "Pentecostal and Charismatic Origins in Malaysia and Singapore." In *Asian and Pentecostal: The Charismatic Face of Christianity in Asia*, edited by Allan Anderson and Edmond Tang, 281–306. Oxford: Regnum.

Tang, Edmond. 2011. "'Yellers' and Healers: Pentecostalism and the Study of Grassroots Christianity in China." In *Asian and Pentecostal: The Charismatic Face of Christianity in Asia*, edited by Allan Anderson and Edmond Tang, 379–394. Eugene, OR: Wipf & Stock.

Tangen, Karl-Inge. 2012. *Ecclesial Identification Beyond Late Modern Individualism? A Case Study of Life Strategies in Growing Late Modern Churches*. Leiden: Brill.

Tangen, Karl Inge. 2017. "Pentecostal Movements in Norway." In *Global Renewal Christianity. Spirit-Empowered Movements: Past, Present and Future. Vol. 4. Europe and North America*, edited by Vinson Synan and Amos Yong, 198–214. Lake Mary, FL: Charisma House.

Tapilatu, M. 1982. "Gereja-gereja Pentakosta di Indonesia: Suatu Tinjauan tentang Sejarah, Organisasi. Ibadah, Kegiatan, Ajaran dan Sikap Terhadap Gereja-gereja Lain." ThM thesis, Jakarta Advanced School of Theology, Jakarta.

Taylor, G.F. 1907. *The Spirit and the Bride*. Falcon, NC: 1–9, 40–49, 90–99.

Teemu T. Mantsinen. 2018. "The Finnish Pentecostal Movement: An Analysis of Internal Struggle as a Process of Habitula Division." In *Charismatic Christianity in Finland, Norway and Sweden: Case Studies in Historical and Contemporary Developments*, edited by Jessica Moberg and Jane Skjoldli, 109–136. Palgrave Macmillan.

"Teodor Codreanu." 2004. *Cuvantul Adevărului*, anul XV, nr. 11, 23.

Thayer, Joseph Henry. 1977 [1886]. *Greek-English Lexicon of the New Testament*. Grand Rapids, MI: Zondervan.

The Editor. 1948. "Harvest Gleanings." *Harvest Grain* 5 (3): 14.

The Washington Times. 2001. "Islamic Country Promotes Tourism." *The Washington Times*. June 15, 2001. Accessed Oct. 3, 2019. https://www.washingtontimes.com/news/2001/jun/15/20010615-023756-3833r/.

Thiselton, Anthony C. 2013. *The Holy Spirit – in Biblical Teaching, Through the Centuries, and Today*. Grand Rapids: Eerdmans.

Thollander, John. 2000. *He Saw a Man Named Mathews: A Brief Testimony of Thomas and Mary Mathews, Pioneer Missionary to Rajasthan*. Udaipur, India: Cross and Crown.

Thomas, John Christopher, ed. 2010. *Toward a Pentecostal Ecclesiology: The Church and the Fivefold Gospel*. Cleveland, TN: CPT Press.

Thomas, Marcus. 2016. *The God of Our Fathers: Belting the Globe with the Gospel*. Belfast: Ambassador International.

Thompson, Livingstone. 2010. "Pentecostal Migrants – A Challenge to the Churches." *Search* 33 (3): 185–193. https://www.academia.edu/8152663/Pentecostalism_in_Ireland.

Thoorens, Jan. [1976]. *L'Union de Prière de Charmes s/Rhône: Mémoire, Maîtrise en théologie*. Institute Catholique de Paris.

Thureson, Birger. 2004. *The Fires of Burma: Biography of Rev. U Myo Chit*, translated by Jami Nordenstam. N.P.

Tiedemann, R.G. 2011. "The Origins and Organizational Developments of the Pentecostal Missionary Enterprise in China." *Asian Journal of Pentecostal Studies* 14 (1): 108–146.

Tiedemann, R.G. 2012. "Protestant Revivals in China with Particular Reference to Shandong Province." *Studies in World Christianity* 18 (3): 213–236.

Togarasei, L. 2005. "Modern Pentecostalism as an Urban Phenomenon: The Case of the Family of God Church in Zimbabwe." *Exchange* 40 (4): 336–350.

Togarasei, Lovemore. 2007. "Modern/Charismatic Pentecostalism as a Form of 'Religious' Secularisation in Africa." *Studia Historiae Ecclesiasticae* 41 (1): 55–66.

Togarasei, L. 2011. "The Pentecostal Gospel of Prosperity in African Contexts of Poverty: An Appraisal." *Exchange* 40 (4): 336–350.

Togarasei, Lovemore. 2012. "Mediating the gospel: Pentecostal Christianity and Media Technology in Botswana and Zimbabwe." *Journal of Contemporary Religion* 27 (2): 257–274.

Togarasei, L. 2017. "The Place and Challenges of Modern Pentecostal Christianity in Botswana." *Botswana Notes and Records* 48: 225–235.

Togarasei, L. 2018. *Aspects of Pentecostal Christianity in Zimbabwe*. New York: Springer.

Tomlinson, A.J. 2011. *The Last Great Conflict*. Cleveland, TN: White Wing Press.

Toppi, Francesco. 1999. *E mi sarete testimoni: Il movimento pentecostale e le Assemblee di Dio in Italia*. Rome: ADI Media

Toppi, Francesco. 2007. *Luigi Francescon: antesignano del Risveglio pentecostale Evangelico Italiano*. Rome: ADI-Media.

Torres, David Ramos. 1992. *Historia de la Iglesia de Dios Pentecostal, M.I.* Río Piedras, Puerto Rico: Editorial Pentecostal.

Torres, Rubén Pérez. 2004. *Poder desde lo Alto: Historia, Sociología y Contribuciones del Pentecostalismo en Puerto Rico, El Caribe y en Los Estados Unidos*, 2nd Edición. Terrassa (Barcelona) Clie.

Trudinger, Ron. 1982. *Built to Last: Biblical Principles for Church Restoration*. Eastbourne: Kingsway Publications.

Tudur Jones, R. 2004. *Faith and the Crisis of a Nation: Wales 1890–1914*. Cardiff: University of Wales Press.

Tupamahu, Ekaputra. 2016. "Tongues as a Site of Subversion: An Analysis from the Perspective of Postcolonial Politics of Language." *Pneuma* 38 (3): 293–311.

Turner, L., H. Adam, and N. Bettcher, eds. 2006. *Legacy: Timeless Truths for a New Generation: A Compendium of Works by Leo Harris*. Seaton, SA: CRC Churches Int.

Tyson, James. 1992. *The Early Pentecostal Revival: History of Twentieth-Century Pentecostals and The Pentecostal Assemblies of the World, 1901–30*. Word Aflame Press.

Ugba, Abel. 2009. *Shades of Belonging: African Pentecostals in Twenty-First Century Ireland*. Trenton NJ: Africa World Press.

Ukah, Asonzeh. 2008. *A New Paradigm of Pentecostal Power: A Study of the Redeemed Christian Church of God in Nigeria*. Trenton, NJ: Africa World Press.

US Department of State. 2008. "International Religious Freedom Report." Accessed May 22, 2018. https://www.state.gov/j/drl/rls/irf/2008/108530.htm.

Usher, John Martin, ed. n.d. "The Polhill Collection Online" pconline.org.uk.

Usher, John Martin. 2012. "Cecil Henry Polhill: The Patron of the Pentecostals." *Pneuma* 34 (1): 37–56.

Usher, John Martin. 2015. "For China and Tibet, and for World-wide Revival: Cecil Henry Polhill (1860–1938) and His Significance for Early Pentecostalism." PhD thesis., University of Birmingham, UK.

Usher, John. 2020. *Cecil Polhill: Missionary, Gentleman and Revivalist*. Leiden: Brill.

Valente, Rubia R. 2015. "Institutional explanations for the decline of the Congregação Cristã no Brasil." *Pentecostudies* 14 (1): 72–96.

Van Beek, Huibert, ed. 2009. *Revisioning Christian Unity: The Global Christian Forum*. Oxford: Regnum.

van de Kamp, Linda. 2016. *Violent Conversion: Brazilian Pentecostalism and Urban Women in Mozambique*. Rochester, NY: Boydell & Brewer.

Van der Laan, Cornelis. 2011. "The development of Pentecostalism in Dutch Speaking Countries." In *European Pentecostalism*, edited by William K. Kay and Anne E. Dyer, 85–112. Leiden: Brill.

Van Klinken, A.S. 2012. "Men in the Remaking: Conversion Narratives and Born-Again

Masculinity in Zambia." *Journal of Religion in Africa* 42 (3): 215–239.

Van Wyk, Ilana. 2014. *The Universal Church of the Kingdom of God in South Africa: A Church of Strangers*. Cambridge: Cambridge University Press.

Vatter, Stefan. 2018. *Finden, Fördern, Freisetzen; Wirksam führen – die Wiederendeckung des apostolischen Dienstes*. 3. Auflage. Schwartzenfeld, Deutschland: Neufeld Verlag.

Vázquez, Carmen Castilla. 1999. "De neófitos a iniciados. El movimiento neocatecumenal y sus ritos de admisión." *Gazeta de Antropología* 15 (febrero). http://www.gazeta-antropologia.es/?p=3443.

Vásquez, Manuel A. 2009. "The Global Portability of Pneumatic Christianity: Comparing African and Latin American Pentecostalism." *African Studies* 68 (2): 273–286.

Veldhuizen, Evert. 1995. "Le Renouveau Charismatique Protestant en France (1968–1988)." PhD diss., University of Paris.

Venn, John Archibald. 1953. *Alumni Cantabrigiensis: A Biographical List of all Known Students, Graduates and Holders of Office at the University of Cambridge, from the Earliest Times to 1900*. Cambridge: Cambridge University Press, s.v. "Polhill-Turner (post Polhill), Cecil Henry."

Verbi, Samuel, and Ben Winkley. 2020. "The Story of BSSM [Bethel School of Supernatural Ministry] Alumni." Accessed April 10, 2020. https://www.eidoresearch.com/wp-content/uploads/2018/02/The-story-of-BSSM-alumni-Web-version.pdf.

Vetter, Ekkehart. 2009. *Jahrhundertbilanz – erweckungsfasziniert und durststreckenerprobt. 100 Jahre Mülheimer Verband Freikirchlich-Evangelischer Gemeinden*. Bremen: MV-Missionsverlag.

Viegas, Fátima. 1999. *Angola e as Religiões*. Luanda.

Villafañe, Eldin. 1993. *The Liberating Spirit: Toward an Hispanic American Pentecostal Social Ethic*. Grand Rapids: Eerdmans.

Villazon, Julio C. 2011. "El movimiento neopentecostal en Bolivia: Crisis economica, reorganizacion simbolica y conservadurismo social." In *fe y pueblo. Nada es imposible para Dios. Una ventana a la fe neopentecostal*, no. 18, 23–34. La Paz, Bolivia: ISEAT.

Voiculescu, Cerasela. 2017. "Nomad Self-Governance and Disaffected Power versus Semiological State Apparatus of Capture: The Case of Roma Pentecostalism." *Critical Research on Religion* 5 (2): 188–208. doi:10.1177/2050303217690894.

Vondey, Wolfgang. 2010. *Beyond Pentecostalism: The Crisis of Global Christianity and the Renewal of the Theological Agenda*. Grand Rapids: Eerdmans.

Vondey, Wolfgang. 2011. "Pentecostals and Ecumenism: Becoming the Church as a Pursuit of Christian Unity." *International Journal for the Study of the Christian Church* 11 (4): 318–330.

Vondey, Wolfgang. 2013. *Pentecostalism: A Guide for the Perplexed*. London and New York: Bloomsbury T&T Clark.

Vondey, Wolfgang. 2017. *Pentecostal Theology: Living the Full Gospel*. London and New York: Bloomsbury T&T Clark.

Vondey, Wolfgang, ed. 2010. *Pentecostalism and Christian Unity: Ecumenical Documents and Critical Assessments*. Eugene: Pickwick.

Wacker, Grant. 1998. "The Pentecostal Tradition." In *Caring and Curing: Health and Medicine in the Western Religious Traditions*, edited by Ronald L. Numbers and Darrel W. Amundsen, 514–38. Baltimore: Johns Hopkins University Press.

Wacker, Grant. 2001. *Heaven Below: Early Pentecostals and American Culture*. Cambridge, MA: Harvard University Press.

Wade, Matthew, and Maria Hynes. 2013. "Worshipping Bodies: Affective Labour in the Hillsong Church." *Geographical Research* 51 (2): 173–179.

Wadkins, Timothy H. 2017. *The Rise of Modern Pentecostalism in El Salvador: From the Blood of the Martyrs to the Baptism of the Spirit*. Waco, TX: Baylor University Press.

Waern, Claes, ed. 2007a. *Pingströrelsen Händelser och utveckling under 1900-talet*. Örebro: Libris Förlag.

Waern, Claes, ed. 2007b. *Pingströrelsen Verksamheter och särdrag under 1900-talet*. Örebro: Libris Förlag.

Wagner, C. Peter. 1973. *Look out! The Pentecostals Are Coming!* Carol Stream, Il: Creation House.

Wagner, C. Peter. 1987. *Signs and Wonders Today*. Portland, OR: Creation House.

Wagner, C. Peter. 1988. *The Third Wave of the Holy Spirit: Encountering the Power of Signs and Wonders Today*. Ann Arbor, MI: Servant Publications, Vine Books.

Wagner, C. Peter. 1996. *Confronting the Powers: How the New Testament Church Experienced the Power of Strategic-level Spiritual Warfare*. Ventura, CA: Regal,

Wagner, Peter, and Pablo Deiros, eds. 1998. *The Rising Revival: Firsthand Accounts of the Incredible Argentine Revival – and How it Can Spread Throughout the World*. Ventura, CA: Renew.

Wahlström, Magnus, ed. 2010. *Pingströrelsens årsbok 2010*. Örebro: Libris Förlag.

Währisch-Oblau, Claudia. 2009. *The Missionary Self-Perception of Pentecostal / Charismatic Church Leaders from the Global South in Europe*. Leiden: Brill.

Wakefield, Gavin. 2007. *Alexander Boddy: Pentecostal Anglican Pioneer*. Milton Keynes: Authentic Media.

Walker, Andrew. 1998. *Restoring the Kingdom: The Radical Christianity of the House Church Movement*. Guildford: Inter Publishing Service Ltd.

Wallis, Arthur. 1981. *The Radical Christian*. Eastbourne: Kingsway.

Walls, Andrew. 2000. "Of Ivory Towers and Ashrams: Some Reflections on Theological Scholarship in Africa." *Journal of African Christian Thought* 3 (1): 1–5.

Walsh, M. 2006. "The Religious Ferment of the Sixties." In *Christianity: World Christianities c.1914–c.2000*, edited by H. McCleod, 304–322. Cambridge: Cambridge University Press.

Wang, Xipeng. 1950. *Documenting the Jesus Family*. Shanghai: The Rural Construction Committee of the National Christian Council of China. (汪锡鹏。《记耶稣家庭》。上海：上海中华基督教协进会上海乡村事业委员会。)

Wanjiru, Gitau M. 2018. *Megachurch Christianity Reconsidered: Millennials and Social Change in African Perspective*. Downers Grove, IL: IVP.

Ward, Kevin, and Emma Wild-Wood. 2010. *The East African Revival: History and Legacies*. Kampala: Fountain Publishers.

Wariboko, Nimi. 2012. "Pentecostal Paradigms of National Economic Prosperity in Africa." In *Pentecostalism and Prosperity*, edited by Amos Yong and Katherine Attanasi, 35–62. New York: Palgrave MacMillan.

Wariboko, Nimi. 2012. *The Pentecostal Principle*. Grand Rapids: Eerdmans.

Wariboko, Nimi. 2014. *Nigerian Pentecostalism*. Rochester, NY: University of Rochester Press.

Warner, Wayne. 1986. *The Woman Evangelist: The Life and Times of Charismatic Evangelist Maria B. Woodworth-Etter*. Metuchen, NJ: Scarecrow Press.

Warner, Wayne E. 1993. *Kathryn Kuhlman: The Woman Behind the Miracles*. Ann Arbor: Servant Publications.

Warner, W.E. 2002. "Pentecostal Fellowship of North America." In *The International Dictionary of Pentecostal Charismatic Movements*, edited by Stanley E. Burgess and Eduard M. Van der Maas. Grand Rapids, MI: Zondervan.

Warrington, Keith, ed. 1998. *Pentecostal Perspectives*. Carlisle: Paternoster.

Warrington, Keith. 2008. *Pentecostal Theology: A Theology of Encounter*. London; New York: T&T Clark.

Watt, James. 2002. Interview by Jim Craig. Pentecostal Assemblies of Canada Archives, May 9.

Watt, P., and W. Saayman. 2003. "South African Pentecostalism in Context: Symptoms of Crisis." *Missionalia* 31 (2): 318–333.

Weaver, C. Douglas. 2000. *The Healer-Prophet: William Marrion Branham: A Study of the Prophetic in American Pentecostalism*. Macon, GA: Mercer University Press.

"Wedding Bells." 1993. *The Pentecostal Testimony* (December): 7.

Wei-Tsing Inouye, Melissa. 2019. *China and the True Jesus: Charisma and Organization in a Chinese Christian Church*. New York: Oxford University Press.

Welch, Tim. 2013. *Joseph Smale: God's 'Moses' for Pentecostalism*. Milton Keynes, UK: Paternoster.

Wesley, Luke. 2004. *The Church in China: Persecuted, Pentecostal, and Powerful*. Baguio, Philippines: AJPS Books.

Westerlund, David, ed. 2009. *Global Pentecostalism: Encounters with Other Religious Traditions*. London: I.B. Tauris.

Whitchurch, Bob. 2002. *The Journey*. Oxford: Salt & Light Publishing.

White, Calvin. 2012. *The Rise to Respectability: Race, Religion, and the Church of God in Christ*. Fayettville, AR: The University of Arkansas Press.

White, Graham. 1977. *Socialization*. London: Longman.

Whitney, E. 2005. "Thesis of Lynn White, (1907–1987)." In *Encyclopedia of Religion and Nature*, edited by B. Taylor, 1735–1737. London: Continuum.

Wiegele, Katharine L. 2005. *Investing in Miracles: El Shaddai and the Transformation of Popular Catholicism in the Philippines*. Honolulu: University of Hawai'i Press.

Wiegele, Katharine L. 2012. "The Prosperity Gospel among Filipino Catholic Charismatics." In *Pentecostalism and Prosperity: The Socio-Economics of the Global Charismatic Movement*, edited by Katherine Attanasi, and Amos Yong, 171–188. New York. Palgrave Macmillan.

Wiegele, Katharine L. 2013. "Politics, Education and Civic Participation: Catholic Charismatic Modernities in the Philippines." In *Global Pentecostalism in the 21st Century*, edited by Robert W. Hefner, 224–250. Bloomington and Indianapolis, IN. Indiana University Press.

Wigglesworth, Smith. 1924. *Ever Increasing Faith*. Various editions including Kindle.

Wightman, Jill, M. 2008. *New Bolivians, New Bolivia: Pentecostal Conversion and Neoliberal Transformation in Contemporary Bolivia*. UMI Microfilm. Diss. University of Illinois at Urbana-Champaign. ProQuest.

Wilkinson, Michael. 2006. *The Spirit Said Go: Pentecostal Immigrants in Canada*. New York: Peter Lang.

Wilkinson, Michael. 2010. "Charles Chawner and the Missionary Impulse of the Hebden Mission." In *Winds from the North: Canadian Contributions to the Pentecostal Movement*, edited by Michael Wilkinson and Peter Althouse, 39–54. Leiden: Brill.

Wilkinson, Michael, ed. 2012. *Global Pentecostal Movements: Migration, Mission, and Public Religion*. Leiden: Brill.

Wilkinson, Michael. 2014. "Sociological Narratives and the Sociology of Pentecostalism." In *The Cambridge Companion for Pentecostal Studies*, edited by Amos Yong and Mel Robuck, 215–234. Cambridge, UK: Cambridge University Press.

Wilkinson, Michael. 2016. "Charismatic Christianity and the Role of Networks: Catch the Fire and the Revival Alliance." *Pneuma* 38 (1/2): 33–49.

Wilkinson, Michael. 2016. "Pentecostals and the World: Theoretical and Methodological Issues for Studying Global Pentecostalism." *Pneuma* 38 (4): 373–393.

Wilkinson, Michael, ed. 2009. *Canadian Pentecostalism: Transition and Transformation*. Montreal & Kingston: McGill-Queen's University Press.

Wilkinson, Michael. 2017. "Pentecostalism, the Body, and Embodiment." In *Pentecostals and *the Body*, edited by Michael Wilkinson and Peter Althouse, 17–35. Leiden: Brill.

Wilkinson, Michael. 2020. "Worship: Embodying the Encounter with God." In *The Routledge Handbook of Pentecostal Theology*, edited by Wolfgang Vondey, 117–128. New York: Routledge.

Wilkinson, Michael. 2021. "Globalization." In *The Wiley Blackwell Companion to the Study of Religion*, Second Edition, edited by Robert A. Segal and Nickolas P. Roubekas, 277–288. Hoboken, NJ: John Wiley & Sons.

Wilkinson, Michael, and Peter Althouse, eds. 2010. *Winds From the North: Canadian Contributions to the Pentecostal Movement*. Leiden: Brill.

Wilkinson, Michael, and Peter Althouse. 2014. *Catch the Fire: Soaking Prayer and Charismatic Renewal*. DeKalb: Northern Illinois University.

Wilkinson, Michael, and Peter Althouse, eds. 2017. *Pentecostals and the Body*. Leiden: Brill.

Wilkinson, Michael and Linda M. Ambrose. 2020. *After the Revival: Pentecostalism and the Making of a Canadian Church*. Montreal & Kingston: McGill-Queen's University Press.

Willaime, Jean-Paul. 1999. "Le pentecôtisme: contours et paradoxes d'un protestantisme émotionnel." *Archives de Sciences Sociales des Religions* 105 (1): 5–28.

Willems, Emilio. 1967. *Followers of the New Faith: Culture Change and the Rise of Protestantism in Brazil and Chile*. Nashville: Vanderbilt University Press.

Williams, Don. 2005. "Theological Perspective and Reflection on the Vineyard Christian Fellowship." In *Church, Identity, and Change: Theology and Denominational Structures in Unsettled Times*, edited by David Roozen and James Neiman, 163–187. Grand Rapids, MI: Eerdmans.

Williams, J. Rodman. 1990. *Renewal Theology: Systematic Theology from a Charismatic Perspective. Salvation, the Holy Spirit, and Christian Living*. Grand Rapids, MI: Academy Books/Zondervan.

Williams, Peter W. 2008. *America's Religions: From their Origins to the Twenty-First Century*. Urbana: University of Illinois Press.

Wilson, B.R. 1961. *Sects and Society*. London: Heinemann.

Wilson, Everett A. 1983. "Sanguine Saints: Pentecostalism in El Salvador." *Church History* 52 (2): 186–198.

Wilson, Everett A. 1998. "Furman, Charles Truman." In *Biographical Dictionary of Christian Missions*, edited by Gerald H. Anderson, 231–232. New York: Macmillan.

Wilson, Lewis F. 2002. "Bible Institutes, Colleges, Universities." In *The New International Dictionary of Pentecostal Charismatic Movements*, edited by Stanley M. Burgess and Eduard M. van der Maas, 372–380. Grand Rapids, MI: Zondervan.

Wilson, William J. 1973. *Power, Racism, and Privilege: Race Relations in Theoretical and Sociohistorical Perspectives*. New York: MacMillan Press.

Wimber, John, and Kevin Springer. 1986. *Power Evangelism*. San Francisco: Harper & Row.

Wimber, John, and Kevin Springer. 1987. *Power Healing*. San Francisco: Harper & Row.

Wiyono, Gani. 2019. "Pentecostalism in Indonesia." In *Asia Pacific Pentecostalism*, edited by Denise A. Austin, Jacqueline Grey, and Paul W. Lewis, 243–270. Leiden: Brill.

Wolde Kidan, Bekele. 2001/2. *Revival Ityopiyana Ye Mechereshaw Mecheresa*. Addis Ababa: Mulu Wongel Church.

Wolff Swatowiski, Claudia. 2015. "Igreja Universal do Reino de Deus em Luanda." In *Ciências Sociais cruzadas entre o Brasil e Portugal: trajetos e investigações no ICS*, edited by Isabel Silva, Simone Frangella, Sofia Aboim, and Susana Viegas, 361–374. Lisbon: Imprensa de Ciências Sociais.

Wolterstorff, Nicholas. 1980. *Art in Action*. Grand Rapids: W.B. Eerdmans.

Wong, Hoover. "Wang Zai." *Biographical Dictionary of Chinese Christianity*. Accessed

November 28, 2019. https://bdcconline.net/en/stories/wang-zai.

Woods, Daniel Glenn. 1997. "Living in the Presence of God: Enthusiasm, Authority, and Negotiation in the Practice of Pentecostal Holiness." PhD diss., University of Mississippi.

World Assemblies of God Fellowship, https://worldagfellowship.org.

Worsfold, James E. 1974. *A History of the Charismatic Movements in New Zealand: Including a Pentecostal Perspective and a Breviate of the Catholic Apostolic Church in Great Britain*. Bradford UK: Julian Literature Trust.

Worsfold, James E. 1991. *The Origins of the Apostolic Church in Great Britain: With a Breviate of Its Early Missionary Endeavours*. Wellington: Julian Literature Trust.

Wu, Silas H. 2002. *Dora Yu and Christian Revival in 20th Century China*. Boston, MA: Pishon River Publications.

Wyllie, Robert W. 1980. *Spiritism in Ghana: A Study of New Religious Movements*. Missoula: Scholars Press.

Wynarczyk, Hilario. 2014. *Tres evangelistas carismáticos. Omar Cabrera, Héctor Aníbal Giménez, Carlos Annacondia*. Buenos Aires: FIET/Prensa Ecuménica.

Xi, Lian. 2010. *Redeemed by Fire: The Rise of Popular Christianity in Modern China*. New Haven, Connecticut: Yale University Press.

Xin, Yalin. 2009. *Inside China's House Church Network: The Word of Life Movement and Its Renewing Dynamic*. Lexington, KY: Emeth Press.

Xing, Fuzeng. 2005. *Fandi, aiguo, shuling ren: Ni Tuosheng yu Jidutu juhuichu yanjiu*. Hong Kong: Christian Study Centre on Chinese Religion and Culture.

Xü, Jia Shu. 1952. *Thirty-one Year of the Jesus Family*. Shandong: Religious Affairs Department of the Culture and Education Committee of Shandong Province. (徐家枢。《耶稣家庭三十一年的历史》。山东：山东省文教委宗教事务处。)

Yang, Fenggang, Joy K.C. Tong, and Allan Anderson, eds. 2017. *Global Chinese Pentecostal and Charismatic Christianity*. Leiden, Brill.

Yip, Jeaney. 2018. "Reaching the City of Kuala Lumpur and Beyond: Being a Pentecostal Megachurch in Malaysia." In *Pentecostal Megachurches in Southeast Asia*, edited by Terence Chong. Singapore: ISEAS.

Yoido Full Gospel Church. "Osanri Cho Jashil Memorial Fasting Prayer Mountain."

Yong, Amos. 2000. *Discerning the Spirit(s): A Pentecostal-Charismatic Contribution to Christian Theology of Religions*. Sheffield, UK: Sheffield Academic.

Yong, Amos. 2005. *The Spirit Poured Out on All Flesh: Pentecostalism and the Possibility of Global Theology*. Grand Rapids, MI: Baker Academic.

Yong, Amos. 2006. *Spirit-Word-Community: Theological Hermeneutics in Trinitarian Perspective*. Eugene: Wipf & Stock.

Yong, Amos. 2008. "Pentecostalism, Science, and Creation: New Voices in the Theology-Science Conversation." *Zygon* 43 (4): 875–77. doi: 10.1111/j.1467-9744.2008.00965.x.

Yong, Amos. 2010. *In the Days of Caesar: Pentecostalism and Political Theology*. Grand Rapids: Eerdmans.

Yong, Amos. 2011. *The Spirit of Creation: Modern Science and Divine Action in the Pentecostal-Charismatic Imagination*. Grand Rapids: Eerdmans.

Yong, Amos. 2012. "Pentecostal Scholarship and Scholarship on Pentecostalism: The Next Generation." *Pneuma* 34 (2): 161–165.

Yong, Amos. 2012. *Spirit of Love: A Trinitarian Theology of Grace*. Waco: Baylor University Press.

Yong, Amos. 2014. *Renewing Christian Theology: Systematics for a Global Christianity*. Waco, TX: Baylor University Press.

Yong, Amos, and Tony Richie. 2010. "Missiology and the Interreligious Encounter." In *Studying Global Pentecostalism: Theories and Methods*, edited by Allan Anderson, Michael Bergunder, André Droogers, and Cornelis van der Laan, 245–67. Berkeley: University of California Press.

Yong-gi Cho, D. 1997. *The Five-Fold Gospel and The Three-fold Blessing*. Seoul: Logos.

Yongmunsan Evangelism, ed. 1969. *The Track of Yongmunsan Movement*. Seoul: Aehyangsook Press.

Yongmunsan Evangelism, ed. 1980. *The 40 Years History of Yongmunsan Movement*. Seoul: Aehyangsook Press.

York, H. Stanley. 2013. *George Floyd Taylor: The Life of an Early Southern Pentecostal Leader*. Maitland FL, Xulon.

Yuasa, Key. 2001. "Louis Francescon: A Theological Biography, 1866–1964." Doctoral diss., University of Geneve.

Yung, Hwa. 2011. "Pentecostalism and the Asian Church." In *Asian and Pentecostal: The Charismatic Face of Christianity in Asia*, edited by Allan Anderson and Edmond Tang, 30–45. Eugene, OR: Wipf and Stock.

Zaplishny, Dionissy M. 1930. "Bulgaria Again Calls the Gospel Call of Russia."

Zarev, Ivan. 1993. *History of the Evangelical Pentecostal Churches in Bulgaria (1920–1989)*. Sofia: self-published.

Zawiejska, Natalia, and Linda van de Kamp. 2018. "The Multi-Polarity of Angolan Pentecostalism: Connections and Belongings." *PentecoStudies* 17 (1): 12–36.

Zeliang, Elungkiebe. 2014. *Charismatic Movements in the Baptist Churches in North East India: A Zeliangrong Perspective*. Delhi: ISPCK.

Zhang, Rongliang, and Eugene Bach. 2015. *I Stand with Christ: The Courageous Life of a Chinese Christian*. New Kensington: Whitaker House.

Zhang, Rongliang. 2015. *The Apostle of Fire: The Acts of Modern China* (火煉的使徒：现代中國使徒行傳). Hong Kong: Kingdom Ministries.

Ziefle, Joshua R. 2012. *David du Plessis and the Assemblies of God: The Struggle for the Soul of a Movement*. Leiden: Brill.

Zielicke, Seth N. 2012. "The Role of American Evangelist Tommy Hicks in the Development of ArgentinePentecostalism." In *Global Pentecostal Movements: Migration, Mission and Public Religion*, edited by Michael Wilkinson, 135–152. Leiden: Brill.

Zillinger, Martin. 2014. "Modernisations chrétiennes: Pratiques circulantes des media le long du Nil." [Christian Modernizations: Circulating Media Practices of the Mission along the Nile.] *L'Année du Maghreb* 11: 17–34.

Zimmerman-Liu, Teresa. 2014. "The Divine and Mystical Realm: Removing Chinese Christianity from the Fixed Structures of Mission Church and Clergy." *Social Sciences and Missions* 27 (2/3): 239–266.

Zimmerman-Liu, Teresa, and Teresa Wright. 2015. "What Is in a Name? A Comparison of being branded a Religious Cult in the United States and the People's Republic of China: Witness Lee and the Local Churches." *Journal of Church and State* 60 (2): 187–207.

Zimmerman-Liu, Teresa. 2017. "From 'Children of the Devil' to 'Sons of God': The Reconfiguration of Guanxi in a Twentieth-Century Indigenous Chinese Protestant Group." *Review of Religion and Chinese Society* 4 (1): 59–86.

Zinov'ev, Alexander Alexandrovich. 1973. *Foundations of the Logical Theory of Scientific Knowledge (Complex Knowledge)*. Dordrecht: D. Reidel Publishing Company.

Zub, Roberto. 1992. "The Growth of Protestantism: From Religion to Politics?" *Envio* 137.

Zucchi, Luigi. 1993. *The Italian Pentecostal Church of Canada: Origin and Brief History*. Montreal: Italian Pentecostal Church of Canada.

Zurlo, Gina A., Todd M. Johnson, and Peter F. Crossing. 2019. "Christianity 2019: What's Missing? A Call for Further Research." *International Bulletin of Mission Research* 43 (1): 92–102.

Index

Note: Main articles are indicated by page ranges in bold. Tables and photographs are indicated by page numbers in italics

Abala, Alexandre Aidini   144
Abraham, K.E.   1–2, 149
Abrams, Minnie   2–4, *3*, 439, 440
Abreu, Emilio   488, 489
abuse   247, 602
Academy for Leadership and Theology (ALT; Sweden)   623
Action Chapel International (Ghana)   12, 252, 253
Adams, Howard   136
Adams, John Archibald Duncan (J.A.D.)   **5–6**, 373
Adams, Leonard P.   136
Adeboye, Enoch Adejare   12, 421, 549, 666
Adelaja, Sunday   421, 450
Administrative Council of the Protestant and Evangelical Religion (ACPER)   57, 58
aesthetics and art   **7–8**
Afghanistan   *xxxii*, 38, 39
Africa   **9–13**. *See also* African independent/initiated/instituted churches; *specific countries*
   about   9, 13
   Anglican Renewal movement and   xxi
   anthropology and   27–28
   appeal of Pentecostalism   602, 613
   Reinhard Bonnke   78–80
   Bread of Life Church (Ling Liang Church)   185
   Classical Pentecostal denominations   10–11
   cosmology and   156
   ecology and   189, 190
   eschatology and   210
   Evangelical, understanding of   222
   healing and   603
   Holy Spirit, experience of   11–12, 602–603
   migration and expansion from   13
   Neo-Pentecostal movements   10, 12, 450–451
   Pentecostal/Charismatic population   xxii, *xliii–xliv*, 601
   politics   522
   Prosperity Gospel   12–13, 210
   worship   11, 12
Africa Evangelical Church (Botswana)   83
African independent/initiated/instituted churches (AICs, Aladura, Zionist churches)
   about   9–10, 60
   Cameroon   96
   definition of Pentecostalism and   175
   ecology and   189
   Ghana   251
   Kenya   627
   Nigeria   9, 461
   South Africa   9, 389, 602
   Tanzania   627
Agape Renewal Ministry (ARM; Taiwan)   **625–626**
Aglow (periodical)   14
Aglow International   10, **14–15**, 252
Agosto Cintrón, Nélida   108
Agüero, Emilio   489–490
Ahn, Ché   326
Akiman, David
   Jesus in Beijing   231
Akindayomi, Josiah   548–549
Akoko, Robert Mbe   97
Aladura. *See* African independent/initiated/instituted churches
Aladura International Church (UK)   641
Albania   *xxxii*, 216, 270
Albrecht, Daniel   614
Aldeia de Oração (Angola)   23
Åleskjær, Åge   466
Alexander, Charles   20, 44, 520
Alexander, Estrelda   544
Algeria   *xxvi, xxviii, xxxii*
All Saints Bible College (USA)   137
Allen, A.A.   **16–17**, 367, 394, 481
"Alliance Evangélique des Eglises de Pentecôte du Tchad" (AEEPT, Evangelical Alliance of Churches of Pentecost in Chad)   113–114
Alm, Daniel   624
Almeda, Wilde and Lina C.   511
Alpha   **17–19**, 301, 302, 641
altar call   146, 239, 614
Althouse, Peter   635
   Pentecostals and the Body (with Wilkinson)   205
Alvarado, Rafael   650
Álvarez, Miguel   307
Alvarez, Tomás   400
American Samoa   *xxvi, xxxii*, 15, 468, 469, 470, 471
Ames, Thomas   44
Ameux, Jean   164

ancestral beliefs and spirits 76, 157, 418
Anderson, Allan viii, xvi, 115, 116, 141, 147, 289, 297, 381
   To the Ends of the Earth 255
Andersson, Axel and Ester 424
Andorra *xxxii*
Anfuso, Francisco 130
Angare, Victorio 132
Angel (periodical) 408
angels 156
Angelus Temple 88, 413, 419
Anglican churches
   apostolic ministry and 30
   Alexander and Mary Boddy 71–74
   in Cape Verde 105
   conservative-liberal tensions 20–21
   Michael and Jeanne Harper xx, 20, 165, 271–273
   Holy Trinity Brompton 18, *301*, 301–302, 641
   liturgical revival 44
   Pentecostal/Charismatics in xix, xx–xxi
Anglican Essentials Canada 20–21
Anglican Renewal Ministries (Canada) **19–21**
Anglican Renewal Ministries (UK) xxi
Anglicans for Renewal Canada (periodical) 21
Anglin, Ava 587
Anglin, Leslie M. 342, 349, 587
Angola *xxvi, xxxii*, **21–23**, 270, 335
Anguilla *xxvii, xxxii*
Anim, Peter **24–25**, 251, 411
animal sounds 634
Annacondia, Carlos **25–27**, 33
anointing 33–34, 209, 303–304, 451, 635, 667
anthropology **27–28**, 259
Antigua & Barbuda *xxxii*
Antioch Network (Belgium) 57
Antoniuk, Józef 517
apostles and apostolic ministry **29–32**
   about 29–30
   Assemblies of God (USA) and 42
   in Australia 31
   debate over 30–31
   in Europe 218
   House Church Movement (UK) 31, **312–313**, 640–641
   Independent Network Charismatic (INC) Christianity and **454–455**
   Jesus is Lord Church Worldwide (Philippines) and 344
   in Latin America 31, 377
   Latter Rain and 381
   in Netherlands 453
   in Nicaragua 460
   regional manifestations 31–32
   Salt & Light **564–565**, 640
   in USA 31–32, 644
   Charles Peter Wagner and 31–32, **654–656**
Apostolic Action (Central African Republic) 112
Apostolic Assembly of the Faith in Christ Jesus (AAFCJ) 477
Apostolic Church 110
Apostolic Church (Australia) 110–111, 152, 468
Apostolic Church (Benin) 60
Apostolic Church (Cameroon) 97, 98
Apostolic Church (Denmark) 68, 69, 178
Apostolic Church (France) 235
Apostolic Church (Germany) 249
Apostolic Church (Ghana) 251, 411
Apostolic Church (Ireland) 332
Apostolic Church (Italy) 335
Apostolic Church (New Zealand) 152, 456, 457–458, 468
Apostolic Church (Nicaragua) 459
Apostolic Church (Slovakia) 590
Apostolic Church (Wales) 30, 216
Apostolic Church in the Czech Republic (Apoštolská církev v ČR) 162
Apostolic Church of Christ (Greece) 261
Apostolic Church of Ethiopia (ACE) 478
Apostolic Church of Ghana 251
Apostolic Church of Jesus Christ (ACJC) 499
Apostolic Church of the Faith in Christ Jesus (Iglesia Apostólica de la Fe en Cristo Jesús; Mexico) 423, 424
Apostolic Churches of Pentecost (Greece) 260, 261
Apostolic Evangel (periodical) 364
The Apostolic Faith (periodical)
   about 48, 578
   Thomas Ball Barratt and 54
   Frank Bartleman and 56
   Bernt Berntsen and 63
   Archibald Cooper and 150
   Abundio and Rosa López and 398
   Mok Lai Chi and 433
   Mukti Revival and 440, 546
   Martin Lawrence Ryan and 563
Apostolic Faith Church (Nigeria) 173, 174
Apostolic Faith Church (UK) 640
Apostolic Faith Mission (Australia) 6, 44, 88, 373, 468. *See also* Good News Hall
Apostolic Faith Mission (Botswana) 83
Apostolic Faith Mission (South Africa)
   Reinhard Bonnke, and 78
   Frank Chikane and 117–118

Apostolic Faith Mission (South Africa) (cont.)
   Archibald Cooper and   150
   David du Plessis and   181
   ecumenism and   193
   establishment   288–289, 369, 383, 602
   Full Gospel Church and   150–151
   Pieter L. Le Roux and   383, 389
   Elias Letwaba and   388–389
   race and   117–118, 289, 383, 388–389
   Redeemed Christian Church of God (Nigeria) and   548
Apostolic Faith Mission (USA). *See* Azusa Street Revival
Apostolic Faith Movement   47, 490, 491, 642–643
Apostolic Light (periodical)   563
apostolic networks   218. *See also* apostles and apostolic ministry
Apostolic World Christian Fellowship   477
Arab Baptist Theological Seminary (ABTS; Lebanon)   386
Arana Cárdenas, Denis   377
Arbeitsgemeinschaft Christlicher Kirchen (Germany)   250
Arbeitsgemeinschaft Pfingstlich-Charismatischer Missionen (Germany)   250
Arbizu, Francisco   415
Archer, Kenneth J.   227, 285, 286, 516
Arevalo, Ruben   422
Argeñal, Misael   306
Argentina   32–34
   Aglow International   15
   Carlos Annacondia   25–27, 33
   anointing movement   33–34
   Apostolic Church of the Faith in Christ Jesus (Mexico) in   423
   beginnings of Pentecostalism   32–33
   Catholic Charismatic Renewal   34
   Charismatic population   *xxvii*
   Christian Assemblies   129–131, 237, 335, 509
   Tommy Hicks   26, 33, 280, 290–291, *291*
   Pentecostal/Charismatic growth rate   *xxvi*
   Pentecostal/Charismatic population   *xxxii*, 34
   Rhema Bible Training Center campus in   270
Argue, Andrew Harvey (A.H.)   34, 35, *35*, 100, 184, 410, 493
Argue, Watson   35
Argue, Zelma   34–36, *35*, 495
Argüello, Francisco (Kiko)   609
Arifin Tedjakusuma, Timotius   320, 464
Armenia   *xxxii*, 39, 40
Arnott, Carol   101
Arnott, John   101, 634, 635

Arrington, French   465
Arslan, Otgontsetseg   434
art and aesthetics   7–8
Aruba   *xxxii*, 108
Arvizú, Francisco   264
Asamblea Cristiana "Dios es Amor" (Argentina)   131
Asamblea Cristiana Evangelica (Argentina)   131
Asamoah-Gyadu, J. Kwabena   450
Ashimolowo, Matthew   13, 421, 450, 641
Ashram movement   196
Asia   37–40. *See also specific countries*
   about   37
   Central Asia   39
   East, Southeast, and South Asia   37–39
   Evangelical, understanding of   222
   Pentecostal/Charismatic population   *xxii*, *xliv*
   West Asia   39–40
Asia Pacific Theological Association (APTA)   293
Asia Pacific Theological Seminary (Philippines)   434
Asian Seminary of Christian Ministries (Philippines)   307
Asociación Teológica de América Latina (ATAL)   293
Assemblea Cristiana (USA)   102, 324
Assemblee di Dio in Italia (ADI)   335
Assemblées de Dieu (France)   216
Assemblies of God
   in Africa   10
   A.A. Allen and   16, 17
   Bernt Berntsen and   63
   David du Plessis and   181
   Prosperity Gospel and   42, 76
   in West Asia   40
   World Assemblies of God Fellowship (WAGF)   103, 267, 335, **670**–**671**
Assemblies of God (American Samoa)   469, 470, 471
Assemblies of God (Angola)   22–23
Assemblies of God (Argentina)   33
Assemblies of God (Australia). *See* Australian Christian Churches
Assemblies of God (Benin)   59, 60
Assemblies of God (Bolivia)   74
Assemblies of God (Botswana)   83
Assemblies of God (Brazil)   89–90
Assemblies of God (Bulgaria)   91, 92, 653, 680
Assemblies of God (Cameroon)   97
Assemblies of God (Canada). *See* Canadian Assemblies of God
Assemblies of God (Cape Verde)   105–106

INDEX

Assemblies of God (Central African Republic)   112
Assemblies of God (Chile)   120
Assemblies of God (China)   122, 438, 587, 624
Assemblies of God (Côte d'Ivoire)   158, 159
Assemblies of God (Cuba)   160
Assemblies of God (El Salvador)   198, 415
Assemblies of God (Fiji)   469, 470, 471, 485
Assemblies of God (France)   235–236
Assemblies of God (Ghana)   251, 253
Assemblies of God (Greece)   260
Assemblies of God (Guam)   470
Assemblies of God (Guatemala)   264
Assemblies of God (Honduras)   306
Assemblies of God (Hong Kong)   308, 438
Assemblies of God (India)   93–94, 149
Assemblies of God (Ireland)   332
Assemblies of God (Italy)   103, 237, 324, 337–338
Assemblies of God (Japan)   152, 353, 354, 675, 676, 677
Assemblies of God (Jordan)   352
Assemblies of God (Liberia)   392
Assemblies of God (Malaysia)   267, 365, 403
Assemblies of God (Marshall Islands)   470
Assemblies of God (Mexico)   422–423, 423–424
Assemblies of God (Mongolia)   434
Assemblies of God (Myanmar)   125–126
Assemblies of God (Netherlands)   453
Assemblies of God (New Zealand)   69, 70, 315–316, 456, 457, 469
Assemblies of God (Nicaragua)   459, 460
Assemblies of God (Papua New Guinea)   469, 471
Assemblies of God (Paraguay)   488, 489
Assemblies of God (Philippines)   511
Assemblies of God (Portugal)   523–524
Assemblies of God (Puerto Rico)   473
Assemblies of God (Rwanda)   562
Assemblies of God (Samoa (Western Samoa))   470, 471
Assemblies of God (Solomon Islands)   470
Assemblies of God (South Africa)   66–67, 602
Assemblies of God (South Korea)   127, 604
Assemblies of God (Spain)   607
Assemblies of God (Taiwan)   624
Assemblies of God (Tanzania)   627, 628
Assemblies of God (UK)   216, 243, 244, 505, 520, 640, 642
Assemblies of God (USA)   **41–43**
    Zelma Argue and   36
    Bethel Church and   64
    Nicholas Bhengu and   66–67
    F.F. Bosworth and   80, 81
    Robert Felix Cook and   149
    ecumenism and   42, 192–193
    establishment   41, 643
    Evangelicalism and   223–224
    in first wave Pentecostalism   ix
    glossolalia and   42, 81, 257
    growth of   42–43
    Kenneth Hagin and   270
    G.T. Haywood and   278
    International Fellowship of Christian Assemblies and   325
    Kong Duen Yee (Mui Yee) and   365
    Latter Rain and   381
    Alice Eveline Luce and   398–399
    Juan León Lugo and   399–400
    media and higher education   41–42, 170, 293
    missionary efforts   42, 293, 399
    Carrie Judd Montgomery and   437
    Nicholas Nikolov and   91, 463
    Francisco Olazábal and   473
    Oneness Pentecostalism and   42, 476, 477, 643
    Charles S. Price and   530
    race and   43
    William Wallace Simpson and   587
    theological challenges and   42
    Ivan Efimovich Voronaev and   653
    Smith Wigglesworth and   662
    Dionissy Michailovitch Zaplishny and   680
Assemblies of God (Vanuatu)   471
Assemblies of God (Venezuela)   649, 650
Assemblies of God (Zimbabwe)   684
Assemblies of God in Queensland (AoGQ)   44, 263
Assemblies of God Theological Seminary   42
Assembly of Christian Churches (AIC)   400
"Association des eglises de Pentecote au Rwanda" (ADEPR; Pentecostal church of Rwanda)   561, 562
Association for Native Evangelism   481
Association for Pentecostal Theological Education in Africa (APTEA)   293
Association of African Earthkeeping Churches   190
Association of Resolute Christians (Czech Republic)   162
Association of Theological Schools   223
Association of Vineyard Churches
    Alpha and Holy Trinity Brompton   18–19, 302
    biblical teaching   665
    Bickle and Kansas City prophets   326, 664
    Central Asia   39
    classification of   ix, xxi
    Malaysia   404
    Netherlands   453

Association of Vineyard Churches (cont.)
  social engagement 665
  Toronto Blessing and 634–635, 664
  John Wimber and **663–666** (*See also* Wimber, John)
Atcho, Albert 159
Atkinson, Maria W. 135
Au, Connie 613, 638
Augustine, Daniela C. 516
Augustine of Hippo 258
Austin, Ray 308
Austin-Sparks, T. 583
Australia **43–46**
  John Archibald Duncan Adams and 6
  Aglow International 15
  apostolic ministry and 31
  beginnings of Pentecostalism 43–44, 468
  Mina Ross Brawner 87–88
  William Cathcart 110–111
  Alexander Thomas Davidson 169–170
  El Shaddai (Philippines) and 648
  Charles L. Greenwood 6, 170, **262–263**, 273, 372
  growth period 44–45, 469
  Leo Cecil Harris 44, 111, 263, **273–275**
  higher education 46, 88, 170, 263, 270, 514
  Hillsong **294–296** (*See also* Hillsong)
  William Francis (Frank) Houston 316
  Italian Transnational Pentecostal Movement and 335
  Jesus People Movement and 347
  Sarah Jane (Murrell) Lancaster 6, 44, 88, 262, **371–373**, 468
  megachurches and international missions 45–46
  National Revival Crusade 111, 274
  Pentecostal/Charismatic population *xxxii, xlv,* 43
  Smith Wigglesworth and 663
Australian Christian Churches (formerly Assemblies of God in Australia (AGA))
  apostolic ministry and 31
  Alexander Thomas Davidson and 169–170
  establishment 44, 263
  Charles L. Greenwood and 262, 263
  Leo Cecil Harris and 273
  higher education 170, 263
  Hillsong and 295
  William Francis (Frank) Houston and 316
  Sarah Jane Lancaster's family and 373
  megachurches and 45
  missionary efforts 45, 469
  radio ministry 169
  Darlene Zschech and 685
Australian Evangel (periodical) 262
Austria *xxxii,* 270
Autero, Esa J. 76
Averill, Lloyd 373
Avila, Yiye 25
Awrey, Daniel 284
Azerbaijan *xxxii,* 39, 40
Azusa Street Revival **46–49**. *See also The Apostolic Faith* (periodical)
  Peter Anim and 25
  Australia and 44
  baptism in the Holy Spirit and 46–47, 577
  Thomas Ball Barratt and 54
  Frank and Anna (Ladd) Bartleman and 56
  beginnings of 46–47, 643
  Bernt Berntsen and 63
  Robert Felix Cook and 148
  Archibald Cooper and 150
  decline and end 48–49, 579
  William H. Durham and 49, 183
  ethics and 211
  Lucy Farrow and 231–232
  first wave Pentecostalism and ix
  glossolalia and 48, 258
  Thomas Hezmalhalch and 288
  Hong Kong and 307
  John G. Lake and 370
  Lucy Leatherman and 384
  Liberia and 391
  Abundio and Rosa López and 397–398
  Charles Harrison Mason and 136
  R.E. McAlister and 408
  Mexico and 422
  miracles, signs, and wonders and 428
  missions and global influence 40, 47–48, 602, 643
  Carrie Judd Montgomery and 437
  origins of Pentecostalism and viii
  Charles Parham and 492
  in Pentecostal historiography 297
  Cecil Polhill and 520
  Charles S. Price and 528
  race and 543, 578–579
  Martin Lawrence Ryan and 563
  William Seymour and viii, 46–47, 48–49, 577–578, 643
  South Africa and 602
  True Jesus Church and 636
  Welsh Revival and 46, 661

Bacani, Teodoro C.   200, 648
Back to Jerusalem Movement   124, 658
Bae, Bu-Geun   604
Bagnall, Diana   685
Bahamas   *xxxii*, 107–108, 135
Bahrain   *xxxii*, 39, 648
Bahtera (the Ark; Indonesia)   537
Baily, Annie L.   138
Baker, Charles E.   497
Baker, David   491
Bakker, Jim   392, 553
Bakker, Tammy Faye   553
Balca, Jan   590
Balcombe, Dennis   50–51, 230–231, 308–309, 682
Ball, Henry (H.C.)   398, 422, 423, 473
Ballesteros, Samuel   375
Ballinger, Julia   472, 473
Bangladesh   *xxxii*
baptism
    believer's baptism   54, 166, 237, 324, 466
    in Christian Congregation in Brazil   132
    conversion and   147
    infant baptism   54, 95, 119, 237, 311
    in Oneness Pentecostalism   63, 278, 409, 476, 477
    in True Jesus Church   637, 659
baptism in the Holy Spirit   51–53
    about   xviii, 51–52, 228, 515
    Peter Anim and   25
    Azusa Street Revival and   46–47, 577
    Dennis Balcombe and   50
    Catholic Charismatic Renewal and   116
    Classical Pentecostalism on   52, 515
    conversion and   147
    cosmology and   155–156
    William H. Durham and   183
    ecclesiology and   187
    first wave Pentecostalism and   ix
    Full Gospel and   239
    glossolalia and other spiritual gifts   xviii, 47, 52, 256–257, 515
    Ha Young Jo on   269
    Holiness Pentecostals and   41, 47, 327
    marginalization of   52–53
    Charles Harrison Mason on   406
    Charles Parham and   ix, 47, 491–492, 642
    Roman Catholic–Pentecostal dialogue and   555, 556
    soteriology and   599–600
    George Floyd Taylor and   631
    in True Jesus Church   637

Baptist Evangelical Churches (Central African Republic)   112
Baptist Mission of Botswana   83
Barbados   *xxvi*, *xxxii*
Barber, Karin   416
Barber, Margaret E.   123, 448, 583
Barbera, Domenico   336
Barnabas Anglican Ministries   20, 21
Barr, James   189
Barr, Rebecca and Edmond S.   107, 135
Barratt, Thomas Ball (T.B.)   53–54
    Azusa Street Revival and   48, 54
    background   53–54
    Alexander Boddy and   72–73
    death   216
    Denmark and   68, 177
    DR Congo and   143
    European Pentecostalism and   215
    Finland and   233
    Germany and   248
    influence of   54
    international Pentecostal union efforts   505
    Joseph H. King and   364
    Lucy Leatherman and   384
    Norway and   54, 466, 467
    Lewi Pethrus and   54, 466, 508, 623
    Charles S. Price and   530
    Sweden and   623
Barrett, David B.
    counting Independent Charismatics   xix, xxi
    counting Pentecostals, early efforts   xiii–xv, *xv*, xvii, 615
    counting Roman Catholic Charismatics   xxii
    critiques of   xv–xvi
    terminology used by   xx
Barros, Valéria   336
Barth, Hattie   209
Barth, N.H.   441
Bartleman, Anna (Ladd)   55–56
Bartleman, Frank   55–56, 72, 284, 496, 542, 661
Barton, Bernadette   575
Basham, Don   581–582
Batterham, David   315
Baugh, Edith   4
Bautista, Juan   650
Baxter, Elizabeth   283, 358–359
Baxter, Ern   86, 581–582
Bays, Daniel   342, 639
Beacham, A.D., Jr.   329
Beacham, Paul   328
Beall, Myrtle D.   380

Bebbington, David   222
Bednar, Milan   590
Belarus   *xxxii*
Belgium   *xxxii*, 15, 57–58, 116, 565, 648
Believer's Voice of Victory (periodical)   153
Belize   *xxxiii*
Bell, Eudorus (E.N.)   41, 136, 184, 653, 669
Bell, J. Wilson   339
Bender, Gottfried (G.F.)   649–651
Benin   *xxxiii*, 59–62
Bennett, Dennis   xix, xx, 20, 404, 582
Benney, Paul
    "Speaking in Tongues"   8
Beretta, Giuseppe   237, 324
Berg, Daniel   89, 184, 523
Berg, David   347
Berg, George   148
Berlin Declaration   249, 517
Bermuda   *xxxiii*
Bernabei, Antonio   510
Berntsen, Bernt   62–64, 123, 636, 659
Berry, Faith Montgomery   437
Bertrand, Louis   258
Bethel Bible Institute (Saskatoon, SK)   275–276
Bethel Church   64–65, 209, 453
Bethel School for Supernatural Ministry (BSSM)   64, 65
Bezalel Evangelistic Mission   4
Bhengu, Nicholas   66–67, 289
Bhutan   xxv, *xxvi, xxviii, xxxiii*
Bially, Geraldo A.   649, 651
Bible. *See also* theology
    on ecclesiology   186
    exegesis   225–227
    experience of God and   229
    on glossolalia   257–258, 610
    hermeneutics   285–288, 376, 516
    homiletics   303–305
    Latter Rain interpretations   380
    on miracles, signs, and wonders   429
    on spiritual gifts   609–612
    theology and   632
Bible College of Malaya   403–404
Bible College of Wales   78
Bible Life Ministries (Botswana)   83
Bible School of Evangelism (Myanmar)   126
Bible-Pattern Church Fellowship (UK)   341
Bickle, Mike   196, 325, 326, 664
Binder, Herbert   415
Biolley, Hélène   235
Bird, Warren   420
Bishau, D.   683

Bjørner, Sigurd and Anna Larssen   67–69, 177–178
Black Consciousness Movement   66, 117
Blaisdell, George and Francisca   422
Blake, Charles Edward, Sr.   138, 501
Blanton, Anderson
    Hittin' the Prayer Bones   205
Blessed Trinity Society   xx
Bloomfield, Ray   69–70, 315
Blue Cross (Modrý kríž; Slovakia)   590
Blue Ocean Faith (USA)   666
Blumhardt, Johann   436
Blumhofer, Edith   595
Boardman, William Edwin   357, 358
Bochian, Pavel   70–71
Boddy, Alexander (A.A.)   71–74
    about and background   71–72
    Thomas Ball Barratt and   54, 72–73
    William Frederick Burton and   95
    Confidence (magazine)   44, 73
    death   74
    European Pentecostalism and   73–74, 215, 249
    George Jeffreys and   340
    Sarah Jane Lancaster and   372
    Pentecostal Missionary Union and   73, 101, 504, 505
    Pentecostalism, first encounters   72–73
    Cecil Polhill and   73, 520
    Sunderland Conventions   72, 73, 215, 340, 505, 520
    Welsh Revival and   72, 359
Boddy, Mary   71–74, 662
body and embodiment   203–205, 633. *See also* aesthetics and art; experience, of God; sexuality
Bokeum Newspaper   527
Bolivia   74–77
    ancestral and traditional beliefs   76
    appeal of Pentecostalism   75
    beginnings of Pentecostalism   74
    Neo-Pentecostalism and Prosperity Gospel   75–76
    Pentecostal/Charismatic population   *xxxiii*, 77
    Rhema Bible Training Center campus in   270
    Julio Cesar Ruibal   74–75, 559–560
    social change and   76–77
    Charles Peter Wagner and   654
Bom Deus Church (Angola)   23, 106
Bongiovanni, Guy   336
Bonnke, Reinhard   78, 78–80, 98, 450, 471, 588, 629
Booth, Herbert   372
Booth, William   315, 437
Bosnia-Herzegovina   *xxxiii. See also* Yugoslavia

INDEX 763

Bosworth, F.F.   6, 42, 80–82, *81*, *82*, 86, 288, 394, 481, 669
Botswana   *xxviii*, *xxxiii*, 82–83, 137
Botswana Pentecostal Protestant Church   83
Bouillon, David   166
Boulos, Ayub   385
Boulos, Nashed   385
Bowie, George   150
Bowler, Kate   190, 270
Braaten, Carl   189
Bracco, Roberto   336
Bradin, Gheorghe   71, 84–85
Bradley, Amos and Effie   198
Braide, Garrick Sokari   9
Branham, William Marrion   82, *85*, 85–87, 156, 276, 367, 393, 394, 481, 644
Brawner, Mina Ross   87–88
Brazil   89–91
   Aglow International   15
   Apostolic Church of the Faith in Christ Jesus (Mexico) in   423
   beginnings of Pentecostalism   89–90
   Catholic and mainline Charismatic renewal   90, 375, 377
   Charismatic population   xxvii, *xxvii*
   Christian Congregation in Brazil   89–90, 130, 131–133, 237, 238, 335
   Evangelicalism and   225
   Louis Francescon and   89, 238
   Independent Charismatic population   *xxviii*
   Edir Macedo   90, 377, 401–402, 451, 645, 647
   media   377, 416
   Neo-Pentecostalism   90–91, 451–452
   Pentecostal (denominational) population   xxvi, *xxvi*
   Pentecostal/Charismatic growth rate   *xxvi*
   Pentecostal/Charismatic population   xxiv, *xxiv*, xxv, *xxv*, *xxxiii*
   Giuseppe Petrelli and   509
   politics   522
   Rhema Bible Training Center campus in   270
   Universal Church of the Kingdom of God   645–647 (*See also* Universal Church of the Kingdom of God)
"Brazil for Christ" Evangelical Pentecostal Church   90
Bread of Life Church (Ling Liang Church)   123, 185, 309, 625, 626
Brelsford, George and Lydia   195
Brenkus, Jozef   220, 590
Brethren Church (Církev bratrská; Czech Republic)   162

Brewster, P.S.   202
Bridegroom's Messenger (periodical)   433
Bright, Bill   348
Brisbin, Lawrence   499
British Apostolic Church   25
British Israelism   44, 82, 111, 168, 202, 273, 274, 341, 468, 491
British Missionary Council   111
British Virgin Islands   *xxxiii*
Britton, F.M.   638
Brooks, Noel   328
Brotherhood of Greek Pentecostal Churches   261
Brown, Candy Gunther   534
Brown, Elisabeth   384
Brown, Jessie   384
Brown, Marie (Burgess)   384, 400
Brown, Robert   400, 463, 679
Brownsville Revival   250
Brunei   *xxxiii*, 648
Bryant, Daniel   383
Bryant, W.F.   134
Buchanan, William Alexander   373
Bucher, Johannes   383
Buciaga, Cesáreo   422
Bueno, John and Lois   198
Buletinul Cultului Penticostal (Pentecostal Bulletin)   566
Bulgaria   91–93
   Anna (Ladd) Bartleman and   56
   beginnings of Pentecostalism   91
   Communist era   92, 216, 680
   higher education   92
   Nicholas Nikolov   91, 463–464, 680
   Oneness Pentecostalism and   478
   Pentecostal/Charismatic population   *xxxiii*
   post-Communist development   92–93
   Ivan Efimovich Voronaev   91, 463, 653, 680
   Dionissy Michailovitch Zaplishny   91, 463, 679–680
Bulgarian Chaplaincy Coalition   92
Bulgarian Christian Coalition   92
Bulgarian Evangelical Alliance   92
Bulgarian Evangelical Theological Institute   92
Bulgarian Pentecostal Union   653
Bullen, Federico   649, 651
Bullock, Geoff   295, 685
Buntain, D. Mark   93–94
Buntain, Daniel Newton (D.N.)   93, 530
Buntain, Huldah   93, 94
Burbidge, Michael   555
Burkhardt, Albert   113
Burkina Faso   *xxvi*, *xxxiii*

Burma. *See* Myanmar
Burnett, Bill 20
Burning Bush Tabernacle (Liberia) 392
Bursey, A. Stanley 497
Burton, William Frederick 95–96, 143
Burundi *xxxiii*
Bustamante, Manuel 422
Bustraan, Richard 347
Butindaro, Giacinto 336
Butler, Eva S. 474
Butticci, Annalisa 336, 337, 338
Byposten (periodical) 54

C3 Church Global (C3 Oxford Falls; Australia) 45, 46
Caballeros, Harold 209–210, 266
Cabo Verde (Cape Verde) *xxxiii*, 105–106
Cabrera, Omar 33, 34
Cacciatore, Nicholas 336
Cahiers du Renouveau 172
Cain, Paul 326, 664
Caine, Christine 296
Calcutta Mercy Ministries 94
Calissi, Mateo 34
The Call (prayer initiative) 326
The Call of the Kingdom Movement (Egypt) 196
Callahan, Lillian 563
Calvary Chapel 346, 663
Calvary Church (Malaysia) 267–268
Calvary Theological College (UK) 137
Cambodia xxvi, *xxvi, xxviii, xxxiii*, 686
The Cambridge Companion to Pentecostalism 186
Cameroon *xxxiii*, **96–99**
Campos, Bernardo 31, 161, 374
Camps Farthest Out 45, 567
Campus Crusade for Christ 268, 677
Canada **99–101**
    Aglow International 15
    Anglican Renewal Ministries 19–21
    Zelma Argue 34–36, *35*, 495
    beginnings of Pentecostalism 100
    Canadian Assemblies of God 102–103, 237, 324, 335, 509
    challenges facing 101
    Church of God in Christ 137
    comparisons to USA 100–101
    demographics, Pentecostal 99–100
    El Shaddai (Philippines) and 648
    Alice Belle Garrigus 240–242, *241*
    George Hawtin 101, 275, 275–277, 379, 379–380, 381
    Ellen Hebden 100, 283–285, 350, 359
    higher education 275–276, 494
    international contributions 101
    R.E. McAlister 101, 408–410, *409*, 476, 493
    Pentecostal Assemblies of Canada **493–495**
        (*See also* Pentecostal Assemblies of Canada)
    Pentecostal Assemblies of Newfoundland and Labrador 99, 493–494, **496–498**
    Pentecostal/Charismatic population *xxxiii*, 99
    Charles S. Price and 529
    Rhema Bible Training Center campus in 270
    Salt & Light 565
    Toronto Blessing (Catch the Fire) 101, 209, 234, 250, 302, 326, 443, **634–635**, 664
Canadian Assemblies of God (formerly Italian Pentecostal Church of Canada) 102–103, 237, 324, 335, 509
Canadian Pentecostal Research Network 595
Cantalamessa, Raniero 104–105
Cantel, Margaret 243
Cape Verde (Cabo Verde) *xxxiii*, 105–106
Capps, Charles 271
Caravela, Manuel José de Matos 523
Carbajal de Valenzuela, Genaro 422
Carbajal de Valenzuela, Romana "Romanita" 422, 423, 477
Caribbean *xliv*, 107–110. *See also specific countries*
Caribbean Netherlands *xxxiii*
Carlson, Raymond 194
Carothers, W.F. 492
Carr, Andrew 488–489
Carter, Howard 44
Cartledge, David 30, 31, 316
Cartledge, Mark J. 593, 635
Cashwell, G.B. 327, 363–364, 643
Castelo, Daniel 612
Castiglione, Mariam 336
Catch the Fire 209. *See also* Toronto Blessing
Cathcart, William 110–111
Catholic Apostolic Church (CAC) 30, 43–44, 381
Catholic Charismatic Renewal (CCR) **115–116**. *See also* Roman Catholic Church
    about xxii, xxvii, 115–116
    Angola 23
    Argentina 34
    baptism in the Holy Spirit and 116
    beginnings and international growth 116
    Belgium 57, 58
    Brazil 90, 375, 377
    Raniero Cantalamessa 104–105
    Communauté de l'Emmanuel 171, 172, 236
    Communauté du Chemin Neuf 172, 236
    Cuba 161

INDEX

Catholic Charismatic Renewal (cont.)
  Albert de Monléon 171–172
  David du Plessis and 181–182
  Egypt 195
  El Shaddai (Philippines) and 200, 648
  France 116, 165, 236
  in global context xxiii
  Guatemala 265, 266
  Hong Kong 309
  India 116, 319
  Indonesia 320–321
  International Catholic Charismatic Renewal Services xxii, 547
  Italy 116, 338
  Kathryn Kuhlman and 367
  Latin America 375, 376, 377
  Messianic Judaism and 116
  Nicaragua 459
  Paraguay 488
  Philippines 37, 116, 512
  Poland 518–519
  Portugal 524–525
  Kevin and Dorothy Ranaghan 546–548
  Spain 609
  Leo Jozef Suenens 57, 272, 547, **617–619**
  Taiwan 625
  United Kingdom 642
Catholic Charismatic Renewal International Service (CHARIS) 547
Cayman Islands xxxiii
Celestial Church of Christ 59, 60, 641
cell churches. *See also* house churches
  Centro Familiar de Adoración 489
  Yonggi Cho and Yoido Full Gospel Church 173, 404, 604, 673
  Deeper Life Bible Church 173
  Holy Trinity Brompton 302
  Malaysia 404
  Mongolia 434, 435
Center for the Study of Global Christianity (CSGC) xvi, xvii
Central African Republic xxxiv, 112–113
Central American Mission (CAM) 415, 459, 460
Central Asia 39. *See also specific countries*
Central Bible Institute (Japan) 677
Central Bible Institute (USA) 16, 42, 463
Central University (Ghana) 483
Centre Evangelique Francophone "La Borne" (DR Congo) 144
Centro Familiar de Adoración (CFA; Paraguay) 488, 489

Cerullo, Morris 537, 651
Ceylon Pentecostal Mission 2, 403
C.H. Mason System of Jurisdictional Institutes 137
C.H. Mason Theological Seminary (USA) 137
Chacko, P.T. 1
Chad xxxiv, 113–115
Chakrabarty, Dipesh 297
Chambe, Juan J. 76
Chan, Ernst 625
Chan, Simon K.H. 446, 516
Channel Islands xxxiv
Chapman, Mary 1, 44, 149
Charisma (Eritrea) 207
Charismatics (Charismatic Movement, Charismatic Renewal). *See also* Catholic Charismatic Renewal
  about xix
  Anglican Renewal Ministries (Canada) **19–21**
  Anglicans xix, xx–xxi
  Argentina 34
  Cameroon 97–98
  Central African Republic 113
  Chad 113
  Émile and Louis Dallière and 165, 166
  ecumenism and 192
  eschatology and 209
  Europe 218
  Germany 249–250
  in global context xxiii
  growth trends xxii
  Michael and Jeanne Harper 271–273
  Hong Kong 308–309
  Indonesia 320
  Netherlands 453
  populations by country xxvii, *xxvii*
  secularization and 572
  Shepherding Movement and 582
  Taiwan 625
  United Kingdom 640, 641–642
  USA 644
Charles, Yvon 236
Chauvie, Aida 510
Chawner, Charles 284
Chemin Neuf (Communauté du Chemin Neuf) 172, 236
Chen, Bixi 349
Cherian, K.C. 1
Chernoff, Marty and Yohanna 116
Cherubim and Seraphim Church 548, 641, 666
Chesnut, Abner 604
Chesnut, R. Andrew 597

Cheung, Joshua   309
Chevreau, Guy   635
Chiesa Evangelica della Riconciliazione (Italy)   335
Chiesa Evangelica Internationale (Italy)   335
Chiese Cristiane Italiane del Nord Europa   335
Chiese Cristiane Pentecostali in Italia   335
Chikane, Frank   117–118
Children of God   347
Chile   118–121
   Minnie Abrams and   4, 440
   Aglow International   15
   appeal of Pentecostalism   120
   beginnings and growth of Pentecostalism   118–120
   Charismatic population   xxvii
   contemporary practices   121, 376
   Willis Collins Hoover   4, 119, 120, 121, **309–311**, 440
   Independent Charismatic population   xxviii
   Mukti Revival and   440
   opposition to Pentecostalism   223
   Pentecostal/Charismatic population   xxv, xxxiv, 121
   Rhema Bible Training Center campus in   270
   social engagement and politics   120–121, 224
China   **122–124**. *See also* Hong Kong; Taiwan
   about   37
   Dennis Balcombe   50–51, 230–231, 682
   Bernt Berntsen   **62–64**, 123, 636, 659
   Charismatic population   xxvii
   Communist era   123–124, 313, 349, 438, 449
   Dzao, Timothy   123, **184–185**
   Fangcheng Fellowship   230–231, 314, 682
   higher education   185, 588, 675
   house churches   124, **313–314**, 658
   Independent Charismatic population   xxvii, xxviii
   indigenous movements   123
   Jesus Family Church   123, **342–343**, 349
   Jing Dianying   123, 124, 342, 343, **348–349**
   Lucy Leatherman and   385
   Li Changshou (Witness Lee)   **389–391**, 449, 583
   missionaries to   122–123
   J. Elmor Morrison   308, **437–438**
   Watchman Nee (Ni Tuosheng)   **447–449** (*See also* Nee, Watchman)
   Oneness Pentecostalism   62, 63, 123, 478
   Pentecostal Missionary Union and   504
   Pentecostal/Charismatic population   xxiv, xxv
   politics   522
   Rhema Bible Training Center campus in   270
   Martin Lawrence Ryan and   564
   Shandong Revival   123, **579–581**, 619
   Shouters (Christian Assemblies, Little Flock, Local Church)   30, 123, 391, 583, **583–584**, 656, 657
   William Wallace Simpson   **586–588**
   Spiritual Gifts Society   123, 580
   John Sung (Song Shangjie)   403, 581, 588, **619–621**
   True Jesus Church   **636–637** (*See also* True Jesus Church)
   William H. Turner   307, **638–639**
   Wang Zai (Leland Wang)   **656–657**, 675
   Weepers   **657–658**
   Paul Wei (Wei Enbo)   63–64, 123, 478, 636, **658–659**
   Yu Cidu (Dora Yu)   123, 448, 583, **674–675**
   Zhang Rongliang   230, 231, **681–682**
China Assemblies of God   122, 438, 587, 624
China Inland Mission (CIM)   73, 504, 519, 520, 587
Chinese Christian Prayer Mountain (Taiwan)   625
Chinese Conversion Fellowship. *See* Fangcheng Fellowship (China)
Chinese Foreign Missionary Union (CFMU)   184, 657
Chinese Gospel Fellowship (China)   230
Chinese-Indonesian Mennonite Churches (GKMI)   621
Chiquete, Daniel   374
Chiquie, Munir   76–77
Chirinos, Martín   650
Chit, Myo   **125–126**
Chitando, E.   684
Cho, Yonggi (David/Paul Yonggi Cho)   **126–128**. *See also* Yoido Full Gospel Church (South Korea)
   background   126–127
   beliefs   127–128, 210, 673
   Jashil Choi and   128, 129
   ecology and   189
   healing and   127
   in Malaysia   404
   in Mongolia   435
   Neo-Pentecostalism and   451
   Petrus Agung Pernomo and   537
   photograph   127
   Prayer Mountain Movement and   527
   Prosperity Gospel and   531
   Yoido Full Gospel Church and   127, 128, 604, 672
Choi, Jashil   127, **128–129**, 527, 604
Chosŏn Pentecostal Church (Chosŏn Osunjŏl Kyohoe; Korea)   152

Chow, Feng Ling   587
Chow, Nathaniel   625
Christ Apostolic Church (Ghana)   25, 251, 253
Christ Apostolic Church Mount Bethel (UK)   641
Christ Apostolic Church of Great Britain   641
Christ Apostolic Churches   10
Christ Chapel International Churches (Cameroon)   98
Christ Citadel International Church   83
Christ Embassy   83
Christ for all Nations (CfaN)   79–80
Christ for the Nations (periodical)   394
Christ for the Nations Inc.   394. *See also* Voice of Healing
Christ for the Nations Institute (USA)   393, 394
Christenson, Larry   189, 272, 273, 567, 582
Christerson, Brad   454, 455
Christian and Missionary Alliance (CMA)   81, 122, 158, 184, 436, 437, 440, 586–587, 651
Christian Assemblies (Argentina)   **129–131**, 237, 335, 509
Christian Assemblies (Little Flock, Local Church, Shouters; China)   30, 123, 391, 583, **583–584**, 656, 657
Christian Assembly "God is Love" (Argentina)   335, 510
Christian Biblical Church (Argentina)   130
Christian Catholic Apostolic Church (CCAC)   30, 383
Christian Catholic Apostolic Holy Spirit Church in Zion (South Africa)   383
Christian Church of North America   102, 130, 323, 509, 509. *See also* International Fellowship of Christian Assemblies
Christian Churches Ireland (CCI)   333
Christian Congregation in Brazil (CCB)   89–90, 130, **131–133**, 237, 238, 335
Christian Congregation in Canada   103
Christian Congregation in France   335
Christian Congregation in Portugal   335, 524
Christian Congregation in the United States   325, 335
Christian Evangel (periodical)   485
Christian Fellowship Joyful Heart (Spoločenstvo kresťanov Radostné srdce; Slovakia)   590
Christian Fellowships (Kresťanská spoločenstvá; Slovakia)   590, 591
Christian Global Network Television (CGNTV)   269
Christian Growth Ministries (USA)   582
Christian Life Assembly (Rwanda)   562
Christian Mission Alliance   352

Christian Outreach Centres (now INC; Australia)   45, 46
Christian Revival Crusade (CRC)   273, 274–275, 456, 468, 470
Christian World Liberation Front   346
Christianity, demographic and growth   vii, xiii
Christology   153, 186, 331, 510, 601
Church, Joe   562
Church Growth movement   654, 655
Church Hymnal   135, 396
Church of Apostles and Prophets (El Salvador)   198
Church of Christ (Nicaragua)   459
Church of Christ in the Congo (Eglise du Christ au Congo, ECC)   143
Church of Christian Fellowship (Czech Republic)   163
Church of Evangelical Faith Christians (Poland)   517, 518
Church of God (Anderson)   1, 470
Church of God (Chile)   120
Church of God (Cleveland)   **134–136**
  about   134
  Angola   22
  Bahamas   135
  beginnings of   134–135, 643
  beliefs   135
  Robert Felix Cook and   1, 149
  El Salvador   198
  Full Gospel Church (South Africa) and   151
  Gereja Bethany Indonesia (GBI) and   464
  Guatemala   264
  higher education   135
  Honduras   306
  India   149
  International Fellowship of Christian Assemblies and   325
  international growth   135
  International Pentecostal Holiness Church and   328
  Jamaica   339
  Liberia   392
  media   135
  Mexico and   135, 424
  Niko Njotorahardjo and   464–465
  Francisco Olazábal and   473–474
  organizational structure   135–136
  Paraguay   488, 489
  Romania   557
  Taiwan   624
  Tanzania   627

Church of God (Nicaragua)   459
Church of God (Palestine)   486–487
Church of God (Philippines)   511
Church of God (South Africa)   150
Church of God Evangel (periodical)   135
Church of God in Christ   41, 83, 108, **136–138**, 405–406, 518, 543, 643
Church of God (Full Gospel) in India   149
Church of God in the Republic of Mexico (Iglesia de Dios en la República Mexicana)   422–424
Church of God Mission International (Nigeria)   98
Church of God of Prophecy   83, 108, 249, 257, 260, 339
Church of God Reformation Movement (Evening Lights Saints)   576–577
Church of Jesus Christ Apostolic (UK)   641
Church of Josafat (Angola)   23
Church of Our Lord Jesus Christ   477
Church of Pentecost (Ghana)
   about   10, 251
   Benin   60
   Cape Verde   106
   Côte d'Ivoire   159
   global expansion   13
   Liberia   392
   James and Sophia McKeown   251, 410–412
   Opoku Onyinah   479–480
   UK   641
The Church of the Candlestick (Eglise du Chandelier; France)   112
Church of the Holy Spirit (Tanzania)   628
Church of the Nazarene   83, 105, 106, 224, 264, 352, 459
Church of the Twelve Apostles (Liberia)   391
church planting   431
Churches of Evangelical Cooperation (Central African Republic)   112
Clark, A.   24
Clark, Mattie Moss   137
Clark, Randy   634, 635, 664
Classical Pentecostalism. *See also specific denominations*
   about   ix, xiv, xviii
   in Africa   10–11
   arts and   7
   Australia   44
   on baptism in the Holy Spirit   52, 515
   Bolivia   74, 76
   Botswana   83
   Brazil   90
   China   122
   on conversion   146
   Côte d'Ivoire   159
   definitions of Pentecostalism and   176
   ethics and   211
   Finland   233
   Ghana   24, 251, 253
   glossolalia and   257
   Greece   260–261
   history of Pentecostalism and   297, 449
   Hong Kong   307–308
   Liberia   392
   New Zealand   456
   Pentecostal World Fellowship and   506
   secularization and   573
   on soteriology   599
   South Africa   602
   spirituality and   612–613
   Taiwan   624–625
   Tanzania   628
   UK   639–640, 642
   World Assemblies of God Fellowship and   670–671
Cleary, Edward   265
Clemmons, Ithiel   500
Clifton, Shane   189
climate change   190, 570
Coady, Ron   456
Coates, Gerald   312
Cobb, John   189
Cobos, Sacramento   650
Codreanu, Teodor   **138–139**
Coe, Jack   394
Coffey, Lillian Brooks   136, 138
Cole, J.A.   585
Coleman, Simon   255, 532
Collins, Archibald   41
Colombia   *xxvi, xxvii, xxxiv*, 270, 375, 423, 477–478, 488, 559–560
colonialism   **140–142**
   about   140
   Asia   37
   Caribbean   107, 109
   counter-imperial possibilities of Pentecostalism   142
   hermeneutics and   287
   India   1–2
   Korea   360, 361, 603, 604, 673
   music and   444
   Neo-Pentecostalism as neocolonialism   141–142
   Nicaragua   459
   Pentecostalism and   140–141
   postcolonial perspectives   141
   secularization and   571–572

INDEX

Colwell, Hollis   567
Colyar, William A. and Edith M.   563
COMIBAM   306
Commonwealth Bible College (Australia)   263
Commonwealth Covenant Church (New Zealand)   468
Communauté de l'Emmanuel   171, 172, 236
Communauté du Chemin Neuf   172, 236
Communauté missionaire chrétienne internationale (Camaroon)   98
Communism
    in Asia   37
    Bulgaria   92, 216, 680
    China   123–124, 313, 349, 438, 449
    Czech Republic   162–163
    Korea   360, 362
    Mongolia   434
    Poland   518
    Romania   71, 84–85, 557–558, 566
    Slovakia   590
    Soviet Union (Russia)   217–218, 560–561, 653–654
Community of Apostolic Churches in Central African Republic   112
Comoros   *xxxiv*
complementarianism   246
Confidence (periodical)   44, 73, 433, 504
Confraternidad Cristiana de Iglesias (Chile)   120
Congo, Republic of the   *xxxiv*. *See also* Democratic Republic of the Congo
Congo Evangelistic Mission (CEM/CEPCO)   143
Congo Protestant Council (Conseil Protestant du Congo)   143
Congregación Cristiana de Goya (Argentina)   131
Congregacion Cristiana en la Argentina   131
Congregación Pentecostal (Cuba)   161
Congregation of New Hope (formerly Nokia Mission Church; Finland)   234
Congregational Holiness Church (USA)   257, 643
Congregazione Cristiana in Italia   335
Congregazioni Cristiane Pentecostali (Italy)   335
Congrès nationale de la Miséricorde (France)   172
Conrad, B.   207
Conseil National des Évangéliques de France (CNEF)   236
Consorte, Antonio   336
Consultative Committee of the Global Pentecostal Conference   69, 566
Continental Theological Seminary (Belgium)   58
conversion   145–148, 331. *See also* soteriology
Cook, Glen   278, 409, 476
Cook, Robert Felix   1–2, **148–149**

Cook Islands   *xxxiv*, 468
Coombs, Barney   564, 565
Cooper, Archibald   **150–151**
cooperation, in inter-religious relations   330
Coote, Leonard Wren   **151–153**, 354, 442
Copeland, Gloria   79, 153, *154*, 530
Copeland, Kenneth   79, **153–155**, *154*, 196, 271, 392, 530, 667
Copley, A.S.   184
Coptic Orthodox and Catholic Churches   40, 195–196. *See also* Orthodox Christianity
Corpeño, Gerardo   451
cosmology   15, **155–158**, 227, 428, 447, 613. *See also* enchanted worldview
Costa, José Placido da   523
Costa Rica   *xxxiv*, 15, 270, 423
Costanza, Daniel   502
Côte d'Ivoire   *xxxiv*, **158–159**
Council of Christian Churches of Angola (CICA)   23
Council of Churches in Sierra Leone (CCSL)   584
Council of Protestant Churches in Nicaragua (CEPAD)   459
Council of Renewal Churches of Angola (CIRA)   23
Couturier, Paul   166
COVID-19 pandemic   133, 556
Cox, Harvey   446
    Fire from Heaven   254
Craig, Robert   473
Crawford, Florence   49, 578
creationism   569–570
CRECES (Renewed Fellowship of Evangelicals and Catholics in the Holy Spirit)   34
Croatia   *xxxiv*, 139, 221. *See also* Yugoslavia
Cross and Crown (periodical)   408
Crouch, Emma Frances   138
Crowther, Samuel Adjai   584
crusades, evangelistic   79, 98, 147–148, 481
Cuba   *xxxiv*, 108, 137, **160–161**, 270
Cullis, Charles   436
Cummine, Charles   148
Cunningham, Blanche   4
Curaçao   *xxxiv*, 15
Currie, Margaret   435
Cyprus   *xxxiv*, 39, 40, 648
Czajko, Edward   518
Czajko, Mieczysław   518
Czech Republic (Czechia)   *xxxiv*, **162–163**, 590
Czechoslovakia   116, 216, 590. *See also* Czech Republic; Slovakia

Dagen (periodical)   623
Dai, Daniel   625
Dalits   149, 318
Dallière, Émile   **164–165**
Dallière, Louis   164, **165–166**
Dallimore, A.H.   **167–168**
Dallmeyer, Heinrich   248–249
Damaris, Stephanus   464
Daniel, S.P.   179
Daniels, David D., III   442, 544
Dansk Oase (Denmark)   178
Darby, John Nelson   209
Darling, Alberto   34
Darnell, Jean   44
Davidson, Alexander Thomas   **169–170**
Dayton, Donald   193, 595
de Marco, Luca   102
de Monléon, Albert   **171–172**
de Walker, Luisa Jeter   649, 650
de Worm, Henri Théophile   166
Deane, Anna M.   307, 433, 503
Deeper Life Bible Church   83, 98, 106, **172–174**, *173*, 641
Deere, Jack   664
definitions, of Pentecostalism   viii–ix, **174–177**, 297, 615–616
Del Colle, Ralph   595
deliverance and exorcism
   about   157–158
   Carlos Annacondia and   26
   Benin   61
   Central African Republic   113
   Côte d'Ivoire   159
   Fuller School of World Missions course on   655
   Leo Cecil Harris and   274
   healing and   279, 281, 282
   William Francis (Frank) Houston and   316
   India   318–319
   Nigeria   461, 462
   Universal Church of the Kingdom of God   402, 452, 646
   use of term   280
Delvecchio, Daniel   336
Demarest, Victoria Booth-Clibborn   496
Dembowski, Bronisław   518
Democratic Republic of the Congo (DR Congo)   **143–145**
   William Frederick Burton   **95–96**, 143
   Congo Evangelistic Mission (CEM/CEPCO)   143
   Fraternité Évangélique Pentecôte en Afrique (FEPACO)-Nzambe-Malamu   144
   Independent Charismatic population   xxviii
   media   418
   Mission libre Norvégienne (Communautés des Eglises Libres de Pentecôte en Afrique (CELPA))   143, 467
   Mission libre Suedoise   144
   Pentecostal (denominational) population   xxvi
   Pentecostal/Charismatic growth rate   xxvi
   Pentecostal/Charismatic population   xxiv, xxv, xxxiv, 143
   Prosperity Gospel   145
   social engagement   144–145
   Swedish missionary work in   623
   unregistered churches   144
   Jacques A. Vernaud   144
demons and demonization (possession)   15, 26, 156–158, 480, 551. *See also* deliverance and exorcism; satan
Dempster, Murray A.
   The Globalization of Pentecostalism (with Klaus and Petersen)   254–255
Denmark   **177–179**
   Aglow International   15
   Apostolic Church and schism   178
   beginnings of Pentecostalism   177
   Bjørner, Sigurd and Anna Larssen   **67–69**, 177–178
   Charismatic Renewal   178
   contemporary revitalization   178
   higher education   178
   missionaries from   178–179
   Pentecostal/Charismatic population   xxxiv, 178
   racism   223
   secularization and   179
Dennis, Annie   44
Depriest, Nina   16
D'Ercole, Eustachio   102
Derstine, Gerald   320
Derstine, Phil   459
Destiny Churches (New Zealand)   458, 469
devil. *See* cosmology; demons and demonization; satan
Dewan Kerjasama Gereja-gereja Kristus Pentakosta Indonesia (DKGKPSI; Collaborative Council of the Pentecostal Churches of Christ in Indonesia)   322
Dewan Pentakosta Indonesia (DPI; Indonesian Pentecostal Council)   322
Dhinakaran, D.G.S.   **179–180**
Di Bella, Maria Pia   336
Di Iorio, Dayana   336
dialogue, in inter-religious relations   330
Dias, João José   105

INDEX

DiBiase, Antonio   102
DiCicco, Albert and Dora   324
Dickson, A.S.   111
Dictionary of Pentecostal and Charismatic Movements   186
Dieter, Theo   194
Dillenbeck, Nora   342, 348, 349
Direction Magazine (formerly *Elim Evangel*)   202
discernment   157, 610–611
DiStaulo, Giuseppe   102
Divine Healing Ministry   83
Djibouti   xxxiv
Doll, Lillian   4
Dominica   xxvi, xxxiv
Dominican Republic   xxxv, 15, 103, 375
dominion theology   13, 31, 381, 570, 622, 655–656
Domoustchief, Christophe   235
Dong, Hengxin   349
Dougherty, Edward   377
Dowie, John Alexander
    John Archibald Duncan Adams and   5
    Apostolic Faith Mission (South Africa) and   289
    apostolic ministry and   30, 31
    in Australia   31, 468
    F.F. Bosworth and   80
    Catholic Apostolic Church and   44
    glossolalia and   258
    John G. Lake and   369
    Pieter L. Le Roux and   383
    Gordon Lindsay and   393, 394
    Charles Parham and   491, 492
    Smith Wigglesworth and   662
Dranes, Arizona   136–137
Drápal, Dan   163
Driver, E.R.   136
Drost, Bill   478
Du Plessis, David   **181–182**
    background   181
    Émile Dallière and   165
    ecumenism and   181–182, 192–193, 194, 244, 554, 555
    legacy   182
    Pentecostal World Fellowship and   505
    on Shepherding Movement   582
    Smith Wigglesworth and   663
Du Plessis, Justus   193, 194, 555
DuBois, W.E.B.   542
Dugmore, W.F.   388
Dumbuya, Dora   585
Duncan, Philip B.   169, 263
Duncan-Williams, Nicholas   12, 252, 253

Durano Seowon (South Korea)   269
Durham, William H.   **182–184**
    about   182–183
    Argue family and   35
    Azusa Street Revival and   49, 183
    Frank and Anna (Ladd) Bartleman and   56
    Bernt Berntsen and   63
    Finished Work perspective   41, 49, 183–184, 476, 643
    Louis Francescon and   32, 237, 324
    Ellen Hebden and   284
    influence of   184
    John G. Lake and   370
    Aimee Semple McPherson and   412
    Lewi Pethrus and   508
    portrait   *182*
    William Seymour and   578
Durkheim, Emile   571, 597, 615
Dutch Pentecostal Missionary Society   122
Dzao, Timothy   123, **184–185**, 625

East African Revival   627–628
East Asia   37–39. *See also specific countries*
East End Mission (Hebden Mission; Canada)   100, *283*, 283–284, 350, 412, 563
Eastern China Seminary   185
Eastern European Mission   517
Eastern Orthodox. *See* Orthodox Christianity
Ecclesia Theological Seminary (Ecclesia Bible Institute; Hong Kong)   308, 438
ecclesiology   **186–188**
    about   186
    baptism in the Holy Spirit and   187
    Full Gospel context   186–187
    future directions   187–188
    House Church Movement and   313
    Latter Rain and   381
    liturgy and   396
    pastor-led approach   316
    in Scandinavia   466
    Shepherding Movement   163, 404, **581–582**
    theological reflections   186
Echoes of Grace (periodical)   273
ecology and ecotheologies   **188–191**, 212, 570
ecopneumatology   189
Ecuador   xxxv
ecumenism   **192–195**. *See also* inter-religious relations
    about   192
    Carlos Annacondia and   26
    Assemblies of God (USA) and   42, 192–193
    Raniero Cantalamessa and   105

ecumenism (cont.)
    Charismatic Renewal and   192
    Church of God in Christ   137–138
    Émile and Louis Dallière and   164–165, 166
    Deeper Life Bible Church   174
    definition   192
    David du Plessis and   181–182, 192–193, 194, 244, 554, 555
    Evangelical–Pentecostal dialogue   223–224
    Global Christian Forum   138, 194
    Walter J. Hollenweger and   300
    International Pentecostal Holiness Church   328
    Italian Transnational Pentecostal Movement and   336
    Lutheran–Pentecostal dialogue   194
    Charles Harrison Mason and   406
    National Councils of Churches and   193
    Opoku Onyinah and   480
    Pentecostal World Fellowship and   194–195
    Reformed–Pentecostal dialogue   194
    Roman Catholic–Pentecostal dialogue   182, 193, 554–556, 595
    Secretaries of Christian World Communions   194
    Society for Pentecostal Studies and   595
    Leo Jozef Suenens and   619
    World Council of Churches   193–194 (*See also* World Council of Churches)
    Darlene Zschech and   686
Eddy, Mary Baker   271
Edel, Eugen   72
Edinburgh Missionary Conference (1910)   40
education. *See* higher education
Edvardsen, Aril   466
Edwards, Ronald   471
egalitarianism   244–245, 246
Église Réformée de France (ERF)   164, 165, 166
Egypt   xxxv, 40, 195–196, 270, 384–385
Ekballo initiative   327
Ekklesia (Bolivia)   75, 559, 560
Ekman, Ulf   196–197, 271, 450, 591
El Pueblo de Dios (The People of God; Paraguay)   488
El Salvador   xxxv, 15, 198–199, 375, 415, 423
El Shaddai (Guatemala)   265
El Shaddai (Philippines)   200–201, 345, 512, 648–649
Elim Bible College (now Regents Theological College; UK)   202, 203, 479
Elim Christian Center (Taiwan)   625
Elim Missionary Assemblies   474
Elim Pentecostal Church (Elim Foursquare Gospel Alliance)   201–203
    in Africa   10
    Australia   44, 468
    Belgium   57
    beliefs   202
    Central African Republic   112
    challenges to and doctrinal revision   202–203, 642
    contemporary position   203
    establishment and growth   201–202, 216, 640
    Guam   470
    Ireland   332
    Italy   335, 337
    George Jeffreys and   202, 340–342
    New Zealand   456, 468
    Tanzania   627
    Welsh Revival and   661
Ellerslie-Tamaki Faith Mission (New Zealand)   69, 315
Ellwood, Robert   347
Embassy of the Blessed Kingdom of God for All Nations (Ukraine)   421, 450
embodiment and body   203–205, 633. *See also* aesthetics and art; experience, of God; sexuality
Emmanuel College (USA)   328, 631
enchanted naturalism   570
enchanted worldview   142, 155, 226, 569, 602. *See also* cosmology
End Time Ministries   83
Engle, Lou   326–327
English, Robert C.   496
ENLACE (El Salvador)   199
Enns, Arno W.   290–291
Enroth, Ronald M.   346
Entente des Eglises et Missions Evangéliques au Tchad (EEMET, Agreement of the Evangelical Churches and Missions in Chad)   114–115
Episcopal Renewal Ministries (USA)   xxi, 20
Equatorial Guinea   xxxv
Ericson, Edward E.   346
Eritrea   xxxv, 206–208
eschatology   208–210
    about   208, 210
    Bethel Church   65
    William Marion Branham and   86–87
    Charismatic Renewal and Neo-Charismatic interpretations   209
    Kenneth Copeland on   154–155
    dispensational ages   209

INDEX

eschatology (cont.)
  ecclesiology and   187
  Full Gospel and   240
  homiletics and   304
  House Church Movement and   312, 313
  Jesus People Movement   347
  Kil Seon Joo on   360
  latter rain   208, 209
  miracles, signs, and wonders and   428
  premillennial dispensationalism   123, 209, 505
  Prosperity Gospel and   13, 209–210
Escobedo, Modesto   422
Eskridge, Larry   347
Esprit et vie (periodical)   166
Estonia   xxxv, 215
Eswatini   xxv, xxvii, xxviii, xxxv
ethics   211–212
Ethiopia   xxvii, xxxv, 137, 213–214, 474, 475, 478
Europe   xliv, 28, 215–219, 502. *See also specific countries*
European Charismatic Consultation (ECC)   272, 273
European Pentecostal Committee   70, 566
European Pentecostal Fellowship (EPF)   502
European Pentecostal Theological Association   220–221, 502
European Research Network on Global Pentecostalism (GloPent)   vii
Evadoc (Protestant Evangelical Archival and Documentation Center)   58
Evangel Bible College (Myanmar)   126
Evangel Church (Myanmar)   125, 126
Evangelical Alliance (Germany)   250
Evangelical Fellowship of Canada   101, 103
Evangelical Fellowship of Sierra Leone (EFSL)   584, 585
Evangelical Pentecostal Church (Chile)   74, 120, 311
Evangelical Pentecostal Church in Angola (EPCA)   22
Evangelical Pentecostal Confederation of Argentina   130
Evangelical Pentecostal Mission of Angola (EPMA)   22
Evangelical Restoration church (Rwanda)   562
Evangelical Theological Seminary (Croatia)   139
Evangelicalism   ix, 30, 42, 221–225, 249, 599–600
Evangelical-Lutheran Church of Finland (ELC)   233, 234
Evangelii Härold (periodical)   623
evangelism. *See* crusades, evangelistic; missiology and missions

Evangelist (periodical)   560
Evans, Andrew   263, 316, 512
Evans, Ida and R.M.   107–108, 135
Evans, Mark   685–686
Evans, Nicholas   7
Evans, Russell   512–513
Evans, Samantha   512
Evans, T.L.   45
Evening Lights Saints (Church of God Reformation Movement)   576–577
evil   156, 204. *See also* deliverance and exorcism; demons and demonization
evolution, biological   569–570
Ewart, Frank   409, 476–477
exclusivism   330, 331
exegesis   225–227. *See also* hermeneutics; homiletics
exorcism. *See* deliverance and exorcism
experience, of God   228–229, 613. *See also* baptism in the Holy Spirit; mysticism; spirituality
Exploits of Faith (periodical)   82

Fabre, Laurent   166
Fabre Street Chiesa Cristiana Pentecostale (Canada)   102
Faeroe Islands   xxxv
Faith Church (Církev víry; Czech Republic)   163
Faith Church – Christian Fellowship Humenné (Cirkev viery – Kresťanské spoločenstvo Humenné; Slovakia)   590
Faith Digest (periodical)   482
Faith Healing Temple of Jesus Christ (Liberia)   392
Faith Mission Pilgrims   411
Faith Movement. *See* Prosperity Gospel
faith principle   674–675
Faith Tabernacle Church   24–25, 411
Falg, Ove   235
Falkland Islands   xxxv
family relations   61. *See also* gender; sexuality
Fangcheng Fellowship (China)   230–231, 314, 682
Fantini, E.   207
Farrow, Lucy   231–232, 384, 491, 577, 643
fasting   129, 326, 379, 527, 562
Faught, Harry   101
Fédération des Églises du Plein Évangile (France)   236
Fédération des Églises et Communautés Baptistes Charismatiques (France)   235
Fédération Nationale des Assemblées de Dieu de France (France)   236
Federation of Evangelical Religious Entities of Spain (FEREDE)   608

Federation of Ministers and Churches International 644
Federation of Pentecostal Churches (Italy) 337
Fee, Gordon 227, 258, 271, 286
Feliciano, Solomon and Dionesia 400
Fellowship for Resolute Christianity (Bund für entschiedenes Christentum; Poland) 517, 518
Fellowship of Faith (Hit Gyülekezete; Hungary) 591
Feng, Tsi-hsin 587
Ferrazzo, Giovanni 510
Fiji xxxv, 270, 468, 469, 470, 471, 484–485
Filadelfia Bible College (FBC; India) 407
Filadelfia Church (Norway) 54, 467
Filadelfia Church (Sweden) 144, 424, 508, 623
Filadélfia Evangelical Church (Portugal) 524
Filadelfia Fellowship Church of India 407
Finished Work Pentecostalism
    about 41, 49, 183–184
    Assemblies of God (USA) and 41, 643
    Bernt Berntsen and 63
    Canadian Assemblies of God and 102
    Christian Congregation in Brazil and 132
    Louis Francescon and 238
    G.T. Haywood and 278
    International Fellowship of Christian Assemblies and 323
    Italian Transnational Pentecostal Movement and 336
    Oneness Pentecostalism and 42, 476, 477
    T.L. Osborn and 481
Finke, Roger 597
Finkenbinder, Frank 400
Finland xxxv, 15, 193, 233, 233–234, 623
    higher education 623
Finney, Charles Grandison 87, 358, 360
Finnish Free Foreign Mission (FFFM) 122, 624, 627
Finnish Pentecostal Mission 26, 206
Finto, D. 116
Fire Baptized Holiness Church of God of the Americas, Inc. 364
Fire Churches 83. *See also* Prosperity Gospel
Fire Conferences 79, 98
Fire-Baptized Holiness Church (FBHC) 134, 327, 363–364, 630, 638, 643. *See also* International Pentecostal Holiness Church
Five-Fold Gospel 186–187. *See also* Full Gospel
five-fold ministry 29–30, 31, 312, 313, 380, 451, 644
Fix, Karl 216
Flaming Fire of God Ministries 98
Flemish Evangelical Alliance 57
Fletcher, John 209
Flock of the Gospel of Jesus Christ (Japan) 153
Flood, Gustaf 74
Flores, Samuel Joaquín 425
Flory, Richard 454, 455
Flower, J. Roswell 42, 399–400, 505
Fockler, B. 388
Fomum, Zacharias 98
Forbes, W. George 170
Ford, Anna Crockett 137
Ford, Henry Louis 138
Fordham, Grace 434
Foreign Missionary Conference of North America 192
forgiveness 534
Forrest, Tom 272–273
Forster, Roger 312
Forum Freikirchlicher Pfingstgemeinden (Germany) 250
Forward in Faith International 83
Foster, Thomas 111, 273
Foucault, Michel 298
Fountain Trust (FT) xx–xxi, 165, 272
Foursquare Church
    about 643
    in Africa 10
    Australia and New Zealand 44, 468
    Benin 59
    Bolivia 74
    Brazil 90
    Côte d'Ivoire 159
    Cuba 160
    Greece 261
    Hong Kong 308
    International Fellowship of Christian Assemblies and 325
    Jesus is Lord Church Worldwide (Philippines) and 344
    Kazakhstan 39
    Liberia 392
    Malaysia 404
    Aimee Semple McPherson and 284, 412–413
    (*See also* McPherson, Aimee Semple)
    Netherlands 453
    Papua New Guinea missions with Leo Cecil Harris 274
    Paraguay 488
    Taiwan 624
    in UK 641
Foursquare Missions International. *See* Foursquare Church

Fox, Lorne   530
France   235–236
    Aglow International   15
    Assemblies of God   235–236
    beginnings of Pentecostalism in   235
    Bread of Life Church (Ling Liang Church)   185
    Catholic Charismatic Renewal   116, 165, 236
    Émile Dallière   164–165
    Louis Dallière   164, 165–166
    Albert de Monléon   171–172
    El Shaddai (Philippines) in   648
    gypsy ministry   236
    Huguenots   258
    Italian Transnational Pentecostal Movement in   335
    Pentecostal/Charismatic population   xxxv
    Rhema Bible Training Center campus in   270
    Salt & Light in   565
Francescon, Louis   32, 89, 129–130, 132, 184, 237–238, 324, 334, 336
Francis (Jorge Bergoglio; pope)   34, 172, 547, 686
Francis Xavier   258
Franklin, A.P.   508
Fraternité de Jésus   171
Fraternité Évangélique Pentecôte en Afrique (FEPACO)-Nzambe-Malamu (DR Congo)   144
Frazee, J.J.   498
Free Apostolic Church (El Salvador)   415
Free Apostolic Church of Pentecost (Greece)   260–261
Free Evangelical Assemblies of Norway   122
Free Friend Movement   466
Freetown Bible Training Centre (Sierra Leone)   585
Freidzon, Claudio   33–34, 635
Freikirchliches Evangelisches Gemeindewerk/International Foursquare Church (Germany)   249
French, Talmadge   478
French Guiana   xxxv
French Polynesia   xxxv, 236, 468, 470
Fresh Streams   641–642
Freston, Paul   452
Friends of Pentecost (Finland)   233
FrikirkeNet (Denmark)   178
Frisbee, Lonnie   348, 429, 663
Fritsch, Cora   563, 564
Full Gospel   186–187, 226, **238–240**, 599, 632–633
Full Gospel Bible Fellowship (Tanzania)   628
Full Gospel Businessmen's Fellowship International in Africa   10, 11
    Aglow International and   14
    Charismatic Renewal and   192
    Ghana   15, 252
    Guatemala   265
    Indonesia   320
    Malaysia   404
    Neo-Pentecostalism and   450
    Kevin and Dorothy Ranaghan and   547
    Oral Roberts and   553
Full Gospel Church of God (Botswana)   83, 135
Full Gospel Church of God (South Africa)   66, 150–151, 602
Full Gospel Mission (Cameroon)   97, 98
Full Gospel Testimony (UK)   216–217
Fuller, W.E.   364
Fuller Theological Seminary
    School of Intercultural Studies (formerly School of World Missions)   654–655, 664
fundamentalism   222, 534
Furman, Charles   264
Futa, Alphonse   144

Gabon   xxxv, 144
Gaines, Margaret   486–487
Gaj, Jan   590
Gallice, Felix   235
Gambia   xxxv
Ganiel, G.   683
García, Miguel C.   423
Garcia-Herreros, Rafael   375
Garippa, Salvatore   510
Garlock, H.B.   223
Garr, Alfred (A.G.)   258, 307, 432, 503, 563
Garr, Lillian   258, 307, 432, 503
Garrigus, Alice Belle   240–242, *241*, 496
Gause, Hollis   594
Gavillas Doradas (*Golden Sheaves*; periodical)   423
Gaxiola-Gaxiola, Manuel   595
Gbagbo, Laurent   159
Gdańsk Bible Institute (Poland)   517
Gee, Donald   166, 192, **243–244**, 341, 359, 505
Geivett, Douglas   32
Gemeinde der Christen Ecclesia (Germany)   249
Gemeinde Gottes/Church of God (Germany)   249
Gemeinschaftsbewegung (Pietistic movement)   223, 248, 249
gender   **244–248**. *See also* family relations; sexuality
    about   244
    Minnie Abrams and   4
    abuse and   247
    Aglow International on   15
    Zelma Argue and   36

gender (cont.)
   Mina Ross Brawner and 88
   Christian Congregation in Brazil 133
   complementarianism vs. egalitarianism 246
   Cuba 161
   egalitarianism in early Pentecostalism 244–245
   Elim Pentecostal Church 203
   femininities and masculinities 246–248, 684
   Finland 233, 234
   Alice Belle Garrigus and Newfoundland Pentecostalism 241–242
   homiletics and 305
   B.H. Irwin and 328, 364
   Italian Transnational Pentecostal Movement 336
   Korea 604, 605
   Sarah Jane Lancaster and 372–373
   missions and 431
   Mukti Revival and Pandita Saraswati Ramabai 439–440, 546
   Opoku Onyinah and 480
   Pentecostal Assemblies of Canada 495
   Pentecostal Assemblies of the World 499
   Pentecostal institutionalization and 245–246
   psychology and 534
   sexuality and 574
   Society for Pentecostal Studies and 595
   True Jesus Church 637
   Maria Woodworth-Etter and 670
   Yoido Full Gospel Church 673
General-Ukrainian Union of Christians of Evangelical Faith 653
generational curses 113
Georgia xxxv, 39, 40
Geredja Bethel Indonesia 135
Gereja Baptist Pelita Cahaya Sabah (Malaysia) 404
Gereja Bethany Indonesia (GBI) 464
Gereja Pantekosta di Indonesia/GPdI (Indonesian Pentecostal Church) 320
Germany 248–250
   Aglow International 15
   beginnings of Pentecostalism in 215–216, 248–249
   Charismatic movement 249–250
   contemporary developments 250
   El Shaddai (Philippines) in 648
   Evangelical, understanding of 221
   Evangelical-Pentecostal relations 223, 249
   interwar and postwar periods 216, 249
   migration to 218
   Neo-Pentecostalism and 250
   Pentecostal/Charismatic population xxiv, xxv, xxxv
   pre-WWI 249
   Rhema Bible Training Center campus in 270
Geyer, Richard 72
Gezahagne, Teklemariam 478
Ghana 250–253. *See also* Church of Pentecost
   Aglow International 15, 252
   Peter Anim 24–25, 251, 411
   Charismatic ministries 251–252
   Charismatic population xxvii
   Classical Pentecostalism 251
   Full Gospel Businessmen's Fellowship International 15, 252
   higher education 253, 480
   Independent Charismatic population xxviii
   James and Sophia McKeown 25, 251, 410–412
   media 252–253, 417
   music 443
   Opoku Onyinah 479–480
   Mensa Otabil 253, 483–484
   Pentecostal (denominational) population xxvi
   Pentecostal/Charismatic growth rate xxvi
   Pentecostal/Charismatic population xxv, xxxvi
   prophetic ministries 252
   Prosperity Gospel and 253
   Rhema Bible Training Center campus in 270
   social engagement 253
   trans-denominational fellowships 252
Ghana Apostolic Church 251. *See also* Church of Pentecost
Ghana Pentecostal and Charismatic Council (GPCC) 25, 251
Gibraltar xxxvi
Gideon Theological Seminary (South Korea) 540
Gifford, Paul 96, 683
Gift Movement 630
Gih, Andrew (Ji Zhiwen) 581, 675
Gil, Segundo 650
Gil, Sunjoo 525
Gitwaza, Paul 562
Gjerme, Øysteim 467
Glad Tidings Tabernacle (New York) 400, 463, 509, 653, 679
Global Awakening 209
Global Christian Forum (GCF) 138, 194
Global Harvest Ministries 655
Global University (formerly International Correspondence Institute) 126, 423
global warming. *See* climate change
globalization ix, 254–256, 282, 444, 450, 598, 635. *See also* migration; transnationalism

glossolalia 256–259. *See also* xenolalia
   angels and 156
   anthropology on 259
   Assemblies of God (USA) 42, 81, 257
   Azusa Street Revival and 48, 258
   baptism in the Holy Spirit and 47, 52, 256–257
   Biblical references 257–258, 610
   F.F. Bosworth and 42, 81
   Chile 119, 311
   in church history 258
   Church of God (Cleveland) 135
   Classical (first wave) Pentecostalism and ix, xviii
   Fangcheng Fellowship 230–231
   first instances of 491, 642
   Donald Gee on 243
   Leo Cecil Harris on 274
   Watchman Nee on 583
   neuroscience on 259
   Pentecostal understandings 258–259
   psychology and 533
   revivals and 551
   socialization and 593
   "Speaking in Tongues" (Benney) 8
   subversion by 142
   John Sung (Song Shangjie) on 620
   True Jesus Church 637
   Zimbabwe 683–684
Glover, Kelso 44
Gnirrep, Anna 319
"God is Love" Evangelical Pentecostal Church (Brazil) 90, 106, 488, 524
Golden Grain (periodical) 529–530
Gomelsky, Jorge 25, 26
González, Avelino 160
González, Eusebio (Aarón) Joaquín 424–425, 477
González, Valente Aponte 424
Good News (periodical) 44, 88, 372
Good News Fellowship (Botswana) 83
Good News Hall (GNH; Australia) 6, 44, 372, 373, 468. *See also* Apostolic Faith Mission (Australia)
Good News Ministry (Egypt) 195
Good Tidings (periodical) 240, 497
Gospel Forum Network 250
gospel music 136–137, 443
Gospel of the Kingdom Church (GKC; Indonesia) 536, 537
The Gospel Times (newspaper) 541
Goss, Howard 41, 184
Goursat, Pierre 171
Grady, Lee 329

Graham, Billy 222, 291, 348, 424, 553, 588, 657
Grant, W.V. 69, 394
Gray, Frank and Mary 152
Great Awakening 456
Greece *xxxvi*, 259–261, 270, 648
Greek Evangelical Alliance 261
Greek Evangelical Charismatic Community 261
Greenland *xxxvi*
Greenwood, Charles L. 6, 170, **262–263**, 273, 372
Greenwood, Elviss 263
Gregersen, Dagmar 249, 466, 467
Greisen, Paul 308
Grenada *xxxvi*
Grimes, Samuel 499
Groesbeek, Cornelius E. 319–320, 322
Groesbeek, Mies 319–320
Gros, Jeffrey 193
Grothaus, Clarence 627
Grudem, Wayne 664
Gruen, Ernie 326
Guadeloupe *xxxvi*
Guam *xxxvi*, 468, 470
Guatemala xxv, xxvii, *xxvii*, *xxxvi*, 15, 224–225, **263–266**, 270, 423
Guillén, Miguel 422
Guimarães, Roberto 524
Guinea *xxxvi*
Guinea-Bissau *xxxvi*
Gulliford, Helen 366
Gulliksen, Kenn 663
Gumbel, Nicky 18, 301, 641
Gummer, W. 235
Guneratnam, Prince **267–268**
Guy, Laurie 168
Guyana *xxxvi*
Gypsy Evangelical Movement (Mission Evangelique des Tziganes) 608
gypsy people. *See* Roma people

Ha, Young Jo **268–269**
Habermas, Jurgen 356
Haggard, Ted 655
Hagin, Kenneth, Jr. 271
Hagin, Kenneth E. **270–271**
   Enoch Adejare Adeboye and 549
   apostolic ministry and 30, 31
   background 270
   beliefs 270–271
   on William Marion Branham 87
   Kenneth Copeland and 155
   critiques of 271
   Ulf Ekman and 196, 271

Hagin, Kenneth E. (cont.)
    influence of   271
    Liberia and   392
    T.L. Osborn and   481
    David Oyedepo and   667
    Petrus Agung Pernomo and   537
    Prosperity Gospel and   270, 530, 531, 644
    Rhema Bible Training Center and   270
    Slovakia and   591
    Eddie Villanueva and   344, 651
Haiti   xxxvi, 108, 109, 137, 270, 335
Hall, A. Walker   308
Hall, Anna   642
Hall, Franklin   379
Hall, William Phillips   476
Halleluya (Eritrea)   207
Hämäläinen, Arto   502
Hamon, Bill   30
Hancock, Samuel N.   499
Hancock, Trenton Doyle   7
Hanegraaff, Hank   271, 635
Hanna, Ghali   195, 384–385
Hansen, Letta and Harold   434
Hardie, Robert A.   539
Härdstedt, Jack   523
Harford-Battersby, Thomas Dundas   357
Harper, Jeanne   271–273
Harper, Michael   xx, 20, 165, 271–273
Harrell, David E.   87
Harris, Iwan   517
Harris, Leo Cecil   44, 111, 263, 273–275
Harris, William Wadé   9, 158, 251, 391
Harvest Grain (periodical)   262
Hatfield, D.B.   486
Haustein, Jörg   207, 298, 478
Hawkinson, Tim
    "Pentecost"   8
Hawtin, Ernest (Ern)   276, 277, 381
Hawtin, George   101, 275, 275–277, 379, 379–380, 381
Hayford, Jack   501
Haywood, Garfield Thomas (G.T.)   277–279, 278, 476, 477, 498, 499, 543
healing   279–282
    about   279, 429
    John Archibald Duncan Adams and   5
    Africa   603
    Aglow International and   15
    A.A. Allen and   16–17
    Australia   44, 45
    beliefs   281–282
    Biblical references   278–279
    Bolivia   74–75, 76
    Reinhard Bonnke, and   79
    F.F. Bosworth and   80, 81, 82
    William Marion Branham and   86, 87, 394, 644
    contemporary practices   282
    A.H. Dallimore and   167, 168
    Deeper Life Bible Church and   174
    D.G.S. Dhinakaran and   180
    ecclesiology and   187
    ecology and   189–190
    Full Gospel and   239–240
    Thomas Hezmalhalch on   289
    Tommy Hicks and   280, 290
    India   318–319
    Keswick movement and   358–359
    Kim Ik-du and   362
    Korea   37
    Kathryn Kuhlman   367
    John G. Lake and   370, 371
    Sarah Jane Lancaster and   372
    LGBTQ people and   575
    Liberia   392
    Gordon Lindsay and   393, 394
    methods and practices   280–281
    Carrie Judd Montgomery and   436
    New Zealand   45, 456
    Nigeria   462
    T.L. Osborn and   481
    Charles S. Price and   529–530
    psychology and   534
    Oral Roberts and   552, 553–554, 644
    Agnes Sanford and   567–568
    science and   569
    Universal Church of the Kingdom of God and   646
    USA   644
    Voice of Healing   17, 80, 82, 393, 394, 481
    Smith Wigglesworth and   216, 662
    John Wimber and   665
    Maria Woodworth-Etter and   670
    Yoido Full Gospel Church and   127, 673
Healing Waters (periodical)   552
Health and Wealth Gospel. *See* Prosperity Gospel
heaven   156
"Heaven's Gates and Hell's Flames" (evangelistic drama)   156
Hebden, Ellen   100, 283–285, 350, 359, 370, 412, 495
Hebden, James   100, 283–284, 350, 370
Hedin, Sten-Gunnar   624
Heeterbry, Adrian and Charlotte   469, 485
Hegba, Meinard   98
hell   156

Hengen uudistus kirkossamme ry (The Spiritual Renewal within Our Church; Finland)   233
Hepner, T.R.   207
Hermandad Cristiana Agraria de Cuba (Cuba)   160
hermeneutics   285–288, 376, 516. *See also* exegesis; homiletics
Hernández, Carmen   609
Heward-Mills, Dag   253
Hewitt, Isaac   111
Hewitt, John   111
Hezmalhalch, Thomas   6, 150, 181, **288–289**, 371, 383, 602
Hicks, Tommy   26, 33, *280*, **290–291**, *291*
Hickson, James Moore   44
higher education   **292–294**
   accreditation and validation   292, 293
   Assemblies of God (USA)   42, 293
   Australia   46, 88, 170, 263, 270, 514
   beginnings of   292
   Belgium   58
   Bethel School for Supernatural Ministry   64, 65
   Bulgaria   92
   Canada   275–276, 494
   China   185, 588, 675
   Church of God (Cleveland)   135
   Church of God in Christ   137
   curriculum and program structure   293–294
   Denmark   178
   education vs. training   293
   European Pentecostal Theological Association   220–221, 502
   Evangelicalism and   223, 224
   Finland   623
   Fuller's School of Intercultural Studies (formerly School of World Missions)   654–655, 664
   Ghana   253, 480
   Greece   261
   Hillsong   46, 296
   Holy Trinity Brompton   302
   Honduras   306
   Hong Kong   292, 308, 438
   India   149, 407
   Ireland   333
   Italian Transnational Pentecostal Movement and   336
   Japan   152, 441, 676, 677
   Jordan   351
   Latin American Bible Institute   399
   Lebanon   386
   Li Changshou (Witness Lee) and   390–391
   Liberia   392
   Malaysia   403–404
   Mexico   423
   missions and   292–293
   Myanmar   125–126
   Netherlands   453
   Nigeria   98
   Pentecostal Assemblies of Canada   494
   Philippines   307, 434
   Planetshakers   514
   Poland   517
   Puerto Rico   400
   Rhema Bible Training Center   270
   Romania   70, 139, 566
   Sierra Leone   585
   South Africa   118
   South Korea   152, 540
   Sweden   197, 623
   UK   95, 137, 202, 203, 244
   USA   135, 137, 270, 290, 399, 400, 436, 463, 553
   Venezuela   650
   World Alliance for Pentecostal Theological Education   221, 293
Hildegard of Bingen   258
Hill, Peter   534
Hillsong   **294–296**
   about   45, 294, 469
   Denmark   178
   denominational affiliation   295–296
   establishment and international growth   46, 294
   Finland   234
   Germany   250
   higher education   46, 296
   Latter Rain and   382
   Lebanon   386
   media   296
   as megachurch   421
   music   294–295, 444
   Netherlands   453
   Norway   467
   popularity of   296
   social engagement   296
   UK   641
   Darlene Zschech   295, **685–686**
Himitian, Jorge   34
Hindle, Thomas and Louise   434, 563
Hines, C. Albert   264
Hinn, Benny   33, 352, 471, 530, 537
Hispanic American Bible Institute (USA)   400
history   **297–299**
Hitch, I.G.   563
Hobbs, Vincent   45
Hocken, Peter   115, 116, 595, 613

Hodges, M.L.
   A Theology of the Church and Its Mission   186
Hoeh, Hong   604
Hogan, Brian and Louise   434
Hogan, J. Philip   293
holiness, and conversion   147
Holiness Movement. *See also* International Pentecostal Holiness Church
   about   358
   baptism in the Holy Spirit and   41, 47, 327
   beginnings of Pentecostalism and   41
   Church of God (Cleveland) and   134
   ethics and   211–212
   faith principle and   674–675
   Pentecostalism and   187, 223, 327, 643
   visual art and   7
Holiness Movement Church   408
Holiness Union Church of Botswana   83
Hollenweger, Walter J.   86, 297, **299–300**, 303, 613
Hollywood Free Paper (periodical)   346
Holocaust   164, 166
Holt, Herrick   101, 275, 276, *379*
Holy See   xxxvi. *See also* Catholic Charismatic Renewal; Roman Catholic Church
Holy Spirit (pneumatology)   **514–516**. *See also* baptism in the Holy Spirit
   Africa and   11–12
   beliefs about   514–515
   ecopneumatology   189
   experience of God and   228–229
   hermeneutics and   287, 516
   homiletics and   303
   miracles, signs, and wonders, and   429
   missiology and   430
   pneumatological imagination   189, 331
   science and   570
   spiritual gifts and   515, 610–612
   theology and   515–516, 632
Holy Spirit Teaching Mission (USA)   582
Holy Trinity Brompton (HTB)   18, *301*, 301–302, 641
Home of Peace (USA)   4
homiletics   303–305. *See also* exegesis; hermeneutics
Honduras   xxxvi, 15, 306–307, 375, 423
Hong Kong   307–309
   about   38, 307
   Assemblies of God/Pentecostal Assemblies of God   308
   Dennis Balcombe   50–51, 308–309
   Bread of Life Church (Ling Liang Church)   309
   Charismatic Renewal   308–309
   Timothy Dzao in   185
   El Shaddai (Philippines) and   648
   Foursquare Gospel Church   308
   higher education   292, 308, 438
   Jesus is Lord Church Worldwide (Philippines) and   344
   Kong Duen Yee (Mui Yee)   308, **365–366**, 403
   Mok Lai Chi   307, 364, *432*, **432–434**, 503
   J. Elmor Morrison   308, **437–438**
   Pentecostal Holiness Church   307–308
   Pentecostal Mission   307, 432, 503
   Pentecostal/Charismatic population   xxxvi
Hood, Ralph   534
Hoover, Mary Anne Hilton   4, 310, 440
Hoover, Willis Collins   4, 119, 120, 121, **309–311**, 440
Hope, John   45
HOPE: Global   686
Hope Unlimited Church (HopeUC; Australia)   686
Hopkins, Evan Henry   358, 359
Horne, Robert   44
Horner, Ralph Cecil   408
Hörnmark, Pelle   624
Horstman, H.E.   322
Hoste, D.E.   587
Houck, Minnie   4
house churches. *See also* cell churches
   China   124, **313–314**, 658
   Ireland   332
   Kuwait   368–369
   UK   203, **312–313**
Houston, Bobbie   294, 685
Houston, Brian   294, 295–296, 316, 382, 469, 685
Houston, Joel   295
Houston, William Francis (Frank)   69, 70, 294, 296, **315–317**, 457
Howard, Chonita Morgan   422
Howard-Browne, Rodney   635
Howy, Martin   44
Huber, Odilo W.   533
Huber, Stefan   533
Hudson, Henry   339
Hughes, Ray   194
Huguenots   258
Hungary   xxxvi, 116, 216, 591
Hunt, Percy   101, 275, 276, *379*
Hunt, Stephen   635
Hunt, William   539
Hunter, Harold   189
Hutchins, Julia   577
Hutchinson, Mark   381–382
   Explorations of Italian Protestantism   336
Hydzik, Michał   518

Iceland   xxxvi, 15
Ichtus (Belgium)   58

INDEX   781

Idahosa, Benson   98, 252, 450, 667
Idahosa Bible College (Nigeria)   98
La Igelsia Apostólica de la Fe en Cristo Jesús (Mexico)   477
Iglesia Biblia Abierta (Cuba)   160
La Iglesia Calvario (Guatemala)   264
Iglesia Congregacional Pentecostal (Cuba)   161
Iglesia Cristiana Biblica (Argentina)   131
Iglesia Cristiana Evangélica Pentecostal (Cuba)   160
Iglesia Cristiana Pentecostal (Cuba)   160
Iglesia Cristiana Vida Eterna (Argentina)   131
Iglesia de Diós (Argentina)   131
Iglesia de Diós (Cuba)   160
Iglesia de Dios, Evangelio Completo (Guatemala)   264
Iglesia de Dios de la Profecía (Cuba)   160
Iglesia de Dios del Paraguay   489
Iglesia de Dios el Evangelio Completo (Cuba)   160
Iglesia de Dios en Cristo Jesús (Cuba)   160
Iglesia de Dios Ortodoxa (Cuba)   161
Iglesia de Dios Pentecostal Movimiento Internacional (Pentecostal Church of God International Movement)   109
Iglesia de Jesucristo Libre (Cuba)   160
Iglesia de la Fe Apostólica (Cuba)   160
Iglesia Evangélica Bethel (Cuba)   160
Iglesia Evangélica Cristiana Reunidos en el nombre de nuestro Señor Jesucristo (Argentina)   131
Iglesia Evangelica de Filadelfia (IEF; Spain)   608
Iglesia Evangélica Getsemaní (Cuba)   160
Iglesia Evangélica Libre (Cuba)   160
Iglesia Evangélica Monte Sinaí (Cuba)   160
Iglesia Evangélica Pentecostal (Cuba)   160
La Iglesia Evangélica Pentecostal, Las Buenas Nuevas (Cuba)   161
Iglesia Evangélica Pentecostal Luz del Mundo (Cuba)   160
Iglesia Evangélica Santa Pentecostés (Cuba)   160
Iglesia La Cosecha (Church of the Harvest; Honduras)   306
Iglesia Liga Evangélica de Cuba (Cuba)   160
Iglesia Misionera Amplias Mundiales (Cuba)   161
Iglesia Misionera de Dios (Cuba)   160
Iglesia Pentecostal in Cuba   160
Iglesias Cristianas Evangelicas Apostolicas (Spain)   335
Igreja Videira   58
Ikoma Bible School (Ikoma Seisho Gakuin; Japan)   152
Ilczuk, Porfiry   517
Imbach, Jeffrey   189

Immanuel Evangelical Church (Palestine)   487
INC (International Network of Churches, formerly Christian Outreach Centres; Australia)   45, 46
inclusivism   330–331
Independent Assemblies of God (Botswana)   83
Independent Charismatics   xix–xx, xxi, xxii, *xxiii*, xxvii, *xxviii*. *See also* Neo-Pentecostalism
Independent Evangelical Church (Iglesia Evangélica Independiente; Mexico)   424
Independent Network Charismatic (INC) Christianity   **454–455**
Independent Pentecostal Evangelical Church Movement (Movimiento Iglesia Evangélica Pentecostés Independiente; Mexico)   424
India   **317–319**
  about   38, 317
  K.E. Abraham   1–2, 149
  Minnie Abrams   2–4, *3*, 439, 440
  Assemblies of God in   93–94, 149
  beginnings of Pentecostalism in   317–318
  Bread of Life Church (Ling Liang Church)   185
  D. Mark Buntain   93–94
  Catholic and mainline Charismatic renewal   116, 319
  Church of God in Christ in   137
  Robert Felix Cook   1–2, **148–149**
  Dalits   149, 318
  D.G.S. Dhinakaran   **179–180**
  El Shaddai (Philippines) in   648
  healing, exorcisms, and evangelism   318–319
  higher education   149, 270, 407
  HOPE: Global and   686
  Independent Charismatic population   *xxviii*
  Italian Transnational Pentecostal Movement in   335
  Barbara Johnston   **349–351**
  Lucy Leatherman and   385
  Alice Eveline Luce and   398
  Thomas Mathews   **407–408**
  Mukti Mission and Revival   2–4, 298, 349–350, 364, **439–440**, 545–546
  Northeast India   318
  Pentecostal/Charismatic population   *xxiv, xxv, xxxvi*
  politics   522
  Pandita Saraswati Ramabai   **544–546** (*See also* Ramabai, Pandita Saraswati)
  Salt & Light in   565
  socio-economic context   318
  Smith Wigglesworth in   663
Indian Pentecostal Church of God (formerly South Indian Church of God)   2, 149

individualism   28, 83, 532
Indonesia   38, 39, 185, **319–321**
   beginnings of Pentecostalism in   319–320
   Catholic Charismatic Renewal   320–321
   Charismatic Renewal   320
   evangelism and conversions   321
   Full Gospel Businessmen's Fellowship International   320
   megachurches   320
   Netherlands churches from   453
   Niko Njotorahardjo   320, **464–465**
   Pentecostal (denominational) population   *xxvi*
   Pentecostal/Charismatic population   *xxvi, xxxvi*
   Petrus Agung Purnomo   *536*, **536–537**
   Rhema Bible Training Center campus in   270
   Adi Sutanto   537, *621*, **621–622**
Indonesian Pentecostal Fellowship of Churches (Persekutuan Gereja-gereja Pentakosta di Indonesia)   321–323
Indrakusuma, Yohanes   320–321
infant baptism   54, 95, 119, 237, 311
Ingram, J.H.   135
Inouye, Melissa Wei-Tsing   478
Institute of Contextual Theology (South Africa)   118
Instituto Bíblico Central (Venezuela)   650
Institutul Teologic Penticostal (formerly Seminarul Teologic Penticostal; Romania)   70, 566
intercultural theology   300
inter-faith   329. *See also* inter-religious relations
International Apostolic Bible College (Denmark)   178
International Assemblies of God (IAG)   67
International Catholic Charismatic Renewal Services (ICCRS; formerly International Catholic Charismatic Renewal Office (ICCRO))   *xxii*, 547
International Central Gospel Church (Ghana)   253, 483
International Charismatic Consultation on World Evangelism (ICCOWE)   272–273
International Christian Assembly (Hong Kong)   434
International Christian Fellowship   250
International Church of the Foursquare Gospel. *See* Foursquare Church
International Coalition of Prophetic Leaders   644
International Correspondence Institute (now Global University)   126, 423
International Council of Apostolic Leaders (ICAL)   31
International Council of Evangelical Theological Education   223
International Fellowship for Christ (Kenya)   475
International Fellowship of Christian Assemblies (IFCA; formerly Unorganized Italian Christian Churches in North America)   103, 130, 237, 238, **323–325**, 334, 335
International House of Prayer (IHOP)   196, **325–327**, 664, 666
International Missionary Conference   181, 192
International Missionary Council   222
International Pentecostal Consultative Council   73, 249, 364
International Pentecostal Holiness Church (formerly Pentecostal Holiness Church)   **327–329**. *See also* Fire-Baptized Holiness Church
   Argentina   33
   background and establishment   327, 364, 643
   beliefs   327–328
   China   122
   ecumenical relations   328
   on glossolalia   257
   Hong Kong   307–308
   Joseph H. King and   364
   media and higher education   328
   social engagement   328–329
   George Floyd Taylor and   328, **630–631**
   William H. Turner and   638, 639
Internationale Jesusgemeinde/Church of God of Prophecy (Germany)   249
inter-religious relations   **329–331**. *See also* ecumenism
intersectionality   543
Intra-textual Fundamentalism Scale   534
Introvigne, Massimo   337
Ippolito, Luigi   102
Iran   *xxvi, xxviii, xxxvi*, 38
Iraq   *xxxvii*, 39, 40
Ireland   *xxxvii*, 201–202, 270, **332–333**, 340, 478
Irish Bible Institute   333
Irving, Edward   30, 590
Irvingites   31, 235, 258, 381, 468
Irwin, Benjamin Hardin (B.H.)   134, 328–329, 363
Isle of Man   *xxxvii*
Israel   *xxxvii*, 39, 40, 648
Italian Christian Churches of North Europe (CCINE)   324
Italian District of the Assemblies of God (USA)   324
Italian Pentecostal Christian Church   337

INDEX 783

Italian Pentecostal Church of Canada. *See* Canadian Assemblies of God
Italians
    Canadian Assemblies of God   102–103, 237, 324, 335, 509
    Christian Assemblies (Argentina)   **129–131**, 237, 335, 509
    Christian Congregation in Brazil and   132
    Louis Francescon   32, 89, 129–130, 132, 184, **237–238**, 324, 334, 336
    International Fellowship of Christian Assemblies (formerly Unorganized Italian Christian Churches in North America)   103, 130, 237, 238, **323–325**, 334, 335
    Italian Transnational Pentecostal Movement   **334–336**
    Giuseppe Petrelli   130, 325, 335, 336, **509–510**
Italy   **337–338**
    about   337
    Aglow International   15
    Assemblies of God   103, 237, 324, **337–338**
    beginnings of Pentecostalism and growth   216, 337–338
    Catholic Charismatic Renewal   116, 338
    El Shaddai (Philippines) in   648
    Jesus is Lord Church Worldwide (Philippines) in   344
    migrant churches   338
    Pentecostal/Charismatic population   *xxxvii*, 219
    Rhema Bible Training Center campus in   270
Izbaşa, Alexandru   139

Jackson, Bill   664
Jackson, John Paul   326
Jackson, Ray   45
Jacobs, Cindy   352, 465
Jaffray, Robert A.   184, 657
Jamaica   *xxxvii*, 15, 283, **339–340**
Jamieson, Robert J.   108
Janes, Burton K.   240, 497
Japan
    Aglow International   15
    Bread of Life Church (Ling Liang Church)   185
    Jashil Choi in   129
    Leonard Wren Coote   **151–153**, 354, 442
    El Shaddai (Philippines) in   648
    Ha Young Jo and   269
    higher education   152, 270, 441, 676, 677
    Italian Transnational Pentecostal Movement in   335
    Carl Fredrick Juergensen   **352–354**, 441, 676
    Jun Murai   152, **440–442**, 676
    Pentecostal/Charismatic population   *xxv*, *xxxvii*
    Martin Lawrence Ryan and   563–564
    Kiyoma Yumiyama   354, **675–677**
Japan Apostolic Mission   152, 153, 442, 624
Japan Bible Church (JBC)   441, 676
Japan Evangelical Church   153
Japan Evangelistic Band   151, 440, 564
Japan Pentecostal Church (Nihon Pentekosute Kyokai)   152, 153
Javanese Mennonite Churches (GITJ)   621
Jeannot, Koudou   158
Jeffreys, George   72, 201–202, 216, **340–342**, 359, 411, 640, 661
Jeffreys, Stephen   44, 340, 341, 468, 661
Jemaat Kristen Indonesia/JKI (Indonesia Christian Fellowship)   622
Jesus Calls (India)   180
Jesus Culture   64, 234, 453
Jesus Family Church (China)   123, **342–343**, 349
Jesus is Lord Church Worldwide (Philippines)   344, **344–346**, 511, 652
Jesus Miracle Crusade International Ministry (Philippines)   511
Jesus People Movement   178, 196, **346–348**, 444, 469, 508, 583, 655
Jesus People USA   347
Jews   164, 166. *See also* Messianic Judaism
Ji, Zhiwen (Andrew Ghi)   581, 675
Jia, Yuming   658
Jiménez Escudero, Emiliano   607
Jing, Dianying   123, 124, 342, 343, **348–349**
Joda, Tunde   98
John Chrystostom   258
John Paul II (pope)   104, 217
Johnson, Bill   64, 65
Johnson, Todd M.   xxii, 29, 615
Johnston, Barbara   **349–351**
Jones, Bob   326
Jones, Bryn   312
Jones, Charles Price   136, 405, 577
Jones, E. Stanley   196
Jones, Jeanette   36
Jones, Ozro Thurston, Sr.   136, 138
Jonson, Berger   33
Jordan   *xxxvii*, 39, 40, **351–352**
Jordán, Edmundo   400, 650
Joshua, Seth   243, 660
Journal of Pentecostal Theology   480
Journal of the European Pentecostal Theological Association (*JEPTA*)   220–221

Juergensen, Agnes   353, 354
Juergensen, Carl Fredrick   **352–354**, 441, 676
Juergensen, Esther   354
Juergensen, Frederike   352, 353, 354, 677
Juergensen, John W.   353, 354, 676
Juergensen, Marie   353, 354, 676, 677
Jugend-, Missions-, und Sozialwerk Altensteig (Germany)   249
Jung, Courtney   543
justification   183, 358, 599, 600

The Kairos Document   118
Kajfosz, Jan   162, 517
Kakobe, Zacharia   628
Kaleta, Karol   517
Kalu, Ogbu   613, 614
Kamiński, Marek   518
Kansas City prophets   326, 664
Kardanov, N.   653
Kashweka, Henry   163
Kassel Declaration   249
Kawasaki, Hajime   441
Kay, William   31, 209, 455, 565
Kazakhstan   *xxxvii*, 39, 478
Kelchner, Charles F.   353
Kelty, Harriet May   160
Kenneth Copeland Ministries   153. *See also* Copeland, Kenneth
Kenya   **354–357**
    African Initiated Churches in   627
    Charismatic population   *xxvii*
    Independent Charismatic population   *xxviii*
    media   354–355, 356
    music   416–417, 443
    Chacha Omahe   **474–475**
    Pentecostal (denominational) population   *xxvi*
    Pentecostal/Charismatic population   *xxiv, xxvi, xxxvii*
    politics   355–356
    Rhema Bible Training Center campus in   270
    Salt & Light in   565
    sociological imagination and   356–357
Kenyon, E.W.   155, 271, 481
Kérékou, Mathew   60, 61
Keryx (periodical)   197
Keswick Movement (Keswick Conventions)   **357–359**
    Minnie Abrams and   3
    Alexander and Mary Boddy and   72
    Canada and   101, 359
    early conferences   357–358
    Evangelicalism and   222
    faith principle and   675
    international influence   44, 358–359
    Watchman Nee and   448
    New Zealand and   456
    Pandita Saraswati Ramabai and   359, 546
    theological views   358
    visual art and   7
    Yu Cidu (Dora Yu) and   675
Kgatle, Mookgo S.   289
Kidok Gongbo (newspaper)   541
Kidson, W.E.   86
Kidula, Jean   443
Kil, Seon Joo   **359–361**, 539
Kileyesus, A.   206, 207
Kim, Ik-du   **361–362**
Kimbangu, Simon   9
King, Joseph H. (J.H.)   328, **363–364**, 433, 630, 639
King, Roy D.   497
The Kingdom of Jesus Christ The Name Above Every Name (Philippines)   511–512
kingdom theology   64–65
Kingsway International Christian Center (UK)   13, 421, 450, 641
Kinnear, Guy   7
Kiribati   *xxxvii*, 468
Kirkland, Jennie   4
Kirkpatrick, Milford   276
Kitonga, Arthur   355
Klaus, Byron D.
    The Globalization of Pentecostalism (with Dempster and Petersen)   254–255
Klikibik, V.   653
Knorr, Werner   97
Kolenda, Daniel   80
Koloi, Senetuli   469–470
Koltovich, V.R.   653
Kong, Duen Yee (Mui Yee)   308, **365–366**, 403
Koré, Moïse   159
Korea. *See also* North Korea; South Korea
    American Presbyterian Mission Annual Meeting   *538*
    Leonard Wren Coote and   152
    Kil Seon Joo   **359–361**, 539
    Kim Ik-du   **361–362**
    Yong Do Lee   **387–388**, 526, 604
    Oneness Pentecostalism in   152
    Prayer Mountain Movement   128–129, **525–528**, 540–541
    Pyongyang Revival   360, 525–526, *526*, **538–540**, 603
Korean Pentecostal Holiness Church   527
Koroma, Abu   585

Kosovo   *xxxvii. See also* Yugoslavia
Kotimma (periodical)   364
Kraft, Charles   656
Krasowski, Grzegorz   517
Kreis Charismatischer Leiter (Germany)   250
Kříž, Jaroslav   591
Krogedal, Jostein   467
Krushnisky, Nicholas   625
Kuhlman, Kathryn   366, **366–368**, 429, 530, 559, 621
Kumuyi, William Folorunso   172–173, 174
Kuttab, George M.   486
Kuwait   *xxvi, xxvii, xxxvii*, 39, 40, **368–369**, 648
Kyrgyzstan   *xxxvii*, 39

Lacho, Ján   590
Ladd, George Eldon   209, 665
Lado, Ludovic   98
Laestadians   622
Laffitte-Catta, Martine   171
Laggah, Julius   585
Lake, John G.   **369–371**
  John Archibald Duncan Adams and   6
  Apostolic Faith Mission (South Africa)   150, 181, 288–289, 369, 371, 383, 602
  Australia and   44
  background   369–370
  Archibald Cooper and   150
  critiques of   371
  A.H. Dallimore and   167
  healing and   370, 371
  international connections   370
  Elias Letwaba and   388
  Gordon Lindsay and   393, 394
Lalou, Marie   158, 159
Lancaster, Sarah Jane (Murrell)   6, 44, 88, 262, **371–373**, 468
Land, Steven
  Pentecostal Spirituality   612–613
Langstaff, Alan   45
Laos   *xxxvii*
Lapa, José da   525
Larkin, Brian   417
Larsen, Verner   477–478
Lathrop, John   336
Latin America   **373–378**. *See also specific countries*
  about   373–374, 377–378
  anthropology and   28
  apostolic ministry and   31
  Catholic Charismatic Renewal   375, 376, 377
  ecology and   190
  eschatology and   209–210
  Evangelical, understanding of   222
  evangelism and missions   376–377
  hermeneutics   376
  media   377
  neoliberalism and religious shifts   375–376
  Neo-Pentecostalism   377, 451–452
  Pentecostal/Charismatic population   *xxii, xliv*
  politics   522
  Julio Cesar Ruibal   **559–560**
  scholarship on Pentecostalism in   374–375
Latin American Bible Institute (USA)   399
Latin American Council of Christian Churches (CLADIC)   398, 473–474
Latter Rain   **379–382**
  apostolic ministry and   30, 381
  Assemblies of God (USA) and   42
  in Australia and New Zealand   31, 45, 456–457, 469
  beginnings of   379–380
  beliefs and Biblical interpretation   380, 644
  Bernt Berntsen and   62–63
  Canada and   101
  eschatology and   208, 209
  George Hawtin and   276–277, *379*, 379–380, 381
  impact of   381–382, 644
  laying on of hands   380–381
  Lewi Pethrus and   508
Latter Rain Evangel (periodical)   36
Latvia   *xxxvii*, 215, 216
Laughing Revival   234, 635
Lausanne Committee for World Evangelization (Lausanne Movement)   222
Law, May   563
Lawler, Homer L. and Emma B.   563
laying on of hands   *281*, 380–381
Layzell, Reg   380, 381
Le Cossec, Clément   236, 608
Le Roux, Pieter L.   **382–383**, 389
Leatherman, Lucy   195, **384–385**, 386, 511, 563
Leaves of Healing (periodical)   369, 383
Lebanon   *xxxvii*, 39, 40, 384, **385–386**, 648
Lee, Bernice   4
Lee, Edward   56, 577
Lee, Edwin   308
Lee, Graham   360, 539
Lee, Ho-bin   387
Lee, Hwan-sin   387
Lee, Sungbong   128, 526
Lee, Witness (Li Changshou)   **389–391**, 449, 583
Lee, Yong Do   **387–388**, 526, 604
Lee, Young-hoon   672
Lee University (USA)   135

Lemiur, J.S.   179
Lemons, M.S.   135
Lencioni, Agostino   102
Leonard, Charles   195
Leonard, T.K.   184, 278
Lesotho   *xxxvii*, 78
Letwaba, Elias   95, **388–389**
Lewini, Anna   68
Lewis, Barbara McCoo   138
Lewis, John   263
Léys, Paulcéus   108
LGBTQ people   575. *See also* queer theory
Li, Changshou (Witness Lee)   **389–391**, 449, 583
Li, Ruth (Li Yuanru)   675
Li, Tien-en   230
Lian, Xi   123
Liberia   *xxvi, xxxvii*, 137, 232, **391–393**
Libres (periodical)   490
Libya   *xxxvii*, 648
Lidman, Sven   508
Lie, Geir   271
Liechtenstein   *xxxviii*
Life Bible School (USA)   290
Light of the World Church (Iglesia La Luz del Mundo; Mexico)   424–425, 477
Lillie, David   312
Lin, Heping   675
Lindhardt, Martin   375, 376
Lindsay, Freda (Schimpf)   393–394
Lindsay, Gordon   17, 82, 315, **393–394**, 481, 482
Lindsey, Hal   86, 347
Ling Liang Worldwide Evangelistic Mission   185. *See also* Bread of Life Church
Lisanti, Felice   102
Lithuania   *xxxviii*, 216
Lithuli, Fred   383
Little Flock (Christian Assemblies, Local Church, Shouters; China)   30, 123, 391, 583, **583–584**, 656, 657
Litton, Fred and Lucille   306
liturgy   239, **395–397**. *See also* worship
Live Coals (periodical)   364
lived dialogue   330
Livets Ord (Word of Life) Church (Sweden)   450
Livets Ord University   197, 234
Living Faith Church Worldwide. *See* Winners Chapel
Living Stream Ministry   583
Living Waters   83
Lixin Fellowship (China)   230, 314

Local Church (Christian Assemblies, Little Flock, Shouters; China)   30, 123, 391, 583, **583–584**, 656, 657
Lombardi, Giacomo   32, 129–130, 184, 238, 337
Londino, Caterina   510
López, Abundio   **397–398**, 422, 577
Lopez, Luis   422
López, Rosa   **397–398**, 577
López, Sixto   160, 550
Lord, Andrew   455
Lorenzen, Alfred   178
love   212, 610
Lovett, Leonard   544, 595
Lü, Xiaomin   231
Lubansa, Billy   98
Luce, Alice Eveline   **398–399**, 422
Lugo, Juan León   108, **399–401**
Lum, Clara   49, 578
Lutheran World Federation   194
Luxembourg   *xxxviii*
La Luz Apostolica (periodical)   399
Lyseight, Oliver   640

Ma, Nathan C.S.   587
Ma, Zhaorui   580
Macao   *xxxviii*, 37
MacArthur, John, Jr.   271
Macchia, Frank D.   187, 336, 516, 600, 601
Macedo, Edir   90, 377, **401–402**, 645, 647
MacGregor, Kirk R.   531
Machingura, F.   683–684
MacNutt, Francis   195, 375, 567, 665
Madagascar   *xxxviii*
Madonia, Elio   103
Madzokere, N.   683
Mafoe, Viliame   470
Magee, Gordon   478
Magowan, Fiona   444
Mahan, Asa   358
Mahoney, Ralph   651–652
Malankara Full Gospel Church (India)   1–2, 149
Malawi   *xxxviii*, 15
Malaysia   **403–404**
 about   38, 39
 beginnings of Pentecostalism in   403
 Charismatic Movement   404
 Chinese-speaking Pentecostalism   404
 East Malaysia   403, 404
 El Shaddai (Philippines) in   648
 Prince Guneratnam   267–268

Malaysia (cont.)
    higher education   403–404
    Kong Duen Yee (Mui Yee)   308, **365–366**, 403
    Pentecostal/Charismatic population   *xxxviii*
Maldives   *xxxviii*
Maldonado, Guillermo   307
Mali   *xxxviii*
Malines Documents   618
Mallory, Arena C.   136
Malta   *xxxviii*
Mambu, Francis   585
Maná Christian Church (Portugal)   23, 106, 524
Mandey, A.H.   323
Mandryk, Jason   75, 488
"manifest sons" doctrine   381
Manna Church (Cirkev Manna; Slovakia)   590
Manna Ministries (India)   335
Manoramabai   3, 4, 439, 545
Mansilla Agüero, Miguel   376
Mantofa, Philip   404
Māori   69–70, 315, 457–458, 469
Margies, Wolfhardt   163
Marino, Domingo   130
Marker, Gordon and Marilyn   423
marriage   574
Marshall, Sunshine   422
Marshall Islands   xxvi, *xxvi, xxxviii*, 468, 470–471
Martin, David   xv–xvi, 255, 597
Martin, Francis   618
Martin, Ralph   582
Martínez Luis, Francisco   161
Martinique   *xxxviii*
Martins, Joaquim Cartaxo   22
Más que Vencedores (MQV; Paraguay)   489–490
Masasu, Joshua   562
masculinity   247, 684
Mason, Charles Harrison   136, **405–406**, 543, 578, 643
Mast, Michel E.   235
masturbation   575
Mathews, Thomas   407–408
Mattson-Boze, Joseph   475
Mauritania   *xxxviii*
Mauritius   xxvi, xxvii, *xxxviii*
Mauss, Marcel   532
Maxwell, David   684
Mayfield, Alex   639
Mayotte   *xxxviii*
McAlister, Robert   90, 401
McAlister, Robert Edward (R.E.)   101, **408–410**, *409*, 476, 493
McArthur, John   635

McCabe, Joshua   111
McConnell, Daniel   271
McConnell, John, Jr.   189
McDonald, Archibald W. and Vinnie M.   563
McDonnell, Kilian   193, 272, 554, 555, 595
McGavran, Donald   407, 654, 655
McGlothen, Mattie C.   138
McIntosh, T.J.   364
McKeown, James   25, 251, **410–412**
McKeown, Sophia   **411–412**
McKinney, Michael   652
McLeod, Sadie Margaret   308
McPherson, Aimee Semple   **412–414**. *See also* Foursquare Church
    Angelus Temple   88, 413, 419
    Zelma Argue and   35, 36
    in Australia   44, 468
    background   412
    Mina Ross Brawner and   88
    controversies and death   413–414
    William H. Durham and   184
    Ellen Hebden and   100, 284, 412
    Tommy Hicks   290
    Hong Kong and   308
    Kathryn Kuhlman and   366, 367
    John G. Lake and   370
    ministry of   412–413
    Pentecostal Assemblies of Canada and   495
    photographs   245, *413, 414*
    Charles S. Price and   529
    scholarship on   414
    Smith Wigglesworth and   663
McTernan, John   335
Mebius, Frederick E.   198, 306, **415**
media   **416–418**
    adaptations to local cultures and   417–418
    A.A. Allen and   17
    Carlos Annacondia and   26
    Assemblies of God (USA)   41–42, 170
    Brazil   377, 416
    Bulgaria   92
    Cape Verde   106
    Myo Chit and   125
    Church of God (Cleveland)   135
    Alexander Thomas Davidson and   169
    definition   416
    Democratic Republic of the Congo (DR Congo)   418
    Egypt   196
    Ethiopia   214
    future research areas   418
    Ghana   252–253, 417

media (cont.)
    Charles L. Greenwood and   262
    Ha Young Jo and   269
    haptic media   418
    Hillsong   296
    homiletics and   305
    House Church Movement and   313
    Jesus is Lord Church Worldwide (Philippines)   344, 652
    Kenya   354–355, 356
    Kathryn Kuhlman and   367
    Latin America   377
    Lebanon   386
    Thomas Mathews and   408
    mediation and   418
    music and   442–443
    Nigeria   462
    T.L. Osborn and   482
    Paraguay   490
    Pentecostal publics and   416–417
    Lewi Pethrus and   508
    politics and   416
    Oral Roberts and   552, 553, 644
    Julio Cesar Ruibal and   559
    Sweden   623
    George Floyd Taylor and   328, 630–631
    Universal Church of the Kingdom of God   402, 417–418, 645
    Mariano Velarde and   648
    Yoido Full Gospel Church and   673
megachurches   419–421. *See also specific megachurches*
    about   419
    Australia   45
    beliefs   421
    Bolivia   75
    future research areas   421
    global distribution and transnational networks   419–421
    Indonesia   320
    Neo-Pentecostalism and   451
    Netherlands   453
    Nigeria   420–421
    Prosperity Gospel and   421
    Singapore   589
    United Kingdom   642
Mei, Paochen   587
Melanesia   *xlv*, 468, 470, 485
Men of Issachar   15
Meng, Mingshi   587
Menna, Lucía   32, 129–130, 238

Mensaje de Salvación (Message of Salvation; Argentina)   26, 33
Menzies, William   594
Mercer, Robert   411
Mercy Ministries   686
Meseret Kristos (Mennonite; Eritrea)   207
Messianic Judaism   116. *See also* Jews
Methodist Pentecostal Church (Chile)   118–119, 120, 309–310, 311, 328
Metropolitan Bible Institute (USA)   463
Mexico   422–425
    Aglow International   15
    apostasy from Pentecostalism   376
    Apostolic Church of the Faith in Christ Jesus   423, 424
    Assemblies of God   422–423, 423–424
    beginnings of Pentecostalism in   422
    Charismatic population   *xxvii*
    Church of God (Cleveland) and   135, 424
    Church of God in the Republic of Mexico   422, 423–424
    higher education   270, 423
    Independent Evangelical Church   424
    Independent Pentecostal Evangelical Church Movement   424
    Light of the World Church   424–425, 477
    Alice Eveline Luce and   398–399
    Oneness Pentecostalism in   477
    Pentecostal Fraternal Association in Mexico   424
    Pentecostal/Charismatic growth rate   *xxvi*
    Pentecostal/Charismatic population   *xxiv, xxxviii*
Meyer, Frederick Brotherson   358
Meyer, Joyce   386, 686
Miccolis, Onofrio   103
Michel, David   544
Micronesia   *xxxviii*, 468, 470–471
Micronesia Islands   *xlv*, 468
Middle East   39–40, 384–385. *See also specific countries*
Middle East Council of Churches   486
migration   425–427. *See also* globalization; transnationalism
    Africa   13
    Bulgaria   92
    China   124
    Christian Assemblies (Argentina) and   130
    Christian Congregation in Brazil and   132
    definition and factors   425–426
    Europe   218–219
    globalization and   255

migration (cont.)
    Greece   260
    Ireland   332–333
    Italy   130, 337, 338
    Kuwait   368
    Malaysia   404
    Netherlands   453
    New Zealand   457
    Norway   467
    Pentecostalism and   426–427
    Portugal   523
    relations with local congregations   225
    Romania   558
    secularization and   572
    Sierra Leone   585–586
    Spain   608–609
    True Jesus Church and   636–637
    United Kingdom   218, 641
    Universal Church of the Kingdom of God and   647
Miguel, Iranilde   336
Millar, Sandy   301
Miller, Donald E.   204, 255, 454–455, 597
Milles, J.N.   362
Milligan, Bertha   563, 564
Million Soul Movement   539
Mills, C. Wright   356
Mills, Verent John Russell   438
Ministry of the Power of the Gospel (Côte d'Ivoire)   159
Miracle Center (Rwanda)   562
Miracle Magazine   17
miracles, signs, wonders   428–430. *See also* baptism in the Holy Spirit; cosmology; deliverance and exorcism; glossolalia; healing; Prosperity Gospel; xenolalia
La Misión Cristiana Elim (Guatemala)   199, 264
Misión del Nazareno (Guatemala)   264
Misión el Verbo (Guatemala)   265
Missão Evangélica de Vista Alegre (Pentecostal Mission; Angola)   22
missiology and missions   430–432. *See also* Pentecostal Missionary Union
    Assemblies of God (USA)   42, 293, 399
    from Caribbean   109
    colonialism and   140–141
    definition   430
    from Denmark   178–179
    ecclesiology and   186
    evangelism, emphasis on   430–431
    flexibility and   431

    Walter Hollenweger on participatory missions   300
    Holy Spirit and   430
    from Honduras   306–307
    indigenization   431
    from Italian Transnational Pentecostal Movement   335
    Jesus People Movement   347
    from Latin America   376–377
    Latter Rain and   380
    Alice Eveline Luce and   398–399
    mass conversions   431
    miracles, signs, and wonders and   428, 430
    from Norway   466–467
    T.L. Osborn and   481–482
    Planetshakers   513–514
    from Sweden   22, 33, 74, 144, 607, 623, 627
    Charles Peter Wagner on spiritual gifts and   654–655, 656
Mission libre Norvégienne (Communautés des Eglises Libres de Pentecôte en Afrique (CELPA); DR Congo)   143, 467
Mission libre Suedoise (DR Congo)   144
Mission Lluvias de Gracia (Guatemala)   265
Mission of Orebro   112
Mission Vie et Lumière (France)   236
Missionary and Apostolic Church of Venezuela   651
missions. *See* missiology and missions
Mix, Sarah (Mrs. Edward)   436
Mizpa Bible Institute (Puerto Rico)   400
Moffet, S.A.   360
Mok, Lai Chi   307, 364, *432*, **432–434**, 503
Moldova   *xxxviii*
Moll, Frank   195
Monaco   *xxxviii*
Mongolia   *xxxviii*, **434–435**
Mongolia Evangelical Alliance   434
Monod, Théodore   358
Monrovia Bible Training Center (MBTC; Liberia)   392
Monsen, Marie   579–580, 658
Montanists   258
Monteiro, Yara   336
Montenegro   *xxxix*. *See also* Yugoslavia
Montgomery, Carrie Judd   4, 88, 385, 422, *435*, **435–437**, 473
Montgomery, George   385, 422, 436–437, 472, 473
Montgomery, G.H.   328
Montreal Declaration of Anglican Essentials   20–21

Montserrat *xxxix*, 108
Moody, Dwight Lyman 358, 360
Mooi, Raymond 537
Moomau, Antoinette 385, 587
Moore, Jack 86, 394
Moore, Jennie Evans 48–49, 577, 578, 579
Mora, G. Cristina 418
morality 534. *See also* sexuality
Morgan, Sister Gertrude 7
Morning Star (newspaper) 92
Morrison, J. Elmor 308, **437–438**
Morrison, Laura Mae 438
Morrison, Louella 438
Morroco *xxxix*
Morrow, Peter 457
Mortomore, Florence (Florrie) 6, 44, 372
Morton, Barry 388
Mosaik (Denmark) 178
Motaung, Edward "Lion" 388
Moule, Handley Carr Glyn 358, 359
Mountain of Fire & Miracles Ministries 159
Moussa, Iya 98–99
Movimento Apostólico do Renovamento Carismático (Angola) 23
Mozambique *xxxix*, 335
Mpofu, S. 683
Mraida, Carlos 34
Mt. Zion Bible Institute (India) 149
Mukti Mission and Revival 2–4, 298, 349–350, 364, **439–440**, 545–546. *See also* Ramabai, Pandita Saraswati
Mukwakwama, L. 683
Mukwege, Denis 623
Mülheim Movement (Mülheim Association (Germany)) 215, 216, 248, 249
multi-faith 329. *See also* inter-religious relations
Mulu Wengel (Full Gospel; Eritrea) 207
Mulu Wongel Church (Ethiopia) 214
Mumba, Nevers 450
Mumford, Bob 581–582
Muñoz, Antonio 424
Muñoz, Gregorio 424
Muñoz, José María 264
Murai, Jun 152, **440–442**, 676
Murray, Andrew 358, 382
Murray, Charlette C. 358
Muse, Dan T. 364
music **442–445**
  about 442, 444–445
  Chile 311
  Church of God in Christ 136–137
  Contemporary Christian Music industry 348, 444
  embodiment and 205
  Ethiopia 214
  Ghana 443
  global roots of Pentecostal music 442
  globalization and 444
  gospel music 136–137, 443
  Hillsong 294–295, 444
  Jesus People Movement and 348, 444, 655
  Kenya 416–417, 443
  media and 442–443
  new forms and styles 443
  Nicaragua 460
  Planetshakers 513, 514
  secular vs. Christian music 443
  senwele (Muslim music genre) 417
  Third Wave Pentecostalism and 655
  worship and 395–396
  Darlene Zschech 295, **685–686**
Mwakasege, Christopher 629
Myanmar
  about 39
  Myo Chit 125–126
  Pentecostal/Charismatic population *xxxix*, 38
  Rhema Bible Training Center campus in 270
  John Sung and 619
Mygind, H.J. 67
Myriam Bethléem 172
mysticism **445–447**. *See also* baptism in the Holy Spirit; experience, of God; spirituality

Næser, Carl 68
Nagashima, Tsuru 441
Nahuway, Jacob 323
Nainggolan, Robinson 323
Nakada, Juji 353, 563
Namibia *xxxix*
Napolitano, Carmine 336
Nardi, Michele 237, 324
narrative theology 299–300
Naso, Paolo 337
National Association of Bolivian Evangelicals (Asociación Nacional de Evangélicos de Bolivia, ANDEB) 76–77
National Association of Charismatic and Christian Churches (Ghana) 251
National Association of Evangelicals (NAE) 42, 192, 222, 224, 328, 500
National Council of Churches (NCC) 138, 181, 193, 223–224, 595
National Evangelical Association 325
National Evangelical Church of Kuwait (NECK) 368–369
National Revival Crusade 111, 273, 274

Native Missionary Movement (NMM)   407–408
Natucci, Narciso   130
Nauru   *xxxix*, 468
Navapur Convention   408
Navarro Martinez, Juan   422
Navigators   196, 677
Nazem, Mohsen   196
Nee, Watchman (Ni Tuosheng)   **447–449**
  about   123, 447–448
  apostolic ministry and   30
  beliefs and influence   448–449
  Li Changshou (Witness Lee) and   389, 390, 449
  persecution by Communists   124, 449
  Shouters and   583
  Wang Zai (Leland Wang) and   656
  Weepers and   658
  Yu Cidu (Dora Yu) and   675
Needham, Hulda   399
Negro, Angel   34
Nelson, Ted   20
Németh, Sándor   591
Neocatechumenal Way (Camino Neocatecumenal)   609
neoliberalism   199, 201, 375–376, 532, 558, 646
Neo-Pentecostalism (Neo-Charismatics, Third Wave)   **449–452**. *See also* Independent Charismatics; Prosperity Gospel; *specific churches*
  Africa   10, 12, 450–451
  Angola   23
  Benin   59–60, 61
  Bolivia   75–76
  Brazil   90–91, 451–452
  characteristics and teachings   451
  on conversion   146, 147
  definition challenges   449–450
  eschatology and   209
  Ethiopia   214
  Finland   233, 234
  Germany   250
  Greece   260
  Guatemala   265–266
  Latin America   377, 451–452
  miracles, signs, wonders   429–430
  as neocolonialism   141–142
  Netherlands   453
  New Zealand   458
  Nicaragua   460
  Paraguay   488
  Portugal   524
  secularization and   572
  sexuality and   575

Spain   609
Taiwan   626
Tanzania   628
Charles Peter Wagner and   654, 655, 664
neo-prophetism   602
Nepal   *xxviii, xxxix*
Netherlands   *xxxix*, 15, 193, 215, 217, 218, 270, **452–453**, 648
networks   **454–455**
neurotheology   533
New Age Herald (periodical)   564
New Apostolic Church (Novoapoštolská cirkev; Slovakia)   590
New Apostolic Reformation. *See* apostles and apostolic ministry
new birth (regeneration)   146–147, 477
New Caledonia   *xxxix*, 468, 470, 485
New Covenant Church   641
New England Bible Institute (USA)   463
New Frontiers   453
New Hope Church (Církev Nová naděje; Czech Republic)   163
New Life Bible Church (Rwanda)   562
New Life Churches of New Zealand   457, 469, 470
New Life Pentecostal Church (Brazil)   90, 401
NEW Missions (Haiti)   335
New Pentecost Movement (Italy)   337
New Song   525
New Testament Church   308, 365–366, 626
New Testament Church of God   339, 640, 642
New Wine (UK)   453, 641, 642
New Wine Magazine   582
New Zealand   **456–458**
  John Archibald Duncan Adams   5–6
  Aglow International   15
  beginnings of Pentecostalism in   456, 468
  Ray Bloomfield   **69–70**, 315
  Mina Ross Brawner and   88
  William Cathcart and   111
  A.H. Dallimore   **167–168**
  El Shaddai (Philippines) in   648
  growth period   456–457, 469
  William Francis (Frank) Houston and   69, 70, 315–316, 457
  Latter Rain and Healing Revival in   45, 456–457
  Māori   69–70, 315, 457–458, 469
  migration to   457
  National Revival Crusade   273
  Neo-Pentecostal megachurches   458
  Pentecostal/Charismatic population   *xxxix, xlv*
  Salt & Light in   565
  Smith Wigglesworth and   663

Newberg, Andrew   533
Newfoundland and Labrador
   Alice Belle Garrigus   240–242, *241*, 496
   Pentecostal Assemblies of Newfoundland and Labrador   99, 493–494, **496–498**
Newman, Joe   544
Next Towns Crusade (Japan)   153
Ngakane, Maurice   117
Ngoloma Ndela Bantu   95, 143
Ni, Tuosheng. *See* Nee, Watchman
Nicandro, Patrizia   336
Nicaragua   *xxvi*, *xxxix*, 270, 423, **458–460**
Nicolle, Pierre   235
Niger   *xxxix*
Nigeria   **461–462**
   about   461
   Aladura (African Independent/Initiated Churches (AICs))   9, 461
   characteristics of Pentecostal/Charismatic churches   461–462
   Charismatic population   *xxvii*
   Deeper Life Bible Church   83, 98, 106, **172–174**, *173*, 641
   higher education   98, 270
   Independent Charismatic population   xxvii, *xxviii*
   influence in Cameroon   98
   media   462
   megachurches   420–421
   Oneness Pentecostalism in   478
   Pentecostal (denominational) population   xxvi, *xxvi*
   Pentecostal/Charismatic population   xxiv, *xxiv*, *xxv*, *xxxix*
   politics   462, 522, 549
   Redeemed Christian Church of God   **548–549** (*See also* Redeemed Christian Church of God)
   senwele (Muslim music genre)   417
   social engagement   462
   Winners Chapel   12, 83, 98, 112, **666–668**
Nikolov, Nicholas   91, **463–464**, 680
Nilsson, Sten   196
Niue   *xxxix*, 468
Njotorahardjo, Niko   320, **464–465**
Nkoyane, Daniel   383
Noble, John   312
Noer, Johny   92
Nokia Mission Church (now Congregation of New Hope; Finland)   234
Nolan, Albert   118

Nongminsungbo (*The Voice of the Farmer*; periodical)   541
Nonini, Rogelio   26–27
Nordquelle, Erik Andersen   466
Norman, Larry   348
North America   *xliv*. *See also* specific countries
North Korea   *xxviii*, *xxxix*, 674. *See also* Korea
North Macedonia   *xxxix*. *See also* Yugoslavia
Northern Mariana Islands   *xxxix*, 468
Norton, Albert   350, 351
Norton, Mary   350
Norton John   350–351
Norway   **466–467**
   Aglow International   15
   Thomas Ball Barratt   **53–54** (*See also* Barratt, Thomas Ball)
   beginnings of Pentecostalism in   215, 216, 466
   contemporary church plants   467
   ecumenism in   193
   global missions and influence   33, 466–467
   Lutheran charismatic renewal   467
   migrant churches in   467
   Pentecostal/Charismatic population   *xxxix*
   racism   223
   Rhema Bible Training Center campus in   270
Norwegian Pentecostal Movement   466, 467
Nouveau, Papa   158
La Nouvelle Jérusalem (Church of God)   57, 58
Novák, Josef   162
Nukida, Jun   153, 442
Nunn, David   394
Nuzum, Clarissa   422
Nyarkoah, Comfort   25
Nyien, David   365
Nyuki, Abraham   143

Oase (oasis) movement (Norway)   467
O'Byrne, Ryan Joseph   606
Oceania   xxii, *xliv*, **468–471**. *See also* specific countries and regions
Ohta, Fukuzo   441
Olazábal, Francisco   398, **472–474**
Olena, Lois   595
Oliveira, Valdemiro Santiago de   402
Oliverio, L. William, Jr.   285, 286
Olson, Ingve   650
Omahe, Chacha   **474–475**
Oman   *xxvi*, *xxxix*, 648
Oneness Pentecostalism   **476–478**
   about   476, 478

INDEX

Oneness Pentecostalism (cont.)
    Assemblies of God (USA) and   42, 476, 477, 643
    on baptism   63, 278, 409, 476, 477
    beginnings and theological development   409, 476–477, 643
    Bernt Berntsen and   63, 659
    Canadian contribution to   101
    in China   62, 63, 123
    on conversion   146
    critiques of   278
    denominational bodies   477
    G.T. Haywood and   278, 476
    international growth   477–478
    Jamaica   339
    Korea   152
    R.E. McAlister and   409–410, 476, 493
    Pentecostal Assemblies of Canada and   493
    Pentecostal Assemblies of the World   498–500
        (*See also* Pentecostal Assemblies of the World)
    Philippines   511
    True Jesus Church and   62, 478, 637, 658, 659
Onething Conferences   196
Onnuri Community Church (South Korea)   268–269
Onyinah, Opoku   479–480
Oommen, K.C.   1
Oparebea, Agnes   25
Open Bible Churches (Open Bible Standard Churches)   88
Opočenský, Milan   194
Opperman, Daniel C.O.   41
Oral Roberts Evangelistic Association   552. *See also* Roberts, Oral
Oral Roberts University (ORU)   553
Order of Saint Luke   45
Origin   258
Orozco, Juan   422
Orozco, Rodolfo   422
Ortega, Rubén   423
Orthodox Christianity. *See also* Coptic Orthodox and Catholic Churches
    apostolic ministry and   30
    glossolalia and   258
    Greece   259–260
    Michael and Jeanne Harper   273
    Middle East   40
    Pentecostalism and   *xxiii*, 211, 216
    Russia   560, 561
Ortiz, Francisco, Sr.   399
Ortiz, Juan Carlos   34, 290, 336

Ortíz, Luis M.   160
Ortiz, Panchito   399, 400
Osanri Choi Jashil Memorial Prayer Mountain (South Korea)   128–129, 527
Osborn, Daisy (Washburn)   481
Osborn, LaDonna   481
Osborn, T.L.   33, 86, 144, 179, 394, 452, **481–482**, *482*, 651
Osborn National Missionary Assistance Program   481
Osinbajo, Yemi   549
Osterberg, Arthur   577
Osterberg, Emma   577
Otabil, Mensa   253, **483–484**
Ottolini, Peter   184, 337
Owens, David Chandler   138
Owiredu, Stephen   25
Oyedepo, David O.   12, 666–668
Ozman, Agnes   491, 642

Pace, Enzo   337, 338
Paddock, Ross   499
Padgett, Carl   135
Page, Albert T. and Lou   **484–485**
Pakistan   *xl*, 38
Palau   *xl*, 468
Palau, Luis   75
Palestine   *xl*, 39, 40, **486–487**
Palma, Alfred   336
Palma, Anthony   336
Palma, Paul   336
Palmer, Phoebe   358, 436
Paloutzian, Raymond   533
Panama   *xl*, 375
Papua New Guinea
    about   468, 469, 471
    Assemblies of God and   45, 170, 469, 471
    Leo Cecil Harris and   274
    Pentecostal (denominational) population   *xxvi*
    Pentecostal/Charismatic population   *xl*
    Planetshakers and   514
    Rhema Bible Training Center campus in   270
Paraguay   *xl*, 15, **488–490**
Pare de Sufrir (Bolivia)   75
Parham, Charles   **490–492**
    about   490
    background and theological development   490 491
    baptism in the Holy Spirit and   *ix*, 47, 491–492, 642
    Lucy Farrow and   231–232, 491–492

Parham, Charles (cont.)
    glossolalia and   258
    John G. Lake and   370
    later career   492
    Lucy Leatherman and   384
    Gordon Lindsay and   393
    photograph   *491*
    William Seymour and   48, 491–492, 577, 578
    Zion City and   80–81, 288
Park, Crystal   533
Park, Gui-Im   604
Park, Seong-San   604
Parsons, Ann   336
Parto, Blanch Elizabeth   308
Patterson, Gilbert Earl   138
Patterson, James Oglethorpe, Sr.   138
Paul, Jonathan   54, 72, 162, 249
Paul VI (pope)   104, 367, 617, 618
Pavia, Carlo   102
Payne, Julie   638
Payne, Leah   414
    Gender and Pentecostal Revivalism   205
Paz, Eleutero   400
Paz, Francisco   473
Pelcé, Paul   235
Penn-Lewis, Jessie   359, 660–661
Pennsylvania United Free Missionary Society   264
Pentecost (periodical)   244
Pentecost University College (Ghana)   480
Pentecostal Assemblies of Canada (PAOC)   493–495
    about   99
    Argentina   33
    D. Mark Buntain and   93
    Canadian Assemblies of God and   103
    China   122
    ecumenism and   507
    establishment   493
    gender and   495
    George Hawtin and   275–276
    higher education   494
    Hong Kong   308
    Indigenous peoples and   495
    institutionalization   494
    Latter Rain and   381
    R.E. McAlister and   409–410, 493
    Pentecostal Assemblies of Newfoundland and Labrador and   493–494, 497
    race and   494–495
    Taiwan   624
    Tanzania   627
Pentecostal Assemblies of China (Taiwan)   624

Pentecostal Assemblies of Newfoundland and Labrador   99, 493–494, **496–498**
Pentecostal Assemblies of the World (PAW)   498–500
    about   498
    beliefs   499
    Bernt Berntsen and   63
    China   122
    Leonard Wren Coote and   152
    Leonard Wren Coote and   152
    gender and   499
    G.T. Haywood and   278, 498
    Jamaica   339
    Liberia   392
    organization and size   499–500
    race and   63, 477, 498–499, 543, 643
    rupture with Assemblies of God (USA)   42, 643
    schisms within   499
Pentecostal Band   152
Pentecostal/Charismatic Churches of North America (formerly Pentecostal Fellowship of North America (PFNA))   500–501
    Assemblies of God (USA) and   42
    Canadian Assemblies of God and   103
    Church of God in Christ and   137
    ecumenism and   192
    establishment   500
    International Fellowship of Christian Assemblies and   325
    International Pentecostal Holiness Church and   328
    race and   43, 329, 500–501
    Society for Pentecostal Studies and   594
Pentecostal Church of Australia (PCA)   44, 262–263
Pentecostal Church of Christ   643
Pentecostal Church of Finland (PCF)   233
Pentecostal Church of God (PCG)   257, *281*, 400, 473, 524, 643
Pentecostal Church of New Zealand (PCNZ)   6, 456
Pentecostal Church of Poland   518, 519
Pentecostal church of Rwanda ("Association des eglises de Pentecote au Rwanda" (ADEPR))   561, 562
Pentecostal Church of Sabah (Malaysia)   404
Pentecostal Churches of the Apostolic Faith (PCAF)   499
The Pentecostal Educator (periodical)   293
Pentecostal European Conference (PEC)   502, 623
Pentecostal European Fellowship (PEF)   221, 261, 502
Pentecostal Evangel (periodical)   36, 41, 88, 92, 399

INDEX

Pentecostal Evangelical Church (Italy)   337
Pentecostal Evangelistic Fellowship of Africa (PEFA)   474, 627
Pentecostal Fellowship of North America (PFNA). See Pentecostal/Charismatic Churches of North America
Pentecostal Fellowship of Sierra Leone (PFSL)   585
Pentecostal Fraternal Association in Mexico (Asociación Fraternal de Iglesias Pentecostales en la República de México)   424
Pentecostal Holiness Advocate (periodical)   328, 364, 630–631
Pentecostal Holiness Association Mission (Tanzania)   627
Pentecostal Holiness Church. See International Pentecostal Holiness Church
Pentecostal Holiness Church in Botswana   83
Pentecostal League   73
Pentecostal Ministerial Alliance (PMA)   499
Pentecostal Mission (Hong Kong)   307, 432, 503
Pentecostal Mission (South Africa)   150
Pentecostal Missionary Union (PMU)   73, 95, 101, 122, 143, 504–505, 520, 564, 586–587, 662
Pentecostal studies   x. See also Pentecostalism, counting
    about   vii
    on body and embodiment   205
    definitions of Pentecostalism   viii–ix, 174–177, 297, 615–616
    on Italian Transnational Pentecostal Movement   336
    perceptions of   614–615
    Society for Pentecostal Studies   vii, 594–596
    statistics   614–617
The Pentecostal Testimony (periodical)   36, 410, 494
Pentecostal Theological Seminary (USA)   135, 465
Pentecostal Times (periodical)   44
Pentecostal Truths (periodical)   307, 433, 503
Pentecostal World Fellowship (PWF; formerly Pentecostal World Conference)   505–507
    background and establishment   192, 505–506
    Church of God in Christ and   138
    critiques of   507
    David du Plessis and   181
    ecumenism and   194–195
    Prince Guneratnam and   267
    headquarters   506
    membership   506–507
    objectives   506

Pentecostal/Charismatic Churches of North America and   500
    Lewi Pethrus and   623
    photograph   506
    Society for Pentecostal Studies and   594
    World Alliance for Pentecostal Theological Education and   293
    World Assemblies of God Fellowship and   506–507, 671
Pentecostalism. See also specific topics
    approach to   vii–viii, x, xi
    definitions   viii–ix, **174–177**, 297, 615–616
    terminology   xx
Pentecostalism, counting
    about   xiii, xxviii
    Anglicans   xx–xxi
    Barrett, critiques of   xv–xvi
    Barrett, early work by   xiii–xv, *xv*, xvii, 615
    challenges of   x
    Charismatics   xix, xxvii, *xxvii*
    countries with fastest growth rates   xxv, *xxvi*
    countries with largest populations   *xxiv*, xxiv–xxv, *xxv*
    global context   *xxiii–xxiv*
    Independent Charismatics   xix–xx, xxi, xxvii, *xxviii*
    methodology   xiii, xvii–xviii
    Pentecostals (denominational)   xviii–xix, xxi, xxvi, *xxvi*
    recent efforts   xvi–xvii
    research results, summary   xxii
    Roman Catholics   xxii
    statistics   **614–617**
pentecostalization   161. See also Charismatics (Charismatic Movement, Charismatic Renewal)
Pentecostals (denominational)   xviii–xix, xxi, xxiii, xxvi, *xxvi*
People of Praise Community (USA)   xxii, 547
Peploe, Hanmer William Webb   358
Perales, José   424
Perez, Brigido   422
Perkins, Noel   463
Perruc, Roman and Carmen   607
Perry, Mattie   80
Perry, Sam C.   108
Persatuan Antar Pendeta-pendeta Seluruh Indonesia (PAPSI; Association of Indonesian Pastors)   322
Persekutuan Pentakosta Indonesia (PPI; Indonesian Pentecostal Fellowship)   322

795

Persekutuan Umat Kristen Pancasila (PUKP; Pancasila Christian Fellowship)   322
Persekutuan Umat Kristen Pentakosta di Indonesia (PUKRIP; Pentecostal Christian Fellowship in Indonesia)   322
Peru   *xl*, 270
Peters, C. Breckinridge   346
Petersen, Douglas
   The Globalization of Pentecostalism (with Dempster and Klaus)   254–255
Pethrus, Lewi   54, 144, 243, 380, 466, 507–509, 530, 622–623
Petites Soeurs des Pauvres   172
Petrelli, Giuseppe   130, 325, 335, 336, 509–510
Pettit, W.H.   168
Petts, David   221
Pew Forum on Religion and Public Life
   Global Christianity (report)   xvi
   "Spirit and Power" (report)   xvi
Pezzi, Mario   609
Pfister, Raymond   221
Pharos (Belgium)   58
Philadelphia Evangelical Church   488
Philip, K.V.   407
Philippine Council of Evangelical Churches (PCEC)   345, 511
Philippines   511–512
   about   37, 38, 511
   appeal of Pentecostalism   512
   beginnings of Pentecostalism   511
   Bread of Life Church (Ling Liang Church)   185
   Catholic Charismatic Renewal   37, 116, 512
   Charismatic population   xxvii, *xxvii*
   El Shaddai   200–201, 345, 512, 648–649
   higher education   270, 307, 434
   Independent Charismatic population   *xxviii*
   Italian Transnational Pentecostal Movement in   335
   Jesus is Lord Church Worldwide   *344*, **344–346**, 511, 652
   The Kingdom of Jesus Christ The Name Above Every Name   511–512
   Pentecostal organizations, overview   511
   Pentecostal/Charismatic growth rate   *xxvi*
   Pentecostal/Charismatic population   xxiv, *xxiv*, xxv, *xxv*, *xl*, 511
   politics   345–346
   Mariano "Mike" Velarde   200, 201, 345, 512, **647–649**
   Eddie Villanueva   344, 345–346, 511, **651–652**
Philippines for Jesus Movement (PJM)   345
Phillips, E.J.   202, 341

Pierson, Arthur Tappan   358
Pietism   7, 233, 248, 517
Pingst (Pentecost), The Swedish Alliance of Independent Churches   624
Pinkster Jongeren Vlaanderen (Belgium)   58
Pinnock, Clark   635
Pinson, Mack M.   41, 398
Piper, William H.   184
Pittman, Rosa   563
Pivec, Holly   32
Planetshakers   512–514, *513*
pluralism, religious   330
Plüss, Jean-Daniel   194
Pneuma (journal)   595
pneumatological imagination   189, 331
pneumatology   514–516. *See also* Holy Spirit
Pneumavita (Portugal)   524–525
Poewe, Karla   151, 254
Poland   *xl*, 15, 116, 216, **517–519**
Polhill, Cecil   47, 72, 73, 504, 505, *519*, **519–521**, 586–587
politics   521–522. *See also* social engagement
   Aglow International on   15
   Benin   60–61
   Reinhard Bonnke and   79
   Brazil   522
   Bulgaria   92
   Chad   115
   Chile   120–121, 224
   China   522
   Côte d'Ivoire   159
   El Shaddai (Philippines) and   200–201
   Eritrea   207–208
   Evangelicalism, Pentecostalism and   224–225, 521
   Guatemala   265–266, 522
   India   522
   Indonesian Pentecostal Fellowship of Churches and   323
   Kenya   355–356
   Korea   360
   Liberia   392
   media and   416
   migration and   426
   Mok Lai Chi and   433
   Nicaragua   459–460
   Nigeria   462, 522, 549
   Pentecostal European Fellowship and   502
   Lewi Pethrus and   508
   Philippines   345–346
   Redeemed Christian Church of God and   549
   Sweden   623

politics (cont.)
  UK   522
  Universal Church of the Kingdom of God
    and   402, 645
  USA   224, 521
  Eddie Villanueva and   652
  Zambia   678–679
  Zimbabwe   684
Pollock, James   372
Polman, Gerrit R.   57, 249, 319, 322, 520
Polman, Wilhelmina   57, 520
Poloma, Margaret   597, 635
polygamy   575–576
Polynesia   xlv, 468, 469, 470, 471
Polynesian Pentecostal Church   470
poor (poverty)   190–191
Popular Gospel Truth (*PGT;* periodical)   63
pornography   574
Portugal   xl, 15, 116, 219, 270, 335, 523–525
Portuguese Evangelical Alliance (Aliança
    Evangélica Portuguesa, AEP)   523, 524
Post, Ansel and Henrietta   195
postcolonial critical theory   141. *See also*
    colonialism
posthumanism   598
post-racialism   543
postsociality   598
prayer
  International House of Prayer (IHOP)   196,
    325–327, 664, 666
  Prayer Mountain Movement (Korea)   128–129,
    525–528, 540–541
  worship and   396
Prayer Book Society of Canada   20, 21
Prayer Mountain Movement (Korea)   128–129,
    525–528, 540–541
preaching. *See* homiletics
premillennial dispensationalism   123, 209, 505
Prentiss, Henry   278
Prevailing Christian Ministries   83
Price, Charles S.   35, 93, 167, 366, 528–530
Price, Frederick K.C.   271, 530
Primera Iglesia Pentecostal (Cuba)   160
Primera Iglesia Pentecostal in Cuba   160
Primitive Apostolic Church of Pentecost (USA)
    260
Primitive Methodist Church USA   264
Prince, Derek   30, 326, 581–582, 591
Principe de Paz (Guatemala)   264
Prison Fellowship Mongolia   435

profession of faith   146
prophecy
  Bible on   610
  Chad   113
  Ghana   252
  Gift Movement   630
  Kansas City prophets   326, 664
  revivals and   551
  John Sung (Song Shangjie) and   620
  Zimbabwe   683
Prosperity Gospel (Health and Wealth, Word of
  Faith)   530–532
  about   530
  Africa   12–13, 210
  Asia   38
  Assemblies of God (USA) and   42, 76
  beginnings and development   531
  Benin   59–60
  Bolivia   75–76
  Botswana   83
  Brazil   90
  Cameroon   97
  Central African Republic   112–113
  conversion and   147
  Kenneth Copeland and   153–155, 155
  critiques of   205, 530–531
  Czech Republic   163
  definition and beliefs   530, 532
  Democratic Republic of the Congo
    (DR Congo)   145
  Denmark   178
  ecology and   190
  El Shaddai (Philippines) and   201
  Eritrea   207
  eschatology and   13, 209–210
  Finland   234
  Ghana   253
  Guatemala   266
  Kenneth Hagin   270–271, 531, 644
  homiletics and   305
  Jesus is Lord Church Worldwide (Philippines)
    and   344
  Latter Rain and   381
  Liberia   392–393
  Edir Macedo and   402
  megachurches and   421
  Neo-Pentecostalism and   451, 452
  Nicaragua   460
  Nigeria   462
  Petrus Agung Pernomo and   537

Prosperity Gospel (cont.)
　　Oral Roberts and　553–554
　　Roman Catholicism on　271
　　secularization and　572
　　Sierra Leone　585
　　social and political empowerment and
　　　　mobility　531–532
　　South Korea　605
　　Tanzania　628–629
　　Universal Church of the Kingdom of God
　　　　and　452
　　USA　644
　　Mariano Velarde and　648
　　Winners Chapel and　667
　　Zimbabwe　683
Prosperity Now (periodical)　98
prosumption theory　598
psychology　533–535
psychotherapy　535
PTL Heritage Church (Liberia)　392
public sphere　356
publishing. *See* media
Puerto Rico　xxv, xxvii, xl, 108, 399–401, 473
Pulepule, Samuelo　469
Pulkingham, Betty　272
Pullin, Thomas　264
Purdie, James Eustace　101, 358
Purdie, Samuel　415
Purinton, William　639
Purnomo, Petrus Agung　536, 536–537
Pyongyang Revival　360, 525–526, 526, 538–540, 603
Pype, Katrien　418

Qale Heywet Church (Eritrea)　207
Qatar　xxv, xxvi, xxvii, xl, 344
queer theory　598. *See also* LGBTQ people
Quiboloy, Apollo　511–512
Quinto Flores, Pio　264

Ra, Woonmong　526, 527, 540–541, 604
race and racism　541–544
　　about　541–542, 544
　　Aglow International and　15
　　A.A. Allen and　17
　　Apostolic Faith Mission (South Africa) and
　　　117–118, 289, 383, 388–389
　　Assemblies of God (USA) and　43
　　Azusa Street Revival and　543, 578–579
　　Reinhard Bonnke, and　79
　　William Frederick Burton and　95–96
　　Church of God in Christ and　136, 406, 543
　　definition of racism　542
　　Evangelicalism and　223
　　exclusion and inclusion　543–544
　　G.T. Haywood and　278
　　ideological approach to　542–543
　　institutional racism　542
　　intersectionality and　543
　　B.H. Irwin and　328, 364
　　Pentecostal Assemblies of Canada and
　　　494–495
　　Pentecostal Assemblies of the World and　63,
　　　477, 498–499, 543, 643
　　Pentecostal/Charismatic Churches of North
　　　America and　43, 329, 500–501
　　Pentecostal history and　543
　　post-racialism and color blindness　543
　　prejudice and　542
　　Oral Roberts and　552–553
　　Romania　558
　　William Seymour and　578–579
　　Society for Pentecostal Studies and　594, 595
　　South Africa　66–67, 117–118
Radano, John　555
radio ministries. *See* media
Raiser, Konrad　194
Rajasthan Pentecostal Church (India)　407
Ramabai, Pandita Saraswati　544–546
　　Minnie Abrams and　2–3
　　background　544–545
　　Barbara Johnston and　350, 351
　　Keswick Movement and　359, 546
　　Joseph R. King and　364
　　Mukti Revival and　4, 439, 545–546
　　Norwegian missionaries and　467
　　photograph　545
Ramaphosa, Cyril　117
Ranaghan, Dorothy　546–548
Ranaghan, Kevin　546–548, 582
Randall, Herbert　195
Randall, John　165
Read, Ralph　170
recommitment　147
Redeemed Christian Church of God (Nigeria)
　　548–549
　　about　12
　　beginnings of　548
　　Cameroon　98
　　Cape Verde　106
　　Central African Republic　112
　　expansion and growth　13, 548–549

INDEX

Redeemed Christian Church of God (cont.)
  Ireland   333
  megachurches and   421
  Redemption Camp   549
  UK   641
Redemption Tidings (periodical)   244
Reformed–Pentecostal dialogue   194
Refresh Rwanda conference   562
regeneration (new birth)   146–147, 477
Regents Theological College (formerly Elim Bible College; UK)   202, 203, 479
Reichel, Alex   45
religious pluralism   330
Renewal (periodical)   272
Renewal in the Spirit Community (Hong Kong)   309
Renewalists   xiv–xv, xvi, xx
repentance   146
restitution   174
restorationist approach   312, 347, 564, 574, 640–641
retribution, theology of   76
Réunion   *xl*, 236
revival   550–551, 613
Revival Chinese Ministries International   51
Revival Christian Church (Hong Kong)   50, 309
Revival Fire Mission (New Zealand)   167, 168, 468
Revival Fire Monthly (periodical)   167, 168
Rhema (Eritrea)   207
Rhema Bible Training Center (RBTC)   196, 270, 392, 466
Rhema Church   83
Richards, Dave   564, 565
Richmann, Christopher J.   183
Richmond Temple (Australia)   262, 263
Right On! (periodical)   346
Riley, Edward   563
Rios Montt, Efraín   265
Rivas, Felipe   423
Rivers, Willie Mae   138
Rivers of Life Ministry (Egypt)   196
Robbins, Joel   27
Robeck, Cecil M., Jr.   viii, 193, 194, 555
Roberts, Bill   585
Roberts, Evan   55, 359, 520, *660*, 660–661
Roberts, Henry   456
Roberts, Oral   **552–554**
  about   552
  Australia and   45
  background and ministry   552–553
  Kenneth Copeland and   155
  Kathy Kuhlman and   367
  media and   552, 553, 644

T.L. Osborn and   481
Pentecostal Fellowship of North America and   328
photograph   *552*
Prosperity Gospel and Full Gospel emphasis   530, 553–554
race and   329
Eddie Villanueva and   651
Voice of Healing ministry and   394
Roberts, Richard   553
Roberts, Thomas   164, 166, 235
Robertson, Pat   459, 582
Robinson, A.E.   630, 631
Robinson, Lizzie Woods   136, 138
Rodríguez, J.L.   473
Rodríguez, Prisciliano   650
Rodríguez Agosto, Francisco   160
Rogers, Kent   17
Roma (gypsy) people   92–93, 236, 335, 524, 558, 607–608, 609
Roman Catholic Church. *See also* Catholic Charismatic Renewal
  apostolic ministry and   30
  Benin   59
  Bolivia   76
  Brazil   89
  Cape Verde   105
  Ulf Ekman and   197, 271, 591
  Holy See, Pentecostal/Charismatic population   *xxxvi*
  Ireland   332
  membership data   xvii
  Nicaragua   460
  on Prosperity Gospel   271
  Roman Catholic–Pentecostal dialogue   182, 193, 554–556, 595
  Vatican II Council   115–116, 192, 459, 617–618
Romania   **557–558**
  beginnings of Pentecostalism in   84, 216, 557
  Pavel Bochian   70–71
  Gheorghe Bradin   71, **84–85**
  Teodor Codreanu   **138–139**
  Communist era   71, 84–85, 557–558, 566
  higher education   70, 139, 566
  Pentecostal/Charismatic population   *xl*, 219, 557
  race and   558
  Trandafir Sandru   71, 84, **565–566**
  social engagement   558
Rosado Rosseau, Leoncia   473
Roslyn City Road Mission (New Zealand)   5–6
Rowlands, J.K.   179

Rubio, Josué and Vanette 306
Ruesga, David and Raquel 422, 423–424
Ruibal, Julio Cesar 74–75, 559–560
Ruiz, Manuel 25
Rumsey, Mary C. 604
Russell, J.R. (Mother) 339
Russia 560–561
    Aglow International 15
    beginnings of Pentecostalism in 215, 216
    Communist era 217–218, 560–561, 653–654
    contemporary era 561
    Ulf Ekman and 197
    Oneness Pentecostalism in 478
    Pentecostal/Charismatic population *xxv*, *xl*, 219, 561
    Ivan Efimovich Voronaev 216, 560–561, 653–654
Russian and Eastern European Mission (REEM) 680
Rwanda *xl*, 15, 561–562, 627
Ryan, Martin Lawrence 562–564
Rybarczyk, Edmund 7
Ryder, Steve 163

sacrifices 402, 646
Saginario, Carmine 336
Saint Helena *xl*
Saint Kitts & Nevis *xl*
Saint Lucia *xl*
Saint Pierre & Miquelon *xl*
Saint Vincent *xxviii*, *xli*
Salbashian, Dirkan 352
Salman, Nihad and Salwa 487
Salmerón, Regla María 160
Salt & Light 564–565, 640
SALT network (Norway) 467
Salter, James 95, 143
salvation. *See* soteriology
Salvation Army 44, 315, 372, 415, 437
Samarin, William J. 593
Samaritan Foundation 103
Sam-Jolly, Akintayo 585
Samoa (Western Samoa) *xli*, 87, 270, 468, 469, 470, 471
Samuelsen, Åge 466
San Marino *xli*
sanctification
    baptism in the Holy Spirit and 52
    Deeper Life Bible Church on 174
    William H. Durham on 183
    ethics and 211–212
    Full Gospel and 239

    Holy Spirit and 147, 514–515
    International Pentecostal Holiness Church and 327
    Italian Transnational Pentecostal Movement and 335–336
    Barbara Johnston on 350
    soteriology and 599
    Smith Wigglesworth on 662
Sanders, Anna 160, 422
Sandford, Frank 258, 491
Sandgren, F.A. 184
Sandidge, Jerry L. 193
Sandru, Trandafir 71, 84, 565–566
Sanford, Agnes xx, 567–568
Sangkakala (Trumpet) Foundation (Indonesia) 621, 622
Santiago, Valdemiro 402
Sao Tome & Principe *xxviii*, *xli*
Saracco, Norberto 34
satan 154, 156. *See also* cosmology; demons and demonization
Saudi Arabia *xxvi*, *xxvii*, *xli*, 39
Savelle, Jerry 271
Saxby, A.E. 72
Schaepe, John 409
School of Intercultural Studies (Fuller Theological Seminary) 654–655, 664
Schvartz, A. and E. 166
science 568–571
Scofield, C.I. 415
Scott, Benjamin McNair 31
Scott, Douglas 57, 164, 166, 216, 235
Scratch, Carman Clare 434
Scripture Union 173, 470, 585, 677
Secord, Charles F. 264
Secours Catholique 172
Secretaries of Christian World Communions 194
secularization 179, 219, 333, 522, 571–573, 597
Seirei (periodical) 441
Self, Kathy 8
Seminario Bíblico Pentecostal de Centro América (SEBIPCA) 306
Seminario Teológico Pentecostal de Honduras (SETEPH) 306
Seminarul Teologic Penticostal (now Seminarul Teologic; Romania) 70, 566
Semple, Robert James 184, 284, 308, 370, 412
Senegal *xli*
Seney, Léon 235
senwele (Muslim music genre) 417
Sepúlveda, Carlos 400
Sepulveda, Juan 374–375

Serbia   xli. See also Yugoslavia
Serrano Elías, Jorge   265
Seventh-day Adventism   340, 637, 658
Séverin, Kacou   159
sexuality   574–576, 598. See also family relations; gender
Seychelles   xli
Seymour, William   576–579
    John Archibald Duncan Adams and   6
    Azusa Street Revival and   viii, 46–47, 48–49, 577–578, 643
    background   576–577
    Archibald Cooper and   150
    death   579
    family life   48–49, 578
    Lucy Farrow and   231–232, 577, 643
    glossolalia and   258
    Thomas Hezmalhalch and   288
    international influence   579
    John G. Lake and   370
    Abundio López and   398
    Mukti Revival and   440, 546
    Charles Parham and   491–492
    photograph   576
    race and   578–579
Shakarian, Demos   192, 530, 553, 582
Shalom Training School (USA)   437
Shalumbo   95–96, 143
Shambach, R.W.   17
Shandong Revival (China)   123, 579–581, 619
Sharing of Ministries Abroad (SOMA)   xxi, 272
Shekina Glory Ministries   159
Shembe, Isaiah   9
Shepherding Movement   163, 404, 581–582
Sherrill, John and Elizabeth   165
Shinsho Church (Japan)   354, 676, 677
Shouters (Christian Assemblies, Little Flock, Local Church; China)   30, 123, 391, 583, 583–584, 656, 657
Shuttleworth, Abigail   65
Sidang Injil Borneo (Malaysia)   403
Siefer, Paul and Rosa   236
Siemans, Renata   627
Sierra Leone   xli, 584–586
Sierra Leone Fellowship of Evangelical Students   585
signs. See miracles, signs, wonders
Silesian Evangelical Church of the Augsburg Confession (Czech Republic)   162
Simon, K.V.   1

Simpson, Albert Benjamin (A.B.)   32, 237, 324, 359, 366, 384, 436, 467, 586
Simpson, Charles   581–582
Simpson, Otilia (Ekvall)   434, 586, 587
Simpson, William Wallace   434, 586–588
Singapore   xli, 38, 270, 365–366, 588–589, 648
Singleton, Andrew   45
Sint Maarten   xli
Sittler, Joseph   189
Siu, Hoi Lei   308
Slager, Abigail   434
Slavic Pentecostal Union   679, 680
Sloan, William   373
Slovakia   xli, 590–591. See also Czechoslovakia
Slovenia   xli. See also Yugoslavia
Smail, Tom   272
Smale, Joseph   46, 55, 638, 661
Small, Franklin   476, 477
Smith, Beulah Argue   35
Smith, Brian   45
Smith, Carrie   264
Smith, Chuck   346
Smith, Hannah Whithall   357
Smith, James K.A.   446, 447, 516
Smith, Mable and Jessie   183
Smith, Oswald   291
Smith, Robert Pearsall   357
Smith, Rodney Gipsy   150
Smith, Rudolph   339
Smith, Sarah   195
Śniegoń, Karol   517
Soares, Romildo Ribeiro   90, 401
social engagement. See also ecology and ecotheologies; politics
    Bolivia   76
    D. Mark Buntain   94
    Calvary Church (Malaysia)   267
    Chile   121
    Church of God in Christ   138
    Cuba   161
    Deeper Life Bible Church   174
    Democratic Republic of the Congo (DR Congo)   144–145
    D.G.S. Dhinakaran   180
    El Salvador   198
    El Shaddai (Philippines)   201
    ethics and   212
    Ethiopia   214
    Ghana   253
    Guatemala   264–265

social engagement (cont.)
    Hillsong   296
    Holy Trinity Brompton   302
    International House of Prayer (IHOP)   326
    International Pentecostal Holiness Church   328–329
    Charles Harrison Mason   406
    Thomas Mathews   408
    Aimee Semple McPherson   413
    Mok Lai Chi   433–434
    Mongolia   435
    Nigeria   462
    Mensa Otabil   483
    Pentecostal European Fellowship   502
    Planetshakers   513
    Pandita Saraswati Ramabai   546
    Redeemed Christian Church of God   549
    Romania   558
    South Korea   605
    Mariano Velarde   649
    Eddie Villanueva   652
    Vineyard churches   665
    Winners Chapel   667–668
    Yoido Full Gospel Church   674
    Darlene Zschech   686
socialization   592–593
Society for Pentecostal Studies (SPS)   vii, **594–596**
sociological imagination   356–357
sociology   596–598
Södermalmskyrkan (Sweden)   197
Soekoto, Leo   320
Solomon Islands   *xli*, 468, 469, 470, 484, 485
Somalia   *xli*
Somosierra, Maximiano   511
Song, Shangjie. *See* Sung, John
Sosa, Exeario   650
Sosulski, Kazimierz   518
soteriology (salvation)   **599–601**
    Reinhard Bonnke, and   80
    Classical understanding of   599
    contemporary views   600–601
    conversion and   **145–148**, 331
    ecclesiology and   187
    ecology and   189–190
    Evangelicalism and   599–600
    Full Gospel and   239, 599
    hermeneutics and   287
    Keswick movement and   358
    miracles, signs, and wonders and   429
    Neo-Pentecostalism on   451
    Oneness Pentecostalism on   477
    of other religions   330–331
    revivals and   550–551
South Africa   **601–603**. *See also* Apostolic Faith Mission (South Africa)
    Aglow International   15
    appeal of Pentecostalism   602–603
    beginnings of Pentecostalism in   602
    Nicholas Bhengu   **66–67**, 289
    Reinhard Bonnke, and   79
    William Frederick Burton and   95
    Frank Chikane and   **117–118**
    Church of God in Christ   137
    Archibald Cooper   **150–151**
    Thomas Hezmalhalch   150, 181, **288–289**, 371, 383, 602
    higher education   118
    Independent Charismatic population   *xxviii*
    Italian Transnational Pentecostal Movement in   335
    John G. Lake   150, 181, 288–289, **369–371**, 383, 388, 602
    Pieter L. Le Roux   **382–383**, 389
    Elias Letwaba   95, **388–389**
    Oneness Pentecostalism in   478
    Pentecostal (denominational) population   *xxvi*
    Pentecostal/Charismatic population   *xxiv, xxiv, xxv, xli*, 601
    race and racism   66–67, 117–118
    Smith Wigglesworth and   663
    Zionist churches   9
South African Council of Churches (SACC)   118, 193
South America. *See* Latin America
South Asia   37–39. *See also specific countries*
South India Full Gospel Church (SIFGC)   149
South Indian Church of God (now Indian Pentecostal Church of God)   2, 149
South Korea   **603–605**. *See also* Korea
    about   37, 38
    Aglow International   15
    beginnings of Pentecostalism in   603, 604
    challenges and schisms   605
    Jashil Choi   127, **128–129**, 527, 604
    Yonggi Cho   **126–128** (*See also* Cho, Yonggi)
    El Shaddai (Philippines) in   648
    gender and   604, 605
    Ha Young Jo   **268–269**
    higher education   152, 540
    megachurches   420
    Pentecostal (denominational) population   *xxvi*
    Pentecostal/Charismatic population   *xxiv, xli*
    Prayer Mountain Movement   128–129, **525–528**, 540–541

INDEX

South Korea (cont.)
    Prosperity Gospel and   605
    Woonmong Ra   526, 527, **540–541**, 604
    social engagement   605
    types of Pentecostal churches   603–604
    Yoido Full Gospel Church (*See also* Yoido Full Gospel Church)
South Korean Central Bible School   152
South Seas Evangelical Church   469
South Seas Evangelical Mission (SSEM)   468, 469
South Sudan   *xli*, **606–607**
Southeast Asia   37–39. *See also specific countries*
Southern Evangelical Mission   44
Soviet Union. *See* Russia
Spadaro, Antonio   271
Spain   *xli*, 15, 116, 216, 270, 335, **607–609**, 648
Sparks, Jack   346
Spencer, Ivan Q.   380
Spetz, Bror   197
Spina, Miguel   132
Spirit baptism. *See* baptism in the Holy Spirit
Spirit of Jesus Church (Japan)   152, 441–442, 478
spirit possession   602–603
spiritual gifts   515, 551, 556, **609–612**, 654–655, 656. *See also* glossolalia; healing; prophecy; xenolalia
Spiritual Gifts Society (Ling'en hui; China)   123, 580
spiritual mapping   655
spiritual warfare   28, 156–158, 282, 377, 460, 575, 646, 655
spirituality   **612–614**, 632. *See also* baptism in the Holy Spirit; experience, of God; mysticism
spontaneous performance Jesus painting   8
Spooner, Kenneth   329
Spurgeon, Charles   372, 419
Spurling, Richard Green   134
Squire, Fred   216–217
Sri Lanka   *xlii*, 38, 663, 686
Stafford, Glenn   125
Stafford, Isaac   136
Stålsett, Gunnar   194
Standard Church of America   408
Stapleton, Nina   339
Stark, Edmond and Pearl   22
Stark, Rodney   597
statistics   **614–617**. *See also* Pentecostalism, counting
Steiner, Leonard   505
Stewart, Don   17
Stewart, Joseph   477
Stiller, Brian   101

Stockmayer, Otto   358, 359
Stott, John R.W.   222, 268, 272
Stronstad, Roger   227
Stube, Edwin Brownell   320, 621
Students for Christ   58
Suarsana, Yan   298
Sudan   *xlii*, 385
Sudan Interior Mission (SIM)   60
Suenens, Leo Jozef   57, 272, 547, **617–619**
Suico, Joseph   652
Sumrall, Lester   45, 197
Sun, Zhanyao   580
Sundaram, G.   180
Sunderland Conventions   72, 73, 215, 340, 505, 520
Sundh, Bengt   475
Sung, John (Song Shangjie)   123, 403, 581, 588, **619–621**
Sung, Sheung Hong   503
Sung, Teng Man   503
Sunrise Educational Foundation   435
Suriname   *xlii*
Sutanto, Adi   537, **621**, **621–622**
Sutton, Geoffrey   534
Sutton, Matthew   414
Suurmond, Jean-Jacques   189
Svartdahl, Egil   467
Svenska Fria Missions (SFM)   144
Swaggart, Jimmy   459, 553
Swallen, W.   361
Swaziland. *See* Eswatini
Sweden   **622–624**
    Aglow International   15
    beginnings of Pentecostalism in   216, 622–623
    ecumenism   193
    Ulf Ekman   **196–197**, 271, 450, 591
    Evangelicalism and   223
    higher education   197, 623
    missionaries from   22, 33, 74, 144, 607, 623, 627
    Pentecostal organizational structure   341, 624
    Pentecostal/Charismatic population   *xlii*, 623
    Lewi Pethrus   54, 144, 243, 380, 466, **507–509**, 530, 622–623
    Smith Wigglesworth and   663
Swedish Free Mission   627
Swenson, Donald S.   115
Swindoll, Orville   34
Swiss Pentecostal Mission (SPM)   112, 299, 300
Switzerland   *xlii*, 15, 270, 565, 648
Sword of the Spirit (periodical)   24
Synan, J.A.   328
Synan, Vinson   328, 594

Syria *xlii*, 39, 40
Syverson, H.S. 415

Tábor Life-Saving Association (Záchranný spolek Tábor; Czech Republic) 162
Tadeu, Jorge 524
Taejŏn Evangelist Tabernacle (Korea) 152
Taiwan 624–626
    about 37, 38
    Bread of Life Church (Ling Liang Church) 123, 185, 625, 626
    Charismatic Renewal and 625
    Classical Pentecostalism 624–625
    contemporary developments 625–626
    defining Pentecostalism challenges and 626
    El Shaddai (Philippines) and 648
    Jun Murai and 441
    Kong Duen Yee (Mui Yee) and 308
    Changshou Li (Witness Lee) and 390
    Pentecostal/Charismatic population *xlii*
    True Jesus Church 626, 637
Taiwan Assemblies of God 624
Taiwan Full Gospel Church 624
Tajikistan *xlii*, 39
Tallman, Matthew 189
Tamaki, Brian 458, 469
Tamaki, Hannah 469
Tanghe (China Gospel Fellowship) 314
Tanzania *xlii*, 626–629
Taste and See (periodical) 21
Tatro, Russ 585
Taylor, George Floyd (G.F.) 328, **630–631**, 638
Taylor, James Hudson 358
Taylor, Mary and William (Japan) 151, 440, 564
Taylor, William (Chile) 310
Tebay, Mary 169
Teen Challenge 470
Telle, Agnes 249, 466, 467
temperance movement 5, 53, 54, 661
Temple of Love Ministries 83
Temple of Restoration 106
Temple Trust 45, 316
Tertullian 258
testimonies 304
Thailand *xlii*, 37, 38, 137, 270
The School of Acts (TSOA; Indonesia) 537
theological education. *See* higher education
theology **632–633**. *See also* Bible; Finished Work Pentecostalism; Oneness Pentecostalism; Trinitarian theology
    Christology 153, 186, 331, 510, 601
    dominion theology 13, 31, 381, 570, 622, 655–656
    eschatology 208–210 (*See also* eschatology)
    Walter J. Hollenweger and 299–300
    intercultural theology 300
    kingdom theology 64–65
    narrative theology 299–300
    Pentecostal characteristics 632–633
    pneumatology **514–516** (*See also* Holy Spirit)
    of religions 331
    soteriology **599–601** (*See also* soteriology)
    on spiritual gifts **609–612**
Thiessen, Johan 319, 322
Third Wave. *See* Neo-Pentecostalism
Thiselton, Anthony C. 515
Thomas, Eloise 534
Thomas, Steve 564, 565
Thomas, William Henry Griffith 358
Thompson, Muri 469
Thompson, William Thomas 7
Thornton, J.B. 151, 440, 441
Three Hills Bible Institute (Canada) 275
Three Wave taxonomy viii–ix, xiv, xvi
Thuvayur Church (India) 149
Tibet 504, 519–520
Tibet Prayer Union 520
Tice, Kenneth 127
Tice, Richard 127
Timor-Leste *xlii*
Tinazzo, Ezio 23
Togarasei, L. 683, 684
Toggs, Laura 295
Togo *xlii*
Tokelau *xlii*
Tokelau Islands 468
Tollefsen, Gunnerius 467
Tomlinson, Ambrose (A.J.) 134–135, 339, 473
Tomlinson, Homer 473
Tonga *xlii*, 468, 470
tongues. *See* glossolalia
Tongues of Fire (periodical) 20
Tony, Daud 404
Toppi, Francesco 336
Toronto Blessing (Catch the Fire) 101, 209, 234, 250, 302, 326, 443, **634–635**, 664
Torrey, Reuben (R.A.) 44, 95, 472, 520
Tosetto, Massimiliano 102
Total Christian Church Group (Japan) 153
Toukea, Nestor 97
transnationalism. *See also* globalization; migration
    Africa and 13
    Italian Transnational Pentecostal Movement **334–336**
    megachurches and 420–421
Trasher, Lillian 195, 385

INDEX

Trinidad & Tobago   *xxiv, xxv, xlii*
Trinitarian theology
    Kenneth Copeland and   153
    A.H. Dallimore and   168
    Louis Francescon and   238
    Oneness Pentecostalism and   42, 409–410, 478, 493, 643
    soteriology and   600
    theology of religions and   331
Triumphs of Faith (periodical)   435, 436, 437
Trudel, Dorothea   436
True Jesus Church   **636–637**
    beginnings of   63–64, 123, 636
    beliefs and practices   123, 478, 637, 659
    Bernt Berntsen and   62, 63–64, 636
    growth and international reach   123, 478, 636–637
    Hong Kong   307
    influence of   637
    Jun Murai and   441
    Malaysia   404
    Oneness Pentecostalism and   62, 478, 637, 658, 659
    Taiwan   626, 637
    Paul Wei (Wei Enbo)   63–64, 123, 478, 636, **658–659**
Truth Bible Institute (China)   588
Tsuge, Fujito   676
Tunisia   *xlii*
Turkey   *xlii*
Turkmenistan   *xlii*, 39
Turks & Caicos Islands   *xlii*
Turner, William H.   307, **638–639**
Tuvalu   *xliii*, 468
Tylor, Irene   160

Uganda   *xxvii, xliii*, 565, 627
Ugba, Abel
    Shades of Belonging   333
Ukraine   *xliii*, 197, 219, 270
Umaña, Manuel   311
Underwood, Bernard E.   329, 500–501
Unión de las Asambleas de Diós (Argentina)   130
Union de Prière de Charmes (France)   166, 236
Union Nationale des Assemblées de Dieu de France (UNADF)   236
Union of Christians of Evangelical Faith (Russia)   560
Union of Elim Evangelical Churches (Central African Republic)   112
Union of Evangelical Pentecostal Churches (Bulgaria)   91, 463, 680

Union of the Assemblies of God (Argentina)   33
Unitas Fratrum in Slovakia (Jednota bratská na Slovensku)   590
United Arab Emirates   *xxvi, xxvii, xliii*, 344, 648
United Christ Church of Japan   441, 676
United Evangelical Church (Poland)   518
United Holy Church (USA)   328
United Kingdom   **639–642**
    Aglow International   15
    beginnings of Pentecostalism in   215, 216
    Alexander and Mary Boddy   71–74 (*See also* Boddy, Alexander)
    Bread of Life Church (Ling Liang Church)   185
    Charismatic Renewal   640, 641–642
    Church of God in Christ   137
    Classical Pentecostal denominations   639–640, 642
    Deeper Life Bible Church   174
    El Shaddai (Philippines)   648
    Elim Pentecostal Church   201–203 (*See also* Elim Pentecostal Church)
    Evangelicalism and   222–225
    Donald Gee   166, 192, **243–244**, 341, 359, 505
    Michael and Jeanne Harper   xx, 20, 165, 271–273
    higher education   95, 137, 202, 203, 244, 270
    Holy Trinity Brompton   18, *301*, 301–302, 641
    House Church Movement   203, **312–313**
    George Jeffreys   72, 201–202, 216, **340–342**, 359, 411, 640, 661
    Jesus People Movement   347
    Keswick Movement   **357–359** (*See also* Keswick Movement)
    megachurches   642
    migration to   218, 641
    Pentecostal networks   640–641
    Pentecostal/Charismatic population   *xxiv, xliii*, 219
    politics   522
    Salt & Light   **564–565**, 640
    Welsh Revival   **659–661** (*See also* Welsh Revival)
    Winners Chapel   667
United Pentecostal Church International (UPCI)
    establishment and Oneness Pentecostalism   477, 643
    Guam   470
    Hong Kong   307
    Jamaica   339
    Japan   152–153, 442
    Marshall Islands   471
    Taiwan   624

United Pentecostal Church of Cape Verde 106
United Pentecostal Church of Colombia 478
United Pentecostal Evangelical Mission (Nicaragua) 459
United States Coalition of Apostolic Leaders 644
United States of America 642–644
  A.A. Allen 16–17, 367, 394, 481
  Alpha 19
  anthropology and 28
  apostolic ministry and 31–32, 644
  Assemblies of God (USA) 41–43 (See also Assemblies of God (USA))
  Azusa Street Revival 46–49 (See also Azusa Street Revival)
  beginnings of Pentecostalism in 642–643
  Bethel Church 64–65, 209, 453
  F.F. Bosworth 6, 42, 80–82, *81*, *82*, 86, 288, 394, 481, 669
  William Marrion Branham 82, *85*, 85–87, 156, 276, 367, 393, 394, 481, 644
  Charismatic population xxvii, *xxvii*
  Charismatic Renewal and 644
  Church of God (Cleveland) 134–136 (See also Church of God (Cleveland))
  Church of God in Christ 41, 83, 108, 136–138, 405–406, 518, 543, 643
  as colonial and neocolonial power 140, 141
  comparisons to Canada 100–101
  Kenneth Copeland 79, 153–155, *154*, 196, 271, 392, 530, 667
  Deeper Life Bible Church 174
  William H. Durham 182–184 (See also Durham, William H.)
  Evangelicalism and 222–225
  Lucy Farrow 231–232, 384, 491, 577, 643
  Kenneth E. Hagin 270–271 (See also Hagin, Kenneth E.)
  Garfield Thomas (G.T.) Haywood 277–279, *278*, 476, 477, 498, 499, 543
  healing and 644
  higher education 135, 137, 270, 290, 399, 400, 437, 463, 553
  Independent Charismatic population xxvii, *xxviii*
  International Fellowship of Christian Assemblies 323–325 (See also International Fellowship of Christian Assemblies)
  International House of Prayer (IHOP) 196, 325–327, 664, 666
  Jesus People Movement 178, 196, 346–348, 444, 469, 508, 583, 655
  Joseph H. (J.H.) King 328, 363–364, 433, 630, 639
  Kathryn Kuhlman 366, 366–368, 429, 530, 559, 621
  Latter Rain and 644
  Gordon Lindsay 17, 82, 315, 393–394, 481, 482
  Alice Eveline Luce 398–399, 422
  Charles Harrison Mason 136, 405–406, 543, 578, 643
  Aimee Semple McPherson 412–414 (See also McPherson, Aimee Semple)
  Carrie Judd Montgomery 4, 88, 385, 422, *435*, 435–437, 473
  Francisco Olazábal 472–474
  Charles Parham 490–492 (See also Parham, Charles)
  Pentecostal/Charismatic Churches of North America 500–501 (See also Pentecostal / Charismatic Churches of North America)
  Pentecostal (denominational) population xxvi, *xxvi*, 644
  Pentecostal/Charismatic population xxiv, *xxv*, *xliii*
  politics 224, 521
  Charles S. Price 35, 93, 167, 366, 528–530
  Prosperity Gospel and 644
  Kevin and Dorothy Ranaghan 546–548, 582
  Oral Roberts 552–554 (See also Roberts, Oral)
  Agnes Sanford xx, 567–568
  William Seymour 576–579 (See also Seymour, William)
  George Floyd (G.F.) Taylor 328, 630–631, 638
  Charles Peter Wagner ix, 30, 31–32, 621, 622, 644, 654–656, 664
  Wimber, John 663–666 (See also Wimber, John)
  Maria Woodworth-Etter 35, 36, 81, 398, 428, *668*, 668–670
United States Virgin Islands *xliii*
Unity of the Brethren Church (Jednota českobratská; Czech Republic) 162
Universal Church of the Kingdom of God (Brazil) 645–647
  about 90, 645
  Angola 23
  beginnings of 645
  beliefs and teachings 377, 451–452, 645–646
  Bolivia 75
  Cape Verde 106
  controversies 646–647
  Côte d'Ivoire 159
  growth 647
  healing, deliverance, and sacrifice 646
  Edir Macedo 90, 377, 401–402, 451, 645, 647

Universal Church of the Kingdom of God (cont.)
   media   417–418
   Paraguay   488
   politics and   402, 645
   Portugal   524
   structure and organization   645
Universal Prayer Group Ministries (UPG)   641
Unorganized Italian Christian Churches in North America   238, 323. *See also* International Fellowship of Christian Assemblies
Upper Room Mission (USA)   4, 152, 289
Uribe, Alfonso   375
Urshan, Andrew   184, 278, 476, 477, 478
Uruguay   *xliii*, 15
Uwai, Otokuma   441
Uzbekistan   *xliii*, 39

Valdez, A.C., Jr.   45
Valdez, Adolpho (A.C.), Sr.   44, 262, 468, 577
Valdez, Susie Villa   577
Valente, Rubia   336
Vallotton, Kris   65
Van Beek, Huibert   193
Van Eyk, Frederick (F.B.)   44, 273
Van Klaveren, Richard D.   319–320, 322
Van Klaveren, Stien   319–320
Vanuatu   *xxv, xxvi, xliii*, 270, 468, 471, 485
Vaters, Eugene   496–497
Vatican II Council   115–116, 192, 459, 617–618
Vatter, Stefan   30, 31
Velarde, Mariano "Mike"   200, 201, 345, 512, **647–649**
Velásquez Pavón, Óscar   460
Velberter Mission   78–79
Venezuela   *xliii*, 15, 225, **649–651**
Vereinigte Missionsfreunde (Germany)   249
Vereinigung Evangelischer Freikirchen (Germany)   250
Vernaud, Jacques A.   144
Vestitorul Evangheliei (The Gospel Herald)   566
Vickers, John   20
Victory Outreach   453
Viens et vois (periodical)   166, 236
Vietheer, Heinrich   72
Vietnam   *xliii*, 37, 50, 185, 367, 686
Viljanen, Alti   26
Villanueva, Eddie   344, 345–346, 511, **651–652**
Vineyard. *See* Association of Vineyard Churches
Vineyard Christian Fellowship (Kresťanské spoločenstvo Vinica; Slovakia)   590

Vingren, Gunnar   89, 184, 523
Visión de Futuro (Vision of the Future; Argentina)   33
visual art. *See* aesthetics and art
Vlaamse Verbond van Pinkstergemeenten (Belgium)   57
Voice in the Wilderness (periodical)   278
Voice of Healing   17, 80, 82, 393, 394, 481
The Voice of Healing (periodical)   86, 394, 644
Voice of Prophecy   474
Volksmission entschiedener Christen (Germany)   216, 249
Vondey, Wolfgang   600–601
Voronaev, Ivan Efimovich   91, 216, 463, 560–561, **653–654**, 680
VPE (United Pentecostal and Gospel Assemblies; Netherlands)   453
Vraie Eglise de Dieu (Cameroon)   97
Vrije Universiteit Amsterdam   453

Wagner, Charles Peter   ix, 30, 31–32, 621, 622, 644, **654–656**, 664
Wagner University (formerly Wagner Leadership Institute)   655
Wahlsten, Julia and Martin   607
Wakkary, Max D.   323
Waldvogel, Hans   649–650
Walker, Andrew
   Restoring the Kingdom   312
Wallace, James   170
Wallis, Arthur   312
Wallis & Futuna Islands   *xliii*, 468
Walsh, M.   115
Waltrip, Burroughs   366–367
Wang, Mingdao   313, 620, 658
Wang, Peace (Wang Peizhen)   390, 675
Wang, Zai (Leland Wang)   **656–657**, 675
Ward, C.M.   36
Ward, Horace   594
Warner, Daniel S.   576
Warnock, George   276, 380, 381
Warren, Joseph   232
Watt, James   276–277
Watt, P.   66
Weber, Max   421, 454, 531, 571, 597, 673
The Weekly Evangel (periodical)   670
Weepers (China)   **657–658**
Wei, Chen-mo   587
Wei, Paul (Wei Enbo)   63–64, 123, 478, 636, **658–659**

Wells, David   194
Welsh Revival   **659–661**
  about   660–661
  Apostolic Church and   110
  Australia and   44
  Azusa Street Revival and   46, 661
  background   659–660
  Bible College of Wales and   78
  Alexander Boddy and   72
  France and   235
  influence of   661
  Italy and   335
  George and Stephen Jeffreys and   340, 661
  Keswick movement and   359
  UK and   640, 661
Wenzhou Yueqing Church (China)   230, 314
Wesley, John   358
Wesleyan Holiness Movement. *See* Holiness Movement
Wesleyan Methodist Church of Brazil   328
West Asia   39–40. *See also specific countries*
West Berlin Fellowship "On The Way" (Společenství na cestě; Czech Republic)   163
Western Sahara   *xliii*
Western Samoa. *See* Samoa
Wheeler, Rob   456
White, Alma   55
White, George and Melvina   339
White, Lynn   188
Whitt, Maude Evans   496
The Whole Truth (periodical)   406
Wigglesworth, Smith   **661–663**
  John Archibald Duncan Adams and   6
  Australia   44, 468
  background   216, 661–662
  Alexander and Mary Boddy and   73
  death   663
  Denmark   177
  healing and   662
  James McKeown and   411
  missionary travels   662–663
  New Zealand   456, 468
  photograph   *661*
  Cecil Polhill and   520
  theology of   662
Wilkerson, David
  The Cross and the Switchblade   192, 347
Wilkes, Paget   184
Wilkinson, Alfred   44
Wilkinson, Michael   635
  Pentecostals and the Body (with Althouse)   205
Willaime, Jean-Paul   236

Willets, Mabel   125
Williams, Daniel Powell (D.P.)   30, 411
Williams, J. Rodman   595
Williams, Rafael D.   264
Williams, Ralph   415
Williams, Riley F.   136
Williamson, Paul   534
Wilson, Bryan   573
Wilson, Robert   357
Wilson, William   506
Wilson, William J.   542
Wimber, John   **663–666**. *See also* Association of Vineyard Churches
  Alpha and   18–19
  background   663
  death   664
  eschatology of   209
  at Fuller Theological Seminary with Charles Peter Wagner   654–655, 664
  Jesus People Movement and   348
  Kansas City prophets and   326, 664
  ministry approach and influence   665–666
  on miracles, signs, and wonders   64, 429
  theology of   664–665
  Third Wave Pentecostalism and   ix
  Toronto Blessing and   634, 664
  worship and   663–664
Winger, Adah   651
Winners Chapel   12, 83, 98, 112, **666–668**
Wirhaspati, Soehandoko   323
witchdemonology   480. *See also* demons and demonization
Wittick, Karl and Marian   627
women. *See* gender
wonders. *See* miracles, signs, wonders
Woo, Tsz Ho   433
Wood, Alice   32–33
Wood, Edward   594
Wood, George O.   352, 671
Woodworth-Etter, Maria   35, 36, 81, 398, 428, *668*, **668–670**
Word and Witness (periodical)   41, 388, 669
Word of Faith. *See* Prosperity Gospel
Word of Faith (periodical)   541
Word of God Community (USA)   xxii
Word of Life (Sweden)   197, 590, 591
Word of Life Church (Církev Slovo života; Czech Republic)   163
World Alliance for Pentecostal Theological Education (WAPTE)   221, 293
World Assemblies of God Fellowship (WAGF)   103, 267, 335, **670–671**

INDEX

World Christian Fundamentalist Association   192
World Church of the Power of God (Brazil)   402
World Council of Churches (WCC)
    Christian Biblical Church (Argentina) and   130
    Church of God in Christ and   138
    David du Plessis and   181, 192
    ecumenical dialogue with   193–194
    Evangelicals and   222
    Donald Gee and   244
    Walter J. Hollenweger and   299
    George Jeffreys and   341
    Opoku Onyinah and   480
    World Assemblies of God Fellowship and   671
World Evangelical Alliance (WEA)   222, 507, 671
World for Jesus International Christian Center and Ministries   652
World Pentecostal Conferences   164, 175, 217, 341, 623, 640
World Prayer Center   655
World Revival Crusade   341
World War I   74, 405
World War II   164, 216–217, 438
World's Faith Missionary Association (WFMA)   88
Worldwide Church of God's Power   524
Worldwide Family of God Churches   83
World-Wide Revival (periodical)   394
worship
    accessibility   431
    aesthetics and art in   8
    Africa   11, 12
    Christian Congregation in Brazil   133
    embodiment and   204
    liturgy   239, **395–397**
    music and   395–396 (*See also* music)
    mysticism and   **445–447**
    Pentecostal Mission (Hong Kong)   503
    spirituality and   613–614
    theology and   633
    John Wimber and   663–664
Wortman, Charles   33
Wray, J.J.   372
Wyatt, Thomas   380
Wyns, Clara   434

xenolalia   4, 232, 258, 284, 563. *See also* glossolalia
Xu, Peter (Xu Yongze)   657

Yamamori, Tetsunao   255, 454–455, 597
Yamanaka, Mankichi   441
Yang, Rulin   580
Yao, Wangmin   681
Yayi Boni, Thomas   61

Yemen   *xliii*
Yingshang Fellowship (China)   230, 314
Ylivainio, Niilo   233
YMCA   68, 433
Yoido Full Gospel Church (South Korea)   **672–674**
    about   604–605, 672
    appeal of and beliefs   672–673
    Yonggi Cho   126–128 (*See also* Cho, Yonggi)
    Jashil Choi   127, **128–129**, 527, 604
    critiques of   673–674
    Deeper Life Bible Church and   173
    ecumenism and   193
    gender and   673
    healing and   127, 673
    William Francis (Frank) Houston and   316
    media   673
    as megachurch   128, 419
    Neo-Pentecostalism and   451
    Prayer Mountain Movement and   527
    social engagement   674
    in Taiwan   624
Yong, Amos   186, 189, 516, 600, 601
Yongmoon Prayer Mountain (South Korea)   527, 540, 541
Yongmun Mountain Bible School (South Korea)   540
Young, D.J.   136
Young Earth Creationism   569–570
Youth for Christ   470
Youth with a Mission (YWAM)   268, 434, 467, 470, 585
Yu, Cidu (Dora Yu)   123, 448, 583, **674–675**
Yu, Ligong (Moses Yu)   581
Yuan, Zhiming
    Cross in China (documentary)   231
Yugoslavia   478. *See also* Bosnia-Herzegovina; Croatia; Kosovo; Montenegro; North Macedonia; Serbia; Slovenia
Yumiyama, Kiyoma   354, **675–677**

Zaccardiani (Italy)   335
Zaffuto, Ferdinando   102
Zambia   *xliii*, 270, 478, **677–679**
Zaplishny, Dionissy Michailovitch   91, 463, 653, **679–680**
Zaplishny, Olga Popova (Kalkandjieva)   463, 679–680
Zeller, Samuel   436
Zelman, Juraj   590
Zhang, Lingsheng   64, 659
Zhang, Rongliang   230, 231, **681–682**
Zhang, Zhongsan   63–64, 659

Zhonghua Guizhu Tuandui (China for Christ Network). *See* Fangcheng Fellowship
Zielicke, Seth N.   290
Zimbabwe   *xxv, xxvi, xxvii, xxviii, xliii,* 224, 565, **682–684**
Zimmerman, Thomas F.   193
Zion Church (South Africa)   289, 383
Zion Church (Taiwan)   624
Zion City (IL)   6, 80–81, 288, 370, 393, 492
Zion Temple (Rwanda)   562
Zionist churches   9. *See also* African independent/initiated/instituted churches
Zoe Ministries International   83
Zschech, Darlene   295, **685–686**
Zschech, Mark   685, 686
Zuo, Shunzhen   349
Zurlo, Gina   29